# Nortel Networks:
# The Complete Reference

James Knapp

Osborne/**McGraw-Hill**

Berkeley   New York   St. Louis   San Francisco
Auckland   Bogotá   Hamburg   London   Madrid
Mexico City   Milan   Montreal   New Delhi   Panama City
Paris   São Paulo   Singapore   Sydney
Tokyo   Toronto

Osborne/**McGraw-Hill**
2600 Tenth Street
Berkeley, California 94710
U.S.A.

For information on translations or book distributors outside the U.S.A., or to arrange
bulk purchase discounts for sales promotions, premiums, or fund-raisers, please
contact Osborne/**McGraw-Hill** at the above address.

**Nortel Networks: The Complete Reference**

234567890 DOC DOC 019876543210
Book P/N 0-07-212271-4   and   CD P/N 0-07-212028-2
parts of
ISBN 0-07-212027-4

| | |
|---|---|
| **Publisher** | **Proofreader** |
| Brandon A. Nordin | Valerie Perry |
| **Associate Publisher and Editor-in-Chief** | **Indexer** |
| Scott Rogers | David Heiret |
| **Acquisitions Editor** | **Computer Designers** |
| Wendy Rinaldi | Jani Beckwith |
| | Roberta Steele |
| | Gary Corrigan |
| **Acquisitions Coordinator** | |
| Monika Faltiss | **Illustrators** |
| | Beth Young |
| **Technical Editor** | Brian Wells |
| Toby Velte | Robert Hanson |
| **Copy Editor** | |
| Bill McManus | |

This book was composed with Corel VENTURA™ Publisher.

For my wife, Kim

## About the Author ...

James Knapp is a System Quality Assurance Engineer at Nortel Networks. He worked for several years as a Senior Support Engineer acting as one of the primary escalation paths for frame, cell, and third-layer switching, with a focus on ATM technologies. He holds Nortel Networks Certification in Routing, Switching, and Shared Media. Mr. Knapp has been involved in the networking industry for six years, during which time he has also had extensive experience with multi-protocol routing, and wide area technologies such as frame relay and ISDN. He can be reached at jknapp@nortelnetworks.com.

# Acknowledgments

I would like to thank everyone in the Technical Support Center over at Technology Park in Billerica, Massachusetts, who assisted on this book—in particular, Kim Moses and David Callahan for their invaluable help in putting together the chapters on routing, Bridget O'Rourke for her input regarding the material on OSPF, Tai Ngo for his assistance reviewing the ATM material, and Ragho Mahalingam for reviewing some of the Token Ring chapters. Thanks also to Toby Velte for reviewing each one of these chapters, which was no small job, and to Dan Tsoukalas and Don Fitzreiter for all the hours of testing they put in with me.

A big nod of thanks to the Nortel Networks legal department for supporting this endeavor and graciously giving permission to use release notes, screen shots, all the product-specific information, and everything else I asked them for. Last, a big thanks to all the women and men over at Osborne/McGraw-Hill, who labored with me on this book; it was a big job, with a lot of effort and understanding on everyone's part over an extended period of time. I believe the end result was well worth our combined efforts.

# Contents

## Part I

### An Overview of Networking

**Part II**

**Ethernet on Nortel Networks**

**Part III**

**The Accelar Layer 3 Switch**

**Part IV**

**ATM Technologies**

**Part VII**

**Internetworking with Nortel Networks**

## Part VIII

## Appendixes

# Introduction

This book is about enterprise switching and internetworking and, specifically, enterprise switching and internetworking on the Nortel Networks enterprise platforms (formerly known as Bay Networks). The book was conceived with a dual mission: to provide an in-depth explanation of some of the LAN architectures and protocols, and also to provide a guide to implementing these networking architectures and configuring the specific protocols on the Nortel Networks equipment. This book was created for anyone owning Nortel Networks enterprise products or anyone planning to implement these products in a production network.

The chapters begin at a basic level, then work their way toward more advanced technologies and more detailed coverage of the different protocols. The first chapters cover networking basics, such as the OSI model; basic ethernet (including bridging, switching, and Spanning Tree); token ring (including basic ring operation and concepts of the Token Ring protocol); third-layer switching technology, including protocol-based VLANs, IP-subnet VLANs, and 802.1Q frame tagging; and ATM switching, including basic ATM technology, Permanent Virtual Circuits (PVC), and concepts of connection-oriented technology. Later chapters go more in depth, covering token ring source-route bridging in a switched and routed environment and internetworking protocols such as Open Shortest Path First (OSPF), the Routing Information Protocol (RIP), and RIP version 2 on both the Nortel router platform as well as the Accelar third-layer switching platform. ATM protocols such as LAN Emulation (LANE), LANEv2, Quality of Service (QoS), and the Interim Inter-Switch Protocol (IISP) are also covered. Discussion of the Private Network to Network Interface (PNNI) includes a detailed description of PNNI functioning at all three levels of hierarchy with examples, and Multi-Protocol Over ATM (MPOA) includes an in-depth description of MPOA virtual routing and internetworking-to-ATM address resolutions. In addition, though not yet implemented on the Nortel Networks ATM platforms, a discussion of the LANE Network to Network Interface (LNNI) is included for future use.

Each topic is first covered as a protocol or technology, and multiple examples, diagrams, example sniffer trace output, and packet formats are included. Configuration sections follow, describing how each protocol is configured on the Nortel Networks platforms using configuration utilities such as Site Manager, Device Manager, and SpeedView. Each configuration section is then followed by a troubleshooting section, which includes such information as useful CLI commands and how to interpret their output, useful Technician Interface (TI) and script commands, as well as numerous tips and suggestions. In addition, the CD contains an archive of release notes for the Nortel router, the Accelar, and the Centillion ATM switching platforms, example configuration files, and example sniffer trace files.

In all cases, unless otherwise specified, the latest code versions and management application versions were used in all examples found in this book at the time the examples were taken. For the Centillion 100/50/5000BH family, code version 4.0 and SpeedView version 4.0 were used; for the router product line, Site Manager 7.10 and BayRS 13.10 were used; and for the Accelar product line, code version 2.0 and Device Manager 2.0 were used. All screen shots and CLI output for these devices reflect these code versions unless otherwise specified.

If you wish to contact me regarding the book for any reason, please do not hesitate to email me at jknapp@nortelnetworks.com.

The Complete Reference

Nortel Networks

# Part I

## An Overview of Networking

# Chapter 1

## Networking
## and the OSI Model

In order for different local area network (LAN) and wide area network (WAN) technologies to interact together, standards need to be in place to ensure interoperability. Vendors of different networking technologies must adhere to these standards so that the multitude of networking equipment functions together correctly. A wide variety of standards are already in place for technologies such as Ethernet, token ring, Fiber Distributed Data Interface (FDDI), and Asynchronous Transfer Mode (ATM), and new standards are being created continually as technology advances.

## The Seven-Layer OSI Model

The Open Systems Interconnection (OSI) model, formulated by the International Standards Organization (ISO), defines the seven different networking layers (see Figure 1-1).

The purpose of this model is to define how information from a user application, such as e-mail or a web browser, should be converted into a physical signal for transport across the LAN or WAN, and then converted back again for use at the application layer on the receiving side. The OSI model describes the seven networking layers and the functions of each, but it doesn't define the specific manner in which these layer functions work, because that varies depending on the networking architecture being used.

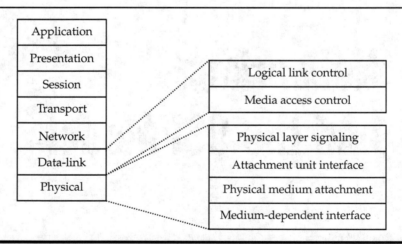

**Figure 1-1.** *The seven-layer OSI model*

# Physical Layer (Layer 1)

The first layer of the OSI model is the *physical layer*, which defines how data should pass over the physical medium, and how that data should be encoded at the bit level. Included in the physical layer are the physical medium, including cabling types and pinouts, voltage levels, and physical transmitters and receivers. Physical mediums include coaxial cable, twisted-pair cable, fiber optics, and wireless.

As is shown in Figure 1-1, the physical layer is divided into four sections:

- **Physical layer signaling (PLS)**   Defines how the signaling should be performed
- **Attachment unit interface (AUI)**   Defines the transceiver cable specifications
- **Physical medium attachment (PMA)**   Defines the actual transceiver specifications
- **Medium-dependent interface (MDI)**   Specifies the actual connection between the transceiver and the specific cable type the transceiver is designed for

An example of a physical layer device is a *repeater*, which simply refreshes the incoming signal and repeats it, increasing the overall distance that the signal can travel before degrading beyond use.

# Data-Link Layer (Layer 2)

The *data-link layer* is responsible for transmission, flow control, and error detection, so that data received by the lower layers is screened for potential problems before being passed to the higher layers. The data-link layer is broken into two sublayers (see Figure 1-1):

- **Logical link control (LLC)**   Handles the interface between the upper layers, and connection to the physical media type. The LLC, which is defined in the Institute of Electrical and Electronics Engineers (IEEE) 802.2 standard, provides a common interface between the upper layers and the particular network architecture.
- **Media access control (MAC)**   Responsible for receiving data from the LLC and actually encapsulating the data into the correct packet format for transmission onto the physical media. The MAC layer first determines whether the physical media is available for transmission, and then determines whether retransmission is necessary, due to a collision or other failure. The receiving MAC is responsible for error checking and passing the data to the LLC.

# Network Layer (Layer 3)

The *network layer* is responsible for *logical addressing*, which involves mapping logical addresses to MAC-layer addresses so that devices can intercommunicate. Layer 3 also is responsible for determining a packet's destination and making sure that packets are correctly routed through the network. The Internet Protocol (IP) is an example of a protocol that exists at the network layer.

# Transport Layer (Layer 4)

The *transport layer* is responsible for repackaging long messages into a series of smaller packages (if necessary), and then sequencing these packages so that they can be reassembled at the receiving end. Layer 4 also is responsible for determining the packet size, based on the amount of data being sent, as well as the network architecture being used (Ethernet, FDDI, and so forth). When the transport layer receives data from the network layer, it makes sure that the frame sequence is in order and that the sequence doesn't have any duplicate or missing frames. Other transport layer responsibilities include error recognition, error recovery, and sending receipt acknowledgements.

# Session Layer (Layer 5)

The *session layer* is responsible for allowing two remote applications to establish a session between them. This includes setting up, maintaining, and ending such a session, as well as regulating data flow for the sending and receiving sides. The session layer defines the rules associated with any such session, as well as determining and monitoring the service type (best effort, required acknowledgements, handshaking, and so forth).

# Presentation Layer (Layer 6)

The *presentation layer* receives information from the application layer and provides intermediary services, such as data compression and data encryption. It also handles the translation between different file formats.

# Application Layer (Layer 7)

The highest layer, the *application layer*, involves the actual applications used across the LAN, which can include e-mail systems and database applications. The application layer represents the actual application manipulated by the user.

# Networking Architectures

A variety of LAN and WAN architectures have been developed over the years to transport network data. Some of the common LAN types include Ethernet, token ring, FDDI, and ATM. Some of the popular WAN methods include frame relay, T-1 lines, Integrated Services Digital Network (ISDN), and digital subscriber line (DSL). Each network type has its own advantages and disadvantages; Ethernet, token ring, and ATM are covered in this book, along with managing LAN traffic with switches and bridges, and internetworking these technologies with routers and routing switches.

## Ethernet

The Ethernet 802.3 standard, which is perhaps the most common networking architecture, began to be developed by Xerox in 1973, as a bus topology data-passing system. Later, in 1980, the first version of Ethernet (as we know it today) was released by a partnership of Digital, Intel, and Xerox (DIX), although the current 802.3 standard wasn't approved until 1983. The original Ethernet network consisted of physical segments of 10Base5 coaxial cable, fitted with transceiver taps, which provided connectivity to individual stations, as well as devices such as repeaters, bridges, and routers in a bus-type architecture.

Since its conception, Ethernet has evolved from the thick-coax backbone to the chassis-based, stand-alone, hub-and-switch implementations that are commonly used today. Ethernet has also grown from its original 10Mbps capacity to include 100Mbps, as well as 1000Mbps, with support for both half-duplex communications (in which data is transmitted and received in turn) and full-duplex communications (in which data is received and transmitted simultaneously). Ethernet has also evolved to run over a very wide variety of media types, such as thin-coax, twisted-pair, fiber optics, and microwave.

Ethernet supports a theoretical maximum of 1,024 end stations per segment. However, depending on the types of network traffic and their bandwidth requirements, you generally are advised to use a more conservative number. You can manage Ethernet traffic by separating individual segments with devices such as bridges, switches, and routers.

## Token Ring

First established in the 1970s, token ring became the network architecture of choice for IBM's Systems Network Architecture (SNA) protocol. As its name implies, token ring is a token-passing, ring-based system, in which an individual station must have possession of a MAC frame, called the *token,* before it can transmit data. Token ring is designed to run at speeds of 4 or 16Mbps, with full-duplex token ring designed to run at speeds up to 32Mbps.

Token ring is rated to run over a variety of different media types, including shielded twisted-pair (STP), unshielded twisted-pair (UTP), and fiber optics. Token ring supports a maximum of approximately 250 stations per ring and, as with Ethernet, rings (segments) can be separated by bridges, switches, or routers to manage network traffic more efficiently.

# Fiber Distributed Data Interface (FDDI)

The Fiber Distributed Data Interface is described in the XT39.5 ANSI specification. Like token ring, FDDI is a ring-based, token-passing system consisting of a dual-ring system in which one ring is primary and the other ring is secondary. Stations in an FDDI network are either single-attached, to the primary or secondary ring only, or dual-attached to both rings simultaneously. In the event of a ring failure, the primary and secondary rings may be wrapped together, ensuring the ring's integrity.

FDDI utilizes a token-passing system that is more efficient than token ring and that has greater bandwidth: 100Mbps compared to token ring's 4, 16, or 32Mbps. For these reasons, as well as the additional cost associated with it, FDDI is generally considered to be a backbone technology.

Despite its name, FDDI is also rated to run over copper (sometimes referred to as CDDI, or FDDI over copper). FDDI rings can be separated by bridges, switches, or routers.

# Asynchronous Transfer Mode (ATM)

ATM is a connection-oriented network architecture, in which point-to-point or point-to-multipoint circuits are built end to end throughout the network, to pass data between two end systems. These circuits consist of pairings of virtual paths and virtual circuits, to identify data flows uniquely throughout the ATM mesh. ATM is, relatively speaking, a recent development, and is still being developed today.

Unlike Ethernet, token ring, and FDDI, ATM doesn't use varying sized frames, but instead uses fixed-sized 53-byte cells to transmit data. ATM connections provide a bandwidth of 155Mbps (OC3), 622Mbps (OC12), 100Mbps (TAXI—Transparent Asynchronous Transmitter/Receiver Interface) and 45Mbps (DS3). Other implementations are being developed to provide even greater bandwidth. ATM is rated to run over fiber optics and twisted-pair, and the possibility of wireless ATM is currently being studied.

ATM functions in a variety of different ways, including the following:

■ **Native ATM**   Devices utilize ATM addresses to route data throughout the switched network.

■ **LAN Emulation (LANE)**   If ATM is being used in conjunction with legacy LAN technologies, such as Ethernet or token ring, LANE may be used to handle the broadcast and multicast functions, which aren't inherent to ATM. LANE currently doesn't support FDDI networks.

## Wide Area

Passing data from one location to another, geographically remote location can be accomplished in a variety of ways; T-1 and fractional T-1, leased 56K or 128K lines, frame relay, DSL, ISDN, E-1 (in Europe), and cable modems, to name a few. ATM can also be utilized as a wide area technology.

# Networking Components

In keeping with the OSI model, different networking components function at different layers. For instance, repeaters operate at the physical layer (Layer 1) of the OSI model, whereas routers operate at the network layer (Layer 3). Some hybrids, such as the routing switch, have the capability of operating at different levels simultaneously. Each networking component has a unique purpose, and each has its own circumstances in which it is best used.

In general, devices such as bridges, switches, and routers are used not only for the transport of network data, but also for the organization and management of LAN and WAN traffic. Each technology has a limited bandwidth; thus, in practice, limiting the scope of network traffic is a good idea, so that it goes only where it specifically needs to go. This reduces unnecessary overhead and prevents bandwidth from being wasted on data that will never be used. Some of the devices used to accomplish traffic management and limiting the scope of network traffic are discussed in the following sections.

## Repeaters

A *repeater* is a Layer 1 device whose only purpose is to revitalize incoming signals and then repeat the signal out one or more ports. Each data impulse can travel only a certain distance before the signal degrades to the point where it can no longer be interpreted at the receiving side; the exact distance depends on the technology being used (Ethernet, token ring, FDDI, and so forth) and the media type over which the signal is traveling (twisted-pair, coax, fiber optics, and so forth). This distance can be increased, in most cases, by positioning a repeater device to clean up and boost the signal, and then send it off again.

The maximum distance that the signal can travel is generally defined by the protocols used by the technology. For instance, an Ethernet impulse must make its round trip (from sender to receiver, and then back to sender) in 51.2μs. This is the window that the Ethernet specification allots for the sender to determine whether a collision has taken place. A collision requires retransmission of the lost frame, so the sender must be able to determine whether the last frame transmitted was received, before it sends the next frame.

Initially, repeaters generally were stand-alone devices, used to increase the distance of transmissions over traditional 10Base5 coaxial backbones, connecting them via unpopulated links known as inter-repeater links (IRL). Today, repeater functionality exists in hubs, switches, and other networking devices.

If a repeater detects 32 consecutive collisions, it partitions the port upon which the collisions were received. This is to protect the rest of the network from the problems occurring on a single port, because a straight repeater normally forwards all traffic, including collisions. If a port enters a partitioned state, it is separated from the rest of the network and no signal will pass through it. Each time that a transmission is destined for the partitioned port, the repeater attempts to send; if a collision occurs on that port, the port remains in a partitioned state. If the transmission is successful, the port automatically "unpartitions" and rejoins the network. The following are the two basic repeater types:

- **Class I repeaters**   Incur a 168-bit time delay between the input and output ports; generally, used when varying physical types are being used, such as 10BaseT in combination with 100BaseT or 100BaseFL.

- **Class II repeaters**   Incur a 92-bit time delay (maximum) between the input and output ports; generally, used when a single physical type is used.

# Bridges

*Bridges* provide a way to expand a LAN beyond the scope of its local limitations. For instance, a token ring may support a maximum of 250 stations. A bridge placed between two such rings enables the maximum number of stations in the network to be doubled, to 500 stations, while still allowing communication between the two rings. Likewise, in an Ethernet network, bridges can be used to establish intercommunication between separate segments, for example, 200 users on a single segment works much less efficiently than four segments of 50 users each, interconnected by Ethernet bridges.

The specifics of how bridges make their forwarding or filtering decisions, as well as the specifics of the Spanning Tree Protocol (STP), used to prevent network loops in bridged networks, are covered in Chapter 2 for Ethernet, and in Chapter 26 for token ring.

## Store-and-Forward Bridges

*Store-and-forward bridges* receive and store the entire packet before forwarding, if the packet is to be forwarded. After the store-and-forward bridge receives a packet in its entirety, it checks the frame for errors before sending it out to the appropriate interface. Consequently, by examining each packet, store-and-forward bridges add an increased propagation delay, but they prevent the possible propagation of errors and corrupted frames.

## Cut-Through Bridges

*Cut-through bridges* forward frames the instant that the filter or forward decision can be made. If the proper entries already exist in the bridge's forwarding table, a cut-through bridge begins forwarding the frame as soon as the destination address is known, without performing any error checking. Cut-through bridges are faster for this reason, but they don't prevent the propagation of potentially corrupt frames.

## Translational Bridges

*Translational bridges* can be used to interconnect LANs of different types, such as Ethernet and token ring. Translational bridges perform frame conversion between the different LAN types and make filter or forwarding decisions for bridges; translational bridges perform these actions in such a way that the bridging functions and the translations are invisible to the end stations on either LAN.

# Switches

In concept, switches are very similar to bridges; each uses a forwarding table of MAC addresses to determine where each address is located and, based on that information, whether incoming frames should be filtered or forwarded. Switches can be regarded in many ways as multiport bridges, although now, they often are positioned more as a concentrator would be. Switches employ the same filter-or-forward method as bridges do, on a port-by-port basis.

Although a switch port usually is similar in appearance to a shared-media hub or concentrator, each switch port acts as a bridge port, and collisions aren't propagated beyond the local bridged port. This places each individual port in its own collision domain, whereas the switch as a whole remains in a single broadcast domain (provided virtual LANs, or VLANs, aren't being used). Each switch port also participates in the Spanning Tree Protocol (if enabled), which means that redundant connections may exist between switches.

Switches generally used to be positioned as core devices, hosting a series of separate hubs (segments). However, as the per-port cost of switches continually declines, switches more commonly are being used to host individual users, replacing shared-media hubs altogether.

## Virtual LANs (VLANs)

Another innovation of switching technology is the concept of the virtual LAN. VLANs are logical broadcast domains, and can be user-configured to allow a single physical switch to be divided into several logical broadcast domains. As with any separate broadcast domains, communicating from one VLAN to another requires a router.

Prior to the 802.1Q frame-tagging standard, VLAN implementation varied from vendor to vendor, resulting in a mix of different, proprietary VLAN methods, including Bay Networks's LattisSpan technology. With the standardization of VLANs, 802.1Q VLAN implementations can function across multiple vendors.

# Routers

Routers operate at the network layer (Layer 3) of the OSI model. Routers are much more complex than bridges or switches, and are used to separate broadcast domains within the network. In a traditional bridged or switched network, broadcasts are propagated out all ports; this is the method used initially to discover unknown destination address locations and to ensure that broadcast traffic is received by all stations in the broadcast domain. Broadcasts are not propagated by routers. A multiport router, upon receiving an Address Resolution Protocol (ARP) broadcast, for example, won't flood the packet. Instead, the multiport router first uses the Layer 3 protocol information (IP in this case) to determine with which network the destination is associated, and then it initiates its own ARP broadcast, if the destination network is associated with one of its local interfaces, or forwards the packet to the next hop on the way to the destination network. This cuts down tremendously on the amount of broadcast traffic in the network as a whole, and directs broadcasts only where they need to go (and no further).

Routers support a variety of Layer 3 protocols, such as IP, IPX, DECnet, and AppleTalk, and provide a way to organize LAN traffic at the network layer. Routers also utilize their own Layer 3 routing protocols, to intercommunicate network information to one another, ensuring that data arrives at its proper destination in the most efficient manner. Such routing protocols include Open Shortest Path First (OSPF), the Routing Information Protocol (RIP), and RIP v2, which are covered in Chapters 32 and 33.

Routers can also facilitate the translation between dissimilar network architectures, such as Ethernet, token ring, FDDI, and ATM. This translation can occur at the network layer or, if bridging services are supported on the router, at the data-link layer.

## Protocol-based Traffic Management

Different protocols operate in different ways, but each provides a logical addressing system that maps to the hardware address at the MAC layer. This allows packets to be routed through the network according to the logical addressing scheme, which, in turn, allows packets to be routed over greater distances while minimizing the amount of broadcast traffic within each domain.

### Wide Area Routing

Routers generally are used for wide area connections, too. However, because wide area bandwidth generally is limited, only traffic that is destined for the remote network should be sent across the connection, which means that broadcast traffic associated with each domain should be excluded, generally speaking. Wide area connections come in a wide variety, including point-to-point connections over T-1 lines, or other leased lines, such as 56K or 128K lines, frame relay connections, and ISDN.

## Layer 3 Switching

Layer 3 switches, sometimes referred to as *routing switches*, are a relatively recent development in networking technology. As its name implies, the Layer 3 switch is a hybrid device, combining the functionality of a router and a Layer 2 switch. The Accelar is an example of a routing switch.

The idea behind Layer 3 switching is to make the device Layer 3 protocol-aware and capable of steering traffic correctly based on Layer 3 information, but prevent it from actually going into the third layer of the packet, thus avoiding the overhead associated with true routing. The Accelar product line also supports true routing and port-based VLANs. Layer 3 switches generally use the 802.1Q frame-tagging specification.

### Port-based VLANs

Layer 3 protocols can be kept separate by issuing them into port-based VLANs. A port-based VLAN is not protocol-aware, but different protocols (including different subnets) can be segmented into these separate broadcast domains, while a router may be used to route between them. By using frame tagging, the traffic can be kept separated, even when passing from switch to switch, to be distributed to the proper VLAN at the receiving switch based on its tag. For example, this allows users on IP subnet 150.50.10.0 in VLAN 1 to communicate with other users on the same subnet, even though they may be on different switches, as long as they are also in VLAN 1.

### Protocol-based VLANs

Protocol-based VLANs actually use Layer 3 information to route packets through the switched network; by examining the Protocol ID in each frame, the VLAN can determine which protocol the frame uses, and thus accomplish frame distribution at Layer 2 of the OSI model based on this Layer 3 information. For example, a Layer 3 switch configured with an IP VLAN, an IPX VLAN, and an AppleTalk VLAN could be configured with a port that is a member of all three VLANs. If a segment containing groups of users (each of which utilizes one of these three protocols) is connected to this port, then incoming traffic on this port will be distributed to the appropriate VLAN based on Protocol ID.

## Layer 3 Switching by IP Subnet

The Accelar routing switch functionality enables traffic to be distributed both by IP Protocol ID (0800) and, after the protocol is identified as IP, by subnet. This allows incoming traffic to be distributed not only into different VLANs, based on their different protocol types, but also within the IP protocol, based on an even more specific designation. For example, IP subnet 150.50.10.0 can be distributed into VLAN 1, and IP subnet 150.50.20.0 can be distributed into VLAN 2, without the use of a router to make that decision. The specifics of this function are covered in Chapter 9.

## Virtual Router Services

The Accelar product line also includes traditional routing services, in the form of an internal virtual routing entity, capable of routing between VLANs, isolated routing ports, and any combination of the two. This entity supports protocol distribution at the second layer, for traffic management between switches, combined with true Layer 3 routing.

The
# Complete
# Reference

Nortel
Networks

# Chapter 2

## Ethernet Basics

15

Ethernet is the most common local area network (LAN) type in existence today; it was conceived in 1973, and officially approved as a standard by the Institute of Electrical and Electronics Engineers (IEEE) standards board in 1983. Its simplicity, flexibility, and overall cost-effectiveness have enabled it to remain in common use, even in today's era of rapid technological change.

## Ethernet Specifications

The specifics of Ethernet are defined in the 802.3 Ethernet specification, in which it is described as *Carrier Sense Multiple Access with Collision Detection (CSMA/CD)*. This means that in Ethernet, unlike a token-passing system or connection-oriented technology such as Asynchronous Transfer Mode (ATM), the transmission medium is shared by all end stations, and stations transmit whenever they detect that the medium is available for use.

Ethernet is a *broadcast medium*, which means that when one station transmits, the transmission is seen by every device on the local segment. For this reason, Ethernet end stations are aware of when another station is transmitting, and when the transmission medium is available for their own use. This is known as *Carrier Sense*; Ethernet stations monitor the wire to sense whether or not they can transmit. If the path becomes available, and the station has something to transmit, it does so at that time. Unlike token ring or other token-passing systems, Ethernet isn't a turn-based system—Ethernet stations transmit the moment the medium becomes available. This is why Ethernet is also referred to as *Multiple Access*, because many stations may access the system simultaneously in a first-come, first-serve fashion.

In a CSMA-CD system, an obvious problem results: Because no rules are in place for any sort of turn-based system, two Ethernet stations may have data to transmit, sense that the wire is available, and transmit simultaneously. Since Ethernet is a broadcast medium, and transmissions reach every portion of the local system, the two transmissions will collide, and the resulting voltage spike, though small, is enough to corrupt each transmission beyond use, causing loss of the data from each station. This is known as a *collision*. Should a collision occur, both signals are lost. A certain amount of collisions are normal in an Ethernet environment; given the nature of Ethernet, it is inevitable that eventually more than one station will attempt to transmit simultaneously. When a collision occurs, it is detected by all stations, and each "backs off" from transmitting for a random period of time to ensure that the line is clear, then data flow resumes. On a busy segment, this may occur frequently; however, unless performance begins to degrade, or collisions begin to approach 10 percent or so of the total network traffic, collisions may be considered a normal part of Ethernet and not necessarily something to be concerned about.

From a physical standpoint, Ethernet networks are divided into groupings called *segments*; this concept goes back to when Ethernet networks consisted of 10Base5 thick-coaxial backbones, where each backbone constituted a segment. An Ethernet end station transmitting onto the backbone was received not only by the destination station, but by every station on the segment—although the transmission was processed only by the destination station. Each Ethernet end station that was connected to the segment received every transmission sent by every other station.

This concept is still true today, and even though the 10Base5 backbone has been replaced with the now-familiar collapsed backbone hubs and switches, the idea of the "segment" as an Ethernet system in which all stations share a common collision and broadcast domain is maintained and commonly used.

# Ethernet Addressing

Ethernet devices are addressed with unique hardware media access control (MAC) addresses, which are used to identify each host on the network at the data-link layer, and are required to ensure that a transmission is received at its destination. The three basic types of addressing schemes are unicast addresses, multicasts, and broadcasts.

## Unicast Addressing

A *unicast* is a frame that is directed to a single, specific destination. During initial Ethernet communications, a broadcast is transmitted first, to determine the MAC address of the destination station. After this address is determined, the specific MAC address is used as the destination address for any further communication to that device.

## Multicast Addressing

*Multicasts* are transmissions that are directed to more than one station, but not to all of them. Multicasts use special multicast group addresses, as do certain routing protocols, such as Routing Information Protocol (RIP) v2 or Open Shortest Path First (OSPF). For instance, the multicast MAC-level address for a RIPv2 packet is 01-00-5e-00-00-09. Multicasts can be identified by the fact that the least significant bit of the first byte will be flipped from a 0 to a 1 (making 00 a 01, as in the previous example).

Multicast addressing can be extremely useful, as in the example with RIPv2 updates. By using the multicast address of 01-00-5e-00-00-09, only router interfaces configured for RIPv2 will process the incoming updates, whereas a broadcast packet, such as a RIPv1 packet, is destined for all destination addresses, and therefore must be processed by all. Other network devices will discard the RIPv1 updates, but the overhead still exists. Likewise, multicasts provide a convenient method for reaching a specific group without unnecessarily involving users for whom the transmission is not meant.

# Broadcast Addressing

A *broadcast* is an address that designates that the packet in question is destined for all devices. A broadcast is indicated by a MAC address of all Fs: FF-FF-FF-FF-FF-FF. Broadcasts are an important part of Ethernet functionality; for instance, in Internet Protocol (IP), the Address Resolution Protocol (ARP) uses a broadcast to determine the MAC address of a destination IP address. By sending a packet to the destination IP address while using the all F's broadcast MAC, every local station receives the packet. The local station possessing the correct IP address responds with its true MAC address.

Too much unnecessary broadcast traffic causes some overhead, so the number and scope of broadcasts can be controlled through network design and the strategic use of routers.

# Ethernet Frame Format

Ethernet frame types come in a few different varieties, which are described in this section. Ethernet frames do, however, share certain traits in common. The basic Ethernet frame consists of the fields shown in Figure 2-1 and described in the following list:

- **Preamble**   A bit pattern of 10101010, which is 7 bytes long. This pattern is recognizable by all Ethernet devices and indicates the beginning of a packet. The Preamble also allows for packet timing at the receiving station.

- **Start Frame Delimiter (SFD)**   Follows the Preamble, and basically indicates that the Preamble portion of the frame has ended, thus commencing the actual frame information. It uses a pattern of 10101011 (1 byte total). The 11 at the end of the SFD indicates the end of the SFD itself and the beginning of the frame information.

- **Destination Address (DA)**   The MAC address of the station to which the frame is destined (6 bytes long).

- **Source Address (SA)**   The MAC address of the station that is sending the frame (6 bytes long).

- **Length (Type)**   Indicates the overall length of the frame's Data field. The Length field itself is 2 bytes long. Depending on the frame type, this may also be referred to as the *Type* field.

- **Data**   The actual data contained in the frame. The Data field can be anywhere from 46 bytes to 1,500 bytes long. With an overhead of 18 bytes, this results in a minimum packet size of 64 bytes and a maximum size of 1,518 bytes. If the frame's data is less than 46 bytes, a *pad bit pattern* is used to fill the rest of the space.

- **Cyclic Redundancy Check (CRC)**   Also referred to as the Frame Check Sequence (FCS), the CRC is 4 bytes long. This field indicates the overall frame size, so that the frame can be checked to ensure that it has not experienced any corruption or loss during transmission.

| Preamble | Start Frame Delimeter (SFD) | Destination Address (DA) | Source Address (SA) | Length (type) | Data | Cyclic Redundancy Check (CRC) |
|---|---|---|---|---|---|---|
| 7 bytes | 1 byte | 6 bytes | 6 bytes | 2 bytes | 46-1500 bytes | 4 bytes |

**Figure 2-1.**   *The Ethernet frame*

# Ethernet Frame Types

The four basic Ethernet frame types are Ethernet_II, 802.3, Ethernet_802.2, and Ethernet_SNAP.

## Ethernet_II

Ethernet_II frames are actually the original Ethernet frame type; the Ethernet_II designation comes from the fact that, although the frame type precedes some of the other frame types, it came after some of the earlier implementations, prior to the IEEE standards committee's standardization of the 802.3 Ethernet specification. Ethernet_II was most notable for the existence of the Type field, which contained the protocol discriminator. This was later abandoned in favor of the Length field, whereas the protocol ID was indicated in an 802.2 header.

## 802.3

The 802.3 frame, sometimes called the 802.3 raw frame, originated with Novell. It doesn't contain a third-level protocol identifier in an 802.2 header and, as a result, can be used only with the Internetwork Packet Exchange (IPX) protocol.

## Ethernet_802.2

The 802.2 frames arrived after the standardization of Ethernet by the IEEE standards body. When this occurred, Ethernet framing was modified slightly; the 2-byte protocol ID (known in Ethernet_II as the Type field) was removed and replaced with the Length field. The protocol ID at that point was moved to the 802.3 packet in an 802.2 header. Because this changed the intrinsic design of the frame, it got a new designation: the Ethernet_802.2 frame.

## Ethernet_SNAP

The Ethernet_SNAP (Sub-Network Access Protocol) packet came about after the arrival of the Ethernet_802.2 frame type. Because the 802.2 header is 3 bytes long, a poor alignment of some third-layer protocols resulted. In addition, because only 7 bits were available for defining the protocol type, an Ethernet_802.2 frame can specify only up to 128 different protocols.

The Ethernet_SNAP frame uses a single 802.2 protocol ID of 0xAA, which labels the frame as being a SNAP frame. The third-layer protocol ID in this case is indicated by a 5-byte header. The first 3 bytes define the organizational unit identifier (OUI), and the last 2 bytes define the actual protocol itself.

# Collision Domains

An Ethernet collision domain is confined to a single segment; whereas a repeater propagates collisions to let other stations know that the collision has occurred, a bridge, switch, or router does not. The *collision domain* defines the boundary of the shared environment—each station within a single collision domain must contend for use of that Ethernet. Once the total number of stations utilizing the segment becomes too great, the number of resulting collisions increases to the point where performance degrades. If collisions begin to approach a significant percentage of network traffic (10 percent), additional segments may need to be added, separated by a bridge, switch, or router, to separate the domains.

# Broadcast Domains

A *broadcast domain* is the extent to which a broadcast will travel in the network. Unlike collisions, a bridge or switch forwards broadcasts. Traffic is managed through filter and forward techniques, but the initial destination location is determined through a broadcast. A broadcast will extend to every portion of the network, blocked only by a router, which will not forward broadcast packets.

# Shared Ethernet

A hub-based environment is often referred to as *shared Ethernet* or *shared media*. A *hub* generally consists of an internal Ethernet segment and possibly several internal segments, depending on the implementation. If more than one segment exists on the backplane, an external bridge or switch is often required to intercommunicate between them; hubs provide repeater functionality on a port-by-port basis, but not bridge functionality. Hub ports do not participate in the spanning tree algorithm.

Each segment in this case remains a single collision domain, so a 24-port, stand-alone, shared-Ethernet hub provides 24 ports that share the same bandwidth and resources. In a hub environment, every attached end station sees every transmission that occurs through the hub. A hub constitutes a single broadcast domain.

# Switched Ethernet

In contrast to the hub, a *switch* provides a series of segments that are interconnected with a switched core; for instance, a 24-port switch provides 24 segments, which are switched between by the core processor. Each port is its own collision domain in the case of a switch, and each port participates in the spanning tree algorithm.

Switched Ethernet can also provide virtual LAN (VLAN) functionality. Although switches, by default, provide a single broadcast domain, many switches may be broken into several VLANs, which constitute logical broadcast domains within a single physical device (see Figure 2-2). VLANs were standardized under the 802.1Q standard.

# Using Routers to Separate Broadcast Domains

*Routers*, regardless of the third-layer protocol they are running, separate physical broadcast domains; a broadcast from one IP subnet, for example, will not be passed on by a router into another IP subnet. For this reason, broadcast traffic can be controlled through the strategic positioning of routers.

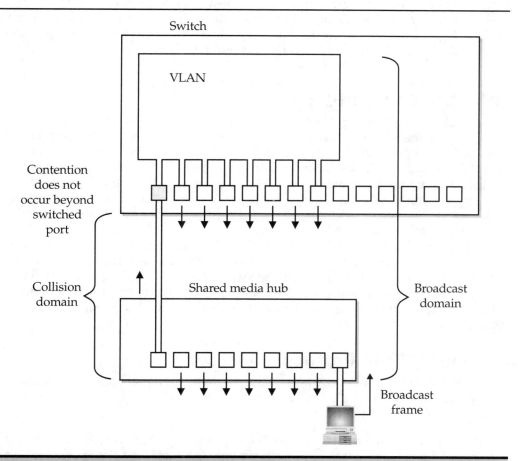

**Figure 2-2.** *Collision vs. broadcast domains. Collisions will not be propagated between collision domains, but broadcasts will. Neither collisions nor broadcasts will be propagated between broadcast domains.*

Some routers may also run *bridging services*, which allow nonroutable protocols to be passed. However, this also allows broadcasts to traverse the router, as long as the protocol in question hasn't been configured specifically on the router. For instance, if a router interface is configured for IP routing, as well as bridging services, it routes any incoming IP packets and bridges anything else.

## Using VLANs to Separate Broadcast Domains

Using a VLAN is another way to reduce the amount of broadcast traffic over the LAN. A VLAN creates a logical broadcast domain on a single physical device, where data from one VLAN will not pass into another VLAN. A router must be used to intercommunicate between VLANs. This concept adds flexibility when managing LAN traffic. In addition, with the advent of the 802.1Q frame-tagging standard, VLANs have significance beyond the local LAN, and separate broadcast domains can be created across the same physical infrastructure without the need for adding any additional devices.

# 802.1d Spanning Tree

When bridging or switching Ethernet, you must take care not to introduce a loop condition into the network. A *loop condition* arises when a packet travels a path that actually forms a physical loop (see Figure 2-3). This causes a condition in which a packet continually circles the Ethernet until its Time to Live (TTL) expires. If the frame is a broadcast frame, each time that it is received on a port, it is flooded out all other ports on the same device; since the packet continually loops, the repeating broadcast that results is referred to as a *broadcast storm*. Broadcast storms are capable of bringing down an entire Ethernet broadcast domain.

The Spanning Tree Protocol (STP) is responsible for the detection and resolution of network loops. If Spanning Tree detects a loop condition, it causes one of the paths involved to stop forwarding, to prevent the loop. If the primary path goes down, the blocked path begins forwarding. This also enables Spanning Tree to provide redundancy; if Spanning Tree is in place, an intentionally introduced network loop will provide a redundant path.

## The Spanning Tree Protocol

The Spanning Tree Protocol (STP) was created to detect and prevent the introduction of physical loops within the network. Loops are detrimental to a LAN environment for several reasons, including the following:

■ Bridges determine device locations by monitoring which port different source addresses are received on. A packet caught in a loop condition may be received on multiple bridge ports, thus associating that particular source MAC with more than one port.

■ Broadcasts may be triggered repeatedly if broadcast frames are caught in a network loop, continually being received on a certain port and therefore causing the receiving bridge or switch to flood the broadcast repeatedly.

The Spanning Tree Protocol uses control packets called *bridge protocol data units (BPDU)* to determine the presence of network loops. These packets are used both to determine the current Spanning Tree topology and to indicate topology changes that may occur in the network. If a loop is detected, the spanning tree algorithm determines which bridge and port should block, in order to break the loop. The blocked link in this case may be used as a redundant path; for example, if the forwarding link fails, the spanning tree algorithm (STA) will rerun, and the formerly blocked port will begin to forward in the event that the loop has been resolved.

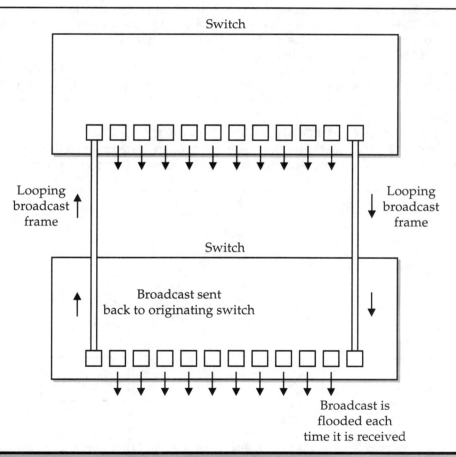

**Figure 2-3.**    *A network loop displaying the broadcast domain*

## Root Bridge

As bridges within the Ethernet network become aware of one another's presence through the distribution of BPDU packets, an election process begins, to determine which bridge will become the root bridge. The root bridge is determined by examining several pieces of information found within the BPDU. The bridge priority is checked first, and the bridge with the lowest priority indicator is automatically selected to be the root. If the priorities are equal, as they are by default, then the MAC address of each bridge is examined, and the bridge with the lowest MAC address is elected to be the root.

The root bridge is significant, because it acts as the root of the Spanning Tree network. When a network loop is detected, each bridge involved first must determine whether it should block. If it determines that it should block, it then must determine which port or ports should be blocked. To help make these determinations, the root bridge is used as a central point, where all bridges attempt to maintain a shortest path to the root. This assists in making blocking decisions, because if two possible paths exist, both of which may be blocked, the path with the shortest (lowest cost) path to the root will be left in a forwarding state.

An example of this is shown in Figure 2-4. Bridge A is the root bridge. Therefore, in the loop that exists between bridges A, B, and C, the connection between bridges B and C will be blocked, because a bridge won't block its direct path to the root bridge.

## Determining the Spanning Tree Topology

After determining the root bridge, the network topology is determined through the exchange of BPDUs, which are issued by the root bridge and propagated through the

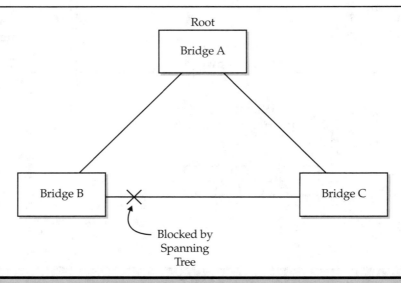

**Figure 2-4.**   *A Spanning Tree network with root bridge and blocking on correct ports*

network by other Spanning Tree bridges. The path cost to the root bridge is determined on a port-by-port basis, where the lowest-cost root path is the most desirable in the case of a loop condition. If two paths to the root exist, one of which must be blocked, and the cost to the root is equal on both ports, then the port ID is used to break the tie.

## Bridge Protocol Data Units (BPDU)

*Bridge protocol data units* are control packets sent by bridges and switches participating in the Spanning Tree Protocol. The unique multicast group MAC address of 01-80-C2-00-00-10 is used to intercommunicate between STP devices. Bridges send BPDUs out each STP interface in intervals of two seconds (by default) to this group address.

BPDUs use the frame format shown in the following illustration for Configuration BPDUs and Topology Change Notification BPDUs, the two BPDU types. The Destination Address is the multicast group address in this case, whereas the Source Address is the unique hardware address of the sending bridge.

| Configuration BPDU |
| --- |
| Protocol ID |
| Protocol Version Identifer |
| BPDU Type |
| Flags |
| Root ID |
| Root Path Cost |
| Bridge ID |
| Port ID |
| Message Age |
| Maximum Age |
| Hello Time |
| Forward Delay |

| Topology Change Notification BPDU |
| --- |
| Protocol ID |
| Protocol Version Identifier |
| BPDU Type |

## Configuration BPDUs

Configuration BPDUs indicate the current Spanning Tree topology. After the root bridge has been determined and the Spanning Tree portion of the network has spanned in accordance with the root bridge's location, Configuration BPDUs are continually sent out to validate the STP state. These messages include the MAC address of the root bridge, the cost associated with the transmitting interface to the root bridge, the bridge and bridge port identifiers, and the Spanning Tree–specific parameters associated with the transmitting bridge. The following are the specific fields:

- **Protocol ID**   Specifies the packet as being an Spanning Tree packet (2 bytes long). The protocol ID for Spanning Tree is 0000 0000 0000 0000.

- **Protocol Version Identifier**   Indicates the current Spanning Tree version. 802.1d Spanning Tree is designated with a version ID of 0000 0000.

- **BPDU Type**   Indicates whether the BPDU is a Configuration BPDU or a Topology Change Notification BPDU.

- **Flags**   Indicates Spanning Tree topology information, such as topology changes in the current STP state.

- **Root ID**   Identifies the current root bridge.

- **Root Path Cost**   Indicates the relative cost from the transmitting STP interface to the root bridge. Because this value is calculated by all transmitting STP interfaces, forwarding or blocking decisions can be made based on this value in the event of a network loop.

- **Bridge ID**   Identifies the transmitting bridge. This unique value is used to help determine whether a loop condition exists in the network.

- **Port ID**   Identifies specific STP interfaces on a particular bridge.

- **Message Age**   Indicates the relative age of the BPDU; if the Message Age reaches the Maximum Age indicator, the BPDU is considered to be no longer valid.

- **Maximum Age**   Indicates the maximum amount of time that a BPDU will be considered valid.

- **Hello Time**   Indicates the amount of time between the transmission of BPDU packets.

- **Forward Delay**   Indicates the amount of time that passes between determining that a port should be in a forwarding state and actually forwarding the data. This interval provides a buffer for the Spanning Tree Protocol to converge completely prior to going into a forwarding state.

## Topology Change Notification BPDUs

In the event that the Spanning Tree topology of the network changes, through the loss of a bridge or the failure of an individual Spanning Tree port, bridges within the network must be notified. A topology change necessitates rerunning the spanning tree algorithm, because the loss of a bridge or bridge port may alter paths to the root, result in a loss of the root itself, or require certain ports to alter their Spanning Tree state (blocking to forwarding, or forwarding to blocking).

A Topology Change Notification BPDU is issued by a designated bridge in response to a change in the Spanning Tree topology. When the root bridge receives this BPDU, it alters the Flags field in its Configuration BPDUs, informing other bridges in the network that a topology change has occurred. When this occurs, remote bridges must respond by clearing their tables and running the spanning tree algorithm again, to learn the new topology.

# Blocking vs. Forwarding

A Spanning Tree bridge attempts to block when it detects its own BPDU; upon seeing its own BPDU come back on another port, the bridge assumes a loop condition exists in the network, and thus begins its algorithm to determine which port should block and which should forward.

## Spanning Tree Port States

Spanning Tree ports transition between several Spanning Tree states during network operation, depending on the current STP state of the network. For instance, a port that is in a blocking state may transition into a forwarding state if a formerly active link goes down, depending on the network topology. The STP port states are as follows:

- ■ **Blocking**   The port will not pass any data. When an STP port first initializes, it enters a blocking state, by default, until the network topology can be determined and an informed decision can be made regarding what the port STP state should ultimately be. A forwarding port may also transition into a blocking state if a network loop is introduced into the network.

- ■ **Listening**   Entered before a blocking or forwarding decision can be made. No packets pass through the port at this time (technically, it's in a blocking state at this time, while the listening phase is executed). During this state, the port is monitored to see whether any Configuration BPDUs are received; if one is received and the port in question is neither defined as a designated port nor connected to the root, the port enters a blocking state. Otherwise, it transitions to the learning state.

- ■ **Learning**   No packets are forwarded by the port in question, but the port does begin to learn station addresses and place them in its database. It remains in this state until the Forward Delay time expires, at which point—unless it receives a Configuration BPDU with new information that may induce a blocking state—the port enters the forwarding state.

■ **Forwarding**    After the learning state is complete, the port begins to forward; in this state, it passes data normally and continues to learn addresses normally. A port remains in the forwarding state until it receives a BPDU that indicates a network loop has been introduced, at which point it immediately enters the blocking state, and the spanning tree algorithm is run again.

# Ethernet Speed and Duplex Modes

Initially, Ethernet ran at 10Mbps only, regardless of the media type. Since its conception, Ethernet has evolved to run at 100Mbps and 1000Mbps, too. Ethernet originally ran at *half-duplex* only, meaning that data could be transmitted and received only in turn, not simultaneously. *Full-duplex* operation is now supported on many Ethernet platforms, allowing devices to both send and receive simultaneously.

## 10Mbps Ethernet

The original Ethernet implementation, prior to standardization, ran at 3Mbps, which was increased to 10Mbps before becoming standardized, resulting in the Ethernet that is in widespread use today. Generally, 10Mbps Ethernet runs at half-duplex, but is capable of running in full-duplex operation. Half-duplex versus full-duplex operation is discussed in "Half-Duplex vs. Full Duplex," later in this chapter.

## 100Mbps Ethernet

100Mbps Ethernet has become very common for both twisted-pair and fiber connections. 100Mbps Ethernet differs from 10Mbps Ethernet only insofar as the bit time has been reduced by a factor of 10; this allows for faster transmission, while leaving the essential framing techniques and basic concepts of 10Mbps Ethernet essentially unchanged.

**802.3U AUTONEGOTIATION**    The advent of 100Mbps Ethernet enabled the development of *autonegotiation*, an optional portion of the Ethernet specification that allows interconnected Ethernet devices to determine one another's capabilities, so that the fastest, most efficient connection can be dynamically determined and then implemented. This includes both the speed at which the link will run and the duplex mode of operation.

Autonegotiation utilizes a *fast link pulse (FLP)*, a variation on the normal Ethernet link pulse used to check line status. The FLP signal is triggered when the link first initializes, and then is generated during times that the link is idle, so that the process is nonintrusive. When the FLP signal is transmitted, it contains information regarding the maximum speed and duplex at which the sending device will run.

**Note**    *Because autonegotiation is defined only for 10 and 100BaseT connections, fiber links do not use it.*

Autonegotiation allows opposite ends of a link to determine dynamically the optimal operating speed and duplex for the connection. However, the FLP information might not synchronize correctly, particularly between different vendors. If this occurs, hard-coding one side of the link to the desired speed and duplex generally enables the opposite side of the link to negotiate correctly. A more permanent fix may come in the form of software or driver patches from the vendors in question.

## 1000Mbps Ethernet

Gigabit Ethernet, defined in the 802.3z standard, supports gigabit speeds while remaining completely compatible with the existing Ethernet standards. Two PHYs are offered to provide Gigabit Ethernet transmission over fiber-optic cabling: 1000Base-SX and 1000Base-LX.

**1000BASE-SX**    1000Base-SX is positioned for shorter distances, generally for multimode fiber installations. Multimode fiber distances can be between 300 and 550 meters. 1000Base-SX utilizes a short-wavelength transceiver, for operation with multimode fiber.

Differential mode delay (DMD) may be a problem in high-speed, laser-oriented technologies that are transmitting over multimode fiber, such as 1000Base-SX. DMD occurs because different light modes actually travel different distances as they traverse the fiber. The DMD solution in 1000Base-SX involves a conditioned laser launch that results in a light pattern similar to the light-emitting diode (LED) launch for which the fiber was initially designed.

**1000BASE-LX**    1000Base-LX provides a longer reach for campus backbones and single-mode fiber implementations. Single-mode fiber reaches distances up to two kilometers. Due to the fact that 1000Base-LX transceivers can be used with either multimode or single-mode fiber, the alteration of the laser launch, as described in the preceding section, doesn't occur at the transceiver. In this case, an external patch cord is used to condition the transmission, so that both multimode and single-mode fiber can be used while still overcoming the DMD effect. The patch cord in this case provides a single-mode fiber that is coupled off-center to a graded-index multimode fiber.

## Half Duplex vs. Full Duplex

*Half-duplex* operation is a medium in which transmission and reception of data doesn't occur simultaneously. For instance, in half-duplex Ethernet, regardless of the speed at which it runs, a device must stop transmitting while it is receiving and, likewise, must not be receiving while transmission is taking place.

*Full-duplex* operation allows for the simultaneous transmitting and receiving of data. In Ethernet, full-duplex operation is intended for use over directly connected links, such as between two switches, or between a station and a switch or hub. Since the link is not shared in the traditional sense in this case, the normal access control and collision detection is not required.

# The Complete Reference

Nortel Networks

# Chapter 3

## Asynchronous Transfer Mode (ATM) Basics

Unlike legacy technologies, such as Ethernet and token ring, Asynchronous Transfer Mode (ATM) is a departure from some of the traditional networking concepts; rather than use varying frame sizes in a broadcast environment, ATM uses neither. Instead, ATM uses directed connections only, and a fixed cell size for all devices using Synchronous Optical Network (SONET) signaling (the Synchronous Digital Hierarchy, SDH, is used in Europe and Japan). From its conception, ATM was designed as a technology that would be able to scale well, to meet the growing bandwidth demands of our growing infrastructure. Using its connection-oriented design, ATM is capable of making high-speed point-to-point connections over great distances without incurring a large amount of overhead. And, in conjunction with legacy local area network (LAN) technologies (using LAN Emulation, or LANE), ATM is able to support numerous users while keeping adds, moves, and changes simple (for more information regarding LANE support for legacy technologies, see Chapter 13). ATM technology has a two-fold design: it is designed to work in an environment that is strictly ATM, and it is designed to work in tandem with legacy LANs, specifically Ethernet and token ring.

# Legacy Technologies vs. ATM

Ethernet, token ring, and ATM represent three basic networking technologies. Ethernet represents the connectionless system, token ring represents the token-passing system, and ATM represents the connection-oriented system. The design of ATM required the capability to interact with each of the other two architectures, despite the fact that they are fundamentally different in nature. This chapter begins by taking a look at these three different systems.

## Connectionless Systems

Chapter 2 explained that Ethernet is a *connectionless* system, sometimes referred to as a *contention-based* system. This means that on an Ethernet segment, all stations share the same wire. If station A needs to transmit onto the wire, it first must check to make certain the wire isn't already in use. Station A must contend for the right to transmit. When it sends its information to the destination station, say station B, station B is *not* the only station to receive the transmission—all stations on the segment receive it. In fact, all stations within the broadcast domain may potentially receive it. Only station B responds, however, because only its media access control (MAC) address matches the destination address. This architecture may be broken up, through the use of switches, bridges, and routers, but within every collision domain, all transmissions are sent onto the wire, and all stations see them.

## Token-Passing Systems

Token ring is a *token-passing system,* which means that all stations depend on a token that traverses the ring to determine which station currently has the right to transmit. No contention exists, because data transmission occurs in a turn-based fashion; whichever station receives a free token may transmit. In token ring, as in Ethernet, all stations on the ring receive every transmission. This means that if station A on a ring transmits to station B further along on the ring, the token with station A's data is received by every station along the way as it travels toward station B, and even after station B receives the data and copies it into its buffer, every station downstream of it receives the data as well, as the token makes its way back toward the originator to be stripped. Again, however, like Ethernet, only station B responds, because it has the only MAC address that matches that of the destination address. All other stations receive the data, but they ignore it and do not copy it.

## Connection-Oriented Systems

ATM is a *connection-oriented system,* which is a departure from legacy LANs in many ways. In a connection-oriented environment, a transmission is treated in exactly the opposite fashion from how it's treated in a legacy LAN. In a pure ATM environment (with no Ethernet or token ring), when stations want to transmit, they communicate the ATM address of the end station to their local switch, and within the switched mesh, the destination address is located, a path plotted, and a circuit for transmission is erected point to point, from the sender to the receiver, before transmission begins. These circuits are known as switched virtual circuits (SVCs), permanent virtual circuits (PVCs), or virtual control channels (VCCs). (These terms and their meanings are discussed at greater length later in this chapter and in Chapter 13) These point-to-point switched virtual circuits, once established, remain up until transmission is over, and then they are torn down. No contention occurs, and even though a circuit may be up on a piece of fiber, other circuits still may be built—in fact, many other circuits can be erected over the same piece of wire, to a variety of ultimate destinations.

# Resolving Differences Between Legacy Systems

To get a sense of the hurdles that needed to be overcome, compare Ethernet's connectionless system to ATM's connection-oriented system (token ring's integration into ATM is covered further in Chapter 25). It is easy enough to say that it's because one is connectionless and one is connection-oriented, and that is true, but what specifically about the two makes their differences difficult to resolve?

# Dissimilar Architectures

Ethernet is a staple in part because it is very simple. Because its concepts are so simple, it adapts and scales well, to a point, and is easy to design and configure. Network optimization generally involves physical design, and traffic management. Ethernet traffic may be segmented with bridges and switches, and broadcast domains may be minimized through the use of routers, but Ethernet always uses the same connectionless format. For that reason, everything about Ethernet has been designed to take advantage of that principle.

If station A wants to talk to station B on an Ethernet LAN, it *broadcasts,* which is somewhat like dialing a phone number and having every phone in town ring. Everyone checks their phone to see whether the number that was called is theirs. If it is, they pick up. If not, they ignore it. Fortunately, ATM was designed to work more efficiently than that. The connection is established by the switches ahead of time, before transmission. Using the telephone analogy, this means that when the phone call is placed, only the destination phone rings.

Pure ATM environments at this time are somewhat rare, but not unheard of (at least for portions of the network). A pure ATM network would require having all ATM switches, and an ATM network interface card (NIC) in every server and end station in the entire network. If nothing but ATM were in place, pure ATM connectivity could occur without LANE or PVCs (this is known as *classical internet protocol,* or *CLIP*). Legacy LANs are in place, however, and have been for a very long time. A lot of effort and money have been committed to building these networks, and it is not realistic to think that they could simply be thrown out and replaced. Creating a technology like ATM wasn't feasible without making it backward-compatible. It had to be able to work with legacy equipment, or else its market would have been severely limited. So, ATM's designers decided that two legacy architectures would be supported, and ATM was designed to work with Ethernet and token ring.

# Broadcasts

ATM, by itself, doesn't recognize what a broadcast is. Broadcasts actually are not utilized in a pure ATM environment, because all circuits are created point-to-point or point-to-multipoint. All of Ethernet is based on the concepts of broadcasts and multicasts, however, to take advantage of the contention-based system. ATM needed to be able to interpret and handle these Ethernet broadcasts, and a method needed to be in place for an ATM switch to receive a broadcast Ethernet frame and make sure that every Ethernet-attached device hanging off every switch received the frame.

The purpose of much of the configuration required by ATM is to resolve these differences; this is the function that LANE serves.

# Cells

A fundamental difference about ATM is the method of data transport that it utilizes; rather than the traditional frame, or packet, ATM uses *cells*. Although the comparison to frames is obvious, cells have some important differences in structure, which are discussed next.

## Cells vs. Frames

Legacy technologies generally have a variety of different packet sizes; in Ethernet, they can be as small as 64 bytes and as large as 1,518 bytes; in token ring, frames will be anywhere from 512 to over 18,000 bytes in length. The maximum length for a legacy frame is defined as the maximum transmit unit (MTU) size, after which the frame must be fragmented. ATM cells, conversely, are always the same size, and always have a length of 53 bytes. This results in an efficient system that can easily outpace Ethernet and token ring.

Each cell consists of 48 bytes of actual data, called the *payload*. The payload is preceded by a 5-byte header:

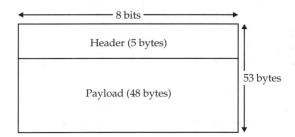

As you can see, cell structure is quite a bit different than legacy frame structure. (More detailed information about cell structure will be presented in "Cell Components," later in the chapter.)

## Converting Between Legacy Frames and Cells

Clearly, even a 64-byte packet won't fit into a 48-byte payload. To accommodate legacy frames, the frames must be cut into smaller pieces, and those divisions must be placed into each cell payload for transport across the ATM. This process is known as *segmentation*.

A packet is segmented into smaller pieces, placed into cells for transport, and then removed at the remote end and rebuilt in a process called *reassembly*. This entire process is known as *segmentation and reassembly* (*SAR*).

# ATM Adaption Layer (AAL)

The ATM adaption layer (AAL) is an addition to the standard Open Systems
Interconnection (OSI) model, relevant to ATM (see Figure 3-1).

For ATM to be able to support a variety of different services, such as voice, video,
and data, all with different requirements and traffic characteristics, a conversion must
take place between the upper layers to the ATM layer. This is the purpose of the ATM
adaption layer. The following is a quick description of the various AAL types:

- **AAL1**   Designed to handle constant bit rates, and have specific timing and
  delay requirements. Timing information must be sent along with data.

- **AAL2**   Supports connection-oriented services that don't require constant bit
  rates. Basically for variable bit rate applications.

- **AAL3/4**   Intended for both connection-oriented and connectionless
  variable-length bit rate services. At one point in time, AAL3/4 was actually two
  AAL types, AAL3 and AAL4, whose characteristics were merged together.
  AAL3/4 was abandoned because it had too much overhead.

- **AAL5**   Supports connection-oriented variable bit rate data services. Although
  it is lean from an overhead standpoint, it loses the error recovery of AAL3/4.
  The advantage in this case is greater speed, less bandwidth requirements, less
  processor time, and ease of implementation. See RFC 1483 for details regarding
  the encapsulation of Layer 3 protocols and bridge protocol data units (BPDUs)
  over AAL5.

**Note**    *RFC means request for comments. Entering "RFC" plus a corresponding number (for
example, "RFC 1483," as mentioned previously) into almost any search engine will
bring up a list of messages on that topic.*

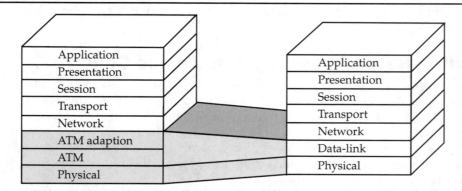

**Figure 3-1.**    *OSI model, including AAL*

The ATM Forum currently is working on AAL6, with added support for MPEG2 video streams.

## The AAL Sublayers

The ATM adaption layer itself consists of three sublayers: the common part convergence sublayer (CPCS), the service specific convergence sublayer (SSCS), and the segmentation and reassembly (SAR) sublayer. The CPCS and SSCS together make up the convergence sublayer (CS) shown in Figure 3-2.

The duties of the different AAL sublayers are as follows (see Figure 3-3):

- **CPCS**   Provides padding (in the event that the remainder of a legacy frame is not enough to fill the 48-byte cell payload) and CRC error checking. Accepts the SSCS-PDU, pads if necessary, and then adds an 8-byte trailer, which consists of 4 bytes (2 bytes packet length, 2 bytes reserved) and 4 bytes CRC.

- **SSCS**   Service-specific and provides such functionality as assured data transmission.

- **SAR**   Segments the higher layer PDUs into 48-byte payloads, which are then transferred to the ATM layer, which generates the 53-byte cells.

## Benefits of a Cell-based System

So, legacy packets are processed by the ATM hardware, segmented into cells for transport, and then reassembled back into their original form on the opposite end; what is gained?

One of the primary benefits of a cell-based system is speed. Cells all share a common size, and this makes them easier to interpret, as opposed to frames, which may be of varying lengths. Since frame sizes vary, their lengths must be determined by the receiving switch (by looking at the length field of the packet), and then calculated

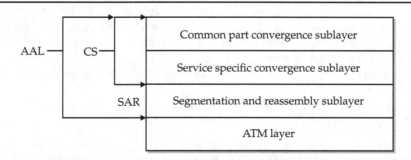

**Figure 3-2.**   *The convergence (CS) and the segmentation and reassemby (SAR) sublayers constitute the ATM adaption layer (AAL)*

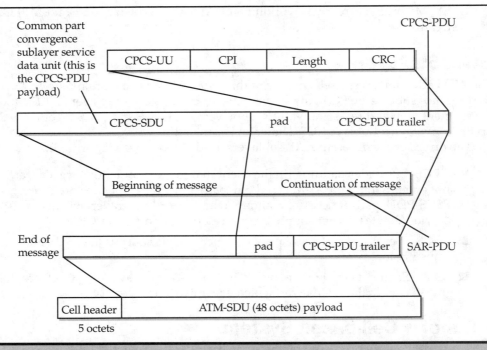

**Figure 3-3.**    *AAL functioning and SAR process*

to be sure that they actually are the correct size. ATM switches don't need to do this, because everything adheres to a common length of 53 bytes. In addition, legacy switches must check the MAC address and compare it against their MAC table, decide whether to filter or forward, and possibly broadcast to find the address, if it's unknown. ATM switches don't need to do this, either, because it is a connection-oriented protocol. The path to the destination has already been determined, and the switches only need to assign virtual path identifier (VPI)/virtual channel identifier (VCI) pairs that will be used in the circuit. All they need to worry about is which VPI/VCI pair the cell is using, and that information sits in the cell header (the 5 bytes preceding the payload).

# Cell Transport

Cells are faster to transport because they share a common size, incurring less overhead on a predetermined point-to-point or point-to-multipoint circuit. Another advantage is that the switching occurs in the hardware as opposed to the software. Each time that a legacy switch receives a packet, it must examine that packet to determine its values, where it needs to go, and whether it knows where that is; if it doesn't know where that destination is, then it must go through a process of discovering it. This entire procedure creates overhead. As you will see in the later chapters on ATM call routing, the call path is largely determined either through a simple hop-by-hop method or via a predetermined source routed path.

# Cell Components

There are three types of ATM cells: data, idle, and OAM. ATM cells are quite a bit simpler than legacy frames; they are smaller, they have fewer fields, and the majority of each cell is the data payload. A closer look at a cell reveals that the header is fairly simple (see Figure 3-4). The following is a description of the fields in the header:

- **Generic Flow Control (GFC)**   This flow control is of a local significance. It is overwritten by the ATM switch.

- **Payload Type (PT)**   The 3 Bit Payload Type field identifies whether the cell is a data cell, idle cell, OAM cell, etc. The following is a list of the different possible payload types:

```
User cell, no congestion encountered, user-to-user indication = 0
User cell, no congestion encountered, user-to-user indication = 1
User cell, congestion encountered, user-to-user indication = 0
User cell, congestion encountered, user-to-user indication = 1
OAM segment associated cell
OAM end-to-end associated cell
Resource management cell
Reserved for future use
```

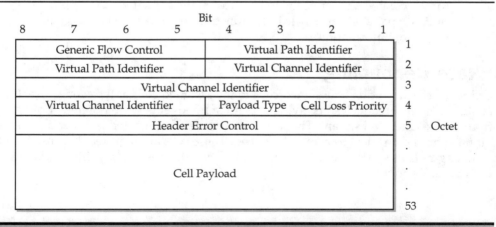

**Figure 3-4.**   *Breakdown of an ATM cell*

Each idle cell is preceded by a special header indicating that it is an unassigned cell and contains no data.

- **Cell Loss Priority (CLP)**   A 1-bit field, and that bit is either on or off. Basically, it can act as an indicator as to whether or not this cell is expendable, should the network start becoming congested.

- **Header Error Control (HEC)**   Physical layer detection/correction of bit errors in the cell header.

# Operations and Management (OAM) Cells

In addition to data cells and idle cells are another variety known as Operation and Management (OAM) cells. The basic formats of OAM cells are called F4 and F5 (see Figure 3-5). OAM cells cover two primary functions:

- **Fault Management**   Encompasses three major tasks:

   *Alarm surveillance*   Looking for virtual path connection (VPC)/virtual control connection (VCC) failures and letting everyone know about them

   *Connectivity verification*   Performing loopback testing on a link

   *Invalid VPI/VCI detection*   Detecting invalid VPI/VCIs in cell headers and reporting them

- **Local Management Interfacing Information**   Exchange of operations information between ATM nodes. The OAM cell flow used for end-to-end management functions are transported transparently through the switch. The F4 flow in this case is used either for the connection between ATM switches on either side of a user network interface (UNI) connection or for the connection between UNI devices at the virtual path (VP) level, utilizing pairs 0/3 and 0/4. These functions use OAM cells to exchange operation information.

# Cell Rate Decoupling

*Cell rate decoupling* adds unassigned cells to the assigned cells at the sender, creating a continuous cell stream. The receiving side must remove these unassigned, or idle, cells from the assigned cell stream. The rate at which they are inserted is dependant on the bit rate and the physical transmission speed. These cells are required, because SONET signaling utilizes synchronous cell time slots. The idle cells are identified as being such in their cell headers.

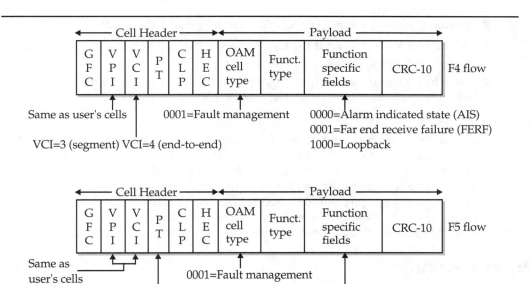

**Figure 3-5.**   *Diagram of F4 and F5 OAM cells*

# Virtual Connections

When you consider the concept of legacy frames being transported through the AAL
and then converted into cells via the SAR process, you can begin to get a picture of how
ATM handles legacy traffic. But how are these cells transported? How is the connection-
oriented, cell-based architecture implemented? In ATM, call setup occurs through the
use of VPI/VCI pairs.

ATM uses many different kinds of virtual connections: VPIs, VCIs, VCCs, PVCs,
SVCs, and so on. The following are some quick definitions:

- **Virtual Path Identifier (VPI)**   Tells each switch along which virtual path the
  circuit will travel.

- **Virtual Channel Identifier (VCI)**   Tells each switch along which virtual
  channel the circuit will travel through the aforementioned virtual path.

- **Virtual Control Channel (VCC)**   The name given to the circuit itself.
- **Permanent Virtual Circuit (PVC)**   A circuit that you define statically. It always remains up.
- **Switched Virtual Circuit (SVC)**   A circuit that is created dynamically. It is called into existence only to service an ATM call, and is torn down when the call is finished.

Essentially, *virtual* is the term given to the concept of connection-oriented data connections; when two ATM-attached stations establish a point-to-point connection between them, it is called a *virtual connection*. The reason for this is because, again, in a scenario where two stations are connected to two different switches, which in turn are connected by a single piece of fiber (see Figure 3-6), in Ethernet, for transmissions to go across the link to the opposite switch, any other data has to wait until the link is free. In ATM, the physical link is divided, logically, into paths and channels.

## VPI/VCI Pairings

A closer look at the physical media in an ATM connection shows a multitude of virtual paths, which in turn are broken into a series of virtual circuits.

Figure 3-7 shows a logical representation of VPI/VCI pairings across a single physical medium. This is not truly representative of how the impulses travel over the wire, but from a logical standpoint, it is accurate. Suffice it to say that, whereas an Ethernet transmission utilizes the whole wire, ATM transmissions travel over interconnected VPIs, and within those VPIs, they travel along individual VCIs. This scheme allows for multiple transmissions to occur simultaneously.

From a physical standpoint, these "virtual paths" and "virtual channels" do not exist. In reality, there are an incredibly dense series of interleaved data, each tagged

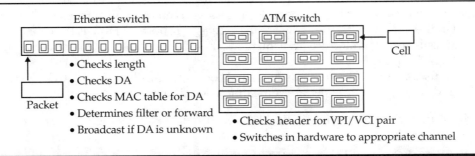

**Figure 3-6.**    *Example of ATM versus Ethernet*

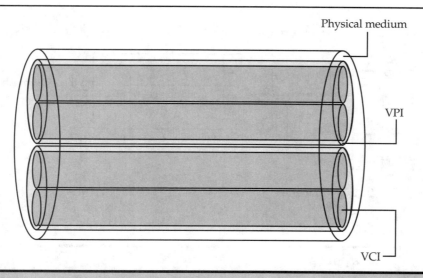

**Figure 3-7.**    *Example of VPI/VCI pairings*

with VPI/VCI values that the ATM switches use to keep track of where they need to go. Rather than a bunch of smaller pipes in a big pipe, it might be more accurately represented in the following manner:

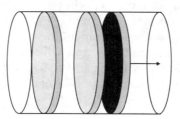

# Edge Devices

An *edge device* may be described as any device that provides an uplink between a legacy LAN (Ethernet or token ring) and the ATM network, thus providing the location where the physical layer, AAL, and ATM layer conversions take place (see Figure 3-8). This conversion, however, differs in many important ways from traditional translational bridging, and actually can be handled in a variety of ways.

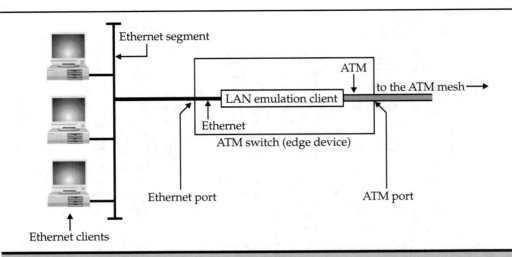

**Figure 3-8.** *ATM edge device in Ethernet network*

Unlike some legacy technologies, ATM can require a fair amount of configuration before any connectivity can take place. Out of the box, an ATM switch will not pass any traffic at all, not even in a pure ATM environment. When positioning ATM in a legacy environment, you need to make some design considerations, such as whether to use PVCs or LAN Emulation, or a combination of the two. In LANE, you need to decide what call routing method to utilize. Will you use a combination of routing types? You must make these decisions before the ATM mesh is put in place, and then you must plan and configure how to implement them.

LAN Emulation, its signaling methods, and call routing mechanisms are discussed in Chapter 13 (LANE) and Chapters 14, 15, and 16 (call routing). For now, only the construction of permanent virtual circuits (PVCs) and soft permanent virtual circuits (SPVCs) will be covered.

## PVCs

One way to create a connection between the legacy portion of a LAN and the ATM mesh is to create a PVC at the edge device. This is the simplest method of integrating the two technologies.

Creating a PVC involves taking a specific, user-defined VPI/VCI pair and statically assigning them to an ATM circuit. This VPI/VCI pair will be used on either end of the ATM link.

A PVC, once built, remains up until it is manually taken down or the link fails. Should the device at either end of the PVC recycle or fail, upon reinitialization, the end

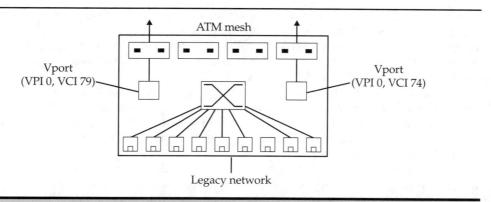

**Figure 3-9.** *PVC as gateway from legacy network to ATM*

nodes will attempt to rebuild the PVC automatically. This PVC, extending from an edge device, acts as a pathway from the legacy network to the ATM mesh (see Figure 3-9).

When building a PVC from one side of a physical link to another, the same VPI/VCI values must be used. However, when extending this PVC further into the ATM mesh, this is not a requirement. The VPI/VCI pairs used may change, when moving from switch to switch (see Figure 3-10).

As long as two termination points exist, any VPI/VCI pairs may be used along the way. For ease of organization, however, since it is also okay to use the same pairs for a single PVC being configured across multiple switches, doing so may be wise, because indiscriminately mapping pairs may make them very difficult to keep track of.

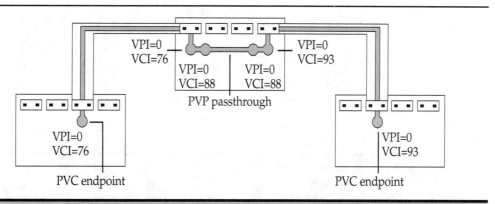

**Figure 3-10.** *PVC extending through network with multiple VPI/VCI pair mappings*

When a legacy broadcast frame is received on the switch in this example, it is flooded out across all other ports, including the PVC, which acts as a virtual port in this case. The broadcast is received by the ATM, undergoes the SAR process, and is flooded across the PVC, to the remote side, where the cells are reassembled, and is flooded to the remote legacy LAN, as well (see Figure 3-11).

While it is true that ATM does not functionally use broadcasts, in this scenario, it is only being asked to transport it across a single circuit to a static destination. The PVC will flood any traffic that it receives to the remote side. Notice that in this example, switch C, and consequently the legacy LAN associated with it, is the only other switch to receive the broadcast in this case.

PVCs may be extended throughout the ATM mesh and, in fact, must be extended to a termination point at every device that is to be reached. PVCs are very literal entities and allow communication only between specific termination points.

Consider an example with three ATM switches: switch A, switch B, and switch C. Using these three switches, a PVC may be built from switch A, passing through switch B, and terminating on switch C. This allows communication between switch A and switch C. It may seem that the circuit that was just built would give switch A access to switches B and C, but in reality, it doesn't. In order for switch A to be able to reach switch B, another PVC must be created from A to B only, and likewise from C to B only. Only then will all three switches have connectivity to each other (see Figure 3-12).

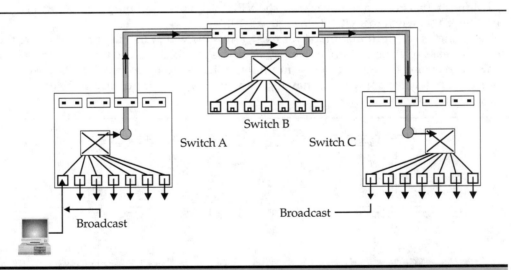

**Figure 3-11.** *Broadcast domain extended across ATM mesh of four switches and across PVC to switch C*

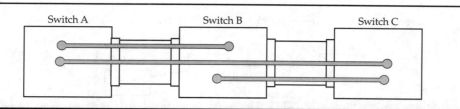

**Figure 3-12.**    *A and B, C and B, and A and C*

The thing to bear in mind with PVCs is that the termination point of the PVC is not necessarily on the next switch over; a PVC doesn't begin at one side of a fiber link and end at the other. It may, but it doesn't have to.

The mechanism used to pass from one switch, through another, to a third is sometimes called a *passthrough*. This is an extension of a PVC not from switch to switch, but between ports on the same switch.

ATM, even when utilizing a PVC, can't flood data quite the way Ethernet can. ATM builds circuits to get from point A to point B; an ATM switch has no way of knowing to pass data on from one PVC to another.

# Soft PVCs

A *soft PVC* is a combination of the PVC concept and that of an SVC. In an SPVC connection, two of the end points are defined statically, while the path between them is determined dynamically (see Figure 3-13).

In this example, the node that houses the server farm has a SPVC set up between it and the node where a group of clients reside. The client node has a statically defined PVC to node 2, and the server node has a statically defined PVC to node 9. The connection between node 2 and node 9 in this case will be determined dynamically, but once in place, will act to complete the PVC between the client node and server node. This dynamically created connection, unlike an SVC, will remain up until it is either torn down or one of the links fails.

The advantage of this connection over a traditional PVC, is that if this were a traditional PVC and node 8 were to fail, the PVC would remain down until either the node was brought back up or the PVC was manually reconfigured to route around it. With a SPVC, if the connection is interrupted (such as in the case of node 4 failing), a new connection will be dynamically reestablished to reconnect node 2 and node 9, and so the connection between the client node and server node is maintained (see Figure 3-14).

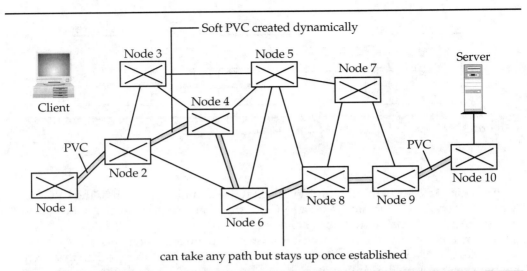

**Figure 3-13.**   *Soft PVC between end nodes*

## Advantages and Disadvantages

Using PVCs to connect ATM nodes has advantages and disadvantages. Some of the advantages follow:

- Traffic going across a PVC has almost no overhead associated with it; the cell destination doesn't need to be determined—cells are simply transported from one end to the other as fast as possible.

- PVCs are simple in concept, and easy to configure.

- PVCs can provide an uplink to either an edge device that doesn't support LANE, or an ATM DSU.

Some of the disadvantages include:

- The connections are static, and can't be rerouted in the event of a failure.

- In large networks, implementing a new switch or switches can be difficult.

- PVC mappings can become extremely difficult to keep track of in a large network, and very difficult to troubleshoot should something go wrong.

At one point in time, PVCs accounted for the majority of ATM networks. However, with the advent of LANE and its more dynamic, scalable features, use of PVCs no longer is nearly as common.

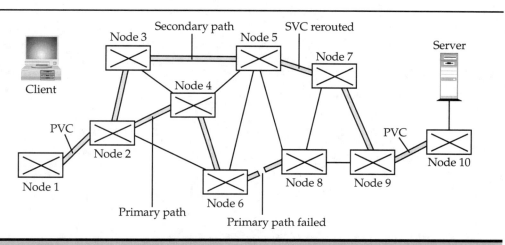

**Figure 3-14.** *SPVC failover*

## ATM Summary

ATM is different from legacy transport protocols, such as Ethernet and token ring. Its connection-oriented protocol requires more consideration and more configuration when positioning it into a legacy LAN environment. However, an ATM implementation can provide many benefits over a legacy LAN implementation, including greater speed, efficiency, and scalability. Note, too, that the topics discussed in this chapter are only a small fraction of what ATM can provide. Understanding the concepts presented in this chapter is paramount to understanding the more advanced concepts of ATM and how these concepts can be put to work in the enterprise network. These features and concepts, as well as Nortel Networks' implementation of them, are discussed in greater detail in Chapter 14, which describes how LAN emulation can be put to work in a legacy environment to increase speed and scalability. Chapter 17 explains how and where to position ATM technology in different types of legacy LAN environments. Chapters 18 through 23 provide an in-depth look at some of the Nortel Networks ATM solutions, as well as how to implement and configure them.

# Chapter 4

## Token Ring Basics

Token Ring is a token-passing protocol, whose concepts were largely developed in the 1970s. The first working model was demonstrated by IBM in Zurich by Olaf Solderblom, whose 1Mbps ring-based system was dubbed Zurich Ring. IBM has, to a large extent, been responsible for the development and refinement of Token Ring, along with Texas Instruments, who jointly developed the chip set. Token Ring, in its present form, first began to gain widespread acceptance in the 1980s, when IBM announced token ring as its local area network (LAN) strategy, alongside its Systems Network Architecture (SNA) protocol. Its token-passing architecture is a departure from that of a contention-based system, such as Ethernet, and as such, its method of transferring data is fundamentally different. To understand how a token ring works, some basic concepts must be understood.

# The Ring

Token ring, as its name suggests, uses a *ring topology*, which behaves quite a bit differently than a traditional bus topology. In an Ethernet environment, as long as everything has a physical connection to one another and the transmission path is clear (putting network-layer considerations aside), all stations should have connectivity to one another. Many devices share a single collision or broadcast domain; things have gotten more complex since the days of 10Base5 thick-coax backbones, but the concepts remain the same. A ring topology, however, is a physical ring; all the stations are connected via a common medium that actually forms a loop, or ring. With the stackables and chassis-based token ring solutions available today, the network doesn't appear as a ring on the surface, but its structure is such when you look inside at the component level. If station A sends a transmission, it eventually sees that transmission again as it travels the ring completely and ends up back at its point of origin.

These rings may be joined together via switches, bridges, and routers. When the number of stations on a ring begins to become unwieldy (the recommended maximum is 250 stations), new rings may need to be created, to distribute the network load more evenly. In such cases, the broadcast domain may either be extended, as in the case of a switched or bridged token ring, or segmented with routers, but each entity remains its own complete individual ring.

## Physical Considerations

In Ethernet, ports may support varying physical mediums and may run at different speeds, from 10MB to 1000MB, but on a conceptual level, they are basically all the same; cable type and bandwidth may change, but Ethernet ports are all used to make physical layer connections between devices and segments, and the same port that connects a switch or hub can just as easily support an end station. Generally, in this case, the straight-through cable used to connect the station will be replaced with a cross-over cable if another switch or hub is connected, but no rule limits what Ethernet device may be connected where, as long as the connector types are compatible. In essence, a 10BaseT Ethernet port on a network interface card (NIC) is no different from a 10BaseT port on an Ethernet switch or hub.

Token ring ports, unlike Ethernet ports, hold specific functions, and must be used only for the specific function for which they were designed. Token ring has different port types and connectors for different types of connections. In many cases, unlike Ethernet, the cabling may actually remain the same (in most but not all cases, a straight-through token ring cable may be used to either connect a station or extend the ring trunk), but the ports differ from one another in architecture. In a token ring, important differences exist between *station ports* (ports that exist on a token ring NIC card, to connect into the ring), *lobe ports* (ports on a ring that you plug a station or server into), and *ring in/ring out (RI/RO) ports* (ports to extend the ring from one device to another), and the connections between these ports may not be thought of as interchangeable (as they are in Ethernet). See Figure 4-1. To understand how the connections between these ports differ and what each connection is used for, you need to understand basic token ring physical-layer architecture.

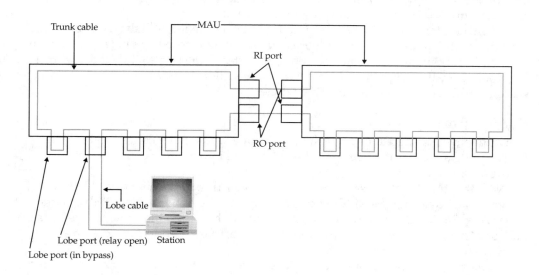

**Figure 4-1.**    *Basic token ring physical layer architecture showing the three types of connections*

## Station Ports

When in an Ethernet environment, a "station" generally is thought of as a workstation, or server. In token ring, "station" has a broader meaning: any device that will be an active member of the ring. This includes end stations and servers, but also router ports, bridge ports, and switch ports. In a ring-based system, any device that is inserted into that ring and actively participating in the token-passing process is considered a station.

## Multistation Access Unit (MAU)

A MAU is another name for a token ring concentrator. In its earliest, simplest form, a MAU basically housed the physical wiring that constituted the ring (see Figure 4-1), along with a varying number of ports that allowed stations access to the MAU. This is the same general concept that is still used in token ring hubs.

From a physical standpoint, the MAU, or concentrator, consists of the ring itself (called the *trunk*), a series of lobe ports for the stations to connect into, and generally a pair of RI/RO ports, to extend the trunk into another MAU, should the need for more lobe ports arise.

## Lobe Ports

In a token ring concentrator, each lobe port contains a relay. When these relays are closed (as they are when the lobe ports are unoccupied), they bridge the ring trunk across the unused connection, keeping the ring intact.

When a station inserts into a lobe port, this relay is opened, and the trunk becomes extended to the station through the lobe cable. The station becomes a part of the ring at this point, and the station's cable and connector extends the ring slightly (see Figure 4-1).

Notice how the ring extends directly into the station. The wire is looped within the station's NIC, as well, keeping the ring whole.

## RI/RO Ports

The ring may be extended even further, to include whole other concentrators. The RI/RO ports are designed to extend the trunk itself into another concentrator (see Figure 4-1).

Note that this is not the same as adding another ring to the network. What is accomplished by using the RI/RO ports is to merge two physical rings into a single, larger ring. Taking this into consideration, the rules become a bit more apparent; each hub, or MAU, is an individual ring, and RI/RO ports are used to extend a ring, to allow more stations to populate it.

Connecting two MAUs or concentrators via lobe ports will not work with a direct connection, because these ports are used to allow stations access to the ring, and are not used for connectivity between the trunks of individual hubs. However, devices other than workstations—namely routers, bridges, and switches—act as stations in a token ring environment, as stated earlier. So, the proper way to connect two rings via lobe ports (see Figure 4-2) is to use one of these devices to do it.

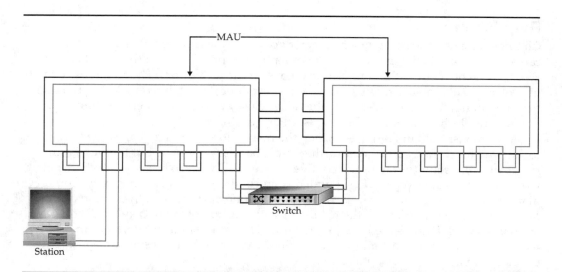

**Figure 4-2.**   *Using a bridge, switch, or router to interconnect MAUs via lobe ports*

In the example shown in Figure 4-2, a switch (which could just as easily be a bridge or router) connects the two rings. The internal switching component will switch between the two rings, but they remain separate, as the figure shows. Each of the two ports on the switch act as stations, one on each of the individual rings.

The important point is that a ring is a self-contained entity—it may be enlarged by using the RI/RO ports to extend it to more MAUs, or shrunk by disconnecting some, or the ring may be divided into multiple rings, but each ring must be complete and unbroken.

The ring must be complete, because the token continuously travels around the ring in a token-passing system, and, in fact, the token's continuous movement in this perpetual loop is the root of any token-based system.

# Ring Behavior

Because all stations on an individual ring depend upon the consistency of that ring, a mechanism must be in place to keep the ring intact, even in the event of a physical failure. In a token ring environment, ring integrity is constantly monitored. Should a portion of it fail, a variety of methods are in place to either clear or, in a worst case scenario, bypass the damaged portion altogether, to preserve the ring as a whole.

## Ring Wrap

Circumstances may arise in which an error occurs on the ring, whether that error is caused by a malfunction in the protocol or a physical problem with the ring itself. *Wrapping* is the method the ring uses to recover from such errors. The ring must remain unbroken, so if a cable actually breaks or a transmitter goes down on a MAU, the ring reacts by initiating a *wrap*. Basically, the relays close at the ports where the link went down, thus closing the gap in the ring (see Figure 4-3).

As demonstrated in Figure 4-3, when the relays close, the ring is preserved; the token now must travel quite a bit further to get back to its source, but the ring is still intact and connectivity is maintained. Even if the cable were to break in another spot, it would wrap again, leaving two separated rings. In this scenario, connectivity would be maintained within each ring; if the servers are on one portion, then the stations on the other ring will be cut off from them, but at least a portion of the network will still have access. Network failures are never a good thing, but at least the network has the ability to recover—even from the failure of an entire MAU or hub—until such time as the problem can be physically repaired.

## Ring Size

A token ring can be quite large; it is recommended that a single token ring host no more than 250 stations, but the ring itself may span many offices and, through the use of fiber optics, may even traverse buildings. However, in keeping with the concept of

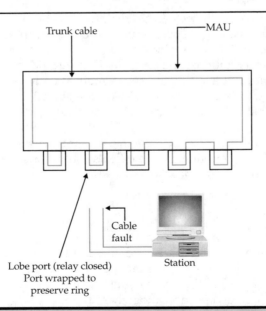

**Figure 4-3.**    *Token ring port in wrapped state*

ring wrapping as a means of recovering from a physical error, always consider that in the event of a wrap, the ring suddenly doubles in size because the token must travel the length of the outermost ring *and* the innermost ring before arriving back at its source (see Figure 4-4). A token ring network must be designed with this in mind. A station must be able to receive its own transmission without data loss, which is known as the *transmission drive distance.*

Recommended drive distances over shielded twisted pair (STP) are 2,500 feet (770 meters) at 4Mbps, and 1100 feet (346 meters) at 16Mbps. Using unshielded twisted pair (UTP) as the main trunk is not recommended. Fiber, of course, supports much greater distances (6,560 feet or about 2km) at both speeds. Sticking to these guidelines, the signal should remain intact even if the ring wraps.

The formula for this is as follows:

*drive limit = (sum of all trunk lengths) + (2×longest lobe cable)*

Of course, this is a single ring. The network may be expanded through the use of bridges, switches, routers, and so forth. Some of these options will be discussed in later chapters.

## Ring Speed

An Ethernet environment can have connections of 10Mbps, 100Mbps, and even 1000Mbps, and standards are in place for each of these speeds. Token ring, likewise, has different ring speeds; its two basic speeds are 4Mbps and 16Mbps, with full duplex

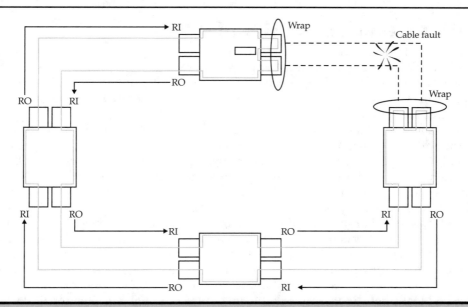

**Figure 4-4.**    *Example of transmission drive distance in the event of a wrap*

support providing 32Mbps. At first glance, this may seem like a low throughput speed. Running at 4Mbps might seem ridiculous when you could run at 100Mbps, but you must consider things other than raw bandwidth when you design a network. If a 4Mbps token ring were likened to a 10Mbps Ethernet segment, it could be argued that in an Ethernet environment, collisions generally begin appearing at approximately 20-percent utilization, and that performance degrades noticeably at 40-percent utilization. Many factors can alter this general rule, such as the number of users, the types of applications being run, and their individual bandwidth requirements, but the bottom line is that Ethernet begins to degrade long before its full bandwidth potential is reached. In a token ring environment, the more efficient token-passing system results in end-users actually seeing most of that 4Mbps or 16Mbps. In addition, the token-passing system ensures that traffic will be consistent, because data is handled much more smoothly than it is with the sporadic bursts of an Ethernet network.

A token ring's ring speed must remain consistent; it is possible to have 4Mbps and 16Mbps rings and mix them in the same chassis, as long as devices of different speeds remain on rings of a like speed. For example, in a switched environment, in which each port is essentially its own segment, this mixing of ring speeds may be done on a port-by-port basis, whereas in a shared media environment, mixing 4Mbps and 16Mbps devices requires support for multiple rings, each running a consistent speed. No intercommunication occurs between a 4Mbps and 16Mbps ring in a shared media environment without the use of an external bridge, router, or switch.

## Stations and State Machines

Token Ring sought to make many improvements over traditional Ethernet; in addition to a ring architecture and a token-passing protocol to ensure efficient data flow, Token Ring was designed to be self-monitoring and, to an extent, self-healing. Token Ring protocol calls for a series of ring entities, known as *finite state machines*, to coordinate and execute these functions.

Finite state machines are an intrinsic part of the Token Ring standard. For the most part, they don't require any user configuration, and are assumed automatically by different stations on the ring. Any station is equally capable of assuming any of the state machine roles; in fact, these roles will be assumed by different stations as individuals insert and deinsert from the ring.

Token Ring constantly monitors itself, checking ring parameters, making notes of ring activity and performance, and looking for errors. It accomplishes this through the use of special frames, called *media access control (MAC) frames*, which are covered in greater detail in Chapter 24. For now, just understand that MAC frames play an active role in the Token Ring protocol—if the ring changes, the stations become aware of it; if a new station inserts, the existing stations learn of it; if a station deinserts, the other stations will take note. If an error or problem occurs, the ring may even repair itself, to a certain degree.

# Finite State Machines

In token ring, you actually join a ring and become part of it—unlike in Ethernet, in which a device may be connected to a segment and (assuming the cable is clean, of the correct type, and the device is running at the correct speed) becomes a member of the segment, immediately ready to begin transmitting data. Again, when a station joins a ring, the other stations become aware of its presence, and the Token Ring protocol outlines certain rules for the joining process. The station first must successfully insert, which requires that it pass a series of tests and be configured with the correct parameters. This ensures that all stations coexist on the particular ring, and prevents an incorrectly configured station from upsetting ring performance.

Token ring maintains itself; a station may not insert at the wrong speed. This is true of Ethernet, as well; you can connect a 100Mbps connection in a 10Mbps port, but you will never establish a valid link. Likewise, you can plug a 4Mbps station into a 16Mbps ring, but the station will never insert. However, token ring does a lot more than just monitor ring speed—token ring stations are in constant communication with each other.

Basically, when all the stations first come onto the ring, they contend for the right to serve as these different state machines. This can be loosely compared to a series of bridges electing a root bridge. The process is different, of course, but it is similar in concept insofar as any station can potentially serve as any of these entities and, should one of them deinsert or experience a failure, any other station is equally competent to pick up the duties of that entity. These functions vary quite a bit and, in some cases, are vital to ring operation.

Seven types of these state machines exist, listed next. The first two listed are the primary state machines, and take perhaps the most active roles in basic ring functionality.

- Active Monitor
- Standby Monitor(s)
- Ring Error Monitor
- Configuration Report Server
- Ring Parameter Server
- LAN Bridge Server
- LAN Reporting Mechanism

Again, for the most part, these are not user-configured; they contend for the positions and assume them automatically. If one goes down, the contention process begins again as soon as the absence is noted, and another station takes over. These functions will not upset performance.

## Active Monitor

The Active Monitor (AM) is the most active token ring entity and is responsible for basic ring housekeeping; every ring has its own Active Monitor. The Active Monitor is responsible for the following ring-related operations:

**PROVIDING THE MASTER CLOCK**    Timing is everything, and on a token ring, this is truer than ever. All stations must be synchronized to a common clock, and the Active Monitor is responsible for providing this clock source.

**MAINTAINING PROPER RING DELAY**    To accommodate the token, ring delay must be introduced sometimes, which is the Active Monitor's responsibility. Because the token is 24 bits long, a 24-bit delay is incurred, when necessary, to prevent the token pattern from converging on itself during transmission.

**HANDLING LOST TOKENS OR FRAMES**    A token must always be on the ring. If the Active Monitor does not detect the token on the ring for 10 milliseconds, it purges the ring and releases a fresh token.

**HANDLING ORPHANED FRAMES**    Because stations in token ring are responsible for stripping the token of its data after transmitting, a mechanism needs to be in place in the event that a station transmits and then fails before stripping the token (for more information regarding token ring data transmission, see Chapter 26). If the token were never stripped by the sending station, the data could potentially traverse the ring endlessly, and the token would never again become available for use. The token contains a bit called the *monitor bit*. The Active Monitor sets this bit to 1 every time that a frame passes by it; this marks the frame as having circled the ring once. If the AM gets a frame with this bit set, then it knows the data was never stripped by the originating station, and that a failure of some kind has occurred. It thus purges the ring and releases a new token.

**INITIATING THE RING-POLL OR NEIGHBOR-NOTIFICATION PROCESS**    In token ring, each station must know the address of its nearest active upstream neighbor (NAUN). Circumstances may arise on the ring in which either a breakdown in the protocol occurs or an actual hard error of some kind exists. In such cases, it may be important for a station to know which station is immediately upstream of it, to help isolate where the problem is coming from. A station or device may be able to associate an error with the MAC of its NAUN. If the upstream neighbor deinserts from the ring, its downstream neighbor notes this and learns its new NAUN. Through this mechanism, stations on a ring are able to maintain a sense of their local surroundings. The ring poll is initiated by the Active Monitor, to update the upstream neighbor address in all stations and to inform the other stations that the AM is still active on the ring. The AM does this by releasing an Active Monitor Present (AMP) frame every seven seconds.

**MONITORING THE NEIGHBOR-NOTIFICATION PROCESS**    If any errors occur during the ring poll, the Active Monitor sends a MAC frame stating this fact to the Ring Error Monitor (REM).

**PURGING THE RING**    Certain failures on a ring will trigger a *ring purge*. If the token is lost or a frame isn't stripped properly, the ring must be stabilized before ring operation can continue. In such a scenario, the Active Monitor can send a *ring purge frame*. This clears the ring of everything, puts it back in a clear state, resets all timers, sets all stations to normal repeat mode, begins neighbor notification, and releases a new token. The AM then announces its presence, again, by sending out an AMP frame every seven seconds.

## Standby Monitors

The Active Monitor's duties must obviously be performed at all times; however, because the AM function is assumed via a contention process (and not preconfigured), the AM can be lost without a failure occurring—it could simply deinsert from the ring. Consequently, after the AM function is assumed, all other stations on the ring become *Standby Monitors*, which monitor the AMP frames issued by the Active Monitor. If they don't see an AMP frame within the specified time, they assume that the Active Monitor has left the ring for whatever reason, and the station whose timer expires first initiates Active Monitor contention. The AM function is contended for again, and a new station (one of the Standby Monitors) resumes the responsibility of being the Active Monitor.

## Ring Error Monitor

The Ring Error Monitor (REM) collects error reports from other stations. These reports include software and hardware errors. Unlike the Active Monitor and Standby Monitors, the REM typically isn't a general station; it is a software function that resides on a station, collecting data sent to its functional address (C0 00 00 00 00 08). The REM is usually a dedicated device. A list of possible token ring errors can be found in Appendix C.

## Configuration Report Server

The Configuration Report Server (CRS) role is given to a station on any ring that needs management functions in a multiple-ring environment. CRS collects statistical information and keeps an eye on configuration changes, such as the current Active Monitor, the new Active Monitor, NAUN address changes, and ring-poll failures.

## Ring Parameter Server

The Ring Parameter Server (RPS) serves a logical function that may reside on each ring in a multi-ring environment. It provides three key services:

- Ring number
- RPS version level
- Soft-error timer value

RPS also makes sure that the stations on the ring adhere to the correct operating values, and sends information to the LAN Manager from new and active stations, including:

- Addresses of ring stations
- Ring station software level
- NAUN address
- Ring number of the RPS
- Current availability of station

## LAN Bridge Server

The LAN Bridge Server (LBS) collects information about data being transferred between rings. This information can be related to the network manager for purposes of monitoring ring efficiency, or for obtaining a baseline, should the need arise.

## LAN Reporting Mechanism

The LAN Reporting Mechanism (LRM) is a ring-management function that keeps up communication between the network management console and any remote management servers.

By working in conjunction, these entities are able to monitor, learn, and propagate a lot of information about the ring environment, such as ring parameters, configuration changes, types of error conditions on the ring, and some traffic analysis. This intercommunication between state machines and stations forms an important basis of the Token Ring protocol.

# Ring Insertion

Ring insertion is initiated by any token ring station upon physical connection. The ring-insertion process has five phases (0 through 4), which, if completed successfully, allow the requesting station to enter the ring.

## Phase 0: Lobe Test

The first thing that a station will test upon detecting a physical connection is the integrity of the cable being used for that connection. The station transmits a series of *lobe media test MAC frames*. Because the lobe port's relay hasn't been opened yet, and access to the trunk hasn't been granted yet, these frames will loop back to the sender. The station examines the frames to see whether any corruption has occurred. If the frames are corrupted or do not come back at all, the insertion process fails at this point.

## Phase 1: Physical Insertion and Monitor Check

Upon successful receipt of the lobe media test MAC frames, the station initiates a DC current to the hub relay (called a *phantom current*). This phantom current basically triggers the opening of the lobe port's relay (an audible snap often accompanies this).

The relay opens, and the station sets the T(Attach) timer, which lasts 18 seconds. At this point, the station is looking to see whether an Active Monitor is present on the ring. If the timer expires, due to no Active Monitor being present, then the station enters the claim token transmit mode.

If the timer doesn't expire (an Active Monitor is present), the station proceeds to Phase 2.

## Phase 2: Duplicate Address Check

The station next sends out a duplicate MAC frame (basically, a packet whose destination address is also the source) to search the ring for a duplicate MAC address. Token ring frames contain a bit known as the *Address Recognized bit* (see Figure 4-5), which is flipped when a station recognizes the destination address (DA) as itself. Therefore, if a station sends out a frame with itself as the DA, and the frame returns with the Address Recognized bit flipped, then another station that is already inserted into the ring must also share the same MAC address. If this occurs, the insertion fails. The following combinations for the Address Recognized bit and the Frame Copied bit show how a station would know whether or not the frame had been received and copied:

| Address Recognized bit | Frame Copied bit | Action |
|---|---|---|
| 0 | 0 | Address not recognized |
| 1 | 0 | Address recognized, frame not copied |
| 1 | 1 | Address recognized, frame copied |

If the frame returns with the Address Recognized bit not set, the station proceeds to Phase 3.

## Phase 3: Ring-Poll Participation

At this point, the station waits for an AMP or an SMP (Standby Monitor Present) MAC frame, to participate in the ring-poll process. On an active ring, an Active Monitor should already be in place. If an AM is not in place, the election process must begin so that one of the stations is assigned the Active Monitor duties.

The ring-poll process basically is used to identify a station during insertion. It provides a reference point in addition to the station address. This process is in continual use and must repeat every 15 seconds to avoid the Active Monitor contention process. This goes back to the concept that in token ring, each neighbor must have certain knowledge of the other participants on the ring.

The Active Monitor initiates this process, which, on an active ring, is in effect at the time the station inserts. The ring poll is initiated by the AM by broadcasting the aforementioned AMP frame (see Figure 4-6).

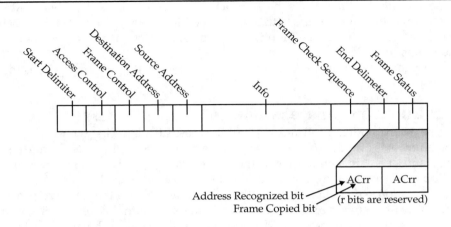

**Figure 4-5.** *Token ring frame with Address Recognized bit blowup*

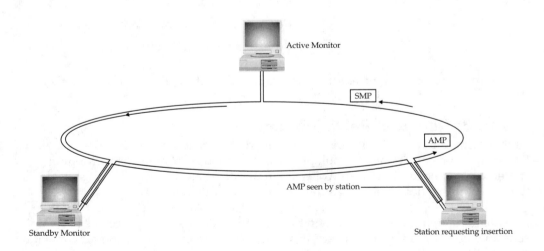

**Figure 4-6.** *Active Monitor issuing AMP frames onto ring*

The station waits for an AMP or SMP MAC frame to participate in the ring-poll process.

- If an interruption in the process occurs, then go to Phase 0.
- If no interruption occurs, then go to Phase 4.

## Phase 4: Request Initialization

The station sends a *request initialization (RI) MAC frame* to the RPS and sets a response timer (2.5 seconds). Once the RI frame is issued, the timer begins and will stop when a response is received:

- If the timer doesn't expire, an RPS is present (a response was sent back) and parameters are received.
- If the timer expires, no RPS is present. The station uses default values.

The RPS response is an *initialize ring station (IRS) MAC frame* containing a ring number and a value for the T(Soft_Error_Report) timer (see Figure 4-7).

The station, at this point, has been given clearance to initialize. It inserts into the ring and becomes an active participant.

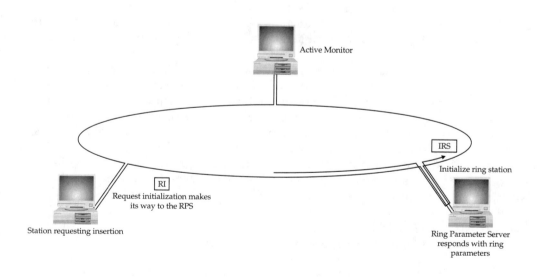

**Figure 4-7.**    *Station receiving initialize ring station MAC frame*

# Station Activities on the Ring

When the stations begin inserting into the ring, certain stations are given specific jobs to do via the contention process outlined earlier. Without these stations, the ring will not function. When token ring stations insert into a quiet ring, they sense the absence of these state machines, and will begin the processes necessary to fill those positions; they contend for the positions, accept them, and then announce their presence so that all the other stations know the contention process is over. Once all the necessary components are present, the ring is initialized and ready to accept network traffic. The entire process should occur so quickly that it is invisible to the user.

## Active Monitor Contention

An Active Monitor will be elected under the following circumstances:

■ The current Active Monitor detects signal loss and its T(Receive_Notification) timer expires.

■ A Standby Monitor detects signal loss and its T(Good_Token) or T(Receive_Notification) timer expires.

■ A station attaches to a ring and detects no Active Monitor.

The Token Ring protocol timers are described in more detail in "Token Ring Timers," later in the chapter.

When one of these situations occurs, the first station to detect the condition enters the claim token transmit mode and transmits a claim token MAC frame addressed to itself. This transmission triggers the token-claiming process, which results in Active Monitor election.

As the MAC frame makes its way around the ring, each station receiving it joins in the process; each station enters claim token repeat mode and compares its address to the address in the MAC frame that it received. If the station's address is higher, then it creates its own claim token transmission (addressed to itself) and sends it onto the ring. The next station looks at the address, compares it to its own, and so on. This process continues until a station receives its own frame successfully three times.

At that point, one station determines that it has the highest MAC address of all the stations on the ring, and thus assumes the role of Active Monitor. The new Active Monitor performs a ring purge to return the ring to a normal condition.

## Neighbor Notification

Four entities commonly are associated with the neighbor-notification process:

■ **MA** My address. This is basically just the unique hardware address each station has.

■ **NAUN** Nearest active upstream neighbor (should be the same as UNA)

- **SUA**  Stored upstream address (should be the same as UNA)
- **UNA**  Upstream neighbor's address

The upstream neighbor is the station that passes the token to a station. The downstream neighbor is the station the token is passed along to. Stations on the ring must be aware of who their upstream neighbor is, and must know its address. Each station on the ring learns of its NAUN during the neighbor-notification process. The station stores this address in its own buffer as the SUA. By doing this, if a station receives a transmission from its NAUN, but the address doesn't equal the SUA, then the station knows that the former upstream neighbor must have left the ring, and that this must be the address of one of the stations behind it (see Figure 4-8).

If an error comes streaming into a station's receiver, it knows that it must have come from the NAUN, because if it had come anywhere further upstream, another station would have already intercepted it. So, if a station receives an error, it will know who it came from and can pass on this information. This concept becomes very useful in troubleshooting token ring problems that may occur.

## Ring Purge

A *ring purge* is another type of token ring MAC frame that purges everything currently on the ring. A ring purge will be initiated under the following three conditions:

- The Active Monitor sees an error condition on the ring, such as a lost token or frame, a token ring process that did not complete properly, or an active timing problem that occurred.
- The T(Any_Token) timer expires (see the upcoming section "Token Ring Timers").
- The Active Monitor sees the M(monitor) bit set to 1 (M=1) in the Access Control field of a frame. This basically states that the data is looping the ring multiple times without being stripped.

Under these conditions, the Active Monitor transmits a ring purge frame and waits for it to return. If it returns, the ring is assumed to have stabilized, all timers are reset, and the neighbor-notification process is initiated to bring the ring back to a normal state. If the ring purge frame does not return, the token-claiming process begins.

A ring purge MAC frame does not require the token for transmission.

## Abort Sequence

If a station receives a free token and begins transmitting, and then detects a failure while in the process of sending, it will issue an *abort sequence* and stop transmitting immediately.

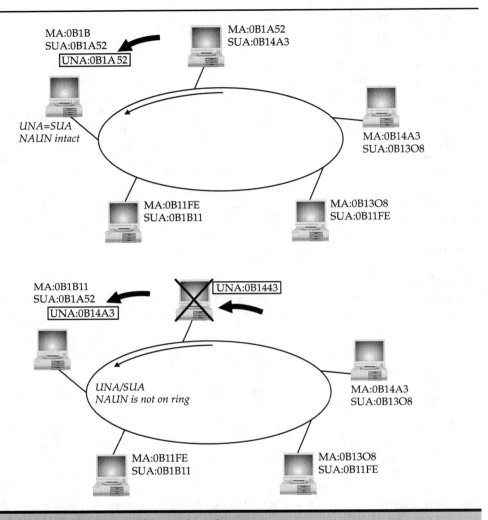

**Figure 4-8.** *NAUN change detected on ring*

The abort sequence consists of a Start Delimiter (SD) and an End Delimiter (ED), marking the beginning and ending of the abort sequence.

## Token Ring Timers

The Token Ring protocol uses a set of timers to keep everything synchronized. Because timing is very important in token ring, this set of timers makes it well-suited for time-sensitive protocols, such as SNA. If the NAUN is not detected, and the timer expires, that station is determined to be off the ring, and the change is noted. If the token hasn't been detected by a station, and the timer expires, the token is assumed to have been lost and a new one must be issued. By adhering to these timers, the token ring protocol is able to detect problems on the ring quickly, adjust for them, and keep data transmission stable and efficient.

The following are the different token ring timers, the names and values for which are taken from the IBM specification:

**T(ANY_TOKEN)**    Dictates how long the Active Monitor will wait to see the SD of a frame or token. Timer begins at the moment the Active Monitor issues the first token. It lasts 10 milliseconds.

**T(ATTACH)**    Dictates how long a station may remain in the ring-insertion process. Timer begins at the beginning of insertion Phase 1, and times out after 18 seconds if insertion still isn't successful.

**T(BEACON_TRANSMIT)**    Dictates how long a station can transmit beacon MAC frames before it removes itself from the ring and performs a series of self-diagnostics. The timer is set to 16 seconds.

**T(CLAIM_TOKEN)**    Dictates how long a station can wait for an Active Monitor to win the token-claiming process (AM election). It lasts one second.

**T(ESCAPE)**    Dictates how long a station should remain in beacon repeat mode before entering the claim token transmit mode. The timer is set when the station first receives a beacon MAC frame. If it doesn't get another one within 200 milliseconds, the timer expires and Active Monitor contention begins.

**T(GOOD_TOKEN)**    Used by Standby Monitors to monitor the ring for problems with the Active Monitor. The duration is 2.6 seconds. If an AMP or data frame is not detected within that time, it enters claim token transmit mode, and a new Active Monitor is elected.

**T(NEIGHBOR_NOTIFICATION)**    Relates to the neighbor-notification process. It is set when the AM sends out an AMP frame, and lasts seven seconds. If an SMP frame isn't seen within that time, another AMP is sent to restart the neighbor-notification process.

**T(NOTIFICATION_RESPONSE)**    Provides a delay of 20 milliseconds between the time that a station sees either an AMP or SMP and the time that it transmits its own SMP.

**T(PHYSICAL_TRAILER)**    Used to detect improperly transmitted frames. It is set when a station transmits. If it does not receive the frame back in 4.1 milliseconds, the lost frame counter is incremented. A soft error is reported to the REM. Ring purge may follow.

**T(RECEIVE_NOTIFICATION)**    Standby Monitors use this to validate the existance of the Active Monitor. It is set to 15 seconds. If an AMP frame does not arrive in that time, claim token transmit time begins again, and a new AM is elected.

**T(RESPONSE)**    Dictates how long a station will wait for a response for a frame that requires one. It lasts 2.5 seconds. If the timer expires, the station will retransmit.

**T(RING_PURGE)**    Dictates how long the Active Monitor may remain in ring purge. It lasts one second. If it expires, it enters claim token transmission.

**T(SOFT_ERROR_REPORT)**    Dictates when a station may generate a report soft error MAC. This allows the error counter to increment at a regular interval. This way, error reports will contain a variety of errors rather than just one, thus reducing traffic. The timer is set to two seconds.

**T(TRANSMIT_PACING)**    Dictates how long a station has to wait before retransmission of a beacon or claim token MAC. It times out in 20 milliseconds, after which the station retransmits.

By using a strict, timing-sensitive protocol and an efficient token-passing, ring-based architecture, Token Ring overcomes some of the latency and scalability problems that are encountered in an Ethernet environment. For this reason, some may argue that token ring handles time-sensitive protocols, such as Internetwork Packet Exchange (IPX) and SNA, better than Ethernet. On the other hand, token ring certainly requires more design considerations, and can be more difficult to troubleshoot if something goes wrong. The actual pros and cons of token ring versus Ethernet is a time-worn debate, one that will continue for some time, thanks to new technologies that involve both architectures.

For more information on token ring and its applications, consult Chapters 26 through 29 of this book. Other topics of interest may be RFC 1231, which covers the Token Ring Management Information Base (MIB). The following are the Institute of Electrical and Electronics Engineers (IEEE) 802.5 subcommittees:

- 802.5Q: 16Mbps Token Ring over UTP
- 802.5i: Early Token Release

- 802.5j: Fiber Optic Station Attachment
- 802.5k: Token Ring Media
- 802.5m: Source Routing

# Token Ring Cabling

Token ring supports a variety of different cable types and connectors; the three basic categories outlined here are UTP, STP, and fiber-optic.

## Token Ring Cable Types

Token Ring is rated to run over a variety of different copper cable types, as well as over fiber-optic cabling using 802.5j signaling.

### UTP (Unshielded Twisted Pair)

UTP cable types include Category 1 and 2, but they are not rated to run Token Ring over them. Categories 3 through 5 are valid cable types, although Cat5 is possibly the most common. The following are the specifications for Categories 3 through 5:

| Cable Type | Data Rate | Impedance | Attenuation | Crosstalk |
|---|---|---|---|---|
| Category 3 | Tested to 10Mbps | 100 ohms | < 40 dB per Km @ 16MHz | < -23 dB between pairs @ 16MHz |
| Category 4 | Tested to 16Mbps | 100 ohms | < 27 dB per Km @ 16MHz | < -38 dB between pairs @ 16MHz |
| Category 5 | Tested to 100Mbps | 100 ohms | < 25 dB per Km @ 16MHz | < -44 dB between pairs @ 16MHz |

**Note**    *Category 3 is tested only for 4Mbps Token Ring.*

Generally, in a token ring environment, a straight-through, RJ-45 connector cable is used when dealing with UTP cable. However, occasionally, a token ring cross-over is used, such as with a Dedicated Token Ring (DTR) connection on a four-port TokenSpeed blade in the Centillion switch.

## STP (Shielded Twisted Pair)

STP is often associated with token ring, because STP was the most common cable type used with token ring for quite a while. The following is a list of different STP types used:

| STP Type | Data Rate | Impedance | Attenuation | Crosstalk |
|---|---|---|---|---|
| IBM Type 1–Data Communication | Tested to 16Mbps (can go to 100Mbps) | 150 ohms +/- 10% @ 3-20MHz | < 45 dB per Km @ 16MHz | < -40 dB between pairs @ 16MHz |
| IBM Type 2–Data and Telephony | Tested to 16Mbps (can go to 100Mbps) | 150 ohms +/- 10% @ 3-20MHz | < 45 dB per Km @ 16MHz | < -40 dB between pairs @ 16MHz |
| IBM Type 6–Data Patch Cable | Tested to 16Mbps | 150 ohms +/- 10% @ 3-20MHz | < 66 dB per Km @ 16MHz | < -34 dB between pairs @ 16MHz |
| IBM Type 8–Flat Cable | Tested to 16Mbps | 150 ohms +/- 10% @ 3-20MHz | < 88 dB per Km @ 16MHz | < -40 dB between pairs @ 16MHz |
| IBM Type 9– Plenum Data Cable | Tested to 16Mbps (can go to 100Mbps) | 150 ohms +/- 10% @ 3-20MHz | < 45 dB per Km @ 16MHz | < -40 dB between pairs @ 16MHz |

## Fiber Optics

Token ring may also run over fiber, using the 802.5j signaling standard:

**62.5/125 Fiber**
**Attenuation:** 3.75 dB/Km 850nm wavelength laser
**Attenuation:** 1.50 dB/Km 1300nm wavelength laser

# Token Ring Connector Types

Token ring STP connectors come in a few flavors; MIC connectors, DB-9 station connectors (such as may be found on the Centillion TokenSpeed blades), and RJ-45 connectors.

## MIC Connectors

Media interface connectors (MICs) sometimes are referred to as "hermaphroditic" connectors, because their design shares the traits of both male and female connector types; they allow for a single connector type for all connections. MIC connectors are rated to have a life of around 15 years, with over 1,000 insertions and deinsertions. MICs were commonly used in IBM MAUs.

## DB-9 Connectors

DB-9 connectors are quite a bit smaller than MIC connectors, and much more common these days, because their smaller design allows for a higher port density. The pinout for a token ring DB-9 connector is as follows:

Pin 1 to TX-
Pin 5 to RX-
Pin 6 to TX+
Pin 9 to RX+

## RJ-45 Connectors

RJ-45 connectors are physically the smallest connectors, and therefore result in the highest port density. Their pinout is as follows:

Pin 3 to TX-
Pin 4 to RX+
Pin 5 to RX-
Pin 6 to RX+

## Fiber-Optic Connector Types

Fiber-optic cable generally uses either of the following connector types:

- **ST**   Each strand locks into place with a spring-locked key.
- **SC**   Each strand locks into place in a keyed port.
- **SMA**   This is an older connector type that is similar to the ST-type connectors, except that each strand utilizes a connector that screws into its connection, much like a BNC connector.

## Media Filters

A *media filter* is a device used to convert an STP connection so that UTP cabling can be used; media filters generally connect with a DB-9 connector to the STP token ring port, and have an RJ-45 UTP port on the opposite end. The device filters any line noise picked up on the UTP end, cleans up the signal, and prevents it from disturbing the STP input.

## Active and Passive MAU Considerations

Token ring MAUs may be referred to as either active or passive. Because each individual station in token ring is responsible for repeating the signals passing on the ring, a token ring MAU does not need any repeater function of its own, in theory. A passive MAU is just that: a MAU that relies on the ring stations to repeat and refresh the signal as it passes through. In fact, a passive MAU does not require electricity. Problems can arise in this scenario, however, because signal degradation may occur, depending on the ring size and station count.

Active MAUs perform repeater functions, and therefore require electricity; however, signal integrity is much more easily maintained.

# The Complete Reference

Nortel Networks

# Part II

## Ethernet on Nortel Networks

The
# Complete
# Reference

# Chapter 5

## Nortel Networks Ethernet Switching

The Nortel Networks frame switches offer both Ethernet and Token Ring switching. Ethernet switching falls mainly onto the BayStack series platform, whereas Token ring switching is mainly covered by the Centillion platform. For this reason, token ring switching is covered in Chapter 25, while switched Ethernet on the Centillion platform is covered in Chapter 6. This chapter covers the BayStack Ethernet switches only.

# BayStack Series Switches

The BayStack series switches fall into three basic categories:

- BayStack 301
- BayStack 302, 303, and 304
- BayStack 350 10/100/1000 and 450 10/100/1000

The switches within these groupings share many design aspects, as well as software functionality and features. This chapter covers each of these categories, describing each switch, and going over some of the most commonly used features.

## BayStack 301

The BayStack 301 is unique among the BayStack product line; although categorized as a BayStack series switch, it actually utilizes the Centillion architecture, using a command-line interface (CLI), and requiring a configuration utility called SpeedView Lite, which is a version of SpeedView that utilizes a minimal feature set.

### SpeedView Lite

SpeedView Lite runs on most Windows-based machines, and is required to configure the BayStack 301. Unlike SpeedView, SpeedView Lite is not able to perform configuration and management across a serial connection, and uses the Simple Network Management Protocol (SNMP) only. For this reason, the BayStack 301 must first be configured with a valid IP address and community strings before any further configuration can take place.

#### PREPARING THE BAYSTACK 301 FOR MANAGEMENT VIA SPEEDVIEW LITE

Configuring an IP address and community strings is accomplished via the CLI. The CLI is accessed by connecting to the console port using either a terminal or terminal-emulation software. If terminal-emulation software is being used, the following parameters should be entered:

| | |
|---|---|
| Baud rate | 9600 |
| Data bits | 8 |
| Stop bits | 1 |
| Parity | none |
| Flow Control | Xon/Xoff or None |

After you initiate a console session, configure the IP address and community strings by using the following commands:

```
Command>config password ikari
```

where **ikari** is the password. This actually sets the password the first time the command is issued, as there is no password by default. This opens Configuration Mode, in which the IP address and mask may be added, and the community strings may be set:

```
Config> ip address 150.50.10.21 gw 0.0.0.0 mask 255.255.255.0
Config> get community melef set community dilandu
```

After you enter the IP address, verify that the management station can ping the BayStack 301. Once the ping is successful, add the 301 into the Switch list. This is accomplished by selecting File | Edit Switch Profile from the main SpeedView Lite window (see Figure 5-1).

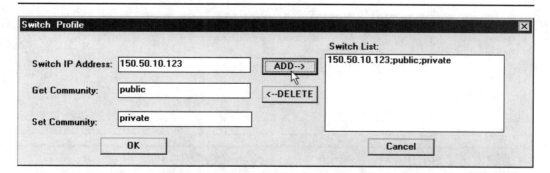

**Figure 5-1.**   *The Switch Profile window*

ETHERNET ON NORTEL NETWORKS

After you complete this task, SpeedView Lite discovers the BayStack 301 and models it using a graphical representation. Users familiar with older versions of SpeedView will recognize the display, because it uses the same format as the pre-3.0 SpeedView. SpeedView Lite displays the BayStack 301 just as SpeedView would a single Ethernet card, and this is effectively what the BayStack 301 is: a stand-alone, 16-port EtherSpeed MCP.

## Configuring the BayStack 301

Configuration of the BayStack 301 is relatively simple, since the switch has only Ethernet ports. These ports can be selected and configured through SpeedView Lite by selecting the port in question (see Figure 5-2).

Of the 24 Ethernet ports, 22 of them are 10BaseT ports, while port 23 and 24 can be configured to run at 100Mbps also. This can be configured from SpeedView Lite; once this configuration change has been made successfully, the LED labeled 100, next to the port 23 and 24 LED, will light to reflect that they are now running at 100Mbps.

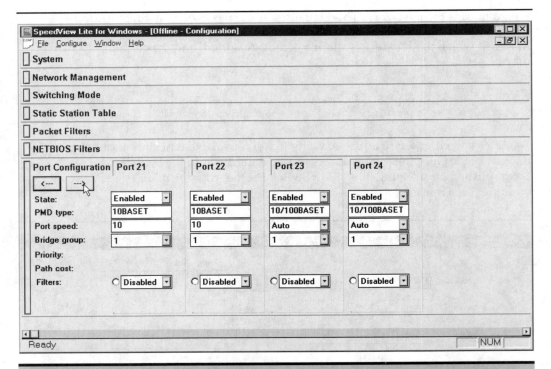

**Figure 5-2.** *Ethernet port selected in SpeedView Lite*

## Upgrading System Software

Upgrading the BayStack 301 is accomplished by using almost the same procedure that is used to upgrade the C100/C50/5000BH, with the exception that it must be done via SNMP and can't be done serially, except in the case of an emergency download, which is covered at the end of this section.

To initiate a normal upgrade, the switch first must be discovered using SpeedView Lite. Once this is done, highlight the switch and then select TFTP Download Software. After you make this selection, another window opens and SpeedView Lite prompts for the image destination and filename. A browse feature is available to assist in finding the file, if necessary. After you select the image file, initiate the download by clicking Start Download.

*It is important not to interrupt the download process once it begins. Halting the upgrade process may corrupt the flash. If this happens, the device may be possible to recover, using the emergency download procedure that is described in the following section.*

**EMERGENCY DOWNLOAD**    A flash corruption may be indicated if a console session is active with the BayStack 301, and the following message appears on the console during bootup:

```
Flash checksum starts…fail
Fatal err!!  Waiting for SpeedView to download code
```

If this message appears, a download may be attempted over the serial connection. With a serial connection still established with the console port, select Switch from the main toolbar and then select Serial Download Software. This initiates the emergency download procedure. A warning appears prior to this, indicating that this type of download should be attempted only in the case of an image corruption on the flash where a normal upgrade is not possible.

# BayStack 303/304

The BayStack 303 and 304 are all high-performance Ethernet switches that provide 10Mbps connections, as well as 100Mbps uplinks and optional media dependent adapter (MDA) connections. Each port supports 802.1u autonegotiation, as well as the 802.1d Spanning Tree Protocol.

## Basic Architecture

The BayStack 303/304 share very similar architectures, with differences being primarily in port density and port types.

**BAYSTACK 303**    The BayStack 303 provides 24 10Mbps RJ-45 Ethernet ports, one 10/100Mbps 100BaseTX RJ-45 Ethernet port, one MDA slot capable of supporting either a 10/100BaseTX or 100BaseFX MDA, and a DB-9 Console connector for establishing a console session with the device.

**BAYSTACK 304**    The BayStack 304 provides 12 10Mbps RJ-45 Ethernet ports, one 10/100Mbps 100BaseTX RJ-45 Ethernet port, one MDA slot capable of supporting either a 10/100BaseTX or 100BaseFX MDA, and a DB-9 Console connector for establishing a console session with the device.

    *Hot-swapping the MDA is not recommended, because this may damage the unit.*

## Connecting to the BayStack 302/303/304

Configuration of the BayStack 302/303/304 can be accomplished by establishing a console session through the device's Console port. The Console port in each case is a male DB-9 connector, using the following pinouts:

| Pin | Signal |
|-----|--------|
| 1 | Not used |
| 2 | Transmit |
| 3 | Receive |
| 4 | Not used |
| 5 | Ground |
| 6 | Not used |
| 7 | Not used |
| 8 | Not used |
| 9 | Not used |

A console session is established by using either a terminal or terminal-emulation software. If terminal-emulation software is used, the following parameters must be configured:

| | |
|---|---|
| Baud rate | 9600 |
| Data bits | 8 |
| Stop bits | 1 |
| Parity | None |
| Flow Control | Disabled |

## Initial IP Connectivity

The BayStack 302/303/304 also utilizes a default IP address, so that it may be reached via SNMP or telnet while still at the factory default settings. The default IP address and mask in this case are as follows:

IP Address: 127.0.0.2
Subnet Mask: 255.255.255.0

    *You should alter this IP address and mask at your earliest convenience.*

## Language Selection

The first time the unit initializes at its factory default settings, you must select a language preference, which you are prompted for prior to accessing the Main Menu:

```
1 --- English
2 --- French/Francais
3 --- German/Deutsche
4 --- Japanese
5 --- Spanish/Espanol
6 --- Italian/Italiano
7 --- Chinese

Current Selection:
Please enter number for selection:
```

After you choose a language preference, the Language Preference screen does not reappear unless the unit is set back to its factory defaults; thus, mistyping the language preference results in having to navigate through the menu system in a potentially unfamiliar language to access and execute the option to reset the device to its factory defaults, so take care when selecting the language to be used.

# Basic Configuration

After you initiate a console session and choose a language preference, the Main Menu is accessed:

```
*****************************************************************
                    Nortel Networks BayStack 303 Ethernet Switch
IP Address:         [150.50.10.21]
Mac Address:        [00:00:81:A2:31:08]
Software Version    [1.0]
System Up Time:     [0d:01h:21m:03s]
```

ETHERNET ON NORTEL NETWORKS

```
Switch Status            [Switching]
**********************************************************************
                                        Main Menu
1 -- System Information
2 -- System Configuration
3 -- Reset System
4 -- Exit Telnet


Enter Command  ([Esc] --- Previous Screen    [Space] --- Refresh Screen)
```

## Web-Based Management

The 303 and 304 series BayStack switches may use Web-based management. This feature must first be enabled from a console session, which is accomplished by selecting Management Access from the Main Menu, and then selecting Web Access. Toggle the feature to Enabled, if it is not already. Once this is accomplished, and the device has been configured with a valid IP address, that IP address may be entered into a Web browser, and the Web-based management will be accessed (see Figure 5-3).

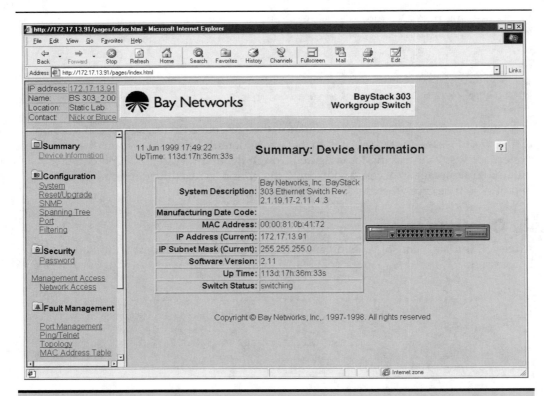

**Figure 5-3.** *Main Menu in Web-based management for 303*

From the Main Menu, you may log in to the switch, at which point you are prompted for a name and password.

## Upgrading System Software

Upgrading the system software on the 303/304 series BayStack switches is accomplished via a console session. To successfully complete the upgrade, a Trivial File Transfer Protocol (TFTP) server must be present on the network, with the appropriate image file stored on it. The upgrade procedure is then initiated by selecting option 5 from the Main Menu, System Reset/Upgrade. This accesses the menu in which the image upgrade parameters may be set:

```
*******************************************************************
                Nortel Networks BayStack 303 Ethernet Switch

IP Address:                          [170.70.10.91]
MAC Address:                         [00:00:81:0b:41:72]
Software Version:                    [2.11 ]
System Up Time:                      [53d:07h:19m:52s]
Switch Status:                       [Switching]
*******************************************************************


                    System Reset/Upgrade

1 ---TFTP Server IP Address [150.50.102.143]
2 ---Default Gateway IP Address [170.70.10.1]
3 ---Software Image File Name [b3032114.img]
4 ---Specify Reset Action [None]
5 ---Set/Clear Reset Action Timer [0 min.]

0 ---Immediate Reset Action




Enter Command ([ESC]-Previous Menu   [Space]-Refresh Screen)
```

The preceding options are accessed by entering the corresponding number. These options should be configured in the following way:

- **TFTP Server IP Address**   Entering 1 at the System Reset/Upgrade menu causes the switch to prompt for an IP address; enter the IP address of the TFTP server.

- **Default Gateway IP Address**   Entering 2 at the System Reset/Upgrade menu causes the switch to prompt for a Default Gateway IP address; this option is only necessary if the upgrade will occur through a router (the TFTP server is on a different network number than the switch). If the TFTP server is local to the switch, a value of 0.0.0.0 may be used. If the upgrade will occur through a router, enter the IP address of the local router interface here.

■ **Software Image File Name**   Entering 3 at the System Reset/Upgrade menu prompts for the image name; this is case-sensitive and should not include the path to the image file.

■ **Specify Reset Action**   Option 4 is where the upgrade is actually initiated from; when selected, the following prompt appears:

```
Enter Reset Action (1:reset 2:download):
```

Option 1 in this case resets the device normally, without initiating the image upgrade, while option 2 actively seeks the download.

# BayStack 350

The BayStack 350 comes in two basic varieties: the standard 350x series BayStack, which uses port-based VLANs, and the 350x 10/100/1000, which is quite a bit more similar to the 450 series BayStack switch. This segment concentrates on the standard 350x series BayStack; for information regarding the 350x 10/100/1000 series switch, consult the section on the BayStack 450 10/100/1000, later in this chapter.

The 350x series switch comes in several different varieties:

■ **BayStack 350T**   Includes 16 802.3u-compliant autonegotiating 10/100BASE-TX Ethernet ports using RJ-45 connectors. These ports are capable of running in full- or half-duplex mode.

■ **BayStack 350F**   Includes 12 802.3u-compliant autonegotiating 10/100BASE-TX Ethernet ports using RJ-45 connectors, as well as two 100BASE-FX fiber-optic ports using SC connectors. The RJ-45 ports are capable of running in either full- or half-duplex mode.

■ **BayStack 350T-HD**   Includes 24 802.3u-compliant autonegotiation 10/100BASE-TX Ethernet ports using RJ-45 connectors. These ports are capable of running in full- or half-duplex mode.

■ **BayStack 350F-HD**   Includes 24 802.3u-compliant 10/100BASE-TX Ethernet ports using RJ-45 connectors, and two 100BASE-FX fiber-optic ports using SC connectors. The RJ-45 ports are capable of running in either full- or half-duplex mode.

## 350x Features

The primary features of the 350x series switch are as follows:

■ **802.1u autonegotiation**   Allows for dynamic selection of the fastest speed and duplex mode.

■ **MultiLink Trunking**   Allows for the grouping of physical ports, to provide a single connection consisting of the aggregate bandwidth of all MLT members.

■ **Port-based VLANs**   Software-configurable logical broadcast domains, grouped by port.

■ **Port mirroring**   Mirroring the input or output from one port and mirroring the same data to another port; used for taking sniffer traces in a switched environment.

# BayStack 450 10/100/1000 and 350 10/100/1000 (350-12T and 350-24T)

The BayStack 350x and 450x series switches historically did not share the same feature set; when the 350x made its first appearance, it used port-based VLANs only, because the 802.1Q specification had not yet been created. With the release of the 350-12T and 350-24T (also designated the 350 10/100/1000 series BayStack switch), these two units adopted many of the same characteristics as the 450 series, and for purposes of this chapter, the material found in this section pertains to both BayStack varieties. All 450 examples in this section utilize 1.10 code.

## 450 and 350 10/100/1000 Features

The primary functions of the 450 and 350 10/100/1000 series switches are as follows:

■ **802.1Q-capable VLANs**   VLANs utilizing the 802.1Q frame-tagging standard.

■ **Gigabit uplinks**   1000BASE-SX/LX MDAs provide gigabit speeds for switch-to-switch or switch-to-server connections.

■ **MultiLink Trunking**   Allows for the grouping of physical ports to provide a single connection consisting of the aggregate bandwidth of all MLT members.

■ **Cascading to form stacks (450 only)**   Allows stacking of up to eight units together, to act as a single unit with a common backplane.

■ **IGMP snooping**   Internet Group Membership Protocol snooping allows for more efficient multicast transmission, by sending multicast streams only to switch ports where IGMP queries were received.

■ **802.1p traffic prioritization**   Traffic prioritization based on priority queuing, as defined in the 802.1p specification.

■ **Autonegotiating ports**   802.1u autonegotiation allows for dynamic selection of the fastest speed and duplex mode.

■ **Port mirroring**   Mirroring the input or output from one port and mirroring the same data to another port; used for taking sniffer traces in a switched environment.

# 802.1Q VLANs

A very common configuration when dealing with the 350 or 450 10/100/1000 series BayStack switches is to configure 802.1Q frame-tagged virtual LANs (VLANs) and then use a trunk connection to connect via a gigabit uplink port to an Accelar routing switch. For information regarding configuring VLANs and trunk connections on the Accelar, consult Chapter 9. To configure the 350 or 450 side of the connection, a console session must be established with the device, for which a menu-based system is used.

## Creating Multiple VLANs on the 350/450 10/100/1000

By default, each 450 and 350 10/100/1000 switch has a single default VLAN configured: VLAN 1. Additional VLANs may be configured by selecting Switch Configuration | VLAN Configuration | VLAN Configuration from the Main Menu. From this menu, select the option Create VLAN to create the new VLAN. Port-tagging options may also be selected from this screen, which is explained in the next section.

## VLAN Tagging Between the 350/450 and the Accelar

In this example, a 450T is connected via a gigabit uplink to an Accelar 1150. Two VLANs have been configured on the Accelar: VLAN_1, with a VLAN ID of 10, and VLAN_2, with a VLAN ID of 100.

On the 350 and 450 switches, VLANs are created differently than they are on the Accelar, though the concept remains the same. Whereas on the Accelar, a VLAN is created and given a VLAN ID (VID), on the 450, ports are assigned to a VLAN and then they are assigned a Port VLAN ID (PVID) on a port-by-port basis.

Unlike VLANs configured on the Accelar, a specific VID isn't assigned to the VLAN at the time of its creation; on the 450/350 10/100/1000 series switches, the VID is assigned at the port level. This is accomplished from the VLAN Port Configuration screen, accessible by selecting Switch Configuration | VLAN Configuration | VLAN Port Configuration from the Main Menu:

```
                      VLAN Port Configuration
                Unit: [ 1 ]
                Port: [ 25 ]
                Filter Tagged Frames: [ No ]
                Filter Untagged Frames: [ No ]
                Filter Unregistered Frames: [ No ]
                Port Name: [ Unit 1, Port 25 ]
                PVID: [ 100 ]
                Port Priority: [ 0 ]
The following parameters specify egress rules for the Gigabit port only:
        Primary VLAN Tagging (with VLAN equal to PVID): [ Untagged ]
        Secondary VLAN Tagging (with VLAN not equal to PVID): [ Tagged ]
Use spacebar to display choices, press <Return> or <Enter> to select choice.
Press Ctrl-R to return to previous menu. Press Ctrl-C to return to Main Menu.
```

In this example, port 25 is being assigned a PVID of 100; this is the same as assigning a VLAN a VID of 100 on the Accelar, the difference being that on the 350/450 10/100/1000, the VID must be assigned on a per-port basis for all ports that will be in the VLAN (see Figure 5-4).

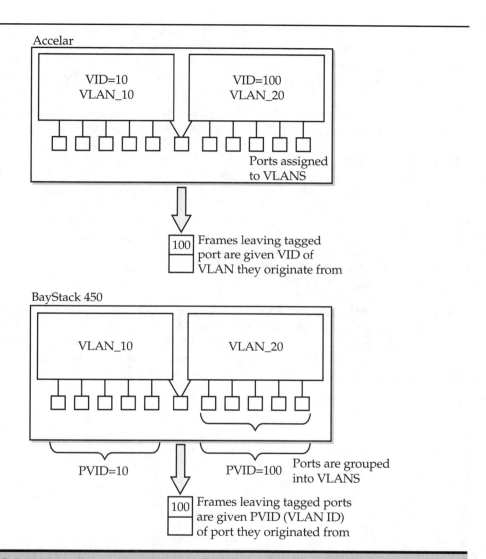

**Figure 5-4.** *VLAN ID assignment on the Accelar versus on the 450*

## VLAN Port Assignment

In the case of the 350/450, then, assigning ports to a VLAN is a two-step process:

    1. The port must be given the specific VID for the VLAN they are in. This VID (called the PVID on the 450/350) is assigned to frames that are transmitted out

a port configured for tagging. Thus, for example, if a frame comes in on port 1, which is configured with PVID 100, and then is transmitted out port 25, which is configured for tagging, the frame will be tagged with a VID of 100 before passing over the trunk. Likewise, any incoming traffic received on port 25 that has a VID of 100 will be transmitted out all ports that have a PVID of 100.

2. In addition, in the VLAN Configuration screen, the port must be set to either tagged (T) or untagged (U) for that VLAN (see the next section for details).

**PORT ASSIGNMENT ON THE BAYSTACK 350/450 10/100/1000**    On the 350 and 450 10/100/1000 series BayStack switches, ports are not designated as access or trunk, as they are in the Accelar. Instead, they are either tagged, untagged, or not members of the VLAN being configured. (The terms *tagged* and *untagged* eventually replaced *trunk* and *access* on the Accelar in the later versions of code.) Ports that are s et to tagged act as trunk ports, while untagged ports act as access ports. The port membership is selected by highlighting the desired port and then toggling through the choices by hitting the SPACEBAR. Pressing the ENTER key selects the currently displayed option. Options are untagged (U), tagged (T), or not a VLAN member (-).

**TAGGING FOR MULTIPLE VLANS**    Just as a trunk port on an Accelar must be made a member of each VLAN that it will carry, a trunk port on the 350 and 450 10/100/1000 series must be configured to tag for each individual VLAN that it will carry. This is accomplished in the VLAN Configuration screen, accessible by following the menu path Switch Configuration | VLAN Configuration from the Main Menu:

```
                         VLAN Configuration
                         Create VLAN: [ 1 ]
                          Delete VLAN: [ ]
                       VLAN Name: [ VLAN #1 ]
                          Port Membership
                1-6        7-12       13-18      19-24       25-28
                ------     ------     ------     ------      ------
Unit #1         UUUUUU     UUUUUU     UUUUUU     UUUUUU      UUTT
Unit #2         ------     ------     ------
Unit #3         UUUUUU     ------
KEY: T = Tagged Port Member, U = Untagged Port Member, - = Not a Member of VLAN
Use spacebar to display choices, press <Return> or <Enter> to select choice.
Press Ctrl-R to return to previous menu. Press Ctrl-C to return to Main Menu.
```

This output, obtained from a stack of three 450 switches, displays the VLAN port information regarding VLAN membership and whether the ports are tagged or untagged. In this example, all the ports in unit 1 are members of VLAN 1, none of the ports in unit 2 are members of VLAN 1, and, in unit 3, ports 1 through 6 are in VLAN 1 and ports 7 through 12 are not. Most of the ports are untagged, and ports 27 and 28 of unit 1 are configured as trunk ports (they are configured to tag). Untagged ports are designated with a U, while tagged ports are designated with a T.

In this example, only ports 27 and 28 in VLAN 1 are configured to tag; for these two ports to truly act as trunk ports, tagging must be enabled for each VLAN that the trunk will serve. This means that if two VLANs are on the 450 (VLAN 1 and VLAN 2), then for the 450 to tag outgoing frames for both VLANs, the option Create VLAN must be selected and toggled to the next VLAN, which causes the VLAN port configuration for the next VLAN to appear. If this is the first time that the device is being configured, all ports will flip back to being untagged (U), because, by default, all ports are untagged; this is a VLAN other than the one that was just configured for tagging on ports 27 and 28, so these ports now are listed as untagged. Toggle ports 27 and 28 to tagged (T) for all additional VLANs that will participate in the trunk (this is the same as assigning a trunk port to more than one VLAN on the Accelar). Otherwise, frames leaving ports 27 and 28 that originated in VLAN 1 will be tagged, but all others will not.

## Tagging on Gigabit Uplinks

In the VLAN Port Configuration screen, in addition to assigning the PVID and other parameters, two options are available that are specific to the gigabit ports:

```
Primary VLAN Tagging (with VLAN equal to PVID): [ Untagged ]
Secondary VLAN Tagging (with VLAN not equal to PVID): [ Tagged ]
```

These options are available because the gigabit uplink ports may be associated with one primary VLAN and several secondary VLANs. For instance, a gigabit uplink port may have a primary VLAN membership of VLAN 1 (this is the default). The gigabit ports may, however, be configured as members of multiple VLANs. These options indicate how the uplink port will behave in this case, using the following rules:

- **Primary VLAN Tagging (with VLAN equal to PVID)**   Indicates that for the VLAN sharing the same PVID as the uplink port, the uplink port may be considered either tagged or untagged. So, if the uplink port is in VLAN 1 with a PVID of 1, then for VLAN 1, it may be either tagged or untagged. The remaining VLANs will follow the rule defined by the second choice.

- **Secondary VLAN Tagging (with VLAN not equal to PVID)**   All other VLANs that the uplink port is a member of but that don't share its same PVID (for instance, the uplink port is in VLAN 1, with a PVID of 1, but is also a member of VLAN 2, with a PVID of 10, and VLAN 3, with a PVID of 100) are considered secondary VLANs. The uplink port may be either tagged or untagged for the secondary VLANs as well; however, whichever option is selected in this field applies to all secondary VLANs.

# Gigabit Uplinks

Both the 350 and 450 10/100/1000 have a single media dependent adapter (MDA) slot for the addition of an MDA module. The addition of an MDA module provides additional ports of varying types, including gigabit uplink ports. The following MDA modules are available for the 350/450 10/100/1000 series BayStack switches:

- **400-4TX:** Four 10/100BASE-TX RJ-45 autonegotiating RJ-45 Ethernet ports.
- **400-2FX:** Two 100BASE-FX ports using SC connectors.
- **400-4FX:** Four 100BASE-FX ports using SC connectors.
- **450-1SR:** A single MAC MDA with separate redundant PHY; two multimode fiber gigabit ports, only one of which is active at a time. The other acts as a standby, triggered by a physical-layer failure.
- **450-1SX:** Single port 1000BASE-SX MDA using multimode fiber.
- **450-1LR:** Single MAC MDA with separate redundant PHY; two long-range gigabit ports, only one of which is active at a time. The other acts as a standby, triggered by a physical-layer failure.
- **450-1LX:** Single port 1000BASE-LX MDA.

Any of the gigabit MDAs will provide 1000Mbps throughput for the 350/450 10/100/1000 series switch. For more information regarding the specifics of gigabit Ethernet connectivity, consult Chapter 2.

*Unlike many Nortel Networks MDA modules, the MDA modules for the 350 and 450 are not hot-swappable; the unit must be powered down prior to removing or adding an MDA module.*

# MultiLink Trunking

MultiLink Trunking is also supported on the 350/450 10/100/1000 series switches. This allows a series of ports to be grouped together and their bandwidth aggregated, so that they act as a single port. In this scenario, four 100Mbps ports grouped together in a MultiLink Trunk provide 400Mbps of bandwidth, for a total of 800Mbps when running in full-duplex mode. For purposes of Spanning Tree, the MLT is considered a single port.

Each MLT may have up to four port members, and each 350/450 10/100/1000 can support up to six MLTs. In the case of a 450 stack, MLTs may also have up to four members, although the limit of six MLTs applies to the whole stack, not to the individual units in the stack.

*In a 450 stack configuration, port members of an MLT grouping must all be on the same unit if the code version is lower than 1.3.0. Distributed MLT (for MLTs whose members span multiple stack units) was introduced in System Image version 1.3.0.*

## Configuring MLT on the 350/450 10/100/1000

MLT configuration is accomplished by selecting Switch Configuration | Multilink Trunk Configuration | Multilink Trunk Configuration. Here, the MLT groupings may be defined as follows:

```
MultiLink Trunk Configuration
Trunk  Trunk Members   (Unit/Port)   STP    Learning   Trunk Mode    Trunk Status
-----  -----------------------------  ------------  ---------------  ------------
1      [ 1/1 ][ 1/2 ][ 1/3 ][ 1/4 ]  [ Normal ]    Basic            [ Enabled ]
2      [ 2/1 ][ 2/2 ][ / ][ / ]      [ Normal ]    Basic            [ Enabled ]
3      [ 3/7 ][ 3/8 ][ 3/9 ][ 3/10 ] [ Normal ]    Basic            [ Enabled ]
4      [ / ][ / ][ / ][ / ]          [ Normal ]    Basic            [ Disabled ]
5      [ / ][ / ][ / ][ / ]          [ Normal ]    Basic            [ Disabled ]
6      [ / ][ / ][ / ][ / ]          [ Normal ]    Basic            [ Disabled ]
Trunk       Trunk Name
-----       ------------------
1           [ U2:T1 to FS1]
2           [ U2:T2 to S2]
3           [ U3:T3 to S3]
4           [ Trunk #4 ]
5           [ Trunk #5 ]
6           [ Trunk #6 ]
    Use spacebar to display choices, press <Return> or <Enter> to select choice.
    Press Ctrl-R to return to previous menu. Press Ctrl-C to return to Main Menu.
```

In this example, a stack of three 450s is configured with three MLT groupings; unit 1 has ports 1 through 4 grouped together, unit 2 has ports 1 and 2 grouped together, and unit 3 has ports 7 through 10 grouped together. Spanning Tree Learning is set to Normal for each MLT, which means that they will participate in 802.1d Spanning Tree, each active MLT is enabled, and each MLT is configured for Basic Mode.

 *The Trunk Mode field is currently a read-only field. A Trunk Mode of Basic indicates that the source MAC addresses will be assigned dynamically to specific trunk members, and from that point on will be associated with that specific member.*

# Cascading the 450

The BayStack 450 switches can also be stacked by using the cascade module (400-ST1), which is housed in a cascade module bay located in the rear of the chassis. To use this feature, the 450 switch must be running system image version 1.1.0 code or greater. This may require a code upgrade; if this is the case, you must follow these procedures:

1. Remove the cascade modules prior to upgrading the code.

   The BayStack 450 400-ST1 cascade modules must be removed prior to upgrading the code to version 1.1.0 or higher. Upgrading the units with the modules installed will prevent the upgrade from completing normally.

2. Upgrade the bootstrap code before upgrading the image code.

   Before the BayStack 450 can be upgraded to code version 1.1.0, the bootstrap must be upgraded. The procedure for doing this is exactly the same as the procedure for upgrading the image code (covered later in this section). This means that two code files must be uploaded to the switch; at the time of publication, the code versions use the naming scheme b4501101.img for the bootstrap code, and b4501102.img for the image code.

*If you are in doubt as to which file is the bootstrap code (which must be uploaded first), the smaller of the two files is the bootstrap file.*

## Managing the 450 Stack

After you upgrade the code and install the cascade modules, you must connect the units via the cascade cables in the following fashion:

1. Connect the cables from the Cascade A Out port to the Cascade A In port in the next switch in the stack (see Figure 5-5).

2. After you connect the last unit in the stack, connect the Cascade A Out port in the last unit in the stack to the Cascade A In port in the first unit in the stack.

*If the maximum of eight units are being stacked, the normal cascade cable will be too short to make the connection from the bottom of the stack back up to the top unit; to complete the stack in this case, a special meter-long (39.27 inches) cascade cable needs to be used (order number AL2018001).*

## Selecting a Base Unit and Stack Numbering

The numbering of the units within a stack of BayStack 450 switches revolves around which unit in the stack is designated the Base Unit. This is accomplished by setting the Unit Select Switch located on the 400-ST1 cascade module to the up position. Unit numbering may also be adjusted through a console session:

```
                    BayStack 450-24T Main Menu
              IP Configuration/Setup...
              SNMP Configuration...
              System Characteristics...
              Switch Configuration...
              Console/Comm Port Configuration...
              Identify Unit Numbers
              Renumber Stack Units...
              Spanning Tree Configuration...
              TELNET Configuration...
              Software Download...
              Display Event Log
              Reset
              Reset to Default Settings
              Logout
     Use arrow keys to highlight option, press <Return> or <Enter> to
select option.
```

ETHERNET ON NORTEL NETWORKS

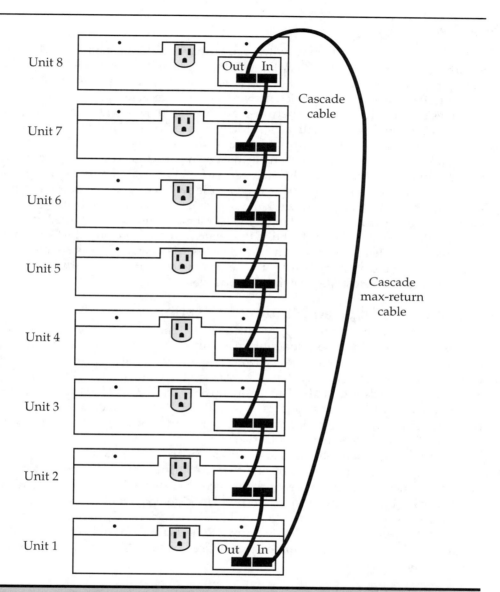

**Figure 5-5.** *Cascade cabling scheme for BayStack 450 cascade modules*

The options to manipulate the unit numbering are presented in bold in the screen output above; these options are only made available from the Main Menu in code version 1.1.0 or higher.

# IGMP Snooping

The 350/450 10/100/1000 series switches are capable of IGMP snooping, which helps to further refine the routing of IGMP multicast streams. When using IGMP, routers configured as IGMP Designated Routers issue Host Membership Queries out each of their interfaces, to determine which networks want to receive a given multicast stream. Hosts residing on the particular network indicate that they want to receive the stream by responding to the query with a Host Membership Report. This limits the scope of the multicast to only those networks containing hosts that need to receive it.

In an IGMP environment, if even one host on a particular network responds to a Host Membership Query, then the multicast stream in question must be directed to that network. IGMP snooping can be used by the switch to filter the mutlicast streams so that not every host on the network receives them. To accomplish this, the 350/450 monitors (snoops) each port, looking for Host Membership Reports issued in response to a Host Membership Query, by hosts that want to receive the multicast stream in question. The switch notes on which ports the Host Membership Reports were received, and then, when the multicast stream is received by the switch, forwards it only to the ports on which the Host Membership Reports were received.

## Proxy Reporting and Multicast Filtering

In addition to "marking" ports that received Host Membership Reports as being ports that need to receive the associated multicast stream, the switch is capable of generating a Proxy Report, which it issues back toward the router that originated the Host Membership Query (this Proxy Report may be sent to an upstream 350/450 if the router is not directly attached). If an upstream 350/450 10/100/1000 series switch does receive the Proxy Report, it generates its own Proxy Report and combines it with the received information. This consolidated Proxy Report makes its way back to the router that issued the Host Membership Query.

The advantages of IGMP are that multicast streams are limited by the router to only networks that need to receive them, and then are further limited by the switches to only the segments within that network that need to receive them. In addition, the router does not necessarily need to interpret Host Membership Reports from every individual host wanting to receive the multicast; instead, it only needs to interpret a much smaller number of consolidated Proxy Reports (perhaps only one, depending on the design). This cuts down on unnecessarily used bandwidth and overhead on both the switch and the router.

## Configuring IGMP Snooping

IGMP snooping is configured on the 350/450 10/100/1000 series switches by selecting Switch Configuration | IGMP Configuration from the Main Menu. This opens the IGMP Configuration screen:

```
                        IGMP Configuration
                VLAN: [ 2 ]
                Snooping: [ Enabled ]
                Proxy: [ Enabled ]
                Robust Value: [ 2 ]
                Query Time: [ 125 seconds ]
                Set Router Ports: [ Version 1 ]
                         Static Router Ports
          1-6      7-12      13-18     19-24     25-28
          ------   ------    ------    ------    ------
Unit #1   ------   -X----    -X----    ------    ----
Unit #2   -X---X   ------    -
Unit #3   ------   ------    -
Unit #4   ------   ------    ---X
KEY: X = IGMP Port Member (and VLAN Member), - = Not an IGMP Member
Use spacebar to display choices, press <Return> or <Enter> to select choice.
Press Ctrl-R to return to previous menu. Press Ctrl-C to return to Main Menu.
```

Here, the IGMP-specific parameters may be set on a VLAN-by-VLAN basis. Certain options available on this screen relate to the VLAN that has been selected, while others are applied to all VLANs. The configurable parameters are as follows:

- **VLAN**   The currently selected VLAN to which the VLAN-specific IGMP parameters will be applied.

- **Snooping**   Enables or disables IGMP snooping; the Snooping parameter applies to all VLANs.

- **Proxy**   Enables or disables the generation of IGMP Proxy Reports, which consolidate all received Membership Host Reports for delivery to the upstream switch or router. To enable this parameter, the Snooping parameter must also be enabled. This parameter is applied to all VLANs.

- **Robust Value**   Enables the user to offset expected packet loss on a specific subnet (VLAN), allowing for varying degrees of robustness in the event of packet loss. This parameter affects only the selected VLAN. The default value is 2, with a range of 1 to 64.

- **Query Time**   Limits the frequency with which IGMP queries will be passed onto the selected VLAN. The default value is 125 seconds, with a range of 1 to 512 seconds.

- **Set Router Ports**   Defines whether the switch will accommodate IGMPv1 or IGMPv2 (see RFC 2236). This change affects all VLANs.

- **Static Router Ports**   The remainder of the IGMP Configuration screen is devoted to the configuration of static router ports. For each VLAN, each port that has a path to a multicast router should be selected by toggling the port indicator from a - to an X. These ports don't have to have a multicast router directly connected; the indicated ports need only have a path to the router.

If an MLT is to be used as a static router port, then all group members of the MLT must be selected as static router ports.

# 802.1p Traffic Prioritization

The 350/450 10/100/1000 series switches have two priority transmit queues on a per-port basis: a high-priority queue and a low-priority queue. Additionally, the switches may be configured with eight different traffic classes (priority 0 to priority 7), which may be assigned either a high or low priority. Once these traffic classes are configured, the different user priorities may be assigned to individual ports.

Once a traffic priority is assigned to a port, traffic coming in on that port is assigned the given priority; this priority indicator is part of the 802.1Q frame tag and, as such, will be carried with the frame throughout the network to its destination, to be interpreted by all 802.1p-capable switches along the path (see Figure 5-6).

Each transmit buffer, then, is divided into a high- and low-priority queue, and each queue is broken down into different priority levels, where the high-priority queue takes precedence over the low-priority queue, and higher priority levels take precedence over lower-priority levels within the individual queues.

## Configuring Traffic Classes and Priority

The configuration of 802.1p traffic prioritization is a two-step process: the traffic classes must be defined, and then priorities must be assigned to individual ports. By default, all traffic classes are set to low, which means that all traffic is initially set for the low-priority transmit queue. This does not mean that the traffic is assigned a low priority by nature; low and high priority are relative values and, by default, because all traffic is assigned the same priority, all traffic is equal if none of the values are changed. Altering the traffic class and priority levels is accomplished through the Traffic Class

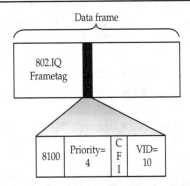

**Figure 5-6.** *802.1p traffic class indicator used to assign priority in 802.1Q frame tag*

Configuration screen, accessible by selecting Switch Configuration | VLAN Configuration | Traffic Class Configuration from the Main Menu:

```
                   Traffic Class Configuration
          User Priority  Traffic Class
          ------------   -------------
          Priority 0:         [ Low ]
          Priority 1:         [ Low ]
          Priority 2:         [ Low ]
          Priority 3:         [ Low ]
          Priority 4:         [ High ]
          Priority 5:         [ High ]
          Priority 6:         [ High ]
          Priority 7:         [ High ]
Changing the priorities of the traffic classes will cause an automatic
Reset to Current Settings to occur across the entire stack.
The current configuration will be adapted to the new set of priorities

Are you sure you want to change priorities to the new settings? [ Yes ]

Use spacebar to display choices, press <Return> or <Enter> to select choice.
Press Ctrl-R to return to previous menu. Press Ctrl-C to return to Main Menu.
```

In this example, priorities 0 through 3 are assigned to the low-priority queue, while priorities 4 through 7 are assigned to the high-priority queue. These priorities may be altered to any combination desired.

**SETTING TRAFFIC PRIORITIES**    After the traffic class of each priority has been set, the different priorities may be configured on each individual port. This is done through the VLAN Port Configuration screen, accessible by selecting Switch Configuration | VLAN Configuration | VLAN Port Configuration from the Main Menu:

```
          Unit: [ 1 ]
          Port: [ 25 ]
          Filter Tagged Frames: [ No ]
          Filter Untagged Frames: [ No ]
          Filter Unregistered Frames: [ No ]
          Port Name: [ Unit 1, Port 25 ]
          PVID: [ 10 ]
          Port Priority: [ 5 ]
```

This output is a snippet from the VLAN Port Configuration screen; port 25 (with a PVID of 10) has been assigned a port priority of 5, which will place it in the high-priority queue in accordance with the traffic class configuration outlined earlier in this section. This information will be placed in the 802.1Q tag along with the VID.

# Port Mirroring on the 350/450 10/100/1000

*Port mirroring* (also called *conversation steering*) is used in a switched environment primarily for purposes of obtaining sniffer traces. Unlike a shared media environment, a switch does not simply propagate all traffic out all ports. For this reason, a sniffer placed on a switched port will not obtain a sample of all traffic passing through the switch—only the traffic passing through its own switched port.

To work around this, port mirroring enables users to define which ports they would like to monitor, and then select the port to which the traffic received and transmitted on the port(s) being monitored will be mirrored. For example, if a sniffer is placed on port 10 and wants to sniff the transfer between a client on port 1 and a server on port 5, port 10 is selected as the monitor port, and ports 1 and 5 are the monitored ports.

## Configuring Port Mirroring

The port mirroring configuration is accomplished in the Port Mirroring Configuration screen, accessible by selecting Switch Configuration | Port Mirroring Configuration from the Main Menu:

```
                        Port Mirroring Configuration
        Monitoring Mode: [ -> Port X or Port Y -> ]
        Monitor Unit/Port: [ 1/10 ]
              Unit/Port X: [ 1/1 ]
              Unit/Port Y: [ 1/5 ]
                  Address A: [ 00-00-00-00-00-00 ]
                  Address B: [ 00-00-00-00-00-00 ]

Port mirroring configuration has taken effect.
                  Currently Active Port Mirroring Configuration
                  --------------------------------------------
Monitoring Mode: -> Port X or Port Y -> Monitor Unit: 1 Port: 10
Unit X: 1 Port 1: 5 Unit Y: 1 Port Y: 5
Use spacebar to display choices, press <Return> or <Enter> to select choice.
Press Ctrl-R to return to previous menu. Press Ctrl-C to return to Main Menu.
```

The preceding screen shows the scenario in which the traffic between ports 1 and 5 (on stack unit 1) is being mirrored to the monitor port, port 10 (also on stack unit 1). In this configuration, all traffic received by port 1 and then transmitted out port 5, is mirrored to port 10. A variety of monitoring modes, listed in Table 5-1, may be selected by altering the Monitoring Mode parameter.

In addition to these monitoring modes, port mirroring may also be configured to specify certain MAC addresses. This is accomplished by entering the MAC addresses of the two communicating stations (the client and server, in the present example) into the fields provided for Address A and Address B. Once this is done, one of the additional address-based monitoring modes, listed in Table 5-2, may be selected.

| Monitoring Mode | Monitors |
|---|---|
| -> Port X | Traffic received by port X |
| Port X -> | Traffic transmitted by port X |
| <-> Port X | Traffic received or transmitted by port X |
| -> Port X or Port Y -> | Traffic received by port X or transmitted by port Y |
| -> Port X and Port Y -> | Traffic received by X destined for Y and then transmitted out Y |
| <->Port X and Port Y <-> | Traffic received/transmitted by port X and port Y |

**Table 5-1.**   *Port Mirroring Port-Based Monitoring Modes*

In the previous example of monitoring traffic between a client on port 1 and a server on port 5, the most efficient option might be to configure the MAC address of each station and then select a Monitoring Mode of Address A <-> Address B, to mirror the entire conversation between the two devices to port 10, the monitor port where the sniffer is connected.

**Note**   *MAC Address A and B may also be configured in the MAC Address Table screen, accessed from the Main Menu by selecting Switch Configuration | MAC Address Table.*

# Upgrading the 350/450 10/100/1000

Upgrading the 350/450 is a straightforward procedure. To complete the upgrade, a TFTP server package is needed, along with the appropriate image/bootstrap code.

| Monitoring Mode | Monitors |
|---|---|
| Address A -> Any Address | Traffic from address A to any MAC address |
| Any Address -> Address A | Traffic from any MAC address destined for address A |
| <-> Address A | Traffic to or from MAC address A |
| Address A -> Address B | Traffic from address A to address B |
| Address A <-> Address B | All traffic between address A and address B |

**Table 5-2.**   *Port Mirroring Address-Based Monitoring Modes*

The switch must be configured with a valid IP address, and must be reachable by the TFTP server (this can be verified by pinging the switch from the TFTP server). A station or laptop can be used as a TFTP server by using the appropriate software package; if you have no TFTP server on site, contact the Nortel Networks Technical Solutions Center (TSC) and one can be made available to you.

Once the necessary elements are in place, the upgrade can be initiated by selecting Software Download from the Main Menu:

```
                                Software Download
Image Filename: [ b4501102.img ]
TFTP Server IP Address: [ 160.60.10.123 ]

Start TFTP Load of New Image: [ Yes ]

The Software Download process has started. Do NOT power down the
switch before the process has completed (approximately 10 minutes).
Enter text, press <Return> or <Enter> to select choice.
Press Ctrl-R to return to previous menu. Press Ctrl-C to return to Main Menu.
```

Here, the upgrade is executed simply by entering the image name (the path is generally outlined in the TFTP server configuration and does not need to be included in the image name) and the IP address of the TFTP server. Once these parameters are configured, toggle the Start TFTP Load of New Image field to Yes, and then press ENTER to initiate the download.

 *Once the upgrade has initiated, do not power down the switch; a power interruption in the middle of a code upgrade may corrupt the image.*

# The Complete Reference

Nortel Networks

# Chapter 6

## Frame Switching on the Centillion Platform

This chapter covers the basic frame-switching parameters related to the Centillion platform. Many of the Centillion features may be found in other chapters that are specific to a particular technology, such as ATM and Token Ring, as well as an appendix on SpeedView, the Centillion configuration utility. This chapter, in contrast, covers the basic frame-switching parameters that are common to most Centillion configurations, and that are not necessarily technology-specific.

## System Information

The System tab which is the default tab in SpeedView 3.0 and higher, provides information regarding the code version, system location, system contact, and so forth that are common to most networking devices. In addition, the password may be set in the System tab, though it will not be displayed (a series of asterisks are displayed in its place). The following fields are also configured from this tab:

- **Admin MAC Address**   A locally administered MAC address that can be used to override the burned-in hardware address, which is the default. The original MAC address can be restored at any time by selecting the Reset MAC Address on config download button. This change will require a switch reset in order to take effect.

- **Token Ring Max Frame Size**   The Token Ring maximum transmit unit (MTU) size for the switch.

- **Station Table Aging Timer**   The amount of time, in seconds, before inactive MAC entries in the forwarding database are aged out. The range is from 10 to 1,000,000 seconds, with a default of 300 seconds (5 minutes).

- **NetBIOS Name Table Aging Timer**   Indicates the amount of time before a NetBIOS name is aged out of the system; this value is only used if NetBIOS Name Proxy is enabled (this is done in the NetBIOS Filters tab, described later in the chapter). The Range is from 1 to 999,999,999 seconds, with a default of 300 seconds (5 minutes).

- **NetBIOS Query Interval**   Indicates the maximum rate at which NetBIOS name queries are passed through the switch. The value used is multiplied by 100 milliseconds. This value is only used if NetBIOS Name Proxy is enabled (this is done in the NetBIOS Filters tab, described later in the chapter). The range is from 0 to 255.

- **Source Route Unknown Frame Flood**   This parameter is only significant if Token Ring LANE is being used in a Source Route Bridging environment; if not, this parameter is ignored and does not need to be configured. Source Route Unknown Frame Flood relates to how Spanning Tree Explorer (STE) frames are handled when received by a token ring LEC; if this feature is disabled, and the explorer frame is received, the learning process is initiated while the explorer frame itself is dropped. If this feature is enabled, upon receipt of an STE, the learning process is initiated and the STE is also sent to the BUS for processing.

■ **Redundant MCP Enabled**   Appears only in code version 3.0 or higher, where more than one MCP card of the same type are configured in the unit. Selecting this box indicates that MCP redundancy is enabled.

# Network Management Information

The Centillion network management information is accessible from the Network Management tab in SpeedView, and includes the IP-related information, such as the IP address, mask, and gateway, as well as the SNMP configuration, such as community strings, trap configuration, and so forth.

## IP Information

The Centillion IP information relates to the IP stack that resides on the Master Control Processor (MCP). This information includes the primary and secondary IP address, mask, and gateway. In addition, if a configuration server is being used by the Centillion to obtain its configuration, the Trivial File Transfer Protocol (TFTP) server address is configured here, as well. The following parameters can be configured from this tab:

■ **IP Address (Primary and Secondary)**   Relates to either the primary or secondary IP address associated with the MCP, depending on which of the two radio buttons is selected. The secondary IP is generally associated with ATMSpeed MCP modules, and is applied to the single Ethernet port mounted on these blades. The secondary IP address can be useful for SNMP transfers in an environment in which no other Ethernet ports are free, or the chassis is entirely populated with ATMSpeed modules.

**Note**   *The primary and secondary IP addresses must be on different networks or subnets; placing both addresses in the same network will cause both to become unreachable.*

■ **Subnet Mask**   The subnet mask associated with the IP address. This value is unique for the primary and secondary IP addresses.

■ **Broadcast Address**   The IP broadcast address that is used by the switch; by default, the broadcast address 255.255.255.255 is used. This value is unique for the primary and secondary IP addresses.

■ **Gateway Address**   The gateway used by the switch. This value is relevant if an image upgrade or TFTP configuration application is being performed that must pass through a router. In this event, the local router interface should be configured here. This value is unique for the primary and secondary IP addresses.

■ **Config Server Address** If the switch is configured to obtain its configuration information automatically via TFTP (see the upcoming section "System Configuration"), then the IP address of the TFTP server should be configured here. If BootP is being used, the BootP server address should be configured here. This parameter applies to the primary IP address only.

■ **IP Enabled** Enables IP for purposes of SNMP and TFTP transfers (enabled by default).

■ **BootP Enabled** Allows the Centillion to obtain IP and configuration information via BootP (disabled by default).

# SNMP Information

The SNMP information is also configured from the Network Management tab in SpeedView. Here, the community strings and trap information may be set.

## Community Strings

Unique community strings can be selected to provide security regarding SNMP communications with the device. By default, the community strings are configured as public, for read-only access, and private, for read/write access.

## Trap Enabled

Selecting Trap Enabled enables the use of SNMP traps for the device; this causes the switch to issue a warning, or trap, to a specified management station (or stations) under certain circumstances. If Trap Enabled is selected, an SNMP trap is issued if the following events occur:

■ **SNMP authentication failures** A user attempts to gain access to the device by using the incorrect community strings. The Auth Trap Enabled box must also be selected to include these traps.

■ **Cold starts** The device undergoes a hard reset.

■ **Link up** A port on the switch becomes active.

■ **Link down** A port on the switch stops functioning.

## Authentication Trap Enabled

Selecting the Auth Trap Enabled box causes the switch to issue a trap whenever someone attempts to control it by using the incorrect community strings. This can be useful for detecting unauthorized access to the switch.

## Multiple Trap Receiver Configuration

The Centillion can be configured to issue traps to several network management stations. This is done by clicking Add under the Multiple Trap Receiver Config section of the Network Management tab, and then filling in the following fields:

- ■ **Trap Community**   The community string used when sending traps to the network management station.

- ■ **Trap Receiver IP Address**   The IP address of one of the management stations the trap will be sent to.

- ■ **Trap Enabled**   Allows the individual entries to be enabled and disabled.

- ■ **Add/Delete**   Allow new entries to be added or currently configured entries to be deleted.

## System Configuration

The System Configuration portion of the Network Management tab is used when the Centillion is to obtain its configuration information via TFTP rather than from its internal flash, when it first boots up. The following fields apply:

- ■ **System Configured via TFTP**   Causes the Centillion to attempt to contact a TFTP server upon bootup, to obtain its configuration information. The TFTP server address that it attempts to contact is the address configured in the Config Server Address field in the IP configuration portion of this tab.

- ■ **Config File Name**   The filename of the configuration file that resides on the TFTP server.

# Switching Mode

The Switching Mode tab includes parameters relating to the bridging method, Spanning Tree method, as well as the configuration of bridge groups or VLAN/Spanning Tree Group combinations.

## Bridge Groups

Prior to code (and SpeedView) version 4.0, the term *bridge group* was used to describe the logical partitions, or broadcast domains, used by the Centillion. A bridge group encompasses both a logical broadcast domain (which is now thought of as a *virtual LAN*, or *VLAN*) and a separate Spanning Tree entity. This means that two bridge groups running in parallel not only constitute two separate broadcast domains, but also do not incur a loop condition from a Spanning Tree perspective:

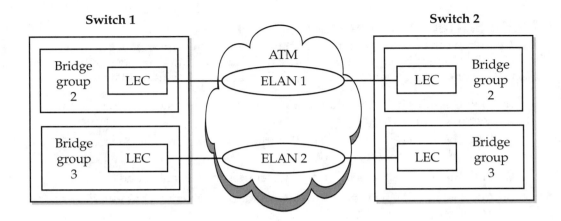

Bridge groups may support either Token Ring or Ethernet, but not both, and are a way of logically breaking up the network. Most commonly, bridge groups are also used to associate different groupings of legacy ports with specific ATM Emulated LANs (ELANs). For example, a C100 containing one ATMSpeed MCP and five EtherSpeed host cards may have each of the five cards associated with five different ELANs. This is accomplished by placing the cards in five different bridge groups, and then associating each of the five LAN Emulation Clients (LECs) with the different bridge groups, as well (see Figure 6-1).

In this example, note also that bridge groups have local significance only. Although the LEC for ELAN 1 is associated with bridge group 03 on switch A, the LEC for ELAN 1 on switch B is associated with bridge group 06. This configuration is supported,

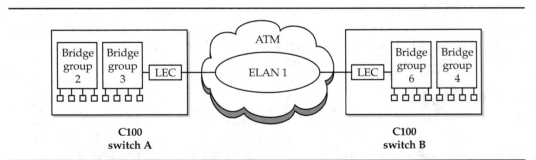

**Figure 6-1.** *Bridge groups used to logically partition switch*

because bridge group information is not passed from switch to switch; the configuration is simply a means of grouping ports on a single switch.

# Virtual Local Area Networks

With the release of code version 4.0, the concept of bridge groups was altered to resemble more closely the Accelar's method of separating VLANs and STGs. Whereas before, with bridge groups, each grouping consisted of an individual broadcast domain (VLAN) and a unique Spanning Tree entity, with code version 4.0, the term "bridge group" has been replaced with two separate groupings: VLANs and Spanning Tree Groups.

# Spanning Tree Groups

VLANs may be thought of in the same way that bridge groups were in pre-4.0 code; the difference being that VLANs, by default, do not utilize separate Spanning Tree entities, so VLANs may not run in parallel without first creating a new STG:

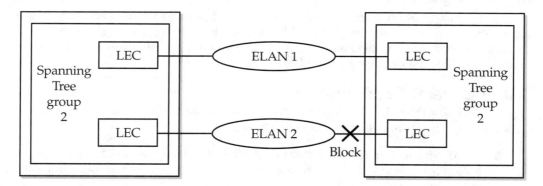

In this example, two VLANs have been associated with two ATM ELANs. However, both VLANs (and therefore both clients for the two ELANs) reside in the default Ethernet STG. A loop is incurred in this scenario, and one of the LECs will go into a blocking state. This is a good example of a common configuration that would have worked when bridge groups were being used (because they separated the Spanning Tree entities automatically), but requires a bit of additional configuration and design consideration when using the new code. However, this new scheme does provide more flexibility of design, and can also help to increase efficiency. For more information regarding the concepts of different VLANs and STGs, consult Chapter 10, which presents the information relative to the Accelar; the concepts remain essentially the same.

# IP Multicast

Starting with code version 3.1, IP multicast support was introduced into the Centillion product line. This allows for what is commonly called *IGMP snooping*, whereby a switch helps to further narrow down the scope of multicast streams, by noting which ports receive queries. When a Centillion configured for IP multicast receives reports from hosts on different ports, indicating in which multicast groups they want to participate, the switch will bundle this information and generate a single IGMP report that it sends to the router, indicating that it wants to participate in each of the IP multicast groups for which it has received host reports. Upon receipt of these multicast streams, the Centillion forwards them to their appropriate destinations, based on which ports the original host reports were received on. The Centillion supports both IGMPv1 and IGMPv2.

**Note** *Code version 3.1 or higher is required to support IP multicast.*

## IGMP Configuration

All IGMP configuration is accomplished from the IP Multicast tab in SpeedView. If the SpeedView version is prior to 3.1, the IP Multicast tab is not present, because the feature was not added until code version 3.1. The following sections describe the fields and parameters that can be configured from this tab.

### IGMP General Configuration

The general IGMP configuration consists of enabling IGMP support and selecting an IGMP mode. The following parameters can be set:

- **IGMP Support Enabled**   Indicates whether IGMP support is active. If this option is not selected, the feature is deactivated and none of the configuration options are accessible.

- **Pseudo Query Mode Enabled**   Enables Pseudo Query mode. This option is used if no router is associated with the bridge group or VLAN/STG grouping. This actually allows the switch to send IGMP queries in the absence of a router. If multiple switches are running Pseudo Query Mode, an election process takes place whereby the switch with the lowest IP address becomes the "querier" and all others are silent. This option is not necessary if an IGMP router is configured within the bridge group or VLAN/STG combination.

- **IRAP Query Mode Enabled**   Enables IGMP Router Advertisement Protocol (IRAP). Used to inform the switch of the router's presence when more than one IGMP router is present. Since only one router in this case issues queries and the rest remain silent, the IRAP feature allows switches to advertise the presence of silent IGMP routers, and not only the querier. The IRAP protocol is used by the

Centillion switches only, and is not recognized by IGMP routers or hosts. If enabled, the switch will send out IRAP packets periodically to other Centillion switches when two or more IGMP router ports are present.

- **Max Groups**   Indicates the maximum number of IGMP multicast groups the switch may support.

## IGMP Timer

The IGMP timer information can be configured on a switch-by-switch basis from the IP Multicast tab. The following parameters apply:

- **Query Interval**   Indicates how often the device should expect to see an IGMP query.
- **Query Response Interval**   Indicates how often the device should expect to see an IGMP response.
- **Robustness**   Indicates the robustness (tolerance to packet loss) the multicast group is configured to handle. A higher value makes a greater amount of packet loss acceptable.

## IGMP Router Port

The IGMP router port is the Centillion port from which the IGMP router is accessible. It is from this router (and therefore, this port) that the router IGMP queries are received. If multiple IGMP routers are connected to the Centillion, all IGMP router ports should be defined, not just the querier. The IGMP router port can be configured by means of a static entry for the port(s):

- **Cards**   Indicates the card (module) with which the IGMP router is associated.
- **Ports**   Indicates the port on the selected card with which the IGMP router is associated.
- **Static Entries**   Indicates which module/port combinations have been statically set. To create a static entry, select the card and port as previously described, and then click the Add button to commit the entry to the Static Entry table.

## IGMP Group Address

The IGMP multicast address groupings can also be defined, by configuring either an Included or Excluded list. Either one or the other must be selected, because both may not be used simultaneously. Multicast group addresses can be added to either list, indicating whether or not streams for these groups should be forwarded. The following parameters are associated with the IGMP group addresses:

- **Static Entries**   Configured by entering the IP multicast address in the field provided, and then clicking Add. The address is then added into either the

Excluded or Included table, depending on which is selected at the time the entry was added.

- **Excluded**   Addresses that are configured in the Excluded table are not forwarded.
- **Included**   Addresses that are configured in the Included table are forwarded to the appropriate ports. All other multicast streams are not forwarded.

# Packet Filters

The Centillion is capable of using *packet filters,* which can be used to limit broadcast traffic, mirror traffic, or block traffic altogether. Packet filtering is achieved by first creating filter templates and then applying those filters to the desired ports.

## Using Packet Filters

Packet filters are configured from the Packet Filter tab in SpeedView. Prior to code version 3.0, all filters had to be configured manually. Beginning with code version 3.0, some of the more commonly used filters have been preconfigured and may simply be selected from a menu. The sections that follow describe how to configure packet filters on the Centillion; these sections do not walk through configuring a variety of specific packet filters, but rather describe how a filter is created. The specific values that relate to the filter you want to create must be entered, using the fields and parameters described next.

### Packet Filter Configuration

The following parameters must be configured for each packet filter; some fields are generated automatically:

- **Name**   The user-defined name associated with the packet filter.
- **ID**   The ID associated with the packet filter. This value is generated automatically at the time the filter is applied.
- **Seq**   The sequence number of the filter. This is used when more than one filtering criterion is associated with a single Filter ID. For instance, a filter with ID 1 may have one criterion that states that a certain type of packet should be accepted, and a second criterion that states that everything should be dropped. In this case, the first criterion should have a sequence of 1 and the second should have a sequence of 2. Reversing the order would cause the switch to first drop everything, leaving nothing to compare against the second criterion. The sequence value is referenced in the Match and Fail functions (described later in this list).

- **Type**  May be set to MAC (the default) or LLC, to indicate where the offset should begin. In most cases, MAC should be selected. However, in a source route bridged (SRB) token ring environment, LLC should be selected, because the presence of the RIF in the frame skews the offset. For this reason, the offset should begin at the start of the LLC header in a token ring SRB network.

- **Offset**  Indicates where the information to be examined by the filter begins. This value is expressed as the number of bytes, starting from the location defined in the Type field, before the information to be examined is reached. For example, to target the destination address with a Type of MAC, a value of 2 would be used.

- **Value (hex)**  Defines the actual value that will be used as the criteria. For example, if the filter were targeting a specific destination MAC address in an Ethernet network, a Type of MAC would be used, the Offset would be set to 2, and the actual destination MAC address would be entered in the Value field.

- **Cond**  Defines what constitutes a match condition for the filter. The condition will either require an exact match or define a range of all possible matches. The following options can be selected as conditions:

| Condition | Meaning |
| --- | --- |
| EQ | Equal to |
| NE | Not equal to |
| LT | Less than |
| LE | Less than or equal to |
| GT | Greater than |
| GE | Greater than or equal to |

- **Match**  If the condition specified in the Cond field is met, the packet may still need to be checked against additional filters. If this is the case, the Match value indicates the sequence number of the next filter that should be used. For example, suppose that only packets that are passing between a specific source and destination MAC are to be targeted by the filter. The filter that checks the source address may have a sequence of 1, while the filter that checks the destination address may have a sequence of 4. In this case, the first filter would have a match value of 4, because after verification is made that the source is the source station being targeted, the destination address must be checked to

ETHERNET ON NORTEL NETWORKS

see whether it also is a match. If no other filters must be checked, a value of 0 is used.

■ **Fail**    If the first filter (the filter within a group that has the first sequence number) does not produce a match for an incoming packet, the Fail field indicates what should be done with the packet next. If a valid sequence number within the Filter ID is entered, then the packet will be compared against that filter next. If the packet should be compared against a new filter group with a different Filter ID, then select a value that exceeds the total sequence numbers within the current group. For example, if the current filter group has four entries, and you want the packet to be checked against the next filter group, select a value of 5 (selecting 255 will also produce this result). If the packet doesn't need to be compared against any additional filters, use a value of 0.

■ **Fwd**    Indicates what should be done with the packet if the match criteria is met. The options in this table apply:

| Value | Meaning |
|-------|---------|
| NORM | Forward the packet normally, as well as to any additional destinations. |
| DROP | Drop the packet. |
| ALT | Forward the packet only to the additional destinations. |

■ **Mon Dest**    Allows traffic matching the filter to be forwarded to a monitor port, where a sniffer or probe may be attached. Module and port numbers are entered with a colon separating them. For example, module 3, port 1 is entered as 3:1. Only one monitor destination may be entered.

■ **Addl Dests**    Indicates additional ports that the packet matching the criteria should be directed to. Module and port numbers are separated by a colon, and multiple ports may be defined by separating them with commas. For instance, to send a packet matching the criteria to module 3 port 1, module 4 port 3, and module 6 port 2, the entry would appear as 3:1, 4:3, 6:2.

## Applying the Filter

Applying the filter, once created, is accomplished through the tabs relating to the specific modules to which the filter will be applied. For example, if a given filter will be applied to port 5 of module 2, first select the tab related to module 2, and then select port 5. Depending on the code version, the filter application field will consist of one of two things; the filters may be applied through the use of radio buttons or, in the more recent code versions (3.0 and later), a button labeled Configure must be selected. Either method opens the Apply Filter window, shown here:

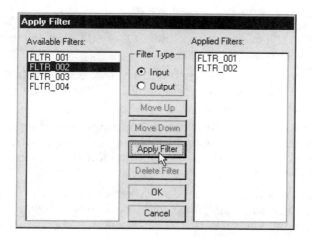

In the Apply Filter window, you can choose the individual filters by selecting them from the Available Filters table, selecting a Filter Type (Input or Output), and then clicking Apply Filter. After you do this, each filter is applied to the port and appears in the Applied Filters table.

# NetBIOS Filters

In addition to the packet filters available in the Packet Filter tab, specific NetBIOS filtering may be achieved from the NetBIOS Filters tab. These filters limit NetBIOS broadcasts and NetBIOS name advertisements. The NetBIOS Filters tab is broken down into several sections, beginning with the selection of the bridge group (or VLAN/STG) with which the filter will be associated:

- **Token Ring Bridge Group (SRB/SRT)**   Bridge groups (or VLANs) that are configured for Token Ring and using either source route bridging or source route transparent (SRT) bridging.

- **Token Ring Bridge Group (TB)**   Bridge groups (or VLANs) that are configured for transparent bridging.

- **Ethernet Bridge Group**   Ethernet bridge groups or VLANs.

## Filter

The filter parameters must be configured as well. This involves determining the module and port number with which the filter will be associated, as well as additional parameters, such as the specific bridge group:

- **Module Number**   The module number to which the filter will apply.

- **Port Number**   The port number of the previously described module to which the filter will apply.

- **Bridge Group**   If the switching mode that is selected is a Token Ring bridge group or VLAN that is running either SRB or SRT, then the bridge group (or VLAN) number must be specified.

- **(V)ring# (hex)**   If the switching mode that is selected is a Token Ring bridge group or VLAN that is running either SRB or SRT, then the ring number or Vring number must be specified in hex.

- **Datagram Broadcast Discard**   Keeps datagram broadcast traffic on the local segment that is associated with the selected port. DATAGRAM_BROADCAST frames are used by NetBIOS to broadcast NetBIOS datagrams to all names on the network.

- **NetBIOS Name Proxy Enabled**   Allows the switch to learn NetBIOS names and then redirect frames destined for those names directly to them rather than broadcasting another query onto the network.

- **Name**   Indicates the actual NetBIOS name that the filter is placed against. Multiple names may be added, and wildcards may be used. If the wildcard appears in the middle of the name, a question mark (?) should be used. For instance, to filter against the names MAIL1SERV, MAIL2SERV, and MAIL3SERV, the single entry MAIL?SERV can be used. The * wildcard is used at the end of a name. For instance, to filter against SALESMSERV, SALESFSERV, and SALESQSERV, the single entry SALES* can be used.

- **Forward/Discard**   Indicates what should be done in the event of a match. Selecting Forward causes those frames matching the filter to be forwarded, and all other frames to be dropped. Selecting Discard causes all frames matching the filter to be discarded, and all other frames to be forwarded.

- **Applied to**   Indicates which filters are applied to which ports.

## MultiLink Trunking

MultiLink Trunking (MLT) was added to the Centillion platform in code version 4.0. A MultiLink Trunk is a port grouping that aggregates the bandwidth of each link into a single logical link. The following rules govern the configuration of MultiLink Trunks on the Centillion:

- MLT ports must be 100Mbps.
- MLT ports must be full-duplex.
- MLT ports must reside on the same module.
- MLT ports must reside in the same VLAN and Spanning Tree Group.
- MLT ports may not have more than four ports in a group.
- MLT ports must be enabled to be added to the group.
- MLT ports will not support static stations.

*MLT support was not added until code version 4.0. Image version and SpeedView version 4.0 or higher are required to configure MLT.*

## Configuring MLT on the Centillion

To configure an MLT on the Centillion, select the Configure MLT tab, in which MLT groups can be added or removed. By default, no MLT groups exist on the Centillion. To add a group, select Add Group, which opens the MLT Group Name window. Here, a name may be associated with the MLT; this is an arbitrary name that allows the administrator to uniquely identify MLT groups. The name is not used by the switch. In addition to the name, you must indicate whether this MLT will be connecting two switches or will extend to a server. This is determined by selecting or deselecting the box labeled Attach Server. This box should be checked if the MLT is extending to a NIC with MLT support, where each of the NIC ports are associated with the same MAC address.

## Selecting the MLT Ports

After you create the MLT group, you need to add the ports to the group, following the rules outlined at the beginning of this section on MLT. To do this, click the first field beneath the header Ports selected for this group. Enter the module and port number for each MLT member. As you do so, the selected ports will be highlighted in yellow on the graphical image of the Centillion that dominates the window.

Once this is done, the MLT configuration is complete. Ports may be removed by using the Del Port button located at the bottom of the window. Likewise, MLT groups can be removed by clicking the Del Group button. Existing MLT groupings can be selected by clicking the arrow in the MLT Group Name field and then selecting the desired MLT name.

ETHERNET ON NORTEL NETWORKS

# The Complete Reference

# Chapter 7

## LattisSpan Switching

L attisSpan is a proprietary VLAN technology that was implemented prior to the development of the 802.1Q frame-tagging specification. Unlike a port-based VLAN implementation, LattisSpan VLANs do not have local significance only, and a VLAN may span different LattisSwitches within the switch community.

## LattisSwitch Technology

In a LattisSpan network, LattisSwitches that are directly connected pass VLAN information to one another. This is accomplished by passing Global MAC tables for each VLAN across the trunk connections that form between LattisSpan switches. The specifics of the LattisSpan protocol are covered in the sections that follow.

### LattisSpan Packets

In a LattisSpan network, switches transmit protocol data units (PDUs) known as *LattisSpan packets*. These packets utilize the multicast addresses 01-00-81-00-02-00 and 01-00-81-00-02-01, which are recognized by all LattisSpan devices. The packets are transmitted out all ports every two seconds and announce the presence of the LattisSwitch to other LattisSwitches that exist within the network.

LattisSwitches are able to form and maintain two basic connection types: trunk ports and feeder ports. Upon receipt of a LattisSpan packet, a LattisSwitch makes the assumption that it is directly connected to another LattisSwitch, and a trunk port is formed between them. If no LattisSpan packets are received over a given link, the connected device is assumed not to be a LattisSpan device, and a feeder port is formed. This occurs dynamically, although the option exists to hard-code the port type.

### Trunk Ports vs. Feeder Ports

The formation of trunk and feeder ports is very important in a LattisSpan network, because each connection type has a specific function. Trunk ports are meant to be interswitch links, whereas feeder ports are meant only for connections to stations and other, non-LattisSpan devices.

**TRUNK PORTS**    Trunks are formed when a port receives a LattisSpan packet. Trunk links are used for sending and receiving VLAN information. For instance, in a scenario in which two LattisSwitches are connected with a trunk, each with two VLANs configured (VLAN 1 and VLAN 2), the trunk behaves in the manner shown in Figure 7-1 and described next.

In this configuration, each LattisSwitch bundles the MAC addresses associated with each VLAN and transports this information across the trunk, so that station A can learn about all MAC addresses associated with VLAN 1, not only on its own local switch, but also on other network switches. This enables a specific VLAN to span multiple switches.

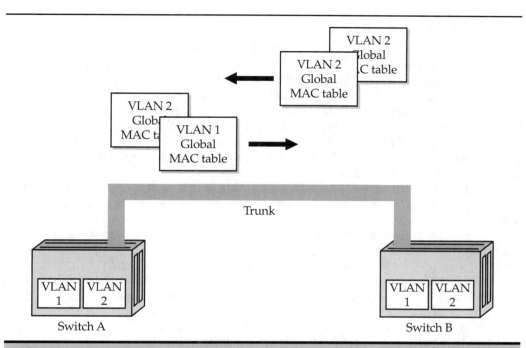

**Figure 7-1.** *LattisSwitches connected by a trunk, with VLAN 1 and VLAN 2 on either switch*

When station A needs to transmit to station B, this also occurs over the trunk, but the trunk does not learn any new MAC addresses dynamically, only those that are bundled in the VLAN information.

**FEEDER PORTS**    Feeder ports are formed when a link is detected but no LattisSpan packets are received on the interface. Feeder ports behave like normal switched Ethernet ports and, unlike trunk connections, *do* dynamically learn MAC addresses.

## Design Considerations and LattisSpan Trunks

When you configure a LattisSpan network, you need to remember two primary factors:

- All LattisSwitches have relatively low MAC address table limitations.
- LattisSpan packets use MAC-layer multicast addresses, and therefore propagate quickly throughout the broadcast domain.

ETHERNET ON NORTEL
NETWORKS

## MAC Address Limitations

LattisSpan switches represent older switching technology, which is evidenced by the presence of a proprietary VLAN mechanism, as well as a MAC address table limit that may be considered low by today's standards. This does not mean that LattisSpan technology—that it is better suited to smaller networks. LattisSwitches have a MAC address learning limit of 1,024 per port and 1,024 per VLAN. In other words, a single VLAN can support up to 1,024 MAC addresses. However, since a single port can only support 1,024, then if multiple VLANs are passing over a trunk link, the sum of each global MAC table cannot exceed 1,024. Depending on the design, this may or may not present a problem in a small to moderately sized network.

The instance in which the MAC address learning limit is most likely to arise is when implementing LattisSpan VLANs. Because a trunk must transport the total bundled MAC addresses for an entire VLAN, which may span multiple switches, the MAC address limit on a trunk port may be exceeded, even though no individual switch has approached the limit.

In Figure 7-2, the trunk port on switch B must handle the aggregate incoming bundled MAC addresses for VLAN1 and VLAN2 from switch A. In switch A, neither VLAN comes close to the 1,024 limit; however, the total bundled addresses for both VLANs does exceed the limit on the incoming trunk for switch B. The extra 76 MAC addresses will be dropped in this case, resulting in intermittent connectivity problems.

## Trunk Considerations

Another consideration that you must make when designing LattisSpan networks is the formation of trunks: how they are formed and how they behave once they are formed. Remember, a LattisSwitch port that receives a LattisSpan packet determines that it is directly attached to another LattisSwitch and transitions into Trunk mode regardless of where the LattisSpan packet really came from. Consider an example in which two LattisSpan devices are attached to a shared media hub that is supporting multiple users (see Figure 7-3). In this scenario, each LattisSwitch is transmitting LattisSpan packets; these PDUs are received by the hub and flooded out all ports. In this case, then, both LattisSpan devices are receiving LattisSpan packets on the ports that connect to the Ethernet hub, and so both ports transition into Trunk mode.

The problem with this scenario is that trunk connections are used only for Global MAC table sharing, and do not dynamically learn new MAC addresses themselves. For this reason, neither LattisSwitch will learn any of the MAC addresses of the users being supported by the Ethernet hub, and users residing on the hub will not be able to communicate outside the hub itself.

Trunks can form inadvertently and can seriously impact the network. If a large portion of the network has become unreachable behind a LattisSpan device, check its

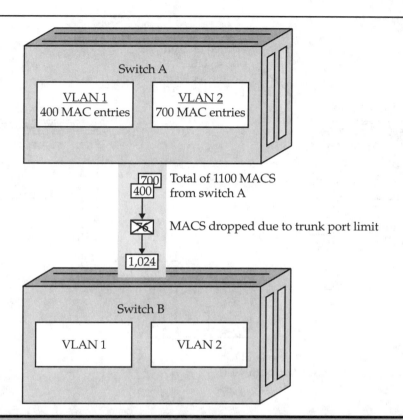

**Figure 7-2.**    *Two LattisSwitches showing bundled MAC addresses approaching the 1,024 limit*

connection to make certain that a trunk hasn't somehow formed. All that is required for a trunk to form is for a LattisSpan device to receive a LattisSpan packet. Such a packet may be received through a hub, a bridge, or even a router that is running bridging services. On one occasion, a trunk actually formed across a WAN connection between two separate sites.

Remember, a trunk will not dynamically learn any MAC addresses—it will only accept Global MAC tables from another LattisSpan switch, so the formation of a trunk

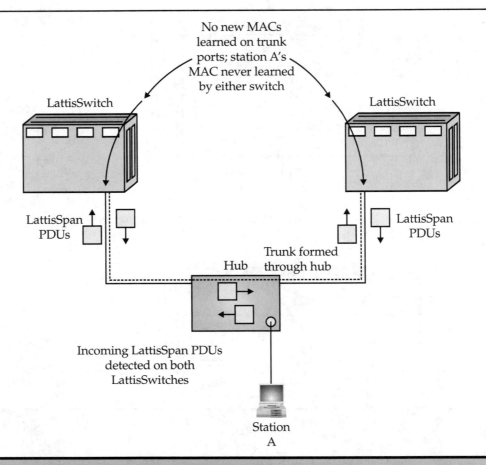

No new MACs
learned on trunk
ports; station A's
MAC never learned
by either switch

LattisSwitch

LattisSwitch

LattisSpan
PDUs

LattisSpan
PDUs

Trunk formed
Hub    through hub

Incoming LattisSpan PDUs
detected on both
LattisSwitches

Station
A

**Figure 7-3.**    *Two LattisSpan devices forming a trunk through a hub*

where it isn't appropriate can seriously upset network performance. Several options are available to work around this potential problem.

## Disable LattisSpan

If VLANs are not being used, disable LattisSpan. The only practical function of LattisSpan is to support the LattisSwitch VLANs, and if they are not being used, no reason exists to run the LattisSpan protocol. All LattisSpan products are capable of also functioning as traditional 802.1d Spanning Tree switches, which may be a viable workaround if VLANs are not required.

Disabling LattisSpan eliminates trunk and feeder port designations, eliminates Global MAC table sharing between LattisSpan devices, and prevents the 80-second delay across all connected switches that is associated with collecting VLAN information and learning the topology each time that a single switch reboots or is added/removed.

## Forced Feeder Ports

If VLANs are being used, a port that would normally be a trunk port can be manually forced to Feeder status; this prevents the formation of a trunk, prevents the sharing of Global MAC tables, and allows the port to learn new MAC addresses dynamically. Ports that are manually set to Forced Feeder will not transition into a trunk state even if LattisSpan packets are received.

To select Forced Feeder Mode, select Configuration Parameters | Switch Parameters | Modify Switch Port Type. From this screen, select the port to alter and then toggle from Trunk to Forced Feeder:

```
System Up Time:  3 D-11H-43M-02S            IP Address:   160.60.20.211   [M]
MAC Address:  000081001532                  Default Gateway:  160.60.20.1
Switch Software Version:  2.0.4             Subnet Mask:  255.255.255.0

                            Switch Port Type
Port  Operational     Current    Next Boot    Port  Operational    Current    Next Boot
1     [Act Feeder]    [Auto]     [Auto]        10    [Act Feeder]   [Auto]     [Auto]
2     [Act Feeder]    [Auto]     [Auto]        11    [Act Feeder]   [Auto]     [Auto]
3     [Act Feeder]    [Auto]     [Auto]        12    [Act Feeder]   [Auto]     [Auto]
4     [Act Feeder]    [Auto]     [Auto]        13    [Act Feeder]   [Auto]     [Auto]
5     [Act Feeder]    [Auto]     [Auto]        14    [Act Feeder]   [Auto]     [Auto]
6     [Act Feeder]    [Auto]     [Auto]        15    [Act Feeder]   [Auto]     [Auto]
7     [Act Feeder]    [Auto]     [Auto]        16    [Act Feeder]   [Auto]     [Auto]
8     [Act Feeder]    [Auto]     [Auto]        MDA P1 [Act Feeder]  [Auto]     [Auto]
9     [Forced Feeder] [Auto]     [Auto]        MDA P2 [Act Feeder]  [Auto]     [Auto]

                       Change port type of port 9.
             Use cursor keys to choose item.  Press <RETURN> to confirm choice.
<CTRL><P>:Main Menu     <CTRL><U>:Previous Menu      <CTRL><L>:Refresh Screen
```

This option takes effect dynamically and thus does not require a reset of the LattisSpan device.

## Filter the LattisSpan PDUs

LattisSpan PDUs use the Layer 2 multicast addresses 01-00-81-00-02-00 and 01-00-81-00-02-01. These packets should be filtered, if possible, particularly on a router running bridging services in a LattisSpan environment.

# Redundant Links in a LattisSpan Environment

LattisSpan devices support redundant links for both trunk and feeder connections. If parallel links are discovered, an algorithm is run based on relative positioning to the Master (M2) switch, similar to the method used in relation to the root bridge in 802.1d Spanning Tree. The redundant link goes into a Standby mode and is designated either Standby Feeder or Standby Trunk.

# LattisSpan Switch Community

A LattisSpan *community*, or *domain*, is a collection of LattisSpan devices that share VLAN information. For multiple switch communities to exist in a single network, some method must be implemented to block the LattisSpan PDUs between communities. A maximum of 32 LattisSpan switches may exist within a single community.

Each LattisSpan switch within a single community has either an M1 or an M2 designation. One switch will hold the M2 status, while the rest remain as M1. The M2 switch is considered the master, and is elected via an algorithm run within the switch community. The responsibilities of the M2 switch include maintaining a view of the VLANs configured within the community. The M2 switch is considered the VLAN management entity, communicating with the network management station for VLAN management. M1 switches function normally; however, if the M2 switch fails or is removed, a new instance of the algorithm is run and a new master is chosen from among the M1 switches.

# Modifying Switch Priority

To ensure that a specific switch becomes the master, the Switch Priority may be altered. This is similar in concept to altering the Bridge Priority for purposes of 802.1d Spanning Tree. You may alter this value through a console session by selecting Configuration Parameters | Switch Parameters | Modify Switch Priority. The Switch Priority may be any hex value between 0 and FFFF (0 being the highest and FFFF being the lowest, in this case), with the default being 8000. The switch with the highest priority is assigned the M2 designation. In the case where all Priority values are equal, the lowest MAC address is the deciding factor.

# LattisSpan VLANs

All LattisSpan VLANs must be configured by using the Bay Networks Network Management utility called *Optivity*. Although VLAN information may be viewed from a console session with the switch, Optivity is required to actually configure the VLANs. A minimum of 18 VLANs may be created within a single LattisSwitch.

After you configure and place the VLANs, you can view the VLAN information via a console session with the LattisSpan device by selecting System Information | Switch Mode, which results in the following display:

ETHERNET ON NORTEL NETWORKS

```
System Up Time:  3 D-11H-43M-02S      IP Address:  160.60.20.211   [M]
MAC Address:  000081001532            Default Gateway:  160.60.20.1
Switch Software Version:  2.0.4       Subnet Mask:  255.255.255.0

                    Local VLAN Information
Port  VLAN ID/Name                    Port  VLAN ID/Name
1     [2/Default]                     9     [2/Default]
2     [2/Default]                     10    [2/Default]
3     [2/Default]                     11    [2/Default]
4     [2/Default]                     12    [2/Default]
5     [2/Default]                     13    [2/Default]
6     [2/Default]                     14    [2/Default]
7     [2/Default]                     15    [2/Default]
8     [2/Default]                     16    [2/Default]
Exp   1     [Trunk]                   Exp   2     [2/Default]

               VLAN ID and name associated with port 1.
     Use cursor keys to choose item.  Press <RETURN> to confirm choice.
<CTRL><P>:Main Menu      <CTRL><U>:Previous Menu      <CTRL><L>:Refresh Screen
```

# Flow Control

Flow Control is an option implemented in code version 2.0 or higher and is used on 100Mbps full-duplex links between LattisSpan switches. When Flow Control is active, if the receive buffer of the remote switch becomes full, a proprietary Flow Control signal is sent to the sending device, which causes it to pause its transmission. Once the receive buffer is no longer full, another signal is sent indicating that the sending switch may resume.

The Flow Control option may be set by selecting Configuration Parameters | Switch Parameters | Modify Switch Port Flow Control Mode:

```
System Up Time:  3 D-11H-43M-02S      IP Address:  160.60.20.211   [M]
MAC Address:  000081001532            Default Gateway:  160.60.20.1
Switch Software Version:  2.0.4       Subnet Mask:  255.255.255.0
```

```
                        Switch Port Flow Control
Port   Flow Control                  Port   Flow Control
1      [Enable]                      9      [N/A]
2      [N/A]                         10     [N/A]
3      [Disable]                     11     [N/A]
4      [N/A]                         12     [Disable]
5      [Enable]                      13     [Enable]
6      [Disable]                     14     [Disable]
7      [N/A]                         15     [N/A]
8      [N/A]                         16     [Disable]
Enable                       Disable
            Enter Y/y to confirm, N/n to ignore:
            Change made will be effective immediately.
                         Press <CTRL><C>: Abort
<CTRL><P>:Main Menu    <CTRL><U>:Previous Menu    <CTRL><L>:Refresh Screen
```

*The LattisSpan Flow Control mechanism is proprietary; although the Flow Control signals should not interfere with network operation if a non-LattisSpan switch is connected to a port using Flow Control, the Flow Control signals generally are interpreted as CRC errors by the receiving switch.*

## Upgrading the LattisSwitch

Upgrading each variety of LattisSwitch involves essentially the same procedure, so the process for all varieties is covered once in this section rather than in each section for each individual device. To perform the upgrade, you will need a few things:

- A TFTP server or BootP/TFTP server software running on a laptop or workstation
- A valid Ethernet connection
- An IP address on both the switch and the TFTP server
- The appropriate system image software

After you assemble these components, you can initiate the upgrade procedure as outlined in the following sections. The LattisSpan switches utilize dual flash banks, so the image upgrade initially is performed to one flash and then to the other, as outlined in the following section.

ETHERNET ON NORTEL
NETWORKS

# Dual Flash Modules

Each LattisSpan switch has two flash banks, to hold different images. Depending on the version of code you are using, you may need to repeat the upgrade procedure if you want both flash banks to hold the same system image software.

Take care not to interrupt the upgrade procedure—if one of the flash banks becomes corrupt, it can potentially prevent any further upgrade from taking properly. The reason for this is that each LattisSpan switch will boot from one flash bank, and then, in the event of an upgrade, will write the new image to the second flash bank. If the second flash bank becomes corrupt and won't take an image, the device will no longer be upgradable.

# Altering the Boot Parameters

To initiate the upgrade sequence, choose Configuration Parameters | Boot Parameters:

```
System Up Time:  3 D-11H-43M-02S        IP Address:  160.60.20.211   [M]
MAC Address:  000081001532              Default Gateway:  160.60.20.1
Switch Software Version:  2.0.1         Subnet Mask:  255.255.255.0

                         Boot Parameters
Modify Boot Mode  [Local]
Modify Image Load Mode  [Network]
Modify Boot Router IP Address  [0.0.0.0]
Modify TFTP Load Server IP Address  [160.60.20.63]
Modify TFTP Retry Count  [5]
Modify Image File Name  [28xxx204.img]




                Change the boot mode to Local or Network.
           Use cursor keys to choose item.  Press <RETURN> to confirm choice.
<CTRL><P>:Main Menu       <CTRL><U>:Previous Menu        <CTRL><L>:Refresh Screen
```

These options should be set in the following fashion:

- **Boot Mode**   Set to Local if TFTP is being used. Setting it to Network causes the device to execute a BootP.

- **Image Load Mode**   Set to Network; after the upgrade is complete and the new system image has been initialized, this mode is automatically set back to Local.

■ **Modify Boot Router IP Address**   In this example, this value is set to all zeros, meaning the TFTP server is on the local network and will not pass through a router. If the TFTP transfer must pass through a router, enter the IP address for the local router interface here. You are recommended to avoid upgrading any LattisSpan device through a router and, if possible, you should set up the TFTP server locally.

■ **Modify TFTP Load Server IP Address**   Enter the IP address of the TFTP server.

■ **Modify TFTP Retry Count**   You may adjust the TFTP Retry Count. The default value of 5 should be fine for most upgrades.

■ **Modify Image File Name**   Enter the image filename, which is case-sensitive. Don't enter the path as part of the string, because the root directory for TFTP transfers is generally defined in the TFTP server software itself.

## Initiating the Upgrade

After you configure the boot parameters, you initiate the upgrade from the Reset System menu, which you can access from the main menu by selecting Reset System:

```
System Up Time:  3 D-11H-43M-02S          IP Address:  160.60.20.211   [M]
MAC Address:  000081001532                Default Gateway:  160.60.20.1
Switch Software Version:  2.0.1            Subnet Mask:  255.255.255.0
                              Reset System
Reset
Reset to Default
Download Image
Select Boot Image Version (Active/Select)  [Image2/Image1]
Schedule Image Reboot (Set/Countdown)   [0D:0H:0M/0D:0H:0M]
Cancel Scheduled Reboot



            Configuration information will be kept after Reset.
Use cursor keys to choose item.  Press <RETURN> to confirm choice.
<CTRL><P>:Main Menu    <CTRL><U>:Previous Menu    <CTRL><L>:Refresh Screen
```

The download can be initiated in either of two ways:

■ Select Download Image, which initiates the download.

■ Select Reset | Hard Reset, which causes the LattisSwitch to boot using the parameters that you defined when you altered the boot parameters and selected Network Image Load Mode.

### Upgrading the 58000

The upgrade procedure for the 58000 is the same as that for the other LattisSpan switches, except that when you upgrade the 58000 to 2.0.*x* or higher, a special upgrade image is required (58k143u2.img). Without the upgrade image version, only one of the two flash banks is verified prior to initiating the upgrade and, under certain circumstances, both flash banks may not be ready. This often results in a flash error and failure of the image upgrade. The 58000 must be upgraded to image version 58k143u2.img before it can be upgraded to any more-recent code version.

## LattisSwitch Architecture

LattisSpan devices come in three basic models: the 281*xx* (which includes the 28115 and the 28104), the 28200, and the 58000. Although these models differ in architecture and may even appear very different physically, they are very similar from a software standpoint.

## The 281*xx*

The 281*xx* family includes the 28115 (ADV) and 28104 series switches. These switches are very similar in architecture, the primary difference being that the 28115 series switch provides RJ-45 Ethernet connections that run at either 10Mbps half-duplex or 100Mbps half- or full-duplex, whereas the 28104 provides 100Base-FX connections that run at either half- or full-duplex. In all other respects, these devices are essentially the same. A description of each follows:

- **The 28115**   A stackable LattisSpan switch that has 16 fixed 10/100Mbps switched Ethernet ports, as well as two fixed cascade ports.
- **The 28104**   Also a stackable LattisSpan switch, it has 8 fixed 100Mbps fiber ports that utilize SC connectors, as well as two fixed cascade ports.

### Configuring for 10Mbps or 100Mbps

The 28104 switch runs at 100Mbps only, although the duplex mode can be toggled between half- and full-duplex. The 28115 is capable of running its fixed RJ-45 Ethernet ports at either 10 or 100Mbps, and any port configured for 100Mbps may also be toggled between half- and full-duplex.

Each RJ-45 port on the 28115 has four LEDs associated with it; when these LEDs are not illuminated, they are not clearly visible through the smoked plastic shield that covers the LED display, but can be discerned if you look at them closely. Table 7-1 describes the different meanings of these LEDs.

| LED | Meaning |
|-----|---------|
| Link (top left) | Valid link has been established. |
| High Speed (top right) | Port is running at 100Mbps. |
| Part (bottom left) | Port is partitioned. |
| Col (bottom right) | Collision is detected on the link. |

**Table 7-1.**    *28115 LEDs*

You can change the port speed and duplex mode from a console session by choosing Configuration Parameters | Switch Parameters | Modify Switch Port Speed and Duplex Mode:

```
System Up Time:  3 D-11H-43M-02S    IP Address:  160.60.20.211   [M]
MAC Address:  000081001532          Default Gateway:  160.60.20.1
Switch Software Version:  2.0.4        Subnet Mask:  255.255.255.0


                    Switch Port Speed and Duplex Mode
Port  Speed(Mb/s)  Duplex Mode        Port   Speed(Mb/s)   Duplex Mode
1     [100Mb/s    Half]                9     [100Mb/s     Half]
2     [10Mb/s     Half]               10     [100Mb/s     Half]
3     [10Mb/s     Half]               11     [10Mb/s      Half]
4     [10Mb/s     Half]               12     [100Mb/s     Full]
5     [10Mb/s     Half]               13     [10Mb/s      Half]
6     [100Mb/s    Full]               14     [100Mb/s     Full]
7     [100Mb/s    Full]               15     [10Mb/s      Half]
8     [100Mb/s    Full]               16     [100Mb/s     Half]
              Change port 4 speed and duplex mode.
         Use cursor keys to choose item.  Press <RETURN> to confirm choice.
<CTRL><P>:Main Menu    <CTRL><U>:Previous Menu    <CTRL><L>:Refresh Screen
```

**Note** *When connecting an autonegotiating switch or station to a 28115 Ethernet port running at 100Mbps, proper speed negotiation may fail, because the 28115 port sends out a 10Mbps link pulse upon initialization. If it is configured for 100Mbps, it then switches over and sends out a 100Mbps link pulse, but the initial link pulse often has already been received and used for autonegotiation purposes.*

## Cascading the 281xx

The 28115 and 28104 can be cascaded together by using the expansion ports. By default, these cascade connections form trunk links between switches if the LattisSpan protocol is being used. The cascade cable used for these connections can be no longer than one meter.

If distances for the cascade need to be longer than one meter, you may use the series 514 transceiver to extend the distance. The 514 transceiver utilizes an expansion port that accepts the cascade cable and then provides a fiber-optic connector so that the cascade can be run over fiber to another 514 transceiver at the remote end. When using the 514 transceiver, you must use speeds of 100Mbps half-duplex or 100Mbps full-duplex.

## Altering the Speed and Duplex Mode of the Cascade Port

You may also change the speed and duplex mode for the expansion ports. The cascade expansion ports may run at either 100Mbps half-duplex, 100Mbps full-duplex, or 200Mbps full-duplex. When a cascade cable is used, the port automatically runs at 200Mbps full-duplex; however, if you use a 514 transceiver, then you must select 100Mbps full- or half-duplex. This is done by selecting Configuration Parameters | Switch Parameters | Modify Switch Expansion Port Transceiver Speed and Duplex Mode:

```
System Up Time:  3 D-11H-43M-02S      IP Address:  160.60.20.211   [M]
MAC Address:  000081001532            Default Gateway:  160.60.20.1
Switch Software Version:  2.0.4       Subnet Mask:  255.255.255.0


            Switch Expansion Port Transceiver Speed and Duplex Mode
                Exp Port            Speed(Mb/s)     Duplex Mode
                   1                [100 Mb/s       Full]
                   2                [100 Mb/s       Half]


            Change selected expansion port 2 transceiver speed and duplex mode.
        Use cursor keys to choose item.  Press <RETURN> to confirm choice.
<CTRL><P>:Main Menu     <CTRL><U>:Previous Menu     <CTRL><L>:Refresh Screen
```

# The 28200

The 28200 is very similar to the 281xx series LattisSpan switches, from a software and configuration standpoint, but is physically very different. Unlike the 281xx series switches, in which all ports are fixed, the 28200 utilizes a modular chassis design that can hold up to four media dependent adapters (MDAs). In addition, the 28200 has redundant power supply unit (RPSU) connectors in the rear of the device, as well as a bay in which to mount an RMON probe.

The front panel LED indicators give a status regarding the port, MDA, RSPU, and Probe. The 28200 LED panel provides the indicators listed in Table 7-2.

## Using Media Dependent Adapters

Media dependent adapters for the 28200 come in several varieties:

- **28200-14** Provides four 10Base-FL connections, utilizing SC connector types.
- **28200-15** Provides eight 10Base-T RJ-45 UTP connections.
- **28200-104** Provides two 100Base-TX RJ-45 UTP connections.
- **28200-105** Provides two 100Base-FX connections, utilizing SC connector types.

| LED | Color | Meaning |
|---|---|---|
| Pwr | Green | Unit is receiving AC power. |
| | Off | Unit is not receiving AC power. |
| Fan1/Fan2 | Green | Fan is working properly. |
| | Amber | Fan is malfunctioning. |
| RPS1/RPS2 | Green | Unit is receiving power from RSPU. |
| | Amber | RSPU is connected, but not providing power. |
| | Off | RSPU is not connected. |
| RMON | Green | RMON probe is present and operating. |
| | Amber | RMON probe present but failed diagnostics. |
| | Off | RMON probe is not present. |
| MDA1 through 4 | Green | MDA is present and operating normally. |
| | Amber | MDA is present but has failed diagnostics. |
| | Off | MDA is not installed. |
| 1-12 | Green | Link is detected on port. |
| | Amber | Specified port is partitioned. |
| | Off | Link is not detected on port. |

**Table 7-2.**   *28200 LED Matrix*

- **28200-109**   Provides a single FDDI uplink, with A and B ports that utilize FDDI MIC connectors.

- **28200-EXP**   Provides two cascade connectors, for cascading 28200 switches with either 281*xx* switches or other 28200 switches at 200Mbps full-duplex.

## Using an RMON Probe

In addition to the standard MDA modules, the 28200 supports an RMON probe that can be mounted in a bay located on the rear panel. RMON probes are used to obtain more detailed management statistics from the unit. RMON probes come with 8MB memory, upgradable to 32MB.

 *The 28200 must be running system software image version 2.0 or higher to support the use of an RMON probe.*

## The 28200-109 FDDI Uplink Module

The 28200 supports the 28200-109 MDA, which provides a single FDDI uplink port. This provides translational bridging between the FDDI and Ethernet portions of the network. The FDDI uplink module is unique in a few ways. Unlike the other MDA modules, which have one MDA slot each, the 28200-109 takes two MDA slots. Also, it has its own upgradable code and its own individual command-line interface (CLI). This interface can be used to gather certain statistics, and it must be accessed to upgrade the FDDI MDA.

The FDDI MDA's CLI is accessible through the DB-9 connector located on the MDA itself. This connection requires a standard RS232 cable, and either a terminal or terminal emulation software using the following settings:

| | |
|---|---|
| Baud rate | 9600 |
| Data bits | 8 |
| Stop bits | 1 |
| Parity | None |
| Flow Control | None |

After you access the console, the following prompt appears:

```
3071>
```

The entire range of commands available through the MDA CLI is not covered in this book; upgrading the code on the FDDI MDA is explained in the following section. The full CLI command set is as follows:

```
arp
    del host_address
    dump
    set host_address hardware_address
clear bstats
di
    agingtime
    bstats
    forward
    ignoredf
    ip
    ttrt
    version
ifconfig
    fd0 address
    fd0 {up | down}
    fd0 broadcast broadcast_address
    fd0 netmask subnet mask
    fd0 netmask subnet mask broadcast broadcast_address
    fd0 address netmask subnet mask broadcast broadcast_address
netstat
    {udp | ip | icmp | routes}
newsmt filename host_address
newswitch filename host_address
ping host_address [size] [count]
route
    add default gateway [hop count]
    add destination gateway [hop count]
    delete destination gateway

set
    agingtime seconds
    filter {on | off}
    ip {up | down}
    ignoredf {on | off}
    forward {on | off}
    ttrt time_value
```

## Upgrading the 28200-109 FDDI Uplink Module

The FDDI uplink MDA actually uses two separate image files: the 3071 image, which is the FDDI switching image, and the 3051 image, which is the SMT protocol image. Either of these images may be downloaded through a sequence of commands executed from the MDA CLI. The download will occur through the FDDI port.

After you access the CLI, you first must configure the IP and FDDI interface information, and then initiate the download. This is accomplished with the following set of commands:

```
3071>set forward on
3071>set ip up
3071>ifconfig fd0 150.50.10.21
3071>ifconfig fd0 mask 255.255.255.0
3071>route add 150.50.20.0 150.50.10.1 [hop count]
```

These commands, in order, set forwarding on the FDDI interface, set IP globally on the MDA, assign an IP address and mask to the FDDI interface, and specify the target network number and the local router interface. The last command is executed if the TFTP server resides on a different subnetwork than the FDDI MDA (network 150.50.20.0, in this case). A hop count must also be specified in this case.

After you execute these commands, the FDDI interface will have an IP and mask assigned to it, with both forwarding and IP activated on that interface. The code may now be downloaded from the TFTP server. The command to download the code varies, depending on whether the code is the FDDI switch code or the SMT protocol image. For the FDDI switch code, the command is as follows:

```
3071>newswitch fddi119.bin 150.50.20.42
```

For the SMT image, use this command:

```
3071>newsmt smt517.bin 150.50.20.42
```

where 150.50.20.42 is the IP address of the TFTP server. After the code is downloaded to the MDA, the new version may be identified by entering the following command:

```
3071>di version
```

This displays the version of both images.

*The IP information that is entered into the FDDI MDA is for the purposes of image upgrading only; after the image is successfully upgraded, the IP information is cleared from the MDA.*

## Cascading the 28200

Multiple 28200 switches may be cascaded together by using a cascade cable, just as the 281*xx* series LattisSwitches can be cascaded. The 28200 has no fixed expansion ports, however, and if you want to use a cascade connection, you must install an expansion MDA to provide the expansion ports. By default, these cascade connections form trunk links between switches if the LattisSpan protocol is being used, just as they do in the 281*xx* series LattisSwitches. The cascade cable used for these connections may be no longer than one meter. These cascade ports and cables are for all intents and purposes the same as those used in relation to the 281*xx* series LattisSwitches, and may be extended by using the 514 fiber-optic transceiver.

## The Boot Main Menu

The Boot Main Menu is a boot monitor that can be accessed in the 28200 by pressing CTRL-C during the normal bootup procedure. The command will interrupt the boot sequence and break out to the boot monitor:

```
Boot Main Menu
MAC: 000081001282

Boot Mode: NVRAM              Image Load Mode: Local
Boot Protocol: IP             Config. Load Mode: Local
Management Protocol: IP       Image Save Mode: WriteIfDiff

m - Toggle Boot Mode                c - System Configuration Menu
p - Toggle Boot Protocol            j - IP Configuration Menu
t - Toggle Management Protocol      e - Load and Execute Boot Files
i - Toggle Image Load Mode          g - Perform Power-up Boot Load Sequence
f - Toggle Config. Load Mode        k - Reset NVRAM to Factory Defaults
d - Toggle Image Save Mode          z - Reset Switch Module
w - Write Boot Config. to NVRAM     x - Configure DCM RMON Probe

Enter Command:
```

The Boot Main Menu can be useful for accomplishing certain tasks, particularly to alter the boot parameters if the unit will not load its system image software successfully. Here, an IP address can be assigned to the switch; the Boot Mode may be set, as well as the Image Load Mode. The Image Save Mode in this case gives the user three options with which to specify whether the image will be overwritten: only if newer, only if different, or always during an upgrade.

# The 58000

The 58000 is actually a module supported by the System 5000 chassis; it requires two slots and provides 20 fixed Ethernet ports, a fixed MDA slot, an expansion slot for an expansion card containing four more slots for different MDA modules, and up to 12 10Mbps Ethernet backplane connections.

## Configuring for Front- or Back-Panel Connectivity

The first 12 fixed Ethernet ports on the 58000 may be configured for either front- or back-panel connectivity. If configured for front-panel connectivity, the port behaves as a normal LattisSpan switched port; if the port is configured for back-panel connectivity, it connects to the corresponding 10Mbps Ethernet backplane segment (1 through 12). For instance, if port 1 is configured for back-panel connectivity, it will connect to 10Mbps Ethernet backplane segment 1. At this point, port 1 on the front panel will be disabled and will not accept a front-panel connection. Be aware that back panel connections still transmit LattisSpan PDUs.

The order of each port's backplane connection is fixed, meaning that port 1 must always connect to backplane segment 1, port 2 must always connect to backplane segment 2, and so forth (see Figure 7-4).

Once a backplane connection is made, that segment has a switched connection to the 58000. Multiple backplane connections enable the 58K to switch between each of the 10Mbps Ethernet backplane segments.

To configure front- and back-panel connections, select Configuration Parameters | Switch Parameters | Modify Switch Front/Back Panel Connection:

```
System Up Time:  3 D-11H-43M-02S      IP Address:  160.60.20.211   [M]
MAC Address:  000081001532            Default Gateway:  160.60.20.1
Switch Software Version:  2.0.1       Subnet Mask:  255.255.255.0


                        Switch Front/Back Connection
Port   Connection            Port   Connection
1      Front                 7      Front
2      Front                 8      Front
3      Back                  9      Front
4      Back                  10     Front
5      Front                 11     Back
6      Front                 12     Front


                  Change port 3 front/back connection
        Use cursor keys to choose item.  Press <RETURN> to confirm choice.
<CTRL><P>:Main Menu     <CTRL><U>:Previous Menu     <CTRL><L>:Refresh Screen
```

ETHERNET ON NORTEL NETWORKS

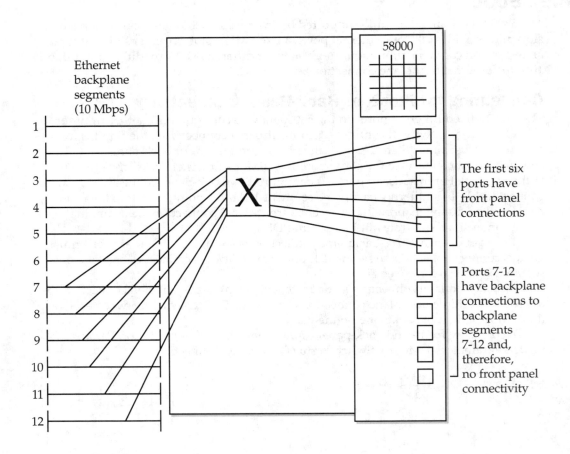

**Figure 7-4.**   *Front- and back-panel connections on the 58000 switch*

## Using Media Dependent Adapters (MDAs)

The 58000 series LattisSwitch also uses MDAs, as does the 28200, although the modules
for the two series differ in their physical architecture and may not be interchanged. The
following MDAs are available for the 58000 switch:

- **58000-104**   Provides two 100Base-FX ports, utilizing SC connectors.
- **58000-105**   Provides two 100Base-TX ports, utilizing RJ-45 UTP connectors.

- **58000-106**   Provides one 100Base-FX port using an SC connector, and one 100Base-TX port using an RJ-45 UTP connector.

- **58000-109**   Provides one A port and one B port utilizing FDDI MIC connectors. For more details regarding the FDDI uplink MDA, consult the section on the 28200, which also utilizes a FDDI uplink; the 28200-109 and 58000-109 vary in physical architecture, but are the same in all other ways.

The 58000 switch comes with three MDA slots, but an expansion board can be optionally installed to provide four more MDA slots, for a total of seven.

# The
# Complete
# Reference

Nortel
Networks

# Part III

## The Accelar Layer 3 Switch

The
Complete
Reference

Nortel
Networks

# Chapter 8

## Basic Accelar
## Architecture

s networks became larger and bandwidth demands increased, new ways
needed to be devised to keep broadcast domains small enough to allow for
smooth traffic flow, while simultaneously keeping throughput high by
decreasing latency. Because limiting broadcast domains involves placing routers—a
Layer 3 device that, by its nature, incurs a relatively high latency—new methods had
to be considered. One of the primary methods settled upon was the development of
third-layer switching technology, such as the Accelar 1000 series routing switch.

# Basics of Layer 3 Switching

Layer 3 switching is a relatively new concept. *Layer 3* refers to the third layer of the OSI
reference model, also known as the *network layer*, where traditional routing decisions
are made. IP, IPX, and a host of other networking protocols sit at Layer 3. Switching
occurs at Layer 2 of the OSI model (see Figure 8-1) and is based on the source and
destination device's hardware address. The purpose of developing Layer 3 switching
was to create a device that was Layer 3 protocol-aware, while at the same time
avoiding the latency normally associated with a third-layer routing decision.

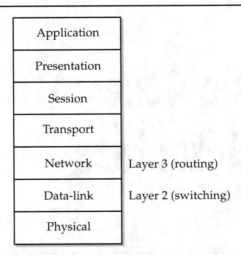

**Figure 8-1.**    *The OSI model showing the second and third layers*

# Switching vs. Routing

The differences in speed between switching and routing are determined by how fast each device can make a forwarding decision. A variety of ways exist to accomplish forwarding; the following are a few examples related to a traditional LAN environment:

- **Cell switching** Cell traffic is extremely fast, because cells are relatively simple entities. They also share a common size (so a switch that uses cells does not need to check packet length, because all packets are the same size).

- **Frame switching** This method is also very fast, though not quite as fast as cell switching. Again, a frame switch has to be concerned only with the MAC layer of the packet to see where it is destined. The size of the packets varies, however, so each packet has to be checked in the Length field to see whether it is the correct size. Forwarding decisions are based on an internal MAC forwarding table.

- **Routing** Router forwarding is slower than both cell and frame switching. First the MAC layer information is checked to see if the router is the destination. Then the 802.2 header is checked to determine the protocol, and once this is done, the packet is handed up to the appropriate protocol (IP, for instance) to determine the third-layer source and destination addressing information. A delay is incurred due to this close examination of the packet. In addition, routing decisions are handled by software rather than by hardware. These factors combined result in increased overhead for router-based forwarding.

## Layer 3 Protocol Awareness

One of the features introduced on the Accelar platform is protocol awareness, even at Layer 2. Although the Accelar can route, it can also be used to create protocol-based VLANs without actually routing.

Packets have a variety of information contained within them, and one such item found in the 802.2 packet header is an identifier stating the packet's protocol type. All protocol types have an identifier, so even without examining the inside of the packet for the Layer 3 information, Accelar can at least determine the protocol type of an incoming packet. In fact, this is how some second-layer devices such as bridges are able to filter on third-layer protocols; they just look at the identifier and base their decisions on that.

The Layer 3 switches accomplishes the same thing; they are capable of distributing traffic into different VLANs based on protocol. This can be done with very little delay. The Accelar can be configured to look for any number of third-layer protocols, and even nonroutable protocols, such as NetBIOS (discussed in more detail in Chapter 9), distributing them to the different VLANs based on their protocol type. This results in a very fast decision-making process.

# Accelar Architecture

The Accelar 1000 series comes in two basic flavors:

- **Stackable unit** Self-contained, with an internal flash and Silicon Switch Fabric (SSF).
- **Chassis-based unit** Uses a central CPU card known as the *Silicon Switch Fabric (SSF)*, which is required for the device to function. The Accelar 1250 uses a single SSF, whereas the Accelar 1200 also supports a redundant SSF.

## Accelar Types

A variety of different Accelar types are available. These vary in appearance, hardware types, and, to a small degree, functionality. Each utilizes the same type of interface, however, whether it be through the runtime command-line interface (CLI), Device Manager, or VLAN Manager. The following is a list of the current Accelar models.

**ACCELAR 1200**  The Accelar 1200 chassis contains eight slots, two of which are dedicated to the SSF cards (one primary and one redundant). These slots may not contain any other card type, which leaves a total of six I/O modules in which to place different host cards. The following modular cards were available at the time of publication:

| Model Number | Card Description |
| --- | --- |
| XLR1202SR-B | 2-port 1000BaseSR/LR with LinkSafe |
| XLR1202SX-B | 2-port 1000BaseSX or LX |
| XLR1208FL-B | 8-port 10BaseFL |
| XLR1208FX-B | 8-port 10BaseFX |
| XLR1216FX-B | 16-port 100BaseFX with MT-RJ connectors |
| XLR1216TF-B | 14-port 10/100BaseTX with two 100BaseFX using MT-RJ |
| XLR1216TX-B | 16-port 10/100BaseTX |

When using redundant SSF cards, it is important to note that configuration changes made on the primary SSF are automatically updated on the redundant SSF, so that the configuration will remain current at all times in the event of a failure.

**ACCELAR 1250**  The Accelar 1250 chassis contains four slots, and may contain only one SSF card, leaving a total of three I/O modules. It supports the same host modules as the Accelar 1200.

**ACCELAR 1100**    The 1100 is a modular stackable unit. The SSF is onboard in this case and has a fixed row of 16 Port 10/100BaseTX (referred to in the runtime CLI as slot 3), as well as two expansion slots over it (referred to as slots 1 and 2). The expansion slots support one of the following modular cards:

| Model Number | Card Description |
|---|---|
| XLR1101SX-B | 1-port 1000BaseSX or LX |
| XLR1102SR-B | 2-port 1000BaseSR/LR with LinkSafe |
| XLR1102SX-B | 2-port 1000BaseSX or LX |
| XLR1102XD-B | 2-port long-distance gigabit module |
| XLR1104FX-B | 4-port 100BaseFX |
| XLR1108FX-B | 8-port 10/100BaseFX with MT-JR connectors |
| XLR1108TX-B | 8-port 10/100BaseTX |

**ACCELAR 1150**    The Accelar 1150 is also a modular stackable unit. Instead of 16 fixed 10/100BaseTX ports as found in the 1100, it has four fixed 1000BaseSX ports (also referred to as slot 3 in the runtime CLI). It has two expansion slots, which support the same modules as the 1100 series.

**ACCELAR 1050**    The 1050 has 12 fixed 10/100BaseTX ports and a Port 1000BaseSX, also fixed.

**ACCELAR 1051**    The Accelar 1051 is identical to the 1050, with the exception that it has a redundant 1000BaseSX LinkSafe port.

# The Silicon Switch Fabric (SSF)

The Silicon Switch Fabric contains the core switch fabric, as well as the unit's CPU, which manages both the switch fabric itself and the I/O host modules. A variety of LEDs located on the SSF will report information regarding the device, as shown in Table 8-1.

Also present is a CPU and Switch bar graph, which measures the utilization of the CPU and switch fabric, respectively.

Depending on the hardware version of the SSF, an RJ-45 10BaseT connector may or may not be located on the front panel. This port gives out-of-band access, and may have an IP address assigned to it in order to model the device via Device Manager or VLAN Manager. Using this diagnostic port as another Ethernet port for purposes of network connectivity is not recommended, because doing so may severely impact the performance of the device, but it is useful for gaining access to the device for management purposes.

THE ACCELAR LAYER 3 SWITCH

| LED | Color | Meaning |
|---|---|---|
| CPU | Off | Unit did not boot. |
| | Red | CPU has faulted. |
| | Solid green | SSF is a redundant SSF, but CPU is functional. |
| | Flashing green | SSF is active and CPU is functional. |
| PS1/PS2 | Off | Power supply 1 or 2 is absent, or device is booting. |
| | Red | Power supply is present but faulting. |
| | Green | Power supply is present and active. |
| FAN | Off | System is booting. |
| | Red | Fan is faulting. |
| | Green | Fan is functioning. |

**Table 8-1.**   *SSF LED List*

## Functions of the SSF

The SSF controls the Accelar and is required for the Accelar to function; each SSF contains the unit's core switch fabric, its CPU subsystem, and a realtime clock. The switch fabric is used to handle all traffic passing through the Accelar, whereas the CPU subsystem is responsible for maintaining the switch fabric and any other I/O modules.

Each SSF module CPU subsystem utilizes a PowerPC CPU and 32MB of dynamic random access memory (DRAM). In addition, the SSF contains 4.5MB of onboard flash, used to store the device's runtime image, boot ROM, and configuration files. The switch fabric itself uses 2MB of shared, high-speed memory, which is dynamically allocated to buffer traffic destined for the I/O modules, in accordance with any traffic-priority queues that may be configured.

 *The earlier version of the SSF (part number XLR1297SF) has neither a realtime clock nor a diagnostic port, and contains only 16MB of DRAM as opposed to 32MB. An upgrade to 32MB of DRAM is available for the older SSF (part number AA0011017).*

### Redundant SSF Modules

The Accelar 1200 routing switch is capable of supporting a redundant SSF module; this enables the redundant SSF to take over network operations in the event that the primary unit fails.

**COMMITTING CHANGES TO THE REDUNDANT SSF**   Any changes made to the primary SSF can be automatically saved to the redundant SSF by issuing the Save command with the **standby** parameter:

```
Accelar# save standby
```

Files such as image files or bootstrap files can also be updated without changing the standby status of the slave CPU. After the file has been updated on the primary SSF, files to the slave SSF can be updated through the CLI, by initiating a Trivial File Transfer Protocol (TFTP) transfer with a variation of the loopback address 127.0.0.1; in this case, the TFTP transfer should be initiated to this address, altering the last octet to reflect the slot number of the redundant SSF module. For example, to update the redundant SSF in slot 5, the TFTP transfer would be initiated to IP address 127.0.0.5. This is done by using the following command:

```
Accelar# copy flash:acc2.0.1 tftp
Enter destination tftp server address [127.0.0.5]: 127.0.0.5
Enter destination file [syslog]: acc2.0.1
tftp starting ... Press any key to abort the operation.
tftp result: success
```

# Storage Mediums

The Accelar has a variety of storage mediums, listed next, which may be used for software image files, configuration files, log files, bootstrap code, and so forth:

### BOOT ELECTRICALLY ERASABLE PROGRAMMABLE ROM (BOOTEEPROM)
Is 512K in size and is divided into three main areas: the bootstrap, the boot monitor image, and the runtime configuration. This is the location from which the bootstrap launches, and where the runtime configuration is stored after being saved to NVRAM.

**FLASH**   Storage location of the runtime image. When the code is upgraded, the image may be stored in flash memory, along with any new bootstrap code that may be required. Older versions of the image and bootstrap code may be stored, as well, for future use. System flash is 4.5MB in size, and may also contain alternate configuration files, and log files.

### PERSONAL COMPUTER MEMORY CARD INTERNATIONAL ASSOCIATION
**(PCMCIA)**   The 1200 and 1250 series Accelar support a PCMCIA Card, as well as flash memory. These may be used to transport images, bootstrap code, and configuration or log files more easily from one Accelar to another, or to store backups. For those with Nortel Networks routers and Accelar routing switches, the router flash cards and the Accelar PCMCIA Cards are not interchangeable; router flash cards run at 3.3 volts, whereas Accelar PCMCIA Cards run at 5 volts. Interchanging these flash units may cause them to become corrupted and unusable.

## File Structure

The storage medium file structure and contents may be viewed by using the **dir** command:

```
Accelar-1100# dir f
Device: flash
FN Name                                    Flags       Length
-- ----                                    -----       ------
1  acc1.3.0                                XZN         1362252
2  test                                    CN          10088
3  syslog                                  LN          131072
4  config                                  CN          6088
5  accboot1.3.0                            XZN         88693
--                                                     ------
5   files                   bytes used=  1769472 free=2424656
Accelar-1100#
```

This example shows the files that are currently contained in flash memory. In this case, item 1 is the runtime image for 1.3.0 code, followed by some config files, log files, and the accboot1.3.0 file, which is the boot code for that image version. Also included is a list of how much space is used and how much is left.

A list of flags follows the filenames, which provides information about each file. Table 8-2 lists these flags and describes what they mean.

**CONFIGURATION FILES**    Files flagged with the designation $C$ contain configuration information. Several may exist simultaneously, and may be pointed to during bootup. This is accomplished either by using the **choices** command in the CLI or by selecting the appropriate file in Device Manager. These options are covered later in this chapter.

**EXECUTABLE FILES**    Files flagged with the designation $E$ are executable files, such as runtime images or boot code.

**COMPRESSED FILE**    Files flagged with the designation $Z$ have been compressed.

**FILES SLATED FOR DELETION**    Files flagged with the designation $D$ have been slated for deletion. They are flagged as $D$ after being deleted from the CLI, but remain on the storage medium and are fully accessible and functional until the space is recovered by issuing the **squeeze** command. At that time, the file is removed from the storage medium, and can't be recovered.

**LOG FILE**    The log can be dumped to a file that can sit on the flash or PCMCIA storage mediums. Log files are flagged with the $L$ designation.

| Flag | Description |
|------|-------------|
| C | Configuration file |
| X | Executable file |
| Z | Compressed file |
| D | File slated for deletion |
| L | Log file |
| N | Directory entry in 1.1 format |
| T | Trace filev |

**Table 8-2.**   *Flash File Extensions*

**TRACE FILE**   The trace log normally isn't active and thus isn't accessed by end users. It refers to a reserved space for diagnostic messages referred to by the file system commands.

## Recovering Storage Space

Recovering the space on a storage medium (the flash, for example) after a file has been marked for deletion involves reclaiming the space with the **squeeze** command, which recovers any space on the flash by deleting files you mark as unwanted. (You do this by setting the *D* flag). The remaining files are reordered so that no space is wasted between them:

```
Accelar-1100# squeeze f
recovering deleted file space ... success
```

This command can be issued against the flash or the PCMCIA Card. Recovering this space can also be accomplished through Device Manager. If you need to recover a file that has been marked *D* for deletion, you can use the **recover** command to remove the *D* flag and recover the file. The **recover** command can't recover files after the space has been reclaimed with the **squeeze** command.

## Transferring Files

File transfer to and from the flash or PCMCIA Card is accomplished through TFTP. A TFTP server package needs to be running on the network; either a dedicated TFTP server or a TFTP application running on a workstation or laptop. Once this is set up, the file may be transferred. This is initiated either from Device Manager, or through the CLI:

```
Accelar-1100# copy tftp pcmcia
Accelar-1100# copy tftp pcmcia
Enter source tftp server address [100.10.10.21]: 100.10.10.21
Enter source file [XLR.cfg]: accboot1.3.0
tftp result: success
Accelar-1100#
```

## Formatting Devices

The flash and PCMCIA mediums may be formatted through use of the **format** command:

```
Accelar-1250# format flash
Accelar-1250# format pcmcia
```

*Any new, unformatted PCMCIA Card needs to be formatted before it can be used in the Accelar.*

# The Runtime CLI

The Accelar routing switches may be configured by using the command-line interface (CLI). The CLI is accessible through either the device's serial port, a telnet session, or a dial-up session using a modem. The CLI can be used to accomplish the same configuration changes that are available through Device Manager.

The evolution of the Accelar 1000 series routing switches resulted in several different CLI command structures; in fact, four different CLI command sets exist; one each for code versions 1.0.*x*, 1.1.*x*, 1.3.*x*, and 2.0.*x*. The CLI used in code version 2.0.*x* mimics the router Bay Command Console (BCC). Only the 2.0.*x* CLI is covered in this book.

## Establishing a Console Connection

To access the CLI, either a telnet, console, or dial-up session must be established with the Accelar. A telnet session is possible after the Accelar is configured with a reachable IP address. A physical serial connection must be used to establish a console session. The serial port on the Accelar is a DTE port, so it requires a null modem cable when connecting via a terminal or terminal-emulation software. If connecting with a modem, a straight-through cable is used. Use the following settings to establish a serial connection:

| Baud rate | 9600 |
|---|---|
| Data bits | 8 |
| Stop bits | 1 |
| Parity | None |
| Flow control | None |
| Terminal type | VT100 |

Because the Accelar serial port is a DTE device, it expects to see Data Set Ready (DSR) and Clear To Send (CTS) signals before it will transmit, so these pins must be present on the cable being used. The following pinouts may be used for either a 9-pin or 25-pin PC connector:

| | | 9 Pin | | 25 Pin |
|---|---|---|---|---|
| 2 | RXD | RXD | 2 | 3 |
| 3 | TXD | TXD | 3 | 2 |
| 4 | DTR | DTR | 4 | 20 |
| 5 | GND | GND | 5 | 7 |
| 6 | DSR | DSR | 6 | 6 |
| 7 | RTS | RTS | 7 | 4 |
| 8 | CTS | CTS | 8 | 5 |

## Levels of Security in the CLI

Once a terminal session is established, the user must log in at one of five security levels; these login options define what sorts of configuration changes (if any) the user can make during the CLI session. The following five levels of permission are available:

**READ-ONLY ACCESS**    Enables the user to view statistics and configuration settings, but not alter parameters. Login for read-only access is **ro,** with a default password of **ro**.

**LAYER 2 READ-WRITE ACCESS**    Enables the user to view statistics and configuration settings, as well as change Layer 2 parameters, such as switching, Spanning Tree Groups (STGs), and VLAN settings that are not related to Layer 3 internetworking protocols. Login for Layer 2 read-write access is **l2,** with a default password of **l2**.

**LAYER 3 READ-WRITE ACCESS**    Enables the user to view statistics and configuration settings, as well as change Layer 3 parameters, such as IP, IPX, and internetworking protocols such OSPF and RIP. Login for Layer 3 read-write access is **l3,** with a default password of **l3**.

THE ACCELAR LAYER 3 SWITCH

**READ-WRITE ACCESS**   Enables the user to view statistics and change any configuration settings that are not related to security, such as password settings. Login for read-write access is **rw**, with a default password of **rw**.

**READ-WRITE ALL ACCESS**   Enables the user to view statistics, as well as make any configuration changes to the device, including the altering of security and password information. Login for read-write all access is **rwa**, with a default password of **rwa**.

After the user enters the password, the command prompt is displayed:

```
Accelar 1250#
```

A variety of configuration options are available through the runtime CLI; in fact, most of the configurable parameters can be configured by using nothing but the CLI. The command set is more cumbersome than using the Device Manager GUI, but has the added advantage of being accessible through the serial port or through a telnet session. The different configuration options are covered in the following chapters.

## Port Assignments

The port numbering scheme for the CLI follows a similar scheme across all Accelar platforms, assigning each port the designation *module/port*. In the case of devices with fixed ports, as well as modules, each module is counted, and the row of fixed ports is considered a single module. For example, to view the port statistics in the CLI for port 5 of slot 3 in an Accelar 1200, you would issue the following command:

```
Accelar-1200# show port info interface 3/5
```

By the same token, in an Accelar 1100, to view the same port statistics for port 8 in the fixed row of ports, you would use this command:

```
Accelar# show port info interface 3/5
=============================================================================
                               Port Interface
=============================================================================
PORT                                       PHYSICAL          STATUS
NUM   INDEX DESCRIPTION  TYPE         MTU   ADDRESS           ADMIN  OPERATE
-----------------------------------------------------------------------------
3/5   52    100BaseTX    iso88023Csmacd 1500  00:00:81:c1:e8:28 up       up
```

This port-naming scheme can also be used in groups, meaning that when you assign a group of ports to a VLAN, you don't need to enter each individual port, because you can group them together. For instance, in an Accelar 1100, to add ports 1 through 5 to a common VLAN (VLAN 100), you would use this command:

```
Accelar-1100# config vlan 100 ports add 3/1-3/5
```

This adds the group of ports 1 through 5, inclusive.

# Boot Monitor CLI

The Boot Monitor CLI is accessible before the runtime image has been executed, and boot options may be configured from this interface. If autoboot is disabled, a prompt appears during initialization:

```
Press any key to stop autoboot
```

Pressing any key at this point halts the initialization procedure and brings up the Boot Monitor CLI. This displays the following prompt:

```
monitor>
```

If autoboot is currently set to true, the option to break out of the boot process is not offered. To set the autoboot option to false, issue the following command from the runtime CLI:

```
Accelar-1250# config sys set flags autoboot false
```

After the Boot Monitor CLI is accessed, a limited set of commands is accessible from the monitor prompt; these may be useful in file manipulation and/or boot instructions if anything goes wrong during the bootup procedure. Table 8-3 lists the Boot Monitor CLI functions.

With these commands, several recovery steps can be taken if, for some reason, the boot process should fail.

Type the following command:

```
monitor> show boot
Primary    = flash:acc1.3.1
Secondary = pcmcia:acc1.1.6
Tertiary   = net
Config     = nvram
Autoboot is disabled
Factory defaults is disabled
Switch port isolation is disabled
```

| Function | Purpose |
|---|---|
| boot | Booting an image from a device |
| choices | Changing boot order |
| copy | Copying a file to device |
| delete | Deleting a file from device |
| devices | Enabling/disabling boot devices |
| directory | Listing files on a device |
| flags | Changing boot flags |
| format | Formatting a device |
| help | Displaying additional information when a user enters the **help** *command* |
| history | Listing the command history |
| ip | Changing ip address information |
| log | Displaying system log file information |
| ping | Pinging an ip address on a network |
| recover | Recovering deleted files on a device |
| reset | Resetting the system |
| save | Saving changes to the boot configuration |
| show | Displaying the boot configuration |
| squeeze | Reclaiming deleted file space on a device |
| tests | Enabling/disabling device boot-up tests |
| tftp | Changing tftp server information |
| trace | Displaying system trace file information |
| quit | Quitting the menu and booting |
| ? | Displaying additional information when a user enters the **help** *command* |

**Table 8-3.** *Boot Monitor CLI Functions*

This displays the current boot configuration. In this example, the primary boot method is the internal flash, the secondary method is the PCMCIA Card, and, if both methods fail, a boot then is attempted off the network. The current configuration file is the one stored in NVRAM. These options can be changed, in the event that the primary image file is corrupted or is the wrong version.

## Accelar Boot Recovery Example

Using the preceding boot parameters, the primary boot method is the flash, using the image file acc1.3.1. However, in this example, the bootstrap code is accboot1.3.0, and due to the inconsistency between the bootstrap and runtime image versions, the initial bootup has failed. By interrupting the boot process and breaking out to the Boot Monitor CLI, the device can be recovered.

The file listed on the PCMCIA Card is acc1.1.6, which likewise is incompatible with the current bootstrap version. Assume that the runtime image file acc1.3.1 must be saved for future use, and that the current flash does not have enough space left to hold a new image. Also, for the sake of this example, assume that only the one PCMCIA Card is available. By following the procedure below, the acc1.3.1 image can be preserved, while still providing the device with a consistent bootstrap and runtime image file.

Because the runtime image has not executed, none of the device's configuration is in place and, therefore, no reachable IP address is associated with it. Since a TFTP transfer is going to be necessary in this case, an IP must be configured. In this instance, it will be configured on the diagnostic Ethernet port, located on the SSF (for the stackable series, this port is located on the rear of the device). Older SSF models may have this port mounted on the circuit board, and an I/O module may need to be removed to allow access via a 10BaseT cable. Once the connection is made between this Ethernet port and the management station, assign an IP to the diagnostic port. Assuming that the management station's IP address is 100.10.20.1 with a 24-bit mask, enter the following:

```
monitor>ip
------CHANGE IP ADDRESS------
Net Devices:
4       Enabled     Serial Port 2 [s2]       hw=ff:ff:ff:ff:ff:ff
                    ip=0.0.0.0    netmask=0x00000000
                    mgmt net=0.0.0.0   gateway=0.0.0.0
5       Enabled     Debug Ethernet [nic]    hw=00:e0:16:ae:31:d3
                    ip=0.0.0.0    netmask=0x00000000
                    mgmt net=0.0.0.0    gateway=0.0.0.0
```

THE ACCELAR LAYER 3 SWITCH

```
Select network device [5]: 5
Enter IP address [0.0.0.0]: 100.10.20.10
Enter netmask [255.0.0.0]: 255.255.255.0
Enter default gateway [0.0.0.0]
Enter Mgmt Network [0.0.0.0]
```

Since no router is involved, a default gateway is not necessary. Likewise, the management network IP address is needed only if the management station is on a different subnet. Here, device 5, the debug Ethernet port, has been chosen and assigned an IP address of 100.10.20.10/24, consistent with the management station's IP address of 100.10.20.1/24. Device 4 refers to a secondary serial port for use with a modem. This device is not supported on earlier versions of the code.

After you assign the IP address, verify connectivity through a ping from the monitor prompt. After a successful ping, launch the TFTP application on the management station. To transfer the image to the Accelar, enter the following command:

```
monitor> copy tftp pcmcia
Enter source tftp server address [0.0.0.0]: 100.10.20.1
Enter source file []: acc1.3.0
```

This transfers the acc1.3.0 runtime image to the PCMCIA Card. Now, copy the bootstrap code to the PCMCIA, as well:

```
monitor> copy flash:accboot1.3.0 pcmcia
```

Although this transfers the bootstrap code to the PCMCIA, the primary boot mode still points to the internal flash. To alter the boot sequence, use the **choices** command:

```
monitor> choices
select boot choice to change [1]: 1
Enter new boot choice: 2
Enter filename:acc1.3.0
```

This selects the primary boot option (1) and points it to the PCMCIA Card (2), specifying the new runtime image code, acc1.3.0.

When using the **choices** command to point to different system devices, the matrix in Table 8-4 may be used.

Save the information by using the **save** command. The device may now be reset either through the Boot Monitor CLI, the Reset button on the SSF, or by powering

| Device Location | Device Name | Device Number |
|---|---|---|
| System memory | dram | 0 |
| On-board flash | flash | 1 |
| PCMCIA flash | pcmcia | 2 |
| Serial port 2 (for modems) | s2 | 4 |
| Debug Ethernet port | net | 5 |
| CPU | cpu | 3 |
| BootEEPROM | booteeprom | 6 |

**Table 8-4.**   *Accelar Device Designations*

down the device and then back on again. Upon reinitialization, the device should point to the PCMCIA Card for bootup, using the 1.3.0 bootstrap code, as well as the 1.3.0 runtime image.

**Note**   *It is a good practice to remove the IP information from the debug port after recovery is completed, to avoid conflicting IP addresses.*

### Boot Flags

The boot flags may also be set from the Boot Monitor CLI. This may be useful for changing the autoboot option, setting the device to factory defaults, or setting the ports to be in isolated mode. Issuing the **flags** command results in a series of simple yes/no prompts:

```
monitor> flags
Do you want to enable autoboot (y/n)? n
Do you want to use the factory defaults (y/n)? n
Do you want to enable switch port isolation (y/n)? n
```

## Using and Viewing the Log

Like the Nortel Networks router platform, the Accelar also has a log function, although its functionality differs from that of the router; this feature can be extremely useful when troubleshooting. The log is capable of logging a variety of different events, from informational events to fatal error events:

```
Accelar# show log level
Log Levels are:
 0 = INFO
 1 = WARNING
 2 = ERROR
 3 = MFG
 4 = FATAL
The Log Level is INFO
```

The log level can be altered through the CLI by using the **config** command and selecting one of the preceding log levels listed. Setting the log level indicates what types of messages will be recorded in the log file, and is used to filter out unwanted messages. For instance, to set the log level to FATAL, so that only fatal log events are recorded, you would use the following command:

```
Accelar# config log level 4
```

This command alters the current log level to the level indicated (4 in this case, which indicates fatal error messages).

**Note**   *Setting the log level to, for instance, FATAL, causes only fatal log events to be recorded; however, changing the log level will not remove log events other than fatal events that were previously recorded. To remove these entries, the log must be cleared by using the* **config log clear** *command, which clears all log entries.*

## Viewing the Log

The Accelar log is viewed by using the **show log file** command, which displays the log file by beginning with the most recent entries. Optionally, you can view the log from the least recent entry back toward the most recent entry, by using the command **show log file tail**, where the **tail** argument indicates that the log should be viewed backward:

```
Accelar# show log file
0: [000 00:00:00:633] INFO: Code=0x0 Task=rcStart: INTERPRET FOLLOWING
                            TIMESTAMPS AS TIME SINCE BOOT
1: [000 00:00:00:900] INFO: Code=0x0 Task=rcStart: System boot
2: [000 00:00:01:166] INFO: Code=0x0 Task=rcStart: Accelar System Software
                            Release 2.0.1
3: [000 00:00:01:433] INFO: Code=0x0 Task=rcStart: System log file flash:syslog:0:3
4: [000 00:00:06:400] INFO: Code=0x0 Task=rcStart: INTERPRET FOLLOWING
                            TIMESTAMPS AS ACTUAL DATES
5: [000 00:00:08:533] INFO: Code=0x0 Task=rcStart: Card Inserted: Slot#=1,
```

```
Serial#=AY5R00XZ, Version=v3.0
6: [000 00:00:11:966] INFO: Code=0x0 Task=rcStart: System is ready
7: [000 00:00:13:900] INFO: Code=0x0 Task=tChassis: Link Up(3/1)
8: [000 00:00:14:300] INFO: Code=0x0 Task=tChassis: Link Up(3/3)
9: [000 00:00:14:700] INFO: Code=0x0 Task=tChassis: Link Up(3/5)
10: [000 00:00:15:100] INFO: Code=0x0 Task=tChassis: Link Up(3/6)
11: [000 00:00:00:366] INFO: Code=0x0 Task=rcStart: INTERPRET FOLLOWING
                               TIMESTAMPS AS TIME SINCE BOOT
12: [000 00:00:00:633] INFO: Code=0x0 Task=rcStart: System boot
13: [000 00:00:00:900] INFO: Code=0x0 Task=rcStart: Accelar System
                               Software Release 2.0.1
14: [000 00:00:01:166] INFO: Code=0x0 Task=rcStart: System log
                               file flash:syslog:0:14
```

## Directing the Log to the Terminal Screen

You can direct the log to the screen rather than to the automatically generated log file, so that you can see log entries as they occur, instead of viewing the log after the messages have been written. This is accomplished with the following command:

```
Accelar# config log screen on
Screen logging is on
```

# Using the Syslog Feature

The syslog feature in the Accelar is used to control the UNIX syslog facility, to log messages relating to the Accelar and to assign these messages different severity levels depending on the message. Configuring the syslog feature requires a specific host ID associated with the UNIX host (this is a value from 1 to 10). The valid syslog commands are as follows:

- **config sys syslog info**   Displays the current syslog settings.
- **config sys syslog host** *ID* **address** *IP address*   Associates the assigned host ID to a specific UNIX system by IP address.
- **config sys syslog host** *ID* **{create | delete}**   Creates a syslog host, or deletes an existing one.
- **config sys syslog host** *ID* **facility** *facility*   Indicates the UNIX facility that will be used in messages to the syslog host (LOCAL0 to LOCAL7).
- **config sys syslog host** *ID* **{enable | disable}**   Enables or disables syslog information for the {host ID indicated.
- **config sys syslog host** *ID* **info**   Displays syslog info for the host ID indicated.

■ **config sys syslog host** *ID* **mapinfo** *level*   Defines the severity level associated with Accelar Info messages. Severity levels are emergency, alert, critical, error, warning, notice, info, or debug.

■ **config sys syslog host** *ID* **mapwarning** *level*   Defines the severity level associated with Accelar warning messages. Severity levels are emergency, alert, critical, error, warning, notice, info, or debug.

■ **config sys syslog host** *ID* **maperror** *level*   Defines the severity level associated with Accelar error messages. Severity levels are emergency, alert, critical, error, warning, notice, info, or debug.

■ **config sys syslog host** *ID* **mapfatal** *level*   Defines the severity level associated with Accelar fatal messages. Severity levels are emergency, alert, critical, error, warning, notice, info, or debug.

■ **config sys syslog host** *ID* **severity** *severity*   Defines the syslog severity levels that should be sent to the syslog host. Severities include info, warning, error, and fatal.

■ **config sys syslog host** *ID* **udp-port** *port*   Indicates the UDP port number over which the messages will be sent to the syslog host (514 to 530).

■ **config sys syslog max-hosts** *maxhost*   Defines the maximum number of syslog hosts that will be supported.

■ **config sys syslog state Penable | disable**   Enables or disables the syslog state.

After you configure the syslog parameters, you can view the settings through the CLI by using the **show sys syslog** command:

```
Accelar-1100# show sys syslog host 1 info
Id : 1
IpAddr : 180.80.10.11
UdpPort : 514
Facility : local2
Severity : info|warning|error|mfg|fatal
MapInfoSeverity : info
MapWarningSeverity : warning
MapErrorSeverity : error
MapMfgSeverity : notice
MapFatalSeverity : emergency
Enable : true
```

This example shows a fairly straightforward configuration for a host with ID 1 and an IP address of 180.80.10.11.

# Using the Trace Feature

The trace feature is another useful troubleshooting tool available from the Accelar CLI. The trace feature enables the user to target certain switch events and log trace information regarding the selected function. For instance, if an OSPF problem is occurring on the Accelar, a trace can be run on OSPF-related functions, and then the trace information can be viewed from the CLI. The following trace information may be gathered:

```
Accelar# trace level
usage: trace level <modid> <level>

Module IDs:                    Trace Levels:
 0 - Common                    0    0 - Disabled
 1 - SNMP Agent                0    1 - Very terse
 2 - RMON                      0    2 - Terse
 3 - Port Manager              0    3 - Verbose
 4 - Chassis Manager           0    4 - Very verbose
 5 - STG Manager               0
 6 - Phase2 OSPF               0
 7 - Hardware I/F              0
 8 - (N/A)                     0
 9 - CP Port                   0
10 - (N/A)                     0
11 - VLAN Manager              0
12 - CLI                       0
13 - Main                      0
14 - Phase2 IP+RIP             0
15 - RCC IP                    0
16 - HTTP Server               0
17 - ASIC I/F                  0
18 - Gigabit                   0
19 - Watch Dog Timer           0
20 - Topology Discovery        0
21 - (N/A)                     0
22 - (N/A)                     0
23 - IGMP                      0
24 - IPFIL                     0
25 - MLT                       0
30 - P2IPX                     0
31 - RCIPX                     0
```

THE ACCELAR LAYER 3 SWITCH

**Caution**    *Utilization of the trace feature may impact network performance.*

This output shows the series of events for which the trace feature can be activated, as well as a series of verbosity levels concerning how detailed the trace information should be that is being accumulated. In the next example, a trace is configured for SNMP events, with the maximum verbosity setting:

```
Accelar# trace level 1 4
```

After you configure this trace, the Accelar will begin to generate a trace file for SNMP events. In this example, once the trace level was configured, a Device Manager session was launched against the Accelar. The following is an excerpt from the trace file output after the SNMP polling of the Accelar was complete:

```
Accelar# show trace file
.
.
.
[001 06:18:12:811] tSnmpd SNMP: In rcCardEntryNext(compc=1, *compl=0x0,
                                 last=2)
[001 06:18:12:811] tSnmpd SNMP: Get first row
[001 06:18:12:811] tSnmpd SNMP: Got row for index=0x1
[001 06:18:12:811] tSnmpd SNMP: In rcCardEntryNext(compc=1, *compl=0x1,
                                 last=2)
[001 06:18:12:811] tSnmpd SNMP: Get next row with index=0x1
[001 06:18:12:811] tSnmpd SNMP: Got row for index=0x3
[001 06:18:12:811] tSnmpd SNMP: In rcCardEntryNext(compc=1, *compl=0x2,
                                 last=2)
[001 06:18:12:811] tSnmpd SNMP: Get next row with index=0x2
[001 06:18:12:811] tSnmpd SNMP: Got row for index=0x3
[001 06:18:13:361] tSnmpd SNMP: In rcSysTrapRecvEntryGet(compc=4,
                                 *compl=0x84, last=5)
[001 06:18:13:361] tSnmpd SNMP: Get exact row with addr=132.245.152.123
[001 06:18:13:378] tSnmpd SNMP: in rcSysTrapTblGet()
[001 06:18:13:378] tSnmpd SNMP: Got row for index
[001 06:18:13:378] tSnmpd SNMP: In systemGet(compc=1, *compl=0x0, last=3)
[001 06:18:13:378] tSnmpd SNMP: In systemGrpGet()
[001 06:18:13:378] tSnmpd SNMP: Got scalar variables
[001 06:18:13:378] tSnmpd SNMP: In ifEntryGet(compc=1, *compl=0x10, last=8)
[001 06:18:13:378] tSnmpd SNMP: Get exact row with index=0x10
[001 06:18:13:378] tSnmpd SNMP: Got row for index=0x10
[001 06:18:13:378] tSnmpd SNMP: In rcCardEntryGet(compc=1,
                                 *compl=0x3, last=6)
[001 06:18:13:378] tSnmpd SNMP: Get exact row with index=0x3
[001 06:18:13:378] tSnmpd SNMP: Got row for index
```

Like the log feature, the trace can be viewed from the last entry, by using the **show trace file tail** command. After you configure the trace, you must disable it from the CLI to stop the trace file from being collected. This is done by setting the verbosity level to 0:

```
Accelar# trace level 1 0
```

After you run a trace, you may need to run a new trace. It may be useful to clear out the trace file before you proceed, so that the entries don't become too cluttered. This is accomplished with the following command:

```
Accelar# trace clear
```

## Running System Tests

A variety of system tests can be run from the Accelar's runtime CLI; the address resolution table can be tested, the switch fabric can be tested, and ports can be tested by using either an internal or external loopback test. These tests must be executed from the CLI, which initiates the test, and then must be stopped. Once this is completed, the results of the test may be viewed. For example, to begin a test of the address resolution table, the command **test artable** is used; then, to stop the test, the command **test stop artable** is used. The **show** command is used to view the test results:

```
Accelar# test artable
Accelar# test stop artable
Accelar/test# show test artable
Currently no test is running.
Last test results:
  IfIndex: 0
    Result: success
PassCount: 185244999
FailCount: 0
```

Likewise, the switch fabric can be tested by using the following commands:

```
Accelar# test fabric
Accelar#
Switch Fabric test is running.  Accelar switch performance
 will be impacted!
Accelar# test stop fabric
Accelar#
Switch Fabric test has been stopped.
Accelar# show test fabric
Currently no test is running.
Last test results:
```

```
   IfIndex: 0
    Result: success
 PassCount: 22419
 FailCount: 0
```

As the preceding sequence indicates, testing the Accelar switch fabric impacts the performance of the Accelar, and thus should be performed at a time when it is least likely to impact the network.

# Accelar MAC Address Assignment

Due to the nature of the Accelar, MAC address assignment takes on a few different forms, depending on what the MAC address is associated with. For instance, each Accelar has a base MAC address, physical MAC addresses, and virtual MAC addresses. Since static Address Resolution Protocol (ARP) entries may need to be configured at some point, it is important to understand how the MAC addresses are generated, and what they are associated with.

## Base MAC Address

The *base MAC address* for the Accelar is a unique MAC address that is associated with the internal flash unit. This is the base MAC address from which all other MAC types are generated. As is the case with any other hardware address, the first three octets comprise the vendor code. Of the last three octets, the first two octets are a unique value associated with the Accelar, and the last octet will vary depending on what the MAC is associated with. The last octet has a valid range of 00 to FF.

## Physical MAC Address

The *physical MAC addresses* are those that are associated with the physical ports; these MAC addresses are assigned to bridge protocol data units (BPDUs), and are also used by the Accelar as the interface MAC when an isolated router port is configured. The last octet of the base MAC address varies depending on the slot and port, using the following scheme:

| Slot \ Port | 1 | 2 | 3 | 4 | 5 | 6 | 7 | 8 | 9 | 10 | 11 | 12 | 13 | 14 | 15 | 16 |
|---|---|---|---|---|---|---|---|---|---|---|---|---|---|---|---|---|
| 1 | 00 | 01 | 02 | 03 | 04 | 05 | 06 | 07 | 08 | 09 | 0A | 0B | 0C | 0D | 0E | 0F |
| 2 | 10 | 11 | 12 | 13 | 14 | 15 | 16 | 17 | 18 | 19 | 1A | 1B | 1C | 1D | 1E | 1F |
| 3 | 20 | 21 | 22 | 23 | 24 | 25 | 26 | 27 | 28 | 29 | 2A | 2B | 2C | 2D | 2E | 2F |
| 4 | | | | | | ← | SSF | → | | | | | | | | |
| 5 | | | | | | ← | SSF | → | | | | | | | | |
| 6 | 30 | 31 | 32 | 33 | 34 | 35 | 36 | 37 | 38 | 39 | 3A | 3B | 3C | 3D | 3E | 3F |
| 7 | 40 | 41 | 42 | 43 | 44 | 45 | 46 | 47 | 48 | 49 | 4A | 4B | 4C | 4D | 4E | 4F |
| 8 | 50 | 51 | 52 | 53 | 54 | 55 | 56 | 57 | 58 | 59 | 5A | 5B | 5C | 5D | 5E | 5F |

The valid range of the last octet for a physical MAC address is 00 to 80.

## Virtual MAC Address

The *virtual MAC addresses* are those that are associated with the different VLANs; the base MAC address is used, with the last octet having a valid range of 81 to FF. Because the default VLAN (VLAN 1) is always present, it uses the value 81 as its last octet.

# Device Manager

The primary method of configuring the Accelar is through an application called Device Manager, a GUI that uses the Simple Network Management Protocol (SNMP) to poll and manage the Accelar.

# Modeling Devices in Device Manager

Device Manager is a Windows 95/98/NT application that enables the Accelar to be monitored and configured. A single copy of Device Manager is capable of modeling each of the Accelar platforms, as well as the 450 series switches.

File management, physical port configuration, VLAN creation and configuration, and routing services (as well as numerous other features) may be configured by using Device Manager. Each of these configuration utilities is described in both this chapter and later chapters as it comes up in discussion.

To model the Accelar in Device Manager, a valid IP first needs to be configured to launch Device Manager against. You need to do this through the CLI, because Device Manager has no serial support.

## Configuring an IP Address on the Accelar

To configure an IP address on the device, first establish a CLI session with the Accelar. You need to log in to the device. Default login and password information is included earlier in this chapter in the section "Levels of Security in the CLI." At the CLI prompt, you have two basic methods for adding an IP:

- Create an isolated router port.
- Create a VLAN and then an IP address associated with that VLAN.

**CREATING AN ISOLATED ROUTER PORT**   Depending on the code version, the method of creating an isolated router port may differ slightly; this text covers code versions 2.0 and above, which implement the BCC interface:

```
Accelar-1200# config ethernet 3/8 ip create 100.10.20.1/24
```

This command automatically sets routing to true, and assigns an IP address of 100.10.20.1 with a 24-bit mask to interface 3/8 on the Accelar. If the managing station is to be directly connected into this port for purposes of initial configuration, no routing protocols need to be configured. Verify connectivity by pinging the management station from the CLI.

THE ACCELAR LAYER 3 SWITCH

**CREATING A VLAN AND ASSOCIATING AN IP WITH THAT VLAN**    A second method for providing initial IP connectivity is to assign an IP address to the default VLAN, of which all ports are a member by default. By doing this, the device can be managed by connecting the management station into any port currently in the default VLAN. This is accomplished through the following command:

```
Accelar-1200# config vlan 1 ip create 100.10.20.1/24
```

which assigns the IP address 100.10.20.1 with a 24-bit subnet mask to the default VLAN. Verify connectivity by pinging the management station from the CLI.

## Modeling the Accelar

After you establish a valid IP address, you are ready to model the Accelar. To do so, follow these steps:

1. Launch Device Manager to bring up the opening window:

2. This small window offers two choices: Device and Help. Choose Device, which opens a pull-down menu that enables you to set up the device that you want to model.

3. Click Open; you are prompted for the IP address of the Accelar that you want to manage, as well as its community strings.

4. Enter the IP address that you configured through the CLI. If the community strings were altered as well, make the appropriate changes in the Community String fields.

5. Click Open, which opens a graphical view of the Accelar:

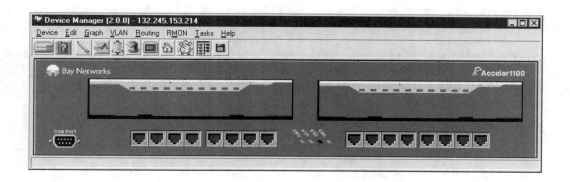

Device Manager automatically detects the device that is being managed, and displays the representation appropriate to that device.

# Web-Based Management

The Accelar can also be managed (though to a lesser degree) through a Web-based interface called the *Accelar Configuration Page*, and is accessible through a Web browser. By entering the IP address of the Accelar in the URL field, an HTTP connection will be established.

The Accelar Configuration Page is a frame-based interface that offers device and port information, as well as statistics. The Web-based management is not as robust as either the CLI or Device Manager, but it is useful for monitoring and managing single devices. The following is a list of the pages available:

**SYSTEM INFORMATION**    Displays the system name, contact, and system up-time. It will display the model of Accelar being managed, as well as the time when the last save was made to NVRAM.

**CHASSIS INFORMATION**    Displays the serial number, the hardware revision level, a text representation of the number of slots and ports, and environmental information, such as the fan and power supply status.

**BOOT CONFIGURATION INFORMATION**    Displays the current running image version, as well as the primary, secondary, tertiary, and configuration boot methods.

**VLAN INFORMATION**    Displays the individual configured VLANs, including the following information: VLAN ID, VLAN Name, whether High Priority is set to true or false, whether routing is enabled, the Spanning Tree Group being used for the individual VLAN (discussed in greater detail in Chapter 10), the VLAN type, and port assignments (covered in Chapter 9). These VLANs may be paged through via hypertext links located at the top of each page.

**SPANNING TREE INFORMATION**    Displays Spanning Tree Protocol information for each individual Spanning Tree Group.

**PERFORMANCE INFORMATION**    Provides a text display yielding a CPU and switch fabric utilization (%), which is also displayed via LEDs on the SSF module.

**SWITCH FABRIC INFORMATION**    Monitors address resolution statistics through the switch fabric. Statistics are monitored for MAC and IP, as well as for VLANs, broken down according to port-based, protocol-based, and IP subnet-based configurations.

**WEB SERVER INFORMATION**    Displays the number of hits the Accelar has received, as well as other access statistics, such as access checks and the number of blocked attempts.

**CONFIG WEB SERVER**    Provides a series of hyperlinks to follow to alter the access permissions and passwords.

# VLAN Manager

VLAN Manager is an application that may be launched separately from Device Manager, but that is also accessible from within Device Manager. You can create VLANs from within VLAN Manager, as well as assign access and trunk ports and reassign ports to different VLANs. However, VLAN Manager's primary function is to monitor existing VLANs.

You may also create and monitor VLANs in Device Manager, but Device Manager is geared toward viewing VLANs on a single device, whereas VLAN Manager enables you to view all VLANs simultaneously. Another important difference is that, whereas Device Manager displays a VLAN's port assignments for a single switch, VLAN Manager displays the port assignments for all ports on each device that are members of each VLAN. Meaning, if a single VLAN spans four devices, then VLAN Manager will display the port assignments for that VLAN on every device simultaneously. This makes viewing VLAN information for an entire network much simpler.

# Creating Domains

To use VLAN Manager, you must initially complete a few tasks. First, you must create a domain. VLAN Manager uses domains as a means of further organizing network VLANs. For example, suppose that a network has three buildings, each with a series of Accelars, and that each building has three VLANs that span multiple switches within that building. In this scenario, because each VLAN spans multiple switches within a building, but no one VLAN actually leaves its building, three separate models may be created, one for each building (see Figure 8-2).

By using this concept, all devices in a single building may be grouped into a common domain. By bringing up a view of a single domain, all devices within that domain may be viewed, so a single VLAN's presence on each switch within that domain may be viewed. Thus, the whole network does not need to be viewed at once, but instead may be viewed on a group-by-group basis. This is valuable for very large or dispersed networks.

## Modeling Devices in VLAN Manager

Launch VLAN Manager in the opening window, which refers to the domains previously mentioned. These are not to be confused with LattisSwitch domains, although the concept is similar. For now, do *not* select Default, because no switches are in the default domain, and selecting Default will cause an error message to appear stating that devices must first be added to the default domain. A *domain* does not have any significance from a network-traffic standpoint; when a domain is created and switches are placed within it, the devices are not affected in any way—it is merely a logical grouping for management purposes.

Follow these steps to define a domain:

1. Click Add. After you define the domain and add the switches to it, you won't need to go through this procedure again until a new domain is added. In this case, the domain Engineering has been added, but no switches have been added to it. Add the necessary devices into the domain by entering the IP address in the appropriate field.

2. Put the IP address in the right-hand field, and change the community strings if needed. Click Add. The switch is now visible in the table, and the community strings have been noted.

3. Highlight the domain that was just created, and click Open. This opens the VLAN Manager window (see Figure 8-3), which displays each VLAN that exists on the network and within that domain. This example has three VLANs and five switches, with each VLAN spanning multiple switches.

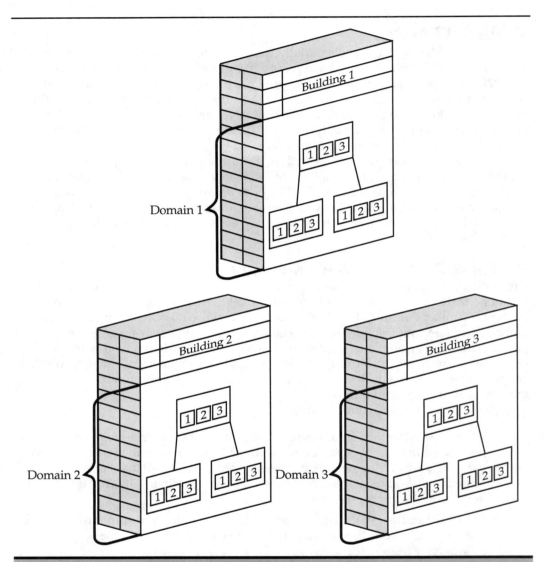

**Figure 8-2.**   *Three buildings with three VLANs each; each building is grouped as a logical domain*

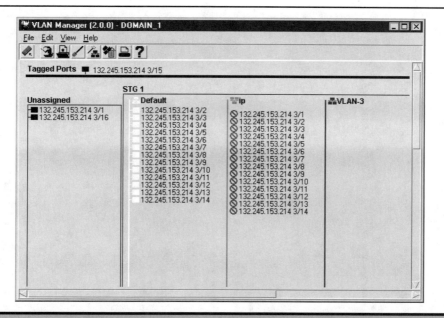

**Figure 8-3.** *The VLAN Manager window*

| Note | *More information on configuring VLANs and managing them, both through Device Manager and through VLAN Manager, can be found in Chapter 9.* |

# The Complete Reference

Nortel Networks

# Chapter 9

## Virtual LANs

One way to solve the problem of managing traffic flow in a flexible way without the need for adding more devices is to use Virtual LANs (VLANs). With the advent of 802.1Q frame tagging (discussed later in this chapter), VLANs also have proven to be an efficient, low-latency method of sorting traffic across the network.

# VLANs

VLAN is a term that is very frequently used, but whose definition is sometimes ambiguous. Part of the reason for this ambiguity is that, until the completion of the 802.1Q specification, no single, defined method of utilizing VLANs existed. Different vendors came up with different ways to accomplish the concept of VLANs, so the mechanics of any particular VLAN may depend on the device, since many devices handle them a bit differently (even ATM ELANs sometimes are referred to as VLANs). However, regardless of the particular vendor and device, VLANs share one definition in common: they are all a logical broadcast domain.

## Building Logical Broadcast Domains

Building a VLAN involves taking a single physical device that normally consists of a single broadcast domain (remember, switches provide a dedicated collision domain on a per-port basis, but it is a single broadcast domain) and creating a series of logical partitions, wherein each partition is its own broadcast domain. The idea is to break up flat networks, without incurring the delay associated with Layer 3 routing. A router is still required to route between VLANs (routers are, to date, still the only way to navigate between different broadcast domains), but VLANs enable a network to be broken up logically in a very versatile way (see Figure 9-1).

In this example, three departments—Sales, Engineering, and Human Resources—share the same device, though each is effectively separated from one

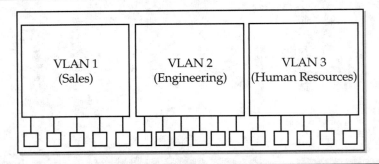

**Figure 9-1.**   *A single physical device broken into multiple logical broadcast domains*

another without the additional expense of a new device or devices. If intercommunication between the departments is required, they must be routed. Likewise, from a logical standpoint, the Sales VLAN could be broken into three smaller VLANs—in this case, Product Marketing, Professional Services, and Systems Engineering—and, with an external device (or, in the case of the Accelar, an internal routing engine), these Sales departments could be interrouted, while having a common routed path to other portions of the corporate intranet (see Figure 9-2).

The preceding example shows how VLANs work and how they might be positioned. As far as what defines each VLAN and makes it different from the others may depend on the device(s) being used. From a technical standpoint, VLANs may differ in execution and functionality, though they accomplish a similar task.

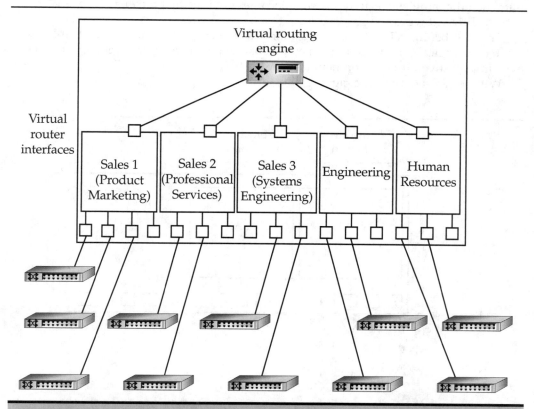

**Figure 9-2.**    *Internetworking among VLANs*

# Port-Based VLANs

Port-based VLANs were one of the first practical applications of VLANs. The concept of port-based VLANs is simple: a grouping of ports—if ports 1 through 5 are in VLAN 1, and ports 6 through 10 are in VLAN 2, then a broadcast on port 1 will be seen out ports 2 through 5, and a broadcast on port 6 will be seen out ports 7 through 10 (see Figure 9-3). Ports 1 through 5 will never see traffic from ports 6 through 10, and visa versa.

This VLAN method is still in common use today, though it is generally now being integrated with 802.1Q frame tagging to increase its functionality (frame tagging is discussed later in this chapter).

Differences in the workings of port-based VLANs may exist; Chapter 5 outlines port-based VLANs on the BayStack 350/450 family of switches, and Chapter 6 discusses port-based VLANs on the Centillion platform. Chapter 7 outlines the VLANs on the LattisSwitch family. All use port groupings to define logical broadcast domains, but when the families are juxtaposed, it becomes obvious that they handle the VLANs in very different ways.

The idea behind VLAN standardization was to make it so that once a VLAN was created, its logical broadcast domain could span many switches and remain a constant, even in a multivendor environment (see Figure 9-4).

With the advent of frame tagging, this functionality is now possible.

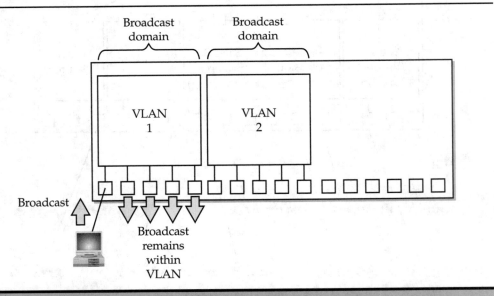

**Figure 9-3.**   *Broadcast traffic in a port-based VLAN environment*

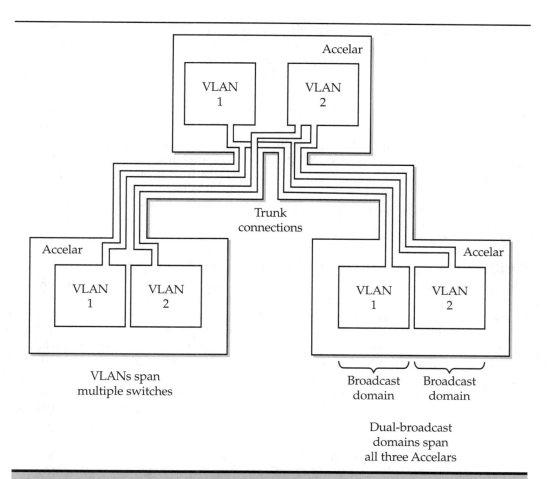

**Figure 9-4.** *Two VLANs spanning many switches*

# Creating Port-Based VLANs on the Accelar

The Accelar supports frame-tagged, port-based VLANs, which are in very common use and, particularly in a single protocol environment, are simple to configure and maintain. The following sections walk through the different methods of configuring port-based VLANs on the Accelar platform.

## Setting Up Port-Based VLANs in the Command Line Interface

Port-based VLANs can be created using the Accelar's command-line interface (CLI); these CLI commands differ depending on which version of code is being used. The following example uses the syntax of the 2.0.*x* code version. To create a port-based VLAN named Vlan 10 on the Accelar from the CLI, with a VLAN ID of 10, in Spanning Tree Group 1, with slot/port 1/1 as a member, enter the following commands:

```
Accelar# config vlan 10 create byport 1 name Vlan10
Accelar# config vlan 10 ports add 1/1
```

The VLAN with an ID of 10 has now been created. In earlier code versions, by default, a VLAN is a port-based VLAN (though this is specified in code version 1.3.1 and later, because policy-based VLANs may, starting at 1.3.1, also be configured through the CLI), and no ports are members. The 1 following "create byport" in the preceding syntax refers to the Spanning Tree Group (STG). For this chapter, examples are limited to the default group of 1. More information regarding setting up multiple STGs can be found in Chapter 10.

## Setting Up Port-Based VLANs in Device Manager

Setting up a new port-based VLAN through Device Manager is easy to do, and, unlike the CLI, the methodology does not differ between code versions. Launch Device Manager and, using a valid IP, model the Accelar.

In the main window, select VLAN | VLANs, which opens the Edit Vlans window. The default VLAN, labeled Default, is in place and is using the default color of white. You want to add another VLAN, so click Insert, which opens the Insert Basic window (see Figure 9-5).

Note the parameters; you can assign a VLAN ID (values may be 1 to 4094), a color, and a priority (covered later in the chapter). Routing is disabled on this VLAN, and its type (port-based) is reflected in the Type field. Because this is a port-based VLAN, you can select the ports that are to be members by clicking them. Then, click Insert.

The new VLAN is now present in the VLAN table dominating the edit VLAN window. The name, color, Spanning Tree Group, and Active Members (in this case, ports 3/7 through 3/9) are visible. A message in the lower-left corner states that the VLAN has been inserted.

## Configuring Port-Based VLANs in VLAN Manager

To configure port-based VLANs through VLAN Manager, first launch the application and configure a domain. This is done in the VLAN Manager - Domain window. These domains are easy to confuse with LattisSwitch domains, because the concept is similar. For now, do not select Default, because it doesn't have any switches, and selecting it will produce an error message stating that devices must first be added to the default domain.

A *domain* does not have any significance from a network traffic standpoint; when a domain is created, and switches are placed within it, this does not affect the devices in any way—it is merely a logical grouping for management purposes. For example, the VLANs in individual buildings may be grouped into domains, making it easier to

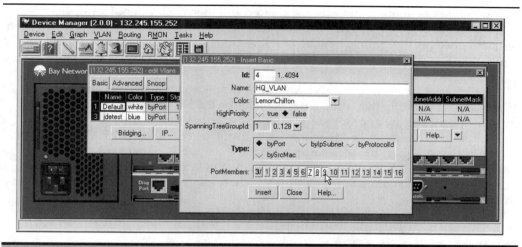

**Figure 9-5.**   *The Insert Basic window*

organize and monitor them. For this example, create a new domain and name it. Click Add. Once the domain is defined and the switches are added to it, you won't need to go through this procedure again until you add a new domain. In the following example, the domain Domain_2 has been added, but initially, no switches have been added to it. Add the switch to the new domain. In the right-hand field, enter the IP address. Change the community strings, if needed. Click Add. The switch is now visible in the table, and the community strings are noted:

Highlight the domain that was just created and then click Open. This opens a window called VLAN Manager. The default VLAN is visible there, along with a bunch of unassigned ports. Create a new VLAN, this time through VLAN Manager, which you can initiate in either of two ways: via the toolbar or via the icon. Click Edit | Create VLAN.

The VLAN Manager - Create VLAN window opens in which you can choose the VLAN type (byPort, in this case). After you choose the VLAN type, you can drag and drop the ports into the appropriate VLAN.

This section has described the three ways to create a port-based VLAN. This is, of course, a single, logical broadcast domain, with a single STG. There are many other variations on how this grouping may now be manipulated, including the use of multiple STGs and routing between VLANs. These concepts are covered further on in this chapter.

# Policy-Based VLANs

Policy-based VLANs sometimes are referred to as *protocol-based VLANs.* The concept of the protocol-based VLAN is at the root of Layer 3 switching, because many of the different protocols sit at the network layer (Layer 3) of the OSI model. By giving VLANs protocol-awareness, you can begin to switch packets using third-layer protocol attributes, performing the switching at Layer 2 and thus avoiding the routing delay normally associated with Layer 3 routing.

A port that's in a policy-based VLAN is only intended to receive traffic for the specified protocol or protocols, if it is a member of more than one protocol-based VLAN. This is accomplished without passing the traffic for examination on the network layer, by examining the packet header to determine which protocol type the packet is, and then sorting the traffic to the appropriate VLAN based on that protocol information.

Protocol distribution may be handled very specifically, and a single uplink port may distribute a large variety of different protocol types to their respective VLANs. Configuring policy-based VLANs is not much different from configuring port-based VLANs, and can be accomplished through either the CLI, VLAN Manager, or Device Manager.

## Setting Up Policy-Based VLANs in Device Manager

Just as before with the port-based VLAN, policy-based VLAN creation is initiated by selecting VLAN | VLANs, which opens the edit VLANs.

This time, however, when choosing the VLAN parameters, instead of leaving the default of byPort, click byProtocolId, which causes the window to enlarge, revealing more choices:

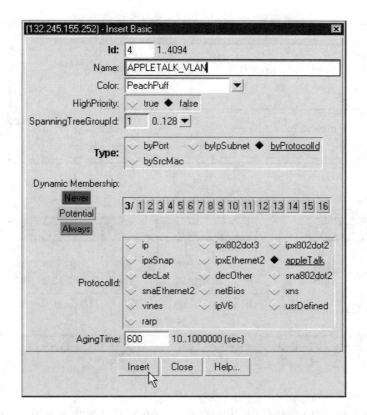

Protocol-based VLANs require a bit more consideration. In this example, because the VLAN is an AppleTalk VLAN, routing will not be active. Notice that an area has opened in which to select your protocol, offering quite a few options. The Accelar recognizes each of these protocols. The last selection in the ProtocolId list is usrDefined. If this option is chosen, a new field appears at the bottom of the window, prompting for the user-defined Protocol ID, in hex format.

After selecting byProtocolId, the Dynamic Membership area appears, which is a bit different from the port-selection tool for the port-based VLAN.

With port-based VLANs, a port either is or isn't a member of a VLAN. With a policy-based VLAN, however, a port has three membership choices (see Figure 9-6):

■ **Always**   The port is a member of this VLAN, regardless of traffic flow.

■ **Potential**   In a policy-based VLAN, a port may have a *potential membership*, which means that if a certain protocol is active in a certain VLAN for only a relatively short amount of time, no real reason exists for the port to be a member of that VLAN all the time. Since any member of the logical broadcast domain will flood its broadcast traffic to every other member of the VLAN, it may be convenient to allow certain protocols membership only at the times

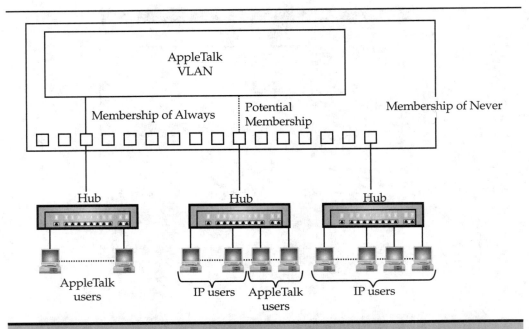

**Figure 9-6.**    *Sample membership arrangement in a policy-based AppleTalk VLAN*

when they have actual data to send. A port with a membership designation of Potential starts off *not* being a member of the AppleTalk VLAN; when that one AppleTalk transmission an hour comes in, then the port becomes a member of the AppleTalk VLAN temporarily. After a certain period of inactivity, the port removes itself from that VLAN until the next packet comes in.

■ **Never**    The port is not a member of this VLAN, nor will it ever be.

A group of ports in this case has been set to Always be a member of the AppleTalk VLAN. However, any one or all of them could be assigned Potential membership from that same window. Click Insert to add the VLAN.

## Setting Up Policy-Based VLANs in VLAN Manager

Setting up a policy-based VLAN through VLAN Manager is very similar to setting up a port-based VLAN in VLAN Manager. You create the protocol-based VLAN domain and then add the switches to it. In this case, the domain AppleTalk/SNA has been added, but no switches have been added to it. Add the switch to the new domain. In the right-hand field, enter the IP address. Change the community strings, if needed, and then click Add. The switch is now visible in the table, and the community strings are noted.

Highlight the newly created domain and then click Open, which opens a window called VLAN Manager. The default VLAN is visible there, along with a bunch of unassigned ports. Create a new VLAN, but this time through VLAN Manager. You can initiate this in either of two ways: via the toolbar or via the icon. Click Create VLAN, which opens the Create VLAN window.

Select the byProtocolId option, which opens a window specific to this VLAN type. Here, you may choose the protocol type (AppleTalk, in this example). Again, the device differentiates between protocols, based on the Protocol ID in the packet. Unlike the port-based VLAN, however, ports may not be dynamically assigned to protocol-based VLANs through VLAN Manager (as of code version 1.3.1). Each port retains its default designation of Potential member, until it is changed in either the runtime CLI or Device Manager.

## Setting Up Policy-Based VLANs in the CLI

Setting up policy-based VLANs via the CLI was introduced in code version 1.3.1. Prior to this code version, it was necessary to use either Device Manager or VLAN Manager to accomplish this. The command syntax used is as follows:

config vlan *vlan-ID* create byprotocol *spanning-tree-group-ID protocol-ID* name *VLAN-name*.

The following is an example of the commands used to create an IPX 802.2 VLAN with a VID of 30 named IPXVlan in STG 1, with port 3/1 through 3/4 always members, and port 3/5 a potential member:

```
Accelar# config vlan 30 create byprotocol 1 ipx802dot2 name IPXVlan
Accelar# config vlan 30 ports add 3/1-3/4 member static
Accelar# config vlan 30 ports add 3/5 member portmember
```

When specifying the protocol that the VLAN will support, the following options are available: ip, ipx802dot3, ipx802dot2, ipxSnap, ipxEthernet2, appleTalk, decLat, decOther, sna802dot2, snaEthernet2, netBios, xns, vines, ipV6, rarp, and usrDefined. These options correspond to the protocols IP, IPX 802.3, IPX 802.2, IPX SNAP, IPX Ethernet_II, AppleTalk, DEC LAT, DEC Other (including MOP), SNA 802.2, SNA Ethernet_II, NetBIOS, XNS, Banyan VINES, IP version 6, Reverse Address Resolution Protocol (RARP), and user defined. These options are accurate as of code version 2.0.1.

# Configuring IP Subnet-Specific Policy-Based VLANs

With the advent of code version 1.3.0, the Accelar can distinguish not only between IP and IPX, and between IPX using 802.3 raw frames and IPX using 802.2 frames, but also between individual IP subnets, despite the fact that they are the same protocol.

# Configuring IP Subnet-Specific Policy-Based VLANs in the CLI

Configuring IP subnet-based VLANs on the Accelar first became available in code version 1.3.0, although the capability to create them from the CLI first became available in code version 1.3.1. To set up an IP subnet-based VLAN with a VLAN ID of 40, in STG 1, with a subnet address of 180.80.10.0 and a subnet mask of 255.255.255.0 (24-bit), enter the following command:

```
Accelar# config vlan 40 create byipsubnet 1 180.80.10.0/24 name Subnet10
```

## Configuring IP Subnet-Specific Policy-Based VLANs in Device Manager

To initiate the IP subnet VLAN creation process, select VLAN | VLANs, which opens the primary VLAN display in the Insert Basic window. When choosing the VLAN parameters, choose byIPsubnet as the Type, which causes the window to enlarge, revealing more choices:

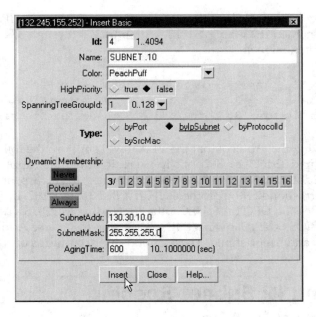

In this example, the IP subnet VLAN is for the .10 subnet in the network 130.30.0.0, with a subnet mask of 255.255.255.0. In the SubnetAddr field, enter **130.30.10.0**, and in the SubnetMask field, enter **255.255.255.0**. In addition to these new fields, the port selection area (labeled Dynamic Membership) is a bit different from that of the port-based VLAN. The port designation of Potential in this case indicates that if incoming traffic matches the IP subnet defined for the VLAN of which the port is a member, the port will temporarilly join that VLAN. After a period of inactivity, the port will remove itself from the VLAN.

Dynamic port membership is accomplished the same way with IP subnet VLANs. Click Insert to add the VLAN.

### Configuring IP Subnet-Specific Policy-Based VLANs in VLAN Manager

Setting up an IP subnet-specific VLAN through VLAN Manager is very similar to setting up a port or policy-based VLAN.

Create the VLAN domain and add the switches to it. In this case, the domain Subnet.10 has been added, but no switches have been added to it. Add the switch to the new domain. To do this, enter the IP address in the right-hand field. Change the community strings, if necessary, and then click Add. The switch is now visible in the table, and the community strings are noted.

Highlight the newly created domain and click Open, which opens a window called Vlan Manager. The default VLAN is visible, along with a bunch of unassigned ports. Create a new VLAN, this time through VLAN Manager, which can be initiated in either of two ways: via the toolbar or via the icon. Click Create VLAN, which opens the Create VLAN window, in which you may select the byIpSubnet option. This opens a window specific to this VLAN type. Here, the IP address can be entered (in this case, 130.30.10.0), along with its subnet mask (255.255.255.0). This specifies that any incoming traffic for the .10 subnet on the 130.30.0.0 network should be routed to this VLAN.

# Configuring MAC-Based VLANs

With the advent of Accelar software version 2.0, source MAC-based VLANs were introduced. These allow for VLAN groupings based on a device's source hardware address. MAC-based VLANs, like the other VLAN types, can be created through Device Manager or the CLI. Source MAC-based VLANs cannot be created through VLAN Manager, though they can be viewed through VLAN Manager.

## Configuring MAC-Based VLANs via Device Manager

To configure MAC-based VLANs through Device Manager, first model the Accelar in Device Manager, and then select VLAN | VLANs from the main Device Manager display. This opens the Edit Vlans window, in which all currently configured VLANs are displayed. To add the new VLAN, click Insert, which opens the Insert Basic window, in which you may select the VLAN type.

Select the bySrcMac option. Select the ports and their membership type by selecting the individual ports from the port list, and then click Insert. This creates the MAC-based VLAN. However, by default, no source MAC addresses are associated with the VLAN, so you must add these.

To add a series of source MAC addresses to the VLAN, click the MAC button in the Edit Vlans window, which opens the Edit MAC (SRC_MAC VLAN) window:

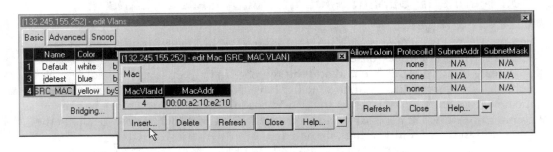

Click Insert to open the Insert MAC window, in which you may enter a source MAC address. You must do this for each individual MAC address that will be associated with the VLAN.

 *MAC addresses must be entered into the Insert MAC field using the format 00:00:A2:21:E2:43. If colons are not used to separate the octets, the error message NoSuchName will appear.*

## Configuring MAC-Based VLANs via the CLI

Through the CLI, source MAC-based VLANs can be created, ports can be added statically or potentially, and individual source MAC addresses can be added to the VLAN. First, the VLAN is created by using the **config vlan** command; in this example, a source MAC-based VLAN is created with a VLAN ID of 200 in STG 1, a port grouping is added as a Potential member, and an example source MAC address is added:

```
Accelar# config vlan 200 create bysrcmac 1 name MACVlan
Accelar# config vlan 200 ports add 3/5 member portmember
Accelar# config vlan 200 srcmac add 00:00:A2:21:34:00
```

The last command in this sequence adds the source MAC address to the VLAN. This command is used to add in any additional source MAC addresses.

# Viewing VLAN Information

VLAN information can be obtained through Device Manager, VLAN Manager, or the CLI. VLAN information viewed through the CLI or Device Manager relate only to the Accelar being viewed, while VLAN information viewed through VLAN Manager displays VLAN information throughout the Accelar network.

## Viewing VLAN Information via Device Manager

Viewing VLANs through Device Manager is accomplished from the same basic windows in which the VLAN configuration is performed. From the main Device Manager display, select VLAN | VLANs to open the Edit Vlans window. Each VLAN configured on the Accelar will be displayed here, across three tabs: Basic, Advanced, and Snoop.

### Basic VLAN Information

The Basic tab in the Edit Vlans window displays basic VLAN information, such as the VLAN name and the VLAN type. The complete list of fields associated with the basic VLAN information is as follows:

- **Name**   Lists the user-assigned name for the VLAN.
- **Color**   Indicates the color selected to be associated with each VLAN; this color is used in VLAN Manager to further differentiate between VLANs.
- **Type**   Indicates the VLAN type: port-based, protocol-based, IP subnet-based, or source MAC-based.
- **StgId**   Indicates the Spanning Tree Group ID for the STG the VLAN is participating in. For more information regarding multiple STGs, consult Chapter 10.
- **PortMembers**   Lists ports that are only potential members of the VLAN; these ports have been associated with the VLAN, but haven't been statically defined. If the port membership type is Potential, then these ports are not necessarily active members of the VLAN.
- **ActiveMembers**   Lists ports that are actively participating in the VLAN.
- **StaticMembers**   Lists ports that have been statically assigned to the VLAN, so they are considered to be actively participating at all times.
- **NotAllowToJoin**   Lists ports that have been assigned a port Dynamic Membership of Never in the Insert Basic window of Device Manager; these ports will not join a protocol, subnet, or MAC-based VLAN even if a packet is received that meets the criteria for that VLAN.

■ **ProtocolId**    Lists the protocol type of the VLAN being viewed if it is a protocol-based VLAN. This will be the protocol name as it is referenced in the CLI (such as ip or ipx802dot2) and not the actual protocol identifier value (such as 0800 for IP).

■ **SubnetAddr**    Lists the IP subnet of the VLAN being viewed if it is an IP subnet-based VLAN.

■ **SubnetMask**    Lists the subnet mask of the VLAN being viewed if it is an IP subnet-based VLAN.

## Advanced VLAN Information

The Advanced tab contains more detailed information regarding the VLAN configuration as well as its current state, such as its MAC address, priority level, and aging time. The full range of values listed in the Advanced tab are as follows:

■ **Name**    Lists the user-defined name for the VLAN.

■ **High Priority**    Indicates whether a high traffic priority has been assigned to the VLAN.

■ **IfIndex**    A value generated and used by the Accelar; it does not need to be used by the administrator.

■ **Aging Time**    Refers to how long a port that has a potential membership in a particular VLAN will remain in that VLAN when idle.

■ **MAC Address**    Lists the MAC address associated with the VLAN; the last octet of this MAC will be within the range 81-FF.

■ **Action**    Clicking this interactive field causes an arrow to appear to its right, which, when selected, opens a list of options (see Table 9-1).

In addition to these tabs, from the main Edit Vlans window, Bridging, IP, IPX, and MAC information can be viewed on a VLAN-by-VLAN basis by selecting each of the options discussed next.

**IP**    Selecting the IP option opens the Edit VLAN_IP window, in which the IP address, subnet mask, broadcast address, and maximum frame size can be viewed. Additional IP information can also be added by clicking Insert. Several other tabs are available in this window:

■ ARP

■ DHCP

■ L3IGMP

■ OSPF

■ RIP

■ VRRP

| Action | Result |
|--------|--------|
| FlushMacFdb | Flushes the forwarding database for that VLAN |
| FlushArp | Flushes the ARP cache for that VLAN |
| FlushIp | Flushes the IP routing table for that VLAN |
| FlushDynMemb | Flushes the VLAN of potential port members that have joined |
| All | Flushes all VLAN tables |
| FlushSnoopMemb | Flushes all Internet Group Membership Protocol (IGMP) snooping members |
| TriggerRipUpdate | Causes the VLAN to issue a RIP update |
| FlushSnoopMRtr | Flushes all multicast routers from the IGMP snooping table |

**Table 9-1.**    *Advanced VLAN Actions and Their Results*

These tabs provide statistics and configurable parameters for each of these protocols. The information found in each of these tabs is covered in Chapter 11 in greater detail, in the sections pertaining to each protocol or function.

**IPX**    This option opens the Edit IPX window, in which information regarding IPX configuration is displayed. The following fields can be viewed:

- **VlanId**    The VLAN ID associated with the VLAN selected.
- **NetAddr**    The IPX network address associated with the VLAN.
- **Encap**    The frame encapsulation type selected for this VLAN (Ethernet_II, Snap, LLC, or 802.3 RAW).

As is the case with the IP selection, IPX information can be added here by clicking Insert. The details concerning IPX configuration are covered in Chapter 11.

**MAC**    The MAC button pertains to MAC-based VLANs only; if a MAC-based VLAN is not highlighted when the MAC button is clicked, a warning message appears stating "The 'MAC…'configuration applies only to bySrcMac vlans." Selecting the MAC button opens the Edit MAC (SRC_MAC VLAN) window, in which you can view, add, and delete source MACs from the VLAN:

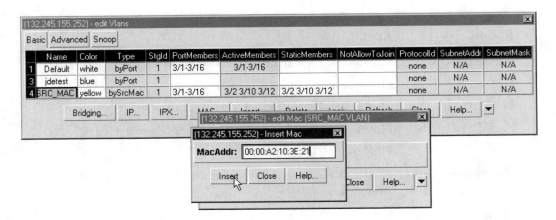

In this example, three source MAC addresses are associated with VLAN ID 101. You can add additional source MAC addresses by clicking Insert and entering them. Source MACs can be deleted by highlighting the MAC address and clicking Delete.

## Viewing VLAN Information from the CLI

The same VLAN information that can be viewed within Device Manager can also be viewed from the CLI. VLAN information can be viewed all at once, or portions of the VLAN configuration can be viewed individually. For instance, to view the entire VLAN configuration for VLAN ID 30, the following command would be used:

```
Accelar# show vlan info all 30

----------- Basic ---------
VLAN                         STG
ID  NAME               TYPE   ID  PROTOCOLID  SUBNETADDR   SUBNETMASK
30  IPXVlan            byProtocolId 1  ipx802dot2  N/A        N/A

----------- Port---------
VLAN PORT            ACTIVE         STATIC          NOT_ALLOW
ID   MEMBER          MEMBER         MEMBER          MEMBER
30   1/1,3/1-3/12

----------- Advance -------
VLAN      IF    HIGH     AGING MAC                              USER
ID  NAME  INDEX PRIORITY TIME  ADDRESS            ACTION RESULT DEFINEPID
30  IPXVlan 263 false    600   00:00:00:00:00:00  none   success 0

----------- Arp -----------

VLAN ID  DOPROXY    DORESP
```

```
30        false      true

----------- Fdb-Entry -----------
VLAN          MAC
ID    STATUS  ADDRESS           PORT MONITOR PRIORITY
30    self    00:00:81:c1:e8:00  -   true    low
30    self    00:00:81:c1:e8:20  -   true    low
30    self    00:00:81:c1:e8:21  -   true    low
30    self    00:00:81:c1:e8:22  -   true    low
30    self    00:00:81:c1:e8:23  -   true    low
30    self    00:00:81:c1:e8:28  -   true    low
30    self    00:00:81:c1:e8:29  -   true    low
30    self    00:00:81:c1:e8:2a  -   true    low
30    self    00:00:81:c1:e8:2b  -   true    low
30    self    00:00:81:c1:e8:30  -   true    low
30    self    00:00:81:c1:e8:31  -   true    low
30    self    00:00:81:c1:e8:32  -   true    low
30    self    00:00:81:c1:e8:33  -   true    low
----------- Fdb-Filter --------
VLAN              MAC                  NOT_ALLOW
ID   STATUS       ADDRESS         PORT FROM

----------- Ip ------------
VLAN        IP              NET           BCASTADDR REASM    ADVERTISE
ID   NAME   ADDRESS         MASK          FORMAT    MAXSIZE  WHEN_DOWN

----------- Dhcp ----------
VLAN IF          MAX  MIN          ALWAYS
ID   INDEX ENABLE HOP  SEC   MODE   BCAST
30   263   false  4    0     both   false

----------- Ospf ----------
VLAN      HELLO    RTRDEAD  DESIGRTR
ID   ENABLE INTERVAL INTERVAL PRIORITY METRIC AUTHTYPE AUTHKEY   AREAID
30   false  10       40       1        0      none               0.0.0.0

----------- Rip -----------
VLAN      ADVERTISE ACCEPT  TRIGGERED AUTOAGG
ID   ENABLE DEFAULT  DEFAULT UPDATE    ENABLE  SUPPLY LISTEN POISON
30   false  false    false   false     false   true   true   false

----------- Snoop ------------
VLAN      IGMP  PROXY         QUERY  MROUTER ACT_RTR LAST       QUERIER
ID   NAME SNOOP ENABLE ROBUST INTVAL PORTS   PORTS   QUERIER    PORT
30  IPXVlan false false  0      0                     0  .0  .0  .0

----------- Vrrp ------------
VLAN VRRP               VIRTUAL
```

```
ID    ID   IPADDR          MAC ADDR


                                MASTER          ADVERTISE  CRITICAL
VID   STATE       CONTROL  PRIORITY  IPADDR      INTERVAL   IPADDR


----------- Ip Dvmrp--------------

VLAN-ID          DVMRP-ENABLE    METRIC
30               disable         1
----------- Ip Igmp--------------

VLAN_ID   QUERY_INTERVAL   QUERY_MAX_RESP   ROBUST     VERSION    LSTMEMBER_QUERY
30        125              10               2          version2   1

----------- Ipx -----------

VLAN-ID VLAN-TYPE       IPXNET      ENCAPSULATION  ROUTING

Accelar#
```

This command results in quite a bit of information; the output gives all information for all aspects of the VLAN configuration. However, in most cases (including the preceding example), many of the VLAN features will not be relevant to the VLAN being viewed. For instance, the VLAN in the preceding example does not participate in the Internet Group Multicast Protocol (IGMP), is not running the Distance Vector Multicast Routing Protocol (DVMRP), and is not configured for the Virtual Router Redundancy Protocol (VRRP). For this reason, VLAN information can be viewed in sections: basic information, advanced information, IP information, and so forth, each can be viewed individually by using the **show vlan info** command:

```
Accelar# show vlan info ?

Sub-Context: vrrp
Current Context:

        advance [<vid>]
        all [<vid>] [by <value>]
        arp [<vid>]
        basic [<vid>]
        dhcp [<vid>]
        dvmrp [<vid>]
        fdb-entry <vid>
```

```
fdb-filter <vid>
l3-igmp [<vid>]
ip [<vid>]
ipx [<vid>]
ospf [<vid>]
ports [<vid>]
rip [<vid>]
snoop [<vid>]
srcmac [<vid>]
fdb-static <vid>
```

For example, the information contained in the Basic tab from the Edit Vlans window in Device Manager can be viewed either for all VLANs, by using the **show vlan info basic all** command, or for a single VLAN only, by using the **show vlan info basic VID** command:

```
Accelar# show vlan info basic 30

==============================================================================
                                  Vlan Basic
==============================================================================
VLAN                            STG
ID   NAME            TYPE       ID   PROTOCOLID SUBNETADDR   SUBNETMASK
------------------------------------------------------------------------------
30   IPXVlan         byProtocolId 1  ipx802dot2 N/A          N/A
```

Port information, however, which would be found under the Basic tab in the Edit Vlans window, must be obtained by using the **show vlan info ports <VID>** command:

```
Accelar# show vlan info ports 30

==============================================================================
                                  Vlan Port
==============================================================================
VLAN PORT            ACTIVE          STATIC          NOT_ALLOW
ID   MEMBER          MEMBER          MEMBER          MEMBER
------------------------------------------------------------------------------
30   3/1-3/5         3/1-3/5         3/1-3/4
```

In the same way, the information contained in the Advanced tab in the Edit Vlans window can be obtained with the **show vlan info advance all | VID** command:

```
Accelar# show vlan info advance 30

========================================================================
                                Vlan Advance

========================================================================
                                                              USER
VLAN    IF     HIGH     AGING MAC
ID  NAME   INDEX PRIORITY TIME  ADDRESS          ACTION RESULT DEFINEPID
------------------------------------------------------------------------
30  IPXVlan 263   false    600   00:00:00:00:00:00 none   none   0
```

In these examples, notice that the protocol type has been specified, and that the PortMembers list indicates that port 3/1 through 3/5 are members. However, on the StaticMembers list, only ports 3/1 through 3/4 are listed.

In the output of the previous example, where the active members are specified, port 3/5 should appear only after 802.2 IPX traffic traverses it, granting it temporary active membership. A variety of identifiers are associated with any one VLAN: the VLAN ID, the IfIndex, and a name. These identifiers have the following significance, in order of importance to the administrator:

- **VlanId**   This value is significant when considering traffic-distribution decisions. The VlanId is the value that is inserted into the 802.1Q frame tag that is inserted into the frame when it passes between switches, and it is by checking this value that the receiving switch knows where to direct the frame in question.

- **Name**   A string assigned to the VLAN by the administrator, such as Sales or Corp_hq. Although these names are not used in any way by the switches themselves, they can make management of VLANs much easier, particularly when the VLANs span multiple switches.

- **IfIndex**   A value generated by the switch and assigned automatically to each VLAN as it is created. These values are used by the Accelar in a variety of circumstances. This value does not need to be used by the administrator.

## Sorting VLAN Traffic

This chapter has outlined port-based VLANs and policy-based VLANs, but these implementations must work together. For instance, an uplink port that is a member of multiple policy-based VLANs may distribute traffic based solely on their respective Protocol ID fields. But what if traffic coming in on that same uplink port includes packets from several port-based VLANs, as well, that are all of a like protocol? To support these kinds of configurations, ports are designated as either access ports or trunk ports (tagged or untagged), each of which has a unique functionality.

# Access Ports vs. Trunk Ports

Access ports and trunk ports may be confused with feeder ports and trunk ports, such as those found in the LattisSwitch family, because they are somewhat similar in concept. However, Accelar has only two different port types, trunk ports and access ports.

## Trunk Ports (Tagged)

*Trunk ports* are just what they sound like—ports that interconnect Accelars; switch-to-switch links. A trunk port can be a member of any and all VLANs and any and all STGs, because if a VLAN or STG needs to span multiple switches, the data for each needs to be able to travel from one switch to another. Since this is done over a trunk link, that trunk must be eligible to be a member of each VLAN and each STG. Trunk ports also recognize 802.1Q frame tags for purposes of VLAN distribution. This is how the Accelar is able to distribute port-based VLANs between multiple switches, even though they are of the same protocol.

## Access Ports (Untagged)

*Access ports* are the ports into which a hub, non-Accelar switch, router, probe, or station connects. Access ports are different from trunk ports in one important way—an Access port can't be a member of two VLANs of the same type, nor can it be a member of more than one STG. This is an important rule, the reason for which will be explained shortly. This doesn't mean that an Access port can't be a member of more than one VLAN; it may be a member of one port-based VLAN, one AppleTalk VLAN, one VINES VLAN, and one IP VLAN simultaneously. However, it cannot then be added into another port-based VLAN, a second AppleTalk VLAN, and so forth, because access ports don't recognize 802.1Q frame tags, and therefore can't distinguish between port-based VLANs, or multiple protocol-based VLANs that rely on tags to make them unique from one another.

This is a configurable option, meaning that a port doesn't automatically become a trunk port when connected to another Accelar, as may occur when dealing with LattisSwitch devices. The port type must be selected.

## Configuring the Port Type in the CLI

To toggle between the access (nontagging) and trunk (tagging) port type on any given port via the CLI, the **config** command is used. Depending on the code version, the port type will be assigned a type of either Access or Trunk (code versions prior to 2.0), or the Perform Tagging option will be set to True or False (code version 2.0 or higher). For this reason, both methods are shown in the following examples. To configure a port as either access or trunk in code versions prior to 2.0, the following command is used:

```
Accelar-1250# config ethernet 1/1 type trunk
```

For code version 2.0 or higher, the following command is used to configure the same port as a trunk port:

```
Accelar# config ethernet 1/1 perform-tagging enable
```

## Configuring the Port Type in Device Manager

Choosing the port type in Device Manager is very simple; double-click the port to be changed, which opens the Edit Port screen. Some basic port parameters are accessable from here, as well as a series of tabs. Select the VLAN tab. From there, chose the port type you want to use.

In code versions prior to 2.0, trunk ports were configured by selecting a port type of Trunk under the VLAN tab of the Edit Port window. With code version 2.0 or higher, the port status is referred to as Perform Tagging, which may be set to either True or False. Setting the Perform Tagging option to True enables 802.1Q frame tagging (causing the port to act as a trunk port). Setting this option to False disables 802.1Q frame tagging (causing the port to act as an Access port).

## Setting Up the Port Type in VLAN Manager

Setting up the port type in VLAN Manager is a little different, but equally simple. Launch VLAN Manager and choose the domain:

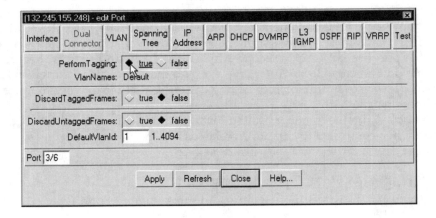

A window opens with the configured VLANs listed, as well as a line going across the top of the screen labeled Tagged Ports (this may be referred to as Trunk in earlier code versions):

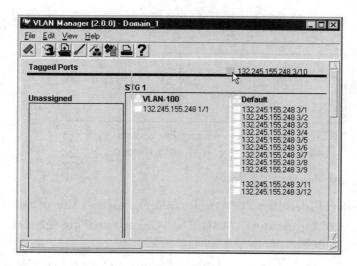

By default, no ports are assigned to be tagged (or trunk) ports in any VLAN; however, any port can be dragged and dropped to the line marked Tagged Ports. Once this is done, another window opens, prompting for which VLANs the port is to be a member of. In this example, both the default white VLAN and the blue engineering VLAN (VLAN 100) are selected. Click OK.

The port remains on the Tagged Ports line at the top of the screen after that. To do a quick check of which VLANs the trunk port is a member of, just right-click it and hold down the mouse button.

# 802.1Q Frame Tagging

The 802.1Q specification (or *frame-tagging*) was the chosen standard for extending VLAN information from one device to the next. Before this, each vendor was left to produce its own interpretation of VLANs, resulting in noninteroperable VLAN types in some cases.

As stated earlier, the tag is a 4-byte field that gets added into the frame. The tag is positioned between the Source Address field and the Protocol Type field:

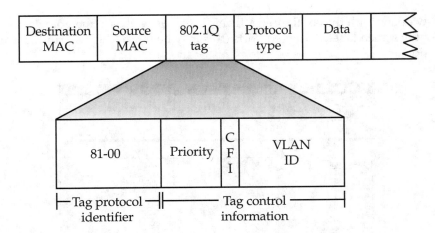

These fields are defined as follows:

■ **Tag Protocol Identifier (TPID)**   Currently, the hex value of 8100 is used.

■ **Tag Control Information (TCI)**   The TCI portion of the 802.1Q frame tag consists of three separate portions:

    **Priority**   A 3-bit field that marks the priority of a frame. Consult Chapter 12 for more information about this field.

    **CFI (Canonical Field Identifier)**   A 1-bit field that basically says whether or not the frame is in canonical format.

    **VLAN ID**   The remaining bits specify the VLAN ID, telling the receiving port the VID of the VLAN where the frame needs to go.

Distributing frames based on something as simple as the tag is very fast. This distributes traffic to the appropriate VLANs very quickly even when loads are heavy. The traffic still needs to find the ultimate destination within that VLAN, but as far as the initial sorting goes, not much overhead is associated with scanning a 4-byte tag.

Frame tagging currently is implemented only between switches that support the 802.1Q standard, which is why most direct attached stations, or hubs and/or non-802.1Q switches that house them, are connected via access (non-tagged) ports, where the frame tag is not applied. Part of the reason for this is that if an Ethernet frame 1,518 bytes in length is transmitted between devices, it has a 4-byte tag added to the overall length when it is tagged by a switch; the maximum size for an Ethernet frame is 1,518 bytes, but the 4-byte addition makes it 1,522 bytes long. This is allotted for by a trunk port on a switch that is 802.1Q-compatible, but it is interpreted as a bad frame by any other device, and subsequently dropped.

This isn't necessarily a problem, but is something to be aware of. Normally, you attach a frame-tagging trunk port only to another trunk port that recognizes frame tags, and all is well. However, it is possible to feed a trunk port into a hub that contains other trunk ports. This will work, and the trunks will all receive the tagged frames, since a shared-media hub will continue to pass the frames regardless of the fact that, from a strict Ethernet standpoint, they are not valid frames. If the hub is managed, however, expect to see giant packets on your management station. These are just the tagged frames.

## Layer 3 Switching Decisions

The Accelar has a simple policy of determining where VLAN traffic goes (see Figure 9-7).

Assuming that the ingress port is a trunk port, capable of interpreting 802.1Q frame tags (if it is not, the frame tag consideration is skipped and the Accelar checks for a policy), the frame is received on the port and is subject to the following decision-making process:

1. The Accelar checks whether the frame is tagged. If it is, it distributes the frame to the appropriate VLAN based on the VLAN ID. Since this is the quickest way of determining the destination VLAN, it does this first.

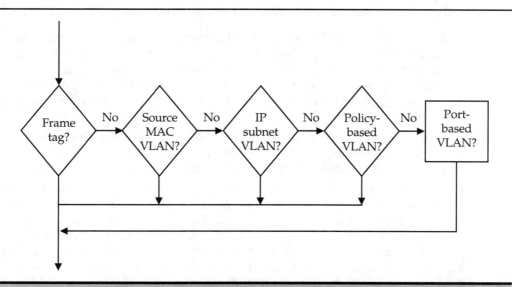

**Figure 9-7.**    *Determining the destination VLAN*

THE ACCELAR LAYER 3 SWITCH

2. The Accelar checks whether the source MAC matches a source MAC that is associated with a MAC-based VLAN. If it does, the packet is sent to the MAC-based VLAN.

3. If the source MAC does not find a match, the IP subnet is checked to see whether it is associated with an IP subnet-based VLAN. If it is, the packet is sent to the appropriate IP subnet-based VLAN.

4. It checks whether this port is a member of a protocol-based VLAN. If it is, it checks whether this frame's protocol type matches the protocol-based VLAN's protocol type. If it does, then it sends the frame to the appropriate VLAN.

5. It checks whether this port is a member of a port-based VLAN. If it is, then the frame goes to that VLAN.

6. If the port is not a member of a port-based VLAN, and the incoming frame is not tagged and its protocol does not match any policy-based VLAN that may exist on the port, then the frame is dropped.

Although this is an efficient means of determining the ultimate destination of a frame, this decision-making procedure must always be taken into account from a design standpoint. An improper implementation can create some odd scenarios, and even a loss of connectivity.

Figure 9-8 illustrates the one-way-connectivity problem that such a mechanism can cause when improperly implemented. In this example, client A must reach server B using the IP protocol. The design outlined in this example will not work. To understand why it will not work, follow the frame from the client to the server.

1. Station A sends out an IP frame destined for station B. Station A is sitting on a segment that is in both a port-based and a policy-based VLAN, as is station B. In this particular case, they are in the same port-based VLAN, but each is also part of a different policy-based VLAN—station A's segment sits on a port that is also in an AppleTalk VLAN, while station B's segment sits on a port that is also in an IP VLAN.

2. Station A's segment's port gets the frame; it is not an AppleTalk frame, so it falls into the port-based VLAN. Since B's segment's port is in the same port-based VLAN, station B gets the frame. Station B responds.

3. The response arrives at the Accelar 2's access port. The Accelar follows its rules of distribution and checks whether the frame is tagged. In this example, these are access ports, so the frame is not tagged. The Accelar then checks whether the frame belongs in a policy-based VLAN. Since the packet is an IP packet, and the ingress port is a member of an IP VLAN, the frame is distributed into the IP VLAN. The frame is sent into the IP policy-based VLAN (of which station A is not a member). Station A never gets the response.

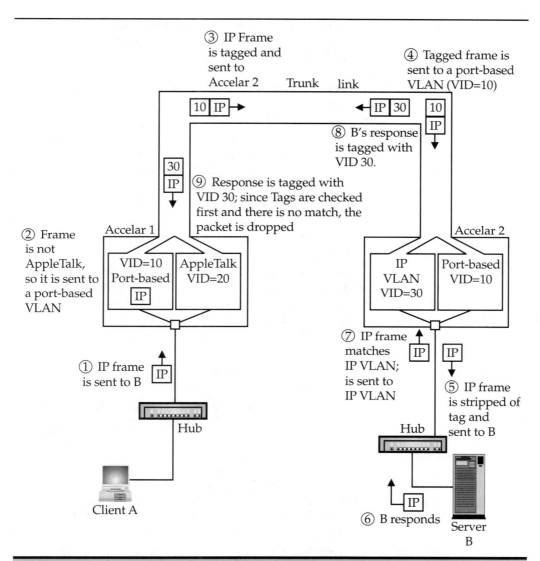

**Figure 9-8.** *Frame hitting Server B's segment's port, and B responding*

## Using Frame-Tagged VLANs Between the Accelar and the 450

To have multiple VLANs span from an Accelar to a 450 series switch, the following steps must be taken. In this example, two port-based VLANs will span the two devices—one VLAN for IP, and one for IPX (do not confuse these with policy-based VLANs). The trunk connection will be over the gigabit uplink. The 450 is running code version 1.1.0.

1. Configure two VLANs on the Accelar, naming one **IP** and the other **IPX**. Assign these VLANs VLAN IDs of 10 and 100, respectively. Select a color for each VLAN (for example, PeachPuff and LemonChiffon). Configure ports 3/1 through 3/5 to be in the IP VLAN, and ports 3/6 through 3/10 to be in the IPX VLAN. These active ports in each VLAN (except the uplink) will be access ports, because this is where the users will be connected, and the end-user stations will not recognized tagged frames. Frames passing over a trunk connection will be tagged.

2. Configure the gigabit port that will be the uplink to the 450 to be a trunk port, and make it a member of both VLANs (remember, only a trunk port can be a member of more than one VLAN).

3. On the 450, create the two VLANs as well. For this example, also name them **IP** and **IPX**. The number next to Create VLAN is not relevant, since it is not the VLAN ID that will be contained in the frame tag, but for ease of configuration, set them to 10 and 100, respectively.

4. Set the PVID on each port on the 450 in the IP VLAN to **10** (ports 1 through 5), and set the PVID on each port on the 450 in the IPX VLAN to **100** (ports 6 through 10). The PVID is actually going to be the VLAN ID when the frames get tagged. As previously discussed, the 802.1Q frame tag has a few fields, but the only field looked at for purposes of VLAN distribution is the VLAN ID, so these must match.

5. Make sure all the ports in each VLAN on the 450 are set to Untagged. This is the equivalent of setting them to be Access ports on the Accelar.

6. On the 450, go to the VLAN Configuration Screen. Toggling between VLANs by using the Create VLAN tab, be sure to set to Tagged the gigabit trunk port that is the uplink to the Accelar. This must be done for both the IP and the IPX VLAN. Unlike the Accelar, on the 450, a port is not configured to be a member of multiple VLANs, since only one PVID can be set per port. Leave the PVID of the trunk port on the 450 to 1, the default. The PVID that will be inserted into the tag will not be that of the PVID on the uplink port, but rather the PVID that is configured on the untagged port associated with each VLAN (see Figure 9-9). By setting this port to Tagged in each VLAN, you are telling it to apply the PVID tag to frames from those VLANs.

When this is configured, frames coming into the IP VLAN on the 450 will be untagged. When going out the uplink port, however, since it is set to Tagged, the frame with the PVID of the port the frame initially came in on will be tagged. The tagged frame traverses the uplink and is received by the Accelar, which checks the VLAN ID in the frame tag (the PVID for the IP VLAN on the 450); it should be set to 10. Because 10 is the VID of the IP VLAN on the Accelar, the frame is sent to that VLAN. The same holds true the other way, and for the IPX VLAN, as well.

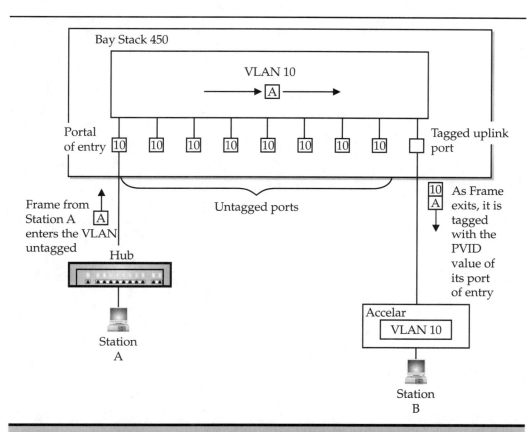

**Figure 9-9.**    *When set to Tagged, the uplink port tags the outgoing frames, using the PVID value as the VLAN ID*

## Routing Between VLANs

You can also route between VLANs, by assigning IP addresses on a VLAN level. This IP assignment will be routed through the Accelar's Virtual Router Engine, to other VLANs (either port-, policy-, source MAC-, or IP subnet-based) or to isolated router ports. These concepts are discussed at greater length in Chapter 11.

# Chapter 10

## Accelar Spanning Tree Groups and MultiLink Trunking

This chapter discusses multiple Spanning Tree Groups (STGs) on the Accelar platform, as well as FastStart, a Spanning Tree enhancement that supports faster convergence times, MultiLink Trunking (MLT), which allows for the aggregation of bandwidth on several links into a single link, and LinkSafe, a physical-layer method of redundancy for gigabit uplink ports.

The Accelar product supports the IEEE 802.1d Spanning Tree Protocol (STP), as well as the configuration of multiple different Spanning Tree Groups, which may exist simultaneously within the network. These STGs can provide options for redundancy that wouldn't otherwise be available with a single Spanning Tree entity. In addition, all Spanning Tree ports support the option for the FastStart protocol, which offers faster Spanning Tree convergence time than normally would be available. For faster cutover times on critical gigabit links, the LinkSafe option also is available, allowing for a physical-layer cutover in the case of link failure without the convergence time associated with Spanning Tree.

In addition, the Accelar platform supports MultiLink Trunking, which aggregates the bandwidth of up to four ports into a single link. The MLT feature supports the Spanning Tree Protocol as well as different STGs.

# Spanning Tree and the Accelar

The Accelar platform supports the standard IEEE 802.1d Spanning Tree Protocol for purposes of detecting network loops and implementing redundancy. In addition, the Accelar platform supports the configuration of multiple Spanning Tree entities, where a Spanning Tree topology is created individually for each entity. Multiple STGs may be required where different virtual local area networks (VLANs) span more than one Accelar, because STP isn't VLAN-specific. Some scenarios in which multiple STGs may be desirable are outlined later in this chapter in "Redundancy and Multiple STGs," as well as how to configure and manage separate Spanning Tree entities, once they are created.

## 802.1d Spanning Tree

Traditional 802.1d Spanning Tree was conceived by Radia Perlman to detect and resolve loops in the network topology. It may also be used to create redundancy, by deliberately introducing parallel links (and therefore a loop) so that the connection that is blocked by Spanning Tree can be used as a redundant link if the primary link fails. This configuration is fairly common in networks today. Spanning Tree can be a useful protocol, but it isn't necessary to network operations; in a network with no physical loops, Spanning Tree is not required at all. However, because it does act as a safeguard against loops that may inadvertently be introduced as the network expands, it is advisable to leave the Spanning Tree Protocol active.

> **Note**
>
> *An exception exists regarding keeping the Spanning Tree Protocol active: ports with directly attached clients who are using the IPX protocol, or who are configured as Dynamic Host Configuration Protocol (DHCP) clients, should have the Spanning Tree Protocol disabled. On a switch, STP is run on each individual port; each time a client becomes active, a link state change is detected on its port. This causes the spanning tree algorithm (STA) to run on the client port. A directly attached client obviously won't introduce a loop, but until this is determined, the port remains in a blocking state. The amount of time the STA takes to run is just long enough, in most cases, that the port is still in a blocking state when Get Nearest Server requests are issued, which also is true for DHCP requests.*

The IEEE 802.1d specification does not account for more than one STG; at the time of 802.1d's creation, VLANs had not been standardized and the possibility of their existence was not accounted for. This means that design considerations must be made when mixing Accelars running multiple STGs with other devices that only support 802.1d Spanning Tree. Some of these considerations are examined later in this chapter in "Redundancy and Multiple STGs."

> **Note**
>
> *As factory defaults, all Accelar routing switches use a single STG for the entire device. The default STG is the traditional 802.1d Spanning Tree and is completely compatible with all 802.1d bridges and switches. The default 802.1d STG may not be deleted.*

## Spanning Tree and VLANs

A common misconception regarding the Spanning Tree Protocol and VLANs is that the Spanning Tree entity maintains a separate Spanning Tree domain for each VLAN; by default, this is not true. The 802.1d specification was written before the first VLAN-based system was created, and thus no inherent mechanism exists in the 802.1d protocol to account for separate VLANs. Consequently, a device that has Spanning Tree enabled on all of its ports—even if it is broken into two VLANs—will flood bridge protocol data units (BPDUs) out of each port from a single source as if there were no VLANs present. To demonstrate, Figure 10-1 shows a scenario in which two switches are present, each configured with two VLANs. For purposes of redundancy, two connections are made between the switches, one for each VLAN. In this scenario, the Spanning Tree Protocol will block one of the ports.

In this example, no traffic passes between switches A and B from VLAN 2. Users in VLAN 1 can communicate back and forth, but VLAN 2 remains separated until STP is disabled on these ports, because switch A is sending BPDUs out each port (port 5 and port 10, in this case). Switch B is doing the same. It is determined that a loop exists in the network. Spanning Tree is invoked and, in this case, port 10 is blocked, cutting off VLAN 2.

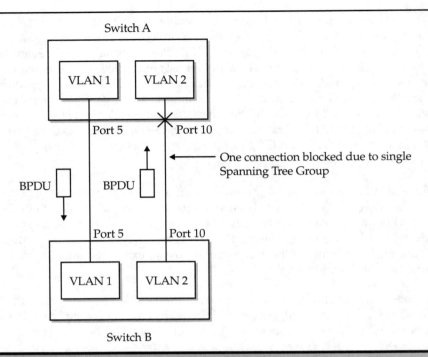

**Figure 10-1.**  *VLAN connection blocked by Spanning Tree due to presence of single Spanning Tree Group*

Although a BPDU sent from switch A out port 5 seemingly should remain in VLAN 1 and not cross over into VLAN 2, this isn't the case. The 802.1d Spanning Tree Protocol is independent of any VLAN configuration, and although no user data ever crosses from one VLAN to another, 802.1d BPDUs will be sent and received as if the VLANs were not in place. This is a limitation of the Spanning Tree Protocol, as outlined by the IEEE. Only by creating a new method of utilizing Spanning Tree can redundant links be created on a VLAN-by-VLAN basis.

## Multiple Spanning Tree Groups

The method selected to support VLAN-independent Spanning Tree entities creates multiple STGs that can be configured on the device and then assigned to individual VLANs. This creates the scenario in which BPDUs are are interpreted only by devices which are participating in the Spanning Tree Group from which the BPDU originated, and each instance of STP truly is independent. By using this method, network loops can be monitored, and redundant links can be created for each VLAN throughout the network. Up to 25 unique STGs may be created on a single Accelar.

## Multiple Spanning Tree Groups and VLANs

Multiple STGs are created by utilizing an 802.1Q frame tag and applying it to BPDUs. This is done only on STG 2 or greater. The default Spanning Tree Group, STG 1, uses the IEEE 802.1d Spanning Tree Protocol, which always remains untagged. This is because the 802.1d specification was written prior to the 802.1Q specification, and thus has no support for frame tagging.

The BPDUs for each STG created beyond the default group, however, will be assigned an 802.1Q frame tag with a VLAN ID indicating which Spanning Tree Group it is assigned to. This tagged BPDU VLAN ID value is assigned by the Accelar at the time the Spanning Tree Group is created. This provides a lot of flexibility when designing network redundancy and traffic management, but it requires some consideration, since any incoming BPDU that doesn't have the proper VLAN ID for the STG receiving it will be dropped. A particular STG does not have local significance only; it must remain constant from switch to switch.

**Note**  *A STG may contain more than one VLAN, but a VLAN may not exist in more than one STG. The default STG (STG 1) is the only STG that uses nontagged BPDUs. Other devices that aren't capable of multiple STG won't recognize BPDUs from a tagged STG. Likewise, 802.1d BPDUs received by a different STG using tags are assumed to be from the incorrect STG and thus are dropped.*

# Redundancy and Multiple STGs

Multiple STGs allow for a wide variety of redundancy, and also load sharing, to a certain degree. Once it is understood how multiple STGs function together, it will be much easier to understand how to use and manage them, as well as how to avoid design problems.

## Multiple STG Redundancy Example

As an example of multiple STG redundancy, consider a scenario in which two switches each have three VLANs configured. The switches are connected by a trunk port, over which traffic for all three VLANs passes. For redundancy, three more connections are made between the switches; one access port connection for each VLAN. The costing is configured such that the trunk connection is the preferred path. Since the trunk connection carries the BPDUs for each STG configured, each of the access port connections go into blocking mode, to be used as redundant backups in the event that the trunk connection fails (see Figure 10-2).

This scenario creates a degree of fault tolerance; for all three VLANs, traffic passes over the gigabit uplink as the preferred path, to be distributed to the destination VLANs based on the 802.1Q frame tags. BPDUs for each STG are also distributed to the appropriate STG over the trunk link. Each STG then detects the presence of the loop condition, and Spanning Tree will be invoked in three separate instances. Due to the port costing, each access port will go into a blocking mode. If the trunk link goes down, each access port shifts into forwarding mode, and traffic for each VLAN still has a dedicated 100MB full-duplex connection to the corresponding VLAN on the remote switch.

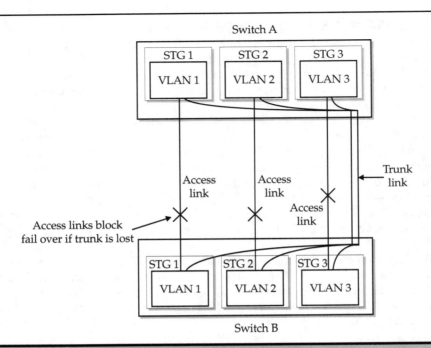

**Figure 10-2.**    *Access ports acting as redundant connections for each of three Spanning Tree Groups connected over a trunk*

**TRUNK AND ACCESS REDUNDANCY EXAMPLE WITH A SINGLE SPANNING TREE GROUP**    To get a better sense of how separate STGs work, this example uses the same physical configuration, access/trunk assignments, and Spanning Tree costs as the prior example, but uses a single STG rather than three separate STGs.

The preferred path is still the gigabit uplink, and frames destined for each VLAN are passed over this connection, to be distributed to the appropriate VLAN based on their 802.1Q frame tags. Likewise, the 802.1d untagged BPDUs from the default STG 1 are passed over the trunk. Since these BPDUs are flooding over each of the three access ports, each switch detects the loop condition, and, due to the costing on each port, the trunk remains in a forwarding state and each access port blocks. This is exactly the same behavior the switches display under the previous scenario, with three STGs; however, the reaction is much different in the case of a trunk failure when only one STG is present (see Figure 10-3).

In the event of a trunk failure, BPDUs now pass over only the access ports; however, since only one STG exists, switches A and B still detect a loop condition. The two switches determine that there are three links between them—one primary and two redundant. One of the ports goes into a forwarding state, while the two other ports remain in a blocking state. Since the access ports now constitute the only connection

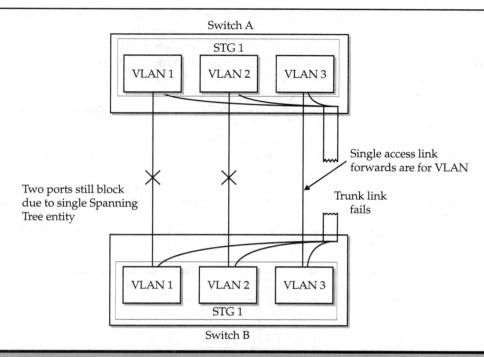

**Figure 10-3.** *A single Spanning Tree Group will result in all redundant paths being blocked regardless of VLAN boundaries*

between each VLAN, two of the three VLANs are cut off from one another, resulting in only one unaffected VLAN.

The preceding examples demonstrate the kinds of considerations that you must make when you decide to implement redundancy over multiple VLANs. In each of the examples, everything works fine upon the initial configuration and appears to be functioning correctly. Only in the event of a trunk failure does the potential problem surface; in one scenario, all connections fail over, as desired; in the other scenario, two-thirds of the network traffic is cut off.

### SAME EXAMPLE WITH AN INCORRECTLY CONFIGURED SPANNING TREE GROUP
This example also uses as its basic scenario the original example of two switches with three VLANs configured, connected by a primary trunk link and three redundant access links. Multiple STGs are configured in this case. Switch A is configured for three STGs: STG 1, STG 2, and STG 3 in VLAN 1, VLAN 2, and VLAN 3, respectively. Switch B is *misconfigured*, with VLAN 1 in STG 1, and VLANs 2 and 3 sharing STG 2.

Remember, STGs have more than just local significance, because they span multiple switches. In this scenario, a problem will surface immediately. The untagged BPDUs for VLAN 1 (in STG 1) traverse the trunk link, and due to the presence of the access link a loop condition is detected. The access link goes into blocking mode, providing redundancy for VLAN 1, which continues to function normally.

VLAN 2, using STG 2, detects on the trunk link incoming BPDUs, which are tagged with STG 2's ID and directed to STG 2 at the receiving trunk port. As with VLAN 1, the presence of the access link results in a loop condition being detected; the access link goes into blocking mode, and VLAN 2 functions normally.

Both VLAN 1 and VLAN 2 are unaffected in this configuration, and even fail over correctly if a trunk failure occurs. VLAN 3, however, is assigned two different instances of STGs: STG 3 and STG 2. All tagged BPDUs from VLAN 3, coming from switch A, actually receive an 802.1Q frame tag associating them with STG 2. When these BPDUs are received on switch B's trunk, they are associated with STG 2. BPDUs from VLAN 3 on switch B have a tag associating them with STG 3, but because STG 3 isn't configured on switch A, these BPDUs are dropped (see Figure 10-4).

Consequently, VLAN 3 on switch B doesn't receive any BPDUs from VLAN 3 on switch A since the BPDUs are forwarded to STG 2, which is associated with VLAN 2;

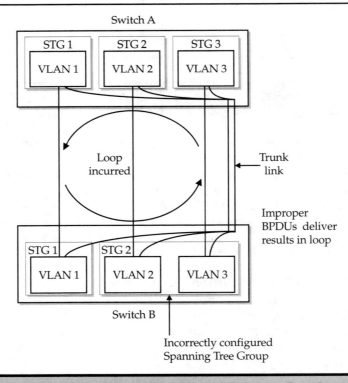

**Figure 10-4.** *Loop incurred due to misconfigured Spanning Tree Groups*

likewise, VLAN 3 on switch A doesn't receive any BPDUs from VLAN 3 on switch B, since they are associated with STG 3, which doesn't exist on switch B, and thus are dropped. VLAN 3 has two connections, however, between switches A and B. VLAN 3 contains a network loop, but Spanning Tree won't ever be invoked, and a broadcast storm will result.

**EXAMPLE OF REDUNDANCY WITH TWO SPANNING TREE GROUPS**    This scenario includes three switches, A, B, and C, each with two VLANs configured. The three switches are interconnected in a triangle formation, with gigabit trunk connections that are configured to be in both VLANs. Two STGs are configured, one for each VLAN, and the trunk ports are members of both STGs. In this case, each STG will detect a loop condition.

By default, all Spanning Tree parameters are equal across STGs for a single switch. However, these parameters (such as Bridge Priority, Hello Time, and so forth) can be configured on a STG-by-STG basis. By default, then, one of the trunk ports will block traffic for both VLANs, to resolve the network loop.

By taking advantage of the ability to configure Spanning Tree parameters for each STG individually, however, the Bridge Priority may be changed for STG 2, so that switch A becomes the root bridge for STG 1, and switch C becomes the root bridge for STG 2. By doing this, a certain degree of load sharing over the trunk links is accomplished (see Figure 10-5).

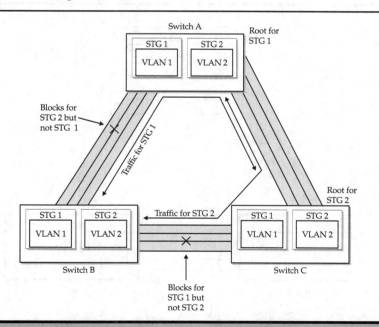

**Figure 10-5.**    *STP blocking accomplished on two links, each for one STG only*

Since there are effectively two different root bridges, each STG will span accordingly:

- **Spanning Tree Group 1**   Since switch A is the root for STG 1, neither switch B nor switch C will block on the connections they share with switch A directly. STP will cause the connection between switches B and C to go into a blocking state for STG 1 only.

- **Spanning Tree Group 2**   Since switch C is the root for STG 2, neither switch A nor switch B will block on the connections they share with switch C directly. STP will cause the connection between switches A and B to go into a blocking state for STG 2 only.

By configuring the switches in this way, only one trunk link bears the burden of two-way traffic for both STGs, while the other two links share the load, and no trunk links go unused.

**REDUNDANCY EXAMPLE WITH A SINGLE SPANNING TREE GROUP**   Using the same example, but with a single STG and one root bridge, redundancy is still in place, and the switches will function normally and fail over correctly in the event of a link going down. However, with only one STG configured, the use of the gigabit uplinks is not as efficient as it could be (see Figure 10-6).

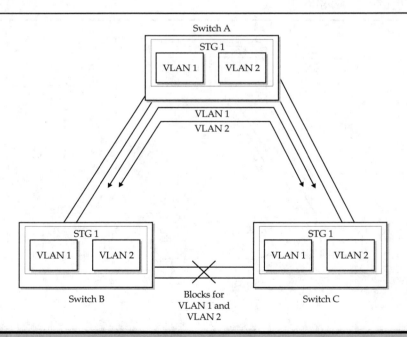

**Figure 10-6.**   *The presence of a single Spanning Tree Group causes both VLAN traffic flows to be blocked across a common link*

Switch A in this case is the root bridge, so the link between switch B and switch C goes into a blocking state. With only a single STG in place, this connection blocks for both VLANs. The links between switches A and B and between switches A and C must support the full network load, while the gigabit connection between switches B and C goes completely unused, except in the event of a failure, at which point it takes on the full load of both VLANs.

**REDUNDANCY EXAMPLE WITH AN INCORRECTLY CONFIGURED SPANNING TREE GROUP**   Using the same example again, the impact of incorrectly configured STGs can be demonstrated. In this example, switches A and B both have VLAN 1 and VLAN 2 configured, positioned in STG 1 and STG 2, respectively. Switch C also has VLAN 1 and VLAN 2 configured, but they both are placed in STG 2.

Consequently, BPDUs from switch A, STG 1, end up in STG 2 when they reach switch C. Likewise, BPDUs from switch C in STG 2 are associated with VLAN 1, which, on two remote switches, is associated with STG 1.

The end result is a mingling of BPDUs from what should be separate STGs, which results in a broadcast storm for each VLAN, across all three switches.

**TRADITIONAL BRIDGE IN A MULTIPLE SPANNING TREE GROUP ENVIRONMENT EXAMPLE**   In this example, two Accelars running three STGs each are integrated with a third switch, which is capable of running only traditional 802.1d Spanning Tree. The Accelars are connected via a single trunk link, while the third switch is connected to both Accelars in VLAN 1.

In this case, VLAN 1 is assigned to STG 1. Traffic will pass normally in this configuration; if switch A is the root in this case, it will see untagged BPDUs flooded back onto its secondary trunk port. The third switch also detects the loop and puts its connection to switch B into a blocking state, to resolve the loop. VLAN 1 now has a redundant link in place, whereas VLAN 2 does not have any redundancy.

**MULTIPLE SPANNING TREE GROUP EXAMPLE WITH INCORRECT POSITIONING OF 802.1D DEVICE**   This example places the same 802.1d-only third switch into the same configuration as the previous example, but connects this switch to VLAN 2 and VLAN 1, which yields different results than the previous example. In this example, redundancy is desired for both VLANs, not just one. Since the third switch isn't 802.1Q-capable, two connections are needed to each Accelar, one for each VLAN.

Using this configuration, STG 1 detects a loop condition as in the previous example. The connection between the third switch and switch B goes into a blocking state, as a redundant link for VLAN 1. However, the connection to VLAN 2 is now receiving tagged BPDUs from each Accelar. These tagged BPDUs will be dropped by the 802.1d-only switch, while, simultaneously, untagged BPDUs are being flooded into VLAN 2, which is assigned to STG 2 on either Accelar. These untagged BPDUs are assumed to have come from VLAN 1 and thus are ignored. VLAN 2, then, never sees the network loop. Although a loop exists, it will never be detected by Spanning Tree on VLAN 2, and a loop condition will occur.

# Configuring Multiple Spanning Tree Groups

Configuring multiple STGs on the Accelar may be done through the Command Line Interface (CLI) or through Device Manager. After a STG is created, it can be attributed to a specific VLAN or to a series of ports. VLANs may be associated with only a single STG at a time. To change the association from one STG to another, the ports must be removed from the original group before they are placed in another.

 *Like VLAN membership, a trunk port may be a member of multiple STGs simultaneously, whereas access ports can be a member of only one STG at a time.*

## Configuring Multiple STGs Through the CLI

Configuring multiple STGs through the CLI is simple to do. From the command prompt, enter the following commands to create a STG 2, and assign ports 3/6 through 3/8 to it. This example was taken from code version 1.3.5:

```
Accelar-1100# config stg 2 create
Accelar-1100# config stg 2 add ports 3/6-3/8
```

The existence of the new STG can be verified with the following command:

```
Accelar-1100# show stg info all 2
-----------Config--------------------
StgId:2
Priority: 32768
BridgeMaxAge: 2000
BridgeHelloTime: 200
ForwardDelay: 1500
EnableStp: true
StpTrapEnable: true
TaggBpduAddress: 01-80-c2-00-00-00
TaggedBpduVlanId: 61346
PortMembers: 3/6-3/8
-------Status--------------------
StgId: 2
BridgeAddress: 00-e0-16-00-50-02
NumPorts: 3
ProtocolSpc: ieee8021d
TopChanges: 0
DesignatedRoot: self
MaxAge: 2000
HelloTime: 200
```

```
HoldTime: 200
ForwardDelay: 1500
Accelar-1100#
```

In the preceding output, some basic Spanning Tree parameters are included, as well as some parameters that are specific to STG 2. Many of these parameters can also be altered through the CLI, such as forward-delay, hello-interval, max-age, priority, add ports, and remove ports. For instance, to create a STG of 5 containing ports 3/5 through 3/10, with a forward-delay of 1500, a hello-time of 200, a max-age of 2000, and a priority of 7999 (to apply a greater priority than the default 8000), the following commands would be issued:

```
Accelar-1100# config stg 5 create
Accelar-1100# config stg 5 add ports 3/10
Accelar-1100# config stg 5 forward-delay 1500
Accelar-1100# config stg 5 hello-interval 200
Accelar-1100# config stg 5 max-age 2000
Accelar-1100# config stg 5 priority 31129
```

Note that the priority is in decimal, where 31129 yields a hex value of 7999.

## Configuring Multiple STGs Through Device Manager

To create multiple STGs through Device Manager, first launch Device Manager and model the Accelar. From the main window, select VLAN | STG to open the edit Stg window, as shown here:

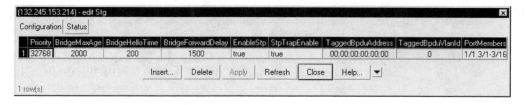

By default, only one STG should be present: the default, STG 1. It has the default Priority of 8000 (32768 in decimal), BridgeMaxAge of 20 seconds, HelloTime of 2 seconds, and ForwardDelay of 15 seconds. The TaggedBpduAddress will be denoted as 00:00:00:00:00:00, because the default 802.1d STG isn't tagged. The TaggedBpduVlanId is set to 0 for the same reason. By default, all ports participating in Spanning Tree are in STG 1, which encompasses the whole device.

To add a new STG, click the Insert button in the edit Stg window, which opens the Insert Configuration dialog box:

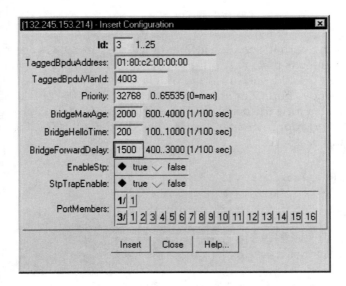

In the Insert Configuration dialog box, you may insert a new STG and configure its parameters. The fields in the Insert Configuration dialog box are defined in the following table:

| Field | Meaning |
| --- | --- |
| ID | The ID number for the STG (the default is 1). |
| TaggedBpduAddress | A media access control (MAC) address specifically assigned to tagged BPDUs. |
| TaggedBpduVlanId | The VLAN tag associated with the STG, given to BPDUs. It does not need to equal the VLAN ID for the VLAN the STG is associated with. |
| Priority | Sets the Spanning Tree bridge priority for this STG; remember, a root bridge can be prioritized on a STG-by-STG basis. This value is in decimal format, where 0 is the highest and 65535 is the lowest. The default is 32768 (which calculates to 8000 in hex, the standard default priority). |
| BridgeMaxAge | The value used by all bridges for MaxAge when the bridge is acting as root. This value is in hundredths of a second, so the default of 2000 equals 20 seconds. |

| Field | Meaning |
|---|---|
| BridgeHelloTime | This value is also in hundredths of a second, and indicates the HelloTime used by all bridges when this bridge is root. The default value is 200 hundredths of a second (two seconds). |
| BridgeForwardDelay | Value in hundredths of a second; indicates the ForwardDelay used by all bridges when this bridge is acting as root. The default value is 1500 hundredths of a second (15 seconds). |
| EnableSTP | Enables STP for this STG. |
| StpTrapEnable | When enabled, this causes a Simple Network Management Protocol (SNMP) trap to be sent each time a Spanning Tree topology event occurs. |
| PortMembers | The ports that are members of this STG; ports being moved from one group to another must be removed from the old STG first. |

Although you may alter these parameters, you must be very cautious in doing so for many of them, because other bridges in the network may rely on them, such as BridgeHelloTime and BridgeForwardDelay. For more information on these parameters and their specific meanings, consult "802.1d Spanning Tree" in Chapter 2.

*The TaggedBpduVlanId value is automatically generated by the Accelar, and is used by other Accelars in the network that are participating in STGs that share the same ID (meaning all STGs with an ID of 2 utilize a common TaggedBpduVlanId). Altering this value on one device necessitates altering it to match on all other Accelars.*

## Editing a Spanning Tree Group in Device Manager

To edit an existing STG, from the main Device Manager window, select VLAN | STG to open the Edit Stg window. Any new STGs that have been created will be visible in this window. Click the field that you want to edit, and a pointer appears to the right of the selected field. Click the pointer to alter the value within the field. After you change the parameters, click the Apply button to commit the changes. STGs may also be removed from the Edit Stg window, by highlighting them and clicking Delete.

*Device Manager doesn't allow a STG to be removed if VLANs are still associated with it. All VLANs and ports must be removed from a STG before it can be deleted.*

THE ACCELAR LAYER 3 SWITCH

## Spanning Tree Status

The Edit Stg window has two tabs:

- **Configuration**   Enables you to edit STGs and their parameters dynamically.

- **Status**   Enables you to view the current status of a functioning STG. When you click the Status tab, it display a variety of Spanning Tree statistics for each STG:

The statistics displayed on the Status tab of the Edit Stg window are defined as follows:

| Field | Meaning |
| --- | --- |
| BridgeAddress | The unique MAC address used by this bridge. |
| NumPorts | The number of ports currently associated with this STG. |
| ProtocolSpecification | The STP used, which is the IEEE 802.1d specification, in this case. |
| TimeSinceTopologyChange | The amount of time, in hundredths of a second, that has passed since the last time a topology change was detected for this STG. |
| TopChanges | Each time a port transitions Spanning Tree states, such as forwarding to blocking, this constitutes a Spanning Tree topology change. A topology change trap may be sent in this event. |
| DesignatedRoot | The bridge ID for the root bridge for this Spanning Tree entity. This value is used as the Root Identifier in this bridge's Configuration Bridge BPDUs. |
| RootCost | The path cost to the root bridge from this bridge. |
| RootPort | The port that offers the lowest path cost to the root bridge. |

| Field | Meaning |
|-------|---------|
| MaxAge | Upon reaching the MaxAge, Spanning Tree information is considered no longer valid and ages out. This value is denoted in hundredths of a second. |
| HelloTime | The amount of time that passes between the transmission of Configuration BPDUs. The default is 200 hundredths of a second (2 seconds). |
| HoldTime | No more than two Configuration BPDUs may be sent within this interval. The default is 100 hundredths of a second (1 second). |
| ForwardDelay | Indicates how long a port will remain in each Spanning Tree state during the transition into a forwarding state. The default is 1500 hundredths of a second (15 seconds). Given that the listening and learning states precede the forwarding state, a port running Spanning Tree should be forwarding in approximately 30 seconds, if no loop is detected. |

# FastStart and LinkSafe

The Accelar routing switches use FastStart to improve Spanning Tree convergence times, and use LinkSafe to add redundancy, with its provision of an extremely fast cutover in the case of a gigabit uplink failure.

## The FastStart Protocol

The FastStart feature, which can be implemented on any port, supports faster Spanning Tree convergence. When FastStart is enabled on a port, that port immediately enters into a forwarding state when it first detects a link. Spanning Tree BPDUs are then transmitted on the port, as normal. The port remains in the forwarding state unless it detects an incoming BPDU, at which point it goes into blocking mode while it runs the spanning tree algorithm.

This allows for a much faster convergence on ports that would not receive BPDUs, and therefore are in no danger of incurring a network loop. It also allows Spanning Tree to be run on ports that either support directly attached clients using the Internetwork Packet Exchange (IPX) protocol, or are configured as DHCP clients, because STP generally blocks initial client queries while the algorithm is being run. This can make managing the network simpler, because all ports have the benefits of Spanning Tree in a nonintrusive way, making moves and changes possible without reconfiguration.

## Configuring FastStart Through the CLI

To configure FastStart on a port through the CLI, simply enter the following command at the CLI prompt:

```
Accelar-1100/config# config ethernet 3/10 stg 1 faststart enable
Accelar-1100/config#
```

This command enables FastStart for port 3/10, in STG 1. This can be enabled on a per-STG basis. The change occurs dynamically on the routing switch and doesn't require a reboot.

## Configuring FastStart Through Device Manager

FastStart may be enabled through Device Manager, as well. To enable or disable this feature, in the main Device Manager window, right-click the port that you want to alter, which presents a drop-down menu in which you can select to enable or disable FastStart on that port:

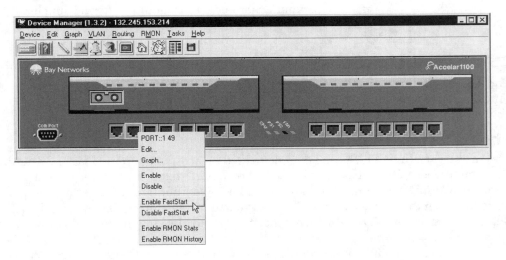

## LinkSafe

LinkSafe is a form of redundancy that is separate from the Spanning Tree Protocol, and is a failover mechanism used on gigabit ports only. Not all gigabit modules support LinkSafe; because LinkSafe is actually a physical-layer cutover, it is present in the module's hardware, so special LinkSafe modules must be purchased to take advantage of this feature.

A LinkSafe module has two gigabit ports, one active and one redundant, and may have only one port active at a time, regardless of how they are attached. While the primary link is active, the secondary link isn't in a blocking state (as would be the case with Spanning Tree), but is actually disabled.

Connections on a LinkSafe module are meant to run in parallel between two LinkSafe modules on two different switches. Although the active port participates in Spanning Tree for purposes of loop detection, LinkSafe ports don't use Spanning Tree to monitor the primary and redundant LinkSafe connections; instead, they monitor the actual physical components. If the primary link fails and the physical signal is lost, then the LinkSafe module immediately cuts over to the secondary link. The advantage to this is that no algorithm needs to be run and no MAC layer protocol is involved, so the failover is extremely fast; as soon as the signal is lost on the primary port, the hardware activates the redundant port and connectivity is restored. In this case, if the failed port becomes active again, the switch isn't prompted to fail back over to the primary port, so even in the case of a connection that cuts in and out, connectivity will be maintained.

**LINKSAFE CONFIGURATION**    LinkSafe isn't "configured" per se; since everything is handled in the hardware, there are no protocol parameters to configure. However, you may select which of the two ports will be active and which will be redundant. This is configured through the Edit Port window in Device Manager. To access this port, right-click the gigabit port in question and select Edit Port. This opens the main Edit Port window, which consists of a variety of tabs. Select the Dual Connector tab.

| Note | *The Dual Connector tab is available only on ports that support LinkSafe.* |

The Dual Connector tab enables you to select the active port, as well as view the current status of the ports, which are described in the following table:

| Field | Meaning |
| --- | --- |
| PrimaryConnector | Selects which connector is to be the primary (by default, the left connector). |
| ActiveConnector | Displays which of the two ports is currently the active port. |
| BackupConnectorStatus | Indicates the redundant connector status. Down indicates that the port is functioning, but not yet active. Up indicates that the port has become the active port. |

## LinkSafe Considerations

When you implement LinkSafe, you must remember that it's a physical-layer backup and doesn't use Spanning Tree. The active port participates in Spanning Tree if it is enabled on that port, but Spanning Tree does not dictate when the LinkSafe link fails over. Only one port may be active at a time, which is true even if there is no network loop to consider.

## Example of LinkSafe Redundancy

This scenario involves three Accelars, each with a gigabit LinkSafe module, arranged in a traditional triangle formation, wherein each port on each LinkSafe module is connected to the two neighboring Accelars. This configuration will not work, as it would if Spanning Tree alone were being used (see Figure 10-7).

In this example, only switches A and B have a valid link. By default, the left connector is the active, primary connector, so the connection between switches A and B remains up. Since the connection between switches A and C exists on the right connector in both cases, this link is inactive. Switch C can't reach switch A through its right link, and its left connector, which normally is active, is connected to the right connector on switch B, which is inactive.

The end result of this configuration is a valid connection between switches A and B, with switch C being cut off completely from the rest of the network. If the link between switches A and B fails, the connection between either switches C and B or switches C and A comes up, but not both, because the LinkSafe module on switch C may have only one active connection. Either way, one switch is always cut off.

To implement LinkSafe properly in a triangle formation, you actually run parallel links between each switch, one primary and one redundant (see Figure 10-8).

# MultiLink Trunking (MLT)

MultiLink Trunking takes a series of ports on a single device and aggregates their collective bandwidth into a single link. MLT is supported on all Accelar routing switches, as well as the 350 and 450 series BayStack switches, and C100/C50/5000BH

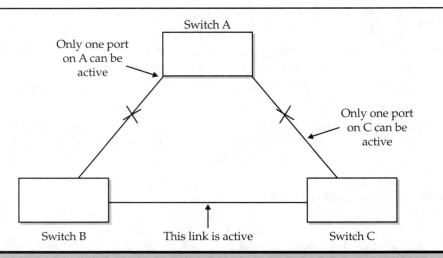

**Figure 10-7.**   *Triangle formation with LinkSafe does not provide redundancy when single links are used*

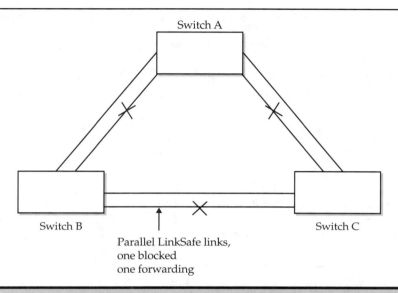

**Figure 10-8.**    *Proper application of LinkSafe connections must run parallel in triangle formation*

platforms. MLT can be used to aggregate bandwidth between switches, or to connect a server or any end station that contains a network interface card (NIC) capable of MLT support.

**Note** *To run MLT on the Accelar, the hardware must be using Address Resolution Unit (ARU) 2 Application Specific Integrated Circuits (ASIC)s. Accelars using the older ARU1 hardware don't offer MLT, and the option is grayed out in Device Manager. MLT is offered only in software release 1.3.1 and higher. MLT is not interoperable with trunking on the LattisSwitch product. Trunk ports on a LattisSwitch use a proprietary trunking method, used to distribute VLAN information, and may not be aggregated.*

## MLT on the Accelar Platform

To configure MLT on the Accelar platform, you must bundle a group of ports into a single MLT connection. You can do this either through the CLI or through Device Manager. A single Accelar is capable of providing up to eight MultiLink Trunks, each with a maximum of four ports in each grouping.

MultiLink Trunk ports don't have to be continuous on a single Accelar module, nor are they confined to a single Accelar module in the case of Accelar models that support multiple cards or netmods. However, MLT ports must be of a like media type and have the same settings for each port. This means that if one port in the MLT is a 100Base-TX port set to half-duplex, then the other members of the MLT must also be 100Base-TX ports set to half-duplex. MLT is supported on 10BaseT, 100Base-TX, 100Base-FX, and gigabit Ethernet ports (see Figure 10-9).

Ports grouped into a single MLT must be within the same Spanning Tree Group, and the single MLT entity is capable of participating in Spanning Tree as a single connection. MultiLink Trunks also support 802.1Q frame tagging, so the MLT can be configured as a trunk port between Accelars for purposes of VLAN distribution.

**Note**   *Each time a MultiLink Trunk is created, it cuts the available number of total VLANs by four, one for each potential port in the MultiLink Trunk, whether the ports are used or not. Given this scenario, an Accelar with four MLTs configured would have a maximum VLAN count of 107 VLANs.*

When dealing with bridged traffic, the algorithm that handles traffic distribution across the MultiLink Trunk is based on the source and destination MAC address; when dealing with routed traffic, the algorithm is based on the source and destination IP address.

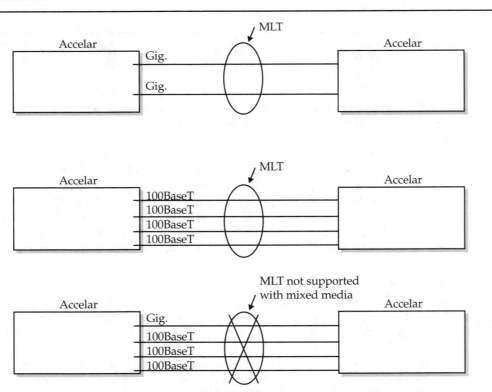

**Figure 10-9.**   *Examples of MLT configuration using 100Base-TX and 1000Base-SX*

## Configuring MLT Through the CLI

To configure MLT through the CLI, gain access to the command prompt with read/write access. You first must create the MLT group and assign an ID to it; then, you must assign the MLT ports. The following commands build an MLT with ID 5 and assign ports 3/10 through 3/12 to it. The following examples were taken from code version 1.3.5:

```
Accelar-1100# config mlt 5 create
Accelar-1100# config mlt 5 add ports 3/10-3/12
```

Verify the configuration with the following "show" command:

```
Accelar-1100# sho mlt info 5

        MltId: 5
         Name: Mlt-5
     NumPorts: 3
  PortMembers: 3/10-3/12
         Type: access
       VlanId: 1
        StgId: 1
   ActivePort:
```

By default, the MLT is an access port, just as is the case with ordinary ports. You can alter this to trunk status and assign the MLT to different VLANs. For instance, to configure MLT 5 to be a trunk port with membership in VLAN 1 and VLAN 2, enter the following commands:

```
Accelar-1100# config mlt 5 type trunk
Accelar-1100# config mlt 5 add vlan 1
Accelar-1100# config mlt 5 add vlan 2
Accelar-1100#
```

Verify the configuration:

```
Accelar-1100# sho mlt info 5

        MltId: 5
         Name: Mlt-5
     NumPorts: 3
  PortMembers: 3/10-3/12
```

THE ACCELAR LAYER 3
SWITCH

```
     Type: trunk
   VlanId: 1
   VlanId: 2
    StgId: 1
ActivePort:
```

## Configuring MLT Through Device Manager

To configure MLT through Device Manager, first model the Accelar in Device Manger and then select VLAN | MLT, which brings up the Edit Mlt window:

By default, no MultiLink Trunks are configured. To add a new MLT, click the Insert button, which brings up the Insert Multi-Link Trunks dialog box:

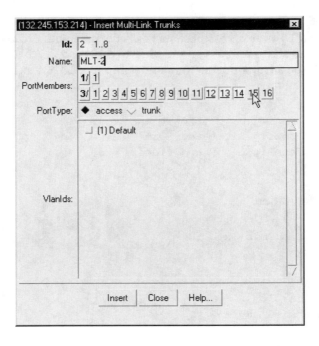

In the Insert Multi-Link Trunks dialog box, you can assign the MLT a unique MLT ID number, which may be a value between 1 and 8 (one for each MLT supported). For easier management, you may also assign the MLT a name that describes its destination switch or server.

You may then select the port members for the MLT that is being configured; remember that these ports must be of a like type and must be members of the same STG. Configure the MLT to be either a trunk or an access port, to select whether or not frames passing over the MLT will be tagged or untagged.

You must then associate the MLT with a VLAN; a list of VLANs with which the MLT may be associated appears in the Insert Multi-Link Trunks dialog box, under the VlanIds heading. Select the VLAN by clicking the box associated with that VLAN.

MLT is a very flexible tool, allowing for an aggregated bandwidth of multiple ports. Since the MLT can act as a trunk port, it may have membership in multiple VLANs, and because it can participate in Spanning Tree as a single link, it can also be created as a redundant link for either a trunk or an access port.

THE ACCELAR LAYER 3
SWITCH

The Complete Reference

Nortel Networks

# Chapter 11

## Routing on the Accelar Platform

235

In addition to Layer 3 switching, the Accelar is capable of traditional routing. Routing may take place between individual ports, individual virtual LANs (VLANs), or a combination of both. Currently, the Accelar platform supports both Internet Protocol (IP) and Internetwork Packet Exchange (IPX) routing, as well as the routing protocols Open Shortest Path First (OSPF), Routing Information Protocol (RIP), and RIPv2.

## Accelar Routing Concepts

Routing on the Accelar is accomplished with a virtual routing engine internal to each unit. This virtual router, at the time of purchase, has no interfaces and is dormant, leaving the Accelar to act as a Layer 2 switch only. Depending on the protocols you want to route, and the port or ports you want to route between, the Accelar's routing services can be configured to activate these services. The routing services on the Accelar can be thought of as an internal router with no physical interfaces; instead, virtual router interfaces are created and then assigned to either single physical ports or VLANs. Within this arrangement, ports grouped into a VLAN can share a virtual router interface, while a single port can also be assigned its own router interface (see Figure 11-1).

This scheme allows for a good deal of flexibility, and additional virtual router interfaces can be added and removed, as necessary.

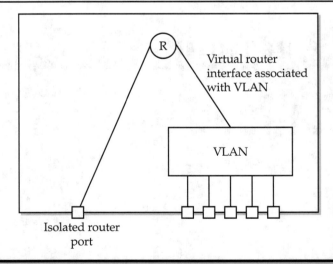

**Figure 11-1.** *The Accelar with virtual router interfaces assigned to both a dedicated port and a VLAN*

# IP Configuration

The Accelar routing switch is capable of routing IP. Also, when running both system software 2.0 or greater and Address Resolution Unit (ARU) version 3 or greater, it is capable of routing IPX. This chapter focuses on IP configuration and troubleshooting at both the global and the interface level.

## Global IP Configuration

The IP configuration on the Accelar can be accomplished either through Device Manager or through the command-line interface (CLI). IP configuration takes place on two levels: the global level and the interface level.

## IP Interface Configuration

IP interface configuration on the Accelar can pertain to either an isolated port or a VLAN. From a conceptual standpoint, the IP configuration is assigned to a virtual router interface in either case; that virtual router interface is simply associated with a single port in one case, and a VLAN in another.

### Configuring IP Interface Parameters for a Single Port

In the case of an isolated router port, the IP interface parameters can be accessed by selecting the port in question and right-clicking it, which opens a new menu, where Edit can be selected. This opens the Edit Port window. Select the IP Address tab:

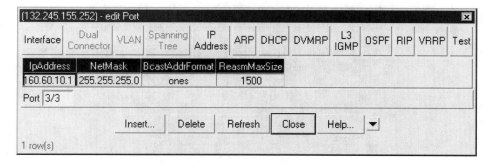

### Configuring IP Interface Parameters for a VLAN

When configuring IP parameters for a VLAN, the configuration still is applied to a single routed interface. The router interface in this case is the virtual router interface associated with the VLAN, which all the physical port members of that VLAN share. For this reason, the actual interface configuration is no different conceptually than it would be when configuring an isolated router port, although the configuration is accomplished from the VLAN selections rather than from those of the actual ports. To configure VLAN IP parameters, select VLAN | VLANs. This will open the edit VLANs window, where the individual VLANs are displayed. Selecting the appropriate VLAN and clicking the IP button will bring up the edit VLAN IP window where the IP parameters are located. Selecting Insert from this window will allow you to configure an IP address and subnet mask for the selected VLAN.

# Viewing and Configuring the IP Host Cache

The Accelar's IP host cache (ARP cache) can be viewed to display the IP-to-MAC address associations currently residing there. From either Device Manager or the CLI, ARP entries can be viewed, added, or removed.

## Viewing the ARP Cache Through Device Manager

The Accelar's IP host cache can be viewed by selecting Routing | IP | IP and then selecting the ARP tab from the main Edit IP window. This displays the current ARP entries:

The fields present in this window have the following meanings:

■ **Interface** Identifies the interface with which the ARP entry is associated, meaning, the interface that resolved the address. Depending on the nature of the interface, it will be displayed differently. For ports that are dedicated routing ports, the slot and port number will be displayed. If the ARP entry is associated with a virtual router interface, which in turn is associated with a particular VLAN, then the slot and port number within the VLAN are displayed, followed by the name of the VLAN itself.

- **MacAddress**   Lists the MAC hardware address associated with the IP address for this entry.
- **IpAddress**   Lists the IP address associated with the MAC address for this entry.
- **Type**   Indicates whether the ARP entry was learned dynamically (dynamic) or configured statically (static).

## Configuring a Static ARP Entry Through Device Manager

To configure a static ARP entry, select Routing | IP | IP from the main Device Manager display, select the ARP tab, and click Insert. This opens the Insert ARP window, where the entry can be added:

Configure the interface with which the static ARP entry will be associated, and then enter the IP address and its associated MAC address.

## Configuring a Static ARP Entry Through the CLI

Static ARP entries can be configured through either the CLI or Device Manager, using the command **config ip arp**. This command must be performed on a port or a VLAN that has an IP address associated with it. For instance, to apply a static ARP entry to an Ethernet port configured with an IP address, the following command is used:

```
Accelar-105X# config ip arp add ports 3/3 ip 210.70.123.10
              mac 00:00:a2:3e:21:0a
```

To apply a static ARP entry to a VLAN that is associated with an IP address (virtual router interface), the following command is used:

```
Accelar-105X# config ip arp add port 3/3 ip 132.245.155.132
              mac 00:00:81:3e:e2:45:01 vlan 1
```

In this example, the ARP entry is associated with port 3/3 in VLAN 1. Of course, the port member listed must be an actual members of the VLAN specified.

## Viewing the ARP Cache Through the CLI

The Accelar's current ARP cache can also be viewed through the CLI, using the following command:

```
Accelar-105X# sho ip arp info

=================================================================
                               Ip Arp
=================================================================
  IP_ADDRESS        MAC_ADDRESS       VLAN  PORT   TYPE     TTL
-----------------------------------------------------------------
170.70.162.250  00:a0:c9:19:af:ee     1    3/3    DYNAMIC  1680
170.70.162.253  00:e0:16:04:5c:81     1    3/6    DYNAMIC  981
170.70.162.249  00:20:af:09:93:fb     1    3/4    DYNAMIC  690
170.70.162.220  00:40:05:a1:8c:8c     1    3/1    DYNAMIC  581
170.70.162.245  00:60:fd:8c:4e:ed     1    3/1    DYNAMIC  449
170.70.162.201  00:00:81:d1:5e:cd     1    3/1    DYNAMIC  448
170.70.162.202  00:00:81:e1:1a:82     1    3/1    DYNAMIC  426
170.70.162.244  02:07:01:14:13:06     1    3/1    DYNAMIC  372
170.70.162.203  00:00:a2:6d:bc:d8     1    3/1    DYNAMIC  370
170.70.162.252  00:e0:16:2b:f1:81     1    3/5    DYNAMIC  236
170.70.162.247  00:00:a2:c3:54:5b     1    3/1    DYNAMIC  2158
170.70.162.208  00:00:a2:09:f2:20     1    3/1    DYNAMIC  2159
170.70.162.207  00:00:a2:06:e5:40     1    3/1    DYNAMIC  2159
170.70.162.193  00:00:a2:09:f5:88     1    3/1    DYNAMIC  2158
170.70.162.255  ff:ff:ff:ff:ff:ff     1     -     LOCAL    2160
170.70.162.248  00:00:81:c1:e8:81     1     -     LOCAL    2160
Total 16
```

In addition to viewing the entire IP ARP cache, you can view the cache entries by subnet; simply use the **–s** switch in association with the **show ip arp info** command. For example, in network 200.20.10.0, subnetted with a 27-bit mask (255.255.255.224), to check only the entries related to subnet .192, the following command would be used:

```
Accelar-105X# show ip arp info -s 200.20.10.192/27


================================================================
                              Ip Arp
================================================================
  IP_ADDRESS        MAC_ADDRESS        VLAN  PORT    TYPE    TTL
----------------------------------------------------------------
200.20.10.208 00:00:a2:31:f7:20  1       3/1   DYNAMIC 2159
200.20.10.207 00:00:a2:06:21:4f  1       3/1   DYNAMIC 2159
200.20.10.193 00:00:a2:e9:f5:00  1       3/1   DYNAMIC 2159
200.20.10.255 ff:ff:ff:ff:ff:ff  1        -    LOCAL   2160
200.20.10.206 00:00:81:c1:e8:81  1        -    LOCAL   2160
Total 5
```

# Routing Between Isolated Router Ports

The Accelar uses the concept of an *isolated router port,* which allows for a single physical port to be configured as though it were a routed interface. By applying an IP address to the Ethernet port itself, and configuring the port with the appropriate routing protocol, the Ethernet port takes on the characteristics of an actual physical router interface. However, the routed interface still isn't the physical interface, but instead is the virtual router interface associated with the single port.

An isolated router port can be a useful way to create an IP connection that Device Manager can use to communicate with the Accelar.

## Configuring an Isolated Router Port Through Device Manager

To apply an IP address to an Ethernet port for routing purposes, simply double-click the desired port in Device Manager; this opens the Edit Port window. From this window, select the IP Address tab. By default, no IP address information is associated with an Ethernet port, so none is listed. To apply the IP address to the port, click Insert to open the Insert IP Address window, where you can configure the IP address and subnet mask.

| Note | *An isolated router port cannot be a member of a VLAN; creating an IP address on a specific Ethernet port will cause it to be removed from any VLANs it may be a member of.* |

## Configuring an Isolated Router Port Through the CLI

An isolated router port can also be configured through the CLI, by using the **config** command against the appropriate Ethernet port. For example, the following command would be used to apply an IP address of 210.70.123.1 with a subnet mask of 255.255.255.0 to Ethernet port 3/3:

```
Accelar-105X# config ethernet 3/3 ip create 210.70.123.1/24
```

The IP information can then be verified by using the **show** command:

```
Accelar-105X# sho ports info ip 3/3

==============================================================================
                                      Port Ip
==============================================================================
PORT     IP_ADDRESS        NET_MASK          BROADCAST   REASM    ADVERTISE
NUM                                                      MAXSIZE  WHEN_DOWN
------------------------------------------------------------------------------
3/3      210.70.123.1      255.255.255.0     ones        1500     disable
```

# Viewing the IP Routing Table

The Accelar's IP routing table can be viewed through either Device Manager or the CLI. This table is comprised of a list of all IP routes that the Accelar is currently aware of, and, therefore, all IP networks and subnetworks that are accessible from the Accelar. In addition to displaying the routes themselves, other route-specific information is provided, such as the method by which the route was learned, the age of the route, and which remote interface is the next hop to that route.

## Viewing the IP Routing Table Through Device Manager

Viewing the IP routing table through Device Manager is accomplished by selecting Routing | IP | IP Route from the Device Manager main menu, which opens the IP Route tab in the Edit IP window, where the routing table is displayed. The following fields are associated with the IP Route tab:

- **Dest**   Displays the IP network that is the destination network for the IP routing entry. For example, if the entry is 150.50.10.0, then the Accelar routing service is aware of the existence of the 150.50.10.0 network.

- **Mask**   Lists the subnet mask associated with the destination network.

- **Interface**   Indicates the virtual router interface associated with the IP route. If this virtual interface is associated with a particular VLAN, then the VLAN name is listed in this field. If the virtual interface is associated with an single routed port, then this field displays the slot and port number of the physical interface.

- **NextHop**   Indicates the next hop through which the IP route is accessible.

- **Type**   Indicates the type of IP route that is being listed; this may be either *direct* or *indirect*.

- **Proto**   Indicates how the IP route was learned: *local* means the Accelar has a virtual router interface configured for that IP network; *netmgmt* means the route is a static route configured through network management; *RIP* means the route was learned via the Routing Information Protocol; and *OSPF* means the route was learned via the Open Shortest Path First routing protocol.

- **Age**   Displays the amount of time, in seconds, that the particular route has been in the routing table without receiving an update. Local and static routes (netmgmt) display an age of 0, because the route wasn't learned and doesn't need to be refreshed.

- **HopOrMetric**   Varies depending on the routing protocol; the *hop* or *metric* refers to the relative distance or desirability of the route. For more information regarding hop or metric values, consult Chapters 31 and 33.

## Viewing the IP Routing Table Through the CLI

Viewing the IP routing table through the CLI is accomplished with the following command:

```
Accelar-105X# show ip route info

===============================================================================
                                 Ip Route
===============================================================================
DST               MASK            NEXT             COST  VLAN  PORT  CACHE  OWNER
-------------------------------------------------------------------------------
0.0.0.0            0.0.0.0        200.20.10.195     1     1    3/1   TRUE   STATIC
200.20.10.192   255.255.255.224 200.20.10.193      1     1    -/-   TRUE   LOCAL
Total 2
---------------------- INACTIVE STATIC ROUTES ----------------------
Total 0
```

In this example, only two routes are present: one locally configured network (the 200.20.10.192 network, associated with the virtual router interface in VLAN 1, which has an IP address of 200.20.10.193) and a static default route (0.0.0.0).

## Adding a Static Route

Adding a static route can be done through Device Manager or the CLI. To configure a static route through Device Manager, select Routing | IP | IP Route from the main Device Manager menu. This opens the Edit IP window, which consists of a series of tabs. Select the IP Route tab, which displays the IP routing table. Here, you can add a static route into the table by clicking Insert, which opens the Insert IP Route window:

THE ACCELAR LAYER 3 SWITCH

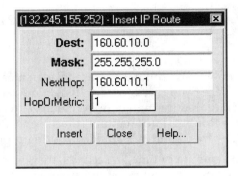

This window consists of four fields: Dest (the destination IP route), Mask, NextHop, and HopOrMetric (the metric associated with the route). A common static route is a *default route*—an IP route described as 0.0.0.0 with a mask of 0.0.0.0, which indicates it is a match for all routes. An incoming packet destined for an IP route that is not specifically in the IP routing table will be sent to the next hop associated with the default route, if a default route is in place.

**Note**    *Once a default static route is in place, it is not advertised to other routers, by default. To change this default in a RIP network, from the main Device Manager window, select the desired interface, choose the RIP tab, and then set AdvertiseDefaultRoute to Advertise the Route 0.0.0.0, and set AcceptDefaultRoute to accept such advertisements from remote routers. Otherwise, from the CLI, use the **config** command. For instance, to set up the Accelar to both supply and listen for the default route, use the following commands: **config vlan 10 ip rip default-supply enable** and **config vlan 10 ip rip default-listen enable**. In addition, a static route other than the default route will not be advertised, by default. In this case, an Announce Policy must be configured to advertise the route. For more information regarding the configuration of Announce Policies, consult the sections on OSPF and RIP later in this chapter.*

## Configuring a Static Route Through the CLI

Configuring a static route through the CLI is done using the command syntax **config ip static-route**. For example, the following commands show how to add a static route to network 10.1.0.0/16 with a next hop of 160.60.162.193 and a metric of 2:

```
Accelar-105X# config ip static-route create 10.1.0.0/16 next-hop 160.60.162.193 cost 2
```

# Dynamic Host Configuration Protocol and the Accelar

In a network where IP addresses are dynamically assigned using the Dynamic Host Configuration Protocol (DHCP), the Accelar may be configured to forward DHCP packets. By default, this capability is not active. Thus, in a network where DHCP is being used and multiple IP networks or subnetworks are configured, the Accelar may need to be configured to pass DHCP packets between these networks, depending on where it is positioned, so that each DHCP client can obtain its IP address (on the correct network or subnet) from its DHCP server even if the server does not reside on its local network.

To do this, the Accelar must be configured for DHCP relay on the virtual router interfaces over which the DHCP packets will need to pass. This function is combined with the forwarding of BootP packets, and is configured in the same way, using the same configuration windows.

## Configuring the Accelar to Handle DHCP

To configure the Accelar for DHCP relay, both the global and interface parameters must be correctly defined. On the global level, the Accelar needs to be informed as to which IP interface will be associated with the DHCP server. This can be either a single port, as in the case of an isolated router port, or a virtual router port associated with a VLAN having multiple port members. In addition, DHCP must be configured on a port level, including every port over which DHCP packets must be relayed on their way from client to server.

### DHCP Globals

The DHCP global parameters are concerned with what sort of packets must be relayed (DHCP packets in this case, though BootP packets can also be specified), what the IP address of the DHCP server is, and which interface is associated with the clients that the server will service.

The following parameters apply to the DHCP relay global settings:

- **Agent Address**   Refers to the IP address that is configured on the local interface. This can be the IP address of a single port, in the case of an isolated router port, or the virtual router interface associated with a VLAN, serving all ports configured for that VLAN. This is the IP address of the interface (or interfaces) that will serve DHCP clients. If multiple interfaces support DHCP clients, each must be specified as an agent address.

- **Server Address**   Indicates the IP address of the DHCP server. If the DHCP server exists on one of the Accelar's locally configured network numbers, then the Accelar unicasts the DHCP packets out of that particular interface to the DHCP server. This is known as *relay-agent* mode. Alternately, the IP address of the IP interface associated with the DHCP server's network may be configured; this will cause the interface to broadcast the DHCP request.

- **Enable**   Enables and disables the current entry.

- **Mode**   Dictates whether the entry pertains to BootP packets, DHCP packets, or both.

**SETTING DHCP GLOBALS THROUGH THE CLI**   The DHCP global parameters can also be configured through the CLI. For instance, to enable DHCP for VLAN 7 with a mode of DHCP relay only, where VLAN 7 is associated with a virtual router interface with the IP address 170.70.20.1/24, which serves a VLAN containing DHCP clients which utilize a DHCP server with IP address 170.70.10.16/24, the following commands would be used:

```
Accelar-105X# config vlan 7 ip dhcp-relay enable
Accelar-105X# config vlan 7 ip dhcp-relay mode dhcp
Accelar-105X# config ip dhcp-relay create-fwd-path agent
170.70.20.1 server 170.70.10.16 mode dhcp
```

## DHCP Port-Level Configuration

In addition to configuring DHCP at the global level, individual ports (virtual router ports) must be configured to actually relay the DHCP packets. For example, an Accelar configured with two VLANs, one of which contains a DHCP server that must receive DHCP requests and respond with DHCP replies, must have the virtual router ports associated with these VLANs configured to execute the relay of the DHCP packets so that they are not blocked from leaving their local VLAN.

When configuring ports for DHCP relay, it is important to make a distinction that arises frequently in dealing with the Accelar routing switch: the port does not refer to a physical Ethernet port per se—it refers to a virtual router port within the Accelar. That virtual router port may, in turn, be associated with a single physical port. So, it may seem as though the physical port is being configured, but conceptually, the virtual router port associated with that port (or VLAN, as the case may be) is actually being configured.

When configuring DHCP parameters at the port level, the following values can be defined:

- **Enable**   Enables or disables DHCP support on the individual port.

- **MaxHop**   Defines how many hops a DHCP packet is allowed to traverse from the client to the server. Values can be set between 1 and 16, with a default value of 4.

- **MinSec**   Dictates how long (in seconds) the Accelar waits between receiving a DHCP packet and forwarding it. The range is between 0 and 65,535, with a default of 0. A value of 0 indicates that the Accelar does not incur any delay, and forwards the packets as soon as they are received.

- **Mode**   Indicates whether the forwarding mode includes BootP packets, DHCP packets, or both.

- **AlwaysBroadcast**   Set to true or false; when set to true, server DHCP replies are broadcast back toward the client.

**CONFIGURING DHCP PORT PARAMETERS THROUGH THE CLI**   To access the same port-level DHCP parameters that are available through Device Manager, the DHCP configuration commands can be invoked from the Accelar's CLI. For instance, to enable DHCP relay for the virtual router port associated with VLAN 10, with a max-hop value of 6, a min-sec value of 0, and a mode that includes BootP packets where all DHCP replies are broadcast back toward the client, the following set of commands would be used:

```
Accelar-105X# config vlan 10 ip dhcp-relay max-hop 6
Accelar-105X# config vlan 10 ip dhcp-relay min-sec 0
Accelar-105X# config vlan 10 ip dhcp-relay mode bootp_dhcp
Accelar-105X# config vlan 10 ip dhcp-relay broadcast enable
Accelar-105X# config vlan 10 ip dhcp-relay enable
```

# User Datagram Protocol Forward

The UDP forward feature was implemented to support UDP broadcasts. UDP broadcasts are sent to a subnet broadcast address or the limited broadcast address, and are used by different applications for purposes such as server discovery. UDP broadcasts are used by DHCP and BootP (which are supported on the Accelar by using the DHCP relay feature, discussed in the previous section), as well as Microsoft Networking NetBIOS over IP for purposes of server discovery in a non-WINS environment. UDP broadcasts are not forwarded through a router by default; to accommodate this function, the UDP forward mechanism must be used.

## Configuring the Accelar for UDP Forwarding

To configure the Accelar to support UDP forwarding, the ingress IP interface(s) must be configured, the egress broadcast interface(s) must be selected, and the appropriate UDP port(s) must be specified. For example, an administrator may want to configure the Accelar to forward Trivial File Transfer Protocol (TFTP) packets from IP interface 160.60.10.1 and broadcast them out IP interface 160.60.20.1, where the TFTP server is positioned. To accomplish this, the following steps must be taken:

- The UDP port 69 must be defined (indicating TFTP).

- The destination IP address must be associated with UDP port 69; in this example, this would be the IP address of the TFTP server or the IP address of the interface through which the TFTP server can be reached. Depending on the UDP broadcast type, there may be multiple addresses, or a limited broadcast address associated with the port number.

- A UDP forwarding list must be assembled, indicating which IP destinations are to be associated with the broadcast interface.

- The broadcast IP interface must be specified, and UDP port 69 configured as the destination port.

After you perform these four steps, the Accelar knows the UDP port for which you want to forward traffic, monitors the IP interfaces specified by the forwarding list for UDP packets received on port 69 (TFTP), and forwards those packets on UDP port 69 either, broadcasting them out of the specified broadcast IP interface onto the network where the TFTP server sits or, if the specific server IP address is configured, a unicast will be sent to that address. The following sections cover these steps in greater detail, by outlining the individual parameters and statistics.

## User Datagram Protocol

Before UDP forwarding can be configured on the Accelar, the UDP protocol ports need to be defined. This is accomplished by selecting Routing | IP | UDP Fwd from the main Device Manager toolbar, which opens the Edit UDP Forward window. This window consists of four tabs: Protocol, UDP Port Forwarding, UDP Port Forward List, and UDP Broadcast Interface. The Protocol tab is the first that you will use, because it is where you define the specific UDP ports. To define a specific protocol, click Insert and then enter the UDP port number and name:

- **Port Number**   Specifies the UDP port number associated with the protocol in question; for instance, UDP port 69 is used for TFTP, and UDP port 161 is used for the Simple Network Management Protocol (SNMP). Any UDP port can be defined here, except for UDP ports 67 and 68, which are used for BootP and DHCP, respectively; forwarding for these UDP packets is configured using the DHCP relay options.

**Note**   *A full list of UDP port numbers can be obtained from RFC 1700.*

- **Name**   Specifies the user-configured name to associate with the UDP port number; for instance, UDP port 161 may use the name *SNMP*. Once the name is configured, it can't be changed without reconfiguring the entry.

After you enter these values, they are added to the protocol table. At this point, the newly defined UDP protocol can be viewed from the Protocol tab.

**CONFIGURING UDP PROTOCOL ENTRIES USING THE CLI**    UDP port protocols can also be added through the CLI, using code version 2.0 or higher. This is accomplished by using the following command syntax:

config ip udpfwd protocol [*UDP-port-number*] create [*protocol-name*]

For example, to configure UDP port 161 with a name of SNMP, the following command would be issued:

```
Accelar# config ip udpfwd protocol 161 create SNMP
```

This information can also be viewed from the CLI, using the following command syntax:

```
Accelar# show ip udpfwd protocol info

================================================================
                          Udp Protocol Tbl
================================================================
UDP_PORT PROTOCOL_NAME
----------------------------------------------------------------
37       Time Service
49       TACACS Service
53       DNS
69       TFTP
137      NetBIOS NameSrv
138      NetBIOS DataSrv
161      SNMP
Accelar#
```

# UDP Port Forwarding

When configuring UDP forwarding, the UDP port forwarding parameters must be configured, including the UDP port number and the associated interfaces; because the specific UDP port being used will need to be referenced, the UDP port must first be defined in the Protocol tab. For example, if the protocol is SNMP, then UDP port 161 must be specified in the UDP Port Forwarding tab; before this can be done, UDP port 161 must be specified in the Protocol tab. Once this is completed, select the UDP Port Forwarding tab and click Insert. This opens the Insert UDP Port Forwarding window, where the following parameters can be defined:

```
(132.245.155.252) - edit UdpFwd                                              ☒
┌──────────┬──────────┬──────────┬──────────────┐
│          │ UDP Port │ UDP port │ UDP Broadcast │
│ Protocol │Forwarding│Forward List│  Interface   │
└──────────┴──────────┴──────────┴──────────────┘
 DestPort  DestAddr   Id FwdListIdListSize  FwdListIdList  NumFwdPackets  NumDropPacketsTtlExpired  NumDropPacketsDestUnreach
   37     160.60.10.1  1        0                             0                    0                          0
   53     160.60.10.1  2        0                             0                    0                          0

              [ Insert... ]  [ Delete ]  [ Refresh ]  [ Close ]  [ Help... ]  [▼]

inserted.
```

- **DestPort**   Identifies the destination UDP port to be used for this UDP port forwarding entry. This UDP port must be defined in the Protocol tab before it can be used. Clicking the arrow located to the right of the DestPort field produces a list of configured UDP ports, as well as their assigned names.

- **DestAddr**   Identifies the destination IP address to which the UDP packets should be sent. This can be a host address (of a server, for instance) or it may be a limited broadcast if a network or subnetwork broadcast address is configured. For instance, to direct the UDP broadcast to a server with IP address 160.60.10.1/24, configure the destination address as 160.60.10.1, which will convert the packet to a unicast to that host. To direct the UDP broadcast to subnetwork 160.60.10.0/24, configure the destination address with the IP address of the IP interface associated with subnet 160.60.10.0.

## ADDING UDP PORT FORWARDING LISTS AND FORWARDING PORTS THROUGH THE CLI

The CLI commands related to configuring forwarding UDP ports and their corresponding destination addresses are combined with the creation of UDP port forwarding lists, or the addition of additional UDP port entries into an existing list. Essentially, this means that the parameters found in the UDP Port Forwarding tab and UDP Port Forward List tab in Device Manager are configured simultaneously in the CLI. To do this configuration, you need to create a port forwarding list and then add the specific UDP port and destination address. For instance, to create a UDP forwarding list with an ID of 10, and then add UDP port 161 (SNMP) with a destination address of 180.80.10.255 (the broadcast address for subnetwork 180.80.10.0), the following commands would be issued:

```
Accelar# config ip udpfwd portfwdlist 10 create
Accelar# config ip udpfwd portfwdlist 10 add-portfwd 161 180.80.10.1
```

This example assumes that IP address 180.80.10.1 is the IP address of the IP interface on the Accelar from which the broadcast should be sent. The commands in the previous example create an entry in both the UDP Port Forwarding tab, describing UDP port 161 with an associated destination address of 180.80.10.1, and the UDP Port Forward List tab, using a default name. The default name uses the naming scheme UDPFWDLIST#*list ID number*, so the default name in this case will be UDPFWDLIST#10. To alter the name from the default by using the CLI, use the following command:

```
Accelar# config ip udpfwd portfwdlist 10 name SNMP
```

## UDP Port Forwarding Statistics

The UDP Port Forwarding tab also contains a series of statistics associated with each UDP Port Forwarding Policy. In addition to the DestPort and DestAddr that were explained in the previous section, these statistics have the following meanings:

- **Id**   Indicates the ID number given to the UDP Port Forwarding Policy. This number is assigned dynamically by the Accelar.

 **Note**   *IDs are assigned in order; however, once the list is refreshed, the entries will be reordered numerically by UDP port number, not ID number. For this reason, the ID numbers may appear out of order.*

- **FwdListIdSize**   Indicates how many forwarding lists each particular policy is a member of.
- **FwdListIdList**   Lists the individual forwarding list ID numbers if the policy in question is a member of one or more forwarding lists. If it isn't a member of any forwarding lists, this field is blank. This value is displayed in hexadecimal format, so UDP Port Forward List ID 10 would be displayed as 00:0a.
- **NumFwdPackets**   Indicates the total number of packets that were forwarded as a result of the particular policy.
- **NumDropPacketsTtlExpired**   Indicates the number of packets that were dropped due to the Time to Live (TTL) expiring.
- **NumDropPacketsDestUnreach**   Indicates the number of packets that were dropped due to the fact that the destination host or network that was defined was unreachable.

## UDP Port Forward List

A UDP port forward list must also be defined, after the protocol entries are complete and the UDP Port Forwarding entries have been filled out. The UDP Port Forward List tab will reference existing entries in each of the former two tabs (the Protocol tab and the UDP Port Forwarding tab), so those must be completed first. Selecting this tab opens the Insert UDP Port Forward List window:

Here, a list ID is generated, but can be changed from its default value. By default, the ID increments by one for each list created. A name can also be assigned to the list. Once this is completed, select the desired entries from the Forward ID List (FwdIdList) that dominates the window, by clicking the entries you want to add. After you select an entry successfully, the gray box associated with it turns solid black. Once all the desired entries are selected, click Insert to add the list.

**ADDING UDP PORT FORWARDING LIST ENTRIES THROUGH THE CLI**    In the CLI, adding UDP port forwarding list entries is accomplished by using the same command that creates the port forwarding entries themselves. This procedure is outlined in the previous section.

## UDP Broadcast Interface

In addition to the UDP port forwarding list, you must configure the actual interfaces that will be participating in UDP forwarding. This is accomplished by configuring the UDP broadcast interface. Select Routing | IP | UDP Fwd to open the Edit UdpFwd window, and then select the UDP Broadcast Interface tab. From this tab, all existing interfaces are displayed (none, by default). To insert an interface, click Insert, which opens the Insert UDP Broadcast Interface window, in which the following fields are configured:

- **LocalIfAddr**   Configures the IP address of the local interface that will participate in UDP forwarding. This is the interface which will receive UDP broadcasts which must be forwarded.

- **UdpPortFwdListId**   Configures the UDP Port Forward List ID. Selecting a value of 0 indicates that no UDP packets will be forwarded. A particular UDP port forward list can be selected by clicking the arrow to the right of this field, which opens a list of all configured UDP port forward list IDs.

- **MaxTtl**   Configures the maximum TTL for received UDP packets. This indicates the maximum number of hops the packet can pass through before being considered invalid. For example, if the MaxTtl is set to 4, and the UDP packet has already been forwarded through four router hops when the Accelar in question receives the packet, its TTL will be considered to have expired, and the packet will be dropped. The Max Ttl range is from 1 to 16 with a default of 4.

**CONFIGURING A UDP BROADCAST INTERFACE THROUGH THE CLI**   UDP broadcast interfaces can also be configured using the CLI. To configure the local interface 180.80.10.1, with UDP port forward list 10, the following command would be issued:

```
Accelar# config ip udpfwd interface 180.80.10.1 udpportfwdlist 10
```

The maximum TTL can also be altered from the CLI. In this example, the TTL is changed from its default of 4 to 10, using the following command:

```
Accelar# config ip udpfwd interface 180.80.10.1 maxttl 10
```

# Distance Vector Multicast Routing Protocol

The Distance Vector Multicast Routing Protocol (DVMRP) is a distance-vector protocol similar to RIP. Unlike RIP, however, where routes to specific destinations are learned with an associated metric, DVMRP allows routes to a multicast source to be determined (also with an associated metric). When using IP multicast groups, and multiple paths exist to common destinations, multicast datagrams may have extra copies sent to the same destination. DVMRP attempts to prevent this by using a reverse path multicasting (RPM) algorithm, exchanging information between routers regarding their reachability of multicast source networks. By doing this, a shortest path first tree can be built, indicating the best path to the multicast source. Since there may be multiple multicast sources, several trees may coexist simultaneously. Each tree begins at the network that is the source of the particular multicast stream.

## DVMRP Concepts

DVMRP utilizes a series of control packets, each of which is sent to the IP multicast group address of 224.0.0.4:

- **DVMRP Probes**   Used by DVMRP to accomplish several things: they are used for DVMRP neighbor discovery, they indicate the protocol version, and they act in a keep-alive capacity to indicate neighbor failures. Probes are issued by DVMRP routers from each interface that is configured to participate in multicast routing. Included in each Probe message is a list of all the DVMRP neighbors from which Probes have been received. This is similar in concept to OSPF Hello messages, where DVMRP routers discover the presence of other DVMRP routers by examining the entries in each Probe message received. The protocol version number is also indicated in the Probe message, allowing DVMRP routers to determine which version each of their neighbors are running.

  If a DVMRP router receives a Probe packet and, upon examining the neighbor list contained within, sees itself listed as one of the DVMRP neighbors for the sender of the Probe for the first time, then it issues a unicast to the Probe's originator, containing the router's entire multicast routing table (a DVMRP report) as it currently stands.

  By default, Probe messages are issued on DVMRP interfaces once every ten seconds. If a Probe message isn't received from a particular neighbor within the specified period of time (defined by the Neighbor Timeout Interval, which is 35 seconds by default), then the neighbor is assumed to have failed and is timed out.

- **DVMRP Reports**   After the DVMRP neighbors are determined by a DVMRP interface, route Report messages are sent to those neighbors. Report messages are used to exchange information about the location of multicast source networks, as well as their metrics.

  The contents of the specific DVMRP Report indicate the source network (the network where the particular multicast stream originates), the mask associated with the network, the upstream neighbor, and the metric (the distance, in hops, to the source network). In addition, an expiration time is given, indicating the time in seconds before the entry will age out. These messages are issued on all DVMRP interfaces that have received Probe messages, indicating at least one DVMRP neighbor is present within that network that will receive the Report. These multicast routing tables are issued in accordance with the Update Interval (which defaults to 60 seconds on the Accelar).

- **DVMRP Prunes and Grafts**    DVMRP utilizes the concept of *pruning and grafting* when creating multicast trees. This means that because multicast clients utilize IGMP to register for specific multicast groups, DVMRP routers can issue Prune messages back toward the source of the multicast if no IGMP hosts register for that multicast stream. Likewise, if a network has no IGMP hosts registered, and then one or more hosts do register at some point, that network can be added to the tree by means of a Graft message.

- **DVMRP Graft Acks**    Because it is essential that a graft takes place successfully, Graft Acknowledgements are used when dealing with Graft messages, to ensure that the Graft is not being lost in transit somewhere along the path toward the multicast source.

## Triggered Updates

DVMRP uses triggered updates, or flash updates, if route information changes prior to the end of the Update Interval. This is intended to quickly update other DVMRP routers if a preferred multicast path suddenly becomes unusable, for whatever reason. The frequency with which flash updates can be issued is defined by the Triggered Update Interval. This parameter defaults to five seconds, indicating that flash updates cannot be sent any more frequently than one per five seconds.

# Configuring DVMRP Through Device Manager

DVMRP can be configured on the Accelar through Device Manager, by selecting Routing | IP | DVMRP from the main Device Manager window. This opens the Edit DVMRP window (see Figure 11-2), which consists of a series of tabs. The contents of these tabs and their individual parameters are described in the sections that follow.

## Globals

Here, DVMRP can be enabled on a global level, and the system-wide parameters can be set:

- **Enable**    Indicates the current administrative state of the DVMRP protocol (set to true or false).

- **UpdateInterval**    Indicates how frequently a multicast routing table update should be sent. The default value is 60 seconds. This can be altered to anywhere between 10 and 2,000 seconds (about 30 minutes). These routing tables are also issued to specific DVMRP routers upon the receipt of a Probe message that contains the receiving router as one of the sending router's neighbors for the first time.

- **TriggeredUpdateInterval**    Indicates how often a triggered update can be sent. By default, this is set to five seconds, meaning the Accelar won't allow a triggered update to be sent more frequently than one every five seconds. The range is from 5 to 1,000 seconds.

THE ACCELAR LAYER 3 SWITCH

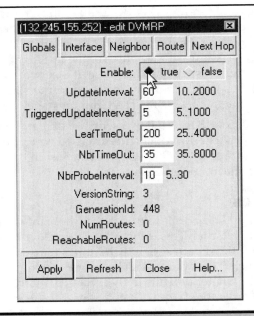

**Figure 11-2.** *The Edit DVMRP window*

- **LeafTimeOut** Indicates how long after sending a DVMRP report the router will wait without receiving a positive response before assuming the network to be a leaf network (containing no DVMRP neighbors).

- **NbrTimeOut** Indicates how much time can pass with no receipt of a report from a neighbor before that neighbor is considered inactive and thus aged out.

- **NbrProbeInterval** Indicates how often a Probe message will be sent. The default is 10 seconds, with a range of 5 seconds to 30 seconds.

- **VersionString** Indicates the version of DVMRP being used.

- **GenerationId** Generated by the Accelar and used to track DVMRP restarts; since a new generation ID is calculated whenever the DVMRP is reset, fluctuations in the generation ID indicate a DVMRP restart.

- **NumRoutes** Indicates the number of multicast routes in the Accelar's multicast routing table.

- **ReachableRoutes** Indicates the total number of multicast routes in the Accelar's multicast routing table that have valid metrics (rather than those with metrics of infinity).

# Interface

DVMRP interface-specific statistics are viewed from the Interface tab in the Edit DVMRP window. Here, the specific interfaces that are participating in DVMRP can be viewed. Essentially, this tab is used to view the current status of DVMRP interfaces, and isn't used to configure, although the Metric parameter can be altered from this tab. The following parameters apply:

- **Interface**   Indicates either the slot and port number of the interface, if the interface is an isolated router port, or the VLAN, if the interface is a virtual router port associated with a VLAN.

- **LocalAddress**   Indicates the IP address of the DVMRP interface described in the previous field.

- **Metric**   Indicates the metric associated with the interface. This is used similarly to how a metric in RIP is used, where the value is viewed as a distance metric. Individual metrics can be altered from the Interface tab by clicking the Metric field and altering the value.

- **OperState**   Indicates the current operational state of the DVMRP interface.

# Neighbor

DVMRP neighbors can also be viewed from the Edit DVMRP window, by selecting the Neighbor tab. This tab displays the following information regarding the individual DVMRP neighbors:

- **Interface**   Indicates the DVMRP interface that is used to reach the DVMRP neighbor. This may be either a specific slot and port number, if the interface is an isolated router port, or a VLAN, if the DVMRP interface is associated with a VLAN.

- **Address**   Indicates the IP address of the DVMRP neighbor.

- **ExpiryTime**   Indicates how much longer (in seconds) before the neighbor is aged out.

- **GenerationId**   Indicates the DVMRP neighbor's generation ID, generated by the system to track DVMRP restarts.

- **MajorVersion**   Indicates the major version number of the DVMRP version used by the neighbor.

- **MinorVersion**   Indicates the minor version number of the DVMRP version used by the neighbor.

- **Capabilities**   Indicates the DVMRP capabilities of the neighbor. Four bits are used in this case: the *leaf* bit (0), which indicates the neighbor has only one DVMRP interface with neighbors; the *prune* bit (1), which indicates the neighbor supports pruning; the *generation ID* bit (2), which indicates the neighbor will send its generation ID along with its Probe messages; and the *mtrace* bit (3), indicating the neighbor can handle incoming mtrace requests.

■ **State**   Indicates the current operational state of the adjacency with the DVMRP neighbor. This may be one-way (meaning a neighbor has been detected but no adjacency has been formed), active (meaning an adjacency exists), ignoring, or down.

## Route

The actual multicast routing table information can be viewed from the Route tab, indicating the following information:

■ **Source**   Masked with the source mask, this identifies the sources for which the specific entry has multicast routing information.

■ **SourceMask**   Used with the source value; the result of the masking identifies the sources for which the specific entry has multicast routing information.

■ **UpstreamNeighbor**   Indicates the upstream Reverse Path Multicasting neighbor from which multicast datagrams from the preceding source(s) were received. Meaning, from which neighbor were the multicast datagrams originating from the specified Source received.

■ **Interface**   Indicates the DVMRP interface on which the multicast datagrams were received from the indicated sources. This may be a slot and port number or, if the interface is associated with a VLAN, the specific VLAN.

■ **Metric**   Indicates the total number of hops to the source subnet.

■ **ExpiryTime**   Indicates the amount of time, in seconds, before the entry is aged out.

## Next Hop

DVMRP next hop information can also be obtained from the Edit DVMRP window. The fields displayed here indicate information about the next hop toward a specific multicast source:

■ **Source**   Masked with the SourceMask value to determine the sources for which the individual entries specify a next hop.

■ **SourceMask**   Used in conjunction with the Source value to identify the sources for which the entry specifies a next hop.

■ **OutInterface**   Indicates the DVMRP interface through which the next hop is reachable.

■ **Type**   Is either *leaf* (0) or *branch*; if no downstream dependent neighbors exist on the outgoing interface, the type is leaf. Otherwise, the type is branch.

## Configuring DVMRP Through the CLI

DVMRP parameters can also be configured from the CLI. To accomplish this, the following command is used:

```
Accelar-105X# config ip dvmrp enable
```

The preceding command enables the DVMRP protocol on a global level. The commands that follow set the Neighbor Probe Interval (the frequency with which Probe messages are sent to DVMRP neighbors) to 15 seconds; the Update Interval to 60 seconds (indicating a routing update will be issued every minute); the Triggered Update Interval to 5 seconds (indicating that triggered updates can occur once every 5 seconds, at a maximum), a Neighbor Timeout Time of 90 seconds (indicating that the neighbor will be considered to have failed if a Probe is not received from it within 90 seconds); and a Leaf Timeout Time of 120 seconds, indicating that if no request for a certain multicast group is received from a leaf within 2 minutes, it is assumed that the leaf no longer requires the multicast stream and thus is pruned:

```
Accelar-105X# config ip dvmrp nbr-probe-interval 15
Accelar-105X# config ip dvmrp update-interval 60
Accelar-105X# config ip dvmrp triggered-update-interval 5
Accelar-105X# config ip dvmrp nbr-timeout 90
Accelar-105X# config ip dvmrp leaf-timeout 120
```

## Viewing DVMRP Information Through the CLI

DVMRP information can be viewed through the CLI on a variety of levels. For instance, to view global DVMRP information, the following command would be used:

```
Accelar-105X# show ip dvmrp info
=============================================================================
                              Dvmrp General Group
=============================================================================
AdminStat             : enabled
Genid                 : 593
Version               : 3
NumRoutes             : 0
NumReachableRoutes    : 0
```

THE ACCELAR LAYER 3 SWITCH

```
UpdateInterval            : 60
TriggeredUpdateInterval   : 5
LeafTimeOut               : 120
NbrTimeOut                : 90
NbrProbeInterval          : 15
```

DVMRP information can be viewed at the interface level, as well, from the CLI, by using the following command:

```
Accelar-105X# show ip dvmrp interface


=============================================================================
                                       Dvmrp Interface
=============================================================================
IF        ADDR           METRIC    OPERSTAT
-----------------------------------------------------------------------------
Vlan1     160.60.15.218  1            up
Vlan10    170.70.211.4   1            up
```

# Internet Group Multicast Protocol and the Accelar

The Accelar routing switch is capable of supporting both Layer 3 IGMP, which can be configured on a routed port, and IGMP snooping at Layer 2.

## Configuring the Accelar for Layer 3 IGMP

The Layer 3 IGMP parameters are associated with the IGMP functions that reside on the router, and not the IGMP snooping functionality often associated with a Layer 2 switch. IGMP at Layer 3 involves determining which routed interfaces require a certain multicast stream. IGMP achieves this through the transmission of Host Query messages, which are issued from each of its interfaces. Clients who want to participate in a certain multicast group being advertised by the router will respond to these messages with a Host Report, indicating that they want to receive multicast traffic for that group. The router, then, forwards traffic for a specific multicast group only through the interfaces that received reports from clients requesting that group. In order to utilize the L3 IGMP functionality, DVMRP must be enabled globally, as well as on the particular IGMP interface.

## Port-Level IGMP Configuration

The port-level IGMP information includes the frequency with which host queries will be made, as well as the IGMP version. You can access these parameters by selecting IP | L3 IGMP from the main Device Manager window, and then selecting the Interface tab. The following parameters apply:

- **QueryInterval**  Indicates the frequency with which IGMP Host Query packets will be sent from this interface. The range is from 1 to 65,535 seconds, with a default value of 125.

- **Version**  Indicates the IGMP version that will be used on the interface. The Accelar is capable of running IGMP version 1 and version 2.

> **Note**    *All routers on a particular network that are running IGMP must run the same version.*

- **QueryMaxResponseTime**  Defines the maximum amount of time, in seconds, advertised as a Query Response Time from the specified interface (IGMPv2 only). The range is from 1 to 255 seconds, with a default of 10. A lower value in this case allows for faster pruning of multicast groups.

- **Robustness**  Indicates how much packet loss will be tolerated on the IGMP interface. If the network in question is likely to experience a certain amount of packet loss due to latency or lack of bandwidth, this value can be set to provide robustness by instructing the interface to expect a certain amount of loss. The number of packets that the interface will tolerate losing is the Robustness value minus one. The range is from 2 to 255, with a default of 2 (indicating only 1 packet may be lost).

- **LastMemberQueryInterval**  Defines how long before a host ages out. Increasing the timer increases the aging time (in seconds). The range is from 1 to 255 seconds, with a default of 10.

# Viewing and Configuring IGMP Parameters

The IGMP parameters can be altered through Device Manager or the CLI, by selecting Routing | IP | L3 IGMP from the main Device Manager display. This opens the Edit IGMP window, which consists of three tabs: the Cache, Interface, and Group tabs.

## Cache

The IGMP cache information can be viewed from Device Manager, but can't be altered.

- **Address**  Indicates the IP multicast group address that relates to the particular entry.

- **Interface**   Indicates the interface from which the associated IP multicast group address is heard.
- **LastReporter**   Contains the source IP address of the most recent membership report received on the interface, for the corresponding IP multicast group address.

**Note**   *If no membership report has been received, then a value of 0.0.0.0 is displayed.*

- **ExpiryTime**   Indicates the amount of time remaining (in seconds) before the entry ages out of the cache.
- **Version1HostTimer**   Indicates the amount of time remaining (in seconds) before the local router assumes no more IGMPv1 members are on the interface's network. This values is refreshed upon receipt of an IGMPv1 membership report. While this field contains a value other than 0, any IGMPv2 Leave messages will be ignored.

**VIEWING IGMP CACHE INFORMATION THROUGH THE CLI**   The same information accessible from the Cache tab of the Edit IGMP window in Device Manager can also be obtained via the CLI, by issuing the following command:

```
Accelar# show ip l3-igmp cache
================================================================================
                                Igmp Cache
================================================================================
GRPADDR          INTERFACE   LASTREPORTER    EXPIRATION V1HOSTTIMER
--------------------------------------------------------------------------------
224.0.0.2        Vlan2       160.60.12.237   117        250
224.0.1.22       Vlan2       160.60.142.3    242        0
224.0.1.35       Vlan2       160.60.142.3    242        0
```

## Interface

The Interface tab of the Edit IGMP window displays interface statistics and provides a means of altering IGMP interface parameters:

- **Interface**   Indicates the interface actively participating in IGMP.
- **QueryInterval**   Dictates how often, in seconds, IGMP Host Query packets are transmitted on the particular interface. The range is from 1 to 65,535, with a default value of 125.

■ **Status** Indicates the interface IGMP status as either *active* or *notInService*. For an interface to have a status of active, it must have an IP address and mask assigned to it, and DVMRP must be enabled.

■ **Version** Indicates the current version of IGMP the interface is running. This can be changed by clicking this field, clicking the arrow that appears, and then selecting either IGMPv1 or IGMPv2 from the drop-down menu that appears. All routers within a common LAN must be running the same IGMP version if IGMP is being used.

■ **OperVersion** Displays the actual operating version of IGMP. This may differ from the configured version, because IGMPv2 is able to shift backward if placed in an IGMPv1 network.

■ **Querier** Displays the IP address of the IGMP querier for the network associated with the specified interface.

■ **QueryMaxResponseTime** Indicates the maximum amount of time advertised in IGMPv2 queries for the specified interface.

■ **WrongVersionQueries** Useful for determining whether IGMP problems stem from a version mismatch. This counter is incremented by one each time an IGMP query is received that is of a different version from what the interface is configured for.

■ **Joins** Indicates the number of successful *joins* for this interface—the number of times an IGMP entry for that interface has been entered into the IGMP cache.

■ **Robustness** Indicates the relative robustness associated with the IGMP interface. *Robustness* refers to how much packet loss the interface should account for if, for whatever reason (congestion, limited bandwidth, and so forth), packet loss is likely to occur. The range is from 2 to 255 packets, with a default value of 2.

**Note** *Robustness is defined as the robustness value minus 1, so a value of 2 actually indicates that 1 packet may be lost.*

■ **LastMembQueryIntvl** Defines the amount of time before aging out IGMP hosts. The value indicates the maximum amount of time that can be inserted into a group-specific query, in response to a Leave Group message. This parameter also indicates the amount of time between group-specific query messages. The range is from 1 to 255 (seconds), with a default value of 10.

**VIEWING AND CONFIGURING IGMP INTERFACE PARAMETERS THROUGH THE CLI** The same information that can be seen from the Interface tab in the Edit IGMP window can also be accessed via the CLI. To view IGMP interface statistics from the CLI, the following command is used:

```
Accelar# show ip 13-igmp int
=======================================================================
                                Igmp Interface
=======================================================================
           QUERY             OPER            QUERY   WRONG              LASTMEM
IF         INTVL STATUS VERS. VERS QUERIER   MAXRSPT QUERY JOINS ROBUST QUERY
-----------------------------------------------------------------------
V4         125   active 1     1    198.152.170.1  10  2     1     2      1
V5         125   inact  2     1    0.0.0.0        10  0     0     2      1
V3         125   inact  2     1    0.0.0.0        10  0     0     2      1
V2         125   active 1     1    135.60.132.1   10  6     5     2      1
```

## Group

IGMP multicast group information is displayed from the Group tab in the Edit IGMP window. This tab contains a series of informational fields, which have the following meanings:

- **IpAddress**   Indicates the IP multicast group address that members can join.
- **Members**   Contains the IP address of a member that has issued a group report, pertaining to the IP multicast group address described in the *IpAddress* field.
- **InPort**   Either contains a slot and port number corresponding to a physical interface, or references a virtual interface associated with a VLAN that has received group reports.
- **Expiration**   Indicates the amount of time remaining (in seconds) before the group report for this port expires. A refresh will reset this timer.

**VIEWING IGMP GROUP INFORMATION THROUGH THE CLI**   The same information accessible from the Group tab of the Edit IGMP window in Device Manager is also accessible through the CLI, by issuing the following command:

```
Accelar# show ip 13-igmp group
=======================================================================
                                Igmp Group
=======================================================================
GRPADDR         INPORT      MEMBER          EXPIRATION
-----------------------------------------------------------------------
224.0.0.2       2/8         160.60.108.218  234
224.0.0.2       2/8         160.60.108.132  107
224.0.1.22      1/4         160.60.114.2    232
224.0.1.35      1/4         160.60.114.2    232
224.0.1.60      2/8         160.60.108.1    234
224.0.1.60      1/8         160.60.109.7    238
```

# IGMP Snooping on the Accelar

IGMP Snooping can also be performed on the Accelar; when this feature is configured, the switching function of the Accelar will monitor its ports for the presence of IGMP queries and reports, so that it can further increase efficiency by passing multicast streams only to ports which received requests for those streams. For instance, in a typical IGMP scenario without snooping, if the Accelar receives a request for a specific group address on a certain VLAN, then the multicast will be sent to that VLAN, including all ports encompased by that VLAN. With snooping in place, the Accelar will make a note of which ports within the VLAN the Host Reports were actually received on, and send the multicast stream only to those specific ports within the VLAN. IGMP Snooping functions only when a multicast router is present in the VLAN, and has been dynamically learned as an IGMP querier.

**Note** | *In order for IGMP Snooping to function, the Accelar must use ARU 2 or higher. In order for the Sender and Access List functionality to work, ARU 3 or higher is required.*

## Configuring IGMP Snooping

IGMP Snooping parameters are accomplished at the VLAN level. To alter the configuration, select VLAN | VLANs from the main Device Manager display. This will open the edit VLANs window, where each VLAN is displayed. Select the Snoop tab to display the following fields:

- **Enable**   Selecting this field will cause an arrow to appear in the right portion of the field. Selecting this arrow will bring up a small drop down menu where IGMP snooping can be set to true or false.

- **ReportProxyEnable**   Selecting this field will cause an arrow to appear in the right portion of the field. Selecting this arrow will bring up a small drop down menu where Report Proxy can be set to either true or false. Setting this option to true (the default) will cause all incoming Host Reports to be bundled and sent to the querying router as a single package.

- **Robustness**   This field indicates the amount of packet loss expected or tolerated on a subnet. The value indicates the number of packets that can be lost.

- **Query Interval**   This value indicates the expected interval between multicast router queries. This value should be the same as that used by the multicast routers in the particular VLAN.

- **MRouter Ports**   This field indicates the ports to which a multicast router is attached, or through which a multicast router is reachable if it is not directly attached. These ports are ports which will receive query packets originated from an IGMP router.

- **Active MRouter Ports**   This field indicates the ports which are connected to an active multicast router. Included here is the querier port, as well as ports in the forwarding state, both static and dynamic.

- **Last Querier**   This field indicates the last router address from which a Host Query packet was received.

- **Querier Port**   This field indicates the port over which queries from the last querier are being received.

- **MRouter Expiration**   This field indicates the time remaining before the multicast querier is aged out. Should the multicast querier age out, all group memberships in the VLAN will be flushed.

In addition to these fields, there is a button labeled Multicast located in the lower portion of the window. Selecting this button will bring up the edit Snoop window, which consists of four separate tabs; the Receiver, Sender, Static, and Access tabs, which are described in turn below:

## The Receiver Tab

The Receiver tab displays information regarding IGMP multicast group receiver information. The following fields apply:

- **VlanId**   The VLAN ID of the VLAN receiving the multicast information (the egress VLAN).

- **GrpAddress**   The multicast group address to which the receiver has subscribed.

- **InPort**   The port over which the multicast group membership was learned.

- **Member**   The IP Address of the source of the membership report received for the multicast group address on this interface. If no membership report has been received, this object has the value 0.0.0.0

- **Expiration**   The age-out time for the entry.

- **Type**   The type of entry; either dynamic (1) or static (2).

## The Sender Tab

In the Sender tab, multicast group information is displayed regarding the sender of multicast information. The following fields and parameters apply to this tab:

- **VlanId**   The VLAN ID of the VLAN where the multicast information originates (the ingress VLAN).

- **GrpAddress**   The multicast group address for the group broadcasted by the sender.

- **InPort**   The port over which the multicast group membership was learned.

- **Member**   The IP Address of the source of the membership report received for the multicast group address on this interface. If no membership report has been received, this object has the value 0.0.0.0

- **Action**   This is the action you wish to apply to the highlighted multicast group; selecting this field will cause a small drop down menu to appear with the following actions; None, which is the default meaning no action is to be applied, flushEntry, which will flush the multicast entry, and flushGrp, which will flush the multicast group entirely.

## The Static Tab

Ports can be given static membership for a given multicast group address. This is done by selecting the Static tab, and clicking the button labeled Insert. This will open the Insert Static window, where the following parameters can be configured:

- **VlanId**   The VLAN ID of the VLAN which will participate in the multicast group address.
- **GrpAddress**   The actual multicast group address for which the static entry is being created.
- **MemberPorts**   The ports which will participate in the multicast group address. (Simply click on the individual ports.) Selected ports must be a member of the VLAN.
- **NotAllowedToJoin**   Selecting ports under the heading Not Allowed To Join will prevent the selected ports from receiving multicast information associated with the defined group address, regardless of whether or not a Host Report is received on that port.

## The Access Tab

The Access tab allows the user to configure a multicast group address or range of multicast group addresses, then apply a certain mode to any entries which match. For instance, a specific host can be denied a certain multicast stream by defining the multicast group address in question, defining the host who is to be denied, then selecting a mode of denyRX. You can create access lists by selecting Insert from the main Access tab. This will bring up the Insert Access window, where the following parameters apply:

- **VlanId**   This is the VLAN ID of the VLAN to which the policy will be applied.
- **GrpAddress**   This is the multicast group address to which the policy relates.
- **Host Addr**   This is the host to which the policy applies.
- **Host Mask**   This is the mask of the host which will be affected by this policy.
- **Mode**   This is the mode which is applied to the policy; the options are denyRX, which means that the the specified host will not be permitted to receive the multicast group address, denyTX, which means that the multicast group information cannot be transmitted, or denyBoth, which stops both transmitting and receiving.

## Configuring IGMP-Snooping Through the CLI

IGMP-Snooping parameters can also be configured via the CLI. For example, to specify port 3/5 as a multicast router port, the following command is used:

```
Accelar-1250# config vlan 1 igmp-snoop mrouter 3/5
```

The following commands go on to set the query-interval to 100 seconds, the robust value to 5, then enable the report-proxy feature:

```
Accelar-1250# config vlan 1 igmp-snoop query-interval 100

Accelar-1250# config vlan 1 igmp-snoop report-proxy enable

Accelar-1250# config vlan 1 igmp-snoop robust-value 5
```

Lastly, the following command enables IGMP snooping itself on VLAN 1:

```
Accelar-1250# config vlan 1 igmp-snoop state enable
```

**CONFIGURING A STATIC ENTRY VIA THE CLI**    Static IGMP port members can also be defined from the CLI. For example, the following command would be used to create a static entry for port 3/5, multicast group 224.0.3.3:

```
Config vlan [vlan id] igmp-snoop static-members [multicast group address] create [port] static.
```

For example:

```
Accelar-1250# config vlan 1 igmp-snoop static-members 224.0.3.3 create 3/5 static
```

This indicates that multicast traffic for group address 224.0.3.3 should be delivered to port 3/5, whether or not any Host Reports are received.

**CONFIGURING ACCESS LISTS VIA THE CLI**    Access lists can be used to control the flow of multicast information from the CLI as well as through Device Manager. For instance, to deny any multicast streaming for group address 224.0.3.3 to or from host 135.25.15.12, the following command would be used:

```
Config vlan [vlanid] igmp-snoop access-list [multicast address] create [host ip address] [host mask] [mode]
```

For example:

```
Accelar-1250# config vlan 1 igmp-snoop access-list 224.0.1.7 create 135.25.15.12 255.255.255.255 denyRX
```

| Note | *ARU 3 or higher is required for IGMP-Snooping Access Lists.* |

# IPX Routing on the Accelar

The routing of the IPX protocol is a new feature enhancement, beginning with system software version 2.0. In addition to running code version 2.0, ARU 3 I/O modules are required to support this feature. This section covers the configuration of the Accelar routing switch to route IPX. It does not cover the IPX protocol itself, except for a brief overview of the protocol functionality. For more information regarding the IPX protocol, consult RFC 1132.

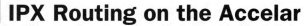 *When converting to I/O units that utilize the ARU 3 chips (thus supporting IPX routing), remember that ARUs dynamically drop back to the least common denominator found in the chassis, which means that if an Accelar 1200 contains six I/O modules, five of which contain ARU 3s and one of which contains ARU 1s, the ARU 3 I/O modules will drop back in functionality so that all I/O modules will effectively run as ARU 1 units.*

## An Overview of IPX

IPX uses a client-server relationship, where servers advertise their presence and function, and clients connect to servers based on their needs. Typically, an IPX client issues a packet known as a *Get Nearest Server (GNS) Request*, which is used to discover the closest server that can provide the requested services. The steps that are generally used are as follows:

1. **Get Nearest Server Request**   Issued by the client, this is a Service Advertising Protocol (SAP) broadcast, and is issued to discover the closest server that can provide the service being requested.

2. **Get Nearest Server Reply**   Issued by the server in response to a GNS Request, this is a SAP reply that is directed back to the client who issued the initial GNS Request. If several servers can provide the requested service, and these servers are local to the client, several GNS Replies are received, and the one that is received first is assumed to have originated from the closest server, and thus is the preferred server for this connection. If the server or servers are not local, the Accelar will respond with a matching entry from its SAP table.

3. **Get Local Target**   If the required service is not local, once the GNS Reply is received from the Accelar, the client issues this IPX RIP packet. This is also a broadcast packet, whose purpose is to determine the location of the service once the name has been determined.

4. **Give Local Target**   The Accelar respond to the Get Local Target packet with this reply RIP packet, which is directed back toward the client. This packet indicates the location and address of the requested service.

5. **Create Connection**   Once the location of the service is determined, the client attempts a connection with the actual server. At this point, the client and server both utilize NetWare Core Protocol (NCP) frames, which are simply forwarded by the Accelar.

## IPX Addressing

IPX addressing is formatted quite a bit differently than IP addressing. Rather than the 32-bit dotted-decimal format associated with IP, IPX utilizes a 32-bit IPX network number combined with a 48-bit IPX Node ID. The resulting address uses a format of *nn.nn.nn.nn.hh.hh.hh.hh.hh.hh*, where *nn* indicates the IPX network number portion of the address, and *hh* indicates the individual Node ID.

## IPX Service Advertising Protocol

IPX SAP provides a method of propagation for upper-layer entities, such as IPX servers. These SAPs are generated by the servers themselves and advertise their presence and functionality to the network's IPX clients. These advertisements include such information as the server name, its IPX network and node address, the service type (file server, print server, and so on), the IPX socket address, and the number of hops it will take to get to the server (the number of router hops that must be traversed).

IPX clients attempt to contact their servers either through the transmission of GNS Requests, which are used to determine where the closest print or file server is, or via a General Service Query (GSQ), to learn of all servers of the type specified. If the desired service exists on a different IPX network, the router will determine the optimum path, based on the SAP table that it has accumulated through the SAPs it has received on its different interfaces. For instance, if one of the Accelar's routed interfaces receives a GNS request, the Accelar consults its SAP table to determine which service is closest; that advertisement (containing the server name, service type, socket number, and so forth) is returned to the requesting client so that it can initiate a connection to that server.

## IPX Routing Information Protocol

IPX routes are propagated through the use of the IPX Routing Information Protocol (RIP), not to be confused with the RIPv1 and RIPv2 route advertisement protocols associated with IP. IPX RIP works similarly, however, in that each IPX RIP router advertises its locally configured routes (IPX networks configured on local interfaces), as well as any statically or dynamically learned routes, by broadcasting RIP advertisements out its interfaces at regular intervals. Like IP RIP, IPX RIP utilizes a Split Horizon algorithm to prevent the propagation of routes that have gone down or become invalid, and also uses triggered updates if the routing information changes, so that remote IPX routers can be updated quickly without having to wait for a scheduled update.

## Varying Frame Types

The IPX protocol uses four different frame types. Using varying frame types can allow a single physical network to support more than one IPX network scheme, where one overlaps the other, each using a different frame type. The four supported frame types are as follows:

- **Ethernet-II**   Use the Ethertype identifier 0x8137. This is the most common frame format for Ethernet.

- **802.2-LLC (SNAP)**   Used in Ethernet and Token Ring networks, and identified by a DSAP/SSAP of 0xE0.

- **802.3 (RAW)**   Use a 2-byte Length field in place of the Type (Ethertype) field. RAW frames are not as commonly used today.

- **802.3 (SNAP)**   The Sub-Network Access Protocol (SNAP) header provides an Ethertype of 0x8137 to identify the payload. A DSAP/SSAP value of 0xAA is used to identify the SNAP frame itself.

The Accelar is capable of recognizing each frame type even when IPX routing is not enabled. When performing Layer 2 switching, these four frame types can be identified by the Accelar for purposes of protocol-based VLAN distribution. When routing, the Accelar is capable of translating between these different frame types. So, although IPX frame encapsulation must remain consistent within a particular IPX network number, the frame type doesn't need to be consistent throughout the entire network.

### Different Encapsulation Methods Across Different Platforms

The four methods of encapsulation described in the preceding list may be referred to differently depending on the platform being used. For instance, the Accelar and the Nortel Networks router platform use different identifiers to describe the same frame encapsulations, which in turn are different from those used by Novell. To eliminate confusion, the matrix set forth in Table 11-1 can be used.

## IPX Configuration on the Accelar

To configure the Accelar for IPX routing, IPX must be enabled globally, and global IPX parameters must be set. Once this is accomplished, the interface-specific parameters

THE ACCELAR LAYER 3
SWITCH

| Frame Type | Accelar Name | Bay RS Name | Novell Name |
|------------|-------------|-------------|-------------|
| Ethernet_II | ethernetii | Ethernet | Ethernet_II |
| 802.3 RAW | raw | Novell | Ethernet_802.3 |
| 802.3 SNAP | snap | SNAP | Ethernet_SNAP |
| 802.2-LLC | llc | LSAP | Ethernet_802.2 |

**Table 11-1.**   *IPX Frame Encapsulation Reference Across Platforms*

and any static route or SAP entries can be set. The Accelar supports basic IPX routing, with support for each of the four IPX frame types.

## Global

IPX must first be enabled on a global level for IPX routing to take place on the Accelar. To do this, select Routing | IPX | IPX from the main Device Manager display. This opens the Edit IPX window, which defaults to the Global tab:

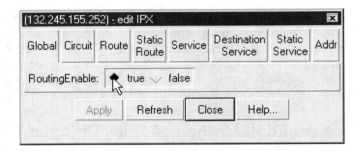

Here, IPX is enabled by selecting true for RoutingEnable. After you do this, you must access the other IPX tabs to complete the configuration.

**ENABLING IPX FROM THE CLI**    IPX can also be enabled and disabled globally from the CLI, by use of the following commands:

```
Accelar# config ipx forwarding enable
Accelar# config ipx forwarding disable
```

The current global IPX forwarding state can be viewed with the following command:

```
Accelar# config ipx forwarding info

Sub-Context: clear config monitor show test trace
Current Context:

        forwarding : disable

           enable :

          disable :
```

## Circuit Statistics

The IPX circuit (IPX Interface) statistics can be viewed from Device Manager; simply select the Circuit tab from the Edit IPX window. The following fields are found in this tab:

- **Index**   Used to reference the IPX circuit. This value is generated automatically when the interface is first created.

- **OperState**   Indicates the current operational state of the IPX circuit. The OperState may indicate up, down, or sleeping, indicating the interface is administratively up, but has no connection.

- **IfIndex**   Indicates the IfIndex associated with the circuit; this relates to the IfIndex associated with the VLAN, which in turn is associated with an Accelar virtual router port.

- **VlanId**   Indicates the VLAN ID of the VLAN that is associated with the Accelar virtual router port. Remember, as of the time of publication, IPX routing can occur only on a virtual router port associated with a VLAN, and cannot be implemented on an isolated router port.

- **NetNumber**   Indicates the IPX network number that is associated with the virtual router interface.

- **Encap**   Indicates the encapsulation method used: none (0), EthernetII (1), LLC (2), RAW (3), or SNAP (4).

## Route Statistics

IPX route statistics can also be viewed, to see which IPX networks the Accelar is currently aware of, as well as their relative distance, in ticks or hops, from the Accelar. The following fields can be viewed:

- **NetNum**   Indicates the destination IPX network number.

- **Protocol**   Indicates the manner in which the IPX route was learned. This will be either *RIP*, meaning that the route was learned dynamically from a remote source, or *local*, meaning that the route is locally accessible from one of the Accelar's IPX interfaces.

- **Ticks**   Indicates the number of ticks to the destination network, where one tick is equal to 1/18 of a second.

- **HopCount**   Indicates the total number of router hops to the destination network.

- **NextHopCircIndex**   Indicates the IPX circuit index of the next hop router.

- **NextHopNICAddress**   Indicates the NIC address of the next hop router.
- **NextHopNetNum**   Indicates the IPX network number associated with the next hop.

## Configuring and Viewing Static Routes

From the Edit IPX window, static IPX routes can be configured and viewed by means of the Static Route tab, which has the following parameters:

- **CircIndex**   Indicates the circuit index associated with the first hop on the way to the destination route.
- **NetNum**   Indicates the IPX network number associated with the destination route.
- **Ticks**   Indicates the number of ticks (1/18 of a second) it takes to get to each route.
- **HopCount**   Indicates the number of hops to the destination route.

**ADDING A STATIC ROUTE**   To add a static IPX route, select Routing | IPX | IPX, and then select the Static Route tab to open the static route display. From there, click Insert to open the Insert Static Route window, where the static route is configured:

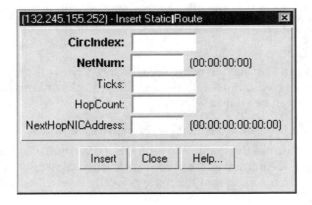

Here, the same parameters that are covered in the previous section must be defined, as well as the additional parameter *NextHopNICAddress*, which refers to the NIC address of the next hop network on the way toward the destination.

**ADDING A STATIC IPX ROUTE THROUGH THE CLI**   An IPX static route can also be configured through the CLI. This is accomplished using the following command syntax:

config ipx static-route create [*IPX-network-number*] [*next-hop address*] [*hops*] [*ticks*]

For example, to create a static route to configure a static IPX route with a network of 00:00:aa:01, and a next-hop of 00:00:aa:02.00:00:81:11:23:9f, which is two hops away and two ticks away, the following command would be used:

```
Accelar-105X# config ipx static-route create 00:00:aa:01 00:00:aa:02.00:00:81:11:23:9f 2 2
```

# Viewing Services

The SAP table can also be viewed from Device Manager, which lists a series of services and their relative distance from the Accelar, in hops. The SAP table indicates the name of each service, the type of service it is, the IPX network number, and the manner in which the service was learned:

- **Type**   Indicates the specific service type, which may include 00:04 (file server), 00:07 (print server), or 02:78 (NetWare Directory Services server).

- **Name**   Indicates the name of the service in ASCII format (maximum of 48 bytes).

- **Protocol**   Indicates the method by which the service was learned; meaning, whether the service was learned from a received SAP or was statically configured.

- **NetNum**   Displays the 32-bit IPX network number of the service (this is generally the server's internal network number).

- **Node**   Displays the 48-bit Node ID of the service. The server's internal network generally utilizes a Node ID of 1.

- **Socket**   Indicates the transport-layer socket address of the specified service (in hex).

- **HopCount**   Indicates the number of router hops that must be traversed to reach the service.

# Destination Services

Destination services can also be viewed from Device Manager. Select the Destination Services tab from the Edit IPX window, and the following fields can be viewed:

- **NetNum**   Indicates the IPX network number of the destination service.

- **Node**   Indicates the IPX Node ID of the destination service.

- **Socket**   Indicates the transport-layer socket address of the destination service.

- **Name**   Indicates the name of the destination service.

- **Type**   Indicates the specific service type; this may include 00:04 (file server), 00:07 (print server), or 02:78 (NetWare Directory Services server).

- **Protocol**   Identifies the method through which the destination service was learned (through a SAP or through a static configuration).

THE ACCELAR LAYER 3
SWITCH

- **HopCount**    Indicates the number of routers that must be traversed on the way to the destination service.

### Configuring a Static Service

To enter a static entry into the SAP table, select Routing | IPX | IPX from the main Device Manager window, and then select the Static Service tab. To add the static service, click Insert. This opens the Insert Static Service window, in which the following parameters are entered:

- **CircIndex**    Indicates the circuit that is used to reach the specified service.

- **Name**    Indicates the service name in ASCII format.

- **Type**    Indicates the specific service type; this may include 00:04 (file server), 00:07 (print server), or 02:78 (NetWare Directory Services server).

- **NetNum**    Indicates the 32-bit IPX network number of the service.

- **Node**    Indicates the 48-bit IPX Node ID of the service.

- **Socket**    Indicates the Layer 4 socket address of the specified service.

- **HopCount**    Indicates the total number of router hops that must be traversed to reach the specified service.

### IPX Addresses

You can view a list of the configured IPX addresses, along with the individual frame encapsulation type, by selecting Routing | IPX | IPX from the main Device Manager window and then selecting the Addr tab:

- **VlanId**    Specifies the VLAN ID; because IPX routing on the Accelar occurs only over virtual router ports associated with different VLANs, in this case, the VlanId refers to the IfIndex value that is associated with a VLAN's virtual router port.

- **NetAddr**    Indicates the IPX address.

- **Encap**    Indicates the encapsulation method used (ethernetii, llc, snap, or raw). These are useful when the VLAN type being used is a port-based VLAN (protocol-based VLANs must select the specific frame type and will only admit that type).

# IPX Interface Parameters

IPX interface parameters apply to the virtual router port associated with a particular VLAN. Isolated router ports cannot, as of the time of this publication, be configured to route IPX. IPX interface parameters, therefore, are accessed through the VLAN options. To access the VLAN IPX parameters, select VLAN | VLANs from the main Device

Manager window. This opens the Edit VLANs window, where VLANs are created and configured. From there, highlight the VLAN whose virtual router interface is to be used as the IPX interface, and click IPX. This opens the Edit IPX window. Here, you can configure the interface-specific IPX parameters by selecting the Addr tab, and clicking Insert, which opens the Insert Addr window:

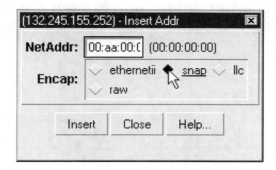

The following parameters are set in the Insert Addr window:

- **NetAddr**   Indicates the 32-bit IPX network number associated with the interface.

- **Encap**   Select one of four encapsulation methods: ethernetii (Ethernet_II), snap (Ethernet_SNAP), llc (Ethernet_802.2), or raw (Ethernet_802.3). This frame type must remain consistent within a particular IPX network, but does not need to be consistent throughout the entire network.

## IPX Address

The IPX address associated with a particular VLAN can be viewed from this tab, as well, once configured. After the IPX configuration information is complete, the following information is available from the Addr tab of the Edit IPX window:

- **VlanId**   Indicates the ifIndex value of the VLAN with which the virtual router interface is associated.

- **NetAddr**   Indicates the 32-bit IPX network number associated with the interface.

- **Enacap**   Displays the encapsulation method used for this IPX network.

## Configuring IPX Interface Parameters Through the CLI

IPX interface configuration can also be accomplished through the CLI, by using the **config vlan** command with the following command structure:

config vlan [*vlan ID*] ipx create [32-*bit IPX-network-number*] [*encapsulation-type*]

For instance, to configure VLAN 10 with IPX network number 00:00:aa:01 and an encapsulation type of Ethernet_II, the following command would be used:

```
Accelar-105X# config vlan 10 ipx create 00:00:aa:01 ethernet-ii
```

### Displaying the IPX Configuration Through the CLI

The current IPX interface configuration on the Accelar can be viewed by using the **show** command, with the syntax **show ipx config**. This command produces the following output:

```
Accelar-105X# show ipx config

================================================================================
                                 Ipx Config
================================================================================
CID NETNUM     ENCAPSULATION  RIP STATUS   UPD HLD DLY SAP STATUS   UPD HLD DLY
--------------------------------------------------------------------------------
1   0x0040aa01 Ethernet-II    RIP Enabled  60  3   20  SAP Enabled  60  3   20
2   0x0050aab2 Ethernet-II    RIP Enabled  60  3   20  SAP Enabled  60  3   20
3   0x0040aabb Ethernet-II    RIP Enabled  60  3   20  SAP Enabled  60  3   20
```

Here, the Circuit ID is displayed, followed by the IPX network number and the encapsulation type. RIP is shown to be enabled, with an Update Interval of 60 seconds, a transmit limit of 3 RIP packets per second, and a delay time of 20 seconds. Similar values are used in relation to SAP updates.

# Open Shortest Path First Configuration

In addition to RIP and RIPv2, the Accelar supports the OSPF routing protocol for IP networks. OSPF parameters include the global parameters, area parameters, and interface parameters, all of which are covered in this section. This chapter covers OSPF configuration as it relates to the Accelar, and does not cover the specifics of OSPF; for more information regarding the OSPF routing protocol, consult Chapter 31. For more detailed information, consult RFC 2178.

## Global OSPF Configuration

Global OSPF configuration is concerned with those parameters that affect OSPF on the entire Accelar, including all areas and interfaces within those areas that can be configured on the unit. Such global parameters include the Router ID, the administrative status (whether OSPF is enabled or disabled), whether the Accelar will be acting as an autonomous system border router (ASBR), and so forth.

## Global OSPF Configuration Parameters

Global OSPF configuration can be accomplished through either Device Manager or the CLI. To configure OSPF global parameters through Device Manager, select Routing | IP | OSPF from the main display, which opens the Edit OSPF window (see Figure 11-3).

This window is where you define the global parameters, including the following OSPF parameters:

- **RouterId**  Indicates the OSPF Router ID associated with the Accelar virtual routing services. By default, this value is calculated randomly, but may be changed to reflect one of the IP interfaces or any unique value that is easy to remember. This value is configured in 32-bit dotted-decimal format.

- **Admin Stat**  Indicates the administrative state of the OSPF protocol, and can be set to either *enabled* or *disabled*.

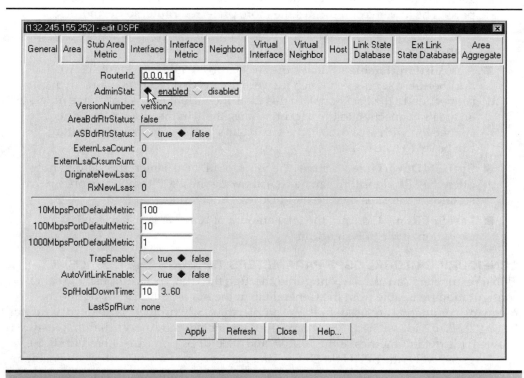

**Figure 11-3.**   *The Edit OSPF window*

- **AreaBdrRtrStatus** Indicates whether the Accelar is acting as an area border router. If it has interfaces configured in more than one area, then it's acting as an ABR.

- **ASBdrRtrStatus** Indicates whether the Accelar is acting as an ASBR.

- **ExternLsaCount** Indicates the total number of external Link State Advertisements (LSA type 5) that have been received and are currently in the Link State Database (LSDB).

- **ExternLsaCksumSum** Indicates a 32-bit sum of all link-state checksums for all external LSAs currently contained in the LSDB. This can be used to determine whether any local changes have occurred in the LSDB, and to compare the LSDBs of two Accelars.

- **OriginateNewLsas** Increments each time an LSA is generated by the Accelar.

- **RxNewLsas** Increments each time an LSA is received by the Accelar.

- **10/100/1000Mbps PortDefaultMetric** Indicate relative costs (metrics) between ports. The lower cost indicates the more preferred route, so the more bandwidth available for a port, the lower its metric should be.

- **TrapEnable** Indicates whether OSPF traps will be sent.

- **AutoVirtLinkEnable** Allows the Accelar to create virtual links between area border routers even when they are not needed (each area already has a connection to the backbone). In this case, the virtual link is not active unless an area's connection to the backbone fails; then, in the absence of a direct connection with area 0.0.0.0, the virtual link becomes active. This feature can be set to true or false.

- **SpfHoldDownTime** Defines the SPF Hold Down Timer; this defines how often the SPF algorithm can be run, allowing the algorithm to run once per $x$ seconds, where $x$ is the SPF Hold Down Timer value.

- **Last Spf Run** Indicates the total amount of time passed since the last execution of the SPF algorithm.

**CONFIGURING GLOBAL OSPF PARAMETERS THROUGH THE CLI** OSPF global parameters can also be configured through the CLI. To accomplish the same configurations available from the General tab in the main Edit OSPF window, the following commands are used. In this example, the OSPF protocol is enabled; a Router ID of 180.80.10.1 is assigned; ASBR capability is enabled; the auto-virtual-link feature is enabled; the default metrics of the 10, 100, and 1000Mbps ports are altered to 50, 10, and 1, respectively; the SPF Hold Down Timer is set to 5; and OSPF traps are enabled:

```
Accelar# config ip ospf admin-state enable
Accelar# config ip ospf router-id 180.80.10.1
Accelar# config ip ospf as-boundary-router enable
Accelar# config ip ospf auto-vlink enable
Accelar# config ip ospf default-metric ethernet 50
Accelar# config ip ospf default-metric fast-ethernet 10
Accelar# config ip ospf default-metric gig-ethernet 1
Accelar# config ip ospf holddown 5
Accelar# config ip ospf trap enable
```

# OSPF Interface Configuration

In addition to the OSPF global parameters, the individual OSPF interfaces must be configured. In addition to being assigned an IP address, OSPF interfaces must be configured with the Hello Interval, Router Dead Interval, router priority (for purposes of electing a Designated Router and Backup Designated Router), and so forth, which are relevant to the particular network the interface is configured in. For example, in a scenario where an Accelar is configured with three interfaces—one configured in area 0.0.0.0, and the remaining two configured in area 0.0.10.21—they can be configured in a variety of different ways (see Figure 11-4).

In this diagram, the three interfaces are set up in the following manner:

- Interface 1 is configured with a Hello Interval, Router Dead Interval, and so forth, that are consistent with the rest of that IP network.

- Interface 2 is configured with a different set of values for the same parameters, but those values are still consistent within its own IP network.

- Interface 3 is configured with a third set of values and, unlike interfaces 1 and 2, is also configured to use OSPF simple password authentication.

This is one example of how OSPF interface configurations may differ, although the global OSPF parameters for the Accelar unit as a whole have not changed. Interface-level OSPF configuration is accomplished by selecting the port or VLAN to be configured; the options are essentially the same, because the OSPF interface parameters apply to a virtual router interface, and not to the front panel interface or VLAN associated with the virtual router interface.

If a singular port is being configured, select the port in question from the main Device Manager display and then click Edit. This opens the Edit Ports window, where the OSPF tab can be accessed. If a VLAN is being configured, select VLAN | VLANs to open the Edit VLANs window, and then click the IP option at the bottom of the window, which opens the Edit IP window, where the OSPF tab can be accessed (see Figure 11-5).

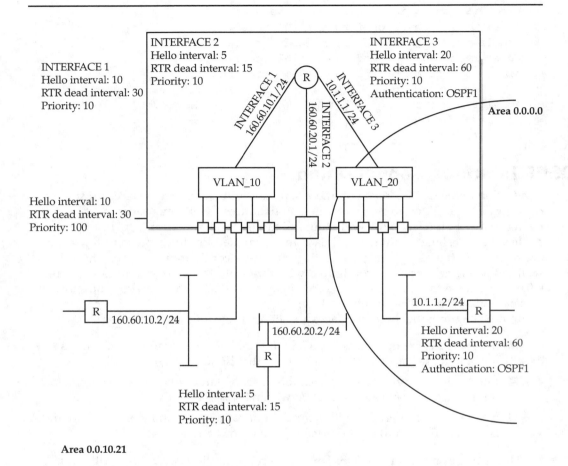

**Figure 11-4.** *Accelar with three OSPF interfaces in two different areas*

## Port-Level OSPF Configuration

OSPF port-level configuration can be accomplished by selecting the interface you want to configure in Device Manager, and then right-clicking the port; while holding down the right-mouse button, click the Edit option, which opens the Edit Port window. (Alternately, double-clicking the port will achieve the same thing.) Select the OSPF tab to alter the interface-level OSPF parameters. These parameters have the following meanings:

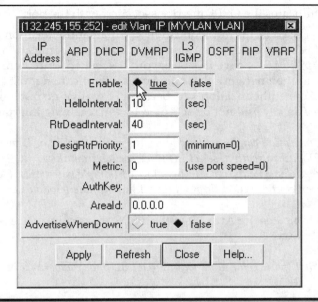

**Figure 11-5.** *The OSPF tab*

- **Enable**  Indicates the administrative state of the OSPF protocol for the interface being configured.

- **HelloInterval**  Indicates the frequency, in seconds, with which the OSPF interface will transmit OSPF Hello packets, which are used to establish neighbor states with other OSPF routers. Since this also indicates the frequency with which the interface expects to receive Hello packets, this value must be consistent for all OSPF interfaces connected to a common network. The default value is 10 seconds.

- **RtrDeadInterval**  Indicates how long a router will wait without receiving a Hello packet from a neighbor before it assumes that router is down. This value should be a multiple of the HelloInterval. For instance, the default value is 40 seconds, and the default Hello Interval is 10 seconds, meaning that four Hello packets can be missed before the remote router will be considered to be down. This value must be consistent for all OSPF interfaces connected to a common network.

- **DesigRtrPriority**  Indicates the OSPF router priority for this interface; router priority is used by OSPF interfaces to elect a Designated Router (DR). A higher value is more desirable than a lower value for purposes of the DR election. A value of 0 indicates that the interface is ineligible to be DR for its network. In the event of a tie, the Router ID is used to break the tie.

- **Metric**   Indicates the OSPF metric associated with the port.
- **AuthKey**   Used as the authentication key if an authentication type of simple password is being used; when simple password authentication is active, all outgoing OSPF LSAs have this password associated with them. All interfaces within a common network that are using authentication must be configured with the same authentication key, because LSAs that do not have the proper authentication key will not be accepted by the receiving interfaces.

**Note**   *OSPF authentication can be activated through either the CLI or Device Manager; to enable OSPF authentication, select the Interface tab from the edit OSPF window and toggle the AuthType field from a 0 (none) to a 1 (simple password). Details concerning authentication configuration through the CLI immediately follows this section.*

- **AreaID**   Indicates the Area ID of the OSPF area the interface is configured to be a member of.

**Note**   *Remember that the Accelar must maintain a LSDB for each area it participates in.*

- **AdvertiseWhenDown**   Indicates whether the Accelar virtual router interface that is configured for OSPF should be notified at the Layer 3 level when a Layer 2 state change occurs on the port(s) it is associated with. For instance, an Accelar virtual OSPF interface may be associated with a VLAN with five port members; toggling this option indicates whether the Layer 3 entity on the virtual router interface should be notified if the port state changes on one or more of the VLAN's five ports.

**CONFIGURING OSPF INTERFACE PARAMETERS THROUGH THE CLI**   OSPF interface parameters can also be configured by using the Accelar CLI. This is accomplished by using the following commands. In this example, the administrative status for the interface is enabled; the interface is configured to be in the backbone area; the Hello Interval is set to 5; the Router Dead Interval is set to 15 (meaning three Hello packets can be missed before reporting a neighboring router as down); the metric is set to 10; the interface is configured to not participate in DR elections; and an authentication type of simple password is configured, with a password key of ospf010:

```
Accelar# config ip ospf interface 180.80.10.1 admin-status enable
Accelar# config ip ospf interface 180.80.10.1 area 0.0.0.0
Accelar# config ip ospf interface 180.80.10.1 hello-interval 5
Accelar# config ip ospf interface 180.80.10.1 dead-interval 15
Accelar# config ip ospf interface 180.80.10.1 metric 10
Accelar# config ip ospf interface 180.80.10.1 priority 0
Accelar# config ip ospf interface 180.80.10.1 authentication-type simple
Accelar# config ip ospf interface 180.80.10.1 authentication-key ospf010
```

# OSPF Area Configuration

The Accelar is capable of assuming each of the different OSPF router roles: a backbone router, area border router, internal router, or ASBR. Each OSPF interface (this will be either an isolated router port or a VLAN associated with a Accelar virtual router port) can be configured to be in a different area, bearing in mind that the Accelar must maintain a LSDB for each area in which it participates.

## Inserting an OSPF Area

An interface can be added to an area through either Device Manager or the CLI. To do so, you first must define on the Accelar the area to which the interface will be added, by selecting Routing | IP | OSPF from the main Device Manager window; this opens the Edit OSPF window. From there, select the Area tab (see Figure 11-6).

The Area tab displays a variety of statistics, which are defined in the next section. By default, area 0.0.0.0 is defined in this window; this is the backbone area. To add additional areas, click the Insert button, which opens the Insert Area window:

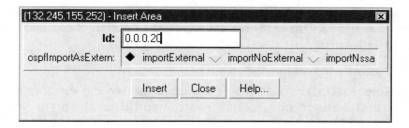

In the Insert Area window, you can add additional OSPF areas. To define the area, you must select an area ID and the method of handling external LSAs. The different OSPF area parameters and their meanings are as follows:

- **Id**   Indicates the OSPF Area ID, configured in dotted-decimal format. Any unique value other than 0.0.0.0 can be used.

- **importExternal**   Indicates that external LSAs are imported into the area. This should be selected if external LSAs are being advertised into the OSPF domain and the area being configured has multiple points of access to the rest of the OSPF areas.

- **importNoExternal**   Indicates that external LSAs are not imported into the area; if the area being configured has only one point of connection to the other OSPF areas (most likely the backbone area), then it is considered a stub area and does not need to import external LSAs.

- **importNssa**   Image version 2.0 and higher supports the existence of Not So Stubby Areas (NSSAs). An NSSA operates similarly to a stub area, but, unlike a stub area, allows routers within the NSSA to originate type 7 external LSAs.

| Id | ospfImportAsExtern | SpfRuns | BdrRtrCount | ospfAsBdrRtrCount | LsaCount | LsaCksumSum | Summary | ImportSummary | ActiveIfCount |
|---|---|---|---|---|---|---|---|---|---|
| 0.0.0.0 | importExternal | 0 | 0 | 0 | 0 | 0 | sendAreaSummary | true | 0 |
| 0.0.0.10 | importNoExternal | 0 | 0 | 0 | 0 | 0 | sendAreaSummary | true | 0 |

**Figure 11-6.** *The Edit OSPF window Area tab*

These type 7 LSAs will be converted by the area border router to type 5 external LSAs before being propagated into the backbone area.

## OSPF Area Statistics

The Area tab of the Edit OSPF window contains a variety of fields that report information and statistics for each area defined on the Accelar. These fields and their meanings are as follows:

- **Id**   Indicates the configured area ID.

- **ospfImportAsExtern**   Indicates the method used by the area for handling external advertisements. The choices are ImportExternal, Import NoExternal, and Import Nssa. This parameter is configured at the time the area is first defined. If you need to change this parameter, click the field and then select the arrow that appears on the right side of the field. This opens a list of the three options, which can be reselected at that time.

- **SpfRuns**   Indicates the total number of times that the SPF algorithm has been run within the area.

- **BdrRtrCount**   Indicates the total number of area border routers contained within the area; this value is recalculated each time the SPF algorithm is run.

- **ospfAsBdrRtrCount**   Indicates the total number of ASBRs that are contained within the area; this value is recalculated each time the SPF algorithm is run.

- **LsaCount**   Indicates the total number of LSAs contained within the Accelar's LSDB for this area. AS external LSAs are not included in this calculation.

- **LsaCksumSum**   Indicates the total checksum of all LSAs within the area, excluding AS external LSAs. This total can be used to determine whether any alteration has occurred to the Accelar's LSDB, and to compare the LSDB of two or more routers.

- **Summary**   Indicates how Area Summaries are handled by stub areas; this field has no bearing on nonstub areas. If the indication is sendAreaSummary, then

Area Summaries will be both sent and propagated; if the indication is noAreaSummary, then only the default route will be used.

- **ImportSummary** Indicates whether summaries will be imported into a stub area. This parameter is available only if the ospfImportAsExtern parameter is set to false.

- **ActiveIfCount** Indicates the number of active interfaces within the area. An area can't be removed if it contains active interfaces.

## Stub Area Metric

The stub area metric refers to the metrics that will be used in advertisements by an area border router, advertised into a stub area.

- **Area ID** Indicates the area ID for the stub area.
- **TOS** Indicates the Type of Service associated with the metric.
- **Metric** Indicates the actual metric that will be applied.
- **Metric Type** Indicates the actual metric type, which is either comparableCost (indicating external type 1) or noncomparableCost (indicating external type 2).

### CONFIGURING OSPF AREA AND STUB AREA PARAMETERS THROUGH THE
**CLI** OSPF area parameters can be configured through the CLI. In the following example, a new area with ID 0.0.0.20 is created, assigned as a stub area, and then configured not to import summaries (the default route is used), and a stub metric has been configured as 10:

```
Accelar# config ip ospf area 0.0.0.20 create
Accelar# config ip ospf area 0.0.0.20 stub true
Accelar# config ip ospf area 0.0.0.20 import-summaries false
Accelar# config ip ospf area 0.0.0.20 stub-metric 10
```

## Interface Parameters

OSPF interface-specific parameters can also be configured from the Edit OSPF window by selecting the Interface tab. The following parameters can be configured:

- **IP Address** Indicates the IP address associated with the OSPF interface.
- **AddressLessIf** Used to differentiate between interfaces, because the virtual router interface sometimes is referenced to an interface with an IP address (an isolated router port), and at other times is referenced to a grouping of ports that themselves do not possess an IP address (a VLAN). Interfaces that have an IP address are given a value of 0, while those that do not are given the corresponding ifIndex value.
- **AreaID** Indicates the area in which the interface will participate.

THE ACCELAR LAYER 3 SWITCH

■ **Type**    Indicates the OSPF routing type; on the Accelar, which currently supports only 10/100/1000Mbps Ethernet, the only available type is broadcast. In a Frame Relay or ATM network, this type would be nonbroadcast multiple access (NBMA). On a point-to-point wide-area link, the type would be point-to-point. For more information regarding different OSPF network types, consult Chapter 31.

■ **AdminStat**    Indicates the administrative status of the OSPF protocol on this interface; meaning, whether OSPF is currently enabled or disabled on this interface.

■ **RtrPriority**    Used in an OSPF domain for purposes of electing a DR for a particular network. A higher router priority indicates a higher desirability to be the DR for the network that the interface is participating in. If the interface should not be considered as DR, setting this value to 0 excludes the interface from the DR election. If two routers have the same router priority, the router ID is used as a tie-breaker.

■ **TransitDelay**    Indicates the number of seconds it takes to transmit an LSA over this interface.

■ **RetransInterval**    Indicates the number of seconds that are to elapse between LSA retransmissions.

**Note**    *The RetransInterval value is also used for the exchange of Database Description packets and Link State Request packets.*

■ **HelloInterval**    Indicates the amount of time (in seconds) that can pass before the interface expects to receive a Hello packet from each of its neighbors.

**Note**    *Within a single OSPF network (a single IP network, not the entire OSPF domain), the Hello Interval must be the same value for all interfaces participating in that network.*

■ **RtrDeadInterval**    Indicates how much time (in seconds) can pass without a Hello packet from one of the interface's neighbors before the interface considers the neighbor to be down. This value should be some multiple of the Hello Interval; for instance, if the Hello Interval is set to 15, the Router Dead Interval can be set to 45, indicating that three Hello messages can be missed before assuming the neighbor to have failed.

**Note**    *Within a single OSPF network (a single IP network, not the entire OSPF domain), the Router Dead Interval must be the same value for all interfaces participating in that network.*

■ **PollInterval**    Indicates the amount of time (in seconds) between Hello packets sent to an inactive NBMA neighbor.

- **State**   Indicates the current OSPF interface state. If the interface in question is the DR or BDR, this fact also is displayed here.

- **DesignatedRouter**   Indicates the IP address of the OSPF interface within the local network that is acting as the DR for that network. This will be either an OSPF neighbor interface or the local interface itself.

- **BackupDesignatedRouter**   Indicates the IP address of the OSPF interface within the local network that is acting as the BDR for that network. As with the DR, this will be either an OSPF neighbor interface or the local interface itself.

- **Events**   Indicates the total number of OSPF state changes and errors for all OSPF interfaces configured on the Accelar.

- **AuthKey**   Indicates the authentication key, if authentication is being used within an area or network.

- **AuthType**   Indicates the authentication type, represented by a numerical value. This value can be altered to change the authentication type. A value of 0 indicates no authentication, and a value of 1 indicates simple password authentication.

- **Status**   Indicates the OSPF interface's current operational status.

## Interface Metric

Interface metrics are used when determining the best possible path to route data through an OSPF network. OSPF may contain multiple paths to a common destination, so interface metrics can be used to indicate which path is the most desirable out of the list of paths available. For example, if there are two paths by which an IP destination is accessible through an OSPF network, and one path traverses a 10Mbps half-duplex connection, while the other traverses a gigabit uplink, the gigabit link is clearly the more desirable path and thus should receive a metric indicating it is the more desirable path (the lower the metric, the more desirable the path is).

**Note**   *The actual metric associated with 10Mbps, 100Mbps, and 1000Mbps connections is configured when configuring OSPF interface parameters (see the previous section).*

The following fields are found in this tab:

- **IPAddress**   Indicates the IP address associated with the OSPF interface.

- **AddressLessIf**   Used to differentiate between interfaces, because the virtual router interface sometimes is referenced to an interface with an IP address (an isolated router port), and at other times is referenced to a grouping of ports that themselves do not possess an IP address (a VLAN). Interfaces that have an IP address are given a value of 0, while those that do not are given the corresponding ifIndex value.

- **TOS**   Indicates the Type of Service associated with the interface metric.

- **Value**   Indicates the value that is advertised into remote OSPF areas, indicating the relative distance from the OSPF router to networks summarized in the network range.

- **Status**   Indicates a status of active or not active, to indicate whether the interface is currently active.

## Neighbor

OSPF interfaces establish neighbor states with remote OSPF interfaces sharing a common IP network. For example, an OSPF interface with IP address 170.70.10.1/24 may share IP subnetwork 170.70.10.0/24 with three other OSPF interfaces: interface 170.70.10.2/24, 170.70.10.3/24, and 170.70.10.4/24. Through the exchange of Hello packets, these interfaces (and, therefore, the routers they are associated with) will learn of each other and form OSPF adjacencies, where appropriate (adjacencies are formed between OSPF interfaces and their DR and BDR). The following fields are present in the Neighbor tab:

- **IPAddr**   Indicates the IP address associated with the particular OSPF neighbor. These values will be the IP addresses of other remote router interfaces participating within the same OSPF network or subnetwork.

- **AddresLessIndex**   Indicates either the ifIndex number associated with an address-less interface, or 0 for OSPF interfaces that are configured with an IP address. This value pertains to the remote neighbor, not the local interface.

- **RtrId**   Indicates the 32-bit dotted-decimal Router ID associated with the OSPF neighbor.

- **Options**   Indicates a bit mask corresponding to the neighbor's Options field.

- **Priority**   Used during the DR and BDR election phase; these values are compared by OSPF neighbors during the exchange of Hello packets.

- **State**   Indicates the neighbor's current operational state.

- **Events**   Indicates the total number of neighbor state changes and errors that have occurred between the two OSPF neighbors.

- **LsRetransQLen**   Indicates the number of seconds that have passed between retransmitting link state information (the same advertisement) to the specified neighbor.

- **HelloSuppressed**   Indicates whether the OSPF interface will transmit Hello messages.

## Virtual Interface

All OSPF areas must border the backbone area of 0.0.0.0. If a scenario arises in which a new area must be added to the OSPF network, and a direct boundary with the backbone area is impossible, a virtual link must be established through the intermediate area to the backbone area so that the new area can receive route summary information from the backbone. You can manually configure these virtual links, or let the Accelar do it, as the Accelar is capable of automatically detecting this condition and establishing the virtual link of its own accord (if the automatic virtual link feature is enabled). The following fields are present in the Virtual Interface tab:

- **AreaID**   Indicates the OSPF Area ID associated with the interface.
- **Neighbor**   Refers to the virtual neighbor, in the case of a virtual link.
- **TransitDelay**   Indicates the amount of time associated with transmitting an LSA across the router.
- **RetransInterval**   Indicates the number of seconds that are to elapse between LSA retransmissions.

**Note**   *The RetransInterval value is also used for the exchange of Database Description packets and Link State Request packets.*

- **HelloInterval**   Indicates the amount of time (in seconds) that can pass before the interface expects to receive a Hello packet from each of its neighbors.
- **RtrDeadInterval**   Indicates how much time (in seconds) can pass without receiving a Hello packet from one of the interface's neighbors before the interface considers the neighbor to be down. This value should be some multiple of the Hello Interval. For instance, if the Hello Interval is set to 15, the Router Dead Interval can be set to 45, indicating that three Hello messages can be missed before assuming the neighbor to have failed.

**Note**   *Within a single OSPF network (a single IP network, not the entire OSPF domain), the Hello Interval must be the same value for all participating interfaces, and so must the Router Dead Interval.*

- **State**   Indicates the current operational state of the virtual link interface.
- **Events**   Indicates the number of times the OSPF interface changed states or experienced an error.
- **AuthKey**   Indicates the authentication key, if authentication is being used within an area or network.
- **AuthType**   Indicates the authentication type, represented by a numerical value. This value can be altered to change the authentication type. A value of 0 indicates no authentication, and a value of 1 indicates simple password authentication.

## Virtual Neighbor

A *virtual neighbor* is an extension of the virtual link concept (see previous section). Within an area, OSPF interfaces sharing a common network form neighbor states between them. Similarly, in a scenario where an area does not have a direct connection to the backbone area, and a virtual link must be established, the OSPF interface in question will form a virtual neighbor relationship with the interface at the remote end of the virtual link. This tab is concerned with the statistics associated with that virtual neighbor or neighbors, and contains the following fields:

- **Area**  Indicates the Area ID of the virtual neighbor.

- **RtrId**  Indicates the 32-bit dotted-decimal Router ID associated with the virtual neighbor at the remote end of the virtual link.

- **IpAddr**  Indicates the IP address associated with the particular OSPF virtual neighbor. These values are the IP addresses of other remote router interfaces participating within the same OSPF network or subnetwork at the remote end of the virtual link.

- **Options**  Indicates a bit mask corresponding to the virtual neighbor's Options field.

- **State**  Indicates the current operational state of the remote virtual neighbor.

- **Events**  Indicates the total number of neighbor state changes and errors that have occurred between the two OSPF virtual neighbors.

- **LsRetransQLen**  Indicates the number of seconds that have passed between retransmitting link state information (the same advertisement) to the specified virtual neighbor.

## Host

The Host tab can also be selected, to view the following information regarding hosts which are directly attached to the router:

- **IPAddress**  Indicates the IP address of the specific host.

- **TOS**  Indicates the Type of Service associated with the route being configured.

- **Metric**  Indicates the metric to be advertised with the host.

- **AreaID**  Indicates the OSPF area in which the host is found.

## Link State Database

The LSDB can be viewed from Device Manager by selecting the Link State Database tab from the Edit OSPF window. This window displays the contents of the Accelar's LSDB for each area in which the Accelar is participating:

- **AreaID**  Indicates the OSPF Area ID of the area from which the LSA was received.

- **Type**   Indicates the LSA type for each LSA in the LSDB. Valid types include Router Links Advertisements (type 1), Network Links Advertisements (type 2), Summary Links Advertisements (type 3), AS Summary Links Advertisements (type 4), AS External Advertisements (type 5), and NSSA Externals (type 7).

- **LSID**   Indicates the Link State ID for each entry, which varies depending on the OSPF network type. For more information regarding the relationships between the LSID and the OSPF network type, consult Chapter 31.

- **RouterID**   Indicates the Router ID of the router that originated the LSA.

- **Sequence**   Indicates the LSA sequence number, used to coordinate LSA entries to ensure they are all current.

- **Age**   Indicates how long (in seconds) the LSA has been in the LSDB.

- **Checksum**   Indicates the checksum of the LSDB.

# OSPF VLAN Configuration

Configuring OSPF within a VLAN or VLANs is essentially the same in concept as configuring an isolated router port for OSPF, the difference being that the parameters now apply to the virtual router interface associated with the specific VLAN rather than to a single physical port.

To access the VLAN OSPF parameters, select VLAN | VLANs from the main Device Manager window. Highlight the VLAN you want to associate with the OSPF interface, and then click IP. This opens the Edit VLAN_IP window. Configure an IP address (if one hasn't already been added) by clicking Insert on the IP Address tab (the tab that is open by default), and then select the OSPF tab from the Edit VLAN_IP window. Here, the OSPF interface parameters can be configured. These parameters are identical to those configured on a physical interface. For a complete description of these parameters, consult the earlier part of this chapter that discusses OSPF interface parameters.

# Viewing OSPF Information

To verify the configuration of the Accelar, you can view the current state of the OSPF interfaces, neighbors, and LSDBs through either the CLI or Device Manager.

You can view OSPF information in Device Manager by selecting Routing | IP | OSPF. This opens the Edit OSPF window, in which you can view and configure OSPF information. The Edit OSPF tabs that relate to OSPF statistics and status are described in the previous sections on OSPF configuration.

## Viewing Global OSPF Information Through the CLI

The global OSPF information can be viewed from the CLI by using the **show ip ospf info** command, whose output is displayed here:

THE ACCELAR LAYER 3 SWITCH

```
Accelar-105X# show ip ospf info
================================================================================
                               Ospf General
================================================================================
            RouterId: 0.0.0.10
           AdminStat: enabled
       VersionNumber: 2
    AreaBdrRtrStatus: false
    ASBdrRtrStatus: false
      ExternLsaCount: 639
  ExternLsaCksumSum: 20521766(0x1392326)
          TOSSupport: 0
   OriginateNewLsas: 10823
          RxNewLsas: 3863349
          TrapEnable: false
  AutoVirtLinkEnable: false
    SpfHoldDownTime: 10
```

## Viewing OSPF Interface Information

OSPF interface information can also be viewed through the CLI. This displays
information such as the interface state, the area in which the interface is configured,
and DR and BDR information. To view the OSPF interface information, the following
command syntax is used:

```
Accelar-1250# show ip ospf interface

================================================================================
                               Ospf Interface
================================================================================
INTERFACE        AREAID      ADMINST IFST METR PRIO DR/BDR     AUTHKEY AUTHTYPE
--------------------------------------------------------------------------------
150.215.52.251   0.0.0.0     enable  DR    10   1    150.215.52.251  none
                                                     150.215.52.11
151.121.43.1     0.0.0.0     enable  DR     0   1    151.121.43.1    none
                                                     151.121.43.61
160.60.10.1      0.0.0.10    enable  DR_OTHER 0 1  160.60.10.4       none
                                                     160.60.10.42
================================================================================
                            Ospf Virtual Interface
================================================================================
AREAID           NBRIPADDR        STATE    AUTHKEY  AUTHTYPE
--------------------------------------------------------------------------------
```

The IFST column indicates that the first two interfaces in the previous output are
acting as the DR for their individual networks; note that their own IP address is listed
under the DR/BDR column as the first entry (the DR). The entry below the DR entry is
the IP address of the BDR. Lastly, the authentication type is listed (no authentication is
being used in this case).

## Viewing OSPF Neighbor Information

A list of all current OSPF neighbors for all OSPF interfaces configured on the Accelar can be viewed by using the **show ip ospf neighbor** command. This command displays each OSPF neighbor for each interface, the IP address of each neighbor, and the current neighbor state:

```
Accelar-1250# sho ip ospf neighbor

===============================================================================
                              Ospf Neighbors
===============================================================================
INTERFACE        NBRROUTERID      NBRIPADDR         PRIO_STATE      RTXQLEN
-------------------------------------------------------------------------------
150.64.155.5     150.64.176.145  150.64.155.2    1     Full        0
150.64.155.5     150.64.155.3     150.64.155.3    1     Full        0
150.64.136.171  141.251.1.133    150.64.136.131  1     Full        0
150.64.136.171  141.251.1.129    150.64.136.132  2     Full        0
150.64.136.171  150.64.136.31    150.64.136.137  1     Full        0
150.64.136.171  150.64.135.3     150.64.136.135  1     Full        0
===============================================================================
                           Ospf Virtual Neighbors
===============================================================================
NBRAREAID        NBRROUTERID      NBRIPADDR         STATE      RTXQLEN
-------------------------------------------------------------------------------
```

## Viewing the Link State Database

Several ways exist to view LSDB information from the CLI. The **show ip ospf lsdb** command produces a complete listing of all LSDB information for each area the Accelar is participating in. However, you can look at more specific LSDB information, by appending arguments to the **show ip ospf lsdb** command. Table 11-2 lists the arguments that can be used.

| Argument | Result |
|---|---|
| area [*Area ID*] | LSDB information for the specified Area ID |
| lsatype (0 – 5) | LSDB listings for the specified LSA type |
| lsid [*Link State ID*] | LSDB listings for specified Link State ID |
| adv_rtr [*Router ID*] | LSDB entries for LSAs received from specified Router ID |
| detail | Detailed LSDB information |

**Table 11-2.**    *Arguments for show ip ospf lsdb* **Command**

For instance, on an Accelar that is configured to participate in multiple areas, you may want to examine the LSDB for a single area, and not all of them together. The following command would be used to view the LSDB for area 0.0.0.20:

```
Accelar# show ip ospf lsdb area 0.0.0.20

        Router Lsas in Area 0.0.0.20

LSType      LinkStateID     Adv Router      Age  Seq Nbr     Csum
---------- --------------- --------------- ---- ---------- ----------
Router      141.23.55.3    141.23.55.3     2    0x8000446a 0xf756
Router      141.23.55.213  141.23.55.213   271  0x800070f5 0xfa50
Router      141.23.55.221  141.23.55.221   1210 0x800071af 0x3edb
Router      141.23.55.225  141.23.55.225   67   0x8000662d 0xb016
Router      141.23.55.245  141.23.55.245   569  0x80004c0f 0x7e55
Router      141.23.51.31   141.23.51.31    1783 0x80003901 0x49e9
Router      141.23.51.33   141.23.51.33    1794 0x8000142e 0x8b92
Router      141.23.51.35   141.23.51.35    1331 0x80000169 0xe852
Router      141.23.51.130  141.23.51.130   1698 0x800091c0 0x8ae8
Router      141.23.51.172  141.23.51.172   1768 0x8000159c 0x41c8
Router      141.23.121.1   141.23.121.1    1790 0x800046bb 0xe2b6
Router      141.23.12.3    141.23.12.3     1232 0x80000205 0x489e
Router      141.23.81.145  141.23.81.145   325  0x800003db 0x2b9b
Router      141.251.1.129  141.251.1.129   1516 0x8000794a 0x998b
Router      141.251.1.133  141.251.1.133   407  0x800022a3 0xa65

        Network Lsas in Area 132.245.128.0

LSType      LinkStateID     Adv Router      Age  Seq Nbr     Csum
---------- --------------- --------------- ---- ---------- ----------
Network     141.23.55.3    141.23.55.3     611  0x80000bb4 0x72eb
Network     141.23.51.3    141.23.55.3     611  0x80000011 0xf8c6
Network     141.23.51.132  141.251.1.129   1525 0x80000c70 0xfb11
Network     141.23.12.5    141.23.51.33    578  0x800003ef 0x78c0

        Summary Lsas in Area 132.245.128.0
LSType      LinkStateID     Adv Router      Age  Seq Nbr     Csum
---------- --------------- --------------- ---- ---------- ----------
Summary     150.64.0.0     141.251.1.129   625  0x80007bff 0x1ab8
Summary     150.64.0.0     141.251.1.133   416  0x80000633 0xe72b
Summary     150.64.64.0    141.251.1.129   625  0x80007ca5 0xa922
Summary     150.64.64.0    141.251.1.133   416  0x80002311 0xb205
Summary     150.64.96.0    141.251.1.129   625  0x80000679 0x90a1
Summary     150.64.96.0    141.251.1.133   416  0x8000066a 0x82bc
Summary     150.64.103.0   141.251.1.129   625  0x8000067c 0xf142
```

```
        AsSummary Lsas in Area 132.245.128.0

LSType      LinkStateID     Adv Router       Age  Seq Nbr     Csum
----------  --------------- ---------------  ---- ----------  ----------
AsSummary   150.64.1.99     141.251.1.129    626  0x8000231e  0xe66e
AsSummary   150.64.1.99     141.251.1.133    417  0x800006ed  0x722e
AsSummary   150.64.13.24    141.251.1.129    626  0x800002be  0xb671
AsSummary   150.64.13.24    141.251.1.133    417  0x800002b1  0xa48e
AsSummary   150.64.13.27    141.251.1.129    626  0x800055b8  0xaa2d
AsSummary   150.64.13.27    141.251.1.133    417  0x800006ef  0xfdef
AsSummary   141.251.1.133   141.251.1.129    626  0x800006b6  0xc7ba
AsSummary   141.251.1.137   141.251.1.129    626  0x800018e2  0x75c0
AsSummary   141.251.1.137   141.251.1.133    417  0x800006d5  0x99b9
AsSummary   141.251.1.141   141.251.1.129    626  0x8000065c  0x7c50
AsSummary   141.251.1.141   141.251.1.133    417  0x80000657  0x5a75


        AS External Lsas
LSType     LinkStateID   Adv Router     E Metric ASE Fwd Addr   Age  Seq Nbr Csum
-------    ------------  ------------ - ----- ----------  ---- --- ---------
AsExternal 0.0.0.0       150.64.13.24 1 1       150.64.4.1 1072 0x8000 0507 x2c01
AsExternal 0.0.0.0       141.251.1.129 1 4      0.0.0.0    1526 0x8000 0524 0xe9b2
AsExternal 0.0.0.0       141.251.1.133 1 4      0.0.0.0    417  0x8000 0521 0xd7c3
AsExternal 10.0.0.0      141.251.1.141 1 1   150.64.103.1 1627 0x8000 02a2 0xa4e7
AsExternal 10.0.164.0 141.23.81.145 0 1      0.0.0.0    337  0x8000 03d3 0xac66
```

These arguments can be strung together, as well; for instance, to view only Router Links Advertisements (type 1 LSAs) for area 0.0.0.10, the command **show ip ospf lsdb area 0.0.0.10 lsatype 1** would be used.

## Detailed LSDB Information

The **show ip ospf lsdb detail** command displays verbose information regarding the specified entries. Again, this command may be used in conjunction with other arguments. In this example, the command is used to display verbose information regarding all Router Links Advertisements (type 1) currently in the LSDB:

```
Accelar# show ip ospf lsdb lsatype 1 detail

Router Link LSA :
Area      : 0.0.0.10 (0x84f58000)
Age       : 1216
Opt       : true (External Routing Capability)
Type      : 1
LsId      : 141.23.55.3 (0x84f58703)
Rtr       : 141.23.55.3
```

```
Seq      : -2147466134 (0x8000446a)
Csum     : 63318 (0xf756)
Len      : 132
ABR      : false
ASBR     : true
Vlnk     : false (endpoint of active Vlink)
#Lnks    : 9
[1]
Id       : 162.27.16.160 (0x84f5a3a0)
Data     : 255.255.255.224 (0xffffffe0)
Type     : (conn-to-stub-net)(Id=Subnet-Prefix, Data=Prefix-Len)
#Tos     : 0
Met      : 10
[2]
Id       : 162.27.16.128 (0x84f5a380)
Data     : 255.255.255.224 (0xffffffe0)
Type     : (conn-to-stub-net)(Id=Subnet-Prefix, Data=Prefix-Len)
#Tos     : 0
Met      : 5
```

This list has been truncated and does not display the entire list of Router Links Advertisements for the specified area.

# RIP and RIPv2 Configuration

The Accelar routing switch is also capable of supporting both the RIP and RIPv2 routing protocols. These can be configured through either Device Manager or the CLI. This section relates to RIPv1 and RIPv2 configuration specific to the Accelar; for more information regarding RIP as a protocol, consult Chapter 33.

## RIP Parameters

RIP must be configured at both the global and the interface level (this includes any virtual router interfaces associated with VLANs that must run the RIP routing protocol). When configuring the Accelar, RIPv1 or RIPv2 does not need to be specified at any sort of global level; rather, the RIP version will be specified at the interface level.

To enable RIP globally from Device Manager, simply select Routing | IP | RIP. This opens the Edit RIP window, which consists of three tabs: Globals, Interface Status, and Interface Configuration. These tabs are discussed in the following sections. The Globals tab, which is displayed by default, is where RIP is enabled at the global level. This is accomplished by clicking Enable and then clicking Apply.

Alternately, RIP can be enabled globally through the CLI, by issuing the command **config ip rip enable**.

# Port-Level RIP Configuration

Port-level RIP configuration is accomplished in the Interface Configuration tab. The following parameters can be configured:

- **Enable**  Enables and disables RIP on the selected interface.

- **Supply**  Indicates whether RIP updates will be supplied by the selected interface. If set to false, no RIP updates will be advertised from the interface.

- **Listen**  Indicates whether RIP updates will be listened for on the selected interface. If set to false, the interface will not accept RIP updates.

- **Poison**  Causes the RIP interface to implement Poison Reverse as a means of preventing routes from being advertised back out the interface they were received on. By default, Accelar RIP interfaces use Split Horizon.

- **AdvertiseDefaultRoute**  Indicates whether a default route of 0.0.0.0 will be advertised. A default route may be introduced into the local routing table, but it may or may not be necessary to advertise the default route into the rest of the network. If the route 0.0.0.0 should be propagated throughout the network, set this option to true.

> **Note**  *Configuring a static default route does not automatically cause it to be advertised; this option must be set for remote RIP routers to learn of the default route.*

- **AcceptDefaultRoute**  Specifies whether the RIP interface will accept a default route as part of its received routing advertisements. By setting this to false, any default route received will not be placed in the routing table.

- **TriggeredUpdateEnable**  Indicates whether the RIP interface will use triggered updates—issuing RIP updates in response to new information (such as a new route)—rather than waiting until the specified update time. This allows for faster convergence.

- **AutoAggregateEnable**  Indicates whether the interface will automatically aggregate subnet information when advertising one IP network number to another, separate one. For example, with Auto Aggregate enabled, a RIP interface configured for IP network 170.70.10.0/24 would advertise learned networks 160.60.10.0, 160.60.20.0, 160.60.30.0, and 160.60.40.0 simply as 160.60.0.0. This parameter has relevance to RIPv2 only, because RIPv1 automatically aggregates this information.

- **AdvertiseWhenDown**  Indicates whether the Layer 3 entity should be informed if a state change occurs in the port or VLAN associated with the RIP interface. This means that if the option is set to true (advertise when down) and the isolated router port or VLAN associated with the virtual router port (RIP interface) goes down (the isolated router port goes down, or all ports in the VLAN go down), then the virtual router port will still be considered up, and the associated route will still be advertised.

## Configuring RIP Port Parameters Through the CLI

RIP port-level parameters can also be configured through the CLI, using the **config** command. For example, you use the following commands to configure a RIP interface (associated with VLAN 10) to both supply and listen for RIP updates; to use Poison Reverse rather than the Split Horizon algorithm; to advertise a default route but not accept them; to utilize triggered updates; to automatically aggregate subnetworks when advertising to a nonlocal IP network number; and to not advertise the interface when the physical ports have gone down:

```
Accelar-105X# config vlan 10 ip rip enable
Accelar-105X# config vlan 10 ip rip supply enable
Accelar-105X# config vlan 10 ip rip listen enable
Accelar-105X# config vlan 10 ip rip poison enable
Accelar-105X# config vlan 10 ip rip default-supply enable
Accelar-105X# config vlan 10 ip rip default-listen disable
Accelar-105X# config vlan 10 ip rip trigger enable
Accelar-105X# config vlan 10 ip rip auto-aggr enable
Accelar-105X# config vlan 10 ip rip advertise-when-down disable
```

# RIP and RIPv2 Status

Once configured and enabled on the appropriate port, the RIP status and statistics can also be viewed through Device Manager. These statistics are viewed by selecting Routing | IP | RIP from the main Device Manager window. This opens the Edit RIP window, which includes the Global tab, the Interface Status tab, and the Interface Configuration tab. These tabs offer the statistics described in the following sections.

## Global RIP Status

Global RIP status refers the RIP status of the entire Accelar. This includes such information as the operational status of the existing RIP interfaces and global timer information:

- **Operation**   Indicates the current operational status of all RIP interfaces; RIP must be enabled globally for specific RIP interfaces to function.

- **UpdateTime**   Indicates the frequency with which RIP updates are sent. By default, this value is 30 seconds.

- **RouteChanges**   Indicates the number of times the IP routing table has undergone a change due to newly learned RIP route information. This field does not increment with the normal refreshing of existing routes.

- **Queries**   Indicates the number of responses sent to RIP queries.

- **HoldDownTime**   Indicates a global RIP Hold Down Time (in seconds).

## Observing the Global Status from the CLI

The same global RIP information specified via Device Manager can be obtained through the CLI by using the **show ip rip** command:

```
Accelar-105X# show ip rip info

================================================================================
                              Rip Global
================================================================================
         Rip : Enabled
 Update Time : 30
HoldDown Time : 120
Route Changes : 1
     Queries : 32
      Domain : 0
```

## Interface Status

The Interface Status tab offers information regarding specific, individual RIP interfaces. This includes such information as the IP address of each RIP interface, and the number of RIP updates sent.

- **Address**  Indicates the IP address associated with a particular RIP interface.
- **RcvBadPackets**  Indicates the number of RIP packets received that were discarded by the interface, for whatever reason, such as an invalid RIP version number.
- **RcvBadRoutes**  Indicates the total number of routes received that arrived in valid RIP updates, but that were not added into the routing table due to an incorrect address type or a metric of infinity (16).
- **SentUpdates**  Indicates the total number of triggered RIP updates issued from the specified RIP interface. This counter increments only when a triggered update is sent, and does not increment when a normally scheduled RIP update is sent.

## Examining the RIP Interface Status Through the CLI

The RIP interface status can also be obtained through the CLI, using the **show ip rip** command. For example:

```
Accelar-105X# show ip rip interfaces

================================================================================
                              Rip Interface
================================================================================
IP_ADDR          RIP_ENABLE      SEND              RECEIVE
--------------------------------------------------------------------------------
```

```
160.60.15.218     true          ripVersion1        rip1OrRip2
2.2.2.2           true          ripVersion1        rip1
```

## Interface Configuration

Specific RIP interface parameters can be configured from the Interface Configuration tab. This includes such information as the IP address of the interface, the authentication type (if any), and the type of RIP update to send or receive. This last parameter is important, because it specifies the RIP version (RIPv1 or RIPv2).

- **Address**   Indicates the IP address of the RIP interface.
- **Domain**   Inserted into the Routing Domain field of each RIP packet sent on this interface.
- **AuthType**   Specifies whether simple password authentication will be used for the interface. If authentication is to be used, all RIP interfaces within a common IP network must use the same case-sensitive, simple password.
- **AuthKey**   Indicates both the password used to authenticate incoming RIP packets and the key that is inserted into outgoing RIP packets, if authentication is being used. This simple password must be consistent within a common IP network. If a RIP interface configured for authentication receives route information bearing a password that does not match its own, the packet will be discarded.

**TYPE OF RIP UPDATE TO SEND**   This parameter indicates the version of RIP updates to be sent; this specifies the version of RIP that will run on the interface:

- **doNotSend**   No updates of either RIP version type will be sent.
- **ripVersion1**   RIPv1 packets will be sent to an all-hosts IP broadcast address for the appropriate network or subnetwork.
- **rip1Compatible**   RIPv2 updates will be broadcast rather than multicast, and will aggregate route information as described in RFC 1058.
- **ripVersion2**   RIPv2 updates will be multicast to the IP group address 224.0.0.9.

**TYPE OF RIP UPDATE TO RECEIVE**   This parameter indicates the type of RIP update the interface expects to receive (RIPv1, RIPv2, or either):

- **rip1**   RIPv1 updates addressed to an all-hosts broadcast for the network or subnetwork will be accepted by the interface.
- **rip2**   RIPv2 updates addressed to the multicast group address 224.0.0.9 or the broadcast address, if sent from a rip1Compatible interface (see the section "Type of RIP Update to Send"), will be accepted by the interface.
- **rip1OrRip2**   Updates of either RIP version will be accepted by the interface.

## Configuring RIP Interface Parameters Through the CLI

The interface-specific RIP parameters can also be configured through the CLI, using the **config** command. For example, the following command would be used to configure the virtual router interface associated with VLAN 10 with IP address 170.70.10.1/24, with a simple password authentication type using a password of rippy, configured to send RIPv2 updates but receive either RIPv2 or RIPv1 updates:

```
Accelar# config vlan 10 ip create 170.70.10.1/24
Accelar# config ip rip send 170.70.10.1 mode rip2
Accelar# config ip rip receive 170.70.10.1 mode rip1-or-rip2
```

## Running RIP on a VLAN Basis

Configuring RIP at the VLAN level is essentially the same as configuring it at the interface level, because the RIP VLAN configuration essentially relates to the virtual router interface associated with that VLAN. The primary difference is in how the parameters are configured.

To configure RIP at the VLAN level, select VLAN | VLANs from the main Device Manager window, which opens the Edit VLANs window. From the Edit VLANs window, highlight the VLAN on which you want to configure RIP, and then click IP. This opens the Edit VLAN_IP window. Select the RIP tab to open a list of RIP interface parameters. These are the same parameters that are configured at the port level by selecting the port and then selecting the RIP tab from the Edit Ports window.

# Configuring a Brouter Port

The concept of the brouter port was introduced with system software version 2.0. A *brouter port* is an interface that performs both IP routing and bridging simultaneously. This is similar to the Nortel Networks router that is configured to route IP, with bridging services also configured.

## Brouter Port Concepts

The result of configuring an Accelar brouter port is that all IP traffic will be routed, and all other traffic will be bridged. Bridged traffic in this case is subject to the rules of Spanning Tree, while the IP traffic is not. A brouter port differs conceptually from an isolated router port in that isolated router ports do not have bridging capability.

### Configuration Requirements for the Brouter Port

To configure a brouter port, a single-port, IP protocol-based VLAN must be created in Spanning Tree Group 0 (prior to code version 2.0, STG 0 does not exist). STG 0 indicates no spanning tree, providing a separate spanning tree instance for the IP portion of the interface, which should not block even if the bridging portion of the interface is blocking. The interface can then be associated with another STG, in which the bridging services will participate.

Once the brouter port is created in STG 0, the interface can be associated with other VLANs for bridging purposes. For example, a brouter port could be configured to route IP between two VLANs and bridge all other traffic between the same two VLANs (see Figure 11-7).

In this diagram, the brouter port is part of STG 0 and also STG 2, which encompasses both VLAN 10 and VLAN 100. However, the brouter port may be active in more than one STG (aside from STG 0) if the port is configured to tag. Since the brouter port is technically a single-port member of a protocol-based VLAN, it has a VLAN ID associated with it that may be used for tagging purposes. If the brouter port is configured to tag, it may participate in multiple STGs.

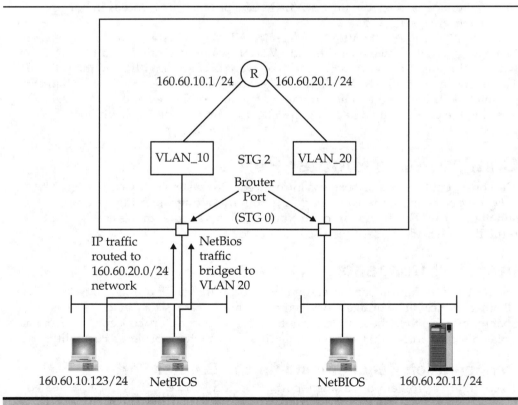

**Figure 11-7.** *Brouter port used to route IP, and bridge all other traffic, between VLANs*

*As of the time of publication, brouter ports support IP only and cannot be configured with IPX. Brouter ports must be single ports only, and can not aggregate ports together using MultiLink Trunking (MLT).*

## Configuring a Brouter Port Through Device Manager

Configuring a brouter port through Device Manager is very similar to creating a VLAN, with a few important differences. The first step to create the VLAN that will contain the brouter port, because it is technically a single-port VLAN, not an isolated router port. To do this, select VLAN | VLANs from the main Device Manager window. This opens the Edit VLANs window. Select Insert to add the new VLAN.

Once the Insert Basic window is open, change the VLAN type from the default of port-based to protocol-based, and select the protocol IP. (This is the default protocol for protocol-based VLANs.) Alter the Spanning Tree Group from the default of 1 to STG 0.

 *A brouter port must be configured in STG 0 so that IP traffic will not be blocked if the bridging portion of the interface transitions into a blocking state.*

Next, alter each port's membership status in the Dynamic Membership portion of the window (see Figure 11-8). By default, all ports are listed as Potential members (yellow) of a protocol-based VLAN. Change this so that the single brouter port is Always a member (green), and all other ports are Never members (red).

Once this is complete, the brouter port can be associated with other STGs, as necessary.

## Configuring a Brouter Port Through the CLI

A brouter port can also be configured through the CLI. The command structure to do this is a bit different from creating a VLAN and adding a single port to it, but the result is the same. To configure a brouter port through the CLI, the following command syntax is used:

config ethernet [*port*] ip create-brouter [*ip address/mask*] [*VID*]

For example:

```
Accelar# config ethernet 3/10 ip create-brouter 170.70.10.1/24 10
```

This command configures port 3/1 as a brouter port with an IP address of 170.70.10.1, a mask of 255.255.255.0, and a VLAN ID of 10 (for 802.1Q frame-tagging purposes). Here, an IP protocol-based VLAN is not specified, nor is STG 0 specified; these are a function of the **ip create-brouter** portion of the command and will be configured automatically when the command is executed.

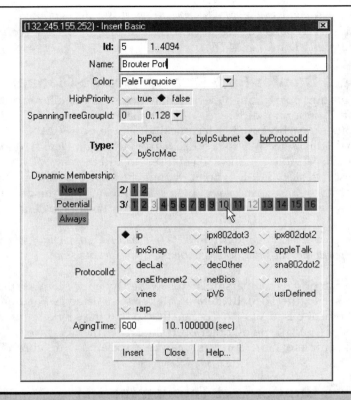

**Figure 11-8.**    *VLAN configuration for a brouter port*

# IP Policies

The Accelar is capable of supporting both Accept and Announce IP policies, for both RIP and OSPF. These IP policies are created by first forming what are called router and network lists, then applying those lists to the different policies as they are created.

## Router and Network Lists

Two preliminary steps that must be taken prior to configuring specific Accept or Announce Policies are the creation of router and network lists, which consist of specific router interfaces and specific networks or ranges of networks. The creation of these lists is accomplished by selecting Routing | IP | IP Policy from the main Device Manager window, which opens the Edit Announce window (although Accept Policies are also configured from this window; see Figure 11-9). The creation of the individual entries and lists are accomplished from the following tabs:

- **Interface/Router Addresses** These entries indicate specific IP interfaces that exist on the local Accelar. The entries in this list constitute a compilation of all router interfaces that may have Announce or Accept Policies associated with them. Creating these entries enables these interfaces to be compiled into lists (described next). These interfaces will be either isolated router ports or a virtual router interface associated with a VLAN.

- **Interface/Router Lists** Once individual IP interfaces have been configured in the Interface/Router Addresses tab, these interfaces can be grouped into lists. This enables the user to apply a single policy to multiple interfaces simultaneously, rather than individually.

- **Network Addresses** These entries indicate addresses or address ranges that are relevant to the specific policies that are being created. For instance, to create an Accept Policy that specifies that any incoming route information for network 160.60.10.0/24 should be ignored, network 160.60.10.0 first needs to be added as a network address, so that it can be selected later when actually configuring the policy.

- **Network Lists** As with interface/router lists, a network list is a compilation of network addresses and/or network ranges to which a specific policy applies. For example, if an interface is to be configured with an Accept Policy to ignore any incoming route information for networks 160.60.10.0/24, 160.100.0.0/16, and 160.60.121.0/24, then each of these addresses can be added in the Network Addresses tab, enabling these three networks to be placed in a single list. That list can then be applied to the policy, so that three individual policies do not need to be created.

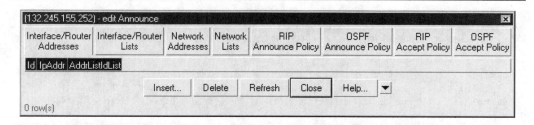

**Figure 11-9.** *The Edit Announce window*

## Compiling and Using Lists

As an example of how such policies would be created, consider an Accelar that has two IP interfaces, both of which are to be configured with an Accept Policy indicating that if any route information is received for three specific networks, it should be ignored. To accomplish this, the following steps are taken:

1. In the Interface/Router Addresses tab, create the two IP interfaces to which the policy will be applied.

2. In the Interface/Router Lists tab, create a list that includes both IP interfaces.

3. In the Network Addresses tab, create the three networks that are to be ignored.

4. In the Networks Lists tab, create a list that includes all three networks added in the Network Addresses tab.

These steps do not, in and of themselves, create the Accept Policy; to do this, the actual policy must be created by using either the RIP Accept Policy tab or the OSPF Accept Policy tab, depending on the routing protocol being used. However, these lists will be referenced when creating these policies, so that, in this case, if the policy were a RIP Accept Policy, when the Accept Policy is being created, the Interface/Router list would be selected as the RIP Interface List ID (indicating that these are the interfaces to which the policy will be applied), and the network list would be selected as the Exact Net List ID (indicating that the three specified networks will be matched by the policy). Alternately, if ranges of networks were specified rather than specific networks, the network list can be selected as the Range Net List ID. More information regarding the configuration of the policy itself is covered later in this section.

## Configuring Router/Interface Address Lists Through the CLI

Router/interface address lists can be configured through either the CLI or Device Manager. To do this, the specific address list can be created using the **config** command:

```
Accelar-1250# config ip policy addrlist 10 create
```

This command creates an empty list with an ID of 10. Then, individual addresses can be added to the existing list, also using the **config** command:

```
Accelar-1250# config ip policy addrlist 10 add-address 170.70.10.0/24
Accelar-1250# config ip policy addrlist 10 add-address 170.70.20.0/24
Accelar-1250# config ip policy addrlist 10 add-address 180.80.10.0/24
```

While creating the list, if an erroneous address is entered, it can be removed from the CLI by means of the following command:

```
Accelar-1250# config ip policy addrlist 10 remove-address 180.80.10.0/24
```

## Configuring Network Lists Through the CLI

Network lists can be created in a similar fashion to interface address lists from the CLI, using the following command structure:

```
Accelar-1250# config ip policy netlist 10 create
```

After the list has been created, the individual networks can be added to the list. The following are two specific networks:

```
Accelar-1250# config ip policy netlist 10 add-network 160.60.10.0/24
Accelar-1250# config ip policy netlist 10 add-network 160.60.122.0/24
```

Next is a range of networks that includes a range of subnets between .128 and .135, inclusive, on the 170.70.0.0 network:

```
Accelar-1250# config ip policy netlist 10 add-network 170.70.128.0/21
```

Lastly, an erroneous entry is removed:

```
Accelar-1250# config ip policy netlist 10 remove-network 160.60.10.0/24
```

# OSPF Accept Policies

After you create the lists described in the preceding sections, you can configure the actual policies and apply them to the Accelar. The first policy type that is examined here are OSPF Accept Policies. These policies can be created through either Device Manager or the CLI. To create an OSPF Accept Policy through Device Manager, select Routing | IP | IP Policy to open the Edit Announce window. Then, assuming the appropriate lists have been created, select the OSPF Accept Policy tab. By default, this tab contains no entries. Configure the policy by clicking Insert, which opens the Insert OSPF Accept Policy window (see Figure 11-10).

Here, the actual OSPF Accept Policy is created, as detailed in the following section.

## Adding an OSPF Accept Policy

To add the OSPF Accept Policy through Device Manager, the following fields and parameters apply:

- **Id**  Uniquely identifies each particular OSPF Accept Policy entry.
- **Name**  Specifies a user-defined name for the policy.

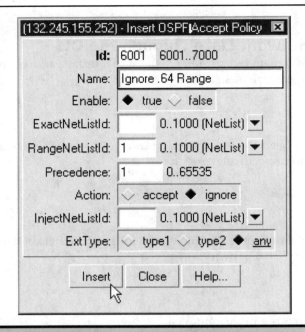

**Figure 11-10.**   *The Insert OSPF Accept Policy window*

- **Enable**   Indicates the current operational state of the policy; in other words, whether or not the specified policy is currently being applied.

- **ExactNetListId**   Indicates the List ID for a list of exact network matches. For example, in a network where all addresses are class B addresses utilizing a 24-bit subnet mask, the entry 160.60.10.0/24 would be considered an exact entry, because it only specifies subnet .10 of the 160.60.0.0 network.

- **RangeNetListId**   Indicates the List ID for a specific range of networks. For example, in a network where all addresses are class B addresses utilizing a 24-bit subnet mask, the entry 160.60.128.0/21 would be considered a range entry, because a range of subnets (.128 to .135, inclusive) are covered by the summary mask and are considered a match, whereas the remaining subnets that fall outside the 21-bit masked range are not considered a match.

- **Precedence**   Enables the administrator to prioritize the order in which the policies are applied, because a specific route may match multiple policy rules. For instance, if one policy is configured to match subnet .10 on the 160.60.0.0

network (with a match criteria of exact), with an action stating that the route should be accepted, and the second policy is configured to drop all routes, then the first policy rule must be implemented first; otherwise, the 160.60.10.0/24 route will be dropped before the Accelar has a chance to apply the second policy (which matches it and states that the route should be accepted). A higher precedence in this case indicates the rule will be examined first. In the event of a tie, the Policy ID is used (the higher value is prioritized).

- **Action**    Specifies what action should be taken if an incoming route matches the policy (accept or ignore).

- **InjectNetListId**    Indicates the List ID of the network list associated with the policy, and injects the route information in the network list into the route table. For example, an OSPF router that is acting as an ASBR may receive route information from the external AS advertising all subnets of the network number 150.50.0.0/24. Rather than advertise each of these subnets individually, a network list aggregates all subnets of the 150.50.0.0/24 network into a single entry of 150.50.0.0. This allows the ASBR to advertise all subnets with a single entry. If the List ID is set to 0, then all incoming routes will be advertised as they normally would, specifying each subnet.

- **ExtType**    Refers to the type of external route that will be considered for this policy:

    **Type 1**    Routes that are connected locally to the ASBR. For example, if an ASBR borders an OSPF domain and a RIP domain, and the ASBR's local RIP interface is configured for network 150.50.10.0/24, then network 150.50.10.0/24 is considered an external type 1 route for purposes of advertising the route information back into the OSPF domain.

    **Type 2**    Routes that are not connected locally to the ASBR. For example, if an ASBR borders an OSPF domain and a RIP domain, and the ASBR's local RIP interface is configured for network 150.50.10.0/24, and this interface has received route information for remote network 150.60.16.0/24, which is two hops away in the RIP domain, then network 150.60.16.0/24 is considered an external type 2 route.

    **Any**    Indicates that either external route type will be considered for this policy.

## Configuring an OSPF Accept Policy Through the CLI

OSPF Accept Policies can be created through the CLI, using the **config** command. The command syntax is as follows:

```
Accelar-1250# config ip policy ospf accept 6001 create
```

The value of 6001 refers to the specific Accept Policy ID. The range for this value is between 6001 and 7000, so this is the first policy being configured.

Now, a series of exact network matches will be specified; these networks have been compiled under Network List ID 10:

```
Accelar-1250# config ip policy ospf accept 6001 exact-net-list 10
```

Next, the external metric type that will be considered a match for this policy is defined as type 2. In this case, only type 2 external routes will be considered:

```
Accelar-1250# config ip policy ospf accept 6001 ext-metric-type type2
```

In this example, incoming routes that match this policy will have a series of networks injected into the route advertisement. These networks are defined in Network List ID 20. So, in this case, you want to set the action to be Accept, and then instruct the policy to inject the routes from network list 20:

```
Accelar-1250# config ip policy ospf accept 6002 action accept
Accelar-1250# config ip policy ospf accept 6001 inject-net-list 20
```

A precedence of 1 is assigned to this OSPF Accept Policy, and the policy itself is enabled:

```
Accelar-1250# config ip policy ospf accept 6001 precedence 1
Accelar-1250# config ip policy ospf accept 6001 enable
```

The Accept Policy configuration can then be verified using the **show** command:

```
Accelar-1250# show ip policy ospf accept info
================================================================================
                                   Policy Ospf Accept Info
================================================================================
PID  NAME                         ENABLE PREC  ACTION    OSPFTYPE
--------------------------------------------------------------------------------
6001 POLICY-6001                  true   1     accept    type2
```

## OSPF Announce Policies

OSPF Announce Policies are configured on Accelar routing switches acting in the capacity of an ASBR; announce Policies may be used to either promote or suppress the advertisement of specific route information, as well as to alter aspects of the route information being advertised, such as route metrics.

## Creating an OSPF Announce Policy

OSPF Announce Policies can be configured on the Accelar, through either the CLI or Device Manager. To configure an Announce Policy through Device Manager, select Routing | IP | IP Policy from the main Device Manager window. This opens the Edit Announce window (although both Announce and Accept Policies can be created from this window), where the individual policies can be created. To create the policy, select the OSPF Announce Policy tab and click Insert. This opens the Insert OSPF Announce Policy window (see Figure 11-11). The following parameters apply:

- **Id**   Uniquely identifies the OSPF Announce Policy.
- **Name**   Specifies a user-assigned name that identifies the specific OSPF policy.
- **Enable**   Indicates whether the configured policy is currently active.

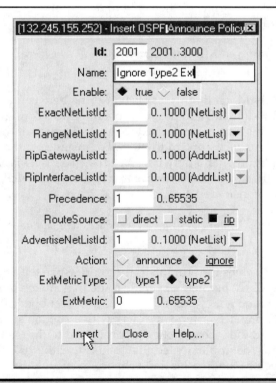

**Figure 11-11.**   *The Insert OSPF Announce Policy window*

THE ACCELAR LAYER 3 SWITCH

- **ExactNetListId**   Indicates the List ID for a list of exact network matches. For example, in a network where all addresses are class B addresses utilizing a 24-bit subnet mask, the entry 160.60.10.0/24 would be considered an exact entry, since it only specifies subnet .10 of the 160.60.0.0 network.

- **RangeNetListId**   Indicates the List ID for a list of network ranges. For example, in a network where all addresses are class B addresses utilizing a 24-bit subnet mask, the entry 160.60.64.0/21 would be considered a range entry, since the subnet range .64-.71, inclusive, is considered a match, whereas the remaining subnets that fall outside the 21-bit masked range are not considered a match.

- **RipGatewayListId**   If RIP is used as a route source, then RIP-sourced routes can be compared against the RIP gateways configured in the specified RIP Gateway List ID. For example, if a specific policy is configured that specifies RIP Gateway List ID 10, and the RIP gateway list configured with ID 10 contains the IP address for RIP interfaces A, B, and C, then only route information sourced from interfaces A, B, and C will be considered a match for the policy.

> **Note**   *A value of 0 indicates all RIP-sourced routes will be considered.*

- **RipInterfaceListId**   If the Accelar is bordering between the OSPF domain and an external RIP domain, and has multiple interfaces configured within that RIP domain, then this parameter is used to indicate which of those RIP interfaces should have the policy applied to them. For instance, if the Accelar has two RIP interfaces configured, and only interface 160.60.10.1/24 is specified in the RIP interface list, then only that interface is considered a match, whereas the other interface is not considered a match.

> **Note**   *An empty interface list indicates that all interfaces will be considered.*

- **Precedence**   Enables the administrator to prioritize the order in which the policies are applied, because a specific route may match multiple policy rules. For instance, if one policy is configured to match subnet .10 on the 160.60.0.0 network (with a match criteria of exact), with an action stating the route should be accepted, and the second policy is configured to drop all routes, then the first policy rule must be implemented first; otherwise, the 160.60.10.0/24 route will be dropped before the Accelar has a chance to apply the second policy (which matches it and states the route should be accepted). A higher precedence in this case indicates the rule will be examined first. In the event of a tie, the Policy ID is used (the higher value is prioritized).

- **Route Source**   Identifies which types of routes will be considered by the policy. More than one type of route can be configured. Route sources that are not specified are not considered by the policy. The following route sources may be considered:

    **Direct**   A route that is configured on one of the Accelar's local interfaces (an external type 1 route).

    **Static**   A route that is configured statically on the local Accelar and has not been learned through any dynamic routing protocol.

    **Rip**   Indicates any RIPv1 or RIPv2 routes.

- **AdvertiseNetListId**   Applies only when the action is set to Announce; indicates the total number of entries configured in the advertise net list that the policy is configured with. This is used to advertise networks that are different than what may actually be in the routing table, which means that if the policy action is set to Announce, and an incoming route matches this policy, then the Accelar advertises the networks listed in the AdvertiseNetList.

- **Action**   Specifies the action that will be applied to routes matching the policy. For example, if the policy is configured to look for an exact match for network 150.50.10.0/24, with an action of Drop, then all incoming route advertisements for 150.50.10.0 will be dropped.

- **ExtMetricType**   Refers to the type of external route that will be considered by this policy:

    **Type 1**   Routes that are connected locally to the ASBR. For example, if an ASBR borders an OSPF domain and a RIP domain, and the ASBR's local RIP interface is configured for network 150.50.10.0/24, then network 150.50.10.0/24 is considered an external type 1 route for purposes of advertising the route information back into the OSPF domain.

    **Type 2**   Routes that are not connected locally to the ASBR. For example, if an ASBR borders an OSPF domain and a RIP domain, and the ASBR's local RIP interface is configured for network 150.50.10.0/24, and this interface has received route information for remote network 150.60.16.0/24, which is two hops away in the RIP domain, then network 150.60.16.0/24 is considered an external type 2 route.

- **ExtMetric**   Indicates the metric that will be associated with an announced external route. For example, if two ASBRs have one interface in the OSPF domain, and one interface in a common RIP domain, and each Accelar is receiving the same RIP route from a remote source, then both ASBRs advertise the route into the OSPF domain as an external type 2 route. One path could be favored over another by configuring one Accelar to attach a more desirable metric to the RIP route. An external metric of 0 indicates that the actual route metric should be used.

**Note**   *This parameter has meaning only if the action of the policy is set to Announce.*

## Configuring an OSPF Announce Policy Through the CLI

OSPF Announce Policies can be created through the CLI, as well. In this example, an Announce Policy is created indicating that certain RIP-sourced routes will be announced into the OSPF domain with an altered metric. First, the policy itself is created:

```
Accelar-1250# config ip policy ospf announce 2001 create
```

The value of 2001 indicates the specific Announce Policy ID; the range is from 2001 to 3000, so this is the first Announce Policy to be created.

Next, the policy is configured so that only RIP-sourced routes are considered:

```
Accelar-1250# config ip policy ospf announce 2001 add-route-source rip
```

Once this is accomplished, the policy is further narrowed by specifying that only certain external RIP networks are considered a match by the policy. These networks are compiled under network list 10:

```
Accelar-1250# config ip policy ospf announce 2001 exact-netlist 10
```

Next, the policy is configured so that only external type 2 metrics are considered by the policy, and only routes that originate from a list of specified RIP gateways are considered. The addresses associated with these RIP gateways are defined in router/interface address list 10:

```
Accelar-1250# config ip policy ospf announce 2001 ext-metric-type type2
Accelar-1250# config ip policy ospf announce 2001 rip-gateway-list 10
```

Lastly, the Announce Policy is configured with an action of Announce, indicating the routes will in fact be advertised by the Accelar. However, an external metric of 5 is configured, indicating the new metric for external routes matching this policy would be set to 5 when being advertised. The policy is then enabled:

```
Accelar-1250# config ip policy ospf announce 2001 action announce
Accelar-1250# config ip policy ospf announce 2001 ext-metric 5
Accelar-1250# config ip policy ospf announce 2001 enable
```

# RIP and RIPv2 Accept Policies

RIP policies are configured using router/interface address lists as well as network lists, as is the case with OSPF policies. Once these lists are assembled, the actual policies can be created. To configure a RIP Accept Policy, select Routing | IP | IP Policy from the main Device Manager window. This opens the Edit Announce window, where the RIP Accept Policy tab can be selected. Then, click Insert to open the Insert RIP Accept Policy window (see Figure 11-12), in which the actual policy is created. The parameters described in the following sections apply.

## Creating a RIP Accept Policy

From the Insert RIP Accept Policy window, the following parameters can be configured:

- **Id**   Indicates a value that uniquely identifies the RIP Accept Policy.
- **Name**   Indicates a user-assigned name that identifies the policy.
- **Enable**   Indicates the operational state of the policy (in other words, whether or not it's being used).
- **ExactNetListId**   Indicates the List ID for a list of exact network matches. For example, in a network where all addresses are class B addresses utilizing a

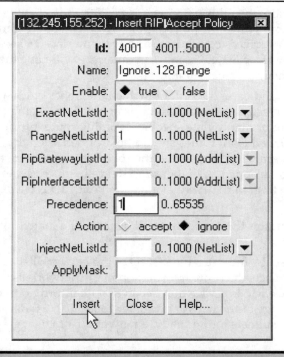

**Figure 11-12.**   *The RIP Accept Policy window*

24-bit subnet mask, the entry 160.60.10.0/24 would be considered an exact entry, since it only specifies subnet .10 of the 160.60.0.0 network.

- **RangeNetListId**   Indicates the List ID for a list of network ranges. For example, in a network where all addresses are class B addresses utilizing a 24-bit subnet mask, the entry 160.60.16.0/22 is considered a range entry, since subnets .16-.19, inclusive, are considered a match, whereas the remaining subnets that fall outside the 22-bit masked range aren't considered a match.

- **RipGatewayListId**   If RIP is used as a route source, then RIP-sourced routes can be compared against the RIP gateways configured in the specified RIP Gateway List ID. For example, if a specific policy is configured that specifies RIP Gateway List ID 10, and the RIP gateway list configured with ID 10 contains the IP address for RIP interfaces A, B, and C, then only route information sourced from interfaces A, B, and C will be considered a match for the policy.

**Note**   *A value of 0 indicates that all RIP-sourced routes will be considered.*

- **RipInterfaceListId**   If the Accelar has multiple interfaces configured within the RIP domain, then this parameter is used to indicate which of those RIP interfaces should have the policy applied to them. For instance, if the Accelar has two RIP interfaces configured, and only interface 160.60.10.1/24 is specified in the RIP interface list, then only that interface will have the policy applied, while the other interface will not.

- **Precedence**   Indicates the order in which the policy rules will be applied; this is useful for specifying the order, for example, of matching criteria. If several policies admit or manipulate specific incoming route information, and the last policy indicates that all routes should be dropped, then the last drop policy must be implemented last, so that the specified routes can be checked for *before* the routes are dropped. A higher precedence in this case indicates the rule will be examined first. In the event of a tie, the Policy ID is used (the higher value is prioritized).

- **Action**   Indicates the action that will be taken if a match condition for the policy is found.

- **InjectNetListId**   Indicates the List ID of the network list associated with the policy, and injects the route information in the network list into the route table. For example, a RIP interface may receive route information that is all within the subnet range of the network number 150.50.0.0/24. Rather than advertise each of these subnets individually, a network list may aggregate all subnets of the 150.50.0.0/24 network into a single entry of 150.50.0.0. If the List ID is set to 0, then all incoming routes will be advertised as they normally would, specifying each subnet.

■ **ApplyMask**   Allows a specific subnet mask to be applied to an incoming route that matches the policy criteria. This can be useful in a RIPv1 network to allow for variable-length subnet masking (VLSM); since RIPv1 does not normally include the subnet mask information, a RIPv1 interface configured in network 150.50.128.0/19, receiving route information from a remote RIPv1 router with an interface configured in network 150.50.10.0/24, will apply its own mask to the incoming route information for network 150.50.10.0/24, and will incorrectly interpret the route as being in subnet 0, because none of the subnet bits fall within the range of the 19-bit mask. The Apply Mask option can be used to apply a 24-bit mask to incoming routes for the 150.50.10.0 network.

## Configuring a RIP Accept Policy Through the CLI

In this example, a RIP Accept Policy is created to apply subnet mask information to incoming RIPv1 routes. First, the policy is created using the following syntax:

```
Accelar-1250# config ip policy rip accept 4001 create
```

The value of 4001 indicates the Accept Policy ID; the range for this ID is 4001 to 5000, so this is the first policy being created.

Next, the policy is configured so that a list of networks that are compiled under network list 10 are considered matches by the policy:

```
Accelar-1250# config ip policy rip accept 4001 exact-netlist 10
```

Since the routes will not be discarded, they will simply have subnet mask information added to them, an action of Accept is configured. Lastly, the subnet mask that will be inserted is specified, and then the policy itself is enabled:

```
Accelar-1250# config ip policy rip accept 4001 action accept
Accelar-1250# config ip policy rip accept 4001 apply-mask 255.255.255.0
Accelar-1250# config ip policy rip accept 4001 enable
```

## Creating a RIP Announce Policy

Creating a RIP Announce Policy through Device Manager is accomplished by selecting Routing | IP | IP Policy from the main Device Manager window, selecting the RIP Announce Policy tab, and then clicking Insert to add the new policy. This opens the Insert RIP Announce Policy window (see Figure 11-13). Here, the following parameters can be configured:

THE ACCELAR LAYER 3 SWITCH

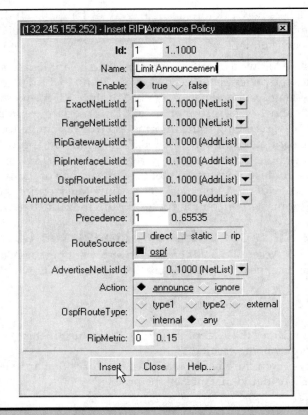

**Figure 11-13.**    *The Insert RIP Announce Policy window*

- **Id**    Uniquely identifies the RIP Announce Policy.
- **Name**    Indicates a user-assigned name that identifies the policy.
- **Enable**    Indicates the operational state of the policy (in other words, whether it's being used or not).
- **ExactNetListId**    Indicates the List ID for a list of exact network matches. For example, in a network where all addresses are class B addresses utilizing a 24-bit subnet mask, the entry 160.60.10.0/24 is considered an exact entry, since it only specifies subnet .10 of the 160.60.0.0 network.
- **RangeNetListId**    Indicates the List ID for a list of network ranges. For example, in a network where all addresses are class B addresses utilizing a

24-bit subnet mask, the entry 160.60.192.0/22 is considered a range entry, since subnets .192–.195, inclusive, are considered a match, whereas the remaining subnets that fall outside the 22-bit masked range are not considered a match.

- **RipGatewayListId**   If RIP is used as a route source, then RIP-sourced routes can be compared against the RIP gateways configured here. For example, if a specific policy is configured that specifies RIP Gateway List ID 10, and the RIP gateway list configured with ID 10 contains the IP address for RIP interfaces A, B, and C, then only route information sourced from interfaces A, B, and C will be considered a match for the policy.

**Note**   *A value of 0 indicates that all RIP-sourced routes will be considered.*

- **RipInterfaceListId**   If the Accelar has multiple interfaces configured within the RIP domain, then this parameter is used to indicate which of those RIP interfaces should have the policy applied to them. For instance, if the Accelar has two RIP interfaces configured, and only interface 160.60.10.1/24 is specified in the RIP interface list, then the policy is applied only to that interface.

- **OspfRouterListId**   Indicates the OSPF routers from which the policy will consider route information. Only OSPF routes learned from the OSPF routers contained in the List ID will be propagated. This is only relevant if a route source of OSPF is selected and the incoming route information was sourced from an OSPF router. A value of 0 indicates all OSPF sourced routes will be considered.

- **AnnounceInterfaceListId**   Indicates which interfaces will be affected by the policy in the event of a match. For example, an Accelar with four interfaces may receive route information on one interface that is a match condition for a specified Announce Policy, whose action indicates the route should have a specific metric applied before being announced. However, it is not desired to have the route advertised out all three of the remaining interfaces with the altered metric; the route should be advertised out only one of the remaining three interfaces. This parameter can be used to specify which interfaces will actually be affected by the policy. A value of 0 indicates all interfaces will be affected.

- **Precedence**   Indicates the order in which the policy rules are applied. This is useful for specifying the order, for example, of matching criteria. If several policies admit or manipulate specific incoming route information, and the last policy indicates that all routes should be dropped, then the last drop policy must be implemented last, so that the specified routes can be checked for *before* the routes are dropped. A higher precedence in this case indicates the rule will be examined first. In the event of a tie, the Policy ID is used (the higher value is prioritized).

THE ACCELAR LAYER 3 SWITCH

■ **RouteSource**   Indicates which types of routes will be considered by the policy. Routes that are from a source not specified by the Announce Policy's route source are ignored by the policy. The following route sources can be selected:

**Direct**   Routes that are directly connected to the local interface.

**Static**   Routes that have been statically configured into the routing table.

**Rip**   Routes that were sourced from a RIPv1- or RIPv2-routed interface.

**Ospf**   Routes that were sourced from an OSPF router.

■ **AdvertiseNetListId**   Applies only when the action is set to Announce; it indicates the total number of entries configured in the advertise net list that the policy is configured with. This is used to advertise networks that are different than what may actually be in the routing table, so that if the policy action is set to Announce, and an incoming route matches this policy, then rather than advertise the received route, the Accelar advertises the networks listed in the AdvertiseNetList.

■ **Action**   Indicates the action that will be taken if a match condition for the policy is found (announce or ignore).

■ **OspfRouteType**   Specifies the OSPF route type, if OSPF is chosen as a route source; the valid options are as follows:

**Type 1 external routes**   Routes that are advertised by an ASBR that has an interface actually configured in the external network. For instance, an ASBR with an OSPF interface in the OSPF domain, and a RIP interface configured in the bordering RIP domain with IP address 150.50.10.1/24, would advertise the 150.50.10.0/24 network back into the OSPF domain as an external type 1 route, because it has a direct connection to that network.

**Type 2 external routes**   Routes that are advertised by an ASBR that has an interface actually configured in the external network. For instance, an ASBR with an OSPF interface in the OSPF domain, and a RIP interface configured in the bordering RIP domain that learned of RIP network 160.60.10.0, which is two hops away, would advertise the 160.60.10.0/24 network back into the OSPF domain as an external type 2 route, because the route is external to the OSPF domain and does not have a direct connection to that network.

**Internal OSPF route**   A route that was learned strictly within the OSPF domain and did not originate external to the local AS.

**Any**   Indicates that all OSPF routes will be considered by the Announce Policy.

■ **RipMetric**   Alters the RIP metric for the route(s) being announced, if the action for the policy is set to Announce. If a value of 0 is used, the actual metric is calculated and used.

## Configuring a RIP Announce Policy Through the CLI

RIP Announce Policies can also be configured through the CLI. In this example, an Accelar is configured with a RIP Announce Policy that matches against OSPF-sourced routes of any kind, so long as the specified networks match. If a match is established, the Accelar will announce the route advertisements from only a subset of its interfaces. First, the policy is created:

```
Accelar-1250# config ip policy rip announce 1 create
```

Next, a route source of OSPF is specified. In addition, it is specified that any OSPF route type is valid, but must match the network information contained in network list 10:

```
Accelar-1250# config ip policy rip announce 1 add-route-src ospf
Accelar-1250# config ip policy rip announce 1 exact-netlist 10
Accelar-1250# config ip policy rip announce 1 ospf-route-type any
```

An action of Announce is specified, because the route information will be advertised—just not out all the interfaces. A subset of the Accelar's interfaces are defined in router/interface address list 10. The policy is then enabled:

```
Accelar-1250# config ip policy rip announce 1 action announce
Accelar-1250# config ip policy rip announce 1 outbound-interface-list 10
Accelar-1250# config ip policy rip announce 1 enable
```

# Virtual Router Redundancy Protocol on the Accelar Platform

Virtual Router Redundancy Protocol (VRRP) support also exists for the Accelar. This allows for *hot router standby*, so that if the default gateway for a series of end stations is lost, a secondary interface may assume this role, using the same IP address as the original gateway. Prior to the failure, the secondary interface remains in a dormant state.

This is accomplished by using a virtual IP address that is shared between two or more routers running VRRP. One router acts as the master in this case, performing the routing functions for the specified IP interface. The backup router remains in a dormant state until such time as the master fails.

The VRRP master and backup routers have the following responsibilities:

- **VRRP master**   Handles the router functions for the IP address or addresses associated with the virtual router. While master, the router must respond to ARP requests for the IP address(es) associated with the virtual router, forward packets with a destination MAC address of the virtual router, and accept all packets that are associated with IP interfaces of the virtual router. It must not accept packets addressed to the virtual router's IP address(es) if it is not the IP address owner. The VRRP master is also responsible for routing advertisements.

- **VRRP backup**   Does not perform any of the functions of the master. It remains in a standby state and listens for advertisements from the master. If it fails to receive these advertisements within a specified time, a dynamic failover occurs and the backup takes on the responsibilities of the master.

## Configuring VRRP

VRRP configuration is initiated by double-clicking a specific isolated router port to open the Edit Port window, in which the VRRP tab can be selected. Alternately, if VRRP is being configured at the VLAN level, select VLAN | VLANs from the main Device Manager window to open the Edit VLANs window, highlight the VLAN, click IP, and then select the VRRP tab in the Edit VLAN_IP window. In either case, the same parameters appear:

- **VrId**   Used in combination with a specific ifIndex value as a unique ID for a virtual router on the VRRP router.

- **IpAddr**   Indicates the IP address that the virtual router will be backing up.

- **Control**   Indicates the current state of the virtual router function; if set to enable, the virtual router is set to back up the primary router. If set to disable, the virtual router returns to an initializing state and no longer acts as backup for the primary router.

- **Priority**   If multiple virtual routers are acting as redundant routers for one or more IP addresses, this parameter determines which virtual router becomes the next in line to assume the router responsibilities if the primary router fails. A higher priority indicates a greater desirability for the backup virtual router.

> **Note**   *The router that actually possesses the IP address that the virtual routers are backing up should be configured with a priority of 255.*

- **AdvertisementInterval**   Indicates the interval, in seconds, between VRRP advertisements sent by the master router.

■ **CriticalIpAddr**   Indicates the IP address of the specific interface that will trigger a shutdown event. This is configured in a scenario where VRRP is configured at the VLAN level rather than on an isolated router port; since it is possible for a link within the VLAN to go down, while others remain up. In this case, a link to a specific router may go down while other links remain up (thus keeping active the virtual router interface associated with the VLAN), meaning that the VRRP interface has not really gone down. By specifying a critical IP address, you can specify a specific IP that, if contact to this IP address is lost, will trigger the VRRP failover.

**Note**    *VRRP support requires ARU2 or greater.*

# The Complete Reference

Nortel
Networks

# Chapter 12

## Traffic Management

In a large and busy network, traffic management becomes very important. When network utilization becomes high, the number of users becomes large, and usage becomes diversified, you may want to prioritize high-level, crucial information over other network traffic. Managing traffic on the Accelar routing switch can be done in several ways. The primary method is to use the different virtual local area network (VLAN) and frame-tagging technologies to minimize broadcast domains, and to direct and distribute networking protocols selectively. The secondary method is to use prioritization and filtering within VLANs. The focus of this chapter is the secondary method, the use of Internet Protocol (IP) traffic filtering to manage more accurately which traffic is permitted to travel where, and the implementation of a certain level of security and prioritization to target mission-critical data and assign it the appropriate weight.

IP filtering can be accomplished on the Accelar platform through either Device Manager or the command-line interface (CLI). These filters, once created, are used as a set of criteria that network traffic is matched against, performing a predefined action after a match is established. Through the use of these filters, traffic can be managed and mirrored, and security can be implemented.

Up to 1,024 filter IDs may be created on a single device (with the numbers being generated by the Accelar), and up to 128 filter lists may be defined. A *filter list* is a bundle of filter IDs that may be applied to a specific port so that each filter ID is applied in turn.

# Filter Types

Two basic filter types can be configured on the Accelar platform:

- **Source/destination filters**   May filter on either a target source/destination IP address or a range of source IP addresses
- **Global filters**   May filter on both source and destination IP addresses, either one alone, or neither

## Source Filters

A *source filter* points to a source IP address and its mask (the mask must be at least 8 bits in length). In the case of both source and destination filters, the IP address and the mask both must be configured, allowing a filter to be placed against a specific subnet, network, or even a specific station network (see Figure 12-1).

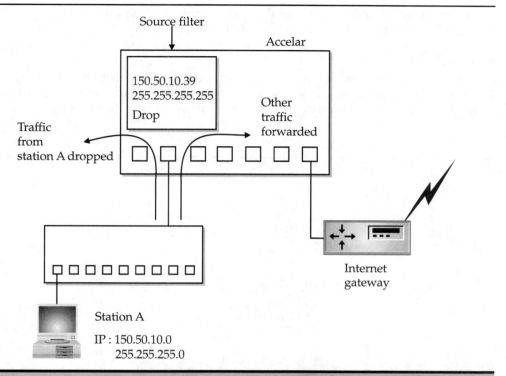

**Figure 12-1.**    *Source filter applied against incoming packet*

A source filter can apply the following actions to a matched packet:

- Drop the packet
- Forward the packet
- Mirror the packet to another port, for monitoring purposes
- Alter the priority level, which marks the packet as being either high priority or normal priority (for more information, consult the sections within "Prioritization," later in this chapter)
- Alter the VLAN tag priority, which sets a priority in the 802.1Q VLAN frame tag for purposes of prioritizing tagged frames

Source and destination filter lists always have a filter ID of 300 or more, because the numbers below that are reserved for global filters.

## Filter Sets

Source filters may be created individually, and then may be described in a list or set. This means that a group of source filters may be defined to a port individually or may be grouped together in a list that is then defined on a port (see Figure 12-2).

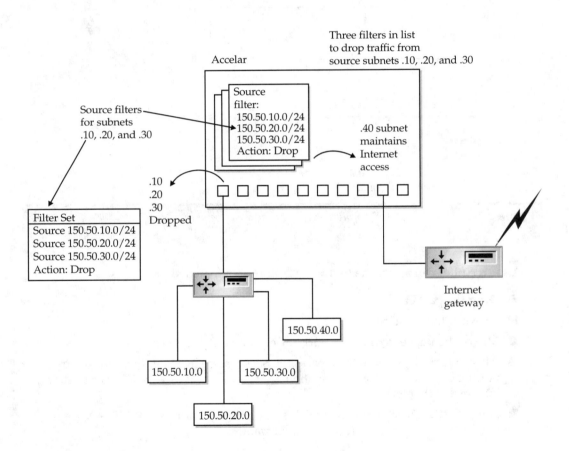

**Figure 12-2.** *Filter list matches and applies action to multiple source addresses*

Multiple lists may be assigned to a single port, but the maximum number of global filters that may be defined is eight, so the sum of the filters in the multiple lists must never exceed eight.

# Destination Filters

*Destination filters* are similar to source filters, except that a destination filter specifies the destination IP address and mask. The mask length must be at least 8 bits, as with a source filter. This allows a filter to be applied against a specific destination network or subnet (see Figure 12-3).

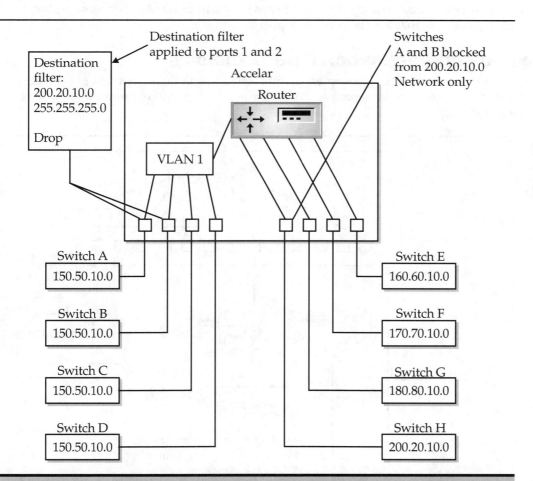

**Figure 12-3.** *Destination filter applied to filter specific IP network*

Like source filters, a destination filter can apply the following actions to a matched packet:

- Drop the packet
- Forward the packet
- Mirror the packet to another port, for monitoring purposes
- Alter the priority level
- Alter the VLAN tag priority

Source and destination filter lists always have a filter ID of 300 or more, as the numbers below that are reserved for global filters.

## Source and Destination Filter Examples

For the purposes of these examples, an intranetwork with three networks of two subnets each is used. An Accelar separates these networks, acting as a core routing switch (see Figure 12-4).

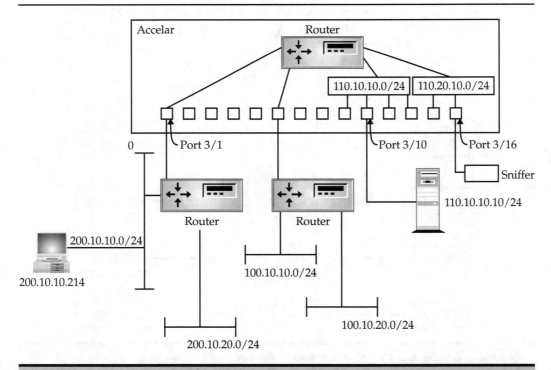

**Figure 12-4.** *Network of three networks of two subnets each, with an Accelar core*

## Example of a Source and Mirror Filter

In this example, a client in subnet 200.10.10.0/24 with an IP address of 200.10.10.214 must communicate with a server in subnet 110.10.10.0/24 with an IP address of 110.10.10.10, connected to port 3/10. A communications problem has occurred. As part of the troubleshooting process, a sniffer is to be used to do a packet capture. To accomplish this, a source filter is applied to port 3/1, specifying the source as 200.10.10.214 with a 255.255.255.255 bit mask, and an action set to mirror, pointing to port 3/16.

**Note** *This could also be achieved using the port mirroring feature of the Accelar, but here we are picking out specific traffic.*

Mirroring traffic is useful, because it ignores all traffic except that specified in the filter (200.10.10.214; that of the problematic client), and only mirrors communications originating from the client and going to the server in question (refer back to Figure 12-4).

## Example of a Destination Filter

In this example, the same client (200.10.10.214/24) is still experiencing a communications issue with its server. The former filter applied against the source showed packets destined for the server going out as expected. As the next step in the troubleshooting procedure, a decision is made to use the same sniffer, to determine what, if anything, the server is sending back. A destination filter is created, specifying an IP address of 200.10.10.214 with a mask of 255.255.255.255, stating that the match must be exact. The action is set to mirror, pointing toward the same sniffer port of 3/16, and is applied to the server port, 3/10.

This filter is useful, because it filters out any traffic pointed toward destinations other than the problematic server, and steers only the desired traffic to the sniffer port.

# Global Filters and Examples

Global filters provide a bit more flexibility when managing traffic. With a *global filter*, neither a source IP address and mask nor a destination IP address and mask are required, although either may be used, and, in fact, both may be used. Also, the minimum mask length of 8 bits does not apply to a global filter.

For purposes of this example, an Accelar is configured with a VLAN (VLAN_10), which supports multiple users and an isolated router port leading to the Internet Gateway (see Figure 12-5).

## Global Filter Used to Monitor Web Access

Using this example, imagine a global filter is applied on ports 3/1–3/5. For this particular filter, no source or destination IP is specified. Rather, a protocol type of TCP is specified, and a source port of 80 (http) is used. An action of mirror is set, so that http

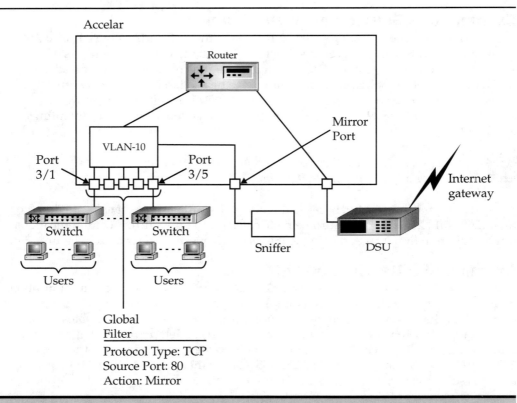

**Figure 12-5.**    *TCP traffic on Port 80 (HTTP) is mirrored*

traffic, once detected, will be mirrored to a sniffer port. Once the filter is defined, add it to a global set and apply that set to ports 3/1–3/5.

## Example 2

Using the same network design as the preceding example, imagine that a global filter is applied on the same port, 3/16 (in place of, not in addition to, the last filter). This filter is given a source IP of 100.10.20.0, with a mask of 255.255.255.0, and a destination IP of 200.20.10.0, also with a 255.255.255.0 mask. In this case, the action is also set to drop.

In this case, because no source or destination IP is specified, traffic to and from any IP address or network will be considered. Since the protocol type is set to TCP, only TCP traffic is considered and, furthermore, only TCP source port 80 is considered a match (the default http port). Http traffic will be mirrored in this case, but nothing else.

# Setting Filters

This section describes the process for setting up filters on the Accelar specifically. Configuring filters on the Accelar is a three-step process: create the filter itself, add the filter or filters into a set, and then apply that filter set to a port or ports. These functions can be accomplished through either Device Manager or the CLI.

## Configuring Source and Destination Filters in Device Manager

Editing IP filters through Device Manager is done by selecting Routing | IP | IP Filters, which opens the Edit Filter window, as shown here:

The Edit Filter window displays a list of all configured filters (none, by default). To the right of the Filters tab, which is the default display, three other tabs are available:

- **Global Set**   Groups the filters into sets for the global filter type
- **Source/Destination Set**   Groups the filters into sets for the source/destination filter type
- **Filtered Ports**   Decides to which ports the filters will be applied

First, you must create a filter. Click the Insert button, which opens the Insert Filters window (see Figure 12-6).

Here, you select the type of filter (global, destination, or source), along with the remainder of the filter parameters. A list of the filter parameters and their descriptions follows:

- **Type**   Choices are global, destination, or source
- **DstAddr**   The destination IP address, configured if the filter is a destination or global filter
- **DstMask**   The destination IP address's subnet mask
- **ID**   The filter ID, assigned by the Accelar
- **Name**   An arbitrary name, selected by the administrator
- **ProtocolType**   Select the IP protocol type.
- **SrcPort**   The Transmission Control Protocol/User Datagram Protocol (TCP/UDP) source port number, not the physical port

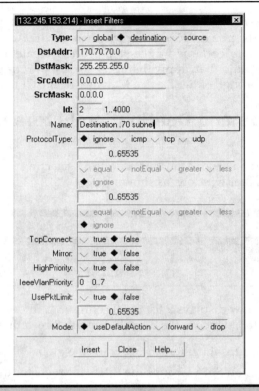

**Figure 12-6.**   *The Insert Filters window*

- **SrcOption**   The TCP/UDP source port option: ignore, equal, less than, greater to, or not equal to (again, this does not refer to the physical port, but the TCP/UDP port)

- **DstPort**   The TCP/UDP destination port number

- **DstOption**   The destination TCP/UDP port option: ignore, equal, less than, greater to, or not equal to

- **TcpConnect**   Setting TCP Connect to true allows only TCP connections from within the network. False allows bidirectional connections.

- **Mirror**   Setting Mirror to true allows for mirroring to the destination port, so that only certain traffic will be mirrored.

- **HighPriority**   Sets the traffic specified in the filter to a priority level of High

- **IeeeVlanPriority**   Alters the priority bits in the 802.1Q frame tag, assuming the value is greater than that found within the tag currently

- **UsePktLimit** By defining a packet limit to a filter, you can define a limit to the number of times that an action is performed against a filter match. For example, if you are using a filter to mirror traffic to a sniffer port, you could assign a packet limit that defines how much traffic should be mirrored before the action is ceased.

- **PktLimit** Defines the packet limit number (0 to 8388607)

- **Mode** Chooses forward, drop, or uses DefaultAction for the selected filter

After you define the filter, click Insert, which causes the filter to appear in the filter list. It is automatically assigned a filter ID, as follows:

- Source and destination filters are automatically assigned a number beginning at 300 and incrementing from there.

- Global filters are automatically assigned a value beginning at 1 and ending at 299.

## Creating a Filter Set

After you create the necessary filters, you must create a filter set. Depending on the type of filters that you intend to use on the port in question, click either the Global Set tab or the Source/Destination Set tab. The procedure for adding filters to the list is the same, regardless of the type. Choose one and click Insert. This brings up the Insert Global Set window, as shown next, or the Insert Source/Destination Set window, depending on which one you choose.

In this window, you may associate a name with the filter list. Each of the configured filters of the same type (global or source/destination) is listed in this window, and you may select them by clicking them. You need to select only one filter, but you may select all the filters (as long as the global filters do not exceed eight). After you choose the appropriate filters, click Insert.

The filter list will now be visible in the index, and may be chosen for application to a port.

## Applying Filter Lists to a Port

After you create the filters and compile them into their appropriate filter lists, you can apply those lists to ports. Filters are not applied to any port by default, so you must apply them specifically to make them function. From the Edit Filter window, choose Filtered Ports, and click Insert to bring up the Insert Filtered Ports window. In the Insert Filtered Ports window, click the Ports button, which brings up a list of ports to choose from, as shown here:

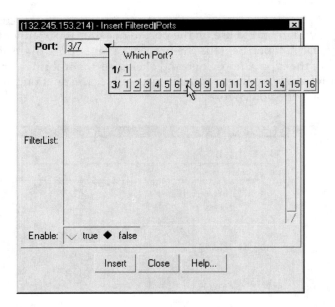

Click the port to which the filter should be applied. After you select the port, choose the filter list or lists that will be applied to the selected ports. Remember that although you may apply several lists, their combined global filter count must not exceed eight.

The filter lists that have been applied to a port may be set to Enabled or, if they are not to be used all the time, may be set to Disabled until they are needed.

After you select the filter lists and either enable or disable them, click Insert, which applies the filter list to the specified port, thus activating the filter.

## Setting Global Filters Through the CLI

IP filters may also be created through the CLI. The procedure is the same as when you configure the filters through Device Manager: create the filters, assign them to a filter list, and then assign that filter list to a specific port.

To create a global filter in the CLI, issue the following command:

```
Accelar-1100# config ip traffic-filter create global src-ip 10.0.0.0/8
Global filter 5 is created
Accelar-1100# config ip traffic-filter filter 5 action mirror enable
Accelar-1100# config ip traffic-filter filter 5 action use-packet-limit
enable
Accelar-1100# config ip traffic-filter filter 5 match packet-limit 50000
```

This creates a global filter on the source IP address of 10.0.0.0 with an 8-bit mask. It has been assigned the Filter ID (FID) of 5. This filter will mirror traffic, using a packet limit that has been set to 50,000 packets.

The other parameters associated with IP filters in Device Manager are also available in the CLI; the syntax of the specific parameters will be offered by entering ? at any point in the command string.

Next, create a global filter set by issuing the following command:

```
Accelar-1100# config ip traffic-filter global-list 100 create
Accelar-1100# config ip traffic-filter global-list 100 add-filter 5
```

This creates a global list with an ID of 100, and filter 5 has been added to it. Assign the filter list to a port by issuing the following command:

```
Accelar-1100# config ethernet 3/11 ip traffic-filter create
```

This command configures the port (3/11 in this case) to accept an IP traffic filter. Then, apply the list and enable it:

```
Accelar-1100# config ethernet 3/11 ip traffic-filter add list 100
Accelar-1100# config ethernet 3/11 ip traffic-filter enable
```

THE ACCELAR LAYER 3 SWITCH

# Configuring Source and Destination Filters Through the CLI

Configuring source and destination filters through the CLI is very similar to setting up a global filter. You must create the filter, assign it to a list, and then apply the list to a port. First, configure the IP filter:

```
Accelar-1100# config ip traffic-filter create source src-ip 10.0.0.0/8
Source filter 2 is created
Accelar-1100# config ip traffic-filter create destination dst-ip
100.205.20.1/32
Destination filter 4 is created.
Accelar-1100# config ip traffic-filter filter 4 action mirror enable
```

In this example, two filters have been created: one source filter, on the source IP of 10.0.0.0 with an 8-bit mask (filter 2), and a destination filter, configured for an exact match on IP address 100.205.20.1 with a 32-bit mask (filter 4). Also, mirroring has been configured to mirror any traffic destined for the IP address 100.205.20.1.

Next, a filter list must be created, and the filters must be added to it:

```
Accelar-1100# config ip traffic-filter list 330 create
Accelar-1100# config ip traffic-filter list 330 add-filter 2
Accelar-1100# config ip traffic-filter list 330 add-filter 4
```

A filter list with an ID of 330 has been created, and both filters added. This filter list may now be applied to a port:

```
Accelar-1100# config ethernet 3/16 ip traffic-filter create
```

This command configures the port to accept an IP traffic filter. Then, apply the list and enable it:

```
Accelar-1100# config ethernet 3/16 ip traffic-filter add list 330
Accelar-1100# config ethernet 3/16 ip traffic-filter enable
```

# Prioritization

Another technique of traffic management available on the Accelar platform is *prioritization*. The two basic modes of priority are best effort and high priority. The difference between the two modes has to do with how the traffic is queued in the output buffers, and which path is taken through the switch fabric (high-priority traffic is routed through a high-priority data path). Priority may be configured on the Accelar in the following manners:

- **By port**  All traffic received on a specific port is assigned a high priority.
- **By VLAN**  All traffic received on a specific VLAN is assigned a high priority.
- **By media access control (MAC) address**  All traffic received from a predefined MAC address is to be given a high priority, regardless of its ingress point.
- **By IP flow**  IP traffic between a specified source and destination may be assigned a high priority. The source and destination port numbers must be defined.

Traffic may also be prioritized by using filters (as described in the "Setting Filters" section earlier in the chapter), which enables you to assign priority to specific IP addresses or ranges, or by altering the priority bits in the 802.1Q frame tag on a VLAN-by-VLAN basis.

## By Port

Setting priority on a port-by-port basis may be accomplished through Device Manager. Bring up the Accelar in Device Manager, and then choose the appropriate port by right-clicking it. A pull-down menu appears with a list of choices; choose Edit, which causes the Edit Port window to appear (see Figure 12-7).

The bottom third of the window presents a choice of setting HighPriority to either true or false. By default, this is set to false, which indicates a best-effort priority. Setting this to true assigns a high priority to any traffic received on that port. Commit the changes by clicking Apply.

## By VLAN

To prioritize traffic received on any active port in a VLAN, model the device in Device Manager. You can assign priority to a VLAN either at the time that you create the VLAN or at a later time, after the VLAN has been established.

THE ACCELAR LAYER 3
SWITCH

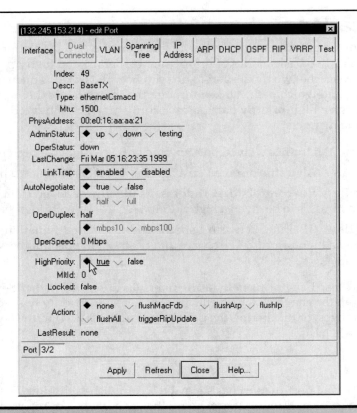

**Figure 12-7.**   *The Edit Port window*

To set priority at the time that you create a VLAN, select VLAN | VLANs and then click the Insert button to bring up the Insert Basic window:

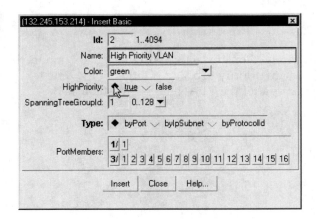

The option to set VLAN priority is located in the lower half of the window. If the VLAN has already been created, then you may alter the priority by selecting VLAN | VLANs to bring up the Edit VLANs window, which displays all configured VLANs. Click the Advanced tab, shown next, to display a list of options, including changing the VLAN priority.

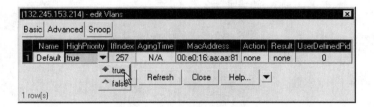

# By MAC Address

Priority may also be configured on a per-MAC-address basis. This can be applied to a MAC address that is currently in the forwarding table, or it can be assigned to a statically assigned MAC address.

To change the priority on a learned MAC address, choose VLAN | VLANs to open the Edit VLANs window. In the Edit VLANs window, choose Bridging, which opens the Edit Bridge window, shown here:

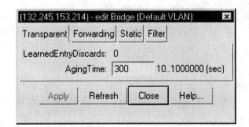

Selecting the Forwarding tab in the Edit Bridge window displays a table of all MAC addresses learned in the specified VLAN; in this table, you may alter the priority of the MAC addresses on an individual basis (see Figure 12-8).

To define priority on a static MAC address, first define the address in the Edit Bridge window. Choose the Static tab, click Insert, enter the MAC address whose priority you want to define, and then assign its priority. You must also define the port with which the MAC address is to be associated.

THE ACCELAR LAYER 3 SWITCH

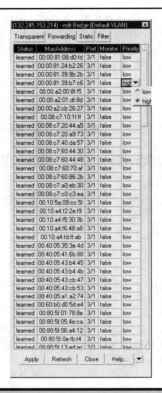

**Figure 12-8.**    *Changing priority on a learned MAC address*

## By IP Flow

Communication between two specific IP devices may also be prioritized at the IP layer or TCP/UDP layer. To access the IP Flow menu, choose Routing | IP, which opens the Edit IP window. Select the IP Flow tab:

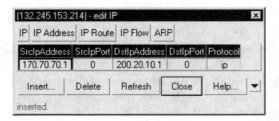

Click Insert to add a source and destination address, as well as the protocol layer. You may also define the source and destination ports, which are specific to the protocol layer (IP, TCP, or UDP).

# The
# Complete
# Reference

Nortel
Networks

# Part IV

## ATM Technologies

The
Complete
Reference

Nortel
Networks

# Chapter 13

## ATM Signaling and LANE

The evolution of Asynchronous Transfer Mode (ATM) moved from the static definition of permanent virtual circuits (PVCs) throughout the ATM mesh, to a dynamic signaling protocol known as LAN Emulation (LANE). LANE allows legacy Ethernet or token ring frames to be dynamically routed through the ATM portion of the network, while the conversion remains invisible to the legacy LAN devices.

LANE is more complex than PVCs, both from a conceptual and configuration standpoint. Once understood, however, LANE makes adds, moves, and changes much easier, and is much more scalable. PVCs, although simple in concept and simple to configure on a singular basis, can become quite laborious in large networks, whereas LANE, although requiring an understanding of the different signaling techniques and LANE components, is easier to configure and manage in a large network. Most ATM networks at this point either have moved away from strict PVC meshes or are in the process of doing so.

A LANE network has two basic types of connections: user-to-network connections, such as directly attached ATM servers or ATM router interfaces, and network-to-network connections, such as connections between ATM switches. User-to-network interfaces, known as UNI connections, utilize different signaling methods than are used between switches. Switch-to-switch connections are accomplished by means of Interim Inter-Switch Protocol (IISP) connections or Private Network-to-Network Interface (PNNI) connections, utilizing static or dynamic call-routing methods, respectively.

# User to Network Interface

The User-to-Network Interface (UNI) specification defines two ATM UNI types:

- **Public UNI**   A connection between a private ATM switch and an ATM switch residing with a public service provider, where the private ATM switch acts as a UNI device.

- **Private UNI**   A connection between an ATM user (such as an ATM router interface or ATM-attached server) and an ATM switch found within the same private ATM network.

The primary differences between the two types are media type (a connection to the public ATM network is often accomplished using a DS3 connection, which utilizes coaxial cable and BNC connectors), and reach, because a public UNI connection most likely will need to span a long distance, whereas the private UNI will cover a relatively short distance. Both UNI types share the same ATM layer specifications. Table 13-1 outlines some of the differences between the two UNI types.

In the ATM UNI specification, an ATM user is defined as an *intermediate system* that encapsulates data into ATM cells and then forwards the cells across an ATM UNI to

| ATM Bearer Service Attribute | Public UNI | Private UNI |
|---|---|---|
| Support for point-to-point VPCs | Optional | Optional |
| Support for point-to-point virtual control channels (VCCs) | Required | Required |
| Support for point-to-multipoint VPCs | Optional | Optional |
| Support for point-to-multipoint VCCs, switched virtual circuits (SVCs) | Required | Required |
| Support for point-to-multipoint VCCs, PVCs | Optional | Optional |
| Support of permanent virtual connection | Required | Required |
| Support of switched virtual connection | Required | Required |
| Support of specified QoS classes | Required | Optional |
| Support of an unspecified QoS class | Optional | Optional |
| Multibandwidth granularities for ATM connections | Required | Optional |
| Peak Cell Rate (PCR) traffic enforcement via UPC | Required | Optional |
| Sustainable Cell Rate (SCR) traffic enforcement via Usage Parameter Control (UPC) | Optional | Optional |
| Traffic shaping | Optional | Optional |
| ATM layer fault management | Required | Optional |
| Interim Local Management Interface (ILMI) | Required | Required |

**Table 13-1.**    *Public vs. Private UNI Parameters*

either a privately or publicly owned switch, or to a private network ATM switch that uses a public ATM network service for the transfer of cells to connect to other ATM user devices (see Figure 13-1).

The C100/C50/5000BH platform, as well as the C1x00 platform, support both public and private UNI connections. In the case of the C100/C50/5000BH, utilizing a port as the user side of a UNI connection (as would be configured if the switch has a public UNI connection), only one UNI port is supported, and the remaining ATM ports will not support any other connections. If this configuration is required, you should use a two-port ATMSpeed module.

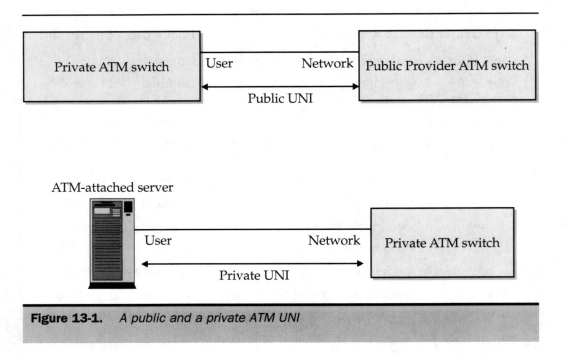

**Figure 13-1.** *A public and a private ATM UNI*

# User-to-Network Interface Protocol Architecture

From a protocol standpoint, the UNI model is broken down into three distinct planes:

- **U-plane** The *user plane* is responsible for the transfer of user application information. Included are the physical layer, ATM layer, and ATM adaption layer (AAL) that are required for different Quality of Service (QoS) users, such as constant bit rate (CBR) or variable bit rate (VBR) services.

- **C-plane** The *control plane* protocol layers handle connection control functions, such as call establishment and release. AAL functions and higher-layer signaling protocols are also included on the C-plane.

- **M-plane** The *management plane* is the mechanism for exchange between the U- and C-planes, providing management functions, as well as information exchange. The M-plane is further divided into two distinct sectors: layer management, which performs layer-specific management functionality, and plane management, which coordinates functions of the whole (see Figure 13-2).

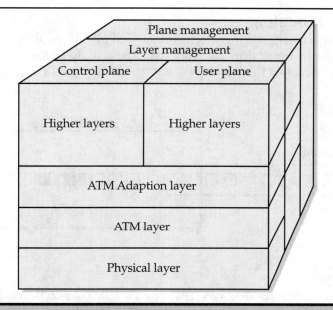

**Figure 13-2.**    *A model of the ATM protocol*

## ATM Layer Functions at the UNI

The ATM layer provides for the transfer of fixed-size cells between the communicating upper-layer AAL entities. Because ATM is a connection-oriented technology, these transfers take place across a preestablished connection, in accordance with its traffic contract. These connections may be either VCCs, which consist of a singular circuit, or VPCs, which consist of a group of VCCs. In either case, the connection may be a point-to-point connection or a point-to-multipoint connection. From the most basic standpoint of ATM cell transfer, the UNI specification defines the multiplexing among different ATM connections, cell rate decoupling, payload type found within the cell stream, cell loss priority, and traffic shaping.

### Multiplexing Among Different ATM Connections

UNI defines the multiplexing of various ATM connections with QoS requirements. These connections may have either a specified or an unspecified QoS class. The QoS that is specified at the time of call setup will remain unchanged for the duration of the connection.

## Cell Rate Decoupling

Traffic bursts may create gaps in the cell stream. Cell rate decoupling is the method by which the gaps in the traffic flow are filled with idle cells, to keep cell flow smooth. Idle cells have a special header that identifies them as fill:

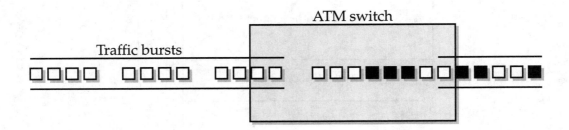

## Payload Type

Switches must check the payload type (PT) of each cell. These cells need to be divided between data cells, Operation and Management (OAM) cells, and their various cell types, as described in Chapter 3.

## Cell Loss Priority

Cell Loss Priority (CLP), also referred to as *cell-tagging*, is often a configurable parameter, though not a required component. CLP may be either on or off. Cell tagging, if enabled, marks cells if the network becomes congested, by flipping the CLP bit. If the bit is set to 0, then it must be kept. If it is set to 1, then it is marked as expendable in times of congestion and a switch may make the decision to drop these marked cells under a heavy network load.

## Traffic Shaping

*Traffic shaping* is a means of regulating cell flow on egress ports, by applying a traffic shaping profile.

# ATM Layer Management

UNI also provides management functions, which have been reduced to a minimal set in order to ease cooperation between ATM users and network equipment. These functions include fault management, which can be broken down into two main categories:

- Alarm surveillance and connectivity verification
- Detection of invalid virtual path identifier (VPI)/virtual channel identifier (VCI) pairings

These functions enable UNI to monitor connections for integrity, and to report any errors that may be encountered.

## Alarm Surveillance

*Alarm surveillance* monitors VPC/VCC failures at the public UNI and propagates this information. These signals are carried via OAM cells over the channel 0/4. The VP or VC Alarm Indication Signal (AIS) is generated by the node at the connecting point, to alert the downstream nodes that a failure has occurred.

## Connectivity Verification

Connectivity may be verified through the use of an OAM loopback mechanism. This loopback can occur on either VPs or VCs, and the connection remains up while the loopback is being performed. Endpoints that receive OAM cells that are indicated to be loopback cells (an indication value of 00000001 and a function value of 1000) will loop back each cell within one second.

## Invalid VPI/VCI Detection

As in the case of statically defined PVCs, the VPI/VCI pairs for a VC must match between nodes, though the ultimate endpoints through the mesh may vary. In a UNI connection, the VPI/VCI pair suggested by the originating UNI port must be available for use by the receiving UNI port.

# UNI Signaling Specifications

Three different UNI specifications are in common use today: UNI 3.0, UNI 3.1, and UNI 4.0. Although this chapter mainly discusses common UNI characteristics, variances between the UNI versions are addressed on a case-by-case basis.

## UNI Call States

A UNI call may transition between several of the following defined states, which may vary slightly depending on whether the call is viewed from the user side of the interface or the network side:

**NULL**   No call currently exists.

**CALL INITIATED**   On the user side of UNI, this call state indicates that an outgoing call exists and that call establishment has been requested from the network. On the network side of UNI, this state indicates that an outgoing call has been initiated and the network side has actually received the call establishment request. At this point, the network side has not responded to the call establishment request.

**OUTGOING CALL PROCEEDING**   On the user side, this state indicates that an acknowledgement has been received from the network side in response to the call establishment request, indicating that it has all the information required to establish the call. On the network side of the UNI, this state is entered once the call establishment request acknowledgement is sent to the user side.

**CALL PRESENT**   From the user side of the UNI, this state is entered when an incoming call is received and a call establishment request is received from the network side. The user side has not responded to the request at this point. From the network perspective, the call establishment request has been sent, but no reply has been received.

**CONNECT REQUEST**   The user side transitions to this state when it has answered the incoming call and is waiting to be awarded the call. The network side transitions to this state when it receives an answer from the user side, but has not yet awarded the call to the user.

**INCOMING CALL PROCEEDING**   The user side assumes this state for an incoming call when it has sent acknowledgement indicating that it has received all the call information necessary to establish the call. The network side assumes this state when it receives acknowledgement that the user has received the call information it requires to establish the call.

**ACTIVE**   This state indicates that either the user or network side, depending on the perspective, has received an indication that the call has been awarded, in the case of an incoming call, or that the call has been answered, in the case of an outgoing call, and that the call is now active.

**RELEASE REQUEST**   This state exists on the user side when it issues a request to the network side for a call to be cleared. On the network side, this state is assumed when such a request is received.

**RELEASE INDICATION**   If the network disconnects an end-to-end connection for any reason, the user side will be requested to disconnect as well. This state is entered if a connection is disconnected and the request to the user to disconnect has been extended.

**RESTART REQUEST**   This state exists when one side has issued a restart request but has not yet received an acknowledgment from the remote side.

**RESTART**   This state exists when a restart request has been received, but not all locally active calls have yet responded.

# UNI 4.0 Features

UNI 4.0 is currently the most recent version of ATM UNI. It has a series of new functionality, some of which is covered in this section. Table 13-2 shows a full list of the UNI 4.0 features.

| Feature | Optional/Mandatory |
|---|---|
| Point-to-point calls | Required |
| Point-to-multipoint calls | Required |
| Signaling of QoS parameters | Mandatory |
| Leaf-initiated join (LIJ) | Optional |
| ATM Anycast | Optional (public); required (private) |
| Available bit rate (ABR) signaling for point-to-point calls | Optional |
| Generic identifier transport | Optional |
| Virtual UNIs | Optional |
| Switched virtual path service | Optional |
| Proxy signaling | Optional |
| Frame discard | Optional (though transport is required) |
| Traffic parameter negotiation | Optional |
| Direct dialing in (DDI) | Optional |
| Multiple subscriber number | Optional |
| Calling line ID presentation | Optional |
| Calling line ID restriction | Optional |
| Connected line ID presentation | Optional |
| Connected line ID restriction | Optional |
| Subaddressing | Optional |
| User-user signaling | Optional |

**Table 13-2.**    *UNI 4.0 Feature Set*

## ATM Anycast

ATM Anycast enables an individual user to request connection to an ATM end system that is part of an ATM group. This connection is a point-to-point connection. The ATM group is a collection of ATM end systems that share the specified group address. In this respect, the ATM Anycast works in a similar fashion to a multicast group address in a legacy LAN.

The ATM Anycast group address is included in the SETUP message when the point-to-point call is made. When received, the ATM end system that receives it may in turn communicate its own ATM address, as well as those of any other registered members.

Registered members in this case must fall within the specified UNI scope (the UNI scope element is described later in this section). If no registered members fall within the defined UNI scope, the call will be cleared with a cause code of 3, "no route to destination."

## Leaf-Initiated Joins

The leaf-initiated join feature enables users to join existing point-to-multipoint calls without intervention from the call's creator. The users in this case are referred to as *leaves,* while the call creator is referred to as the *root.* Two basic types of LIJs exist:

- **Network LIJs**    The network adds new leaves to an ongoing call automatically, at the leaf's request.
- **Root LIJs**    The root adds each leaf manually.

**CREATION OF INITIAL LIJ CALL**    The root initiation of an LIJ call is essentially the same procedure for initiating a point-to-multipoint call, the difference being that the SETUP message includes additional information elements that indicate the point-to-multipoint call will be LIJ-capable. Each LIJ call is assigned a unique call identifier, used to distinguish it from other LIJs that may originate at the same root. In addition, each LIJ call identifier is paired with the root address, so that each LIJ instance maintains uniqueness within the network, as well.

**NETWORK LIJ**    A leaf initiates its join to an active network LIJ call by issuing a LEAF SETUP REQUEST message. This message contains the root's address, the LIJ call identifier, and a leaf sequence number, which will be echoed when the call is initiated to the leaf (assuming it is not rejected) so that the leaf is able to associate the reply with its own request and not that of another leaf. Unlike in a normal point-to-multipoint call, the call initiator is not informed when new leaves join the call, or drop from it. The root in the case of an LIJ does not receive any notification, nor does it screen potential additions to the call, as is the case with a point-to-multipoint call, such as the Control Distribute VCC, initiated by the LES, or the Multicast Forward VCC, initiated by the BUS. Likewise, the root can't drop certain leaves.

In the case where a leaf attempts to join a call that is no longer active, a LEAF SETUP REQUEST message is sent, and the network uses the root's address, LIJ call identifier and sequence number. Upon receipt by the root, the root has two options available: send back a LEAF SETUP FAILURE message, with a failure code, or elect to create the call and allow the leaf to join.

**ROOT LIJ** When a leaf attempts to join a root LIJ, it sends a LEAF SETUP REQUEST message, as would be the case with a network LIJ. However, because the root in this case must add each leaf requesting membership, the root has two options available:

- Disallow the leaf, in which case it sends a LEAF SETUP FAILURE message.
- Add the leaf, at which point an ADD PARTY message is issued, with the LIJ sequence number included, and the ADD PARTY setup proceeds as it normally would.

## Virtual UNIs

UNI 4.0 includes support for multiple virtual UNI devices to share a common physical UNI connection. A series of users connected to a VP multiplexer (MUX) may be assigned a series of VPI values to be used with the default VCI values of 5 for the signaling channel and 16 for the ILMI channel. These alternate VPI values are translated from the original value of 0 by the UNI, which acts as proxy for the virtual UNIs.

## Individual Quality of Service Parameters

QoS parameters are supported by UNI 4.0. (The specifics of the QoS implementation are covered in detail in Chapter 14.)

## UNI Scope

The UNI membership scope indicates how far into the routing hierarchy the UNI's membership should be recognized. By using this optional feature, a client may initiate a call to a group address and reach members also included within the specified range, while clients outside the defined scope will not receive the call. The scope is indicated over the ILMI channel, during the address registration procedure.

The scope used by the UNI is not directly related to the scope utilized by the network; instead, an indirect mapping is used between the UNI scope and the routing scope used, such as in the PNNI routing hierarchy. Currently, 15 levels of UNI scope are outlined in the UNI 4.0 specification.

The first four designations map to a physical network, such as a lowest-level peer group, with gradations for other ATM subnetworks that do not include wide area connections:

1. local network
2. localPlusOne
3. localPlusTwo
4. siteMinusOne

The next three intrasite gradations may possibly map to further layers of the routing hierarchy that are still local from a geographic standpoint, up toward ATM networks that may be separated by different buildings or wide area links:

5. intraSite

6. intraSitePlusOne

7. organizationMinusOne

The next three organization designations refer to an autonomous ATM system that may be separated geographically. Further gradations indicate possible groupings of autonomous systems:

8. intraOrganization

9. organizationPlusOne

10. communityMinusOne

The following four values may be used to identify groupings of autonomous systems organized by a provider:

11. intraCommunity

12. communityPlusOne

13. regional

14. interRegional

The last designation indicates all branches of the private ATM, whether separated by buildings on a campus or geographic location:

15. global

The UNI scopes just outlined are to be user-configured, not only to make mappings easier to the network routing scope, but also to make changes in the routing scope simpler without upsetting the scope of the UNI.

## Example of UNI Signaling

The following is an example of a communication between a remote LEC and a router LEC; the capture was taken on the router's UNI interface:

```
Q2931: ----- UNI Signaling -----
Q2931:
Q2931: Protocol discriminator   = 09
Q2931: Length of call reference = 3 bytes
Q2931: Call reference flag      = 0... ....(message sent from call
reference originator)
```

```
Q2931: Call reference value     = 7
Q2931: Message type             = 05 (Setup)
Q2931: Message type Flag/Action = 80
Q2931:                ...0 .... = flag
Q2931:                .... ..00 = action (Clear call)
Q2931: Message Length           = 94
Q2931:
Q2931: Info element id          = 58 (ATM adaptation layer parameters)
Q2931: Coding Standard/Action = 80
Q2931:  1... .... =             ext
Q2931:  .00. .... =             code stand(ITU-T standardized)
Q2931:  ...0 .... =             flag(not significant)
Q2931:  .... .000 =             IE instruction field(clear call)
Q2931: Length of info element = 9 byte(s)
Q2931:   AAL type          = AAL type 5
Q2931: Forward max CPCS-SDU
Q2931:                 id   = 140
Q2931:                 size = 1536
Q2931: Backward max CPCS-SDU
Q2931:                 id   = 129
Q2931:                 size = 1536
Q2931: SSCS type
Q2931:    id   = 132
Q2931:    type = Null
Q2931:
Q2931: Info element id          = 59 (ATM traffic descriptor)
Q2931: Coding Standard/Action = 80
Q2931:  1... .... =             ext
Q2931:  .00. .... =             code stand(ITU-T standardized)
Q2931:  ...0 .... =             flag(not significant)
Q2931:  .... .000 =             IE instruction field(clear call)
Q2931: Length of info element = 9 byte(s)
Q2931: Forward peak cell rate (CLP = 0+1)
Q2931:            id    = 132
Q2931:            rate  = 365566 cells/sec
Q2931:                    154999984 bps
Q2931: Backward peak cell rate (CLP = 0+1)
Q2931:            id    = 133
Q2931:            rate  = 365566 cells/sec
Q2931:                    154999984 bps
Q2931:    Best effort indicator  =  190
Q2931:
Q2931: Info element id          = 5E (Broadband bearer capability)
Q2931: Coding Standard/Action = 80
Q2931:  1... .... =             ext
Q2931:  .00. .... =             code stand(ITU-T standardized)
Q2931:  ...0 .... =             flag(not significant)
Q2931:  .... .000 =             IE instruction field(clear call)
Q2931: Length of info element = 3 byte(s)
```

```
Q2931:   Bearer class          = BCOB-X
Q2931:   ATM transfer capability= Non-real time VBR
Q2931:   Suscept to clipping   = Not susceptible to clipping
Q2931:   User plane conn config = Point-to-point
Q2931:
Q2931: Info element id        = 5F (Broadband low layer information)
Q2931: Coding Standard/Action = 80
Q2931:  1... .... =            ext
Q2931:  .00. .... =            code stand(ITU-T standardized)
Q2931:  ...0 .... =            flag(not significant)
Q2931:  .... .000 =            IE instruction field(clear call)
Q2931: Length of info element = 1 byte(s)
Q2931:   Layer 2 protocol
Q2931:  1... .... =   ext
Q2931:  .10. .... =   layer 2 id
Q2931:  ...0 1100 = User info layer 2 protocol(LAN logical link
control (ISO 8802/2))
Q2931:   Layer 3 protocol
Q2931:  0... .... =   ext
Q2931:  .11. .... =   layer 3 id
Q2931:  ...1 0000 = User info layer 3 protocol(User specified)
Q2931:  1... .... =   ext
Q2931:  .00. .... =    mode(invalid)
Q2931:  ...0 0000 =   spare
Q2931:    Default packet size = invalid
Q2931:    Packet window size = 21
Q2931: *** 4 byte(s) extra
Q2931:
Q2931: Info element id        = 70 (Called party number)
Q2931: Coding Standard/Action = 80
Q2931:  1... .... =            ext
Q2931:  .00. .... =            code stand(ITU-T standardized)
Q2931:  ...0 .... =            flag(not significant)
Q2931:  .... .000 =            IE instruction field(clear call)
Q2931: Length of info element = 21 byte(s)
Q2931:  1... .... =            ext
Q2931:  .000 .... =            type of num(Unknown)
Q2931:  .... 0010 =            addressing/num plan id(ATM Endsystem
Address)
Q2931: 39:2000:0000 0000 0000 0000 0000:020B481F2000:00
Q2931:
Q2931: Info element id        = 6C (Calling party number)
Q2931: Coding Standard/Action = 80
Q2931:  1... .... =            ext
Q2931:  .00. .... =            code stand(ITU-T standardized)
Q2931:  ...0 .... =            flag(not significant)
Q2931:  .... .000 =            IE instruction field(clear call)
Q2931: Length of info element = 21 byte(s)
Q2931:  1... .... =            ext
```

```
Q2931:    .000 .... =             type of num(Unknown)
Q2931:    .... 0010 =             addressing/num plan id(ATM Endsystem
Address)
Q2931: 39:2000:0000 0000 0000 0000 0000:WllfltCB2BE7:03
Q2931:
Q2931: Info element id        = 5C (Quality of Service)
Q2931: Coding Standard/Action = 80
Q2931:    1... .... =             ext
Q2931:    .00. .... =             code stand(ITU-T standardized)
Q2931:    ...0 .... =             flag(not significant)
Q2931:    .... .000 =             IE instruction field(clear call)
Q2931: Length of info element = 2 byte(s)
Q2931: QoS class
Q2931:    QoS forward  =  QoS class 0 - Unspecified QoS class
Q2931:    QoS backward =  QoS class 0 - Unspecified QoS class
```

# Processing ATM Calls

The UNI specification details the methods by which calls are established and maintained. The procedure and control parameters for the ATM UNI call are partially determined by the type of call being made. These call formats are broken down into three main categories:

- **Point-to-point CAC**   In this case, may refer to a unidirectional LANE control connection, such as a Control Direct VCC or a Data Direct VCC (discussed in greater detail later in this chapter, in the section regarding LANE).

- **Point-to-multipoint CAC**   In this case, may refer to a bidirectional LANE control connection, such as a Multicast Forward VCC (also discussed in greater detail in the section regarding LANE).

- **Global call references**   Relate to global procedures, such as restarting a call or global call status.

## Point-to-Point Call Control Indications

The UNI call control for point-to-point connections can be broken down into three basic categories: call establishment, call clearing, and miscellaneous control messages.

### Call Establishment Messages

These control messages are related to the establishment of point-to-point calls through the ATM network. These messages can be viewed in an ATM sniffer trace, to track point-to-point calls across the ATM UNI.

**SETUP**   This message is sent to initiate call establishment, whether from the user to the network or from the network to the user.

**CALL PROCEEDING**   This message may involve user-to-network calls, as well as network-to-user calls. The CALL PROCEEDING message is sent either by the called user to the network or by the network to the calling user. Call establishment has begun at this point and, until its resolution, no more call establishment information will be accepted.

**CONNECT**   The CONNECT message is sent either by the called user to the network or by the network to the calling user, depending on the direction of the call. This message indicates that the call has been accepted.

**CONNECT ACKNOWLEDGE**   This is an acknowledgement either from the network to the called user or from the user to the network acknowledging that the call has been accepted.

## Call Clearing Messages

These messages are related to the normal tear-down of established calls and the release of resources associated with those calls to be allocated for reuse.

**RELEASE**   The user may send this message to request that the network clear the end-to-end connection, meaning that if the user side of the UNI wants to tear down a connection, the network side is notified so that the entire end-to-end call is released. This message may also be sent by the network to the user, indicating that it should release its virtual channel if the end-to-end connection is cleared.

**RELEASE COMPLETE**   This message is sent by the network side if the remote end of the end-to-end connection indicates that the virtual channel has been released and is available for reuse; it is sent by the user side if those resources are released. The receiver must release the call at this point.

## SVC Status Messages

The SVC status can be checked through the use of status enquiries and their associated responses, to determine whether a connection is still viable. Although a STATUS ENQUIRY is not specifically required, a status response is required if an enquiry is made.

**STATUS ENQUIRY**   A STATUS ENQUIRY may be sent by the network or the user to check the integrity of a call state. Once the STATUS ENQUIRY has been made, the T322 timer begins in anticipation of receiving a Status message in response. If the T322 timer expires before receiving a STATUS message, then the call is cleared with a cause code of 41, indicating a temporary failure.

**STATUS**   The STATUS message must be sent in response to a STATUS ENQUIRY, to indicate the current condition of the call. The Status response to this enquiry is mandatory.

# Global Call Reference Messages

These messages are global messages, indicating either a call restart and clearing of resources or the validation of a current call state. These messages may be sent by either the user or the network side of the UNI.

## RESTART

This message is sent when a request is being made to the recipient to release all resources associated with a particular call.

## RESTART ACKNOWLEDGE

In response to a RESTART message, a RESTART ACKNOWLEDGE is sent to indicate to the sender that the requested resources have been released, and that the restart is completed.

# Point-to-Multipoint Call Control

A point-to-multipoint call may include a fixed number of endpoints, or, as is the case with certain LANE control channels, new endpoints may be added dynamically. For example, in a LANE network with three LAN Emulation Clients (LECs), a LAN Emulation Server (LES) may have a point-to-multipoint Control Distribute VCC connection with itself as the starting point, and each LEC as one of the three remote end points. If a new LEC is configured or added to the existing ATM network, the point-to-multipoint control connection is not released and reestablished, rather, the new LEC is added as an endpoint to the existing point-to-multipoint circuit. LANE, as well as these control connections, are covered in greater detail later in this chapter. The following messages are utilized in this regard:

## ADD PARTY

This message is sent if a new party needs to be added to an existing point-to-multipoint connection, such as is the case whenever a new LEC joins its LES or BUS.

## ADD PARTY ACKNOWLEDGE

Upon the successful addition of the party to the existing call, this message is sent to indicate that the addition of the new party was successful.

## ADD PARTY REJECT

If the ADD PARTY request is unsuccessful for any reason, then the call is rejected and an ADD PARTY REJECT message is sent to indicate this.

## DROP PARTY

This message is sent to clear an existing party from a point-to-multipoint connection. The receiving party must clear its connection upon receipt of this message.

ATM TECHNOLOGIES

## DROP PARTY ACKNOWLEDGE

This message is sent in response to the DROP PARTY message to indicate that the requested party has been dropped from the point-to-multipoint connection.

## LEAF SETUP REQUEST (UNI 4.0)

This message is specific to UNI 4.0 and may be extended from the user or network side. This message is used to initiate the leaf joining procedure.

## LEAF SETUP FAILURE (UNI 4.0)

This message is sent to the leaf attempting a leaf-initiated join to a point-to-multipoint call. This message is generated either by the root or by the network.

### UNI Cause Codes

A failed UNI call is accompanied by a cause code, describing the reason for the call failure or the call release. Table 13-3 describes these cause codes.

| Cause Code | Reason for Failure/Release |
|:---:|:---|
| 1 | Unallocated or unassigned number |
| 2 | No route to specified transit network |
| 3 | No route to destination |
| 16 | Normal call clearing |
| 17 | User busy |
| 18 | No user responding |
| 21 | Call rejected |
| 22 | Number changed |
| 23 | User rejects all calls with calling line ID restriction |
| 27 | Destination out of order |
| 28 | Invalid number format (address incomplete) |
| 30 | Response to STATUS ENQUIRY |
| 31 | Normal, unspecified |
| 35 | Requested VPI/VCI not available |
| 36 | VPI/VCI assignment failure |

**Table 13-3.** *UNI Cause Codes*

| Cause Code | Reason for Failure/Release |
|:---:|:---|
| 37 | User cell rate not available |
| 38 | Network out of order |
| 41 | Temporary failure |
| 43 | Access information discarded |
| 45 | No VPI/VCI available |
| 47 | Resource unavailable, unspecified |
| 49 | Quality of Service unavailable |
| 57 | Bearer capability not authorized |
| 58 | Bearer capability not presently available |
| 63 | Service or option not available, unspecified |
| 65 | Bearer capability not implemented |
| 73 | Unsupported combination of traffic parameters |
| 78 | AAL parameters cannot be supported |
| 81 | Invalid call reference value |
| 82 | Identified channel does not exist |
| 88 | Incompatible destination |
| 89 | Invalid endpoint reference |
| 91 | Invalid transit network selection |
| 92 | Too many pending Add Party requests |
| 96 | Mandatory information element missing |
| 97 | Message type nonexistent or not implemented |
| 99 | Information element nonexistent or not implemented |
| 100 | Invalid information element contents |
| 101 | Message not compatible with call state |
| 102 | Recovery on timer expiry |
| 104 | Incorrect message length |
| 111 | Protocol error, unspecified |

**Table 13-3.**   *UNI Cause Codes* (continued)

ATM TECHNOLOGIES

# ATM Signaling Timers

ATM signaling has a series of timers associated with it; these timers are referred to in the format T3*xx*. These timers ensure that the ATM signaling protocols remain synchronized. Also, in the event of a failure, they ensure that errors are detected and reported in a consistent way. Sometimes these timers are configurable, and other times not; this depends largely on the vendor and the specific product line. These timers have the following meanings and values:

- **T303**   Setup Sent timer value. Begins when a call request is initiated by sending a SETUP message over the signaling VC, and stops when a CONNECT, CALL PROCEEDING, or RELEASE COMPLETE message is received. If the timer expires without the receipt of any of these messages, a second attempt is made. If the timer expires a second time, the connection is cleared.

- **T308**   Release Sent timer. Begins when a RELEASE message is sent to clear an SVC, and stops when a RELEASE or RELEASE COMPLETE message is received (the receipt of a RELEASE message in this case indicates simultaneous transmission of a RELEASE message). If no message is received prior to expiration, then the RESTART procedure is initiated.

- **T309**   SAAL Data Link Connect timer. Begins when an SAAL malfunction occurs, and stops when the Signaling AAL is reestablished.

- **T310**   Call Proceeding Received timer. Begins when a CALL PROCEEDING message is received, and stops when either a CONNECT or RELEASE message is received. If one of the follow-up messages is not received prior to the timer's expiration, the call is cleared.

- **T313**   Connect Send timer. Begins when a CONNECT message is sent, and stops when a CONNECT ACKNOWLEDGE message is received. If the timer expires without receiving the CONNECT ACKNOWLEDGE message, the call is cleared.

- **T316**   Restart Request Sent on Interface timer. Initiated by a RESTART message where the interface is to be cleared, and stops when a RESTART ACKNOWLEDGE message is received. If the timer expires prior to receiving this message, additional messages may be sent. If the maximum number of retries is reached and still no response is received, the circuit enters a NULL state.

- **T317**   Restart Request Send on Channel timer. Initiated by a RESTART message where a single VC is to be restarted rather than the whole interface, and stops when a RESTART ACKNOWLEDGE message is received. If the timer expires prior to receiving this message, additional messages may be sent. If the maximum number of retries is reached and still no response is received, the VC enters a NULL state.

- **T322**   Status Enquiry Sent timer. Begins when a STATUS ENQUIRY message is sent, and stops when a STATUS message is received. If no STATUS message is received, then additional STATUS ENQUIRY messages may be sent. If still no response is received, the call is cleared.

- **T331**   Leaf Setup Request Sent timer. Begins when a LEAF SETUP REQUEST is issued, and stops when a SETUP, ADD PARTY, or LEAF SETUP FAILURE message is received. If one of these messages is not received before the expiration of this timer, an additional LEAF SETUP REQUEST may be sent. If, after the second instance, a valid response is not received, the call is cleared and a NULL LIJ state is entered.

- **T398**   Drop Party Sent timer. Begins when a DROP PARTY message is sent, and stops when a DROP PARTY ACKNOWLEDGE or RELEASE message is received. If no such messages are received prior to the timer's expiration, the call is cleared. This timer applies to multipoint circuits only.

- **T399**   Add Party Sent timer. Begins when an ADD PARTY message is sent, and stops when either an ADD PARTY ACKNOWLEDGE, ADD PARTY REJECT, or RELEASE message is received. If the timer expires without such a control message being received, the call is cleared. This timer applies to multipoint circuits only.

# Interim Local Management Interface (ILMI)

ILMI is an integral component of UNI signaling. ILMI signaling occurs over the reserved VPI/VCI channel 0/16, and is responsible for the following:

- **Transmission type**   ILMI keeps track of the ATM framing method (in other words, SONET, STS-3, DS-3, 100Mbps TAXI, OC-3, and so on).

- **Media Type**   Refers to the cable type, such as coaxial cable, UTP, Multi- or Single-Mode fiber.

- **Physical Layer Operations**   Refer to the current port state, indicating whether the port in question is in service, out of service, or looped back.

- **Adjacency Information**   A table is maintained of adjacent systems in order to facilitate autodiscovery and tracing of ATM connections by network management.

ILMI may also keep track of the maximum number of VPCs, the maximum number of VCCs, as well as the transmit and receive QoS.

ATM TECHNOLOGIES

## Address Registration

Address registration is one of ILMI's primary functions. It is through ILMI that ATM UNI-attached devices register their addresses with the switch they are attached to. A device such as an ATM-attached server, connected to a switch, must register its address with its host switch. Once the port initializes, the LEC will attempt to bring up the ILMI channel to make this registration.

In a legacy network, the device's MAC address is the vital portion; the hardware address is needed before any communication can occur to or from the device. ATM uses MAC addresses as well, in the case of LANE, but as a native technology, it is mainly concerned with ATM addresses:

- **ATM Address** 39:00:10:31:00:00:00:00:00:00:00:11:00:40:00:01:E3:F0:A8:01
- **MAC Address** 00:00:A0:19:BD:E8

ATM addresses are 20 octets in length, and consist of 4-byte nibbles. The following are their component parts:

| | |
|---|---|
| Address | 39.00.10.31.00.00.00.00.00.00.00.11.00.40.00.01.E3.F0.A8.01 |
| NSAP prefix | 39.00.10.31.00.00.00.00.00.00.00.11.00 |
| ESI | 40.00.01.E3.F0.A8 |
| Selector byte | 01 |

## Network Service Access Point Prefix

The first 13 bytes of the ATM address are known as the Network Service Access Point (NSAP) prefix. This is the portion of the ATM address that describes a logical identification for a particular ATM node. The NSAP prefix may vary, depending on whether the switch is in a private or public network, as well as on the method of call routing that is chosen.

In a private network, the administrator can assign the NSAP prefix to whatever they wish, bound only by the call routing method used. (IISP demands each NSAP prefix varies with no concessions to level or scope, while nodes in a common peer group in a PNNI environment share a commonly masked prefix portion, and PNNI nodes in separate peer groups will each have a uniquely masked portions of the prefix. For more information on these routing protocols and their addressing requirements, consult Chapters 15 and 16.)

In the preceding example, the switch prefix is 39.00.10.31.00.00.00.00.00.00.00.14.00.00. In a private network, this can be simplified, and often is, to use only the first few octets. An NSAP address could be simplified to just 39.10.00.00.00.00.00.00.00.00.00.00.00, for instance. In private networks, this address is very likely in common use. As in IP, it is okay to use an arbitrary addressing scheme as long as the switches are not a part of the public ATM network. In the public forum, the NSAP prefix must adhere to the scheme that has been standardized as follows:

39.CCCC.RR.AAAAAA.WW.WW.XX.XX.XX.XX.YYYYYYYYYYYY.ZZ

| Field | Description |
| --- | --- |
| 39 | Defines the address as a DCC ATM Format |
| CCCC | Country Code; 840F indicates US (840 plus an F for pad) |
| RR | Registering body; 80 defines registration with ANSI |
| AAAAAA | The Administrative Authority (the organization that requested the registered NSAP) |
| WW.WW | Reserved |
| XX.XX.XX.XX | Routing Domain (RD) and Area; the field defined to be used in addressing your switches |
| YYYYYYYY... | End Station Identifier (ESI) |
| ZZ | Selector byte |

The NSAP prefix is provided by the switch. It can be statically defined on a UNI device attached to the switch, but in such a case, the prefix must match that of the switch.

The 6 bytes that follow the prefix are known as the End System Identifier (ESI). The ESI can be manually configured, like the NSAP; if it isn't manually configured, it will be automatically generated by the device, based on its MAC address. Like a MAC address, it is 6 bytes long. This field is common to all ATM devices, and will be generated by any LEC, regardless of whether it resides on a switch, a router, or an end station.

The ESI is either generated automatically or statically defined on the client; again, regardless of where that client resides. The last byte, the selector byte, is a unique identifier and is not used for routing purposes. It is a single byte long.

These portions of the ATM address are a way of identifying where in the network a call originates. The two major portions of the address, the NSAP prefix and ESI, indicate the switch and the end system, respectively.

## Address Registration Over ILMI

When the ATM-attached UNI device first initializes, it does not require an NSAP prefix to be preconfigured. In accordance with the UNI specification, it only needs a MAC address. The end device and the switch to which it is attached communicate over the ILMI channel to exchange address information, so that the UNI device may receive a valid ATM address.

The exchange of address information takes place over the ILMI channel of 0/16. The UNI device contacts the switch and communicates its MAC address or, if the ESI

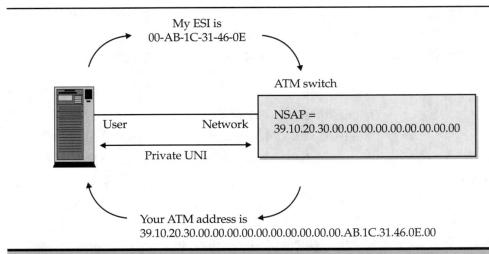

My ESI is
00-AB-1C-31-46-0E

ATM switch

User        Network

NSAP =
39.10.20.30.00.00.00.00.00.00.00.00.00.00

Private UNI

Your ATM address is
39.10.20.30.00.00.00.00.00.00.00.00.00.00.AB.1C.31.46.0E.00

**Figure 13-3.**   *A prefix/ESI exchange between the end device and the switch*

portion has been statically configured on the device, this value is sent. The switch then takes the 6-byte ESI and adds its NSAP prefix to it, as well as the selector. This becomes the UNI device's ATM address. This full ATM address is communicated back to the UNI device, and it is now a part of the ATM network (see Figure 13-3). This is the primary function of ILMI.

# LAN Emulation Version 1

LAN Emulation was created to resolve the inherent differences between legacy networking technologies and ATM. In the case of Ethernet, a connectionless technology, a way needed to be devised to make the connection-oriented architecture of ATM invisible to the legacy network. In the case of Token Ring, likewise, the cell-switched, connection-oriented ATM mesh needed to be made to seem like just another part of the token-passing, ring-based architecture. The mechanism that was decided upon is LANE.

ATM in and of itself does not require LANE; in fact, it works more efficiently without it. Legacy networks are already in very common and extensive use, however, and it is unrealistic that the legacy infrastructure be removed and replaced with native ATM in the majority of cases. LANE is a necessity, then, if ATM is to function dynamically in a practical environment.

ATM is a connection-oriented technology, meaning that all communications are processed over a channel that is created strictly for that transfer. This is true whether the environment is LANE or native ATM. In a strictly ATM environment, all calls are processed point-to-point or point-to-multipoint, and this connection takes us all the way from sender to receiver:

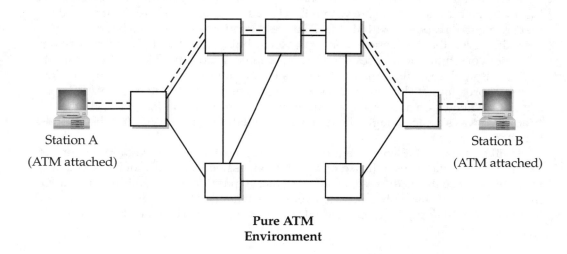

**Pure ATM
Environment**

However, in a LANE environment, the circuit begins at the local edge of the ATM mesh and takes us only to the remote edge of the mesh:

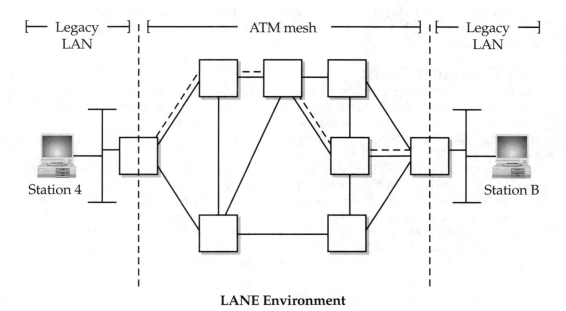

**LANE Environment**

For example, if an IP client on an Ethernet segment initiates a transmission to another IP Ethernet device—one that it either hasn't communicated with before or has communicated with but has aged out of its ARP cache—it first must ARP to resolve the destination station's hardware address. An ARP request is, of course, a broadcast, and is seen by all the clients who are within that broadcast domain. If the client is local to that segment, it responds with its MAC address, and transmission can begin.

If, however, the destination client is not local, but is in fact on the other side of an ATM network, a problem arises. An Ethernet client has no way of knowing the ATM network is in place at all, let alone that it is a connection-oriented protocol that makes no use of broadcasts. The station does what it always does: it broadcasts an ARP request. (When PVCs had been erected, prior to the implementation of LANE, the procedure was simple enough: the ARP was flooded across the PVC, and the response was flooded back.)

Unlike PVCs, LANE was meant to be dynamic insofar as, once configured and set in place, calls could be established and torn down as needed instead of being cemented in place. Because this is the case, no circuit exists to pass station-to-station traffic across initially, because it hasn't been created yet. The challenge of LANE was to do this, and to make the entire operation transparent to the legacy network, which has no way of allowing for ATM.

# LANE Components

To implement the idea of an Emulated LAN (ELAN), several components or entities were decided on to handle the legacy traffic. The sections that follow provide a brief description of each of the LANE components and its primary functions. These descriptions are meant to be fairly simple, as a prelude to how they interact with each other and, ultimately, how they work together in a live network to route legacy communications.

## LAN Emulation Client

The LEC is the entity that handles the transition between the legacy network and the ATM network, and back again. Two types of LEC exist: 802.3 Ethernet and 802.5 Token Ring. This section will concentrate on the Ethernet variety. For more information regarding Token Ring LECs, consult Chapter 25, which describes source routing over Token Ring LANE.

To understand how the LEC works, it helps to think of it as a virtual switched port on the switch. In reality, it is a more complex entity than that, but for purposes of understanding how Ethernet transmissions are received by the ATM network, the LEC does serve in this capacity. An Ethernet transmission goes through two basic phases: finding its destination via a broadcast, and then being switched along the appropriate path after it has been established. By creating this entity, you are effectively creating virtual port that will receive any Ethernet broadcasts coming in to that switch.

For example, a station (station A) is connected directly to a switched port on a switch that is both Ethernet- and ATM-capable, in a network containing only one ELAN (see Figure 13-14). Each switch has a single Ethernet LEC configured on it, each of which is a member of the ELAN. The LEC is the legacy network's gateway to the ATM mesh, and each switch has its own gateway, including the one station A is connected to. Station A initiates a transmission to another station elsewhere in the network. Station A ARPs to gain the remote station's hardware address. The switch receives this broadcast and floods it out all of its ports, hoping to reach the destination. The broadcast hits every switched port including the LEC.

The LEC doesn't handle the broadcast in the same way the legacy Ethernet ports do. It does, however, make it appear to the switch and the rest of the Ethernet network as though this is what it has done. Once the call has been processed, it appears to station A as though the remote station is on its local segment. This is covered in more detail a bit further on. For now, just understand the LEC's basic function in LANE, which is to receive incoming legacy frames, and then determine where across the ATM network the destination lies and erect a circuit to the LEC associated with that destination in such a way that is invisible to the legacy clients.

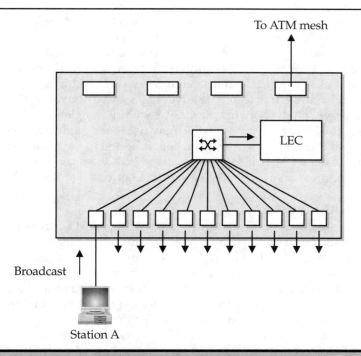

**Figure 13-4.** *A broadcast hitting the LEC*

## LAN Emulation Configuration Server

The LECS plays a relatively minor role in LANE, and, in fact, is optional in LANE version 1. LANE version 2, with the advent of MPOA, may require the use of a LECS if MPOA clients and servers are to obtain their configuration dynamically. The LECS has one primary purpose, which is to supply LECs with the ATM address of the LES that serves their ELAN.

In essence, the LECS acts as a database of ELAN names and the LES addresses associated with those ELANs. It is a static entity that, once created, remains active to serve any new LECs.

When a LEC first initializes, if it is configured to use a LECS, the first thing that it does is initiate a call to the LECS. Once the connection is established, the LEC will request to join the ELAN it has been configured for. It will communicate the ELAN name to the LECS, which in turn checks whether the ELAN is found in its table. If it is, the LECS then checks whether the LEC's Time, Length, and Value (TLV) parameters match those configured for that ELAN (for example, the ELAN in the LECS table is configured for 802.3 Ethernet, so it must check to make sure the LEC is an 802.3 client not an 802.5 client). If the parameters match, the LECS matches the ATM address of the ELAN's LES to the name of the ELAN requested, and transmits that address to the LEC, so that it may in turn initiate a call to the LES.

After this exchange of information takes place, the LEC and the LECS do not need to communicate any further. The connection between the LEC and the LECS is torn down, and doesn't need to be reestablished unless the LEC reinitializes.

Again, in many cases, the LECS is optional. If desired, an ATM client may be configured to not use the LECS, and instead have the ATM address of its LES statically entered so that it bypasses this step. The advantages and disadvantages to using an LECS depend largely on the network, and LECs within a single ELAN do not need to use the LECS exclusively or bypass it; some may use it and some may not. The LECS is a convenient mechanism, however, since clients added in the future need only be given their ELAN name. Also, if for any reason a LES address is changed, having to reconfigure the address on every switch across the network would be time-consuming.

## LAN Emulation Server

The primary function of the LES is to assist in resolving ATM address-to-MAC address pairings. This is similar in concept to an ARP, and in fact, the method used to resolve these addresses is called an LE_ARP (LAN Emulation ARP). In a legacy network, two devices must know each other's MAC address to communicate; in an ATM environment, each device must know the other's ATM address if they are to initiate a call. In a LANE environment, because the legacy clients will be looking for the destination's MAC, and because the ATM clients will be looking for the destination LEC's ATM address, a mechanism is needed to make a MAC-to-ATM address association.

When the LEC receives traffic destined for a station behind a remote LEC, two things may happen. If it is a broadcast, such as an initial ARP, the broadcast will be forwarded to the Broadcast and Unknown Server (BUS) for processing. If the destination address is known by the sending station, the LEC will issue an LE_ARP control frame to the LES to see whether it knows which remote LEC the MAC address is associated with (see Figure 13-5). If the MAC-to-ATM address association is not currently registered with the LES, it forwards the LE_ARP_REQUEST over its control channels to each LEC which has joined to it. The remote LEC which is associated with the destination MAC address responds with an LE_ARP_RESPONSE and the LES forwards the LE_ARP_RESPONSE to the originating LEC. The originating LEC notes the remote LEC's ATM address, and places this MAC-to-ATM address mapping in its table so that further attempts to reach that destination can be directed there immediately. If the LES already has the mapping in its table when the LE_ARP_REQUEST comes in, it may reply to the LEC with an LE_ARP_RESPONSE.

## Broadcast and Unknown Server

The BUS is responsible for handing any broadcast traffic that enters the ATM mesh from the legacy LAN. If a broadcast comes in, it must be flooded to every LEC common to that ELAN, so that it is seen within the entire broadcast domain. This operation is handled by the BUS. Likewise, if a transmission to a client whose destination MAC is known by the sender, but not known by, or aged out of, the switch receiving it, then the frame must be flooded to determine where the destination address lies. The BUS processes these frames as well, until such time as the MAC-to-ATM mapping of the destination station is determined.

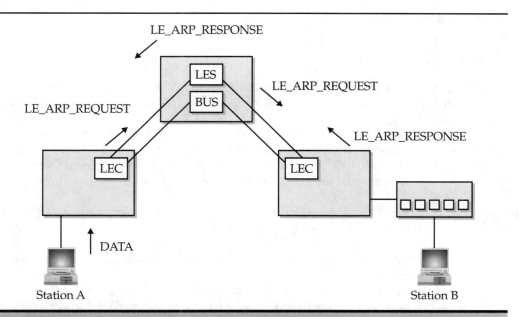

**Figure 13-5.** *An LE_ARP_REQUEST and the subsequent LE_ARP_RESPONSE*

# Emulated LANs

The LANE processes need to initialize and join together correctly before any traffic can flow from the legacy network across the ATM mesh. In the LANE scenario, this constitutes the establishment of an ELAN. The ELAN is a *logical broadcast domain* in that, although ATM doesn't broadcast per se, traffic from one ELAN will never cross over into another ELAN unless routed there. An ATM network may contain many ELANs, both for Ethernet and Token Ring. Ethernet and Token Ring ELANs can coexist simultaneously in the LANE environment.

The individual LANE components described previously make up different ELANs together. Each ELAN is serviced by a single LES and a single BUS, unless a vendor-specific method is in place to allow LES/BUS cooperation. A LES/BUS pair will service multiple clients, or LECs, each of which is a member of that ELAN.

## Connecting an ELAN

In the following example, a LEC utilizes a LECS to obtain its LES address. The LEC, once initialized, enters the LECS connect phase. At this point, the LEC attempts to establish a connection with the LECS.

### Connecting to the LECS

The LEC obtains the address of the LECS in one of the following ways:

- Find the LECS via ILMI
- Use the well-known address (WKA)
- Use the LECS PVC

If the LEC uses ILMI, then it issues an ILMI Get to find the address over its UNI connection. If it fails, it has the option of doing another ILMI Get to find any additional Configuration Servers that may exist.

If the LEC uses the WKA, then the address is preconfigured and already known. The WKA is the common, reserved address 47.00.79.00.00.00.00.00.00.00.00.00.00.00. A0.3E.00.00.01.00 that all ATM switches recognize. If the LEC doesn't use either of these choices, it must use the reserved signaling channel of 0/17 for the connection.

 *Due to the possibility of multiple active LECS entities in accordance with the LNNI specifications, the option of using signaling channel 0/17 was removed in LANE 2.0.*

The initial connection between the LEC and its LECS is called the Configuration Direct VCC (Figure 13-6).

During the configuration phase, the LEC attempts to find the address of the LES serving the ELAN that it wants to join, as well as exchange TLVs. Two basic types of control frames are utilized during this procedure: the LE_CONFIGURE_REQUEST

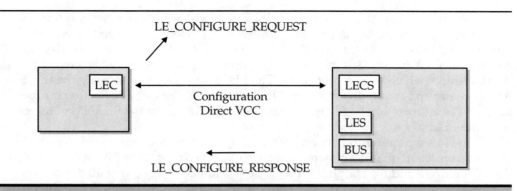

**Figure 13-6.**    *The Configuration Direct VCC*

and the LE_CONFIGURE_RESPONSE. The LEC sends the LE_CONFIGURE_REQUEST to the LECS to obtain information regarding the LES. This control frame includes the ELAN name of the ELAN that the LEC wants to join, as well as a series of control TLVs. For example, the following is an excerpt from an ATM sniffer trace, taken during the join phase, which shows the LE_CONFIGURE_REQUEST:

```
LANE: ----- LAN EMULATION CONTROL FRAME -----
LANE:
LANE: Marker        = FF00
LANE: Protocol      = 01
LANE: Version       = 01
LANE: Opcode        = 0001 (CONFIGURE_REQUEST)
LANE: Status        = 0 (Success)
LANE: Trans ID      = 181272849
LANE: Request ID    = 0
LANE: Flags         = 0000
LANE: Src LAN Dest  = 0000000000000000
LANE:   Tag         = 0000(not present)
LANE:    MAC Adr    = 000000000000(not present)
LANE: Tar LAN Dest  = 0000000000000000
LANE:   Tag         = 0000(not present)
LANE:    MAC Adr    = 000000000000(not present)
LANE: SRC ATM ADDR  = 39:2000:0000 0000 0000 0000 AA00:DDDDDDDDDDDD:FF
LANE: LAN-TYPE      = 01 (Ethernet/IEEE 802.3)
LANE: MAX FRAME SIZE= 01 (1516)
LANE: NUMBER TLVs   = 0
LANE: ELAN NAME SIZE= 5
LANE: TARG ATM ADDR = 00000000000000000000000000000000000000000
LANE: ELAN NAME     = "Sales"
```

The LAN type is included (Ethernet/IEEE 802.3), as well as the maximum frame size. The ATM address of the LEC that is attempting to join is included, as well (ATM address 39.20.00.00.00.00.00.00.00.00.AA.00.DD.DD.DD.DD.DD.DD.FF). The ELAN name, "Sales," is included at the end of the frame, and just above that is the target ATM address, which is currently all 0's. The LEC in this case is informing the LECS of its parameter and requesting membership in the ELAN "Sales." The 0 value for the target ATM address will be filled in when the LES address for the ELAN is obtained from the LECS.

If, due to a misconfiguration, any of the TLV parameters do not match up (the MTU size is inconsistent, the ELAN name is incorrect, and so forth), the LEC will be denied the LES address and the configuration phase will fail. Assuming that all the control parameters are consistent with those configured on the LECS, the LECS will then issue an LE_CONFIGURE_RESPONSE back to the LEC. The following is another excerpt taken from the same ATM sniffer trace, capturing the LE_CONFIGURE_RESPONSE:

```
LANE: ----- LAN EMULATION CONTROL FRAME -----
LANE:
LANE: Marker         = FF00
LANE: Protocol       = 01
LANE: Version        = 01
LANE: Opcode         = 0101 (CONFIGURE_RESPONSE)
LANE: Status         = 0 (Success)
LANE: Trans ID       = 181272849
LANE: Request ID     = 0
LANE: Flags          = 0000
LANE: Src LAN Dest   = 0000000000000000
LANE:    Tag         = 0000(not present)
LANE:    MAC Adr     = 000000000000(not present)
LANE: Tar LAN Dest   = 0000000000000000
LANE:    Tag         = 0000(not present)
LANE:    MAC Adr     = 000000000000(not present)
LANE: SRC ATM ADDR   = 39:2000:0000 0000 0000 0000 AA00:DDDDDDDDDDDD:FF
LANE: LAN-TYPE       = 01 (Ethernet/IEEE 802.3)
LANE: MAX FRAME SIZE= 01 (1516)
LANE: NUMBER TLVs    = 0
LANE: ELAN NAME SIZE= 5
LANE: TARG ATM ADDR = 39:2000:0000 0000 0000 0000 0000:BBBBBBBBBBBB:01
LANE: ELAN NAME      = "Sales"
```

The target ATM address has been specified in the response, indicating the LES address for the "Sales" ELAN. After the control parameters are communicated and verified, the LECS sends back the LES address associated with that ELAN as per its user-configured table. At this point, the Configuration Direct VCC will be dropped.

## LANE Version 2 LECS Enhancements

In a LANEv2 environment, other TLV information is encoded in both the
LE_CONFIGURE_REQUEST and LE_CONFIGURE_RESPONSE. If the LEC initiating
the Control Distribute VCC is LANEv2-capable, it will communicate this fact to the
LECS during this exchange. Included with this information will be the ELAN ID for
the V2-capable ELAN.

In addition, if MPOA is being used, and the LEC in question is V2-capable, then the
presence of an MPOA Client (MPC) may also be communicated to the LECS at this
time if the MPC wishes to obtain its configuration information from the LECS. If so
configured, the LECS will respond with the configuration TLVs requested by the MPC in
the configuration response, and those values will be passed on to the MPC by the LEC.

## Initiating Connection to the LES

After the LEC has its parameters verified as a viable client in the ELAN that it wants
to join, and has obtained the LES address for that ELAN, it must initiate a connection
to that LES. This is the join phase. During the join phase, the LEC attempts to establish
a connection with its LES. This procedure has two types of control frames: the
LE_JOIN_REQUEST and the LE_JOIN_RESPONSE (Figure 13-7).

The LEC initiates signaling procedures to establish a bidirectional, point-to-point
connection, known as the Control Direct VCC, between itself and the LES. It is over this
connection that the LE_JOIN_REQUEST will be sent. The following is an example
LE_JOIN_REQUEST frame, issued from a LEC during its join phase:

```
LANE: ----- LAN EMULATION CONTROL FRAME -----
LANE:
LANE: Marker        = FF00
LANE: Protocol      = 01
LANE: Version       = 01
LANE: Opcode        = 0002 (JOIN_REQUEST)
LANE: Status        = 0 (Success)
LANE: Trans ID      = 181272850
LANE: Request ID    = 0
LANE: Flags         = 0000
LANE: Src LAN Dest  = 0000000000000000
LANE:    Tag        = 0000(not present)
LANE:    MAC Adr    = 000000000000(not present)
LANE: Tar LAN Dest  = 0000000000000000
LANE:    Tag        = 0000(not present)
LANE:    MAC Adr    = 000000000000(not present)
LANE: SRC ATM ADDR  = 39:2000:0000 0000 0000 0000 AA00:DDDDDDDDDDDD:FF
LANE: LAN-TYPE      = 01 (Ethernet/IEEE 802.3)
LANE: MAX FRAME SIZE= 01 (1516)
LANE: NUMBER TLVs   = 0
LANE: ELAN NAME SIZE = 5
LANE: TARG ATM ADDR = 000000000000000000000000000000000000000000000000
LANE: ELAN NAME     = "Sales"
```

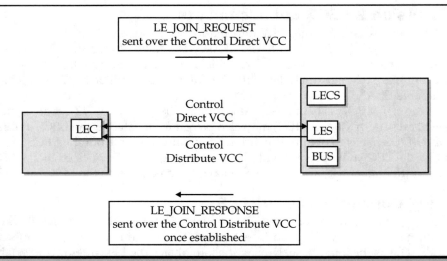

**Figure 13-7.**   *An LE_JOIN_REQUEST and the LE_JOIN_RESPONSE*

The target ATM address has reverted to all 0's in this frame, because the LES is already being contacted in this case, and the value is ignored upon receipt.

Once the Control Direct VCC is established, the LES may attempt to set up a point-to-multipoint unidirectional connection called the Control Distribute VCC. This connection is optional, but if it is utilized, the LEC must accept it. It is considered point-to-multipoint because, unlike the Control Direct VCC, the LES maintains this connection not only with one LEC, but with every LEC that is a member of its ELAN. It is unidirectional in that the LEC may not send any data across this connection; it is for the sole use of the LES.

The LES will check for a duplicate MAC address. If two clients share the same MAC, the new client will not be allowed to join.

If the LES extends the Control Distribute VCC, and the LEC for whatever reason fails to accept it, the LES will terminate that ELAN membership, because its control frames will pass over this connection.

Since the use of the LECS is optional, the LES will also look at the same client values that the LECS will look at. LAN Type must either match or be "Unspecified." Likewise, MTU must be either "Unspecified" or less than or equal to the LES MTU size. If the join fails, the LEC must terminate the ELAN membership

If a Control Distribute VCC is used and accepted, then the LE_JOIN_RESPONSE will be sent over that channel. If it is not used, then the LE_JOIN_RESPONSE may alternately be sent back over the Control Direct VCC. If all the parameters are acceptable, then the

LES will issue the LE_JOIN_RESPONSE, indicating to the LEC that the join was successful. The following is a captured LE_JOIN_RESPONSE control frame:

```
LANE: ----- LAN EMULATION CONTROL FRAME -----
LANE:
LANE: Marker         = FF00
LANE: Protocol       = 01
LANE: Version        = 01
LANE: Opcode         = 0102 (JOIN_RESPONSE)
LANE: Status         = 0 (Success)
LANE: Trans ID       = 181272850
LANE: Request ID     = 11
LANE: Flags          = 0000
LANE: Src LAN Dest    = 0000000000000000
LANE:   Tag          = 0000(not present)
LANE:   MAC Adr      = 000000000000(not present)
LANE: Tar LAN Dest    = 0000000000000000
LANE:   Tag          = 0000(not present)
LANE:   MAC Adr      = 000000000000(not present)
LANE: SRC ATM ADDR    = 39:2000:0000 0000 0000 0000 AA00:DDDDDDDDDDDD:FF
LANE: LAN-TYPE       = 01 (Ethernet/IEEE 802.3)
LANE: MAX FRAME SIZE= 01 (1516)
LANE: NUMBER TLVs    = 0
LANE: ELAN NAME SIZE= 5
LANE: TARG ATM ADDR = 39:2000:0000 0000 0000 0000 0000:BBBBBBBBBBBB:01
LANE: ELAN NAME      = "Sales"
```

## Initiating Connection to the BUS

Now the LEC must join the BUS (see Figure 13-8). All LECs must join the BUS. The BUS address is determined by issuing an LE_ARP_REQUEST. The LEC sends an LE_ARP_REQUEST to the LES for an all F's broadcast MAC address to find this address, and the LES in turn responds with an LE_ARP_RESPONSE containing the ATM address of the BUS.

The following is a capture of this specific LE_ARP_REQUEST, as the LEC attempts to resolve its BUS address:

```
LANE: ----- LAN EMULATION CONTROL FRAME -----
LANE:
LANE: Marker         = FF00
LANE: Protocol       = 01
LANE: Version        = 01
LANE: Opcode         = 0006 (ARP_REQUEST)
LANE: Status         = 0 (Success)
LANE: Trans ID       = 181272851
LANE: Request ID     = 11
LANE: Flags          = 0000
LANE: Src LAN Dest    = 0000000000000000
```

```
LANE:    Tag         = 0000(not present)
LANE:    MAC Adr     = 000000000000(not present)
LANE: Tar LAN Dest   = 0001FFFFFFFFFFFF
LANE:    Tag         = 0001(MAC address)
LANE:    MAC Adr     = FFFFFFFFFFFF
LANE: SRC ATM ADDR   = 39:2000:0000 0000 0000 0000 AA00:DDDDDDDDDDDD:FF
LANE: Reserved       = 0000
LANE: NUMBER TLVs    = 0
LANE: Reserved       = 00
LANE: TARG ATM ADDR  = 000000000000000000000000000000000000000000
LANE: Reserved       = 0043454E0101FFFF000000006D794D5900000000000000000000000000000000000000
```

The target ATM address is all 0's in this case, because the BUS address is not yet known. The LES then replies with an LE_ARP_RESPONSE containing the BUS address, as shown in the following response frame:

```
LANE: ----- LAN EMULATION CONTROL FRAME -----
LANE:
LANE: Marker         = FF00
LANE: Protocol       = 01
LANE: Version        = 01
LANE: Opcode         = 0106 (ARP_RESPONSE)
LANE: Status         = 0 (Success)
LANE: Trans ID       = 181272851
LANE: Request ID     = 11
LANE: Flags          = 0000
LANE: Src LAN Dest   = 0000000000000000
LANE:    Tag         = 0000(not present)
LANE:    MAC Adr     = 000000000000(not present)
LANE: Tar LAN Dest   = 0001FFFFFFFFFFFF
LANE:    Tag         = 0001(MAC address)
LANE:    MAC Adr     = FFFFFFFFFFFF
LANE: SRC ATM ADDR   = 39:2000:0000 0000 0000 0000 AA00:DDDDDDDDDDDD:FF
LANE: Reserved       = 0000
LANE: NUMBER TLVs    = 0
LANE: Reserved       = 00
LANE: TARG ATM ADDR  = 39:2000:0000 0000 0000 0000 0000:BBBBBBBBBBBB:02
LANE: Reserved       = 0043454E0101FFFF000000006D794D5900000000000000000000000000000000000000
```

Notice that the target ATM address is the same as that of the LES, except that the selector byte is 02 rather than 01. This is the default addressing scheme if the LES and BUS are co-located, as they are in this example. The LEC uses this address to initiate a call to the BUS, to establish a bidirectional, point-to-point connection called the Multicast Send VCC. All multicast and broadcast traffic will be transmitted to the BUS from the LEC over this VCC (see Figure 13-8).

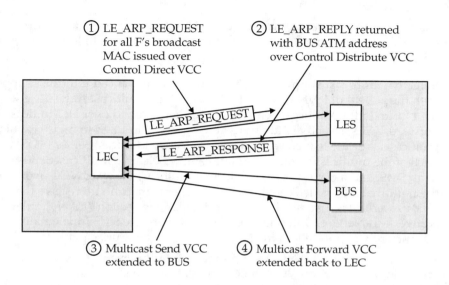

① LE_ARP_REQUEST for all F's broadcast MAC issued over Control Direct VCC

② LE_ARP_REPLY returned with BUS ATM address over Control Distribute VCC

③ Multicast Send VCC extended to BUS

④ Multicast Forward VCC extended back to LEC

**Figure 13-8.** *A call initiated to the BUS*

At this point, the BUS automatically initiates the setup of a point-to-multipoint, unidirectional connection to the LEC, called the Multicast Forward VCC, which the LEC must accept. It is over this connection that broadcasts and unknown frame floods will be sent. If at any time the Multicast Send VCC drops, the LEC will drop the Multicast Forward VCC, and vice versa; if the Multicast Forward VCC is dropped by the LEC, the BUS will drop the Multicast Send VCC.

Once these connections are in place, the configuration is complete, and the LEC transitions into an operational state. It is now a member of that ELAN.

## LANE Version 2

The LANEv2 specification was created as an enhancement and continuation of the LANEv1 specification. It includes enhancements to the existing LANE components, as well as the specific functionality of the LAN Emulation User to Network Interface (LUNI) and the LAN Emulation Network to Network Interface (LNNI).

## LANEv2 Features

LANEv2 is not an overall drastic change from LANEv1, but it does have some important added functionality and new features. Specifically, the following enhancements have been made:

- **Selective multicast support**    LANEv2 provides enhanced multicast support with the advent of LNNI. Unlike LANEv1, where multicast frames are sent by the LEC over the Multicast Send VCC and then flooded over all Multicast Forward VCCs, selective multicasts allow for certain LECs to register which multicasts they are to receive, by using a Selective Multicast Server (SMS) entity. Each of the multicast instances initiates a new Selective Multicast Send VCC to an SMS, and a corresponding Selective Multicast Forward VCC over which the multicast data is delivered only to the clients that should receive them. This procedure is discussed in greater detail in the section "LAN Emulation Network-to-Network Interface." LNNI, and therefore SMS functionality, are not currently supported on the Nortel Networks enterprise platforms.

- **LLC multiplexing**    LANEv1 supported nonmultiplexed VCCs only, meaning that a single Data Direct VCC could carry data for one LEC only. LANEv2 supports LLC multiplexing for VCCs, allowing multiple LAN emulation clients to share the same VCC. LLC multiplexing is supported on Data Direct VCCs only.

- **Quality of Service (QoS)**    QoS parameters may be attributed to Data Direct VCCs in LANEv2. The exact methods by which this is accomplished, and the details of call setup, are covered in Chapter 14.

- **Multiprotocol Over ATM (MPOA) support**    LANEv2 is a required component of MPOA; LANEv2 is necessary because its components support the additional TLVs required by MPOA, as well as MPOA Client (MPC) and MPOA Server (MPS) awareness on the part of the LEC.

# LANE User-to-Network Interface and LANE Network-to-Network Interface

In addition to the ATM UNI, which is concerned with the interaction between the ATM user (generally an end-system, such as an ATM-attached router or server) and the ATM network (an ATM switch), and ATM NNI, which is concerned with the interaction between ATM switches, LUNI and LNNI incorporate the same concepts into the ELAN services. LUNI, in this case, is concerned with the interaction between the LEC, which is considered the user in this instance, and the LANE services (such as the LECS, LES, and BUS), which are considered the network side. Likewise, the ATM LNNI is concerned with the interaction between LANE server entities, such as the LECS, LES, and BUS, in which no client is involved.

## ATM LANE User-to-Network Interface

Also referred to as LUNI 1.0 in LANEv1, ATM LUNI refers to the control functions between the LEC and both LANE services components, as well between LECs. LUNI is the control interface, with the LEC as the source or destination. Likewise, the LNNI constitutes the control connections that may exist between LANE services where the LEC is not involved, such as may exist between two LES entities (see Figure 13-9).

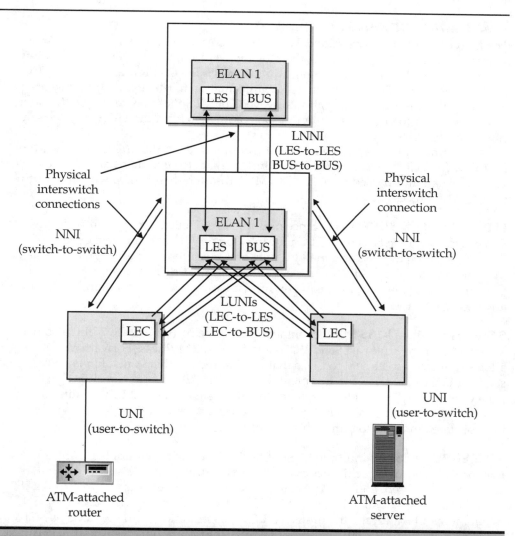

**Figure 13-9.**   *LUNI and LNNI vs. UNI and NNI interfaces*

ATM TECHNOLOGIES

## Maximum Frame Size

LANEv2 utilizes a larger maximum frame size than LANEv1 for 1580- and 1592-octet frames. This value is designated X"05" or simply X5. All LANEv2-capable components accept the X5 maximum frame size values; however, because V1 and V2 clients may coexist within not only the same network, but also the same ELAN, a conversion must take place when communicating between V1 and V2 LECs so that the maximum frame size is not exceeded.

## LEC Enhancements

The LANEv2 LEC supports added TLVs for MPOA; if an MPC exists on the same switch as a LANEv2-capable LEC, then the LEC will support this entity in a variety of functions. At the time of LECS registration, when the Configuration Direct VCC is established, the LEC will obtain its LES information for the ELAN that it wants to join. At this time, it will also allow any MPC or MPS that may reside on the same switch or router to obtain its configuration parameters from the LECS over the same control channel.

At the time of LES registration, the LEC communicates the presence of the MPC (or MPS, if the client exists on a router interface that also maintains an MPS) to the LES. This information is passed from MPC to MPS, through their respective LECs, during the LE_ARP process.

**LLC MULTIPLEX SUPPORT**    Since multiple LANE clients may share a single Data Direct VCC with the advent of LLC multiplexing on ATM Data Direct circuits offered in LANEv2, both the LES and the LEC may be configured with an ELAN ID. This value provides a unique identification for data flows originating in a specific ELAN, and prevents cells originating in one ELAN from crossing over to a client in another ELAN after being multiplexed.

**SELECTIVE MULTICAST**    In conjunction with the BUS, a LANEv2 LEC also may support Selective Multicast Send VCCs and Selective Multicast Forward VCCs. This allows multicasts to be sent to LECs that need to receive them only. For example, a series of LECs in a RIPv2 environment that have no RIPv2 routers residing on their legacy LANs may opt not to receive multicasts destined for the RIPv2 multicast group address. LNNI and its associated Selective Multicast Server (SMS) function must be incorporated in order to utilize this function.

**PREFERRED LES**    If multiple LES entities are used within a single ELAN, a LEC may be directed to a specific *preferred LES*. This address must be attempted first, is statically configured, and must be communicated to the LECS as the preferred LES if a LES address is obtained from the LECS. In the case where a LEC uses the LECS to obtain the LES address, the preferred LES is communicated to the LECS as a TLV embedded in the LE_CONFIGURE_REQUEST control frame. This is useful, because as part of the ATM LNNI (covered in the upcoming section, "LAN Emulation Network-to-Network Interface") involves the LECS dynamically monitoring each LES regarding its current operational status; the LECS in this case knows of each LES serving the ELAN and attempts to assign the requesting LEC to its preferred LES, provided it is operational. If the preferred LES is not operational, one of the cooperating LESs will be selected.

Once the LES address is obtained, a LEC indicates to the LES that it is V2-capable during the join process. The following is a control frame captured with a sniffer during the join phase of a V2 LEC while in the process of joining its LES:

```
LANE: ----- LAN EMULATION CONTROL FRAME -----
LANE:
LANE: Marker        = FF00
LANE: Protocol      = 01
LANE: Version       = 01
LANE: Opcode        = 0002 (JOIN_REQUEST)
LANE: Status        = 0 (Success)
LANE: Trans ID      = 181272850
LANE: Request ID    = 0
LANE: Flags         = 0002  A flag indicator of 0002 indicates V2 capability
LANE: Src LAN Dest  = 0000000000000000
LANE:    Tag        = 0000(not present)
LANE:    MAC Adr    = 000000000000(not present)
LANE: Tar LAN Dest  = 0000000000000000
LANE:    Tag        = 0000(not present)
LANE:    MAC Adr    = 000000000000(not present)
LANE: SRC ATM ADDR  = 39:2000:0000 0000 0000 0000 AA00:DDDDDDDDDDDD:FF
LANE: LAN-TYPE      = 01 (Ethernet/IEEE 802.3)
LANE: MAX FRAME SIZE= 01 (1516)
LANE: NUMBER TLVs   = 1
LANE: ELAN NAME SIZE= 7
LANE: TARG ATM ADDR = 0000000000000000000000000000000000000000
LANE: ELAN NAME     = "ELAN_V2"
```

## Selective Multicast Groupings

With LANEv2, if a LEC resolves a multicast address and determines that it is associated with a certain ATM address, a Selective Multicast Send VCC and Selective Multicast Forward VCC may be initiated to the SMS that serves that multicast group address. In this scenario, if the LES (providing it is V2-capable) receives an LE_ARP_REQUEST for a multicast MAC address, and this request originates from a LEC that both indicated V2 capability and had the Selective Multicast flags set in its LE_JOIN_REQUEST, then it responds with either the address of the particular SMS associated with that multicast address, so that the Selective Multicast control channels may be established for that group address (see Figure 13-10), or the ATM address of the BUS, if no SMS is in place to service that multicast address. For more information on the functionality of the SMS, consult the upcoming section, "LAN Emulation Network-to-Network Interface."

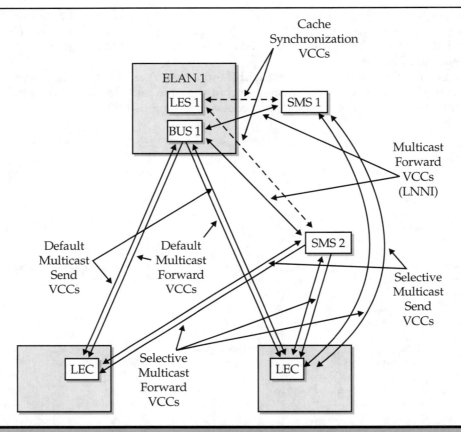

**Figure 13-10.** *A Single BUS with two Selective Multicast servers*

The LEC, upon receiving the address of the BUS for establishment of these control channels, may request validation that the BUS address is a valid BUS address for that ELAN. This is accomplished by the client issuing an LE_VERIFY_REQUEST frame to the LES. The LES, upon receipt of the control frame, issues an LE_VERIFY_RESPONSE back to the client, validating the BUS address.

## Quality of Service
QoS is supported in LANEv2, although it is not required. The specifics of the LANEv2 QoS implementation are covered in detail in Chapter 14.

## LECS Enhancements

The LECS supports additional TLVs in LANEv2, including a V2 designation for all LES addresses that are V2-capable and configured as such. An ELAN ID is also associated with these addresses, to prevent entities that use the LECS from registering with an incorrect ELAN ID.

Although not specifically part of the LANEv2 specification, MPOA support exists, of which LANEv2 is a required component. MPC and MPS configuration TLVs can be transferred to their corresponding LECs during the configuration phase. These TLVs can be communicated in the LE_CONFIGURE_RESPONSE, over the Configuration Direct VCC. The LECS will interpret whether a LEC is V2-capable by examining the LE_CONFIGURE_REQUEST, which may also contain TLVs indicating V2 capability.

Table 13-4 shows a list of all the TLVs that can be defined in the LECS LE_CONFIGURE_RESPONSE frame.

## LES Enhancements

With LANEv2, each LES is configured to be either V1- or V2-capable. A V2 LES must be assigned a specific ELAN ID, to keep possible LLC-multiplexed cell flows separate. As an additional part of V2 enhancement, the LES may receive TLVs from a LEC, indicating the existence of an MPC or MPS that resides on the same switch or router as the client. This occurs during the join phase. The LES in this case facilitates the MPC and MPS discovery of one another, by adding this information into the LE_ARP_REQUEST and LE_ARP_RESPONSE, respectively. For example, a V2 LEC configured on a switch also hosting an MPC will register this fact with the LES during the join phase. Once the LEC is joined, any LE_ARP_REQUEST issued by that client will have the MPC information appended to it before being flooded by the LES. A LEC that is configured on a router also hosting an MPS will communicate the existence of the MPC to the MPS when the LE_ARP_REQUEST is received. Likewise, the LEC that issued the request will receive an LE_ARP_RESPONSE with the presence of the MPS included and, by this method, will learn of the presence of the MPS.

Additionally, a LES may respond to a LEC's LE_ARP_REQUEST for a multicast group address with either the BUS address (if no SMS is in place to service the multicast group address) or the ATM address of an SMS that services that multicast address.

 **Note**    *In LANEv1, no LE_ARP_REQUEST is associated with a multicast group address; all multicast traffic is sent directly to the BUS.*

## BUS Enhancements

LANEv2-enhanced multicast support is orchestrated largely between the LEC, its LES, and an associated SMS that handles the multicast group address being requested. The SMS in turn maintains Multicast Forward VCCs to the BUS, to use in the event that LECs need to receive multicast traffic but are unable to participate with an SMS. Selective Multicast VCCs are established to the appropriate SMS, while the Default Multicast

ATM TECHNOLOGIES

| TLV | LANE Version |
|---|:---:|
| Control Timeout | V1 |
| Max Unknown Frame Count | V1 |
| Max Unknown Frame Time | V1 |
| VCC Timeout Period | V1 |
| Max Retry Count | V1 |
| Aging Time | V1 |
| Forward Delay Time | V1 |
| Expected LE_ARP Response Time | V1 |
| Flush Timeout | V1 |
| Path Switching Delay | V1 |
| Local Segment ID | V1 |
| Default Multicast Send VCC Type | V1 |
| Default Multicast Send VCC average rate | V1 |
| Default Multicast Send VCC peak rate | V1 |
| Connection Completion Timer | V1 |
| Configuration Fragmentation Info | V2 |
| ELAN ID | V2 |
| X5 Adjustment | V2 |
| Preferred LES | V2 |

**Table 13-4.**    *LECS TLVs*

Send/Forward VCCs are maintained with the BUS. The Selective Multicast Send VCCs are bidirectional, point-to-point control connections initiated by clients who will be participating in a specific multicast group address.

## LLC Multiplexing

Data Direct VCC LLC multiplexing (MUXing) is supported as of LANEv2; this functionality is available only on Data Direct VCCs that connect two V2-capable LECs. A LANEv2 LEC is either capable or incapable of implementing LLC MUXing. If a V2

LEC initiates a Data Direct VCC to a remote LEC that doesn't offer a TLV indicating its V2 capability, then LLC MUXing must not be used; likewise, if a Data Direct VCC is received on a V2 LEC that originated from a remote LEC that isn't V2-capable, LLC MUXing must not be used.

# LAN Emulation Network-to-Network Interface

In addition to the ATM LUNI of LANEv2, the ATM LNNI is specified. LNNI offers a standard means of establishing cooperating LES/BUS pairs, configuration and dynamic configuration of LES and SMS entities, and intercommunication between LESs, SMSs, and a combination of the two so that cooperating LES entities synchronize cache information and forward control frames, as well as share multicast group address cache entries.

## LNNI Overview

LNNI uses SMS entities, as well as a series of LNNI control connections that extend between different LANE server entities (LECS, LES, BUS, and SMS). The ATM LNNI is concerned with the intercommunication between LANE server entities, rather than between LECs and their services, as is the case with LUNI. This intercommunication between server entities allows for more flexibility of configuration, the dynamic learning of the different servers, and, ultimately, load sharing, LANE redundancy, and increased multicast support. For example, through the use of the ATM LNNI, two cooperating LES entities are able to synchronize databases and exchange control frames so that both may serve a common ELAN. Prior to the creation of LNNI, many vendors (Nortel Networks included) had already implemented a form of this. A LES may also, upon receipt of an LE_ARP for a multicast group address, direct a LEC to a specific SMS that serves that address, using LNNI control connections with that SMS to share cache information.

Each of these functions, including the SMS entity, along with the individual LNNI control connections and their associated control functions, is covered in this section.

# The Selective Multicast Server

With the advent of LANEv2 LUNI and LNNI, a new LANE entity was conceived: the *Selective Multicast Server*. The SMS is an entity that serves a certain multicast group address or addresses. The purpose of creating the SMS was to refine the manner in which multicast addresses were serviced by LANE; formerly, multicasts were sent over the Multicast Forward VCC, just as broadcasts are. This can result in quite a few of the LECs within the network receiving the multicast, regardless of whether there are any hosts residing on their legacy LAN that need to receive it. The concept of the SMS is that a series of entities can now exist that serve one or more multicast group addresses, so that only the LECs that need to receive the multicast data do in fact receive it.

Multiple SMSs may exist within a single ATM network, and multiple SMSs may exist within a single ELAN. An SMS is a sort of hybrid between the LES functionality and the BUS functionality: like the LES, it maintains a database of which LECs are associated with which addresses (multicast group addresses, in this case), and, like the BUS, it forwards multicast streams. However, unlike the LES, a LEC does not go through an actual join procedure with the SMS, nor is the SMS associated with any particular LES, as a BUS would be (see Figure 13-11).

To understand better how the SMS functions and its relationship to the other LANE entities, you first must understand the specifics of LNNI and its associated control connections.

## LNNI Control VCCs

Just as LUNI is concerned with the interaction between LECs and LANE services, LNNI is concerned with the interaction among LANE services themselves. To this end,

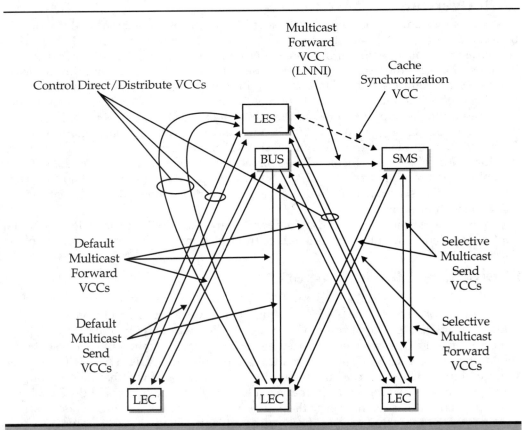

**Figure 13-11.**   *A SMS serving a particular multicast group address within an ELAN*

LNNI uses several new LANE control VCCs that interconnect different LANE services. The LNNI control VCCs are as follows:

- **LECS Synchronization VCC**   Extends between a LECS and all other LECSs that exist within the ATM network. It is used by the LECS entities to ensure that each LECS has a common view of network configuration data, as well as the status of all LANE services.

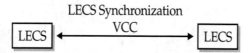

- **Configuration Direct VCC**   Extends between a LECS and one or more LES and/or SMS entities. Although it is used in the ATM LUNI between a LEC and a LECS, the Configuration Direct VCC used in LNNI is different from its LUNI counterpart in that it remains up at all times. It is used in LNNI for the LES and SMS to obtain their configuration; the LECS may also use it to make dynamic configuration changes to the LES or SMS.

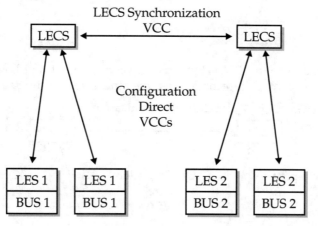

- **Cache Synchronization VCC**   Extends between a LES and another neighboring LES, or between a LES and a neighboring SMS. This VCC is used to synchronize database information. For instance, two cooperating LES entities that are both serving the same ELAN would use this control VCC to ensure that the database information that each has for the clients in that ELAN is identical. Likewise, an SMS keeps its cache synchronized with the LES to keep a current database of which multicast addresses are associated with which clients (unicast data from the LES in this case is not required by the SMS, because it does not process unicast traffic).

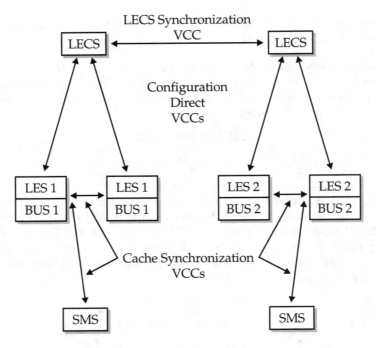

■ **Control Coordinate VCC** Extends between cooperating LES entities, and is used to pass control information between those cooperating servers.

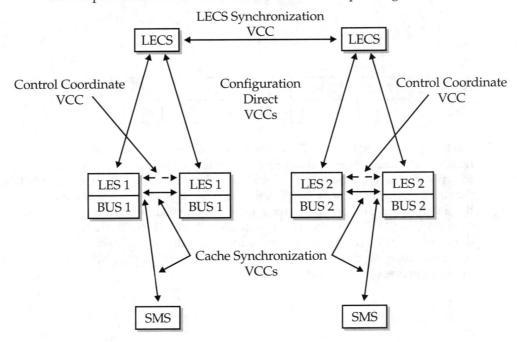

- **Multicast Forward VCC** In the ATM LNNI, extends between cooperating BUS entities, to allow broadcast traffic to propagate to all local LECs, regardless of which BUS is serving them. Multicast Forward VCCs may also extend between BUS and SMS entities.

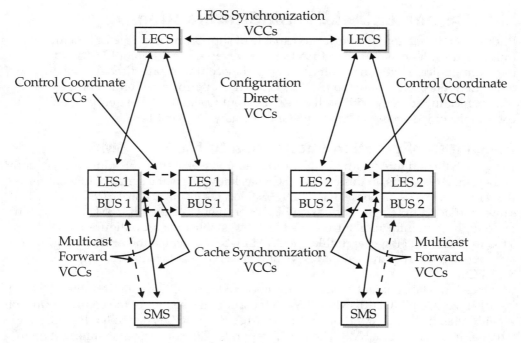

- **Selective Multicast Send/Forward VCC (LUNI)** In addition to the Default Multicast Send/Forward VCCs, Multicast Forward VCCs and Multicast Send VCCs may extend between a LEC and a given SMS. While technically a LUNI connection, it is important to distinguish between these connections and those that interconnect cooperating BUS entities in the LNNI.

# LANE Server Functions Under the ATM LNNI

To better serve LECs, the LNNI allows intercommunication between LANE servers, using the control connections described in the previous section. Multiple servers (such as a LES and BUS) may exist within a single ELAN to both load-share and add redundancy. Under the LNNI, the LES, BUS, LECS, and SMS entities are capable of sharing control information (such as between two cooperating LES entities over the Control Coordinate VCC), synchronizing database information (such as between two

LECS entities over the LECS Synchronization VCC, or between LES/SMS entities over the Cache Synchronization VCC), and monitoring server status and obtaining configuration information (such as between a LECS and a LES/SMS over the LNNI Control Direct VCC).

# LECS-LECS and LECS-LES/SMS Interaction

Prior to LNNI, a LANE network was capable of supporting multiple LECS entities (this functionality exists even in LANEv1); however, these different LECSs did not intercommunicate with one another, nor did they communicate directly with any of the LES functions. Using the LNNI, a LECS must perform both functions: communicating directly with both other LECS entities in the ATM network, and communicating directly with the LES (and possibly SMS) entities.

## Passing Configuration Information to the LES/SMS

Each LECS is configured with ELAN information, as well as the LES address(es) of each of those ELANs. Thus, in this case, a LECS has knowledge of a series of LES entities that are found in its database. Each LES/SMS locates its particular LECS by using the same methods a LEC does, and, like a LEC over the LUNI, the LES/SMS must obtain its configuration information from the LECS by establishing a Configuration Direct VCC to the LECS. However, unlike the ATM LUNI, for which the LECS configuration is optional, it is a requirement of LNNI, and all server entities must configure using the LECS.

Once the establishment of the Configuration Direct VCC is complete, the LES/SMS issues an LE_CONFIGURE_REQUEST to the LECS; the sender of the control frame will set either the IS_LE_SERVER flag or the IS_MCAST_SERVER flag to let the LECS know whether it is a LES or an SMS. The LECS responds with configuration information in an LE_CONFIGURE_RESPONSE control frame. This includes the following information:

- A list of cooperating LES and SMS entities. This could be any combination of LES-LES, LES-SMS, or SMS-SMS, depending on which entity is requesting configuration. For instance, a LES with a cooperating LES needs to know the address of that LES. Likewise, if that cooperating LES has an associated SMS, the LES needs that information as well. An SMS requesting configuration needs the ATM address of any remote neighbor SMS entities. This information is required, because cooperating server entities will need to synchronize their databases by erecting a Cache Synchronization VCC.

- A unique server ID, uniquely identifying the server within its ELAN.

- For LES only, a range of LECIDs, which the LES may assign to its local LECs. This is requested through a LECID Range TLV in the LE_CONFIGURE_REQUEST.

## Dynamic Configuration of the LES/SMS Using the Trigger Function

In addition to configuration information obtained through the exchange of the LE_CONFIGURE_REQUEST and LE_CONFIGURE_RESPONSE at the time each Configuration Direct VCC is established, each LES and SMS may obtain configuration changes dynamically. This process is similar to the trigger mechanism used in MPOA. The LECS in this case does not impose the information on the LES, but rather triggers the server entity to request its configuration information again. The LECS in this case issues an LNNI_CONFIGURE_TRIGGER control frame over the Configuration Direct VCC. Upon receipt of this control frame, the LES entity issues an LE_CONFIGURE_REQUEST frame, and the new configuration information is imparted through an LE_CONFIGURE_RESPONSE control frame.

### LECS Keep-Alive Messages

The LNNI Configuration Direct VCCs must remain up at all times, and the LECS must receive constant updates from each LES/SMS as to their operational status, so that it knows which servers are currently active. In LANEv1, a LECS could be configured with multiple LES addresses for a single ELAN, indicating cooperating LES/BUS pairs, but the LANEv1 LECS had no way of knowing whether or not any of the LESs listed was operational. A LEC would attempt to join the first LES on the list, and then each in turn until a join was successful. Through the LNNI, a LECS is constantly updated as to the operational status of each server entity, because it constantly receives Keep-Alive control frames over each Configuration Direct VCC.

Each Keep-Alive sent indicates the sender's ATM address, and indicates to the LECS that the server in question is operational. In response to each Keep-Alive Request, the LECS sends a Keep-Alive Response; each response indicates a Keep-Alive time to the server. The Keep-Alive time indicates how much time can pass before the LECS will expect a new Keep-Alive from the server; the LECS will consider each server entity to be functional for at least the duration of the Keep-Alive time. If the Keep-Alive time expires and no Keep-Alive has been received by the LECS, then that server is considered nonoperational; the Configure Direct VCC is severed by the LECS, and the LECS will no longer assign any registering LEC to that LES/SMS until the Configuration Direct VCC is reestablished and the server has reconfigured.

### Remaining Synchronized with Other LECSs

Multiple LECSs find one another in one of two ways: they may be configured statically with the ATM addresses of the remote LECS(s), or they may learn of the existence as well as the ATM addresses of the remote LECS(s) via ILMI.

Once a LECS learns of the existence of one or more remote LECSs, a LECS Synchronization VCC must be built between the LECS and each of the remote LECSs.

ATM TECHNOLOGIES

The reason is that, given the existence of more than one LECS combined with the required LNNI Control Distribute VCC connections between each server and a LECS, the scenario can easily arise in which different groups of LES/SMS entities have established Control Distribute VCCs to different LECSs (see Figure 13-12).

This scenario has two LECSs, each of which maintains a control connection to two groups of LES/SMS entities. In this case, a LEC may initially establish its Configuration Direct VCC to either LECS, and so both LECSs must know of the existence of all LESs serving each ELAN, as well as the operational state of each. Since each group of two LESs is connected to only one of the LECSs, each LECS requires a method of intercommunicating so that one LECS can learn of any server entities, as well as their operational states, from any other LECSs that may exist. This is accomplished over the LECS Synchronization VCC.

## Interaction Between the LES and LES/SMS Entities

The ATM LNNI between the LES entities, SMS entities, and LES and SMS entities exists to serve two primary functions: to provide a standard method of load-sharing LES/BUS pairs as well as multiple SMS entities, and to assist in providing enhanced multicast support by allowing a LES to be associated with specific SMS instances.

For instance, in a scenario where more than one LES is configured to serve a single ELAN, LECs need to be able to reach remote LECs that have joined to either LES, not

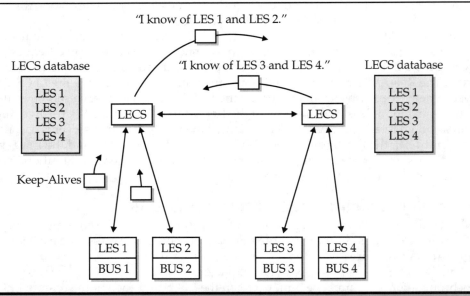

**Figure 13-12.**   *Two LECSs serving two groups of LESs and synchronizing their databases to establish a single list of all LESs*

just the local one, and LES databases must remain synchronized so that the two servers can function as one. This is accomplished through the LNNI.

## Remaining Synchronized with Cooperating LES Entities

Upon establishing the Configuration Direct VCC with the LECS, a LES learns of any other LES entities that may be serving the same ELAN; if multiple LESs do exist to serve a common ELAN, then each LES must establish a Cache Synchronization VCC with all other LESs serving that ELAN. All LESs must have a direct connection to all other cooperating LESs in a full mesh. In addition, each LES must establish a Control Coordinate VCC to all other cooperating LES entities, also in a full mesh (see Figure 13-13).

Although this example shows each control VCC individually, in reality, both a Cache Synchronization VCC and a Control Coordinate VCC aren't always necessary (although both may exist). A single VCC can serve both functions, since in the case of LES-to-LES communication (as opposed to LES-to-SMS communication or SMS-to-SMS

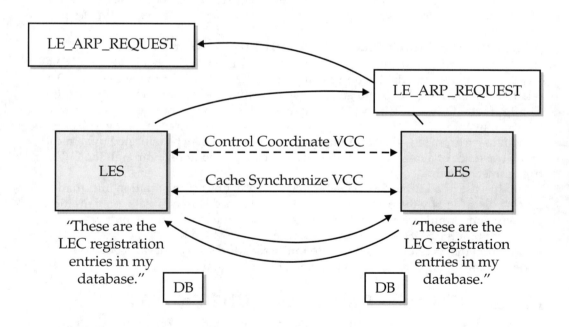

**Figure 13-13.**    *Cooperating LES entities connected via Cache Synchronization VCCs and Control Coordinate VCCs*

communication), both types of control VCCs must be in place between the same two LESs at all times.

Once in place between the cooperating LESs, the Cache Synchronization VCC is used to synchronize database information. This is done using the Server Cache Synchronization Protocol (SCSP), which is explained in greater detail later in this chapter. The Control Coordinate VCC is used by cooperating LESs to exchange control frames. For example, in a case where there are two cooperating LES/BUS pairs, and a LEC joined to LES-1 issues an LE_ARP_REQUEST to its local LES for an address that is associated with the legacy LAN behind a LEC joined to LES-2, the LE_ARP_REQUEST frame needs a way to reach LES-2. This is done by passing the request across the Control Coordinate VCC to all cooperating LES entities, so that the destination can be resolved regardless of which LES received the request.

The Control Coordinate VCC is also used to forward control frames, such as LE_FLUSH_RESPONSE frames, and LE_REGISTER and LE_UNREGISTER frames, so that a LEC destination that is registered with one cooperating LES will be propagated to all cooperating LESs for that ELAN. These control frames are flooded by the receiving LES only; a LES receiving a control frame from another cooperating LES will not in turn flood the frame to any other LES entities. Because the Control Coordinate and Cache Synchronization VCCs are both established in a full mesh, the originating LES is responsible for forwarding any control frames to all other cooperating LESs.

### Remaining Synchronized with Neighbor SMS Entities

SCSP is also used to synchronize the database of a LES entity with an associated SMS, which takes place over the Cache Synchronization VCC between the two servers. The relationship between a LES and an SMS can be communicated to each entity over the Configuration Direct VCC to a LECS where the association is configured. For instance, a LECS may inform a LES at the time of its configuration of any cooperating LES or SMSs it should synchronize with. Additionally, the LES or SMS may be informed dynamically of the existence of a new server with which it should synchronize through the LECS trigger mechanism.

In the case of a LES-to-SMS synchronization, any unicast registration information may be discarded by the SMS, because it does not process unicast data, only multicasts. Likewise, any multicast information that does not relate to the group multicast addresses that the SMS serves is also discarded. The SMS in this case will accept information that is relevant to its group multicast address(es), but does not have to flood this information to its own neighbors, though it may.

## Interaction Between Cooperating BUS Entities

Like the LESs, each BUS using the LNNI is interconnected in a full mesh; each BUS establishes a Multicast Forward VCC with each other cooperating BUS, for the forwarding of control frames. Like the LES, a BUS is responsible for forwarding a frame to all other cooperating BUSs, and a BUS will not forward a control frame received by a cooperating BUS.

## BUS Handling of Multicast Data

In LANEv1, the BUS was responsible for handling all multicast traffic. In LANEv2, using the LNNI, a BUS handles multicast data differently depending on whether the Selective Multicast flag is set at the time the sending LEC joined (this is set in the LE_JOIN_RESPONSE, to inform the LEC that the LES it has joined has one or more associated SMS entities). If this flag is set, the LEC is considered an SMF-LE Client, meaning that it may use one or more SMSs.

A multicast received by an SMF-LE Client then must be forwarded to all other SMF-LE Clients registered for the particular multicast group address, all non-SMF-LE Clients (such as LANEv1 clients, who can't share in SMS distribution but may need to receive the multicast), and all cooperating BUS entities.

## Connections to the SMS

A BUS that must serve both SMF-LE Clients and non-SMF-LE Clients, and that also has control connections to other, cooperating BUS entities, potentially requires multiple sets of Multicast Forward VCCs:

- A set for forwarding data to all clients (used to forward frames received by a cooperating BUS).

- A set that extends to all LECs and to all BUSs (used to forward frames received by one of its LECs).

- A set that extends only to non-SMF-LE Clients (used to forward frames received from an SMS, such as the example in the previous section wherein an SMS must forward multicast frames to SMF-LE Clients that are registered for the multicast address, as well as to any non-SMF-LE Clients that may require the multicast but don't have the functionality to register for one).

# Functions of the Selective Multicast Server

Each SMS is able to determine the complete database for a complete ELAN via SCSP. When an SMF-LE Client registers multicast group address information with its local LES, the LES must decide to which SMS (if any) the LEC should be directed to serve the multicast. The ATM address of the appropriate SMS is returned to the SMF-LE Client with the LE_ARP_RESPONSE.

All relevant SMSs are informed that an SMF-LE Client has been assigned during the database synchronization process (the information regarding a LEC registering for a multicast group address is communicated to each SMS by the LES receiving the registration).

## SMS Assignment

In LANEv2, when implementing both the ATM LUNI and LNNI, a LEC may send an LE_ARP_REQUEST to its local LES for a multicast group address. Formerly, in

ATM TECHNOLOGIES

LANEv1, multicast addresses were directed to the BUS to be forwarded over the Multicast Forward VCC indiscriminately. In LANEv2, each LES knows of each SMS needed by the LECs it is serving; this may be determined at the time the configuration is downloaded from the LECS. The LES that receives the LE_ARP_REQUEST for an address that is a multicast group address then returns the address of the SMS that serves that multicast address, rather than the BUS address. The LEC initiates a Selective Multicast Send VCC to that address; then, if required, the SMS may add the LEC as a leaf onto its Selective Multicast Forward VCC.

 *Unlike the BUS control connections, a LEC that is using an SMS may need to either send only, receive only, or both, so it is possible that either only the Selective Multicast Send VCC, only the Selective Multicast Forward VCC, or both may be present between a LEC and an SMS.*

## Server Cache Synchronization Protocol

SCSP consists of two sublayers: one that is protocol-dependent, and one that is not. The protocol-independent sublayer is concerned with the Hello Protocol (used to maintain the SCSP connection to the neighboring server), the Cache Alignment Protocol (used to synchronize the actual database information), and a portion of the Client State Update (CSU) protocol (used to monitor LEC information and bindings that may become obsolete if the client fails or is removed). The protocol-dependent sublayer of SCSP is concerned with the server-specific (LES/SMS) portion of the CSU protocol, coordinating LES-to-LES, LES-to-SMS, and SMS-to-SMS synchronizations.

Databases must be synchronized between server systems. For instance, an SMS that is serving multiple SMF-LE Clients must be made aware if one of the clients is no longer participating in a multicast group address and no longer requires multicast traffic for that group.

### Client State Update Protocol

Upon the establishment of a Cache Synchronization VCC, each server system begins issuing Hello messages, allowing the remote server to recognize it as being SCSP-capable. Caches are then synchronized by using the Cache Alignment Protocol that coordinates the exchange of cache information. After the databases are synchronized, the CSU protocol is used to ensure that the information received by each server system is still up to date. This is accomplished through the exchange of CSU Request and CSU Reply messages, each of which contains one or more Client State Advertisements (CSAs). Each CSA indicates the current LEC state and registration information, allowing server entities to learn rapidly of any information that changes.

## Summary of LANEv2 Features

Table 13-5 gives a brief summary of the LANEv2 features.

| LANEv2 Feature | Required at LEC | Required at LES |
|---|---|---|
| Changes to configuration variables | Yes | Yes |
| Extended set of TLVs | Yes | Yes |
| ARP-based TLVs | Yes | Yes |
| Extended API to higher layers | Yes | N/A |
| Quality of Service | No | N/A |
| Multicast services | No | No |
| LLC multiplexing | No | N/A |
| Support for UNI 4.0 | No | No |
| Targetless LE_ARP and no source LE_NARP | Yes | Yes |

**Table 13-5.**   *LANEv2 Features*

## Processing Calls Through a LANE Network

After the LEC successfully joins its services, it is ready to service the legacy network that it borders. Until the client is joined, no legacy traffic will traverse the ATM mesh. Assuming an ATM cloud around which three legacy networks border, each with its own LEC and all part of the same ELAN, with station A on one side of the mesh and station B on another, what actually occurs when station A transmits to station B? The answer is the focus of this section.

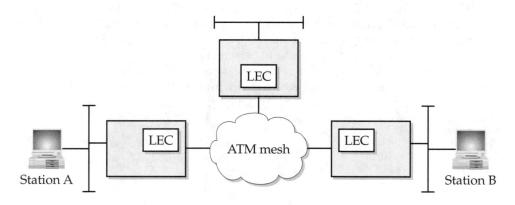

# Resolving Legacy Destinations Across the ATM Mesh

Station A in this case has no knowledge of the ATM network. It wants to communicate with station B, and, if it has its MAC in its ARP cache, it sends. Station B obviously won't respond locally, though it will appear to. The data destined for station B will hit everything on the local segment, including the LEC for that ELAN.

More than one remote LEC exists behind which station B could reside, and the LEC receiving the data has no way of knowing which one it is. Whichever remote LEC it is, the local LEC will ultimately need to create a point-to-point connection with it, so that it can send traffic destined for station B across it. To determine the remote ATM address, the LEC sends an LE_ARP_REQUEST to the LES, over the Control Direct VCC, to try and resolve which ATM address station B is associated with.

## LE_ARP

After issuing the LE_ARP_REQUEST, the LEC also begins forwarding the data from station A to the BUS, which floods it out of every LEC over the Multicast Forward VCC. While this is not ideal, it is only meant to maintain connectivity between the end stations until a direct connection can be made between the two LECs, because some protocols will not tolerate the delay involved in finding the correct LEC. The BUS will accept station B's responses, as well, coming back the other way for this period. The BUS was not intended to maintain this type of traffic flow for extended periods of time, however.

In the meantime, if the LES has the MAC-to-ATM address mapping for station B in its table, it responds to the LE_ARP with the ATM address of the remote LEC. The local LEC initiates a call to that address, whereupon a Data Direct VCC is established between the two LECs. Data between station A and station B is then passed across this connection.

If this is the first time station A has ever attempted communication with station B, however, then the LES does not have the MAC-to-ATM mapping in its table; nor may any remote LEC. When the LES receives the LE_ARP, it forwards the LE_ARP_REQUEST to each of its associated LECs, to see if any responds (see Figure 13-14).

If station B's MAC address is not currently registered with any LEC, there will be no response. The originating LEC continues to send LE_ARP_REQUESTs, while at the same time it forwards the data across the BUS (see Figure 13-15).

Since station B has, by this time, responded and is sending its responses back across the BUS, the remote LEC associated with station B now has B's MAC address registered, and responds to the incoming LE_ARP_REQUESTs with an LE_ARP_RESPONSE. The originating LEC initiates a Data Direct VCC to the remote LEC at this point.

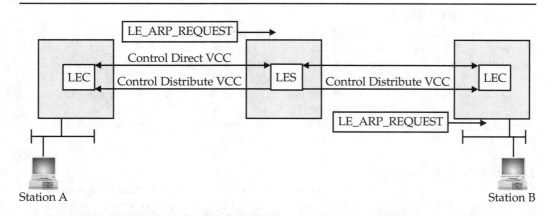

**Figure 13-14.**   *The LEC issues an LE_ARP_REQUEST to the LES*

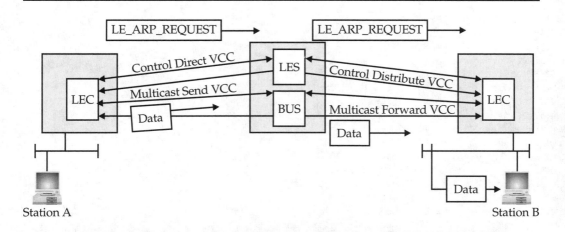

**Figure 13-15.**   *The LEC sends the LE_ARP_REQUEST to the LES, which forwards it to all remote LECs*

ATM TECHNOLOGIES

## Data Direct VCCs

Station A's LEC will now, while still flooding its data across the BUS, initiate a call to the remote LEC's ATM address. Once the call is established, the Data Direct VCC is established between the two LECs. It is over this connection that the rest of station A and station B's communication will pass (Figure 13-16).

Regardless of the size of the transmission, once initiated, the Data Direct VCC will be built, and it will remain in place until it times out in accordance with the administrator's configuration. If stations A and B need to talk again prior to the VCC timeout, they will automatically utilize this same VCC.

## LE_FLUSH_REQUEST

Since each LEC will begin flooding data across the BUS prior to establishing a Data Direct VCC if the remote LEC's ATM address is not known, the possibility exists for two data streams to be happening simultaneously and for data to arrive out of order. To eliminate this possibility, the LEC uses the *flush protocol*.

The flush protocol sends a control cell, referred to as an LE_FLUSH_REQUEST, across the BUS Multicast Send VCC immediately following the establishment of the Data Direct VCC. The following is an LE_FLUSH_REQUEST captured with an ATM sniffer:

```
LANE: ----- LAN EMULATION CONTROL FRAME -----
LANE:
LANE: Marker        = FF00
LANE: Protocol      = 01
LANE: Version       = 01
LANE: Opcode        = 0007 (FLUSH_REQUEST)
LANE: Status        = 0 (Success)
LANE: Trans ID      = 1605
LANE: Request ID    = 1
LANE: Flags         = 0000
LANE: Src LAN Dest  = 0000000000000000
LANE:   Tag         = 0000(not present)
LANE:   MAC Adr     = 000000000000(not present)
LANE: Tar LAN Dest  = 0000000000000000
LANE:   Tag         = 0000(not present)
LANE:   MAC Adr     = 000000000000(not present)
LANE: SRC ATM ADDR  = 39:1000:0000 0000 0000 0000 0000:EEEEEEEEEEEE:00
LANE: Reserved      = 0000
LANE: NUMBER TLVs   = 0
LANE: Reserved      = 00
LANE: TARG ATM ADDR = 39:2000:0000 0000 0000 0000 0000:W11f1t0D749E:00
LANE: Reserved      = 000000000000000000000000000000000000000000000000000000000000000000
```

The Flush Request is sent by the LEC (indicated as the source ATM address in the preceding listing, with an ESI of all E's) across the control channels to the destination

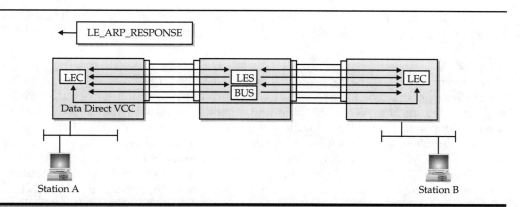

**Figure 13-16.**   *A Data Direct VCC is created after the ATM address of the remote LEC is resolved*

LEC (a Bay Networks ATM router interface, in this case). After dispatching the LE_FLUSH_REQUEST, the LEC sends no more data across the BUS. During this time, no data is forwarded across the newly established Data Direct VCC either. When the flush request is received by the remote LEC for station B, it knows not to expect any more data across the Multicast Forward VCC. Upon receipt, the remote LEC issues back an LE_FLUSH_RESPONSE:

```
LANE: ----- LAN EMULATION CONTROL FRAME -----
LANE:
LANE: Marker        = FF00
LANE: Protocol      = 01
LANE: Version       = 01
LANE: Opcode        = 0107 (FLUSH_RESPONSE)
LANE: Status        = 0 (Success)
LANE: Trans ID      = 1605
LANE: Request ID    = 1
LANE: Flags         = 0000
LANE: Src LAN Dest  = 0000000000000000
LANE:    Tag        = 0000(not present)
LANE:    MAC Adr    = 000000000000(not present)
LANE: Tar LAN Dest  = 0000000000000000
LANE:    Tag        = 0000(not present)
LANE:    MAC Adr    = 000000000000(not present)
LANE: SRC ATM ADDR  = 39:1000:0000 0000 0000 0000 0000:EEEEEEEEEEEE:00
LANE: Reserved      = 0000
LANE: NUMBER TLVs   = 0
LANE: Reserved      = 00
LANE: TARG ATM ADDR = 39:2000:0000 0000 0000 0000 0000:W1lf1t0D749E:00
LANE: Reserved      = 000000000000000000000000000000000000000000000000000000000000000000
```

Once the local LEC receives the flush response, it knows that any data it has sent across the BUS is clear, and it will then begin sending traffic across the Data Direct VCC.

## LE_NARP

Given the preceding scenario, problems may arise if the target MAC address is moved for any reason. Since the Data Direct VCC remains in place until it times out, defaulting to 20 minutes, and the ATM/MAC binding remains associated with this VCC, it is a severely impacting delay if the location of the MAC does not remain constant.

An example of such a scenario might be a roaming, handheld wireless device that has its own MAC. Devices such as these are not uncommon in retail firms, hospitals, and other large facilities, and generally pick up different access points throughout the building or campus; thus, the MAC will jump from location to location. In a LANE environment, a LEC may generate a control frame called an LE_NARP_REQUEST if the ATM/MAC binding becomes invalid. It will do this if a MAC address that was formerly associated with a remote LEC in its LE_ARP cache is suddenly registered locally. This control frame is unsolicited. The LEC issuing the frame must include its own ATM address in the LE_NARP_REQUEST and the ATM address previously associated with the target destination LAN.

LECs may update their LE_ARP cache from the binding information included in an LE_NARP_REQUEST as the receiving LES forwards the LE_NARP_REQUEST to all LECs over the Control Distribute VCC.

## Targetless LE_ARP

LANEv2 introduced the targetless LE_ARP_REQUEST, which is an LE_ARP_REQUEST that has a target LAN destination of '"not present,"' but contains the source LAN destination and source ATM address. This accomplishes the advertising of an LE_ARP cache binding, so that if a LEC elsewhere in the network already possesses the same LE_ARP cache binding, it deletes that entry from its own table and updates it accordingly. This is a replacement of the LE_NARP protocol, and it supports any MAC address that has roamed in such a way that it is now associated with a new LEC instead of its original LEC. Targetless LE_ARP provides a method of quickly updating all other LECs within the ELAN as to the new MAC location.

# The Complete Reference

Nortel Networks

# Chapter 14

## ATM Quality of Service

The concept behind ATM Quality of Service (QoS) is to allocate bandwidth dynamically as new circuits are built and torn down, and to have the different circuits negotiate traffic contracts, depending on their specific bandwidth requirements, on a per-call basis. For example, an application such as a video conference application is much less fault-tolerant than a data transfer; even a high-priority data transfer is capable of recovering from a certain amount of latency and/or congestion. A video conference that encounters too much latency results in poor video and voice quality. QoS was designed so that bandwidth-intensive, delay-intolerant applications may contract for a greater amount of bandwidth than is required by a more fault-tolerant or less critical transfer, and be guaranteed that bandwidth when it is needed.

# Functions of QoS

To accomplish the goal of QoS, several QoS functions have been developed by the ATM Forum. These functions are intended to assist in the establishment of QoS traffic contracts, the maintenance of such contracts after they are established, and the monitoring and enforcement of such contracts to ensure adherence. These functions of QoS are defined as follows:

- **Call Admission Control (CAC)**    Indicates the set of actions taken at the time of the ATM call's setup, to determine whether or not the connection request can be accepted. The CAC function may take QoS traffic contracts into account; for instance, a node receiving a connection request that indicates a bandwidth requirement the node can't currently support may elect to refuse the connection, because the contract can't be honored.

- **Usage Parameter Control (UPC)**    Monitors connections once they are in place, to ensure that negotiated traffic contracts are being adhered to. If a violation is detected, UPC may discard cells or tag them for discard eligibility, in the event they threaten to breach another existing contract.

- **Cell Loss Priority (CLP)**    Involves using cell-tagging to help maintain QoS when network loads are high; lower-priority traffic may be tagged, indicating the cells are eligible for discard if a connection becomes too congested. Such cells are "tagged" by flipping the CLP bit in the cell header; this bit may or may not be acknowledged by the network, depending on the implementation.

- **Frame discard**    Involves dropping traffic at the frame level rather than at the cell level. In a scenario in which a frame is divided into multiple cells, the loss of one cell within the frame effectively corrupts the entire frame; therefore, ATM nodes may elect to discard all cells associated with the frame rather than just one, or a portion of them.

- **Traffic shaping**    Involves adjusting egress cell flow, smoothing it into a more efficient transfer, and further ensuring that QoS service classes are adhered to.

■ **Network Resource Management**   Helps to ensure that the different connections remain logically bound with their service requirements, and that the resources they require are available.

# QoS Parameters

The different QoS service classes may have different relevant parameters. Some of these parameters are negotiated at the time the traffic contract is made, while others are not negotiated. QoS parameters involve such things as how much delay a connection can tolerate, how much cell loss a connection can withstand, and so forth. These parameters are defined as either negotiated or nonnegotiated, as discussed next.

## Negotiated Parameters

The following QoS parameters are *negotiated,* meaning the application may request specific values for these parameters, and the network in turn must determine whether or not the request can be honored. Three parameters may be negotiated:

■ **Peak-to-peak Cell Delay Variation (peak-to-peak CDV)**   The peak-to-peak CDV indicates the amount of variation that can occur in cell transfer delay; in other words, the range of delay that is tolerable to the service requirements of the application requesting the call.

■ **Maximum Cell Transfer Delay (maxCTD)**   The CTD measures the amount of time that passes between a cell leaving the UNI source and arriving at the UNI destination (the amount of time that passes while the cell travels from one end of an established connection to the other). The maxCTD is the maximum amount of delay that a specific traffic contract can withstand. For a video or voice application, this delay may be very small, whereas other applications may be more delay-tolerant. The maxCTD parameter applies to CBR and rt-VBR contracts.

■ **Cell Loss Ratio (CLR)**   The CLR parameter indicates how much cell loss can be tolerated by the application requesting the service class. The CLR may apply to all cells in a network where CLP tagging is not used or is not significant to the network (the CLP bit is not examined), or only to cells that have not been subject to discard due to CLP.

## Nonnegotiated Parameters

Certain QoS parameters are not negotiated. The following three parameters are statically defined:

■ **Cell Error Ratio (CER)**   The CER defines the acceptable ratio of successfully transmitted cells to errored cells. CER is defined by the ATM Forum as follows:

CER = Errored Cells / Successfully Transferred Cells + Errored Cells

**ATM TECHNOLOGIES**

- **Severely Errored Cell Block Ratio (SECBR)** Within a certain size of cell block, a certain number of bad cells indicates a Severely Errored Cell Block; in other words, in a cell block that has $x$ number of cells, if $y$ number of cells are errored, the block is considered to be severely errored. For recommendations as to cell block size (the number of cells constituting a block), refer to ITU-T Recommendation I.610.

- **Cell Misinsertion Rate (CMR)** The CMR indicates the rate at which cells are misinserted into the cell flow; this can be caused by corruption in the cell header, which may cause the VPI/VCI destination to become misinterpreted.

## QoS Service Classes

Several QoS service classes have been defined in a range from the highest-priority traffic to the lowest-priority traffic. These service classes are designed to function together yet remain logically separated, to ensure that the most efficient use of bandwidth is made. To help define these different service classes, a series of metrics were devised, including the following:

- **Peak Cell Rate (PCR)** The highest rate at which traffic will run for any length of time (defined in cells per second).

- **Sustainable Cell Rate (SCR)** The mean rate at which traffic ideally will travel (defined in cells per second).

- **Maximum Burst Size (MBS)** The largest cell burst that will be tolerated by the traffic contract (defined in cells per second).

By defining a PCR, SCR, and MBS, a traffic contract may indicate the fastest cell rate, the average cell rate, and the maximum traffic burst size the connection can be expected to tolerate.

Cell Loss Priority may be applied to the PCR and to the SCR. In other words, cells marked for discard eligibility in times of network congestion or due to a UPC parameter violation may be so tagged in relation to either PCR or SCR cell flows. Nodes within the ATM network are considered to be either *CLP-transparent,* where the CLP bit is ignored regardless of its setting (in this case, CLP=0+1, meaning both cells, where CLP=1 and CLP=0 receive equal treatment), or *CLP-significant,* meaning the CLP bit is interpreted by the network (where CLP=1 and CLP=0 are differentiated). In the latter case, the network may make a best effort to deliver CLP=1 cells, or it may simply discard them.

## QoS Service Classes

The functions and parameters described in the previous sections work together to fashion a series of distinct QoS service classes. These service classes are designed to serve many different traffic requirements and levels of priority, from critical transfers which require dedicated bandwidth, to transfers which may be executed on a best-effort basis. Different service classes may, in some cases, have their ranges administratively defined, while others may seek to utilize as much bandwidth as possible given the current network load. Six distinct service classes have been defined:

- **Constant Bit Rate (CBR)**    The CBR service class reserves a certain amount of bandwidth (configured by the network administrator) for traffic negotiating a CBR contract. The amount of bandwidth assigned is defined by a PCR, and this bandwidth is reserved strictly for these connections; it may not be reallocated to other service classes. CBR connections may execute transfers at the PCR or below at any time, for any length of time, with no constraints. Video and voice applications generally fall into this category.

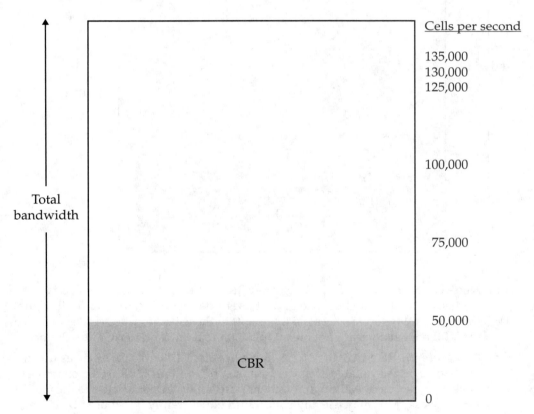

- **Real-time Variable Bit Rate (rt-VBR)**    Variable Bit Rate indicates that the rate defined for the service class is not constant, as it is with CBR, but that it must fall within certain specified parameters; each rt-VBR service class is given a

PCR, SCR, and MBS. Since an rt-VBR connection is intended to run in real time, a maxCTD is defined so that network latency does not compromise the service class.

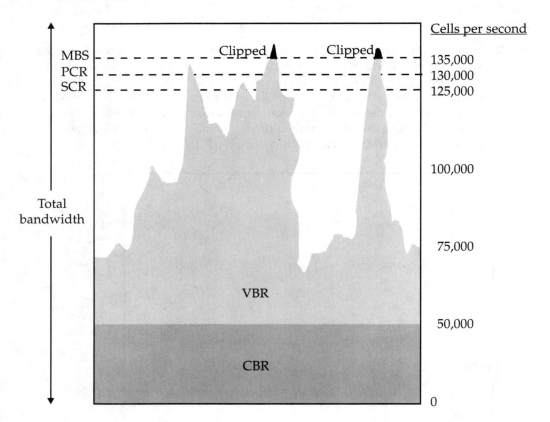

- **Non-real-time Variable Bit Rate (nrt-VBR)**   The nrt-VBR service class is similar to the rt-VBR class insofar as it uses a defined PCR, SCR, and MBS, and traffic with this service class must fall within those boundaries. However, since nrt-VBR connections are not meant to run in real time, no maxCTD is defined.

- **Available Bit Rate (ABR)**   The ABR service class attempts to utilize as much bandwidth as is available after the CBR, rt-VBR, and nrt-VBR traffic contracts have been satisfied. Although it may not use bandwidth allocated to the CBR service class, ABR may use any bandwidth not currently being used by either of the VBR classes. Because the amount of bandwidth used by VBR connections fluctuates, the amount of bandwidth available to the ABR class changes dynamically to the point where fluctuations may occur after the connection has been established. The ABR class is defined by a PCR and a Minimum Cell Rate (MCR). ABR connections utilize a flow control feedback mechanism to monitor changes in the available bandwidth and to ensure that the bandwidth used does not rise above the PCR or fall below the MCR. The ABR service class generally is intended for data transfers and is not well-suited to real-time applications such as voice and video.

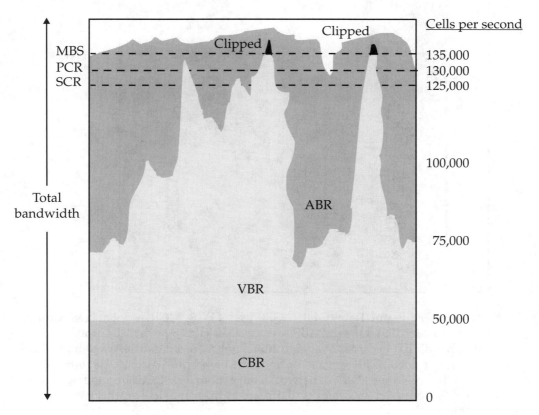

■ **Unspecified Bit Rate (UBR)**   UBR traffic is delivered on a best-effort basis, utilizing whatever bandwidth remains after all other traffic contracts have been satisfied. All other service classes take precedence over UBR, and bandwidth allocated to one UBR connection may or may not be available the next time such a connection is made. The UBR traffic class is intended for data transfers.

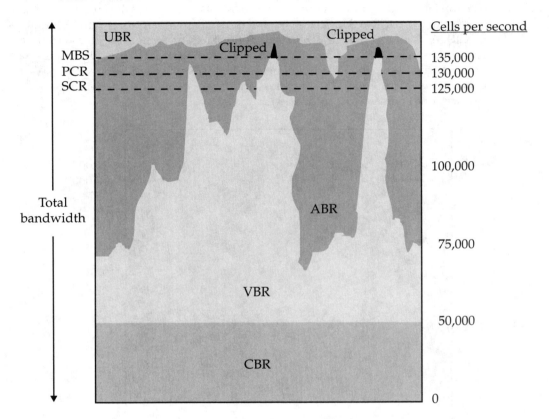

- **Guaranteed Frame Rate (GFR)**   GFR uses a PCR, MCR, MBS, and Maximum Frame Size (MFS). Like the ABR service class, GFR may use additional bandwidth if it becomes available, but is not required to utilize a defined flow control protocol. GFR service contracts are based on AAL-5 PDUs rather than on cells, and in the event of network congestion, if discards become necessary, the GFR service class attempts to discard at the frame level rather than at the cell level.

# QoS Application

The manner in which ATM QoS contracts may be negotiated is defined in User-to-Network Interface (UNI) 4.0 and Private Network-to-Network Interface

(PNNI) 1.0. In a practical scenario, traffic requirements may be requested at the time a call is initiated—for instance, when a Lan Emulation Client (LEC) initiates a Data Direct VCC with a remote LEC. PNNI may take such traffic contracts into account when a source node calculates a Designated Transit List (DTL) to a destination node (for more information regarding PNNI and DTLs, consult Chapter 16).

The Lan Emulation (LANE) 2.0 specification defines a method for applying QoS parameters to circuits created by LECs within a LANE environment. In this scenario, a LEC may indicate the service levels it offers by encoding Service Category TLVs into its LE_REGISTER_REQUESTS and LE_ARP_RESPONSES. By including TLVs which advertise its QoS capabilities, a LEC can let a remote, calling LEC know what types of service contracts it is capable of providing.

## QoS Sets and Bindings

QoS traffic contracts in a LANE environment must be applied in some way to Data Direct VCCs as they are constructed between LECs; the LANE 2.0 specification describes the use of QoS sets and QoS bindings to achieve this. A QoS set in this case is a portion of the QoS requirements; a group of QoS sets may be bundled together for use as a qos_handle, while that qos_handle in turn is bound to a particular connection by using a QoS binding (see Figure 14-1).

The example in Figure 14-1 indicates two different qos_handles bound to two different Data Direct VCCs. In this case, both Data Direct connections extend between the same two endpoints. Whether or not a specific VCC may be used for a specific transfer will depend on the service requirements of the application making the request, the QoS bindings which are currently in place, and whether a current QoS binding indicates a connection may be shared, or if it is dedicated. Should a connection be requested with a certain service contract, the LEC must decide if an existing connection may be used, or if a new connection with a new QoS binding must be created (if it can indeed be supported). LANEv2 offers LLC Multiplexing for VCCs, so any LEC may

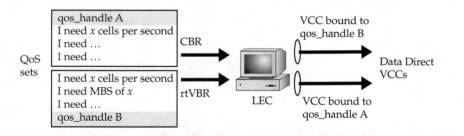

**Figure 14-1.**   *QoS sets and bindings*

potentially have a series of existing Data Direct VCCs to select from. To determine if one can be used, a LEC may use the following decision-making process:

1. Is there already a QoS binding to a VCC extending to the remote address that is being requested? If so and a VCC is defined, but the qos_handle bound to it cannot satisfy the service level being requested, the LEC cannot use the existing VCC.

2. If there is a VCC in place with the correct binding, does it allow for sharing, or multiplexing? In certain scenarios, even if a match is discovered, the service class defined may not allow multiplexing over the VCC (as may be the case with a CBR connection), in which case the LEC still may not use the existing VCC.

3. Is there a VCC in place to the destination which has either no QoS binding, or the default QoS binding? In this case, the LEC may initiate the new binding. In the event that such multiple VCCs exist, the LEC will select the one which was created first.

QoS has long been a goal of ATM, as well as that of other technologies; ATM can function without the presence of QoS service classes (in fact the default UBR traffic class is commonly used), however traffic prioritization in accordance with policed traffic contracts serves to further increase the efficiency of ATM. For more information regarding ATM QoS and traffic management, consult the ATM Forum Traffic Management specification version 4.1.

# Chapter 15

## Call Routing via IISP

To reach their destinations, Asynchronous Transfer Mode (ATM) calls that are not passing over statically configured permanent virtual circuits (PVCs) require a call routing method. If a data-direct virtual control channel (VCC) needs to be built between two LAN Emulation clients, that VCC must be routed to the proper switch that hosts the destination LEC. Interim Inter-Switch Protocol (IISP) was the initial method of achieving this, and consists of user-defined static routes configured for every route to every switch through the mesh.

IISP, sometimes referred to as PNNI phase 0, was created as an interim solution to support multivendor switch interoperability. In the absence of a pure PVC mesh, the dynamic signaling methods of LANE required a method of routing calls through the ATM network. IISP was always intended to be an interim solution until the dynamic routing capability of the Private Network to Network Interface (PNNI) phase 1 was completed.

Static routing has advantages and disadvantages. It has low overhead, because each switch is responsible for routing only to the next hop and is not required to learn routing information or maintain a topology database. However, static routes can be difficult to implement, particularly with redundancy, and they do not scale very well. IISP was built upon the user network interface (UNI) 3.1 specification, and this was done specifically with the idea of implementing a call routing mechanism while making minimal changes to the existing specification.

# IISP Signaling

The reference model illustrated in Figure 15-1 (per the IISPv1.0 specification) outlines the relative positioning of the Interim Inter-Switch Protocol.

IISP uses the same cell format as the ATM UNI 3.1 (refer to Chapter 13), and its physical layer and ATM adaption layer (AAL) specifications follow those outlined in UNI 3.1, as do its traffic management procedures (outlined in Chapter 14).

## Signaling Considerations

IISP signaling effectively determines the next route hop and then initiates a UNI connection to that hop. Therefore, although an IISP connection is defined separately from a UNI connection, a version of UNI signaling must still be selected to complete this task. In addition to the UNI 3.1 specification it was built upon, the IISP specification includes optional support for the UNI 3.0 signaling protocol. Because the UNI specification discriminates between the User and Network side of any given link, these roles must be assumed at either end of an IISP connection, which is why the ends of each individual IISP link must be defined as User and Network; the call, as it traverses the network, will actually be set up as a user-to-network connection.

The User and Network sides of an IISP link are configured manually, by the administrator. These roles may be chosen and defined on a link-by-link basis, and no

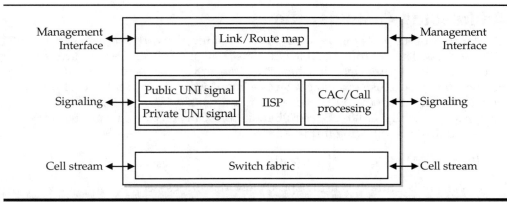

**Figure 15-1.** *IISP reference model*

rules exist regarding which links must serve which roles. Note, however, that to eliminate the possibility of call collision due to two calls attempting to utilize the same VPI/VCI pair, only the Network side of an IISP link is permitted to assign the VPI/VCI values. As is outlined further in the chapters on ATM configuration, this fact could become important when considering VPI/VCI bit masking in a multivendor environment.

## ILMI

Although IISP is based on the UNI 3.1 specification and adopts the roles of User and Network for each IISP link, the Interim Local Management Interface (ILMI) isn't used over these links, and no address registration occurs between nodes over an IISP connection. This is due to the fact that, unlike an ATM-attached UNI device, the ATM switch is already in possession of a full, 20-octet ATM address and does not need to register to obtain an ATM prefix. ILMI may be disabled on these links.

## IISP Routing

In IISP, no actual exchange of route information occurs between switches. IISP routes are static routes, and routing is performed on a hop-by-hop basis, through the consultation of user-defined call routing tables. Calls routed through an IISP network are routed very quickly, because little overhead is associated with the protocol; an incoming call destined for a specific address need only be processed to discover which port on the receiving switch is associated with the call routing entry for the destination system.

# IISP Addressing Considerations

The IISP protocol supports the use of any portion of the Network Service Access Point (NSAP) address. The call routing table will consist of an NSAP address, which is a 20-octet string; the address length, which is an integer value between 0 and 104 inclusive, and 152, exclusive; and an interface index, which is an identifier for the interface through which the ATM address in question may be reached.

For example, on the C100/C50/5000BH platform, an entry using a partial ATM prefix will utilize the following format:

39.10.04.11    Module1, Port1    Cost:10

In this example, and when using SpeedView, the address length is implied when the partial prefix is entered, meaning that a partial prefix of 39.10.04.11 is 32 bytes in length (each digit being a 4-byte hex nibble); thus, a length of 32 does not need to be configured against the entire ATM address, because it is assumed, and the rest of the address is ignored for purposes of matching against the IISP route index. Note that a length of 0 will constitute a match for any incoming call, and a default route will utilize an address length of 0. In this example, the address 39.10.04.11 is reachable out of module 1, port 1, with a cost of 10. IISP route costing is discussed later in this chapter.

When configuring the IISP call routing table, a complete address may be specified, but this isn't necessary. Inputting a partial prefix is enough, but care must be taken to ensure enough of the prefix is included to make it unique, depending on the circumstance (see Figure 15-2).

In the example shown in Figure 15-2, prefixes of different lengths are utilized, depending on the location of the node in question, and the addresses that are reachable from it. Switch A, for instance, uses two prefixes only in its routing table: 39.10 and 47. This makes sense in this case, because switch A has only one connection to the rest of the ATM mesh. Each route may have been individually described, but since each node beyond it shares the prefix 39.10, the single entry will suffice. In this scenario, because the well known address (WKA) is the only address using the first octet of 47, this entry will suffice for the WKA. Alternately, in a situation where an ATM switch has only a single connection to the rest of the network, a default route may be used.

After a call passes from switch A into the mesh, however, routes must become more specific. Switch B's call routing table must accurately reflect the three switches that are connected to it. An incoming call on switch B that is destined for switch A must be routed to that switch specifically. Therefore, station B's routing table contains routes that are more specific; 39.20, 39.10.02, and 39.10.03.

Moving to switch D, routes must become even more specific. In this example, because the addressing scheme is such that switches E, F, and G share in common a larger portion of the prefix, that again must be reflected in the routing tables; switch D's entries of 39.10.06.01, 39.10.06.02, and 39.10.06.03 prevent confusion when an

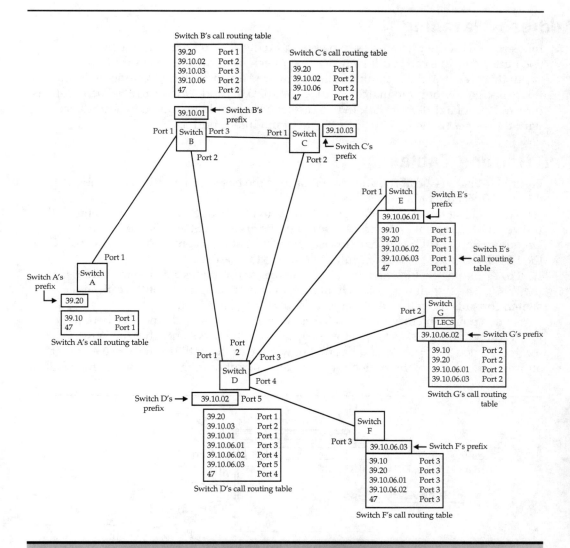

**Figure 15-2.**  *ATM mesh with call routes, with varying degrees of prefix masking*

incoming call is destined for one of those addresses. Also note, however, that since switches E, F, and G are all accessible from port 2 on switch C, only a prefix of 39.10.06 is required.

# Address Matching

In keeping with the previous examples, a call request coming into a switch may encounter multiple call routing entries that match its address (see Figure 15-3).

In this scenario, the incoming call is compared against the call routing table, and three entries are found to match; 39.10.05, 39.10.05.01, and 39.10.05.01.99. Each prefix is directed out of a different port. In this case, the call would be routed in accordance with the longest match; 39.10.05.01.99 out of module 1, port 3.

# Call Routing Tables

Figure 15-4 shows a call routing table that uses the basic format utilized in the C100/C50/5000BH platforms.

This routing table also includes the WKA; in this example, the LANE clients will utilize an LECS to obtain their LAN Emulation Server (LES) and Broadcast and Unknown Server (BUS) information, so clients initiating a configuration-direct VCC to the LECS will need a series of routes in place to that address.

For example, the LEC on switch A initializes and initiates a call to the LECS, using the WKA. The switch that is the client's host is the starting point of the call, so the switch consults the call routing table, as shown in Figure 15-4.

At this point, an entry for the WKA is confirmed; the switch knows where to forward the call for *its next hop*. However, the switch knows only that the WKA is located at module 1 port 2, and has no knowledge of the path taken to arrive at that address after that. So, the switch forwards the call out of module 1, port 2, and awaits a

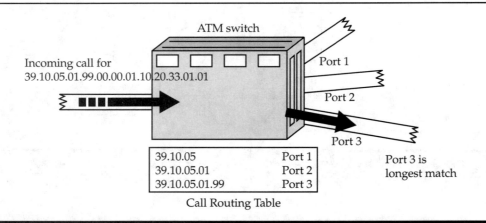

**Figure 15-3.**   *Incoming call compared against a routing table in which multiple entries match*

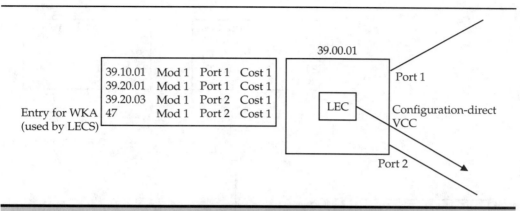

**Figure 15-4.**   *The call routing table is consulted to resolve the location of the WKA*

successful connection. At this point, if either an error occurs, a route to the next hop is not in place, or the link described in that next hop is inactive or has failed, the originating switch (39.00.01 in this case) has no way of knowing this, and no method exists by which the switch might learn this information and use it.

The IISP specification states that if an incoming call is received for which no match is found in the receiving node's routing table, a RELEASE COMPLETE message is generated, with a rejection cause #3, "No route to destination." Likewise, if a match exists in the call routing table, but the specified link is not active, a RELEASE COMPLETE message is generated with a rejection cause #38, "Network out of order." However, neither the switch that initiated the call nor any of the switches along the path will note this fact and account for it; the call will simply fail.

Before releasing the call, the switch that was the point of failure will consult the call routing table again, to see whether any other routes are in place by which it may get to the desired address. If no other such route is in place, then the call fails, as illustrated in Figure 15-5.

The originating switch has no way of knowing where the call broke down, which path it took, or whether or not it was forced to take an alternate path. The switch has knowledge only of its next hop. For this reason, IISP routes must be defined carefully.

In this example, when the setup of the VCC fails, switch 39.10 attempts a new call to switch 39.50. It will consult the call routing table again and, unless the damaged portion of the route is repaired, the call will continue to fail as the originating switch continually forwards the call down a dead path. Switch 39.10 would need another entry, costed differently, for switch 39.50 pointing to port 2, and switch 39.30 would need a valid entry for route 39.50 in order for an alternate path to be taken.

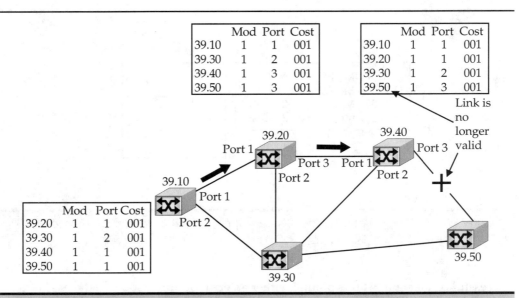

**Figure 15-5.**    *Call failure due to a bad link*

## Redundant Routes

To take into account the possibility of a link failure, multiple routes to the same destination may be defined. In these cases, the cost may be incremented for each link, as shown in Figure 15-6, to describe the paths' order of desirability.

If redundant routes are going to be used, they must be defined in the static routing table. In the preceding example, the originating switch 39.10 has multiple ways of reaching switch 39.20, the primary route being module, 1 port 1 with a cost of 001. If the secondary route (from module 1, port 2 with a cost of 002) and the tertiary route (from module 1, port 3 with a cost of 003) were not defined, and the primary route of module 1, port 1 were to fail, then the LEC located on switch 39.10 would be unable to reach a remote LEC configured on switch 39.20. The cost ensures that, unless the link fails, switch 39.10 will take the shortest path to 39.20, using the longer paths only as backup routes.

By utilizing cost, a series of redundant routes may be established. A node receiving an incoming call will attempt to use the path with the lowest cost first. If that link is down, the node will attempt to transport the call again by using the next-highest-cost route.

Great care must be taken when using redundant, multicosted routes to avoid call routing loops. *Call routing loops* appear when a static route somewhere in the path between two destinations routes the call back toward some previous point within the path, which in turn routes it back toward the loop, and the call never finds the destination.

In Figure 15-7, switch F houses a server farm. Because these servers must maintain their connection to the network, the decision is made to implement a redundant IISP route from the servers' ATM switch back to the core. By following its call routing table, switch A finds a direct route to switch F and back again, using the primary IISP links. Trouble occurs, however, if the primary IISP connection between switches A and F fails. Follow the IISP routes in this new scenario carefully. Switch B still has a valid route to switch F, and back again, but switch A, switch C, and switch D, however, no longer have a valid route to switch F.

With the link connecting switch A and switch F down, switch A is forced to use its secondary path (to switch C). Switch C routes to switch D, as its call routing table indicates. Switch D's routing table indicates switch F can be reached from module 1 port 2 (to switch A). If switch A's primary path to F were still in place, this would work; since it is not, the secondary path is used, and switch A sends its own call back to switch C, looping the call.

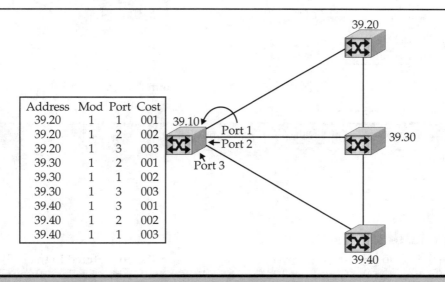

| Address | Mod | Port | Cost |
|---------|-----|------|------|
| 39.20 | 1 | 1 | 001 |
| 39.20 | 1 | 2 | 002 |
| 39.20 | 1 | 3 | 003 |
| 39.30 | 1 | 2 | 001 |
| 39.30 | 1 | 1 | 002 |
| 39.30 | 1 | 3 | 003 |
| 39.40 | 1 | 3 | 001 |
| 39.40 | 1 | 2 | 002 |
| 39.40 | 1 | 1 | 003 |

**Figure 15-6.**   *Redundant routes and their different costing*

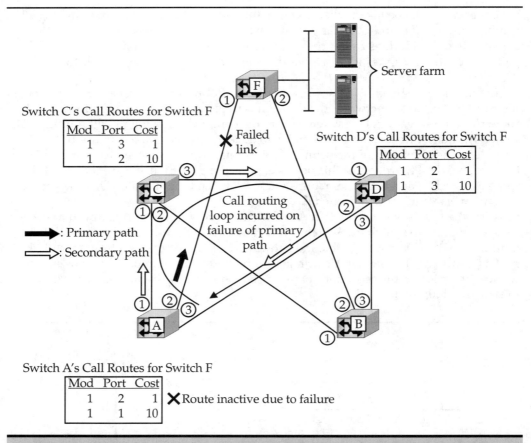

Switch C's Call Routes for Switch F

| Mod | Port | Cost |
|-----|------|------|
| 1 | 3 | 1 |
| 1 | 2 | 10 |

Switch D's Call Routes for Switch F

| Mod | Port | Cost |
|-----|------|------|
| 1 | 2 | 1 |
| 1 | 3 | 10 |

Server farm

Failed link

Call routing loop incurred on failure of primary path

➤: Primary path

⇨: Secondary path

Switch A's Call Routes for Switch F

| Mod | Port | Cost |
|-----|------|------|
| 1 | 2 | 1 |
| 1 | 1 | 10 |

✗ Route inactive due to failure

**Figure 15-7.**   *Routing loop incurred by failover route*

# Parallel Links

Parallel links in IISP are supported, although not specifically defined in the IISP specification. On the Centillion 100/50 and 5000BH platforms, parallel links may be achieved through the use of *Link Groups*. Link Groups cause two parallel links to behave as a single link, with bandwidth equal to the number of links combined. IISP Link Groups on the Centillion may be configured in groups of up to four links.

# Link Failure

In the event of an IISP link failure, all SVC calls currently active on or through that link are cleared. If redundant call routes are in place, the calls may be rerouted. If no redundant path exists, the calls will drop until the link state is repaired.

# CAC Support

Call Admission Control (CAC) support is optional in IISP, and the use of CAC over IISP links does not guarantee QoS (Quality of Service) from end to end; it is of significance only when passing from node to node. When utilizing CAC with IISP, incoming calls are first compared against the call routing table to see whether a match exists. If the interface does have requirements that must be matched, and those requirements have been met, or if the call has no special requirements, the call is forwarded to the next hop. If any requirements have not been matched, the call is rejected.

IISP functions very well; it is a fast, reliable method of routing calls throughout an ATM mesh. However, after the network becomes larger (20+ switches), designing and maintaining the network becomes difficult. The difficulties can be minimized through proper design; edge switches with only a single connection to the core may utilize a default route, cutting down tremendously on the number of routes configured in the routing table, and address groupings; summarizing 39.10.01, 39.10.02, and 39.10.03 as 39.10 can be done, as long as 39.10 is unique from other portions of the network. Redundant routes may be built in for fault tolerance, so that if the primary link fails that an ATM LANE client is using for its LANE control channels, the client can reconnect to its services over the redundant link.

# Chapter 16

## Private Network-to-Network Interface

P rivate Network-to-Network Interface (PNNI) is an ATM protocol that provides dynamic call routing throughout the ATM mesh. Unlike the Interim Inter-Switch Protocol (IISP), which uses a hop-by-hop-based system of routing ATM calls based on static routes of varying costs, PNNI call routes are determined by the ATM node from which the call originates, making it a source-routed protocol.

To accomplish this, each PNNI node must determine the network topology of the ATM mesh and its relative positioning within that mesh. PNNI utilizes many of the same concepts as the Open Shortest Path First (OSPF) routing protocol, and, in fact, is based heavily upon OSPF. For more information regarding OSPF, consult Chapter 31.

## Concepts of PNNI

The PNNI routing protocol is an inter-switch protocol, used to determine dynamically the best path through which to route ATM calls. It is a source-routing protocol, which means that the node that originates the call is responsible for determining an end-to-end path that the call will take. Although similar to OSPF insofar as each PNNI node maintains a database of the entire network topology, to serve its source-routing requirements, some fundamental differences exist:

- PNNI is a Layer 2 protocol, whereas OSPF is a Layer 3 protocol
- Unlike a traditional routed environment, PNNI nodes share actual physical connections, rather than common networks.
- OSPF (or any routing protocol) will run on top of PNNI, not in place of it.

PNNI uses the concept of logical groupings of interconnected nodes, called *peer groups*, which are similar in concept to OSPF areas; this requires PNNI nodes to maintain only specific topology information for their own peer group, while remote peer groups may be viewed as summarizations of addresses.

## PNNI Features and Requirements

PNNI phase 1 was designed to support a certain set of features, described in the following list. However, a subset of these features (known as Annex G) are deemed to be required features in a PNNI implementation.

The current features supported by PNNI phase 1, in accordance with the PNNI 1.0 specification, are as follows:

- **Supports all UNI 3.1 and some UNI 4.0 capabilities**   The PNNI routing protocol supports all the capabilities of ATM UNI 3.1; this doesn't mean that UNI 3.0 may not be supported as well. Some of the capabilities of ATM UNI 4.0 also are supported.

- **Supports hierarchical routing**   The PNNI environment may be broken into peer groups. PNNI nodes may share advertisements on different hierarchical levels with nodes in other peer groups that are on a like hierarchical level. These higher-level routing advertisements (remote peer groups) may be communicated down to nodes within the same peer group as logical group nodes (LGNs).

- **Supports QoS**   PNNI phase 1 supports variable QoS requirements and takes QoS parameters into consideration for purposes for dynamic route determination.

- **Supports multiple routing metrics and attributes**   PNNI supports path costing (referred to as *administrative weight*) for purposes of dynamic route determination, as well as total bandwidth and bandwidth availability.

- **Utilizes a source-routed call setup**   In a PNNI environment, the circuit path to the destination is determined end to end by the source node. If the initial path fails for any reason (such as unavailability of required resources or link failure), the source node becomes responsible for calculating a new path. In the case of a multiple peer group environment in which the circuit must traverse multiple peer groups, the source node is responsible for devising a path to the proper border node, bordering the next peer group in the overall path.

- **Operates in the presence of partitioned peer groups**   If a peer group becomes *partitioned* (the peer group is divided into two logical groups due to link failure, yet the two groups still share the same Peer Group ID), the PNNI protocol continues to function. This is done by ensuring that nodes retain uniqueness even when summarized at higher levels as LGNs.

- **Provides dynamic routing that responds to changes in resource availability**   PNNI routes are determined dynamically, based on an ATM mesh topology derived from shared link state information. In addition to physical availability of the path, factors such as resource availability may be considered when determining the viability of a route.

- **Keeps routing protocol in different peer groups separate**   Nodes within a single peer group need not maintain a database of the topology in other peer groups. These are viewed only as LGNs, communicated to nodes within a peer group by their Peer Group Leader (PGL).

- **Interoperates with external routing domains**   PNNI peer groups may exist alongside IISP within the same network; IISP may be used to separate PNNI peer groups, or PNNI may be used as a dynamic core serving other IISP portions of the network. In these cases, IISP routes are advertised as external routes to the rest of the PNNI network by the connected node.

- **Supports soft PVCs**   Soft PVCs (SPVCs) are supported by PNNI, whereby remote nodes act as termination points for a dynamically determined path that,

ATM TECHNOLOGIES

once erected, remains static. In the event of link failure, these connections are recalculated and reestablished. SPVCs are used by the PNNI protocol in some instances, such as the connections maintained between Peer Group Leaders in a multihierarchical routing environment.

# PNNI Overview

Like OSPF, PNNI is a link state protocol, where individual nodes maintain a database of the network topology. In the case of a local area (peer group), a database of the full network topology is maintained, while remote peer groups are summarized as a PNNI address range. PNNI nodes discover one another through the distribution of control packets, and topology information is communicated and maintained through the flooding of link state advertisements within specific peer groups.

## Lowest Hierarchical Level

In the lowest hierarchical PNNI level, each node is required to maintain a full topological database of every node, link state, and reachability information within the network. This is a viable solution for networks that are not overly large. PNNI nodes are able to maintain these databases and routing information as long as the number of nodes does not become too great. Depending on the processing power of the switches used within the mesh, maintaining the topological database begins to become too processor-intensive after a point. The solution to this problem is to create multiple PNNI hierarchies, whereby nodes are broken into logical groupings (peer groups). Nodes in this scenario need only maintain a full topological database for their own peer group (see Figure 16-1).

## PNNI Nodes

PNNI nodes are considered logical entities residing on a physical device, although in common use, nodes and the switches they reside on are used more or less interchangeably. Unlike legacy Layer 3 routing protocols that are based on broadcasts and multicasts, PNNI nodes share common physical attachments rather than common networks, and their routing information is passed point to point to one another.

Each PNNI node has an awareness of the other nodes it is directly attached to. By receiving information over these links from its neighboring nodes and sending information regarding its own link state, each PNNI node is able to share with other nodes the information regarding its links.

## Peer Groups and Logical Nodes

Logical nodes at the lowest hierarchical level are referred to simply as *nodes* and are organized into peer groups. The interaction between separate peer groups is covered later in this chapter, in the sections "Further Up the PNNI Hierarchy" and "Highest Hierarchical Level." For purposes of this section, only interaction within a single peer group is studied (see Figure 16-2).

The example shown in Figure 16-2 has six nodes, all interconnected. Each node has a unique, identifying Node ID, as well as a common Peer Group ID (PG ID). The Node ID in this case enables nodes to identify one another as unique entities within the PNNI

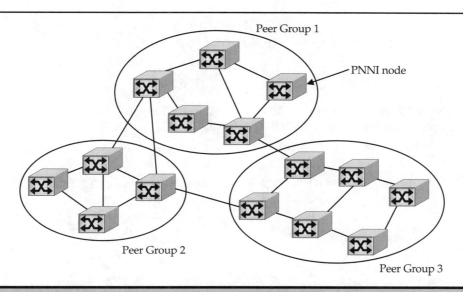

**Figure 16-1.**  *PNNI nodes broken into peer groups*

environment, while the common PG ID enables each node to determine that each of its five neighboring nodes are within its same peer group.

## Level Indicators

The level indicator acts as a sort of "mask" for the PNNI PG ID; the level indicator is a string of bits ranging in length from 0 to 104 bits (0 to 13 octets), and defines the number of significant bits used in the PG ID. For example, consider the following two NSAP prefixes:

Node A: 39.00.00.10.00.20.01.00.32.41.00.00.00
Node B: 39.00.00.10.00.30.01.00.68.41.00.00.00

In the NSAP address, each digit is a 4-bit hex nibble. Using the preceding two nodes and their specific NSAP prefixes, depending on the level indicator assigned, they may be within either the same or different peer groups. For instance, if both nodes are given a level indicator of 32, this would place them within the same peer group:

Node A: 39.00.00.10
Node B: 39.00.00.10

Notice that the level indicator defines the first 32 bits as significant, which results in the first 4 octets (eight 4-bit hex nibbles = 32). This results in a PG ID of 39.00.00.10.00.00.00.00.00.00.00.00.00, which both nodes share in common. At the lowest

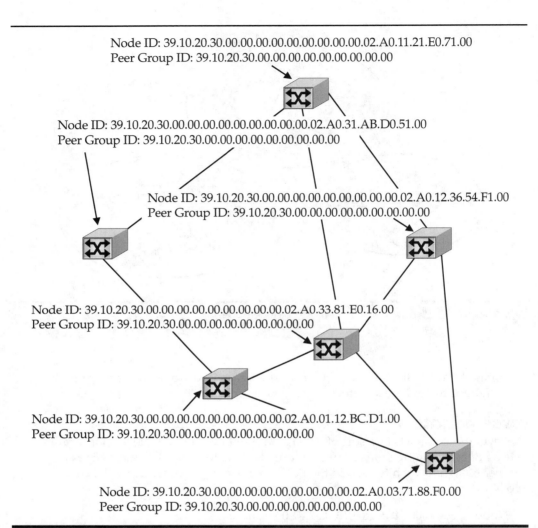

Node ID: 39.10.20.30.00.00.00.00.00.00.00.00.00.02.A0.11.21.E0.71.00
Peer Group ID: 39.10.20.30.00.00.00.00.00.00.00.00.00

Node ID: 39.10.20.30.00.00.00.00.00.00.00.00.00.02.A0.31.AB.D0.51.00
Peer Group ID: 39.10.20.30.00.00.00.00.00.00.00.00.00

Node ID: 39.10.20.30.00.00.00.00.00.00.00.00.00.02.A0.12.36.54.F1.00
Peer Group ID: 39.10.20.30.00.00.00.00.00.00.00.00.00

Node ID: 39.10.20.30.00.00.00.00.00.00.00.00.00.02.A0.33.81.E0.16.00
Peer Group ID: 39.10.20.30.00.00.00.00.00.00.00.00.00

Node ID: 39.10.20.30.00.00.00.00.00.00.00.00.00.02.A0.01.12.BC.D1.00
Peer Group ID: 39.10.20.30.00.00.00.00.00.00.00.00.00

Node ID: 39.10.20.30.00.00.00.00.00.00.00.00.00.02.A0.03.71.88.F0.00
Peer Group ID: 39.10.20.30.00.00.00.00.00.00.00.00.00

**Figure 16-2.**  *Six PNNI nodes within a single peer group showing Node ID and PG ID*

hierarchical level, PNNI nodes in the same peer group must use a common level indicator. However, using the same two NSAP prefixes as the previous example, if the level indicator is set to 48, then the number of significant bits is extended to include octets that are unique to each NSAP prefix:

Node A: 39.00.00.10.00.20
Node B: 39.00.00.10.00.30

The first six octets are now defined as significant (twelve 4-bit hex nibbles = 48), which results in two unique PG IDs:

Node A: 39.00.00.10.00.20.00.00.00.00.00.00.00
Node B: 39.00.00.10.00.30.00.00.00.00.00.00.00

This variance in PG IDs places nodes A and B logically within separate peer groups.

## Peer Group Identifiers

Peer Group IDs are a result of masking the level indicator (see the previous section) against the NSAP prefix for purposes of defining which nodes exist in which peer group. The PG ID in this case appears as a 14-octet string; 1 octet indicating the actual level, and 13 octets defining the PG ID itself:

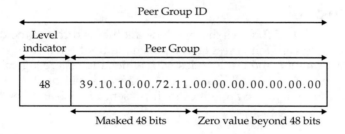

The value of the level indicator must be 0 to 104 bits. The value sent in the identifier information field is encoded with the 104-$n$ (where $n$ is the level) rightmost bits set to 0. Therefore, an NSAP prefix of 39.10.31.14.00.73.00.00.10.21.53.22.10 with a level of 72 would yield a PG ID of 48.39.10.21.14.00.73.00.00.10.00.00.00.00.

## Node Identifiers

The PNNI Node ID is a value that uniquely defines a node among members of its own peer group. Nodes within the same peer group share a common PG ID, but have unique Node IDs. The PNNI Node ID is 22 octets in length. The first octet is a level indicator, which is consistent with the level of the node's peer group, followed by a 21-octet value. Note that the level of the node is consistent with that of its peer group; this is true of parent as well as child peer groups, meaning that if a node is participating on a higher hierarchical level (for instance, it is PGL in a multiple peer group environment), then its level will be consistent with the level of that parent peer group. This is discussed later in the chapter as hierarchical PNNI routing is examined. For the purposes of a node participating in the lowest-level hierarchy, the following rules apply to the Node ID:

■ The level indicator specifies the level of the node's peer group. This indicates that the node exists within a particular peer group.

■ The second octet has a value of 160 (A0 in hex); this makes the ID unique from those assigned to nodes existing at higher levels (such as parent peer groups).

■ The remainder of the Node ID contains the 20-octet ATM address of the system on which the logical node resides (the switch itself).

## Logical Links

PNNI nodes are connected by *logical links*. Links between nodes within the same peer group are *horizontal links*, whereas links between two peer groups are *outside links*.

Once a logical link has been established between nodes, Hello packets may be passed over these links. It is through the Hello protocol that PNNI nodes periodically advertise their presence to one another, including what kind of node they are, and which peer group they are in.

# The Hello Protocol

The method by which PNNI nodes discover one another is through the distribution of control packets known as Hello messages. By exchanging these messages, nodes are able to collect information about the nodes with which they share logical links. These Hello messages consist of a PNNI header, followed by a series of nodal information, and are used by PNNI nodes to announce their presence to one another over their logical links:

| State |
| --- |
| Port ID |
| Remote node ID |
| Remote Peer Group ID |
| Remote port ID |
| Hello interval |
| Hello timer |
| Inactivity factor |
| Inactivity timer |
| Version |

PNNI hello message

The transmission and receipt of these messages enables nodes to determine the current link state between them.

## Hello States

PNNI nodes transition between a variety of Hello states as they transmit and receive Hello messages over their logical links. The information they receive from neighboring peers within the Hello messages indicates the type of node they are. The example shown in Figure 16-3 has two PNNI nodes that are directly attached to each other and exist within the same peer group.

**DOWN** Prior to initialization, both nodes exist in a *Down* state, which means that neither node has received or transmitted any Hello messages at this point. When a logical link is established and the nodes initialize, node A detects that the connection between itself and node B has come up, which node B also detects.

**ATTEMPT** With the establishment of a logical link, the transmission of Hello packets begins. Both nodes begin transmitting Hello messages. After a node has transmitted a Hello message but has yet to receive one, the interface has transitioned into the *Attempt* state.

Contained within these Hello messages being transmitted by each node are pieces of information about the sending node. Specifically, the Hello message contains the following information:

- **State**   The sending node's current state.

- **Node ID**   Because each node in this case is within the same peer group, the Node ID consists of a common level indicator, followed by the value 160.

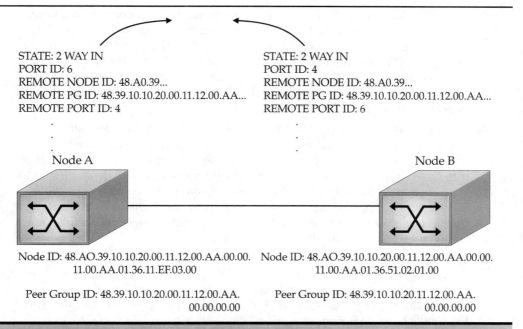

STATE: 2 WAY IN
PORT ID: 6
REMOTE NODE ID: 48.A0.39...
REMOTE PG ID: 48.39.10.10.20.00.11.12.00.AA...
REMOTE PORT ID: 4

STATE: 2 WAY IN
PORT ID: 4
REMOTE NODE ID: 48.A0.39...
REMOTE PG ID: 48.39.10.10.20.00.11.12.00.AA...
REMOTE PORT ID: 6

Node A

Node B

Node ID: 48.AO.39.10.10.20.00.11.12.00.AA.00.00.
11.00.AA.01.36.11.EF.03.00

Node ID: 48.AO.39.10.10.20.00.11.12.00.AA.00.00.
11.00.AA.01.36.51.02.01.00

Peer Group ID: 48.39.10.10.20.00.11.12.00.AA.
00.00.00.00

Peer Group ID: 48.39.10.10.20.11.12.00.AA.
00.00.00.00

**Figure 16-3.**   *Node A and node B exchanging Hello messages*

ATM TECHNOLOGIES

The remainder of the Node ID is the 20-octet address of the switch each node resides on.

- **ATM address**  The 20-octet ATM address associated with the logical node. This information is necessary because any calls actually placed will be to an ATM End System Address (the ATM address associated with the physical switch), not the PNNI Node ID.

- **Peer Group ID**  The node's NSAP prefix, as masked against the level indicator. In this case, node A and node B both advertise a PG ID of 39.00.10.00.00.00.00.00.00.00.00.00.00, because they are within a common peer group, node A has an ATM NSAP prefix of 39.00.10.00.20.00.11.15.00.00.00.00.00, node B has an ATM NSAP prefix of 39.00.10.00.20.00.11.15.00.01.00.00.00, and both have a level indicator of 24.

- **Remote PNNI Node ID**  The PNNI Node ID of the neighboring peer. In this case, because the nodes are still within an Attempt state, this value is 0. Once node A receives a Hello message from node B containing node B's PNNI Node ID, node A will insert that value under the Remote PNNI Node ID header. By doing this, each node is able to determine whether its Hello messages have been received, by seeing whether its Node ID is listed as the Remote PNNI Node ID in the incoming Hello message.

- **Port ID**  A dynamically assigned unique value that is associated with the port over which the Hello messages are being sent. In the case where PGLs are sending Hellos over a switched virtual control channel (SVCC) rather than over the PNNI signaling channel of 0/18, this is indicated by assigning the value of 0xFFFFFFFF to the Port ID. For more information regarding PGLs and their control connections, consult the sections on Peer Group Leaders, later in this chapter.

- **Remote Port ID**  Again, while two nodes are still in an Attempt state, this value is set to 0, since the remote port value is not yet known. When node A receives a Hello message from node B, it inserts node B's Local Port number into the Remote Port header in its own Hello messages. This is another method for peer nodes to identify that their Hello messages are being received over the proper link; once node A sees its own Local Port number listed as Remote Port in node B's Hello message, then it knows that its own Hello message was received by node B from the port it was sent.

- **Hello Interval**  Indicates how often the node will transmit a Hello message. If the receiving peer does not receive a Hello message within the time allotted in the Hello Interval, it assumes that the remote node has experienced a failure. If no Hello messages are received before the expiration of the inactivity timer, the link is brought down.

**1-WAY INSIDE**    After node A receives a Hello message from node B, it examines it; if it doesn't see its own Node ID or Local Port listed in the Hello message, then it transitions into a *1-Way* state. This indicates that it has received a Hello message from a neighboring peer, but that it hasn't received any indication yet that the remote peer has received its Hello messages. Node A examines the Hello message that it received, and checks the Peer Group ID. Because the PG ID in this case matches its own, it determines that the remote node is a member of its peer group. The 1-Way state it enters into then is a *1-Way Inside* state. If the PG ID didn't match its own, it would enter into a *1-Way Outside* state, indicating the neighboring peer is in a different peer group.

**2-WAY INSIDE**    Once node A receives a Hello message from node B and sees its own Node ID listed as the Remote PNNI Node ID and its own Local Port listed as the Remote Port, then it determines that its Hello messages are being received by node B. Two-way communication is now established between two nodes within the same peer group.

If no Hellos are received on a link over which Hellos are being transmitted, the link remains in an Attempt state, and the transmission of Hello messages continues.

Outside links are covered in the sections of this chapter dealing with multiple peer groups and border nodes.

## PNNI Hello Timers

PNNI Hello messages have a series of timers to ensure that neighbor state information remains accurate, and that topology information is synchronized. By maintaining timers, the PNNI protocol insures that logical links remain stable once established. The PNNI Hello timers are defined as follows:

- **Hello Interval**    The amount of time, in seconds, that passes before a node sends a Hello message
- **Hello Timer**    Set whenever a Hello message is sent
- **Inactivity Factor**    The amount of time declared by the neighbor node in its most recent Hello packets (the amount of time which has passed since the neighbor node last received a Hello on that link)
- **Inactivity Timer**    If no Hello is seen in this interval, the link is lost and the state returns to Attempt
- **SVCIntegrity Timer**    The amount of time, in seconds, that this node waits for a routing control channel (RCC) to reach 2-Way Inside state before release
- **SVCIntegrity Timer**    The amount of time before the RCC (an SVCC) is unusable
- **Horizontal Link Inactivity Timer**    The amount of time, in seconds, a node keeps advertising a horizontal link when no LGN horizontal link information group (IG) is being received

■ **Horizontal Link Inactivity Timer**    Timer that, should it expire, indicates that no LGN horizontal link IGs have been received from the neighbor

## Sending and Receiving Hellos

Hello messages are sent over each PNNI link that exists on a node, to determine bidirectional communication with neighbor peers. The frequency with which these Hello messages are transmitted is defined by the HelloInterval. Hello messages are also sent every time a state change occurs on a logical link between nodes, except in the following circumstances:

■ A 1-Way Inside or 1-Way Outside transition to 2-Way Inside or 2-Way Outside. This transition is due to the fact that the 2-Way state is the normal progression from the 1-Way state.

■ A 1-Way Outside or 2-Way Outside transition to Common Outside. Again, if two border nodes share a common parentage (they exist on the same hierarchical level above the lowest hierarchical level), the Common Outside state is the normal progression. This is described in detail later in this Chapter in the section "Multilevel Architecture."

■ A Common Outside state transition to a 2-Way Outside.

In the case of a multilevel routing environment, a nodal hierarchy list is also included in the Hello information whenever the Hello message is being passed over an outside link.

Upon receipt of a Hello message on a logical link, the receiving node stores the information about its neighboring peer node.

## Triggered Updates

A topological change within the ATM mesh or a change of a link or peer neighbor state may occur that necessitates the exchange of Hello messages outside the time specified in the Hello Interval. Under these circumstances, Hello messages may be sent outside the specified time. These are known as *triggered updates*.

# PNNI Information Exchange

Once the exchange of Hello messages determines the current neighbor states between nodes, the exchange of link information begins over any link that is 2-Way (bidirectional) or Common. A PNNI node then gathers together all the information it has learned about its neighbors, including their PG IDs, their Node IDs, and the status of each link it shares with these neighbors. This information is bundled in the form of *PNNI Topology State Elements (PTSEs)*.

## PNNI Topology State Elements

PTSEs are generated by a single PNNI node, to be flooded to all other nodes within the same peer group. If a node shares an outside link (a link with another node that isn't within its same peer group) with another node, it doesn't flood its PTSEs across that link, because at the lowest hierarchical level, PNNI nodes only need to maintain a topology database of their own local peer group.

PTSEs are small advertisements about local link states only. Each PTSE generated by a PNNI node contains nodal information that describes itself, its Node ID, its PG ID, and other information regarding its capabilities, such as eligibility for Peer Group Leadership. PTSEs also contain information about the topology state; the current status of the logical links the sending node shares with its neighbor nodes, possible QoS capabilities, and the desirability of a specific link. Links may have a static costing, called *administrative weight*, for purposes of route preference; or, the desirability of a path may be based on bandwidth. Fluctuation of bandwidth may cause a link to be reported in varying ways each time a PTSE is generated and flooded.

## PNNI Topology State Packets

To exchange database information during database synchronization (covered later in this Chapter in the section titled "Database Synchronization"), PNNI nodes bundle the PTSE packets into another packet, known as *PNNI Topology State Packets (PTSPs)*. These PTSPs are generated whenever the node in question originates a new PTSE, whenever the node performs a retransmission of an existing PTSE with a higher sequence number, in response to a PTSE Request during database synchronization (see the upcoming section on database synchronization), in response to a PTSE requested, or when the node receives a PTSE from a remote node that wasn't formerly found in its database.

A PTSP may contain one or more PTSEs. When a node receives a PTSP, each PTSE contained within is examined. If any of the PTSEs within do not exist within the current database, then the PTSE is added to a list called the *Peer Delayed Acks List*, which means that the packet requires an acknowledgement, but that the response doesn't have to be immediate. The PTSE is then added into the node's existing database. This triggers the node to generate a new PTSP of its own, containing the new PTSE that it just installed. The PTSP is then flooded to all neighboring peers, except the peer that sent the new PTSE that initiated the new PTSP.

This scheme allows for rapid propagation of topology state information, and since acknowledgements are required for each topology element, the flooding occurs in a reliable manner.

## Reachability Information

PTSEs also inform other nodes about reachability information; this consists of the actual addresses of the other nodes within the peer group. Each node within the peer group needs to acquire this information, because PNNI is a source-routed protocol, and any node may be required to initiate a call to any other node at any time. PTSE reachability information may fall into one of two categories:

■ **Internal addresses**   Assigned to PNNI nodes that exist and are active within the PNNI mesh. These addresses are dynamically communicated among nodes through the flooding of PTSEs. Internal addresses are advertised by nodes within the PNNI domain.

■ **Exterior addresses**   Assigned to nodes that may exist outside the PNNI domain, such as ATM switches running IISP that are connected to the PNNI network. Exterior addresses aren't learned dynamically by PNNI nodes, and aren't dynamically advertised. For nodes outside the PNNI environment to become reachable from within the PNNI mesh, the PNNI node that is connected to both environments may need to be manually configured to advertise the external addresses as reachable through itself (see Figure 16-4).

In the scenario in Figure 16-4, node A, which connects the PNNI and IISP portions of the network, advertises its own nodal information, as well as the reachability of switches 1, 2, and 3 as exterior addresses.

## Building a Network Topology

As each node floods PTSEs over its interface, it begins to piece together a view of the network as a whole. By piecing together the information contained within the PTSEs, each node begins to assemble the PNNI topology (see Figure 16-5).

In this example, node A is connected to node B and to node C. Node A knows that its own PG ID is 39.10.00.00.00.00.00.00.00.00.00.00.00 and that its Node ID shows a level indicator of 16, followed by the value 160 (indicating this is a lowest-level node and this is the Node ID; see the section on hierarchical routing for more details). These values are followed by the 20-octet address of node A's system, 39.10.00.20.11.00.00.00.00.30.00.12.03.57.E1.FA.08.AA.11.00. Node A also knows that it has two logical links, both of which are in a 2-Way Inside state (one to node B and one to node C). Due to the exchange of Hello messages, node A knows that node B has a PG ID of 39.10.00.00.00.00.00.00.00.00.00.00.00, placing it within its same peer group (determined when the two-way link was formed), and that its Node ID is 10.A0.39.10.00.20.11.00.00.00.00.40.00.12.03.21.02.66.AE.09.31.00. Node A also knows that node C, to whom it is also connected, has a PG ID of 39.10.00.00.00.00.00.00.00.00.00.00.00, placing it within its peer group, and that its Node ID is 16.160.39.10.00.20.11.00.00.00.00.50.00.12.03.BB.DA.12.07.54.23.00.

Each node will receive one another's PTSPs containing their individual PTSEs, but for the sake of this example, node A receives a PTSP containing the PTSE originating from node B. It examines the PTSE and learns several things:

■ Node B has three logical links to three nodes, one of which is the link over which the PTSE passed, the link to node A.

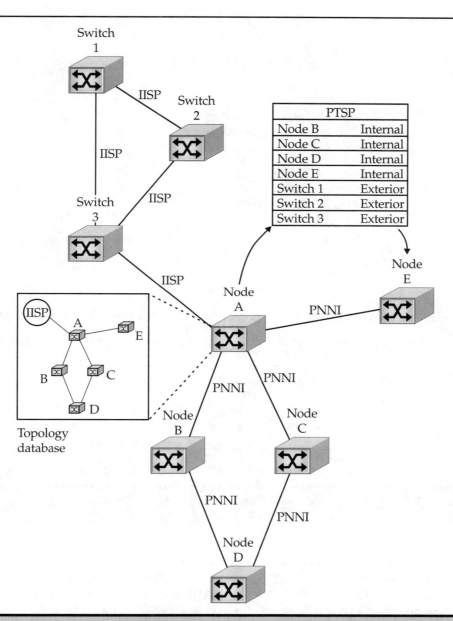

| PTSP | |
|------|--------|
| Node B | Internal |
| Node C | Internal |
| Node D | Internal |
| Node E | Internal |
| Switch 1 | Exterior |
| Switch 2 | Exterior |
| Switch 3 | Exterior |

Topology
database

**Figure 16-4.**    *PNNI and IISP networks connected, and IISP switches advertised as exterior addresses*

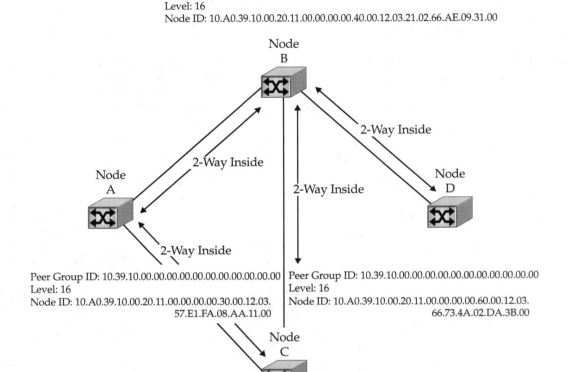

Peer Group ID: 10.39.10.00.00.00.00.00.00.00.00.00.00.00
Level: 16
Node ID: 10.A0.39.10.00.20.11.00.00.00.00.40.00.12.03.21.02.66.AE.09.31.00

Node
B

2-Way Inside

2-Way Inside

Node
A

2-Way Inside

Node
D

2-Way Inside

Peer Group ID: 10.39.10.00.00.00.00.00.00.00.00.00.00.00
Level: 16
Node ID: 10.A0.39.10.00.20.11.00.00.00.00.30.00.12.03.
57.E1.FA.08.AA.11.00

Peer Group ID: 10.39.10.00.00.00.00.00.00.00.00.00.00.00
Level: 16
Node ID: 10.A0.39.10.00.20.11.00.00.00.00.60.00.12.03.
66.73.4A.02.DA.3B.00

Node
C

Peer Group ID: 10.39.10.00.00.00.00.00.00.00.00.00.00.00
Level: 16
Node ID: 10.A0.39.10.00.20.11.00.00.00.00.50.00.12.03.BB.DA.12.07.54.23.00

**Figure 16-5.** *PNNI topology determined by nodes A, B, C, and D*

■ Node B has a link to the following Node ID:
10.A0.39.10.00.20.11.00.00.00.00.50.00.12.03.BB.DA.12.07.54.23.00
which is in PG ID 39.10.00.00.00.00.00.00.00.00.00.00.00.00. Node A recognizes this
information as belonging to node C, with whom it also shares a link.

■ Node B has a link to the following Node ID:
10.A0.39.10.00.20.11.00.00.00.00.60.00.12.03.66.73.4A.02.DA.3B.00
which is also in peer group 39.10.00.00.00.00.00.00.00.00.00.00.00.00.

Node A at this point realizes that it has a connection with node B, that both itself and node B share a connection to node C, and that node B has another connection to node D, which node A doesn't share a connection with. Node A also knows that all four nodes exist within the same peer group, sharing a common level indicator of 16 (see Figure 16-6).

Node A might also learn other pieces of information from the PTSE received from node B; node B might advertise that it has an OC-12 connection to node C, or that its connection to node D is an OC-3 link, half the bandwidth of which has been reserved for a constant bit rate (CBR) connection and isn't available for dynamic use. Indicators such as this are supported within the PNNI specification, although they aren't required by Annex G of that specification, which outlines the minimum subset of required PNNI features.

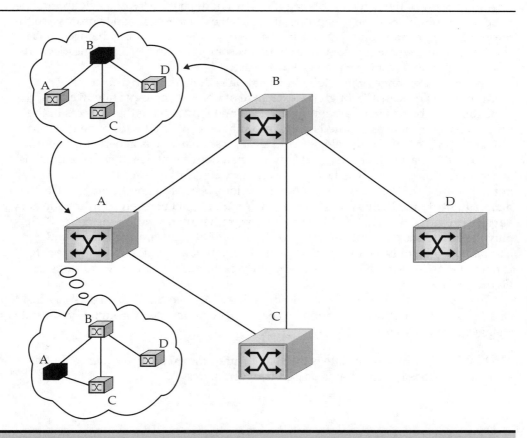

**Figure 16-6.**   *Node A's view of the network based on PTSE received from node B*

# Database Synchronization

In the PNNI environment, each node must maintain a synchronized database of the network topology. The first step in accomplishing this is the flooding of PTSEs containing nodal and topology information. As the PNNI nodes collect PTSEs, they begin to piece together a view of the ATM network as a whole.

The database synchronization procedure occurs between two neighboring PNNI nodes, the first time they learn of one another's existence. The ATM switch nodes—after going through the Hello exchange previously outlined and determining their neighbor states and local link information—now need to generate and maintain a full database of all the links within their peer group, to perform PNNI source-routing through the ATM mesh. To make accurate routing decisions and choose the best path, each node must have a common view of the network topology. When a node first learns of a neighboring peer node that is within its same peer group, it begins the database exchange process, so that this database synchronization can occur. The two basic steps in doing this are database synchronization, where topology information is compared, and PTSE Request, where any missing topology information is requested.

The initial exchange of topology information is done through a *database synchronization* process. Through the exchange of PNNI Topology State Events, a node topology begins to be assembled by each node. By placing these pieces in the proper configuration, as dictated by the information contained within the PTSEs, a more complete picture is developed, and a *Database Summary* is generated. These Database Summaries are exchanged between neighboring nodes during the database synchronization process. The Database Summary contains a list of PTSE headers only, not the entire PTSEs. This is to keep overhead low, because a good chance exists that many, if not all, the PTSEs found in the DB Summary packet received by a node are already present in its database. For this reason, rather than sending the entire PTSE, only the headers are initially exchanged. This list of headers are exchanged and compared, so that PNNI nodes can determine whether any link information exists that is not yet known to it. The Database Summary exchange involves several steps (see Figure 16-7).

The connected nodes (nodes A and B) in this case have established a 2-Way Inside state, and database synchronization has begun. The nodes pass through several state changes during this process:

**NPDOWN**   The NPDown state is the state prior to the exchange sequence. In this state, no database information is passed between nodes.

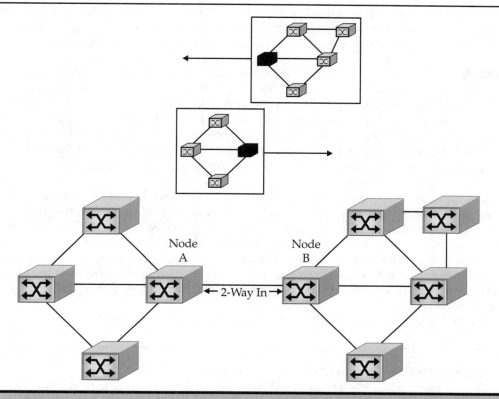

**Figure 16-7.**   *Two nodes, each with attached peers exchanging database information*

**NEGOTIATING**   Database Summary exchange requires that the PNNI peers establish a master/slave relationship, to assure that the synchronization procedure stays in sequence. Since the exchange process has just begun, the two nodes must negotiate to see which node will be designated master and which will be designated slave.

During the negotiation phase, the two nodes involved each sends an initial DB Summary that doesn't contain any summary information. The DB Summaries still contain information regarding the nodes themselves, however, and are used to establish a master and slave:

When the initial empty Database Summaries are exchanged, the Initialize (I) bit is flipped, as is the More (M) bit (because more Database Summaries are exchanged after the master/slave contention is resolved).

Upon receipt of the first DS, each node checks to see which of the two nodes has the larger Node ID. The node with the smaller Node ID, node B in this case, becomes the slave, and node A becomes the master. Node B sets the Master bit to 0, and node A, being the master, sets the DS sequence number. The slave increments this sequence number upon receipt of a DS from the master, when it returns its own Database Summary.

**EXCHANGING** During the exchange process, the actual exchange of DB Summary packets occurs. The master initiates this exchange by selecting the DS sequence number and sending the first DB Summary packet that contains database information. There may be a series of such packets, depending on how large the database is. The slave expects to see the DS sequence number incremented by one (once the DS sequence number has been established), while the master expects to see a return packet with the last DS sequence number that it used. If the receiving node is the master, the DS sequence number is incremented by one.

DB Summary packets are exchanged and processed, each in turn, by the master and slave nodes. When a node accepts the packet as having a valid sequence number, it compares the contents of the DB Summary packet with its own; each PTSE header in the packet is looked up in the receiving node's own database, to see whether it already has an instance of the PTSE in its own database. If it does, it goes on to the next in the list. If it does not already have knowledge of the PTSE, it will need to request the whole PTSE (remember, DB Summary packets contain PTSE headers only) from the neighboring node.

The information included in the PTSE header is shown in Table 16-1.

| Offset | Octets | Name | Function |
|--------|--------|------|----------|
| 0 | 2 | Type | Type=64 (PTSE) |
| 2 | 2 | Length | |
| 4 | 2 | PTSE Type | Indicates which restricted information groups may appear in the PTSE |
| 6 | 2 | Reserved | |
| 8 | 4 | PTSE Identifier | Identifies multiple PTSEs from a single node |
| 12 | 4 | PTSE Sequence | PTSE Sequence number |
| 16 | 2 | PTSE Checksum | Includes the logical Node ID and the originating node's PG ID |
| 18 | 2 | PTSE Remaining Lifetime | The amount of time PTSE information is still considered valid. |

**Table 16-1.** *PTSE Header Information*

These missing PTSEs are placed on a PTSE Request list, to be requested from the remote node. These requests may be issued during the exchanging phase and during the loading phase.

**LOADING**   After the master node receives a DB Summary packet from the slave, with the expected DS sequence number and the More bit set to 0 (indicating the slave has no more information to send), and the master has completed transmitting all of its own DB Summary packets, then the master generates the event indicating that the exchange process is over. If outstanding PTSEs remain on the PTSE Request list, then the event ExchangeDone is generated. No more DB Summary packets should be exchanged at this point. If no PTSEs are on the PTSE Request list, then the event SynchDone is generated, indicating that the databases are in synch currently.

Once the exchange process is complete, assuming there are PTSE Requests outstanding, the loading procedure begins. During this phase, each node transmits PTSE Request packets to its neighboring peer. Only one of these packets may be outstanding at any one time by either peer. When the neighbor receives a PTSE Request packet with its list of PTSEs required by the transmitting node, it looks up each PTSE being requested, bundles the PTSEs into a PTSP, and sends the PTSP to the requesting node. If any of the PTSEs on the list are not in the receiving node's database, then something has gone wrong; a node should only request a PTSE sent to it by its neighbor in the form of a PTSE header, contained in the Database Summary packet. If a request comes in for a PTSE that a node is unaware of, a BadPTSERequest is generated and the database synchronization must be run again.

Once the requesting node receives the PTSP, the PTSEs contained within are removed from its PTSE Request list and a PTSE acknowledgment is transmitted back to the sender for each PTSE instance. At that point, another PTSE Request packet is transmitted if PTSEs are still outstanding on the PTSE Request list. Once the PTSE Request list is empty, an event of LoadingDone is generated.

**FULL**   The Full state is entered when the DB Summary packets have been exchanged and the PTSE Requests generated by both nodes have been satisfied. At this point, the databases are considered to be synchronized.

## Exchanging Database Summary Packets

The sending of DB Summary packets follows implicit rules; only one DB Summary packet may be outstanding at any one time. When two nodes are in the Negotiating state, the DB Summary packets are empty and are used solely for the purpose of determining the master/slave relationship. Once this has been decided, the rules for sending DB Summary packets vary between the master and the slave.

The master sends the first DB Summary packet and assigns the initial DB sequence number. After it sends the first packet, it must wait for an Acknowledgement packet to return from the slave. It will know it has received its initial packet when it receives a packet using the same sequence number (because the slave node can't increment the sequence number—only the master can). If this doesn't occur for a certain amount of time (defined by the DBRxmitInterval), then the master retransmits the same DB Summary packet. The slave sends DB Summary packets only in response to those it receives from the master. Once either the master or the slave has exhausted the DB Summary packets to be sent, the More bit must be flipped to 0 to indicate that no more packets are to follow.

*The last DS Summary packet sent by the slave peer will be an empty packet with the More, Initialize, and Master bits all set to 0, using the same sequence number as the master node's last packet.*

Upon receipt of a DB Summary packet, the receiving node must follow certain rules regarding its processing. If the neighboring peer state is NPDown, then the packet is ignored and dropped. If the state is Negotiating, then the master/slave relationship may not have been determined yet. If the received DB Summary packet is empty, and the Initialize and Master bits are set to 0, then the Node ID of each node is compared. If the node receiving the DB Summary packet has the higher Node ID, then it assumes the role of master. If this happens, the DB Summary packet is processed and a new one is sent out, this time with a portion of the topology database included, with the DB sequence number incremented by one. If the received DB Summary packet is empty, the Initialize, More, and Master bits are all set to 1, and the sending node's Node ID is higher than the node receiving the packet, then the neighbor peer node is the master. The receiving node assumes the role of slave and issues a NegotiatingDone event to signal the end of the negotiation process. It sets its own Master bit to 0 and sends a DB Summary packet using the DS sequence number defined by the master node.

Once the Negotiating state is finished, the Exchange state begins. When DB Summary packets are received in the Exchange state, they are handled differently depending on whether the receiving node is designated the master or slave. If the receiving node is the master, then the incoming DB Summary packet is processed and the DS sequence number is incremented by one. If any DB Summary packets remain to send, then the master sends the next one on the list. If no more remain to be sent, then the master doesn't transmit except to acknowledge incoming DB Summary packets from the slave (who might not be finished). Once both the master and slave have set the More bit to 0, indicating no more DB Summary packets exist to exchange, then the master signals the end of the exchange process by generating an ExchangeDone event.

In this case, if the receiving node was the slave, then it is compared to the current DS sequence number; it should be incremented by one. If it isn't, then the packet is considered a duplicate. Slaves respond to duplicates with their own duplicates; they resend their last DB Summary packet, which carries the same DS sequence number.

## Neighbor Peer State Changes

The peer state may change between two neighboring peers; this may be triggered by either the Database Summary exchange or the Hello states that exist between them. The following are the possible state changes between two neighboring PNNI nodes, and their causes:

- **AddPort**   A logical link between two neighboring peers has just entered the 2-Way Inside state. This makes the link eligible for PTSE flooding. PTSEs aren't flooded by lowest-level nodes to other nodes that exist outside their peer group (nodes with which it shares an outside link). Once this state is reached, this port is added as part of the peer data structure described in the previous section.

- **NegotiationDone**   The master/slave contention has completed. A master and slave now exist, and the master has generated an initial DS sequence number.

- **ExchangeDone**   The DB Summary packets have all been sent and received. A list of the PTSEs needed has been assembled.

- **SynchDone**   The last DB Summary packet has been sent, and the last DB Summary packet has been received. The list of needed PTSEs is empty, indicating that all the needed PTSEs have been provided, and the databases are now synchronized.

- **LoadingDone**   A node has received the last PTSE on its list of PTSEs to request after Database Summary exchange.

- **DSMismatch**   Either a DB Summary packet has been received that is out of sequence (the sequence number isn't what was expected), a DB Summary packet has been received with the Initialize (I) bit flipped when it shouldn't be, or the node designated as master has received a DS Summary packet with the Master bit flipped.

- **BadPTSERequest**   A PTSE has been received that is actually older than one already in the database, or a PTSE Request has been received for a PTSE that doesn't exist in the database.

- **DropPort**   If a peer state changes from 2-Way Inside to any other peer state, then PTSEs aren't to be flooded over the logical link and the port is considered dropped.

- **DropPortLast**   If multiple ports exist to the neighboring peer, and all of them exit the 2-Way Inside state, this state is entered.

## Peer Data Structure

Each node must maintain a single neighboring peer data structure for each neighboring peer node. If multiple links between two nodes exist, only one is necessary to maintain the neighbor peer relationship. Each link connecting a separate neighboring peer node, however, must run an individual instance of the Hello machine.

Once the peer neighbor state has left the NPDown state, the two nodes are said to have an *adjacency* with each other. In this scenario, each node must maintain a model of all relative information for that adjacency. A list of required information follows:

- **State**   The current peer state between neighboring peer nodes. This state may be Negotiating, Exchanging, Loading, or Full.

- **Remote Node ID**   The Node ID of the neighbor peer node. Because this is an adjacency over a 2-Way Inside link, the Node ID includes a level indicator and

ATM TECHNOLOGIES

a value of 160, followed by the End System Address for the ATM switch upon which the node resides.

- **Port ID list**   A list of all ports (these may be physical links or virtual links) between the node and its neighboring peer that are currently in the 2-Way Inside state. For purposes of PTSE flooding, DB Summary exchange, or PTSE Requests, any ports listed may actually be used. The Port ID chosen in one instance doesn't have to be used in each case; any port between the neighbors that is in the 2-Way Inside state is valid.

- **Master/slave**   During the Database Summary exchange Negotiating state, the two neighboring peer nodes contend to form a master/slave relationship. Once established, the PNNI peer maintains this knowledge. The master peer initiates the first DB Summary exchange packet and also assigns the initial DS sequence number.

- **DS sequence number**   Initiated by the master and incremented by one each time the master issues a Database Summary packet. Upon receipt of the slave's Database Summary packet utilizing the same sequence number, the master node determines that its last packet was received, since the slave will not increment the DS sequence number.

- **Peer Retransmission List**   PTSEs that are flooded, but that aren't acknowledged by the neighboring peer node, are placed on the Peer Retransmission List. These PTSEs continue to be flooded periodically, as defined by the PTSERetransmissionInterval, until they are acknowledged or the adjacency fails.

- **PTSERetransmissionInterval**   The amount of time, in seconds, that will pass between retransmitting PTSEs that haven't been acknowledged yet by a neighboring peer.

- **Peer Delayed Acks List**   A list of all PTSEs for which a delayed acknowledgement will be sent.

- **PeerDelayedAckInterval**   The interval between which the Peer Delayed Acks List will be checked.

- **Peer Delayed Ack Timer**   Upon expiration of this timer, any PTSEs from the Peer Delayed Acks List that haven't been acknowledged are placed in an Acknowledgement packet and transmitted to the neighbor.

- **PTSE Request List**   During the Database Summary exchange process, if a node compares a received DS packet with its current database and finds PTSE headers for PTSEs that it doesn't yet have, each of those PTSEs is placed on the PTSE Request list. For each instance on the list, the node will request the full PTSE from the neighbor peer.

- **DSRxmtInterval** After a DB Summary packet is sent, a packet should come back. The node waits DSRxmtInterval number of seconds before retransmitting the DB Summary packet.

- **DS Rxmit Timer** This timer fires after the DSRxmitInterval expires. It will be stopped upon receipt of a valid DB Summary packet.

- **RequestRxmtInterval** Once the PTSE Request list has been formulated, the node issues a PTSE Request and then waits RequestRxmtInterval seconds before assuming the Request wasn't received, and resending it.

- **Request Rxmit Timer** This timer fires after the RequestRxmitInterval timer expires. It stops when each of the PTSEs included in the PTSE Request has been received.

Note that neighboring peer nodes in separate peer groups will not form an adjacency, because they will never enter the 2-Way Inside state and thus will never initiate Database Summary exchange between them.

## PTSE Sequence Numbers

Each PTSE has a sequence number attributed to it, so that the receiving node can determine the relative age of an incoming PTSE. If a node receives an incoming PTSE that already exists within its database, a comparison of the PTSE sequence number occurs.

In this case, the PTSE with the higher sequence number is considered the more recent, so it will replace the PTSE with the older sequence number, even if the information contained within is the same.

## Flushing PTSEs

PTSEs have a finite age, after which they are considered invalid. All PNNI nodes must monitor the PTSE age of each PTSE they have entered into their topology database. To accomplish this, each PTSE has a PTSE Remaining Lifetime, which indicates how long it has been since the PTSE was entered into the topology database. A PTSE can either age out naturally, after reaching the limit defined by the ExpiredAge value found in the PTSE, or, if the information in the PTSE becomes invalid, the PTSE can be aged out prematurely by the advertising node. This is done by setting the PTSE Remaining Lifetime value to the ExpiredAge value, immediately invalidating the PTSE.

Once the PTSE has aged out, it is flushed. This is done by deleting the PTSE from each neighboring peer's Peer Retransmission List and Peer Delayed Ack List, setting the PTSE Remaining Lifetime to ExpiredAge, and then flooding the PTSE with no topology description in it to each neighbor. At this point, the expired PTSE is added to the Peer Retransmission List.

The PTSE must then be removed from the topology database, because the information it formerly described is considered to be invalid. PTSEs may be removed from the topology database if they are shown to have aged out, and if the PTSE is no longer listed on any of the node's Peer Retransmission Lists or Peer Delayed Ack Lists. As these entries are removed during the flushing process, the PTSE, at that point, may be safely removed from the topology database.

## Flooding

The flooding of PTSEs throughout the ATM mesh must be done continually to ensure that each node maintains an identical topology database. Each node takes each PTSE it has received so far, and encapsulates it in a PTSP. These PTSPs are transmitted to the neighboring peers. Upon receiving a PTSP, the PTSEs contained within are examined, and an Acknowledgement packet is sent for each individual PTSE. If a received PTSE either isn't already in the database, or an instance of the PTSE is present but is older than the one just received, then the more recent PTSE is installed into the database.

## Database Synchronization Example

This example has two interconnected nodes, nodes A and B (see Figure 16-8), each of which has already learned about a certain portion of the network (node A knows of three other nodes; node B knows of nine other nodes).

Node A and node B transmit Hello messages. Node A receives a Hello message from node B and examines it; node B's PG ID indicates it is in the same peer group as node A. Node A makes a note of node B's Node ID and Port ID and then transitions into a 1-Way Inside state. When it sends its Hello message, it includes node B's Node ID as the Remote Node ID, and its Port ID as the Remote Port ID.

Node A then receives a Hello message from node B again, and this time sees its own Node ID and Port ID listed as Remote Node ID and Remote Port ID. Node B is receiving node A's Hello messages, so bidirectional communication exists. The link between node A and node B transitions into a 2-Way Inside state.

Once a 2-Way Inside state is reached, the nodes will attempt to synchronize their databases. Node A sends an empty DB Summary packet to node B. The Initialize bit and More bit are flipped. Node B also sends an empty DB Summary packet with the Initialize and More bits flipped. Each node compares the Node ID in the received DB Summary packet. In this case, node A has the higher Node ID, so it will be the master. It selects a DS sequence number and transmits a new DB Summary packet, this time containing the first portion of information from its database of PTSEs. The new DB Summary packet has the Initialize bit set to 0, the Master bit flipped to 1, and the More bit flipped to 0, because it only has three nodes to describe, all of which fit in one DB Summary packet.

Node B receives this packet and accepts it as the slave node. It sends an Acknowledgement to node A, so that node A doesn't retransmit the DB Summary packet. Node B then examines the contents of the packet and sees PTSE headers for nodes C, D, and E. Node B at this point has no knowledge of nodes C, D, and E, so it

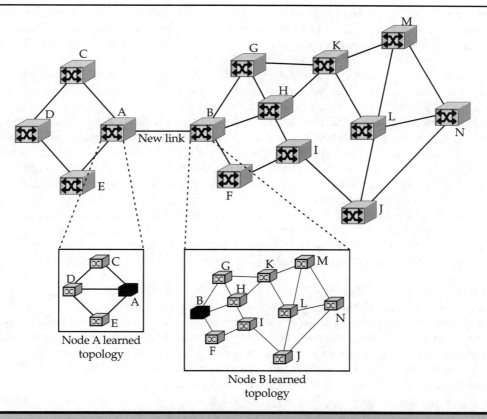

**Figure 16-8.**    *Node A and node B along with their learned nodes*

places each of these nodes on its PTSE Request list. It also knows that this will be the only DB Summary packet to be received from node A, since the More bit is set to 0. Node B then transmits a DB Summary packet of its own, utilizing the same DS sequence number selected by node A. This packet contains the PTSE headers for nodes F, G, H, I, J, K, L, M, and N. Since this is the sum of the nodes that node B is aware of, it sets the Initialize, More, and Master bits to 0.

Because the last DB Summary packet node B received had the More bit set to 0, and the DB Summary packet that it just sent also had the More bit set to 0, node B must generate either an ExchangeDone event or a SynchDone event; it checks its PTSE Request list and finds that there are outstanding PTSEs still in the Request list, so it generates an ExchangeDone event. Node A receives the DB Summary packet from node B and sends back an Acknowledgement. The DS sequence number is equal to the one it attributed to the last DB Summary packet, so the packet is valid; it processes the contents of the packet and finds PTSE headers for the nine nodes. Because node A currently has no knowledge of any of these nodes, it places all nine headers on its PTSE Request list.

The ExchangeDone event has been generated, and no more DB Summary packets remain to exchange. The state between the nodes transitions to Loading. Node A examines its list of PTSE headers and transmits a PTSE Request for nodes F, G, H, I, J, K, L, M, and N. Node B likewise sends a PTSE Request for nodes C, D, and E. Node A receives node B's Request and reads the PTSE headers that are being requested. It bundles the full PTSEs for nodes C, D, and E into a PTSP and transmits the PTSP to node B. Node B receives node A's PTSE Request, processes it, and then bundles the full PTSEs for nodes F through N into a PTSP and transmits it to node A. Upon receipt of the PTSP, node A examines the PTSEs inside and removes nodes F through N from its PTSE Request list, since it has now successfully received the full PTSE for each. A PTSE acknowledgment is returned for each PTSE received. Node B has also received and examined the PTSP from node A, and has removed each PTSE from its PTSE Request list. Because nodes A and B no longer have any PTSEs to request, and the neighboring peer state is Loading, a LoadingDone event is generated.

Both node A and node B now have a common view of the network as it currently stands. The Full state is entered, and the databases are synchronized. Bear in mind that, although in this example nodes A and B had an already established view of two different portions of the network, in an actual environment where many nodes are all discovering one another at the same time, the DB Summary exchange can be quite dynamic until all neighbor states are settled. In this example, once node A and node B learn each other's databases, the PTSE flooding process continues and all nodes in the peer group are updated.

The following is an example of a PTSP packet, obtained from an ATM sniffer trace:

```
PNNIR: ----- PNNI Routing -----
PNNIR:
PNNIR: Packet type                = 2(PTSP)
PNNIR: Length                     = 168
PNNIR: Protocol version           = 1
PNNIR: Newest version supported   = 1
PNNIR: Oldest version supported   = 1
PNNIR: Reserved                   = 0
PNNIR: Originating Node ID=
58A03900000000000000000000004018260000000000000
PNNIR: Node's peer group ID= 58390000000000000000000000000
PNNIR: IE type                    = 64(PTSE)
PNNIR: Length                     = 49328
PNNIR: PTSE type                  = 24640
PNNIR: Reserved                   = 124
```

```
PNNIR: PTSE identifier          = 18874368
PNNIR: PTSE sequence number     = 42
PNNIR: PTSE checksum            = 0
PNNIR: PTSE remaining lifetime  = 4
PNNIR: IE type                  = 288(Horizontal links)
PNNIR: Length                   = 3598
PNNIR: Flags            = 288
PNNIR:   0... .... .... ....  VPCs not supported
PNNIR: Remote node ID    =
0068800058A03900000104000200000000402828500
PNNIR: Remote port ID           = 0
PNNIR: Local port ID            = 50331649
PNNIR: Aggregation token        = 1660944388
PNNIR: IE type                  = 0(invalid)
PNNIR: Length                   = 0
PNNIR: IE type                  = 96(Nodal state parameters)
PNNIR: Length                   = 28672
PNNIR: Flags
PNNIR:   VP capability flag     = 1... ....
PNNIR: Reserved                 = 8416
PNNIR: Input Port ID            = 0
PNNIR: Output Port ID           = 1290240
PNNIR: IE type                  = 97(Nodal information group)
PNNIR: Length                   = 51320
PNNIR: ATM endsystem address
PNNIR: 0000C8780000003C0000000B0014001400800020
PNNIR: Leadership priority          = 8
PNNIR: Nodal flags
PNNIR:   I am leader            = 1... ....(I am PGL)
PNNIR:   Restricted transit     = .1.. ....(I am a restricted
transit node)
PNNIR:   Nodal representation   = ..1. ....(complex node
representation)
PNNIR:   Restricted branching   = ...1 ....(cannot support
additional
branch points)
PNNIR:   Non-transit for PGL    = .... 1...(no connectivity through
this node for PGL)
PNNIR: Preferred PGL node ID          =
00FF80180000000000013B00000EBD90000C878000000
PNNIR: IE type                  = 192(Next higher level binding
information)
```

```
PNNIR: Length                    = 45216
PNNIR: IE type                   = 224(Internal reachable ATM
addresses)
PNNIR: Length                    = 53392
PNNIR: Flags                      = 15360
PNNIR:    0... .... .... ....  VPCs not supported
PNNIR: Reserved                   = 0
PNNIR: Port ID                    = 184584037
PNNIR: Scope of advertisement     = 87
PNNIR: Address information length  = 151
PNNIR: Address information count   = 1
PNNIR: Prefix length             = 5 bits
```

# Building the Designated Transit List

The Designated Transit List (DTL) is the source-routed path determined by the sending node between itself and the destination node within a single peer group. Each time a call must be initiated, for instance, whenever a LEC must initiate a call to a remote LEC, the source node (known as the *DTL originator*) is responsible for determining the best path to the destination node. This destination node may be located within the same peer group or in another peer group. If it is within the same peer group, then a DTL must be generated to that node. If it is outside the peer group, then a DTL index must be formed, with the first DTL in the index targeting the border node of the next peer group in the overall path. The source node always selects a destination node in this case with the longest NSAP prefix that matches the destination address.

## The DTL Originator

Because PNNI is a source-routed protocol, the node from which the call originates must determine the path it is to take, and then must initiate the circuit along the predetermined route. This node is the DTL originator (see Figure 16-9).

In this example, the LEC residing on node 39.10.10.01 receives data destined for a MAC address that is currently residing on node 39.10.10.07. Node 39.10.10.01 must then initiate a Data Direct VCC to the remote LEC. The call will be routed there via PNNI signaling, and node 39.10.10.01 is the DTL originator.

Node 39.10.10.01 examines its topology database and discovers there are several routes to get to the destination node; however, because the OC-12 connection has been given a more desirable path cost (defined as the administrative weight), it determines that the best path should take advantage of this particular link. It builds the DTL, describing a path from itself, node 39.10.10.01, to 39.10.10.03, to 39.10.10.04, to 39.10.10.08, to the destination, 39.10.10.07. This DTL not only describes the path, but also contains a pointer, showing where along the path the call currently is, which means that when the DTL is first created, the previously listed path is indicated, with a pointer pointing to 39.10.10.01. The

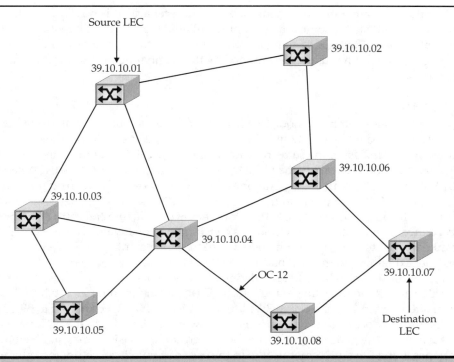

**Figure 16-9.**   *A single peer group with eight nodes, 39.10.10.01 through 39.10.10.08*

call is then initiated to the next node listed in the DTL, and the DTL itself is passed along to the next node. The next node in the list, node 39.10.10.03, receives the DTL, alters the pointer to point to its own entry (to indicate to upstream nodes where in the overall path the call is), and knows by examining the DTL's contents that node 39.10.10.04 is the next node in the path. Node 39.10.10.03 initiates a call to node 39.10.10.04, sending the DTL along. Node 39.10.10.04 receives the call, alters the DTL pointer, and checks the DTL to see which node is next in the path.

By following this procedure, the call ends up at the destination node 39.10.10.07. The destination node examines the DTL and sees that its entry is the last in the list, meaning that it must be the destination node. Since the call in question is actually destined for a LEC residing on that switch, the call has been successfully routed to the proper LEC, and the Data Direct VCC is established.

The originating node in this case has no way of knowing ahead of time that all the links along the path are still available; it only knows that, in accordance with the topology database it has constructed, all the links should be available. Since link state changes are quickly propagated throughout the mesh, nodes are updated quickly if there are any link state changes, but in this scenario, it is possible that the ideal route isn't viable for some reason (a physical link goes down, the requested QoS is unavailable at one of the nodes along the path, and so forth). In this case, the call is rejected and a new path must be determined by the originating node. This mechanism is called *crankback*.

## Crankback

Using the previous example, if node 39.10.10.01 attempts to route a call to destination node 39.10.10.07 using the OC-12 link, but this link has failed sometime after the initiation of the call. Using the same routing method, the call is sent to node 39.10.10.03, which examines the DTL, alters the pointer, and sends it to node 39.10.10.04. When node 39.10.10.04 receives the call, it also examines the DTL and sees that the next node in the path is node 39.10.10.08, by way of the 622Mbps OC-12 link. This link has gone down and isn't available. Node 39.10.10.04 therefore rejects the call; the call can't be completed in accordance with the current DTL, so it is considered to be invalid. In this case, the call is "cranked back" to the originating node. Crankback is accompanied by a crankback cause code, explaining to the originating node why the call was refused.

Node 39.10.10.04 also has full knowledge of the network topology; thus, it knows that an alternate route exists to get to 39.10.10.07 (the destination node). This could be accomplished by sending the call to 39.10.10.06, which in turn is connected to 39.10.10.07. Node 39.10.10.04 does not make this decision, however. All nodes in the DTL path must always adhere to the path outlined in the DTL. Rerouting decisions may not be made by other nodes along the path dynamically. In the case of a failed call setup, the call must be cranked back to the originating node, so that the DTL can be recalculated.

Node 39.10.10.04 then refuses the call and cranks back the call to node 39.10.10.01, with a crankback cause code describing the failed link. The originating node recalculates the DTL, excluding the OC-12 link between 39.10.10.04 and 39.10.10.08. It chooses a new path from itself to 39.10.10.03, to 39.10.10.04, to 39.10.10.06, and then to 39.10.10.07, the destination. The call is initiated a second time, using the new route. Because all the links are valid along this path, it is successfully routed to its destination, and the Data Direct VCC is established between the two LECs (see Figure 16-10).

The call must be cranked back to the originating node in this case, because if node 39.10.10.04 were able to dynamically alter the DTL path to steer around a link failure, the current DTL would no longer be valid, since the path described within would no longer be accurate (the new path takes it to node 39.10.10.06, which isn't described in the original DTL). Node 39.10.10.06 would find no entry for itself in the DTL. Thus, node 39.10.10.06 would need to determine how to get to node 39.10.10.07, the destination node. Since multiple paths to get there from node 39.10.10.06 may exist, the possibility arises for call looping if rerouting is permitted from any node along the DTL path. To prevent these loops, only the originator may reroute a call.

Keep in mind that this path recalculation occurs very quickly, and that the flooding of link state changes also causes a very fast reconvergence of the nodes when a link failure

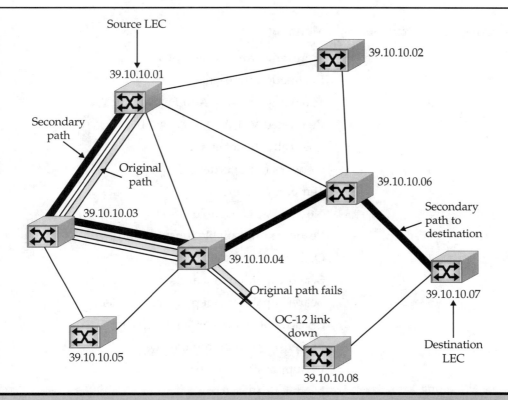

**Figure 16-10.**    *Data Direct VCC between two LECs routed via PNNI with crankback*

ATM TECHNOLOGIES

occurs. By the time node 39.10.10.01 is receiving the crankback cause code, it may be receiving or have already received updated information describing the OC-12 link as being down. PNNI calls are routed and rerouted dynamically; the originating node, in the event of multiple link failures, will attempt to route the call along any combination of nodes through which there is a valid path. It continues to attempt to reroute the call until its topology database indicates there is no path from itself to the destination.

**Note**    *All switches must obey the DTL. They may not decide to reroute if a link is down. If they can't honor the DTL, they report that back to the originating switch, which must try again with a different route that it calculates.*

The different crankback cause codes that may appear are listed in Table 16-2.

| Cause Code Number | Meaning |
|:---:|:---|
| 2 | Transit network unreachable |
| 3 | Destination unreachable |
| 32 | Too many pending Add Party requests |
| 35 | Requested VPI/VCI not available |
| 37 | User cell rate not available |
| 38 | Network out of order |
| 41 | Temporary failure |
| 45 | No VPI/VCI available |
| 47 | Resource unavailable (unspecified) |
| 49 | QoS unavailable |
| 57 | Bearer capability not authorized |
| 58 | Bearer capability not presently available |
| 63 | Service not available (unspecified) |
| 65 | Bearer service not implemented |
| 73 | Unsupported traffic parameters |
| 128 | Next node unreachable |
| 160 | DTL transit not my Node ID |

**Table 16-2.**   *Crankback Cause Codes*

# Further Up the PNNI Hierarchy

The PNNI routing hierarchy emerges when multiple peer groups exist within the network. At the lowest level of PNNI routing, nodes are responsible only for maintaining a topology database within their own peer group. Therefore, any node should be capable of plotting a path from itself as the source, to any other node within its peer group. The routing hierarchy allows a call originated from a node in one peer group to be correctly routed to a destination node in another peer group elsewhere in the ATM network.

# Multilevel Architecture

In an environment with a second layer of the PNNI hierarchy, multiple peer groups are interconnected. Nodes within a single peer group maintain a topology database for their own peer group, while remote peer groups are summarized and advertised as LGNs (see Figure 16-11).

In this example, node 39.10.01.01 in peer group A is aware of the other four nodes within its own peer group, their link states, and its relative placement in the network topology. Node 39.10.01.01 will also have an awareness of peer groups B, C, D, and E, but not of their specific contents. Node 39.10.01.01 will see these peer groups as LGNs, advertised as follows:

Peer Group B: 39.10.02
Peer Group C: 39.10.03
Peer Group D: 39.10.04
Peer Group E: 39.10.05

Therefore, if node 39.10.01.01 needs to initiate a call to the destination node 39.10.05.02, it will not know of the destination node's relative placement in the network topology; it will only know that the call is destined for LGN 39.10.05 (peer group E), which, according to the address specified, should contain node 39.10.05.02.

To accommodate the setup of a call that must span multiple peer groups, the nodes in peer group A must have a way to learn of the existence of other LGNs within the network, and also where to direct a call that is known to be destined for a node outside the local peer group. Multihierarchical PNNI routing has three new nodal designations:

- **Peer Group Leader**  An entity that is elected for each peer group; any node that supports PGL capability is eligible to become the PGL, which is responsible both for advertising its local peer group to other peer groups as a logical group node and for accepting LGN advertisements from remote peer groups, to inform the nodes within the local peer group of the remote LGNs.

- **Border node**  A node that interconnects two peer groups. Since nodes are members of specific peer groups, and peer group membership may not be assigned on an interface-by-interface basis, two border nodes are involved: one in each peer group, connected by a logical link. These links are known as outside links.

- **Logical group node**  Present when multiple hierarchical layers exist; the LGN is the sum of nodes within a peer group, representing them as a single, logical node. The LGN functions with the Peer Group Leader for purposes of aggregating route information for a single peer group and flooding this information to other peer groups.

ATM TECHNOLOGIES

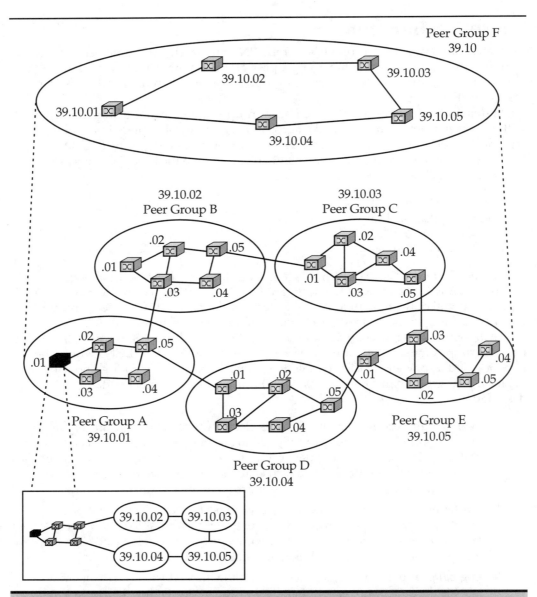

**Figure 16-11.** *Five peer groups, A, B, C, D, and E, each with five nodes, with sixth peer group (F) at higher level containing LGNs*

## Peer Group Leaders

In a multiple peer group environment, a PGL is elected for each peer group. It becomes the PGL's function to make nodes within its peer group aware of remote peer groups (in the form of LGNs), and advertise its own peer group as an LGN to remote peer groups. The PGL doesn't have any other special functions, and any node may serve in this capacity, assuming it is PGL-capable. Only one PGL may exist per peer group, and in a single peer group environment, a PGL isn't required.

## PGL Election States

A PGL election takes place within any peer group configured for more than one hierarchical level. This occurs automatically and is initiated by the transmission of a *Nodal Information PTSE* on the part of all nodes participating in the election (all nodes within a single peer group that are PGL-capable). The "I am leader" bit is initially set to 0. These Nodal Information PTSEs are flooded and compared by all receiving nodes. The first thing examined is the priority, and the node with the highest priority becomes the PGL. Nodes incapable of becoming the PGL will advertise their Nodal Information PTSE with a leadership priority of 0.

Each node compares its own priority, as well as the priorities of all the other nodes, against any incoming Nodal Information PTSE. Based on the information it receives, each node then announces to its surrounding nodes which node has the highest priority based on what it's seen. By doing this, each node ultimately agrees on who the PGL should be (a switch may determine that *it* should be the PGL and announce itself). In the event of equal priorities, the nodes sharing an equal priority compare Node IDs, and the highest Node ID wins.

The following lists the different PGL election states, which don't necessarily occur in order:

- **HelloFSMStarted**  The first Hello state machine started on this link. For a more detailed description of the Hello protocol and its associated link states, consult the earlier section in this chapter regarding the Hello protocol.

- **PeerFound**  Two peer nodes have discovered each other through the Hello protocol. Through the examination of Hello messages received from the peer, each node has verified bidirectional communication, and a 2-Way Inside state has been reached.

- **LostAllPeers**  The last remaining Hello state machine that was in the 2-Way Inside state has left that state. This indicates no bidirectional communication exists anywhere on the node.

- **SearchPeerTimerExpired**  The SearchPeer timer has fired. No peer has been found yet and the PGL election starts immediately.

- **DBReceived**  PNNI nodes have completed the Database Summary exchange process and have reached a Full state.

- **PGLInitTimerExpired**  The PGLInit timer has fired. At this point, nodes begin comparing Hello information to see which node has the highest priority. Once determined from the information a node currently possesses, it begins advertising which node is most eligible to become PGL.

- **PreferredPGLNotSelf**  The node determines, after tallying up the priority values, that it can't be the PGL because a neighboring peer has a higher priority. If a node's leadership priority value is set to 0, excluding it from the election, the PreferredPGLNotSelf is automatically set.

- **Unanimity**  A node determines itself to be the PGL. All other nodes indicate in their PTSEs that the node in question is the preferred PGL.

- **OverrideUnanimitySuccess**  The OverrideUnanimity timer has begun. The node's preferred PGL is itself, and at least two-thirds of the other nodes agree that this node should be PGL (this prevents one faulty switch from holding up the election indefinitely).

- **OverrideUnanimityFailure**  The OverrideUnanimity timer has begun. The node's preferred PGL is itself, but less than two-thirds of the other nodes agree.

- **TwoThirdReached**  The node's preferred PGL is itself. Two-thirds of the other nodes in the peer group are now indicating in their PTSEs that they agree that the node in question should be elected PGL.

- **PreferredPGLSelf**  Node has entered Calculating state; the node determines it should be PGL because, given its current received Hello information, it has the highest priority.

- **ChangePreferredPGL**  During initialization, a node may select a preferred PGL, only to receive a Hello message containing a higher priority. Under these circumstances, the preferred PGL must be changed.

- **LoseConnectivityToPGL**  Connectivity to the PGL has been lost.

- **ReestablishConnectivityToPGL**  Connectivity to the PGL has been reestablished.

- **ReElectionTimerExpired**  There was no successful election, so the PGL election must be rerun.

To understand better the processes behind the PGL election states, consult the flow chart in Figure 16-12.

## Higher-Level Peer Groups

The PGL elections, at a common level of the hierarchy, result in a higher-level peer group in which each LGN becomes a member, rather than the individual nodes that are

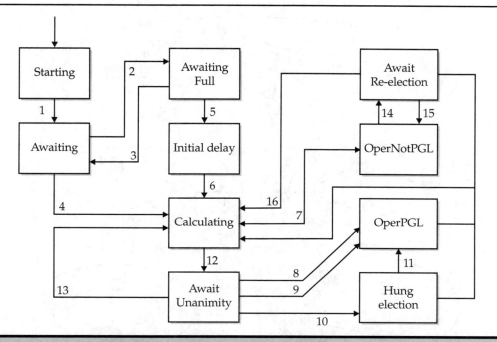

**Figure 16-12.** *PGL election state flow chart*

the members of the lowest-level peer group (see Figure 16-13). This is the beginning of the PNNI hierarchy.

## Border Nodes

When two nodes in different peer groups are interconnected, they become aware of their border node status through the exchange of Hello messages (see Figure 16-14).

In this example, nodes A and B are border nodes between peer groups 39.10.10.00.00.00.00.00.00.00.00.00.00 and 39.10.20.00.00.00.00.00.00.00.00.00.00. During the initial exchange of Hello messages, node A will receive node B's Hello message. Node A examines the contents and discovers the Remote Node ID and Remote Port ID to be 0, indicating that node B hasn't yet received its Hello message. Node A also determines that, through examining the Peer Group ID contained within the Hello message, that node B is, in fact, in a different peer group. At this point, the node transitions to a 1-Way Outside state, indicating it has received a Hello message from a node outside its peer group.

The next Hello message that node A receives from node B includes its own Node ID and Port ID as the Remote Node ID and Remote Port ID, so it determines that bidirectional

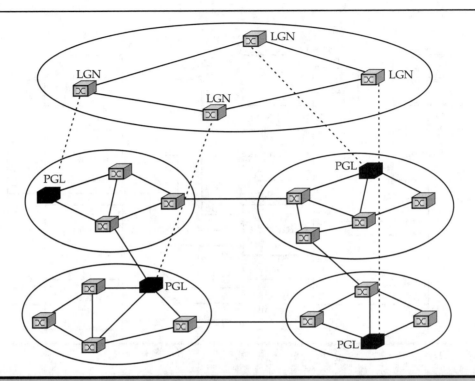

**Figure 16-13.**    *Multiple LGNs as members of higher-level peer group*

communication exists between the two nodes. The state transitions to a 2-Way Outside state. Furthermore, assuming the nodes in the two peer groups are configured with a common layer in the PNNI hierarchy, the border node's link will transition to Common Outside, indicating each has an LGN participating at a common hierarchical level. (This is covered in the next section in greater detail.) Since a common layer of hierarchy is required for lowest-level nodes to learn of remote peer groups, the 2-way outside state is considered a transitive state. Nodes A and B are aware of being border nodes at this point. This information is injected by each node into its individual peer groups, so that the individual nodes within each peer group become aware that there is an uplink to another peer group and can determine which node in the local peer group is acting as the border node.

The advertisement of these uplinks by either border node occurs through the border node's Hello messages, and not through PTSEs, which must be confined to their local peer group. The uplink information is communicated throughout a border node's local peer group when the border node includes the information regarding the outbound link

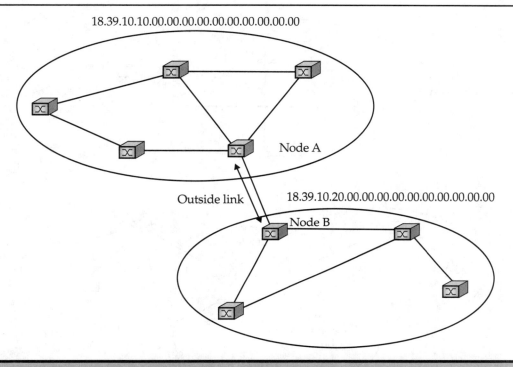

18.39.10.10.00.00.00.00.00.00.00.00.00.00

Node A

Outside link    18.39.10.20.00.00.00.00.00.00.00.00.00.00

Node B

**Figure 16-14.** *Node A and node B as border nodes*

in its PTSEs. The border node receiving a Hello message containing this information learns both that the node sending the Hello is a border node (and therefore it is a border node also), and which peer group it borders. Since Hello messages only pass between individual nodes, the receiving border node must bind this information to its topology state parameters for propagation throughout its local peer group.

## Communicating Hierarchy Between Border Nodes

After the PGL is elected and announces its presence within the peer group by setting the "I am leader" bit to 1 in its Nodal Information PTSE, the border nodes within that peer group must include Higher Level Binding information in their nodal hierarchy list, which is included in their Hello messages on outside links. This higher level binding information is communicated to the border node from the PGL. This information allows two border nodes sharing an outside link to determine which level peer group the two have in common (see Figure 16-15).

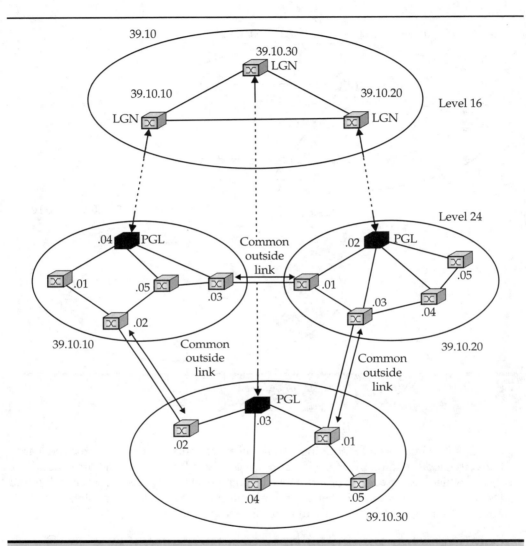

**Figure 16-15.** *Three peer groups, each with LGNs represented on a common level*

The example in Figure 16-15 has three peer groups: 39.10.10, 39.10.20, and 39.10.30. Each peer group contains five nodes. In this case, a PGL is elected for each peer group, and each is summarized as a single LGN:

Nodes 39.10.10.01 – 39.10.10.05  =  LGN 39.10.10
Nodes 39.10.20.01 – 39.10.20.05  =  LGN 39.10.20
Nodes 39.10.30.01 – 39.10.30.05  =  LGN 39.10.30

These LGNs participate on a common level: 39.10. Therefore, each of the three peer groups shares a common layer of hierarchy. Border nodes will communicate that they have a hierarchical peer group level in common, as well as which LGNs are represented within the higher-level peer group. Border nodes between peer groups in this case will determine that they all share peer group 39.10 in common. Once this occurs, the former state of 2-Way Outside between the border nodes transitions to Common Outside, indicating that although the two peer groups are separate, they do share a peer group in common at a higher level.

## Uplinks

In the previously described scenario, nodes learn of their local topology within their own peer group, as well as the existence of neighboring peer groups as summarizations. Nodes must learn which border nodes have connectivity to which remote peer groups. These inter-peer group links are called uplinks.

For instance, when the border node in peer group 39.10.20 has a connection with LGN 39.10.30, border nodes 39.10.20.03 and 39.10.30.01 have exchanged Hello messages, and since both have received Nodal Information PTSEs from their respective PGL with the "I am leader" bit flipped, they are also exchanging nodal hierarchy lists. They have determined that they share a common peer group level, at 39.10, where their peer groups are summarized as 39.10.20 and 39.10.30, respectively.

At this point, node 39.10.20.03 realizes that its outside neighbor node 39.10.30.01 is actually represented as an LGN in higher-level peer group 39.10 as LGN 39.10.30. Border node 39.10.20.03 then advertises an uplink between itself and LGN 39.10.30 (see Figure 16-16).

In this scenario, LGN 39.10.30 is known as the *upnode*, and the advertised link between 39.10.20.03 and 39.10.30 is known as the *uplink*. This association is also made between border node 39.10.30.01 and LGN 39.10.20.

These border nodes will then advertise these uplinks in their PTSEs, flooded within their respective peer groups. Using this scheme, lowest-level nodes are able to learn not only about the summarized topology of the neighboring peer group from their PGLs, where a lowest-level node in peer group 39.10.10 knows of the existence of a remote peer group summarized as 39.10.20 in the higher-level peer group 39.10, but also from which border node the remote peer group is accessible.

## Interaction of Multiple Peer Group Leaders

In a scenario with five peer groups and two levels of hierarchy, five PGLs exist, one for each peer group. These PGLs also participate at the lowest level of the hierarchy, for purposes of PTSE and Database Summary exchange with the nodes in their local peer

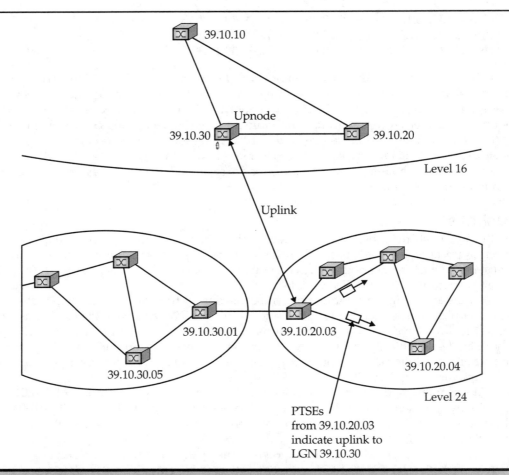

39.10.10

Upnode

39.10.30    39.10.20

Level 16

Uplink

39.10.30.01    39.10.20.03

39.10.30.05

39.10.20.04

Level 24

PTSEs
from 39.10.20.03
indicate uplink to
LGN 39.10.30

**Figure 16-16.**    *Node 39.10.20.03 forming uplink with LGN 39.10.30*

groups. As such, the PGL of each group is aware of the presence of multiple peer groups, and thus multiple PGLs.

After the existence of multiple peer groups is established, each leader has been elected (election takes place automatically when multiple layers of hierarchy are configured), common layers of hierarchy are determined by border nodes, and uplinks are formed, PGLs must form a routing control channel (RCC) between the higher-level LGNs. Lowest-level nodes utilize the reserved signaling channel VPI/VCI 0/18 for their RCC, but in the case of higher-level LGNs, a Switched Virtual Control Channel (SVCC) will be used.

Using the previous example (refer to Figure 16-15), an RCC must be formed between LGNs 39.10.10 and 39.10.20. This is accomplished when PGL 39.10.10.04 receives a PTSE from border node 39.10.10.03, which describes that border node's uplink to upnode 39.10.20. PGL 39.10.10.04 examines the PTSE and determines the common peer group the two peer groups share (39.10 in this case), as well as the ATM End System Address of upnode 39.10.20, since the address will be needed to place the call for SVCC establishment. PGL 39.10.10.04 communicates this as LGN (39.10.10).

LGN 39.10.10 determines at this point that both itself and upnode 39.10.20 are logical nodes in the same higher-level peer group 39.10. An RCC must be formed between them (more specifically, between the PGLs of each peer group, which are acting as LGNs). Using the ATM End System Address, the SVCC is initiated from one LGN to its upnode. At this point, all lowest-level nodes within each peer group should have a complete topology of their own peer group, as well as the advertised uplinks in order to successfully route the SVCC.

## Node Interaction at a Higher Level

The previous examples have all yielded a higher-level peer group, peer group 39.10. The LGNs within this peer group have formed RCCs between them, providing each with connectivity to each LGN for which an uplink exists (see Figure 16-17).

Once this relationship is established, the same kinds of neighbor relationships and database synchronization must occur between nodes at the higher level as occurred between nodes at the lowest level. This DB exchange only includes information from the current peer group level, which means that LGN 39.10.20 in this case is only going to exchange database information regarding peer group 39.10. For instance, LGN 39.10.20 is actually a logical representation of nodes 39.10.20.01, 39.10.20.02, 39.10.20.03, 39.10.20.04, and 39.10.20.05, but it will not communicate any of this information, or any of the topology or link state information regarding those nodes, with the other LGNs (39.10.10 and 39.10.30) in peer group 39.10. LGN 39.10.20 will only communicate information regarding the links within its own local peer group, just as holds true at the lowest level of PNNI routing; it will advertise that it has a connection to LGN 39.10.10 and LGN 39.10.30.

LGNs effectively become neighbors in the higher-level peer group, and this occurs through the exchange of Hello messages between the LGNs. The LGN Hello protocol is very similar to the Hello protocol used by lowest-level nodes, except that it occurs over the SVCC-based RCCs created between LGNs, and not over the PNNI control channel (0/18).

One of the purposes of the LGN Hello protocol is to ensure that the RCCs are still up and active; from a logical, higher-level peer group perspective, the RCCs are direct connections, but even though they are point-to-point circuits, they may traverse many intermediary nodes. For this reason, it is important to be sure that these connections are maintained. If LGN Hello messages aren't seen over these connections in the time defined by the HelloInterval, then the RCC may need to be reestablished. In the event of an RCC failure, it will be reestablished dynamically, because it is an SVCC-based circuit.

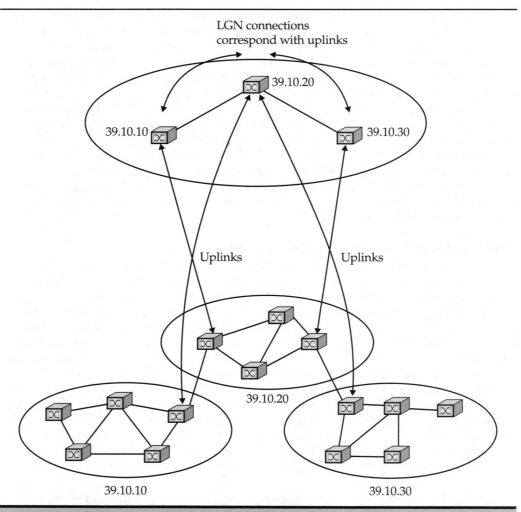

**Figure 16-17.**   *LGN interconnectivity at the higher-level peer group corresponding to uplinks at lower level*

## LGN Hello Protocol over the RCC

Monitoring the RCC is one of the two jobs the LGN Hello protocol is responsible for; the other is to communicate horizontal links to the other LGNs and agree on which should be mutually advertised.

Just as with the lowest-level nodes, LGN entities issue their Hello messages over the RCCs. In the higher-level peer group, however, the LGNs are always considered to be within the same peer group; although the RCCs traverse multiple lowest-level peer groups, they never actually leave the higher-level peer group. For this reason, Outside states are never reached between LGNs. The Port ID, included in the Hello message, always holds a value of 0xFFFFFFFF when that Hello message originates from an LGN and is passed over the RCC.

**NODE IDENTIFIERS IN LGN HELLO MESSAGES**   The PNNI Node ID in an LGN Hello message is 22 octets in length, and represents a child peer group being advertised within a parent peer group. For instance, a lowest-level node in peer group 39.10.10.01.00.00.00.00.00.00.00.00.00 may advertise itself within its local peer group by using its unique Node ID, whereas in a higher-level peer group, the LGN for peer group 39.10.10.01.00.00.00.00.00.00.00.00.00 will advertise its child peer group to other nodes within the parent group (39.10.10). Under these circumstances, the LGN Node ID, as defined in the LGN Hello message, adheres to the following rules:

- The level indicator specifies the level of the parent peer group (16, in the prior example, yielding parent peer group 39.10.00.00.00.00.00.00.00.00.00.00.00). This is the peer group containing the LGN.

- The following fourteen octets are the encoded Peer Group ID of the child peer group (39.10.10.00.00.00.00.00.00.00.00.00.00, in the prior example). The encoded PG ID will not be preceded by a value of 160, such as is the case with lowest-level nodes.

- The following six octets represent the End Station Identifier (ESI) of the physical system that is implementing the LGN functionality. This unique ID ensures lowest-level peer individuality in the case of a peer group partition (covered later in this chapter).

- The last octet of the Node ID is 0.

**THE AGGREGATION TOKEN**   The *aggregation token* is a four-octet identifier whose purpose is to identify links that can be aggregated at the next level; meaning, for example, that three parallel links between the same two peer groups are configured with a common aggregation token value, so that they are identified as being eligible for aggregation at the higher level as a single link. The aggregation token is included in the PTSEs that describe uplinks; as such, the PGL will learn of multiple, parallel links between common peer groups and will advertise them as a single, logical link via the LGN at the higher-level peer group.

## LGN Peer States

To determine the horizontal logical link states between them, LGNs first establish neighbor states with one another; they send Hello messages over the newly formed SVCCs. In this case, however, each Hello that is sent contains a *LGN Horizontal Link Extension* information group. This piece of information indicates all the existing horizontal links between the sending node and the neighboring peer node, including the Local Port ID, the Remote Port ID, and the aggregation token. The structure of the LGN Hello message differs slightly from that of the lowest-level peer Hello message. A description of the LGN Hello structure follows:

- **Aggregation Token**   The aggregation token associated with the particular link between LGNs. Two LGNs participating in a higher-level peer group may have two or three parallel physical connections connecting their child peer groups. Those links that share the same value defined in their aggregation token are aggregated as a single logical link for purposes of LGN logical link advertisement.

- **State**   The current operational status of the logical link between LGNs.

- **Port ID**   In the case of Hellos passed over an RCC, the Port ID is 0xFFFFFFFF. This will be true of all ports participating in the higher-level peer group.

- **Remote Node ID**   The Node ID of the remote LGN; a 22-octet value that includes the encoded Node ID of the Peer Group Leader.

- **Remote Port ID**   Initially, this value is set to 0. Upon receiving a successful Hello message from its neighboring LGN, this value is replaced with the common RCC Hello message Port ID value of 0xFFFFFFFF.

- **Inducing Uplinks List**   An *induced uplink* occurs between LGNs if a lowest-level node establishes an uplink with a higher-level LGN and bypasses a hierarchical level. This may occur if a border node connects to a remote peer group that only operates at a higher level. In this case, an uplink forms between the lower-level node and the higher-level LGN, and the LGN at the hierarchical level that was bypassed then forms an uplink with the higher-level LGN, as well, which is an induced uplink. This is covered in more detail in the sections involving the highest hierarchical level, later in this chapter.

When a PTSE containing an uplink is received, the LGN for that peer group is assigned a logical Port ID (0xFFFFFFFF) and given a state machine in the Down state. The aggregation token is checked, because multiple instances of the token value may exist, indicating these are in fact parallel logical links that may be aggregated. Once this uplink is identified, it is advertised in the Hello message sent to the neighboring LGN. At this point, the neighboring peer state between LGNs transitions into the Attempt state.

An LGN indicating an induced uplink in its Hello message from its child peer group to the LGN with which it has a connection should see information in its neighbor's Hello message indicating the uplink from the neighbor's child peer group to itself.

Once the LGN receives a Hello message from its neighbor describing this uplink, the state transitions into 1-Way if the Remote Port ID is still set to 0, and 2-Way if the Remote Port ID is that of the receiving LGN.

A summarization of the LGN neighboring peer states follows:

- **Down** When an uplink PTSE is received by the Peer Group Leader, a logical port is assigned to the LGN, but no information has been exchanged with the neighbor yet.

- **Attempt** The LGN has indicated the induced uplink in its Hello message, but hasn't received like information from the neighbor LGN, which also describes an induced uplink to itself.

- **1-Way** A Hello message has been received from the neighboring peer LGN that indicated the presence of an induced uplink to the receiving LGN, where the receiving LGN has also indicated in its own Hellos an induced uplink to the sending LGN. In the 1-Way state, the Remote Port ID is still set to 0.

- **2-Way** A Hello message has been received from the neighboring peer LGN that indicated the presence of an induced uplink to the receiving LGN, where the receiving LGN has also indicated in its own Hellos an induced uplink to the sending LGN. In the 2-Way state, the Remote Port ID in the received Hello has been assigned the value of 0xFFFFFFFF.

## Aggregating PNNI Topology

The information advertised by LGNs at the higher-level peer group represents an aggregation of the actual, physical topology. This aggregation occurs on two different levels: the nodes themselves are aggregated as a single summary address (represented by the LGN), and parallel links that connect the same two peer groups are aggregated. Advertisements among higher-level nodes should be kept as concise as possible, so that at the next level of the hierarchy, multiple links that are parallel between peer groups are viewed as a single, next-level logical link (see Figure 16-18).

The scheme shown in Figure 16-18 allows for a higher-level view of the PNNI topology, where the path from node 39.10.10.01 to node 39.10.50.02 can be determined in its simplest form; since the nodes do not share a common peer group, which peer groups must be traversed to reach the destination peer group, and therefore the destination node? Although multiple links may exist between the source peer group and its neighboring peer group, for purposes of determining a higher-level path, the source node really only needs to know whether the peer groups are connected, not how many connections they have or where they are. When generating the DTL, it will know which nodes border the next-hop peer group, based on the fact that they are advertising uplinks to the proper LGN. Once the source node determines how the peer groups are laid out and which ones are connected by border nodes, it will be able to determine which peer group is next in the path to the destination, and which other peer groups it may have to traverse to get to the destination.

## Communicating Information from Different Hierarchical Levels

Information must pass between higher-level and lower-level peer groups. For an LGN to advertise the sum of its child peer group to other LGNs, the PGL must have that information communicated to it from its surrounding peers at the lowest-level;

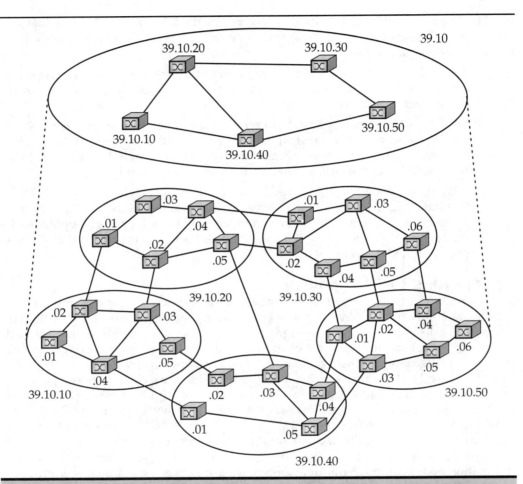

**Figure 16-18.** *Five peer groups with five nodes each connected with parallel links, and then as LGNs with single higher-level connections*

likewise, once the LGNs have determined their topology, this information must in turn be passed down to the lowest-level nodes, so that a node in one peer group is able to successfully route a call to a destination residing in another peer group.

The PGL plays the instrumental role in this procedure, because it acts as representative of its peer group, aggregating links and nodes to be advertised on the LGN level, and also communicates to the lowest-level nodes the information learned about the higher-level peer group LGN topology. Once the topology of the lowest-level peer groups has been determined, and every node within its peer group has a complete view of the ATM mesh topology, as well as all LGNs, then any single node within a peer group should have the information it needs to plot a Designated Transit List (DTL) Index to any destination node in any other remote peer group that is reachable.

## Operation in the Absence of a PGL

Even in a PNNI environment utilizing more than one hierarchical level, a peer group may exist without representation by a PGL. In the absence of a PGL, lowest-level nodes within the peer group still function normally and still maintain a topology database for that peer group. They will not have representation as an LGN at the next layer of hierarchy, however, so a call will not be routed using only PNNI from a peer group with no PGL to any other peer group.

Reachability information may still be advertised into the PNNI routing domain from a leaderless peer group, however, as exterior addresses. This may be done if there is a mixed environment of IISP and PNNI; IISP links do not share or learn routing information, because they are statically configured hop-by-hop routes. The addresses found within an IISP domain may be advertised by the connecting PNNI node as external addresses.

# Building a Designated Transit List Index

To build a DTL across multiple peer groups, a DTL Index needs to be created by the source node (see Figure 16-19). From the source node perspective, a DTL through the local peer group must be determined, as well as an overall route to the destination that traverses all peer groups in that path.

The example in Figure 16-19 has five peer groups: 39.10.10, 39.10.20, 39.10.30, 39.10.40, and 39.10.50. Each peer group contains five nodes. Station A, which is connected to node 39.10.10.02 in peer group 39.10.10, transmits to station B, which is connected to node 39.10.50.04 in peer group 39.10.50. Node 39.10.10.02 must create a DTL to the destination node.

The source node compares PG IDs and determines that node 39.10.50.04 isn't in its local peer group. This means that the call must traverse a border node to reach the destination. Node 39.10.10.02 examines its topology database and finds link information for the four other nodes within its local peer group. It also finds that node 39.10.10.03 is advertising an uplink to upnode 39.10.20, and that node 39.10.10.05 is advertising an uplink to upnode 39.10.30.

By examining its topology database, node 39.10.10.02 determines that, in addition to its peer group, four other LGNs exist: LGNs 39.10.20, 39.10.30, 39.10.40, and 39.10.50. Of these LGNs, there are only border nodes within its local peer group advertising uplinks to two of those LGNs, 39.10.20 and 39.10.30. Since neither of these LGNs represents the destination node's peer group, it must be determined which LGN should be the next hop on the way to destination node 39.10.50.04.

In this case, LGN 39.10.50 is actually reachable via either border node, but, according to the topology passed down from the PGL, the path through LGN 39.10.20 is actually the shorter route. Node 39.10.10.02 can only plot a node-specific DTL through its own peer group, because it only has specific link information regarding

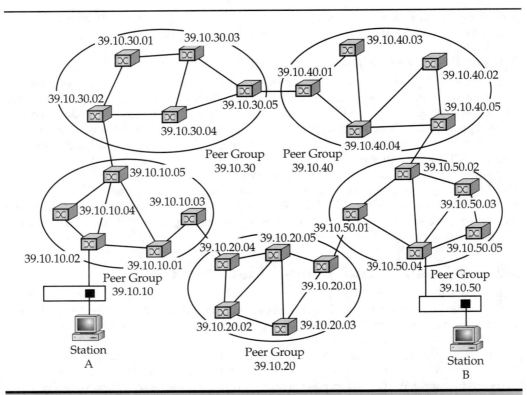

**Figure 16-19.**   *Five peer groups interconnected with five nodes each*

those nodes. In this case, then, the source node must create a *DTL Index,* which describes the path to the destination node in several steps. First, it determines the path at its highest level, which in this case will be a path from its own peer group, to LGN 39.10.20, to LGN 39.10.50, where the destination node resides. Next, because LGN 39.10.20 is its next hop on the way to the destination, it must chart a path to this LGN. Node 39.10.10.03 is advertising an uplink to upnode 39.10.20, so the call must be routed to border node 39.10.10.03.

The source node examines its local peer group link information and builds a specific DTL to border node 39.10.10.03, and since it knows it will be traversing more than one peer group, it gives it an index, to denote the different hierarchical levels it must traverse. The index it gives the DTL within its own peer group is an index of 0.

> *The DTL of the node's current peer group is always 0. Other hierarchical levels are designated 1, 2, and so on, in order of ascension.*

Node 39.10.10.02 knows it must get to a destination node in LGN 39.10.50. It knows the path through the LGNs it must take (39.10.10 to 39.10.20 to 39.10.50) and keeps that overall path in mind (as index 1), while plotting the path through its own peer group (index 0) (see Figure 16-20).

In the example shown in Figure 16-20, the Pointer column designates the call's current location in the path; index 1 points to 39.10.10, because that is the current position in the overall LGN path, and index 0 points to 39.10.10.02, because that is the current node in the local DTL.

Using the DTL Index, the source node sends the call to the next node in the path to border node 39.10.10.03; each node in the path will increment the pointer to point to the next node in the path (in index 0) and will leave the pointer alone for the LGN path (in index 1), because the call hasn't left the local peer group yet.

The call reaches border node 39.10.10.03, which passes the call into the next LGN (39.10.20), by way of border node 39.10.20.04. Border node 39.10.20.04 takes the DTL Index, strips off index 0, and creates a new index 0, because index 0 always represents the current local peer group and describes a lowest-level node path through that peer group. Node 39.10.20.04 knows by examining the DTL Index that the next LGN in the path is LGN 39.10.50, and also knows, by examining the topology database of its local peer group, that border node 39.10.20.01 is advertising an uplink to upnode 39.10.50, which is the destination LGN.

| Index level | Position 1 | Position 2 | Position 3 | Position 4 | Position 5 | Pointer |
|---|---|---|---|---|---|---|
| 0 | 39.10.10.02 | 39.10.10.01 | 39.10.10.03 | | | 1 |
| 1 | 39.10.10 | 39.10.20 | 39.10.50 | | | 1 |

DTL Index

**Figure 16-20.**    *DTL Index showing Index 0 and Index 1*

ATM TECHNOLOGIES

The call has now become the responsibility of border node 39.10.20.04, which must successfully route the call to the border node advertising the uplink (node 39.10.20.01). Using its topology database, border node 39.10.20.04 plots a path to node 39.10.20.01, under index 0, with the index 1 path remaining 39.10.10 to 39.10.20 to 39.10.50, except with the pointer adjusted to point at LGN 39.10.20, which is the call's current location. Border node 39.10.20.04 does basically the same thing node 39.10.10.02 did, but for its own peer group. Node 39.10.20.04 passes the call along to the other nodes within its intra-peer group path, each of which examines the index and alters the pointer within index 0 to indicate the call's current position in the relative path. When the call reaches the destination border node, it passes the call into peer group 39.10.50, by way of node 39.10.50.01.

Node 39.10.50.01 takes the DTL and strips index 0, because this was the path through the previous peer group and thus is no longer valid. It redesignates index 1 as index 0, and then bumps the LGN path back to index 1 as it plots its own path to the destination node, marking that index 0, because the path remains within its local peer group.

Border node 39.10.50.01 knows that the destination node 39.10.50.04 resides within its local peer group, since in index 1, the pointer has now reached the end of the path, LGN 39.10.50. Border node 39.10.50.01 sends the call along the path indicated in index 0; the intermediary nodes pass the call along, altering the pointer in index 0 to indicate the relative placement in the overall path, until the call ends up at its destination, node 39.10.50.04, where station B resides.

## Crankback in a PNNI Hierarchy

A failed PNNI call must still be cranked back to its source, so that the source can build a new DTL to the destination. This holds true even in the presence of a PNNI hierarchy. Using the PNNI topology outlined in the previous section (refer to Figure 16-19), station A, connected to node 39.10.10.02, needs to communicate with station B, connected to node 39.10.50.04. In the previous example, this call was established starting at peer group 39.10.10, then passing through peer group 39.10.20, and ending in peer group 39.10.50, where the destination node resides. For the sake of this example, the call will fail at peer group 39.10.20.

Using the methodology described in the previous section, the LEC on node 39.10.10.02 must build a Data Direct VCC to node 39.10.50.04; by looking at the destination address and level indicators, the source node knows the destination is outside the local peer group. The source node examines its topology information and finds that two ways exist to get to the destination peer group: local peer group to LGN 39.10.20 to LGN 39.10.50, or local peer group to LGN 39.10.30 to LGN 39.10.40 to LGN 39.10.50. The former of the two routes is shorter, so it is selected.

The source node determines which border node is advertising an uplink to the appropriate LGN (39.10.20), so a DTL Index is built, describing a path to the border node in index 0, and the LGN path of 39.10.10 to 39.10.20 to 39.10.50 in index 1. The call is initiated to the border node, which receives it.

Border node 39.10.10.03 then passes the call to 39.10.20.04, its neighboring border node in LGN 39.10.20. Border node 39.10.20.04 adjusts the DTL Index and plots a path to border node 39.10.20.01.

A link failure has occurred, however, on one of the links, making it impossible to follow the DTL, so the call must be cranked back at this point. In this case, the call isn't cranked back to the original source node, 39.10.10.02; it is cranked back to the source node for the current peer group, node 39.10.20.04. The LGN path may still be valid and thus may not need to be recalculated, and the original source node has already successfully routed the call to the next peer group in the DTL Index. Border node 39.10.20.04 receives a crankback cause code and attempts to build a new DTL for Index 0.

By this point, however, node 39.10.20.04 has received updated topology information that reflects the failed link. In this example, this failed link has ocurred between border nodes 39.10.20.01 and 39.10.50.01, which was the only connection into peer group 39.10.50 from peer group 39.10.20. An uplink to LGN 39.10.50 is no longer being advertised anywhere in peer group 39.10.20. Node 39.10.20.04 determines that it will not be able to honor the current DTL Index.

All nodes must honor the DTL Index created by the original source node. Only when the DTL Index can't be followed is the call then cranked back all the way to the source peer group. The call is cranked back to node 39.10.10.02 with a crankback cause code.

Node 39.10.10.02 reexamines its topology information. It must create a new DTL Index regardless of whether its topology has been updated, but ultimately, the logical link between LGNs 39.10.20 and 39.10.50 will disappear from the topology database. The source node now must make a new calculation based on this information. Looking at the higher-level topology, the source node determines that there is, in fact, another path to the destination: the local peer group to LGN 39.10.30 to 39.10.40 to 39.10.50. It examines the topology database for its own peer group and discovers that border node 39.10.10.05 is advertising an uplink to LGN 39.10.30. It builds a new DTL Index, in which index 0 describes a path to the border node, and index 1 describes a path across the LGNs.

Once the call reaches the border node, it is passed into the next peer group, and the DTL Index is adjusted, with a new DTL at index 0 describing a path across peer group 39.10.30. This time, with no failed links along the path, the DTL Index can be honored, and the Data Direct VCC between nodes 39.10.10.02 and 39.10.50.04 is created, using the alternate path.

## Operating in a Partitioned State

A single peer group may become partitioned in the case of a link failure or switch failure, as in the example shown in Figure 16-21.

In this example, a single connection has failed between nodes in a single peer group. The absence of this link, however, effectively separates the peer group into two halves. This is known as a *partitioned state* in the PNNI environment. In this case, peer group 39.10.10 has been partitioned; one portion of the partition (partition A) contains the PGL for the original peer group. The nodes within partition A recalculate their topology, with the nodes in the other partition removed from their databases. The

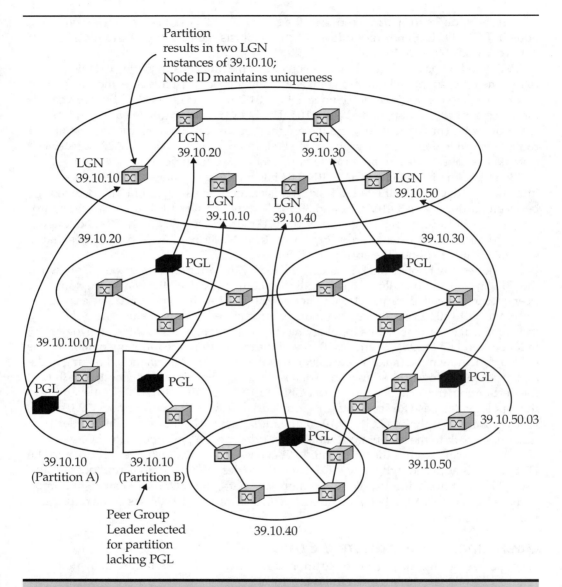

Partition results in two LGN instances of 39.10.10; Node ID maintains uniqueness

LGN 39.10.20

LGN 39.10.30

LGN 39.10.10

LGN 39.10.10

LGN 39.10.40

LGN 39.10.50

39.10.20

39.10.30

PGL

PGL

39.10.10.01

PGL

PGL

PGL

39.10.50.03

PGL

39.10.10 (Partition A)

39.10.10 (Partition B)

39.10.50

Peer Group Leader elected for partition lacking PGL

39.10.40

**Figure 16-21.** *Partitioned peer group with LGN at parent peer group level*

nodes in partition B are separated from their PGL, so they must elect a new one. The PGL election is held and a new PGL is elected.

The network topology in this example now has six functioning peer groups, instead of the original five. Each of these peer groups has a PGL, which represents the individual peer groups at the next-highest peer group level: LGNs 39.10.20, 39.10.30, 39.10.40, 39.10.50, and two instances of 39.10.10. For these LGN entities to retain uniqueness, their individual Node IDs must be considered. Remember that at the LGN level, the Node ID consists of a level indicator, specifying the level of the peer group containing the LGN, the encoded PG ID of the child peer group, and the ESI of the physical switch the PGL resides on. This is to maintain a unique identity in the case of a partition. Partitions A and B are each represented at the higher-level peer group by LGNs that are unique (refer to Figure 16-21).

The network topology is now altered from its original layout; there are now six peer groups, and whereas each peer group formerly was connected in a sort of "ring" topology, now the physical layout is more linear. Partition A maintains an uplink to LGN 39.10.20, and partition B maintains an uplink to LGN 39.10.40; however, partitions A and B have no connection to each other. This will not present a problem for calls routed between the nonpartitioned peer groups, even if those calls traverse either partition (although this would not occur in this example's topology), since each partition LGN has a unique identifier. However, if a call is actually destined for a node that resides in either partition, then problems may arise.

If node 39.10.50.03 needs to establish a connection with node 39.10.10.01, for example, it examines the destination node address and determines that it doesn't reside in its local peer group. It checks its topology at the next layer of the hierarchy, looking for an LGN representing the destination node, and finds two such LGNs. Peer group 39.10.10 actually has two instances in the parent peer group, one for each partition. Although they are identified as being unique entities due to their unique ESIs, for purposes of making a PNNI routing decision, this doesn't indicate in any way which partition 39.10.10.01 resides in. In this situation, the source node (39.10.50.03) must arbitrarily select an LGN path, even though it may be incorrect. Once the call reaches the partition's border node, that node will have a full topology of the partition contained in its database, so the border node will be able to determine, once the call reaches it, whether or not the destination node resides within its partition. If it does, the call is processed normally. If it doesn't, then the border node rejects the call and it is cranked back to the originating source node. The source node, at this point, must build a new DTL, this time with the other partition's LGN as its destination.

While this may result in failed call attempts, it does allow for PNNI routing to continue unhampered throughout most of the network, and, even in the case of the partitioned peer group, the destination should be still reachable, even though some failed route computations may occur initially.

# Highest Hierarchical Level

The third and final level of the PNNI routing hierarchy is an extension of the concepts covered so far in this chapter. The highest hierarchical level exists in a scenario where multiple lowest-level peer groups have spawned not one but several higher-level peer groups. In a configuration where three levels of PNNI routing hierarchy have been specified, the LGNs themselves in the higher-level peer groups are aggregated to the next-highest-level peer group.

This is accomplished through user configuration, as well; in this example (see Figure 16-22), the LGNs of each of the six peer groups are represented by an LGN, in the next-highest layer of the hierarchy. Of the two groups of three LGNs that result from this, each is aggregated as a single LGN at the highest level of the hierarchy.

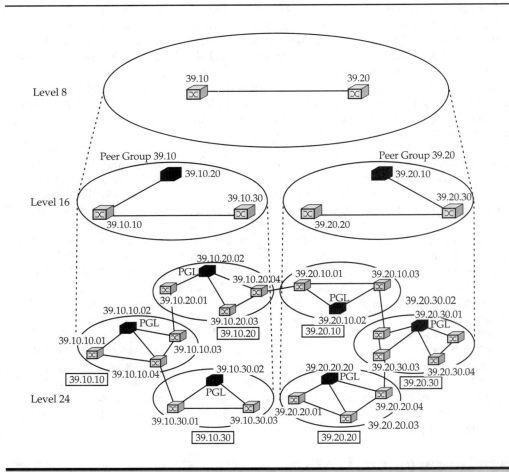

**Figure 16-22.** *Nodes and LGNs in six peer groups in three PNNI levels*

## Uplinks

Uplinks in a hierarchically complete PNNI network occur in much the same way as they do at lower levels. In the case of multiple peer groups spawning multiple higher-level peer groups, which are themselves aggregated at a still higher level, uplinks exist between border nodes at the lowest level, and their corresponding upnodes. At the highest hierarchical level, induced uplinks also exist between the LGNs at the midlevel and highest-level LGNs (see Figure 16-23). For the sake of clarity, only the uplinks and induced uplinks between peer groups 39.10.20 and 39.20.10 are displayed. In actuality, such uplinks also exist between the other connected peer groups.

The example in Figure 16-23 has six peer groups: 39.10.10, 39.10.20, 39.10.30, 39.20.10, 39.20.20, and 39.20.30. These peer groups are aggregated under two higher-level peer groups, peer groups 39.10.10 and 39.20.10. The 39.10.10 peer group contains LGNs 39.10.10, 39.10.20, and 39.10.30, and peer group 39.20.10 contains LGNs 39.20.10, 39.20.20, and 39.20.30. Each of these two higher-level peer groups, in turn, is aggregated in the highest-level peer group as LGNs 39.10 and 39.20, respectively, in the highest-level peer group, 39.

Uplinks are created between these peer groups in the following manner:

- **At the lowest level under parent peer group 39.10**    Border node 39.10.10.03 forms an uplink with upnode 39.10.20 in the parent peer group. Likewise, an uplink forms between border node 39.10.20.01 and upnode 39.10.10 in the parent peer group. Uplinks will also form between border node 39.10.20.04 and LGN 39.20, and between border node 39.10.30.01 and LGN 39.10.10.

- **At the lowest level under parent peer group 39.20**    Border node 39.20.10.03 forms an uplink with LGN 39.20.30, and border node 39.20.30.02 forms an uplink with LGN 39.20.10. Border node 39.20.20.04 forms an uplink with upnode 39.20.30, and border node 39.20.30.03 forms an uplink with upnode 39.20.20.

**Note** *In this case, uplinks do not form between border node 39.10.20.04 and upnode 39.20.20, because LGN 39.20.20 is in peer group 39.20, and not in 39.10, the parent peer group of border node 39.10.20.04. The uplinks are actually formed between border node 39.10.20.04 and upnode 39.20 at the highest hierarchical level, since it is the only level the two share in common. Likewise, an uplink is formed between 39.20.10.01 and upnode 39.10. Induced uplinks are formed then between LGN 39.10.20 and upnode 39.20, and between LGN 39.20.10 and upnode 39.10.*

- **At the higher-level peer groups**    Since the LGNs in peer group 39.10 and 39.20 share a common layer of hierarchy, uplinks form between their nodes, as well. In this case, an induced uplink forms between LGN 39.10.20 and its upnode, 39.20. Likewise, an induced uplink forms between LGN 39.20.10 and its upnode, 39.10.

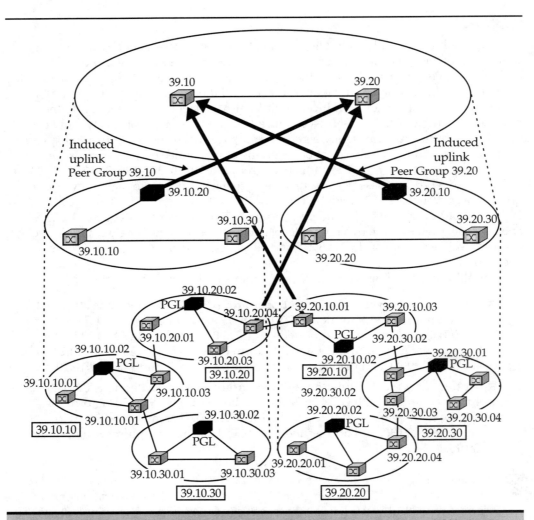

**Figure 16-23.**   *Six peer groups with two parent peer groups that have LGNs in a single peer group*

## Induced Uplinks

Add to this example the existence of a seventh peer group, peer group 39.30.10, which is connected via a border node to peer group 39.20.30. Notice that the new peer group actually is configured to exist only at the lowest level and highest hierarchical level, 39. This is dictated by the node's level indicators and scope values. The new peer group, however, does have a direct connection to peer group 39.20.30, between border nodes

39.20.30.05 and 39.30.10.01. In this case, although they do not share a common layer of hierarchy at the second level, they do share a common layer of hierarchy at the highest level. Border node 39.20.30.05 forms an uplink with upnode 39.30 at the highest level. At the same time, an induced uplink is formed between LGN 39.20.30 at the second hierarchical level and upnode 39.30 (see Figure 16-24).

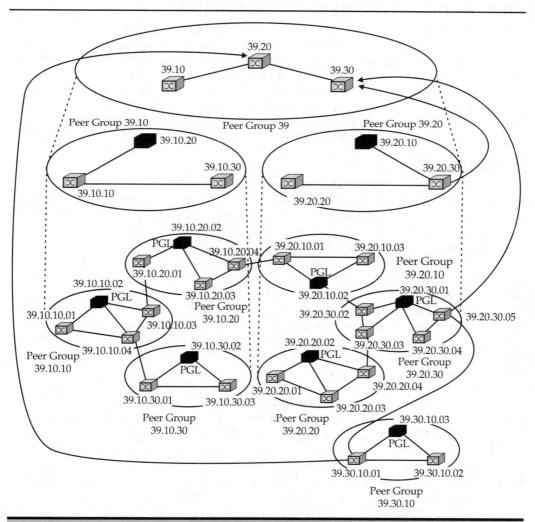

**Figure 16-24.** *Induced uplinks with seventh peer group existing only at highest level*

ATM TECHNOLOGIES

This scenario is possible because of the level indicator that nodes in peer group 39.30 have been configured with: they are configured to advertise only at the lowest and highest levels. The PGL in peer group 39.30 is configured with a level causing it to only represent the group as an LGN at the highest level, so their advertisements will only be shared with other LGNs in peer group 39.

# Address Summarization and Reachability

*Address summarization* relates to the idea of nodal aggregation; using a single prefix to denote a larger range of node addresses. A node may be configured to advertise a series of address summarizations, allowing access to a series of address ranges. By default, a PNNI node advertises a single address summary equal to its 13-octet prefix. This is considered its internal summary address. A node with a level indicator of 104 (the lowest level) does not summarize. At higher peer group levels, LGNs will, by default, advertise a summary address equal to the PG ID that it represents at the higher level. Additional summary addresses may also be configured.

## Address Suppression

PNNI address summaries may also be suppressed. In this scenario, the defined address summary will not be advertised further into the PNNI hierarchy. This can be useful for security purposes, where a certain peer group may contain sensitive network traffic. By configuring an address summary and indicating that the address should be suppressed, it will not be propagated by the LGN (see Figure 16-25).

The example in Figure 16-25 has four peer groups: 39.10.10, 39.10.20, 39.20.10, and 39.20.20. These peer groups are aggregated at two higher-level peer groups, 39.10 and 39.20, which in turn are aggregated at a common highest layer, 39. Peer group A (39.10.10) contains sensitive network traffic. Users within peer group A need to be able to route calls within their local peer group, as well as reach remote peer groups. Peer groups B, C, and D, however, are to be restricted from accessing peer group A. At the second level, each peer group is represented by an LGN in two higher-level peer groups: 39.10.10 and 39.10.20 in peer groups 39.10, and 39.20.10. The LGNs contained within the two parent peer groups are themselves part of peer group 39 as LGNs 39.10 and 39.20. LGN 39.10's default address summary would be to summarize all lower-level addresses as 39.10; however, in this case, there are two address summaries, 39.10.10 and 39.10.20, with address summary 39.10.10 (peer group A) suppressed.

The address range 39.10.10 in this case isn't advertised and peer groups B, C, and D never learn of this address range as being accessible through the uplink advertised by the border node in peer group 39.20.10, so nodes in peer groups B, C, and D will not be able to reach peer group A, although they will be able to reach one another.

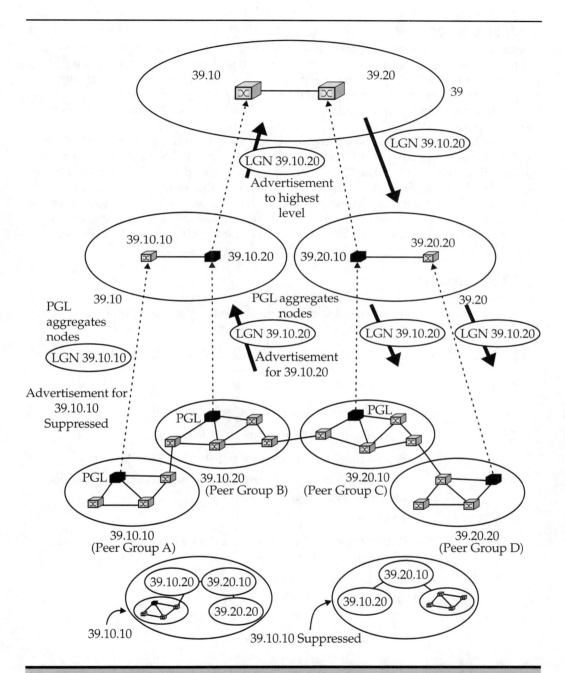

**Figure 16-25.** *Four peer groups in two higher-level peer groups and a common highest level*

## Address Scope

Logical nodes always have a scope value associated with them that instructs them as to how high into the PNNI hierarchy an address should be advertised. Consider the previous example of four peer groups and three layers of hierarchy. In this example, the goal is that peer group A must be able to reach all peer groups, peer group B must be able to reach peer group A, and peer groups C and D must be able to reach peer group B but not peer group A.

No address suppression takes place in this scenario; the nodes in peer group A are configured with a scope of 16, indicating that their reachability information is not to be advertised any higher up in the PNNI hierarchy than the level of peer group 39.10 (four 4-byte hex nibbles = 16). So, LGN 39.10.10 will advertise the peer group to the other LGN in peer group 39.10, but this address information will not be advertised up to peer group 39, since that peer group rests at level 8, and the scope value configured on the nodes in peer group A indicates the address information should only go up to level 16 (see Figure 16-26).

## ATM Addressing

ATM addresses are 20 octets long. Each of the 20 octets serves a different function. Review the following example and then consult the following corresponding chart (these examples are directly from the *C100/5000BH Reference Guide*):

39.CCCC.RR.AAAAAA.WW.WW.XX.XX.XX.XX.YYYYYYYYYY.ZZ

| Field | Description |
|---|---|
| 39 | Defines the address as a DCC ATM format |
| CCCC | Country code; 840F indicates U.S. (840 plus an F for pad) |
| RR | Registering body; 80 defines registration with ANSI |
| AAAAAA | The administrative authority (the organization that requested the registered NSAP) |
| WW.WW | Reserved |
| XX.XX.XX.XX | Routing domain (RD) and area; the field defined to be used in addressing your switches |
| YYYYYYYY… | End Station Identifier (ESI) |
| ZZ | Selector byte |

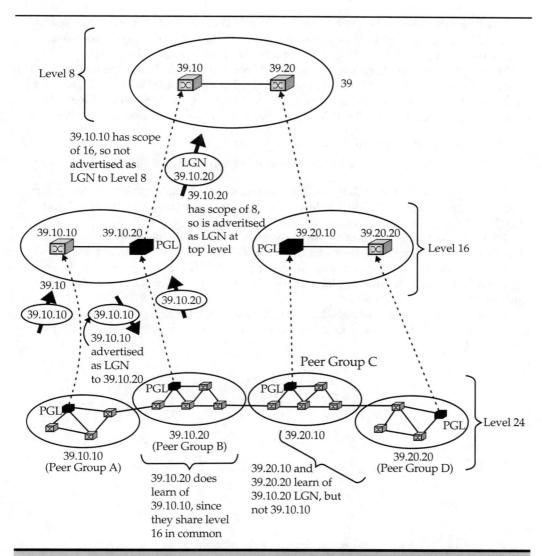

**Figure 16-26.**  *Node advertisement range controlled through scoping*

Much of an ATM address to be used in the public domain is fixed; the address portion 39.CCCC.RR.AAAAAA.WW.WW is assigned in the public network, and the remainder may be user-configured. In a PNNI environment, the default scope value is 96.

The scope value denotes a level in the PNNI hierarchy and indicates the highest level at which this address can be advertised or summarized. If an address has a scope indicating a level lower than the level of the node itself, the node will not advertise that address. This means that in a peer group of 39.10.20, the PGL will advertise its address in two ways:

- **In its own peer group**   It will advertise as 39.10.20.xx.
- **To the other LGNs**   It will advertise its group as LGN 39.10.20.

The purpose of this is so that the PGLs can quickly calculate the inter-peer group routes through the mesh, while the lower-level nodes calculate paths through their individual peer groups.

PNNI phase 1 is a vast improvement over IISP. Dynamic link state discovery, along with dynamic route determination, makes PNNI much easier to maintain and can make adds, moves, and changes much simpler. PNNI is also very fault-tolerant, with crankback mechanisms in place, and with optional rerouting support even in multihierarchical environments.

Although the concepts of PNNI are much more complex than those of IISP, it is a very robust protocol, it reconverges very quickly, and it is surprisingly easy to implement.

# The Complete Reference

Nortel Networks

# Chapter 17

## MultiProtocol Over ATM and the Next Hop Resolution Protocol

The function of MPOA is to identify data flows between host devices as they pass through a router, determine when they have exceeded a predefined threshold, and then determine the information required to eliminate the router hop(s) and initiate a direct connection between the ATM entities serving those hosts (LAN Emulation Clients, or LECs, for our purposes). This direct connection is called an *MPOA shortcut*, sometimes referred to as virtual routing.

Several components are required to accomplish these tasks:

- MPOA Client (MPC)
- MPOA Server (MPS)
- Next Hop Resolution Protocol (NHRP)
- NHRP Server (NHS) and NHRP Client (NHC)

The function of these components and how they interact to accomplish virtual routing are covered in this chapter, which includes both MPOA and the Next Hop Resolution Protocol that it utilizes.

MPOA was designed to support virtual routing involving higher-layer protocols; presently, however, only IPv4 shortcuts are supported on the Nortel Networks platform. For this reason, references within this chapter often refer to IP-to-ATM address associations, or the monitoring of IP traffic flow; in actuality, this eventually may be taken to mean any third-layer protocol.

# MultiProtocol over ATM

For MPOA to function, the LAN Emulation Services being used must all be LANEv2-compliant; LANEv2 supports the presence of MPCs and MPSs, which use the LECs to intercommunicate.

In addition to the concept of MPCs and MPSs, MPOA uses the concepts of ingress and egress MPCs, and ingress and egress MPSs. Although an MPOA shortcut may be a unidirectional or a bidirectional VCC, they are established by first using an address resolution process which is initiated by the ingress MPC. The ingress MPC communicates with its MPS (which acts as the ingress MPS). When the MPS communicates with the MPC which will act as the remote end of the shortcut, it acts as the egress MPS, and the MPC it communicates with is then acting as the egress MPC. Whether the shortcut is a unidirectional or bidirectional circuit, the address resolution procedure must be completed twice, once for each direction of the IP flow, before two-way communication can occur over the shortcut. Thus, important differences exist between, for example, the roles of the ingress MPC and the egress MPC. These differences are explained in the sections that follow, and throughout this chapter.

# MPOA Components

MPOA uses several components: LANEv2, the MPC, the MPS, and NHRP, which utilize an NHRP server (NHS) and an NHRP client (NHC). The terms *ingress* and *egress* are used in relation to the MPC and MPS, to indicate from where the MPOA shortcut is being initiated and to where it is destined. For example, an MPC that initiates an MPOA shortcut is known as the *ingress MPC*. An ingress MPC can also be an *egress MPC* if a remote MPC attempts to extend a shortcut to it. Using this scheme, the MPOA components can be broken down in the following manner:

- **LANEv2**   Necessary to support MPOA components and functionality.
- **Ingress MPC**   Any MPC detecting a data flow that exceeds the defined threshold, thus initiating a request to its MPS to resolve the destination ATM address associated with the destination third-layer address.
- **Ingress MPS**   Any MPS receiving a Resolution Request from an MPC.
- **Next Hop Resolution Protocol**   Used by the MPOA router function to locate a remote egress MPS.
- **Egress MPS**   The MPS that is associated with the destination network; meaning, the MPS that is mapped to a LEC, configured as an interface in the destination IP network. The ingress and egress MPS may be the same MPS.
- **Egress MPC**   Any MPC associated with the LEC that, in turn, is associated with the destination host; meaning, the MPC that exists on the node also containing the LEC serving the destination host.

Bear in mind that although the terms "ingress" and "egress" are associated with both the MPC and the MPS, this does not necessarily imply that an ingress MPC and egress MPC, or an ingress MPS and egress MPS, are always two separate components. The ingress MPS and egress MPS might well be the same MPS. For example, suppose that an MPS is mapped to two V2-capable LECs on an ATM router interface, and those LECs are members of two separate Emulated LANs (ELANs). If an MPC serving one ATM switch that has a LEC joined to the first ELAN initiates a shortcut to another MPC on another switch that serves a LEC in the second ELAN, then the single MPS acts as both the ingress and egress MPS.

Likewise, an MPC may be both the ingress and egress MPC; taking the previous example, but putting a second LEC in the second ELAN on the first switch, the MPC that serves both LECs may find itself both the ingress and egress MPC (see Figure 17-1).

## Bidirectional vs. Unidirectional MPOA Shortcuts

MPOA shortcuts may be bidirectional or unidirectional. For instance, if an ingress MPC initiates a shortcut to an egress MPC, data begins to pass toward the egress MPC over the shortcut, while the egress MPC, at first, continues to pass its traffic via the router.

ATM TECHNOLOGIES

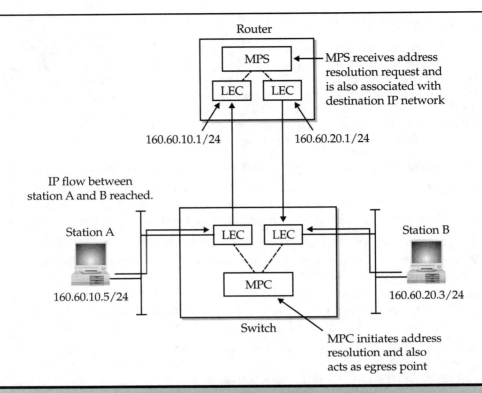

MPS receives address resolution request and is also associated with destination IP network

MPC initiates address resolution and also acts as egress point

**Figure 17-1.**    *MPS and MPC as both ingress and egress points*

Once the egress MPC detects the traffic flow as having reached the threshold, it acts as the ingress MPC and initiates its own MPOA Resolution Request.

After the address is resolved, and the egress MPC has had the appropriate DLL header information imposed, the ingress MPC will find a shortcut to the destination already in place, and may use the existing shortcut. Alternatively, the MPC may elect to create a new, dedicated shortcut. In this scenario, when a shortcut is created, data flows in only one direction over the shortcut, while the return path occurs through the router as normal, until a second shortcut can be built to accommodate the return traffic (see Figure 17-2).

**Note**    *Another common point of confusion regarding the terms "ingress" and "egress" in relation to MPOA is that "ingress" refers to data that is incoming to the MPC from the local side, not from the remote side; ingress is often thought of as data that is incoming from a remote source, but, in this instance, the remote MPC that is receiving the data over the shortcut is actually the egress MPC.*

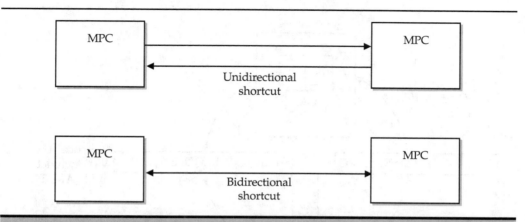

**Figure 17-2.** *Dual unidirectional MPOA shortcuts vs. a single bidirectional shortcut*

# Discovery of the MPC and MPS

For MPOA to function, each MPC must locate its MPS, and the MPS must, in turn, locate each MPC that it serves.

## Using Time, Length, and Value Indicators

To accomplish the dynamic discovery of the MPC and MPS, each uses its associated LEC or LECs. The MPC and MPS each communicates its control ATM address to each LEC with which it is associated. Each LEC then includes this information in its LE_ARP messages as encoded TLVs contained within the LE_ARP. These TLVs indicate the presence of the MPC or MPS, as well as the associated control ATM address of each.

Since all LECs must send an LE_ARP_REQUEST for an all-F's broadcast address to the LES during the LANE join phase, to obtain their BUS address, these TLVs will be communicated at that time. Likewise, because the LES then responds with an LE_ARP_RESPONSE containing the BUS address, the MPC and MPS information is quickly propagated among each LEC (see Figure 17-3). Those that are not learned during the join phase—due to the fact that, for instance, not all LECs had initiated their LE_ARP_REQUEST (containing their TLVs) prior to certain LECs receiving their LE_ARP_RESPONSE messages—will quickly be learned as LE_ARP messages are exchanged as part of normal LANE operations.

When the LE_ARP_RESPONSE is received by a LEC, the TLVs associated with remote MPCs or MPSs are communicated to the MPC or MPS the LEC is bound to. By using this procedure, the MPS and MPC quickly learn of one another's presence.

ATM TECHNOLOGIES

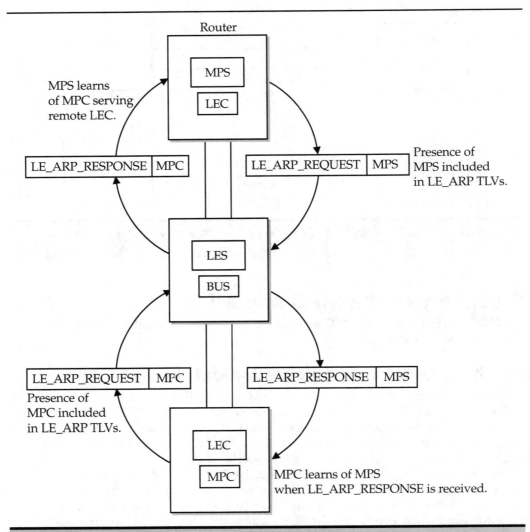

**Figure 17-3.**    *The MPC and MPS discovery process through LE_ARP TLVs*

## MPOA Overview

The goal of MPOA is to eliminate the router when hosts on different networks or subnetworks are communicating over ATM. This is done by establishing MPOA shortcut VCCs directly between the source and destination LECs, through LANEv2

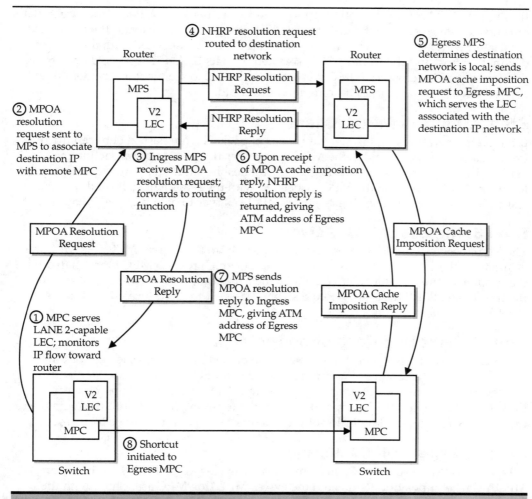

**Figure 17-4.** *Establishment of MPOA shortcut VCC*

and its support for the MPOA components, as well as NHRP. In basic terms, this is accomplished by using the following components and steps (see Figure 17-4).

## Step 1. Exceeding The IP Threshold

LECs in a LANEv2 ATM network are associated with the MPC that resides on their same ATM node. In a scenario where a legacy host in one ELAN is communicating through an ATM router to another legacy host in another ELAN, two Data Direct VCCs are created—one between the LEC associated with the source host and the router LEC associated with its ELAN, and another between the LEC associated with the destination host and the router LEC associated with its ELAN. The MPC monitors the flow of traffic across each LEC it is associated with, to see whether the data flow between two IP hosts reaches a predefined threshold.

## Step 2. Ingress MPOA Client

If the predefined threshold is met ($x$ number of packets were passed between the IP hosts in $y$ number of seconds), the MPC determines that this data transaction may benefit from an MPOA shortcut. The MPC initiates the shortcut by first attempting to learn the ATM address of the MPC associated with the remote host; it sends a request (called an *MPOA Resolution Request*) to its MPOA Server to obtain this ATM address.

## Step 3. Ingress MPOA Server

The MPS receives the MPOA Resolution Request from the ingress MPC (the MPC that is initiating the shortcut). It must then determine which remote MPC is associated with the destination host IP address. To do this, the MPS translates the MPOA Resolution Request to an NHRP Resolution Request, and passes it to its co-located next hop server (NHS).

## Step 4. Next Hop Resolution Protocol

The NHRP Resolution Request may need to be passed on through the network in the event that the receiving MPS is not mapped to a LEC which is associated with the destination network. Alternatively, if a single ATM router is routing between all ELANs, and a single MPS is mapped to each, the receiving MPS is both the ingress and the egress MPS, and the NHRP Resolution Request does not need to be forwarded.

## Step 5. Egress MPOA Server

When the NHRP Resolution Request reaches the egress MPS, this MPS initiates an MPOA Cache Imposition Request to the egress MPC (the MPC associated with the destination LEC), informing it of the DLL encapsulation information that it needs to be able to accommodate the MPOA shortcut. This is necessary because the source host will be sending frames to the destination IP address, but will use its default gateway router's MAC address as the destination MAC. The egress MPC needs the information required to ensure the data gets to the destination host; specifically, it needs the destination's default gateway router MAC address, and the destination MAC with the actual destination host's MAC address. This information is imposed on the egress MPC through the MPOA Cache Imposition Request. The egress MPC responds to this request with an MPOA Cache Imposition Reply, indicating that the information has been successfully cached, and that it is able to support an incoming VCC.

### Step 6. NHRP Revisited

When the egress MPS receives the Cache Imposition Reply from the egress MPC, it issues an NHRP Resolution Reply back towards the ingress MPS, indicating the destination ATM address of the MPC serving the LEC associated with the destination host.

### Step 7. Ingress MPS Revisited

Upon receipt of the NHRP Resolution Reply, the Ingress MPS is able to respond to the ingress MPC with the destination MPC's ATM address. The ingress MPC does not need to know the DLL information associated with the transfer, because the egress MPC will add the DLL header. At this point, the ingress MPC may initiate its shortcut.

### Step 8. Virtual Routing

The ingress MPC initiates either a bidirectional or unidirectional VCC directly to the egress MPC, bypassing the router altogether. This MPOA shortcut will be used either for traffic passing both ways, between the two communicating hosts, or as a one-way channel; either way, for the destination MPC to communicate directly with the source MPC without the use of the router, the remote MPC must detect the IP flow reaching the threshold, and initiate its own MPOA Resolution Request so that the appropriate DLL header information can be placed in each MPC's egress cache. The only difference between the two types of shortcuts in this case is that if a unidirectional shortcut is used, a new VCC must be built going back the other way, whereas if a bidirectional shortcut is used, the single VCC will be used for traffic flow in both directions.

## Functions of MPOA

The overview given in the previous section describes in loose terms what occurs in an ATM network configured to utilize MPOA; however, for MPOA to function, several key points must be addressed.

Consider what occurs in a scenario in which two hosts residing on different IP networks must communicate (see Figure 17-5), whereby station A is configured with IP address 160.60.10.123/24 and station B is configured with IP address 170.70.10.123/24, each residing in a different ELAN with an ATM router routing between them. Station A is aware that station B is on a different network, because of the IP address and subnet mask information it is configured with. Station A will not ARP for station B's MAC address, then, it will ARP for the MAC of its default gateway (if the default gateway's MAC isn't already in its ARP cache). Then Station A will send its data to station B using B's destination IP, with its own MAC as the source MAC address, and its local router interface's MAC (the local router LEC) as the destination MAC address. A Data Direct VCC is built between the LEC serving station A and the router LEC.

The local router LEC, upon receiving the data, routes it to the LEC that serves station B's ELAN (determined by the destination IP). Station B's local router interface

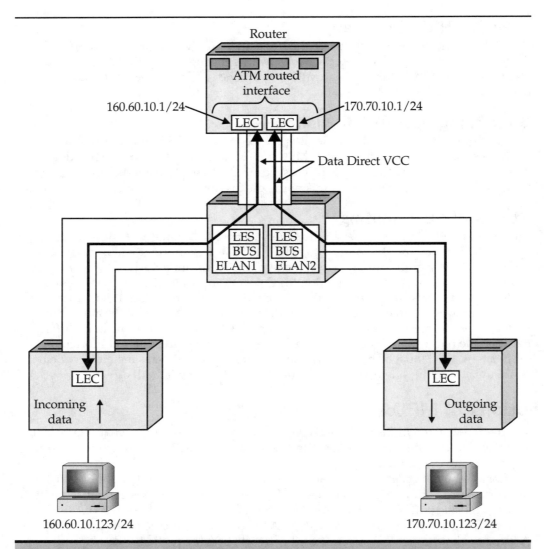

**Figure 17-5.**    *Station A communicating with station B through an ATM router*

(router LEC) then issues an LE_ARP_REQUEST to find the LEC serving station B. The address is resolved and station B's MAC address is obtained. The router LEC initiates a Data Direct VCC to the LEC serving station B. Data is then passed to station B, using a source IP of station A and a destination IP of station B, with a source MAC of station B's local router interface, and a destination MAC of station B.

Thus, station A never actually learns station B's MAC address. As this is the case, it can't simply send its data to station B across the newly formed MPOA shortcut that was described in the previous sections. More steps must occur to make this work correctly, which are part of the functionality of the MPC and MPS. The two main points that must be addressed are as follows:

■ The LEC serving station A builds a Data Direct VCC to the router LEC without the use of MPOA; it never learns the ATM address of the LEC that serves station B, so it can't request a VCC to that LEC without first determining which LEC address is associated with the destination IP.

■ Station A sends its data using its default gateway MAC as the destination MAC address, and never learns station B's MAC directly; it can't send directly to station B unless some mechanism is in place to resolve this fact.

MPOA resolves both of these problems by using the MPC, the NHRP protocol, and the MPS. The sections that follow describe exactly how the MPC and MPS function, as well as how they provide the information necessary to bypass the router altogether, and allow two hosts on different IP networks to intercommunicate directly across the ATM network.

## The MPOA Client

MPCs exist on ATM switches and will serve any number of LECs that may also exist on that same switch. An MPC supports all local LANEv2-capable LECs, regardless of which ELAN they are a member of. The MPC's function is to detect data flows that may benefit from an MPOA shortcut, and then initiate those connections.

Each MPC communicates with its MPS, which is configured on a router; by communicating with this MPS, the MPC is able to obtain the information it requires to accomplish the MPOA shortcuts it must build (see Figure 17-6).

The MPC acts as an intermediary between the LEC and the upper-layer protocols. A single MPC entity will serve all local LECs, and no one LEC may be bound to more than one MPC. Like a LEC, the MPC entity has a control ATM address that is associated with it specifically, though in the case of the MPC, the control ATM address may be the same as that of one of the LECs it serves. The MPC communicates this control address with each of its corresponding LECs, because the LECs must communicate the presence of the MPC in the TLV of each LE_ARP_RESPONSE message, letting the other MPOA and LANE components know of the presence of the MPC, as well as its control ATM address.

## MPC Addressing

Each switch has a variety of ATM addresses associated with its MPC. Each MPC has an *MPC control ATM address,* which is the primary address associated with the MPC entity

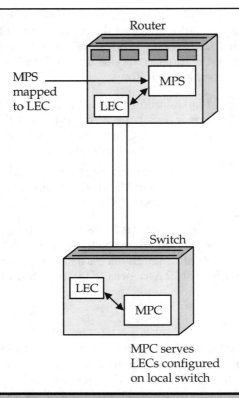

**Figure 17-6.**    *MPC relationship to LEC and MPS*

itself. In addition to this control address, each MPC has a series of *MPC data ATM addresses*; in the Centillion switch, these refer to the different cards that may be present (see Figure 17-7).

The reason for this scheme is that once the MPOA shortcut is initiated, it will extend from the ingress MPC to the egress MPC, not from the source LEC directly to the destination LEC. The MPCs still use the LECs, but the shortcut itself will be extended to the egress MPC data ATM address that is associated with the card on which the destination host resides.

## Using the LECS to Obtain Configuration Information

An MPC may be configured manually, or it may obtain its configuration information from a LAN Emulation Configuration Server (LECS). The LECS, as part of its LANEv2 enhancements, may be configured with both MPC and MPS configuration information,

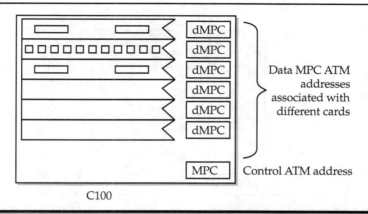

**Figure 17-7.**   *MPC control ATM address vs. MPC data ATM addresses*

so that multiple MPC and MPS entities may obtain their configuration information from a central source. The LECS in this scenario may be configured with any number of individual MPC and MPS configuration parameters, just as it may be configured with any number of individual ELAN entries. If the MPC (or MPS) is configured to use an automatic configuration mode, it will attempt to get this information from the LECS.

## The Role of the LANEv2 LECS

For a LECS to support the added TLVs utilized by MPOA, it must be LANEv2-capable; LANEv1 has no functionality to provide configuration information to MPOA components. In addition, at least one of the LECs served by the MPC must be LANEv2-capable, because the MPC will actually use the LEC to obtain its configuration. When a V2-capable LEC initiates the Configuration Direct VCC to the LECS, and an MPC is present on the switch that's housing the LEC, *and* the MPC residing on the switch is configured to obtain its configuration information from a LECS, the MPC will request this configuration information as part of the LE_CONFIGURE_REQUEST control frame. The LECS, upon receiving this request, returns the MPC configuration TLVs in the LE_CONFIGURE_RESPONSE frame sent back to the LEC (see Figure 17-8).

Once these TLVs are obtained by the MPC, no need exists to repeat the process; therefore, only one of the LECs being served by the MPC needs to be V2-capable, and only one LEC needs to utilize the LECS to receive its LES address.

## MPC Configuration TLVs

The TLVs that may be included in the MPC configuration portion of the V2-capable LECS include information required for protocol detection, as well as threshold

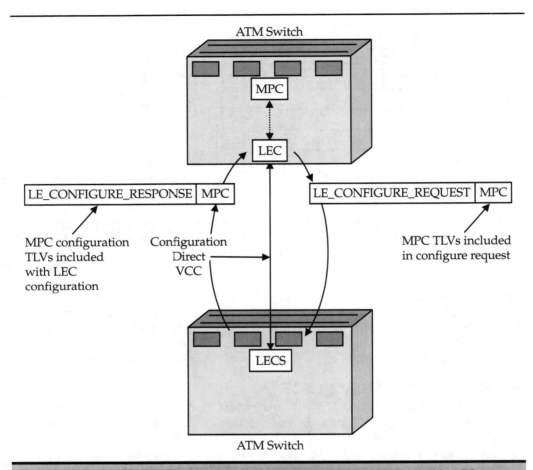

**Figure 17-8.** *MPC obtains configuration TLVs from LECS via V2 capable LEC*

monitoring for purposes of determining when a shortcut is appropriate and when it is not. The MPC TLVs are as follows:

- **Shortcut Setup Frame Count**   Used in conjunction with the Shortcut Setup Frame Time TLV; these values are used to define the threshold associated with the flow control of the specific internetworking protocol being monitored by the MPC. This TLV indicates the number of frames between the same source and destination internetworking address that must be detected prior to initiating an MPOA shortcut. These frames must be received within the defined Shortcut Setup Frame Time.

- **Shortcut Setup Frame Time**   Used in conjunction with the Shortcut Setup Frame Count; this value defines the amount of time in which the number of frames defined by the Shortcut Setup Frame Time must be detected. This means that $x$ frames must be detected in $y$ seconds, where $x$ is the Shortcut Setup Frame Count and $y$ is the Shortcut Setup Frame Time.

- **Flow Detection Protocols**   Defines which internetworking protocol flows will be monitored by MPOA for purposes of detecting whether or not the defined threshold has been met. Presently, the Nortel Networks platform is capable of monitoring IPv4 only.

- **MPC Initial Retry Time**   Indicates how long the MPC waits after sending a Resolution Request before assuming it has failed and reissuing another request.

- **MPC Retry Time Maximum**   Defines the longest period of time an MPC spends retrying a Resolution Request for which no Resolution Reply has been received.

- **Hold Down Time**   Indicates how long an MPOA shortcut remains in place before it needs to be refreshed.

# Inbound vs. Outbound Data Flows

The manner in which data is handled will differ depending on whether the MPC in question is the ingress MPC or the egress MPC:

- The ingress MPC detects the IP flow between the source and destination, and monitors this traffic flow to determine whether or not an MPOA shortcut is required. It also checks its ingress cache to make determinations regarding the specific MPS associated with a destination, as well as the destination IP and ATM address.

- The egress MPC is responsible for accepting the shortcut initiated by the ingress MPC, and caching the DLL header information imposed on it by the egress MPS. Since each MPC may act as both an ingress MPC and egress MPC, each MPC maintains both an ingress and egress cache.

## Ingress Traffic

Traffic originating from the internetworking layer toward a router LEC is monitored by the MPC to determine how much traffic is passing between a particular source and destination. To do this, the MPC first examines the destination MAC address to see whether this is the MAC address of an MPS entity (this information is learned at the time of MPS discovery, covered later in this chapter). Data with a destination MAC address of the MPS (in other words, the local router interface) is not local and must be bound for another network or subnetwork. The MPC then examines the upper-layer protocol associated with the traffic (the IP address or other internetworking protocol) to determine the destination address.

The MPC needs to know the destination Layer 3 address to monitor the IP flow, and because eventually it may need to build a shortcut to the LEC associated with that destination address. The first step in doing this is to find the MPS that is mapped to a LEC that serves that network or subnetwork. Once this is accomplished, the MPC can obtain, for instance, the IP-to-ATM address association and initiate a connection directly to the remote LEC.

The first thing that the MPC does, however, upon detecting that the traffic flow being monitored has reached the defined threshold and will require a shortcut, is to check its ingress cache to see whether the IP-to-ATM address association is already there.

## The MPC Ingress Cache

The MPC ingress cache contains information regarding which MPSs are associated with which destination IP hosts, and the destination MPC ATM address associated with each grouping. Once an MPOA address resolution has taken place, the MPC will have obtained the ATM address of the MPS associated with the destination IP network, and the ATM address of the MPC associated with the destination IP address (the MPC associated with the LEC serving that IP host). Should the ingress MPC need to establish a shortcut connection to a remote MPC, it checks to see if the destination IP host address and its associated MPS are located in its ingress cache; if it is, the MPC may initiate a shortcut to the egress MPC address associated with that ingress cache entry. If the ATM address of the egress MPC for the destination IP address is not currently in the ingress cache, then the MPC must resolve this address by using an MPOA Resolution Request; this procedure is covered in the sections that follow.

## Determining the MPS Control ATM Address

If the MPC does indeed detect data flow using the MPS destination MAC, it determines which MPS control address the MAC is associated with. It does this so that the MPS and MPC may serve multiple LECs that are all members of different ELANs. Each router LEC in this case has its own MAC address, so a series of destination MAC addresses may be related to a single MPS; however, since multiple MPSs may exist on a router, it doesn't make sense that the MAC address of each router LEC (MPS destination MAC) is associated with the same MPS (see Figure 17-9), although each may be.

This information is determined by examining the LE_ARP cache; since each LEC indicates in its LE_ARP messages the control ATM address of its associated MPS, the MPC can determine which MPS is associated with which LEC. Once the specific MPS control address is determined, the ingress cache is checked to see whether the specific

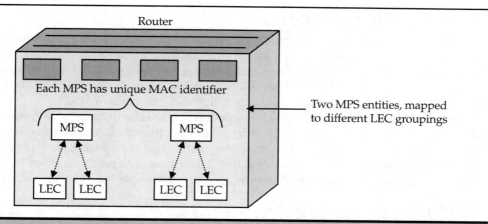

**Figure 17-9.**    *Different MPS destination MAC addresses associated with individual MPSs*

MPS control address is associated with the destination IP address. A typical entry in the ingress cache contains the following information:

- **MPS Control ATM Address**    Multiple MPS entities may exist within a single network; this ingress cache information defines which MPS is mapped to a LEC serving the destination IP host's network or subnetwork.

- **Destination IP Address**    The destination IP address of the destination host, associated with the MPS control ATM address.

- **Destination ATM Address**    Address associated with one of two things: if the destination host is a legacy host, then this address is the ATM address of the egress MPC associated with that host; if the destination host is actually an ATM-attached device, then this address is the actual ATM address of the destination host. If a VCC is already built to this address (an MPOA shortcut has already been created, but is currently idle), then the specific VCC is indicated here.

- **Encapsulation Information**    Defines the encapsulation method and type used if the data flow is transmitted over a formed MPOA shortcut (RFC 1483 LLC encapsulation for routed protocols by default).

- **Other Configuration Information**    Indicates the specific parameters and configuration information used by the MPC, such as timing information and flow count.

# MPOA Resolution Requests

After the ingress MPC detects that the traffic threshold has been reached, if there is no related entry in its ingress cache, it issues an MPOA Resolution Request control frame. This frame, like all MPOA control and data protocol data units (PDUs) may be sent over any valid VCC that extends to the MPS; this may be an existing VCC that was already in place, or, if no suitable VCC exists, the MPC may initiate one.

After the VCC is in place, the MPOA Resolution Request is sent to the MPS, to resolve the internetworking address-to-ATM address binding. In this case, the internetworking address is the IP address of the destination host, and the ATM address is the egress MPC data ATM address that is associated with that legacy host. The fields included in the MPOA Resolution Request contain the following information, with the following meanings:

- **Source Protocol Address**   Can be either a null value or, alternatively, the protocol address associated with the MPC.

- **Destination Protocol Address**   Indicates the destination host IP address.

- **Source NBMA Address**   Indicates the ingress MPC's (the MPC initiating the MPOA Resolution Request) data ATM address.

- **Extensions**   Include an empty MPOA Egress Cache Tag extension and an MPOA ATM Service Category extension.

When captured in a sniffer trace, these individual details can be interpreted. For instance, the following example shows an MPOA Resolution Request that was initiated by in ingress MPC when the data flow between a source station, and destination host 180.80.17.12 reached its threshold. The destination IP address is given to the MPS, asking for address resolution, and the source nonbroadcast multiaccess (NBMA) address is also given (the ingress MPC ATM address).

```
SUMMARY    Destination        Source        Summary
  133      DTE              DCE.0.43        MPOA Resolution Request

MPOA: ----- MPOA -----
MPOA:
MPOA: MPOA fixed header
MPOA:    Link layer type      = 3
MPOA:    Protocol type        = 0800
MPOA:    SNAP                 = 0000000000
MPOA:    Hop count            = 5
MPOA:    Packet size        = 72
MPOA:    Checksum           = 6F42
MPOA:    Extension offset   = 64
MPOA:    Op version         = 1(NHRP)
MPOA:    MPOA packet type   = 86x(Resolution Request)
```

```
MPOA:    NBMA address
MPOA:       Reserved              = 0... ....
MPOA:       Address type          = .0.. ....(NSAP)
MPOA:       Address length        = 20
MPOA:    NBMA subaddress
MPOA:       Reserved              = 0... ....
MPOA:       Address type          = .0.. ....(NSAP)
MPOA:       Address length        = 0
MPOA:
MPOA: Source protocol address length      = 0
MPOA: Destination protocol address length = 4
MPOA: Flags       = 0(unused)
MPOA: Request ID = 2
MPOA: Source NBMA address         =
3920000000000000000000AA00020E09EF2000F2
MPOA: Destination protocol address = [180.80.17.12]
```

**Note**

*In the preceding code section, the source MPC (source NBMA address) is listed, as well as the IP address of the destination station. This indicates that this MPC wants to initiate a shortcut to the MPC associated with the destination station, and a Resolution Request is sent to determine the egress MPC data ATM address.*

```
MPOA:
MPOA: CIE
MPOA:    Code                  = 0(Successful Registration)
MPOA:    Prefix length         = 0
MPOA:    Unused                = 0
MPOA:    Max transmission unit = 0(invalid)
MPOA:    Holding time          = 0 seconds
MPOA:    Client address
MPOA:       Reserved           = 0... ....
MPOA:       Address type       = .0.. ....(NSAP)
MPOA:       Address length     = 0
MPOA:    Client subaddress
MPOA:       Reserved           = 0... ....
MPOA:       Address type       = .0.. ....(NSAP)
MPOA:       Address length     = 0
MPOA:    Client protocol length = 0
MPOA:    Preference            = 0
MPOA:
MPOA: Compulsory bit    = 0... ....
MPOA: Extension type    = 1001x(MPOA Egress Cache Tag Extension)
MPOA: Length            = 0
MPOA: Valid end of extensions
```

*In the preceding section of code, the Egress Cache Tag associated with this particular data flow is included, so that this data flow can be uniquely identified at the egress MPC.*

# Outbound Traffic

The egress MPC is responsible for accepting the VCC shortcut initiated by the ingress MPC; however, it can't forward any packets until it has established the proper egress cache entry for the transfer. This goes back to the problem outlined in the sections that overview the MPOA protocol: a host on one IP network can't communicate directly with a host on another IP network without some kind of intervention, because when communicating across IP networks, the sending station sends its data using its default gateway MAC address as the destination MAC, and never learns the destination host MAC directly. The destination host's local router interface learns its MAC, since it is the local router interface that, in the absence of MPOA, sends the data on to the destination host.

In a LANE environment, because the sending host is most often a legacy device, there is no way to prevent it from sending data with a destination MAC of its default gateway; the MPOA protocol must resolve this, and it does so by placing an entry in the egress MPC's egress cache containing the necessary DLL header information. This cache entry, called an *egress cache entry*, is actually originated by the egress MPS by issuing an MPOA Cache Imposition Request. This control frame provides the egress MPC with the MAC-layer information necessary to allow the sending station's data to be sent directly to the destination station. Upon receiving an MPOA Cache Imposition Request, the egress MPC must return an MPOA Cache Imposition Reply, indicating the information was cached and that it is capable of accepting a shortcut VCC.

## The MPC Egress Cache

The egress MPC, upon receiving data over a shortcut, checks its egress cache for a matching IP-to-ATM address binding, or it looks for a matching egress cache tag. An egress tag can be used to differentiate between egress cache entries that sport the same source and destination ATM address but different DLL header information. An MPOA egress cache tag can also be uniquely assigned to every egress cache entry, in which case each entry can be distinguished by its tag alone.

A match for an egress cache entry must include the source and destination ATM addresses, as well as the destination IP address. The actual egress cache entry consists of several pieces of information, which are listed here:

- **Destination IP Address**   The IP address of the destination IP host.
- **Source ATM Address**   The ATM address of the ingress MPC.
- **Destination ATM Address**   The egress MPC data ATM address, associated with the destination internetworking address.

- **Tag (if used)**   May be used either to provide a unique identity to cache entries that share the same source and destination ATM address but different DLL header information, or to provide a unique identity for every individual cache entry, allowing them to be identified by the tag value alone.

- **LEC**   This is the LEC associated with the egress MPC. It is used in the event that an egress cache hit occurs, but the destination MAC address included in the DLL header information is no longer associated with the destination host's LEC. Should this occur, the egress MPC may forward packets received over the shortcut to the LEC, to refresh the bridge entry.

- **DLL Header Information**   Includes the MAC-layer address of the destination host's local router interface (default gateway), as well as the MAC-layer address of the actual destination host. Also included is a Protocol ID defining which internetworking protocol is being used.

- **Other Configuration Information**   Includes configuration information, such as the Holding Time, and other MPC-specific parameters.

### Utilizing the Egress Cache Entry

The egress MPC must use its egress cache entries to resolve the MAC-layer addressing between the source and destination hosts; remember that data passing over the shortcut to be received by the egress MPC has a source IP address of the source host, a destination IP address of the destination host, a source MAC address of the sending host, and a destination MAC address of the source host's local router interface. The egress MPC must use the appropriate egress cache entry to encapsulate the incoming frames with the appropriate DLL header information: the IP source and destination remain the same, while the source MAC address is changed to that of the destination host's local router interface, and the destination MAC address is changed to the MAC address of the destination host (see Figure 17-10).

## Sending MPOA Cache Imposition Replies to the MPS

Once the egress MPC receives an MPOA Cache Imposition Request from the egress MPS (covered in the next section, "The MPOA Server"), it must respond with an MPOA Cache Imposition Reply, indicating that the cache entry has been made and that the incoming shortcut VCC can be accommodated by the egress MPC. The MPOA Cache Imposition Reply contains the following information:

- **Source Protocol Address**   The protocol address (IP) of the egress MPS (the MPS to which the MPOA Cache Imposition Reply is being sent).

- **Destination Protocol Address**   The protocol address (IP) of the destination host.

- **Source NBMA Address**   The ingress MPC data ATM address.

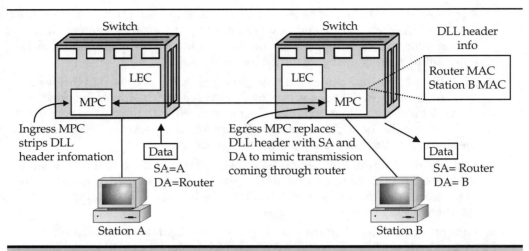

**Figure 17-10.**    *Egress MPC using imposed DLL header information to allow direct internetwork communication*

- ■ **Client NBMA Address**    The egress MPC's (the MPC issuing the MPOA Cache Imposition Reply to the MPS) data ATM address.
- ■ **Extensions**    Any received extensions.

The following is an example of an MPOA Cache Imposition Reply sent to the egress MPS (using source protocol address 180.80.17.1) by an egress MPC that is associated with destination address 180.80.17.12:

```
SUMMARY     Destination  Source        Summary
   169      DTE          DCE.0.45          MPOA Cache Imposition Reply

MPOA: ----- MPOA -----
MPOA:
MPOA: MPOA fixed header
MPOA:   Link layer type      = 3
MPOA:   Protocol type        = 0800
MPOA:   SNAP                 = 0000000000
MPOA:   Hop count            = 5
MPOA:   Packet size        = 127
MPOA:   Checksum           = 71A2MPOA:   Extension offset    = 88
MPOA:   Op version         = 1(NHRP)
MPOA:   MPOA packet type   = 81x(Cache Imposition Reply)
MPOA:   NBMA address
MPOA:      Reserved          = 0... ....
```

```
MPOA:       Address type          = .0.. ....(NSAP)
MPOA:       Address length        = 20
MPOA:    NBMA subaddress
MPOA:       Reserved              = 0... ....
MPOA:       Address type          = .0.. ....(NSAP)
MPOA:       Address length        = 0
MPOA:
MPOA: Source protocol address length   = 4
MPOA: Destination protocol address length = 4
MPOA: Flags      = 0
MPOA: Request ID = 0
MPOA: Source NBMA address          = 39200000000000000000000AA00020E09EF2000F2
MPOA: Source protocol address      = [180.80.17.1]
MPOA: Destination protocol address = [180.80.17.12]
MPOA:
MPOA: CIE
MPOA:    Code                = 0(Successful Registration)
MPOA:    Prefix length       = 0
MPOA:    Unused              = 0
MPOA:    Max transmission unit = 1516
MPOA:    Holding time        = 0(unused)
MPOA:    Client address      = 20
MPOA:    Client subaddress   = 0(not present)
MPOA:    Client protocol length= 0(not present)
MPOA:    Preference          = 0
MPOA:    Client NBMA address     = 39200000000000000000000000E09A2020001F0
MPOA:
MPOA:    Compulsory bit   = 1... ....
MPOA:    Extension type   = 1000x(MPOA DLL header extension)
MPOA:    Length           = 23
MPOA:    Cache ID         = 2
MPOA:    ELAN ID          = 2
MPOA:    DLL header length = 14
MPOA:    DLL header        = 0008L7606A800000A2LB2BE70800
MPOA:
MPOA:    Compulsory bit   = 1... ....
MPOA:    Extension type   = 1000x(MPOA DLL header extension)
MPOA:    Length           = 23
MPOA:    Cache ID         = 2
MPOA:    ELAN ID          = 2
MPOA:    DLL header length = 14
MPOA:    DLL header        = 0008C760BA800000A2CB2BE70800
MPOA: Compulsory bit    = 0... ....
MPOA: Extension type    = 1001x(MPOA egress cache tag extension)
MPOA: Length            = 4
MPOA: Egress cache ID   = 4194305
MPOA: Valid end of extensions
```

ATM TECHNOLOGIES

# The MPOA Server

The role of the MPS is to field MPOA Resolution Requests from individual MPCs, resolve internetworking-to-ATM address information, and make egress cache impositions on egress MPCs to resolve MAC-layer addressing, in order to allow hosts on different networks or subnetworks to communicate directly. The MPS is also responsible for passing MPOA Resolution Requests for hosts on networks which are not local up to the co-located Next Hop Server (NHS) as NHRP resolution requests.

The MPS resides on a router and is mapped to a series of LECs. The MPS, like the MPC, may act as either the ingress MPS, the egress MPS, or both simultaneously. Unlike the MPC, however, multiple MPS entities may be configured on a single router, with different groupings of LECs mapped to them.

To fulfill its role in resolving destination internetwork layer addresses to their associated egress MPC data ATM addresses, the MPS uses NHRP; this is in part used to determine whether or not the MPS receiving the MPOA Resolution Request is in fact the egress MPS, and, if it is not, to determine which MPS in the ATM network is the egress MPS. Each MPS, then, uses a co-located Next Hop Server (NHS), which is a component of the NHRP protocol, to make these determinations (see Figure 17-11).

The MPS is able to interpret both MPOA Requests and Replies from its remote MPCs, as well as NHRP Requests and Replies from both its local and any remote NHS entities.

## Using the LECS to Obtain Configuration Information

Like the MPC, the MPS may also obtain its configuration information automatically from a LECS; this function occurs in essentially the same way as with an MPC. The MPS receives its configuration TLVs from the LECS at the time one of the V2-capable LECs establishes the Configuration Direct VCC with the LECS and

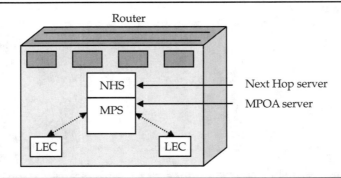

**Figure 17-11.**    *The MPS and its relation to the NHS and other MPOA components*

the LE_CONFIGURE_REQUEST and LE_CONFIGURE_RESPONSE control frames are exchanged.

The following configuration information may be attributed to the MPS:

■ **Keep-Alive Time**    Indicates how frequently the MPS expects to receive Keep-Alive messages. This TLV works in conjunction with the Keep-Alive Lifetime TLV, and should be a value consistent with the Keep-Alive's lifetime. For instance, if the Keep-Alive Lifetime is set to 20 seconds, and the Keep-Alive Time is set to 25 seconds, connection to the MPS will continually time out. It is a good idea to keep the ratio between the two values at least 2:1; the MPS should be able to miss at least one Keep-Alive without assuming something has gone wrong.

■ **Keep-Alive Lifetime**    Indicates the amount of time the MPS considers a Keep-Alive message to be valid. This TLV works in conjunction with the Keep-Alive Time. The Keep-Alive Lifetime should exceed the Keep-Alive Time by at least 50 percent, so that a single missed Keep-Alive message does not automatically indicate a failure.

■ **Internetwork-Layer Protocols**    Indicates which internetworking protocols the MPS supports; presently, the Nortel Networks platform supports IPv4 only.

■ **MPS Initial Retry Time**    Indicates the period the MPS waits before retrying a Resolution Request for which it has not received a response.

■ **MPS Retry Time Maximum**    Indicates the cumulative amount of time the MPS attempts to retry Resolution Requests for which it has not received a response. The number of actual retries that occur is determined both by this value and by the Initial Retry Time.

■ **MPS Give-up Time**    Indicates the minimum amount of time the MPS waits without receiving a Resolution Reply before it assumes it to be lost and gives up on it.

■ **Holding Time**    Indicates the default holding time to be used in NHRP Resolution Replies.

## Mapping the MPS to a LEC or LECs

An MPS configured on a router may be mapped to one or more LECs; an MPS may be mapped to all local LECs, or it may be mapped only to a subset of them, if more than one MPS is desired. Once mapped to a LEC, the MPS maintains a status for all ingress and egress cache entries for each MPC it serves within that ELAN.

By doing this, the MPS is able to keep track of which cache entries are associated with which MPCs, and therefore has knowledge of which MPCs need to be updated in the event that one of the cache entries becomes invalid and needs to be purged. For more information regarding cache maintenance and cache purges, consult the sections on cache maintenance later in this chapter.

ATM TECHNOLOGIES

# MPS Processing of MPOA Resolution Requests

When an MPC has monitored the IP flow between a specific source and destination and the defined traffic threshold has been met, it issues an MPOA Resolution Request to the MPS if there is no current ingress cache entry for the destination. The purpose of this frame is to determine the ATM address associated with the destination IP address (the egress MPC data ATM address). The MPS takes this Resolution Request and, in turn, uses NHRP to make the actual address resolution so that it can formulate a Resolution Reply to the requesting MPC.

## Using NHRP to Make Address Resolutions

Two pieces of information are crucial to setting up an MPOA shortcut:

- The ingress MPC must know to which destination ATM address to build the VCC.

- The egress MPC must learn the appropriate DLL header information, to ensure that the data sent to the destination is properly addressed at the MAC layer.

However, the proper egress MPS must also be located as a precursor to discovering the destination ATM address. This is accomplished by using NHRP.

NHRP is used after an MPS receives an MPOA Resolution Request from an ingress MPC; at this point, the MPS is aware that an MPOA flow control threshold has been reached, and that the ingress MPC wants to build a VCC directly to the destination ATM address, bypassing the router. If multiple MPSs exist, the MPS receiving the MPOA Resolution Request may not be mapped to any LEC that serves the destination's IP network. If this is the case, then the appropriate egress MPS must be discovered. To do this, the MPOA Resolution Request is translated into an NHRP Resolution Request and is sent along to be routed toward the destination network.

### Translating the MPOA Resolution Request

After an MPOA Resolution Request frame is received from the ingress MPC, the ingress MPS translates it into an NHRP Resolution Request, in an attempt to resolve the address information on behalf of the MPC. It then forwards the request via the Next Hop Server along the routed path to the MPS associated with the destination IP network; alternatively, the destination network may be local and the NHRP Resolution Request may not need to be forwarded.

### Translating the NHRP Resolution Request and Making the Cache Imposition

After the NHRP Resolution Request is received by the remote NHS and handed down to the egress MPS (the MPS serving the destination host's network or subnetwork), the egress MPS must determine which remote LEC is associated with the destination IP address; if the information is already cached, it checks the router's current ARP cache to determine the DLL header information associated with the destination host. If it does not currently know which remote LEC is associated with the destination host, this must be determined through an LE_ARP_REQUEST.

Additionally, after the remote LEC associated with the destination host is discovered, the MPS must check to make certain the destination LEC is V2-capable and is being served by an MPC. If these criteria are met, then the egress MPS translates the NHRP Resolution Request into an MPOA Cache Imposition Request, which in turn is sent to the egress MPC. This Cache Imposition Request includes the DLL header information that the egress MPC will need to correctly encapsulate the incoming shortcut frames. The egress MPC responds with an MPOA Cache Imposition Reply, sent back to the egress MPS. This Cache Imposition Reply includes the data ATM address of the egress MPC.

### Translating the Cache Imposition Reply into an NHRP Resolution Reply

The egress MPS at this point translates the MPOA Cache Imposition Reply into an NHRP Resolution Reply; the destination ATM address has been acquired, and the egress MPC has been given the DLL header information it requires. The egress MPC, in return, has indicated that it received and cached the information, and is able to accept an incoming VCC from the ingress MPC.

### Translating the NHRP Resolution Reply into the MPOA Resolution Reply

After the ingress MPS receives the NHRP Resolution Reply, indicating the destination ATM address associated with the destination host's internetworking address, the NHRP Resolution Reply is translated into an MPOA Resolution Reply, to indicate to the ingress MPC the destination ATM address for the MPOA shortcut. Part of the reason this conversion is necessary is that NHRP is primarily concerned with the internetworking protocol next hop, for purposes of locating the destination host internetworking address. Since LECs (and MPCs) do not utilize third-layer addressing schemes, the NHRP Resolution Reply can't be sent directly to the MPC, so the MPS that resides on the router handles the translation.

## Making MPOA Cache Imposition Requests

After the MPS receives the NHRP Resolution Request from the co-located NHS (indicating that one of the LECs it serves is associated with the destination internetworking address), the egress MPS must determine which particular remote LEC is associated with the destination host. Once this is accomplished (via LE_ARP), the egress MPS must insert information into the egress MPC's egress cache; this is accomplished through a control frame called an *MPOA Cache Imposition Request*.

This MPOA Cache Imposition Request informs the egress MPC of the DLL header information it requires for the shortcut; remember, the sending station does not know of the destination host's MAC-layer address, because it sends data to its default gateway's MAC-layer address, not the actual destination host's address. The egress MPC will receive the frames that are destined for the destination host, and add the new DLL header information (the original DLL header is stripped by the ingress MPC prior to forwarding over the shortcut), indicating the destination MAC address is that of the destination host and the source MAC address is that of the local (to the destination host) router interface (LEC). The MPOA Cache Imposition Request contains the following information:

- **Source Protocol Address**  The protocol (IP) address of the egress MPS.
- **Destination Protocol Address**  The destination IP address of the destination host device.
- **Source NBMA Address**  The ingress MPC's data ATM address.
- **Holding Time**  Defined in the MPOA specification as a value greater than or equal to the holding time multiplied by 2. This is the amount of time the receiving egress MPC may consider the information given to it by the egress MPS to be valid; the egress MPS in this case guarantees that the information given will be updated or purged if it changes prior to the expiration of the Holding Time, so the egress MPC may use the information without validation for the duration of that time, unless something on its local end occurs that invalidates the information.
- **Extensions**  Include any received extensions, along with the MPOA DLL header information the egress MPC requires to receive the MPOA shortcut and process the incoming frames; this information includes the Cache ID, the ELAN ID, and the DLL header information itself.

Below is an example of a sniffer trace, capturing the MPOA Cache Imposition Request as it is issued to the egress MPC by the MPS:

```
SUMMARY    Destination   Source        Summary
   168     DCE           DTE.0.45         MPOA Cache Imposition Request

MPOA: ----- MPOA -----
MPOA:
MPOA: MPOA fixed header
MPOA:    Link layer type      = 3
MPOA:    Protocol type        = 0800
MPOA:    SNAP                 = 0000000000
MPOA:    Hop count            = 99
MPOA:    Packet size        = 103
```

```
MPOA:    Checksum              = 056F
MPOA:    Extension offset      = 68
MPOA:    Op version            = 1(NHRP)
MPOA:    MPOA packet type      = 80x(Cache Imposition Request)
MPOA:    NBMA address
MPOA:      Reserved                = 0... ....
MPOA:      Address type            = .0.. ....(NSAP)
MPOA:      Address length          = 20
MPOA:    NBMA subaddress
MPOA:      Reserved                = 0... ....
MPOA:      Address type            = .0.. ....(NSAP)
MPOA:      Address length          = 0
MPOA:
MPOA: Source protocol address length    = 4
MPOA: Destination protocol address length = 4
MPOA: Flags      = 0
MPOA: Request ID = 0
MPOA: Source NBMA address       =
3920000000000000000000AA00020E09EF2000F2
MPOA: Source protocol address    = [180.80.17.1]
MPOA: Destination protocol address = [180.80.17.12]
```

| Note | *In the preceding code section, the source MPC ATM address is given as the source NBMA address; however, the source protocol address is the IP address of the router. The destination protocol address (the IP address of the destination station) is listed as well. This indicates to the receiving MPC the source MPC, the MPS router IP, and the destination host IP.* |
| --- | --- |

```
MPOA:
MPOA: CIE
MPOA:    Code                  = 0(Successful Registration)
MPOA:    Prefix length         = 32
MPOA:    Unused                = 0
MPOA:    Max transmission unit = 1514
MPOA:    Holding time          = 2400 seconds
MPOA:    Client address
MPOA:    Reserved              = 0... ....
MPOA:    Address type          = .0.. ....(NSAP)
MPOA:    Address length        = 0
MPOA:    Client subaddress
MPOA:    Reserved              = 0... ....
```

```
MPOA:    Address type          = .0.. ....(NSAP)
MPOA:    Address length        = 0
MPOA:    Client protocol length = 0
MPOA:    Preference            = 0
MPOA:
MPOA: Compulsory bit     = 1... ....
MPOA: Extension type     = 1000x(MPOA DLL Header Extension)
MPOA: Length             = 23
MPOA:    Cache ID        = 2
MPOA:    ELAN ID         = 2
MPOA:    DLL Header Length = 14
MPOA:    DLL Header       = 0008C7606A800000A2CB2BE70800
```

> **Note**  *In the preceding code section, the ELAN ID is given for this ELAN, along with the data-link layer (DLL) header information required. The first six octets of the DLL header string are the MAC address of the destination station. The next six octets are the MAC address of the router. The remaining value of 0800 indicates the Protocol ID for the IP protocol.*

```
MPOA:
MPOA: Compulsory bit     = 0... ....
MPOA: Extension type     = 1001x(MPOA Egress Cache Tag Extension)
MPOA: Length             = 0
MPOA: Valid end of extensions
```

## Issuing MPOA Resolution Replies

After the MPS resolves the IP-to-ATM address binding for the destination IP host, it translates the NHRP Resolution Reply into an MPOA Resolution Reply and sends it to the ingress MPC. This is the final step before the ingress MPC actually initiates the shortcut VCC to the egress MPC, or, if a bidirectional shortcut is being used and is already in place, the ingress MPC begins sending data over the existing shortcut.

The MPOA Resolution Reply contains the same information as the NHRP Resolution Reply, but is in a slightly different format, because it will be delivered to a second-layer component only. The MPOA Resolution Reply contains the following information:

- **Source Protocol Address**   May be a null value or, alternatively, may be the ingress MPC address taken from the original MPOA Resolution Request.
- **Destination Protocol Address**   The destination host's protocol address (IP).
- **Source NBMA Address**   The ingress MPC's data ATM address.

- **Client Protocol Address**   The protocol address (IP) associated with the egress MPS.

- **Holding Time**   The shortcut holding time.

- **Client NBMA Address**   The egress MPC data ATM address.

- **Extensions**   Include any received extensions.

The following is an example of an MPOA Resolution Reply, as captured in a sniffer trace:

```
SUMMARY     Destination    Source        Summary
   187      DCE            DTE.0.43           MPOA Resolution Reply

MPOA: ----- MPOA -----
MPOA:
MPOA: MPOA fixed header
MPOA:    Link layer type       = 3
MPOA:    Protocol type         = 0800
MPOA:    SNAP                  = 0000000000
MPOA:    Hop count             = 5
MPOA:    Packet size           = 127
MPOA:    Checksum              = F630
MPOA:    Extension offset      = 88
MPOA:    Op version            = 1(NHRP)
MPOA:    MPOA packet type      = 87x(Resolution Reply)
MPOA:    NBMA address
MPOA:       Reserved           = 0... ....
MPOA:       Address type       = .0.. ....(NSAP)
MPOA:       Address length     = 20
MPOA:    NBMA subaddress
MPOA:       Reserved           = 0... ....
MPOA:       Address type       = .0.. ....(NSAP)
MPOA:       Address length     = 0
MPOA:
MPOA: Source protocol address length      = 0
MPOA: Destination protocol address length = 4
MPOA: Flags        = 0(unused)
MPOA: Request ID = 2
MPOA: Source NBMA address
               = 3920000000000000000000AA00020E09EF2000F2
MPOA: Destination protocol address = [160.60.10.123]
MPOA:
```

```
MPOA: CIE
MPOA:    Code                  = 0(Successful Registration)
MPOA:    Prefix length         = 0(unused)
MPOA:    Unused                = 0
MPOA:    Max transmission unit = 1516(unused)
MPOA:    Holding time          = 1200(unused)
MPOA:    Client address        = 20(invalid)
MPOA:    Client subaddress     = 0(not present)
MPOA:    Client protocol length= 0(not present)
MPOA:    Preference            = 0
MPOA:    Client NBMA address=
MPOA:            = 39200000000000000000000000000E09A2020001F0
MPOA:
MPOA: Compulsory bit    = 0... ....
MPOA: Extension type    = 1001x(MPOA Egress Cache Tag Extension)
MPOA: Length            = 0
MPOA: Valid end of extensions
```

# MPOA Keep-Alive Protocol

To further maintain existing cache entries, an MPS must periodically let each of its MPCs know that it is still operational and still maintaining its active entries. To accomplish this, each MPS must issue MPOA Keep-Alive messages at regular intervals to each MPC with which it is associated.

MPOA Keep-Alive messages may be transmitted over any existing LLC/SNAP VCC between the MPS and an MPC, or alternatively, the MPS may create a point-to-multipoint VCC to each MPC specifically for the purpose of sending Keep-Alive messages (although the Keep-Alive messages should generally keep the circuit up regardless, provided the Keep-Alive Lifetime does not exceed the VCC timeout period).

## Receiving MPOA Keep-Alive Messages

Each MPC expects to receive MPOA Keep-Alive messages within the amount of time, specified within the MPOA Keep-Alive itself. Each Keep-Alive message sent by the MPS contains the following information:

- **Control ATM Address**   The control ATM address of the sending MPS.

- **Keep-Alive Lifetime**   Indicates for how long the MPOA Keep-Alive is valid, which means the amount of time that may pass before the MPC should expect to see another MPOA Keep-Alive.

- **Sequence Number**   A sequence number used to identify possible interruptions in the Keep-Alive protocol.

Each MPC interprets each received Keep-Alive message, looking for any possible discrepancies. If an MPC does not receive an MPOA Keep-Alive within the amount of time specified by the Keep-Alive Lifetime, it assumes the MPS to have failed. Likewise, if there is an interruption in the order of the sequence number, the MPC interprets this as an indication of an MPS failure that may have caused it to reinitialize; this is considered a failure of the MPS, as well, and even though Keep-Alive messages are still being received after the interruption, the MPC must behave as though the information received from the MPS is no longer valid.

### Detecting an MPS Failure

If an MPC does detect a failure of the MPS (no Keep-Alive is received within the Keep-Alive Lifetime, or an interruption in the sequence number occurs), then it must invalidate all entries given to it by that MPS. Cache entries based on this information must then be redetermined.

## Next Hop Resolution Protocol

NHRP is used by a host or router in an NBMA environment to determine the internetworking (IP) address and NBMA subnetwork address (ATM address, in this case) of the next hop toward a particular destination host.

NHRP is used by MPOA to determine where on the network the egress MPS resides in relation to the ingress MPS; as explained in some of the previous sections, the ingress and egress MPS may be the same MPS, but the NHS is still used in this instance to make that third-layer determination.

## The NHRP Server

The NHS is an entity that serves a set of destination hosts; each NHS maintains a cache of internetworking address IP-to-NBMA address information. This information is collected through the exchange of NHRP Resolution Requests and NHRP Resolution Replies. Each NHS works with its co-located MPS in this case both to determine which MPS is the egress MPS and to cache address resolution information. Each MPC in this case is seen a Next Hop Client (NHC)

In a scenario where the ingress MPS is not also the egress MPS, however, the specific function of NHRP may be easier to understand. In an ATM network in which multiple MPSs are configured on multiple routers, the NHS may determine, after receiving an NHRP Resolution Request and examining the destination internetworking destination address, that the egress MPS is not located locally. In this case, it must check the router function and determine whether the next hop toward the destination address is known (see Figure 17-12).

The incoming MPOA Resolution Request in this example was intended for destination IP address 214.21.17.72; this was translated into an NHRP Resolution Request, whereupon the local NHS determined that the 214.21.17.0 network is not local

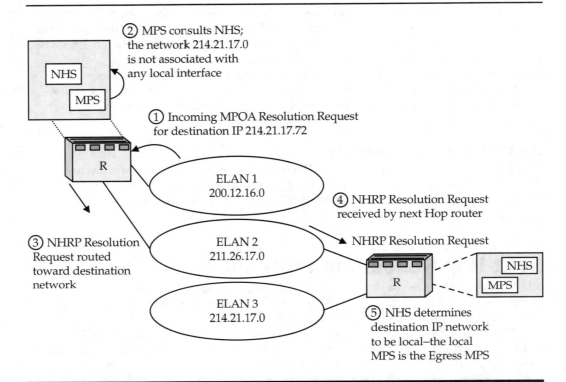

② MPS consults NHS;
the network 214.21.17.0
is not associated with
any local interface

NHS

MPS

① Incoming MPOA Resolution Request
for destination IP 214.21.17.72

R

ELAN 1
200.12.16.0

④ NHRP Resolution Request
received by next Hop router

③ NHRP Resolution
Request routed
toward destination
network

ELAN 2
211.26.17.0

NHRP Resolution Request

NHS

R

MPS

ELAN 3
214.21.17.0

⑤ NHS determines
destination IP network
to be local–the local
MPS is the Egress MPS

**Figure 17-12.**   *NHS entities resolving location of egress MPS*

to it. In this case, the NHRP Resolution Request must be forwarded to the proper
remote NHS.

The 214.21.17.0 network is not local to the receiving router, but the router does
have the next hop to that network in its routing table. The NHRP Resolution Request
is forwarded onto ELAN 2, because this is the path to the next-hop router that serves
that network. The exact manner in which the NHRP Resolution Request is routed to its
destination depends on the routing protocol being used in the network; this could be
RIP, RIPv2, OSPF, and so on. The request (and its associated reply) will be routed back
and forth between the ingress MPS and egress MPS in accordance with whichever
routing protocol is being used.

After the NHRP Resolution Request arrives at the remote NHS, the receiving NHS
determines that the destination host lies on one of the local networks served by its
router. The packet is accepted and the egress MPS forms an MPOA Cache Imposition
Request that it sends to the egress MPC.

# MPOA Shortcuts

In this section, the process of determining an MPOA shortcut must be built, resolving the necessary address information, and then building the actual MPOA shortcut is followed in sequence, from beginning to end. The process described in this section charts the shortcut from the ingress MPC to the egress MPC. Bear in mind that this procedure will most likely be followed again, going back the other way, because the egress MPC also detects the IP flow meeting its threshold, and either initiates a shortcut of its own back the other way or uses an existing shortcut once the address resolution procedure is complete. When this occurs, both MPCs will be sending and receiving data over the MPOA shortcut(s), and both MPCs will be simultaneously acting as both ingress and egress MPC.

## Building the MPOA Shortcut

In the following scenario, a source IP device initiates a large transfer with a destination IP device. This transfer occurs across an ATM core, where the source and destination devices are in two different IP networks, across two different ATM ELANs. The sections that follow describe the shortcut setup procedure in a step-by-step fashion (see Figure 17-13).

### The Ingress MPC

The ingress MPC begins the procedure by monitoring any frames that are destined for the MAC-layer address associated with the MPS (the MAC address of the LEC VPort the MPS is mapped to). This indicates to the ingress MPC that the data is being sent to a router interface and is therefore ultimately destined for a host that lies on a separate network or subnetwork. Since more than one MPS exist on the destination router, the MAC is checked to see which MPS it is associated with.

Once this is done, the ingress MPC places the destination IP address into its ingress cache and then begins counting each frame that is destined for the same MAC-layer destination address, along with the same destination IP address; this constitutes traffic flow that may be eligible for an MPOA shortcut. After counting the frames, if the ingress MPC receives a number equal to that defined in the Setup Frame Count, and within the amount of time specified in the Setup Frame Time, then the predefined threshold has been reached; the ingress MPC responds by issuing an MPOA Resolution Request control frame to the appropriate MPS. The MPOA Resolution Request is sent to determine the egress MPC data ATM address, so that an MPOA shortcut can be initiated. Without the correct destination ATM address, the VCC can't be requested.

### The Ingress MPS

The ingress MPS, upon receiving the MPOA Resolution Request, must translate the Request into an NHRP Resolution Request, so that the appropriate egress MPS can be located.

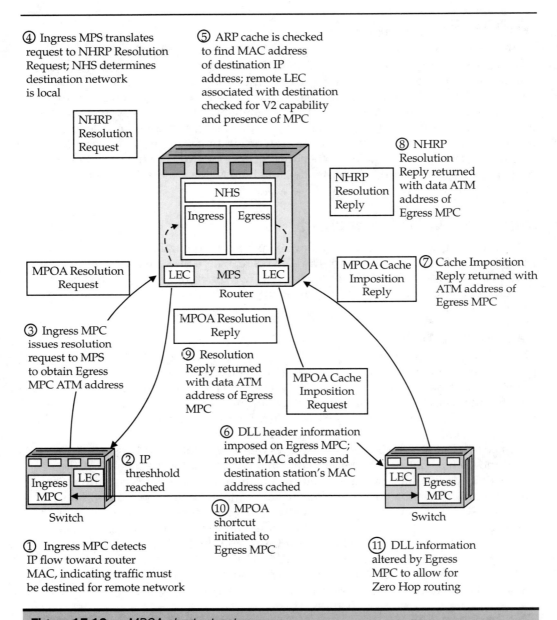

④ Ingress MPS translates request to NHRP Resolution Request; NHS determines destination network is local

⑤ ARP cache is checked to find MAC address of destination IP address; remote LEC associated with destination checked for V2 capability and presence of MPC

NHRP Resolution Request

⑧ NHRP Resolution Reply returned with data ATM address of Egress MPC

NHRP Resolution Reply

NHS

Ingress   Egress

MPOA Resolution Request

MPOA Cache Imposition Reply

⑦ Cache Imposition Reply returned with ATM address of Egress MPC

LEC   MPS   LEC
Router

③ Ingress MPC issues resolution request to MPS to obtain Egress MPC ATM address

MPOA Resolution Reply

⑨ Resolution Reply returned with data ATM address of Egress MPC

MPOA Cache Imposition Request

② IP threshhold reached

⑥ DLL header information imposed on Egress MPC; router MAC address and destination station's MAC address cached

LEC
Ingress MPC
Switch

LEC
Egress MPC
Switch

⑩ MPOA shortcut initiated to Egress MPC

① Ingress MPC detects IP flow toward router MAC, indicating traffic must be destined for remote network

⑪ DLL information altered by Egress MPC to allow for Zero Hop routing

**Figure 17-13.**   *MPOA shortcut setup*

## The NHRP Resolution Request

The ingress MPS translates the MPOA Resolution Request into an NHRP Resolution Request and hands it to the co-located NHS to determine which MPS is mapped to a LEC associated with the destination IP network. The NHS examines the third-layer protocol information associated with the local LEC instances, and discovers that one of the local LECs is configured for the IP network that also contains the destination host. As this is the case, the ingress MPS is, in fact, also the egress MPS.

## The Egress MPS

The egress MPS, upon receiving the NHRP Resolution Request, checks its associated LECs to see which is associated with the destination's IP network or subnetwork; it must now determine two things: the MAC address associated with the destination IP host, and the egress MPC data ATM address associated with the destination IP host.

The egress MPS checks the router's ARP cache to determine the MAC address of the destination IP host. Because communication is currently taking place between the source and destination hosts, this entry should already be present; likewise, because a Data Direct VCC already exists between the router's LEC and the LEC associated with the destination IP host, the MPS also has knowledge as to which remote LEC is associated with the destination. It checks the LEC to make certain it is V2-capable and is being served by an MPC. If the remote LEC is V2-capable and associated with an MPC, the egress MPS issues an MPOA Cache Imposition Request that includes the DLL header information it will need to put into its egress cache (the destination IP host's MAC address, pulled from the router's ARP cache, and the MAC address of the local router interface).

## The Egress MPC

The egress MPC, upon receiving the MPOA Cache Imposition Request from the egress MPS, places the information in its egress cache for the duration of the Holding Time described by the egress MPS. The egress MPC makes sure that it is able to accept an incoming shortcut VCC, and then issues to the egress MPS an MPOA Cache Imposition Reply that contains the egress MPC data ATM address associated with the destination IP host.

## The NHRP Resolution Reply

Upon receiving the MPOA Cache Imposition Reply from the egress MPC, the egress MPS notes this in its egress cache and then takes the destination NBMA address (the egress MPC's data ATM address that the shortcut will be built to) and translates this information into an NHRP Resolution Reply.

## The MPOA Resolution Reply

Upon receiving the NHRP Resolution Reply, the ingress MPS makes a note of this in its ingress cache and then translates this information into an MPOA Resolution

Reply, which in turn is issued back to the ingress MPC that originally requested the address resolution.

### Building the MPOA Shortcut

Upon receiving the MPOA Resolution Request, the ingress MPC uses the information it contains to complete its ingress cache entry. It now knows the destination MPC data ATM address and can request a VCC to that address; at the receiving side (the egress MPC), the egress cache entry for the destination IP address contains the DLL header information required to accommodate the MPOA shortcut.

## MPOA Cache Management

In an ATM network utilizing MPOA, information must be cached at both the ingress and egress MPC, as well as at the MPS. This information must be monitored and validated periodically to ensure that the cache entries are still accurate. If an entry is found to be no longer valid, the entry must be purged from the cache in question, and the other MPOA components must be notified of this change.

Cache maintenance occurs in relation to the ingress MPC's ingress cache, the egress MPC's egress cache, the ingress MPS, and the egress MPS.

### Ingress MPC Ingress Cache Management

The ingress MPC caches information regarding particular internetworking destination addresses, as well as their associated destination MPC data ATM addresses. Once cached, MPC ingress cache entries are maintained through an aging process; the aging time is dictated by the source holding time from the last MPOA Resolution Reply that was received in relation to the particular destination IP address. To prevent an ingress cache entry from aging out of the table, an ingress MPC must periodically issue a new MPOA Resolution Request to refresh the entry and make certain it is still valid. The exact amount of time between refreshing these entries is not specified, but should be less than the Holding Time, to prevent idle shortcuts from being torn down that may still be usable.

### Fielding NHRP Purge Requests

In addition to the aging process, ingress cache entries may be removed from the ingress cache through an NHRP Purge Request, issued by the ingress MPS to the ingress MPC (discussed in more detail in the following sections on MPS cache maintenance). This control frame indicates to the ingress MPC that the ingress cache entry associated with the destination internetworking address is no longer valid and that any data being sent across an MPOA shortcut to that destination host must cease at once. Under these circumstances, the ingress MPC purges the ingress cache entry and may immediately issue a new MPOA Resolution Request to attempt to relocate the destination host.

Additionally, in the event that the egress MPS becomes inactive or fails to find an egress cache entry for data received over a shortcut, the egress MPC may issue an NHRP Purge Request over the shortcut.

# Egress MPC Egress Cache Management

When the egress cache entry is imposed on the egress MPC by the egress MPS, the MPOA Cache Imposition Request contains a Holding Time that is provided by the egress MPS; the egress MPC will not use the egress cache entry after the time indicated by the Holding Time has been exceeded without the entry first being refreshed (the ingress MPC periodically refreshing its own ingress cache entries by reissuing MPOA Resolution Requests should accomplish this).

For the egress MPC to consider an egress cache entry valid, the destination MAC address (contained in the DLL header information included in the MPOA Cache Imposition Request, which now resides in the egress cache entry for the destination internetworking address) must be present as both the associated LEC's Local Unicast MAC Address(es) variable (LEC variable C6, as defined in the LANE specification) and the Remote Unicast MAC Address(es) variable (LEC variable C27); essentially, this indicates that for the egress cache entry to be considered valid by the egress MPC, the LEC that serves the legacy LAN where the destination host resides must still be associating that host's MAC address with itself, and must be able to respond to LE_ARP_REQUESTs for that address.

If the MAC address associated with the destination host IP address moves to a different LEC (the destination host was moved to either a different ELAN or a different physical location within the same ELAN), or disappears altogether from its LEC table (the destination host went down or is not reachable), then the egress MPC can no longer consider the DLL header information in the egress cache entry valid, and must inform the egress MPS of this fact.

## Egress Cache Purges

If the egress MPC has an egress cache entry whose Holding Time has reached 0, has lost contact with its MPS, or if has received data over a shortcut whose egress cache entry specifies a destination MAC address that is no longer found in any of the associated LEC's variables (the MAC address is no longer associated with that LEC), then the egress cache entry is considered invalid, and the egress MPC must take steps to remove the entry.

The first step the egress MPC may take is to forward the packets coming over the shortcut to the bridging function; this causes the packets to appear as though they are actually coming in over the LEC, and may result in the MAC being relearned by the LEC (indicating the destination host is still associated with the same LEC). This occurs for about 30 seconds; if the egress cache entry can't be validated within that time, the egress MPC must invalidate the entry, by issuing an MPOA Egress Cache Purge Request.

ATM TECHNOLOGIES

## MPOA Egress Cache Purge Requests

By sending an MPOA Egress Cache Purge Request to the egress MPS, the egress MPC notifies the MPS that an egress cache entry that was formerly imposed on it has been found to be no longer valid. This Purge Request contains the following information:

- **Destination Protocol Address**   The protocol address (IP) associated with the egress MPS.

- **Source NBMA Address**   The egress MPC's (the MPC issuing the MPOA Egress Cache Purge Request) data ATM address.

- **Client Protocol Address**   The protocol address (IP) of the destination host; this protocol address is to be purged as a result of this Purge Request.

- **Prefix Length**   The destination's prefix length.

- **Client NBMA Address**   The egress MPC's (the MPC issuing the MPOA Egress Cache Purge Request) data ATM address.

- **Extensions**   Include the DLL header information as well as any other received extensions.

Upon receiving an MPOA Egress Cache Purge Request, the egress MPS must generate its own NHRP Purge Request for the entry specified by the egress MPC. An MPOA Egress Cache Purge Reply is optional, and the egress MPC will indicate in the original MPOA Egress Cache Purge Request whether it expects to receive a Purge Reply. If a Reply is expected, it will be issued by the egress MPS *after* it receives an NHRP Purge Reply in response to its own NHRP Purge Request.

# Ingress MPS Cache Maintenance

The ingress MPS maintains an ingress cache that keeps track of which ingress MPCs are utilizing shortcuts to which destination internetwork-layer addresses/ATM addresses. This information is used if the ingress MPS receives an NHRP Purge Request for one or more of its entries; in this event, the MPS forwards the Purge Request to the appropriate MPCs.

In addition, the ingress MPS may itself monitor traffic flow, and may also make a determination as to whether or not an MPOA shortcut is required; if this is the case, the ingress MPS may, in the absence of an MPOA Resolution Request from the ingress MPC, initiate or provoke one by using an *MPOA Trigger*.

## MPOA Trigger

Because of the methodology of the MPOA protocol, the ingress MPS must receive an MPOA Resolution Request from the ingress MPC to initiate the address resolution process; it can't simply issue an NHRP Resolution Request as if it had received the MPOA Resolution Request. An MPOA Trigger is issued by an ingress MPS to an ingress MPC to provoke an MPOA Resolution Request from the ingress

MPC, if it has not issued one of its own accord. The MPOA Trigger contains the following information:

- **Ingress MPS Control ATM Address**   Required by the ingress MPC so that it can identify which packets will be sent over the MPOA shortcut. This information will be placed in its ingress cache.

- **Destination Internetworking Address and Address Prefix**   This information is also required by the ingress MPC, so that it can formulate the MPOA Resolution Request that is actually triggered by the MPOA Trigger.

### Responding to NHRP Purge Requests

If an egress MPC issues an MPOA Egress Cache Purge Request to the egress MPS, the egress MPS in turn forwards an NHRP Purge Request to the ingress MPS. In this situation, the ingress MPS must forward the NHRP Purge Request to all relevant MPCs, informing them that the destination internetworking address-to-ATM address binding (and therefore, their ingress cache entry for that destination internetwork-layer address) has been determined to be no longer valid. An NHRP Purge Request sent by the ingress MPS to each MPC may or may not require a Purge Reply, depending on what the sending MPS asks for in the Request.

## Egress MPS Cache Maintenance

The egress MPS also maintains egress cache information regarding the state for all MPOA and NHRP Resolution Replies, as well as each successful MPOA Cache Imposition Request. The egress MPS considers to be an active entry any entry that resulted in a successful MPOA Cache Imposition Request and NHRP Resolution Reply to an NHRP Resolution Request.

Such entries are considered valid for the duration of time defined by the Holding Time; while the Holding Time is still in effect, the egress MPS will notify all relevant parties if any of the information in the entry changes. The implication of this is that an egress MPC, for instance, that has received an egress cache entry via an MPOA Cache Imposition Request from the egress MPS may consider this information valid for the duration of the Holding Time (included by the egress MPS in the MPOA Cache Imposition Request), since the MPS has contracted to update the information or purge it if the information changes during this time. The egress MPC then needs to be concerned only with whether the information is still valid from a local standpoint (the MAC of the destination is still listed in the same local LEC).

### Egress MPS Cache Purges and Updates

The egress MPS may at some point detect a change involving one of its active entries; this may occur if an internetwork-layer next-hop has changed, which may direct an NHRP Resolution Request to the wrong MPC, or if an egress LEC has changed, so that the destination egress MPC data ATM address has changed. If the egress MPS detects

ATM TECHNOLOGIES

information that conflicts with one of its active egress cache entries, it must do one of two things:

- Send an NHRP Purge Request to the ingress MPCs that would be affected by this change (ingress MPCs that either have established shortcuts to the destination or are in the process of doing so), and then issue an MPOA Cache Imposition Request to the egress MPC that holds the now-invalid egress cache entry; this new MPOA Cache Imposition Request will have a Holding Time of 0, which will cause it to be purged by the egress MPC.

- Send an MPOA Cache Imposition Request with updated DLL header information to reflect the change. In this situation, as long as the MPOA Cache Imposition Reply contains the same information as it did previously (the egress MPC data ATM address hasn't changed, the tag hasn't changed, and so forth), then the update may be considered successful. If anything has changed, however, the entry must be purged, because no way exists to dynamically update the ingress MPC of this new information, and the MPOA Resolution procedure must be repeated.

If an egress cache entry in the egress MPC needs to be updated, the egress MPS issues a new MPOA Cache Imposition Request with a non-zero holding time, using the same Cache ID as the former entry, but with an updated DLL header or other relevant information.

# The Complete Reference

Nortel
Networks

# Part V

## ATM on Nortel Networks

# Chapter 18

## ATM on the Nortel Networks Platforms

There are two primary families of Centillion ATM switches: the C100/C50/5000BH product line, and the C1200/C1400/C1600 product line. All switches have a chassis-based architecture, with a native ATM backplane, processor control cards, and host cards to provide a variety of ATM connections and connector types.

## Centillion Varieties

The Centillion family consists of two basic groupings: the C100/C50/C20/5000BH platforms, and the C1x00 series switches. These switches have the following basic architectures:

- **C100**  A six-slot chassis, designed for the wiring closet or for the core of small to moderately sized networks.

- **C50**  A smaller, more cost-effective cousin of the C100, with three slots rather than six. It is designed primarily for the wiring closet or for small offices. Older versions of this switch were outfitted with a single, nonremovable MCP module.

- **5000BH**  An upright chassis with a total of 14 slots, 12 of which may be used for Centillion switch cards. Its ATM backplane is split into two sets of six slots each. It is designed for core networks, or for the wiring closet in large ATM networks.

- **C1200**  A four-slot chassis; it is primarily designed for the core in small to moderately sized networks. It provides up to 16 OC-3 ports.

- **C1400**  A ten-slot chassis, two of which may contain controller cards (one primary, one redundant). It is a core switch to be used in moderately sized networks, providing up to 32 OC-3 ports.

- **C1600**  A 16-slot chassis, with 2 slots for primary and redundant controller cards. It is designed as a core switch in large, heavily utilized networks and can provide up to 64 OC-3 ports.

### Options for Services

The Centillion family offers the following ATM components and services.

**C100/C50/5000BH**    The C100/C50/5000BH family of ATM switches supports LANE services and all standard call routing methods. The C100/C50/5000BH switches are designed for edge and core positioning. The following features are supported:

- **OC-3, OC-12, and DS-3 connections**    155Mbps OC-3, 622Mbps OC-12, and 45Mbps DS-3 ports are now available for the C100/C50/5000BH family. OC-3 is available in multimode fiber, single-mode fiber, or copper. A single-port OC-12 module is available in both single- and multimode fiber. Media-dependent adapter (MDA) MCPs and host cards now support DS-3 MDAs for wide-area connectivity up to 45Mbps.

■ **Centillion LAN Client (CLC) PVC connections**   CLCs exist in two varieties: Circuit Saver, which allows for a greater number of simultaneous connections, and Turbo (GIGArray), which supports a fewer number of simultaneous connections, but with greater speed.

■ **Soft PVC (SPVC) support**   With the advent of PNNI support, the C100/C50/5000BH support SPVCs beginning with code version 4.0

■ **Full LANEv1 services**   The entire C100/C50/5000BH family supports full LANEv1 services, including LAN Emulation Clients (LECs), LAN Emulation Configuration Server (LECS), LAN Emulation Server (LES), and Broadcast and Unknown Server (BUS).

■ **Full LANEv2 services**   LANEv2 support is also available, beginning with code version 4.0, including Multi-Protocol Over ATM (MPOA) support for MPOA Clients (MPCs), LUNI 2.0 functionality for each LEC, LANEv2 functionality for each LES, and added MPOA configuration TLV support for both MPOA Clients (MPCs) and MPOA Servers (MPSs) within the LECS functionality.

■ **LEC-only UNI functions**   The C100/C50/5000BH may act as a LEC-only device, with a single, user-side UNI connection to the network.

■ **UNI 3.0, UNI 3.1**   Both UNI 3.0 and UNI 3.1 User to Network Interface connections are supported. Presently, UNI 4.0 is not supported on this platform.

■ **Cooperating LES/BUS pairs for up to four redundant, load-sharing pairs**   LES/BUS pairs servicing a single ELAN can be grouped for up to four total pairs. This provides redundancy if one pair fails, as well as load-sharing capabilities.

■ **Interim Inter-Switch Protocol (IISP) call routing method**   IISP is supported in all code versions. IISP addresses may be advertised into a PNNI domain as exterior addresses.

■ **Link groups for bandwidth aggregation of up to four OC-3 links**   IISP connections can be logically bound together for bandwidth aggregation. Up to four links on a single module can be bound in a link group, for a total bandwidth of up to 620Mbps.

■ **PNNIv1 call routing method with support for multiple hierarchical layers**   Beginning with code version 3.0, PNNI phase 1 is supported for a single layer of hierarchy only. Code version 4.0 and higher support multiple layers of the PNNI routing hierarchy, although C100/C50/5000BH nodes cannot act as Peer Group Leaders (PGLs), as of the time of publication.

- **MPOA Client services**   Beginning with code version 4.0, the C100/C50/5000BH supports MPOA Client (MPC) services, for the creation of MPOA shortcuts. An MPS, which resides on the router, is required for MPOA services.

- **IP Verification feature for MPOA**   This feature allows for a range of IP addresses to be defined, for either inclusion or exclusion from MPOA shortcuts. This feature can be used to prevent an MPC from attempting to create shortcuts to destinations outside the private network.

**C1200/C1400/C1600**   The C1200/C1400/C1600 family of Centillion switches is positioned as core switches in large, heavily utilized networks. As of the time of publication, the C1x00 is positioned as a core transit switch, and LANE is not offered on the switches themselves. The following feature sets are available:

- **OC-3, OC-12, and DS-3 connections**   155Mbps OC-3 ports, 622Mbps OC-12 ports, and 45Mbps DS-3 ports are available on all C1x00 models.

- **UNI 3.0, UNI 3.1, and UNI 4.0 signaling support**   UNI 3.0, 3.1, and 4.0 are supported on all C1x00 platforms.

- **Soft PVC (SPVC) support**   As a function of PNNI, SPVCs are supported on all C1x00 platforms.

- **IISP call routing method**   PNNI phase 0, or IISP, is supported on all C1x00 platforms. IISP and PNNI can be run simultaneously, with IISP links advertised as exterior addresses. Additional support for IISP split-horizon and restricted transit are also available. These features are covered in Chapter 22.

- **PNNI 1.0 call routing method with support for multiple hierarchical layers**   Multihierarchical PNNI routing is supported on all C1000 platforms, with support for advertising IISP addresses into the PNNI domain as exterior addresses. Crankback is supported.

- **PGL support for PNNI**   The C1000 platform supports PGL functionality for all nodes, to aggregate nodal information as a logical group node (LGN) in the PNNI hierarchy. In a mixed C100/C50/5000BH–C1000 environment, PGL functions are assumed by the C1000 nodes.

- **Border node capability for PNNI**   Full border node functionality is supported, including crankback, as well as uplinks to upnodes at multiple hierarchical layers.

- **Traffic Shaping and Traffic Policing for cell-flow control**   Traffic Shaping and Traffic Policing profiles can be created on a port-by-port basis, to manage ingress and egress cell flow.

- **Tunneling support for Wide Area connections**   SVC tunneling is supported, for tunneling ATM signaling over a single PVC for wide area connections.

# C100

The C100 is a core/edge ATM switch that is capable of supporting up to 24 OC-3 connections. It is capable of both IISP and PNNI call routing methods, as well as support for full LANE services, and utilizes a chassis-based architecture.

## Basic Chassis Architecture

The C100 utilizes a six-slot chassis architecture, with an ATM backplane and up to two redundant power supplies. The C100 supports Ethernet, token ring, and ATM boards; each media type utilizes a variety of front panel connections, as well as an ATM backplane connector to attach to the ATM backplane. All communication between boards takes place across the ATM backplane, regardless of the media type.

The C100 uses a controller card called the *Master Control Processor (MCP)*, which serves as the processor for the other host cards. The MCP can be placed in any of the six slots, and comes in three different varieties: ATM, token ring, and Ethernet. Prior to code version 3.0, only one MCP module is permitted to exist in a single chassis; however, with code version 3.0 or higher, redundant MCPs can also be placed in the chassis. In this scenario, the redundant MCP acts as a host card until such time as the primary MCP fails, at which point the redundant MCP becomes active.

### ATM Backplane

The C100 utilizes an ATM backplane, which all switched modules use, including the EtherSpeed and TokenSpeed blades. This backplane spans all six slots of the C100 chassis, and provides up to 3.2Gbps of throughput. Combined with the 1.2Gbps of throughput provided by each additional ATMSpeed module, the aggregate throughput for the C100 exceeds 10Gbps.

### ATMSpeed MCPs

The ATMSpeed MCP is the Master Control Processor ATMSpeed card. At least one MCP must be present in the Centillion chassis for the host blades to function. Without an MCP, host blades will not initialize. The ATMSpeed MCP provides controller functions for other ATMSpeed, EtherSpeed, or TokenSpeed host modules, while providing ATM front panel connectivity itself.

The ATMSpeed MCP also houses a 10-pin round DIN connector for establishing serial communication with the device. This serial connection may be used to manage the Centillion via SpeedView, or to access the Command Line Interface (CLI). In addition to the serial connector, the MCP houses a single RJ-45 Ethernet port for Ethernet connectivity. This Ethernet connector is not intended to provide connectivity to Ethernet clients or servers; it provides a means of configuring the Centillion via SNMP if no EtherSpeed or TokenSpeed modules are present.

ATM ON NORTEL
NETWORKS

*The RJ-45 connector on the MCP requires its own IP address, which is configured as the secondary (as opposed to the primary) IP address in both SpeedView and the CLI. The secondary IP must be on a different subnet than the primary IP address, or else communication with both IP addresses will be lost.*

**NETWORK CENTER MCPS**    The Network Center ATMSpeed MCP is a variation of the fixed-port ATMSpeed MCP module, providing 16MB of processor memory and four OC-3 ports for better performance in the network core. Both multimode and single-mode connector types are available. Most ATMSpeed MCPs in use today are Network Center MCPs.

**TWO-PORT MCPS**    Prior to the release of the MDA ATMSpeed MCP, a fixed, two-OC-3-port model was produced and is still in existence today. It functions exactly as the four-port variety, but is less expensive than the four-port version.

**MEDIA DEPENDENT ADAPTER MCPS**    In the more recent ATMSpeed implementations, ports are no longer fixed, but instead are modular, in the form of MDAs. The ATMSpeed MCP in this case has no ports, by default, instead having two MDA slots that may each contain one two-port MDA. This provides more flexibility, allowing for two or four ports, and also allowing a migration from two to four ports without necessitating the replacement of the entire MCP. MDA types include multimode OC-3 connectors, single-mode OC-3 connectors, UTP, and DS-3 connectors for Wide Area connectivity.

**ONE PORT OC-12 MCPS**    A one-port variety of ATMSpeed MCP also exists, providing a single OC-12 port for a 622Mbps Synchronous Optical Network (SONET) or Synchronous Digital Hierarchy (SDH) connection. Multimode and single-mode varieties are available.

## Host Modules

ATM host modules are also available. Host modules are controlled by the MCP, and do not have any core CPU functionality in and of themselves. Host modules are unable to function, or even initialize, in most cases, in the absence of an MCP. They're in many cases similar, if not identical, to their MCP counterparts, except for the absence of a CPU and the absence of a front panel Ethernet connector.

**FOUR-PORT HOST MODULES**    The four-port ATMSpeed host module is a variation of the fixed-port ATMSpeed module, without MCP functionality. It is outfitted with four OC-3 ports; both multimode and single-mode connector types are available. Prior to the release of the MDA host module, fixed OC-3 UTP connectors were also available, though they're not commonly encountered today.

**TWO-PORT HOST MODULES**    Prior to the release of the MDA ATMSpeed host, a fixed, two-OC-3-port model was produced and is still in existence today. It functions exactly as the four-port variety, but is more cost-effective with only two ports.

**MDA HOST MODULES**    In the more recent ATMSpeed implementations, ports are no longer fixed, but instead are modular, in the form of MDAs. The ATMSpeed host in this case has no ports, by default, and instead has two MDA slots that may each contain one two-port MDA. This provides more flexibility, allowing for two or four ports, and also allowing a migration from two to four ports without necessitating the replacement of the entire host module. MDA types include multimode OC-3 connectors, single-mode OC-3 connectors, UTP, and DS-3 connectors for Wide Area connectivity.

**ONE-PORT OC-12 HOST MODULES**    A one-port variety of ATMSpeed host module also exists, providing a single OC-12 port for a 622Mbps SONET or SDH connection. Multimode and single-mode varieties are available.

## C50

The C50 is a smaller, more cost-effective version of the C100. Two versions of the C50 exist: an older version, in which the MCP controller module is fixed in the chassis, with support for a host card, and the three-slot version, which is used today. Generally, the C50 is simply a smaller version of the C100, and shares the same feature set.

# 5000BH

The 5000BH is a variety of the System 5000 chassis which contains an ATM backplane. The System 5000 is capable of supporting not only Centillion-based switching modules, but also shared-media products, routing modules, and remote access products. For the purposes of this chapter, only the ATM-specific Centillion switch modules are covered.

## Basic Chassis Architecture

The System 5000 chassis provides a variety of backplane connections: 12 Ethernet segments, 12 Fast Ethernet segments, up to nine token rings, up to 5 FDDI ring paths, a switched backplane, a Parallel Packet Exchange (PPX) backplane for Nortel Networks router modules, and an ATM backplane.

The ATM backplane in this case is used almost exclusively by the Centillion modules, with the one exception being the 5782 ATM router module. The presence of this backplane gives the System 5000 its "BH" designation.

## Split Backplane

The ATM backplane in the 5000BH is a split backplane, with the split occurring between slots 7 and 8. No ATM backplane communication will extend beyond the split, and a front panel connection must be made to connect the two halves, if desired. Alternately, two 5782 ATM router modules residing on opposite sides of the backplane split may also intercommunicate across the PPX backplane, thus eliminating the need for a front panel connection between the two halves of the chassis.

## Slot Selection

Unlike the other backplanes, the ATM backplane in the 5000BH doesn't extend the entire length of the chassis; the ATM backplane extends from slot 2 to slot 13, with a split occurring between slots 7 and 8. ATM modules are not supported in slot 1 or slot 14 of the 5000BH chassis. This allows for a total of six slots available for use by Centillion blades. Because all Centillion blades utilize the ATM backplane, this includes even non-ATM Centillion switch modules.

**5724M**    The 5724M is the ATMSpeed MCP controller card for the 5000BH chassis. It has four fixed OC-3 ports, as well as a single RJ-45 Ethernet port for SNMP configuration via SpeedView. In addition, a 25-pin serial connector is present to allow for serial configuration through SpeedView, and also access to the CLI.

**5720M**    The 5720M is similar to the 5724M, except that its ports are not fixed. Instead, two MDA slots are present, each capable of supporting a single, two-port MDA. MDA types include OC-3 ports, both multimode and single-mode, UTP ports, and DS-3 ports for Wide Area connectivity.

**5720-622M**    The 5720-622M provides MCP functionality, as well as a single 622Mbps OC-12 connection for both multimode and single-mode fiber.

*The RJ-45 connector on all MCPs requires its own IP address, which is configured as the secondary (as opposed to the primary) IP address in both SpeedView and the CLI. The secondary IP must be on a different subnet than the primary IP address, or else communication with both IP addresses will be lost.*

**5724**    The 5724 has four fixed OC-3 connectors for SONET or SDH connections.

**5720**    The 5720 is similar to the 5724, except that its ports are not fixed. It supports two two-port MDA modules, for a total of four ports. MDA types include OC-3 for both multimode and single-mode fiber, UTP, and DS-3.

**5720-622**    The 5720-622 provides a single 622Mbps OC-12 connection, in both multimode and single-mode varieties.

## Redundant MCPs

Prior to code version 3.0, two MCP modules were not permitted to be in the same chassis or, in the case of the 5000BH, in the same side of the chassis. In that scenario, neither MCP will initialize and, therefore, none of the host modules will ever initialize. Beginning with code version 3.0, however, more than one MCP may be installed, for purposes of redundancy. One MCP will initialize as master in this case, and the redundant MCP will come up as a host module, assuming MCP functionality only if the primary MCP fails.

# C1x00 Basic Architecture

The C1x00 series ATM switches have a different architecture than the C100/C50/5000BH platform, and are not configured using SpeedView. The C1x00 series switches are also chassis-based, however, and the components do utilize a CPU controller card/host module relationship, as does the C100/C50/5000BH.

## C1200

The C1200 is a desktop ATM switch with a core switch fabric providing 2.5Gbps throughput, capable of supporting up to 4 622Mbps OC-12 connections, or up to 16 155Mbps OC-3 connections.

### C1200 Chassis Architecture

The C1200 contains four slots for line cards, which provide front panel ATM connectivity. In addition, the C1200 supports a single power unit, a single CPU card containing an RS-232C 9-pin D-Sub connector for initiating terminal sessions with the device, and two PCMCIA slots located in the CPU card, which may be used to house either an ATA flash card for storing software and system files or an Ethernet PCMCIA card for Ethernet connectivity.

*An Ethernet PCMCIA card is necessary for the C1x00 switch to support Telnet sessions if the device is not being managed over an RFC 1483-compliant PVC.*

The CPU card has a series of LEDs located on the front panel, which are described in Table 18-1.

The C1200 CPU card also provides a Reset button, which initiates a soft reset of the chassis.

### Chassis Configuration

Unlike the C100/C50/5000BH product, the C1x00 product utilizes a slot and port number of 0. In addition, unlike the C100, which is similar in physical design, the

| LED | Color | Meaning |
|-----|-------|---------|
| Power | Green | Device is currently receiving power. |
|  | Off | No power is reaching the device. |
| Ready | Green | Equipment is functioning properly. |
|  | Off | Equipment failure has occurred. |
|  | Flashing | Diagnostics are being run. |
| Alarm | Red | Equipment failure has occurred. |

**Table 18-1.**    *C1200 LED Indicators*

C1200 numbers its slots from bottom to top, not top to bottom (see Figure 18-1). Port numbering occurs from left to right.

Each slot/port location is identified by a single, two-digit number, which is also a departure from the C100 architecture. For instance, in the C100, slot 1, port 1 would be signified in the CLI as two separate values:

```
C100:Command>show port 1 1
```

In the C1200, the same port would be identified as follows:

```
C1200# show atmsig 11
```

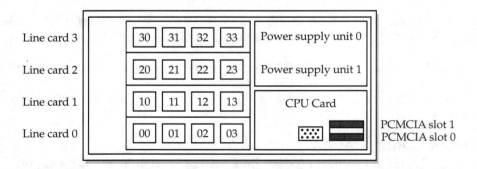

**Figure 18-1.**    *Slot and port numbering scheme on the C1200*

## Using a PCMCIA Card

The C1200 is capable of supporting a PCMCIA LAN card and a PCMCIA ATA flash card. Two PCMCIA slots are located on the front of the C1200 chassis, one positioned over the other. The top slot is considered slot 1 and is generally used for the LAN card, while the slot below it, slot 0, is generally used for the PCMCIA flash. The LAN card in this case is used as an Ethernet connection, allowing the device to be reached via telnet, and also allowing Trivial File Transfer Protocol (TFTP) transfers of image code or configuration information.

# C1400

The C1400 ATM switch provides a switched core with 5Gbps throughput. It is capable of supporting up to 8 622Mbps OC-12 connections, and up to 32 155Mbps OC-3 connections.

## C1400 Chassis Architecture

The C1400 provides a total of eight slots for various line cards, as well as two slots for CPU cards in a redundant configuration. In addition, the C1400 has dual power supplies for added redundancy, as well as dual fan trays.

## CPU Switch Card

The redundant CPU cards offer a high degree of reliability; although the C1400 can function normally with only one CPU card, the presence of a second CPU card enables one CPU card to be active while the other is in standby mode. The CPU card has the LEDs shown in Table 18-2.

| LED | Color | Meaning |
| --- | --- | --- |
| Link | Green | Link is detected on Ethernet port. |
| INS | Red | CPU card is currently in service. |
|  | Green | Firmware or hardware error has occurred. |
|  | Off | CPU card is not receiving power. |
| ACT | Green | CPU card is currently primary and active. |
|  | Off | CPU card is functional, but not active. |
| ALM | Red | Hardware error has occurred. |
|  | Off | CPU is functioning normally |

**Table 18-2.**   *C1400 LED Indicators*

Each CPU card is fitted with an RS-232C 9-pin D-Sub connector for establishing terminal sessions with the device, as well as a Reset button for initiating a soft reset of that particular CPU card. In addition, each CPU card is fitted with an RJ-45 Ethernet port, used to download software and to support telnet sessions.

## Chassis Configuration

Unlike the C100/C50/5000BH product, the C1x00 product utilizes a slot and port number of 0. Unlike the C1200, however, the C1400 numbers its slots from top to bottom, not bottom to top (see Figure 18-2). Two columns of slots exist in this case, the left column beginning with slot 0, and the right column beginning with slot 4. Port numbering occurs from left to right.

Each slot/port location is identified by a single, three-digit number, as opposed to the two-digit value used in the C1200. For instance, slot 0, port 1 in the C1200 is referred to in the following manner:

```
C1200# show atmsig 01
```

while in the C1400, the same port would be referred to as follows:

```
C1400# show atmsig 001
```

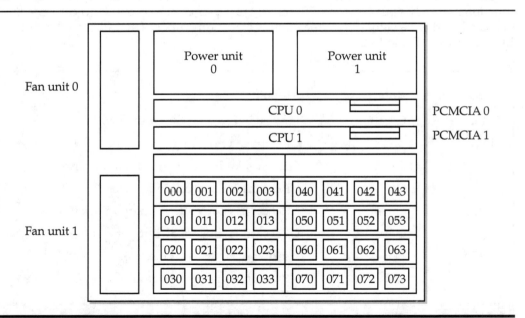

**Figure 18-2.** *C1400 slot and port numbering scheme*

Also notice in Figure 18-2 the presence of an additional card in the slot located just above slot 0; this is known as the LED card, which is used to indicate failures in different hardware components. The slot that contains this card has no official designation, and cannot be used to contain any other line cards. The LED card is optional. Its indicators have the meanings listed in Table 18-3.

## Using a PCMCIA Card

Like the C1200, the C1400 has two PCMCIA slots (two per CPU module), providing support for both a PCMCIA LAN card and a PCMCIA flash card. As is the case with the C1200, the top PCMCIA slot is considered slot 0 and is generally used for the LAN card, while the slot beneath it (slot 1) is generally used for the PCMCIA flash.

# C1600

The C1600 is the largest core Centillion switch currently available from Nortel Networks. The C1400 ATM switch provides a switched core with 10Gbps throughput. It is capable of supporting up to 16 622Mbps OC-12 connections, and up to 64 155Mbps OC-3 connections.

## C1600 Chassis Architecture

The C1600 provides a total of 16 slots for various line cards, as well as two slots for CPU cards in a redundant configuration. In addition, the C1600 has dual power supplies for added redundancy, as well as dual fan trays.

## CPU Switch Card

The redundant CPU cards offer a high degree of reliability; although the C1400 may function normally with only one CPU card, the presence of a second CPU card enables one CPU card to be active, while the other is in standby mode. For a list of the LEDs and their meanings, consult Table 18-2.

| LED | Meaning |
|-----|---------|
| PWR | Device has power. |
| ALM | Hardware failure has occured. |
| FAN0 | Fan 0 is present and active. |
| FAN1 | Fan 1 is present and active. |
| PWR0 | Power supply 0 is present and active. |
| PWR1 | Power supply 1 is present and active. |

**Table 18-3.**   *LED Card Indicators*

Each CPU card is fitted with an RS-232C 9-pin D-Sub connector for establishing terminal sessions with the device, as well as a Reset button for initiating a soft reset of that particular CPU card. In addition, each CPU card is fitted with an RJ-45 Ethernet port, used to download software and to support Telnet sessions.

## Chassis Configuration

Unlike the C100/C50/5000BH product, the C1x00 product utilizes a slot and port number of 0. The C1600 numbers its slots from left to right, moving from top to bottom, not bottom to top (see Figure 18-3). The slots are arranged in four quadrants, with the the bottom-left quadrant beginning with slot 0, and the top-right quadrant beginning with slot 12. Port numbering occurs from left to right.

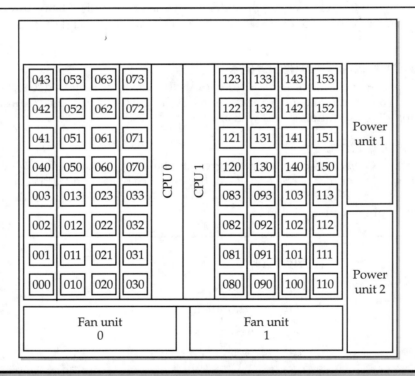

**Figure 18-3.**    *C1600 slot and port numbering scheme*

Each slot/port location is identified by a single, three-digit number, as opposed to the two-digit value used in the C1200. For instance, slot 0, port 1 in the C1200 is referred to in the following manner:

```
C1200# show atmsig 01
```

In the C1600, the same port would be referred to as follows:

```
C1400# show atmsig 001
```

## Using a PCMCIA Card

Like the C1200 and C1400, the C1600 also has two PCMCIA slots (two per CPU module), providing support for both a PCMCIA LAN card and a PCMCIA flash card. As is the case with the C1200, the top PCMCIA slot is considered slot 0 and is generally used for the LAN card, while the slot beneath it (slot 1) is generally used for the PCMCIA flash.

# The
# Complete
# Reference

Nortel
Networks

# Chapter 19

## Configuring PVCs and SPVCs on the C100/C50/5000BH Platforms

The Centillion family is broken down into two main categories; the C100/C50/5000BH platform, and the C1200/C1400/C1600 platform. This chapter covers the first group of products, and Chapter 22 covers the C1x00 line. The C100/C50 and 5000BH have different hardware architectures, but from a configuration standpoint, they are very similar. Each uses SpeedView as its configuration tool, and each uses the same set of command-line interface (CLI) commands for statistics gathering and troubleshooting. For this reason, the configuration and troubleshooting outlined in this chapter are not specific to any one model, except in cases where the information applies only to a specific device, which will be noted accordingly.

## Configuring ATM on the Centillion Switch

Configuration of the Centillion switch is primarily accomplished through SpeedView; this creates a configuration template that will be uploaded to the switch. A word of advice before getting into the specifics of ATM configuration on the Centillion switches: save your configuration. Once the switch has been discovered in SpeedView and has been brought up in Configuration mode, the configuration file can be saved by selecting File | Save Configuration. This saves any configuration information to the hard drive of the SpeedView station in CFG format. Configuration files typically take only 4KB to 15KB of drive space; keeping a backup copy is highly recommended. If the MCP of a switch fails for any reason and can't be recovered, the configuration will be lost if no backup was made, and even if a configuration needs to be rebuilt completely, it's helpful to have a template to work from.

**Note**   *Passwords are not revealed in Offline Configuration mode, so they can't be determined simply by looking at a stored configuration file. If a password is lost, however, a Nortel Networks engineer can recover the password if the configuration file is made available to them. If not, recovering the password is still possible, but will be much more difficult and time-consuming.*

### Configuring CLCs

A Centillion LAN Client (CLC) basically functions as a permanent virtual circuit (PVC), and may be thought of as a PVC for design purposes. CLCs are statically defined ATM circuits, which remain up between switches permanently, until such time as they are removed from the configuration. CLCs come in two varieties; Circuit Saver CLCs and Turbo CLCs. These both are discussed in this section.

Prior to LAN Emulation (LANE) v1, PVCs were the primary method of configuring an ATM mesh. With the advent of LANEv1, Interim InterSwitch Protocol (IISP), Private Network-to-Network Interface (PNNI), LANEv2, and finally MultiProtocol Over ATM (MPOA), not as much call exists for static PVCs any longer, but they are still necessary in some circumstances. For instance, when connecting to a provider's switch, the network administrator generally is given a virtual path identifier/virtual channel identifier (VPI/VCI) value to be used for a static PVC assignment.

## Initial CLC Configuration

CLCs are created exactly as a PVC would be; the CLC is configured with two endpoints, which establish a point-to-point connection between two or more switches. Since a PVC does not necessarily directly connect two switches, and may pass through intermediate switches on the way to the ultimate destination, a Circuit ID is assigned to indicate that the PVC is part of the same circuit, even though it may utilize different VPI/VCI pairs between switches.

A CLC is configured by first selecting ATM Configuration in SpeedView and then clicking Configure CLC. This causes the Centillion LAN Client Configuration window to appear, which will be grayed out for the most part when it first appears. The first thing that you must do is select the CLC type: Circuit Saver or Turbo.

**CIRCUIT SAVER CLC MODE**    With Circuit Saver CLC mode, incoming packets from the legacy portion of the network that are destined for a CLC ATM Vport are first sent to a high-speed packet serializer onboard the MCP, before being transmitted onto the PVC. This process minimizes the number of actual PVCs that must be used by the switch. The added overhead of packets being processed by the packet serializer causes a slight decrease in speed, but allows more simultaneous connections.

**TURBO CLC MODE**    Turbo CLC mode, or GIGArray, utilizes the full virtual path configured for each circuit, and incoming legacy traffic does not go through the added process of the MCP packet serializer. This allows for a faster connection than otherwise would be available in Circuit Saver CLC mode, but it does utilize a greater number of PVCs, and thus fewer simultaneous connections are possible. A total of 15 PVC circuit entries can be made per Turbo Vport.

## Configuring a Vport

From a configuration standpoint, the primary differences between Circuit Saver and Turbo Vports is the VPI/VCI ranges used for each, and the total number of circuits allowed on a single Vport. Both types of Vport are covered in the following sections when discussing Vport configuration.

From the main Centillion LAN Client Configuration window, select a Vport type. This causes the Inter Switch PVC/PVP (permanent virtual path) table to appear, in which the individual circuits can be entered (see Figure 19-1).

A Vport ID also is assigned; this is a value assigned to the Vport by SpeedView, and is only used by SpeedView for purposes of making the Vports unique. In addition, a field appears that allows the Vport to be Enabled or Disabled (with a default of Enabled). A third field appears, allowing a Bridge Group to be selected.

ATM ON NORTEL
NETWORKS

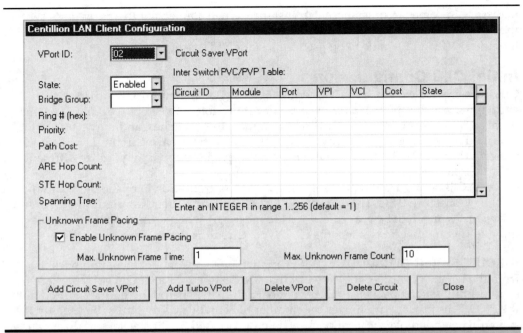

**Figure 19-1.** *Centillion LAN Client Configuration window with active fields*

Clicking the arrow to the right side of the Bridge Group field causes a drop-down menu to appear containing all Bridge Groups configured on that switch. In code version 4.0 or greater, SpeedView refers to Bridge Groups as VLANs, so the Vport needs to be associated with a VLAN, not a Bridge Group.

Depending on whether the Bridge Group (or VLAN) supports token ring or Ethernet, different options appear beneath the Bridge Group (VLAN) field. For the sake of this example, token ring is selected. After a Token Ring Bridge Group (or VLAN) is selected, the following fields appear:

- **Ring#** The ring number, in hex, associated with the PVC. When ATM and Token Ring coexist, the CLC is viewed as a virtual ring, and the Vports that constitute either endpoint of the CLC are viewed as stations on that ring. Both ends of the CLC must be configured with the same ring number.

- **Priority** The port priority associated with 802.1d Spanning Tree. The range is between 0 and 255, with a default of 128.

- **Path Cost** The path cost, used for purposes of determining which ports will block and which will forward in the event of a Spanning Tree loop. Lower-cost ports are favored over higher-cost ports. For this reason, ATM Vports should be given a lower cost than legacy ports, so that in the event of a Spanning Tree loop involving both an ATM link and an Ethernet or token ring link, the slower legacy port will block and the ATM Vport will continue to forward. The range for this value is between 1 and 65535, with a default of 7. Legacy ports default to 10.

- **ARE Hop Count**   Indicates how many hops an All Routes Explorer (ARE) is allowed to traverse before being dropped. Each time an ARE is switched between two rings, it is considered a single hop. This parameter can be set between 1 and 13, with a default of 7. Hop count is checked on the outbound port.

- **STE Hop Count**   Indicates how many hops a Spanning Tree Explorer (STE) is allowed to traverse before being dropped. Each time an STE is switched between two rings, it is considered a single hop. This parameter can be set between 1 and 13, with a default of 7. Hop count is checked on the outbound port.

- **Spanning Tree**   May be set to On, Off, or Block. On and Off, respectively, enable and disable Spanning Tree on that LAN Emulation Client (LEC) Vport. Setting this parameter to block causes the LEC Vport to block all data and all bridge protocol data units (BPDUs), as well as STEs in IBM Spanning Tree mode.

After you select these parameters, the individual circuits must be built for that Vport; these circuits are added directly into the Inter Switch PVC/PVP table.

| Note | *The total number of Turbo and/or Circuit Saver Vports that may exist on a single physical port is 15.* |

**PVC VS. PVP**   Although the Inter Switch PVC/PVP table refers to both PVCs and PVPs, and the main ATM Configuration tab has a Configure PVC/PVP button, these refer to different things, despite having the same name. The Configure PVC/PVP option is used to extend a PVC between ports; this means that a PVC coming in port 1 and then going out port 2 must be configured with a "'passthrough'" PVC/PVP between ports 1 and 2. This indicates that the circuit will continue from port 1 to port 2, and does not terminate on that switch. The Inter Switch PVC/PVP table makes reference to PVC/PVPs because in the case of Circuit Saver Vport, a PVC will be configured, whereas a Turbo Vport circuit will be a PVP.

The Inter Switch PVC/PVP table consists of seven fields:

- **Circuit ID**   Gives a unique identifier to a circuit as a whole; from endpoint to endpoint. For instance, when configuring a CLC between two switches, a VPI/VCI value is assigned, and the same VPI/VCI pair is used at either end of the connection. However, if that CLC is extended further into the network, the VPI/VCI pairs used may change between each interswitch connection (see Figure 19-2).

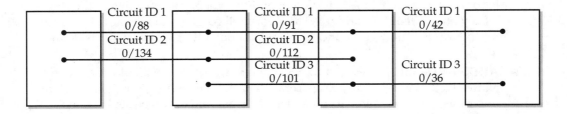

**Figure 19-2.** *Four C100s with three CLCs configured with circuit IDs*

This example includes four C100s, with three CLCs configured; two Circuit Saver and one GIGArray. Notice that although circuit 2 begins using VPI/VCI pair 0/88, this changes as the circuit extends through the network. Since circuits 1 and 3 also extend into the network, on the same links in some cases, some indicator is needed that at switch B, the traffic coming in on VPI/VCI pair 0/88 should be sent over VPI/VCI pair 0/91, and not over 0/42 or 0/101. This indicator is provided though the use of a unique Circuit ID for each PVC in the chain; 0/88 is configured with Circuit ID 2, as is 0/91 on switch B.

- **Module**   Indicates which module the CLC circuit will be built on. This may be any ATM module, and may be either an MCP or a host.

- **Port**   Indicates which port on the defined module the CLC circuit will actually be built on. This may be any ATM port on the previously defined module.

- **VPI**   The VPI to be used for this circuit. If the Vport being configured is a Circuit Saver Vport, then this field automatically defaults to 0. All Circuit Saver Vports use a VPI value of 0 by default, but may be configured with other values between 0 and 15. If the Vport being configured is a Turbo Vport, then this field must be configured with a non-0 value between 1 and 255. The field will default to 1.

- **VCI**   The VCI to be used for this circuit. If the Vport being configured is a Circuit Saver Vport, then this field automatically defaults to 32, because on VPI 0, the first 31 virtual channels have been reserved for signaling purposes by the ATM Forum. The VCI value may be between 32 and 1024. If the Vport being configured is a Turbo Vport, then this field, depending on the code, may still default to 32; however, the first 31 channels technically are reserved only on VPI 0. Values lower than 32 are allowed with a non-0 VPI.

- **Cost**   A reference to the path cost for this virtual connection. Valid values are between 1 and 65535, with a default of 128.
- **State**   The administrative state of the circuit on the Vport. It is possible to have a Vport enabled while some of the circuits configured on that Vport are disabled. Values are enabled and disabled.

To configure a single CLC between two switches, then, you implement the following steps:

1. Select a CLC type, Circuit Saver or Turbo, and create the Vport.
2. Associate the Vport with a Bridge Group, or VLAN, depending on the code version.
3. Configure Vport Spanning Tree and ring parameters (if necessary).
4. Create the circuit itself, by choosing a Circuit ID number. This may be any value between 1 and 256. This number is used to identify this circuit and make it unique from other circuits. For this example, a Circuit ID of 1 is used.
5. Select the module and port numbers; in this case, the module and port number of the connection to the remote switch.
6. Select a VPI/VCI pair in accordance with the rules previously outlined. The cost may be left at default, or, if need be, may be adjusted. The default state of Enabled is accepted in this example.

On the remote switch, the same procedure is followed, using the same Circuit ID (because these are two endpoints of the same circuit) and the same VPI/VCI pair. When the configuration is finished, a single endpoint should look something like the example in Figure 19-3.

This is an example of a token ring Circuit Saver Vport in Bridge Group 1, configured for ring number 0E, and default Spanning Tree and explorer characteristics, with a Circuit ID of 10, and a VPI/VCI assignment of 0/88 on module 1 port 1.

## PVC/PVP Configuration (PVP Passthrough)

In a situation in which a CLC is being built between two switches, and a third switch is positioned between them as a transit switch, then a PVP passthrough must be created, connecting the two ports on the transit switch so that the CLC remains uninterrupted (see Figure 19-4).

In this example, switch A is connected to switch B on module 1, port 1, and switch C is connected to switch B on module 1, port 4. The CLC that is being created extends from switch A to switch C, and does not have a termination point on switch B. To accomplish this, first a circuit must be built from switch A to switch B, as described in the previous section. This circuit may be either a Circuit Saver or a Turbo Vport. Likewise, a circuit must be built between switch C and switch B. This may also be

**Centillion LAN Client Configuration**

VPort ID: `02` ▾   Circuit Saver VPort

Inter Switch PVC/PVP Table:

State: `Enabled` ▾

| Circuit ID | Module | Port | VPI | VCI | Cost | State |
|------------|--------|------|-----|-----|------|-------|
| 10 | 1 | 1 | 0 | 88 | 128 | Enabled |

Bridge Group: `01` ▾

Ring # (hex): `0E`

Priority:

Path Cost: `7`

ARE Hop Count: `7`

STE Hop Count: `7`

Spanning Tree: `On` ▾

Enter an INTEGER in range 1..256 (default = 1)

┌─ Unknown Frame Pacing ──────────────────────────────────
☑ Enable Unknown Frame Pacing

Max. Unknown Frame Time: `1`      Max. Unknown Frame Count: `10`

| Add Circuit Saver VPort | Add Turbo VPort | Delete VPort | Delete Circuit | Close |

**Figure 19-3.** *Centillion LAN Client Configuration window with Vport configured*

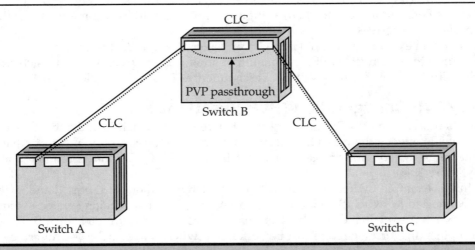

**Figure 19-4.** *PVP passthrough example*

either a Circuit Saver or Turbo Vport, but because these will be two endpoints of the same circuit, ultimately, they must be consistent.

At this point, circuits have been defined from switch A to switch B, and from switch C to switch B; now, they must be connected so that the path is complete from switch A to switch C. Select the ATM Configuration tab in SpeedView and then click the button labeled Configure PVC/PVP. This brings up the ATM PVC/PVP Configuration window (see Figure 19-5).

This window is broken down into a few sections: a field for selecting the Circuit ID; a graph for defining circuit endpoints; a list of configuration options, including circuit enabling/disabling, priority, and Virtual Path; and a graphical representation of the switch and its current contents.

First, you must enter the circuit; click Add Circuit, which causes a Vport ID to be generated and displayed in the field in the top-left corner of the window. This Vport ID is used by SpeedView to distinguish Vports from one another, but it does not need to be consistent with the Vport ID configured on the CLCs going between switches.

Clicking Add Circuit also causes the cursor to jump to the graph in which the passthrough circuits are configured. Select the appropriate module and port number for the first port (module 1, port 1, in this case, the port that switch A is connected to), as well as the appropriate VPI/VCI value. After you do this and select the next row, the port—as displayed in the graphical representation of the switch—becomes highlighted to indicate that this is one of the two ports that are to be connected via the PVC/PVP. Below the first entry, in the row immediately following, add the same information for the destination module and port number (module 1, port 4, in this case, the port connected to switch C). After you do this, the second port also becomes highlighted.

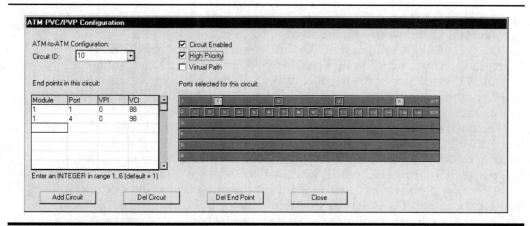

**Figure 19-5.**  *ATM PVC/PVP Configuration window*

When configuring a PVC/PVP between two ports, both ports are defined under the same Circuit ID; a new circuit is created only if more than one actual circuit will be passing between the two ports. By default, the circuit is enabled.

**CIRCUIT ENABLED**    This indicates whether or not the circuit is administratively enabled or disabled.

**HIGH PRIORITY**    The High Priority option may be checked on a circuit-by-circuit basis. Selecting this option on a circuit places a priority for that circuit, in case network congestion occurs. Circuits configured with High Priority are favored over other circuits.

**VIRTUAL PATH**    When a circuit is added, by default, a VPI of 0 is used, as is the case of a Circuit Saver circuit. If you want a Turbo circuit, selecting Virtual Path causes the VCI to default to 0, and the VPI to be incremented to 1.

## Building SPVCs

Soft permanent virtual circuits (SPVCs) are similar to PVCs, but with an important difference. With a PVC, the circuit is manually created from endpoint to endpoint, which means that each switch the circuit traverses must have the entry for that circuit configured on it, as well as any PVC/PVP passthrough circuits. With an SPVC, the endpoints are defined, and the circuit is created dynamically. Unlike a switched virtual circuit (SVC), however, the SPVC remains up permanently after it is established. Once the circuit is in place, if a link that the circuit traverses fails, the SPVC will reestablish the connection with the destination switch, routing around the failed link. To achieve this, the ATM network through which the SPVC will pass must use PNNI as its call routing method.

SPVCs may be built on the Centillion 100/50/5000BH by selecting Configure SPVC from the ATM Configuration tab in SpeedView. This opens the ATM SPVC Configuration window (see Figure 19-6).

The ATM SPVC Configuration window consists of a main SPVC Entry Configuration area, which in turn has Source Border Switch, Destination Border Switch, and Retry Setting areas. Initially, much of this window is grayed out. The first circuit may be created by clicking the Add Circuit button, which causes the configuration fields to become active.

The goal of creating an SPVC is to select a *source border switch*, the switch from which the SPVC will be initiated, and a *destination border switch*, the switch that is actually called by the source border switch. The source border switch is the switch that currently is being configured, which will have the Network Service Access Point (NSAP) of the destination border switch(es) defined, as well as the module number, port number, and VPI/VCI pair associated with the SPVC that will act as the first endpoint. After this first endpoint is defined, no other VPI/VCI pairs need to be defined, although they may be.

Configuration for an SPVC occurs on the source border switch only, except that the destination border switch must have the ingress port configured with a status of

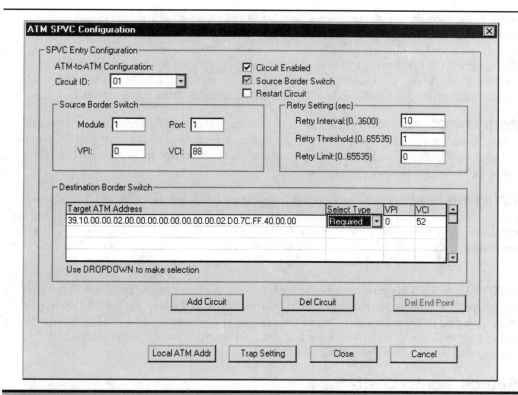

**Figure 19-6.** *ATM SPVC Configuration window*

Enabled, so that it is ready to receive the SPVC; the destination border switch is the called party, and requires no actual configuration other than enabling the correct port. It will accept the SPVC call, once received.

 *Any port that is associated with an SPVC must be configured with PNNI signaling. SPVCs are not supported over non-PNNI links. In addition, the status for the appropriate port on both the source and destination switches must be enabled; this is done by clicking Local Address and then setting the correct Module and Port status to Enable.*

## SPVC Entry Configuration

This portion of the ATM SPVC Configuration window displays the Circuit ID, which is a value generated by SpeedView for purposes of maintaining uniqueness between

SPVCs. By default, the circuit is enabled, and the Circuit Enabled box is checked. The box immediately beneath the Circuit Enabled box is the Source Border Switch box, which is grayed out, but checked—the destination border switch requires no actual SPVC configuration (except to set the addresses as enabled to make them reachable), so the switch being configured for an SPVC is automatically assumed to be the source border switch, and thus the Source Border Switch box is checked by default.

**RETRY INTERVAL**    If the initial SPVC call setup fails, this indicates the amount of time, in seconds, that the switch will wait before attempting to set up the SPVC again. A value of 0 in this case is used if no retry attempts are to occur. The range for this value is between 0 and 3600 seconds.

**RETRY THRESHOLD**    By setting the Retry Threshold, the switch can be configured to not consider every failed SPVC setup an error and log it as such, and instead log an error only if a certain threshold is actually reached. If the number of failed SPVC setups exceeds the Retry Threshold, a failure is indicated in the Statistics screen. The range for this value is 0 to 65535, and a value of 0 actually disables the SPVC alarm.

**RETRY LIMIT**    This parameter defines how many attempts the switch will make to set up an SPVC before assuming that all viable paths to the destination are down, and thus make no more attempts. This value may be set between 0 and 65535. Setting this value to 0 indicates that no retry limit is set, and that the switch will never stop attempting to establish the SPVC.

## Source Border Switch

The configuration applying to the source border switch includes the module and port number that the SPVC will be originated from, as well as the VPI/VCI pair that will serve as the first SPVC endpoint (the other endpoint will be established on the destination border switch).

## Destination Border Switch

The destination border switch is the switch that will be the remote endpoint for the SPVC. The full 20-byte ATM address of the target switch must be configured in the Destination Border Switch table. The ATM address that must be inserted into this field can be determined by bringing up the configuration of the destination switch and clicking Local Address from the main SPVC Configuration window. There, the individual addresses are listed according to slot and port. In addition, the Select Type field must be configured; clicking this field causes a drop-down arrow to appear in the right side of the field; clicking this arrow presents drop-down menu options of Required or Any.

Setting the Required option indicates that the receiving switch must utilize a specific VPI/VCI pair when receiving the SPVC. If this option is selected, that VPI/VCI pair must be configured in the VPI and VCI fields following the Select Type field. The Any option indicates that the destination border switch may use any VPI/VCI pair that is available.

> *As of the time of this publication, SPVCs may be created between the C100/50/5000BH and the C1200/1400/1600. However, the C100/50/5000BH must initiate the call, because it doesn't currently support UNI4.0, which the C1x00 uses when initiating the SPVC call. The C100/50/5000BH supports point-to-point SPVCs only, and not point-to-multipoint.*

**TRAP SETTING**   Clicking the Trap Setting button at the base of the ATM SPVC Configuration window brings up the SPVC Trap Setting dialog box, which has two parameters to set:

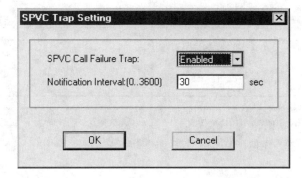

- ■ **SPVC Traps**   May be either Enabled or Disabled. If Enabled, the Notification Interval may be set to indicate how often traps should be sent.

- ■ **Notification Interval**   May be set between 0 to 3,600 seconds, with a default of 30 seconds.

# Troubleshooting CLCs and SPVCs

Troubleshooting CLCs can be relatively straightforward; perhaps the easiest way to determine the current state of a CLC is to bring up the Statistics window in SpeedView. From the main Statistics window, select the ATM PVC tab. This displays the InterSwitch PVC Status table, which includes all configured PVCs, as well as their current status (see Figure 19-7).

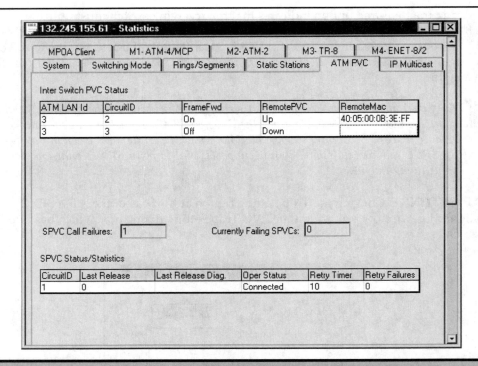

**Figure 19-7.**   *Statistics window displaying PVC status*

The information displayed includes a unique LAN identifier, the Circuit ID for each circuit, the frame forwarding state, the status of the remote PVC, and, if the PVC is up and functioning properly, the registration of the remote MAC address of the destination switch. This is not necessarily the MAC address of the directly connected switch, but of the switch that the PVC terminates at.

If the CLC is functioning correctly, the FrameFwd state should be On, the RemotePVC field should be Up, and the RemoteMac should be listed.

## CLC Errors

The ATM port-level statistics are another thing to check if a CLC is not coming up correctly. From the Statistics window, select the appropriate module, and then Rcv errs. This causes the tab to expand, displaying two error counters:

- **Hdr CRC errs**   Indicates the number of times a cell failed its Header Error Check (HEC), indicating that the cell's header is corrupted and therefore the cell is invalid. This generally indicates either a physical-layer problem, such as a bad fiber or bad remote transmitter, or a signaling mismatch.

- **Unknown vpi/vci** Indicates the number of times a PVC was attempted to be built between the receiving port and the remote port, but the remote port requested a VPI/VCI pair that the receiving port was not configured for. This indicates the VPI/VCI pairs on either end of the connection do not match, and must be set to the same values.

## Troubleshooting SPVCs

The current SPVC status can be viewed from the CLI by issuing the following command:

```
WiringCloset_K:Command>show spvc all
***Num SPVCs configured = 1, Operational SPVCs = 1, Failing calls = 0
***Soft PVC traps = DISABLE,  Trap notification interval = 30

ID = 1,  Circuit = ENABLE,  Status = CONNECTED, Border switch = SOURCE
Source ATM addr = 39.10.10.00.00.00.00.00.00.00.00.00.53.10.3A.E0.43.55.01

Module:port = 1:1,  vpi:vci = 0:71,  Target endpoints = 1

Target ATM addr = 39.20.20.00.00.00.00.00.00.00.00.00.D2.31.29.88.35.E2.01

Target sel = REQUIRED,  vpi:vci = 0:100
```

The preceding SPVC is the only one currently configured on the switch, and is in an operational state. The switch from which the CLI command was issued is the source border switch 39.10.10.00.00.00.00.00.00.00.00.00.53.10.3A.E0.43.55.01, with a target address of 39.20.20.00.00.00.00.00.00.00.00.00.D2.31.29.88.35.E2.01. It is enabled and connected. The output indicates the module and port number the SPVC is associated with on the source border switch, as well as the VPI/VCI pair selected for the originating endpoint. This particular example uses a required VPI/VCI pair for the destination border switch (0/100), which is also listed.

A summary of all SPVCs configured on a certain switch, as well as their current states, can be obtained by issuing the following command from the CLI:

```
WiringCloset_J:Command>show spvc atmaddr all
Card port        ATM address                          user config state
1    1    39.10.00.00.00.00.00.00.00.00.00.00.11.21.92.01.3E.22.01 enable REACHABLE
1    1    39.11.00.00.00.00.00.00.00.00.00.00.32.A2.E0.11.28.76.01 enable REACHABLE
1    2    39.20.00.00.00.00.00.00.00.00.00.00.87.35.23.82.E2.AA.01 enable REACHABLE
```

This indicates the ATM address associated with the SPVC, as well as the module and port the address is accessible through. *User config* indicates the administrative state of the SPVC (enabled in this case), whereas *state* indicates the actual state of the SPVC (REACHABLE or UNREACHABLE). If the User config state is disabled, the port can be enabled by clicking Local Address from the main SPVC Configuration window.

If an ATM address is listed as being UNREACHABLE, make sure that port level signaling is correct, that PNNI is configured, and that the full path between source and destination is clear.

The
Complete
Reference

Nortel
Networks

# Chapter 20

## Configuring LANE on the C100/C50/5000BH Platform

The main components of LAN Emulation (LANE) that must be configured are the LAN Emulation Server (LES), the Broadcast and Unknown Server (BUS), any LAN Emulation Clients (LECs) that are to service the different Emulated LANs (ELANs), and, optionally, a LAN Emulation Configuration Server (LECS). The details of how these entities interact together is detailed in Chapter 13.

This chapter deals primarily with the configuration of LANE on the Centillion platform. The order of configuring these services does not really matter, but beginning configuration with the LES/BUS pair is suggested, simply because the LES address must be referenced in the LECS (if used), and, if a LECS is not being used, the LES address needs to be statically configured in the LEC. Either way necessitates generating a usable LES address for any ELANs that are to be configured, so it makes sense to begin with the LES/BUS pair.

# Configuring ATM Signaling

Most ATM networks in production today are running LANE, which requires configuring a variety of services, beginning with activating ATM signaling on the switch itself. When signaling is configured, the administrator is prompted to configure an NSAP prefix for the switch, which will be used by all ATM LANE, IISP, PNNI, and MPOA services.

ATM signaling is first activated through SpeedView, by selecting the ATM Configuration tab from the main Configuration window. From this tab, select the first button, Configure Signaling, which opens the Configure Signaling dialog box.

```
┌─────────────────────────────────────────────┐
│ Configure Signaling                          │
│                                              │
│  ☑ ATM Forum                                 │
│         ⊙ Full LANE Services                 │
│         ○ LEC only - No IISP                 │
│         ○ ATM switch only                    │
│      ATM Prefix:                             │
│      ┌─────────────────────────────────────┐ │
│      │39.10.00.00.01.00.00.00.00.00.00.00.00│ │
│      └─────────────────────────────────────┘ │
│  ☑ Status Enquiry                            │
│                                              │
│     Status Enquiry Period    ┌──────────┐    │
│                              │600        │    │
│                              └──────────┘    │
│        ┌────────────┐   ┌────────────┐       │
│        │    OK      │   │   Cancel   │       │
│        └────────────┘   └────────────┘       │
└─────────────────────────────────────────────┘
```

Here, signaling may be activated by clicking the ATM Forum box. This causes the other fields to become active, and sets a default 13-byte NSAP prefix of 39, followed by all 0s. Alter the NSAP prefix to the desired prefix. If this is the first time the prefix is being configured, all other services on the switch (LES/BUS, PNNI Node ID, and so forth) will use this prefix. If services are built on the switch and then the prefix is changed at some point, a window pops up, warning that the prefix is different from that configured on any other LANE or call-routing services, and asking whether other instances of the NSAP prefix should be changed to match the new value.

## Selecting a Service Type

The Centillion 100/50/5000BH can serve in a variety of ways within the ATM mesh. Once ATM signaling is active, a service type must be selected from the following three options:

- **Full LANE Services**   Allows the switch to support full LANE services; a LES/BUS, LECS, LEC, or any combination of these services may be configured on the switch.

- **LEC Only – No IISP**   When a switch is configured for LEC only, it will support only a LANE Client, and none of the other services. However, if this LEC is not connected to the rest of the LANE network via an IISP or PNNI link, its connection will actually be a UNI connection, configured for the user side. When this configuration is used, the entire switch acts as a UNI device. Because only one UNI user-side port is permitted on any one switch, the remaining ports on any other ATMSpeed modules may not be used.

- **ATM Switch Only**   This configuration may be used if the switch will be a transit switch only and will not host any LANE services nor any LANE Clients. A switch configured in this way will not support any LANE services, but will support call routing mechanisms such as IISP or PNNI.

After ATM signaling is activated and the switch type is selected, the rest of the LANE services may be configured.

*Beginning with SpeedView 4.0, the Status Enquiry option is present beneath the ATM NSAP Prefix field. This indicates whether SVCs will be checked by the switch to see if they are still operational. If this option is selected, the Status Enquiry Period must be defined; this is the amount of time, in seconds, between checking the SVC status.*

# Creating ELANs

An ELAN consists of a LES and a BUS. LAN Emulation Clients join these services, and all LECs that join a common LES and BUS are considered to be in the same ELAN. Before proceeding, you should decide how many ELANs you will use, and which switches will require representation in which ELANs.

All ELANs may be configured either on the same switch or dispersed among different switches. For purposes of fault tolerance, LES/BUS pairs may be distributed over several switches, so that the loss of any one switch does not cause all ELANs to stop functioning, or, cooperating LES/BUS pairs can be configured for redundancy and load sharing.

## Configuring the LES/BUS

LES/BUS pairs on the Centillion 100/50 or 5000BH platforms are always co-located, meaning they can be configured only as a pair on the same switch. If redundancy is desired, a cooperating pair may be configured to act as a fail-over and to load-share.

To configure the LES/BUS pair, first model the switch they are to be built on in SpeedView. From the main configuration window, select ATM Configuration. From the main ATM Configuration tab, select Configure LES/BUS, which opens the LAN Emulation Server (LES/BUS) window (see Figure 20-1).

Upon the initial configuration, this window is blank. Click Add LES/BUS, which automatically generates an ATM address for the LES and the BUS, using the Network Service Access Point (NSAP) prefix defined in the ATM Signaling window, along with an automatically generated End System Identifier (ESI). The NSAP prefix and ESI for the LES and BUS will be identical; by default, the selector byte will always be 01 for the LES and 02 for the BUS. A LES Internal ID, a unique ID associated with this LES, also is generated automatically. This ID increments each time a LES/BUS pair is added on the switch.

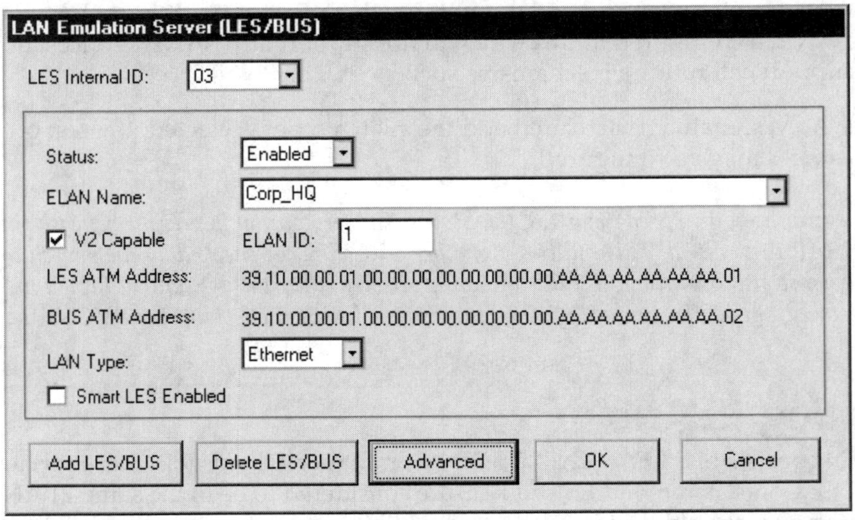

**Figure 20-1.**    *LAN Emulation Server (LES/BUS) window*

Clicking the ELAN Name field enables you to configure a case-sensitive name of up to 32 characters that will be associated with this ELAN. This name must match exactly the name that will be configured on a LECS, if used, as well as for any LECs that will join this ELAN.

A LAN type must also be chosen. Clicking the arrow to the right of the LAN Type field causes a drop-down menu to appear, from which Ethernet or Token Ring may be selected, depending on the type of legacy LAN this ELAN is to support.

Beneath the LAN Type field is a box to select Smart LES Enabled. When enabled, this causes the LES to look up the LAN destination for every LE_ARP that it receives. If the LAN destination has previously been registered with the LES, then the LES forms the LE_ARP response and sends it to the requesting LEC. If the LAN destination has not been previously registered, then the request is flooded over the control channels to each LEC, to resolve the address. When this feature is disabled, each incoming request is flooded for address resolution.

## Advanced LES Parameters

From the main LES/BUS Configuration window, the advanced LES parameters can be accessed by clicking Advanced, which opens the LES/BUS Advanced Configuration window (see Figure 20-2).

This window is broken into four basic parts: alteration of the LES/BUS addresses, LES/BUS Control Parameters, the Unique Server ID, and Other Cooperating LES/BUS pairs.

The top portion of the window contains four fields: two for LES ATM Address and two for BUS ATM Address. The leftmost of the two fields in either case represents the 13-octet NSAP prefix. This prefix may be altered here, but remember that the LES and BUS NSAP prefix must match the prefix of the switch on which they are configured. If the NSAP prefix is altered in this window, then all other instances of that NSAP prefix configured on that switch must also be changed. Previously configured call routes may also become invalid, making the LES/BUS services unreachable, so if a change is made here, be sure to update everything.

The rightmost field is the ESI and selector byte. These can be altered without concern for the prefix of the switch. As long as the new ESI and selector byte are reflected to match the change in the LECS, or, if the LEC will point directly at the LES, the LEC must be configured with the new ESI and selector byte.

> **Note** *One method of keeping LES/BUS services recognizable at a glance during troubleshooting is to alter the ESI of each to something easy to recognize, such as all A's, as in this example:*
>
> *39.10.10.00.00.00.00.00.00.00.00.00.AA.AA.AA.AA.AA.AA.01.*

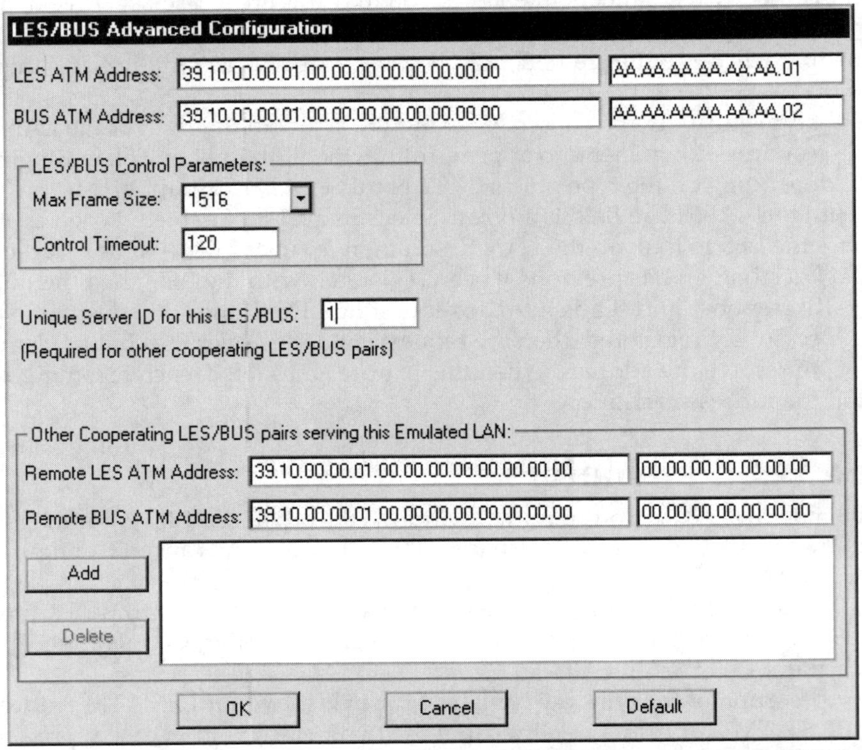

**Figure 20-2.** *LES/BUS Advanced Configuration window*

The LES/BUS Control Parameters consist of two fields: the Max Frame Size, and the Control Timeout field. The Max Frame Size field indicates to the LES the maximum transmit unit (MTU) size that is associated with the legacy frames. This value defaults to 1516 in an Ethernet ELAN, and 4544 in a token ring ELAN. Be certain that this value does not exceed the actual MTU size configured for the legacy network; although the frames will go through the segmentation and reassembly (SAR) process when being transported over the ATM portion of the network, the LANE components need to be aware of what the maximum frame size will be when the frames are reassembled.

## LANE Version 2 Capability

If Multi-Protocol Over ATM (MPOA) is going to be configured, then the LES for each ELAN that will participate in MPOA must be LANE 2-capable. Beginning with code version 4.0, each LES must be designated as V1 or V2, defaulting to LANEv1.

When using code version 4.0, a check box labeled V2 Capable appears just below ELAN Name in the LAN Emulation Server (LES/BUS) window. Checking this box indicates that the LES will be V2-capable, and causes another field to appear next to it, labeled ELAN ID. This ID uniquely identifies the ELAN, and this value is obtained from the LECS as a Time Length Value (TLV) by each LEC joining the ELAN. This parameter is used in conjunction with LANEv2's LLC-Multiplexing support; because a single virtual control channel (VCC) is capable of carrying traffic for multiple ELANs, the ELAN ID is compared against the value obtained from the LECS during the join phase. If the values do not match, then the LEC is considered a mismatch for that ELAN and is discarded.

> **Note**    *Remember, a V2-capable ELAN and LEC are required for MPOA to function correctly.*

## Configuring Cooperating LES/BUS Pairs

The lower portion of the LES/BUS Advanced Configuration window consists of a field for a Unique Server ID, as well as two fields each for a Remote LES ATM Address and Remote BUS ATM Address (each ATM Address field is broken into a field for the NSAP prefix and a field for the ESI and selector byte).

To configure cooperating LES/BUS pairs, first the cooperating pair must be built on another switch, following the procedures previously outlined in this chapter. The remote pair will have a different NSAP prefix (the NSAP prefix of whatever switch they were built on) and may or may not have a different ESI; the unique NSAP prefix is enough to establish uniqueness, so the ESI may be the same, if this makes managing them easier. Whatever the addresses associated with the remote LES/BUS pair are, the ELAN name must be the same, as well as any other control parameters.

Enter the remote LES and BUS address in the fields provided under the heading Other Cooperating LES/BUS pairs serving this Emulated LAN. After you enter both addresses, click Add to add the cooperating pairs into the LES/BUS table. The reason for this setup is that an ELAN is not limited to a single cooperating pair; up to four cooperating pairs may be used, each configured on a different switch. Whether a single cooperating pair or multiple cooperating pairs are being used, the concept is the same. Each LES/BUS pair, in the LES/BUS Advanced Configuration window, must have the LES/BUS addresses of each cooperating pair entered into its table. These pairs consult this table upon initialization, and attempt to contact each remote pair described there. Cooperating pairs will form a VCC between them, so each pair must know the addresses of any other cooperating pairs.

### Unique Server ID

Each LES/BUS pair in a set of cooperating pairs must be assigned a Unique Server ID. The exact values to use in this field sometimes is a point of confusion. The rule is as follows: each LES/BUS pair in a cooperating pair must have a different value for the

ATM ON NORTEL
NETWORKS

Unique Server ID, but LES/BUS pairs on the same switch that are not cooperating may share the same value. This means that if two switches with a single ELAN are configured, with two cooperating LES/BUS pairs, one on each switch, then one pair might be configured with a Unique Server ID of 1, and the other pair might be configured with a Unique Server ID of 2. It doesn't matter what the values are as long as they differ. If the same two switches had three ELANs configured, each with two cooperating LES/BUS pairs, one on each switch, then each LES/BUS pair on the first switch could be given a Unique Server ID of 1, and each pair on the second switch could be given a Unique Server ID of 2. In that scenario, each ELAN has two LES/BUS pairs cooperating, one with a Unique Server ID of 1, and the other with a Unique Server ID of 2 (see Figure 20-3).

**Note**  *If cooperating LES/BUS pairs are configured, then each pair must be defined for that ELAN in the LECS, if one is being used, or on the LEC, if the LECS is to be bypassed. If only one pair is configured on the LECS or LEC, and the pair that is defined fails for any reason, the LEC will never gain knowledge of the cooperating pair, and will never join the redundant services.*

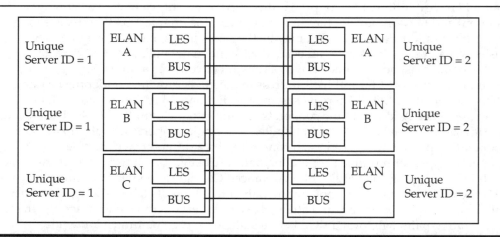

**Figure 20-3.**   *Two switches directly connected showing cooperating pair assignments and Unique Server IDs*

## Configuring the LECS

Although a LECS is not required, you may want to utilize one. To build a LECS, select the ATM Configuration tab and then click the Configure LECS button. This opens the main LECS Configuration window (see Figure 20-4).

This window is broken into two basic sections: the LECS ATM Address information, located at the top of the window, and the ELAN information, located below that, about a third of the way down.

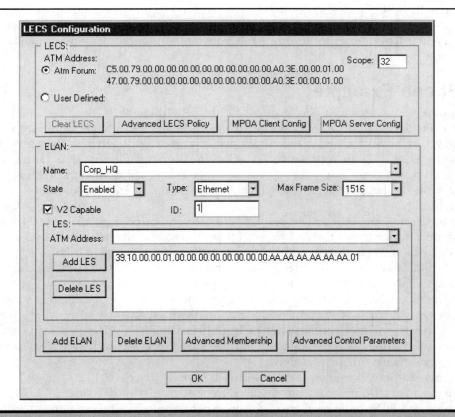

**Figure 20-4.** *The LECS Configuration window*

The LECS address information consists of a LECS Address field, and, in code version 3.0 or greater, the Scope field, located in the upper-right corner. By default, the LECS Address field is blank. Clicking this Address field causes the well-known address (WKA) to appear, because this is the address used by default. If this address is used, be certain to reflect this when configuring any LEC that will use the LECS; this is outlined in greater detail later in this chapter, under the section "Configuring a LEC." The LECS address may also be changed from the WKA to a user-defined address. This may be done as long as the address is also reflected in the LEC configuration.

The Scope field is only of relevance in a Private Network to Network Interface (PNNI) network with multiple hierarchies. This field indicates how high into the hierarchy the LECS address should be advertised. By limiting how far up the hierarchy a particular LECS address should be advertised, certain peer groups can be prevented from using it. This allows for multiple LECS instances, whereby each is accessible only by certain peer groups.

## LECS Scope Example

This example includes four peer groups: 39.10.10, 39.10.11, 39.20.20, and 39.20.21, and three levels of PNNI hierarchy. Peer groups 39.10.10 and 39.10.11 are represented as logical group nodes (LGNs) in the parent peer group of 39.10, whereas peer groups 39.20.20 and 39.20.21 are represented as LGNs in parent peer group 39.20. The LGNs from each parent peer group are represented themselves as LGNs at the highest hierarchical level in peer group 39, which all peer groups share as a common hierarchical level.

In this situation, at the lowest level, nodes are configured with a level of 24, because the significant portion of their addresses for peer group membership falls into a masked level of 24 (six 4-byte nibbles equals 24). The next-highest parent peer groups consist of LGNs with a level of 16, while the highest peer group level, peer group 39, consists of LGNs configured with a level of 8 (see Figure 20-5).

In this example, nodes from each peer group must be able to reach every other node in every other peer group. For this reason, their advertisements must reach the highest hierarchical level, because that is the only level all peer groups share in common; therefore, the scope of each node is set to 8, because this is the highest level at which the advertisements must be received.

In this example, however, the ELANs used in peer groups 39.10.10 and 39.10.11 are, for the most part, different from those used in peer groups 39.20.20 and 39.20.21, and so two separate LECSs have been created; one in peer group 39.10.10 and one in 39.20.20. Each LECS uses the WKA, but each is configured with different ELANs. As the LECs configured on nodes in peer groups 39.10.10 and 39.10.11 are attempting to connect with their LECS to obtain LES information, they must be prevented from inadvertently being routed to the LECS in peer group 39.20.20, because that group doesn't contain the correct ELAN information for the 39.10.10 and 39.10.11 peer groups.

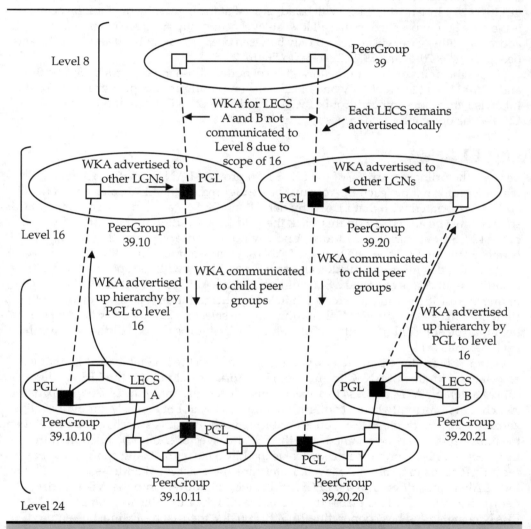

**Figure 20-5.**    *LECS address being advertised only with a scope of 16*

One solution in this case is to set the scope of each LECS to 16, which avoids having the LECS (configured in peer group 39.10.10) from ever being advertised in peer group 39; it will be advertised as high as peer group 39.10, and no higher. The same holds true for the LECS configured in peer group 39.20.20; it will be advertised only as high as peer group 39.20. Since neither LECS will be advertised at the highest hierarchical level, which is the only parent peer group that all lowest-level peer groups share in common, the LECS address in either case will be passed only between peer groups 39.10.10 and 39.10.11, and peer groups 39.20.20 and 39.20.21 (refer to Figure 20-5).

From the point of view of the lowest-level nodes, those in peer groups 39.10.10 and 39.10.11, will learn of only one LECS—the one configured in peer group 39.10.10. Likewise, the nodes in peer groups 39.20.20 and 39.20.21 will learn of only one LECS—the one configured in peer group 39.20.20.

# Adding ELANs

Because the primary purpose of the LECS is to provide LAN Emulation Clients with their LES information, each ELAN must be configured on the LECS, along with the LES address associated with that ELAN. By default, no ELANs are configured on the LECS, so they must be added. To do this, click the Add ELAN button in the bottom-left corner of the LECS Configuration window. A new window appears, prompting for the ELAN Name. Enter the ELAN name for the ELAN that you want to add to the LECS.

Entering this information adds an entry for an ELAN with the specified name; by default, the ELAN is assigned a State of Enabled, a LAN Type of Ethernet, and a Max Frame Size of 1516. You can alter these fields by clicking the drop-down arrow to the right of each. A LAN Type of Token Ring may be selected, and the Max Frame Size field may be adjusted (default for Token Ring is 4544, the same MTU that the switch itself defaults to).

After you set these parameters, you must enter into the LES table the LES that is associated with this ELAN. Clicking the ATM Address field under the LES header causes a default ATM address to appear. This address is simply the NSAP prefix of the switch that is currently being configured, followed by an ESI and selector byte of all zeros. If the LES for the ELAN you are entering is on the same switch as the LECS, then the NSAP prefix may be retained, and the ESI and selector should be filled in. If the LES does not reside on the same switch as the LECS currently being configured, then the NSAP needs to be altered as well. Determine the exact ATM address of the LES for the ELAN being added into the LECS, and enter that address into the ATM Address field. Click Add LES. This places the LES entry into the LES table for that ELAN. If the ELAN being added has cooperating LES/BUS pairs, then each LES must be entered into this table.

| Note | *If cooperating pairs for the ELAN are being configured, add the LES addresses in order of preference, beginning with the LES that each LEC should attempt to join first. Each LEC first attempts to join the first LES on the list, and then, if the first attempt fails, tries each in turn. If all attempts fail, the LEC begins again with the first LES listed.* |

## LANEv2 Capability

Beginning with code version 4.0, each ELAN configured in the LECS must be specified as being either LANEv1- or LANEv2-capable. By default, all ELANs comply with LANEv1. When using code version 4.0, a check box is available in the LECS Configuration window, labeled V2 Capable. By selecting this box, the ELAN being configured is noted as being V2-capable, and another field appears, labeled ELAN ID. This ELAN ID should match the value configured on the V2 LES itself in the LES/BUS Configuration window. This value will be passed along as a TLV to any LEC joining the ELAN in question, contained in the LE_CONFIGURE_RESPONSE over the Configuration Direct VCC during the join phase. The LEC will use this value and compare it against any incoming traffic; anything not matching the specified value is discarded.

LANEv2 capability, as well as individual ELAN IDs, are configured on an ELAN-by-ELAN basis within the LECS. Not all ELANs are required to utilize the same version of LANE.

## Advanced LECS Policy

Beneath the LECS Address field is the Advanced LECS Policy button, which you click to bring up the LECS Policy window (see Figure 20-6).

This window consists of three check boxes, labeled By ATM Address, By MAC Address, and By Token Ring Route Descriptor. Selecting any of these boxes causes the selection to appear in the large field that dominates the window. These options relate to the LEC registration with the LECS. When a LEC initializes, if using a LECS, it will initiate a Configuration Direct VCC to the LECS. Over this control channel, the LEC will communicate information about itself to the LECS, including the ELAN name for the ELAN that it wants to join. The LECS examines the information given to it by the LEC, to see whether it is viable for membership in the ELAN that it is requesting. For instance, a LEC attempting to join can be denied membership with its LES by the LECS if its ELAN name is incorrect or the MTU size on the switch is inconsistent with that of the ELAN. The Advanced LECS Policy selections enable you to configure additional parameters regarding LEC registration. These choices are used in conjunction with the LECS Advanced Membership options, accessible by clicking the LECS Advanced Membership button from the main LECS Configuration window:

- **By ATM Address and Mask**   Indicates that only LECs configured with certain ATM addresses are permitted to join the selected LES. The list of allowed ATM addresses is configured in the LECS Advanced Membership window.

- **By MAC Address**   Indicates that only LECs with certain MAC addresses are allowed to join the selected LES address.

- **By Token Ring Route Descriptor**   Indicates that only LECs configured for the appropriate ring number and using the appropriate Bridge ID are allowed membership in the selected LES.

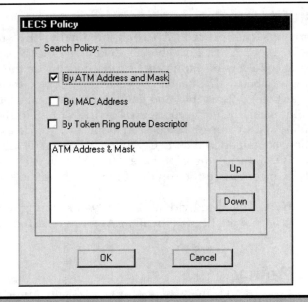

**Figure 20-6.** *LECS Policy window*

## LECS Advanced Membership

The LECS Advanced Membership options are used in conjunction with those configured in the Advanced LECS Policy window. For instance, if you select the By ATM Address option in the Advance LECS Policy window, then the actual ATM addresses that are allowed registration with the specified LES are configured in the LECS Advanced Membership window.

To access the LECS Advanced Membership window, first select the LES with which these control parameters will be associated, by selecting the appropriate ELAN from the drop-down menu in the ELAN field and then highlighting the LES address in the LES table. After you do this, click Advanced Membership, which brings up the LECS Advanced Membership window (see Figure 20-7).

The ELAN name and the LES address that were selected in the main LECS Configuration window will appear at the top of the LECS Advanced Membership window. Beneath that are the three Advanced Membership options discussed next.

**TOKEN RING ROUTE DESCRIPTOR** This option has two fields: Ring # (hex), which should be configured in hex, and the Bridge # (hex), which is also in hex. The ring number should match the number associated with the ELAN that the LEC is attempting to join. This information can be obtained from the LAN Emulation Client Configuration window, from the main ATM Configuration tab. The bridge number is the Bridge ID associated with the switch the LEC is configured on. To obtain this information, go to the switch the LEC is configured on, and select the Switching Mode tab from the main Configuration view. When the correct bridge group (or VLAN, in code version 4.0 and higher) configured for source route bridging or source route transparent bridging is selected, the bridge number is displayed (in hex) about midway down the window. After you configure these parameters, click Add to cause the configured route descriptors to be added to the route descriptor table.

**MAC ADDRESS**    Clicking the MAC Address field causes a default MAC address of all zeros to appear. This MAC must be altered to match the MAC of a LEC that is permitted to join this LES. Clicking Add causes the configured address to be added to the MAC address table.

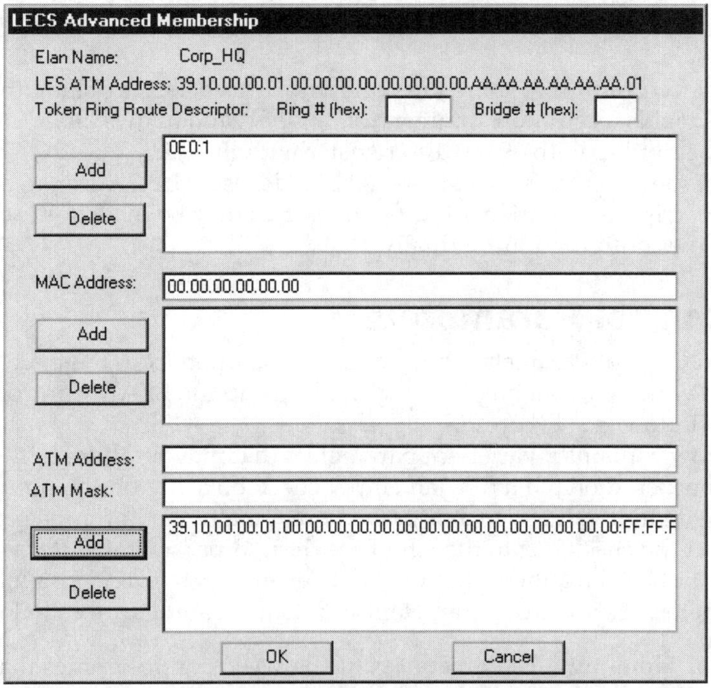

**Figure 20-7.**    *LECS Advanced Membership window*

**ATM ADDRESS**    This option has two fields associated with it: the ATM Address field and the ATM Mask field. Clicking the ATM Address field causes a default ATM address of all zeros to appear. This ATM address can be altered to match the ATM address of any LEC that will be allowed to join this LES. To allow a range of ATM addresses to be used, the ATM Mask may be placed against the address. For example, in a network in which the following LEC addresses are used:

```
39.00.01.00.00.01.01.00.21.00.00.00.00.A2.6B.C4.AF.00.00.00
39.00.01.00.00.02.01.00.21.00.00.00.00.A2.6B.C4.AF.00.00.00
39.00.01.00.00.02.02.00.21.00.00.00.00.A2.6B.C4.AF.00.00.00
39.00.01.00.00.02.02.00.22.00.00.00.00.A2.6B.C4.AF.00.00.00
39.00.01.00.00.01.02.00.11.00.00.00.00.A2.6B.C4.AF.00.00.00
```

All addresses may be summarized by a single entry, by configuring the following ATM address and ATM mask:

```
39.00.01.00.00.00.00.00.00.00.00.00.00.00.00.00.00.00.00.00
FF.FF.FF.00.00.00.00.00.00.00.00.00.00.00.00.00.00.00.00.00
```

Because all five addresses share the same first three octets, masking the first 24 bits of the address yields a common summary of 39.00.01, and allows all LECs utilizing an NSAP prefix beginning with 39.00.01 to register with this LES.

For each of the preceding selections—ATM Address, MAC Address, and Token Ring Route Descriptor—a variety of different entries may be made for each LES, and each LES may be configured individually.

# Advanced Control Parameters

The Advanced Control Parameters button may be selected from the main LECS Configuration window. Selecting this option brings up the ELAN Control Parameter (TLV Table) window (see Figure 20-8).

This window contains a variety of parameters that may be altered. By default, each parameter is bordered on the left by an empty check box, and on the right by a field containing the default value, which is grayed out. To alter any of these parameters, you must select the check box to the left of the desired parameter. After you select the parameter's check box, the rightmost field becomes active, and you may alter the default parameter. The control parameters and their meanings are as follows:

■ **Control Time-out**    The timeout value between control frames that require responses to be altered. This may be set between 10 and 300 seconds, with a default timeout period of 120 seconds.

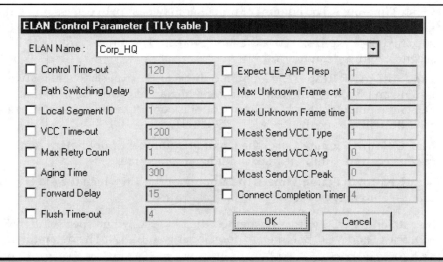

**Figure 20-8.**   *ELAN Control Parameter (TLV table) window*

- **Path Switching Delay**   The amount of time that passes between sending a frame to the BUS, and the LEC determining that this frame was either received or discarded. This can be used to bypass the Flush protocol. The range is 1 to 8 seconds, with a default of 1.

- **Local Segment ID**   The Local Segment ID (ring number) associated with this ELAN. This parameter is used only with token ring ELANs in a source route bridged environment. This value is in decimal.

- **VCC Time-out**   The amount of time that passes between a Data Direct VCC becoming idle and it being torn down due to inactivity. The range is 1 to 500 minutes, with a default of 20 minutes.

- **Max Retry Count**   The maximum number of times a LEC may reissue an LE_ARP_REQUEST when no LE_ARP_RESPONSE has come back. The range is 0 to 2, with a default of 1.

- **Aging Time**   The maximum amount of time a LEC will maintain an entry in its LE_ARP cache without verification that the MAC to ATM relationship is still valid. The range is from 10 to 300 minutes, with a default of 300.

- **Forward Delay**   The amount of time a nonlocal MAC address will remain in the LEC's LE_ARP cache without being refreshed.

- **Flush Time-out**    The amount of time that may pass between issuing an LE_FLUSH_REQUEST and receiving an LE_FLUSH_RESPONSE. If the specified time expires, recovery action is taken. The range is from 1 to 30 seconds, with a default of 1.

- **Expect LE_ARP Resp**    The amount of time a LEC expects to wait between issuing an LE_ARP_REQUEST and receiving an LE_ARP_RESPONSE. Depending on what the Max Retry Count is configured for, if this timer expires, the LEC will reissue the LE_ARP_REQUEST.

- **Max Unknown Frame Cnt**    The maximum number of unknown frames that can be receivedwithin the Max Unknown Frame time.

- **Max Unknown Frame Time**    The amount of time in which the Max Unknown Frame count may be received.

- **Mcast Send VCC Type**    The method the LEC uses when specifying the Multicast Send VCC parameters upon joining an ELAN. The default is 1.

- **Mcast Send VCC Avg**    The forward and backward sustained cell rate the LEC will request when initiating the Multicast Send VCC control connection with the BUS.

- **Mcast Send VCC Peak**    The forward and backward peak cell rate the LEC will request when initiating the Multicast Send VCC control connection with the BUS.

- **Connect Completion Timer**    The amount of time expected during connection establishment before which a READY_IND message, or data, is received from the calling party. The range is between 1 and 10 seconds, with a default of 4.

Remember that these values must, in many cases, match those configured on an individual LEC, before that LEC is permitted to join its ELAN. Altering these parameters may result in a LEC being unable to join its services.

# Redundant LECS Services

Multiple LAN Emulation Configuration Servers may be used within the ATM network, and may be accomplished in one of two ways:

- Each LECS may be uniquely addressed, by using user-defined addresses for each LECS. These addresses must be individually defined, in order of priority, in the LANE Services to Use configuration window of the LAN Emulation Client Configuration screen.

- The well-known address (WKA) may be used by all redundant LECSs.

If all LECS instances are to use the WKA in an Interim Inter-Switch Protocol (IISP) environment, then call routes must be defined to each instance of the LECS. However, to avoid confusion during LEC initialization, either different costing should be used for each WKA entry in the Interim Inter-Switch Protocol call routing table or varying degrees of specificity should be used. For instance, if three LECS instances exist, available out ports 1, 2, and 3 of a single ATM module on a single switch, the call routing table might be similar to this:

| Partial Prefix | Module | Port | Cost |
| --- | --- | --- | --- |
| 47 | 1 | 1 | 10 |
| 47 | 1 | 2 | 20 |
| 47 | 1 | 3 | 30 |

## LECS MPOA Parameters

Beginning with code version 4.0, the LECS may be configured with Multi-Protocol Over ATM (MPOA) TLVs, used to provide MPOA Clients (MPCs) and MPOA Servers (MPSs) with their configurations. Beginning with SpeedView 4.0, two new options, *MPOA Client Config* and *MPOA Server Config,* are available. Selecting these options enables you to define TLVs for each service. The specific configurations for each are covered in Chapter 21.

# Configuring a LEC

A LAN Emulation Client is associated with an ELAN, and a LEC must be created on each switch that will require representation in that ELAN. A single switch can support up to 15 LECs, distributed over 32 ELANs. The number of LECs that a single ELAN can support is highly dependent on the network load that each LEC imposes on its LES/BUS services; however, a single Centillion ELAN is capable of supporting up to

255 LECs. If the configured number of LECs on a specific ELAN gets to the point where performance begins to degrade, segmentation may be accomplished either by creating more ELANs to support additional clients, while an ATM router routes between them, or by creating a cooperating LES/BUS pair, or series of pairs, to help balance the load.

To configure a LEC on the Centillion switch, select the ATM Configuration tab and click Configure LEC. This opens the LAN Emulation Client Configuration window (see Figure 20-9), which is largely blank until a LEC is configured.

## Initial Configuration of the LEC

The initial LAN Emulation Client Configuration window is broken into three main sections. The first section is located at the top of the window and indicates the circuit type (once selected), the VPort ID (once generated), and the ELAN name with which the LEC is to be associated. The second section is the lower-left portion of the window, labeled Bridging, and the third section is the lower-right portion, labeled Advanced.

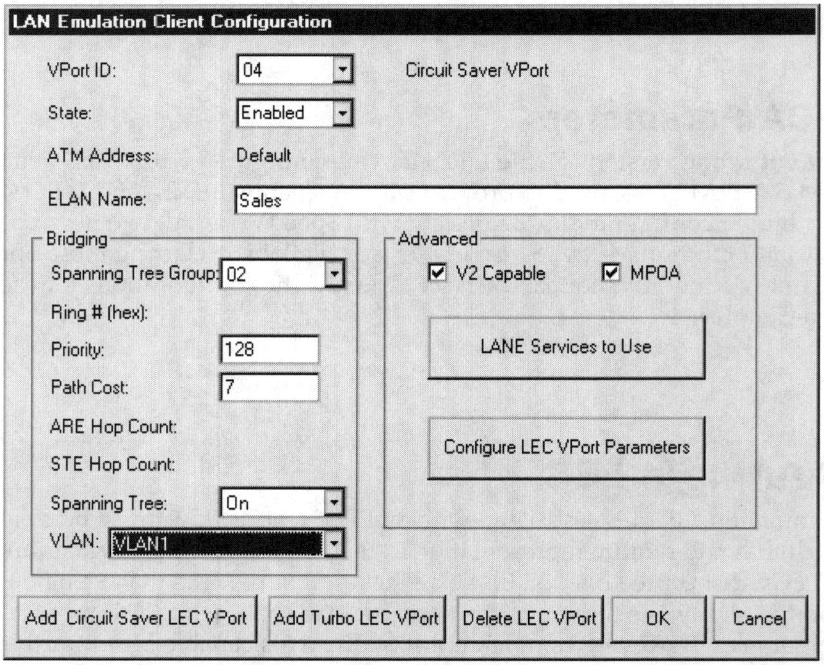

**Figure 20-9.**    *LAN Emulation Client Configuration window*

When you first create a LEC, you must select a LEC type. The following are the different options:

- **Circuit Saver LEC VPort**   Terminates all Control and Data Direct VCCs at the MCP rather than on a slot-by-slot basis. This allows a single port to handle more circuits simultaneously than it would otherwise be able to.

- **Turbo LEC VPort**   Maximizes throughput by eliminating the MCP when building circuits, and by terminating all Control and Data Direct VCCs at the slot level. This reduces the number of overall circuits a single board can handle, but increases performance.

After you select a LEC type, other fields in the LAN Emulation Client Configuration window become active. The circuit type is displayed at the top of the window, and a VPort ID is automatically generated. The VPort ID is a unique identifier for the VPort on the switch being configured. These VPort values are not configurable, are used only by SpeedView, and are not transferred as configuration information to any LANE components. By default, the State setting of the LEC VPort is Enabled.

In addition, either a Bridge Group, or a Spanning Tree Group and VLAN must be selected, depending on the version of code being run.

## Using Code Prior to Version 4.0

The Bridge Group field in the Bridging portion of the LAN Emulation Client Configuration window will be present; clicking the drop-down arrow to the right of this field causes a list of all configured bridge groups to appear. Choose the bridge group in which the newly configured LEC is to be placed.

## Using Code Version 4.0 or Higher

In code version 4.0 or higher, instead of selecting a bridge group, you must select the VLAN that you want the LEC to be a member of. VLANs are added in the Switching Mode tab, and are added into individual Spanning Tree Groups.

For the sake of this example, the LEC is a Circuit Saver LEC, which is a member of the token ring ELAN Token1 (see Figure 20-10).

A token ring ELAN is specified to illustrate the Bridging parameters that appear when a token ring ELAN is used. The fields listed and described next do not appear if the LEC is configured for an Ethernet bridge group or VLAN:

- **Ring#**   The ring number with which this LEC is associated. A token ring LEC VPort is considered another switched token ring port on the Centillion; it is part of the switched core and must be configured with an external ring number. In this case, the ring number is the number associated with the virtual ring that represents the ELAN of which the LEC is a member. All LECs configured for a common token ring ELAN must be configured with the same ring number associated with that ELAN.

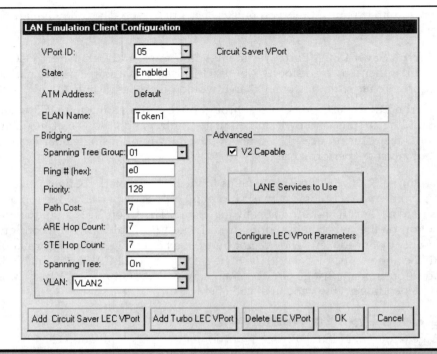

**Figure 20-10.**    *LAN Emulation Client Configuration window with token ring ELAN selected*

- **Priority**    The bridge priority used by the 802.1d Spanning Tree Protocol.
- **Path Cost**    The path cost associated with the LEC VPort for purposes of determining which ports should block and which should forward in the event of a network loop. A lower cost in this case indicates a more desirable path, so the port with the higher path cost will block. For both Ethernet and token ring LECs, the default path cost is 7. For both token ring and Ethernet ports, the default cost is 10. Therefore, in the case of a network loop involving both legacy ports and LEC VPorts, the ATM port will not be the one to block.
- **ARE Hop Count**    The number of hops an All Routes Explorer is allowed to traverse before being dropped. A single hop is considered to occur each time an ARE is switched between two rings. This field can be set between 1 and 13, with a default of 7. The hop count is checked on the outbound port.
- **STE Hop Count**    The number of hops a Spanning Tree Explorer is allowed to traverse before being dropped. A single hop is considered to occur each time an STE is switched between two rings. This field can be set between 1 and 13, with a default of 7. The hop count is checked on the outbound port.

■ **Spanning Tree**   May be set to On, Off, or Block. On and Off enable and disable Spanning Tree on that LEC VPort, respectively. Setting this parameter to Block causes the LEC VPort to block all data and all bridge protocol data units (BPDUs), as well as STEs in IBM Spanning Tree mode.

# Associating the VPort with a Bridge Group and Spanning Tree Group

The LEC is associated with a *virtual port,* or *VPort,* on the Centillion switch. This VPort will act as another port within whichever broadcast domain it is placed.

## Using Code Prior to Version 4.0

In code prior to version 4.0, the broadcast domain will be the bridge group; on a switch, a single VPort services a single bridge group. The bridge group within which the LEC VPort is placed has local significance only, and LECs configured on remote switches may reside in different bridge groups (see Figure 20-11).

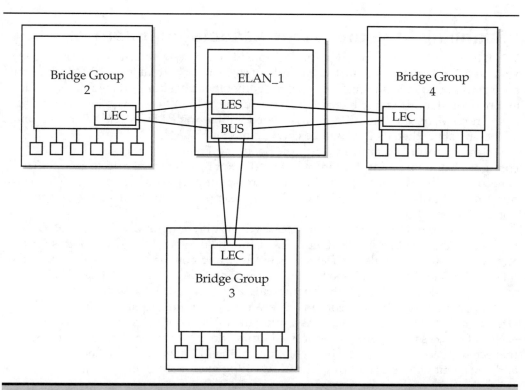

**Figure 20-11.**   *Multiple Centillion network in which LECs in a single ELAN are mapped to different bridge groups*

Since the bridge group simply represents a broadcast domain, the bridge group number doesn't need to match from switch to switch, although organizing them in this way may make network maintenance and troubleshooting simpler.

## Code Version 4.0 or Higher

Beginning with code version 4.0, the term "bridge group" was discarded, because multiple Spanning Tree Group support was added to the Centillion architecture, as well as VLAN support. Since a bridge group essentially is a logical broadcast domain, which basically defines a VLAN, the term "bridge group" was replaced with "VLAN," and the new term "Spanning Tree Group" was added.

When dealing with code version 4.0 or higher, VLANs may be considered the same as bridge groups; they serve exactly the same function and work in the same way. Spanning Tree Groups are separate Spanning Tree entities, which run separately. In the same way that different Spanning Tree Groups may be associated with different VLANs on the Accelar, they may be associated with different VLANs on the Centillion. For more information on Accelar Spanning Tree Groups, consult Chapter 10.

# LEC Spanning Tree and VLAN Association Example

When configuring different LECs for multiple ELANs between switches running code version 4.0 or higher, you must be careful not to create a "virtual loop." ATM LECs are subject to the same Spanning Tree rules that any other physical ports would be, and any network loops that are incurred will cause one of the VPorts to go into a blocking state. In ATM, because the VPort is associated with a single LEC, if the VPort goes into a blocking state, then its LEC will be cut off from that ELAN.

In code versions prior to 4.0, multiple Spanning Tree Groups could not be configured, and Spanning Tree information did not pass between bridge groups. The concept of adding multiple Spanning Tree Group support in conjunction with VLANs offers more flexibility of design, but it also creates potential problems if the design is not implemented correctly.

This example has three C100 switches. Switch A is configured with two LES/BUS pairs servicing two ELANs: the Sales ELAN and the Engineering ELAN. Both switch B and switch C have a single connection to switch A, and both have two clients configured: one for the Sales ELAN and one for the Engineering ELAN. The Sales ELAN is associated with VLAN 2, and the Engineering ELAN is associated with VLAN 3.

Once configured, the switches in this example will initialize, and each LEC will attempt to join its LANE services. Assuming the LANE configuration to be correct, each LEC successfully joins its services and transitions into an operational state. After this occurs, in code version 4.0 or higher, one of the LECs will go into blocking mode and one client will be cut off from the ELAN altogether (see Figure 20-12).

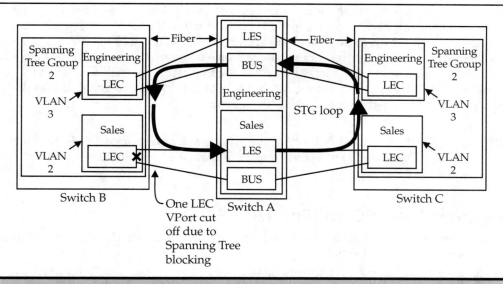

**Figure 20-12.**    *Virtual Spanning Tree loop*

This happens because, by default, all VLANs are associated with a single Spanning Tree Group, which means that both LECs—and, therefore, both VPorts—are associated with a single Spanning Tree Group even though they are in different VLANs. BPDUs from the Sales LEC VPort will be received by the Engineering LEC VPort. Since the Spanning Tree protocol operates independently of VLANS, a Spanning Tree loop condition is incurred.

Upon receiving its own BPDUs, the LEC VPort will determine a network loop exists, and one of the VPorts will go into blocking mode to resolve it. To implement this configuration correctly in version 4.0 or higher software, each LEC (and, therefore, each ELAN) needs to be configured with a different Spanning Tree Group.

## LANEv2 LEC Capabilities

Beginning with code version 4.0, LANE version 2 is supported. LANEv2 is a requirement of MPOA, and must be configured on each LEC per switch that is to participate in MPOA.

Because the MPOA Client (MPC) obtains TLVs from the LECS via a LANEv2-capable LEC, and because a single MPC serves all LECs on a single switch, each LEC that wants to advertise Layer 3 capability must be configured to be V2-capable, and to participate in the MPOA protocol. This configuration is performed in the LAN Emulation Client Configuration window, in the Advanced section (refer to Figure 20-9). There, a check box labeled V2 Capable is present in code version 4.0 and higher. Selecting this box sets the currently selected LEC VPort to be LANEv2-compliant. After selecting this box, another check box appears next to it, labeled MPOA. Checking this box indicates that the LEC should also participate in the MPOA protocol.

*If V2 Capable is checked, but the MPOA box does not appear, check the LES with which the LEC is associated to make certain that it is configured to be LANEv2-compliant, as well.*

## Configuring the LEC to Find Its LES

Each LEC must be configured with a method of finding its LES address. Four methods are available to accomplish this:

- If a LECS is being used, the LECS address can be obtained via the Interim Local Management Interface (ILMI).
- If the LECS is configured with the WKA, the LEC can be configured to point to that address.
- If the LECS is configured with a user-defined address, the LEC can be configured to use that specific address.
- If a LECS is not being used, the LES address may be statically configured on the LEC. This causes the LEC to bypass the LECS entirely and immediately attempt to contact the LES and join its ELAN upon initialization.

These options are accessible from the main LAN Emulation Client Configuration window, by clicking the LANE Services to Use button in the Advanced area.

## Using a LECS

A LEC may use a LAN Emulation Configuration Server to obtain its LES address, although a LECS is not required. If MPOA is being used, then at least one LEC per switch must use the LECS to register and obtain the type, length, and value (TLV) information required by the MPOA protocol, if a manual MPC and MPS configuration is not being used.

Assuming a strictly LANE configuration, however, the LECS is not implicitly required. To configure a LEC to use a LECS, from the main LAN Emulation Client Configuration window, click LANE Services to Use, which brings up the LAN Emulation Client – LANE Services Configuration window (see Figure 20-13).

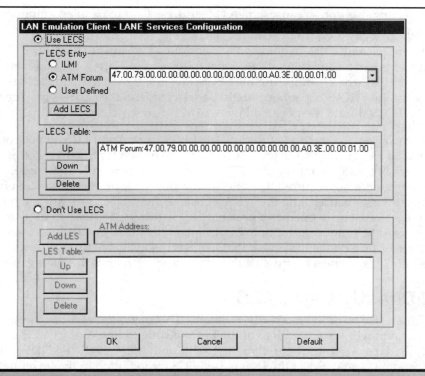

**Figure 20-13.**   *The LANE Services Configuration window*

Here, you may specify the method of obtaining the LES address for the configured ELAN. You can choose to have a LEC obtain the LES address from a LECS, or you can define it statically by selecting the radio button for either Use LECS or Don't Use LECS. If you decide to use a LECS, then you can choose one of the following three options regarding the LECS entry:

- **ILMI**   A client can obtain its LECS address over the ILMI channel, if one is configured (ILMI is selected for the port-level signaling). Once the address is obtained, an actual call can be initiated to the LECS. This initiates the construction of the Configuration Direct VCC.

- **ATM Forum**   Instructs the LEC to place its initial call to the WKA of 47.00.79.00.00.00.00.00.00.00.00.00.00.00.A0.3E.00.00.01.00, or, in addition, the C9.00.79.00.00.00.00.00.00.00.00.00.00.00.A0.3E.00.00.01.00 address in code version 4.0 or higher, in accordance with the LANE specification. This option should be selected if the LECS is using the WKA as its own address.

Selecting this option causes the ATM Address field to be filled automatically with the WKA.

- **User Defined**   You may assign a user-defined address to the LECS. This address can be any unique value that follows the 20-octet ATM addressing format. If, when configuring the LECS, it was assigned a unique address that is not the WKA, this option should be selected, and the address assigned to the LECS should be specified in the ATM Address field provided.

After you select the method of finding the LECS, click Add LECS, which causes the configured address to appear in the LECS table. The reason for the presence of a table is that you may configure multiple LECSs. If the WKA is being used for all LECS, then multiple entries are not required; the LEC in question will simply use the first LECS that it encounters when seeking the WKA. If user-defined addresses are being used, however, each must be defined as a possible LECS address, because all user-defined addresses must be unique. If multiple LECSs are in the LECS table, the LEC attempts to reach the first LECS on the list first; if that LECS is not available (for whatever reason), then the LEC tries the next address on the list, and so forth until the list is exhausted.

## Pointing Directly to the LES

The LEC may also be pointed directly at its LES. This may require more configuration overall, but removes the added step of the LEC needing to first contact a LECS successfully. This is also configured in the LAN Emulation Client – LANE Services Configuration window. Select the Don't Use LECS radio button in the lower portion of this window, which causes the top portions of the window under Use LECS to become grayed out, and causes the bottom portion of the window to become active.

Click the field labeled ATM Address, next to the Add LES button. This causes an address to appear within the field. This address is the NSAP prefix of the switch being configured, with an ESI and selector byte of all 0s. This is not a valid LES address and must be changed. The address in this field must match the actual LES address exactly; the ESI and selector byte must be altered and, if the LES is located on a different switch, the NSAP prefix must be changed, as well, to reflect this.

**Note**   *In code version 4.0 or higher, if the LES is local, the actual LES address may be selected from the ATM address field.*

After you configure the proper LES address in this field, click Add LES. This causes the LES to appear in the LES table located directly underneath the ATM Address field. Multiple LES addresses may be added here; if cooperating pairs are being used, these entries will indicate to the LEC which LES address is the primary and which address is the secondary, tertiary, and so forth. The LEC will attempt to reach the LES addresses configured in the LES table beginning with the top entry first. If the first attempt fails in this case, then the next LES on the list will be tried. After every address has been exhausted, if a successful join still hasn't occurred, the LEC begins again at the first

LES and attempts to join, cycling through the other LES addresses until it is able to join successfully.

## Advanced VPort Parameters

Beneath the LANE Services to Use button is the Configure LEC VPort Parameters button. Clicking this button causes the LEC VPort Configuration Parameters window to appear (see Figure 20-14).

This window is broken into four main parts: the ATM Address field (top of screen), a grouping of VPort parameters (middle left), the LEC Port section (middle right), and the Unknown Frame Pacing section (bottom).

The ATM Address field in this case indicates the ATM address associated with the LEC that is being configured. If this is an offline configuration that hasn't yet been downloaded to the switch, this field initially is blank, because this information is generated by the switch, and thus is not added into the configuration file until after the configuration file has been uploaded to an active switch. The ATM Address field is broken into two sections: the NSAP prefix, and the ESI and selector byte. Either field may be altered, but be aware that a LEC ATM prefix must match that of the switch it resides on; therefore, the NSAP portion of the LEC should not change unless the NSAP prefix of its switch has also been altered. The ESI and selector byte portion of the address also may be altered, although this is not necessary.

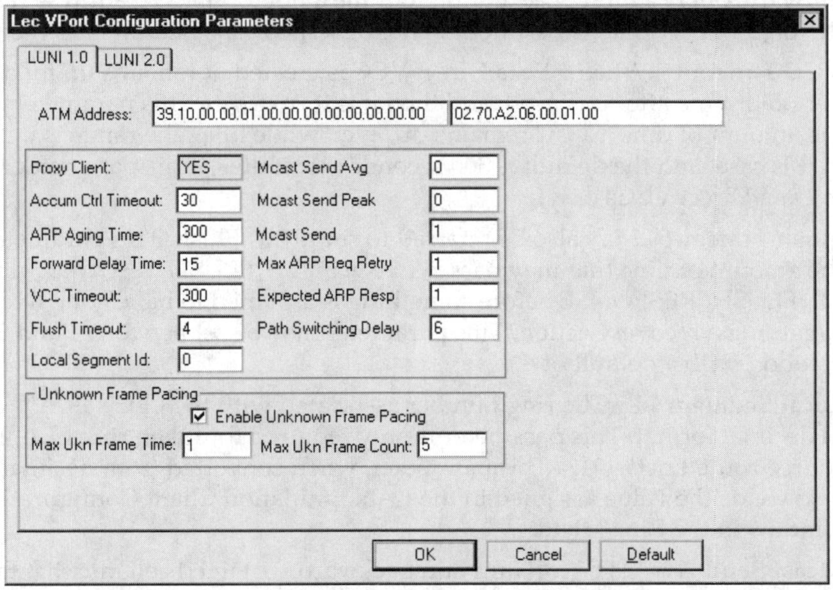

**Figure 20-14.** *LEC VPort Configuration Parameters window*

*As with the LES, altering the ESI can be a useful tool to keep LEC addresses recognizable at a glance should they need to be viewed through the CLI. By changing the ESI portion of the address to all As, all Bs, and so forth, the LEC addresses become easy to distinguish from one another.*

The VPort parameters found to the left, below the ATM Address field, allow some of the more advanced control functions of the LEC to be manipulated. These fields, and their meanings, are as follows:

- **Proxy Client**   Allows the LEC to act as an information proxy for other LECs in the ATM network. This field is read-only and is always set to YES.

- **Accum Ctrl Timeout**   May also be referred to simply as Control. This parameter allows alteration of the timeout value between control frames that require responses. For instance, a Call Connect message must receive a Call Connect Acknowledge in response. This may be set between 10 and 300 seconds, with a default timeout period of 30 seconds.

- **ARP Aging Time**   A LEC maintains an LE_ARP cache, consisting of entries that indicate which legacy MAC addresses are associated with which ATM LEC addresses. The ARP Aging parameter dictates how long (in seconds) an entry remains in the LE_ARP cache without being refreshed. This parameter may be set between 10 and 300, with a default of 30 seconds.

- **Forward Delay Time**   The amount of time a nonlocal MAC address remains in the LEC's LE_ARP cache without being refreshed. The default is 15 seconds.

- **VCC Timeout**   When a Data Direct VCC is created, it remains up for a certain period of time after it is used, and then it is torn down. This parameter dictates the amount of time a VCC remains up, even while idle. The range is unlimited in this case, and the default is 300 seconds (5 minutes). This parameter applies to Data Direct VCCs only.

- **Flush Timeout**   May also be referred to simply as Flush. This parameter is the amount of time that may pass between an LE_FLUSH_REQUEST and an LE_FLUSH_RESPONSE before something is assumed to have gone wrong, thus triggering a recovery action. This parameter may be set between 1 and 30 seconds, with a default of 4.

- **Local Segment Id**   The ring number associated with the LEC's ELAN. It is in decimal format. This parameter is only required for token ring ELANs in source-routed networks. This parameter, when converted from decimal into hex, yields the value assigned in the LAN Emulation Client Configuration window in the Ring# field.

- **Mcast Send Avg**   The forward and backward sustained cell rate that the LEC requests when setting up a Multicast Send VCC with the BUS, if using variable bit-rate coding. By default, this parameter is given a value of 0.

- **Mcast Send Peak**   The forward and backward peak cell rate that the LEC requests when setting up a Multicast Send VCC with the BUS, if using variable or constant bit-rate coding. By default, this parameter is given a value of 0.

- **Mcast Send**   In some versions of code, also referred to as the Mcast Send Type. This indicates the traffic parameters used by the LEC when building a Multicast Send VCC to the BUS. This value should be set to 1.

- **Max ARP Req Retry**   The number of LE_ARP_REQUESTS that a given LEC will attempt without receiving an LE_ARP_RESPONSE back. This parameter may be set between 0 and 2, with a default of 1.

- **Expected ARP Resp**   The amount of time a LEC will wait, in seconds, before assuming an LE_ARP_RESPONSE is not coming. This timer, once expired, triggers the LEC to resend the LE_ARP_REQUEST. It repeat this sequence for a number of times that is defined in the Max ARP Req Retry field (see the preceding description).

- **Path Switching Delay**   The amount of time that will pass after a frame to the BUS before the frame is assumed to have either been delivered to its destination or dropped.

These parameters, for the most part, will not have to be altered, and, in some cases, can severely impact the performance of the switch.

The portion of the LAN Emulation Client Parameters window labeled LEC Port is not, at the time of this publication, fully implemented and does not provide any functionality. In later versions of SpeedView, this section was omitted.

## LANEv2 LEC VPort Parameters

Beginning with code version 4.0, LANEv2 is supported on the Centillion. If the LEC being configured is set up to be LANEv2-capable, then clicking the Configure LEC VPort Parameters button from the main LAN Emulation Client Configuration window causes the LEC VPort Configuration Parameters window to appear, as before, except when the LEC is V2 capable, it consists of two tabs: LUNI 1.0 and LUNI 2.0. The LUNI 1.0 tab contains the same parameters described in the preceding list, which are available on any LANEv1 LEC VPort. Clicking the LUNI 2.0 tab accesses four new options:

- **Initial Control Time-out**   The amount of time, in seconds, the LEC waits after issuing its first LE_JOIN_REQUEST to the LES, before resending. This value is used in conjunction with the Control Time-out Multiplier. The range for this value is between 1 and 10 seconds, with a default of 5 seconds.

- **Forward Disconnect Time-out**   After the Multicast Send VCC is established, this option indicates how long the LEC will wait for the Multicast Forward VCC to be initiated. If this timer expires, the LEC disconnects from the BUS. The range for this value is between 10 and 300 seconds, with a default of 60 seconds.

■ **Control Time-out Multiplier**    After the timeout period has expired, as defined by the Initial Control Time-out parameter, this option allows a LEC to resend LE_JOIN_REQUESTS for a number of times, specified by this value. These requests are sent further and further apart, also calculated by using this value.

■ **Targetless LE_ARP**    Activates the Targetless Address Resolution Protocol, used when a MAC address must be relearned at different areas of the network dynamically, such as with a wireless handheld unit or any mobile device that utilizes a roaming MAC address. This function allows for accurate MAC address learning in these scenarios.

# Unknown Frame Pacing

As Chapter 13 explains in detail, when a LEC must send data to a remote LEC, it attempts to determine which specific LEC the data should be sent to. To do this, the LEC issues an LE_ARP_REQUEST and awaits a response. While the response is still pending, however, the LEC sends the data over the BUS Multicast Send VCC, which in turn floods the data to all LECs configured for that ELAN over its point-to-multipoint Multicast Forward VCC control connection. This is done to prevent a lag or timeout while waiting for the MAC-to-ATM address resolution.

The BUS has a control mechanism in place called *Unknown Frame Pacing*, also referred to as *BUS Pacing*, to prevent the BUS from being overwhelmed during this process. Unknown Frame Pacing controls how fast this data is sent over the BUS control connections while awaiting an LE_ARP_RESPONSE. After the response is received, the Data Direct VCC is built and the control channels are flushed. By default, this parameter is enabled. The Max Ukn Frame Time defines how often the number of frames indicated in the Max Ukn Frame Count parameter will be sent. So, the default values of Max Ukn Frame Time = 1 and Max Unk Frame Count = 5 indicate that, while awaiting an LE_ARP_RESPONSE, the BUS will forward five frames every one second over the Multicast Forward VCC.

| Note | *Connectivity problems in ATM are sometimes related to a Data Direct VCC not being correctly established. In accordance with the LANEv1 specification, if the Data Direct VCC is not built, the data will pass over the BUS channels entirely. This manifests itself as very slow performance, with probable session timeouts. Ping tests may indicate that connectivity exists, because a ping is small enough to pass over the BUS control channels without timing out. If all other LANE parameters and functions have been checked and everything seems to be joined and working properly, yet the preceding symptoms are displayed, select a time where the impact of network testing is minimal, and disable Unknown Frame Pacing. This allows data to travel over the BUS control channels as fast as possible. If this feature is disabled and performance improves dramatically, it could indicate that Data Direct VCCs are not being built properly. This generally should be considered a method of testing only—leaving BUS Pacing turned off is not advised, because the control channels are needed for other functions, as well, and during production hours, turning off BUS Pacing may seriously impact the network.* |

# Troubleshooting LANE

The method with which you troubleshoot LANE connectivity problems will vary depending on the type of LANE configuration that you are using. In LANE, a LECS may or may not be used, cooperating LES/BUS pairs may or may not be used, and a LEC may be Ethernet or token ring. Many basic methods of troubleshooting LANE connectivity problems are available, regardless of the network design.

When confronted with a LANE connectivity problem, you first need to determine whether a LANE component is actually the problem. In a LANE environment, if two switches are connected directly, and end-station 1 on switch A is attempting to transmit to end-station 2 on switch B, then a variety of things must happen:

1. End-station 1 ARPs for end-station 2.

2. The ARP request is received by Switch A.

3. Switch A broadcasts the ARP request out all ports in that VLAN or bridge group, including the VPort associated with the LEC serving the ELAN shared by switches A and B.

4. Since the ARP is a broadcast packet, the LEC on switch A forwards the request to the BUS, which floods the request over the Multicast Forward VCC, where it will be received by the LEC on switch B.

5. The LEC on switch B forwards the request out all ports in its VLAN or bridge group, where it will be received by end-station 2.

This scenario clearly shows that if one or all of the proper control channels haven't been established between the LEC and its LANE services, the two end-stations will never communicate. Because this is the case, perhaps the first thing to check is whether or not the appropriate LECs have joined their services.

## Checking the Registration Status of the LEC

To check the registration status of the LEC, first determine how many LECs should be registered with the ELAN that is having the connectivity problem. Then, establish a console session with the switch that is running the LES/BUS services for that ELAN. This needs to be either a serial connection or a Telnet session. Older versions of 2.0.x code may not support a Telnet session, but this will be the case only with very old versions of image software.

After you log in to the Command prompt, issue the following command:

```
Core_A:Command > show les
LES/BUS 1  ElanType=AF-LANE802.3  ElanName=Finance  Status=Up
   SmartLES=Enabled  ControlTimeOut=120  MaxFrameSize=1516
   LES Addr=39:00:10:00:00:00:00:00:00:00:11:00:00-AA:AA:AA:AA:AA:AA-01
   BUS Addr=39:00:10:00:00:00:00:00:00:00:11:00:00-AA:AA:AA:AA:AA:AA-02
   Redundant/Coop LES/BUS Pairs=1  SetStatus=FullyOperational
```

ATM ON NORTEL NETWORKS

```
      Remote LES 1  Status=FullyOperational
        Addr=39:00:20:00:00:00:00:00:00:00:11:00:00-BB:BB:BB:BB:BB:BB-01
      Remote BUS 1  Status=FullyOperational
        Addr=39:00:20:00:00:00:00:00:00:00:11:00:00-BB:BB:BB:BB:BB:BB-02
    LES Clients=3
      Client=1  CtlDirect=[Internal LEC]  Module=2  Port=0
        Addr=39:00:10:00:00:00:00:00:00:00:11:00:00-83:97:BA:01:00:00-FF
      Client=2  CtlDirect=[0:32]  Module=2  Port=4
        Addr=39:00:10:20:00:00:00:00:00:00:11:00:00-83:97:BA:0D:00:00-FF
      Client=3  CtlDirect=[0:33]  Module=3  Port=1
        Addr=39:00:10:30:00:00:00:00:00:00:11:00:00-00:00:A2:F9:9F:E7-00
    BUS Clients=3
      Client=3  MultiSend=[0:35]  Module=3  Port=1
        Addr=39:00:10:30:00:00:00:00:00:00:11:00:00-00:00:A2:F9:9F:E7-00
      Client=1  MultiSend=[Internal LEC]  Module=2  Port=0
        Addr=39:00:10:00:00:00:00:00:00:00:11:00:00-83:97:BA:01:00:00-FF
      Client=2  MultiSend=[0:34]  Module=2  Port=4
        Addr=39:00:10:20:00:00:00:00:00:00:11:00:00-83:97:BA:0D:00:00-FF
Core_A:Command >
```

The output from this example shows that this is an Ethernet ELAN named Finance, with an MTU of 1516. Its operational status is Up, Smart LES is enabled, and the Control Timeout is 120. For a description of these parameters, consult the section "Configuring the LES/BUS," earlier in this chapter.

## Interpreting the CLI Output

To get a sense of how to interpret what you see, examine the output carefully in this example. The Finance ELAN has its LES and BUS addresses listed. In this case, this LES/BUS pair has a cooperating pair configured that is Fully Operational, meaning that the two cooperating pairs have successfully found one another and are load-sharing. Notice that the primary pair uses all A's in its ESI, whereas the cooperating pair uses all B's in its ESI.

Each LES client is then listed, followed by a list of all BUS clients. There are three clients in each case, in this example, one of which is an Internal LEC, which means that the LEC is configured on the same switch as its LES/BUS pair. Each LEC is assigned a client number and is displayed by its ATM address. Take a closer look at a specific LES/BUS client from the preceding example; for client 2, the module and port number on which the control connection to the LEC exists is identified as module 2, port 4, for both the LES and the BUS. For the LES, the Control Direct VCC VPI/VCI pair is displayed (0/32). For the BUS, the Multicast Send VCC VPI/VCI pair is displayed (0/34).

Examine the list of clients; each client is displayed by its ATM address so that it can be traced back to its source. If you are unsure about the ESI of a particular LEC, try looking for its NSAP prefix in the client list. The client should be listed in both the LES client list and the BUS client list. In the two-switch example, in which switch A is directly connected to switch B, with a single ELAN configured and two clients, both the LES clients and the BUS clients should equal 2.

## CLI Output in Code Version 4.0 or Higher

The output from this same command issued from the CLI in code version 4.0 or higher provides slightly different information:

```
Core_B:Command > sho les
LES/BUS 1   ElanType=AF-LANE802.3   ElanName=Engineering ElanID: 1 Status=Up
    SmartLES=Disabled  ControlTimeOut=120  MaxFrameSize=1516
    LES Addr=39:20:00:00:00:00:00:00:00:00:00:00:00-AA:AA:AA:AA:AA:AA-01
    BUS Addr=39:20:00:00:00:00:00:00:00:00:00:00:00-AA:AA:AA:AA:AA:AA-02
    Redundant/Coop LES/BUS Pairs=0
    LES Clients=1
      Client=9  Flags: (V2) CtlDir=[0:34]  Module=1  Port=1
        Addr=39:20:00:00:00:00:00:00:00:00:00:00:00-00:00:A2:CB:2B:E7-00
    BUS Clients=1
      Client=9  MultiSend=[0:36]  Module=1  Port=1
        Addr=39:20:00:00:00:00:00:00:00:00:00:00:00-00:00:A2:CB:2B:E7-00
LES/BUS 2   ElanType=AF-LANE802.3   ElanName=Sales ElanID: 2 Status=Up
    SmartLES=Disabled  ControlTimeOut=120  MaxFrameSize=1516
    LES Addr=39:20:00:00:00:00:00:00:00:00:00:00:00-BB:BB:BB:BB:BB:BB-01
    BUS Addr=39:20:00:00:00:00:00:00:00:00:00:00:00-BB:BB:BB:BB:BB:BB-02
    Redundant/Coop LES/BUS Pairs=0
    LES Clients=2
      Client=3  Flags: (V2) CtlDir=[Internal LEC]  Module=1  Port=0
        Addr=39:20:00:00:00:00:00:00:00:00:00:00-02:D0:12:F8:00:01-FF
      Client=10  Flags: (V2) CtlDir=[0:39]  Module=1  Port=1
        Addr=39:20:00:00:00:00:00:00:00:00:00:00:00-00:00:A2:CB:2B:E7-01
    BUS Clients=2
      Client=10  MultiSend=[0:41]  Module=1  Port=1
        Addr=39:20:00:00:00:00:00:00:00:00:00:00:00-00:00:A2:CB:2B:E7-01
      Client=3  MultiSend=[Internal LEC]  Module=1  Port=0
        Addr=39:20:00:00:00:00:00:00:00:00:00:00-02:D0:12:F8:00:01-FF
```

In this example, LANEv2 is being used, and MPOA is configured. The LES clients are listed with a flag indicating (V2). This indicates that the LES is LANEv2-capable, as is the client associated with it. Each LANEv2-capable LEC will be followed by the (V2) flag, under the LES entry only. In addition, the ELAN ID associated with this LES/BUS pair is indicated next to the ELAN name.

# Displaying LES Information in Code Version 4.0 or Higher

More advanced LES statistics and information are available in image software version 4.0 and higher. The **show les summary** command provides a brief, concise summary of the LES in question:

```
Wiring_Closet_L:Command > show les summary
LES/BUS 1 ElanType=AF-LANE802.3 ElanName=CorpHQ ElanID: 1 Status=Up
Num LES_Clients:3 Num BUS_Clients:3
```

This primarily indicates whether or not the correct number of LECs have joined their LES and BUS services, as well as the ELAN type and its current operational state.

LES statistics are also available, beginning with code version 4.0, and can be obtained with the following command:

```
Wiring_Closet_L:Command > show les stats
LES/BUS 1 ElanType=AF-LANE802.3 ElanName=CorpHQ ElanID: 1 Status=Up
LES Stats:
JoinOk:3 InvalidParams:0 DupLANDest:0 DupATMAddr:0
InvalidReqId:0 InvalidLANDest:0 InvalidATMAddr:0
InBadPkts:0 OutRegFails:0 LeArpsIn:3 LeArpsFwd:0
NoResources:0 AccessDenied:0 VersionNotSupported:0
BUS Stats:
InDiscards:0 InOctets:17997 InUcastFrms:0
InMcastFrms:223 FrmTimeOuts:0 McastSendRefused:0
McastFwdFailure:0
```

These statistics provide a good indication of the current behavior of the LES and any clients that may have joined the LES/BUS pair, or that are attempting to join these services. These statistics have the following meanings:

- **JoinOK**   The number of JoinOK signals received, meaning a LEC successfully completed the join phase and now has established the necessary control connections with its LANE services.

- **InvalidParams**   The number of times an invalid destination was received during the join phase.

- **DupLANDest**   Increments each time that a duplicate LAN destination is received. A single LEC is permitted to serve any one LAN destination for a single ELAN.

- **DupATMDest**   The number of instances in which a duplicate ATM destination address was received. This goes back to the fact that, for a single ELAN, only one LEC instance per switch is required to serve that ELAN.

- **InvalidReqId**  The number of invalid Request ID messages that were received by the specified LES.

- **InvalidLANDest**  The number of invalid LAN Destination messages received, meaning that the indicated legacy LAN destination does not exist on the current network.

- **InvalidATMAddr**  An invalid ATM address has been indicated in the control frame.

- **InBadPkts**  The number of bad or corrupted packets received.

- **OutRegFails**  Increments each time that a Registration Failure message is sent after a LEC fails registration.

- **LeArpsIn**  The number of LE_ARP control frames that have been received.

- **LeArpsFwd**  The number of LE_ARP forwarded messages.

- **NoResources**  The number of failures that occurred due to lack of resources. This may indicate a lack of memory or that a necessary VCC could not be established.

- **AccessDenied**  The number of times a LEC was denied access to the LES. In accordance with the LANE specification, a LEC may be denied access to an ELAN for reasons of security, with an AccessDenied control frame sent to indicate this. This counter indicates the number of these occurrences.

- **VersionNotSupported**  The number of times a LEC requested to join an ELAN that doesn't support the necessary version, such as when a V2 LEC attempts to join a non-V2-capable LES.

- **InDiscards**  The number of incoming messages that were discarded.

- **InOctets**  The total number of incoming octets received.

- **InUcastFrms**  The total number of incoming unicast frames received.

- **InMcastFrms**  The total number of incoming multicast frames received.

- **FrmTimeOuts**  The total number of frame timeouts received, meaning that no response was made to a control frame that expected a response, such as an LE_ARP_REQUEST that received no LE_ARP_RESPONSE.

- **McastSendRefused**  The number of times the BUS rejected a request to set up the Multicast Send VCC. Failure to set up this VCC will result in the failure of a LEC to join. This connection is initiated by the LEC.

- **McastFwdFailure**  The number of times the setup of the Multicast Forward VCC failed. If this control connection is initiated by the BUS; if it is not accepted by the LEC, the join process will fail.

ATM ON NORTEL
NETWORKS

LEC statistics for an individual LES may also be obtained by using the following command, where the first number indicates the LES, and the second number indicates the LEC VPort being polled:

```
Wiring_Closet_L:Command > show les lecstat 1 3
LES/BUS 1 ElanType=AF-LANE802.3 ElanName=CorpHQ ElanID: 1 Status=Up
LESLEC Stats:
Recvs:2 Sends:1 InRegReq:0 InUnReg:0
InLeArpUcast:0 InLeArpBcast:1
InLeArpResp:0 InNarp:0
BUSLEC Stats:
  BusLecRecvs:16 BusLecFwds:16 BusLecDiscards:0
```

The output from this CLI command may help to indicate what the specific interaction is between a certain LES and a specific individual LEC. The output gives the following indications:

- **Recvs**   The number of control frames that were received by the indicated LES from the indicated LEC.

- **Sends**   The number of control frames sent from the LES to the indicated LEC.

- **InRegReq**   The number of times an LE_REGISTER_REQUEST was received by the LES from the specified LEC.

- **InUnReg**   The number of times the specified LES received an LE_UNREGISTER_REQUEST to deregister from the indicated ELAN.

- **InLeArpUcast**   The number of LE_ARP_REQUESTS received for a unicast address.

- **InLeArpBcast**   The number of LE_ARP_REQUESTS directed to the BUS that were received.

- **InLeArpResp**   The number of LE_ARP_RESPONSEs to the specified LEC that were originated by the specified LES.

- **InNarp**   The number of LE_NARP_REQUESTS received by the specified LES. This occurs when a MAC-to-ATM address binding becomes invalid due to the specified MAC appearing on a remote LEC. (Chapter 14 discusses the LE_NARP protocol in detail.)

- **BusLecRecvs**   The number of frames received from the LEC over the Multicast Send VCC.

- **BusLecFwds**   The number of frames forwarded to the LEC over the Multicast Forward VCC.

- **BusLecDiscards**   The number of frames passing over the BUS control channels that have been dropped, possibly due to either BUS Pacing or lack of resources.

## If All LECs Are Joined

If both LECs are present, monitor them for a bit to make certain neither one is dropping from its services intermittently. If every LEC that should be joined to the ELAN is joined, and all LECs are stable, then the problem may not be an ATM problem. It may still be, but at this point, it probably is more efficient to verify the rest of the Centillion configuration:

- Is the LEC VPort for this ELAN in the same VLAN or bridge group as the stations it will be serving? A VLAN or bridge group constitutes a broadcast domain and won't include the LEC VPort if it is in a different domain.

- Verify that the bridge group (or VLAN) configured is appropriate for the legacy LAN it serves; prior to code version 4.0, bridge group 1 is a token ring bridge group, by default.

- Verify that the MTU size configured for the LES is consistent with that configured for the switch. If it is a smaller value, data may be lost.

- If the ELAN is a token ring ELAN running source route bridging, verify that the LEC VPorts have the proper ring assignments.

- If the station is a token ring station, make certain it has inserted. If the station is an Ethernet station, make certain that the port is configured for the proper speed and duplex.

- If code version 4.0 or higher is being used, and the LEC is V2-capable, verify that the ELAN ID associated with its ELAN in the LECS matches the value the LES is using. If any incoming traffic is associated with an ELAN ID of 1, and the LEC has received an ELAN value of 2 for that same ELAN via TLVs from the LECS, then the traffic will be considered to be a mismatch and thus discarded.

Other things may be tried in this case; depending on the circumstances, the station itself may require a configuration change, such as a different default gateway, or a conflicting IP address may be configured on a secondary network interface card (NIC) or dial-up adapter. Generally, if a connectivity problem occurs in a LANE environment, it is a problem between the LEC and its services, or a problem with the services themselves, so if all clients are joined to their services, ATM connectivity often isn't the root of the problem. A ping issued from the Command prompt in the MCP often can verify whether the issue lies with the LANE services or the legacy LAN.

## If a LEC Is Not Joining

If one or more of the LECs is not joining its services, then you must determine which LECs are not joining, and why they are not joining. The following text and examples assume that a LECS is being used, but also covers potential problems that may arise if a LECS isn't being used.

# Determining What Is Failing

Examining the LES/BUS pair revealed that one or more LECs did not join their services. The next step is to determine why the LEC did not join. The following are some possible reasons:

- The LEC is misconfigured.
- The LECS is misconfigured.
- No IISP route exists from the LEC to the LECS.
- No IISP route exists from the LEC to the LES/BUS.
- No IISP route exists to the LEC from the LECS.
- No IISP route exists to the LEC from the LES/BUS.
- The PNNI node addresses are configured incorrectly.

# Determining Possible LEC or LECS Misconfigurations

If the LES/BUS services are listed as being in an Up state after issuing the **show les** command at the Command prompt, then determine whether the LEC is using a LECS. If it is, then the LEC must first communicate with the LECS. Using the information obtained from the LECS, the LEC will attempt to join the LES and the BUS, so the first thing to examine is the LECS, if one is being used, and then the LEC.

# Examining the LECS

If a LECS is being used, you should check it after you examine the LES/BUS and determine that certain clients are not joining. The reason for this is that the LECS records whether or not the LEC ever reached it, and, if it did, it records whether or not the LEC successfully received its LES information. Issue the following command at the Command prompt of the switch running the LECS:

```
Core_A:Command > sho lecs
LECS 0  Status=Up
   ATM Address=47:00:79:00:00:00:00:00:00:00:00:00:00-00:A0:3E:00:00:01-00
   ELAN 1  ElanName=Finance  ElanType=AF-LANE 802.3  MaxFrameSize=1516
   LES Address=39:00:10:00:00:00:00:00:00:00:11:00:00-AA:AA:AA:AA:AA:AA-01
   LES Address=39:00:20:00:00:00:00:00:00:00:11:00:00-BB:BB:BB:BB:BB:BB-01
   NumOfSuccess 3  InvalidFaram=0  InsufficientRes=0
   AccessDenied=0  InvalidReq=0  InvalidDest=0
   InvalidAddr=0  NoConfig=0  ConfErrors=0
   InsufficientInfo=0
Core_A:Command >
```

This example is for a LECS serving a single ELAN—the Finance ELAN from the last example. Because the Finance ELAN has a cooperating LES/BUS pair, two LES entries for that ELAN are listed in the LECS; the primary one first and the secondary following that.

Beneath the LECS address, ELAN name, and the associated LES address(es) is a list of counters. These counters have the following meanings:

- **NumOfSuccesses**   Increments by one after a successful transaction, at which point the LEC that initiated the communication should have its LES address. A transaction is considered "successful" after a LEC establishes a Configuration Direct VCC with the LECS, the ELAN is requested, the LES information is transferred, and the Configuration Direct VCC is torn down.

- **InvalidParam**   Indicates the number of times a LEC requested to join an ELAN for which it was not properly configured.

- **InsufficientRes**   Indicates that the LECS was contacted successfully, but was unable to respond due to the inability to establish a VCC or due to insufficient table space.

- **AccessDenied**   Indicates that LEC registration with the specified ELAN has been denied for security reasons.

- **InvalidReq**   Increments due to an incorrect LEC ID.

- **InvalidDest**   Indicates either the route descriptor information was included in an 802.3 Ethernet ELAN, or the LAN destination address in this case is a multicast address.

- **InvalidAddr**   Indicates the ATM address of either the source or the target system is not in the correct format.

- **NoConfig**   Indicates the number of times a joining LEC was not recognized as a valid LEC.

- **ConfErrors**   Indicates that the parameters supplied by the LEC were not consistent with those of the specified ELAN; may also be used if service was refused and no specific reason was given.

- **InsufficientInfo**   Increments by one if some portion of the LEC configuration is missing, such as the ELAN name. If this increments, verify the LEC configuration.

The first thing to look for is the NumOfSuccesses. This counter can give a lot of information about the registration progress of a LEC. First, check whether the NumOfSuccesses has incremented at all; this may be difficult to determine if many LECs are configured in the network, but the number should reflect the total number of clients—one success for each client.

ATM ON NORTEL
NETWORKS

## If NumOfSuccesses Has Not Incremented

If NumOfSuccesses has not incremented, then the LEC is not reaching the LECS, or its parameters are misconfigured. If the LEC never contacts the LECS, it will never obtain its LES address and therefore will not join. The signaling should be checked on the switch housing the problematic LEC, to be sure that the port-level signaling is correct. If the LEC exists on an external device, such as a server or router, then this should be a user network interface (UNI) connection, and the proper UNI version should be verified. If the LEC exists on another Centillion switch, then the connection type, IISP or PNNI, should be checked.

## IISP Port-Level Signaling

In an IISP environment, check the port-level signaling on the switch, as well as the switch it is connected to; one side should be set to User, the other to Network. In general, it does not matter which side is set to which. The practical difference between the two is that the Network side is the side that proposes the VPI/VCI pair to use when a call must traverse that connection. ILMI should be disabled, because one switch does not need to register its address with another. The UNI types should match, since, although this isn't technically a UNI connection, IISP essentially issues a UNI call from one switch to another, where one side acts as the User, and the other acts as the Network.

## Check the IISP Call Routes

If the IISP port-level signaling is correct, then most IISP problems generally are due to a lack of a valid call route either to the LECS or back from the LECS to the LEC. If the LECS is using the WKA, verify that each switch in the path between the LECS and the problematic LEC has an entry in its call routing table to reach the LECS.

In a PNNI environment, check the connection between the switches—particularly the connection between the problem switch and the rest of the network—to be sure that a valid link exists between nodes. Determine whether this link should be an inside or an outside link and verify that it is correct. Check the PNNI routing table to verify that a route listing exists for the WKA, if the LECS is using the WKA. For more information on troubleshooting a PNNI connection, consult the section on troubleshooting PNNI, found in Chapter 21.

## If NumOfSuccesses Is Incrementing

Another possibility that may arise is that the NumOfSuccesses has gone up, but it is continually incrementing. This can be determined by issuing the **show lecs** command from the Command prompt and then repeating it few minutes later. After all LECs are joined, the NumOfSuccesses should not continue to increment, because after the LES address for a desired ELAN has been obtained, a LEC has no reason to initiate another Configuration Direct VCC with the LECS.

If a LEC is not joining its ELAN, and the LECS NumOfSuccesses counter continually increments, this indicates that the LEC is finding the LECS, initiating a

Configuration Direct VCC, obtaining its LES address, and the Configuration Direct VCC is torn down. These are the criteria for the NumOfSuccesses counter to increment by one, indicating that the LEC is actually receiving its LES address.

After this happens, the LEC initiates the Control Direct VCC to the LES by placing a call to the LES address. If the NumOfSuccesses continually increments, this means the call to the LES is failing for some reason or the connection to the BUS is failing. Once a control connection fails to be established, the LEC will eventually reinitialize. The first thing that it does upon reinitialization is contact the LECS to obtain its LES information; so, the NumOfSuccesses keeps going up. If this happens, then the same port-level signaling and call routing statistics should be checked, as previously outlined, except this time the path from the LEC to the LES should be examined.

## Examining the LEC VPort

The LEC itself can also be examined to get a sense of how far along in the join process it is getting, and what state it is currently in. To examine the LEC VPort, issue the following command at the Command prompt:

```
WiringCloset_K:Command > show vport status all

ELAN Index=1    Type=ATM Forum Turbo AF-LANE 802.3
    State=Operational   STP_State=forwarding   BridgeGroup=4
    ElanName=Corp_1
    LEC Address=39:10:00:00:00:00:00:00:00:00:01:01:00-83:97:BA:01:00:00-00
    LECS Address=47:00:79:00:00:00:00:00:00:00:00:00-00:A0:3E:00:00:01-00
        ConfigDirect=[Not connected]
    LES Address=39:10:22:00:00:00:00:00:00:00:01:01:00-AA:AA:AA:AA:AA:AA-01
        ControlDirect    =[0:52]
        ControlDistribute=[0:53]
    BUS Address=39:10:22:00:00:00:00:00:00:00:01:01:00-AA:AA:AA:AA:AA:AA-02
        BusSend    =[0:54]
        BusForward=[0:55]
    ArpReqOuts=158589  ArpReqIns=505097  ArpRespOuts=14206 ArpRespIns=296312
    TotalCtlOuts=1727961  TotalCtlIns=8014136  svcFailures=0
    TotalErrs=0  TotalReqInDrops=1513824 TotalRespInDrops =8901544
WiringCloset_K:Command >
```

In this example, only one LEC is configured on the switch; if more LECs were configured, the **show vport status all** command would display information for each LEC configured. The output from this command tells several things about the current state of the LEC. The VPort is currently in an Operational state and its Spanning Tree state is forwarding. It is a member of an ELAN named Corp_1 and it is assigned to bridge group 4.

The LES and BUS address that are currently being used are also displayed, along with the exact control connections being used for each:

```
Control Direct: [0:52]
Control Distribute: [0:53]
Multicast Send: [0:54]
Multicast Forward: [0:55]
```

The Multicast Send and Multicast Forward are referred to as the BUS Send and BUS Forward, but these are the BUS control channels. Immediately following this information is a series of statistic counters, which have the following meanings:

- **ArpReqOuts**   The number of LE_ARP_REQUESTs that have been issued to resolve a MAC-to-ATM address association.

- **ArpReqIns**   The number of LE_ARP_REQUESTS that have been received by the LEC.

- **ArpRespOuts**   The number of LE_ARP_RESPONSEs issued by the specified LEC VPort.

- **ArpRespIns**   The number of LE_ARP_RESPONSEs received by the specified LEC VPort.

- **TotalCtlOuts**   The number of control frames issued by the specified LEC VPort.

- **TotalCtlIns**   The number of control frames received by the specified LEC VPort.

- **SvcFailures**   The number of times a switched virtual circuit (SVC) failed to be established (Data Direct VCC). Failure of Data Direct VCCs to be built results in unnecessary data flow over the BUS control channels, and is manifested as extremely slow performance and session timeouts.

- **TotalErrs**   The total number of invalid or corrupted frames received by the specified LEC VPort.

- **TotalReqInDrops**   The number of LE_ARP_REQUESTS sent by the specified LEC VPort, flooded back over its Control Distribute VCC.

- **TotalRespInDrops**   The number of LE_ARP_RESPONSEs received by the specified LEC VPort over its Control Distribute VCC that were not specifically destined for it.

These constitute the VPort status information for a healthy LEC VPort; however, depending on the join state of the LEC, this output may vary, as explained below.

**STATE**   When a LEC is functioning properly, the State should read Operational. If the join phase is not completing successfully, however, this will most likely read either Joining or Unknown. The LEC may be in a joining state, and then transition into an unknown state if the join is unsuccessful. Upon reinitializing, it may reenter the joining state. To get a sense of how far along the join process it is getting, observe the LES/BUS information.

**LES/BUS ADDRESS**   The LES and BUS addresses are listed in the output of the **show vport status all** command. Depending on how the LEC is configured, this can indicate a lot about how far into the join phase the LEC is getting. Remember, if a LECS is being used, the LEC does not have the LES address upon initialization. It must first obtain its LES address from the LECS; then, the BUS address is found via an LE_ARP and given to the LEC by the LES. If a LECS is being used, check whether the LES or BUS address is present. If neither is present, then the LEC is never receiving the LES address from the LECS, and that is the area that you should focus on. If the LES address is present but the BUS address is not, then the LEC has successfully obtained its LES address from the LECS, but the BUS address is never getting resolved for some reason.

   Generally, situations in which the LES address is being found but not the BUS aren't due to misconfiguration; a few things might cause a situation like this, such as a control channel being refused by a transit switch, a misconfigured Mcast Send Type in the Advanced LEC VPort parameters, configuration corruption, or a software problem on one of the switches.

# LANEv2 LEC VPort Status

The output associated with VPort status differs slightly in code version 4.0 and higher when the LEC is V2-capable and is participating in MPOA. The following output results from a LEC VPort configured on a switch that also hosts an MPOA Client:

```
Building4:Command > show vport status all

ELAN Index=2    Elan=enabled    Type=ATM Forum Circuit Saver AF-LANE 802.3
    State=Operational   STP_State=forwarding   VLAN ID=3
    LEC Configured Version=V2   LEC Operational Version=V2
    Uptime = [00d01h11m13s]MPC substate = MpcCfgComplete
 MPC device
    MPC Device Address=39:20:00:00:00:00:00:00:00:00:00:00-02:0B:48:1F:20:00-00
    ElanName=Sales   ElanID=2
    LEC Address=39:20:00:00:00:00:00:00:00:00:00:00-02:D0:12:F8:00:01-00
    LECS Address=47:00:79:00:00:00:00:00:00:00:00:00-00:A0:3E:00:00:01-00
       ConfigDirect=[Not connected]
    LES Address=39:20:00:00:00:00:00:00:00:00:00:00-BB:BB:BB:BB:BB:BB-01
       ControlDirect    =[Internal LES]
       ControlDistribute=[Internal LES]
    BUS Address=39:20:00:00:00:00:00:00:00:00:00:00-BB:BB:BB:BB:BB:BB-02
```

```
      BusSend   =[Internal BUS]
      BusForward=[Internal BUS]
   ArpReqOuts=13  ArpReqIns=11  ArpRespOuts=10  ArpRespIns=13
   TotalCtlOuts=2119  TotalCtlIns=27  svcFailures=0
   TotalErrs=0  TotalReqInDrops=4198 TotalRespInDrops =0
Building4:Command >
```

In this example, the LEC is configured to be LANEv2-capable and is operating as such. Its VLAN association is listed (formerly the bridge group), as well as its ELAN name, LES/BUS addresses, and the ELAN ID (2, in this case). The LEC uptime is now displayed as well.

In addition to these statistics, information regarding the MPC is present; this indicates the presence of an MPC on the switch also hosting the LEC VPort. The MPC state is listed as MpcCfgComplete, indicating that the MPC has successfully obtained its MPC parameters through TLVs exchanged with the LECS. Below this, the actual MPC control ATM address is listed as MPC Device Address. This is the MPC associated with this LEC VPort.

## VPort Statistics

The statistics associated with the LEC VPort can also be examined to indicate traffic flow, excessive errors, and possible resource problems:

```
WiringCloset_L:Command > sho vport statistics 1 1

Virtual port 1 on module 1:

Port Statistics:
InOctet:        17942  InUcastPkt:        0  InDiscard:        0  InErrors:  0
OutOctet:      155124  OutUcastPkt:       0  OutDiscard:       2  OutErrors: 0
MulticastsTransmittedOk:        2502  BroadcastsTransmittedOk:        0
MulticastsReceivedOk:              0  BroadcastsReceivedOk:         173
InNUcastPkt:                     173  OutNUcastPkts:               2502
InNoResources:                     0  OutNoResources:                 0
VlanMismatches:                    0
```

## Examining the LES/BUS Pairs

Examining the LES/BUS pairs may reveal more information than the simple fact that a LEC is not joining; by observing the LES/BUS pairs over a period of time, you may find that the LEC is joining the LES, but never joins the BUS. If this occurs, it is generally best to focus on the LEC VPort itself, which will provide more in-depth information than the LES and BUS will. These procedures are outlined in the previous sections regarding the LEC VPort.

# Example Sniffer Trace Summary of LANE Registration

The following sniffer trace summarization captures the successful registration between a LEC and its LANE services. This capture was taken with an ATM sniffer placed on an interswitch PNNI link, while a C100 LEC joined its services on the adjoining C100. These are the normal steps of the join process for a single LEC to its services:

1. The LEC (with an ESI of all Ds) initiates a call to the LECS, which uses the WKA (line 8):

```
SUMMARY    Destination    Source         Summary

      1    DCE            DTE.signaling  SSCOP BGN(Request Initialization)
      2    DTE            DCE.signaling  SSCOP BGN(Request Initialization)
      3    DCE            DTE.signaling  SSCOP BGAK(Request Acknowledgement)
      4    DCE            DTE.signaling  SSCOP POLL PDU(Trans Stat Info)
      5    DTE            DCE.signaling  SSCOP STAT PDU(Receiver State Info)
      6    DTE            DCE.signaling  SSCOP POLL PDU(Trans Stat Info)
      7    DCE            DTE.signaling  SSCOP STAT PDU(Receiver State Info)
      8    DCE            DTE.signaling  PNNI Setup CRN=8 called=47:0079:0000
0000 0000 0000 0000:ATMfrm000001:00
                       calling=39:2000:0000 0000 0000 0000 AA00:DDDDDDDDDDDD:FF
```

2. The Configuration Direct VCC is initiated via PNNI:

```
      9    DTE            DCE.signaling  PNNI Call proceeding CRN=8
     10    DTE            DCE.signaling  PNNI Connect CRN=8
```

3. The LES address (and any TLVs) is obtained via an LE_CONFIGURE_REQUEST and an LE_CONFIGURE_RESPONSE across the Configuration Direct VCC:

```
     11    DCE            DTE.0.32       LANE CTRL CONFIGURE_REQUEST
XID=181272849 RID=655360
     12    DTE            DCE.0.32       LANE CTRL CONFIGURE_RESPONSE
XID=181272849 RID=720896
```

4. The Configuration Direct VCC is torn down, as is normal after the exchange of TLVs and LES information:

```
     13    DCE            DTE.signaling  PNNI Release CRN=8 cause=normal,
unspecified
     14    DTE            DCE.signaling  PNNI Release complete CRN=8
cause=normal, unspecified
```

5. The LEC initiates a call (the Control Direct VCC) to the LES address obtained from the LECS. The call is established via PNNI, and the LEC issues an LE_JOIN_REQUEST. After this occurs, a call is initiated from the LES to the LEC (the Control Distribute VCC); the call is connected via PNNI, and an LE_JOIN_RESPONSE is issued to the LEC. At this time, if the LEC is

V2-capable and configured for MPOA, the presence of an MPC or MPS is also registered with the LES:

```
    15    DCE             DTE.signaling    PNNI Setup CRN=9 called=39:2000:0000 0000
0000 0000 0000:BBBBBBBBBBBB:01
                          calling=39:2000:0000 0000 0000 0000 AA00:DDDDDDDDDDDD:FF
    16    DTE             DCE.signaling    PNNI Call proceeding CRN=9
    17    DTE             DCE.signaling    PNNI Connect CRN=9
    18    DCE             DTE.0.33            LANE CTRL JOIN_REQUEST XID=181272850
RID=1114112
    19    DTE             DCE.signaling    PNNI Setup CRN=5 called=39:2000:0000 0000
0000 0000 AA00:DDDDDDDDDDDD:FF
                          calling=39:2000:0000 0000 0000 0000 0000:BBBBBBBBBBBB:01
    20    DCE             DTE.signaling    PNNI Call proceeding CRN=5
    21    DCE             DTE.signaling    PNNI Connect CRN=5
    22    DTE             DCE.0.33            LANE CTRL JOIN_RESPONSE XID=181272850
RID=1376267
```

6. Upon receiving the LE_JOIN_RESPONSE, an LE_ARP_REQUEST is issued, looking for the BUS address. An LE_ARP_RESPONSE is returned and, immediately following that, a call is initiated from the LEC to the BUS (note the selector byte of 02, indicating this is the BUS, not the LES). This is the Multicast Send VCC, and it is routed to the BUS via PNNI. Once established, a call is initiated from the BUS to the LEC (the Multicast Forward VCC), which is routed via PNNI, and connected:

```
    23    DCE             DTE.0.33            LANE CTRL ARP_REQUEST XID=181272851
RID=1441803
    24    DTE             DCE.0.33            LANE CTRL ARP_RESPONSE XID=181272851
RID=1507339
    25    DCE             DTE.signaling    PNNI Setup CRN=10 called=39:2000:0000 0000
0000 0000 0000:BBBBBBBBBBBB:02
                          calling=39:2000:0000 0000 0000 0000 AA00:DDDDDDDDDDDD:FF
    26    DTE             DCE.signaling    PNNI Call proceeding CRN=10
    27    DTE             DCE.signaling    PNNI Connect CRN=10
    28    DTE             DCE.signaling    PNNI Setup CRN=6 called=39:2000:0000 0000
0000 0000 AA00:DDDDDDDDDDDD:FF
                          calling=39:2000:0000 0000 0000 0000 0000:BBBBBBBBBBBB:02
    29    DCE             DTE.signaling    PNNI Call proceeding CRN=6
    30    DCE             DTE.signaling    PNNI Connect CRN=6
```

# General Port-Level Signaling Parameters

From the main configuration screen in SpeedView, a module's individual ports can be configured by clicking the tab for that module. This brings up the module-specific tab, which displays the module type, type of ports, number of ports, and their settings. It is in this tab of the ATM module where port-level signaling may be altered.

Prior to SpeedView 3.0, all ports are visible, as well as their associated signaling, from the main module tab. Beginning with SpeedView 3.0, the ports are displayed on the left side of the tab, while the signaling for the selected port is visible on the right side of the tab (see Figure 20-15).

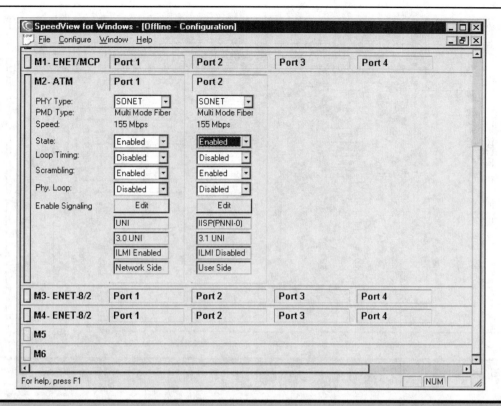

**Figure 20-15a.**    *SpeedView 3.0 vs. pre-3.0 SpeedView display of ATM module*

This tab displays the following fields:

■ **PHY Type**    The type of physical-layer signaling that will be used on this port. By default, the Centillion utilizes SONET signaling. Whereas the Centillion automatically adopts whichever signaling method is incoming on a port, the outgoing signaling method must be selected. In North America, this will be the default choice of Synchronous Optical Network (SONET). Centillion ATM ports also support the Synchronous Digital Hierarchy (SDH), used in much of Europe and Japan.

■ **PMD Type**    The physical media type that is supported on the port. Depending on the type of port, this will be either multimode fiber (Multi Mode Fiber), single-mode fiber (Single Mode Fiber), or unshielded twisted pair (UTP), which is available as one of the port options in the media dependent adapter (MDA) modules.

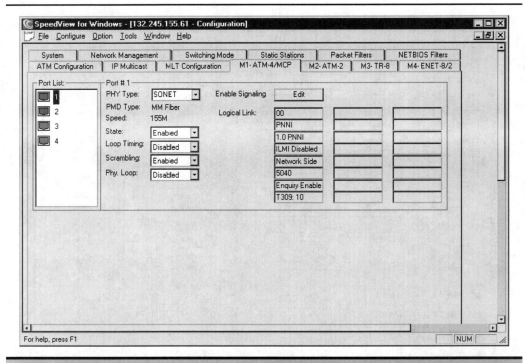

**Figure 20-15b.**    *SpeedView 3.0 vs. pre-3.0 SpeedView display of ATM module*

■ **Speed**    Currently, the speed of the selected port will be either 155Mbps, 622Mbps, or 45Mbps, depending on whether the module type supports OC-3, OC-12, or DS3, respectively.

■ **State**    The current administrative state of the port. Options are Enabled and Disabled.

■ **Loop Timing**    May be set to either Enabled or Disabled (the default). If Enabled, the port derives its timing source on its receive port. If Disabled, the port either uses an internal timing source or receives its timing on the port specified in the External Timing field, also located on the main module tab.

■ **Scrambling**    Enabling this feature scrambles the ATM payload. Options are Enabled (the default) and Disabled.

■ **Phy. Loop**    This parameter has four options: Local—loops back cells internally, without ever sending them out onto the fiber; Remote—takes incoming cells and loops them back toward the source, without accepting them at the receiving port; Local and Remote—performs both loopback functions simultaneously, where no cells are accepted or transmitted, but looped back in both directions; Disabled—causes the port to transmit and receive cells normally.

- **External Timing**   This option is available only if the Loop Timing option is set to Disabled; otherwise, it isn't present. This option is available as of code version 3. Prior to that, all timing that was not taken from the receive port (loop timing) was obtained from an internal, local oscillator. Options now include the Local Oscillator (which is the default option if Loop Timing is not being used) or receiving the timing locally, where it is incoming on another port. For instance, port 1 could be configured with Loop Timing Disabled, while receiving its timing information from port 2, which is receiving timing from an external source.

> **Note**    *The Scrambling option defaults to Enabled. In general, this setting is fine. Circumstances may arise where this option needs to be disabled, however. When connecting to a Nortel Networks ATM router port, this option should be set to Enabled.*

## Troubleshooting at the Port Level

Whenever an ATM connectivity problem occurs, you should quickly check the port statistics to be sure the problem doesn't exist at the port level. You potentially could spend a lot of time looking for a problem, only to find the port itself was the cause. This section describes a few quick things that you can check from the CLI.

### Checking the Port

Before going too far, it doesn't hurt to check the port that physically connects the switch to the rest of the network. You can do this by issuing the following command:

```
Core_A:Command > sho port 2 1
Information and Statistics for port 2,1:

rx_cell_drop_cnt: 20    rx_cell_good_cnt: 401736182  bad_cell_cnt: 0
tx_cell_drop_cnt: 0     tx_cell_good_cnt: 1854892940  sig detected: 1
Frame mode: sonet
Core_A:Command >
```

The output from this command indicates several things, including data transfer statistics and some error counters. These counters have the following meanings:

- **rx_cell_drop_cnt**   The receive cell-drop count; this error is equivalent to the error Unknown VPI/VCI under SpeedView statistics. Seeing a few of these errors isn't unusual, but a large number of them may be cause for some concern. This counter basically indicates that the remote side attempted to erect a circuit by using a VPI/VCI pair that either wasn't configured (in a Centillion LAN Client, or CLC, environment) or was already in use (in a LANE environment). In a CLC environment, this usually indicates that one of the two sides of the connection is configured for the wrong VPI/VCI pair; the remote side attempts to bring up a pair that the local side is not configured for, and the rx_cell_drop_cnt increments. In a LANE environment, SVCs are built dynamically, and a link should never request a VPI/VCI pair that is already in use. If a link does request a VPI/VCI pair already in use, it usually indicates that, due to a signaling mismatch, SVCs are being torn down incorrectly, leaving one side of the link with the impression that the SVC has been torn down and that the VPI/VCI pair is now available for use again, and leaving the other side of the link with the impression that the SVC is still up and that the VPI/VCI pair is not available. Each time this occurs and the VPI/VCI pair is requested by the side that believes it to be available, the side that has the resource still listed as being in use increments this error. This sometimes may occur if the versions of code being run by the two switches are drastically different.

- **tx_cell_drop_cnt**   The number of cells dropped on the transmitting port. This might be an indication that the transmitting interface is experiencing a hardware problem, or that the port buffer is becoming full and some cells are being dropped because they can't be buffered.

- **rx_cell_good_cnt**   The number of good cells received on the port.

- **tx_cell_good_cnt**   The number of good cells that were transmitted by the port.

- **bad_cell_cnt**   The number of incoming cells that were actually corrupted. This may be due to a bad transmitter at the remote end, or a bad fiber connection between the two switches. Corrupted cells are discarded, and the entire frame will need to be retransmitted.

- **sig detected**   Indicates whether or not signaling is detected on the port. A value of 0 indicates that no signal is detected; check the fiber, and also the remote port to be certain both ports are enabled, and that the signaling is set correctly on both ports. A value of 1 indicates a good signal is detected on the line.

In the preceding example, the line looks fine: it has a few rx_cell_drop_cnt (20), but this is within normal thresholds; traffic is being transmitted and received; no cell corruption exists; and a valid signal is detected.

## CLI Output in Code Version 4.0 or Higher

The ATM port statistics differ slightly in code version 4.0 and higher:

```
Edge_A:Command > sho port 1 1
Information and Statistics for port 1,1:
port_state: up
rx_cell_drop_cnt: 3      rx_cell_good_cnt: 2125    bad_cell_cnt: 0
tx_cell_drop_cnt: 0      tx_cell_good_cnt: 5882    sig detected: 1
path ais: no             line ais: no              section los: no
path rdi: no             line rdi: no              section lof: no
path lop: no             sectionbip8errs: 0
Frame mode: sonet
Edge_A:Command >
```

# The
# Complete
# Reference

Nortel
Networks

# Chapter 21

## Configuring Call Routing and MPOA on the C100/C50/5000BH Platform

Two basic call routing methods are currently used in ATM: the Interim Inter-Switch Protocol (IISP), covered in Chapter 15, and the Private Network to Network Interface (PNNI), covered in Chapter 16. IISP is a hop-by-hop protocol consisting entirely of static routes. Conversely, PNNI is a dynamic source-routing protocol; it is more complex, but it also is very robust, very fault-tolerant, and very scalable.

Selecting the call routing method best suited for your ATM network will depend greatly on the number of nodes, the configuration of those nodes, and the type of traffic that the call routing method will service. If only a small number of switches are in a network with little or no redundancy, and the number is not likely to increase, then IISP will work fine and remain manageable. PNNI has many advantages over IISP, but PNNI dynamic route computations make less sense when the destination node will never be more than two hops away, or if there is only one path available to reach each destination. On the other hand, if the network is likely to grow, it may be best to begin using PNNI early. The exact call routing method that is best suited for the network will depend on the network itself.

**Note** *PNNI was first introduced as an ATM call routing protocol on the Centillion 100/50/5000BH platform in code version 3.0. However, the functionality to accept information from a peer group leader (PGL) was not introduced until code version 4.0. The full implications of this are outlined in Chapter 16, but the foremost limitation of PNNI nodes existing without a PGL is that only one peer group can exist, because PGLs act as logical group nodes (LGNs) at the next level of the hierarchy and pass down LGN node aggregations from remote peer groups to the lowest level. To establish multiple peer groups on the Centillion 100/50/5000BH prior to code version 4.0, an IISP link must be configured between the two peer groups, and a summary of the remote peer group nodes must be advertised into the local peer group as exterior reachable addresses.*

## Configuring IISP

When configuring IISP, the primary thing to remember is that no route information is passed along or learned between switches. This means that every switch must have some route configured for every other potential destination in the ATM mesh. This includes the return trip; not only must A have a route to B, but B must also have a route to A. If, at any junction, an incoming call arrives at a switch that has neither a route to the destination defined nor a default route configured, the call will be rejected. The call will be reattempted, but it will never succeed until the missing route is configured.

Configuring IISP is simple in concept, but the simple rule of ensuring that every switch has some kind of route configured pointing to every potential destination can begin to become quite difficult if the ATM network is very large. Implementing redundancy on top of that can be even more difficult, and it becomes crucial to accurately document which call routes point where, which are primary, which are redundant, and how they are costed. You are advised to implement the primary call routes first in these cases, and then, after confirming that no call routing loops or other errors exist, insert the redundant routes. When a network has many switches with many routes, with secondary and sometimes tertiary routes built in for redundancy, tracking down a call routing loop can become extremely time-consuming and difficult.

Unfortunately, no easy formula exists for determining when IISP should be abandoned in favor of PNNI. Unlike a hop-based routing protocol, such as the Routing Information Protocol (RIP), no precise rule (such as exceeding a hop count of 15) defines how large the network should be before switching to PNNI. However, I advise that once IISP routes begin to be difficult to manage, or additions to the ATM network begin to be very difficult to implement, it may be time to consider switching over to PNNI. Remember, PNNI is a dynamic protocol, requiring no static routes, and is fully redundant by nature. In a network where IISP call routes are still manageable, however, IISP is a very fast, stable protocol.

## IISP Addressing Considerations

In an IISP environment, each switch must have a unique Network Service Access Point (NSAP) prefix. No user-configured mask is configured, and the entire 13 bytes of the prefix are considered, so as long as the prefixes are unique to some degree, no conflict occurs. However, bear in mind that the prefixes are masked in the call routing table (for more information, consult Chapter 15), enabling a series of switches to be summarized by a single call routing entry. For instance, the following NSAP prefixes

```
39.10.10.00.00.00.53.19.00.00.11.31.01.AA.3E.21.09.83.41.01
39.10.10.01.20.00.53.19.00.00.22.31.01.E0.32.51.34.90.87.01
39.10.20.00.00.00.53.19.00.00.33.31.01.08.35.86.AB.42.17.01
```

could be summarized with a single entry of

```
39.10
```

This would be configured as a partial prefix in the Centillion's call routing table. Although a specific mask is not configured, it is implied by the partial prefix (a 16-bit mask in the previous example). For this reason, switch addresses in an IISP environment should lend themselves to easy summarization.

## Configuring IISP Signaling for a Connection

To configure a connection for IISP, first select the tab in SpeedView for the specific module on which you want to create the IISP connection. Clicking this tab displays all available ports and their associated signaling. By default, no signaling is configured and all signaling fields are blank. To configure specific signaling parameters, first click Edit Signaling. Prior to code version 3.0, this opens the ATM Signaling window, with all parameters available. In code version 3.0 and greater, where the code is the

Advanced version, the signaling parameters initially are grayed out, and a new button labeled Add Logical Link is available in the bottom-left corner of the ATM Signaling window. This parameter relates to PNNI, although the option must still be selected regardless of the connection type. Clicking Add Logical Link causes a small window labeled Specify VPI to be added:

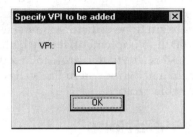

In an IISP environment, select the default value of 0. Once a VPI value is selected, the port-level signaling can be edited:

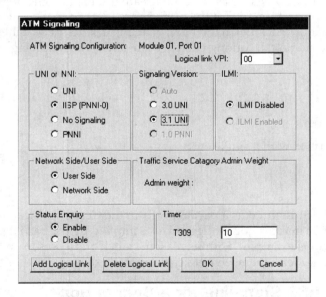

The ATM Signaling window is broken down into four basic parts: UNI or NNI, Signaling Version, ILMI, and Network Side/User Side. In code version 3.0 or greater, running the Advanced version, a fifth part is present, Traffic Service Category Administrative Weight. In code version 4.0 or greater, Advanced version, a sixth part was added, which includes the Status Enquiry function and the T309 timer.

**UNI OR NNI**    This section contains the signaling options, selected by clicking the radio button next to the preferred signaling method. This option will be set to either UNI, IISP (PNNI-0), No Signaling, or PNNI, if the Advanced code is being run.

 *IISP is also referred to as PNNI phase 0, while the dynamic, source-routed version of PNNI sometimes is referred to as PNNI phase 1. This is why IISP is listed as PNNI-0 in the ATM Signaling window.*

In this case, select the radio button next to IISP (PNNI-0). After you select this option, certain options become active, whereas others remain grayed out, because they are not applicable in an IISP environment; for instance, the option to enable Interim Local Management Interface (ILMI) may be grayed out (depending on the code version), because ILMI is not used on IISP connections.

**SIGNALING VERSION**    When IISP is selected as the connection type, you must select a UNI type of either 3.0 or 3.1. You should keep this consistent throughout the network.

**ILMI**    Because ILMI is not utilized on IISP links, the ILMI option should be set to Disabled. Earlier code versions allow this option to be either Enabled or Disabled, but later code versions automatically set ILMI to Disabled and remove the Enabled option.

**NETWORK SIDE/USER SIDE**    All IISP connections require one side of the link to be designated the User side, and the other side to be designated the Network side. No rule defines which side should be given which role, nor does any rule state that once a port on one module is configured for a certain role then all ports on that module must be given the same role. Ports can be assigned as User or Network, in any combination, as long as one side of each connection is set to User and the other is set to Network. Which side is set to User and which side is set to Network makes no practical difference; the Network side is responsible for selecting the VPI/VCI pair to be used when forming a circuit, however.

**TRAFFIC SERVICE CATEGORY ADMINISTRATIVE WEIGHT**    This parameter actually relates to PNNI, and assigns a user-defined weight to the link being configured, for purposes of determining the link's relative desirability when making dynamic route computations. This parameter is not used in IISP.

**STATUS ENQUIRY**    Beginning with SpeedView version 4.0, SVC Status Enquiry can be set to Enabled or Disabled on a port-by-port basis in SpeedView. Status Enquiry checks SVCs periodically (as defined by the Status Enquiry Period in the Configure Signaling window, reached by selecting the ATM Configuration tab, then selecting the Configure Signalling button) to ensure they are still operational.

**T309 TIMER**    Beginning with code version 4.0, the T309 timer can also be configured, which is the Signaling ATM Adaption Layer (SAAL) timer; it begins when a Signaling

AAL problem occurs and the circuit is interrupted. If the circuit is not reestablished before the timer expires, the circuit is cleared. The default value is 10 seconds.

## Building a Call Routing Table

Next, the call routing table must be built. To do this, bring up the ATM Configuration tab in SpeedView and select Configure Call Routing. If the code version is 3.0 or greater, the possibility exists that PNNI may also be running; since this is the case, a small window pops up upon selecting the Configure Call Routing option, warning that in a mixed IISP and PNNI environment, all IISP call routes must be configured with costs greater than zero. Click OK to proceed; this brings up the Configure Call Route window (see Figure 21-1).

The Configure Call Route window is broken down into two main parts: Route Entry and Route Table. The Route Entry portion of the window allows you to select a route type, add an ATM address, associate the route with a specific module and port, and apply a specific cost to the configured route. If the code version is 3.0 or greater, using the Advanced version, fields also are present for Scope and VPI.

The first thing to do is select what type of route is being configured. The route specified in the Route Type area indicates a prefix against which any incoming call will be compared and, if a match is found, which module and port the call should be routed out, at what cost, and at what scope. The following are the four options available under the Route Type header:

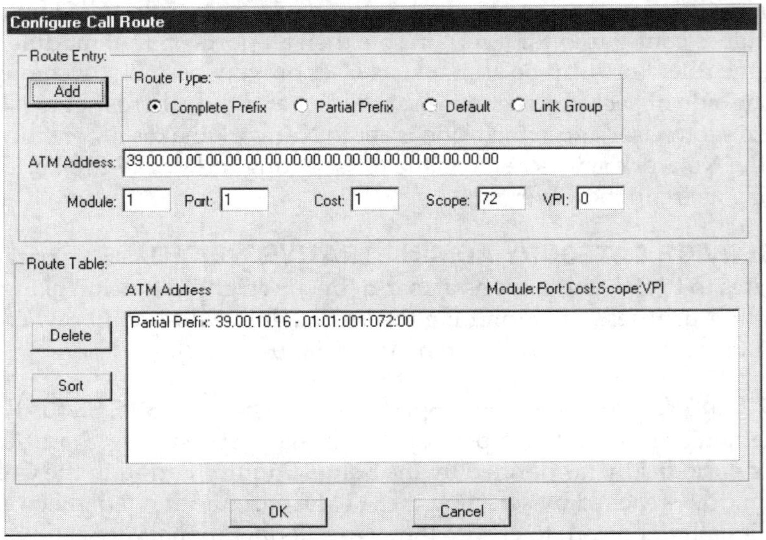

**Figure 21-1.**    *The Configure Call Route window*

**COMPLETE PREFIX**   This specifies that no summarization will take place, and that the entire NSAP prefix must be specified. If this option is selected, then the entire 13-octet NSAP prefix must be entered into the ATM Address field, and any incoming call must match all 13 bytes to be considered a match.

**PARTIAL PREFIX**   Here, only a portion of the NSAP prefix is configured. Configuring a partial prefix accomplishes two things at once: it defines how much of the NSAP prefix will be examined to determine a match, and it defines what portion of the NSAP prefix must be in order to be considered a match. For instance, consider the following partial prefix:

```
39.10.00.20.00.01
```

An incoming call being placed against this partial prefix will be masked in the following manner:

```
39.10.00.20.00.01.01.11.90.00.00.43.00     NSAP prefix of incoming call
FF.FF.FF.FF.FF.FF.00.00.00.00.00.00.00     Mask placed for purposes of
                                           match
39.10.00.20.00.01                          Route matched against
```

Since the first 6 octets were used in the partial prefix, a 48-bit mask is placed against incoming calls when checking for a mask *against that particular call route*. In the preceding example, a match is established, because the masked portion of the destination's prefix matches the partial prefix configured in the IISP call routing table. If it had not matched and the prefix were compared to the next call routing entry that was 8 octets long, then an 64-bit mask would be used against the destination NSAP.

**DEFAULT**   This configures a default route for a specific module and port. No portion of an NSAP prefix must be associated with a default route, because a default route causes an incoming call to be masked in the following way:

```
39.10.00.20.00.01.01.11.90.00.00.43.00   NSAP prefix of incoming call
00.00.00.00.00.00.00.00.00.00.00.00.00   Mask placed for purposes of match
```

Since no portion of the incoming call is considered relevant for purposes of establishing a match condition, all incoming calls are considered to be matches for a default route. As a result, no prefix portion needs to be configured. When a default route is in place, any incoming call that does not match any other call routing entry will match the default route and be sent out the specified module and port.

ATM ON NORTEL
NETWORKS

**LINK GROUP**    A *link group* enables the bandwidth of two separate IISP links to be aggregated into one. If two parallel IISP links exist and are not part of a link group, then a call routing loop may be incurred. By combining the two connections, they are considered a single connection for purposes of determining IISP destination hops.

To create a link group, the two links that are to be aggregated must first be configured. For instance, a link group between switch A, configured with an NSAP prefix of 39.10.10.00.00.00.00.00.00.00.00.00, and switch B, configured with a prefix of 39.10.20.00.00.00.00.00.00.00.00.00.00, with parallel links on module 1, port 1 and module 1, port 2, would be created in the following manner:

Switch A, after the port-level signaling is correctly configured for IISP, must have a call route established pointing to switch B. Two connections to switch B exist, so both must be configured:

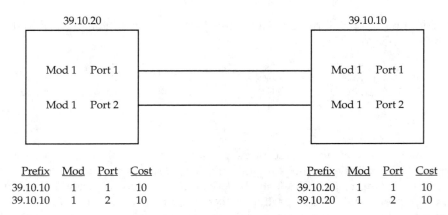

| Prefix | Mod | Port | Cost |
|--------|-----|------|------|
| 39.10.10 | 1 | 1 | 10 |
| 39.10.10 | 1 | 2 | 10 |

| Prefix | Mod | Port | Cost |
|--------|-----|------|------|
| 39.10.20 | 1 | 1 | 10 |
| 39.10.20 | 1 | 2 | 10 |

In this example, a partial prefix is used. Two entries are made: one entry for partial prefix 39.10.20, pointing out module 1, port 1, with a cost of 10, and another entry for partial prefix 39.10.20, pointing out module 1, port 2, also with a cost of 10. These parallel connections will be grouped, so the cost must be equal on both links. Switch B must also have two call routes defined, pointing back to switch A on its two links.

The link group is not created automatically in this case. To signify that the two connections should be combined, two link group entries must also be made. A new entry is made, this time by clicking the radio button labeled Link Group. When this option is selected, the ATM Address field disappears, because no actual ATM address will be defined, having already been defined in the previous step. The options for Module, Port, and Link should be active. For Module and Port, enter the module and port numbers for the first link in the group; module 1, port 1, in this case. Assign a Link number; 10 in this example, although it could be any value. Click Add, and the link group entry appears in the table below. Repeat this step for the second link—module 1, port 2, in this example—and assign it the same Link number of 10, indicating that module 1, port 1 and module 1, port 2 are both members of a link group, and are both members of link group 10 (see Figure 21-2).

Each new link group must be assigned a unique link group number. A single link group can have up to four connections, for a total aggregate bandwidth of 620Mbps, the basic equivalent of an OC-12 connection.

# Troubleshooting IISP

Troubleshooting IISP connections almost always involves one of two things:

■ A call route is missing somewhere along a specific path, causing a call to fail either on the way to the destination or on its way back to the source.

■ A call routing loop has inadvertently been introduced somewhere in the mesh.

## Detecting Call Loops

Call routing loops generally make their presence somewhat obvious, because the presence of a call routing loop can seriously impact the ATM network, causing whole portions of the mesh to lock up completely. Unfortunately, however, it is not always obvious *where* the call routing loop has been incurred.

No actual error is associated with a call routing loop. Call routing entries are user-configured, and, from an IISP standpoint, even if a loop condition is present, as long as all the individual routes are configured correctly, nothing warrants any kind of error. Remember, in an IISP environment, switches don't learn or pass on any route information,

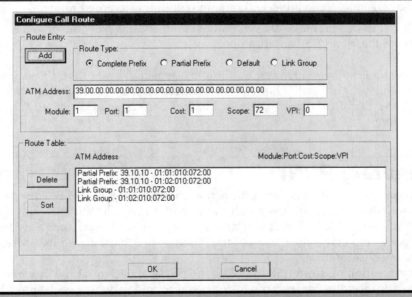

**Figure 21-2.**  *The Configure Call Route window with link groups defined*

so no one switch has any way of even knowing whether a loop exists in the network; the administrator must make sure that no loops exist. The Spanning Tree Protocol is applied to LEC VPorts, not to IISP links, so Spanning Tree will not resolve an IISP loop.

### Bit-Masking Problems with the C1*x*00

When creating a link between the C100/C50/5000BH and the C1*x*00 switches, the VPI/VCI bit masking must be taken into consideration. By default, the C1*x*00 switch utilizes a VPI/VCI mask of 6/8. This potentially can create a problem when connecting to a C100/50/5000BH, because when the C100 uses a VPI value of 0, a total of 1,024 VCI values can be used. However, when the C100 uses a VPI value greater than 0, some of the VCI bits are used, and the total number of VCI values drops to 255. In this scenario, with a VPI/VCI bit mask of 6/8, the C1*x*00 may possibly use VCI values that fall outside the range accepted by the C100 (greater than 255). If this happens, the following error may appear from a console session with the C100:

```
rm_reserve_connId: vpi/vci x/y out of range
```

where the values *x* and *y* are hex values, indicating a VPI/VCI pair. This can be resolved in two ways:

■ If an IISP link is being used, then the network side is responsible for determining the VPI/VCI pair that will be used; by making the C100 the network side, VCI values will remain within the accepted range.

■ The VPI/VCI bit mask can be changed on the C1*x*00; a value of 4/8 is acceptable in an IISP environment.

*In a PNNI environment, where the C100 acts as network side, the C100 may request a pair outside the C1x00's range. If this occurs, a mask of 0/10 should be used. This will keep the VPI at 0, with a possible 1,023 VCI values, which is within the range of both units.*

## Configuring PNNI

PNNI, in contrast to IISP, has very little actual configuration. PNNI is a *dynamic* routing protocol, so it does not require as much static configuration as IISP. As with Open Shortest Path First (OSPF), PNNI is relatively simple to configure from a switch or an interface perspective; it is the design of the PNNI network itself, and its addressing, that requires consideration.

When transitioning from IISP to PNNI, the physical network topology may or may not still be appropriate. For instance, using a star topology, where each spoke has a default route back to the core, should probably be reconsidered if PNNI is going to be implemented; PNNI makes little sense in a star topology that has no redundant connections, because PNNI's two main functions—dynamic route determination, and dynamic rerouting in the case of a link failure—both become irrelevant if there is effectively only one route to get to each destination.

## PNNI Addressing Considerations

In an IISP environment, each NSAP prefix must be unique. This also is true in PNNI, but PNNI addressing requires a bit more consideration. PNNI nodes are given an address, and also a level, which is basically a mask defining how much of the NSAP prefix is considered relevant for peer group membership. This relationship could be likened to an IP address and its mask, although PNNI is a Layer 2 protocol, not a network layer (Layer 3) protocol. Take the following example where an IP address and ATM address are compared from a masking standpoint:

```
160.60.10.215                           IP Address
255.255.255.0                           Subnet Mask
160.60.10.0                             Network/Subnetwork
215                                     Host
39.10.20.00.00.45.31.01.00.21.88.00.00  NSAP prefix
FF.FF.FF.FF.FF.FF.00.00.00.00.00.00     Level (48)
39.10.20.00.00.45.00.00.00.00.00.00     Peer Group ID
31.01.00.21.88.00.00                    Unique portion of Node ID Prefix
```

This example shows the general concept. In reality, the Node ID is expressed using the hex-format level, followed by a value of 160 to indicate the next 20 bytes are the actual Node ID, followed by the full NSAP prefix, the ESI, and the selector. The Node IDs of the lowest-level PNNI nodes, LGNs, are also preceded by their hex-format level, but not by a value of 160. The full Node ID appears as follows:

```
30.A0.39.10.20.00.00.45.31.01.00.21.88.00.00.AE.31.53.90.74.E3.00
30                  =       Level 48 in hex
A0                  =       Hex equivalent of 160, indicating the next 20
                            bytes are to be considered the Node ID
39.10.20.00.00.45   =       Peer Group portion as defined by Level
31.01.00.21.88.00.00 =      Unique portion of prefix
AE.31.53.90.74.E3   =       ESI
00                  =       Selector byte
```

Given this addressing format, switches that were previously in an IISP environment may or may not require readdressing. Remember that a node's level indicator dictates its peer group membership; all nodes on a common level of the hierarchy must share the same level indicator, and if the Peer Group ID of two nodes varies as a result of this, then they have been placed in different peer groups.

## Cutting Over from IISP

If the PNNI network is not a new installation, and is a cut-over from IISP, then addressing is something that you may need to consider. Consider, for example, the NSAP prefix of the following five switches, formerly configured for IISP and now being converted to PNNI:

```
39.10.00.00.00.00.00.00.00.00.00.00
39.20.00.00.00.00.00.00.00.00.00.00
39.30.00.00.00.00.00.00.00.00.00.00
39.40.00.00.00.00.00.00.00.00.00.00
39.50.00.00.00.00.00.00.00.00.00.00
```

From an IISP perspective, these NSAP prefixes are very easy to work with; call routes can be configured with very short partial prefixes, and the routes are very easy to distinguish from one another and keep track of when building a static route table. This addressing scheme is not completely uncommon in private ATM corporate networks. From a PNNI perspective, however, this addressing scheme may or may not cause a problem. When PNNI signaling is configured on five switches using the preceding prefixes and the default level of 72, the following are the Peer Group IDs that result:

```
39.10.00.00.00.00.00.00
39.20.00.00.00.00.00.00
39.30.00.00.00.00.00.00
39.40.00.00.00.00.00.00
39.50.00.00.00.00.00.00
```

This places each of the five nodes in a different peer group, each peer group containing one node only. This means that none of the connections between the nodes will be inside links, and a second layer of hierarchy actually needs to be configured for the PNNI network. In this situation, a peer group leader (PGL) needs to be added to each peer group.

 *Currently, the Centillion 100/50/5000BH family is not PGL-capable. Beginning with code version 4.0, Centillion 100/50/5000BH nodes will interpret LGN aggregated nodal information regarding remote peer groups from a PGL, but can't themselves act as the PGL. A Centillion 1x00 series switch is required for multihierarchical PNNI routing.*

Using the previous addressing scheme, the only way to place each of the five nodes in a common peer group without altering each prefix is to place each PNNI node at a level of 8. This results in only the first octet being considered for peer group membership, placing each node in peer group 39.00.00.00.00.00.00.00.00.00.00.00.00. Although this will work, remember that it may present certain problems if multihierarchical PNNI routing is being considered for the future; a higher layer of the PNNI hierarchy contains nodes with a lower-level indicator than those nodes at a lower level of the PNNI hierarchy. For example, a lowest-level node configured with NSAP prefix 39.10.10.45.32.30.00.00.00.00.21.90.44, might be summarized at the next-highest hierarchical layer as 39.10.10.45.32.30, with a level of 48 (see Figure 21-3).

To configure a higher layer of the hierarchy, LGNs are configured with a lower level indicator; thus, beginning the lowest-level nodes with a level of 8 doesn't leave much room to expand the hierarchy. Taking this into account, you must determine whether the existing IISP addresses can be used, or whether the addressing scheme needs to be reconfigured.

**Note**    *Since PNNI nodes discover one another dynamically and call routes don't need to be built, nor do legacy devices use ATM addresses, simply reconfiguring the addresses may be prudent, because the impact of the changed addresses to the rest of the network is most likely minimal or nonexistent.*

## Configuring PNNI Port-Level Signaling

To configure PNNI signaling on the port level, first select the tab for the module to be configured in SpeedView. This brings up the module-specific configuration parameters,

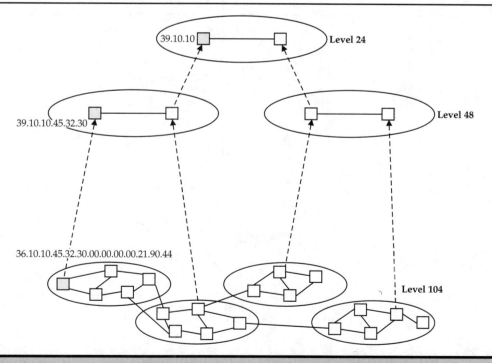

**Figure 21-3.**    *Three hierarchical layers displaying a level/layer relationship*

including the port-level signaling. Select the port to be configured and choose Edit Signaling. This opens the ATM Signaling window, where you can configure the signaling parameters. When you are running the Advanced version of code 3.0 or greater, the signaling options are grayed out, by default, and no signaling is configured. To make the signaling options active, you first must add a logical link, by clicking the Add Logical Link button, located in the bottom-left corner of the ATM Signaling window.

## Selecting a Logical Link Value

If the connection on a given port is simply a direct connection to another switch, then the default logical link value of 0 should be used. The purpose of making more than one logical link configurable on a port-by-port basis is that a connection to a public provider may be required; multiple sites may need to be connected over the ATM cloud via PNNI. This option allows multiple logical links to be configured over a single connection, so that each logical link can carry PNNI signaling to separate locations without necessitating more than one physical connection to the provider (see Figure 21-4).

## PNNI Node-Level Parameters

Configuring PNNI node-level parameters is done by first selecting the ATM Configuration tab. If the code version is 3.0 or greater, then the Configure PNNI option

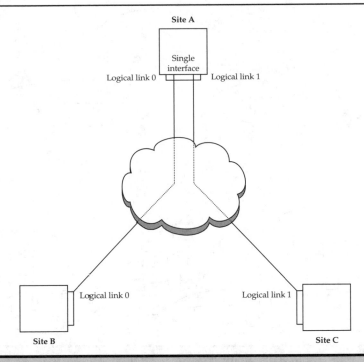

**Figure 21-4.**    *Multiple sites connected via PNNI, using logical links on a single port*

is available in the top half of the main ATM Configuration tab. If the code version is not the Advanced version, then the Configure PNNI button will be present, but grayed out.

Click the Configure PNNI button to bring up the PNNI (Private Network to Network Interface) window, which consists of four fields: Node level, Node ID, Node ATM Address, and Peer Group ID.

**NODE LEVEL**   The node level is configured by entering the desired value in this field. This value is in decimal format and indicates both the layer of the PNNI hierarchy that the node will participate at, and the portion of the NSAP prefix that is considered relevant when determining peer group membership.

When this value is altered, the first field (which is grayed out) of both the Node ID and the Peer Group ID also changes, though not to the same value configured in the Node level field. The grayed-out value is the level indicator, but it is expressed in hex rather than in decimal.

**NODE ID**   This is the individual Node ID for the node being configured. As per the PNNI 1.0 specification, the Node ID for a lowest-level node is expressed as a 22-octet value: the level indicator, in hex, as the first octet, a value of 160 (also represented in hex as A0) to indicate the next 20 octets are to be considered the Node ID, and then the 20-octet ATM address of the node itself. The Node ID is generated automatically, because all of its information is derived from other sources (the level indicator, NSAP prefix, ESI, and selector of the node). If the NSAP prefix of the node itself is altered, this alteration is reflected in the Node ID; however, if the Node ID is altered, this is not reflected anywhere else.

**NODE ATM ADDRESS**   This is the ATM address of the switch itself. This can be used to uniquely identify LGN nodes if a partitioned state occurs and two LGN PGLs are summarizing the same LGN address range. For instance, if peer group 39.10.10.20 is partitioned, the PGL remains active in its portion of the partition, while the secondary partition elects its own PGL. This results in two PGLs at the common layer of hierarchy, both in parent peer group 39.10.10, but both advertising as LGN 39.10.10.20. Since these LGNs must share information via LGN Hello messages, the Node ATM Address field allows each to maintain uniqueness.

| Note | *Currently, Centillion 100/50/5000BH switches do not support the functionality to hold the PGL position, and thus a C1x00 series switch is required to operate as PGL. PGL capability in the Centillion 100/50/5000BH may be implemented at a future time.* |
|---|---|

**PEER GROUP ID**   This value indicates the peer group in which the node is to be a member. It consists of the portion of the node's NSAP prefix that is indicated by the configured level, followed by all zeros. For example, a node with a level of 32 will result in the following Peer Group ID:

```
39.10.20.01.33.48.00.01.00.29.11.32.00          =    Node NSAP prefix
32                                              =    Level
20.39.10.20.01.00.00.00.00.00.00.00.00          =    Peer Group ID
```

> **Note**
>
> *The Peer Group ID includes the level indicator, expressed in hex, and the relevant portion of the NSAP prefix is trailed by all zeros. If a portion of the Peer Group ID is altered that falls outside the range specified by the level indicator, then a warning appears stating "Rightmost x bits of Peer Group ID is not 0" (the value of x varies depending on what the level is configured for). This warning appears because a node's peer group is defined, in part, by its level indicator, so the Peer Group ID cannot fall outside that range.*

## Configuring Summary Addresses

*Address summarization* is a method by which the number of PNNI-advertised addresses can be kept small, particularly when advertising exterior addresses; this reduces overhead and limits the number of overall addresses that must be learned by each switch (see Figure 21-5).

In this example, a single PNNI peer group is bordered by an IISP ATM network. Node A borders the PNNI and IISP portions of the network, and so node A advertises the IISP to the PNNI peer group as the exterior address. In this case, node A can be configured with a summary address of 39.10.10, to summarize IISP nodal information when advertising to the PNNI portion of the network. The addresses can be summarized in the following way for node A:

| | |
|---|---|
| Summarized nodes | 39.10.10.30.20.20.00.00.00.00.00.00.00, |
| | 39.10.10.30.30.30.00.00.00.00.00.00.00, |
| | 39.10.10.40.30.30.00.00.00.00.00.00.00, |
| | 39.10.10.50.20.30.00.00.00.00.00.00.00 |
| Summarized as | 39.10.10 |
| Address type | Exterior |

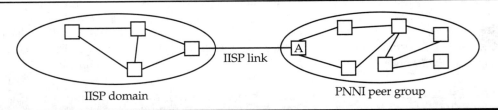

**Figure 21-5.** *A single peer group with a bordering IISP network*

If summarization were not used, each address would need to be advertised individually. Summarization reduces configuration, as well as the amount of route information that must be advertised over the network.

Using the same concept, address ranges can be suppressed. Using the preceding example, certain nodes can be excluded from being advertised into the PNNI portion of the network from node A:

| | |
|---|---|
| Summarized nodes | 39.10.10.30.20.20.00.00.00.00.00.00.00, |
| | 39.10.10.30.30.30.00.00.00.00.00.00.00, |
| | 39.10.10.40.30.30.00.00.00.00.00.00.00, |
| | 39.10.10.50.20.30.00.00.00.00.00.00.00 |
| Suppressed range | 39.10.10.30 |
| Address type | Exterior |

This scheme causes all addresses in the defined range (39.10.10.30) not to be advertised into the PNNI domain. This would exclude the first two node entries on the list, and these nodes would be unreachable from the PNNI portion of the network. This can be useful for implementing security, because nodes serving departments containing sensitive information can be configured such that they cannot be advertised into the rest of the network.

## Configuring Address Summarization and Suppression

Address summarization and suppression is configured from the main ATM Configuration tab, by clicking the Configure PNNI button. From the main PNNI (Private Network to Network Interface) window, select the Config Summary Address button. This brings up the PNNI Summary Group Address Table window (see Figure 21-6).

To add an address summary, click Add. This brings up the PNNI Summary Address window, where the summary is defined. The address does not need to be masked—the mask is implied by entering only a partial prefix or by entering the relevant portion of the address, trailed by all zeros. Click OK after you define the address.

The address must then be defined as either an interior or exterior address; if the address is a summary of nodes within the peer group, then the address is considered to be an interior (internal) address. If the address range is for addresses outside the PNNI domain (such as IISP routes), then the address is considered an exterior address.

Next, you must select or deselect the Suppress option, to indicate whether to advertise the configured address range into the rest of the PNNI domain as a nodal summary. If you select the Suppress option, the configured address range is not advertised into the rest of the PNNI domain.

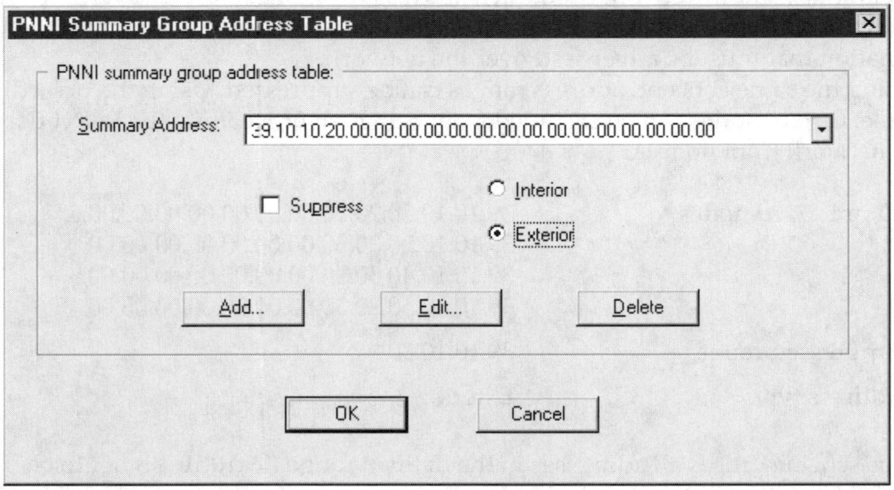

**Figure 21-6.**   *PNNI Summary Group Address Table window*

## Forming Peer Groups

Forming separate peer groups within the C100/50/5000BH involves addressing the nodes and setting the level indicator such that each node participates in the correct peer group. For instance, the following two nodes are in the same peer group:

```
30.A0.39.10.00.33.00.01.00.00.00.00.12.02.11.A3.E0.22.10.02.11.00
30.A0.39.10.00.33.00.01.00.01.00.00.13.03.22.A3.E0.22.21.EA.58.00
```

The level indicator for both addresses is 48 (30 in hex), which indicates that the first 6 octets should be considered when generating the Peer Group ID. Both nodes fall into the following peer group:

```
30.39.10.00.33.00.01.00.00.00.00.00.00
```

In contrast, the following two nodes are in separate peer groups:

```
40.A0.39.10.00.33.00.01.00.10.00.00.12.02.11.A3.E0.22.10.02.11.00
40.A0.39.10.00.33.00.01.00.20.00.00.13.03.22.A3.E0.22.21.EA.58.00
```

The level indicator for both addresses in this case is 64 (40 in hex), which indicates that the first 8 octets should be considered when generating the Peer Group ID. Each node falls into a different peer group:

```
40.39.10.00.33.00.01.00.10.00.00.00.00.00
40.39.10.00.33.00.01.00.20.00.00.00.00.00
```

Recall that when you configure peer groups in the C100/50/5000BH family, only a single layer of the PNNI hierarchy is supported, thus limiting the options for a multipeer group environment. Beginning with code version 4.0, C100/50/5000BH nodes can interpret LGN information from the PGL, but the nodes themselves can't act as PGL.

## Connecting Peer Groups

Two methods exist for connecting separate peer groups with the C100/50/5000BH platform. PGL support wasn't yet implemented prior to code version 4.0, so LGN nodal aggregation for remote peer groups could not be learned by lowest-level nodes. Consequently, dynamic, hierarchical PNNI routing was impossible, and the only way to connect two peer groups was via an IISP connection.

**CONNECTING PEER GROUPS VIA IISP**    In the scenario in which PNNI peer groups are connected via an IISP link, what would normally be the PNNI border nodes in a pure PNNI environment are now configured with an IISP link between them (rather than forming an outside link). In this confguration, the IISP call routing table is built on the border nodes (see Figure 21-7), indicating a route to each node in the remote peer group. These addresses will be advertised into the local PNNI peer group as exterior addresses. Both node A and node B must have IISP call routes configured in their IISP call routing table, pointing to all nodes in the remote peer group. This can be accomplished with a single entry on each side; since the Peer Group IDs differ, configuring a partial prefix entry pointing to the relevant portion of the Peer Group ID for the remote peer group is

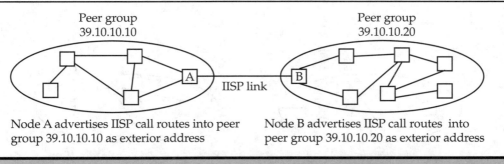

Node A advertises IISP call routes into peer group 39.10.10.10 as exterior address

Node B advertises IISP call routes into peer group 39.10.10.20 as exterior address

**Figure 21-7.**    *Two PNNI peer groups connected via IISP with domains and IISP routes*

necessary. This indicates that any incoming call that is destined for the remote peer group should first be sent to the node advertising the exterior addresses; then, once the call arrives at that node, any call destined for the remote peer group should, in fact, be routed over the IISP link.

**CONNECTING PEER GROUPS VIA HIERARCHICAL PNNI ROUTING** Beginning with code version 4.0, although C100/50/5000BH nodes can't act as PGLs, they can interpret the LGN information coming from a PGL. Using this scenario, a C1x00 series node (or other PGL-capable node) must be used to act as PGL, one in each separate peer group.

More than one hierarchical layer must be configured, with some common layer of hierarchy that the LGNs share (see Figure 21-8).

This example has two peer groups. Each peer group has a lowest level of 48, while the two share a common upper-hierarchy layer of level 16. The specifics of configuring a second and third layer of hierarchy on the C1x00 family of switches is covered in detail in Chapter 22. From the C100/C50/5000BH perspective, the two things to bear in mind are the following:

- The nodes must be grouped into the two peer groups by creating two groups of two different NSAP prefixes (as masked by the level indicator).

- The nodes must advertise their addresses, information up to the common layer of hierarchy (level 16, in this case).

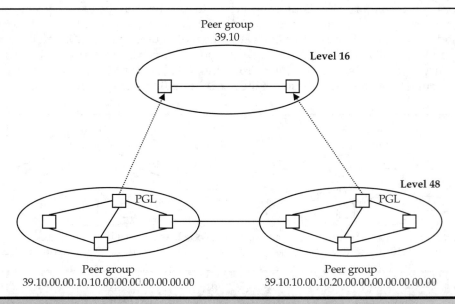

**Figure 21-8.** *Two peer groups with two layers of hierarchy, level 48 and level 16*

In the preceding example, then, a lowest-level node might use the following addressing scheme:

### Peer Group 1:

| | |
|---|---|
| 39.10.00.00.10.10.00.00.33.00.11.01.00 | NSAP Prefix |
| 48 | Level |
| 39.10.00.00.10.10.00.00.00.00.00.00.00 | Peer Group ID |
| 30.A0.39.10.00.00.10.10.00.00.33.00.11.01.00.11.01.A2.32.96.01.00 | Node ID |
| 16 | Scope |

### Peer Group 2:

| | |
|---|---|
| 39.10.10.00.10.20.00.00.33.00.22.02.00 | NSAP Prefix |
| 48 | Level |
| 39.10.10.00.10.20.00.00.00.00.00.00.00 | Peer Group ID |
| 30.A0.39.10.10.00.10.20.00.00.33.00.22.02.00.14.51.A2.07.01.11.00 | Node ID |
| 16 | Scope |

The common level of 48 (the lowest level) placed against the NSAP prefix of each group results in two distinct values:

    39.10.00.00.10.10
    39.10.10.00.10.20

This places the nodes in separate peer groups. The scope of 16 indicates that the address information for the lowest-level nodes should be advertised up to level 16, which is where the common layer of hierarchy sits. This ensures that nodes in peer group 1 will learn of the existence of the nodes in peer group 2 as a single LGN aggregation. If the scope were instead set to 48, then the lowest-level node information would be advertised only at their own level and would never be advertised up the hierarchy.

 *Make certain that if a single LECS is being used, its scope is also set to 16. Otherwise, the LECS address will not be advertised up to the common layer of hierarchy, and only the nodes within the peer group containing the LECS will be able to access it.*

# Troubleshooting PNNI

Part of troubleshooting PNNI connections is knowing what kind of link the connection should be. The type of logical link that exists between any two nodes will vary depending on the configuration of the PNNI network, the type of node being examined, the number of hierarchical layers, and possible common layers of hierarchy. Nodes that exist within a peer group and do not border any other peer group should establish *Inside links*. Border nodes establish *Outside links*.

## Examining Link States and Neighbor States

If it is suspected that two PNNI nodes are not communicating as they should be, or if a new node does not appear to be communicating with its neighbor, then you must examine the link state. Issue this command from the CLI:

```
Core_B:Command > show pnni link
```

You'll see output that resembles the following:

```
PNNI Link Information
*********************
Node Index:     1  Port Id:      3  State: 2-Way In
Remote Node ID:  0x58a03900000000000000000aa01018397ba0dc00100
Remote Port:    3  Rcv Hello: 104219  Tx Hello: 103731

Node Index:     1  Port Id:      4  State: 2-Way In
Remote Node ID:  0x58a03900000000000000000aa02008397ba0ec00100
Remote Port:    4  Rcv Hello: 103755  Tx Hello: 103731

Node Index:     1  Port Id:      5  State: 2-Way In
Remote Node ID:  0x58a03900000000000000000aa102018397ba3cc00100
Remote Port:    3  Rcv Hello: 104211  Tx Hello: 103731

Node Index:     1  Port Id:      6  State: 2-Way In
Remote Node ID:  0x58a03900000000000000000aa12008397ba0ec00100
Remote Port:    6  Rcv Hello: 103755  Tx Hello: 103731

Core_B:Command >
```

This example shows a series of 2-Way Inside links; this is correct for a link between nodes that are in the same peer group. *2-Way Inside* refers to the current neighbor state between the two nodes, established through the exchange of Hello messages; an *Inside* state occurs when a node sees a Hello message from its neighbor, and their Peer Group IDs indicate that the two nodes share a common peer group. *2-Way* indicates that the node received Hellos from its neighbor, and it saw itself listed within those Hello messages as the Remote Node ID. This indicates 2-Way communication on an Inside link. Included in this output is the Port ID of each node. This is an arbitrary number, and in a few cases in the preceding example, the Port ID and Remote Port ID are equal. The number of Hello messages, both sent and received, are also listed. These increment as time goes on, because the Hello protocol runs constantly in a PNNI network.

This example also shows the remote nodes associated with each PNNI link; notice that each Node ID is preceded by its level indicator:

```
Remote Node ID:  0x58a039000000000000000000aa12008397ba0ec00100
```

Remember that the level indicator is given in hex format, so the value of 58 actually indicates a level of 88, the first 11 octets of the NSAP prefix. The value A0 is the hex equivalent of 160, indicating that the next 20 bytes represent the Node ID.

If the nodes are not communicating, the following neighbor states may be seen:

- **1-Way Inside**  Indicates that the node is receiving Hello messages from its neighbor, but does not see itself referenced in them for either the Remote Node ID or the Remote Port ID. For some reason, the remote node is not receiving its Hellos. During the initial Hello exchange, it is normal for a node to transition into this state; it is only a problem if the node remains in this state.

- **1-Way Outside**  Indicates that the node is receiving Hello messages from its neighbor, and the two nodes are in different peer groups. It also indicates that the neighbor node is not receiving its Hello messages, because it is referenced for neither the Remote Node ID nor the Remote Port ID.

- **2-Way Outside**  Indicates that the node is receiving Hello messages from its neighbor, the neighbor is receiving its Hello messages, and the two nodes are in different peer groups.

**Note**  *Because the Centillion 100/50/5000BH do not support PGL functionality, a C1x00 series switch needs to be present if different peer groups are going to be configured. If two Centillion 100/50/5000BH nodes are not communicating via PNNI correctly and no C1x00 is present, then only Inside links should be configured. If a node is reporting a 1-Way or 2-Way Outside state, then either the level indicator or the NSAP prefixes must be altered to place all nodes within the same peer group.*

The neighbor information can also be displayed with this command:

```
Core_A:Command > show pnni nbrinfo
```

The output will resemble the following:

```
PNNI Neighbor Peer Information
******************************
Node                                            Port
Index         Remote Node ID                    State         Count
-----  ---------------------------------------  -----------   -----
1      0x58a039000000000000000000aa01018397ba0dc00100  Full    1
1      0x58a039000000000000000000aa02008397ba0ec00100  Full    2
1      0x58a039000000000000000000aa02018397ba3cc00100  Full    1
Core_A:Command >
```

This indicates that three remote PNNI neighbors exist, and that the current state between them is Full. A Full neighbor state indicates that the database synchronization is complete between the two PNNI nodes, and that any outstanding PNNI Topology State Elements (PTSEs) have been exchanged and loaded. A Full state is a good indication, indicating a stable PNNI neighbor state where the topology databases are in synch.

Another statistic to check is the current neighbor statistic, using this command:

```
Core_C:Command > sho pnni nbrstat
```

The output resembles the following:

```
PNNI Neighbor Peer Statistics
*****************************
Node                                                    DB          PTSE  PTSE
Index        Remote Node ID                    Dir Summs PTSPs ACKs  REQs
-----  ---------------------------------------- --- ----- ----- ----- -----
    1  0x58a039000000000000000000aa1018397ba0dc00100 Rcv    5  3609  3639     2
                                               Xmt    4  4291  2950     4
    1  0x58a039000000000000000000aa2008397ba0ec00100 Rcv    2  3894  3295     1
                                               Xmt    2  4015  3251     1
    1  0x58a039000000000000000000aa2018397ba3cc00100 Rcv    5  3722  3682     0
                                               Xmt    4  4251  2984     3
Core_C:Command >
```

This output indicates that three neighbors exist, and also indicates how often Database Summaries have been exchanged, as well as the number of PNNI Topology State Packets (PTSPs) that have been exchanged between the nodes. This exchange will occur in normal network operations as nodes keep one another updated of their current link states. An acknowledgement is required for each PTSE contained within a received PTSP.

If a node receives a PTSP containing a PTSE header that it does not have an entry for, then it requests the PTSE. These instances are tracked under the PTSE REQ counter. In the preceding example, the number of PTSE REQs is very low, because only four nodes in the test network are used. The number of PTSE REQs actually transmitted
and received will vary from node to node; the figure in the preceding example is the number of requests received from and transmitted to each remote node, as seen from the node being examined. It is possible that a listed node made other requests to the other remote nodes. This is seen only by examining the individual remote nodes.

## PTSE Exchange

PNNI nodes learn about topology information through the exchange of PTSEs. Examining the PTSE information that is being exchanged between nodes indicates what types of connections exist between them. Use this command:

```
Core_A:Command > show pnni ptseinfo
```

You'll see output that resembles the following:

```
PNNI PTSEs
**********

                                             PTSE                      Life-
              Node ID                        ID        Type     Seq #  time
------------------------------------------   -----  --------------- ----- -----
0x58a039000000000000000000aa01008397ba01c00100    1  Nodal Info       2546  2650
0x58a039000000000000000000aa01008397ba01c00100    2  Internal Addr    2547  2650
0x58a039000000000000000000aa01008397ba01c00100    3  Internal Addr    2549  2650
0x58a039000000000000000000aa01008397ba01c00100    4  Internal Addr    2547  2650
0x58a039000000000000000000aa01008397ba01c00100    5  Horizontal Link  1362  2650
0x58a039000000000000000000aa01008397ba01c00100   10  Horizontal Link  1362  2650
0x58a039000000000000000000aa01008397ba01c00100   11  Horizontal Link  1358  2650
0x58a039000000000000000000aa01008397ba01c00100   12  Horizontal Link  1358  2650
0x58a0390000000000000000000101008397ba01c00100   13  Internal Addr    1300  2650
0x58a039000000000000000000aa01018397ba0dc00100    1  Nodal Info       5139  3408
0x58a039000000000000000000aa01018397ba0dc00100    2  Internal Addr    5139  3408
0x58a039000000000000000000aa01018397ba0dc00100   18  Internal Addr    1439  3408
0x58a039000000000000000000aa01018397ba0dc00100   20  Horizontal Link  1435  3408
0x58a039000000000000000000aa01018397ba0dc00100   21  Horizontal Link  1431  3408
0x58a039000000000000000000aa02008397ba0ec00100    1  Nodal Info       5023  2771
0x58a039000000000000000000aa02008397ba0ec00100    2  Internal Addr    5007  2771
0x58a039000000000000000000aa02008397ba0ec00100    3  Internal Addr    5046  2771
0x58a039000000000000000000aa02008397ba0ec00100    4  Internal Addr    5007  2771
0x58a039000000000000000000aa02008397ba0ec00100    7  Horizontal Link  1386  2771
0x58a039000000000000000000aa02008397ba0ec00100    8  Horizontal Link  1386  2771
0x58a039000000000000000000aa02008397ba0ec00100    9  Horizontal Link  1386  2771
0x58a039000000000000000000aa02008397ba0ec00100   10  Horizontal Link  1386  2771
0x58a039000000000000000000aa02018397ba3cc00100    1  Nodal Info       5001  3434
0x58a039000000000000000000aa02018397ba3cc00100    2  Internal Addr    4998  3434
0x58a039000000000000000000aa02018397ba3cc00100   14  Internal Addr    1352  3434
0x58a039000000000000000000aa02018397ba3cc00100   16  Horizontal Link  1348  3434
0x58a039000000000000000000aa02018397ba3cc00100   17  Horizontal Link  1346  3434
Core_A:Command >
```

In the preceding example, several different types of PTSEs are being exchanged: Nodal Info, Internal Addr, and Horizontal Links. These are only some of the PTSE types involving PNNI nodes that are within the same peer group. The following is a full list of the different PTSE types, as well as their meanings, that you might encounter:

- **Nodal Information**  Information regarding the node itself rather that a specific link.

- **Uplink**  Indicates that the node has an uplink to an upnode and therefore is a border node to a remote peer group.

- **Internal Addr**   Can indicate the address of a directly attached ATM server or router, or any address that is associated with the node itself and not with a link or uplink.

- **Exterior Addr**   A non-PNNI address being advertised by a PNNI node as an exterior address. A separate IISP domain advertised into the PNNI domain by a node as an exterior address would be described in this way.

- **Horizontal Link**   Indicates a link to another PNNI node within the same peer group.

- **System Cap**   Indicates an unrestricted information group (IG).

- **Non-PNNI**   Indicates an IG that isn't specified in the PNNI specification or that isn't recognized by the switch.

## Checking the PNNI Routing Table

Another useful CLI command for troubleshooting a PNNI problem is the **show pnni rouaddr** command:

```
Core_A:Command > show pnni rouaddr
```

This displays the current PNNI routing table, listing all node addresses that have been learned by a particular node:

```
PNNI Routable Addresses
*************************
Address: 0x39000000000000000000aa01000000a2f99fe7   Prefix Length: 152
Advertising Node ID: 0x58a0390000000000000000aa01008397ba01c00100
Address type: Internal Addr Scope: 88 Port ID: 7  VP Capable: 0  PTSE ID: 13

Address: 0x39000000000000000000aa01008397ba010000   Prefix Length: 152
Advertising Node ID: 0x58a0390000000000000000aa01008397ba01c00100
Address type: Internal Addr Scope: 88 Port ID: 2  VP Capable: 0  PTSE ID: 3

Address: 0x39000000000000000000aa01008397ba01c001   Prefix Length: 152
Advertising Node ID: 0x58a0390000000000000000aa01008397ba01c00100
Address type: Internal Addr Scope: 88 Port ID: 1  VP Capable: 0  PTSE ID: 2

Address: 0x39000000000000000000aa0100aaaaaaaaaaaa   Prefix Length: 152
Advertising Node ID: 0x58a0390000000000000000aa01008397ba01c00100
Address type: Internal Addr Scope: 88 Port ID: 2  VP Capable: 0  PTSE ID: 3

Address: 0x39000000000000000000aa01018397ba0d0000   Prefix Length: 152
Advertising Node ID: 0x58a0390000000000000000aa01018397ba0dc00100
Address type: Internal Addr Scope: 88 Port ID: 2  VP Capable: 0  PTSE ID: 18
```

```
Address: 0x3900000000000000000000aa01018397ba0dc001   Prefix Length: 152
Advertising Node ID: 0x58a03900000000000000000000aa01018397ba0dc00100
Address type: Internal Addr Scope: 88 Port ID: 1  VP Capable: 0  PTSE ID: 2

Address: 0x3900000000000000000000aa02008397ba0e0000   Prefix Length: 152
Advertising Node ID: 0x58a03900000000000000000000aa02008397ba0ec00100
Address type: Internal Addr Scope: 88 Port ID: 2  VP Capable: 0  PTSE ID: 3

Address: 0x3900000000000000000000aa02008397ba0ec001   Prefix Length: 152
Advertising Node ID: 0x58a03900000000000000000000aa02008397ba0ec00100
Address type: Internal Addr Scope: 88 Port ID: 1  VP Capable: 0  PTSE ID: 2

Address: 0x3900000000000000000000aa0200aaaaaaaaaaaa   Prefix Length: 152
Advertising Node ID: 0x58a03900000000000000000000aa02008397ba0ec00100
Address type: Internal Addr Scope: 88 Port ID: 2  VP Capable: 0  PTSE ID: 3

Address: 0x3900000000000000000000aa02018397ba3c0000   Prefix Length: 152
Advertising Node ID: 0x58a03900000000000000000000aa02018397ba3cc00100
Address type: Internal Addr Scope: 88 Port ID: 2  VP Capable: 0  PTSE ID: 14

Address: 0x3900000000000000000000aa02018397ba3cc001   Prefix Length: 152
Advertising Node ID: 0x58a03900000000000000000000aa02018397ba3cc00100
Address type: Internal Addr Scope: 88 Port ID: 1  VP Capable: 0  PTSE ID: 2

Address: 0x47007900000000000000000000000a03e000001   Prefix Length: 152
Advertising Node ID: 0x58a03900000000000000000000aa01008397ba01c00100
Address type: Internal Addr Scope: 72 Port ID: 2  VP Capable: 0  PTSE ID: 4


Core_A:Command >
```

The preceding output is from the same four-node test network. Although it has only four nodes total, quite a few more entries are in the PNNI routing table, because all reachable addresses are advertised, not just the nodes themselves. For instance, the last entry indicates the well known address, which is associated with the LECS (notice it is at the default level of 72. Because these are lowest-level nodes in a single layer of hierarchy, this is fine, since 72 represents a higher, not lower, scope than the bottommost layer of 88. In a multihierarchical PNNI environment, this would indicate the LECS will be advertised up to level 72, but no further). The two ATM address entries with an ESI of all A's indicate the LES addresses of two cooperating LES/BUS pairs. LAN Emulation Client addresses are also present.

Checking the PNNI call routing table is a good way to determine whether a lack of connectivity is related to a link problem or to a missing entry or entries in the routing table. If a LEC is not getting to its LECS, for instance, check to make certain that the LECS address is listed in the routing table.

The entries in the preceding example are all internal addresses, because they are all advertised by the individual nodes within the PNNI domain. IISP nodes, or PNNI nodes on the remote side of an IISP link, must be advertised into the PNNI domain as exterior addresses, and would be listed as such in the routing table.

## Examining the Current Call List

Calls that are currently active through the PNNI network can be observed with this command:

```
Core_B:Command > show pnni pqcall
```

The output will resemble the following:

```
******************************
CALL ORIG : Source 0x39000000000000000000aa0100aaaaaaaaaaaa01
CALL INFO : Call Ref 2  PMP  EndPtCount 3
PORT INFO : EndPtCount 1  PNNI Port Id 2 Ifindex 73 Card 1 Port 32 Vpi 0
ENPT DEST : Dest    0x39000000000000000000aa01008397ba010000ff
ENPT INFO : State ConnRcvd    Role DTLorig
ENPT ATTR : mpt (0, edf038) blkN (0, 0), blkL (0, 0), blkP (0, 0)
PORT INFO : EndPtCount 1  PNNI Port Id 6 Ifindex 4 Card 1 Port 4 Vpi 0
ENPT DEST : Dest    0x39000000000000000000aa01018397ba0d0000ff
ENPT INFO : State ConnRcvd    Role DTLorig
ENPT ATTR : mpt (92, fca178) blkN (0, 0), blkL (0, 0), blkP (0, 0)
PORT INFO : EndPtCount 1  PNNI Port Id 7 Ifindex 5 Card 2 Port 1 Vpi 0
ENPT DEST : Dest    0x39000000000000000000aa01000000a2f99fe700
ENPT INFO : State ConnRcvd    Role DTLorig
ENPT ATTR : mpt (0, ede660) blkN (0, 0), blkL (0, 0), blkP (0, 0)
******************************
CALL ORIG : Source 0x39000000000000000000aa0100aaaaaaaaaaaa02
CALL INFO : Call Ref 6  PMP  EndPtCount 3
PORT INFO : EndPtCount 1  PNNI Port Id 2 Ifindex 73 Card 1 Port 32 Vpi 0
ENPT DEST : Dest    0x39000000000000000000aa01008397ba010000ff
ENPT INFO : State ConnRcvd    Role DTLorig
ENPT ATTR : mpt (0, edefa8) blkN (0, 0), blkL (0, 0), blkP (0, 0)
PORT INFO : EndPtCount 1  PNNI Port Id 6 Ifindex 4 Card 1 Port 4 Vpi 0
ENPT DEST : Dest    0x39000000000000000000aa01018397ba0d0000ff
ENPT INFO : State ConnRcvd    Role DTLorig
ENPT ATTR : mpt (92, fcd2ec) blkN (0, 0), blkL (0, 0), blkP (0, 0)
PORT INFO : EndPtCount 1  PNNI Port Id 7 Ifindex 5 Card 2 Port 1 Vpi 0
ENPT DEST : Dest    0x39000000000000000000aa01000000a2f99fe700
ENPT INFO : State ConnRcvd    Role DTLorig
ENPT ATTR : mpt (0, ede5d0) blkN (0, 0), blkL (0, 0), blkP (0, 0)
******************************
```

```
CALL ORIG : Source 0x3900000000000000000000aa0100aaaaaaaaaaaa02
CALL INFO : Call Ref 18  PMP  EndPtCount 1
PORT INFO : EndPtCount 1  PNNI Port Id 6 Ifindex 4 Card 1 Port 4 Vpi 0
ENPT DEST : Dest   0x3900000000000000000000aa0200aaaaaaaaaaaa02
ENPT INFO : State ConnRcvd   Role DTLorig
ENPT ATTR : mpt (64, fcb50c) blkN (0, 0), blkL (0, 0), blkP (0, 0)
*******************************
CALL ORIG : Source 0x3900000000000000000000aa0100aaaaaaaaaaaa01
CALL INFO : Call Ref 22  PMP  EndPtCount 1
PORT INFO : EndPtCount 1  PNNI Port Id 4 Ifindex 2 Card 1 Port 2 Vpi 0
ENPT DEST : Dest   0x3900000000000000000000aa0200aaaaaaaaaaaa01
ENPT INFO : State ConnRcvd   Role DTLorig
ENPT ATTR : mpt (64, fd07f8) blkN (0, 0), blkL (0, 0), blkP (0, 0)
*******************************
CALL ORIG : Source 0x3900000000000000000000aa0200aaaaaaaaaaaa02
CALL INFO : Call Ref 24  PMP  EndPtCount 1
PORT INFO : EndPtCount 1  PNNI Port Id 2 Ifindex 73 Card 1 Port 32 Vpi 0
ENPT DEST : Dest   0x3900000000000000000000aa0100aaaaaaaaaaaa02
ENPT INFO : State ConnRcvd   Role Transit
ENPT ATTR : mpt (0, edec48) blkN (0, 0), blkL (0, 0), blkP (0, 0)
*******************************
CALL ORIG : Source 0x3900000000000000000000aa0200aaaaaaaaaaaa01
CALL INFO : Call Ref 26  PMP  EndPtCount 1
PORT INFO : EndPtCount 1  PNNI Port Id 2 Ifindex 73 Card 1 Port 32 Vpi 0
ENPT DEST : Dest   0x3900000000000000000000aa0100aaaaaaaaaaaa01
ENPT INFO : State ConnRcvd   Role Transit
ENPT ATTR : mpt (0, edec00) blkN (0, 0), blkL (0, 0), blkP (0, 0)
*******************************
Total PQ call count        : 6
Total PQ egress port count : 10
Total PQ endpoint count    : 10
Core_B:Command >
```

This output can indicate a lot about what is currently going on in the PNNI domain. The preceding example lists a series of calls connected through the PNNI network. The calls themselves are separated by a series of asterisks (*), for a total of six calls, summarized at the end of the command's output. Though this list has many more than six entries, bear in mind that each call is a point-to-multipoint circuit. This is indicated by the CALL INFO, immediately following the call source:

```
CALL ORIG : Source 0x3900000000000000000000aa0100aaaaaaaaaaaa01
CALL INFO : Call Ref 2  PMP  EndPtCount 3
```

PMP indicates a point-to-multipoint call. The prior address with the ESI of all A's is, in this case, actually the LES address. So the call reference actually indicates the control connections for a group of remote LECs. As indicated by the endpoint count (EndPtCount) entry, the LES has a PMP connection to three endpoints:

```
* * * * * * * * * * * * * * * * * * * * * * * * * * * * * * *
CALL ORIG : Source 0x39000000000000000000aa0100aaaaaaaaaaaa01
CALL INFO : Call Ref 2  PMP  EndPtCount 3
PORT INFO : EndPtCount 1  PNNI Port Id 2 Ifindex 73 Card 1 Port 32 Vpi 0
ENPT DEST : Dest   0x39000000000000000000aa01008397ba010000ff
ENPT INFO : State ConnRcvd   Role DTLorig
ENPT ATTR : mpt (0, edf038) blkN (0, 0), blkL (0, 0), blkP (0, 0)
PORT INFO : EndPtCount 1  PNNI Port Id 6 Ifindex 4 Card 1 Port 4 Vpi 0
ENPT DEST : Dest   0x39000000000000000000aa01018397ba0d0000ff
ENPT INFO : State ConnRcvd   Role DTLorig
ENPT ATTR : mpt (92, fca178) blkN (0, 0), blkL (0, 0), blkP (0, 0)
PORT INFO : EndPtCount 1  PNNI Port Id 7 Ifindex 5 Card 2 Port 1 Vpi 0
ENPT DEST : Dest   0x39000000000000000000aa01000000a2f99fe700
ENPT INFO : State ConnRcvd   Role DTLorig
ENPT ATTR : mpt (0, ede660) blkN (0, 0), blkL (0, 0), blkP (0, 0)
```

There are a total of three remote LECs, and in the preceding listing, the PMP call from the LES extends to each of the three clients and gives each of their addresses. In each case, since the call initiated from the node where the LES resides and was source routed to the destination from that point, the source node is listed as the DTL originator.

The third call entry indicates a call between two different BUS addresses:

```
* * * * * * * * * * * * * * * * * * * * * * * * * * * * * * *
CALL ORIG : Source 0x39000000000000000000aa0100aaaaaaaaaaaa02
CALL INFO : Call Ref 18  PMP  EndPtCount 1
PORT INFO : EndPtCount 1  PNNI Port Id 6 Ifindex 4 Card 1 Port 4 Vpi 0
ENPT DEST : Dest   0x39000000000000000000aa0200aaaaaaaaaaaa02
ENPT INFO : State ConnRcvd   Role DTLorig
ENPT ATTR : mpt (64, fcb50c) blkN (0, 0), blkL (0, 0), blkP (0, 0)
* * * * * * * * * * * * * * * * * * * * * * * * * * * * * * *
```

This is due to the fact that cooperating LES/BUS pairs are configured in the test network, which indicates the VCC that exists between cooperating pairs. Although there are only two BUS addresses, and thus only one circuit between them, the call is still a PMP call, because cooperating LES/BUS pairs support up to four redundant pairs.

The **show pnni pqcall** command can be an excellent way to determine which services are connected and which aren't, as well as which nodes have circuits between them and which don't. If you suspect that a call is not succeeding between two nodes, this command offers a quick way to verify whether or not the call is present. Remember, however, that a PNNI call is dynamically routed and can take many different potential paths, so tracking down a particular call may be difficult, depending on how many possible paths exist.

## PNNI Routing Statistics

The PNNI routing statistics can be viewed with this command:

```
Core_A:Command > show pnni roustat
```

The output will resemble the following:

```
PNNI Version Supported
----------------------
        Newest Version Supported:       1
        Oldest Version Supported:       1
Statistics for Operation as a DTL Originator
--------------------------------------------
                 DTLs Generated:      374
     DTLs Cranked-back to here:        0
     Alternate Routes Attempted:       0
          Failed Route Computes:      13
Destination Unreachable Failures:     11
Statistics for Operation as an Entry Border Node
------------------------------------------------

                 DTLs Generated:        0
     DTLs Cranked-back to here:         0
     Alternate Routes Attempted:        0
          Failed Route Computes:        0
Destination Unreachable Failures:       0
Core_A:Command >
```

The output from this command indicates the version of PNNI being run (currently, only version 1), as well as call route statistics for the node in two capacities: the node as a Designated Transit List (DTL) originator, and the node as an Entry Border Node, meaning that it borders two separate peer groups.

The preceding statistics relate only to the node as a DTL originator, because the node is not a border node and only one peer group is configured. A counter showing how many DTLs have been created from this source node is displayed, showing a total of 374. In the event that a DTL is generated, but for some reason can't be honored, such as a link failure, and the call is cranked back to the source node, this is noted under the DTLs Cranked-back to here counter. A call that is cranked back to the source is attempted again with a new DTL that follows a different path; evidence of this would appear under the counter for Alternate Routes Attempted.

In this example, there are 13 Failed Route Computes and 11 Destination Unreachable Failures. This is not necessarily an indication that something is wrong; unless they are incrementing, these errors may simply indicate that some of the LANE control connections have failed their initial setups because the PNNI nodes have not yet finished learning their topology and synchronizing their databases.

If these counters are incrementing, or if they constitute a large percentage of the total DTLs, then this may indicate a problem with the PNNI network. A Destination Unreachable Failure may indicate a misconfigured PNNI node; the source node has attempted to build a DTL to the destination address, but could not find a corresponding node in its topology database. This could be because the node was inadvertently placed in the wrong peer group, that it has become unavailable due to a link failure that has totally cut it off from the PNNI domain, or that a failure has occurred within the node itself. A Failed Route Computation may indicate a problem with the PNNI functioning within the network itself, and it may need to be reinitialized.

## Configuring MPOA

Configuring Multi-Protocol Over ATM (MPOA) on the C100/C50/5000BH platform involves adding new MPOA-specific parameters, as well as altering portions of the existing LANE component configurations. The switch hosts the MPOA Client (MPC), while the MPOA Server (MPS) resides on the router. When running Advanced code of version 4.0 or higher, the MPC is always active on the switch. To function correctly, however, the MPC needs to obtain a configuration; furthermore, because the MPC needs to work in conjunction with the existing LANE services, those services must be able to recognize and support MPOA as well.

Each ATM switch hosts a single MPC:

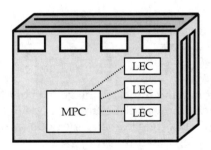

That MPC, in turn, serves each LEC that is configured on the switch, where a single MPC entity will serve multiple ELANs.

 *The current MPOA implementation supports 802.3 Ethernet LANE only. 802.5 Token Ring Emulated LANs are not supported as of the time of publication.*

# MPOA Requirements

In the existing LANE environment, several components are required for MPOA to function:

### EACH MPC REQUIRES A LANEV2-CAPABLE LEC FOR EACH ELAN PARTICIPATING IN MPOA

The MPC and each LEC that it serves work in conjunction with one another. At the time of initialization, when the LEC communicates with the LECS over the Configuration Direct VCC to obtain its LES, the MPC or MPS that serves that client may also obtain its configuration Time, Length, Values (TLV) from the LECS during that same exchange. Likewise, for the MPS and MPC to learn about the existence of one another, their existence must be registered with the LES; this is done by the LEC being served by the MPC or MPS during the join phase. When a LEC joins the LES, it registers the existence of its MPC or MPS with the LES, and this information is communicated client-to-server and server-to-client during LE_ARP resolution. For these reasons, each LEC participating in MPOA must be LANEv2-capable, to support the additional TLVs, and configured to participate in MPOA.

### THE LES FOR EACH ELAN THAT WILL PARTICIPATE IN MPOA MUST BE LANEV2-CAPABLE

Since the MPC and MPS are registered with the LES by the LECs that they serve, the LES must be able to learn this information, as well as propagate the presence of the MPC and MPS, along with their TLVs, during LE_ARP resolution. For this reason, the LES must be LANEv2-capable.

### AT LEAST ONE OF THE LANEV2-CAPABLE LECs MUST UTILIZE THE LECS FOR THE EXCHANGE OF TLVs IF THEIR CONFIGURATION INFORMATION IS TO BE OBTAINED FROM THE LECS

If the MPC or MPS has its TLVs configured locally, it may not be required to communicate with the LECS. If it doesn't have its TLVs configured locally, however, then at least one LEC on the switch the MPC serves must be configured to use the LECS, because that is where the MPC and MPS TLVs are configured. The LEC must also be LANEv2-compatible, to support the added TLVs. Since the MPC and MPS configuration are not ELAN- or LEC-specific, the LECS must be contacted only once. For this reason, it is sufficient that only one V2-capable LEC is configured to use the LECS.

### THE LECS MAY REQUIRE THAT MPC AND/OR MPS TLVs BE CONFIGURED

If the MPC and MPS TLVs are not configured locally, then the TLV parameters must be configured on the LECS. In LANEv2 and MPOA, the LECS is the source of not only the ELAN LES table and LANEv1 TLVs, but also the configuration parameters for the MPC and MPS, including a default configuration for each.

### AT LEAST ONE MPS MUST EXIST TO SERVE THE MPCs

For MPOA to function, the ATM network must contain at least one MPS, to perform MPOA address resolutions.

# LANEv2 Configuration

The following sections outline the new LANEv2 functionality introduced into the LEC, LECS, and LES. These entities must be LANEv2-capable for MPOA to function properly.

## MPOA Settings for the LECS

Beginning with code version 4.0, each ELAN configured in the LECS must be specified as being either LANEv1- or LANEv2-capable. By default, all ELANs comply with LANEv1. When using code version 4.0, a check box is available in the LECS Configuration window, labeled V2 Capable. By selecting this check box, the ELAN being configured is noted as being V2-capable, and another field appears labeled ELAN ID. This ELAN ID should match the value configured on the V2 LES itself in the LES/BUS Configuration window. This value is passed along as a TLV to any LEC joining the ELAN in question, contained in the CONFIGURE_RESPONSE over the Configuration Direct VCC during the join phase. The LEC uses this value and compares it against any incoming traffic; anything not matching the specified value is discarded.

 *LANEv2 capability, as well as individual ELAN IDs, are configured on an ELAN-by-ELAN basis within the LECS. Not all ELANs are required to utilize the same version of LANE.*

With code version 4.0, the LECS Configuration window contains three new options: the MPOA Client Config and MPOA Server Config buttons, located beneath the LECS address field, and a check box labeled V2 Capable, located just above the LES ATM Address field (see Figure 21-9).

These options allow the necessary MPOA parameters to be configured on the LECS for the MPC, the MPS, and the LES associated with each individual ELAN.

# MPOA Client Configuration Within the LECS

Click the button labeled MPOA Client Config to open the LECS MPOA Client Configuration window. By default, much of this window is grayed out until the Add MPC Config button is clicked, at which point the fields become active (see Figure 21-10).

This window is devoted to the MPC configuration. At the top of the window, an MPC config Internal ID is generated. This is a value selected by SpeedView to maintain uniqueness among LECS MPC information. In addition, the following parameters can be set:

- **Default MPC config TLV** This check box in the upper-right corner indicates whether or not a default MPC TLV configuration should be maintained. This ensures that an MPC with an unrecognized ATM address still receives TLV values (the defaults). An MPC that is configured to use the LECS but that does not obtain TLV information from the LECS will not successfully function. For this reason, you are recommended to leave the Default MPC config TLV enabled.

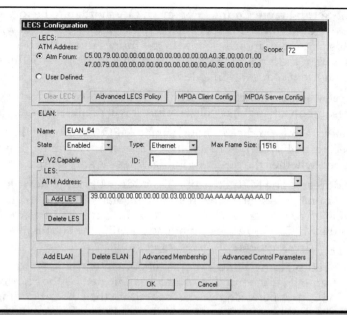

**Figure 21-9.** *The LECS Configuration window in code version 4.0*

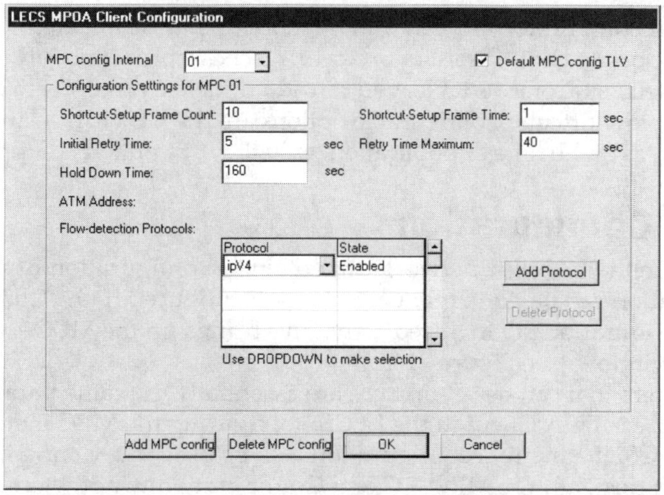

**Figure 21-10.** *The LECS MPOA Client Configuration window*

- **Shortcut-Setup Frame Count**   For an MPOA shortcut to be formed, a certain number of frames must pass between a source and destination within a certain time. This parameter indicates how many frames must pass between two devices within the amount of time defined by the Shortcut-Setup Frame Time, before a shortcut request is initiated.

- **Initial Retry Time**   Indicates the minimum amount of time an MPC will wait after a resolution attempt has failed, before it will reinitiate the resolution process.

- **Hold Down Time**   Indicates how long an MPOA shortcut will remain up after it has been established, before it must be refreshed, meaning it must be determined whether the destination IP address is still valid.

- **ATM Address**   The MPC control ATM address. Prior to downloading the configuration to the switch, this field will be blank. Once the configuration has been transferred, and the switch generates the control address which will be used by the MPC in its requests made to its MPS, the address will appear in this field. The address appears as a read-only value.

- **Shortcut-Setup Frame Time**   Works in tandem with the Shortcut-Setup Frame Count parameter; if the number of frames indicated by the Shortcut-Setup Frame Count pass between two devices within the amount of time (in seconds) specified by the Shortcut-Setup Frame Time, then a shortcut request is issued. The default value is one second.

- **Retry Time Maximum**   Indicates the amount of time (in seconds) that the MPC will attempt to build a shortcut, before it stops issuing shortcut requests. The default value is 40 seconds.

- **Flow-detection Protocols**   An MPOA shortcut may be initiated when the flow of traffic, associated with a certain protocol, reaches a predefined threshold. From the Flow-detection Protocols table, you can add or delete protocols to be monitored for possible shortcuts. Configurable options are IPv4, IPv6, IPX, and AppleTalk; however, as of the time of publication, only the IPv4 option is supported.

# MPOA Client Configuration

Each MPC within the LANEv2 network can obtain its configuration from the LECS, or the configuration can be done manually. Click Configure MPOA Client from the main ATM Configuration tab in SpeedView. This brings up the MPOA Client Configuration window (see Figure 21-11).

The parameters that can be set up here are essentially the same parameters configured for the MPOA Client in the LECS; configuring the MPC manually simply bypasses the LECS. If a manual configuration is to be used, the Config Mode, located in the upper-left corner of the MPOA Client Configuration window, must be changed from its default value of Automatic to Manual.

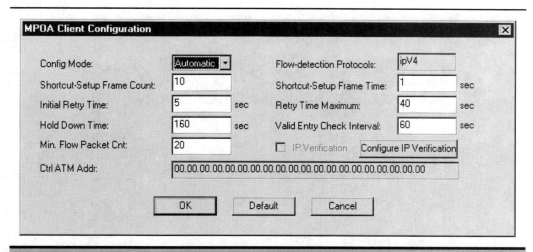

**MPOA Client Configuration**

| | | | |
|---|---|---|---|
| Config Mode: | Automatic ▾ | Flow-detection Protocols: | ipV4 |
| Shortcut-Setup Frame Count: | 10 | Shortcut-Setup Frame Time: | 1 sec |
| Initial Retry Time: | 5 sec | Retry Time Maximum: | 40 sec |
| Hold Down Time: | 160 sec | Valid Entry Check Interval: | 60 sec |
| Min. Flow Packet Cnt: | 20 | ☐ IP Verification | Configure IP Verification |
| Ctrl ATM Addr: | 00.00.00.00.00.00.00.00.00.00.00.00.00.00.00.00.00.00.00.00 | | |

[ OK ]    [ Default ]    [ Cancel ]

**Figure 21-11.** *The MPOA Client Configuration window*

## IP Verification

Selecting this box enables a function called IP Verification. This is a proprietary protocol that allows the user to configure a range of IP addresses that the MPC will service. Any IP address falling outside the specified range or ranges will not be serviced by the MPC.

The purpose of IP Verification is to prevent the MPC from attempting to create an MPOA shortcut to an address that will not support one. For example, a private, routed ATM network with five ELANs will allow MPOA shortcuts to be created between LECs on different IP subnets; however, many (if not most) private networks also have an Internet gateway (see Figure 21-12).

In this example, an MPC serving a LEC in ELAN A, subnet 150.50.10.0/24 may create an MPOA shortcut to a LEC in ELAN B, subnet 150.50.20.0/24. However, if a user being served by that same LEC in ELAN A attempts to make a transfer over the Internet to IP address 134.176.10.132/24, some wasted overhead may result as the MPC serving the LEC in ELAN A attempts to create a shortcut to IP address 134.176.10.132, which obviously won't succeed.

To prevent MPCs from attempting to build shortcuts to addresses that are clearly outside of the private network, MPOA Client IP Verification may be used. When enabled, the MPC will attempt to build an MPOA shortcut only if the destination IP address falls within the range defined by the administrator.

Configuring IP Verification is done by clicking the Configure IP Verification button in the main MPOA Client Configuration window. This brings up the IP Verification Table window (see Figure 21-13).

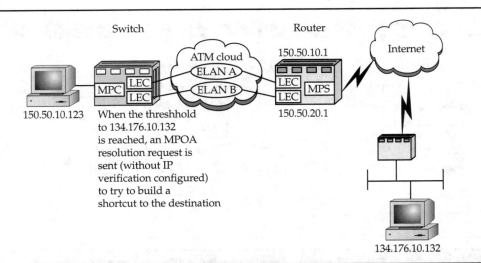

**Figure 21-12.** *Private ATM network with an Internet gateway*

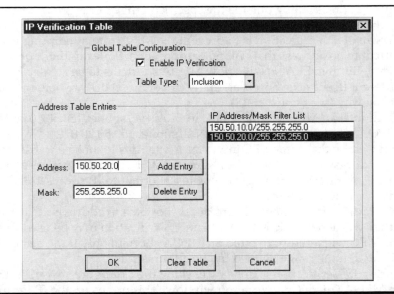

**Figure 21-13.** *The IP Verification Table window*

Within this window, the following IP Verification specifics can be configured:

- **Table Type**  Two types of IP Verification tables can exist: Exclusion tables and Inclusion tables. Setting the table type to Exclusion specifies that the defined IP ranges in the table will not be serviced by the MPC. Setting the table type to Inclusion indicates that the specified IP ranges in the table will be serviced by the MPC. This allows some flexibility of configuration; if the IP range to be included far outweighs those to be excluded, an Exclusion list may be easier and quicker to configure.

- **Address**  The IP address used in conjunction with the configured mask to indicate which range of IP addresses is to be either included or excluded. Individual networks or subnets can be configured.

- **Mask**  The mask associated with the preceding IP address range.

- **IP Address/Mask Filter List**  As the IP address and mask entries are configured, they appear in this table. Each address or range of addresses present in this table will be checked before attempting to create MPOA shortcuts to any destination IP address.

## MPOA Server Configuration

Although the MPOA Server itself is not configured on the switch, its parameters can be configured on the LECS, so that the MPS can obtain its TLVs at the time the router's LEC initiates the join process. These parameters are configured by selecting the ATM Configuration tab in SpeedView, and then clicking Configure LECS, to bring up the LECS Configuration window. This window includes buttons labeled MPOA Client Config and MPOA Server Config. Click MPOA Server Config to bring up the LECS MPOA Server Configuration window (see Figure 21-14).

By default, the screen mostly is grayed out. Clicking Add MPS config causes the following configuration fields to become active:

- **MPS config Internal**  A value generated by SpeedView to keep the MPS configurations unique, because multiple MPS configurations can be resident on the LECS at any one time, to serve multiple MPSs that may exist in the network.

- **Default MPS config TLV**  Checking this box indicates that the default MPS configuration TLVs should be used for any MPS attempting to obtain configuration information from the LECS whose ATM address is not recognized. This ensures that any new MPS at least receives the default values, even if it is not recognized.

- **Keep-Alive Time**  Indicates how frequently keepalive messages will be sent to the MPS. This parameter works in conjunction with the Keep-Alive Lifetime parameter, and should be a value consistent with the Keep-Alive's lifetime. For instance, if the Keep-Alive Lifetime is set to 20 seconds, and the Keep-Alive Time is set to 25 seconds, connection to the MPS will continually time out.

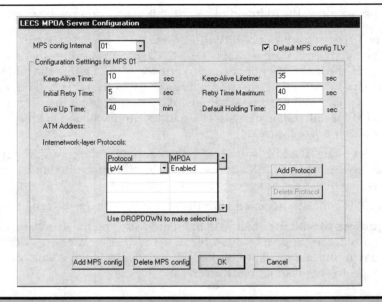

**Figure 21-14.** *The LECS MPOA Server Configuration window*

Keeping at least a 2:1 ratio between the two values is a good idea; the MPS should be able to miss at least one Keep-Alive without assuming something has gone wrong. The range is from 1 to 300 seconds, with a default of 10 seconds.

- **Initial Retry Time**  The period the MPS will wait before retrying a resolution request for which it has not received a response. The range of this value is between 1 and 300 seconds, with a default of 5 seconds.

- **Give Up Time**  The minimum amount of time the MPS will wait without receiving a resolution reply before it assumes that it is lost and gives up on it.

- **ATM Address**  The control ATM address associated with the MPS. As with the MPC, this field remains blank until the information is actually received from the MPS. It is a read-only field.

- **Keep-Alive Lifetime**  The amount of time the MPS considers a Keep-Alive message to be valid. This parameter works in conjunction with the Keep-Alive Time. The Keep-Alive Lifetime should exceed the Keep-Alive Time by at least 50 percent, so that a single missed Keep-Alive message does not automatically indicate a failure. The range is between 3 and 1000 seconds, with a default of 35 seconds.

- **Retry Time Maximum**  The cumulative amount of time the MPS will attempt to retry resolution requests for which it has not received a response. The number of actual retries that will occur is determined both by this value and by the Initial Retry Time. For instance, if the Initial Retry Time is set to 5 seconds, and the Retry Time Maximum is set to 40 seconds, then a resolution request will be attempted eight times.

- **Default Holding Time** The default holding time to be used in Next Hop Resolution Protocol (NHRP) resolution replies. The range is between 1 and 120 seconds, with a default of 20 seconds.

- **Internetwork-layer Protocols** Here, the protocol types that are to be served by the MPS can be added and deleted. By default, IPv4 is selected. As of the time of publication, only IPv4 is supported.

Like the MPC, the TLVs can also be configured manually on the router, when configuring the MPS, and are not required to be configured on the LECS.

# Configuring the LES for MPOA

If MPOA is going to be configured, then the LES for each ELAN that will participate in MPOA must be LANEv2-capable. Beginning with code version 4.0, each LES must be designated as V1 or V2, defaulting to LANEv1.

In code version 4.0, a check box labeled V2 Capable appears just below the ELAN Name in the LAN Emulation Server (LES/BUS) window. Checking this box indicates that the LES will be V2-capable, and causes another field to appear next to it, labeled ELAN ID. This value uniquely identifies the ELAN, and is obtained from the LECS as a TLV by each LEC joining the ELAN. This parameter is used in conjunction with LANEv2's LLC-multiplexing support. Since a single VCC is capable of carrying traffic for multiple ELANs, the ELAN ID is compared against the value obtained from the LECS during the join phase. If the values do not match, then the ELAN is discarded.

## LANEv2 LEC Capabilities

Beginning with code version 4.0, LANEv2 is supported. LANEv2 is a requirement of MPOA, and must be configured on each LAN Emulation Client per switch that is to participate in MPOA.

Because the MPC obtains TLVs from the LECS via a LANEv2-capable LEC, and because a single MPC serves all LECs on a single switch, each LEC that wants to advertise Layer 3 capability must be configured both to be V2-capable and to participate in the MPOA protocol. This is configured in the LAN Emulation Client Configuration window, in the Advanced section. There, a check box labeled V2 Capable is present in code version 4.0 and greater. Selecting this box sets the currently selected LEC VPort to be LANEv2-compliant. Once this is selected, another check box appears next to it, labeled MPOA. Checking this box indicates that the LEC is also to participate in the MPOA protocol.

**Note** *If V2 Capable is checked, but the MPOA box does not appear, check the LES the LEC is associated with, and make certain that it also is configured to be LANEv2-compliant. If the LEC and LES reside on the same switch, and the LES is non-V2-capable, the MPOA option will not appear.*

# Troubleshooting MPOA

Problems with MPOA often occur for one of two reasons: either the MPC and MPS are not communicating or they are communicating but MPOA shortcuts are not being built.

## Examining MPOA Information from the CLI

MPOA information can be viewed from the CLI. Issue the following command:

```
Edge_A:Command > show mpoa info
```

The result will look something like this:

```
MMPC State      MMPCStaRunning

MpcCtrlAddr     39:20:00:00:00:00:00:00:00:00:00:00-02:0B:48:1F:20:00-00
MpcDataAddr
    card  2     39:20:00:00:00:00:00:00:00:00:00:00-02:0B:48:1F:20:00-F1

                        Configured                  Actual
ConfigMode                 auto                       auto
SCSetupFrameCount           10                         10
SCSetupFrameTime             1                          1
InitialRetryTime             5                          5
InitialRetryTimeMax         40                         40
HoldDownTime               160                        160
ValidCheckInterval          60
MinFlowPacketCount          20

Edge_A:Command >
```

In the preceding output, the Master Control Processor MPOA Client (MMPC) instance is shown to be Running, and the MPC control address is shown, along with that of the MPC data address that is associated with the Ethernet switch module (listed as card 2 in this example, because the Ethernet card in this test resides in slot 2). The Config Mode for the MPC is set to Automatic, and the configuration parameters that were configured on the LECS are listed.

## Checking for a Valid Connection with the MPS

If MPOA does not appear to be functioning properly, perhaps the first thing to check is whether the MPC has even learned of the existence of the MPS. You can do this by issuing the following command from the CLI:

```
Edge_A:Command > show mpoa mps
```

The result will look something like this:

```
MpsATMAddr    39:20:00:00:00:00:00:00:00:00:00:00-00:00:A2:CB:2B:E7-03
```

```
MpsState         dis&imp    TimeStamp                   4023
MpsMacCnt             1     ImposedIngressEntryCnt         0
Circuit              10     ImposedEgressEntryCnt          1
KeepAliveTime        35     KeepAliveSeqNumber            23

Edge_A:Command >
```

In this example, a single MPS is being used, which, in fact, has been discovered by the MPC. The MPS control address is given, indicating that of the MPS configured on the router. The current MPS state is listed as dis&imp, which is the normal operating state of an MPS that is correctly communicating with the MPC. The following MPS states may be listed:

- **discovr**   Indicates that the MPS has been discovered by the MPC through an LE_ARP_RESPONSE that indicated the MPS's presence.
- **imposed**   Indicates that the MPC has been learned by the MPS.
- **dis&imp**   Indicates that the MPC is aware of the MPS, and vice versa.

If no MPS has been learned through any means, the command will not produce any output. If multiple MPSs are used on the remote router, all MPS instances will be listed.

This command may be used in conjunction with the **show rllcx** command; the circuit number (10 in this case) will correspond to the circuit number for the connection between the MPC and the MPS. The **show rllcx** command, covered later in this section, will display a circuit number of 10 for the circuit connecting to the router.

Evidence of a valid connection with the MPS can also be obtained from the forwarding database. Use this command:

```
Edge_A:Command > show fdb mcp all
```

The result will look something like this:

```
*** Maximum FDB entries: 10239 Currently in use: 4 Internal entries: 0
*** Number of HASH buckets: 4096, longest list since reset: 1

ILSDTB3  VID Key value      age type st  md/pt vprt phdr ickt umsk irif
1110000    1 02A000D012F8     0 res  rdy 1   0 n/a  n/a  n/a  n/a
1110000    2 4005000B481F     0 res  rdy 1   0 n/a  n/a  n/a  n/a
1000000    3 0008C7606A80     0 enet rdy 2   1 n/a  n/a  n/a  n/a
1110101    3 0000A2CB2BE7    13 enet rdy n/a     2 x000    0  x02
remoteX  n/a 160.60.10.123  n/a  icac vld 0008 <ECTag=00480001> X 4
Edge_A:Command >
```

The preceding output indicates that the MPS has been discovered, and that a shortcut is currently in place. Prior to code version 4.0, the forwarding database included the following bit headers:

| I | In use bit; the entry is currently being used |
|---|---|
| L | Local bit; the address was learned locally |
| S | Static bit; the entry has been statically configured |
| D | Duplicate bit; the same address was received on different ports in the same bridge group or VLAN |
| T | Trunk bit; the address was learned on a VPort |
| B | Backplane extension bit; indicates whether the address was learned on a Turbo VPort (1) or Circuit Saver VPort (0) |

The previous output from a switch running 4.0 code has an additional bit, designated 3. This indicates a Layer 3 device, such as the MPS. An entry with the 3 bit flipped indicates the existence of the MPS:

```
1110101    3 0000A2CB2BE7    13 enet rdy n/a      2 x000    0  x02
remoteX   n/a  160.60.10.123  n/a  icac  vld 0008 <ECTag=00480001> X 4
```

Below the entry for the router's MAC address is a listing beginning with remoteX, which indicates that a shortcut is in place. The entries have the following meanings:

| remoteX | The shortcut originates on a remote switch rather than on another card or port in the same chassis. |
|---|---|
| 160.60.10.123 | The destination station address. |
| icac | The entry is an ingress cache entry, indicating the shortcut originated on the remote switch. |
| vld | The current state of the shortcut. A vld listing indicates that the shortcut is valid and that data is traversing the shortcut. A list of alternate shortcut states follows this list. |
| <ECTag=00480001> | The Egress Cache tag. This keeps data flows unique when being multiplexed over the shortcut circuit. |

The state can indicate a lot about the current operation of a shortcut, if one exists. The possible states a shortcut can be in are as follows:

| | |
|---|---|
| cac (Cache) | A destination IP address has been seen for which no shortcut exists, but the flow control criteria hasn't been met. |
| qry (Query) | The flow threshold has been crossed and the MPC has been requested to resolve the address. |
| rsl (Resolved) | The requested address has been resolved, but the MPC does not currently have data to send over the shortcut. |
| fdp (Flow Pending) | The target IP has been resolved, and there is outstanding data to send. A shortcut has been requested but not yet established. |
| vld (Valid) | The target IP has been resolved, a shortcut has been established, and data is currently using the shortcut. |
| rfr (Refreshing) | The cache entry is being refreshed. Data still passes over the shortcut at this time. |
| hdn (Hold Down) | The cache entry is in a hold down state because the route has not been resolved after repeated attempts. |
| del (Delete) | The cache entry is no longer necessary, and a request has been made that the entry be removed. |

## Examining the Ingress Cache

A shortcut can be traced back to its source by examining the ingress cache of the MPC. Bear in mind that "ingress," in this case, does not actually refer to the incoming shortcut connection, but rather to the MPC itself: the ingress MPC is the MPC that data is flowing into from its local switch; the egress MPC is the MPC that is receiving the data across the shortcut, as this data flows from that MPC to the LEC and from there to the legacy LAN that it serves. Therefore, the ingress cache actually refers to outgoing data.

The ingress cache can be viewed with the following command:

```
Edge_G:Command>show mpoa icache mcp
```

The cache will look something like this:

```
*** FDB MCP Icache entries:
EgressMPCType      remoteX     EgressIPAddr    140.40.10.218    State          rsl
EgressCacheTag     00480001    Timestamp       2012             RetryCount     0
UseMask            x04         HoldingTime     1200             RslRequestID   3
eDatMpcATMAddr     39:20:00:00:00:00:00:00:00:00:00:00-02:0B:3D:32:01:20-F2
Edge_G:Command>
```

This information can indicate quite a bit about each ingress cache entry; although this example has only a single entry, many more may exist in reality. Here, the EgressMPCType is listed as remoteX, which indicates that this is the ingress MPC, and the remote MPC resides on a remote switch (X), and not on another card within the same chassis:

| | |
|---|---|
| remoteX | SVC between two switches |
| cardX | Connection between two cards in the same chassis |
| portX | Connection between two ports in the same Ethernet card |

The IP address of the destination station is displayed (140.40.10.218), with an Egress Cache tag of 00480001. Each separate data flow that uses an individual MPOA shortcut will be assigned an Egress Cache tag, to keep the flows unique when being multiplexed over the shortcut VCC.

The ATM address that is listed next to the header eDatMpcAtmAddr is that of the MPC, but it is not the control MPC address in this case. In this instance, it is the Data MPC associated with the Ethernet card in the remote switch. A list of the following states of the ingress cache entries is defined as follows:

| | |
|---|---|
| qry (Query) | A resolution request has been sent to the MPS but a response has not been received yet. |
| rsl (Resolved) | The MPC has received an MPOA resolution reply from the MPS. |
| rfr (Refreshing) | Two-thirds of the holding time has expired and an MPOA resolution request has been sent to the MPS to refresh the cache entry. A reply has not yet been received. |
| hdn (Hold Down) | The MPC is in a hold down state due to repeated resolution failures. |

This information can be used to determine a lot about the current ingress cache entries: the type of egress point—whether that be an MPC on a remote switch or on a different card or port—the destination IP address associated with each entry, and the current state. With these three pieces of information, the cache can be examined to see whether entries for specific IP addresses exist within the MPC, whether the resolution request has been correctly responded to by the MPS, and where the egress point resides. If the egress MPC resides on a remote switch (remote X), the Data MPC ATM Address can be examined to determine which remote switch the egress MPC is associated with.

## Examining the Egress Cache

The egress cache of an MPC can also be examined, by means of the following command:

```
Edge_E:Command> show mpoa ecache mcp
```

The cache will look something like this:

```
*** Maximum Egress Cache entries: 1024, currently in use: 1
IngressMpcType    remoteX    EgressIPAddr    140.40.10.218    State      actv
CacheID           2          TimeStamp       2004             ElanID     2
FwdRecIndex       1          HoldingTime     2400             VID        1
eDatMpcCardNum    2          eMpsIPAddr      140.40.10.1
iDatMpcATMAddr    39:20:00:00:00:00:00:00:00:00:00:00-02:04:3B:31:35:82-F2
Edge_E:Command>
```

This output is taken from the egress point of an MPOA shortcut. It indicates that the ingress MPC is found on a remote switch (X), and that the data that will egress this local MPC (associated with this particular egress cache entry) is destined for the destination station with IP address 140.40.10.218. The eMpsIPAddr shows the IP address associated with the egress MPS. The current state is Active.

The FwdRecIndex refers to the Forwarding Record Index, which is covered in the next section; the index number cited in the **show mpoa ecache mcp** command will correspond to the index number in the forwarding table, to see the exact DLL header associated with this cache entry.

An egress cache entry is the end result of a successful Cache Imposition Request made by the egress MPS, and the Cache Imposition Reply returned by the egress MPC; it contains all information relevant to the Cache Imposition Request, except the DLL header information, which can be obtained through the process described in the next section.

## Examining the LLC Header Table

For the MPOA shortcut to function properly, the destination station must see the router's MAC address as the source address for incoming packets, and its own MAC address as the destination address. The source station, however, will be sending packets with its own MAC address as the source address, and the router's MAC address as the destination address, since the destination station is not on its local network. To accomplish the conversion of the DLL information, the forwarding record must contain the MAC addresses of both the destination station and the router (the source address must be replaced with the MAC of the router, and the destination address must be replaced with the MAC of the actual destination station, if the router is to be bypassed). This information can be viewed with the following command:

```
Edge_A:Command > show mpoa fwdrec mcp
Mod/Usage  2/1
Mod   Indx   UseCnt   Len   DllHdr
```

```
   2     1     1    14   0008 C760 6A80 0000 A2CB 2BE7 0800
Edge_A:Command >
```

In the preceding example, the output comes from a C100 with an ATMSpeed MCP in slot 1, and an Ethernet card in slot 2, hosting a single station. For this reason, the Mod/Usage indication is 2/1, one device using the record, located on module 2. The DLL header information (DllHdr) is listed as follows:

```
0008 C760 6A80 0000 A2CB 2BE7 0800
```

This entry can be broken down as follows:

| | |
|---|---|
| 0008 C760 6A80 | The destination station's MAC address |
| 0000 A2CB 2BE7 | The router's MAC address |
| 0800 | Protocol identifier (IP) |

At the time the data is forwarded, the IP datagram receives an MPOA tag indicating the egress cache, and the DLL header is appended to the beginning of the IP datagram. Once the frame arrives at its destination via the newly formed shortcut, the MPOA tag is stripped and replaced with the DLL information, indicating the datagram came from the router's MAC, addressed to the destination station's MAC.

## Verifying an MPOA Shortcut

To verify the existence of an MPOA shortcut, the **show rllcx** command can be used from the CLI. The command's syntax stands for *show Remote LLC muX*:

```
Edge_A:Command > show rllcx
 Dst.ATM addr :39:20:00:00:00:00:00:00:00:00:00:aa:00:02:0e:09:ef:20:00:f2
 No. of Ckts  : 1
 Src.Card   Circuit   VPI/VCI   Mod/Port   No. of Users   State   Preferred
    2         11       0/40      1/4            1          OUT        Y

 Dst.ATM addr :39:20:00:00:00:00:00:00:00:00:00:00:00:00:a2:cb:2b:e7:03
 No. of Ckts  : 1
 Src.Card   Circuit   VPI/VCI   Mod/Port   No. of Users   State   Preferred
    1         10       0/45      1/1            1          OUT        Y
Edge_A:Command >
```

This shows all existing shortcuts (one, in this case) from the perspective of the MPC residing on the switch being examined. Because this actually includes the connection to the router, there should always be at least a single entry in the table. In the preceding output, the first entry is the egress MPC data ATM address, and the second entry is the connection to the router.

The two connections exist via two different ports in this case: The router is accessed through module 1, port 1, using VPI/VCI pair 0/45 (the router is actually directly attached to this port, in this case), whereas the shortcut is accessed through module 1, port 4, which is a direct connection to the switch hosting the destination LEC. In this case, then, the router has been successfully bypassed, and communication is taking place between the two switch LECs across the MPOA shortcut. Because only one data stream is utilizing the shortcut currently, the number of users is listed as 1.

At this point, the MPS has issued the Cache Imposition Request. A reply comes back from the destination MPC.

# Chapter 22

## Configuring the C1x00 Series ATM Switches

The C1x00 product line includes the C1200, C1400, and C1600 core ATM switches. Unlike some of the other Nortel Networks switching products, particularly the C100/C50/5000BH ATM switch family, the C1x00 series ATM switches are configured using the command-line interface (CLI) only and do not utilize a graphically based configuration utility. This chapter outlines some basic configuration parameters, as well as some troubleshooting strategies involving the CLI.

# Basic C1x00 Configuration

Configuration of the C1x00 product line falls into four very general categories for the purposes of this book:

- Basic device management
- Port-level signaling
- Call routing methods
- Traffic shaping/policing

These devices are configured primarily with the CLI, which is, for all practical purposes, identical across the C1200, C1400, and C1600; any differences are noted in the text that follows.

## Device Management Configuration

Device management configuration includes such things as configuring the PCMCIA card to accept a telnet session, configuring the local profile information, storing and manipulating files, and upgrading the code.

### The Command-Line Interface

The C1x00 family utilizes an advanced, extensive CLI. At the time of publication, no graphical user interface (GUI) exist, but the C1x00 CLI is extremely versatile and, with a little practice, can be quite easy to use.

The CLI can be reached in either of two ways:

- If a PCMCIA Ethernet network interface card (NIC) is present and configured with an IP address, the device can be reached through a telnet session.

- If a LAN card is not present, the CLI can be accessed through the RS-232C serial connector.

Because the CLI needs to be accessed serially, at least at first (long enough to configure the PCMCIA card with an IP address), this method is covered first.

## Connecting to the Serial Port

To connect serially, an RS-232C crossover cable is required. The C1x00 uses a 9-pin D-Sub connector. Depending on the type of serial connector used by the PC that will manage the device, the following pinouts are used:

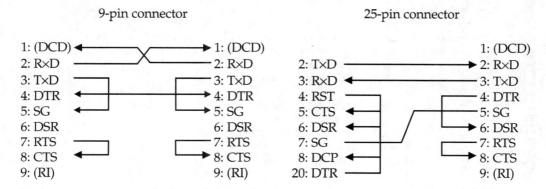

Once the physical connection has been established, the CLI can be accessed by means of terminal or terminal emulation software. The following terminal settings apply whenever you connect to the C1x00:

| | |
|---|---|
| Line rate | 9600 |
| Data bits | 8 |
| Stop bits | 1 |
| Parity | None |
| Flow control | Xon/Xoff |

After the CLI is accessed, the command prompt appears either as a greater-than symbol (>), indicating nonprivileged mode, or as a hash symbol (#), indicating privileged mode. By default, the CLI is accessed in nonprivileged mode, with no name assigned to the switch. Thus, the initial command prompt should appear simply as >.

To make configuration changes, privileged mode must be accessed, by means of the **enable** command. The first time this command is issued, the device prompts for a password to be assigned. This password will be used in future CLI sessions to access privileged mode:

```
ATM_Edge> enable
  Input enable password:
ATM_Edge#
```

## CLI Command List

The output of the C1x00 CLI command set appears as follows:

```
ATM_Core# ?
BACKUP<cmd>       Backup configuration data
CLEAR<cmd>        Clear configuration data (Type "clear ?" for list.)
DEBUG<cmd>        Debug protocol (Type "debug ?" for list.)
DELETE<cmd>       Delete configuration data (Type "delete ?" for list.)
DIAGNOSIS<cmd>    Diagnose hardware (Type "diagnosis ?" for list.)
DISPLAY<cmd>      Display configuration data (Type "display ?" for list.)
ENABLE            Enable privileged commands (Password required)
EXIT              Exit from privileged mode or close current telnet session
GENERATE<cmd>     Generate OAM cells (Type "generate ?" for list.)
?/HELP            Show available commands
INSTALL           Install system files or configuration data
PASSWD            Change password
PVC<cmd>          PVC commands (Type "pvc ?" for list.)
RESET<cmd>        Reset switch/line card (Type "reset ?" for list.)
ROUTE<cmd>        Configure SVC routing table (Type "route ?" for list.)
SAVE              Save configuration data to flash memory
SET<cmd>          Set configuration data (Type "set ?" for list.)
SHOW<cmd>         Display configuration data (Type "show ?" for list.)
SOFTPVP<cmd>      Softpvp commands (Type "softpvp ?" for list.)
TELNETPASSWD      Change telnet password
```

These commands are available on all C1x00 platforms.

## Setting the Date and Time

The date and time on the C1x00 is set with the command **set time** [*yy-mm-dd*]
[*hh:mm:ss*]. The following example sets the date and time for 6:00A.M.,
December 23, 1999:

```
ATM_Core# set time 99-12-23 06:00:00
```

## Configuring Passwords

Passwords can be configured on the C1x00 product line for privileged mode access for
either console sessions, telnet sessions, or both. During initial configuration, the first
time privileged mode is accessed with the **enable** command, a password is prompted
for and must be configured. This can be overridden later with the **passwd** command:

```
ATM_Core# passwd
```

The output will look something like this:

```
Input old enable password:
Input new enable password:
Retype new enable password:

[OK]
ATM_Core#
```

The telnet password can be configured from the CLI with the following command:

```
ATM_Core# telnetpasswd
```

The output will look something like this:

```
Input old telnet password:
Input new telnet password:
Retype new telnet password:

[OK]
ATM_Core#
```

**Note**   *Enable passwords and telnet passwords must consist only of alphanumeric characters. Passwords are case-sensitive.*

## Setting the Local Profile

Now that the password has been assigned, the local profile can be configured. The local profile includes an identifying name for the switch, an IP address and mask for the ATM network, and the ATM address itself. The IP address and mask in this case are accessible through the ATM portion of the network and do not apply to the Ethernet PCMCIA card (if present). The ATM address configured here is the 13-byte Network Service Access Point (NSAP) prefix that will be associated with the switch. If only a portion of the 13-byte prefix is defined, the remainder of the prefix will default to all zeros. Setting the local profile utilizes the following command structure:

```
#set local ATM_Edge 150.50.10.213 255.255.255.0 39102030
ATM_Edge#
```

This command sets the host name to ATM_Edge, which is reflected after the command is entered, and assigns an IP address of 150.50.10.213/24 and an ATM NSAP prefix of 39.10.20.30.00.00.00.00.00.00.00.00.00.

If an Ethernet PCMCIA is also being used for telnet access, management, and upgrades, an IP address can be assigned to it as well, so that telnet sessions can be established with the device. This is accomplished with the following command:

```
ATM_Edge# set ether 150.50.20.142 255.255.255.0
```

*In the preceding examples, notice that the ATM IP address and the Ethernet IP address are on different subnets; this is a requirement. The ATM and Ethernet IP addresses must be on different networks or subnetworks.*

# Upgrading System Software

Upgrading the C1x00 system software can be accomplished in a variety of ways, each of which is covered in the following sections. These methods may necessitate the presence of a PCMCIA flash card or, in some cases, an Ethernet PCMCIA NIC. The switch in question should be powered down if one of these cards must be inserted, and then powered back on to begin the download instructions.

## C1x00 System Software

The C1x00 has three basic software groupings, each of which is stored internally. These groupings include the boot ROM, the configuration information, and the system image software itself.

**BOOT ROM**   The boot ROM is stored on the CPU card and contains the bootstrap software responsible for the unit's initial bootup. At the time of this book's publication, the boot ROM isn't field-upgradable and requires a physical swap. Thus, no reason currently exists to upgrade the boot ROM, because no image features currently require a boot ROM upgrade.

**CONFIGURATION DATA**   The device's configuration changes can be saved with the **save** command. This data can be saved internally or to a PCMCIA flash card or a TFTP (Trivial File Transfer Protocol) server.

**SYSTEM IMAGE SOFTWARE**   The system image software is responsible for all switch operations. System image upgrades can be transferred to the C1x00 switch in either of two basic ways:

- Obtaining a PCMCIA flash containing the new system software from a Bay Networks sales representative.
- Obtaining the system files in the form of a ZIP file, which can be placed on a TFTP server for transfer via a PCMCIA Ethernet LAN card.

## Setting Up System Image Files for TFTP

After you obtain the ZIP file containing the software image files, transfer the ZIP to the TFTP server and unzip the files into the TFTP root directory. A series of files will be unzipped; each of these files is necessary for the upgrade to complete successfully. Once the files are in the TFTP root directory, use a text editor to update the boot file. The boot file contains a list of the load modules for the system software, and may need to be updated to reflect where the software load modules currently reside.

After you complete these steps, you can begin the upgrade process. There are six different methods for achieving this:

**FLASH MODE**   This upgrade option loads the system software from a PCMCIA flash card. No configuration information is loaded using this method, so the unit will return to its factory default settings.

Because this is the default mode, no configuration needs to be done to utilize this method. Power down the unit, mount a PCMCIA flash card containing the system software, and power the unit back up. If the boot mode is changed and needs to be set back to the default mode, access the boot monitor during software initialization by pressing ESC when prompted. From the boot monitor, enter the following commands:

```
BOOT# set boot flash
BOOT# quit
```

**FLASH_UP MODE**   The Flash_up option requires that two PCMCIA cards be used: the PCMCIA card in slot 0 is the flash from which the system software will be loaded, whereas the card in slot 1 is the flash from which the configuration data will be loaded. The configuration in this case is not saved.

To accomplish this, the C1x00 must be powered down, and both PCMCIA cards inserted. Power the unit up, and press ESC when prompted to enter the boot monitor. After you access the boot monitor, enter the following command:

```
BOOT# set boot flash_up
BOOT# quit
```

**FLASH_UP_SAVE MODE**   This option is similar to the Flash_up option, but in this case, after the system software is loaded from the PCMCIA in slot 0, and the office data is loaded from PCMCIA slot 1, the office data is actually saved to the PCMCIA card in slot 0.

As in the previous case, you must power down the device, insert both flash cards, and then power up the unit again. Access the boot monitor by pressing ESC when prompted during the system software initialization, and then issue the following command:

```
BOOT# set boot flash_up_save
BOOT# quit
```

**INITIALIZE MODE**    Initialize mode configures the C1x00 switch to obtain its system software from an Ethernet-attached TFTP server. This is accomplished via a PCMCIA Ethernet LAN card. You must power down the unit, place the Ethernet LAN card in slot 1, and then power up the unit. Access the boot monitor by pressing ESC when prompted during software initialization. After you access the boot monitor, you must assign a local IP address to the LAN card, define the TFTP server, configure a local router IP (if the file transfer must occur through a router), and alter the boot mode. These steps are accomplished with the following commands, respectively:

```
BOOT# set local 150.50.10.123 255.255.255.0
BOOT# set server 150.50.20.52 *****.bootfile
BOOT# set route 150.50.10.1
BOOT set boot initialize
BOOT# quit
```

In this case, the system software and office data is loaded from the TFTP server. Neither is saved, so using this method requires that the server remain available, so that the unit can obtain its system image in case of a reboot.

**INITIALIZE_SAVE MODE**    The Initialize_save option is similar to the Initialize method, except that the system image and data files are loaded and then actually saved to a PCMCIA flash card residing in slot 0.

You must power down the unit, mount a PCMCIA Ethernet card in slot 1, and mount a PCMCIA flash card with the data files in slot 0. Power the unit back on and access the boot monitor by pressing ESC when prompted during software initialization. After you access the boot monitor, issue the following commands:

```
BOOT# set local 150.50.10.123 255.255.255.0
BOOT# set server 150.50.20.52 *****.bootfile
BOOT# set route 150.50.10.1
BOOT set boot initialize_save
BOOT# quit
```

**NETWORK MODE**    This option loads the system software from a TFTP server via an Ethernet PCMCIA LAN card in slot 1, and loads the office data i from the PCMCIA flash card in slot 0. The software is not saved when using this option.

You must power down the unit, mount a PCMCIA Ethernet card in slot 1, and mount a PCMCIA flash card with the data files in slot 0. Power the unit back on and access the boot monitor by pressing ESC when prompted during software initialization. After you access the boot monitor, issue the following commands:

```
BOOT# set local 150.50.10.123 255.255.255.0
BOOT# set server 150.50.20.52 *****.bootfile
BOOT# set route 150.50.10.1
BOOT set boot network
BOOT# quit
```

# The Debugging Tools

The C1x00 series switches utilize a series of debugging tools, which can be invaluable in troubleshooting problems or errors that may arise during configuration or network operation. These tools are not covered in great length in this chapter, but examples are given regarding their use, as well as some suggestions as to how to use them and interpret their output.

Using the debugging tools involves setting a specific debug flag in relation to a specific slot and port number; the debug flag that is set will indicate the level of debugging that will be used. After you set the debug flag, output will be sent to the terminal. This output is not directed to a telnet session, so use of the debug utility necessitates a console session. The protocols described in the following sections use the debug function.

## ATM Signaling

ATM signaling debugging can be very useful, particularly when you need to troubleshoot LANE connectivity problems through the switch. ATM signaling debugging has seven levels (with the first level, level 0, indicating that all debugging is disabled). These different levels provide the following details:

```
ATM_Core# debug sig ?
00|disable      errorflag & packetflag & eventflag OFF
01|event                                  eventflag ON
02|packet                   packetflag              ON
03                          packetflag & eventflag ON
04|error        errorflag                           ON
05              errorflag              & eventflag ON
06              errorflag & packetflag              ON
07              errorflag & packetflag & eventflag ON
```

These are activated by means of the command **set sig debug** [*debug level*] [*slot*] [*port*]:

```
ATM_Core# debug sig 07 00
```

This command turns on debugging at level 7 on slot/port 00.

## Private Network-to-Network Interface

PNNI debugging can be set on a port-by-port basis, with up to 30 different levels of debugging. These different levels provide the following levels of detail:

```
ATM_Core# debug pnni ?
00|disable   packetflag & errorflag & dataflag & processflag & eventflag OFF
01|event                                                        eventflag ON
02|process                                         processflag            ON
03                                                 processflag & eventflag ON
04|data                                dataflag                            ON
05                                     dataflag &                eventflag ON
06                                     dataflag & processflag            ON
07                                     dataflag & processflag & eventflag ON
08|error               errorflag                                          ON
09                     errorflag &                                eventflag ON
10                     errorflag &             processflag                ON
11                     errorflag &             processflag & eventflag ON
12                     errorflag & dataflag                              ON
13                     errorflag & dataflag &                  eventflag ON
14                     errorflag & dataflag & processflag                ON
15                     errorflag & dataflag & processflag & eventflag ON
16|packet    packetflag                                                  ON
17           packetflag &                                       eventflag ON
18           packetflag &                        processflag            ON
19           packetflag &                        processflag & eventflag ON
20           packetflag &            dataflag                           ON
21           packetflag &            dataflag &                eventflag ON
22           packetflag &            dataflag & processflag            ON
23           packetflag &            dataflag & processflag & eventflag ON
24           packetflag & errorflag                                     ON
25           packetflag & errorflag &                          eventflag ON
26           packetflag & errorflag &           processflag            ON
27           packetflag & errorflag &           processflag & eventflag ON
28           packetflag & errorflag & dataflag                         ON
29           packetflag & errorflag & dataflag &              eventflag ON
30           packetflag & errorflag & dataflag & processflag           ON
31      packetflag & errorflag & dataflag & processflag & eventflag ON
```

These are activated by means of the command **set pnni debug** [*slot*] [*port*] [*debug level*]:

```
ATM_Core# debug pnni 21 00
```

This command turns on debugging at level 21 on slot/port 00. This provides advanced PNNI debugging for PNNI packet, data, and event messages.

## Interim Local Management Interface

ILMI debugging is also available on a port-by-port basis, at varying levels. These levels can be used to view the specific functions of ILMI, such as address registration, and system information obtained through ILMI sets and gets. The ILMI debug levels are as follows:

```
ATM_Edge# debug ilmi ?
0|off           ILMI all flag OFF
1|manager       Manager  flag ON
2|agent         Agent    flag ON
3|all           ILMI all flag ON
```

## SSCOP

SSCOP (Signaling Specific Connection Oriented Protocol) interface functions can also be examined with the debug utility, for the purpose of monitoring and reporting events and errors. SSCOP signaling can be debugged at the following severity levels:

```
ATM_Core# debug sscop ?
00|disable      errorflag & packetflag & eventflag OFF
01|event                                  eventflag ON
02|packet                   packetflag              ON
03                          packetflag & eventflag  ON
04|error        errorflag                           ON
05              errorflag               & eventflag ON
06              errorflag & packetflag              ON
07              errorflag & packetflag & eventflag ON
```

Different types of debugging can be used on a port-by-port basis. The following is an example of SSCOP debugging during a link bounce:

```
ATM_Edge# debug sscop 00 20
SSCOP: interfaceReset - port 20 vpi 0
SSCOP(I) (port/vpi 20/0): 00 00 00 01 01 00 00 20          . . . . . . .
```

```
SSCOP(20): i Begin pdu, Active state, length = 8
SSCOP: receive window in Begin Pdu = 32
SSCOP: o Begin Ack pdu, Active state, rcv window v(mr) = 779
SSCOP(O) (port/vpi 20/0): 00 00 00 00 02 00 03 0B          ........
SSCOP(I) (port/vpi 20/0): 00 00 00 01 0A 00 00 00          ........
SSCOP(20): i Poll pdu, Active state, length = 8
SSCOP(20-0): i Poll pdu, ns = 0. nps = 1
SSCOPERR(20): ns 0 is less than vrh 747 - fatal protocol error
SSCOP: o Er pdu, Active state
SSCOP(O) (port/vpi 20/0): 00 00 00 0A 09 00 00 20          .......
SSCOP: state changed from Active to Outgoing Recover Pending
SSCOP(I) (port/vpi 20/0): 00 00 00 00 0F 00 00 20          .......
SSCOP(20): i Er Ack pdu, Outgoing Recover Pending state, length = 8
SSCOP: state changed from Outgoing Recover Pending to Active
SSCOP(I) (port/vpi 20/0): 00 00 00 01 0A 00 00 00          ........
SSCOP(20): i Poll pdu, Active state, length = 8
SSCOP(20-0): i Poll pdu, ns = 0. nps = 1
SSCOP(20-0): o Stat pdu, state = Active, n(r) = 0, n(mr) = 32, n(ps) = 1
SSCOP(O) (port/vpi 20/0): 00 00 00 01 00 00 00 20 0B 00 00 00   ....... ....
```

## LANE Signaling Debug Example

This section presents an extensive example of the C1x00 debugging tools; for the purposes of this example, two C100 switches have been connected to a C1200, with each link running PNNI. One C100 has been configured with a LEC, which is to join its LANE services configured on the second C100.

Because the join must occur through the C1200, this process can be viewed through signaling debugging. For the purposes of this example, debugging is set for level 07 on the port connecting to the C100 that is housing the LEC. After the LAN Emulation Client (LEC) initializes and the join process begins, the debug is captured, displaying each step of the join procedure (bold indicates the address of the LECS as the LEC attempts to create the Configuration Direct VCC):

```
ATMSIG(I) (port/vpi 20/0): F0 03 00 00 42 05 80 00 CB 58 80 00 09 05 8C 05   p...B...KX......
ATMSIG(I) (port/vpi 20/0): EC 81 05 EC 84 00 59 80 00 09 84 05 93 FE 85 05   l..l..Y......~..
ATMSIG(I) (port/vpi 20/0): 93 FE BE 5E 80 00 03 10 80 80 5F 80 00 09 6B 40   .~>^......_...k@
ATMSIG(I) (port/vpi 20/0): 80 80 C0 A0 3E 00 01 70 80 00 15 82 47 00 79 00   ... >..p....G.y.
ATMSIG(I) (port/vpi 20/0): 00 00 C0 00 00 00 00 00 00 00 00 A0 3E 00 00 01 00   .......... >....
```

Again, in bold, is the address of the calling party (the LEC on the C100, in this case). Note that the LEC is configured with an End System Identifier (ESI) of all C's:

```
ATMSIG(I) (port/vpi 20/0): 6C 80 C0 15 82 39 20 00 00 00 00 00 00 00 00 00   l....9 ........
ATMSIG(I) (port/vpi 20/0): AA 00 CC CC CC CC CC CC FF 5A 80 00 05 88 00 00   *.LLLLLL.Z......
```

In the following code block, the three PNNI nodes involved are set apart in bold; the top address is that of the C100 where the calling LEC is configured, the middle address is that of the C1200 that the call must pass through, and the bottom address is the Node ID of the destination node, the C100 where the LES/BUS pair are configured. Notice each Node ID begins with a hex value of 48; this is 72 in decimal, and indicates the level. The A0 that follows works out to 160 in decimal, which is the value following the level indicator, indicating that the following 20 bytes are to be used for the Node ID. This is the expected format for lowest-level PNNI nodes.

```
ATMSIG(I) (port/vpi 20/0): 00 20 5C 80 00 02 00 00 63 80 00 01 8A E2 E0 00    . \.....c....b`.
ATMSIG(I) (port/vpi 20/0): 53 00 1B 01 48 A0 39 20 00 00 00 00 00 00 00 00    S...H 9 ........
ATMSIG(I) (port/vpi 20/0): 00 AA 00 02 70 90 F7 C0 01 00 00 00 00 08 01 48    .*..p.w@.......H
ATMSIG(I) (port/vpi 20/0): A0 39 20 00 00 00 00 00 00 00 00 00 00 00 00 00     9 ...........
ATMSIG(I) (port/vpi 20/0): 32 25 45 F6 00 00 00 00 02 01 48 A0 39 20 00 00    2%Ev......H 9 ..
ATMSIG(I) (port/vpi 20/0): 00 00 00 00 00 00 00 00 00 02 D0 12 F8 C0 01 00    ..........P.x@..
ATMSIG(I) (port/vpi 20/0): 00 00 00 02                                        ....
```

In the following section, **i** indicates an incoming message:

```
ATMSIG: This is LOCAL SCOPE message:
ATMSIG: index = 66, callref = 66, lic = FALSE
enter Hash: index = 66, call ref = 66, lic = FALSE
PNNISIG: i Rcvd Setup msg in CallInitiated(NN1) length 203, call ref 66
```

In the next section, **o** indicates an outgoing message:

```
PNNISIG: mynode state is Intermediate Node in PeerGroup
PNNISIG: from logical port=2 ==> get out port=21 out vpi=0
ATMSIG: o Call Proc msg, Call Initiated(NN1) state, length 24, call ref 66, pad 2
```

The call is being initiated in the following section. The port where the request is coming in is listed as 20. (This is the port where the calling C100 is attached.) The VPI to be used is 0.

```
ATMSIG(O) (port/vpi 20/0): F0 03 80 00 42 02 80 00 09 5A 80 00 05 88 00 00   p...B....Z......
ATMSIG(O) (port/vpi 20/0): 00 20 00 00                                        . ..
ATMSIG: index = 13, callref = 13, lic = TRUE
enter Hash: index = 13, call ref = 13, lic = TRUE
ATMSIG: User Cell Rate IE Best Effort, size = 1
ATMSIG: User Cell Rate IE size = 9
ATMSIG: o Setup msg, Call Present(NN6) state, length 208, call ref 13, pad 1
ATMSIG: open svc request in progress
```

In the following section, the Configuration Direct VCC is now in an Active state. Although LE_CONFIGURE_REQUEST and LE_CONFIGURE_RESPONSE control frames are not specifically seen in the debug messages, they will pass over the connection at this point. An ATM sniffer needs to be used to capture the individual frames.

```
PNNISIG: state changed from Call Initiated(NN1) to Call Proceeding Sent(NN3)
ATMSIG: This is LOCAL SCOPE message:
ATMSIG: index = 13, callref = 13, lic = TRUE
PNNISIG: i Rcvd Call Proceeding msg in CallPresent(NN6) length 9, call ref 13
PNNISIG: state changed from Call Present(NN6) to Call Proceeding Received(NN9)
ATMSIG: This is LOCAL SCOPE message:
ATMSIG: index = 13, callref = 13, lic = TRUE
PNNISIG: i Rcvd Connect msg in CalProceedingReceived(NN9) length 0, call ref 13
```

```
ATMSIG: o Connect msg, Call Proceeding Sent(NN3) state, length 16, call ref 66, pad 3
ATMSIG(O) (port/vpi 20/0): F0 03 80 00 42 07 80 00 00 00 00 00          p...B.......
PNNISIG: DTL/BTL free in Endpoint
PNNISIG: state changed from Call Proceeding Received(NN9) to Active(NN10)
ATMSIG(I) (port/vpi 20/0): F0 03 00 00 42 4D 80 00 06 08 80 00 02 81 9F     p...BM.........
```

Next, the Configuration Direct VCC is released, because the control frames have been successfully exchanged:

```
ATMSIG: This is LOCAL SCOPE message:
ATMSIG: index = 66, callref = 66, lic = FALSE
PNNISIG: i Rcvd Release msg in Active(NN10) length 6, call ref 66
ATMSIG: o Rel Complete msg, Active(NN10) state, length 20, call ref 66, pad 1
ATMSIG(O) (port/vpi 20/0): F0 03 80 00 42 5A 80 00 06 08 80 00 02 83 9F 80    p...BZ..........
ATMSIG: freeSvcBlock(case1 : Active state), release connection.
ATMSIG: o Release msg, Release Request(NN11) state, length 20, callref 13, pad 1
ATMSIG: close svc request in progress
PNNISIG: DTL/BTL free in Endpoint
PNNISIG: DTL/BTL free in Endpoint
```

In the following block, the LES is called by the LEC. The LES address (distinguished by an ESI of all A's) has been obtained from the LECS, and is now called by the LEC whose address immediately follows that of the LES.

```
ATMSIG: removeHashEntry: svc removed from hash table
ATMSIG(I) (port/vpi 20/0): F0 03 00 00 43 05 80 00 CB 58 80 00 09 05 8C 05    p...C...KX......
ATMSIG(I) (port/vpi 20/0): EC 81 05 EC 84 00 59 80 00 09 84 05 93 FE 85 05    l..l..Y......~..
ATMSIG(I) (port/vpi 20/0): 93 FE BE 5E 80 00 03 10 80 80 5F 80 00 09 6B 40    .~>^......_...k@
ATMSIG(I) (port/vpi 20/0): 80 80 00 A0 3E 00 01 70 80 00 15 82 **39 20 00 00**    ... >..p....9 ..
ATMSIG(I) (port/vpi 20/0): 00 00 00 00 00 00 00 00 00 **AA AA AA AA AA AA 01**    .........******.
ATMSIG(I) (port/vpi 20/0): 6C 80 00 15 82 **39 20 00 00** 00 00 00 00 00 00 00    l....9 .........
ATMSIG(I) (port/vpi 20/0): **AA 00 CC CC CC CC CC CC FF** 5A 80 00 05 88 00 00    *.LLLLLL.Z......
```

The following shows that the three PNNI nodes are involved once again, as the Control Direct to the LES is attempted:

```
ATMSIG(I) (port/vpi 20/0): 00 21 5C 80 00 02 00 00 63 80 00 01 8A E2 E0 00    .!\.....c....b`.
ATMSIG(I) (port/vpi 20/0): 53 00 1B 01 48 A0 39 20 00 00 00 00 00 00 00 00    S...H 9 ........
ATMSIG(I) (port/vpi 20/0): 00 AA 00 02 70 90 F7 C0 01 00 00 00 00 08 01 48    .*..p.w@.......H
ATMSIG(I) (port/vpi 20/0): A0 39 20 00 00 00 00 00 00 00 00 00 00 00 00 00    9 ...........
ATMSIG(I) (port/vpi 20/0): 32 25 45 F6 00 00 00 00 00 02 01 48 A0 39 20 00 00    2%Ev......H 9 ..
ATMSIG(I) (port/vpi 20/0): 00 00 00 00 00 00 00 00 00 02 D0 12 F8 C0 01 00    ........@...H .2
```

The following message indicates that this node has other PNNI nodes connected to it, and is not itself a border node:

```
ATMSIG(I) (port/vpi 20/0): 00 00 00 02                                       ....
ATMSIG: This is LOCAL SCOPE message:
ATMSIG: index = 67, callref = 67, lic = FALSE
enter Hash: index = 67, call ref = 67, lic = FALSE
PNNISIG: i Rcvd Setup msg in CallInitiated(NN1) length 203, call ref 67
PNNISIG: mynode state is Intermediate Node in PeerGroup
PNNISIG: from logical port=2 ==> get out port=21 out vpi=0
ATMSIG: o Call Proc msg, Call Initiated(NN1) state, length 24, call ref 67, pad 2
ATMSIG(O) (port/vpi 20/0): F0 03 80 00 43 02 80 00 09 5A 80 00 05 88 00 00    p...C....Z......
ATMSIG(O) (port/vpi 20/0): 00 21 00 03                                       .!..
ATMSIG: index = 14, callref = 14, lic = TRUE
enter Hash: index = 14, call ref = 14, lic = TRUE
ATMSIG: User Cell Rate IE Best Effort, size = 1
ATMSIG: User Cell Rate IE size = 9
ATMSIG: o Setup msg, Call Present(NN6) state, length 208, call ref 14, pad 1
ATMSIG: open svc request in progress
PNNISIG: state changed from Call Initiated(NN1) to Call Proceeding Sent(NN3)
ATMSIG: This is LOCAL SCOPE message:
ATMSIG: index = 13, callref = 13, lic = TRUE
PNNISIG: i Rcvd Release Complete msg in ReleaseRequest(NN11) length 6, call ref 13
ATMSIG: freeSvcBlock(case0 : non Active), release resources.
PNNISIG: DTL/BTL free in Endpoint
PNNISIG: DTL/BTL free in Endpoint
ATMSIG: removeHashEntry: svc removed from hash table
ATMSIG: This is LOCAL SCOPE message:
ATMSIG: index = 14, callref = 14, lic = TRUE
PNNISIG: i Rcvd Call Proceeding msg in CallPresent(NN6) length 9, call ref 14
PNNISIG: state changed from Call Present(NN6) to Call Proceeding Received(NN9)
ATMSIG: This is LOCAL SCOPE message:
ATMSIG: index = 14, callref = 14, lic = TRUE
PNNISIG: i Rcvd Connect msg in CalProceedingReceived(NN9) length 0, call ref 14
ATMSIG: o Connect msg, Call Proceeding Sent(NN3) state, length 16, call ref 67, pad 3
ATMSIG(O) (port/vpi 20/0): F0 03 80 00 43 07 80 00 00 00 00 00               p...C.......
PNNISIG: DTL/BTL free in Endpoint
PNNISIG: state changed from Call Proceeding Received(NN9) to Active(NN10)
ATMSIG: This is LOCAL SCOPE message:
ATMSIG: index = 5, callref = 5, lic = FALSE
enter Hash: index = 5, call ref = 5, lic = FALSE
PNNISIG: i Rcvd Setup msg in CallInitiated(NN1) length 210, call ref 5
PNNISIG: mynode state is Intermediate Node in PeerGroup
```

In the following section, the LEC is called by the LES, as the Control Distribute VCC is established. The called party is listed first, followed by the calling party.

```
PNNISIG: from logical port=1 ==> get out port=20 out vpi=0
ATMSIG: o Call Proc msg, Call Initiated(NN1) state, length 32, call ref 5, pad 3
ATMSIG: index = 15, callref = 15, lic = TRUE
enter Hash: index = 15, call ref = 15, lic = TRUE
ATMSIG: User Cell Rate IE Best Effort, size = 1
ATMSIG: User Cell Rate IE size = 9
ATMSIG: o Setup msg, Call Present(NN6) state, length 216, call ref 15, pad 2
ATMSIG(O) (port/vpi 20/0): F0 03 00 00 0F 05 80 00 C9 58 80 00 09 05 8C 05   p.......IX......
ATMSIG(O) (port/vpi 20/0): EC 81 05 EC 84 00 59 80 00 09 84 05 93 FE 85 00   l..1..Y......~..
ATMSIG(O) (port/vpi 20/0): 00 00 3E 5E 80 00 03 10 80 81 5F 80 00 09 6B 40   ..>^......_...k@
ATMSIG(O) (port/vpi 20/0): 80 80 00 A0 3E 00 01 70 80 00 15 82 39 20 00 00   ... >..p....9 ..
ATMSIG(O) (port/vpi 20/0): 00 00 00 00 00 00 00 AA 00 CC CC CC CC CC CC FF   .......*.LLLLLL.
ATMSIG(O) (port/vpi 20/0): 6C 80 00 15 82 39 20 00 00 00 00 00 00 00 00 00   l....9 .........
ATMSIG(O) (port/vpi 20/0): 00 00 AA AA AA AA AA AA 01 5C 80 00 02 00 00 54   ..******.\.....T
```

The following are the three PNNI nodes:

```
ATMSIG(O) (port/vpi 20/0): 80 00 03 00 00 00 63 80 00 01 8A E2 E0 00 53 00   ......c....b`.S.
ATMSIG(O) (port/vpi 20/0): 36 01 48 A0 39 20 00 00 00 00 00 00 00 00 00 00   6.H 9 ..........
ATMSIG(O) (port/vpi 20/0): 00 02 D0 12 F8 C0 01 00 00 00 00 03 01 48 A0 39   ..P.x@.......H 9
ATMSIG(O) (port/vpi 20/0): 20 00 00 00 00 00 00 00 00 00 00 00 00 00 32 25   .............2%
ATMSIG(O) (port/vpi 20/0): 45 F6 00 00 00 00 01 01 48 A0 39 20 00 00 00 00   Ev......H 9 ....
ATMSIG(O) (port/vpi 20/0): 00 00 00 00 00 AA 00 02 70 90 F7 C0 01 00 00 00   .....*..p.w@....
```

In the following section, the BUS address, having been obtained through the LE_ARP process, is now called by the LEC. Notice the address with an ESI of all A's, and a selector byte of 02, indicating the BUS in this case.

```
ATMSIG(O) (port/vpi 20/0): 00 02 90 F7                                       ...w
ATMSIG: open svc request in progress
PNNISIG: state changed from Call Initiated(NN1) to Call Proceeding Sent(NN3)
ATMSIG(I) (port/vpi 20/0): F0 03 80 00 0F 02 80 00 10 5A 80 00 05 88 00 00   p........Z......
ATMSIG(I) (port/vpi 20/0): 00 22 54 80 00 03 00 80 00                        ."T......
ATMSIG: This is LOCAL SCOPE message:
ATMSIG: index = 15, callref = 15, lic = TRUE
PNNISIG: i Rcvd Call Proceeding msg in CallPresent(NN6) length 16, call ref 15
PNNISIG: state changed from Call Present(NN6) to Call Proceeding Received(NN9)
ATMSIG(I) (port/vpi 20/0): F0 03 80 00 0F 07 80 00 07 54 80 00 03 00 80 00   p........T......
ATMSIG: This is LOCAL SCOPE message:
ATMSIG: index = 15, callref = 15, lic = TRUE
PNNISIG: i Rcvd Connect msg in CalProceedingReceived(NN9) length 7, call ref 15
ATMSIG: o Connect msg, Call Proceeding Sent(NN3) state, length 20, call ref 5, pad 0
PNNISIG: DTL/BTL free in Endpoint
PNNISIG: state changed from Call Proceeding Received(NN9) to Active(NN10)
ATMSIG(I) (port/vpi 20/0): F0 03 C0 00 44 05 80 00 CB 58 80 00 09 05 8C 05   p...D...KX......
```

```
ATMSIG(I) (port/vpi 20/0): EC 81 05 EC 84 00 59 80 00 09 84 05 93 FE 85 05    l..l..Y......~..
ATMSIG(I) (port/vpi 20/0): 93 FE BE 5E 80 00 03 10 80 80 5F 80 00 09 6B 40    .~>^......_...k@
ATMSIG(I) (port/vpi 20/0): 80 80 00 A0 3E 00 04 70 80 00 15 82 39 20 00 00    ... >..p....9 ..
ATMSIG(I) (port/vpi 20/0): 00 00 00 00 00 00 00 00 00 AA AA AA AA AA AA 02    .........******.
ATMSIG(I) (port/vpi 20/0): 6C 80 00 15 82 39 20 00 00 00 00 00 00 00 00 00    l....9 .........
ATMSIG(I) (port/vpi 20/0): AA 00 CC CC CC CC CC CC FF 5A 80 00 05 88 00 00    *.LLLLLL.Z......
ATMSIG(I) (port/vpi 20/0): 00 23 5C 80 00 02 00 00 63 80 00 01 8A E2 E0 00    .#\.....c....b`.
```

The three PNNI Node IDs are present again in the following, as the call is formed:

```
ATMSIG(I) (port/vpi 20/0): 53 00 1B 01 48 A0 39 20 00 00 00 00 00 00 00 00    S...H 9 ........
ATMSIG(I) (port/vpi 20/0): 00 AA 00 02 70 90 F7 C0 01 00 00 00 00 08 01 48    .*..p.w@.......H
ATMSIG(I) (port/vpi 20/0): A0 39 20 00 00 00 00 00 00 00 00 00 00 00 00 00    9 ...........
ATMSIG(I) (port/vpi 20/0): 32 25 45 F6 00 00 00 00 02 01 48 A0 39 20 00 00    2%Ev......H 9 ..
ATMSIG(I) (port/vpi 20/0): 00 00 00 00 00 00 00 00 00 02 D0 12 F8 C0 01 00    ..........P.x@..
ATMSIG(I) (port/vpi 20/0): 00 00 00 02                                        ....
```

In the following section, the LEC is the called party, called by the BUS, as the Multicast Forward VCC is established:

```
ATMSIG: This is LOCAL SCOPE message:
ATMSIG: index = 68, callref = 68, lic = FALSE
enter Hash: index = 68, call ref = 68, lic = FALSE
PNNISIG: i Rcvd Setup msg in CallInitiated(NN1) length 203, call ref 68
PNNISIG: mynode state is Intermediate Node in PeerGroup
PNNISIG: from logical port=2 ==> get out port=21 out vpi=0
ATMSIG: o Call Proc msg, Call Initiated(NN1) state, length 24, call ref 68, pad 2
ATMSIG(O) (port/vpi 20/0): F0 03 80 00 44 02 80 00 09 5A 80 00 05 88 00 00    p...D....Z......
ATMSIG(O) (port/vpi 20/0): 00 23 05 EC                                       .#.1
ATMSIG: index = 16, callref = 16, lic = TRUE
enter Hash: index = 16, call ref = 16, lic = TRUE
ATMSIG: User Cell Rate IE Best Effort, size = 1
ATMSIG: User Cell Rate IE size = 9
ATMSIG: o Setup msg, Call Present(NN6) state, length 208, call ref 16, pad 1
ATMSIG: open svc request in progress
PNNISIG: state changed from Call Initiated(NN1) to Call Proceeding Sent(NN3)
ATMSIG: This is LOCAL SCOPE message:
ATMSIG: index = 16, callref = 16, lic = TRUE
PNNISIG: i Rcvd Call Proceeding msg in CallPresent(NN6) length 9, call ref 16
PNNISIG: state changed from Call Present(NN6) to Call Proceeding Received(NN9)
ATMSIG: This is LOCAL SCOPE message:
ATMSIG: index = 16, callref = 16, lic = TRUE
PNNISIG: i Rcvd Connect msg in CalProceedingReceived(NN9) length 0, call ref 16
ATMSIG: o Connect msg, Call Proceeding Sent(NN3) state, length 16, call ref 68, pad 3
ATMSIG(O) (port/vpi 20/0): F0 03 80 00 44 07 80 00 00 00 00 00              p...D.......
PNNISIG: DTL/BTL free in Endpoint
PNNISIG: state changed from Call Proceeding Received(NN9) to Active(NN10)
ATMSIG: This is LOCAL SCOPE message:
ATMSIG: index = 6, callref = 6, lic = FALSE
enter Hash: index = 6, call ref = 6, lic = FALSE
```

```
PNNISIG: i Rcvd Setup msg in CallInitiated(NN1) length 210, call ref 6
PNNISIG: mynode state is Intermediate Node in PeerGroup
PNNISIG: from logical port=1 ==> get out port=20 out vpi=0
ATMSIG: o Call Proc msg, Call Initiated(NN1) state, length 32, call ref 6, pad 3
ATMSIG: index = 17, callref = 17, lic = TRUE
enter Hash: index = 17, call ref = 17, lic = TRUE
ATMSIG: User Cell Rate IE Best Effort, size = 1
ATMSIG: User Cell Rate IE size = 9
ATMSIG: o Setup msg, Call Present(NN6) state, length 216, call ref 17, pad 2
ATMSIG(O) (port/vpi 20/0): F0 03 00 00 11 05 80 00 C9 58 80 00 09 05 8C 05    p.......IX......
ATMSIG(O) (port/vpi 20/0): EC 81 05 EC 84 00 59 80 00 09 84 05 93 FE 85 00    l..l..Y......~..
ATMSIG(O) (port/vpi 20/0): 00 00 BE 5E 80 00 03 10 80 81 5F 80 00 09 6B 40    ..>^......_...k@
ATMSIG(O) (port/vpi 20/0): 80 80 00 A0 3E 00 04 70 80 00 15 82 39 20 00 00    ... >..p....9 ..
ATMSIG(O) (port/vpi 20/0): 00 00 00 00 00 00 00 AA 00 CC CC CC CC CC CC FF    .......*.LLLLLL.
ATMSIG(O) (port/vpi 20/0): 6C 80 00 15 82 39 20 00 00 00 00 00 00 00 00 00    l....9 .........
ATMSIG(O) (port/vpi 20/0): 00 00 AA AA AA AA AA AA 02 5C 80 00 02 00 00 54    ..******.\.....T
```

The three PNNI Node IDs are utilized once again in the following section as the call is established via PNNI signaling:

```
ATMSIG(O) (port/vpi 20/0): 80 00 03 00 00 00 63 80 00 01 8A E2 E0 00 53 00    ......c....b`.S.
ATMSIG(O) (port/vpi 20/0): 36 01 48 A0 39 20 00 00 00 00 00 00 00 00 00 00    6.H 9 ..........
ATMSIG(O) (port/vpi 20/0): 00 02 D0 12 F8 C0 01 00 00 00 00 03 01 48 A0 39    ..P.x@.......H 9
ATMSIG(O) (port/vpi 20/0): 20 00 00 00 00 00 00 00 00 00 00 00 00 00 32 25     .............2%
ATMSIG(O) (port/vpi 20/0): 45 F6 00 00 00 00 01 01 48 A0 39 20 00 00 00 00    Ev......H 9 ....
ATMSIG(O) (port/vpi 20/0): 00 00 00 00 00 AA 00 02 70 90 F7 C0 01 00 00 00    .....*..p.w@....
ATMSIG(O) (port/vpi 20/0): 00 02 00 00                                        ....
```

At this point, the LEC has contacted the LECS, received its LES address, established the Control Direct VCC, accepted the Control Distribute VCC, used LE_ARP to resolve the BUS address, established the Multicast Send VCC, and accepted the Multicast Forward VCC. This completes the join process.

```
ATMSIG: open svc request in progress
PNNISIG: state changed from Call Initiated(NN1) to Call Proceeding Sent(NN3)
ATMSIG(I) (port/vpi 20/0): F0 03 80 00 11 02 80 00 10 5A 80 00 05 88 00 00    p........Z......
ATMSIG(I) (port/vpi 20/0): 00 24 54 80 00 03 00 80 00                         .$T......
ATMSIG: This is LOCAL SCOPE message
ATMSIG: index = 17, callref = 17, lic = TRUE
PNNISIG: i Rcvd Call Proceeding msg in CallPresent(NN6) length 16, call ref 17
PNNISIG: state changed from Call Present(NN6) to Call Proceeding Received(NN9)
ATMSIG(I) (port/vpi 20/0): F0 03 80 00 11 07 80 00 07 54 80 00 03 00 80 00    p........T......
ATMSIG: This is LOCAL SCOPE message
ATMSIG: index = 17, callref = 17, lic = TRUE
PNNISIG: i Rcvd Connect msg in CallProceedingReceived(NN9) length 7, call ref 17
ATMSIG: o Connect msg, Call Proceeding Sent(NN3) state, length 20, call ref 6, pad 0
PNNISIG: DTL/BTL free in Endpoint
PNNISIG: state changed from Call Proceeding Received(NN9) to Active(NN10)
```

The preceding example gives an indication of the level of information that can be recorded regarding the ATM protocol procedures. Although this is only one example of how the debugging feature can be used, other examples later in this chapter are presented regarding debug information recorded in different troubleshooting scenarios.

Again, the full functionality of the C1x00 debugging tool is outside the scope of this book, but, if the protocol being observed is well understood, the debug output can be interpreted with some patience. Even in the absence of an ATM sniffer, it can be quite useful if used correctly.

**DISABLING DEBUGGING**   As a last word on the debugging feature, there are times when debugging has been enabled and the amount of text that begins scrolling as a result can interfere with attempts to actually disable the feature. Just keep entering the command, despite the fact that the text can't really be seen; it may take a few seconds for the scrolling to wind down, but the command will be accepted as long as there are no typos. Setting the debug level to 00 deactivates debugging in all cases.

## The Boot Monitor

You can access the boot monitor by pressing the ESC key during the normal bootup process. As the initial boot commences, a prompt will appear to enter the boot menu:

```
ATM_Core# reset switch
Are you sure? [Y or N] y

The system is coming up now.
If you want to enter boot program, push [ESC] key immediately.
If the [ESC] key is detected within 3 seconds, boot program is loaded.
Otherwise, online program will be loaded from the flash memory.
```

If you press ESC at this time, the normal bootup sequence is interrupted, and the boot CLI is accessed. This can be useful for performing file manipulation if the device is not booting normally or not completing its normal bootup sequence, for whatever reason.

```
BOOT# ?
Available commands and required parameters :

Commands        Parameters                        Explanation
-------------------------------------------------------------------------
display | show  information_type               : Information display
exit | quit     None                           : Exit boot moniter program.
                                                 Online software is loaded.
read            access_address size access_type: Memory read
set             information_type information    : Set up information
write           access_address value access_type: Memory write

PARAMETERS
```

```
access_address  Address to bo accessed.
access_type     -w : word access, -h : half word access,
                -b : byte access, -s : access SRAM in the real time clock
information_type
                ether  : Switch(Ether Port) IP address
                mac    : Switch MAC address
                server : Server IP address & [Rboot File Name]
                router : Default router IP address
                boot   : boot mode (flash | network | initialize)
[Hit return|space|q]
size            Number of words/half words/bytes to be displayed


INFORMATION
IP address      Specified by decimal value.(ex.133.101.10.5)
flash           Online software in the flash memory is loaded.
initialize      Online software is loaded from the network. All the
                configuration data is initialized and default value is set up.
network         Online software is loaded from the network. All the
                configuration data is unchanged.
flash_up        Online software is loaded from the PCMCIA#0 flash memory.
                Configuration data loaded from the PCMCIA#1 flash memory.
                All the configuration data is unchanged.
initialize_save Online software is loaded from the network. All the
                configuration data is initialized and default value is set up.
                Online software and configuration data stored to the flash
                memory.
network_save    Online software is loaded from the network. All the
                configuration data is unchanged.Online software and
                configuration data stored to the flash memory.
flash_up_save   Online software is loaded from the PCMCIA#0 flash memory.
                Configuration data loaded from the PCMCIA#1 flash memory.
                All the configuration data is unchanged.Configuration data
[Hit return|space|q]
                stored to the PCMCIA#0 flash memory.
```

## Diagnostics

Diagnostics can be run from the CLI on any of the C1x00 products. They can be run on a slot, the CPU, or the switch fabric, or on all three. The diagnostics may take considerable time to run, and the switch should not be disturbed during this time. Once complete, the diagnostics will report any failures that are encountered. The following is an example of diagnostics being run on a C1200 switch:

```
ATM_Edge# diagnosis all
Are you sure? [Y or N] y
Diagnosis in progress...
ATM_Edge#
 Diagnosis Slot 1 OK:

 Diagnosis Slot 2 OK:

 Diagnosis Switch OK:

Diagnosis CPU OK:
```

In this example, the switch is healthy, so no error messages are returned. In the event of a diagnostic failure, a more detailed message regarding the nature of the failure can be obtained through use of the **display alarm** command:

```
ATM_Core# display alarm
Hardware Alarm
99.04.23        03:15:21  -  Environment000001
99.04.26        01:42:01  -  FAN 1
21:17:34        Power Unit 0
```

 *Running diagnostics causes all traffic flow to stop until the diagnostics are complete. You should run them at a time when network impact will be minimal.*

# Configuring Static Connections

The C1x00 product line support both permanent virtual circuits (PVCs) and soft permanent virtual paths (SPVPs). These PVCs and SPVPs extend between ATM switches.

 *Referred to as soft permanent virtual circuits (SPVCs) on the C100/C50/5000BH series switches, SPVCs currently can't be created between the C100/C50/5000BH and the C1x00 switches unless the C100/C50/C5000BH is the source border node, and the C1x00 is the destination. This is due to the fact that when the C1x00 acts as the source node, it utilizes UNI 4.0 signaling specifications, which the C100/C50/5000BH cannot interpret.*

## Configuring PVCs

PVCs are assigned to the C1x00 by means of a single command string. This string utilizes a series of parameter indicating the PVC type, VPI/VCI, etc. The full syntax for the command is as follows:

pvc establish [*traffic-direction*] [*traffic-type*] [*originating-slot-number*] [*originating-port-number*] [*vpi*] [*vci*] [*destination-slot-number*] [*destination-port-number*] [*vpi*] [*vci*] [*orig-dest-UPC-mode*] [*orig-dest-shaper-number*] [*profile-name*] [*dest-orig-UPC-mode*] [*dest-orig-shaper-number*] [*profile-name*]

The following is a practical example of this command, using all possible variables:

```
ATM_Edge# pvc establish 0 4 00 0 88 01 0 88 0 1 ToCore 0 1 ToCore
```

This command creates a bidirectional (indicated by the value 0) unspecified bit rate (UBR, indicated by the value 4) PVC between slot/port 00 and 01, utilizing VPI/VCI pair 0/88 in both cases. The orig-dest usage parameter control (UPC) mode is 0, and the shaper is set to 1, indicating that the shaper profile to core is to be used. The UPC

modes in this case can be set with numeric codes between 0 and 5. To determine the code you wish to use, refer to the following table:

| UPC Mode | Code |
|---|---|
| Off (no UPC) | 0 |
| PCR(CLP0+1) (used for ABR, CBR, and VBR ) | 1 |
| PCR(CLP0+1)/SVR(CLP0+1)/MBS for rtVBR and nrtVBR | 2 |
| PCR(CLP0+1)/SVR(CLP)/MBS no tagging for rtVBR and nrtVBR | 3 |
| PCR(CLP0+1)/SVC(CLP)/MBS tagging yes for rtVBR and nrtVBR | 4 |
| PCR(CLP0+1)/tagging yes for UBR | 5 |

To determine the code to use for *traffic direction*, refer to the following table:

| Traffic Direction | Code |
|---|---|
| Bidirectional | 0 |
| Point-to-multipoint | 1 |
| Unidirectional | 2 |

To determine the code to use for *traffic type*, refer to this table:

| Traffic Type | Code |
|---|---|
| Constant bit rate (CBR) | 1 |
| Non-real-time variable bit rate (nrt-VBR) | 2 |
| Real-time variable bit rate (rt-VBR) | 3 |
| Unspecified bit rate (UBR) | 4 |

## Adding a PVC Leaf to a Multipoint PVC

If the PVC type created uses a direction mode of multipoint, individual PVC leaves can be added with the **pvc add** command, which uses the following syntax:

pvc add [*ingress-line-number*] [*ingress-VPI*] [*ingress-VCI*] [*egress-line-number*]
[*egress-VPI*] [*egress-VCI*]

For example, the following commands would be used to create a multipoint PVC coming in on slot/port 00 and going out slot/port 01, and then adding two PVC leaves that egress slot/port 02 and 03:

```
ATM_Edge# pvc establish 1 4 00 0 88 01 0 88 0 1 ToCore 0 1 ToCore
ATM_Edge# pvc add 00 0 88 02 0 88
ATM_Edge# pvc add 00 0 88 03 0 88
```

The first command establishes a multipoint PVC that utilizes a UBR, VPI/VCI 0/88, coming in on slot/port 00 and leaving slot/port 01. The next two entries create one leaf each; each begins on slot/port 00, with VPI/VCI 0/88, because this is the starting point of the multipoint PVC that each leaf will share.

## Configuring SPVPs

SPVPs are created on the C1x00 by means of the **softpvp establish** command, which utilizes the following syntax:

softpvp establish [*traffic-type*] [*slot*] [*port*] [*vpi*] [*vci*] [*target-ATM-address*] [*target-device*] [*target-slot*] [*target-port*] [*target-vpi*] [*target-vci*] [*UPC-mode*] [*shaper-number-on-local-side*] [*profile-name*] [*target-UPC-mode*] [*target-shaper-number*] [*target-profile*] [*retry-count*]

To determine the code to use for *traffic type,* refer to the following table:

| Traffic Type | Code |
| --- | --- |
| Constant bit rate (CBR) | 1 |
| Non-real-time variable bit rate (nrt-VBR) | 2 |
| Real-time variable bit rate (rt-VBR) | 3 |
| Unspecified bit rate (UBR) | 4 |

To determine the code to use for *target device,* use this table:

| Target Device | Code |
| --- | --- |
| Centillion 1200 | 1 |
| Centillion 1400 | 2 |
| Centillion 1600 | 3 |

ATM ON NORTEL
NETWORKS

This command can become quite lengthy if used to its full capacity. As a beginning example, a portion of the command is used to define an SPVP on line 00, set for UBR, with a C1400 as a target switch, using VPI/VCI pair 0/88 on both the source and target sides of the connection:

```
ATM_Edge# softpvp establish 4 00 0 88 391020304000000000000000 1 03 0 88
```

This command establishes a SPVP configured with a value of 4 (indicating UBR) for slot/port 00, with a VPI/VCI value of 0/88 for the source switch, and the NSAP prefix of the remote switch. A value of 1 is indicated next, (indicating that the remote switch is a C1400), the receiving port on the remote switch is defined (slot 0 port 3 in this example), as well as the VPI/VCI value to be used on the destination switch (also set to 0/88).

UPC modes can also be set with this command. The addition of UPC parameters to the existing SPVP, as outlined in the previous example, are accomplished as follows:

```
ATM_Edge# softpvp establish 4 00 0 88 391020304000000000000000 1 03 0 88 1
0 SPVP1 1 0 SPVP1 infinite
```

This example repeats the command in the previous example, while adding UPC information. In the preceding example, the UPC mode is set to 1, with a shaper number of 0 and a profile name of SPVP1. These parameters are repeated for the target switch. Lastly, a retry count of **infinite** is used, specifying that the SPVP is to be attempted indefinitely, until it is successfully established. The retry count may be a numeric value as well, specifying how many attempts should be made before quitting. The default retry count is 2.

## Troubleshooting PVCs and SPVCs

The first step in troubleshooting a problem with a PVC or SPVP is to verify that the circuit was successfully created. This can be done with the **show** command. PVCs can be viewed with the following command syntax:

show pvc [*line-number*] [*VPI*] [*VCI*]

Likewise, SPVPs can be viewed with this syntax:

show softpvp [*line-number*] [*incoming-VPI*] [*incoming-VCI*]

The VPI/VCI pair does not need to be specified; if it isn't, then all the SPVPs configured on the specified slot and port will be displayed:

```
ATM_Edge# show softpvp 00
Line: 00
                                   Local              Remote
        --------------------------------------
Endpoint     VPI/VCI              Line    VPI/VCI              Traffic
F-profile    B-profile
Calling                   0/88      01    0/88       UBR          ubr
ubr
```

PVC problems often result due to misconfigured VPI/VCI pairs. This can be determined by utilizing the signaling debugging feature on the C1x00. In the following example, a C100 configured with a CLC using VPI/VCI pair 0/100 is configured. However, the PVC configured on the attached C1200 is configured for the incorrect pair, resulting in the following output:

```
ATMSIG: This is LOCAL SCOPE message:
ATMSIG: index = 6, callref = 6, lic = FALSE
enter Hash: index = 6, call ref = 6, lic = FALSE
PNNISIG: i Rcvd Setup msg in CallInitiated(NN1) length 203, call ref 6
PNNISIG: mynode state is Intermediate Node in PeerGroup
PNNISIG: from logical port=2 ==> get out port=21 out vpi=0
PNNISIG: CAC rejected call in CallInitiated(35)  Requested VPI/VCI not available
```

In the preceding section, the requested pair for the configured PVC is reported as being not available. This indicates that there is no corresponding pair to terminate the PVC configured.

The call is dropped and the resources are released.

```
PNNISIG: Spni_node_to_port() failure
PNNISIGERR: get out port number failure
ATMSIG: o Rel Complete msg, Call Initiated(NN1) state, length 76, call ref 6, pad 2
ATMSIG: freeSvcBlock(case0 : non Active), release resources.

PNNISIG: DTL/BTL free in Endpoint
PNNISIG: DTL/BTL free in Endpoint
ATMSIG: removeHashEntry: svc removed from hash table
ATMSIG: This is LOCAL SCOPE message:
ATMSIG: index = 20, callref = 20, lic = TRUE
PNNISIG: i Rcvd Release Complete msg in ReleaseRequest(NN11) length 6, call ref 20
ATMSIG: freeSvcBlock(case0 : non Active), release resources.
PNNISIG: DTL/BTL free in Endpoint
PNNISIG: DTL/BTL free in Endpoint
ATMSIG: removeHashEntry: svc removed from hash table
```

# Configuring Signaling

The C1x00 family supports signaling for the public and private User-to-Network Interface (UNI), Interim Inter-Switch Protocol (IISP), and PNNI. Because these switches are positioned primarily as core and edge transit switches, Nortel Networks currently does not offer LANE services on the C1x00 product line. LANE services can instead exist on the C100/C50/5000BH platform, working in conjunction with the C1x00 product.

The C1x00 also supports PVCs, SPVCs, and SVC tunneling, all of which are covered in this chapter.

## Different Signaling Types

The C1x00 family offers signaling for UNI 3.0, UNI 3.1, UNI 4.0, IISP, and PNNI. Unlike the C100/C50/5000BH, the individual channels that are specific to the signaling method are not established automatically and must be configured. For instance, the PNNI routing channel of 0/18 is not set up by default when a routing method of PNNI is selected—it must be built. In addition, changes in the interface type generally necessitate removing all PVC channels (the signaling channel 0/5, the ILMI channel 0/16, and so on) and then suspending the SVC line on the slot/port being configured. These connections must be rebuilt and the SVC line must be resumed before the port will become active again.

### UNI Signaling

UNI signaling can be configured for either public or private UNI, at version 3.0, 3.1 or 4.0. This is accomplished with the **set interface** command. Prior to altering the UNI type, you can use the **show atmsig** command to determine the type currently being used:

```
ATM_Core# show atmsig
Line   VPI U/N    301 303 308 309 310 313 316 317 322 397 398 399 UNIver
  20     0 Network 180   4  30  10  10   4 120  60   4 180   4  14 4.0( - )
  21     0 Network 180   4  30  10  10   4 120  60   4 180   4  14 3.1(4.0)
  22     0 Network 180   4  30  10  10   4 120  60   4 180   4  14 4.0( - )
  23     0 Network 180   4  30  10  10   4 120  60   4 180   4  14 4.0( - )
```

The output describes the different lines that are present; in this case, only slot 2 is occupied, so only slot 2, ports 0 through 3 are included. The user or network side is specified; because these are all private UNI connections, each port acts as the network side. The T3xx signaling timers are listed, with their current settings. Finally, the UNI version that is configured is listed, followed by the actual UNI type being used. This distinction is made because of the UNI 4.0 capability for autonegotiating the UNI version. Slot 2, port 1 in this case is attached to a device configured for UNI 3.1, so although the port is configured for UNI 4.0, it is actually utilizing UNI 3.1 currently.

**Note**

*One of the features of UNI 4.0 is that it is capable of autosensing and autonegotiating the UNI version with the switch at the remote end of the connection. In the case where the remote switch is a C100/C50/5000BH running UNI 3.1, a C1x00 port configured for UNI 4.0 will automatically drop back to UNI 3.1, although it remains configured for UNI 4.0. Likewise, two C1x00 switches interconnected for the first time will autonegotiate to UNI 4.0 for both sides of the connection.*

## Port-Level Configuration of ATM Signaling

To configure the C1x00 family switch for UNI signaling, a serial connection or telnet session must first be established to access the CLI. Once this is accomplished, enter privileged mode by typing **enable** and then entering the correct password, if one exists. Port-level signaling can now be configured.

To get an idea of how the ports are currently configured, display the port parameters by entering the **show interface** command:

```
ATM_Edge# show interface
Line Interface Physical layer        Forum/ITU Unassigned/Idle Valid VPI/VCI
    20 pri_UNI  OC-3C/STM1(MMF)        ATM Forum Unassigned       6/8
    21 pri_UNI  OC-3C/STM1(MMF)        ATM Forum Unassigned       6/8
    22 pri_UNI  OC-3C/STM1(MMF)        ATM Forum Unassigned       6/8
    23 pri_UNI  OC-3C/STM1(MMF)        ATM Forum Unassigned       6/8
```

In this example, none of the ports have currently been configured, and are operating with the factory default settings. A single, 4-port OC-3 multimode fiber line card is present in slot 2, configured as private UNI ports with a VPI/VCI bit mask of 6 and 8.

To change the port-level signaling on the C1x00 product line, the port line must first be suspended and the existing PVCs must be removed. PVCs, in this case, refer to the signaling channel of 0/5 and the ILMI channel of 0/16, both of which exist by default on all ports. In this example, because the UNI type will be altered, first suspend the line:

```
ATM_Core# set svcline 00 0 sus
 SVC status of line interface  00/0 : Suspended
```

This takes port 0 in slot 0 (designated by the value 00) and suspends the line so that no SVCs can be established for VPI 0. This basically disables the line so that the static signaling channels can be removed. Remove the signaling and ILMI channels by issuing the following commands:

```
ATM_Edge# delete sig 00 0
ATM_Edge# delete ilmi connection 00 0
```

These commands remove channels 0/5 and 0/16 on slot/port 00. In both cases, the value of 0 that follows the slot/port number indicates VPI 0. In each case, the value of 0 may be followed with the actual VCI number (5 and 16, respectively); however, this is not necessary, because these are implied by the entries **sig** and **ilmi** in the command structure.

If any other PVCs exist on the line, remove them as well. For instance, if PNNI has been configured, the PNNI routing channel must be torn down manually:

```
ATM_Edge# delete pnni connection 00 0
```

Any remaining PVCs that are not specific control channels can also be flushed from the port:

```
ATM_Edge# pvc flush 20
Are you sure? [Y or N] y
 All connections on the line interface have been deleted.
```

After all PVCs have been removed, the port-level signaling can be changed:

```
ATM_Edge# set interface 20
 Interface (pri_uni|0  pri_nni|1  pub_uni|2)? 0
 Forum/ITU (forum|0  itu|1)? 0
 IDLE cell (unassigned|0  idle|1)? 0
 Valid VPI (0-8[bit])? 0
 Valid VCI (0-14[bit])? 10
 VPI filter mask range (0-8[bit],default=Valid VPI)? 0
 VCI filter mask range (10-16[bit],default=Valid VCI)? 10
 Line interface  20 has been registered.
```

As the preceding example shows, the **set interface** command initiates a subroutine where the user is prompted to fill in a series of values. These values have been configured for a direct attached ATM server NIC, but could represent any UNI device, such as an ATM router interface. The preceding configuration can be broken down in the following manner:

- **Interface**   Indicates the type of interface the port is to be configured as. The options are for private UNI, public UNI, and private NNI. Because this is a direct attached ATM server, the port must be configured for private UNI, so option 0 has been selected. If the port itself were acting as the user side of a UNI connection to the public ATM network, then this would represent a public UNI connection; likewise, if this were to be an interswitch connection, private NNI would have been selected, for use with IISP or PNNI.

- **Forum/ITU**   Indicates whether the interface will be set as ATM Forum or ITU; ATM Forum generally is used in private networks.

- **IDLE Cell**  Specifies whether idle cells are assigned the designation idle or unassigned.

- **Valid VPI/VCI**  Defines the valid VPI/VCI bit mask. This defines the valid range for individual VPI and VCI values. For instance, in this case, the VPI/VCI bit mask has been set to 0/10. This indicates that only VPI 0 is valid, and that the VCI range is up to 1,023. The 1,023 value is arrived at by adding the total of the 10 bits as binary values (512, 256, 128, 64, 32, 16, 8, 4, 2, 1). These values may be set differently, depending on the supported VPI/VCI ranges of the attached device (an ATM NIC, in this case). In this instance, the NIC itself has also been configured with a bit mask of 0/10.

## Changing the ATM Signaling and UNI Version for a UNI Connection

As in any UNI connection, one side must act as user, and the other side as network. This fact has also carried over into the IISP connection, which relies heavily on the UNI specifications. With a UNI connection, however, the roles of user and network are clearly defined; in a private UNI connection, the switch acts as network and the attached device, whether it be a server, router, or so forth, acts as the user side. In a public UNI connection, because the switch is connecting to the public network, the private switch acts as the user side, and the public switch acts as the network side. Due to this fact, the UNI connection being configured must be set to either User or Network, depending on the connection type specified in the **set interface** command, along with the timing parameters; these settings are made with the **set atmsig** command. The actual UNI type that will be used (3.0, 3.1, or 4.0) is also defined, as in this example:

```
ATM_Core# set atmsig 00 0
  Interface (network|0  user|1)? 0
  T301 (1-511,default=180)?
  T303 (1-255,default=4)?
  T308 (1-511,default=30)?
  T309 (1-511,default=10)?
  T310 (1-255,default=10)?
  T313 (1-255,default=4)?
  T316 (1-511,default=120)?
  T317 (1-255,default=60)?
  T322 (1-255,default=4)?
  T397 (1-511,default=180)?
  T398 (1-255,default=4)?
  T399 (1-511,default=14)?
  UNI version (UNI3.0|0  UNI3.1|1 UNI4.0|2,default=4.0)? 1
  Q.2931 parameters have been set.
ATM_Core#
```

ATM ON NORTEL
NETWORKS

Here, the private UNI is configured as the network side, with the default timer values, and the UNI version is set to UNI 3.1. Each timer value plays a different role in the port-level ATM signaling. For the most part, these can be left at the factory defaults, although they are configurable if special cases arise. These timers and their values are covered in detail in Chapter 13.

Once these changes have been made, the line must be rebuilt. Rebuild the control channels and resume the line by issuing the following commands:

```
ATM_Edge# set sig 00 0
Signaling connection has been set.
ATM_Edge# set ilmi connection 00 0
ILMI connection has been set.
ATM_Edge# set svcline 00 0 resume
SVC status of line interface  00/0 : Resumed
```

At this point, the UNI signaling method has been changed, the control connections are back in place, and the line is once again ready to accept and initiate SVCs.

# Configuring a Call Routing Method

The C1x00 series switches are capable of routing via PNNI, IISP, or a combination of both. The call routing method selected will vary depending on the network.

## Choosing a Call Routing Method

Depending on which call routing method is chosen, the existing method may need to be changed. By default, the C1x00 switch utilizes IISP as its call routing method. To check the device's current call routing method, use the **show pnni method** command:

```
ATM_Edge# show pnni method
  Routing method: HOPBYHOP
```

IISP is considered PNNI phase 0, and the C1x00 switch treats it as a form of PNNI in its CLI. Therefore, if the PNNI method displayed is **hopbyhop** in response to the **show pnni method** command, this refers to IISP, which is a hop-based routing protocol, while PNNI 1.0 is referred to as **SOURCE**.

### Configuring Inter-Switch Signaling

When using UNI signaling, the user and network roles of each end of the connection are easily defined. In a private UNI, the switch always acts as the network side, whereas in a public UNI connection, the private switch acts as the user side of the UNI connection to the public provider. When two switches are connected together, regardless of the call routing method, the user and network sides must be chosen.

# Configuring IISP

Configuring straight IISP on the C1x00 switch is relatively simple: the interface in question must be configured as private NNI, and then the appropriate NSAP call routing entries must be created. These IISP call routing entries can be configured with varying prefix lengths, and redundant paths can be configured.

## Port-Level Configuration of IISP Links

In IISP routing, the first thing that must be done is to set the PNNI method to IISP, if it isn't already; this is referred to by the C1x00 as *hopbyhop routing*:

```
ATM_Edge# set pnni method hopbyhop
Routing method: HOPBYHOP
```

**Note**    *If the switch being configured is to be configured for both IISP and PNNI 1.0, then the PNNI method must be set to SOURCE, which is PNNI 1.0. The IISP links in that case are configured as such, without the PNNI routing channel, and advertised into the PNNI 1.0 portion of the network as exterior addresses. The specifics of this are covered later in this chapter.*

After you select the appropriate PNNI method, you must configure the static IISP call routes.

## Configuring IISP Call Routes

IISP call routes are configured on the C1x00 series switches by means of the **route** command, which uses the following syntax:

route add [*address-type (NSAP or E.164)*] [*destination-ATM-address*]
[*first-choice-slot/port*] [*first-choice-tunneling-VPI*] [*second-choice-slot/port*]
[*second-choice-tunneling-VPI*] [*third-choice-slot/port*] [*third-choice-tunneling-VPI*]
[*fourth-choice-slot/port*] [*fourth-choice-tunneling-VPI*] [*fifth-choice-slot/pot*]
[*fifth-choice-tunneling-VPI*] [*sixth-choice-slot/port*] [*sixth-choice-tunneling-VPI*]
[*seventh-choice-slot/port*] [*seventh-choice-tunneling-VPI*]

As is the case with the C100/C50/5000BH switches, varying lengths can be used for the NSAP prefix, depending on how specific the route should be. Up to seven redundant paths can be configured for each route.

Depending on the network type, a prefix type of NSAP or E.164 must be specified. NSAP refers to the Network Service Access Point address, whose prefix is 13 bytes long, while the total address length is 20 octets. The E.164 format utilizes an address that can be up to 8 octets in length.

To configure a single static IISP route for an NSAP prefix of 39.10.20.30.00.00.00.00.00.00.00.00.00, accessible through slot/port 01, issue the following command:

```
ATM_Edge# route add nsap 39102030 01
```

To configure the same route with two redundant paths, accessible through slot/ports 02 and 03, issue the following command:

```
ATM_Edge# route add nsap 39102030 01 - 02 - 03
```

The dash (-) symbol in this case indicates the default tunneling VPI. Tunneling isn't being used in this case, so this value is fine. As the preceding example demonstrates, specific costing for each path is not configured, as is the case with the C100/C50/5000BH; instead, an order of priority is configured (slot/port 01, 02, and then 03).

Installed static IISP routes can be verified with the **show route** command, which uses the following syntax:

show route [*slot*] [*port*]

Here is an example:

```
ATM_Core# show route 01
Destination                   Type   Line   VPI
39102030                      NSAP   01      0
```

## Loopcheck

The C1x00 series switches offer a feature called *loopcheck*, which allows the maximum number of hops for a SETUP message to be defined. If an IISP call routing loop occurs, the loopcheck feature causes a call that falls into a looping state to travel only so far before being cleared, instead of looping indefinitely and impacting the ATM network.

The IISP loopcheck feature is configured with the following command syntax:

set iisp loopcheck [on | off] [*hop-count (1-64, default 7)*]

The following command activates the loopcheck functionality and defines a maximum hop count of 10:

```
ATM_Edge# set iisp loopcheck on 10
```

## Swaproute

*Swaproute* refers to a method of cranking back SETUP messages in an IISP environment, which is specific to the C1x00 series switches. With swapping active, if the SETUP message detects a failed link, it will dynamically reestablish the SVC and automatically change the priority of the IISP routing tables to account for the missing path. This feature uses the following command syntax:

set iisp swaproute [on | off] [*resume-timer-value (1-20min, default 10min)*]

The following example activates the **swaproute** function, with the SVC resume timer set to five minutes:

```
ATM_Edge# set iisp swaproute on 5
```

 *This feature only functions in a mesh consisting of C1x00 switches only.*

## IISP Split Horizon

IISP Split Horizon can also be configured on the C1x00 series switches. This prevents a SETUP message between the originating switch and a specific destination from being forwarded back over the link it was received on. This feature should be used only on IISP links, and not on UNI connections, because under some circumstances, a UNI connection needs to set an SVC to itself, and this is prevented by split horizon. The split horizon feature uses the following command syntax:

set iisp splithorizon [on | off] [*slot*] [*port*] [*VPI*]

The following command sets IISP split horizon for slot/port 00 on VPI 0:

```
ATM_Edge# set iisp splithorizon on 00 0
```

# Troubleshooting IISP Connections

Generally, IISP problems arise either from misconfigured IISP connections, such as when both sides of the link have been identically configured to network or user, or, more often, from IISP call routing loops or dead ends, wherein a call arrives at a switch that has no route to the destination. A quick check of the interface will state whether it is set to the user or network side. The detection of call routing loops or missing call routes is a bit more difficult.

Call routing loops, by default, loop endlessly through the ATM mesh and generally impact the network, sometimes severely. If a call routing loop is suspected, using the loopcheck feature may help to identify this; configure IISP loopcheck on the switches in question, and set the maximum hop count to a value appropriate to the size of the network. Thus, if the network consists of five switches, a maximum hop count of 7 should suffice; if the network consists of 20 switches, set the maximum hop count higher. After configuring this option, if the network disturbance resolves itself, it could be an indication that a loop is present.

To avoid the presence of call routing loops, IISP call routes must be very specifically documented prior to implementation. This makes them easier to configure, and also makes troubleshooting easier if something fails. It is generally best to configure a single series of routes first, and then implement any redundancy after the initial configuration has been tested and connectivity has been verified. Entering in three or four layers of redundancy during the initial configuration can make troubleshooting extremely difficult if something goes wrong.

Debugging can also be used to observe the integrity of an IISP connection. The following output is captured from a debug on an incorrectly configured IISP link:

```
PNNISIG: i Rcvd Setup msg in CallInitiated(NN1) length 176, call ref 10
PNNISIG: mynode state is Last Node in PrivateNetwork
```

This indicates that the node is a PNNI node, and no other PNNI nodes are attached to it other than this one. The following indicates that the destination port is port 21, out VPI 0 (this is an IISP link in this case):

```
PNNISIG: from logical port=2 ==> get out port=21 out vpi=0
```

In the following section, the node recognizes that the designated transit list (DTL) can't be used to reach the IISP switch, and that it is the last PNNI node in the source DTL. The call must be handed over the IISP link into the hop-based routing environment.

```
ATMSIG: o Call Proc msg, Call Initiated(NN1) state, length 24, call ref 10, pad 2
ATMSIG: index = 84, callref = 84, lic = TRUE
enter Hash: index = 84, call ref = 84, lic = TRUE
ATMSIG: User Cell Rate IE Best Effort, size = 1
ATMSIG: User Cell Rate IE size = 9
ATMSIG: Designated transit list IE is not supported on this link.(UNI/IISP)
```

In the following section, the LEC (signified by an ESI of all C's) is requesting connection to the LECS (utilizing the well known address):

```
ATMSIG: o Setup msg, Call Initiated(U1) state, length 116, call ref 84, pad 1
ATMSIG(O) (port/vpi 21/0): 09 03 00 00 54 05 80 00 66 58 80 00 09 05 8C 05    ....T...fX......
ATMSIG(O) (port/vpi 21/0): EC 81 05 EC 84 00 59 80 00 09 84 05 93 FE 85 05    l..l..Y......~..
ATMSIG(O) (port/vpi 21/0): 93 FE BE 5E 80 00 03 10 80 80 5F 80 00 09 6B 40    .~>^......_...k@
ATMSIG(O) (port/vpi 21/0): 80 80 00 A0 3E 00 01 70 80 00 15 82 47 00 79 00    ... >..p....G.y.
ATMSIG(O) (port/vpi 21/0): 00 00 00 00 00 00 00 00 00 00 00 A0 3E 00 00 01 00    .......... >....
ATMSIG(O) (port/vpi 21/0): 6C 80 00 15 82 39 20 00 00 00 00 00 00 00 00 00    l....9 .........
ATMSIG(O) (port/vpi 21/0): AA 00 CC CC CC CC CC CC FF 5C 80 00 02 00 00 00    *.LLLLLL.\......
```

The call is initiated:

```
ATMSIG: open svc request in progress
PNNISIG: state changed from Call Initiated(NN1) to Call Proceeding Sent(NN3)
```

In the next section, the debug on port 21 (the IISP link) shows that an incoming message (signified by the **i** at the beginning of the fourth line) was received, indicating a Release Complete while still in the Call Initiated state, and then the resources associated with the connection were released:

```
ATMSIG(I) (port/vpi 21/0): 09 03 80 00 54 5A 81 00 07 08 80 00 03 80 E0 5A    ....TZ........`Z
ATMSIG: This is LOCAL SCOPE message:
ATMSIG: index = 84, callref = 84, lic = TRUE
ATMSIG: i Rcvd Release Complete msg in callInitiatedState (U1) length 7, call ref 84
ATMSIG: freeSvcBlock(case1 : non Active), release resources.
```

In the final section that follows, an outgoing Release message is sent, and the SVC is dropped. The reason for the failure in this case is that both sides of the IISP connection (between the C1200 and the C100) are set as the user side. Therefore, the normal signaling procedure can't be followed, so the call fails almost as soon as it initiates.

```
ATMSIG: o Release msg, Release Request(NN11) state, length 20, callref 10, pad 0
ATMSIG: close svc request in progress
PNNISIG: DTL/BTL free in Endpoint
PNNISIG: DTL/BTL free in Endpoint
ATMSIG: removeHashEntry: svc removed from hash table
```

# Configuring PNNI

The C1x00 series switches are capable of participating at multiple levels of the PNNI routing hierarchy. They may act as border nodes, and may also act as Peer Group Leaders (PGLs), to aggregate nodal and PNNI logical link information as logical group nodes (LGNs) at the upper layers. At the onset, then, you must determine how many levels of PNNI hierarchy will exist within the network, how many levels of the hierarchy the individual nodes will be participating at, which peer group each node will be in, and what the node's PGL priority should be, indicating its relative desirability to be PGL (if it is participating in PGL election at all).

## PNNI Configuration Considerations

Since the C1x00 is capable of participating at all levels of the PNNI hierarchy, and also as PGL, the examples in this section show nodes configured both to participate in the full range of the hierarchy and to contend for PGL election.

## Configuring the PNNI Control Channel

As is the case with other control channels on the C1x00, the line must first be suspended before any such changes can take place. In addition, the existing PVCs need to be removed, because the interface type must be changed from the default setting of private UNI to private NNI. This is accomplished with the following commands:

```
ATM_Edge# set svcline 00 0 suspend
ATM_Edge# delete sig 00 0
ATM_Edge# delete ilmi connection 00 0
ATM_Edge# set interface 00
Interface   (pri_uni|0    pri_nni|1    pub_uni|2)?  1
Forum/ITU   (fcrum|0    itu|1)?   0
IDLE Cell  (unassigned|0    idle|1)?   0
Valid VPI  (0-8 bit])?   0
Valid VCI  (0-8 bit])?   10
Line Interface 00 has been registered
ATM_Edge# set sig 00 0
Signaling connection has been set.
ATM_Edge# set ilmi connection 00 0
ILMI connection has been set.
ATM_Edge# set pnni connection 00 0 18 5040 0 0
PNNI connection has been set.
ATM_Edge# set atmsig 00 0
Interface (network|0    user|1)?   0
T303      (1-255,default=4)?    4
T308      (1-511,default=30)?   30
T309      (1-511,default=90)?   90
T310      (1-255,default=10)?   10
T313      (1-255,default=4)?    4
T316      (1-511,default=120)?  120
T317      (1-255,default=60)?   60
T322      (1-255,default=4)?    4
T398      (1-255,default=4)?    4
T399      (1-511,default=4)?    4
UNI Version (UNI3.0|0    UNI3.1|1  UNI4.0|2)?  1
ATM_Edge# set svcline 00 0 resume
```

These commands accomplish the following: the svcline for slot/port 00 is suspended, and the signaling and ILMI channels are removed. Once this is done, the interface type is changed to private NNI, and a bit mask of 0/10 is applied. Then, the signaling and ILMI channels are rebuilt, along with the PNNI routing channel of 0/18. The ATM signaling is altered so that UNI version 3.1 is used, along with the default timer values. The svcline is then resumed.

The setup of the PNNI routing channel is a bit different from the others, utilizing the following syntax:

set pnni connection [*slot*] [*port*] [*vpi*] [*vci*] [*administrative-weight*] [*aggregation-token*] [*UBR-secure-band*]

The following is the isolated command:

```
ATM_Edge# set pnni connection 00 0 18 5040 0 0
```

This command sets the PNNI routing channel for slot/port 00, on VPI/VCI 0/18 (the default). Next, an administrative weight of 5040 is assigned to the connection, while the following two values of 0 and 0 refer to the aggregation token and UBR secure band, respectively. The *aggregation token* defines the number of divisions of the logical link between LGNs in upper layers of the PNNI hierarchy, and can be set between 0 and 255. For more information regarding the aggregation token and PNNI link aggregation, refer to Chapter 16.

# Configuring the PNNI Hierarchy

The C1x00 series switches are all capable of supporting multilevel hierarchical PNNI routing, as either internal or border nodes. Depending on the network in question, a PNNI hierarchy may or may not be desirable. Developing a hierarchy can be useful in several ways, including keeping topology databases at a manageable size, as well as providing more efficient management of a large PNNI network.

In a network of C1x00 series switches, you are recommended to have no more than 11 nodes within a single peer group. This refers to each peer group at each hierarchical level, not to the entire hierarchy. So, when considering a three-level hierarchy, up to 11 nodes can be in the highest-level peer group, each acting as a logical group node (LGN) for 11 separate midlevel peer groups below them, which may consist of up to 11 nodes each, which in turn act as LGNs for the lowest level. Using these guidelines, it is possible to create a very large ATM network without exceeding 11 nodes in any one peer group. For more details regarding the PNNI hierarchy, consult Chapter 16.

## Levels of Hierarchy

The example in Figure 22-1 has three levels of PNNI hierarchy: the lowest level, which is 72, the upper level, which is 24, and the highest level, which is 16. Two nodes will be configured to participate in this hierarchy: node A, which will participate in all three levels of the hierarchy, and node B, which will participate at only the lower two layers.

Since node A has a scope of 16, it is accessible to everything from level 16 downward. (In this example, then, node A can be accessed by all other nodes.) Node B, however, has a scope of 24; it can only reach level 24, and is only accessible to peer groups A and B.

ATM ON NORTEL
NETWORKS

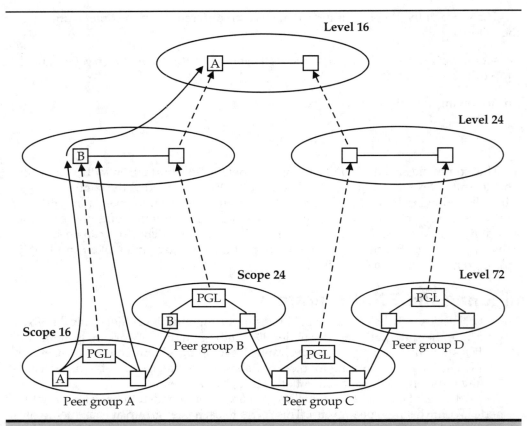

**Figure 22-1.**   *Node A and node B participating at various hierarchical levels*

This arrangement requires that all nodes in peer group B be configured with a scope of 24. If any nodes within the group are configured for a scope of 16, then aggregation of the peer group will occur at level 16 and peer group B will at that point be accessible to all peer groups.

**Note**   *When configuring PNNI nodes, keep in mind that the scope of each node's advertisement is implied by what level it is configured for. (As an example, if a node is configured to operate at two layers of hierarchy, 24 and 16, then the node will be summarized up to level 16 unless another node in the group is configured to summarize at an even higher level.)*

## Peer Group Leader Considerations

The C1x00 series switches are also capable of participating as PGLs for individual peer groups. PGL desirability is dictated largely by PGL priority, which is configured as part of the PNNI nodal information; however, individual nodes may be configured not to participate in the PGL election.

## Configuring Nodal Information

The node levels of the PNNI hierarchy are configured with the **set pnni nodal** command, which uses the following syntax:

set pnni nodal [*number-of-hierarchical-layers*] [*PGL-participation-flag*]

Issuing this command initiates a subroutine that prompts for further information about the PNNI routing hierarchy. This subroutine will be executed for each level of the PNNI hierarchy. This configuration begins at the lowest layer of the hierarchy and works its way up. For example, the following entries allow node A to participate in three levels of the hierarchy (level 72, 24, and 16) and participate in the PGL election process with a priority of 255, ensuring PGL election on all levels:

```
ATM_Edge_1# set pnni nodal 3 1
Level indicator   (1-104)?  72
Restricted transit bit   (on|1     off|0)?  0
Restricted branching bit    (on|1     off|0)?  0
Leadership priority   (0-255)?  255
Peer Group ID    ([ENTER], up to 28 hexadecimal characters)?
LGN ID    ([ENTER], up to 44 hexadecimal characters)?

Level indicator   (1-104)?  24
Restricted transit bit   (on|1     off|0)?  0
Restricted branching bit    (on|1     off|0)?  0
Leadership priority   (0-255)?  255
Peer Group ID    ([ENTER], up to 28 hexadecimal characters)?
LGN ID    ([ENTER], up to 44 hexadecimal characters)?

Level indicator   (1-104)?  16
Restricted transit bit   (on|1     off|0)?  0
Restricted branching bit    (on|1     off|0)?  0
Leadership priority   (0-255)?  255
Peer Group ID    ([ENTER], up to 28 hexadecimal characters)?
LGN ID    ([ENTER], up to 44 hexadecimal characters)?
 Hierarchy1 : UNI scope(1-13)?6
 Hierarchy2 : UNI scope(2-14)?12
 PNNI node information have been set.
```

Notice that there are no entries after being prompted for the Peer Group ID and LGN ID in any instance of the hierarchy; in the absence of any input, these values will be generated automatically. The defaults in these cases are acceptable, but can be altered, although doing so is not recommended. Also note that upon configuring more than one layer of hierarchy, the user is prompted for the UNI scope of the lower two layers. (The top layer includes everything above the first two.) This associates the different layers of hierarchy with different UNI scope values. UNI scope is a function of UNI 4.0 and is covered in greater detail in Chapter 13. For purposes of configuring the C1x00 switches, this feature relates to the UNI scope of ATM Anycast and does not affect the node's PNNI address scope (which is indicated by defining at which levels the node will participate).

Node B is configured similarly, although it will not participate at all in the PGL election state:

```
ATM_Edge_2# set pnni nodal 2 0     Note the PGL participation bit set to 0
Level indicator  (1-104)?  72
Restricted transit bit  (on|1    off|0)?  0
Restricted branching bit   (on|1     off|0)?  0
Leadership priority   (0-255)?  0
Peer Group ID    ([ENTER], up to 28 hexadecimal characters)?
LGN ID   ([ENTER], up to 44 hexadecimal characters)?

Level indicator   (1-104)?  24
Restricted transit bit   (on|1     off|0)?  0
Restricted branching bit   (on|1     off|0)?  0
Leadership priority   (0-255)?  0
Peer Group ID    ([ENTER], up to 28 hexadecimal characters)?
LGN ID   ([ENTER], up to 44 hexadecimal characters)?
Hierarchy2 : UNI scope(2-14)?6
PNNI node information has been set.
```

In this example, the initial command indicates only two levels of hierarchy, and the PGL participation bit is set to 0 (off).

# Troubleshooting PNNI

When troubleshooting a PNNI problem in a C1x00 environment, many steps can be taken prior to resorting to port-level debugging. Certain things must be in place if PNNI is to function correctly, and many aspects of the PNNI environment can be determined through the CLI.

One of the first things to do when facing a potential PNNI problem is to determine whether the nodes are being learned correctly, because a fully synchronized topology database needs to be in place for calls to be correctly routed. A good first step is to determine whether or not the immediate neighbor nodes have been correctly learned, which can be accomplished by viewing the known PNNI nodes, described next.

## Examining the Node List

The first thing that you must determine if PNNI nodes do not appear to be synchronizing correctly is whether or not all the expected PNNI neighbors are listed in the node table.

This can be done with the **show pnni node** command, which lists all the PNNI nodes that are directly connected to the switch being viewed (the neighboring nodes):

```
ATM_Edge# show pnni node
                Destination nodeID                Administrative
weight
    0: 48.A0.3920000000000000000000000000.0000322545F6.00           0
    1: 48.A0.3920000000000000000000000000.02D012F8C001.00        5040
    2: 48.A0.39200000000000000000000AA00.027090F7C001.00        5040
```

This list will not include nodes that are not direct attached neighbors. In this example, two C100 switches are connected to a C1200, so three entries are present: one for the C1200 itself, and one for each of the two C100 switches. Notice the local node address has an Administrative Weight of 0, while the other two have equal weights of 5040 (the default value).

**ADMINISTRATIVE WEIGHT**    Administrative weight defines the relative desirability of a path; for instance, in a scenario where there are multiple paths to the same destination (which is preferable in a PNNI environment), administrative weight can help determine the paths that can be taken. For instance, in the preceding example, if the switches were connected in a loop, and the C1200 connection to one C100 was an OC-3 link, and the connection to the other C100 was an OC-12 link, then a lower (more desirable) weight might be assigned to the OC-12 link, therefore causing the other nodes to favor that path when building a DTL.

The administrative weight can be altered when configuring the PNNI connection:

```
ATM_Edge# set pnni connection 00 0 18 5040
PNNI connection has been set.
```

## Examining All Learned PNNI Addresses

If the PNNI nodes seem to be learned correctly, yet there is still a loss of connectivity or a failure in a LEC join state, take a closer look at the PNNI learned addresses. The command to use is **show pnni longestmatch**:

```
ATM_Edge# show pnni longestmatch
     Length            Reachable address
    0:    152 3920000000000000000000000000020B481F200000
    1:    152 3920000000000000000000000000002D012F8000100
    2:    152 3920000000000000000000000000002D012F8C00100
    3:    152 392000000000000000000000000000AAAAAAAAAAAA00
    4:    152 392000000000000000000000000000BBBBBBBBBBBB00
    5:    152 3920000000000000000000AA00CCCCCCCCCCCC00
    6:    152 470079000000000000000000000000A03E00000100
    7:    152 C50079000000000000000000000000A03E00000100
    8:    104 3920000000000000000000000000000000000000
```

(The command can be abbreviated to **show pnni long**.)

Notice in this example that, in addition to the three nodes still present in the **show pnni node** command, five other addresses are present. These additional addresses are ATM addresses represented by each node, but not necessarily the Node ID itself. For instance, entry 3 is that of the LES address configured on one of the PNNI nodes, entry 4 is that of one of the LEC VPorts, and entry 5 is another LEC VPort. Entries 6 and 7 are the addresses associated with the LECS. The output from this command also includes any exterior addresses or internal addresses that are being advertised into the PNNI domain. An example of this might be if IISP were being used in conjunction with PNNI, where IISP routes were being advertised as exterior addresses.

## Verifying the Nodal Information

Particularly when dealing with a PNNI hierarchy, PNNI routing problems can occur due to incorrectly configured nodal information. If the neighbors apparently are being learned correctly, and other nodes seem to be present, verify the PNNI nodal information with the following command:

```
ATM_Edge# show pnni nodal

Level indicator:          72
Restricted transit bit:   OFF
Restricted branching bit: OFF
ATM end system address:   39.200000000000000000000000.0000322545F6.48
Leadership priority:      255
LGN ID:                   48.A0.392000000000000000000000.0000322545F6.00
Peer group ID:            48.392000000000000000000000

Level indicator:          24
Restricted transit bit:   OFF
Restricted branching bit: OFF
ATM end system address:   39.200000000000000000000000.0000322545F6.18
Leadership priority:      255
LGN ID:                   18.48.392000000000000000000000.0000322545F6.00
Peer group ID:            18.392000000000000000000000

Level indicator:          16
Restricted transit bit:   OFF
Restricted branching bit: OFF
ATM end system address:   39.200000000000000000000000.0000322545F6.10
Leadership priority:      255
LGN ID:                   10.18.392000000000000000000000.0000322545F6.00
Peer group ID:            10.392000000000000000000000

UNI scope1  : PNNI Hierarchy1  (Level 72)
UNI scope2  : PNNI Hierarchy2  (Level 72)
UNI scope3  : PNNI Hierarchy2  (Level 72)
UNI scope4  : PNNI Hierarchy2  (Level 72)
UNI scope5  : PNNI Hierarchy2  (Level 24)
```

```
UNI scope6  : PNNI Hierarchy2  (Level 24)
UNI scope7  : PNNI Hierarchy2  (Level 24)
UNI scope8  : PNNI Hierarchy2  (Level 24)
UNI scope9  : PNNI Hierarchy2  (Level 24)
UNI scope10 : PNNI Hierarchy2  (Level 24)
UNI scope11 : PNNI Hierarchy3  (Level 24)
UNI scope12 : PNNI Hierarchy3  (Level 16)
UNI scope13 : PNNI Hierarchy3  (Level 16)
UNI scope14 : PNNI Hierarchy3  (Level 16)
UNI scope15 : PNNI Hierarchy3  (Level 16)
ATM_Edge#
```

This example has three layers of hierarchy, and the node is configured to participate in all three. UNI scope for the lowest level (72) is set to 6, and the second layer (level 24) is set to 12.

## Debugging PNNI

PNNI debugging can also be used to determine possible problems in the PNNI network. PNNI debugging is quite extensive and, again, is not fully covered in this book. To give a sense of the type of output that can be gathered from the PNNI debugging tool, a debug level of 31 has been set on an active PNNI link, and PNNI Hello information has been captured:

```
PNNIDAT: com_packet_decoder - PNNIPACKETTYPE_HELLO
PNNIDAT: com_packet_decoder - hellopacket->RPortID=1
PNNIEVT: sch_select - >>> ===================================== <<<
PNNIEVT: sch_select -            calling hl_hellorecv no(1)
PNNIEVT: sch_select - >>> ===================================== <<<
PNNIPRO: hl_hellorecv - port(1) is used by physical hello
PNNIPRO: hl_phy_recv - called portid 1
```

In the preceding output, the port is listed as being used by physical hello (this is not an LGN connection), and a Remote Port ID is listed. In the following section, no UpNode is present, because there is only a single layer of hierarchy:

```
PNNIEVT: hl_phy_recv - newest_version >= packetoldver
PNNIPRO: hl_phy_recv - --- inside/outside link ---
PNNIPRO: hl_phy_recv - State=4, PortID=1
PNNIPRO: hl_phy_recv - RemoteNodeID_setflag=1, RemotePortID=3
PNNIPRO: hl_phy_recv - HelloInterval=15, InactFactor=5
PNNIPRO: hl_phy_recv - InactTimerID=1, Version=1
PNNIPRO: hl_phy_recv - --- outside link ---
PNNIPRO: hl_phy_recv - TxULIASeqNo=0, RxULIASeqNo=0
PNNIPRO: hl_phy_recv - TxNodalHierSeqNo=1, RxNodalHierSeqNo=0
PNNIPRO: hl_phy_recv - UpNodeID_setflag=0, CommonPGID_setflag=0
PNNIPRO: hl_phy_recv - UpNodeATMAddr_setflag=0
```

ATM ON NORTEL
NETWORKS

Next, the Aggregation Token is listed; because only a single layer of hierarchy is defined in this case, the value is set to 0:

```
PNNIPRO: hl_phy_recv - DerivedLinkAggToken=0, ConfiguredLinkAggToken=0
PNNIPRO: hl_phy_recv - RemoteLinkAggToken=0
```

The Port ID, Remote Port ID, Hello Interval, and possible Information Group (IG) elements are listed next:

```
PNNIDAT: hl_phy_recv - --- packet---
PNNIDAT: hl_phy_recv - packettype=1, packetleng=100
PNNIDAT: hl_phy_recv - packetver =1, packetnewver=1, packetoldver=1
PNNIDAT: hl_phy_recv - packet->Flags=0x0
PNNIDAT: hl_phy_recv - packet->PortID=3, packet->RPortID=1
PNNIDAT: hl_phy_recv - packet->HelloInterval=15, packet->IGs=0x0
```

In the final section, a state of 2-Way Inside is indicated:

```
PNNIDAT: hl_phy_recv - ----------------------------------
PNNIDAT: hl_phy_recv - comhier? : uliaptr=0,      aggtokenptr=0x0
PNNIDAT: hl_phy_recv - comhier? : nodalhierptr=0,nhlptr=0x0
PNNIEVT: hl_phy_recv - -------- 2-WayInsideReceived portID=1
```

The following is another example of PNNI debugging (at level 10), taken on a PNNI port where the neighboring node has been misconfigured to be in a different peer group in which there is neither a common layer of hierarchy nor a PGL for the remote peer group. This is not an unusual misconfiguration, particularly since the addressing scheme of PNNI varies from that of IISP.

```
PNNIPRO: hl_12 - called portid 1
PNNIPRO: sch_del_timer - (id=1) delete ok
PNNIPRO: sch_set_timer - (sec=75, func=0x814fef94, funcarg=0x1) new id=1
PNNIPRO: hl_phy2pgl_PeerFound - called
PNNIPRO: hl_phy2pgl_PeerFound - current status is `PeerFound'
PNNIPRO: hl_phy_recv - phyhl[1].RxULIASeqNo = 0
PNNIPRO: hl_phy_recv - phyhl[1].RxNodalHierSeqNo = 0
PNNIPRO: sch_del_timer - (id=10) delete ok
PNNIPRO: hl_15 - called portid 2
PNNIPRO: hl_phy_hellosend - start portid 2
PNNIPRO: sch_set_timer - (sec=1, func=0x814fa22c, funcarg=0x2) new id=4
PNNIPRO: hl_phy_hellosend - State is outside(1WAYOUT or 2WAYOUT or COMOUT)
```

In the preceding code section, an outside state is indicated; this should happen only if the nodes are in two different peer groups. In this case, the nodes should be in the same peer group. Though the specific outside state is not listed, the presence of an outside state is enough to indicate the misconfigured node.

# Mixing IISP and PNNI

PNNI and IISP can run simultaneously on the C1x00 series switches. In this situation, the C1x00 switch is configured for PNNI routing (source), and the IISP connections are advertised into the PNNI domain as exterior addresses. Four main things will need to be configured in this case: the PNNI nodal information, the PNNI connection, the IISP connection, and the exterior address to be advertised.

## Exterior vs. Interior Addresses

*Interior addresses* are internal to the PNNI domain and are to be advertised individually. *Exterior addresses* come from another source outside the PNNI domain (such as IISP). Since IISP is a hop-based routing protocol, where no actual route information is exchanged or learned, any IISP addresses must be advertised as being accessible by the PNNI node to which the IISP connections are attached (see Figure 22-2).

### Configuring the C1x00 for Source and Hop-by-Hop Routing

Configuring the C1x00 to do a combination of PNNI and IISP routing requires that the node itself be configured for PNNI (source) routing. The IISP connections in this case are configured exactly the same as they would be if the routing method were HOPBYHOP:

1. Suspend the line.

2. Configure the connection as either the network or user side of the connection.

3. Select a UNI version.

4. Reestablish the signaling channel.

5. Resume the line.

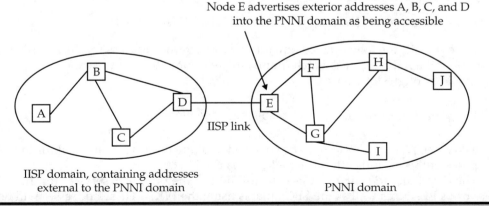

Node E advertises exterior addresses A, B, C, and D
into the PNNI domain as being accessible

IISP link

IISP domain, containing addresses
external to the PNNI domain

PNNI domain

**Figure 22-2.**   *A mixed IISP and PNNI environment, showing internal and exterior addresses*

ILMI and PNNI channels are not required for IISP links, so the 0/16 and 0/18 channels do not need to be configured on the IISP links.

Once the IISP links are in place, the addresses of the switches in the IISP domain, as well as any other addresses associated with that switch (the LES address, LECS address, and so forth), must be advertised into the PNNI domain as exterior addresses.

## Configuring Exterior Addresses

Once the IISP connection is in place, the PNNI node to which it is connected must be configured with an exterior address that will be advertised into the PNNI domain. To do this, you must access the PNNI submenu. Issue the **set pnni address** command:

```
ATM_Edge# set pnni address
PNNI>
```

The command prompt changes to reflect the PNNI submenu, and the hash mark (#) that previously indicated privileged mode reverts back to the original greater-than sign (>). This does not indicate that the permission level has changed; the PNNI submenu does not have different permission levels, and if it has been accessed, you are assumed to be in privileged mode. The PNNI submenu itself has a short command list:

```
PNNI> ?
add             Addition
change          Change
.               Exit
```

From the PNNI submenu prompt, the exterior address can be configured. This involves choosing the address type (exterior or internal), the scope, the bit length, the ATM address itself, the slot and port number the address is accessible from, and the VPI to be used. The command utilizes the following syntax:

add external [*scope*] [*bit-length*] [*ATM-address*] [*slot*] [*port*] [*VPI*]

For example, the following command adds an external address for the full ATM address of the IISP attached switch (minus the selector byte), with a scope of 0, accessible through slot 2 port 1:

```
PNNI> add ext 0 152 39300000000000000000000000002D012F8C001 21 0
```

In reality, the ATM address could be specified as a much shorter value, but for the purposes of this example, the entire address is used.

The IISP attached switch in this case also houses the LES/BUS services for the network's ELAN, as well as the LECS that is using the WKA. These addresses will not be learned dynamically, so, just as in the C100/C50/5000BH, entries for these addresses need to be configured manually. The two addresses can be added by means of the following commands:

```
PNNI> add ext 0 8 47 21 0
PNNI> add ext 0 152 39300000000000000000000000000AAAAAAAAAAAA 21 0
```

The first entry includes only the first octet of the WKA, 47, because the bit length is specified as 8, which only covers the first octet. Since the first octet of 47 is enough, in this network, to ensure uniqueness for that address, it is all that is required. The second address references the LES address (whose ESI has been configured as all A's), and, because the selector byte has been left off, this entry will also be used for the BUS address.

In reality, the IISP switch and its LES/BUS address could have been covered by a single entry of 3930 with a bit length of 16, because they both share this portion of the address, but for the sake of this example, a bit length of 152 was used for the IISP switch address, to show how the exterior address entries interrelate.

After you enter these addresses, exit the PNNI submenu, which will commit the exterior address entries:

```
PNNI> .
PNNI reachable address has been set.
```

The address, once in place, can be verified with the following command:

```
ATM_Edge# sho pnni addr
Exterior reachable address
Address                                    length  Scope  Line  VPI
              /Transit network ID data  Transit network ID
39.2000000000000000                         72     0     21    0
              /            -

39.300000000000000000000000.02D012F8C001   152     0     21    0
              /            -

39.300000000000000000000000.AAAAAAAAAAAA    152     0     21    0
              /            -

47                                           8      0     21    0
              /            -
```

## Exterior Address Scope

The scope value that is specified in the exterior address entry indicates how far up into the PNNI hierarchy the address should be advertised. In the previous examples, the scope for each address has been set to 0, which indicates that there is no limit to how far the address should be advertised. For instance, in a PNNI network with three levels of hierarchy—levels 72, 24, and 16—an exterior address with a scope of 24 would be advertised only at levels 72 and 24, not at level 16. For more information regarding PNNI address scope, consult Chapter 16, which offers specific examples.

## Verifying LANE Connectivity

Once the LANE join process occurs successfully through the C1x00 series switch, the ports through which the LANE connections take place can be viewed to make certain that the control connections are in place. This can be done with the following command:

```
ATM_Edge# sho svc 21
 Line:  21
 Bandwidth Available (Forward/Backward/Line Rate): 353207/353207/353207 cell/s
 Tunneling bandwidth available              : 0/0/0 cell/s
 Existing connections: 4

                                    Incoming        Outgoing
                              ---------------+---------------
 Traffic type   Connection type  Line  VPI/VCI   Line  VPI/VCI
 UBR            P-to-P            20    0/33      21    0/126
 UBR            P-to-M           21    0/127     20    0/34
 UBR            P-to-P           20    0/35      21    0/128
 UBR            P-to-M           21    0/129     20    0/36
```

The preceding example is slot/port 21 on a C1200, with a C100 attached. The C100 has a single LEC configured, and is joining services on a remote C100, also connected to the C1200. The SVCs in place show two point-to-point connections (the Control Direct VCC and the Multicast Send VCC), as well as two point-to-multipoint connections (the Control Distribute VCC and the Multicast Forward VCC). Although these are technically SVCs, these connections should remain up at all times.

# Tunneling

SVC Tunneling is a method of taking signaling VCs and tunneling them over a nonzero VPI value. This is useful when attempting to span a LANE network across a wide area, where transport over a public provider network is necessary. In general, when connecting to a public provider, the private network administrator is given a VPI/VCI pair with which to establish the PVC connection with the provider switch. For example, if a VPI/VCI pair of 2/132 were given, then tunneling could be used to transfer the signaling and PNNI control channels of 0/5 and 0/18 across the PVC 2/132 to connect the remote ATM network (see Figure 22-3).

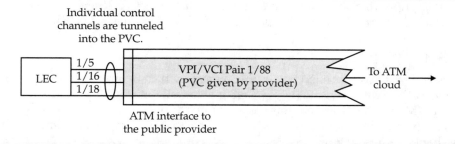

**Figure 22-3.** *An example of SVC tunneling*

## Configuring Tunneling

Tunneling is accomplished with the **set tunneling** command, which uses the following command syntax:

> set tunneling [*line-number*] [*VPI-over-which-to-tunnel*] [*tunneling-bandwidth (1-353,207 (OC-3) or 1-1412830 (OC-12)*] [*UPC-function-mode (0 | off, 1 | on)*] [*shaper-number (off(0) or 1-8)*]

For instance, if a VPI/VCI pair of 2/132 has been specified by the provider and configured on line number 020, the following command could be used to configure the tunneling parameters:

```
ATM_WAN# set tunneling 020 2 353207 0 1
```

In this case, a shaper (shaper 1) has been defined. It is generally a good idea to use a shaper when dealing with a connection to a public provider; this will assist in keeping the cell flow steady across the wide area connection. Traffic shaping and the configuration of shapers is covered in the following sections of this chapter.

# Traffic Shaping and Policing

Traffic parameters can be configured on the C1x00 series switches for both traffic shaping and traffic policing. *Traffic shaping* refers to the defined cell rates for outgoing cell flows; this allows the switch to take an incoming series of traffic bursts and smooth out the cell flow on the egress port. *Traffic policing* actually checks the ingress traffic flow to make certain the applied traffic parameters are adhered to.

*When tunneling on an interface, be sure to set the correct VPI value. For instance, when tunneling over VPI 2, set the signaling channel to 2/5, as opposed to 0/5.*

# Traffic Shaping

Traffic shaping is accomplished by creating a *shaper,* which defines a set of egress traffic parameters: the Peak Cell Rate (PCR), Sustainable Cell Rate (SCR), and Maximum Burst Size (MBS). Once defined, this shaper can be applied to a port or series of ports. Egress traffic passing over a port to which the shaper has been assigned must adhere to the shaper values.

## Setting Up Traffic Shaping Profiles

The first step in configuring traffic shaping is to define the shaper(s) that is to be applied. This is accomplished with the following command syntax:

set shaper [*slot*][*port*] [*shaper-number (1-8)*] [*peak-cell-rate*] [*sustainable-cell-rate*] [*maximum-burst-size*]

The following example creates shaper 1, applied to slot/port 00, with a PCR of 250000, a SCR of 100000, and a MBS of 300000:

```
ATM_Core# set shaper 00 1 250000 100000 300000
```

The valid values for these parameters will differ depending on the interface type, with the following ranges available:

| | |
|---|---|
| OC-3 | PCR (1-353207) |
| | SCR (1-353207) |
| OC-12 | PCR (1-1412830) |
| | SCR (1-1412830) |

# Traffic Policing

Traffic policing is accomplished by creating a *profile,* which defines a set of ingress traffic Quality of Service (QoS) parameters: the PCR, SCR, and MBS. In addition, an Early Packet Discard flag can be set. Once defined, the profile can be applied to a port or series of ports. Ingress traffic on a port to which the specific profile has been assigned must adhere to the traffic policing parameters, or else they are dropped.

## Setting Up Traffic Policing Profiles

Traffic policing profiles are set with the **set profile** command, which uses the following command syntax:

set profile [*traffic-type (0=ABR, 1=CBR, 2=nrt-VBR, 3=rt-VBR, 4=UBR)*] [*profile-name*]

Executing this command initiates a subroutine in which specific policing parameters are prompted for:

```
ATM_Core# set profile 1 CBR
PCR (1-353207 [cell/s]) ?  20000
     Peak cell rate
SCR (1-353207 [cell/s])  ?  10000
     Sustainable cell rate
MBS (1-353207 [cell/s]) ?  90000
     Maximum burst size
EPD (off|0  on|1)  ? 1
     EPD function flag
```

This creates a profile called CBR, with a traffic type of CBR. The PCR is set to 20000, the SCR is set to 10000, and the MBS is set to 90000. The Early Packet Discard flag is set to on.

The
# Complete
# Reference

# Chapter 23

## Configuring ATM on the Nortel Networks Router Platform

**729**

# The Nortel Networks ATM Router Platform

The Nortel Networks ATM router platform consists mainly of Intelligent Link Interface (ILI) combinations of an ATM Routing Engine (ARE) processor and ATM Link Module, FRE2/ATM Link Module ILIs, or the System 5000 5782 series router. Although these options may differ in processing power (the ARE processor card is recommended over the FRE2 for purposes of ATM routing) and design (the 5782 series is a single slot card for the System 5000 chassis, much like the 5380 Ethernet router or 5580 token ring router card), the configuration of each is essentially the same from an ATM standpoint, and each shares essentially the same feature and command set.

The ARE generally is used to route between LAN Emulation Clients (LECs), which allows for ATM routing between different Emulated LANs (ELANs) in a LAN Emulation (LANE) environment. This chapter concentrates on the configuration and troubleshooting of LECs, as well as the configuration and troubleshooting of permanent virtual circuit (PVC) connections.

## Configuring Permanent Virtual Circuits

Configuring a PVC on the Nortel Networks router begins by selecting the appropriate ATM interface from the primary Configuration Manager window. For the purposes of this example, a Backbone Link Node (BLN) router is used, with an ARE/OC-3 Multi-Mode fiber ILI module inserted in slot 5. To begin the PVC configuration, click the ATM interface for that module (see Figure 23-1).

Clicking this interface opens the Add Circuit window. By default, the ATM circuit being created is associated with the interface that was clicked to open the Add Circuit window. The circuit is assigned a name; by default, this name is in the following format: *Axy*, where *A* indicates ATM, *x* indicates the slot number, and *y* indicates the port number. So, for slot 5, port 1 (in the case of ATM, only one port is present on each link module), the default circuit name is A51.

If the defaults are to be used, simply click OK, at which point Site Manager returns to the primary Configuration Manager window. Notice that the ATM connector that was selected has now changed color from blue to white, indicating that it has been configured with a circuit.

After you complete these initial steps, click the ATM connector again. This opens the Select Connection Type window. The options in this window include ATM and MPLS (*Multi-Protocol Layer Switching*, which is not used in this configuration). Select ATM to open the Initial ATM Signaling Config window:

```
Initial ATM Signaling Config                                    [X]

      Configuration Mode: local                    [ Cancel ]
              SNMP Agent: LOCAL FILE                [   OK   ]
                                                    [ Values...]
                                                    [ Help... ]

      Enable ATM Signaling                 [DISABLE              ]
      Max Number of SVC Applications       [                     ]
      Max Point to Point Connections       [                     ]
      Max Point to MultiPoint Connections  [                     ]
      Max Parties In MultiPoint Connections[                     ]
      Protocol Standard
```

This is where the initial signaling parameters are set up.

By default, ATM Signaling is Enabled. Later in this chapter, when a LEC is being created, this parameter will remain enabled. PVCs do not use ATM signaling, however, so this option should be set to Disable, by highlighting the option Enable ATM Signaling and then clicking Values; signaling is disabled by clicking the radio button labeled Disable.

```
Configuration Manager                                     [_][□][X]
Configuration Mode: local
        SNMP Agent: LOCAL FILE
         File Name: C:\WF\CONFIG\ATM.CFG
             Model: Backbone Link Node (BLN)
       MIB Version: 13.10

                                   Color Key:  [ Used ]  [ Unused ]

Slot            Description                    Connectors

 5    [ AG13110112 ARE, OC-3 MM, STS-3 ]                    [ ATM1 ]

 4    [      5450   Quad Ethernet     ]  [XCUR4][XCUR3][XCUR2][XCUR1]

 3    [      5450   Quad Ethernet     ]  [XCUR4][XCUR3][XCUR2][XCUR1]

 2    [ 5710   Dual Token Ring (4/16Mb) ]        [ TOKEN2 ]  [ TOKEN1 ]

 1    [   System Resource Module      ]  [ CONSOLE ]
```

**Figure 23-1.** *The ATM connector in the main Configuration Manager window*

Once this is done, all the other LANE-specific parameters are grayed out, because disabling signaling tells the router that the default ATM connection type will be PVCs and thus, at least for this circuit, the signaling parameters are irrelevant.

Clicking OK brings up the Edit ATM Connector window. Here, the Service Attributes, the Multi-Protocol Over ATM (MPOA) parameters, and the ATM signaling parameters can be accessed. Since neither MPOA nor signaling will be used to construct the PVC, click Service Attributes, which brings up the ATM Service Records List window. At first, this window is mostly grayed out, because no service record currently exists. To create a new service record, click Add, which brings up the ATM Service Record Parameters window:

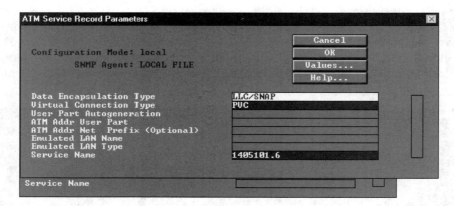

The service record is a logical entity to which the internetworking protocols will be associated; for instance, in a LANE environment, the LEC would be part of the service record.

*Prior to code version 13.10, MPOA was not supported on the router platform. The feature made its first appearance in Site Manager version 7.10. Depending on the Site Manager version and Bay RS version being used, the feature may not be available, even though the option is available in Site Manager.*

## Configuring the PVC

The PVC is created and configured from the ATM Service Record Parameters window. Notice that since ATM Signaling was set to Disable back in the Initial ATM Signaling Config window, the default Virtual Connection Type is set to PVC. Had signaling been enabled, the Virtual Connection Type would have defaulted to switched virtual circuit (SVC). Leave the default of PVC.

## PVC Encapsulation Types

A PVC encapsulation type must also be selected. By default, LLC/SNAP encapsulation is used. The available encapsulation types have the following significance:

■ **LANE**    Refers to LAN Emulation encapsulation, and should be used only if ATM signaling is enabled and LANE is being used. This option is selected if a LEC is being configured.

■ **LLC/SNAP**    Used with ATM PVCs and provides LLC encapsulation, which is required if multiple routed or bridged protocols are being used, because the protocol identifier (PID) is included in the 802.2 LLC header. This is the default option and is used for most PVC applications.

■ **NLPID (Network Layer Protocol ID)**    Indicates that a protocol ID will be attributed to the frame in the encapsulation.

■ **NULL**    Indicates virtual-channel-based multiplexing, which does not support bridging.

Again, for most applications, the default encapsulation type of LLC/SNAP is appropriate. After you select the encapsulation type, click OK. This opens the Select Protocols window.

## Selecting a Protocol

After you build the PVC, you can configure additional protocols on the PVC VPort. For the sake of this example, the PVC being configured will be configured for both bridging and IP routing. Select the following protocols from the Select Protocols window: Bridge, Spanning Tree, IP, and OSPF/MOSPF. After you select the protocols, click OK.

Since Spanning Tree was selected as one of the protocols to be run on this PVC, clicking OK from the Select Protocols window brings up the Spanning Tree Autoconfiguration window. Here, Spanning Tree can be enabled or disabled, the Bridge Priority can be set, and the Max Age, Hello Time, and Forward Delay can be set. For more information regarding these parameters, consult Chapter 2.

Bear in mind that the lowest Bridge Priority results in the associated bridge becoming the root bridge in the Spanning Tree network; most bridges and switches utilize a default Bridge Priority of 8000 in hex, which calculates to 32,768 in decimal.

Clicking OK causes Site Manager to prompt "Do you want to edit the Spanning Tree Interface details?" Clicking Yes brings up another window, labeled Edit Spanning Tree Interface: A51 (though the interface designation may vary, depending on the slot and port of the ATM interface). Here, the specific Spanning Tree interface can be enabled or disabled, and the port priority and path cost associated with that interface can be altered. Clicking OK brings up the IP Configuration window.

## Configuring IP

From the IP Configuration window, add the IP address associated with this PVC, as well as the subnet mask. You must specify a broadcast address; by default, this is set to 0.0.0.0, which indicates that the host portion of whatever IP address and mask were configured will be set to all 1's. So, in the case of the address 150.50.10.1/24, the broadcast address would be 150.50.10.255.

After you configure the IP parameters, click OK. In this case, because Open Shortest Path First (OSPF) is the routing protocol that was selected in the initial Select Protocol window, the OSPF Global Parameters window opens. OSPF, RIP, and RIPv2 configuration are covered in Chapters 32 and 34, so the specific OSPF configuration is not covered in this chapter.

## Assigning the VPI/VCI Pair

After you configure the protocol-specific parameters, the ATM Virtual Channel Link window opens, in which you must add a PVC. By default, before any PVCs have been built, the options associated with this window are grayed out. To add the new PVC, click Add. This opens a smaller window, labeled ATM Virtual Channel Link Parameters (see Figure 23-2). Here, a VPI/VCI pair must be assigned.

Remember that the first 31 VCI values on VPI 0 are reserved for LANE signaling, and thus are not available for use when building PVCs. Select an appropriate VPI/VCI pair and then click OK. This returns you to the ATM Virtual Channel Link window, in

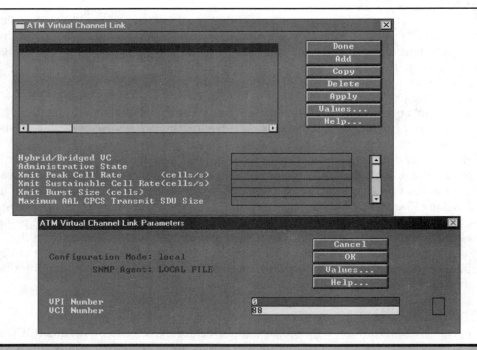

**Figure 23-2.**    *ATM Virtual Channel Link (background) and ATM Virtual Channel Link Parameters (foreground) windows*

which the parameters that were formerly grayed out are now accessible. The following parameters can be set:

■ **Hybrid/Bridged VC**   Indicates whether the PVC being configured will be a hybrid/bridged PVC.

■ **Administrative State**   The administrative state of the PVC; setting this option to Disabled keeps the PVC up, but it will not pass data.

■ **Xmit Peak Cell Rate**   The Peak Cell Rate (PCR) defined on the particular PVC, configured in cells per second. The default value is 2,358, but it may be configured between 128-353,207 for an OC-3 connection and 128-96,000 for a DS-3 connection. This parameter defines the maximum cells/second rate that the PVC can support.

■ **Xmit Sustainable Cell Rate**   The Sustainable Cell Rate (SCR) defined on the particular PVC, configured in cells per second. The default value is 2,358, though the SCR can be set between 128-353,207 for an OC-3 connection and 128-96,000 for a DS-3 connection. This parameter indicates what the average cell rate for the PVC should be. This value should not exceed the PCR.

**Note**   *When using ATM/FRE2 ILI combinations, the SCR value should be set no lower than 300 cells per second.*

■ **Xmit Burst Size**   The maximum burst size (MBS) for the PVC being configured. By default, this value is set to 40. This indicates the maximum cell burst the VC is configured to handle. This parameter relates to ATM/FRE2 ILI combinations and is ignored when using either ATM/ARE ILI combinations or the 5780 series ATM routers.

■ **Maximum AAL CPCS Transmit SDU Size**   The maximum ATM adaption layer (AAL) common part convergence sublayer (CPCS) transmit service data unit (SDU) size that the PVC will accept. This is the maximum packet size the PVC will use. The default is 4,608 bytes.

■ **Maximum AAL CPCS Receive SDU Size**   The maximum ATM adaption layer common part convergence sublayer receive service data unit size that the PVC will accept. This is the maximum packet size the PVC will use. The default size is 4,608 bytes.

■ **Data Encapsulation Type**   You select the data encapsulation type here. The default value is LLC/SNAP encapsulation. For more information regarding the data encapsulation type, consult the earlier sections of this chapter.

■ **OAM Loopback Enable**   Toggles whether Operation and Management (OAM) cells are looped back over the PVC, for purposes of monitoring PVC integrity.

ATM ON NORTEL
NETWORKS

If multiple PVCs exist on a single service record and this feature is to be used, then OAM loopback should be enabled on all PVCs within that service record.

- **OAM Loopback Cell Interval**   Indicates how often OAM loopback cells are transmitted across the PVC.

- **OAM Loopback Threshold 1**   Threshold 1 defines how many consecutive OAM loopback cells can be lost before the PVC is considered to be nonoperational.

- **OAM Loopback Threshold 2**   Threshold 2 defines how many consecutive OAM loopback cells must be received on a PVC that has been deemed nonoperational due to exceeding threshold 1 before that PVC is considered to have entered back into an operational state.

- **OAM Alarm Enable**   When enabled, causes the upper-layer protocols to be notified in the event of an OAM loopback alarm (if the device the router is connected to supports it). If disabled, the upper-layer protocols are not informed of any such failures.

## Troubleshooting PVCs on the Router Platform

Troubleshooting ATM PVCs on the Nortel Networks router platform can be accomplished by using the **show atm vcs** and **show atm stats vcs scripts** commands, if the ATM scripts have been loaded (see Chapter 31). PVCs can also be viewed in detail by using the MIB from the Technician Interface (TI). The following is some of the output from polling the wfAtmAlcDrvEntry MIB; remember that this command results in many more entries than are shown here—for this example, some of the more relevant entries are targeted specifically:

```
[1:2]$ g wfAtmAlcDrvEntry.*.3.1
wfAtmAlcDrvEntry.wfAtmAlc.wfAtmAlcState.3.1 = 1
wfAtmAlcDrvEntry.wfAtmAlc.wfAtmAlcXmtPacketClips.3.1 = 0
wfAtmAlcDrvEntry.wfAtmAlc.wfAtmAlcMadr.3.1 = x00 x00 xA2 x14 xFE x01
```

The preceding entries describe, in order, the interface state (where 1 indicates that the interface is up), the amount of cells clipped due to lack of resources in the transmit buffer, and the MAC address associated with the interface. Particular VPI/VCI pairs also can be specifically targeted through the TI.

The following entry indicates slot 5 (of a BLN in this case):

```
[1:2]$ g wfAtmizerIntfStatsEntry.*.5.1
wfAtmizerIntfStatsEntry.wfAtmizerIntf.5.1 = 5
```

The following entry indicates port 1 of slot 5:

```
wfAtmizerIntfStatsEntry.wfAtmizerPort.5.1 = 1
```

A status of 1 in the following entry indicates that the interface is active:

```
wfAtmizerIntfStatsEntry.wfAtmizerIntfLastChange.5.1 = 1831
wfAtmizerIntfStatsEntry.wfAtmizerIntfOutQLen.5.1 = 0
wfAtmizerIntfStatsEntry.wfAtmizerIntfStatus.5.1 = 1
```

The number of received (good) packets on the interface is listed in the following entry:

```
wfAtmizerIntfStatsEntry.wfAtmizerIntfIndex.5.1 = 2
wfAtmizerIntfStatsEntry.wfAtmizerIntfOcdEvents.5.1 = 0
wfAtmizerIntfStatsEntry.wfAtmizerIntfTcAlarmState.5.1 = 1
wfAtmizerIntfStatsEntry.wfAtmizerIntfRxRacketsOkWrap.5.1 = 0
wfAtmizerIntfStatsEntry.wfAtmizerIntfRxPacketsOk.5.1 = 102182938
```

The following entry indicates the total number of received good cells:

```
wfAtmizerIntfStatsEntry.wfAtmizerIntfRxCellsOkWrap.5.1 = 0
wfAtmizerIntfStatsEntry.wfAtmizerIntfRxCellsOk.5.1 = 204593882
wfAtmizerIntfStatsEntry.wfAtmizerIntfRxOamCount.5.1 = 0
wfAtmizerIntfStatsEntry.wfAtmizerIntfRxFlowCtrlCount.5.1 = 0
wfAtmizerIntfStatsEntry.wfAtmizerIntfRxInvalidHeaders.5.1 = 0
```

The preceding entry could potentially be related to a misconfigured PVC; although it counts the number of cells with a bad value in the header field (which could be caused by an invalid Payload Type Identifier (PTI), or corruption in the header itself), this also includes invalid VPI/VCI values that could result if two ends of a PVC connection are mismatched.

Oversized SDUs, indicated in the following entry, may be a result of a misconfigured MTU size somewhere across the PVC:

```
wfAtmizerIntfStatsEntry.wfAtmizerIntfRxOverSizedSDUs.5.1 = 0
```

The following counter indicates the number of CRC errors during the cell reassembly into frames. This could be due to missing cells clipped along the way or lost due to line corruption.

```
wfAtmizerIntfStatsEntry.wfAtmizerIntfRxCrcErrors.5.1 = 0
```

The following entry is the total number of good packets transmitted on the interface:

```
wfAtmizerIntfStatsEntry.wfAtmizerIntfRxCrc10Errors.5.1 = 0
wfAtmizerIntfStatsEntry.wfAtmizerIntfRxLackBufCredits.5.1 = 0
wfAtmizerIntfStatsEntry.wfAtmizerIntfRxLackPageCredits.5.1 = 0
wfAtmizerIntfStatsEntry.wfAtmizerIntfRxLackBufResc.5.1 = 0
wfAtmizerIntfStatsEntry.wfAtmizerIntfRxLackPageResc.5.1 = 0
wfAtmizerIntfStatsEntry.wfAtmizerIntfTxPacketsOkWrap.5.1 = 0
wfAtmizerIntfStatsEntry.wfAtmizerIntfTxPacketsOk.5.1 = 102183938
```

The following entry is the total number of good cells transmitted on the interface:

```
wfAtmizerIntfStatsEntry.wfAtmizerIntfTxCellsOkWrap.5.1 = 0
wfAtmizerIntfStatsEntry.wfAtmizerIntfTxCellsOk.5.1 = 204594882
```

The following entry is the number of OAM cells transmitted:

```
wfAtmizerIntfStatsEntry.wfAtmizerIntfTxOamCount.5.1 = 0
```

The following entry is definitely something to look for if a PVC is not being established as expected; the counter indicates the number of times that cells were dropped because the requested VPI/VCI pair was invalid:

```
wfAtmizerIntfStatsEntry.wfAtmizerIntfTxFlowCtrlCount.5.1 = 0
wfAtmizerIntfStatsEntry.wfAtmizerIntfTxBadVcs.5.1 = 0
```

# Configuring a LAN Emulation Client

Because a router connection into a switched environment constitutes a User to Network Interface (UNI), a LEC must be built to serve a LANE network. It is this LEC that will act as the ATM routed interface. The sections following describe how to configure a LEC, as well as how to fine-tune several more advanced control parameters. Before beginning this section, be aware that not every parameter covered needs to be altered, and that some, if not most of them, can be left at their defaults and still result in a functional LEC. The conclusion of this section provides a brief walkthrough of the minimum required LEC configuration.

Configuring a LEC on the Nortel Networks router is accomplished by first selecting the appropriate ATM interface from the primary Configuration Manager window. For purposes of this example, a BLN router is used, with an ARE/OC-3 Multi-Mode fiber ILI module inserted in slot 3. To begin the LEC configuration, click the ATM interface for that module.

Clicking this interface opens the Add Circuit window. By default, the ATM circuit being created is associated with the interface that was clicked to open this window. The circuit is assigned a name; by default, this name is in the following format: *Axy*, where *A* indicates ATM, *x* indicates the slot number, and *y* indicates the port number. So, for slot 3, port 1, the default circuit name is A31.

If the defaults are to be used, simply click OK. Site Manager then returns to the primary Configuration Manager window. Notice that the ATM connector that was selected has now changed color from blue to white, indicating that it has been configured with a circuit.

After you complete these initial steps, click the ATM connector again. This opens the Select Connection Type window. The options in this window include ATM and MPLS. MPLS will not be used in this configuration. Click ATM to open the Initial ATM Signaling Config window, which is where the initial signaling parameters are set up:

By default, the Enable ATM Signaling parameter is set to Enable. Since ATM signaling must be active to support LANE, this parameter should be left at its default. The remaining parameters are some of the LANE-specific signaling parameters:

- **Max Number of SVC Applications**   Defines how many applications that use SVCs are supported on the ATM interface. In this context, the LEC itself is considered an SVC application, because it will generate and receive SVCs in the course of network operation. The default value for this parameter is 20; this effectively means that, while utilizing the default value, only 20 LEC entities will be supported on a single interface. This parameter can be set between 1 and 32,767 (although, in reality, far fewer than 32,767 LECs will be configured). This parameter is directly related to the Max Point to MultiPoint Connections parameter and the Max Point to Point.

- **Max Point to Point Connections**   Defines the maximum number of point-to-point connections that can exist on a single interface. Point-to-point connections include control channels to the LES and BUS, as well as Data Direct VCCs to other remote LECs. The default value is 1000, but it can be changed to any number between 0 and 32,767.

- **Max Point to MultiPoint Connections**   Defines the maximum number of point-to-multipoint connections that can exist on a single interface. Point-to-multipoint connections primarily consist of the LANE control channels to the LES and BUS—the Control Distribute VCC and the Multicast Forward VCC. For this reason, the default value for this parameter is 40, which is twice that of the Max Number of SVC Applications parameter default value—if 20 LEC entities are to be supported, those LECs need 40 point-to-multipoint connections, two for each LEC. This value should always be set to at least twice that of the Max Number of SVC Applications parameter.

- **Max Parties in MultiPoint Connections**   Indicates the maximum number of other parties that may be members of a point-to-multipoint connection. Bear in mind that this means point-to-multipoint connections originating at the router, so this does not include point-to-multipoint connections such as the Control Distribute VCC and Multicast Forward VCC, which originate at the LES and BUS, respectively. The default value is 1.

- **Protocol Standard**   Select the UNI version here. Currently, UNI 3.0 and UNI 3.1 are supported.

For this example, the defaults are used, except that the UNI version used will be UNI 3.1. Highlight the Protocol Standard and click Values to change the UNI type. Click OK, which brings up the Edit ATM Connector window.

## Configuring the Service Attributes

After configuring the initial parameters, the specific service attributes must be defined. From the Edit ATM Connector window, click Service Attributes, which will display the ATM Service Records List window. By default, this window is grayed out until a new service record is added. Click Add to bring up the ATM Service Record Parameters window:

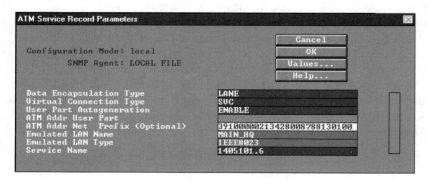

A default Data Encapsulation Type of LANE is selected, because ATM Signaling was set to Enable back in the Initial ATM Signaling Config window, indicating LANE will be used. Likewise, the Virtual Connection Type has defaulted to SVC in this case, whereas if signaling had been disabled, the Virtual Connection Type would default to PVC.

The rest of the parameters all have to do with the LEC's ATM address registration, as well as the ELAN it is being configured to join:

- **User Part Autogeneration**   Can be enabled or disabled. By default, it is enabled, and instructs the router to automatically generate a 6-byte End System Identifier (ESI) for the LEC ATM address. It does this by using the MAC address as the ESI (clients maintain uniqueness, as the selector byte is incremented for each new LEC). Alternately, this parameter can be disabled, and the ESI manually configured (see the following parameter).

- **ATM Addr User Part**   If the previous field, User Part Autogeneration, is set to Enable, then this field is grayed out, because the ESI will be automatically generated by the router. If User Part Autogeneration is set to Disable, then the ESI must be manually configured here.

**Note**

*From a technical standpoint, although no difference exists between automatically generating the ESI and manually configuring one, manually configuring an ESI can make tracking LEC entities simpler in the event of troubleshooting. For instance, a LEC with an ESI of AA.AA.AA.AA.AA.AA is easier to identify in a switch's LES or BUS client table than a MAC address. If this technique is used consistently, key router LECs can be quickly targeted and their presence or absence from the LES or BUS table can be quickly determined.*

- **ATM Addr Net Prefix (Optional)**   The 13-byte ATM NSAP prefix may be defined. This parameter is considered optional, because the NSAP prefix will be obtained from the switch to which the router is attached in the event that this field is left blank. This occurs over the Interim Local Management Interface (ILMI) channel during the normal address registration process. Alternately, the prefix can be manually configured. If the prefix is statically defined, it must match the NSAP prefix of the switch to which it is attached.

- **Emulated LAN name**   The name of the ELAN the LEC will join. ELAN names are case-sensitive.

- **Emulated LAN Type**   The ELAN type is specified. Three options are available: IEEE8023, which indicates an Ethernet 802.3 ELAN, IEEE8025, which indicates a token ring 802.5 ELAN, or Unspecified, in which case the LAN type is dynamically determined.

After configuring these parameters, click OK to bring up the Select Protocols window, which is used to select the various protocols that will run over the LEC interface.

## Configuring Protocols for the LEC

After you create the LEC, you are prompted to assign which protocols will be configured on the LEC. From the Select Protocols window, select the protocols the LEC will use. For this example, IP will be configured, along with Bridging Services and the Spanning Tree Protocol. The routing protocol will be OSPF. Select these protocols from the provided list, and click OK. Since one of the selected protocols is the Spanning Tree Protocol, the Spanning Tree Autoconfiguration window opens. In this window, Spanning Tree can be enabled or disabled, the Bridge Priority can be set, and the Max Age, Hello Time, and Forward Delay can be set. For more information regarding these parameters, consult Chapter 2.

Remember that the lowest Bridge Priority results in the associated bridge becoming the root bridge in the Spanning Tree network; most bridges and switches utilize a default Bridge Priority of 8000 in hex, which calculates to 32,768 in decimal.

Clicking OK causes Site Manager to prompt "Do you want to edit the Spanning Tree Interface details?" Clicking Yes brings up another window, labeled Edit Spanning Tree Interface: A31 (though the interface designation may vary, depending on the slot and port of the ATM interface). Here, the specific Spanning Tree interface can be enabled or disabled, and the port priority and path cost associated with that interface can be altered. Clicking OK invokes the IP Configuration window.

## Configuring IP

From the IP Configuration window, add the IP address associated with this LEC, as well as the subnet mask. A broadcast address must be specified; by default, this is set to 0.0.0.0, which indicates that the host portion of whatever IP address and mask were configured will be set to all 1's. So, in the case of the address 150.50.10.1/24, the broadcast address would be 150.50.10.255.

After configuring the IP parameters, click OK. In this case, because OSPF is the routing protocol that was selected in the initial Select Protocol window, the OSPF Global Parameters window opens. OSPF, RIP, and RIPv2 configuration are covered in Chapters 32 and 34, so the specific OSPF configuration will not be covered in this chapter.

## Further Configuration of the LEC

Upon completing the specific protocol configuration of the LEC, the ATM Service Records List window opens:

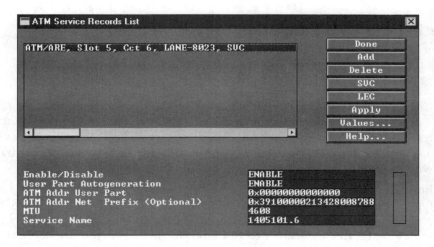

Here, the newly created LEC is present in the display box, specifying the circuit number, the LAN type, and the virtual connection type.

A series of options appears to the right of the service record list, as well as a series of parameters in the lower portion of the window. These parameters mostly echo the parameters configured in the ATM Service Record Parameters window, with the addition of the MTU parameter, described as follows:

- **MTU**   The maximum transmit unit (MTU) that the LEC will accept must also be defined; although the incoming packets will undergo segmentation into cells, these cells must be reassembled at each destination LEC, so MTU sizes must be kept consistent. The default value is 4,608 bytes.

  The buttons to the right of the display window allow additional LECs to be configured, existing LECs to be deleted, the current configuration to be applied to the router ATM interface, or the ATM Service Records List window to be exited by clicking Done. Two other options appear:

- **SVC**   Clicking this button opens the ATM Switched Virtual Circuit List window; during an offline configuration, where the router isn't being specifically communicated with via Site Manager, this window is blank. If the router is being actively polled, however, a list of all existing SVCs associated with this LEC is displayed. In addition to viewing the SVCs, they can be individually removed from the service record by selecting the desired circuit and clicking Delete.

- **LEC**   Clicking this button brings up the LAN Emulation Parameters window, which allows for more specific LEC configuration.

## Targeting the LAN Emulation Server

From the LAN Emulation Parameters window, the method of finding the LAN Emulation Server (LES) may be defined. This is accomplished by configuring the following parameters:

- **Configuration Mode**    By default, set to Automatic, indicating that the LEC will obtain its LES address from a LECS. Also by default, if Configuration Mode remains set to Automatic, the LECS address targeted by the LEC will be the well known address (WKA). The WKA is the address to which LECSs default when configured on a switch.

- **Emulated LAN Type**    If a LECS is being used, the LEC can obtain the LAN type from the LECS during the exchange of the LE_CONFIGURE_REQUEST and LE_CONFIGURE_RESPONSE control frames. Alternately, the LAN type can be configured statically. If a LECS is not being used, the LAN type should be specified here.

- **Maximum Data Frame Size**    The maximum data frame size can be statically defined here, or, if a LECS is being used, this Time, Length, Value (TLV) can be obtained dynamically.

- **Emulated LAN Name**    The ELAN name must be configured here, if it hasn't been defined already. If the ELAN name was previously defined, it appears in this field. ELAN names are case-sensitive.

If a LECS is not being used (the Configuration Mode parameter is set to Manual), then the LES button must be clicked so that the LES address can be statically defined.

## Statically Defining the LAN Emulation Server

Clicking the LES button brings up a window labeled ATM LES List. By default, no LES addresses are present, and the individual address or series of addresses must be added. Click the Add button to bring up the window you see here:

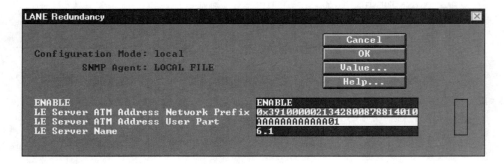

This window is referred to as the LANE Redundancy window for a couple of reasons:

■ A LES address can be statically configured so that a LECS isn't necessary, or to provide redundancy in the event that the LECS can't be reached.

■ It allows multiple LES addresses to be entered in the event that redundant or cooperating LES/BUS pairs are being used.

In this window, the use of the LES address can be enabled and configured. The NSAP prefix must be defined, followed by the User Part, which includes the ESI and selector byte. For example, the NSAP prefix might be 39102030000000000000000000, and the User Part might be configured as AAAAAAAAAAAA01. These values are not arbitrary; they must match exactly the NSAP prefix and ESI/selector byte of the actual LES configured in the switched portion of the ATM network. The LE Server Name defaults to a numeric value; the default can be used in this case. This parameter does not refer to the ELAN name.

**ADDING MORE LES INSTANCES**   After you define the LES address, click OK to return to the ATM LES List window, in which the newly configured LES will now be listed. The Add button at this point is immediately followed by a new option, Add After, which allows additional LES addresses to be defined, to be added after the first instance. This is used in a scenario where multiple redundant or cooperating LES addresses are configured in the network; the LEC attempts to reach the LES that was defined first, and if it is unable to reach the primary LES for any reason, it then tries the next LES in the LES list.

After each of the individual LES addresses have been defined and added to the LES List, click Apply and then click Done to return to the LAN Emulation Parameters window.

## Configuring Advanced LEC Parameters

Also available from the LAN Emulation Parameters window are some of the more advanced LEC parameters. These options are available from the parameter list in the lower portion of the window:

■ **Control Timeout**   Defines how long (in seconds) the LEC will wait after issuing a request frame, such as an LE_CONFIGURE_REQUEST to the LECS or an LE_JOIN_REQUEST to the LES, before expecting the corresponding response frame. This value can be set to between 5 and 32,3767, with a default of 5.

■ **Max Unknown Frame Count**   Works in conjunction with the Max Unknown Frame Time, and defines how many unknown frames can be issued within the time period defined in the Max Unknown Frame Time. This helps to limit the number of unknown frames sent to the BUS for processing.

■ **Max Unknown Frame Time**   Works in conjunction with the Max Unknown Frame Count, and defines the interval of time in which the number of unknown frames defined in the Max Unknown Frame Count parameter can be sent. This helps to limit the number of unknown frames sent to the BUS for processing.

**Note**

*The Centillion C100/C50/5000BH series switches also utilize a parameter called Unknown Frame Pacing, which provides similar protection to the BUS to prevent it from becoming overwhelmed with unknown frames. Unknown frames are considered any frame for which the destination LEC has not been determined and, therefore, must be sent over the BUS control channels. As a troubleshooting tool, Unknown Frame Pacing, or BUS Pacing, may be disabled on the switches to remove the flow control over the BUS. This will help you determine whether performance problems are caused by the failure of one or more LECs to properly build a Data Direct VCC, therefore causing data transfers to occur across the BUS entirely. Recall that if one of the LECs in question exists on the router, then disabling Unknown Frame Pacing on the switches alone will not provide an accurate test, because the Max Unknown Frame Count and Max Unknown Frame Time may still be controlling the flow to the BUS. In this circumstance, these parameters may need to be altered as well.*

■ **VCC Timeout Period**   Can be set to Enable or Disable. If enabled, idle Data Direct VCCs will time out and be torn down after the specified timeout time (the default for both the router and the Centillion series switches is 1,200 seconds). If disabled, idle VCCs never time out.

■ **Max Retry Count**   Defines the number of times a LEC will reissue an LE_ARP_REQUEST if it does not receive a response. This can be set to 1 or 2 times, with a default of 1.

■ **Aging Time**   Defines the amount of time (in seconds) that an entry remains in the LEC's LE_ARP cache before aging out. This can be set to between 10 and 300 seconds, with a default of 300 seconds (5 minutes).

■ **Forward Delay Time**   Indicates how long a nonlocal MAC address remains in the LEC's LE_ARP cache without being refreshed.

■ **Expected LE_ARP Response Time**   Defines the amount of time (in seconds) that the LEC waits for an LE_ARP_RESPONSE before determining that the response is not coming and that the LE_ARP_REQUEST must be reissued in accordance with the Max Retry Count parameter. This parameter can be set to a value between 1 and 30 seconds, with a default of 3.

■ **Flush Timeout**   Once a Data Direct VCC has been built, to ensure that cells do not arrive at the destination out of order, an LE_FLUSH_REQUEST is sent over the BUS control channel, and data flow stops until the LE_FLUSH_RESPONSE is returned, at which point data flow resumes over the Data Direct VCC. If no response frame is received within the Flush Timeout time, data flow resumes over the BUS control channel. The timeout value can be set to between 1 and 4 seconds, with a default of 4.

- **Path Switching Delay**   Can be used to bypass the Flush Protocol; rather than depend on the sending and receiving of LE_FLUSH control frames, the Path Switching Delay simply defines a waiting period between when a LEC stops sending over the BUS control channel and begins sending over a newly formed Data Direct VCC, to ensure the BUS control channel is clear. This delay can be set to between 1 and 8 seconds, with a default of 6. This parameter is observed only if the Flush Protocol is disabled.

- **Emulated LAN Segment ID**   The ring number associated with the LEC's ELAN. It is in decimal format. This parameter is only required for token ring ELANs in source-routed networks.

- **Flush Protocol**   Enables or disables the Flush Protocol. If the Flush Protocol is disabled, the Path Switching Delay determines the amount of time between stopping a data flow over the BUS control channels and resuming that flow over a newly formed Data Direct VCC.

- **LE Config Server ATM Address**   In the switched portion of the network, a LECS address may be user-defined. In this scenario, the user-defined LECS address can be defined here. If left blank, the WKA is used.

- **LAN Emulation Version 2**   Determines whether the configured LEC is LANE version 2-capable. LANEv2-compatibility is required if MPOA is to be used.

## ATM LEC Signaling Parameters

After configuring the initial LEC parameters, Site Manager returns to the Edit ATM Connector window. Here, other ATM parameters can be accessed. You may further alter LANE-specific signaling by clicking ATM Signaling, which opens the ATM Signaling Parameters window:

The initial parameters available in this window were previously defined when the LEC was first created; values such as the UNI version and the maximum number of SVC applications, point-to-point VCCs, point-to-multipoint VCCs, and parties allowed as part of a point-to-multipoint VCC have all been defined previously, but may be altered here. In addition, several other parameters can be adjusted here:

- **Min Memory Threshold**   Defines the minimum percentage of memory required to enable a new call; this percentage will be between 10 and 100 percent, in multiples of 10. The default value is 20 percent.

- **VPI/VCI values**   Set to 0/5 by default. This is the standard ATM signaling channel, and generally should be left at its default VPI/VCI value.

- **T3$xx$ timers**   Each of the T3$xx$ timers can also be adjusted here; for the specific purpose of each timer, consult Chapter 13, which describes each in detail.

- **Num Restarts ReXmitted**   Defines how many RESTART messages can be transmitted before the link is considered to have failed. This will be set to between 1 and 100, with a default value of 3.

- **Num Stat Enquiries ReXmitted**   Defines the number of STATUS ENQUIRY messages that can be sent before the link is considered to have failed; although a STATUS ENQUIRY is not required, if one is used, a STATUS message in response is required. This value can be set to between 1 and 100, with a default of 3.

- **Num Messages/Sec for Call Pacing**   Defines the number of signaling messages that can be sent in one second over the interface. By default, this value is set to 0, which actually disables call pacing and allows the router to negotiate a value with the switch. This parameter can be set to between 0 and 2,147,483,647.

   *If connecting to a switch utilizing the Connection Management System (CMS), this value should be set to 2.*

## Configuring the ATM Signaling Channel

The ATM signaling channel is reserved VPI/VCI channel 0/5 and is used for the basic LANE port-level signaling. From the ATM Signaling Parameters window, the signaling channel VC can be configured specifically by clicking the Sig VC button, which brings up the ATM Control VC for Signaling window, in which the traffic rate and SDU size can be defined. These parameters reflect the signaling channel 0/5 (or another value, if the signaling channel has been changed for some reason) only:

- **Xmit Peak Cell Rate**   The PCR defined on the ATM signaling VC, configured in cells per second. The default value is 2,358, but can be configured between 128-353,207 for an OC-3 connection and 128-96,000 for a DS-3 connection. This parameter defines the maximum cells/second rate that the VC can support.

- **Xmit Sustainable Cell Rate** The SCR defined on the signaling VC, configured in cells per second. The default value is 2,358, but can be set to between 128-353,207 for an OC-3 connection and 128-96,000 for a DS-3 connection. This parameter indicates what the average cell rate for the signaling channel should be. This value should not exceed the PCR.

**Note** *When using ATM/FRE2 ILI combinations, set the SCR value no lower than 300 cells per second.*

- **Xmit Burst Size** Indicates the MBS for the signaling VC. By default, this value is set to 40. This indicates the maximum cell burst the VC is configured to handle. This parameter relates to ATM/FRE2 ILI combinations and is ignored when using either ATM/ARE ILI combinations or the 5780 series ATM routers.

- **Maximum AAL CPCS Transmit SDU Size** Indicates the maximum ATM adaption layer common part convergence sublayer transmit service data unit size the signaling PVC will accept. This is the maximum packet size the signaling channel will use. The default is 4,608 bytes.

- **Maximum AAL CPCS Receive SDU Size** Indicates the maximum ATM adaption layer common part convergence sublayer receive service data unit size the signaling channel will accept. This is the maximum packet size the PVC will use. The default size is 4,608 bytes.

## SAAL Configuration

From the main Edit ATM Connector window, the System-Specific Connection-Oriented Protocol (SSCOP) parameters can be configured. These parameters are concerned mainly with port-level signaling and timing, and can generally be left at their defaults:

- **Link Connection Arbitration** Will be set to either Active or Passive; an active state indicates that this interface is capable of initiating connections. Because this is the desired state for most LANE networks, this should usually be left Active, but can be set to Passive if the interface should accept connections but not initiate them.

- **Poll Timer** Defines how long (in tenths of a second) after a Poll PDU is sent that a response is expected. For each Poll PDU sent, a Stat PDU is expected in response from the receiver. This mechanism allows for quick error recovery if something goes wrong during transmission. This value can be set to between 1 and 120, with a default of 7.

- **Keep Alive Timer** Indicates how often the Poll PDU is sent, defined in tenths of a second. This value can be set to between 1 and 120, with a default of 20.

- **No Response Timer** Defines how long (in tenths of a second) an interval may exist between each Stat PDU received on the interface. This timer works in tandem with the Poll Timer, because not every Poll PDU requires a Stat PDU in response. By running together, a link failure is considered to have occurred if either the Poll Timer or No Response Timer expires. The No Response Timer can be set to between 1 and 120, with a default of 70.

- **Connection Control Timer**   Defines the amount of time (in tenths of a second) that can pass between the transmission of SSCOP control PDUs.

- **Max Connection Control**   Defines the maximum number of each SSCOP control PDU that can be sent without response before an error is indicated. The range is 1 to 20, with a default of 4.

- **Max PD Before Poll**   Defines the maximum value of the poll data state variable before a Poll PDU is transmitted.

- **Max STAT PDU Elements**   Defines the maximum number of elements that can exist within a single STAT PDU. If the number of total elements exceeds this value, the PDU will be segmented. This value can be set to between 3 and 119, and can include odd integers only.

- **Idle Timer**   Indicates how long SSCOP can remain idle. Defaults to 150 tenths of a second, with a range of 1 to 400.

# Configuring Interim Local Management Interface Parameters

UNI connections use ILMI for purposes of ATM address registration with the connected switch, as well as possibly to find a valid LECS. By default, on a router UNI connection, the ILMI state is enabled. ILMI parameters can be accessed from the main Edit ATM Connector window by clicking the Interim Local Management Interface (ILMI) button, which opens the ATM ILMI Signaling Parameters window:

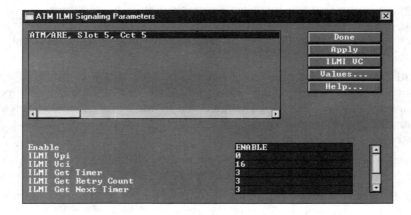

Here, the ILMI state is defined (Enabled, by default), as well as the VPI/VCI pair to be used for ILMI signaling. By default, the ILMI channel uses VPI/VCI pair 0/16; under most circumstances, these should not be altered.

ILMI uses a series of MIB sets and gets; this is, in part, how the ATM address registration takes place, when the ATM NSAP prefix is assigned to the UNI device by the ATM switch it is connected to. The timers associated with these sets and gets can be altered here:

- **ILMI Get Timer**   Indicates the amount of time (in seconds) that can pass between issuing a GET_REQUEST and receiving the expected GET_RESPONSE. The range is between 1 and 120, with a default of 3.

- **ILMI Get Retry Count**   If the ILMI Get Timer expires, this value defines how many additional attempts to send the GET_REQUEST will be made before assuming the line to be down. The range is between 1 and 100, with a default of 3.

- **ILMI Get Next Timer**   Indicates the time (in seconds) that can pass between issuing a GET_NEXT_REQUEST and receiving the expected GET_NEXT_RESPONSE. The range is between 1 and 120, with a default of 3.

- **ILMI Get Next Retry Count**   If the ILMI Get Next Timer expires, this value defines how many additional attempts to send the GET_NEXT_REQUEST will be made before assuming the line to be down. The range is between 1 and 100, with a default of 3.

- **ILMI Set Timer**   Indicates the time (in seconds) that can pass between issuing a SET_REQUEST and receiving the expected SET_RESPONSE. The range is between 1 and 120, with a default of 3.

- **ILMI Set Retry Count**   If the ILMI Set Timer expires, this value defines how many additional attempts to send the SET_REQUEST will be made before assuming the line to be down. The range is between 1 and 100, with a default of 3.

## Configuring the ILMI Channel

From the ATM ILMI Signaling Parameters window, the ILMI channel PVC (0/16, by default) can be configured specifically by clicking the ILMI VC button, which brings up the ATM Control VC for ILMI window, in which traffic rate and SDU size can be defined. These parameters reflect the signaling channel 0/16 only:

- **Xmit Peak Cell Rate**   The PCR defined on the ILMI channel, configured in cells per second. The default value is 2,358, but it can be configured between 128-353,207 for an OC-3 connection and 128-96,000 for a DS-3 connection. This parameter defines the maximum cells/second rate that the ILMI channel can support.

- **Xmit Sustainable Cell Rate**   The SCR defined on the ILMI channel, configured in cells per second. The default value is 2,358, though the SCR can be set between 128-353,207 for an OC-3 connection and 128-96,000 for a DS-3 connection. This parameter indicates what the average cell rate for the ILMI channel should be. This value should not exceed the PCR.

> **Note** When using ATM/FRE2 ILI combinations, set the SCR value no lower than 300 cells per second.

- **Xmit Burst Size** Indicates the MBS for the ILMI channel. By default, this value is set to 40. This indicates the maximum cell burst the VC is configured to handle. This parameter relates to ATM/FRE2 ILI combinations and is ignored when using either ATM/ARE ILI combinations or the 5780 series ATM routers.

- **Maximum AAL CPCS Transmit SDU Size** Indicates the maximum ATM adaption layer common part convergence sublayer transmit service data unit size the ILMI channel will accept. This is the maximum packet size ILMI will use. The default is 4,608 bytes.

- **Maximum AAL CPCS Receive SDU Size** Indicates the maximum ATM adaption layer common part convergence sublayer receive service data unit size that the ILMI channel will accept. This is the maximum packet size ILMI will use. The default size is 4,608 bytes.

## ATM Interface Parameters

After configuring the LEC, you can access individual ATM interface parameters may be accessed from the Set Connection Type window by clicking the Interface Attributes button. This displays the ATM Interface Attributes window:

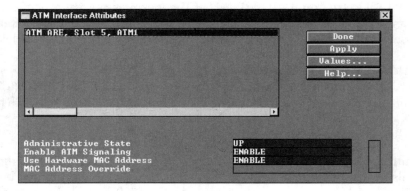

From this window, ATM Signaling may be enabled or disabled, and the ESI portion of the LEC ATM address altered.

- **Enable ATM Signaling** Enables and disables ATM signaling on the interface. ATM signaling is a required component of LANE.

- **Use Hardware MAC Address**    Determines whether the router MAC address will be used in generating the ESI portion of the LEC ATM address. If set to Disable, the MAC Address Override field must be completed.

- **MAC Address Override**    If the ESI portion of the LEC ATM Address is not being generated automatically, then the manually configured ESI must be entered here. This is the ESI only and does not include the selector byte.

## ATM Line Attributes

Specific ATM line driver attributes can also be configured after the initial LEC parameters have been set; these parameters deal primarily with the interface MTU size, SVC timeout values, clocking, and framing. This is accomplished from the Select Connection Type window by clicking Line Attributes, which brings up the ATM/ARE Line Driver Attributes window:

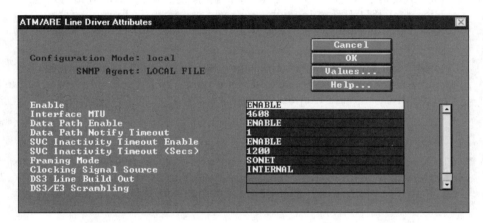

From this window, several line-specific parameters can be set:

- **Interface MTU**    Defines the maximum transmit unit the interface will accept.

- **Data Path Enable**    Defines whether or not the interface between the line driver and the higher-level software is checked in the event that the connection becomes disconnected. If this parameter is enabled, a Data Path Notify Timeout must be defined. If disabled, the driver will not disconnect.

- **Data Path Notify Timeout**    If the Data Path Enable parameter is set to Enable, this parameter is used to determine how long after the interface becomes disconnected the driver itself is disconnected. The range is 0 to 3,600 seconds, with a default of 1.

- **SVC Inactivity Timeout Enable**    Indicates whether inactive SVCs will time out. If set to Disable, individual SVCs will never time out once they are established. This can cut down on setup time, but may eventually cause the number of point-to-point connections to exceed the maximum number defined in the ATM Signaling Parameters window. If this parameter is set to Enable, then an SVC Inactivity Timeout must be defined.

- **SVC Inactivity Timeout (Sec)**   Indicates the amount of time an idle SVC will remain up before it times out and is torn down. This value is ignored if the SVC Inactivity Timeout Enable parameter is set to Disable. The valid range for this parameter is 60 to 3,600 seconds (1 to 60 minutes), with a default of 1,200 seconds (20 minutes).

- **Framing Mode**   Here, the ATM framing mode can be selected. The valid framing types are SDH, SONET, CBIT, M23, G751, and G832. The type of framing that should be used depends on the type of ATM interface being configured:

  **OC-3/OC-12**   OC-3 or OC-12 interfaces use either Synchronous Digital Hierarchy (SDH) framing, which is used primarily in Europe, or the Synchronous Optical Network (SONET) framing that is used in North America.

  **DS-3**   DS-3 interfaces use either the CBIT or the M23 framing mode. DS-3 connections are for wide area ATM support, and the proper framing mode is generally assigned by a public provider.

  **E3**   E3 interfaces use either the G751 or G832 framing mode. E3 interfaces are generally used in Europe.

- **Clocking Signal Source**   Dictates whether the clocking source will be internal or external. If an internal clocking source is being used, this parameter should be set to Internal. If external clocking is being used, this value should be set to Loop.

- **DS3 Line Build Out**   For use only with DS-3 interfaces, and relates to the amount of attenuation a signal is created to withstand; depending on the length of the line being used, the Line Build Out must be set to Short or Long. A Short line is considered a line that is 225 feet or less, whereas any line exceeding 225 feet is considered Long.

- **DS3/E3 Scrambling**   Activating scrambling on a DS-3 or E3 interface causes the interface to scramble the ATM cell payload of individual cells, which aids in maintaining cell synchronization. This parameter must be consistent between interfaces; if scrambling is enabled on one side of the connection, it must be enabled for both sides.

- **Per-VC Clipping**   Enables *clipping* (the dropping of cells that can't be buffered) on a VC-by-VC basis.

# Minimum LEC Configuration Walkthrough

The previous sections covered many of the detailed ATM parameters; depending on the implementation, more or less configuration may be required, and which specific parameters need to be altered varies according to the design. In general, however, a minimal configuration is enough to at least allow the LEC to initialize. The minimum configuration required for a LEC is very brief.

## Configuring the LEC

Configuring a LEC on the router platform involves five main steps:

1. Adding the circuit.

2. Configuring ATM signaling.

3. Adding the LEC.

4. Defining how the LES will be reached.

5. Assigning the appropriate protocols to the LEC.

Each of these steps is covered in the sections that follow. The first thing that needs to be done when configuring the router to route between ELANs is to build two LECs, one for each ELAN. Since the configuration for each is essentially the same, only one LEC is configured in this example, and the process can be repeated for the second LEC.

## Add the Circuit and Select the Connection Type

In the Site Manager main Configuration Manager window, select the ATM interface the LEC will be built on, and then click OK in the Add Circuit window when it appears. This brings up the Select Connection Type window. Click ATM.

## Configure the Signaling

The Initial ATM Signaling Config window opens at this point. By default, ATM Signaling is enabled; since ATM signaling must be enabled for LANE to function, this can be left at its default setting. All other parameters can be left at their default settings, with the possible exception of changing the default Protocol Standard from UNI 3.0 to UNI 3.1, which is more commonly used today. It doesn't matter which it uses, as long as the UNI version matches that of the switch it is connected to. Click OK to bring up the ATM Service Records List window.

## Add a LAN Emulation Client

By default, although signaling has been enabled and a circuit has been added, no actual LEC exists on the interface. From the ATM Service Records List window, click Add to create the new LEC. This opens the ATM Service Record Parameters window. By default, the Data Encapsulation Type is set to LANE, and the Virtual Connection

Type is set to SVC. Both of these defaults are appropriate for LANE, so leave them at their defaults. By default, User Part Autogeneration is set to Enabled, which is also fine. The ATM Addr Net Prefix is blank; this parameter can be left undefined, because the router will obtain the NSAP prefix from the switch it is attached to over the ILMI channel. The Emulated LAN Type is set to Unspecified by default; this parameter does not need to be defined, because the LEC can also obtain its LAN Type from the LANE services built on the switch it is attached to, but you can specify 802.3 Ethernet or 802.5 Token Ring here. Enter the ELAN name in the field provided next to Emulated LAN Name, bearing in mind that ELAN names are case-sensitive.

Basically, the only required parameter is the ELAN name. After configuring this name, click OK to open the Select Protocols window.

### Assigning the Proper Protocols

From the Select Protocols window, choose the protocols that will run on the LEC. Click OK. Fill in the protocol information when prompted. Once this is complete, Site Manager returns to the ATM Service Records List window.

### Optionally Configuring a Static LES Entry

After you complete the preceding steps, if a LECS is being used as the LEC's method of obtaining its LES address, then no further configuration needs to be done as long as the LECS is using the WKA. By default, the router LEC is set up to use a LECS using the WKA. If a LECS is not being used, however, one last parameter must be configured. From the ATM Service Records List window, click LEC, which opens the LAN Emulation Parameters window.

Here, a Configuration Mode of Automatic (the default) indicates that a LECS will be used. If one is not being used, change this parameter to Manual, indicating the LES will not be obtained dynamically. Next, click the button labeled LES to open the ATM LES List window.

Click Add to insert the LES address. This brings up a window labeled LANE Redundancy, which has four parameters; fill in the LE Server ATM Address Network Prefix to the NSAP prefix of the LES address serving the ELAN that the LEC will join, and then fill in the LE Server ATM Address User Part to reflect the ESI and Selector Byte of the LES address. Once this is complete, click Apply and then click Done to exit the LANE Redundancy window. Click Apply and Done again in the LAN Emulation Parameters window to exit the LEC-specific configuration.

## Configuring the 5782 Series ATM Router

The Series 5000 5782 ATM router is treated a bit differently than a typical ATM Routing Engine (ARE) in a BLN or BCN, due to its different architecture, but it is configured essentially the same as any other ARE. The 5782 series router does not have any front panel ports; instead, ATM connections are made across the ATM backplane to a 5724M,

5720M, or 5720-622M ATM Master Control Processor (MCP) module in the System 5000 chassis.

Because the System 5000 ATM backplane is split between slots 7 and 8, the 5782 router must be placed on the appropriate side of the chassis, so that it can communicate with the MCP that is running the LANE services. The connection formed across the backplane is considered a UNI connection, just as any other ATM router connection. The LANE services don't need to be running on the MCP to which the 5782 is connected, as long as a path from the MCP is available to the LES/BUS pair the router LECs must join.

## Installation of the 5782 Series Router

Installation of the 5782 series router is similar to that of any other Nortel Networks router. However, when running the install.bat file to achieve initial SNMP communication between Site Manager and the router, a LEC must be built, rather than configuring a legacy interface for IP.

This is achieved first by connecting to the service port of the 5000BH chassis (this is the nine-pin serial connector). From the main connection menu, select the slot where the VNR resides to access the Technician Interface (TI):

```
Model 5000 Slot Selection Menu 01/12/98, 11:47:30AM
Slot Status Module Description
1 On-Line 5308P Ethernet Host
2 On-Line 5308P Ethernet Host
3 On-Line 5724M 4 Port MMF ATM MCP Host Module
4 On-Line 5782 Virtual Net Router
5 On-Line 5308P Ethernet Host
6 On-Line 5328 16 Port 10BT Enet Switch Module
7 On-Line 5328 16 Port 10BT Enet Switch Module
8 On-Line 5328 16 Port 10BT Enet Switch Module
9 On-Line 5328 16 Port 10BT Enet Switch Module
10 On-Line 5328 16 Port 10BT Enet Switch Module
11 On-Line 5724M 4 Port MMF ATM MCP Host Module
12 On-Line 5380 Ethernet Router
13 On-Line 5308P Ethernet Host
14 (Removed) 5580 Token Ring Router
c - Connect to slot [Press CTRL-T to break connection]
s - Select Supervisory Module main menu r - Reset module
Enter selection:
```

Enter the 5782 slot and then press CTRL-Y when prompted. This deposits the user in the following menu:

```
1*5782 SERVICE PORT MAIN MENU*
t Technician interface
e Engineering diagnostics
q Quit
Enter command:
```

Enter **t** to enter the TI, and then prepare to run the Quick Start installation script; make certain the necessary files are present and then boot from ti5000.cfg by entering the following command:

```
VNR> boot - ti5000.cfg
```

After you do this, the install.bat installation script file can be run. This guides the user through a series of prompts, to get the initial LEC up and running with the appropriate IP address.

**Note** *The appropriate LES/BUS pair must be accessible through the Centillion switch portion of the network, and the ATMSpeed MCP must have its backplane connection interface configured as a UNI interface with the proper UNI version, before the installation script should be run. If no ELAN is present for the 5782 LEC to join, or the ATMSpeed MCP has not had its backplane connection configured correctly so that the 5782 can form a connection with it, the LEC built through the install script will not be able to join its services and will never come up. If the IP circuit never comes up, it will never be reachable via Site Manager.*

After the installation script completes, a summary of the configuration is presented to the terminal screen:

```
---------------------------------------------------------------------------
Configuration Summary
Net Module: ATM_VNR_BH
Module Number: 2
Connector: 1
Slot: 9
Circuit Name: ATMSR_1410301.6
IP address: 150.50.10.24
IP subnetwork mask: 255.255.255.0
Routing Protocol: RIP1
Default Rt. Listen: No
TFTP Default Volume: 7:
TI TELNET: Yes
HTTP Server: No
NOTE: The Connector value in the above Configuration Summary
```

is the Connector number of the 5782 Module backplane ATM port.
Note, however, that within the event log and the MIB browsing
utilities such as Site Manager's Quick Get and the Technician
Interface's debug scripts, connectors are numbered by a
combination of their Connector number and Module number. The
interface you have selected will henceforth be referred to
as Connector 31

-------------------------------------------------------------------

## Configuring the Switch Backplane Connection in SpeedView

If a 5782 is present in the System 5000 chassis, its presence will be noted by SpeedView.
When brought up in Configuration Mode and the 5782 module tab is selected, it
appears as a normal ATM module, with the port and the signaling characteristics
displayed. Only one port will be present, however (see Figure 23-3).

This port is not the backplane port for the 5782, though this is a somewhat common
point of confusion: it is the backplane port for the MCP. The backplane port for the 5782 is
configured via Site Manager, and the signaling properties, as well as the parameters
relevant to any LECs, are configured at that time.

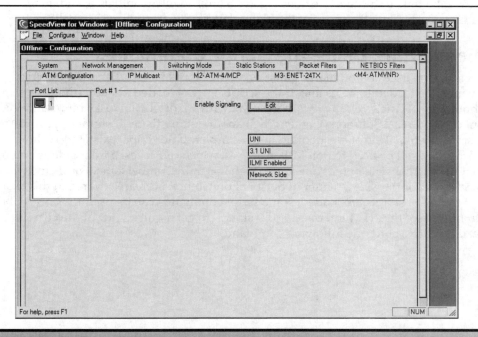

**Figure 23-3.**   *The 5782 as seen through SpeedView*

Click Edit, and then add the default Logical Link value. Notice what the signaling defaults to in this case: only UNI is available as an option, and only the Network Side option is available and selected. The reason why only a network-side UNI connection is available is because only the 5782 will utilize this connection. This is always a UNI connection, and since it is a router attachment it is by nature a Private UNI connection; therefore the switch must act as Network Side of this link. Select the appropriate UNI version (3.0 or 3.1).

*By default, in some code versions, ILMI may be set to Disabled. This option may need to be changed to Enabled.*

# Troubleshooting LANE on the Nortel Networks Router

One of the primary problems that occurs while configuring LANE on the Nortel Networks router (or any ATM LANE device, for that matter) is a misconfiguration of the LEC that doesn't allow it to join its services. Getting the LEC to join its services is paramount when configuring the router to route between ELANs; a LEC that hasn't yet initialized can be likened to a legacy interface, such as an Ethernet connection, that doesn't have a valid link; if the interface doesn't have a link, it will not initialize, and if the interface doesn't initialize, none of the higher-layer protocols will ever initialize either.

## Troubleshooting Using the Script Commands

Scripts can be used to poll many statistics on the Nortel Networks router platform; they must be loaded to be usable. If the scripts are not loaded already (they are technology-specific), you may want to speak with a Nortel Networks representative from the Technical Solutions Center (TSC) about getting them. If storage space permits, the scripts can make troubleshooting much simpler. If no scripts exist, the Technician Interface can still be used to poll MIB instances, which can reveal a tremendous amount about the current state of the router, although it is more cumbersome. For many, whether to use scripts or the TI is a matter of personal preference; both are covered in this chapter.

If the ATM scripts are loaded, some script commands can be used to observe the current state of the ATM interface. For instance, to get a quick view of the current interface status, enter the following command:

```
[12:2]$show atm services

ATM Service Record Table
------------------------
Line.Circuit    Encaps    State   Type           ATM Address
```

```
   ------------ ------------ ------ ----
   ----------------------------------------
   1412101.18   LanEmulation Up     SVC
   39.00.00.10.01.00.00.00.00.00.00.11.00
   .00.A2.CB.2D.12.00
   1412101.19   LanEmulation Up     SVC
   39.00.00.10.01.00.00.00.00.00.00.11.00
   .00.A2.CB.2D.12.01
   1412101.25   LanEmulation Up     SVC
   39.00.00.10.01.00.00.00.00.00.00.11.00
   .00.A2.CB.2D.12.02
   1412101.26   LanEmulation Up     SVC
   39.00.00.10.01.00.00.00.00.00.00.11.00
   .00.A2.CB.2D.12.03
   Total entries: 4
```

Four LECs are configured in this example, all of which are joined and in an operational state.

A more detailed view of the LEC can be seen by using the **show lane clients** script command, which is not available if the scripts are not loaded:

```
   [12:2]$show lane clients

   ATM LAN Emulation Client Running Config Info
   --------------------------------------------

   Cct#      Circuit Name      LecID     State      Fail Code Cfg Src
   -----  ------------------- ----- ----------- --------- --------
   10     ATMSR_1414101.10    36     OPERATIONAL NONE      KNOWNADR

          LAN type   Max Data Frm Size ELAN Name  Proxy
          ---------- ----------------- ---------- -----
          IEEE8023   1516              Sales          1

   Primary    addr 39.00.00.10.0C.60.01.01.02.0A.0A.0A.0A.00.00.A2.CB.23.2D.03
   Cfg Server addr 47.00.79.00.00.00.00.00.00.00.00.00.00.00.A0.3E.00.00.01.00
   LE Server  addr 39.00.00.10.0C.10.01.0B.01.0A.0A.0A.0A.BB.BB.01.51.00.00.01

   ----------------------------------------------------------------------
   Total entries: 1
```

Here, only one LEC is displayed, but quite a bit of information is available: the circuit number and name, the LEC ID, the current state, and the last failure code. The configuration source (cfg src) is listed as KNOWNADR, which indicates the WKA. This indicates a LECS is being used by the LEC. A LAN Type is given, the MTU is listed, and the ELAN name is shown. In addition, three address variables are listed:

- **Primary address**   The address of the LEC itself.
- **Config Server address**   The address used for the LECS.
- **LE Server address**   The address of the LES. If the LES address is not statically defined, the correct LES address appears here only after the LEC has successfully created the Configuration Direct VCC, and the LEC and LECS have exchanged the LE_CONFIGURE_REQUEST and LE_CONFIGURE_RESPONSE control frames.

## Checking the LANE Server States

If you suspect a problem is occurring sometime during the join phase, you can check the status of a LEC's connection to its services through the script commands. The **show lane servers** command indicates the status of the control connections, and what VPI/VCI they exist on:

```
[12:2]$show lane servers

ATM LAN Emulation Client Server VCC Table
-----------------------------------------
                            Config Direct       Control Direct
Cct#       Circuit Name     Line#   VPI  VCI    Line#   VPI  VCI
-----  -------------------  -------- --- -----  -------- --- -----
10      ATMSR_1414101.10    1414101  0   92     1414101  0   93

        Control Distributed    Multicast Send      Multicast Forward
        Line#   VPI  VCI       Line#   VPI  VCI     Line#   VPI  VCI
        -------- --- -----     -------- --- -----   -------- --- -----
        1414101  0   94        1414101  0   96      1414101  0   97


--------------------------------------------------------------------------
Total entries: 1
```

Determining the VPI/VCI pairs for the Control Direct VCC, Control Distribute VCC, Multicast Send VCC, and Multicast Forward VCC can be very useful if ATM sniffer traces need to be analyzed and these pairs are referenced. This command will also reveal whether the join completed successfully. Another script command that can be useful in this regard is the **show lane data_vcs** command, which includes similar information, as well as the VPI/VCI pairs of any Data Direct VCCs that can exist on that client:

```
[12:2]$show lane data_vcs

  LAN Emulation control VCS and data VCS
_____


            Config   Control  Control  Multi  Multi    Data
  Line#.Cct Direct   Direct   Distrib  Send   Forward  Direct
  _____   _____   _____   _____   _____  _____  _____
  1414101.10 0/92     0/93     0/94     0/96   0/97     0/104
                                                        0/106
                                                        0/111
```

## Checking ATM Signaling Through the Scripts

Another valuable ATM script command is the **show atmsig sig** command, which displays a lot of useful information regarding the ATM signaling parameters on the port:

```
[12:2]$show atmsig sig

ATM Signaling Entry Table (Q.93B)
----------------------------------


                     Max#of Max     Max     MaxParties Min Buf
  Line   Circuit State SvcApps Pt-Pt   Pt-Mp   In-MultiPt Threshold
  ------ ------- ----- ------- ------- ------- ---------- ---------
  1412101 -       Init  20      1000    40      1          2

                     # of   # of Stat
         VPI VCI Version Restart Enquiries T303 T308 T309 T310 T313 T316
         --- ----- ------- ------- --------- ---- ---- ---- ---- ---- ----
          0   5    UNI_V31 3       3         4    30   10   10   4    120

         T316C T322 TDisc T398 T399
         ----- ---- ----- ---- ----
         120   4    4     4    14
```

The output from this command shows a lot of the information included in the ATM Signaling Config window in Configuration Manager. The maximum number of SVC applications (LECs) is listed, along with the maximum number of point-to-point and point-to-multipoint connections.

**Note**   *The maximum number of point-to-multipoint connections is twice that of the maximum number of SVC applications, because two point-to-multipoint connection are present for each LEC—the Control Distribute VCC and the Multicast Forward VCC. So, if a maximum of 20 LECs are present, 40 point-to-multipoint connections are allowed, two for each.*

ATM ON NORTEL
NETWORKS

In addition, the T3*xx* timer values are listed. For a description of the purpose of these timers, as well as their individual definitions, consult Chapter 13.

## Checking ILMI Through the Scripts

ILMI statistics for individual LECs can be viewed by using the ATM scripts, which will indicate the VPI/VCI pair being used (0/16, by default), as well as some statistics regarding how many ILMI Sets and ILMI Gets have been issued so far. This is done by issuing the following command:

```
[12:2]$show atmsig ilmi

ATM ILMI Entry Table (UME/ILMI)
-------------------------------

                      Low  Up             Get   Get  GetNext       Set
    Line   Circuit State Thre Thre VPI  VCI  Get Retry Next Retry   Set Retry
    ------- ------- ------ ---- ---- --- ----- --- ----- ---- ------- --- ----
    1412101 -       Up    2    2    0   16    3   3     3    3       3   3

--------------------------------------------------------------------------
Total entries: 1
```

# Troubleshooting LANE by Using MIBs

Using the MIB from the TI can be time-consuming and requires patience. However, since it polls MIB values directly and reports them in text format, this tool is very extensive and can be extremely useful for viewing small details.

Only a fraction of the MIB attributes that could be viewed are covered here; to attempt to cover all of them would be well beyond the scope of this book. Instead, some of the most useful entries have been included, commonly used by Nortel Networks's Technicians when troubleshooting ATM LANE problems on the router.

## Observing the Current Interface State

One of the first things to do when troubleshooting a connectivity problem is to check the interface to see how it is being reported; the interface itself could be down. If an ATM interface has not initialized, none of the clients built on it are going to initialize. The interface state can be examined by using the following command (MIB lists, Sets, and Gets are case-sensitive):

 **Note**    *In the examples which follow, the wfAtmAlcDrvEntry MIB refers to the ATM ILIs which utilize a FRE2 processor card, while the wfAtmAlcDrvEntry MIB should be used when polling an ATM Routing Engine (ARE) ILI.*

```
1:2$ g wfAtmAlcDrvEntry.*.3.1
wfAtmAlcDrvEntry.wfAtmAlc.wfAtmAlcState.3.1 = 1
```

```
wfAtmAlcDrvEntry.wfAtmAlc.wfAtmAlcXmtPacketClips.3.1 = 0
wfAtmAlcDrvEntry.wfAtmAlc.wfAtmAlcMadr.3.1 = x00 x00 xA2 x14 xFE x01
```

In the preceding MIB string, the final entries of .3.1 indicate slot 3, port 1. The entries previously described indicate, in order, the current line state (where a value of 1 indicates the ATM interface is up), the number of packets that are potentially being dropped due to lack of resources (not enough space in the transmit buffer), and the MAC address of the interface. The MAC address entry can be useful in a LANE environment, because if User Part Autogeneration is being used, it will be based on this MAC value.

Likewise, the interface statistics can be examined. The following output indicates slot 5, port 1:

```
1:2$ g wfAtmizerIntfStatsEntry.*.5.1
wfAtmizerIntfStatsEntry.wfAtmizerIntf.5.1 = 5
```

Slot 5:

```
wfAtmizerIntfStatsEntry.wfAtmizerPort.5.1 = 1
```

Port 1:

```
wfAtmizerIntfStatsEntry.wfAtmizerIntfLastChange.5.1 = 1831
wfAtmizerIntfStatsEntry.wfAtmizerIntfOutQLen.5.1 = 0
```

A status of 1 indicates that the interface is up.

```
wfAtmizerIntfStatsEntry.wfAtmizerIntfStatus.5.1 = 1
wfAtmizerIntfStatsEntry.wfAtmizerIntfIndex.5.1 = 2
wfAtmizerIntfStatsEntry.wfAtmizerIntfOcdEvents.5.1 = 0
wfAtmizerIntfStatsEntry.wfAtmizerIntfTcAlarmState.5.1 = 1
wfAtmizerIntfStatsEntry.wfAtmizerIntfRxRacketsOkWrap.5.1 = 0
```

The following counter indicates the total number of good packets received on this interface:

```
wfAtmizerIntfStatsEntry.wfAtmizerIntfRxPacketsOk.5.1 = 102182938
wfAtmizerIntfStatsEntry.wfAtmizerIntfRxCellsOkWrap.5.1 = 0
```

The following counter indicates the total number of good cells received on this interface:

```
wfAtmizerIntfStatsEntry.wfAtmizerIntfRxCellsOk.5.1 = 204593882
```

If OAM cells are being used, the following counter indicates the number of OAM cells received by this interface:

```
wfAtmizerIntfStatsEntry.wfAtmizerIntfRxOamCount.5.1 = 0
.
wfAtmizerIntfStatsEntry.wfAtmizerIntfRxFlowCtrlCount.5.1 = 0
```

Invalid headers (listed in the following counter) may include requests for invalid VPI/VCI pairs. In a LANE environment, because VPI/VCI pairs are determined dynamically, confusion should not occur between two ends of a physical connection as to which pair should be used. If the preceding counter increments in a LANE environment, this may indicate that SVCs are not being torn down properly and that confusion is arising concerning which VPI/VCI pairs are and aren't available for use.

```
.wfAtmizerIntfStatsEntry.wfAtmizerIntfRxInvalidHeaders.5.1 = 0
```

In the following entry, oversized service data units (SDUs) may be indicative of a mismatched MTU size:

```
wfAtmizerIntfStatsEntry.wfAtmizerIntfRxOverSizedSDUs.5.1 = 0
```

CRC errors, such as in the following entry, can result during a packet's reassembly. This may be due to cell loss or cell corruption, and may indicate a problem either in the line or with the remote transmitter or local receiver.

```
wfAtmizerIntfStatsEntry.wfAtmizerIntfRxCrcErrors.5.1 = 0
wfAtmizerIntfStatsEntry.wfAtmizerIntfRxCrc10Errors.5.1 = 0
wfAtmizerIntfStatsEntry.wfAtmizerIntfRxLackBufCredits.5.1 = 0
wfAtmizerIntfStatsEntry.wfAtmizerIntfRxLackPageCredits.5.1 = 0
wfAtmizerIntfStatsEntry.wfAtmizerIntfRxLackBufResc.5.1 = 0
wfAtmizerIntfStatsEntry.wfAtmizerIntfRxLackPageResc.5.1 = 0
wfAtmizerIntfStatsEntry.wfAtmizerIntfTxPacketsOkWrap.5.1 = 0
```

The following counter indicates the total number of good packets transmitted from this interface:

```
wfAtmizerIntfStatsEntry.wfAtmizerIntfTxPacketsOk.5.1 = 102183938

wfAtmizerIntfStatsEntry.wfAtmizerIntfTxCellsOkWrap.5.1 = 0
```

The following counter indicates the total number of good cells transmitted on this interface:

```
wfAtmizerIntfStatsEntry.wfAtmizerIntfTxCellsOk.5.1 = 204594882
```

If OAM cells are being used, the following counter indicates the total number transmitted from this interface:

```
wfAtmizerIntfStatsEntry.wfAtmizerIntfTxOamCount.5.1 = 0
```

Lastly, instances where flow control was invoked, and bad VCs are counted:

```
wfAtmizerIntfStatsEntry.wfAtmizerIntfTxFlowCtrlCount.5.1 = 0
wfAtmizerIntfStatsEntry.wfAtmizerIntfTxBadVcs.5.1 = 0
```

## Observing the Current Status of the LEC

To observe the current LEC status, the MIB can be polled from the TI. Because multiple LECs may exist in this case, you should first determine how many LECs are configured and what each circuit number is (since this circuit number will need to be polled). The following command lists the different LEC instances:

```
[12:2]$1 -i wfAtmLecStatusEntry
inst_ids = 10
           12
           16
```

The preceding output lists three circuit numbers, indicating that three LECs are configured. To determine which circuit number is the LEC you want to view, it may be helpful to use the **show ip circuits** command:

```
[12:2]$show ip circuits
Circuit    Circuit #   State     IP Address        Mask
--------   ---------   -------   ---------------   ---------------
ATMSR_1- 10            Up        150.50.10.1       255.255.255.0
414101.-
10
ATMSR_1- 12            Up        150.50.20.1       255.255.255.0
413101.-
12
ATMSR_1- 16            Up        150.50.30.1       255.255.255.0
```

```
412101.-
16
3 circuit(s) found
```

In the preceding output, the line number for each LEC interface is listed, along with the circuit number. By determining the IP address of the LEC you want to view, the circuit number can be cross-referenced. The specific circuit number is needed because it will be used in the following command when the LEC status is viewed:

```
[12:2]$g wfAtmLecStatusEntry.*.10
wfAtmLecStatusEntry.wflecStatusCct.10 = 10
wfAtmLecStatusEntry.wflecPrimaryAtmAddress.10 =
        x39 x00 x0C x10 x0C x60 x01 x01 x02 x0A x0A x0A x0A x00
x00 xA2
        xCB x23 x2D x03
wfAtmLecStatusEntry.wflecID.10 = 36
wfAtmLecStatusEntry.wflecInterfaceState.10 = 7
```

A LEC interface state is listed in the last line of the preceding listing. The following codes apply in this case:

**(1) Initial**   An initializing state. At this point, the LEC is initializing and hasn't yet attempted to contact any of its services.

**(2) LECS Connect**   The LEC is attempting to establish the Configure Direct VCC with the LECS, but has not succeeded in doing so yet.

**(3) Configure**   Establishment of the Configuration Direct VCC with the LECS was successful, and the LE_CONFIGURE_REQUEST and LE_CONFIGURE_RESPONSE control frames are being exchanged between the LEC and the LECS.

**(4) Join**   The LEC has obtained its LES address from the LECS (if one is being used) and the exchange of LE_JOIN_REQUEST and LE_JOIN_RESPONSE control frames is occurring between the LEC and the LES.

**(5) Register**   The LEC has registered with the LES and is attempting to resolve the BUS address.

**(6) BUS Connect**   The LEC has obtained the BUS address via an LE_ARP_REQUEST and is attempting connection.

**(7) Operational**   The LEC has successfully joined both the LES and the BUS, and has transitioned into an operational state.

In the preceding instance, the state is 7, indicating that the LEC is operational. This instance is of particular importance, however, because it can reveal a lot about how far into the join process the LEC is getting. If this MIB is polled and a LEC state is determined, continue to poll the MIB periodically. The state that it lists may change, and it is important to see how many states it transitions through prior to reinitializing.

The remainder of the output from the **g wfAtmLecStatusEntry.\*.10** command is as follows. Here, the last failure code is listed (1 in this case, indicating no failure). A more detailed description of this MIB instance is covered later in this section.

```
wfAtmLecStatusEntry.wflecLastFailureRespCode.10 = 1
```

The following indicates the protocol being used on the LEC (IP in this case):

```
wfAtmLecStatusEntry.wflecLastFailureState.10 = 0
wfAtmLecStatusEntry.wflecProtocol.10 = 1
```

The following output indicates that the LECS address being used by the LEC is listed. In this case, it is using the WKA, and the LECS is not user-defined.

```
wfAtmLecStatusEntry.wflecVersion.10 = 0
wfAtmLecStatusEntry.wflecTopologyChange.10 = 0
wfAtmLecStatusEntry.wflecConfigServerAtmAddress.10 =
      x47 x00 x79 x00 x00 x00 x00 x00 x00 x00 x00 x00 x00 x00 xA0 x3E
      x00 x00 x01 x00
```

The following output is an entry for the ELAN name of which the LEC is a member:

```
wfAtmLecStatusEntry.wflecConfigSource.10 = 2
wfAtmLecStatusEntry.wflecActualLanType.10 = 2
wfAtmLecStatusEntry.wflecActualMaxDataFrameSize.10 = 2
wfAtmLecStatusEntry.wflecActualLanName.10 = "Engineering"
```

The following output is the full ATM address of the LEC; this can be very useful, because the ATM address of a LEC must be known if it is to be located in the LES table of the ELAN to which it has joined (this is achieved by using the command **show les** at the C100/C50/5000BH command prompt).

```
wfAtmLecStatusEntry.wflecActualLesAtmAddress.10 =
      x39 x00 x00 x10 x0C x10 x01 x0B x01 x0A x0A x0A x0A xBB xBB x01
      x51 x00 x00 x01
```

**DETERMINING THE CAUSE OF REGISTRATION FAILURE**    If the LEC interface state is not transitioning into an operational state (7), several causes are possible. Although a lot can be determined from how far into the join process the LEC is getting, a more detailed idea of the failure cause can be determined by polling the following MIB:

```
[12:2]$g wfAtmLecStatusEntry.5.10
wfAtmLecStatusEntry.wflecLastFailureRespCode.10 = 1
```

The cause code associated with the failure will be between 1 and 15. These codes indicate the reason for the registration failure, using the list that follows:

**(1) None**    No failure has occurred.

**(2) Tmo**    Timeout. A timeout has occurred during the exchange of control information or while a connection request was pending.

**(3) Undef**    The reason for the failure is undefined.

**(4) Vrsnotsup**    The version not supported. Check to make sure the LEC is not attempting to join an ELAN for which it is the wrong version (for example, the LEC is configured for LANEv1, but the LES is configured for LANEv2).

**(5) Invreq**    An invalid request control frame was received. This could be a LE_CONFIGURE_REQUEST, LE_JOIN_REQUEST, or LE_ARP_REQUEST.

**(6) dupdst**    A duplicate destination LAN was discovered. In LANE, only one local LEC is required to service a particular LAN.

**(7) dupatmadr**    The LEC was determined to have duplicated another existing ATM address.

**(8) insufres**    Insufficient resources were available to fully execute the join process.

**(9) accdenied**    The LEC was denied membership in the ELAN it was requesting because of a security constraint.

**(10) invreqid**    The LEC attempted to join the LES using an invalid request ID, and was denied access.

**(11) invdst**    Invalid destination; the destination legacy LAN does not exist on the network currently.

**(12) invatmadr**    Invalid ATM address. The ATM address of the LEC is not configured in the proper format.

**(13) nocfg**    No configuration. The LEC attempting to join does not have a valid configuration recognizable by the service it is attempting to communicate with.

**(14) lecfgerr**    Some portion of the LEC's configuration is not consistent with the rest of the LANE network. This could be due to an inconsistent MTU size or LAN type.

**(15) insufinfo**    The LEC did not provide the minimum number of parameters to allow membership in the ELAN. Although many parameters can be obtained dynamically, the LEC must have some static configuration, including the ELAN name.

## LEC Statistics

Viewing the LEC statistics can indicate current LEC behavior; this command is useful only if the LEC has already joined its services, but may be useful in determining problems that are occurring after the join phase is complete.

```
[12:2]$g wfAtmLecStatisticsEntry.*.16
wfAtmLecStatisticsEntry.wflecArpRequestsOut.16 = 36567
```

The preceding counter indicates the total number of LE_ARP_REQUESTs issued by this particular LEC.

```
wfAtmLecStatisticsEntry.wflecArpRequestsIn.16 = 92236
```

The preceding counter indicates the total number of received LE_ARP_REQUESTs.

```
wfAtmLecStatisticsEntry.wflecArpRepliesOut.16 = 969
wfAtmLecStatisticsEntry.wflecArpRepliesIn.16 = 169705
```

The preceding counters indicate the number of LE_ARP_RESPONSE frames that have been both incoming and outgoing on this virtual interface.

```
wfAtmLecStatisticsEntry.wflecControlFramesOut.16 = 37538
wfAtmLecStatisticsEntry.wflecControlFramesIn.16 = 261944
```

The preceding counters indicate the total number of incoming and outgoing LANE control frames for this LEC.

```
wfAtmLecStatisticsEntry.wflecSvcFailures.16 = 0
wfAtmLecStatisticsEntry.wflecStatisticsCct.16 = 16
wfAtmLecStatisticsEntry.wflecUnknownFramesDropped.16 = 379
```

The preceding output indicates the number of SVC failures (SVCs that were attempted, but not completed successfully), the circuit number (16 in this case), and the number of unknown frames that dropped.

```
wfAtmLecStatisticsEntry.wflecInDataFrames.16 = 0
wfAtmLecStatisticsEntry.wflecInUnicastFrames.16 = 0
```

ATM ON NORTEL
NETWORKS

```
wfAtmLecStatisticsEntry.wflecInUnicastOctets.16 = 0
wfAtmLecStatisticsEntry.wflecInMulticastFrames.16 = 0
wfAtmLecStatisticsEntry.wflecInMulticastOctets.16 = 0
wfAtmLecStatisticsEntry.wflecInBroadcastFrames.16 = 0
wfAtmLecStatisticsEntry.wflecInBroadcastOctets.16 = 0
wfAtmLecStatisticsEntry.wflecOutDataFrames.16 = 0
wfAtmLecStatisticsEntry.wflecOutUnknownFrames.16 = 0
wfAtmLecStatisticsEntry.wflecOutUnknownOctets.16 = 0
wfAtmLecStatisticsEntry.wflecOutMulticastFrames.16 = 0
wfAtmLecStatisticsEntry.wflecOutMulticastOctets.16 = 0
wfAtmLecStatisticsEntry.wflecOutBroadcastFrames.16 = 0
wfAtmLecStatisticsEntry.wflecOutBroadcastOctets.16 = 0
wfAtmLecStatisticsEntry.wflecOutUnicastFrames.16 = 0
wfAtmLecStatisticsEntry.wflecOutUnicastOctets.16 = 0
```

The preceding output gives octet and frame statistics for broadcasts, unicasts, and multicasts for the configured LEC VPort.

## Checking ILMI

The ILMI entries can also be polled from the TI. The command **get wfAtmIlmiEntry.*.1413101** (get may be abbreviated to **g**, as shown in the screen output which follows) polls a particular MIB, a wildcard for the instance indicating all instances of that MIB, and then indicates the value 1413101. This value is the line number and is accessible either through Site Manager or by entering the command **show ip circuits** from the TI. The circuit and line numbers will both be listed there:

```
[12:2]$g wfAtmIlmiEntry.*.1413101
wfAtmIlmiEntry.wfAtmIlmiDelete.1413101 = 1
wfAtmIlmiEntry.wfAtmIlmiDisable.1413101 = 1
wfAtmIlmiEntry.wfAtmIlmiLineNumber.1413101 = 1413101
wfAtmIlmiEntry.wfAtmIlmiAtmCct.1413101 = 0
wfAtmIlmiEntry.wfAtmIlmiState.1413101 = 1
wfAtmIlmiEntry.wfAtmIlmiLowThreshold.1413101 = 2
wfAtmIlmiEntry.wfAtmIlmiUpThreshold.1413101 = 2
```

The VPI and VCI are 0/16, indicated in the following screen output, which is the default. In general, these values should not be changed.

```
wfAtmIlmiEntry.wfAtmIlmiVpi.1413101 = 0
wfAtmIlmiEntry.wfAtmIlmiVci.1413101 = 16
```

The following output lists the ILMI Get timer and ILMI Get Retry timer values. These are accessible through Site Manager by accessing the Interim Local Management Interface (ILMI) option from the Edit ATM Connector window in Configuration Manager.

```
wfAtmIlmiEntry.wfAtmIlmiInterfaceType.1413101 = 1
wfAtmIlmiEntry.wfAtmIlmiLocalPort.1413101 = 0
wfAtmIlmiEntry.wfAtmIlmiRemotePort.1413101 = 0
wfAtmIlmiEntry.wfAtmIlmiGetTimer.1413101 = 3
wfAtmIlmiEntry.wfAtmIlmiGetRetryCnt.1413101 = 3
```

The following timers are also accessible through the Edit ATM Connector window in Configuration Manager:

```
wfAtmIlmiEntry.wfAtmIlmiGetNextTimer.1413101 = 3
wfAtmIlmiEntry.wfAtmIlmiGetNextRetryCnt.1413101 = 3
wfAtmIlmiEntry.wfAtmIlmiSetTimer.1413101 = 3
wfAtmIlmiEntry.wfAtmIlmiSetRetryCnt.1413101 = 3
```

Lastly, in the output below, the ILMI local Object Identifier (OID) is displayed, as well as whether debugging is active (2 indicates no), and the NetPrefixTimer, indicating how long the router LEC will wait in seconds to be given its prefix by the switch it is attached to:

```
wfAtmIlmiEntry.wfAtmIlmiLocalOid.1413101 = 4.1.18.3.4.23.1.9.1
wfAtmIlmiEntry.wfAtmIlmiDebug.1413101 = 2
wfAtmIlmiEntry.wfAtmIlmiNetPrefixTimer.1413101 = 8
```

**DETERMINING THE NSAP PREFIX**    If the NSAP prefix of the LEC is not being configured statically, then the LEC must obtain it via ILMI from the switch. If an ILMI problem is suspected, then the router can be checked to see whether the NSAP prefix has been received. This is done by issuing the following command:

```
[12:2]$g wfAtmNetPrefixEntry.*.1413101.57.0.0.16.12.96.1.1.2.10.10.10.10
wfAtmNetPrefixEntry.wfAtmNetPrefixPort.1413101.57.0.0.16.12.96.1.1.2.10.10.10.10 =
1413101
wfAtmNetPrefixEntry.wfAtmNetPrefixPrefix.1413101.57.0.0.16.12.96.1.1.2.10.10.10.10 =
       x39 x00 x00 x10 x01 x00 x00 x00 x00 x00 x00 x11
wfAtmNetPrefixEntry.wfAtmNetPrefixStatus.1413101.57.0.0.16.12.96.1.1.2.10.10.10.10 = 1
```

In the preceding output, the port is listed, followed by an entry for the NSAP prefix itself (39.00.00.10.01.00.00.00.00.00.00.11).

**EXAMINING THE CONTROL CONNECTIONS** The individual LANE control connections can be examined via the MIB also; the entry covered next shows control connections to the LES and BUS, as well as the VPI/VCI pair for each. This can be very useful in determining how far into the join phase a LEC is getting, if it is not initializing correctly.

The LEC being examined in the output below has a circuit number of 19:

```
[12:2]$g wfAtmLecServerVccEntry.*.19
```

The Configuration Direct interface is identified as the line number for this circuit, as shown in the following output:

```
wfAtmLecServerVccEntry.wflecConfigDirectInterface.19 = 1413101
```

In the following entry, the Configuration Direct VCC VPI/VCI pair of 0/39 is displayed:

```
wfAtmLecServerVccEntry.wflecConfigDirectVpi.19 = 0
wfAtmLecServerVccEntry.wflecConfigDirectVci.19 = 39
```

The following output displays the point-to-point Control Direct VCC to the LES on VPI/VCI pair 0/42:

```
wfAtmLecServerVccEntry.wflecControlDirectInterface.19 = 1413101
wfAtmLecServerVccEntry.wflecControlDirectVpi.19 = 0
wfAtmLecServerVccEntry.wflecControlDirectVci.19 = 42
```

The following output displays the point-to-multipoint Control Distribute VCC from the LES on VPI/VCI pair 0/45:

```
wfAtmLecServerVccEntry.wflecControlDistributeInterface.19 = 1413101
wfAtmLecServerVccEntry.wflecControlDistributeVpi.19 = 0
wfAtmLecServerVccEntry.wflecControlDistributeVci.19 = 45
```

The following output displays the point-to-point Multicast Send VCC to the BUS on VPI/VCI pair 0/52:

```
wfAtmLecServerVccEntry.wflecMulticastSendInterface.19 = 1413101
wfAtmLecServerVccEntry.wflecMulticastSendVpi.19 = 0
wfAtmLecServerVccEntry.wflecMulticastSendVci.19 = 52
```

The following output displays the point-to-multipoint Multicast Forward VCC from the BUS on VPI/VCI pair 0/53:

```
wfAtmLecServerVccEntry.wflecMulticastForwardInterface.19 = 1413101
wfAtmLecServerVccEntry.wflecMulticastForwardVpi.19 = 0
wfAtmLecServerVccEntry.wflecMulticastForwardVci.19 = 53
wfAtmLecServerVccEntry.wflecServerVccCct.19 = 19
```

## Examining the LEC Parameters

LEC parameters can also be verified. These parameters can be verified through Site Manager or by opening the .cfg file for the router being examined in Site Manager. The advantage to using the MIB is that the following entry displays the actual operating parameters of the LEC, and not the configured parameters; many LEC parameters can be automatically obtained, and these values may not show up in Site Manager. If the LEC has negotiated any of its parameters, the values that were negotiated will be displayed in the MIB.

```
[12:2]$g wfAtmLecOperConfigEntry.*.21
wfAtmLecOperConfigEntry.wflecOperConfigCct.21 = 21
wfAtmLecOperConfigEntry.wflecOperConfigControlTimeout.21 = 5
```

The preceding is the Control Timeout Value. This value and many others that follow are described in "The Nortel Networks ATM Router Platform," earlier in this chapter, and are accessible via Site Manager's Configuration Manager in the LAN Emulation Parameters window.

The following entry refers to the idle VCC timeout period. It is using the default of 1,200 seconds (20 minutes):

```
wfAtmLecOperConfigEntry.wflecOperConfigMaxUnknownFrameCount.21 = 1
wfAtmLecOperConfigEntry.wflecOperConfigMaxUnknownFrameTime.21 = 1
wfAtmLecOperConfigEntry.wflecOperConfigVccTimeoutPeriod.21 = 1200
```

The following output describes the maximum retry count, aging time, and forward delay time:

```
wfAtmLecOperConfigEntry.wflecOperConfigMaxRetryCount.21 = 1
wfAtmLecOperConfigEntry.wflecOperConfigAgingTime.21 = 300
wfAtmLecOperConfigEntry.wflecOperConfigForwardDelayTime.21 = 15
```

The following output indicates the number of topology changes which have occurred, the ARP response time (expected within 3 seconds), as well as the flush timeout. The flush timeout is used if a timer is selected, rather than the exchange of LE_FLUSH_REQUEST and LE_FLUSH_RESPONSE frames. The default is 4 seconds:

```
wfAtmLecOperConfigEntry.wflecOperConfigTopologyChange.21 = 0
wfAtmLecOperConfigEntry.wflecOperConfigExpectedArpResponseTime.21 = 3
wfAtmLecOperConfigEntry.wflecOperConfigFlushTimeOut.21 = 4
```

The remainder of the output describes the switching delay, segment ID, and information regarding multicast traffic (traffic passing over the Multicast send/forward VCCs):

```
wfAtmLecOperConfigEntry.wflecOperConfigPathSwitchingDelay.21 = 6
wfAtmLecOperConfigEntry.wflecOperConfigLocalSegmentID.21 = 0
wfAtmLecOperConfigEntry.wflecOperConfigMulticastSendType.21 = 3
wfAtmLecOperConfigEntry.wflecOperConfigMulticastSendAvgRate.21 = 0
wfAtmLecOperConfigEntry.wflecOperConfigMulticastSendPeakRate.21 = 0
wfAtmLecOperConfigEntry.wflecOperConfigConnectionCompleteTimer.21 = 4
```

## Checking the Log Entries

The log is perhaps one of the most useful tools available on the Nortel Networks router platform, and can be particularly useful when troubleshooting ATM problems. The log can be polled in a few different ways, as outlined in Chapter 29. ATM events can be screened, and different severity levels can be specified. The actual log messages will not be covered here; they are far too extensive and, in many cases, vary from code version to code version. You can obtain a text containing all the current log messages and their meanings from Nortel Networks via the Web (**www.nortelnetworks.com**).

This section concentrates primarily on which log entries are useful when troubleshooting an ATM LANE problem. The main things to consider in this scenario are ATM LANE event messages, ATM interface and signaling messages, and the base ATM messages that relate to general protocol functions.

The following command brings up log events for ATM events only, for all Fault, Trace, Warning, Info, and Debug events. Note that ATM LANE events are different from strictly ATM events:

```
2:1$ log -eATM -fftwid
```

The following command targets LANE events specifically, again for Fault, Trace, Warning, Info, and Debug events:

```
2:1$ log -eATM_LE -fftwid
```

In addition, ATM interface events can be viewed separately:

```
2:1$ log -eATMINTF -fftwid
```

The ATM signaling messages can be targeted with the following command:

```
2:1$ log -eATM_SIG -fftwid
```

Or, a series of event groups can be appended together, as they are in the following command. In addition to the severity flags that have been selected, notice that the following command also displays log messages for slot 5 only, by using the -s5 flag:

```
2:1$ log -eATM -eATM_LE -eATMINTF -eATM_SIG -fftwid -s5
```

Depending on the circumstance, different levels of severity may be used. Bear in mind when polling the log that, particularly with debug messages, sometimes normal ATM functioning can generate a tremendous amount of log messages, which may be difficult to dicipher. Depending on what is being looked for, not displaying debug or informational messages sometimes can help to consolidate the log entries that are displayed.

# Configuring a Multi-Protocol Over ATM Server

Starting with Bay RS version 13.01, Multi-Protocol Over ATM is supported. MPOA allows two LECs serving two different IP networks or subnetworks to bypass the router and form a Data Direct VCC (called an MPOA shortcut) between them directly. In an MPOA environment, the router's role is to host the MPOA Server (MPS), which will field MPOA requests from the MPOA Clients (MPCs) located on remote switches within the ATM network. For more-detailed information regarding the exact workings of MPOA, as well as the Next Hop Resolution Protocol (NHRP) that is used by MPOA, consult Chapter 19.

## Initial MPS Configuration

After clicking the MPOA Server Attributes button in the Edit ATM Connector window in Configuration Manager, you are first prompted for the configuration mode for the

MPS control ATM address. This is the ATM address that will be associated with the MPS being configured. By default, this address is generated automatically. Leave the default, or change the MPS Address Generate Mode to Manual, and then configure the ATM address in the fields provided:

- **Ctrl ATM Addr Network Prefix (Optional)**   If Manual is selected as the Configuration Mode, then the NSAP prefix of the MPS control ATM address must be configured here. The MPS control ATM address is simply the ATM address associated with the MPS being configured.

- **Ctrl ATM Addr User Part**   If Manual is selected as the Configuration Mode, then the ESI and Selector Byte must also be configured. This is the ESI of the MPS control ATM address.

Once this is configured, click OK to open the MPOA Service Record window. Another opportunity to alter the MPS control ATM address generation mode is offered, and the MPOA Server service record is listed in the upper-left portion of the window. Now that the service record has been added, select the MPS option to create the MPS. Clicking this option displays the MPS List window. Click Add to create the MPS; the MPS Configuration Parameters window will open, in which the primary MPS configuration takes place:

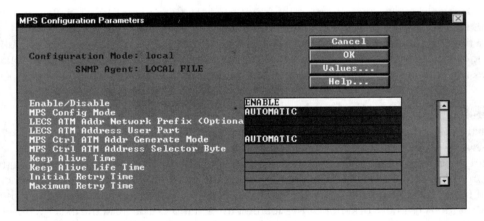

Many of the parameters listed in this window are grayed out initially because, by default, the MPS is configured to obtain its configuration automatically from a LANEv2-capable LECS. In this case, many of the parameters listed also exist on the LECS and can be configured there, enabling many MPS entities to access their configuration from a single source. The primary MPS parameters are as follows:

■ **MPS Config Mode**    An MPS can obtain its configuration in one of two ways: it can contact the LECS and receive its configuration parameters from there, or it can be manually configured with its parameters. The MPS configuration parameters are exchanged when the LEC (or series of LECs) the MPS is mapped to contacts the LECS to obtain its LES address. Included in the LANEv2 TLVs are the configuration parameters for the MPS. If a LECS is not being used, then these parameters should be configured manually. Only one LEC to which the MPS is mapped needs to contact the LECS for Automatic mode to be used. If no LEC is using an LECS, select Manual.

■ **LECS ATM Addr Network Prefix (Optional)**    If a Config Mode of Automatic is being used, the MPS will look to obtain its configuration information from the LECS. If a LECS is being used in the network, but it is not using the WKA, then the user-defined address must be configured. Here, the 13-byte NSAP prefix of the user-defined LECS address must be entered.

■ **LECS ATM Address User Part**    If a Config Mode of Automatic is being used, and the network's LECS is not using the WKA, then the ESI of the user-defined LECS address must be specified here.

■ **MPS Ctrl ATM Addr Generate Mode**    The MPS Control ATM Address Generate Mode was set when the MPOA Service Record was first created, and the address was either generated automatically or configured manually. Here, if the MPS Ctrl ATM Addr Generate Mode is set to Automatic, it will obtain its information from the LECS. If set to Manual, the address will be taken from the MPS control ATM address that was specified at the time the service record was built. If, at that time, an Address Generation Mode of Automatic was selected, Configuration Manager will not permit Manual to be selected at this time, because it would be attempting to draw upon information that was never configured.

■ **MPS Ctrl ATM Address Selector Byte**    If an MPS Ctrl ATM Address Generate Mode of Manual is being used, then the MPS will use the information previously configured. However, because multiple instances of MPSs may exist simultaneously, they cannot have the exact same ATM address. For this reason, a unique Selector Byte must be entered to ensure uniqueness among MPS entities (this must be done even if only one will be configured). The selector byte is a single-octet value, formatted as two 4-byte hex nibbles.

**Note**    *All the following parameters except the last two are available only if the MPS is not obtaining its configuration information from a LECS. If a LECS is being used, the MPS will obtain these parameters from there.*

ATM ON NORTEL
NETWORKS

- **Keep Alive Time** The MPOA protocol uses Keep Alive packets to maintain communication with any possible MPC entities. The Keep Alive Time dictates how often these Keep Alive packets are issued. The range is from 1 to 300 seconds, with a default of 10 seconds.

- **Keep Alive Life Time** Indicates how long a Keep Alive message is considered valid. The range is from 3 to 1,000 seconds, with a default value of 35 seconds.

- **Initial Retry Time** Indicates the amount of time the MPS will initially wait before reattempting a Resolution Request or other control frame, if there is no response to the first one transmitted. The range is 1 to 300 seconds, with a default of 5 seconds.

- **Maximum Retry Time** Indicates the maximum amount of time that can pass between the MPS not receiving an expected response and retransmitting the original request. The range is from 1 to 300 seconds, with a default of 40 seconds.

- **Give Up Time** If the MPS issues a control frame (such as a Resolution Request or Cache Imposition Request) and does not receive an expected response, this parameter dictates how long the MPS waits before assuming the request will not be responded to and giving up. The range is from 5 to 300 seconds, with a default of 40 seconds.

- **Default Holding Time** Defines the time (in minutes) used for Next Hop Resolution Protocol (NHRP) Resolution Replies. The range is from 1 to 120 minutes, with a default of 20 minutes.

- **Initial Cache Size** Indicates the initial cache size in MB the MPS is configured with. By default, this value is set to 100KB, with a range of 50 to 500KB.

- **Maximum Cache Size** Indicates the maximum cache the MPS can maintain, in KB; by default, this is set to 200KB, and can be set from 50 to 500KB.

## Mapping an MPS to a LEC

After the MPS is added and the initial configuration is complete, the MPS must be mapped to each LEC that will be served by it. The MPS will only be able to serve MPCs whose LECs are joined to the same ELANs that the LECs the MPS is mapped to (see Figure 23-4).

After the initial MPS configuration is complete, Site Manager returns to the MPS List window. Here, the newly created MPS is visible in the top-left portion of the window:

**MPS #1    Slot #5  —>**

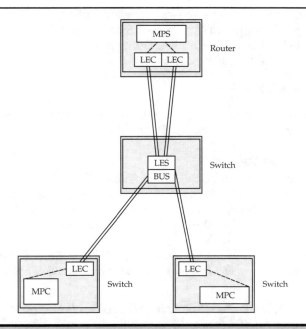

**Figure 23-4.**   *The MPC and MPS using their associated LECs to communicate*

A new option, labeled Mapping, has also been added to the buttons located on the right side of the window. Click this option to open the Lec Mps Mapping List window:

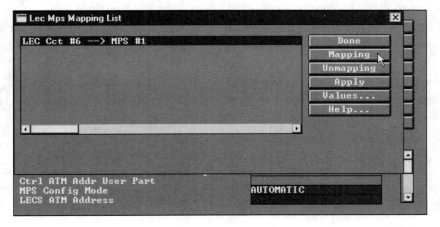

A list of available LEC entries appears in the top-left part of the window. To the right, click the Mapping option to map the MPS being configured to the LEC that is currently highlighted in the LEC entry list. Doing so causes the mapped relationship between the MPS and the LEC to be displayed:

**LEC Cct #2 —> MPS #1**

This should be done for each LEC that will be served by the MPS being configured. Once the mapping is complete, click Apply and then click Done.

## Selecting a Protocol

In addition to the Mapping option, the MPS List window has a second new option after the creation of the first MPS: the Protocol option, which appears just below the Mapping option. Clicking the Protocol option brings up the MPS Protocol Parameters window, in which you can select the protocols that will use MPOA.

*Currently, only IPv4 is supported by MPOA. Thus, no reason currently exists to access the MPS Protocol Parameters window, except to temporarily disable the protocol.*

# Configuring the Next Hop Resolution Protocol

The MPS uses NHRP to help resolve the Nonbroadcast Multiaccess (NBMA)-to-internetworking protocol address (IP-to-ATM in this case); therefore, each LEC that will be served by a particular MPS must have NHRP configured as one of its protocols, in addition to any others that can be run, so that each LEC can provide the third-layer information required.

## Configuring NHRP Parameters

When NHRP is selected as a protocol for one of the LECs, the NHRP configuration information will be prompted for after the IP information (as well as any other routing protocol information, such as OSPF) has been configured. At this time, the NHRP Network Configuration window will open, accessing the NHRP parameters for the router:

- **NHRP Request Path (View Only)**    Determines whether the NHRP client uses the routed path to determine the next hop or, alternatively, uses a Next Hop Server. Currently, the only available option is ROUTED.

- **Client Enable**    Enables and Disables NHRP client capability.

- **Client Reg Interval**    Defines how often the NHRP client must send a registration request to the NHRP server to refresh an entry currently listed in the NHRP cache. This value should not exceed the Client Hold Time parameter.

- **Client Hold Time**   Indicates how long an NHRP cache entry is considered valid. For this reason, this value should exceed the Client Reg Interval, because the NHRP client should be allowed to refresh an entry prior to its timing out and being removed.

- **Client Request Timeout**   Indicates how long an NHRP client will wait for a reply in response to a request made to the NHRP server. The range is from 1 to 100 seconds, with a default value of 10.

- **Client Request Retry**   If an expected reply is not received in response to a request, this indicates how many times the NHRP client will retransmit the request. The range is from 1 to 20, with a default of 3.

- **Client Max Pending Request Entries**   Indicates the total number of incoming Resolution Requests the NHRP client can handle at any one time. The range is from 1 to 100, with a default of 100.

- **Server Enable**   Enables and disables NHRP server capability.

- **Server Forward Enable**   If multiple NHRP servers exist, this option allows an NHRP server to forward a request to other servers if the requested information is not cached. This feature is enabled by default.

- **Server Max Next Hop Entries**   Indicates how many Next Hop entries can be maintained at any one time. The range is from 1 to 20, with a default of 5.

- **Server Max Pending Request Entries**   Indicates the maximum number of outstanding NHRP server requests this NHRP server will service. The range is from 1 to 100, with a default of 100.

- **DNS Proxy Port**   Specifies the DNS proxy port for QoS translation queries. The default is 500.

- **Override NBMA Address**   Indicates whether the router replaces the NBMA source address of incoming client registration messages with the NBMA address associated with the source protocol address.

- **Max Next Hop Cache Size**   Defines the maximum number of Next Hop entries that can be cached at any one time. The range is from 16 to 1,024, with a default value of 16.

- **Max QoS Cache Size**   The maximum number of QoS entries that can be cached.

- **Server Load Balancing**   Enabling this parameter causes the NHRP server to cycle through existing Next Hop cache entries in a round-robin fashion for the NHRP clients that are currently utilizing the information. This creates a sort of "load balancing" for the server.

■ **Server Negative Caching**    Negative caching relates to DNS record caching; if an NHRP server has attempted to query the DNS in the past and got no response, negative caching allows the NHRP server to take note of this, and not continually query the DNS.

■ **Server Negative TTL**    The Negative TTL parameter relates to the Server Negative Caching parameter and indicates (in seconds) the amount of time the NHRP server will note a missing DNS record before it begins querying the DNS again. The range is from 1 to 65,535 seconds, with a default of 10.

# The Complete Reference

# Part VI

## Token Ring on the Nortel Networks Platform

# The
# Complete
# Reference

Nortel
Networks

# Chapter 24

## Token Ring Frames

In a token ring environment, a station can glean many things by looking at a frame. A frame has flippable bits that let stations know the current status of the frame, such as whether it has arrived at its destination yet, whether it is traversing many rings or just one, and so on. These individual fields may also be useful to the network administrator if the ring is behaving erratically, because they may reveal useful information.

When a failure occurs in a token ring environment, obtaining packet traces often is beneficial, which can be accomplished in several ways, depending on the device that is being analyzed. A *sniffer*—some sort of sniffer software running on a station, can take a sampling of data from a ring and write it to a file for later analysis. When doing so, bear in mind the following rules:

- Using a sniffer to obtain traces from a local ring in a shared media environment requires only that the sniffer be connected to a free port on the appropriate ring.

- Using a sniffer to obtain traces from a token ring switched port requires the use of some sort of packet filter or port-mirroring configuration, or an intermediary MAU, because in switched token ring, each port actually connects to a different ring, so placing a sniffer on one port will not show data for any other ports. If a MAU to which the sniffer can attach isn't already in place on the port, then either one needs to be inserted or the traffic needs to be redirected through some sort of filter to another port on the same switch to which the sniffer is connected. The configuration of these filters on the Centillion switch is outlined in Chapter 6.

- Similarly, sniffer traces can't be taken through a router. Routers generally do not have any sort of port-mirroring option to steer the traffic to an available port, so a MAU may need to be positioned on the port to be analyzed, to connect the sniffer and take a viable trace.

Learning to interpret token ring sniffer traces can prove invaluable when managing a token ring network; the specifics of learning how to do this depends in part on the sniffer package being used. This chapter doesn't go into the specifics of reading token ring sniffer traces, but it does review the specific token ring frame types, and frame information, to help familiarize you with the token ring protocol at the frame level.

## Token Functionality

In a token-passing architecture, a token traverses the ring, passing each station on the ring as it does so. Only by receiving the token while it is free may a station transmit data; this keeps ring usage efficient, and more uniform than a contention-based system, which is subject to traffic bursts. The token is, in reality, a pattern of bytes that traverses the ring in a counterclockwise fashion. This entity remains constant, and all token ring devices recognize it.

The token is the basis for any token-passing system, as opposed to a contention-based, or connection-oriented, system. This means that all the stations in a token ring environment neither monitor the wire and wait until it's clear to transmit, nor do they establish direct circuits. They wait until they receive the token and then transmit, if the token does not already have data appended to it. This is why a token-passing system is more efficient than a contention-based system; a series of stations, all part of the ring, transmit and receive in an orderly, turn-based fashion. A station can transmit only after receiving the token, and then can transmit only if the token is free.

The token, diagrammed here, contains a series of fields, each one octed in size:

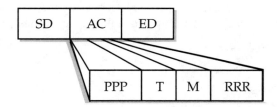

SD is the Starting Delimiter and ED is the Ending Delimiter; in between is AC, the Access Control field, which contains a specific series of bits: PPP T M RRR. These bits can be flipped by different stations, which in turn communicates the status of the token to other stations on the ring. The meanings of the bits are as follows:

P  Priority bits (000 through 111)

T  Token bit (a value of 0 means the token is free; 1 means it is in use)

M  Monitor bit (set to 1 if it has cycled past Active Monitor)

R  Request Priority bits (000 through 111)

The P and R bits relate to token prioritization and reservation, covered further on in this chapter.

# Token Ring Frame Format

Here is a representation of the basic token ring frame format:

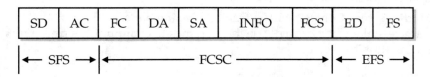

Token ring frames are similar to Ethernet frames in many ways, but they also have some important differences. For example, the size of token ring frames is much larger, ranging from 4544 bytes to as large as 18,000 bytes, and their structure is a bit different than that of Ethernet frames. The meanings of the individual fields are as follows:

| | |
|---|---|
| SFS | Start of Frame Sequence |
| SD | Starting Delimiter (indicates the beginning of a frame) |
| AC | Access Control |
| FCSC | Frame Check Sequence Coverage |
| FC | Frame Control (indicates frame type, data or MAC, which can be important, because many types of token ring frames exist that aren't data) |
| DA | Destination Address |
| SA | Source Address |
| INFO | The data itself |
| FCS | Frame Check Sequence (CRC check) |
| EFS | End of Frame Sequence |
| ED | Ending Delimiter |
| FS | Frame Status |

Note that the frame in this example is a local token ring frame in a nonsource-routed environment. Source-route bridging is part of the token ring protocol, which enables stations to determine a source-routed path to their destination, when in a multi-ring environment. It is an optional configuration, because token ring may also utilize nonsource-routed transparent bridging. A source-routed frame contains a field (not represented in the preceding table) known as the Routing Information Field (RIF), which is inserted between the Source Address and the INFO field. For a closer examination of source-routed token ring and the RIF field, consult Chapter 25.

The following are the two basic types of token ring frames:

- **Logical Link Control (LLC) frames**  Data frames—user information transferred from station to station.

- **Media Access Control (MAC) frames**  Maintenance and control frames—token ring devices use these frames to communicate ring status and information to each other.

Different frames have different meanings, and by examining the bits in certain portions of the frame, the type of frame can be determined. Certain frames may trigger events. A station on the ring needs to know what kind of frame it is dealing with when it sees it. Examine the token ring frame again:

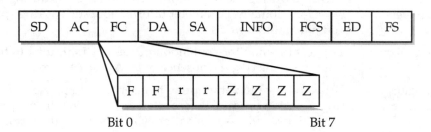

In this diagram, the Frame Control field (FC) has been highlighted, because this is the portion of the frame that communicates the frame type. The first two bits (FF) indicate which type of frame it is, using the following scheme:

| | |
|---|---|
| 00 | MAC frame |
| 01 | LLC (data) frame |
| 10 and 11 | Reserved for future use |

The third and fourth bits (rr) are reserved; these are always set to 0. The remaining bits (ZZZZ) are control bits.

## MAC Frames

MAC frames are part of the token ring protocol and do not contain user data. They are used to monitor and maintain the ring. MAC frames are confined to an individual ring—they don't pass through switches or routers onto other rings. To get an idea of what they do, consult the sections that follow.

| MAC Frame | Description |
|---|---|
| Active Monitor present | Issued by the Active Monitor (AM) during ring poll, letting other stations on the ring know that an AM is present. Under normal circumstances, this frame is issued by the AM every seven seconds. |
| Beacon | Generated by a station that has detected a hard error upstream (see Appendix C, "Token Ring Errors"). Used both to alert other stations on the ring of the error condition and to try to isolate where the error originated from. |

| MAC Frame | Description |
|---|---|
| Change parameters | Received during the request-initialization process during insertion. Contains parameter information, such as ring speed and maximum frame size. |
| Claim token | Triggers the monitor-contention process by indicating to the stations on the ring the absence of an Active Monitor. |
| Duplicate address test | Issued by a station attempting to insert during phase 2 of the ring-insertion process. Before allowing insertion, it ensures that the station's address is not already in existence on the ring. |
| Initialize ring station | Grants ring initialization in response to a request initialization frame from a station. It is issued by the Ring Parameter Server (RPS). |
| Lobe media test | Issued by a station attempting insertion during phase 0 of the ring-insertion process. The frame does a bit error rate test from the NIC to the port it is connecting to. It may also be issued during the beacon-resolution process. |
| Remove ring station | May be sent by the network manager to cause a forcible deinsertion of a station from the ring. |
| Report error | Created and sent to the Ring Error Monitor (REM) if the soft error report timer expires and the station has accumulated errors. |
| Report Error Monitor | Sent by the Active Monitor to the REM if it detects an error within itself, such as determining itself to be the cause of a beacon state. |
| Report NAUN change | Sent by a station to the Configuration Report Server (CRS) when a new NAUN (nearest active upstream neighbor) address is received. This usually occurs during the neighbor-notification process, and will also occur as stations leave and enter the ring. |
| Report new monitor | Sent to the CRS when a station becomes the new Active Monitor. |
| Report ring poll failure | Sent by the Active Monitor to the REM in the event of a ring poll failure. |
| Report station address | Sent by a station when its address is requested by the CRS. |

| MAC Frame | Description |
|---|---|
| Report station attachment | Sent by a station to the CRS in response to a request ring station attachment. Tells which token ring functions are active on the new station. |
| Report station state | Sent in response to a request station state MAC frame. It contains information about the status of the NIC. |
| Report transmit forward | Transmitted to the network manager in response to a transmit forward MAC frame. It shows that the station's communication path is open. |
| Request station address | Issued by the CRS to get a report station address MAC. |
| Request station attachment | Sent by the CRS to get a report station attachment MAC frame. |
| Request station state | Sent by the CRS to get a report station state MAC. |
| Response | A positive frame acknowledgement. |
| Ring purge | Sent by the AM during the ring-purge process. Causes all frames on the ring to be purged so that monitor contention can begin and the ring reinitialize is in a known good state. |
| Ring station request initialization | Occurs during phase 4 of the ring-insertion process to inform the Ring Parameter Server that it is ready to receive its parameters. |
| Standby Monitor present | Used by all stations during ring poll. Notifies stations of their NAUN address. |
| Transmit forward | Used by the network manager function to test the path between it and a station. |

Unlike the frames just described, the following three MAC frames do not require a free token to be transmitted:

- Beacon
- Claim token
- Ring purge

# Ring Purge

A ring purge is basically another type of token ring MAC frame that purges everything that is currently on the ring. A ring purge will be initiated under the following three conditions:

- The Active Monitor sees an error condition on the ring, such as a lost token or frame, a token ring process that did not complete properly, or that an active timing problem occurred.
- The T(Any_Token) timer expires.
- The Active Monitor sees the M(monitor) bit set to 1 (M=1) in the Access Control field of a frame. This basically states that the data is looping the ring multiple times without being stripped.

Under these circumstances, the Active Monitor transmits a ring purge frame and waits for it to come back. If it returns, the ring is assumed to have stabilized. All timers are reset, and the neighbor-notification process is initiated to bring the ring back to a normal state. If the ring purge frame does not come back, the token-claiming process begins.

# Beaconing

A beacon frame usually indicates a hardware error or fault, and this function is designed to be able to narrow down the fault domain. It causes the station that transmitted the beacon and its NAUN to perform self-tests, to determine whether either station may have itself caused the fault.

Hard-error recovery uses the beacon process to recover the ring when a hard error stops transmission on a ring. When a station sees a hard error come in, it enters beacon transmission mode—it sends a warning signal, called a *beacon MAC frame*, which helps define the fault domain. The fault domain consists of the beaconing station, its NAUN, the network equipment (NICs, or other station port), and the cable between them. A beacon MAC frame has three fields: the address of the station that initiated the beacon, the address of that station's NAUN, and the beacon type. The following are the four types of beacon MAC frames, used to narrow down the type of fault:

- **Set recovery mode** Can only be originated by the attached device acting as a recovery station. This mode is vendor-specific, and its purpose is dealing with advanced fault correction.
- **Signal loss** Sent when a station is in monitor contention transmit mode and the T(Claim_Token) timer expires (no new monitor was elected within the

allotted time), and the contention mode was entered because a signal loss was detected. This may be caused either by a 4Mbps station attempting to insert into a 16Mbps ring or by a cable fault. If a signal is detected during the transmission of a type 2 beacon, it is changed to type 3.

- **Bit streaming**   A station experienced monitor contention timeout while in monitor contention transmit mode, as in the signal loss beacon MAC, except it was not initiated by signal loss; if a loss of signal is detected during a type 3 beacon, it is changed to type 2 (signal loss).

- **Contention streaming**   Claim token MACs were received, but contention could not be resolved before T(Claim_Token) timer expired (1 second). If signal loss is detected during this beacon, it is changed to a type 2 (signal loss).

There are a few different types of beaconing and their causes, but they all behave in a common way once the beacon MAC has been transmitted:

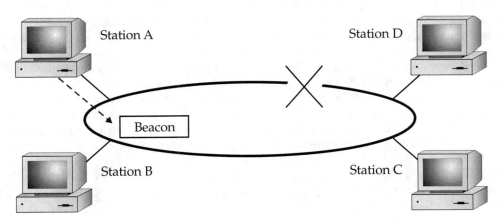

In this example, station A detects a hard error and transmits a beacon MAC frame that causes all other stations to broadcast over 20 milliseconds for the duration of the T(Beacon_Transmit) timer. This beacon frame is a broadcast and will be read by all stations. Within its INFO field, it contains the address of station A's NAUN; in this case, this is station D.

As the beacon traverses the ring, the other stations pass it on, entering beacon repeat mode. As each station detects the beacon frame, it checks to see whether it is, in fact the originator's NAUN, as described within the MAC itself:

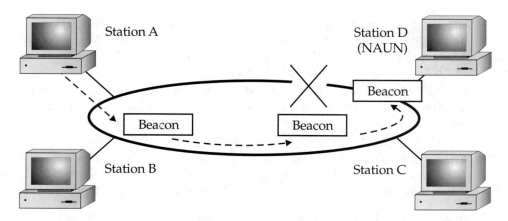

In our example, station D sees its address in the INFO field of the beacon frame, which tells it that it is the NAUN of the station that has transmitted the beacon. Station D determines that somewhere between its transmitter and station A's transmitter, a problem has occurred (a hard error) causing station A to beacon. (Station D also sees what kind of beacon it is by looking at the beacon MAC.)

At this point, station D passes the beacon along, just as the other stations did. The underlying idea is that if station A receives its beacon frame back, then the ring must have recovered and is now stable. At this point, the station that originated the beacon enters claim token transmit mode to initiate the monitor-contention process. A new Active Monitor is chosen, the ring is purged, and a new token is released; the ring now is back to a known, stable condition. However, if the originator of the beacon does not get its beacon frame back, it sends another one.

Station D will continually see beacon MAC frames come in with its address as the NAUN address of the beaconing station. This means the ring isn't recovering, and station D realizes that its repeated beacon frames are not, for some reason, getting to station A.

After station D receives eight consecutive beacon frames with itself as the NAUN of the originator, it determines that the ring is not going to recover and that something has failed. It recognizes that the fault domain lies between itself and station A, so either station has a bad transmitter, or the cable itself is bad. At this point, station D checks the easiest thing that it can—it deinserts from the ring, to make sure that it isn't the actual cause of the problem, and runs self-diagnostics to make sure its transmitter is okay:

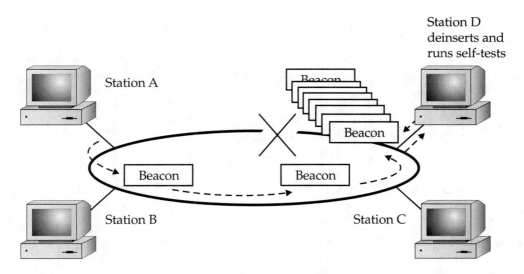

If it fails, of course, it remains off the ring. The next beacon frame should, without the faulty transmitter, make it to station A, which, upon seeing its own beacon, enters contention mode. If station D passes its tests, it reinserts (it does not need to go through the ring-insertion process to do this).

While this process is occurring, station A is running the T(Beacon_Transmit) timer, which lasts 16 seconds. This timer defines how long a station may remain in beacon transmit mode, before stopping, deinserting, and running its own self-diagnostics, to prevent the beacon condition from lasting indefinitely.

If station A fails its diagnostics, it remains out of the ring. If it passes as well, then both stations A and D can be reasonably sure that the hard error wasn't due to a fault in their transmitter or receiver. Station A reinserts (without repeating the ring-insertion process) and notifies network management. At this point, the problem is likely hardware related, and thus human intervention is required; a limit exists to how much the beacon can accomplish. The idea is to prevent one bad transmitter from bringing down the whole ring, and to maintain some degree of ring stability until the administrator can step in.

## Token Ring Addressing

Token ring hardware addresses utilize a format known as *canonical format*, which is different from the format used by Ethernet. This means that the MAC, or hardware, address of token ring devices is bit-flipped; the least significant bit becomes the most significant bit, in a sort of mirror image.

Single out an octet of the basic hardware MAC address, 5E. Token ring takes this octet and canonically flips the bits of each octet, causing the octet 5E to become 7A:

Here, each 4-byte hex nibble is canonically flipped, with the binary bits mirrored to create the new hex values. This is done on an octet-by-octet basis, and once completed, the new canonical format is created.

Since all token ring devices utilize this method, in a pure token ring environment, you don't need to worry about conversions. If, however, translational bridges are in place, ethernet MAC addresses will be canonically flipped when converted to the token ring frame format, and an ethernet address in a sniffer trace will change as it travels from ethernet to token ring.

The following are the two basic forms of addressing in token ring:

■ **Universally administered addresses (UAAs)**   The MAC that comes on the device (also known as the *burned in address*, or *BIA*).

■ **Locally administered addresses (LAAs)**   MACs that you input in place of the UAA. LAAs may be administered to reflect some sort of internal organization, and may ease troubleshooting or, in a secure environment, ease the organization of MAC filters. If LAAs are used, however, they must be strictly documented and updated, because the possibility of duplicate MAC addresses arises.

Either way, the fields within the frame of relevance are the Destination Address (DA) field and the Source Address (SA) field.

## DA: The Destination Address

The DA lets devices know where the frame is going, as its name suggests, but it also has a few other functions in token ring, as later sections will outline. To accomplish its primary function, the DA is divided into its component bits, as follows:

■ **Bit 1 (I/G)**   Identifies whether the destination is an individual or group address (meaning a unicast or a multicast, respectively). If this bit is set to 1, it's a group address; if 0, it's an individual address.

- **Bit 2 (U/L)**   Differentiates between a UAA and a LAA. If the bit is set to a 1, it's an LAA; if 0, it's a UAA.
- **Bits 3 through 48**   Identify the ring/station or group node address. Within this remaining 46 bits is found a specific ring or station address, with control info called *function addressing*. These addresses refer to certain functions, such as the Active Monitor (management functions):

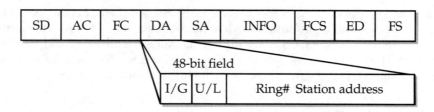

## Broadcast DA

When looking at a token ring trace, variations on the all-Fs broadcast destination address may appear:

| | |
|---|---|
| FF FF FF FF FF FF | Broadcast to all local stations |
| C0 00 FF FF FF FF | Broadcast MAC frame |

The following addresses may also be seen, and are the control frame addresses used in communication between machine states:

| | |
|---|---|
| C0 00 00 00 00 01 | Active Monitor |
| C0 00 00 00 00 02 | Ring Parameter Server |
| C0 00 00 00 00 08 | Ring Error Monitor |
| C0 00 00 00 00 10 | Configuration Report Server |

## SA: The Source Address

The SA identifies the station that has transmitted the frame:

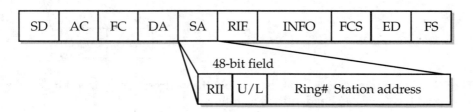

The SA is divided into its component bits, as follows:

- **Bit 1 (RII)**   If this bit is set to 1, it's a source-routed frame; if 0, it's an 802.1 transparently bridged frame.
- **Bit 2 (U/L)**   If this bit is set to a 1, it's an LAA; if 0, it's a UAA.
- **Bits 3 through 48**   Identify the ring/station or group node address.

In this example, notice the presence of two fields, one within the SA and one within the frame itself. The Routing Information Identifier (RII) portion of the SA indicates the presence of a Routing Information Field (RIF) in the frame (identifying it as a source-routed frame). The RIF is present only in source-routed frames. For more information on source-route bridging and the functionality of the RIF, consult Chapter 25.

## The Information Field

The INFO field contains the following frame vectors that show the function of the LLC (data) and MAC (management) frames:

- **LLC frame format**   If the frame is a data frame, it will be formatted with LLC entities, such as a Destination Service Access Point (DSAP) address, Source Service Access Point (SSAP) address, and higher-level data.
- **MAC frame format**   The MAC INFO field will be formatted with a Major Vector and SubVector fields. These fields basically contain the info the MAC management frame needs to communicate to the devices.
- **FCS: Frame Check Sequence**   Checks the frame to make sure that it is intact, by making certain it is the same size that is defined in the length field. Also known as the Cyclic Redundancy Check (CRC).
- **FS: Frame Status field**   When passing data frames, the LLC frames travel around the ring just like MAC frames. When one station sends data to another station, they both must know whether or not that data was received. This is accomplished through the Frame Status Field:

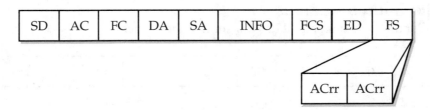

The FS field contains a series of bits, notably the address-recognized bit and the frame-copied bit. They can be identified as follows:

| A | C | Meaning |
|---|---|---|
| 0 | 0 | Address not recognized. |
| 1 | 0 | Address recognized; frame not copied. |
| 1 | 1 | Address recognized; frame copied. |

Together, the address-recognized and frame-copied bits serve two crucial functions:

- The address-recognized bit is flipped if a station sees a frame go by with its address as the DA.
- The frame copied bit is flipped if the frame destined for that station is successfully copied into its buffer.

The remaining bits (r) are reserved.

# Communication Between End Stations

Token ring has no contention in the same sense that Ethernet does, so things happen quite a bit differently. As mentioned earlier, in token ring, no station can transmit without first taking possession of the token; this is the essence of the turn-based system

Consider the following diagram, in which station A has data to transmit to station C, and station C has data that it wants to transmit to station B. The token, which is not in use, is moving around the ring and, for the sake of this example, is received by station A first. Station A examines the token and, observing that the T bit set to 0, realizes that it isn't currently in use. Station A appends its first frame of data to the token, addressed to station C. It then releases the token.

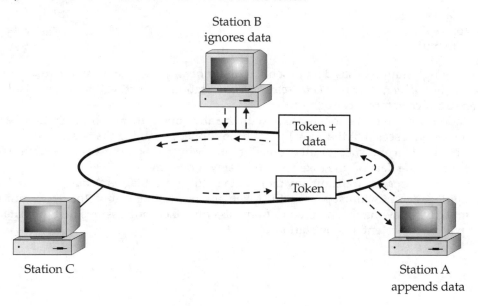

Station B
ignores data

Token +
data

Token

Station C

Station A
appends data

The amount of data attached depends on the MTU size configured on the devices. The token is next received by station B, which has nothing to send at the moment and thus isn't concerned with token availability. It checks the token (with its appended data), sees that the data is not destined for it, and releases the token.

Station C then receives the token. Station C has data that it wants to send but, observing that the T bit is set to 1, determines that the token is currently in use. Station C also identifies itself as the designated destination for the data currently held by the token, so it copies the data into its buffer. It then flips a bit, called the *copy bit*, in the FS (Frame Status) portion of that frame, and releases the token with the data still appended.

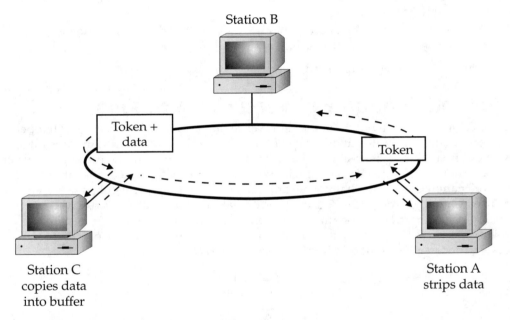

(Even though station C has data to send, it does not strip the data from the token. *Only the sending station can strip its data from the token.* Station C must wait for an available token to arrive before it can send.)

Station A receives the token, along with the attachment that it sent to station C. Upon receipt, it sees that the copy bit has been flipped, meaning that station C has received the data and successfully copied it into its buffer. Station A is now responsible for stripping the data off the token and releasing it once more.

Station A does not transmit any more data at this time. Station A has just transmitted, and now must pass on the token, giving another station the opportunity to transmit. By following this method of transmission, token ring assures that the data flow will be consistent among stations.

Station A releases the token. Station B receives it and still has nothing to transmit. The token is passed to station C, which is still waiting to send. The token is free now, so station C appends its data, and the process begins anew.

## Token Reservation and Prioritization

The token ring system is fair and achieves a smooth data flow, but sometimes data is critical and must be prioritized. For such a case, a function is in place within the token ring specification called *reserving the token*, or *priority control protocol*.

This process consists of a station appending data to the token and then marking the token in such a way as to let all the other stations on the ring know that the station is requesting an increased priority to have the token.

The token frame's Priority (P) and Reservation (R) bits, which work in tandem, are utilized at this point.

Each P and each R is actually a 4-byte nibble, allowing values between 0 and 7 for each field. The lowest is 0 and the highest is 7. If station A needs to transmit to station C and must utilize an increased priority (this is configured on the station itself), it manipulates these bits:

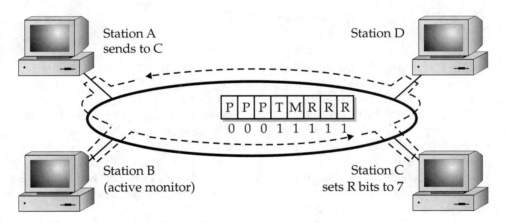

In this example, it sends at a priority of 0. The token, by default, has a priority of 0, so station A grabs the token and sends its data to station C. Station C also has data ready to go, and it wants to attach the highest priority to this extremely sensitive data. It basically wants to reserve the token by marking it so that other stations will know to ignore the token, even if it is free—so Station C reserves the token with the highest level, 7, by altering the reservation bits.

The token passes station D, which has nothing to transmit, and then returns to station A. Station A receives the token, strips its data from it, and notes that the reservation bits have been set to 7, so it sets the priority bits to reflect this, flips the reservation bits back down to 0, and releases the token.

Station B then receives the token and wants to transmit. Station B, for the sake of this example, has data ready, but it is set at a priority level of 5, which is superceded by the priority level of 7. Station B is denied the token, even though it is next in line to transmit. However, station B can also make a reservation; it sets the reserve bits to reflect its priority level 5:

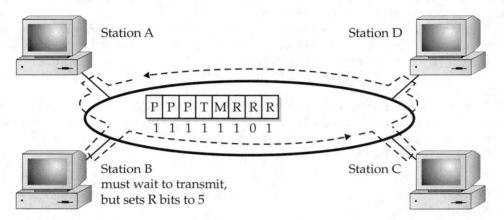

Station C now gets the token at priority 7 (its own priority) and sends it along. When it receives the token back, it strips it, sets the priority to 5 to reflect station B's reservation, sets the reservation bits back to 0, and then releases the token.

Station B receives the token next (assuming no other station had reserved the token with a higher priority before C received it), strips it, releases the token with all zeros (assuming no other reservations have taken place), and the token is back on the ring at its default priority.

Through this technique, high-priority data can be favored in a fair way, because the prioritization is bumped back down to its original state when transmission has occurred, so that no single station monopolizes the ring.

## Early Token Release

As a general rule, only one frame is on a token ring at any one time. However, a mechanism (found in 16Mbps token ring only) called *Early Token Release* enables more than one frame to be on the ring simultaneously.

In Early Token Release, the originating station releases the token right after its frame is transmitted onto the wire. This token is available to be used by any other station, before this data frame returns to the originating station. After the originating station gets its frame back and strips it, it does not release the token, because it has already done so directly following the transmission. This procedure allows for more than one frame on the ring, but only one token. Only one token can be on the ring at any time.

## Dedicated Token Ring

A direct-attached token ring station uses *dedicated token ring (DTR)*. This function often is related to switched token ring ports, whereby a server or router port is attached directly, instead of being a member of a concentrator that is attached. Under these circumstances, the device does not share the token with any other devices, because its connection forms its own dedicated ring with the switched port. It is assured use of the token on every pass, and therefore never competes with other stations for bandwidth.

## Full-Duplex Token Ring

With the advent of DTR came *full-duplex token ring*. Normally in token ring, a station must have possession of a free token to be able to transmit, and the data must be stripped by that station for the token to be available for further transmission. In full-duplex operations, however, a station transmits and receives at the same time. This is at odds with the traditional token-passing system, but when a station is the only station on the ring, the need for the token becomes less important. Because the only two entities on the ring in this situation are the station and the concentrator port, no incoming data exists that needs to be repeated—only data destined for the station—so the station never accidentally overwrites anything if it doesn't wait for the token to transmit. In full-duplex token ring, the DTR station does not wait for the token. They are rated for a full 32Mbps.

Token ring frames, both LLC data frames and MAC frames, can communicate a lot about what is transpiring on the ring at any given time. MAC frames show much information regarding the protocol state, and LLC frames can tell a lot about the current frame state, their type, where they came from, where they're going, and—in many cases—where they've been. This is an intercommunication between devices, and can also be used as a means of analysis and troubleshooting when the frames are captured for viewing. In a moderate-to-large token ring network, some means of frame capture can prove invaluable.

# The Complete Reference

Nortel
Networks

# Chapter 25

## Bridging and Switching Token Ring

Token Ring is an efficient protocol, but like Ethernet, once the number of users begins to increase, performance begins to degrade as more and more stations compete for the ring's resources. When traffic becomes too heavy on a single ring, it is time to begin *segmenting* traffic, breaking up stations into smaller, interconnected rings. Each ring is similar in concept to different Ethernet segments, in this case.

Before the advent of token ring switching, a limited number of ways were available to segment traffic; due to a chip limitation, token ring bridges could consist of only two ports, bridging between two adjacent rings. This becomes an issue mainly when bridging token ring traffic on a router with multiple token ring interfaces, though from a logical standpoint, the two-port rule is, in fact, still adhered to in token ring bridges. The method used to work around the two-port limitation was to attribute an internal ring to the device, whereas in the case of switched token ring (which may also consist of many ports on a single device), each ring is switched through a common core, which, for the purposes of source-route bridging, introduces a single hop between any two rings using a single, common bridge ID.

Later in the chapter, in the segments on internetworking, you'll see other devices using this same concept.

# Transparent Bridging

Of the different bridging methodologies available in the token ring environment, transparent bridging is the simplest. Transparent bridges learn addresses of devices on a port-by-port basis, and build tables to keep track of that information, so that they know which traffic to block, which to forward, and where to forward it.

The term "transparent bridging" is used because it is transparent to the end station; there is no need for the end station to know that its data is being bridged elsewhere in the network, because the bridges handle the business of deciding where the packets are going. The concept works the same as in Ethernet, with segments taking the place of rings.

## Spanning Tree

Spanning Tree is a protocol designed to prevent network loops. This basically is accomplished by detecting redundant paths and then placing one of the paths in a "blocking" state, allowing traffic to pass over only the primary, forwarding path. If the forwarding path fails and the loop is broken, the blocking path becomes active.

In Token Ring, two types of Spanning Tree are available: IEEE 802.1d Spanning Tree, and IBM Spanning Tree (used with source-route bridging).

## IEEE 802.1d Spanning Tree

When configured for 802.1d Spanning Tree, bridges monitor incoming bridge protocol data units (BPDUs) to detect network loops. If a loop is detected, one of the bridge ports blocks incoming traffic, thus resolving the loop. For more information on the 802.1d Spanning Tree Protocol, consult Chapter 2.

## Source-Route Bridge Spanning Tree (IBM Spanning Tree)

The source-route bridging implementation of Spanning Tree is similar in concept, except that when a loop is detected, the port in question doesn't block all incoming and outgoing traffic—it blocks a type of packet called a Spanning Tree Explorer (STE). This packet is used exclusively in a source-route bridged environment, and it is the method end stations use to find remote stations on other rings (this is covered in the next section). If a bridge blocks these packets, then the route through it is effectively blocked, since discovery of the remote node will never occur along that path. In the SRB Spanning Tree scenario, one bridge becomes the designated bridge (the one that will pass STEs) the other blocks, just like in IEEE Spanning Tree, except that data is not blocked, just STE packets.

# Source-Route Bridging

Source routing is another method that token ring utilizes so that two stations can find each other across multiple rings. As the name suggests, the route to the destination is determined by the source station. Meaning, if a station A must reach a remote station B, station A is responsible for determining a route to station B, after which it uses this information to send its transmission with the route already in place.

In this example, the first thing station A must do is determine whether or not station B resides on its local ring. So, station A sends out an initial frame, which traverses the ring and returns to station A.

When the frame comes back, station A examines it to see whether the address recognized bit is set. If it is, then station B is local, and transmission may begin. If it isn't set, then station A determines that station B resides on a remote ring elsewhere in the network, but has no way of determining where at this point. In a source-routed environment, because station A must discover the route to station B itself, it is responsible for initiating this discovery. Station A sends out another type of packet called an explorer packet:

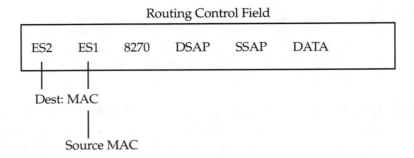

## Explorer Packets

The job of an explorer packet is to traverse the multiple rings, and find the destination station (station B, in this example).

When using source route bridging, bridge IDs are added for each bridge. These IDs will also be used in calculating the best route to station B. These IDs do not have to follow any specific scheme, unless there are two bridges in parallel, in which case their IDs must be unique. Aside from that, the numbering scheme is of no consequence, and all bridges may in fact utilize the same ID number. These bridge IDs will be added, along with the ring numbers, to the route descriptors in the explorer frame, to build a path to the destination.

There are two types of explorer packets: All Routes Explorers (ARE), and Single Route Explorer, often called a Spanning Tree Explorer (STE) or Single Route Broadcast (SRB). The type used depends on the network interface card (NIC), and may in some cases be manually configured. The difference between the explorer types lies in how they are handled by the bridged ports that they are received on.

### All Routes Explorer (ARE)

In a multiring environment, if an ARE traverses a ring that is host to three bridges, it will be forwarded at each bridge. If it encounters a switch, it will be forwarded onto the internal ring, and then out each switched port (see Figure 25-1).

### Spanning Tree Explorer (STE)

In a multiring environment, if an STE traverses a ring that is host to multiple bridges, it will be forwarded only at each bridge that is not in a Spanning Tree blocking state. In a source-routed environment, Spanning Tree will block the passage of Spanning Tree Explorers, therefore invalidating any route along that path. This cuts down on overhead and prevents Spanning Tree loops (refer to Figure 25-1).

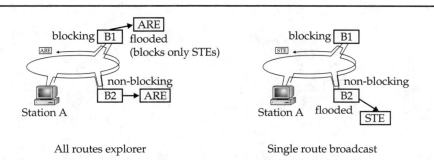

**Figure 25-1.**   *All Routes Explorer (ARE) vs. Spanning Tree Explorer (STE) explorer packets*

Either way, when an explorer packet is received by a bridge, switch, or router, the packet is copied out at least one port along the path to the destination, so that it may travel each ring in the network to find the destination station. These explorer packets quickly propagate throughout the network (see Figure 25-2).

As the explorer packets travel through the network, they are calculating a route. Each time an explorer encounters a bridge or other such device, information is added to that packet. Each bridge that receives such a packet inserts into it both its own bridge number and the ring number of the ring it is flooding it onto. For a switch, the ring number in the route descriptor will be different for each port, though the bridge ID will remain constant.

A device will not copy the packet onto a ring it has already traversed, this information having been inserted into the packet already. This prevents the explorer packet from being received on the interface it initially came in on, and then being copied out every port again.

Eventually, the explorer packet makes its way to station B, which receives it and determines, by examining the Destination Address (DA) field, that it is the destination station. At this point, station B sends an ARE back to station A in response.

In this case, there are two paths, so as the AREs get flooded through the rings, two distinct paths emerge. This results ultimately in two AREs returning to the originating ring. The one that gets there first is accepted by station A, and the latecomer is discarded. The idea behind this is that the ARE that gets there first must have taken the best route, so this is the one that is used (refer to Figure 25-2).

Station A now has a route to station B. It extracts this route information from the ARE and traces backward the path the ARE initially took. Station A now has the information it needs to send data to station B.

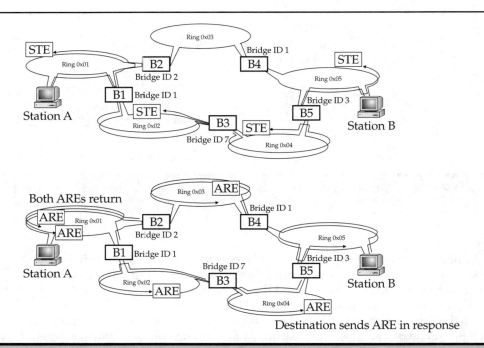

**Figure 25-2.**   *Explorer packets determining path to destination and building a Routing Information Field (RIF)*

# Alternate Explorer Methods

There are two other methods of route discovery, but they follow the same concept of RIF building through the exchange of explorer packets between source and destination.

## All Routes Broadcast/Nonbroadcast Return

Using this method, an ARE is initiated by the sending station rather than an STE. The AREs are flooded out each bridged port on the way to the destination station, determining the shortest route on the way there, as opposed to on the way back. The destination station in this scenario follows the route indicated by the ARE it receives first, and sends a single route broadcast back to the source, based on that information.

## Single Route Broadcast/Single Route Return

Using this method, a Spanning Tree Explorer is sent, and rather than dispatch an ARE back to the source, a single route broadcast is sent back along the same path indicated in the received STE.

Whichever method is used, station A discovers a valid path to station B, two rings away, and knows the shortest path to get there. This will be a logical link control (LLC) transfer, so no third-layer information is added, and the information determined through the explorer frames is added to the LLC frame.

# The Routing Information Field

The Routing Information Field (RIF), which is built through explorer packet exchange, indicates the source-routed path. This field is not always present in a token ring frame. In a transparently bridged environment, there is no need for the RIF, so it is not inserted. Only in a source-routed environment where explorer packets are utilized and multiple rings are traversed is the RIF added into the packet. Whether or not the frame is source-routed will be noted in the Source Address field of the frame:

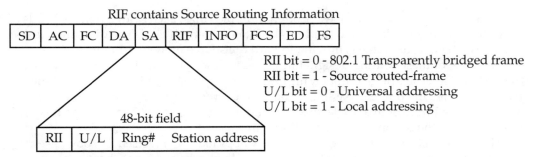

Note: The RII (Routing Information Indicator) flags the presence of a Routing Information Field (RIF).

The Routing Information Indicator (RII) will be flipped to a 1 if the frame is to be source-routed. This is how devices know to look for a RIF field in an incoming packet. Seeing the bit flipped to a 1 tells the devices that they are in a source-routed environment and are now dealing with a source-routed frame. The RIF is inserted, the route contained within, and these two elements combined allow devices to determine where the frame needs to go.

The RIF contains the route the ARE took from the DA back to the source, which is then traced backward. The RIF contains a series of fields:

RIF contains Source Routing Infomation

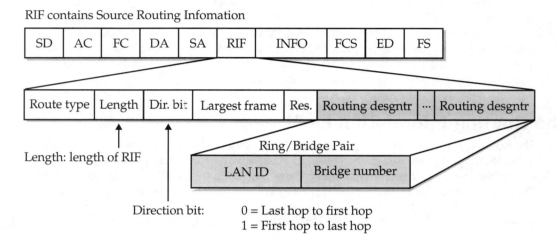

Length: length of RIF

Direction bit:  0 = Last hop to first hop
1 = First hop to last hop

As an explorer frame traverses through multiple rings, each bridge it passes adds an additional routing designator and recalculates the length field. The direction bit indicates whether the frame is moving toward the source or away from it.

Each one of these routing designators or route descriptors will include two things: the LAN ID and the bridge number, meaning the ring the frame is going to, and the ID of the bridge the frame is passing through to get there. By piecing these together, a path is traced from source to destination, and, by reading it backwards, a path is followed from the destination back to the source.

There is a limit, as in Ethernet, to how many hops may be traversed. In some cases, this parameter may be altered, but the maximum is seven hops (due to the maximum number of route descriptors that may be contained in the RIF).

## Source-Route Transparent

In a source-route transparent environment, the bridges and switches involved will source-route any frame that is marked as a source-routed frame (as indicated in the RII portion of the Source Address, or SA, field), and will transparently bridge any frame that is not. This is beneficial, because both types of traffic may coexist within the same network. Also, certain end stations support this dual scheme, transparently bridging frames at first to make faster connections, and then running the explorer in the background, finding the best route, and then, once this route is established, source routing the remainder of the data for speedier transmission.

# Translationally Bridging and Switching Token Ring

Token ring can coexist with a number of other networking architectures, some that are ring-based, token-passing architectures, and some that are not. In a transparently bridged network, this integration is relatively easy, because ring numbers and bridge IDs do not play an active role. However, certain considerations must be made if the token ring network is source routed, or is a source-routed transparent environment.

The main thing to remember is that token ring has no mechanism in place to understand anything except a ring-based architecture. When network types are mixed, such as with Token Ring and Ethernet, the conflicting architecture must be made to *appear* to the native token ring to be ring-based.

## Token Ring and Ethernet

There are many reasons why token ring and Ethernet may coexist within the same network: a network may be cutting over from token ring to Ethernet, or vice versa (though perhaps less likely), from Ethernet to token ring. Ethernet may provide an inexpensive solution if a new group of nodes needs to be added into an existing token ring network; or conflicting network types may be found on either side of a wide area network.

Of course, Ethernet and token ring are very different. One can't be connected to the other without some device in place to resolve the differences between them. Basically, two ways exist to handle the conversion between the dissimilar architectures:

- A translational bridge, which is covered in the next section
- Route between them

Remember, however, that source-routed traffic can't be routed, so for all intents and purposes, a router must be configured as a translational bridge in these cases.

## Translational Bridging

Token Ring flips its address bits around in a canonical format; because of this, a problem with translation may potentially arise. With a translational bridge, this is not difficult to accomplish; a translational bridge may easily be made to check the SA and DA fields in the MAC frame and flip them back again, because they must examine the Layer 2 MAC information anyway. Problems begin to arise when routing between dissimilar topologies like this because SA and DA information also gets inserted into the INFO field, where it can become more problematic. This concept will be discussed at greater length in the section on Token Ring routing.

Translational bridging between Ethernet and token ring is relatively simple in a transparently bridged environment; with no source routing in place, there are no explorer frames, and no RIF information to worry about, and only the frame type needs to be considered. If the network is a source-routed network, however, then some mechanism has to be in place to accommodate the RIF route descriptors when the frame is passing to and from an environment in which no physical ring exists.

In a transparently bridged network, when a frame passes from token ring to Ethernet, the translational bridge handles the frame conversion (from 802.3 or 802.2 frame format to the 802.5 Token Ring frame format), frame lengths (the max MTU size for Ethernet is 1518, while token ring supports much larger frame sizes), and MAC address formats (canonical versus noncanonical).

### Encapsulation

In a strictly Ethernet environment, unless running IPX and utilizing different frame types simultaneously, generally a common Ethernet frame type is running on an Ethernet network. This frame type may need to be specified on the translational bridge as the encapsulation method. Token ring encapsulation will be 802.5.

### MTU

Each networking architecture generally supports a variety of frame sizes (with the exception of certain technologies such as ATM, which uses a fixed cell size), and each has a minimum and maximum frame size that is supported. Depending on the network types being translated between, this may require some consideration. For instance, if a frame comes in at 18,000 bytes on the token ring side of a translational bridge, it would have to be fragmented before undergoing Ethernet encapsulation, where the frame may only be 1518 bytes long.

## Source Routing with Translational Bridging

Since Ethernet is a contention-based system that doesn't use bridge IDs or ring numbers, there are some considerations which must be made when attempting to send source-routed traffic across a translational bridge.

In this environment, since an entry needs to be made into the RIF for the Ethernet segment(s) the data will pass through, the entire Ethernet portion of the network is considered a single *virtual ring* that will be assigned its own ring number (see Figure 25-3).

The translational bridge uses its own bridge ID, as well as the ring ID of the virtual ring, to make its route descriptor entry. By doing so, the existence of the Ethernet segment becomes transparent to the source-route bridged environment.

## Token Ring and FDDI

Token ring may be translated to FDDI, and back again. In fact, FDDI uses a canonical frame format, as well, and is also a ring-based, token-passing system. From a token ring perspective, however, Token Ring views the FDDI ring in the same way that it

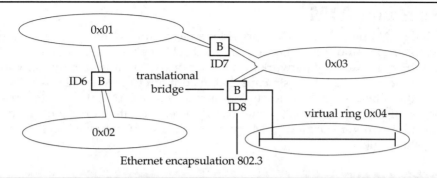

**Figure 25-3.**    *Explorer traversing virtual ring, which is added with bridge ID into the route descriptor field*

views the Ethernet portion of a translationally bridged source-routed network—as a virtual ring. The translational bridge will encapsulate the frame in the appropriate FDDI encapsulation (see Figure 25-4).

FDDI-to-Token Ring translational bridges generally take the form of routers arranged around a FDDI backbone, which must also support source-routed token ring traffic that is nonroutable and, therefore, must be translationally source-route bridged.

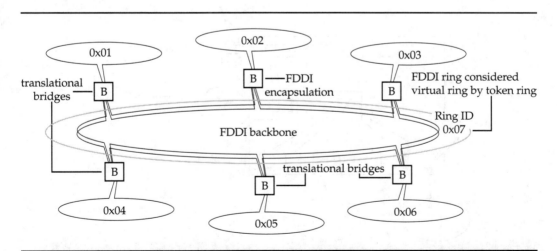

**Figure 25-4.**    *Token rings orbiting a FDDI backbone with virtual token ring ID*

## Token Ring and ATM

Token ring LAN Emulation (LANE) provides a means for resolving the differences between token ring and the connection-oriented ATM network. As in Ethernet, the job of LANE in a token ring network is to render the ATM portion of the network invisible to the legacy LAN. This means that in addition to processing the unknown frames, and multicasts and broadcasts common to legacy LANs, it needs to have the functionality to accommodate a ring-based system and its source-routed traffic. For more information regarding ATM and LANE, consult Chapter 13, in Part IV, "ATM Technologies."

## Token Ring LANE

Token ring LANE provides a virtual port (via the ATM edge device) on the ring in question. In these cases, the LAN Emulation Client (LEC) may be thought of as a station on the ring for purposes of receiving legacy frames (see Figure 25-5).

In this case, the virtual port receives all token ring traffic for the ring of which it is a member (the ATM ELAN, in this case, which acts as a virtual ring), and from that point, handles all broadcasts, multicasts, or unknown frames exactly as it normally would, as long as the frames are transparently bridged.

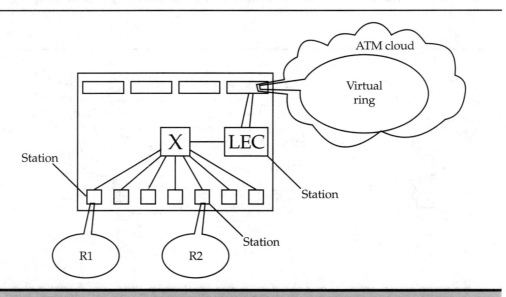

**Figure 25-5.**    *LEC as station on token ring*

If the legacy network is a source-routed network, however, then this must be taken into consideration when implementing the ATM core. For instance, in a source-route environment, one of the frames received by the LEC may be an explorer frame, whether that be an ARE or an STE. This means that source-route information must be added to the route descriptors.

In token ring LANE, a LEC has to support address resolution of those aforementioned route descriptors, in order to position ATM in a source-routed environment. Just as in Ethernet, ATM, as a connection-oriented technology, must resolve the inherent differences between itself and connectionless Ethernet. Likewise, it must resolve the differences between its own connection-oriented environment and a token-based one. So, again, as with Ethernet, token ring LANE must make its existence look like just another portion of the legacy network. In a source-routed token ring network, the ATM cloud appears to the legacy LAN as a ring. Everything in source-routed token ring is thought of in this way, and ATM is no exception to this rule.

This example has three switches, each with its own existing legacy rings. Each is connected via ATM, utilizing a single ELAN (see Figure 25-6). In this example, by placing each LEC in the virtual ring of ring 0x06, and assigning each to ELAN1, each device is given ATM connectivity, while emulating the backbone ring that links them. By doing this, it is possible to create many ELANs, each with a unique ring number (refer to Figure 25-6).

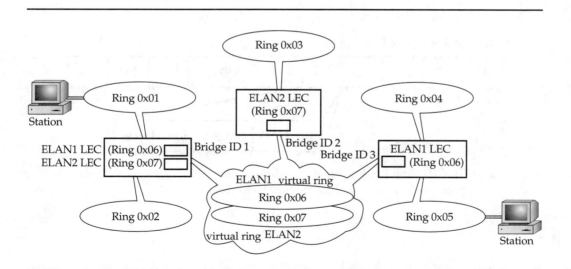

**Figure 25-6.**    *Multiple ELANs with multiple clients in an SRB network*

Following the path from a station on ring 0x01 to ring 0x05, the RIF might show the path ring 0x01 to bridge 1 to ring 0x06 to bridge3 to ring 0x05. Likewise, to go from ring 0x02 to ring 0x03, the RIF would indicate ring 0x02 to bridge 1 to ring 0x07 to bridge 2 to ring 0x03.

If the token ring frame is a non-source-routed frame, the LEC is going to send the frame across the appropriate Virtual Control Channel (VCC) for the destination address specified in the frame. If it doesn't know which VCC that is yet, it does an LE_ARP for the destination address. The frame will be sent across the BUS control channel at this point until the address is resolved, as would normally be the case. If the frame is a multicast, it will be sent to the BUS. These are the same concepts that are seen in Ethernet LANE.

## ATM and Explorer Frames

If an ATM client receives an explorer frame, it is sent to the BUS. At this point, the appropriate route descriptor is added to the RIF, and the length of the frame is recalculated. A LEC determines the type of frame it is dealing with in much the same way as any other device would—it examines the RII field in the SA:

RII bit = 0 - 802.1 Transparently bridged frame
RII bit = 1 - Source Routed Frame
U/L bit = 0 - Universal addressing
U/L bit = 1 - Local addressing

RIF contains Source Routing Infomation

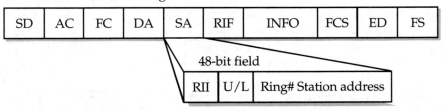

Note: The RII (Routing Information Indicator) flags the
presence of a Routing Information Field (RIF).

Again, the RII may indicate a source-routed frame and point to a RIF. The LEC will use certain fields within the RIF when determining how to handle the frame.

RIF

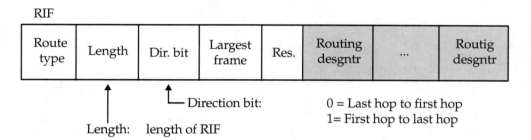

| Route type | Length | Dir. bit | Largest frame | Res. | Routing desgntr | ... | Routig desgntr |

Length: length of RIF

Direction bit:
0 = Last hop to first hop
1 = First hop to last hop

Several things occur once a LEC determines that the frame is a source-routed data frame:

■ Since the ATM client is aware that a RIF is present, it knows it must determine where in the hop count it stands, so it must observe the route descriptors (RDs).

■ If the LEC receives a frame with a RIF field whose length is less than 6 bytes, this indicates that there are no hops. In this case, the LEC must send the frame along the VCC to the destination address. Again, if this is not known, an LE_ARP is generated to find the LEC associated with that token ring address. The frame may be sent to the BUS for processing.

■ If the LEC determines that the last hop is the ELAN of which it is a member, then the frame is passed along the VCC to the DA. If it isn't known, an LE_ARP is used to resolve the address.

Of course, situations will occur in which the length of the RIF exceeds 6 bytes, indicating multiple hops exist, and the ELAN of which the particular LEC is a member isn't the last hop. When this occurs, the LEC locates where in the sequence of route descriptors its own ring ID is located, then sends the frame along the direct VCC for the next_RD (next route descriptor), meaning it will send the frame over the Data Direct VCC leading to the next hop described in the RIF. If it is unknown, an LE_ARP is generated.

The next_RD basically equates to the segment ID and bridge number to the next LAN segment, as the RI is built by sending an explorer frame through the bridged network. A LEC must determine at this point if its ELAN is the last hop (see Figure 25-7).

If the D (direction) bit = 0, and the client's ELAN is located in the last route descriptor in the list, then there are no further route descriptors, and the last hop must be this ELAN.

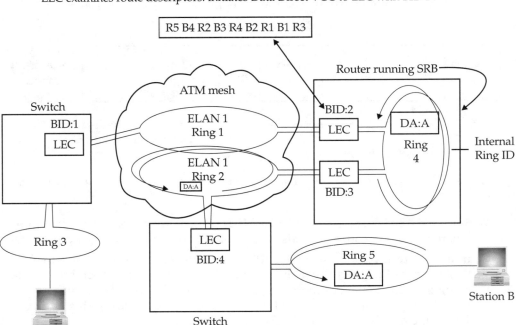

**Figure 25-7.** *Source-routed path determination through ATM*

Likewise, if the D bit = 1, and the client's ELAN is located in the first route descriptor, then there are no further route descriptors and, again, the last hop is this ELAN. If the client's ELAN is located anywhere else in the sequence of route descriptors, then the LEC's ELAN can't be the destination ELAN, and the next hop in the overall path must be determined.

The RD prior to RDn is RDn-1, containing {Segment_IDn-1, BRn-1}. The RD just after RDn is RDn+1, containing {Segment_IDn+1, BRn+1}. When the D bit=0, then the next_RD is the Segment_ID from RDn+1, and the bridge number is RDn. When the D bit=1, the next_RD is the Segment_ID and bridge number from RDn-1.

The LEC looks at the direction bit and determines whether it is following the route descriptors forward, toward the source, or backward away from it. It next attempts to determine whether its hop is the last hop; if it is, then the frame has been delivered to the last hop in the path. If it is not the last hop, then it must be determined where in the source-routed path the ELAN sits, so that it will be delivered to the correct next hop destination.

Tables 25-1 and 25-2 describe token ring frames and how they are handled in an ATM environment. This is from the LANE 1.0 specification.

| *Frame Type | Destination Address Unicast | Multicast |
|---|---|---|
| Non-source-routed | VCC(DA) | BUS |
| Explorer (ARE or STE) | BUS | BUS |
| Specifically routed (SRF) | See Table 25-2 | BUS |

**Table 25-1.**   *LAN Destination of Token Ring Frames*

# Other ATM Considerations

You won't run into MTU problems in Ethernet LANE; all the clients should be running the same maximum frame size (1518) in an Ethernet environment. In token ring, of course, you may select the MTU size you are going to use, and this must be taken into consideration in an ATM network, because a mismatched MTU size is one of the things that causes a LEC to be refused by either the LECS, if it is requesting the LES address from it, or the LES itself, which will deny a successful join if the client is pointed directly at the LES.

Although the legacy frame size may seem irrelevant, because the frames are being segmented into cells, a frame that is 9,234 bytes in length, which is then segmented into cells, can't be reassembled at a remote client whose MTU is set to 4544. LANE helps to avoid this problem by not allowing a client to join if its MTU is not consistent with the rest of the ELAN.

| Routing Information | Destination |
|---|---|
| No hops | VCC(DA) |
| Last hop | VCC(DA) |
| Not last hop | VCC(next_RD) |

**Table 25-2.**   *LAN Destination for Unicast SRF*

In accordance with the LANE 1.0 specification, the AAL-5 max octet size is as follows:

| | |
|---|---|
| 1516 | IEEE 802.3 Ethernet (LANEv1) |
| 4544 | IEEE 802.5 Token Ring 4Mbps |
| 9234 | RFC 1626 (RFC 1626 "Default IP MTU for use over AAL5") |
| 18190 | IEEE 802.5 Token Ring 16Mbps |

# Token Ring Routing

Routing in token ring is really no more complicated than routing in Ethernet; in a non-source-routed environment, the ring ID and bridge ID are not needed, and so the only real routing considerations are those imposed by the protocol that is being routed.

Generally, in token ring internetworking, the complexities arise when using nonroutable protocols, such as source-route bridging.

## Source-Route Bridging

Source-route bridging is not a routable protocol; if source-routed traffic occurs in a token ring network, and routers are involved in the mix, then other traffic may be routed normally, but SRB must be configured on the routers to accommodate anything that is being source-route bridged. Because source-route bridging works quite a bit differently than transparent bridging, some intrinsic problems are encountered when interoperating with third-layer devices.

In the case of a router separating token ring broadcast domains, when the source station sends an explorer packet to determine the route to the destination station, it will be dropped when the router receives it, if SRB has not been configured. Explorer packets are nonroutable, and a device routing at Layer 3 will not add RIF information. The packet gets dropped, and the source never finds the destination. Likewise, with bridging configured on the router, a transparent bridge (even a translational one) will not add RIF information to a frame.

When going LAN to LAN, and source-route bridging across a router, explorer packets must be bridged. Since the environment is source routed as well, the interfaces must be configured for source-route bridging.

A router circumvents the two-bridge port chip limitation by creating an internal ring; each SRB interface in this case bridges between its external ring and the internal ring. All incoming ports in this scenario utilize a common bridge ID. The router ports in question are configured for source-route bridging in addition to any other protocols that are relevant, and the ring numbers are assigned (since source-route bridging is loaded and they are now needed for use in the RIF route descriptors—see Figure 25-8).

In this scenario, a bridge is being emulated for the purposes of transporting source-routed data. Stations using a network layer protocol simply are routed in the

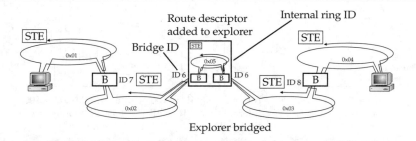

**Figure 25-8.**    *Source-route bridging from LAN to LAN across a router*

normal way and, likewise, transparently bridged token ring traffic may be handled by the router's transparent bridging services, because no explorer packets or RIF information exist to be concerned about.

## Source-Route Bridging on the Nortel Networks Platform

By default, source-route bridging on the Nortel Networks platform utilizes a proprietary scheme, to minimize the perceived SRB hops when source-routed traffic passes through the routed portion of a network, though the traditional method may also be used (incurring more source-route bridge hops). The advantage to reducing the hop count is, in the RIF field of a source-routed frame, a limited number of route descriptors may be added (a total of seven, maximum). Since the router effectively uses two separate token ring interfaces to emulate two token ring bridges on a single internal ring, source-route bridged traffic passing through multiple router hops could potentially incur numerous source-route hops. To get around this, a mechanism was implemented to make the router's source-route hops invisible to the rest of the source-routed network. This method is described in the next section, "Explorer Frames in the Nortel Networks Source-Route Bridged Enviornment."

Depending on its position in the source-routed network, a Nortel Networks router performing source-route bridging may handle incoming packets in different ways; a Nortel Networks router running source-route bridging uses a bridge ID, an internal LAN ID (the internal ring number), and a group LAN ID (see Figure 25-9). The bridge ID must have a common value, and the group LAN ID, by default, will have a value of FFF. To understand the reason for these values and the role that they play, consult the following examples, in which an explorer frame passes through several router hops to determine the source-routed path, and then, once the RIF information is complete, a Specifically Routed Frame is sent to the destination.

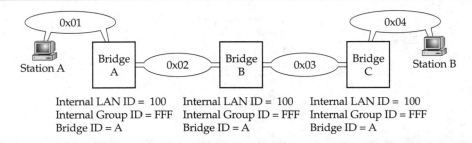

**Figure 25-9.**   Nortel Networks SRB example with two stations, three bridges and four rings

## Explorer Frames in the Nortel Networks Source-Route Bridged Environment

In this example, station A wants to talk to station B, and must traverse a traditional source-route bridge, as well as being source-route bridged across several routers in the core (see Figure 25-10).

Station A sends an explorer frame to determine the route to station B. The explorer frame is received by the traditional source-route bridge, and the route descriptors are

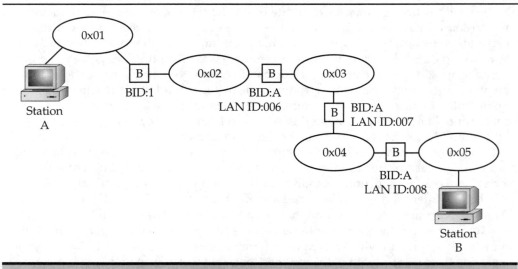

**Figure 25-10.**   Source-routed network with traditional bridges and routers in core

inserted into the RIF field. The frame is next received by router 1, which has SRB configured. Router 1 determines that the explorer has passed through another bridge elsewhere in the network, but that the bridge was not a Nortel Networks router running SRB. At this point, it inserts into the RIF the incoming ring ID and bridge ID, its own internal LAN ID and bridge ID, as well as the outgoing ring ID and a bridge ID of 0.

Router 2 is the next device to receive the explorer frame. To eliminate the added source-route hops that would be introduced by the routers, router 2 takes the explorer frame and removes the last internal LAN ID from the RIF. It replaces the bridge ID that was defined as bridge ID 0 by router 1 with its own bridge ID, and then adds its own internal LAN ID and bridge ID, and adds the outgoing ring ID and, again, gives it a bridge ID of 0 (see Figure 25-11).

Router 3 will follow the same steps as router 2. This effectively makes the journey through the core routers look as though it is only one hop.

## Specifically Routed Frames in a Nortel Networks Source-Routed Environment

Once the RIF has been established, the SRF is transmitted. Following the RIF back, it traverses the traditional bridge and is received by router 1. Router 1 at this point changes the destination system's MAC to a Nortel group address, which will be

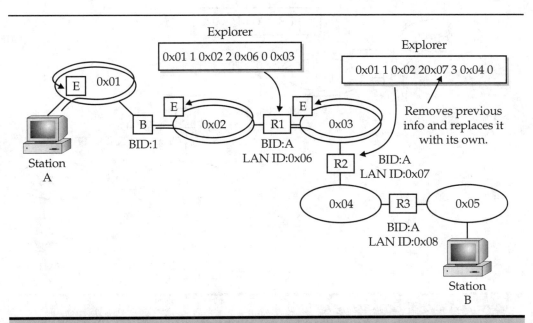

**Figure 25-11.** *Router 2 altering RIF information to eliminate source-route hops*

interpreted as C000A2FFFFFF*x* (where *x* is the bridge ID of the next bridge in the RIF). Next, it strips its own internal LAN ID and puts the group LAN ID (FFF) before the last incoming ring and bridge ID. It then copies the destination MAC address into the Data field of the frame (see Figure 25-12).

Router 2 then receives the frame. It determines that it has passed at least one other Nortel Networks router, due to the presence of the group LAN ID. Due to the information contained in the RIF, router 2 also determines that it is not the last Nortel Networks router that is in the data path. At this point, router 2 changes the bridge ID at the end of the group address (C000A2FFFFFF*x*, looking at the *x* at this point) to the next bridge ID in the chain. Because they are all the same, there isn't anything to change.

Router 3 is the next hop in the path; by examining the frame, it realizes that the frame has passed through other Nortel Networks routers, and that it is the last Nortel

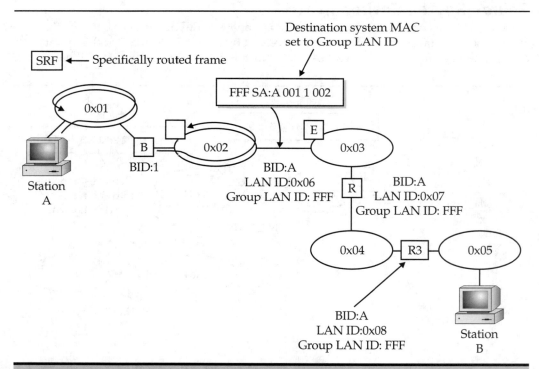

**Figure 25-12.** *SRF traversing router 1*

Networks router in the source-routed path. Router 3 then replaces the group address with station B's MAC (copied from the Data field, where it was inserted by router 1). It then replaces the group LAN ID with its own internal LAN ID (see Figure 25-13).

By doing this, an explorer frame may pass through any number of Nortel Networks routers and appear as though only one hop was traversed.

> **Note** *When using Nortel Networks routers configured for source-route bridging, be sure to assign a common bridge ID to each Nortel Networks router, and be sure that that bridge ID is not in use elsewhere in the source-route bridged network. This is necessary, because if a series of Nortel Networks routers receive a frame from a traditional bridge whose bridge ID is the same, it will determine that the frame originated from another Nortel Networks router running source-route bridging, and will attempt to convert the RIF information in the manner previously described. The only exception to the rule of using a common bridge ID for all routers is if the devices are running in parallel, which is described next.*

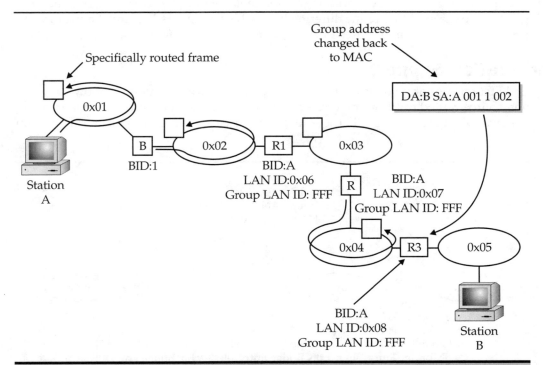

**Figure 25-13.** *SRF traversing router 3*

## Parallel Router Connections in an SRB Environment

By default, since the bridge ID of each Nortel Networks router will have a common value, and should this value be changed, care should be taken that all routers use the same bridge ID. The exception to this rule is if two Nortel Networks routers are running source-route bridging and are running in parallel.

Since running two bridges in parallel with the same bridge ID in a source-route bridged network is not a valid configuration, different bridge IDs must be used in this case. However, because the common bridge ID is one of the ways that Nortel Networks routers running source-route bridges perform their implementation of source-route bridging, the Nortel Networks routers must be made aware of the conflicting bridge IDs.

In this scenario, the internal LAN ID, internal group ID, and bridge ID must all be configured for each router. The bridge ID on router 4 (running parallel to router 2) is altered to a value other than AA, the bridge ID of the parallel bridge (0E, in this example). However, to make the routers aware that they are still Nortel Networks routers running source-route bridging, a Bridge Entry must be created in each router to alert it to the existence of the differing bridge ID. So, routers 1, 2, and 3 must have a Bridge Entry for AA, and router 4 must have a Bridge Entry for 0E (see Figure 25-14).

## End Station Support

End Station Support may be configured on Nortel Networks routers, to allow non-source-routed traffic to traverse a source-route bridged portion of the network. For example, a group of IP Ethernet clients must access a server on a token ring portion

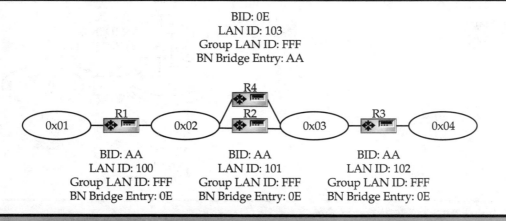

**Figure 25-14.**   *Bridge Entries created for differing bridge IDs*

of the network, the token ring environment is source routed, and the IP traffic must traverse one or more SR bridges.

In this scenario, the IP client is an Ethernet client, and will not issue an explorer frame; however, a source-routed path to the server needs to be established. By configuring End Station Support on router 1's token ring interface, when traffic must pass between an Ethernet and token ring station, the router interface will act as a token ring end station (as proxy for the Ethernet station) and will send an explorer packet to determine the source-routed path to the server. It will use this RIF information to reach the server from that point on (see Figure 25-15).

Once the data is received back at the ESS router interface, it is passed along normally to the Ethernet client, to whom the source-route bridged portion of the network is transparent.

 **Note**    *Source Route End Station Support must be configured for each individual protocol for which it is required, on a per-circuit basis; it is supported for IP, IPX, Xerox Network Systems (XNS), AppleTalk, and VINES.*

## Source Routing over a WAN

There are several methods of transporting SRB traffic across wide area networks using the Nortel Networks Router Platform. A brief outline of the available options—IP encapsulation, source-route bridging, and DLSw (Data Link Switching)—is covered in the following section.

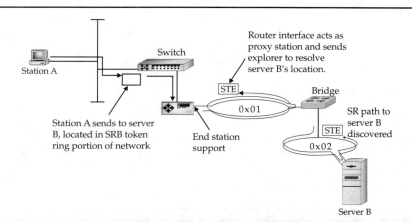

**Figure 25-15.**    *End Station Support used to determine path to destination*

# IP Encapsulation

IP encapsulation can be used to transport SRB traffic over an IP routed WAN. The Nortel Networks routers, acting as IP encapsulating bridges, make the whole process invisible to the source-routed networks on either side of the WAN. In this case, since the hop associated with the WAN is effectively going to be eliminated, the rings on either side of the WAN must have the same ring ID, rendering this portion of the network as flat, or a single ring.

IP encapsulation works in the following way: an explorer frame is received by a Nortel Networks router acting as an IP encapsulating bridge, and the source-routed frame is encapsulated within an IP header and then sent on to the WAN. At the peer bridge (the remote router/IP encapsulating bridge), the encapsulation is stripped and the source-routed frame is forwarded out the appropriate interface token ring or interfaces.

Each Nortel Networks router utilizing IP encapsulation maintains a dynamic table of IP addresses-to-source route bridge bridge IDs and ring numbers. The IP encapsulating bridge builds this table by sending all frames to all IP addresses configured in its IP explorer list.

In Figure 25-16, station A transmits to server A. Since the path to server A has not yet been determined, an explorer frame is sent. It traverses the local source-route bridged network (bridge ID 1) and reaches the wide area router, which is, in this case, acting as an IP-encapsulating bridge (bridge ID 2). The explorer frame is encapsulated in an IP packet and then routed to the remote side, where the IP encapsulation is

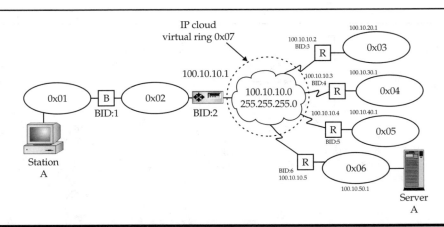

**Figure 25-16.**    *Routers acting as encapsulating bridges in frame relay network with four spokes*

stripped. Since the IP cloud is defined with a single ring ID (virtual ring ID 0x07), the RIF reflects only a single hop.

The path has now been determined, and station A transmits. At this point, the frame is directed toward the bridge, which checks the frame's RIF for the ring and bridge ID following the IP cloud's assigned ring and bridge ID in the RIF. Once it determines this, it does a lookup of the IP address corresponding to that ring and bridge ID (100.10.50.1 in this case). It then encapsulates the frame in an IP packet with the destination IP address and sends it (see Figure 25-17).

IP encapsulation is a straightforward solution; however, due to the extra delay incurred with traversing the IP cloud, the routers encapsulating and then stripping the frames going both ways, time-sensitive protocols may suffer in an environment like this.

## Source-Route Bridging

True source-route bridging may be performed across the WAN; configuring source-route bridging in this scenario is not much different in concept from configuring source routing over a token ring LAN or, more similarly, source routing across the ATM cloud. The

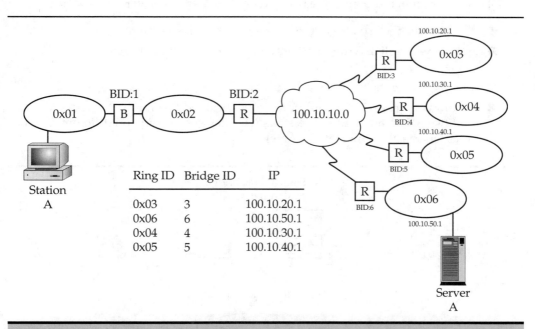

| Ring ID | Bridge ID | IP |
|---------|-----------|-----------|
| 0x03 | 3 | 100.10.20.1 |
| 0x06 | 6 | 100.10.50.1 |
| 0x04 | 4 | 100.10.30.1 |
| 0x05 | 5 | 100.10.40.1 |

**Figure 25-17.**    *Source routed frame encapsulated in IP and sent to appropriate FR spoke*

WAN cloud in this case may be viewed as a sort of "virtual ring," as far as the devices on either side are concerned (see Figure 25-18).

Notice in Figure 25-18 that the SRB bridge ID for all Nortel Networks routers are the same. Nortel Networks routers utilize a proprietary mechanism for doing source routing between one another. When a router examines the RIF of a packet and sees that the next bridge hop ID matches its own, it maintains the proprietary encapsulation method. Should a SR bridge other than a Nortel Networks router configured for SRB be present in the network, its SR bridge ID must differ from those used by the routers, since the proprietary SRB encapsulation method won't be correctly interpreted by any other device. Source route briding across the WAN, like IP encapsulation, may incur more delay than some time-sensitive protocols can tolerate.

# Data Link Switching (DLSw)

Data Link Switching is perhaps the most common method currently used for transporting SRB traffic across a WAN. DLSw caters to time-sensitive protocols, ensuring sessions stay up while providing data link-level conversion. It can be used in many scenarios, but for the purposes of this section, the focus will be on source-route bridged traffic.

DLSw is useful in a source-route bridged environment for several reasons:

- It minimizes the broadcast traffic when establishing sessions.

- It provides a reliable transport and local session termination to keep sessions stable.

- It helps reduce the SRB hop count, which has a limit of seven hops.

- It allows devices residing on source-route bridged token ring networks to establish SNA and NetBIOS sessions with devices residing on different network types (such as Ethernet 802.3 LANs).

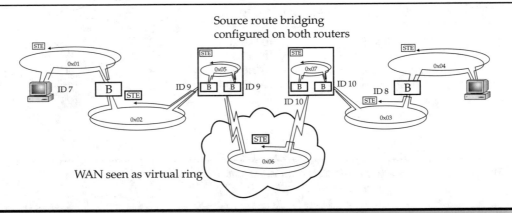

**Figure 25-18.** *Source-route bridging across a wide area network*

## Single vs. Dual Switch Services

DLSw offers *single switch services* and *dual switch-to-switch services*. Basically, the difference between the two is that in a single switch network, a single router renders the DLSw services between multiple interfaces.

However, in a dual switch-to-switch network, two routers are involved—each serving local DLSw connections, while at the same time exchanging DLSw information with each other across an IP network in order to establish SNA or NetBIOS sessions with remote devices.

## DLSw Peers

DLSw establishes a peer relationship between two routers, whereby each router is peered to a *slot IP* associated with its remote, peer router. This slot IP is an IP address configured in the remote peer's slot IP table.

In Figure 25-19, a hub router in a frame relay network is shown peered with three separate spoke routers. While the example here shows the peering over a frame relay WAN, the WAN IP network could be PPP (point-to-point), ATM LANE X.25, or SMDS.

Once DLSw is configured and a peer relationship is established, each router will attempt to establish two TCP connections with its peer. The routers will each monitor TCP ports 2067 and 2065 for these purposes. TCP port 2067 is typically called the "write" channel and 2065 is known as the "read" channel. Much like transmit and receive, these ports are mapped to each other in a crosswise fashion; write to read and read to write, or 2067 to 2065, and 2065 to 2067 (see Figure 25-20). Once established, it is over these TCP connections that the DLSw traffic will be transported.

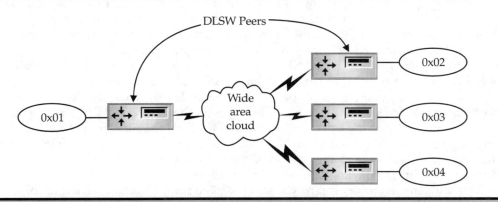

**Figure 25-19.** *FR network hub with three spokes showing DLSw peers*

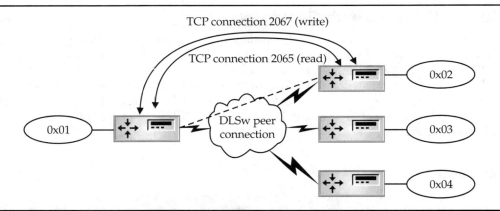

**Figure 25-20.**   *DLSw peer TCP connections established*

## DLSw Source-Route Bridge Example

In Figure 25-21, station A, which resides behind the hub router, needs to communicate with station B, which resides behind spoke router 2. Station A sends an explorer packet to determine station B's location. The explorer packet is received by the hub router (router 1).

Router 1's local token ring interface has been configured for DLSw and it has established peer relationships with each spoke, meaning, the dual TCP connections with each remote peer router are up.

Rather than forward the explorer packet, Router1's local DLSw interface responds as station B's proxy, letting station A believe that station B is actually on its local ring. This is called locally terminating the session. In the meantime, the router sends a control packet over its TCP control write channels (port 2067) to all known DLSw routers. This control packet is known as a CANUREACH packet.

At the remote routers, the CANUREACH packets are received and then translated back into explorer packets, so that the destination station can be located

Station B receives the explorer packet and responds to its local router. The local router then responds to the peer that originally sent the CANUREACH control packet with its own control packet response, known as the ICANREACH packet. Once the originating DLSw peer receives the ICANREACH packet, it then knows which peer to transmit station A's data to, and will transmit and receive only over the TCP connections associated with that peer (see Figure 25-21).

If more than one router can reach station B, then router 1 will receive multiple ICANREACH control packets, and will use the first packet received to determine which peer to send to.

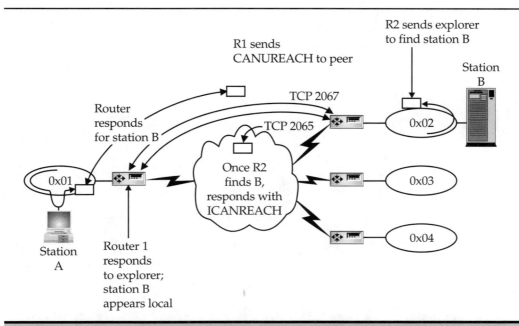

**Figure 25-21.**    *CANUREACH and ICANREACH used to set up station to station communication*

## Summary

The three options just presented are some of the methods that can be used to transport source-route bridged token ring traffic, over a variety of different network types. For more information regarding source-route bridging, consult the IEEE 802.5m specification. For further information on DLSw, consult RFC 1434, RFC 1795, and RFC 2166.

# The
# Complete
# Reference

Nortel
Networks

# Chapter 26

## Configuring
## Token Ring on the
## C100/C50/C20/5000BH
## Platform

**839**

The C100/C50/C20/5000BH platforms support Token Ring switching; a Token Ring Master Control Processor (MCP) may be used to control the host cards, but is not required. In fact, with the demands of a moderate to large modern network, ATMSpeed MCP modules are generally used in favor of the TokenSpeed MCPs, because they have more processing power. Regardless of the MCP type, however, the token ring configuration is essentially the same; therefore, in this chapter, different MCP types are not specified unless there is a limitation specific to that MCP type.

# The Centillion and Token Ring

The Centillion platform offers a variety of Token Ring switching solutions, allowing Token Ring to run in a transparently bridged environment, a source-route bridged environment, or a source-route transparent environment (a hybrid of both bridging types). TokenSpeed modules exist in a 4-port variety, 8-port variety, and 24-port, high-density model. The 4- and 8-port modules are available with unshielded twisted pair/shielded twisted pair (UTP/STP) or fiber-optic connectors, and all TokenSpeed modules are capable of running at 4Mbps or 16Mbps, as well as running in full-duplex mode.

TokenSpeed modules may be used as host cards, and TokenSpeed controller cards are also available.

## Using the TokenSpeed Master Control Processor

Each Centillion switch uses an MCP card to control the host modules. There are two varieties of TokenSpeed MCPs: the 4-port model and the 8-port model. Each is capable of running a fully loaded chassis, although if LAN Emulation (LANE) is going to be used, using an ATMSpeed MCP as the controller is highly recommended, instead of using a TokenSpeed MCP used in conjunction with an ATM host card.

### 4-Port TokenSpeed Modules vs. 8-Port TokenSpeed Modules

The 4-port TokenSpeed MCP module was the predecessor to the 8-port variety; thus, it came with less onboard memory and was less powerful. In fact, the highest system software image version the 4-port TokenSpeed MCP is capable of supporting is code version 2.1.075. The 8-port TokenSpeed MCP, on the other hand, is currently capable of running the same system image versions as the ATMSpeed MCPs, which support up to the most recent image version.

Most of the early 4-port TokenSpeed modules shipped with 2.0.$x$ code, and some are still running these early image versions. Upgrading the image version from 2.0.$x$ to a higher version on the 4-port MCPs requires some special considerations, which are covered in the following sections.

## Upgrading the System Software

For a typical system software upgrade, simply discover the switch to be upgraded. For a 4-port TokenSpeed MCP, this will most likely be done serially, because Simple Network Management Protocol (SNMP) support was not introduced into the Centillion until image version 2.1.070, which is the highest major release supported by the 4-port MCP (although it also supports up to the last maintenance release of 2.1.070, which was 2.1.075). Data Link Control (DLC) existed at that time as an option, as well, for managing and upgrading the Centillion switch, although this option was removed in later releases after the introduction of SNMP support.

To upgrade the MCP, discover the switch using SpeedView, and then highlight the appropriate icon (if you are doing this serially, you will see only one icon). Once this is done, select Switch | Download Software, which opens a window prompting for the image name and location (an option to browse for the image is offered, too). If the upgrade is from release 2.1.070, or the upgrade is being performed on an 8-port MCP, you will be prompted for the Trivial File Transfer Protocol (TFTP) server address (if SNMP is being used). If this is the case, enter the IP address of the station that will act as the TFTP server. After you enter this information, select Start Download to initiate the file transfer.

**Note** *A serial image download takes anywhere from 12 to 20 minutes, depending on how large the image is. The switch will be nonoperational during this time.*

## Upgrading from Image Version 2.0.*x* on the 4-port TokenSpeed MCP

If a 4-port TokenSpeed MCP is being upgraded from 2.0.*x* code to 2.1.*x* code, some special considerations must be made if the unit in question is a C100 or C50. Primarily, the MCP must have enough memory to support the new image version, and if the MCP is running an image version lower than 2.0.3, then the 2.0.3 image needs to be loaded prior to upgrading the system image to 2.1.*x*.

**VERIFYING FLASH SPACE**   Each 4-port C100/C50 TokenSpeed MCP can house either one or two flash memory chips. To upgrade past 2.0.*x* code, both flash chips are required. To determine how much flash memory the MCP currently contains, you need to remove it from the chassis. When the time can be scheduled, remove the module from the chassis, keeping the component side facing upward, toward you. With the front panel of the module facing you, examine the lower-right quadrant of the board (see Figure 26-1).

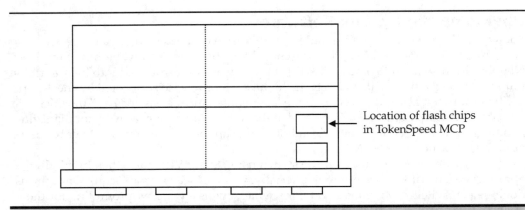

Location of flash chips
in TokenSpeed MCP

**Figure 26-1.**   *Flash memory location on TokenSpeed MCP*

Depending on the age of the TokenSpeed MCP, the lower-right quadrant will have one of the following instances:

- **One soldered flash chip**   Older versions of the C100 TokenSpeed MCPs used a single socketed flash chip; there is no way to upgrade the flash memory on this variety of MCP, and the code version may not be upgraded beyond 2.0.*x*.

- **One socketed flash chip and one empty socket**   If there are two brown plastic flash sockets present on the board and only one of them contains a memory chip, a second flash memory chip must be obtained from Nortel Networks before performing the upgrade.

- **Two socketed flash chips**   If two brown plastic flash sockets are present and both sockets are occupied, then the memory upgrade has already been performed, and the MCP has enough memory to handle the upgrade.

**UPGRADING TO 2.0.3 USING THE LOADER FILE**   Once the flash memory has been upgraded, the system image may also be upgraded. If the code version is prior to 2.0.3, however, the unit must be brought to image version 2.0.3 before proceeding to 2.1.*x*.

Upgrading to image version 2.0.3 is a two-step process. Included with the image file is a smaller loader file that must be uploaded to the switch prior to doing the actual code upgrade. The procedure for uploading the loader file is identical to the procedure for upgrading the code; when prompted to browse for the image file, however, simply select the loader file and click Start Download. Once the loader file transfer is complete, repeat the procedure, but this time using the actual 2.0.3 image file. After you successfully upgrade the switch to 2.0.3, the switch is ready to receive image version 2.1.0*x*.

## Replacing 4-Port TokenSpeed Modules with 8-Port or 24-Port TokenSpeed Modules

Many administrators have opted to replace existing 4-port TokenSpeed modules with 8-port or 24-port modules; one common reason being the image version limitation associated with a 4-port TokenSpeed MCP. When replacing a 4-port MCP with an 8-port MCP, or when replacing a 4-port host card with an 8-port or 24-port host card, you must remember that the (UTP/STP) connector pinout was changed when the 8- and 24-port modules were created, and this potentially involves recabling some of the connections. Any 4-port TokenSpeed connection that has been configured as a hub connection (meaning a station—end-station, server, router, and so on—is attached to it directly) requires a token ring crossover cable. With the advent of the 8-port and 24-port modules, the pins are crossed over internally and a token ring straight-through cable is required for the same kind of connection.

# Token Ring System Parameters

The first thing that must be done when configuring Token Ring on the Centillion platform is to set up the system-level parameters. This involves setting up some of the global token ring parameters, such as the bridging method and maximum frame size. The following sections cover the configuration of basic system-level parameters, including some of the configuration required if SRB is going to be used as a bridging method.

## System Parameters

The initial token ring system parameters are available from the System tab in SpeedView. If the version of SpeedView you are using is prior to version 3.0, then the System tab is the first menu option. If the SpeedView version is 3.0 or greater, the System tab is selected by default when the switch is first brought up in configuration mode. You may configure are a few token ring-specific parameters here (see Figure 26-2), as described in the following sections.

### Token Ring Max Frame Size

The token ring maximum frame size can also be specified in the System tab; by default, a value of 4,472 is used for the Token Ring Max Frame Size setting, which is the maximum frame size for SRB over 4Mbps token ring. This value can be altered to a variety of different sizes; depending on the code version, these frame sizes may include 516, 1,500, 2,052, 4,472, 8,144, 11,407, and 17,800.

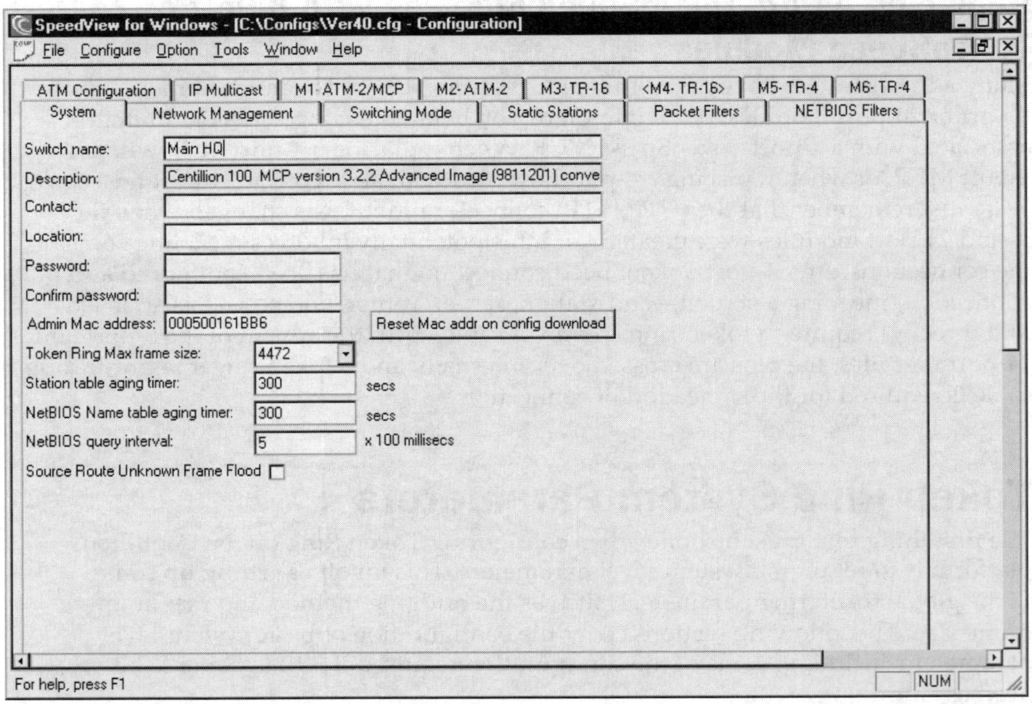

**Figure 26-2.** *The System tab in SpeedView*

## Admin MAC Address

The MAC address for the Centillion switch may be altered administratively; token ring can use either the burned-in hardware address or locally administered addresses (LAAs). In this field a user-defined MAC address may be configured. The following sections describe options that allow an LAA to be assigned on a port-by-port basis, as well.

## Source Route Unknown Frame Flood

One of the available options from the System tab is a check box labeled Source Route Unknown Frame Flood, located at the bottom of the tab. This option is set to either on or off. This parameter is only significant if Token Ring LANE is being used in a source-route bridging (SRB) environment; if either Token Ring LANE or SRB is not being used, this parameter is ignored and does not need to be configured.

The Source Route Unknown Frame Flood option relates to how Spanning Tree Explorer (STE) frames are handled when received by a token ring LAN Emulation

Client (LEC). If this feature is disabled, and the STE frame is received, the learning process is initiated while the STE frame itself is dropped. If this feature is enabled, upon receipt of an STE frame, the learning process is initiated and the STE is sent to the BUS for processing.

The primary reason for this option is that the latency introduced in the first scenario just described can be enough with certain time-sensitive protocols, such as Systems Network Architecture (SNA), to cause session drops. Intermittent connectivity problems in an environment using source-route bridged SNA over token ring LANE may be solved by enabling this parameter.

## Switching Mode Parameters

The second tab that involves basic system configuration is the Switching Mode tab. In versions of SpeedView prior to 3.0, this tab is located just below the Network Management tab. In SpeedView version 3.0 and later, the Switching Mode tab is located just to the right of the Network Management tab (see Figure 26-3).

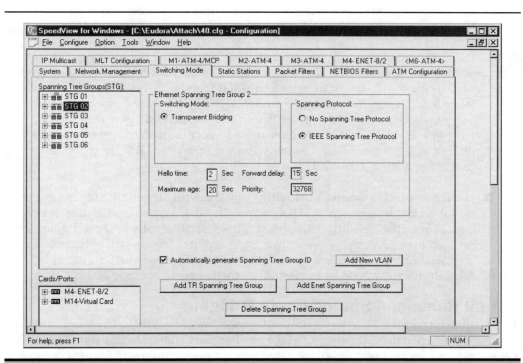

**Figure 26-3.**  *The Switching Mode tab*

Selecting this tab enables you to select several key options: the type of token ring bridging used, the type of Spanning Tree Protocol used, and the assignment of a bridge ID that will be associated with the switch.

## Selecting a Bridging Type

The following are the bridging options included in this tab; a bridging mode is selected by clicking the appropriate radio button:

- **Transparent Bridging**   Used if no source-routing stations or systems are in the token ring network. If this bridging mode is used, all STE frames will be dropped. In this scenario, ring numbers do not need to be assigned to any of the ports, Centillion LAN Clients (CLC), or LECs.

- **Source Route Bridging**   If this option is selected, another series of options appears beneath the selected bridging mode, involving spanning tree parameters and the assignment of a Bridge ID. In a source-routed environment, all ports, CLCs, and LECs must be configured with the appropriate Ring ID, and because SRB uses Ring ID/Bridge ID combinations for purposes of determining the source-routed path to the destination, a Bridge ID must also be assigned. This Bridge ID is used by all rings configured on the switch.

> **Note**   *Bridge IDs do not need to be unique, unless two bridges are running in parallel. Unless the network configuration is such that multiple Centillion switches are bridging between rings in parallel, the default value may be used (the default is 1 in hex). Take care to ensure that if Nortel Networks routers configured for SRB are also involved in the source-routed path, the Bridge ID configured on the Centillion differs from those configured on the Nortel Networks routers, to prevent the routers from becoming confused as to whether or not the switch is part of their same LAN group. This is described in detail in Chapter 27.*

- **Source Route Transparent Bridging**   If the existing token ring environment contains both transparent and source-routing stations or systems, this option may be selected. Selecting this option allows transparently bridged frames to be bridged transparently, while source route explorer frames will be accepted, as well, and processed as they normally would be. The same SRB rules apply for this selection as would be in effect in a strictly source-routed system.

## Virtual Rings and Source-Route Bridging

The Centillion platform also uses a proprietary technique for SRB, when duplicate ring numbers are involved. Normally, in an SRB environment, duplicate ring numbers should not be used; recurring instances of the same ring number within an SRB network can cause a great deal of confusion when route descriptors are being assembled to form a frame's routing information field (RIF). On the Centillion platform, however, if duplicate ring numbers exist on the same switch, they form a single virtual ring, which is viewed in the SRB environment as a single ring. The individual rings within the virtual ring will be transparently bridged between, so that a frame received by one is received by all. This allows a single, overused ring to be broken into multiple rings, for better traffic management, while still appearing as a single ring to the SRB devices (see Figure 26-4).

## Selecting a Spanning Tree Type

A Spanning Tree Protocol type must also be selected. If transparent bridging is being used, then only IEEE Spanning Tree or None can be selected. If SRB or source-route transparent bridging is being used, however, a Spanning Tree Protocol type must be selected: IEEE Spanning Tree or IBM Spanning Tree.

**IEEE SPANNING TREE**   IEEE Spanning Tree detects network loops and then makes a forwarding or blocking decision based on the network topology. If a port is blocked in this scenario due to a loop in the network, then that port blocks all traffic, and no data or MAC control frames will pass over the blocked port.

**IBM SPANNING TREE**   IBM Spanning Tree is used specifically by the SRB protocol. Like IEEE Spanning Tree, IBM Spanning Tree detects network loops and then makes forwarding or blocking decisions based on the network topology; however, a port that is in a blocking state as a result of IBM Spanning Tree does not block all data—it blocks STE frames only. This effectively removes certain paths from the network without actually cutting off the path completely. Since an STE frame can't take a certain path to the destination, because it is dropped at the blocked port, the destination station can't use that path when the return Explorer frame is sent back toward the source.

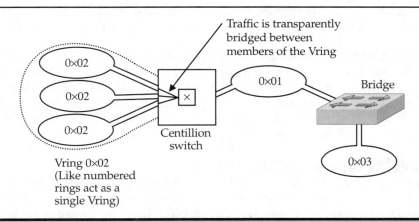

**Figure 26-4.**   *Virtual ring example in SRB environment*

Bear in mind that this blocking mode affects STEs only. In a scenario where the STE is sent to the destination, which then returns an All Routes Explorer (ARE) frame, the ARE frames are not blocked by IBM Spanning Tree, so the blocked path may be used for data.

## Spanning Tree Parameters

Whichever Spanning Tree Protocol type is selected, the spanning tree parameters are also configured in the Switching Mode tab. These options appear just below the Switching Mode and Spanning Tree Protocol options:

- **Hello Time**    Indicates how frequently Spanning Tree bridge protocol data units (BPDUs) are transmitted. The default is every two seconds.

- **Forward Delay**    Indicates how long the switch waits before forwarding data on any port that has entered a forwarding state after running the spanning tree algorithm (STA). This delay is incurred to allow the network's spanning tree state to stabilize prior to forwarding any data. If IEEE Spanning Tree is being used, the default value for this parameter is 15 seconds. IBM Spanning Tree uses a default time of 4 seconds.

- **Maximum Age**    Defines how long a spanning tree port can wait without receiving a BPDU before it determines that a bridge has failed and declares a Spanning Tree Topology Change. For IEEE Spanning Tree, the default is 20 seconds (indicating the loss of ten BPDUs). IBM Spanning Tree uses a default value of 6 (indicating the loss of three BPDUs).

- **Priority**    Determines the root bridge in a Spanning Tree environment, which is the path cost to the root bridge being used by Spanning Tree to make forwarding and blocking decisions. By default, this value is 32,768 in decimal, which calculates to 8,000 in hex, the typical default priority for most bridges and switches. A lower priority takes precedence in this case.

**ASSIGNING A BRIDGE NUMBER**    A bridge number (Bridge ID) must also be assigned if either Source Route Bridging or Source Route Transparent Bridging is selected as the Switching Mode. This value is in hex, and may be duplicated throughout the network as long as two Centillions are not bridging in parallel between the same two rings. If this is the case, the bridge numbers must be unique. Otherwise, any hex value between 1 and F, inclusive, is acceptable.

## Port-Level Bridging Parameters

From the Switching Mode tab in SpeedView 3.0 or greater, if a specific port within a bridge group (or Spanning Tree Group, in code version 4.0 or greater) is selected rather than the bridge group or Spanning Tree Group (STG) itself, then in addition to the spanning tree parameters, a series of port-level bridging parameters appear under the heading Bridge Port Property for $x{:}y$, where $x$ is the slot number and $y$ is the port number (see Figure 26-5).

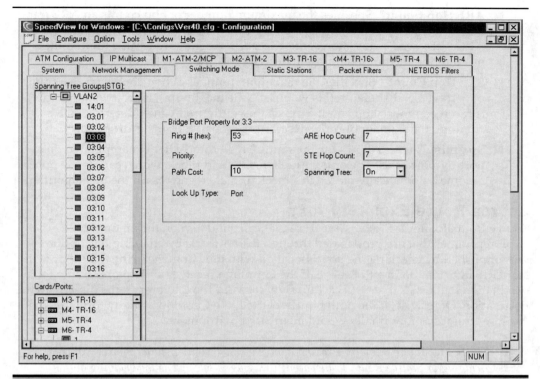

**Figure 26-5.**    *The Bridge Port Property fields*

The parameters that are included under this new heading may also be accessed by selecting the tab for the associated module and then selecting the specific port. However, the Switching Mode tab provides an easy way to access these parameters for all ports across all modules from a single tab. The following are the Switching Mode tab parameters:

- **Ring # (hex)**    Used only in a SRB environment and is not available if the Switching Mode used is Source Route Transparent Bridging. This value is in hex and may be between 1 and FFF, inclusive. Bear in mind that if ports are assigned to a common ring number in the Centillion SRB implementation, they will form a virtual ring and all traffic will be transparently bridged between those rings.

- **Priority**    Specifies the port priority used by IEEE Spanning Tree; this field is not used if IBM Spanning Tree is being used.

- **Path Cost**    Indicates the path cost to the root associated with this port.

- **ARE Hop Count** Specifies the maximum number of hop counts an ARE frame may traverse. By default, this value is 7 (the maximum); if set lower and an ARE is received whose hop count exceeds the configured value (determined by counting the number of route descriptors), the ARE frame is dropped.

- **STE Hop Count** Specifies the maximum number of hop counts an STE frame may traverse. By default, this value is 7 (the maximum); if set lower and an STE is received whose hop count exceeds the configured value (determined by counting the number of route descriptors), the STE frame is dropped.

- **Spanning Tree** Allows the Spanning Tree Protocol to be manipulated on a port-by-port basis. The options are On, Off, and Block, which causes the port to become automatically placed in a blocking state regardless of the STP algorithm.

### Source Route Explorer Proxy

Source Route Explorer Proxy is a feature that can cut down on the amount of Explorer frames that are propagated through the network; by enabling this option (accomplished by checking the box associated with the parameter), the Centillion will store RIF information in a RIF cache. If the Centillion receives an Explorer frame for a destination that exists in its RIF cache, it will forward the Explorer frame directly to the destination. Otherwise, if the option is deselected, the Centillion simply forwards the Explorer frames as it normally would in an SRB environment.

*The Source Route Explorer Proxy option is available only if either Source Route Bridging or Source Route Transparent Bridging is selected as the bridging option.*

### Source Route Frame Forward

Source Route Frame Forward is used to forward Explorer frames in a transparent bridging environment. Rather than dropping STE or ARE frames, the Centillion simply forwards them.

*The Source Route Frame Forward option is available only if Source Route Transparent Bridging is selected as the bridging mode, and either IEEE or IBM Spanning Tree is selected.*

# Management Parameters and Static Station Configuration

Other network management parameters, as well as static station configuration, may also be accomplished via SpeedView. These options are accessible from two separate tabs:

- **Network Management tab** Network management parameters, such as the internal management ring ID and IP information, are configured here.

- **Static Station tab** Static RIF entries are entered here.

# Token Ring Management Parameters

The Network Management tab is used primarily for configuring an IP address, subnet mask, default gateway, broadcast address, and a variety of SNMP parameters. Two token ring-specific parameters are also located on this tab: the Internal Management Ring Number, and the option to enable or disable LAN Network Manager support.

## Assigning an Internal Management Ring Number

The Internal Management Ring Number is used by the switch for purposes of network management; this ring number must be unique if SRB is being used within the network. This rule applies to remote switches as well: the Internal Management Ring Number must be unique throughout the entire network, and must also be different from other remote Internal Management Ring Numbers. The valid values for this internal ring are between 1 and FFE, inclusive.

## Using LAN Network Manager

Support for IBM's LAN Network Manager (LNM) can be enabled or disabled through SpeedView. By default, this option is disabled. LNM is a tool used to ensure compatibility between IBM bridges and different token ring management types. To the LNM, the Centillion appears as a series of bridges connected to an internal ring. The LNM feature, once enabled, allows the LNM to access each of these rings orbiting the internal ring, and view the network topology as if IBM bridges were being used.

If the LNM Enabled box has been checked, the following two radio buttons will appear, each with its own option for how the Centillion bridge groups will be displayed:

- **Display Bridge Groups as Separate Internal Management Rings** If this option is selected, individual bridge groups within the Centillion network will appear to the LNM as separate internal management rings, one for each bridge group.

- **Display Bridge Groups as One Aggregate Internal Management Ring** If this option is selected, individual bridge groups within the Centillion network will appear to the LNM as individual rings connected to a single, common internal management ring.

## Other LAN Network Manager Considerations

To configure the LNM, the locally administered address (LAA) associated with the switch needs to be used to set up a bridge definition. For the switch, this can be obtained by using the command **show port** $x$ $y$, where $x$ is the slot number and $y$ is the port number. Two addresses will be listed in the topmost portion of the command's output; the BIA, which is the burned-in-address, and the LAA. By default, the LAA is a variation on the BIA; the LAA value, however, will reflect the configured value in the Admin MAC Address field in the System tab of SpeedView.

# Configuring a Static Station

In an SRB environment, the sending station must dynamically learn the path to the destination station. Stations that are accessed frequently may be statically defined on Centillion token ring ports, along with their RIF path, to cut down on the number of Explorer packets traversing the network.

Statically defining a station is accomplished through SpeedView, by opening the switch in configuration mode and then selecting the Static Stations tab, which is broken down into three basic sections:

- **Station Address list**   Lists the MAC addresses associated with the statically defined stations.

- **MAC address and RIF fields**   Displays the MAC address of the static station and the associated RIF path.

- **A graphical representation of the chassis and its modules**   Indicates the port associated with the static station.

## Adding a Static Station and Configuring the Routing Information Field Entries

The first step in configuring a static station is to obtain the MAC address of that station. After you obtain this address, enter the address into the MAC field, without adding any colons or dashes to separate the octets.

| Note | *This MAC address must be configured in noncanonical format (where the most significant bit is first, rather than the least significant).* |
|------|------|

Once this is complete, you must define the RIF path to the static station; this consists of the individual Ring and Bridge IDs that make up the individual route descriptors in the RIF. Enter the Ring ID and Bridge ID of each hop to the station being defined, with each value in hexadecimal format. This allows incoming Explorer packets that are destined for the static station to be discarded in favor of the precached RIF information, so that the station can be reached more directly.

After you enter the MAC address and RIF information, select the port from which the static station will be reached. The port will be highlighted yellow after you select it.

Beneath the static station MAC list are two buttons labeled Add and Del. After you complete the preceding steps, click Add; the MAC address will appear in the list. If additional stations need to be added, replace the MAC address in the MAC field, click the Clear RIF Path button, and then configure the new RIF.

# Module-Specific Token Ring Parameters

After you configure the global token ring parameters, you may also need to configure the individual module and port parameters; these parameters may include ring speed, spanning tree parameters, or the token ring connection type.

## Connection Parameters

Centillion token ring ports can assume a variety of roles in a token ring environment, depending on how they are configured. No port is statically designed as a lobe port, or as a ring in/ring out port; instead, any individual port may be assigned to perform whichever function is required. The following list of parameters represents a total of all added features up to image and SpeedView version 4.0, though not all features and options were introduced simultaneously. In particular, code version 2.1.1 introduced the ability of the System 5000, 5525, and 5525M Centillion TokenSpeed modules to connect to both the ATM backplane and to the shared media token ring backplane; thus, beginning with SpeedView version 2.1.1, the layout of the individual TokenSpeed modules was altered to account for this new feature.

- Switch Connect
- Backplane Connection
- Fr Port Mode
- Fr Port

In addition, the Management Wrap parameter was added in code release 2.1.1. The new layout for the TokenSpeed modules in SpeedView carried over into the C100/C50/C20, as well, since the modules are essentially modeled the same by SpeedView. The preceding list of parameters apply only to the System 5000, though they are always present, even when the Centillion modeled is a C100 or C50.

### Switch Connect

This parameter indicates whether or not the TokenSpeed module will be connected to the ATM backplane. Since the modules may also connect to the shared media token ring backplane, there may be no actual need to connect the device to the ATM backplane to communicate with other Centillion TokenSpeed modules. The options are either Enabled, indicating there is a connection to the ATM backplane, or Disabled, indicating that there is no ATM backplane connection.

## Front Port Mode

This parameter indicates how the TokenSpeed port should behave in the token ring environment; since the Centillion TokenSpeed ports do not have a statically defined port type, they must be individually assigned. Depending on the type of TokenSpeed module being used, the options may vary. The following is a list of the possible options, their meanings, and the TokenSpeed modules on which they are available:

**Note**  *TokenSpeed modules that use fiber-optic ports will have their Front Port Mode options followed by the designation of either 802.5j or SNPX. 802.5J is the standard token ring over fiber-optic signaling method, whereas SNPX indicates the connection will be made to a Synoptics token ring fiber port. The Synoptics signaling method for token ring over fiber-optic cabling differs slightly from the 802.5j specification. Generally, however, an option is given to change the signaling from Synoptics to 802.5J within the Synoptics token ring hub itself.*

■ **Hub (all modules)**   Enable the TokenSpeed port to act as a concentrator port; it detects phantom current and accepts direct attached stations. In early versions of software, Hub mode was referred to as DTR (Dedicated Token Ring). If a station is being attached to the port, set it to Hub.

**Note**  *If the TokenSpeed module is a 4-port module, a token ring crossover will be required for the connection; if it is an 8-port or 16-port module, a token ring straight-through cable is used.*

■ **Station (all modules)**   Enables the TokenSpeed port to act as a station; it sources phantom current and is used to connect the TokenSpeed port to a concentrator. If a hub or another TokenSpeed module is being attached to the port, Station mode should be selected.

■ **RIRO Phtm (4-port modules)**   Allows the Centillion port to be connected to a Ring In or Ring Out port on a token ring concentrator that uses Phantom Drive. If the port is connecting to the Ring In port of a concentrator, then a token ring crossover cable must be used for the connection. For a port connecting to a Ring Out connector, a token ring straight-through cable must be used.

■ **RIRO Nophtm (4-port modules)**   Allows the Centillion port to be connected to a Ring In or Ring Out port on a token ring concentrator that does not use Phantom Drive. This option should be selected if the Centillion is being attached to the RI or RO port of an IBM 8228 or compatible hub. If the port is connecting to the Ring In port of a concentrator, then a token ring crossover cable must be used for the connection. For a port connecting to a Ring Out connector, a token ring straight-through cable must be used.

■ **RI/Other (8-port and 16-port modules)**   Used if the TokenSpeed port is connected to the Ring Out port of a non-Nortel Networks token ring hub. It does not use phantom current.

■ **RO/Other (8-port and 16-port modules)**   Used if the TokenSpeed port is connected to the Ring In port of a non-Nortel Networks token ring hub. It does not use phantom current.

■ **RO/SNPX (8-port modules)**   Used if the TokenSpeed port is connected to the Ring In port of a Nortel Networks hub (SNPX stands for the old Synoptics designation). Phantom current is sourced in this case.

■ **FDTR Hub (8-port modules)**   Causes the port to act as a concentrator port in full-duplex mode; this allows full-duplex-capable stations to connect at the maximum speed.

■ **FDTR Station (8-port modules)**   Allows the port to act as a station, to be connected to a concentrator. Useful for connecting to another Centillion module, with the station and hub both configured for full-duplex mode.

■ **Auto Station/Hub (16-port modules)**   Allows the TokenSpeed port to autodetect whether the connection is a station or a concentrator, and dynamically assume the appropriate role.

## Mgmt Wrap

The Management Wrap option is used for troubleshooting purposes only; setting this option to Wrapped causes the backplane ring, internal switch (ATM backplane), and front panel ring to become wrapped or isolated.

## Bk Plane

Alternately labeled Bk plane Att (backplane attachment), this field is grayed out in all modules except the 5525, or 5525M in the System 5000 chassis. This field indicates whether the 5525 series TokenSpeed module is attached to the shared media token ring backplane. This field also isn't available if any of the first three ports are selected, because the backplane token ring to which each port connects is static; which ring each port connects to is dependent on whether or not the token ring backplane is split, and, if it is split, into which side of the System 5000 chassis the 5525 module is inserted (see Figure 26-6).

In this case, if the backplane is not split, 5525 modules on either side of the 5000 chassis will connect port 4 to ring 1, port 5 to ring 2, port 6 to ring 3, port 7 to ring 4, and port 8 to ring 5. If the backplane is split, then port 4 of a 5525 inserted into the left side of the 5000 (slots 2-7) will connect to ring 1, port 5 will connect to ring 2, port 6 to ring 3, port 7 to ring 4, and port 8 to ring 5. A 5525 inserted into the right side of the 5000 (slots 8-13) will connect port 4 to ring 6, port 5 to ring 7, port 6 to ring 8, port 7 to ring 9, and port 8 also to ring 5, which extends the entire length of the backplane, even while in split mode.

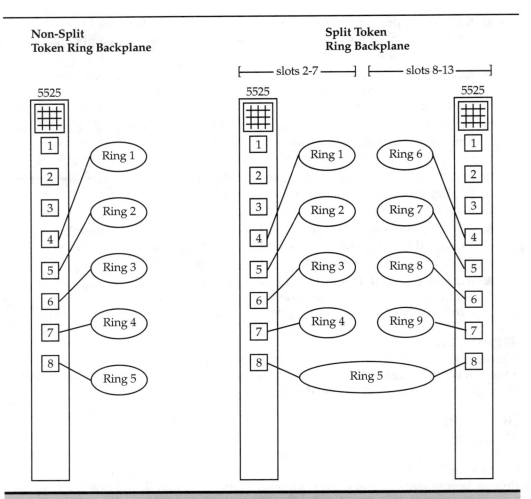

**Figure 26-6.** The 5525 series TokenSpeed module connecting to backplane rings in split and nonsplit configuration

| Note | *Splitting the shared media token ring backplane is accomplished through the Supervisory Module of the 5000 chassis.* |

## Fr Port

Also referred to in some code versions as Front Port Connect, this parameter may be enabled or disabled, which administratively activates or deactivates the front panel port, respectively.

*If a token ring backplane attachment is also being used, then a valid link must be established with the front panel port before the module will insert into the backplane ring.*

## Ring Speed

Depending on the module type, the ring speed can be set in any of the following ways (bear in mind that not all options are available on all modules):

- **4**   The port will run at 4Mbps.
- **16**   The port will run at 16Mbps.
- **Auto (station mode only)**   The port will autodetect the ring speed and adopt the correct speed.
- **32**   The port will run at 32Mbps (full-duplex mode).
- **Auto 16/32**   The port will autonegotiate between 16Mbps and 32Mbps.
- **Auto 4/16/32**   The port will autonegotiate between 4Mbps, 16Mbps, and 32Mbps.

### Speed Sense

The Speed Sense option can be enabled or disabled, and is used if the Auto option is selected for 4-port TokenSpeed modules. If the speed has been hard-coded, this parameter must be set to Disabled.

## Spanning Tree Parameters

The spanning tree parameters for the Centillion switch are located in the Switching Mode tab; this is where the spanning tree type is selected, as well as the configuration of some of the spanning tree parameters. In addition, the Switching Mode tab is where additional bridge groups may be added, or, if code version 4.0 or greater is being used, where additional STGs and VLANs may be added.

### Adding Bridge Groups in Code Prior to 4.0

If the system image version and SpeedView version are prior to 4.0, then logical groups are added to the Centillion in the form of bridge groups; a *bridge group* can be thought of as a VLAN with its own STG (for more information regarding this concept, consult Chapter 10). Individual VLANs are added from the Switching Mode tab; click the button labeled Add TR Bridge Group, located at the bottom of the screen. Once the bridge group is added, by default, it will contain no ports. In code version 3.0 or higher, ports may be selected from the Cards/Ports list box, located near the bottom of the window, and then dragged up to the Bridge Groups list box and dropped into the appropriate bridge group.

## Adding STGs and VLANs in Code Version 4.0 or Higher

Beginning with code version 4.0, the STGs and VLANs are separated, as opposed to the pre-4.0 concept of bridge groups, which were each a VLAN with its own STG automatically assigned. Separating these entities allows for greater design flexibility, particularly when interoperating with the Accelar routing switch, which utilizes the same concept.

To add a new STG, from the Switching Mode tab, click the button labeled Add TR Spanning Tree Group, located near the bottom of the window. This adds the new STG, which, by default, does not contain any VLANs. Once the STG is created, highlight the STG and then click the button labeled Add New VLAN, located to the right of the box labeled Automatically Generate Spanning Tree Group ID. This opens a new window in which SpeedView prompts for three pieces of information:

- **VLAN Name**  This is an arbitrary name, selected by the administrator. By default, new VLANs will be named VLAN *x*, where the *x* value increments with each new VLAN instance.

- **VLAN ID**  By default, the VLAN ID matches the default VLAN number that is generated when the VLAN is created; however, this is not an arbitrary number and must be configured correctly if frame tagging is to be used, so it may need to be altered. If frame tagging is used, the value configured in this field will be the VLAN ID assigned to the 802.1Q frame tag, and will be used to determine a frame's VLAN destination in a frame-tagged environment.

- **VLAN Type**  This defines the VLAN type. As of the time of publication, only port-based VLANs may be configured.

Once the VLAN configuration is complete, click the Add VLAN button. This creates a new VLAN within the selected STG. However, by default, the new VLAN does not contain any ports. The desired ports must be selected from the Card/Ports list box, located at the bottom of the window, and then dragged up to the Spanning Tree Group (STG) list box and dropped into the appropriate VLAN.

# Port-Level Spanning Tree Parameters

In addition to the spanning tree parameters associated with different bridge groups or STGs, you may configure port-level spanning tree characteristics, described next.

## Ring # (hex)

If SRB is being used in the token ring network, then each port must have a ring number associated with it, which is assigned in the Ring # (hex) box, in hexadecimal format. Duplicate ring numbers may be used in an SRB environment on the Centillion switch, provided the ports with which the ring numbers are associated are on the same switch. If two or more ports on the same switch are assigned the same ring number in an SRB environment, those rings form what a virtual ring. Traffic is transparently bridged between the rings. This is useful for segmenting rings that contain frequently accessed devices (such as servers), while still allowing them to appear as a single ring to the SRB systems.

## Path Cost

This indicates the path cost associated with the port, describing its relative relationship with the root bridge. Path cost is used by the spanning tree algorithm to make forwarding or blocking decisions. By default, token ring ports are configured with a path cost of 10. This can be altered, however, if the network is a mixed token ring/ATM environment. It is a good practice to make sure the path cost exceeds the path cost associated with a CLC or LEC VPort, to prevent the ATM port from blocking in the event of a loop condition.

## ARE Hop Count

This parameter indicates the maximum number of hop counts an ARE frame may pass before being discarded. By default, this value is set to 7, which is the maximum for traditional source routing. This value may be set as high as 13, which is the maximum for extended source routing. If an ARE is received with more than the allotted number of hops traversed (determined by examining the total number of route descriptors accumulated so far), the frame is dropped.

## STE Hop Count

This parameter indicates the maximum number of hop counts an STE frame may pass before being discarded. By default, this value is set to 7, which is the maximum for traditional source routing. This value may be set as high as 13, which is the maximum for extended source routing. If an STE is received with more than the allotted number of hops traversed (determined by examining the total number of route descriptors accumulated so far), the frame is dropped.

## Spanning Tree

This field indicates the spanning tree state for the port being configured. Options include On, where Spanning Tree is enabled on the port, Off, where Spanning Tree is disabled, or Block, where Spanning Tree is enabled, but administratively placed in a blocking state.

## MAC Address

The MAC address of the port is also listed (beginning with code version 3.0) in the module-specific tab. The MAC address is displayed in a box labeled MAC Address and, by default, is the Universally Administered Address (UAA).

**USE DEFAULT** By selecting the Use Default radio button, the UAA is used by the token ring port.

**USE LAA ADDRESS**    If the Use LAA Address radio button is selected, an LAA must be configured. Once selected, a new field will appear to the right of the option and just beneath the UAA, in which to configure the locally administered MAC address.

# Token Ring and ATM Parameters

The Centillion also supports 802.5 token ring LANE. If LANE is being used, or if CLCs are being used within a token ring environment, you may need to make certain configuration considerations, described in the following sections.

## Token Ring LAN Emulation Parameters

Token ring LANE considerations come into play mainly when Source Route Bridging or Source Route Transparent Bridging is selected as the Switching Mode option. When transparent bridging is being used, there are no ring and bridge ID information to consider, and virtual ring numbers do not need to be associated with the token ring ELANs. Care must be taken in either case, however, that the LAN type used by the ATM LANE components is correctly configured an 802.5 ELAN.

## Configuring the LAN Emulation Configuration Server

There are three main areas in the LECS configuration where token ring-specific parameters may be configured: the main Configure LECS tab, where the LAN type and MTU size may be configured, the Advanced LECS Policies, and the Advanced Membership policies.

### Selecting a LAN Type and MTU Size

From the main LECS Configuration window, a specific LAN type and MTU size may be specified. When creating an entry in the LECS for a specific ELAN that will support token ring users, a LAN Type of either Token Ring or Unspecified must be selected. If a value of Unspecified is used, the LEC will obtain the LAN Type from the LES.

Next to the LAN Type option is the Max Frame Size parameter. By default, if a LAN Type of Token Ring is selected, this parameter is set to 4544, the maximum frame size for 4Mbps token ring. The Frame Size options may vary depending on the version of system software and SpeedView being used. Using system software version 4.0, the available token ring frame sizes that may be defined in the LECS are 1516, 4544, 9234, 18190, and Unspecified. Again, if Unspecified is selected, the LEC obtains this information from the LES (if it hasn't been statically defined on the LEC itself).

### Advanced LECS Policies and Advanced Membership Parameters

ELAN membership can be controlled through the use of LECS policies. By using these policies, certain parameters must be matched beyond those specified by LANE before a

LEC is permitted to join the ELAN. Such a policy can include the token ring route descriptor associated with the joining LEC.

Configuring this policy involves two parts:

1. Indicating that the token ring route descriptor will be used by the LECS as a means of screening potential ELAN members.

2. Selecting the LES address or addresses that will be associated with the policy, and defining the actual route descriptor or descriptors that will be used.

 *Although the Advanced LECS Policy and Advanced Membership buttons were introduced in SpeedView 3.1, they were not actually functional until SpeedView 3.2. Earlier version of system software do not support this feature.*

**CONFIGURING THE ADVANCED LECS POLICY**   Clicking the Advanced LECS Policy button opens the LECS Policy window. In this window, the LECS simply is being made aware that the selected options in this window must be examined. Select the option labeled By Token Ring Route Descriptor; the selection will appear in the box below it.

**ASSOCIATING THE POLICY WITH A LES, AND DEFINING THE ROUTE DESCRIPTOR**   After you select the Advanced LECS Policy, highlight the LES with which the policy will be associated in the LES table of the main LECS Configuration window. Then, click the Advanced Membership button, which opens the LECS Advanced Membership window, where you define the specific route descriptor.

Insert the Ring Number and Bridge ID number, both in hexadecimal format, and then click Add to add the route descriptor to the table. Multiple entries can be made, allowing LECs associated with each RD to join.

## Configuring the LAN Emulation Server

When configuring the LES, a LAN Type must be defined when the ELAN is first defined; in this instance, unlike that of the LEC or LECS, a value of Unspecified is not listed as an option, because any LANE entity with a value of Unspecified for the LAN Type will obtain that parameter from the LES. The LAN Type parameter is accessible from the main LAN Emulation Server (LES/BUS) window.

In addition, an MTU size must be selected. This is done by clicking the Advanced button to open the main LES/BUS Advanced Configuration window. In the upper-left corner is a box labeled LES/BUS Control Parameters, which contains two fields:

- **Control Timeout**   Refers to the timeout time associated with the LANE control connections if they are unable to connect.

- **Max Frame Size**   As is the case with the LAN Type field in the main LECS configuration window, no value of Unspecified exists for the Max Frame Size, because, like the LAN Type, any LANE entity configured with a value of

Unspecified for the Max Frame Size will obtain the frame size from the LES. As of code version 4.0, valid frame sizes include 1516, 4544, 9234, and 18190. In addition, if the LES is LANEv2-capable, an additional frame size of 1580 is available; the new maximum frame size for Ethernet was introduced in LANEv2.

# Configuring the LAN Emulation Client

In a token ring environment, a LEC behaves as a station on the virtual ring that is associated with the ELAN it is joined to; in a transparently bridged environment, the LEC does not require additional configuration beyond what is required by LANE. If SRB is being used, however, the LEC VPort must be treated like any other token ring port on the Centillion.

## Configuring Bridging Parameters

If Source Route Bridging or Source Route Transparent Bridging is selected as the Switching Mode, the following ring and bridge parameters will be present when the LEC Configuration button is accessed:

- **Spanning Tree Group (Bridge Group)**   In code version 4.0 and later, the STG with which the LEC will be associated must be selected. If the code version is prior to 4.0, a bridge group must be selected. If an STG must be selected, the option to select a specific VLAN will be available as the last option of this set of parameters. A bridge group consists of a VLAN and an individual STG, so if a bridge group is being selected, the VLAN option will not be present.

- **Ring# (hex)**   Indicates the ring number associated with the ELAN of which the LEC is a member. All LECs that are a member of the same ELAN must have the same Ring ID. This value is entered in hexadecimal format.

- **Path Cost**   Indicates the path cost associated with the port, describing its relative relationship with the root bridge. Path cost is used by the STA to make forwarding or blocking decisions. By default, ATM ports are configured with a path cost of 7. This can be altered, however, if the network is a mixed token ring/ATM environment. It is a good practice to make sure the path cost is less than the path cost associated with the actual token ring ports, which are given a path cost of 10 by default. This prevents the ATM port from blocking in the event of a loop condition.

- **ARE Hop Count**   Indicates the maximum number of hop counts an ARE frame may pass before being discarded. By default, this value is set to 7, which is the maximum for traditional source routing. This value can be set as high as 13, which is the maximum for extended source routing. If an ARE is received with more than the allotted number of hops traversed (determined by examining the total number of route descriptors accumulated so far), the frame is dropped.

■ **STE Hop Count**   Indicates the maximum number of hop counts an STE frame may pass before being discarded. By default, this value is set to 7, which is the maximum for traditional source routing. This value can be set as high as 13, which is the maximum for extended source routing. If an STE is received with more than the allotted number of hops traversed (determined by examining the total number of route descriptors accumulated so far), the frame is dropped.

■ **Spanning Tree**   Indicates the spanning tree state for the port being configured. Options include On, where Spanning Tree is enabled on the port, Off, where Spanning Tree is disabled, or Block, where Spanning Tree is enabled, but administratively placed in a blocking state.

■ **VLAN**   If the switch being configured is running system software 4.0 or greater, a specific VLAN within the selected STG must be configured. A drop-down field will display a list of VLANs that exist within the chosen STG.

**CONFIGURING A LOCAL SEGMENT**   From the LAN Emulation Client Configuration window, select Configure LEC VPort Parameters to access the LEC VPort Configuration Parameters window. This window has two columns of parameters; the last parameter in the left column is labeled Local Segment ID, which is the ring number of the virtual ring associated with the LEC's ELAN. This value is also specified in the previous window, under the heading Ring# (hex), the difference being that the value must be configured in decimal in the Local Segment ID field.

# Configuring Centillion LAN Clients for Token Ring

Centillion LAN Clients are also viewed as virtual rings in an SRB environment. Here, the same port-level bridging information that would be associated with a token ring port, or LEC VPort, must be configured for the CLC. These options are as follows:

■ Spanning Tree Group (Bridge Group)

■ Ring# (hex)

■ Path Cost

■ ARE Hop Count

■ STE Hop Count

■ Spanning Tree

■ VLAN (4.0 or higher only)

These parameters hold the same meanings as the port-level bridging parameters that are associated with a LEC VPort. The exact definition of each parameter is given in the preceding section on configuring token ring parameters on a LEC.

# Troubleshooting Token Ring on the C100/C50/C20/5000BH Platform

Troubleshooting token ring problems on the Centillion platform can be done through the Statistics window in SpeedView, or through the CLI. While it is often true that the Centillion CLI offers more detailed analysis of the switch than the Statistics window can offer, in the case of token ring, the statistics that are available are largely the same when obtained from either source.

The two main things to check when dealing with a token ring issue on the Centillion platform are the port-level statistics and the forwarding database.

## Port-Level Information

A lot of information can be obtained from the CLI, using the **show port** command. This command uses the following syntax:

show port *module number port number*

The following is sample output from using the **show port** command:

```
C100:Command > show port 4 1

Information and Statistics for port 4,1:


port_state: up  media_type: tr  vsegment_type: tr  filter_mask: 0xE
ring #: 0x41  vsegment_index: 0x2  insertion_speed: force 16M
connection_mode: station  ring_speed: 16M
bridge_group id: 1  bridging_type: SRT
stp_protocol: IBM  stp_state: forwarding
BIA: 0005000830A0  LAA: 0005000830A0

PortState: forwarding PortConfig: 0x89
vlan_dtag: 0x114  vlan_id: 0x41  hw_id: 0x1
lfbits: 0x3
are_hop_count: 7  ste_hop_count: 7

Port Statistics:
InOctet:  521672753  InUcastPkt:  1591627  InDiscard:  1     InError: 0
OutOctet: 435257228  OutUcastPkt: 1628993  OutDiscard: 0
MulticastsTransmittedOk: 3902714  BroadcastsTransmittedOk: 0
MulticastsReceivedOk:    2163688  BroadcastsReceivedOk:    1860650
InNUcastPkt:             4024338  OutNUcastPkts:           3902714
InNoResources:           0        OutNoResources:          0
```

```
LineError: 59     BurstError: 2246   ACEError: 0        TokenError: 124
SoftError: 398    HardError: 0       Recovery: 2        SignalLoss: 0
TransmitBeacon: 0    LobeWire: 0       Removes: 0        Singles: 0
LostFrameError: 0    FrameCopiedError: 0      ReceiveCongestion: 0

SrSpecInFrames: 0      SrSpecOutFrames:  0        SrApeInFrames:       540922
SrApeOutFrames: 557531  SrSteInFrames:     544908  SrSteOutFrames:     557531
SrSegMismatchDiscards:      6        SrDupSegDiscards:  0
SrHopCountExceededDiscards: 0        SrLanIdMismatches: 0
```

This output can be broken down into three basic sections:

■ The spanning tree and port state information

■ The port-level statistics

■ The SRB statistics

To give you an idea of what this output offers, each of these three sections is examined next relative to the preceding example output.

**SPANNING TREE AND PORT STATE INFORMATION**  The following output is the result of the **show port** command. It is issued to the terminal screen in the same format as in the preceding section, but it has been broken up in this section to illustrate better what the different statistics indicate, beginning with the spanning tree and port state information:

```
C100:Command > show port 4 1
Information and Statistics for port 4,1:

port_state: up  media_type: tr  vsegment_type: tr  filter_mask: 0xE
```

Notice that the port state is up, and the media type is token ring (tr).

The following output indicates that the Ring ID is 0x41, which is the default ring number assigned to module 4, port 1. The vsegment_index is used internally to identify one virtual ring from another. The insertion speed is set at 16Mbps, and the designation force 16M indicates that speed sense is not being used, and that the port has been manually set to 16Mbps.

```
ring #: 0x41  vsegment_index: 0x2  insertion_speed: force 16M
```

A connection mode of station is listed in the following output; this indicates that the device connected to the port is a token ring concentrator. *Station mode* means the port is acting as a station, connecting into a hub. The ring speed is also displayed; this is the actual running speed, as opposed to the configured speed in the insertion speed field that appears in the preceding code line.

```
connection_mode: station   ring_speed: 16M
```

In the following line of output, the port is in bridge group 1 (indicating the device is running pre-4.0 system software, which references STGs), and the bridging mode is set to Source Route Transparent Bridging:

```
bridge_group id: 1  bridging_type: SRT
```

The following indicates that IBM Spanning Tree is being used, and that the STP state is forwarding:

```
stp_protocol: IBM  stp_state: forwarding
```

The following line indicates the burned-in address, as well as any locally administered address that may be used. In this case, because the values are equal, an LAA is not being used.

```
BIA: 0005000830A0  LAA: 0005000830A0
```

The port is currently in a forwarding state:

```
PortState: forwarding PortConfig: 0x89
```

The following entries give information regarding specific VLAN and hardware parameters. Of note is the vlan_id, which is set to the same value as the SRB ring ID.

```
vlan_dtag: 0x114  vlan_id: 0x41  hw_id: 0x1
lfbits: 0x3
```

The ARE and STE hop counts are both at the default value of 7:

```
are_hop_count: 7  ste_hop_count: 7
```

**PORT-LEVEL STATISTICS**    The following is the continuation of the **show port** output, dealing with the token ring port-level statistics. The first set of statistics shows the total number of octets in and out of this port, as well as any frames that have been discarded on the ingress or egress:

```
Port Statistics:
InOctet:  521672753  InUcastPkt:  1591627  InDiscard:  1     InError: 0
OutOctet: 435257228  OutUcastPkt: 1628993  OutDiscard: 0
```

The following set of statistics takes the total packets coming in and breaks them down to show the total number of unicasts, multicasts, and broadcasts. These are counted by packet, not octet. These statistics will also indicate the number of InNoResources and OutNoResources, which indicate packets that were dropped either on ingress or egress because no room was left in the transmit or receive buffer. This generally indicates a congestion problem.

```
MulticastsTransmittedOk: 3902714  BroadcastsTransmittedOk: 0
MulticastsReceivedOk:    2163688  BroadcastsReceivedOk:     1860650
InNUcastPkt:             4024338  OutNUcastPkts:            3902714
InNoResources:                 0  OutNoResources:                0
```

The following set of statistics indicates the number and types of token ring errors reported on the port. For a complete list of token ring errors, as well as their specific meanings, consult Appendix C.

```
LineError: 59      BurstError: 2246  ACEError: 0       TokenError: 12
SoftError: 398     HardError:  0     Recovery:  2      SignalLoss: 0
TransmitBeacon: 0  LobeWire: 0       Removes: 0        Singles: 0
LostFrameError: 0  FrameCopiedError: 0     ReceiveCongestion: 0
```

**SOURCE ROUTE BRIDGING STATISTICS**    The last portion of the token ring **show port** output indicates the SRB statistics. The statistics that follow are relevant only if Source Route Bridging or Source Route Transparent Bridging has been selected as the bridging mode:

```
SrSpecInFrames: 0      SrSpecOutFrames: 0      SrApeInFrames:    540922
SrApeOutFrames: 557531 SrSteInFrames:    544908 SrSteOutFrames:   557531
SrSegMismatchDiscards:      6      SrDupSegDiscards: 0
SrHopCountExceededDiscards: 0      SrLanIdMismatches: 0
```

The preceding statistics indicate the following:

- **SrSpecInFrames**  The total number of specifically source-routed frames received on the interface.

- **SrSpecOutFrames**  The total number of specifically source-routed frames transmitted on an interface.

- **SrApeInFrames**  The total number of ARE frames (also known as All Paths Explorer frames, accounting for the APE designation) received on the interface.

- **SrApeOutFrames**  The total number of ARE frames (also known as All Paths Explorer frames).

- **SrSteInFrames**  The total number of STE frames received on the interface.

- **SrSteOutFrames**  The total number of STE frames transmitted from the interface.

- **SrSegMismatchDiscards**  The total number of source-routed frames discarded due to an incorrect Ring ID, which means that the frame indicated it was sourced from a ring other than the Ring ID the port is a member of.

- **SrDupSegDiscards**  The total number of source-routed frames dropped due to a duplicate Ring ID in the RIF.

- **SrHopCountExceededDiscards**  The total number of source-routed frames dropped because they have exceeded the maximum number of source-route hops permitted in the network.

- **SrLanIdMismatches**  The number of source-routed frames dropped due to a LAN ID being inconsistent.

# The Complete Reference

Nortel Networks

# Chapter 27

## Configuring SRB on the Nortel Networks Router Platform

The Nortel Networks router platform supports bridging, source-route bridging (SRB), translational bridging and routing over Token Ring. This chapter is designed to give a basic understanding of the configuration parameters and design considerations associated with these protocols.

The Token Ring router configuration depends largely on the protocols being utilized, and the specific network design. This chapter deals mainly with SRB parameters in both strict Token Ring environments (where SRB occurs between different Token Rings only) and environments where SRB takes place between Token Ring and other technologies, such as Ethernet and WAN. The next section starts by examining SRB configuration parameters in a strictly Token Ring environment.

# Source-Route Bridging

Some networking protocols cannot be routed (such as NetBIOS and SNA). In order to forward non-routable traffic across a router, the router must act as a bridge. In order to bridge over Token Ring, SRB must be selected as a protocol when configuring the router's interfaces using Site Manager. SRB is selected from the Protocols menu when the interface is first configured; both SRB and bridging services are listed in the Select Protocols window. When configuring SRB, select SRB and not Bridging Services, which is only used to configure Translational Bridging.

## Source-Route Bridging on the LAN

The Nortel Networks router platform supports both standard SRB and a proprietary method of hop-count reduction. This hop-count reduction method is described in detail in Chapter 25. The configuration of SRB involves configuring a series of source-routing parameters and SRB spanning tree parameters at both the global and interface level.

### Global Source-Route Parameters

The first time SRB is selected, Site Manager will automatically bring up the Source Routing Global Parameters window; after the initial global SRB configuration, this window can be accessed from Configuration Manager by means of the Protocols | Source Routing | Global command. This opens the Source Routing Global Parameters window:

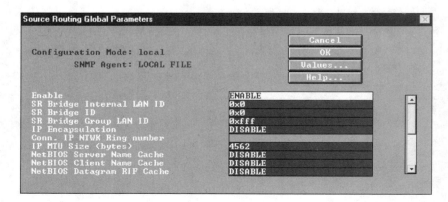

Here, the source-route parameters that apply on a global level can be manipulated. These parameters have the following meanings:

- **Enable**   Enables and disables source-routing on all SRR interfaces.
- **SR Bridge Internal LAN ID**   Defines the Internal LAN ID (in hex). This is the value assigned to the virtual SRB ring that is used by the router when performing SRB between its own SRB interfaces. This value must be unique among all other LAN IDs, as well as among all other Group LAN IDs and Bridge IDs.
- **SR Bridge ID**   Indicates the Bridge ID assigned to the router being configured. The Bridge ID should be the same hex value for all Nortel routers within the network. The exception to this rule is when two bridges are running in parallel (two SRB bridges connect the same two rings), in which case the two associated Bridge IDs must be different.

**Note**   *When bridges are running in parallel, and unique Bridge IDs are being used, the new, unique Bridge ID entry must be added to the Bridge Entry List on all other Nortel Networks routers in the network that are running SRB.*

- **SR Bridge Group LAN ID**   Indicates the ID associated with the Nortel Networks routers running SRB within the same SRB domain. It is used to manipulate the Routing Information Field (RIF) to keep the number of SRB hops low. This is useful, because it reduces the extra hops that a router's internal ring would normally introduce when running SRB. For more details regarding the Group LAN ID and Nortel Networks SRB services on the router platform, consult Chapter 25.
- **IP Encapsulation**   Enables or disables IP encapsulation. If the source-route portions of the network are separated by an IP network, source-routed packets can be encapsulated in IP to traverse the IP network and reach a remote SRB network. Enabling this feature necessitates configuring the Conn. IP NTWK Ring Number parameter.
- **Conn. IP NTWK Ring Number**   Indicates the "virtual ring number" that is associated with the IP cloud when IP encapsulation is employed (see Figure 27-1). This ring number (configured in hex) must be the same for all SRB routers bordering the cloud.
- **IP MTU Size (bytes)**   Indicates the maximum transmit unit size for the IP network, in cases where IP encapsulation is being used. This value should reflect the smallest MTU size present in the IP portion of the network.
- **NetBIOS Server Name Cache**   Enables the router to cache the source name, MAC address, and RIF for each NetBIOS server.
- **NetBIOS Client Name Cache**   Enables the router to cache the source name, MAC address, and RIF for each NetBIOS client.
- **NetBIOS Datagram RIF Cache**   Enables the router to cache source names, MAC addresses, and RIF for NetBIOS datagrams.

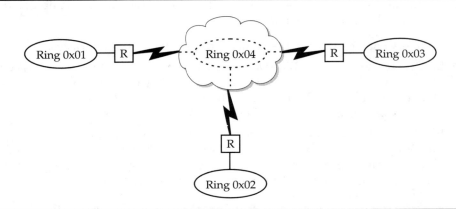

**Figure 27-1.** *The connecting IP network ring number*

- **15-Character NetBIOS Name Caching** Setting to Enable causes the router to treat NetBIOS names as 15-character entries. Setting to Disable causes the router to treat NetBIOS names as 16-character entries.

- **Create MIB Instances for Cached Name** Enabling this parameter allows the router to create specific MIB entries for each cached NetBIOS name, aging these entries out after a period of disuse.

- **Max Name Cache Entries** Indicates the maximum number of NetBIOS names that can be cached; the default value is 100, with a range of 1 to 2,147,483,647.

- **Name Cache Age (secs)** Indicates the amount of time that a NetBIOS name cache entry can remain inactive in the cache before being aged out. The default value is 300 seconds (5 minutes), with a range of 1 to 2,147,483,648 seconds.

- **Hash Entry Count** Indicates the number of entries that will be allowed in the hash table. The range is from 253 to 2,147,483,648. The default value is sufficient to support up to 2,500 NetBIOS client and server names.

- **NetBIOS Query Cache** Enabling this global parameter allows the router to cache the names, MAC addresses, and RIF information for each Add Name Query and Add Group Name Query received.

- **Create MIB Instances for Cached Queries** Enables the router to create individual MIB instances for each cached NetBIOS name query. This also enables the router to age out such queries after a period of disuse. Setting this parameter to Disable frees up the memory associated with the function.

- **Max Number Query Cache Entries**   Indicates the maximum number of NetBIOS name query cache entries that are supported on the router. The range is from 1 to 100, with a default of 100.

- **NetBIOS Query Cache Age (secs)**   Indicates the amount of time, in seconds, before a NetBIOS name query that has been cached will be aged out if it remains inactive. The range is from 1 to 2,147,483,648, with a default of 15.

- **SR Spanning Tree Protocol Version**   Assigns the source-route spanning tree type being used. Options are IEEE802.1D (802.1d Spanning Tree), DECLB100, or Unknown.

## Source-Route Interface Parameters

The SRB interface-specific parameters can be selected from Configuration Manager by selecting Protocols | Source Routing | Interfaces (upon initial configuration of the interface, these parameters are brought up automatically when SRB is selected as a protocol) from the pull-down menus. This brings up the SR Interface List window:

A list of all configured source-routed interfaces appears in this window, and you can select an interface by clicking on it. After you select the desired SRB interface, you can alter the individual SRB parameters for that interface.

The following SRB interface-specific parameters apply:

- **Enable**   Enables and disables SRB on the specified interface.

- **Max Number of RDs**   Indicates the maximum number of route descriptors that can be associated with an incoming explorer packet. Explorers whose route descriptors exceed the maximum number will be dropped; this technique can be used to limit access to certain portions of the source-routed network. The range is from 1 to 7, with a default of 7.

- **Source Routing Ring Number**    Defines the SRB ring number (in hex) associated with the SRB ring this source-routed interface connects to. Ring numbers must be unique within the source-routed network.

- **Outbound STEs**    Used only if source-route Spanning Tree is not being used. Once this parameter is set to Block, all outgoing Spanning Tree Explorer (STE) frames will be dropped, just as they would be by a source-routed interface that is running spanning tree and is in a blocking state. This feature allows a sort of "static Spanning Tree" topology to be built, allowing the network administrator to control the path SRB traffic will take through the network.

- **Inbound STEs**    Setting this parameter to Block causes the interface to drop any incoming STEs. This does not prevent outgoing STEs from being transmitted on the interface. This parameter is not used if source-route Spanning Tree is active since Spanning Tree will use an algorithm to determine which interfaces will block.

- **Frames with IP Ring**    Setting to Block causes the interface to drop any incoming Explorer frames that have already traversed the IP network in an IP encapsulation SRB environment. This can be employed to restrict networks across the IP cloud from accessing portions of the network.

- **IP Address**    Used in IP encapsulation SRB environments to map ring numbers to IP addresses; configured with a standard 32-bit IP address.

- **NetBIOS Server Name Cache**    Enables the selected interface to cache the source name, MAC address, and RIF for each NetBIOS server.

- **NetBIOS Client Name Cache**    Enables the selected interface to cache the source name, MAC address, and RIF for each NetBIOS client.

- **NetBIOS Datagram Cache**    Enables the selected interface to cache the source name, MAC address, and RIF for each NetBIOS datagram.

- **WAN Broadcast Address**    Used when source routing over a WAN.

- **Encapsulation Format**    Refers to the encapsulation format that will be used on the interface. If the SRB interface is a Frame Relay interface, consult Table 27-1 for the proper encapsulation setting.

If the interface is an FDDI interface, the rules in Table 27-2 apply.

## Source-Route Spanning Tree Parameters

If source-route Spanning Tree is selected as one of the protocols in the Select Protocols window at the time the interface is first configured, the Spanning Tree global parameters window will be brought up automatically. Thereafter, the source-route Spanning Tree

| Remote Router RS Version | Select |
|---|---|
| Third-party router supporting RFC 1490 | Standard |
| Bay RS version 5 | Proprietary |
| Bay RS version 7 | Standard |
| Bay RS version 8 | Can be either, but each side must match |

**Table 27-1.**   *Frame Relay Encapsulation Methods*

parameters can be accessed from Configuration Manager by selecting Protocols | Source Route | Spanning Tree | Global from the pull-down menus.

The primary difference between source-route Spanning Tree and 802.1d Spanning Tree is what occurs when a loop condition is detected. In source-route Spanning Tree, instead of having a port enter a blocking state, as in 802.1d Spanning Tree, whereby the port doesn't forward data, the port doesn't forward STEs, which prevents STE frames from looping back during the RIF path discovery. Ports that are blocking in source-route spanning tree do not block All Routes Explorer (ARE) frames, so multiple paths may be considered in a scenario where STEs are used to find a path to the destination, and then AREs are dispatched from the destination to discover the best path back. The following global parameters apply to source-route spanning tree:

■ **Spanning Tree Enable**   Enables and disables source-route Spanning Tree.

| Remote Router RS Version | Select |
|---|---|
| Token Ring endstation to FDDI endstation | Standard |
| Third-party router via FDDI | Standard |
| Bay RS version 5 or 7 via FDDI | Proprietary |
| Bay RS version 8 | Can be either, but each side must match |

**Table 27-2.**   *FDDI Encapsulation Methods*

- **Bridge Priority**   Defaults to 128 (in decimal), and is used in conjunction with the Bridge MAC address to form a unique spanning tree identification for purposes of root bridge election. The lower the bridge priority, the greater the chance the SRB will be elected as root. The root bridge should be centrally located in the SRB network.

- **Bridge MAC Address**   If configured in Local Mode, this field is blank by default; if configured in Dynamic Mode, it indicates a unique MAC address, generated by the router, that is based on the backplane ID. This MAC address is used in conjunction with the Bridge Priority to form a unique Bridge ID that is used by Spanning Tree for root bridge election. During the root bridge election, if two routers have equal SRB priorites, the MAC addresses are compared, and the lowest MAC address has the highest priority.

- **Max Age**   Indicates the amount of time, in hundredths of a second (so the default of 2000 actually indicates 20 seconds), that the bridge will consider information obtained from a BPDU to be valid. After this amount of time, the information is discarded. If the Max Age parameter is altered, it should also be changed to the same value on all other source-route bridges running source-route spanning tree.

- **Hello Time**   Indicates the amount of time, in hundredths of a second, between the transmission of each BPDU by the source-route spanning tree interface. The default value of 200 indicates a 2-second interval.

- **Forward Delay**   Indicates the amount of time, in hundredths of a second, that the source-route spanning tree interface spends in each of its spanning tree states (listening, learning, forwarding/blocking). The default value of 1500 indicates 15 seconds. The range is between 4 and 30 seconds (400 and 3000, respectively).

## Source-Route Bridging in Parallel

Typically, in a SRB environment all SR Bridges and routers configured as SR Bridges will share a common Bridge ID. However, if two SR Bridges are running in parallel, the SR Bridge ID of the two parallel bridges must differ from one another. One SR Bridge ID in this case may match those of the rest of the SRB network, but one must be unique (see Figure 27-2).

In this scenario, routers A, B, and D share the same Bridge ID (0x0A), while router C, which runs in parallel, must have a unique ID (0x0B). In addition to this configuration consideration, due to the proprietary SRB method of hop reduction performed by Nortel Networks routers, each router (acting as a source-route bridge in this case) must also be informed of the Bridge ID associated with any Nortel Networks routers running in parallel and vice versa. So, in this example, routers A, B, and D must have an entry of Bridge ID 0x0B in their bridge entry list tables, and router C, which actually has a Bridge ID of 0x0B, must have an entry for Bridge ID 0x0A in its bridge entry list table.

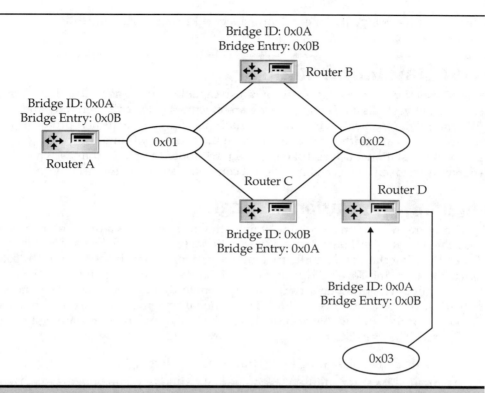

Bridge ID: 0x0A
Bridge Entry: 0x0B

Router B

Bridge ID: 0x0A
Bridge Entry: 0x0B

Router A

0x01

0x02

Router C

Router D

Bridge ID: 0x0B
Bridge Entry: 0x0A

Bridge ID: 0x0A
Bridge Entry: 0x0B

0x03

**Figure 27-2.**  *Two routers running SRB in parallel*

The SRB Bridge ID can be added to the bridge entry list table by selecting Protocols |
Source Routing | Bridge Entry from the pull-down menus in Site Manager's Configuration
Manager Utility. This opens the Source Routing Bridge IDs window:

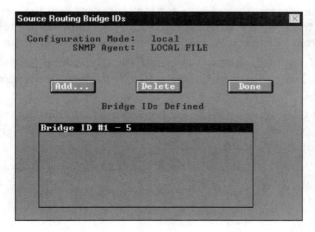

Here, enter the Bridge IDs of any Nortel Networks routers running SRB.

# Translational Bridging

The Nortel Networks router platform is also capable of running translational bridging services between dissimilar networking architectures (such as Token Ring and Ethernet). This enables devices that use dissimilar frame formats and protocols to intercommunicate, with the router handling the necessary frame encapsulation and protocol translation (such as Token Ring source-routed Explorer frames, when source-route token ring end stations must communicate with Ethernet devices).

## Configuring Translational Bridging

To configure translational bridging, it must first be selected as a protocol on one of the associated interfaces. For instance, if translational bridging is to be used between a Token Ring interface and an Ethernet interface, translational bridging must be selected as a protocol on the Token Ring interface. The Ethernet interface in this case should only be configured with bridging services (transparent bridging). The Token Ring interface only must also be configured for SRB. Translational bridging may be configured in the Select Protocols window that appears when the individual interfaces are first configured. The translational bridging window has the following parameters:

- **Enable**   Enables and disables translational bridging.

- **Virtual LAN ID**   Indicates a ring number that is assigned to the non-Token Ring virtual ring. This may be an Ethernet segment or a WAN connection. The Token Ring portion of the network will view the Ethernet or WAN network as a single ring for purposes of source routing. The value given to the virtual ring should be unique from any other LAN ID, Group LAN ID, or Internal LAN ID.

- **Max Translation Entries**   Indicates the maximum number of RIF entries the router will store; stored RIF entries enable the translational bridge to forward source-route frames to common destinations more rapidly. However, for each RIF entry made by the translational bridge, the router-bridging function also makes a transparent bridge entry, which consumes more memory.

- **Aging Value**   Indicates how long a RIF remains stored if inactive. The default value is 300 seconds (five minutes), after which inactive RIF entries are aged out of the table.

- **Broadcast Conversion**   When enabled, causes the router to translate 802.3 broadcasts (FF:FF:FF:FF:FF:FF) to 802.5 broadcasts (C0:00:FF:FF:FF:FF), and translate 802.5 broadcasts to 802.3 format.

- **Ethernet Type**   Specifies whether an Ethernet version 2 frame format or an 802.3 frame type should be used when translating from Token Ring to Ethernet.

| Note |

*Although only one Ethernet frame type can be specified for Ethernet Type, additional frame types may be defined if more than one frame type is being used within the network. To specify additional frame types for specific Ethernet stations, select Protocols | Global Protocols | Translation Bridge | Ethernet Type List from Configuration Manager, which opens the Ethernet Station Type List window. By default, this list is blank. Click Add to open the Translation Bridge Address Mapping window, in which individual Ethernet MAC address may be specified, and a specific frame type may be associated with those addresses.*

- **Source Route Explorer Type**    Indicates the type of source-route Explorer frame that will be used when, for example, an Ethernet station is attempting to reach a source-route token ring station whose location is not yet known. In this case, the source-route interface must issue an Explorer frame to locate the station. The Explorer options are STE or ARE. AREs propagate throughout the entire source-route bridged network, so the optimum path to the destination will be found, but at the cost of increased overhead. STEs follow a single path (dictated by Spanning Tree), so the optimum path may not be discovered, but they incur less overhead, because they don't propagate as thoroughly as do AREs.

- **SAPS**    Indicates the types of (Service Advertisement Protocol) SAPs the translational bridge will accept and translate. By default, the translation bridge will accept NetBIOS, Systems Network Architecture (SNA), and LAN Network Manager (LNM) SAPs.

## Translational Bridging Address Mapping

When running translational bridging, you may also map certain token ring functional addresses to Ethernet multicast addresses. To do this, select Protocols | Global Protocols | Translational Bridging | MAC Addr Conversions from Configuration Manager. This opens the Address Mapping List, which is blank by default. To add an entry, select Add to open the Translation Bridge Address Mapping window, which has two fields: the Token Ring Functional Address, in which you enter the MAC address of the Token Ring functional frame type, and the Ethernet Multicast Address, in which you enter the specific Ethernet multicast address that the token ring address will be mapped to.

## End Station Support

Nortel Networks routers also support a feature called *end station support,* which allows a Token Ring interface to behave as a token ring end station for purposes of source-route determination. This is useful, for example, in a routed environment where an Ethernet client and source-routed Token Ring server must communicate with one another, as depicted in Figure 27-3.

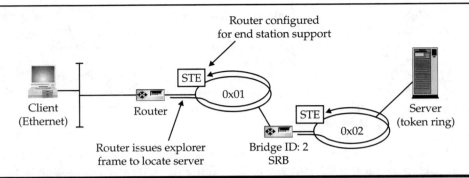

**Figure 27-3.**    *Token ring end station support*

In Figure 27-3, the router borders both an Ethernet network and a Token Ring network that is using SRB.

The Ethernet client attempts to ping the Token Ring server that is configured for source routing. The Ethernet client determines that the Token Ring server resides on a different IP network, so it sends the ping to its default gateway (the local router interface). Before forwarding the ping to the server, the router must ARP to determine its MAC address. By default, however, the router's routing process will not add a RIF to an IP packet's frame before forwarding it, and so the ARP will be issued onto the Token Ring SRB network without a RIF. In this case the router is in fact configured with SRB, but since the packet initially came in as an IP packet it is handled by the router's IP routing engine and not the SRB engine. In this example (see Figure 27-3), if the server resided on Ring 0x01, it would receive the ARP, and reply to it. However, since it resides on Ring 0x02, the packet must traverse a SR bridge. Since no RIF was inserted into the frame, the SR bridge will drop it and it will never be received by the server. Enabling End Station Support causes the router to first generate an explorer frame to discover the server, cache the RIF information, and insert a RIF into the frame destined for that server. Once the RIF is generated, it is stored on the router and inserted into packets destined for that end station, when data destined for that end station is received from the Ethernet portion of the network.

## Configuring End Station Support

In the scenario outlined in the previous example, the router's issuing of the Explorer frame and gathering of RIF information is invisible to the original client.

Configuring end station support consists of enabling the feature on the Token Ring interface, and then selecting the type of Explorer frame that will be used by the interface when assuming the role of an end station for purposes of source-route path determination.

Both of these parameters are configured under the interface-specific parameters for a given routed protocol. For instance, if the interface is an IP interface that is also a token ring interface, then select Protocols | IP | Interfaces from the Main Menu bar in Site Manager's Configuration Manager Utility. The parameters that apply are as follows:

- **TR End Station**    Enables and disables token ring end station support.
- **TR End Station ARP Type (IP Only)**    If token ring end station support is selected, this parameter indicates the Explorer type that will be issued by the interface, if an ARP destined for a source-routing station is received from the non-source-routing station. The options are STE or ARE.

# The Complete Reference

Nortel Networks

# Part VII

## Internetworking with Nortel Networks

The Complete Reference

# Chapter 28

## The Nortel Networks Router Platform

The Nortel Networks router platform exists in two basic groups: the *access nodes* and the *backbone nodes*. As their names indicate, the access node family is suited for edge sites and locations, or smaller offices, whereas the backbone node family is better suited for use in a network backbone or core. Each family has different models, and each is described in this chapter.

# Access Node Routers

The access node family includes the access node (AN), the access node hub (ANH), the access remote node (ARN), and the access stack node (ASN). These are modular, standalone units, where all processing occurs on the motherboard. Each AN product provides a series of LAN connections, as well as WAN connectivity for WAN protocols such as frame relay, ISDN, PPP, Wellfleet Standard, and so forth. The AN family of routers is ideal for connecting small offices to a WAN, or for connecting a series of remote sites to a central office.

## Access Node

The AN has a fixed configuration, though some flexibility is provided in the choice of configuration. All AN routers have a single Ethernet interface, a single token ring interface (STP DB-9), or a combination of the two, in addition to two synchronous interfaces. The Ethernet routed interface offers two Ethernet port types (AUI, and 10BaseT UTP), though only one of these interfaces is active at any one time. The sync interfaces can be used for either two sync connections (such as a PPP link), or one sync connection and one ISDN Basic Rate Interface (BRI).

The AN also has a single console/modem port. This port can be used for local console connections or, alternatively, to affix a modem to provide dial-in access to the router.

### Access Node Interfaces

The AN interfaces adhere to the following specifications:

- **Ethernet interfaces**   Each Ethernet interface is either an AUI connection or a 10BaseT RJ-45 connection. All Ethernet interfaces support IEEE 802.3 and Ethernet version 2 frame format.

- **Token Ring interfaces**   Token ring interfaces are DB-9 STP connectors, capable of ring speeds of 4 or 16Mbps.

- **Synchronous interfaces**   All sync interfaces support V.35, RS-232, RS449/422 balanced, and X.21. They operate from 1,200bps to 2,048Mbps full-duplex.

- **ISDN Basic Rate Interface (BRI)**   A standard ISDN BRI interface, offering two 64Kbps B channels, and one 16Kbps D channel for signaling purposes.

The AN may also optionally be factory configured or field upgraded with the following options:

- **A third synchronous interface**
- **A data collection module (DCM)**    This device gathers Remote Monitoring (RMON) statistics. The DCM is supported only in Ethernet AN configurations, and is not supported in a Token Ring/synchronous, or Ethernet/Token Ring/ssynchronous configuration.

## Access Node LEDs

The AN router has a series of LEDs located on the front panel; these LEDs give information regarding the status of the AN. Table 28-1 details the LED indications that may appear.

The diagnostic test may last one to two minutes following cold boot, after which the Diag LED should go out. If the diagnostics aren't passed, the router may not boot. If the Diag LED remains red for an extended period of time, an internal component may have failed its diagnostic test and may require hardware maintenance.

The AN also has a series of LEDs located on the rear of the unit; these are detailed in Table 28-2.

**AN1 VS. AN2**    The AN exists in two varieties: the older AN1, and the AN2 commonly used today. The AN1 is the predecessor to the AN2 and is different than the AN2 insofar as it does not possess a flash memory card slot, but instead has an internal SIMM flash.

While the AN1 and AN2 are distinguishable at a glance due to the presence or absence of the external flash, they appear the same from a dial-in or Telnet session. (The SIMM flash volume is accessed in the same way as an external flash card.) To distinguish one from the other while accessing the device remotely, enter the following command at the Technician Interface (TI):

```
[1:1]$ g wsFsVolEntry.wfFsRemoveable.*
```

| LED | Color | Status |
| --- | --- | --- |
| Power | Green | Power supply is active. |
| Run | Green | System software is executing. |
| Boot | Green | System is initializing. |
| Diag | Red | Diagnostic test in progress. |

**Table 28-1.**    *LEDs on the AN Front Panel*

INTERNETWORKING WITH NORTEL NETWORKS

| LED | Color | Status |
|-----|-------|--------|
| R | Green | Data being received from Token Ring LAN. |
| N | Green | Station has been inserted into token ring. |
| F | Red | Wire/lobe fault has occurred. |
| RLS | Green | Received Line Signal detected on synchronous port. |
| RX | Green | Data being received on Ethernet LAN. |
| TX | Green | Data being transmitted on Ethernet LAN. |
| CL | Red | Collision has occurred. |

**Table 28-2.**   *LEDs on the AN Back Panel*

If the value returned is 1, the unit is an AN2; if the value is 0, the unit is an AN1. For more information of the TI, consult the section on the TI later in this chapter. For more information regarding the polling of the Management Information Base (MIB), consult Chapter 29 "The TI and the Router MIB."

## Access Node Hub

Like the AN, the ANH also has a fixed configuration, though its architecture is quite different. The ANH is a stand-alone unit with a cluster of Ethernet ports. The variety of Ethernet ports will vary depending on the model of ANH used (8 ports in the ANH-8, and 12 ports in the ANH-12). The port groupings in both the ANH-8 and the ANH-12 act as a shared Ethernet segment that is managed. This segment accesses an internal routed Ethernet port. The ANH also possesses two synchronous ports and, as with the AN, these interfaces can support either two sync connections or one sync and one ISDN BRI connection.

The Ethernet segment found on the ANH can be polled via SNMP for statistic monitoring and configuration on a port-by-port basis. The ANH-8 supports SNMP as well as the option for RMON, whereas the ANH-12 supports SNMP only.

**Note**   *The ANH-8 is fitted with one cooling fan at the factory; with the use of the optional RMON module, a second cooling fan is required.*

## ANH-8

The ANH-8 has eight RJ-45 UTP ports and one AUI port. All Ethernet ports connect in the front of the unit, while the sync connectors are located in the rear of the device. The ANH-8 contains one MDI-X port.

The ANH-8 is outfitted with three switches:

- A power switch, located in the rear of the device, which toggles the power on and off.

- A MDI-X/MDI switch, which toggles port 1 between the MDI and MDI-X states. In MDI-X mode, the transmit and receive connections are reversed, meaning the port is effectively crossed over, while in MDI mode, the port transmits and receives in a straight-through configuration.

- A Reset button, which can be used to reset the device. When you press the Reset button quickly, the ANH executes a warm boot (it resets, but no hardware diagnostics are run). Holding down the Reset button for three seconds or more causes the device to do a cold boot (it resets and runs hardware diagnostics prior to booting).

## ANH-12

The ANH-12 has 12 RJ-45 UTP ports. All connections exist in the front of the unit, including the sync connections. All 12 of the Ethernet connections are MDI-X ports. Like the AHN-8, the ANH-12 has a power switch and a Reset button, which serve the same functions as those on the ANH-8. The ANH-12 does not have an MDI/MDI-X toggle switch.

### ANH LEDs

Each ANH model has a series of LED status indicators, detailed in Table 28-3 and Table 28-4, respectively.

# ARN

The Advanced Remote Node (ARN) is designed to be a scalable router solution for smaller offices. The ARN has a modular design, capable of supporting a single base module, as well as an expansion module and two adapter modules.

The base unit, in this case, provides a LAN connection to the existing network, for either Ethernet or Token Ring. The Ethernet base module provides one AUI and one 10BaseT RJ-45 connection (one active at a time), while the token ring base module provides a single token ring DB-9 interface, STP only. Each of these units is available with DRAM configurations of 8MB, 16MB, or 32MB.

The ARN expansion modules provide either WAN connectivity or, optionally, more LAN interfaces. The following options are available:

- Tri-serial expansion module, with three serial interfaces

- Ethernet expansion module, with one AUI and one 10BaseT RJ-45 Ethernet connection (one active at a time)

- Token ring expansion module, with one DB-9 STP token ring interface

- Ethernet/tri-serial expansion module, with one AUI and one 10BaseT RJ-45 Ethernet connection (one active at a time), and three serial interfaces

- Token ring/tri-serial expansion module, with one DB-9 STP token ring connection and three serial interfaces

| LED | Color | Status |
|---|---|---|
| Power | Green | Power supply is active. |
| Fault | Amber | Bootup diagnostics in progress. If light remains lit, diagnostics have failed. |
| Boot | Green | System is initializing. |
| Run | Green | System software is executing. |
| DCM | Green | Data Collection Module has been installed. |
| AUI Port | Amber | AUI port has partitioned due to excessive collisions. |
| DCD1 | Green | Data Carrier detected; valid signal detected on port 1 (COM1). |
| DCD2 | Green | Data Carrier detected; valid signal detected on port 2 (COM2). |
| <LAN> | Green | Data is passing through internal repeater. |
| Col | Amber | Collision has occurred. |
| Partition | Amber | Associated 10BaseT port has partitioned due to excessive collisions. |
| Link | Green | Valid link state detected on the port. |
| TX (back panel) | Green | Data being transmitted onto LAN. |
| RX (back panel) | Green | Data being received from LAN. |
| COL (back panel) | Amber | Collision has occurred. |
| ISDN BRI (back panel) | Green | S/T interface is active. |

**Table 28-3.**    *LEDs on the ANH-8*

The ARN can also optionally support a DCM for collecting RMON statistics for the Ethernet interfaces only. The ARN can support up to two DCMs: one for the Ethernet base unit, and one for an Ethernet expansion module.

| LED | Color | Status |
| --- | --- | --- |
| TX | Green | Data being transmitted. |
| RX | Green | Data being transmitted. |
| CL | Amber | Collision has occurred. |
| RLSD2 | Green | Received Line Signal detected on COM1. |
| RLSD1 | Green | Received Line Signal detected on COM2. |
| Link | Green | Valid link detected. |
| Part | Amber | Port is partitioned. |

**Table 28-4.**    *LEDs on the ANH-12*

The ARN also supports two adapter modules, which can be factory configured or upgraded in the field. The following adapter module options are available:

- Serial adapter module, providing a single serial interface.

- ISDN BRI S/T interface, with a single ISDN BRI interface. The S/T interface does not include an NT-1.

- ISDN BRI U interface, with a single ISDN BRI interface. The U interface includes an NT-1.

- 56Kbps/64Kbps data service unit (DSU)/channel service unit (CSU) adapter module, providing a single DSU/CSU interface.

- V.34 modem adapter module, with a single V.34 modem adapter interface. Available in North America only. This modem connection can provide remote out-of-band management, for system management and remote troubleshooting.

The ARN may be fitted with a redundant power supply unit (RPSU) to increase fault tolerance.

# Access Stack Node

The ASN is a stackable, stand-alone router module. Up to four of these units can be placed in a common stack. This stack will behave as a single router, which will support up to 40 interfaces.

The ASN is more modular in design than the other AN products; it consists of a processor module that can support up to four network modules (netmods).

In addition to the four slots available for netmods, the ASN comes equipped with a console port, a hardware diagnostic switch and diagnostic port, and a Slot ID switch. The console port is used for terminal access, and the Slot ID switch is for assigning slot numbers to the various units when stacking them. The hardware diagnostic port is used for factory testing, and is not intended for field use.

The ASN processor is based on the BN-FRE2 design (covered in the "Backbone Node Routers" section of this chapter); the unit supports 8MB, 16MB, or 32MB of memory. At least 32MB of memory should be used if all four netmod slots will be occupied, if there are more than four LAN interfaces, or if a Fiber Distributed Data Interface (FDDI) module is being used. In addition, a 256Kbps Fast Packet cache can be purchased to increase forwarding performance. This is recommended if there are more than four Ethernet interfaces present, more than two Token Ring interfaces, one FDDI interface, or if the units are being stacked. The netmod slots may be fitted with a number of router modules:

- 10BaseT dual Ethernet
- 100BaseT Ethernet
- Dual synchronous
- ISDN BRI/dial synchronous
- Quad BRI
- Single-mode fiber, multimode fiber, and hybrid FDDI
- Dual Token Ring
- Multichannel E-1 (MCE1)
- Hardware compression (for use in WAN modules)
- Stack Packet Exchange (SPEX)
- SPEX-Hot Swappable (SPEX-HS)

The modules can be used in any combination; however, if the unit is to be used in an ASN stack, then one of the modules must be a SPEX module or a SPEX-HS module, and this module must always reside in slot 4. SPEX modules as interconnected via a SPEX cable, which acts as the backplane for the ASN stack. The SPEX cable provides a 160Mbps channel between the units.

## Stacking ASN Routers

Each SPEX netmod houses two ports, an IN port and an OUT port. When the SPEX cable is affixed to cascade the units, the connections are made IN to OUT. In this case, you should begin cabling with the OUT port located in the SPEX module of the ASN that is lowest in the stack. When ASN routers are stacked, each must have a unique Slot ID. The lowest ASN in the stack should be assigned a Slot ID of 1, using the Slot ID switch located on the back of the unit. The Slot IDs should then be incremented by 1 for each unit in the stack, moving upward from the bottom.

To accomplish this, you must install one SPEX module for each ASN that will participate in the stack (again, always in netmod slot 4). Any SPEX connector that is unused (on the top or bottom unit of the stack) must be terminated with a SPEX terminator plug:

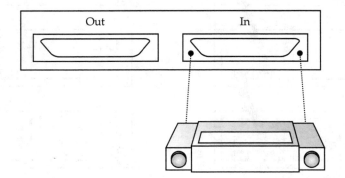

It is recommended that all units in the stack be powered up within 30 seconds of one another, beginning with the bottom-most ASN in the stack.

 *Unless you are using the SPEX-HS modules, be sure to power down an existing stack of ASN routers before adding any new units to the stack.*

## SPEX-HS

The SPEX-HS module allows ASN units in a stack to be added or removed without powering down the entire stack. Rather than being designated IN and OUT, the ports are designated A and C; however, these ports are connected A to A and C to C, unlike the scheme used in the SPEX modules (OUT to IN). The reason for this is due to a difference in the physical cable itself, wherein the SPEX-HS cable is a single unit rather than a series of cables (see Figure 28-1).

Begin with port A of the first (bottom) ASN in the stack, and work up. The same rules for Slot ID and stacking apply to the SPEX-HS as apply to the SPEX module.

 *Although it allows for the dynamic addition of an ASN into an existing stack, the new ASN must be powered down when the SPEX-HS cable is attached, and then powered up; otherwise, the new ASN's diagnostics will fail.*

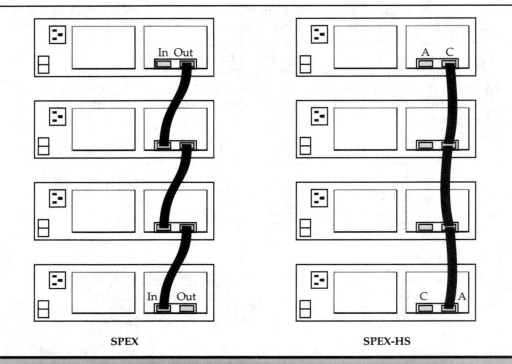

**Figure 28-1.** *SPEX cable vs. SPEX-HS cable*

The C port of the SPEX-HS module is used for a redundant cascade cable. The SPEX-HS also provides a throughput of 256Mbps, as opposed to the 160Mbps offered by the traditional SPEX module. The SPEX module in a dual-bus configuration offers a throughput of 512Mbps.

**Note** *When used with the SPEX-HS module, the ASN must be running Router software, and BootPROM software version 8.10 or greater. With a dual-bus configuration, the Router and BootPROM software must be version 10.0 or greater.*

## ASN LEDs

The ASN has a series of front panel LEDs, detailed in Table 28-5.

| LED | Color | Status |
|---|---|---|
| Remote Power | Green | System is receiving power from high-output power redundant power supply unit (HRPSU). |
| Power | Green | System is receiving power from primary power unit. |
| Run | Green | One or more units in stack is executing system software. |
|  | Flashing | System is initializing, or system failure has occurred. |
| Boot | Green | One or more units in stack is initializing and loading system software. |
| Diag | Amber | Diagnostics have failed. |
|  | Flashing | SPEX has failed. |
|  | Off | System is initializing, or operation is normal. |

**Table 28-5.**    *LEDs on the ASN Front Panel*

**Caution**    *If the Diag and Run LEDs are alternately flashing, it generally indicates a problem with the backplane (SPEX) cabling. This could mean a bad or missing terminator, or a faulty SPEX module or cable. Unlike some of the other units, the Diag LED in the ASN does not light or flash during normal bootup; if the Diag LED flashes or illuminates steadily, some failure has occurred.*

## FlashEEPROM Memory

The flash memory card is the standard local load device for all AN family products, though some of the older AN units may contain onboard SIMMs that act as the local load device. The flash memory card is housed in a Personal Computer Memory Card International Association (PCMCIA) flash socket, accessible from the front of the device. The flash contains 2MB, 4MB, or 8MB of electrically erasable programmable ROM (EEPROM) for file storage. The runtime image software will be housed on this flash memory.

The format of the PCMCIA flash is specifically for the router's Gate Access Management Entity (GAME) operating system; this is not a DOS-compatible format. Files can be transferred via Trivial File Transfer Protocol (TFTP) to and from the flash card once it is in place and the router has booted. Configuration files can be stored on the flash, as can event log files, alias files, and script files.

## Access Feeder Node

The AFN is an older product. It is a single-board, multiprotocol router/bridge with a fixed physical configuration. It comes with one or two LAN interfaces, with options for one Ethernet interface, one token ring, or two token rings. In addition, the AFN includes two synchronous interfaces, capable of supporting T1/E1 via an external DSU/CSU, RS 449, RS-422, RS-232, V.35, X.21, and V.28.

The AFN can utilize a 1.2MB 3.5-inch floppy disk drive (model numbers 1515-1518 and 1520-1521). Newer AFNs use flash memory cards (model numbers 1525-1530). AFNs utilizing flash memory cards must run at software version 7.56 or higher.

| Note | *Software versions 7.8x and higher are not available on floppy disk.* |

## Versa Module Eurocard

The Versa Module Eurocard (VME) product line was Wellfleet's first router architecture in 1988 to around 1992. These products are no longer developed by Nortel Networks, although they still exist today. The product line used a VME bus in a symmetric multiprocessing architecture where link modules and processor modules connect to the VME bus at the chassis midplane; this architecture is discussed in more detail later in the chapter in the sections on the backbone node series. The VME family utilizes link modules as processor cards (known as *Advanced Computing Engines,* or ACEs) to form Intelligent Link Interfaces (ILIs), much as the BN family does, with the difference being that the BN family uses a processor card known as a *Fast Routing Engine,* or FRE.

The VME product line is broken into three basic units:

- **Feeder node (FN)**   A two-slot chassis, where one slot is used for a system I/O module, which provides a console, modem, and printer interface for accessing the device. It has a system controller that can optionally support two flash cards, and, like the AFN, has an onboard 1.2MB 3.5-inch floppy disk drive. The presence of the system I/O module leaves one slot available for a single-link module/ACE module pairing.

- **Link node (LN)**   Has a total of five slots, supporting four processor slots and one slot reserved for the system I/O module, allowing for up to 16 LAN/WAN interfaces. Like the FN, the LN system I/O module provides a console, modem, and printer interface, and also has an onboard 1.2MB 3.5-inch floppy disk drive. This unit could be thought of as the predecessor to the BLN and BLN-2, which are covered in the upcoming sections on the backbone node product line.

- **Concentrator node (CN)**   Has a total of 14 slots, with the first slot reserved for the system I/O module. The CN can contain up to 13 ILIs, with a link module connecting with an ACE processor at the VME midplane. The CN can support a total of 52 LAN/WAN interfaces. Like the FN and the LN, the CN has an onboard 1.2MB 3.5-inch floppy disk drive.

Bear in mind that these products, while still in existence, do not have any further software updates in development (the last code version created being version 12.00, and the last version of Site Manager that supports VME is 6.0). Upgrading to any software version beyond 12.0 will necessitate upgrading the router hardware to a non-VME platform.

# Backbone Node Routers

The backbone node family consists of chassis-based routers, for use in heavily utilized, backbone portions of the network. The BN family has three main flavors: the backbone link node (BLN), the backbone link node 2 (BLN2), and the backbone concentrator node (BCN).

BNs utilize a symmetric multiprocessor architecture, in which each BN utilizes a set of link modules, as well as a FRE module that accompanies it. These modules are inserted in the front and back of the chassis, interconnecting at the midplane where the Parallel Packet Express (PPX) rails sit. The combination of link modules and their associated FRE module are known as *Intelligent Link Interfaces*, or ILIs. It is over the PPX rails that the ILI combinations intercommunicate with other ILIs within the chassis, at throughput rates of up to 1Gbps (see Figure 28-2).

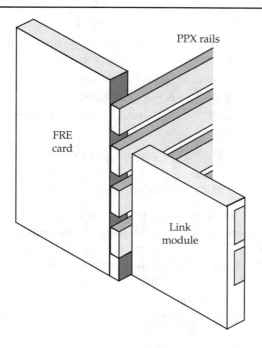

**Figure 28-2.**  *An ILI meeting at the PPX midplane*

# Parallel Packet Exchange

Each BN houses a Parallel Packet Express; the PPX provides fast processor-to-processor transport of data packets across the midplane interconnection at a total throughput of 1Gbps. The PPX consists of four redundant data paths, or rails, and each rail is composed of a series of data and signaling lines. The ILIs connect to the PPX rails to transmit and receive data to and from other ILIs, and all processors on the PPX act as peers, able to transmit and receive data to and from one another (see Figure 28-3).

Each of the four PPX rails consists of eight data lines, as well as multiple signaling lines. Data travels each rail an octet at a time in parallel, where a random path selection algorithm is utilized to accomplish load balancing across the PPX.

The PPX midplane is controlled by system resource modules (SRMs), which provide central arbitration for the PPX rails (see the section "System Resource Module," later in this chapter).

## Link Modules

*Link modules* account for half of the ILI pair. The link module provides the physical network interface to the existing LAN or WAN. Each link module houses the following components:

- Physical port or series of ports, for connection to the existing LAN or WAN
- Line driver chips to translate transistor-to-transistor logic (TTL) signal levels to signal levels appropriate to the media type being used
- Link controllers responsible for the encoding and decoding of packets, performing direct memory access (DMA) transfer of packets to global memory
- A global bus connector, which is used to mate the link module to its associated FRE card, to form the ILI

Though different link modules have different LED indicators, all link modules have a Fail LED, which is located on the right side of the module's surface. The Fail LED, when red, may indicate one of the following things:

- A diagnostic test is in progress. This occurs whenever the link module is cold-started, which may occur if the router is rebooted; the **diags** command is issued from the TI, pointing to the link module in question; or the module is hot-inserted into the slot. Under these circumstances, the LED should blink three times and then go out when the diagnostics are passed.
- Power-up diagnostic testing has failed.
- There has been a hardware failure.

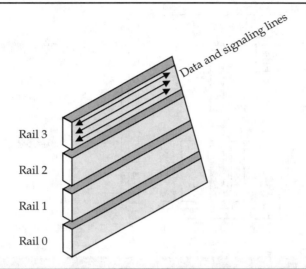

**Figure 28-3.**  *Breakdown of the PPX plane*

## Fast Routing Engine

The Fast Routing Engine (FRE) is a processor card, designed for use with a corresponding link module. These modules together form an ILI, which interconnects at the chassis midplane. The FRE card contains a 33MHz processor—either MC68040 (FRE2-040) or MC68060 (FRE2-060)—with a 4K onboard instruction and data cache, and a high-speed packet buffer for use with the routing processor.

Each FRE card contains a module called the *Parallel Packet Express Interface (PPXI)*, which manages traffic passing to and from the PPX rails. Each PPXI transmitter has four PPX connections (one for each of the four rails), although only one is actually active at any one time. Likewise, each PPXI receiver has four PPX connections, and can receive data from all four rails simultaneously. In addition, each contains a processor link interconnect, for connection with a corresponding link module to form the ILI (see Figure 28-4).

The basic FRE unit contains 8MB of dynamic RAM (DRAM) for task handling, buffering, and maintaining routing tables, event logs, configuration data, and the MIB. A FRE processor is available with either a 33MHz MC68040 microprocessor (FRE2-040), a 60MHz MC68060 microprocessor (FRE2-060), or a 60MHz MC68060 microprocessor with an Accelerated Compression Coprocessor card (FRE2-060E). Each FRE card contains a PCMCIA slot that can house a standard flash memory card, for the storage of the system image, configuration files, event logs, script files, and so forth.

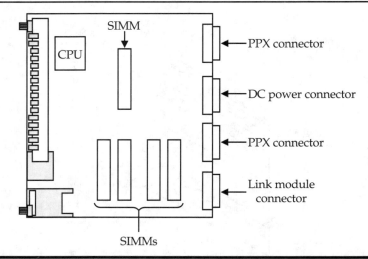

**Figure 28-4.**    *An FRE card with PPXI connections and ILI link connections*

## FRE-2

FRE-2 is the next generation Fast Routing Engine. It is compatible with FRE modules and can coexist in the same chassis with them. FRE-2 contains onboard SIMMs that can be field-upgraded to 8MB, 16MB, or 32MB. Unlike the original FRE, which contains a daughterboard, all FRE-2 components reside on the motherboard. FRE-2 cards come in two flavors: FRE2-040 and FRE2-060. Each variation also houses a PCMCIA for a standard flash memory card.

**FRE2-040**    The FRE2-040 processor utilizes a 68040 microprocessor and provides improved throughput and performance on the PPX bus. It requires software version 7.70 or greater in order to function in the BN chassis.

**FRE2-060**    The FRE2-060 processor utilizes a 68060 microprocessor and is the second generation routing engine for the BLN and BCN families; it has superior forwarding performance and is geared toward the more processor-intensive, higher-bandwidth ILIs, such as the ATM, FDDI, and HSSI interface modules. It is fully compatible with the FRE2-040 ILIs, and they can coexist within the same chassis. A BCN that has been fully populated with FRE2-060 ILIs can achieve forwarding rates of up to one million packets per second. FRE2-060 fully supports all routing and bridging protocols utilizing software version 8.10 or greater. It supports up to 64MB of DRAM.

**FRE2-060E**    The FRE2-060 processor utilizes a 68060 microprocessor also, with the addition of an onboard Accelerated Compression Coprocessor for use with all WAN link modules (except the HSSI interface). The coprocessor allows compression to be used across all WAN modules, increases the dictionary histories to 256, and implements multiple compression algorithms (WCP and Hi/fn).

**ATM ROUTING ENGINE**    The ATM Routing Engine (ARE) is designed for use specifically with an ATM link module. It has two Motorola PowerPC 604 microprocessors and two LSI Logic ATMizer cell processors. The ARE processor performs segmentation and reassembly (SAR) functions for the conversion between legacy frames and ATM cells. The ATM link module in this case performs the transfer of ATM cell data between the physical media and the ARE processor.

The ARE supports DRAM configurations of 8MB, 16MB, and 32MB, and static RAM (SRAM) configurations of 1MB, 3MB, and 6MB. Unlike the FRE processor, the ARE utilizes DRAM only for local memory purposes, such as image storage and routing table maintenance, while the SRAM is used for global memory (buffering). ARE modules support an 8MB onboard flash memory card for storage of additional image and configuration files. The ARE requires software version 9.01 or greater.

**LED INDICATORS ON THE FRE AND FRE-2 CARDS**    Each FRE card has a series of LEDs mounted along its edge, along with a button called the Harpoon Diagnostic Console Monitor (HDCM), and another button that ejects the flash card from the PCMCIA socket (see Figure 28-5).

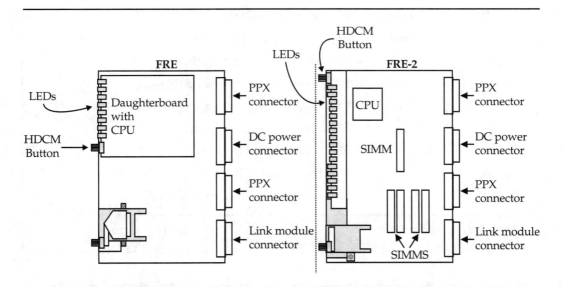

**Figure 28-5.**    *The FRE and FRE-2 processor cards*

Though not specifically labeled, the LED indicators on the FRE card will give an indication as to the processor's status and functioning. Table 28-6 lists and describes the LEDs located on the edge of a standard FRE card.

In addition to the LEDs that are located on its edge, the FRE contains a daughtercard that has its own bank of LEDs, detailed in Table 28-7.

The FRE-2 LEDs differ from those on the FRE card, and have different meanings as well; these are listed in Table 28-8.

| LED | Color | Status |
|-----|-------|--------|
| 16 (A) | Green | System is initializing. If light remains lit, backbone is held in reset due to a hardware or software error. |
| 15 (B) | Green | PPX DMA logic is accessing DRAM. |
| 13 (C), 14 (D) | Green | Diagnostic test in progress. |
| 12 (E) | Red | Diagnostic code is executing. |
| 11 (F) | Green | System software is executing. |
| 10 (G) | Green | CPU is accessing DRAM. |
| 9 (H) | Amber | Hardware is resetting. |
| 8 (I) | Green | FRE module is executing on PPX rail 0. |
| 7 (J) | Green | FRE module is executing on PPX rail 1. |
| 6 (K) | Green | FRE module is executing on PPX rail 2. |
| 5 (L) | Green | FRE module is executing on PPX rail 3. |
| 4 (M) | Green | FRE is executing flow control on PPX 0. |
| 3 (N) | Green | FRE is executing flow control on PPX 1. |
| 2 (O) | Green | FRE is executing flow control on PPX 2. |
| 1 (P) | Green | FRE is executing flow control on PPX 3. |

**Table 28-6.** *LEDs on the FRE*

| LED | Color | Status |
|---|---|---|
| 9 | Green | Reset has been sent to CPU. |
| 8 | Green | Diagnostic testin progress. |
| 8 (F LED also lit) | Green | FRE processor is booting or PROM read/write protection is disabled. |
| 7 -1 | Green | Diagnostic test number is executing |
| 7 (F LED also lit) | Green | Slot is running the TI. |
| 6-1 (F LED also lit) | Green | Indicates the least significant digits of the second counter, as expressed in binary. |

**Table 28-7.**   *Alternate Meanings for FRE-2 LED 15 and Lower*

| LED | Color | Status |
|---|---|---|
| 31 | Amber | System is initializing. If light remains lit, backbone is held in reset due to a hardware or software error. |
| 30 | Green | PPX DMA logic is accessing DRAM. |
| 29, 28 | Green | Diagnostic test in progress. |
| 27 | Green | Diagnostic code is executing. |
| 26 | Green | GAME operating system is running. |
| 25 | Green | CPU is accessing DRAM. |
| 24 | Amber | Hardware is resetting. |
| 23-20 | Green | FRE-2 is transmitting on BNs A through D. |
| 19-16 | Green | BNs A through D are asserting flow control. |
| 15-8 | Green | Diagnostic test in progress. |

**Table 28-8.**   *LEDs on the FRE Daughter Card*

If LED 26 is lit (indicating that the GAME operating system is executing), then LEDs 15 and downward hold the meanings listed in Table 28-9.

**HARPOON DIAGNOSTIC CONSOLE MONITOR**    The HDCM button located on the FRE and FRE-2 cards can be used to cold-start the FRE when pressed for more than one second and then released.

 *If the HDCM is pressed for less than a second and then released, an HDCM session is established. This is for internal testing and diagnostics by Nortel Networks technicians, and is not supported in the field. Pressing the HDCM for less than a second and then releasing it while the HDCM session is in progress causes the FRE to execute a warm-boot.*

## Flash EEPROM Memory

The flash memory card is the standard local load device for all BN family products. It contains 2MB, 4MB, or 8MB of EEPROM for file storage. The runtime image software will be housed on this flash memory, and at least one FRE card within the BN chassis must contain a flash with a software image file to successfully boot.

The format of the PCMCIA flash is specifically for the router's GAME operating system; this is not a DOS-compatible format. Files can be transferred via TFTP to and from the flash card once it is in place and the router has booted. Configuration files can be stored on the flash, as can event log files, alias files, and script files.

## System Resource Module

The SRM is necessary to each BN; in the BLNs, it rests in slot 1, while in BCNs, it rests in slot 7. This unit is inserted into the rear of the chassis, and is known as the *system resource module*-link (SRM-L).

| LED | Color | Status |
|-----|-------|--------|
| 15 | Green | FRE-2 processor is booting, or PROM read/write protection is disabled. |
| 14 | Green | Slot is running the TI. |
| 13-8 | Green | Indicates least significant digits of second counter, as expressed in binary. |
| 7 | Green | Slot is running the TI. |
| 6-4 | Green | Link module is requesting access to DRAM. |
| 3 | Green | Link module interface is accessing DRAM. |
| 2, 1 | Green | States information regarding link module interface. |

**Table 28-9.**    *LEDs on the FRE2*

**SRM-L** The SRM-L provides arbitration control over two of the four PPX rails, for a total of 512Mbps of bandwidth available. The BN functions with only one SRM (the SRM-L), but provides only 512Mbps of its potential throughput, because only two of the data rails will be controlled. The SRM-L also provides an RS-232 interface, for connecting a terminal, or modem, as well as providing access to the TI. Usage of the TI, and ways the TI can be used advantageously, is discussed in Chapter 29, "The TI and the Router MIB." It also has a connector marked JTAG, which is currently not used. Once the SRM-L is in place, an optional SRM-F can be installed. The SRM-L's LEDs are detailed in Table 28-10.

**SRM-F** The SRM-F (system resource module-FRE) can be inserted into the front portion of the chassis, to provide arbitration over the remaining PPX rails, for a total of 512Mbps of bandwidth. Combined with the SRM-L, the SRMs provide 1Gbps bandwidth. The SRM-F's LEDs are set forth in Table 28-11.

Some models of the SRM-F also possess ON/OFF switches, which should be in the ON position.

## Backbone Link Node

The BLN is a rack-mountable, chassis-based unit, and contains five slots on both the link module and FRE module sides. Slot 1 uses the SRM-L and SRM-F modules for PPX control functions, leaving a total of four slots for LAN/WAN-based ILIs. The BLN comes equipped with one 620W power supply, which is surge protected to prevent damage to internal components, but does not offer redundancy.

## BLN-2

The BLN-2 is quite similar to the BLN, with a few modifications. BLN-2 is a bit larger in size, to accommodate a redundant power module; each BLN-2 has a 620W power supply,

| LED | Color | Status |
|-----|-------|--------|
| 12V1 | Green | Positive 12V DC detected/ |
| | Off | Fuse F7 is blown (BLN), or Fuse F9 is blown (BCN). |
| 12V2 | Green | Positive 12V DC detected. |
| | Off | Fuse F6 is blown (BLN), or Fuse F12 blown (BCN). |
| VCC | Green | Power supplies are within normal limits. |

**Table 28-10.** *LEDs on the SRM-L*

| LED | Color | Status |
|-----|-------|--------|
| CR2 | Green | 5V is available to SRM-F. |
| CR1 | Red | Board has been held in reset due to hardware failure. |

**Table 28-11.**    *LEDs on the SRM-F*

with the option of adding an additional redundant, hot-swappable power supply (see Figure 28-6). In addition, the BLN-2 comes outfitted with three hot-swappable fan trays for cooling system redundancy and easy field replacement. Power modules used in the BLN-2 can also be used in the BCN chassis.

## Backbone Concentrator Node

The BCN is a rack-mountable upright chassis, with a total of 14 slots. Slot 7 is reserved for the housing of the SRM-L and accompanying SRM-F modules, leaving a total of 13 slots for different ILI modules. The BCN can hold a total of four 620W surge-protected power supplies, for both load-sharing and redundancy. These power supplies are arranged vertically, in the rear of the unit, numbered 1 through 4, from the bottom up. A fully loaded BCN requires a total of three power supplies, with a fourth available for load-sharing and redundancy. Power modules for BLN-2 and the BCN are fully interchangeable.

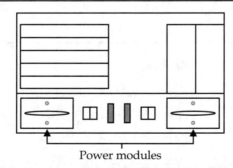

Power modules

**Figure 28-6.**    *A BLN-2 equipped with redundant power modules*

# Intelligent Link Interfaces

The BN series of routers supports a large variety of ILI link module/FRE combinations, providing a large degree of flexibility. The following ILIs are available for the BN series routers:

## FRE2-060(E) ILIs

The Nortel Networks BN router platform supports a variety of FRE2-060 ILIs, including WAN, Ethernet, Token Ring, FDDI, and ATM link modules:

**WAN**   The following WAN ILIs are available with the FRE2-060 series processor cards:

- **Quad port synchronous link module/FRE2-060**   Provides four synchronous ports. Available with 16, 32, or 64MB of memory.

- **Octal port synchronous link module/FRE2-060**   Provides eight synchronous ports. Available with 16, 32, or 64MB of memory.

- **Octal port synchronous link module with 32-context hardware compression/ FRE2-060**   Provides eight synchronous ports with onboard hardware compression for 32 contexts. Available with 16, 32, or 64MB of memory.

- **Octal port synchronous link module with 128-context hardware compression/ FRE2-060**   Provides eight synchronous ports with onboard hardware compression for 128 contexts. Available with 16, 32, or 64MB of memory.

**Note**   *The compression algorithm used in the 32- and 128-context hardware compression modules is called Magnalink Scalable Algorithm (MSA), which is based on the LZ-77 algorithm. The "context" refers to compression and decompression on a single VC (such as a Frame Relay PVC), where compression hardware maps a context to specific regions of compression and decompression memory. A 32-context compression board can run compression over 31 continuous packet compression (CPC) contexts, each with an 8K history size and a shared 8K packet-by-packet context. A 128-context compression board can run over 127 CPC contexts, with 8K history and 8K packet-by-packet context. The FRE2-060E is recommended for any modules using compression.*

- **HSSI link module/FRE2-060**   Provides a single High-Speed Serial Interface (HSSI). Available with 16, 32, or 64MB of memory.

- **MCT1 link module/FRE2-060**   Provides a single multichannel T-1 (MCT1) port. Available with 32 or 64MB of memory.

- **Dual MCT1 link module/FRE2-060**   Provides dual MCT1 ports. Available with 32 or 64MB of memory.

- **Quad MCT1 link module/FRE2-060**   Provides four MCT1 ports (DB15 version). Available with 32 or 64MB of memory.

- **Single 75Ω MCE1 link module/FRE2-060** Provides a single 75ohm multichannel E-1 (MCE1) port. Available with 32 or 64MB of memory.

- **Dual 75Ω MCE1 link module/FRE-060** Provides two MCE1 ports. Available with 32 or 64MB of memory.

- **Dual 120Ω MCE1 link module/FRE2-060** Provides two MCE1 ports. Available with 32 or 64MB of memory.

**LAN** The following LAN ILIs are available using the FRE2-060 processor:

- **Quad Ethernet link module/FRE2-060** Provides four Ethernet connections. Available with 16, 32, or 64MB of memory.

- **Quad Ethernet link module with high-speed filters/FRE2-060** Provides four Ethernet connections with an onboard high-speed filter. Available with 16, 32, or 64MB of memory.

- **Dual Ethernet/dual synchronous link module/FRE2-060** Provides two Ethernet connections and two synchronous connections. Available with 16, 32, or 64MB of memory.

- **Dual Ethernet/dual synchronous with filters link module/FRE-060** Provides two Ethernet connections and two synchronous connections with filters. Available with 16, 32, or 64MB of memory.

| **Note** | *Both versions of the Ethernet/dual synchronous link modules are capable of supporting Unbalanced RS-232, Rs-423, V.28, Balanced X.21, or RS-422. These options are configured through the use of jumper straps located on the module itself. An optional V.35 daughterboard is also available.* |

- **Dual 100BaseT link module/FRE2-060** Provides two fast Ethernet connections. These ports are capable of running at full- or half-duplex. Available with 16, 32, or 64MB of memory.

| **Caution** | *Though both ports are capable of running at full-duplex, it is not a good idea to run both at full-duplex simultaneously. The processor/link interconnect has an approximate bandwidth of 180Mbps, and a dual full-duplex configuration will cause a contention for resources that will degrade performance.* |

- **Dual Token Ring link module/FRE2-060** Provides two DB-9 STP token ring ports capable of 4 or 16Mbps ring speeds. Available with 16, 32, or 64MB of memory.

- **Token Ring/dual synchronous link module/FRE2-060** Provides a single token ring port (DB-9 STP, 4/16Mbps) and two synchronous ports. Available with 16, 32, or 64MB of memory.

**Note** *Both versions of the Ethernet/dual synchronous link modules are capable of supporting Unbalanced RS-232, Rs-423, V.28, Balanced X.21, or RS-422. These options are configured through the use of jumper straps located on the module itself.*

■ **Quad Token Ring link module/FRE2-060**   Provides four token ring ports. Available with 16, 32, or 64MB of memory.

**Note** *The High Speed filter option available on all ILIs consists of a programmable memory cache at the chip level. Once the filters are configured, the hardware is programmed with the parameters and is responsible for the filtering process.*

**FDDI**   The following FDDI ILIs are available using the FRE2-060 processor card:

■ **Multimode FDDI link module/FRE2-060**   Provides a single multimode fiber Dual Attached Station (DAS) connection. Available with 16, 32, or 64MB of memory.

■ **Multimode FDDI link module with filters/FRE2-060**   Provides a single multimode fiber DAS connection with filters. Available with 16, 32, or 64MB of memory.

■ **Single-mode FDDI link module/FRE2-060**   Provides a single single-mode fiber DAS connection. Available with 16, 32, or 64MB of memory.

■ **FDDI hybrid single-mode/multimode link module/FRE2-060**   Provides a single FDDI DAS interface, with single-mode fiber on PHY A, and multimode fiber on PHY B. Available with 16, 32, or 64MB of memory. Also available with filters.

■ **FDDI hybrid multimode/single-mode link module/FRE2-060**   Provides a singe FDDI DAS interface, with multimode fiber on PHY A, and single-mode fiber on PHY B. Available with 16, 32, or 64MB of memory. Also available with filters.

■ **Single-mode FDDI link module with filters/FRE2-060**   Provides a single single-mode fiber DAS interface with filters. Available with 16, 32, or 64MB of memory.

**Note** *The High Speed filter option for all ILIs consists of a programmable memory cache at the chip level. Once the filters are configured, the hardware is programmed with the parameters and is responsible for the filtering process.*

## FRE2-040 ILIs

The BN platform also supports a wide variety of FRE2-040 ILIs; these are quite similar to those associated with the FRE2-060 ILIs, but with a slightly lower-end processor and less onboard memory.

**WAN**    The following WAN ILIs are available with the FRE2-040 processor card:

- **Quad port synchronous link module/FRE2-040**    Provides four synchronous ports. Available with 8, 16, or 32MB of memory.

- **Octal port synchronous link module/FRE2-040**    Provides eight synchronous ports. Available with 8, 16, or 32MB of memory.

- **Octal port synchronous link module with 32-context hardware compression/ FRE2-040**    Provides eight synchronous ports with onboard hardware compression for 32 contexts. Available with 8, 16, or 32MB of memory.

- **Octal port synchronous link module with 128-context hardware compression/ FRE2-040**    Provides eight synchronous ports with onboard hardware compression for 128 contexts. Available with 8, 16, or 32MB of memory.

- **HSSI link module/FRE2-040**    Provides a single HSSI. Available with 8, 16, or 32MB of memory.

- **MCT1 link module/FRE2-040**    Provides a single multichannel T-1 (MCT1) port. Available with 8 or 32MB of memory.

- **Dual MCT1 link module/FRE2-040**    Provides dual MCT1 ports. Available with 8 or 32MB of memory.

- **Quad MCT1 link module/FRE2-040**    Provides four MCT1 ports (DB15 version). Available with 8 or 32MB of memory.

- **Single 75Ω MCE1 link module/FRE2-040**    Provides a single 75ohm multichannel E-1 (MCE1) port. Available with 8 or 32MB of memory.

- **Dual 75Ω MCE1 link module/FRE-040**    Provides two MCE1 ports. Available with 8 or 32MB of memory.

- **Dual 120Ω MCE1 link module/FRE2-040**    Provides two MCE1 ports. Available with 8 or 32MB of memory.

**LAN**

- **Quad Ethernet link module/FRE2-040**    Provides four Ethernet connections. Available with 8, 16, or 32MB of memory.

- **Quad Ethernet link module with high-speed filters daughtercard/ FRE2-040**    Provides four Ethernet connections with an onboard high-speed filter. Available with 8, 16, or 32MB of memory.

- **Dual Ethernet/dual synchronous link module/FRE2-040**    Provides two Ethernet connections and two synchronous connections. Available with 8, 16, or 32MB of memory.

- **Dual Ethernet/dual synchronous with filters link module/FRE-040**    Provides two Ethernet connections and two synchronous connections with filters. Available with 8, 16, or 32MB of memory.

- **Dual 100BaseT link module/FRE2-040**   Provides two fast Ethernet connections. Available with 8, 16, or 32MB of memory.

**Caution**   *The same restrictions on the FRE2-060 cards apply to the FRE-040: Avoid running both 100BaseT ports at full-duplex simultaneously, even though full-duplex mode is supported on both. Simultaneous full-duplex will tax the processor and degrade network performance.*

- **Dual Token Ring link module/FRE2-040**   Provides two token ring ports. Available with 8, 16, or 32MB of memory.
- **Token Ring/dual synchronous link module/FRE2-040**   Provides a single token ring port and two synchronous ports. Available with 8, 16, or 32MB of memory.
- **Quad Token Ring link module/FRE2-040**   Provides four token ring ports. Available with 8, 16, or 32MB of memory.

**Note**   *The High Speed filter option for all ILIs consists of a programmable memory cache at the chip level. Once the filters are configured, the hardware is programmed with the parameters and is responsible for the filtering process.*

### FDDI

- **Multimode FDDI link module/FRE2-040**   Provides a single multimode fiber Dual Attached Station (DAS) connection. Available with 8, 16, or 32MB of memory.
- **Multimode FDDI link module with filters/FRE2-040**   Provides a single multimode fiber DAS connection with filters. Available with 8, 16, or 32MB of memory.
- **Single-mode FDDI link module/FRE2-040**   Provides a single single-mode fiber DAS connection. Available with 8, 16, or 32MB of memory.
- **FDDI hybrid single-mode/multimode link module/FRE2-040**   Provides a single FDDI DAS interface, with single-mode fiber on PHY A, and multimode fiber on PHY B. Available with 8, 16, or 32MB of memory. Also available with filters.
- **FDDI hybrid multimode/single-mode link module/FRE2-040**   Provides a single FDDI DAS interface, with multimode fiber on PHY A, and single-mode fiber on PHY B. Available with 8, 16, or 32MB of memory. Also available with filters.
- **Single-mode FDDI link module with filters/FRE2-040**   Provides a single single-mode fiber DAS interface with filters. Available with 8, 16, or 32MB of memory.

**ATM ROUTING ENGINE ILIS**    The BN platform also supports a variety of ATM connectivity. Generally, the ATM ILIs use the ARE rather than a FRE card, although the higher-end FRE-2 processor cards can support some of the ATM functionality, as well. The following ARE ILIs are available:

- **STS-3/STM-1 multimode fiber link module/ARE**    Provides a single multimode fiber OC-3 connection. Available with 8MB/1MB, 16MB/3MB, or 32MB/6MB of DRAM/SRAM.

- **STS-3/STM-1 single-mode fiber link module/ARE**    Provides a single single-mode fiber OC-3 connection. Available with 8MB/1MB, 16MB/3MB, or 32MB/6MB of DRAM/SRAM.

- **DS-3 link module/ARE**    Provides a single 45Mbps DS-3 link with BNC connectors. Available with 8MB/1MB, 16MB/3MB, or 32MB/6MB of DRAM/SRAM.

- **E3 link module/ARE**    Provides a single E3 link. Available with 8MB/1MB, 16MB/3MB, or 32MB/6MB of DRAM/SRAM.

**HARDWARE VS. SOFTWARE COMPRESSION**    Data compression can be a very useful feature when dealing with a WAN connection; compressing data for transport across the WAN can increase throughput and reduce costs.

Compression utilizes a "dictionary," which is a history of the data being passed. Each side of the WAN link maintains a compression and decompression history, where each history keeps a record of the data that has already been sent. History size is specified by the user (for 8K or 32K). A lookup table is maintained on either side of the link, where pointers are kept to redundant strings, and the offset/length tokens that actually replace the redundant strings. In these cases, a router finding a match in subsequent data will pass a pointer across the link rather than the actual data.

Compression can be implemented on either a packet-by-packet compression (PPC) or a continuous packet compression (CPC) scheme. PPC resets the history after each packet, giving it a lower overall compression ratio, but it does prevent retransmissions if the line quality is low. CPC offers a higher compression ratio overall, but the line quality must be very reliable as histories are maintained for the continuous stream and must remain synchronized at either end.

As previously outlined, the Nortel Networks WAN ILIs support both software and hardware compression. Software compression is supported on all Nortel Networks routers, and is supported over dial-up lines (including ISDN), and leased lines using PPP, frame relay, and X.25, for a compressed throughput of approximately 1.2Mbps full-duplex over a 512Kbps link. Data compression is negotiated between two end points on a per PVC basis. Hardware compression requires an ILI that is hardware-compression-capable. The FRE2-060E provides an onboard Accelerated Compression Co-processor that handles this function for maximum throughput.

The compression algorithms supported are the Telco Systems Magnalink Scalable Architecture (MSA) (based on the LZS algorithm), and the Wan Compression Protocol (WPC).

## Series 5000 Routers

The System 5000, and 5005 chassis, in addition to the Ethernet segments, Token Rings, ATM, and FDDI/Fast Ethernet backplanes, also support a PPX backplane for use with the System 5000 router modules (see Figure 28-7).

The System 5000 chassis can support three basic router types: an Ethernet router (5380), a token ring router (5580), and an ATM router (5780). These units can be placed in any slot within a chassis that supports the appropriate backplane, with the exception of the 5780, which must be placed only in slots 2 to 7 or 8 to 13, because it must connect to the ATM backplane, which is split and extends only between slots 2 and 13.

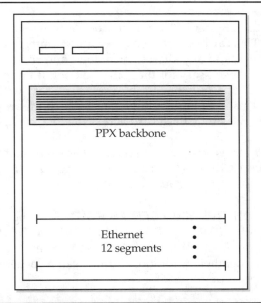

**Figure 28-7.**   *System 5000 chassis equipped with a PPX backplane*

**Caution**   *An exception to the preceding rule is the 5000AH, an older version of the System 5000 chassis; in the case of the 5000AH, router modules must only be installed in slots 6 through 14 (except the 5780, which cannot be placed in slot 14) of a chassis that supports the approptiate backplane. Installing a router module in slot 1 will actually damage the chassis clock module, and installing a router module in slot 4 will actually damage the router's power supply.*

Each System 5000 router module has a PPX connector to connect to the PPX backplane (if present), a connection to the Ethernet, Token Ring, or ATM backplane (depending on the model), and a connection to the Common Management Bus (CMB) so that the router can be accessed through the chassis console port and monitored by the supervisory module.

In each case, the System 5000 router modules provide routing capability between LAN segments across the backplane, as well as intercommunication between router modules across the PPX backplane. In addition, the 5380 and 5580 may be outfitted with additional netmods to provide front-panel connectivity via a variety of routed LAN and WAN interfaces. System 5000 router modules utilize the same technology used in the AN and BN families, and are configured with Site Manager. All System 5000 router modules also provide a technician interface (TI).

**FLASH MEMORY**   Each System 5000 router module contains a flash memory socket to house a flash card. This card, as with the other router units, will contain the system image, configuration files, and any aliases, event logs, and so forth. This flash card, and its accompanying files, is necessary for the router to boot. If multiple router modules exist within the same chassis, only one flash card is necessary with the system software; as in an ASN stack, or a BLN, BLN-2, or BCN configuration, other router modules can boot from the single flash card across the PPX backplane.

**Note**   *If BayStream software is being used to collect Frame Relay Switch billing information, there must be a PCMCIA SRAM card dedicated to that function, and another card elsewhere in the chassis must contain the system files.*

**INSTALLING SIMMS ON THE 5000 SERIES ROUTER**   The System 5000 router modules also contain either 8MB, 16MB, or 32MB of DRAM. This SIMM memory is field-upgradeable (see Figure 28-8). These SIMM modules must be of a like memory size when being paired together. Additional SIMMs can be ordered from Nortel Networks in the form of an upgrade kit.

**NET MODULES**   The 5380 and 5580 have two slots available for the installation of net modules. To install these modules, the protective plates must first be removed from the unit's face (see Figure 28-9). Net modules are inserted at an angle, and then the connector plug is aligned with the connector on the baseboard. Seat the module firmly once the connection is made. The same net modules are compatible with both the 5380 and the 5580, and allow for scalability and WAN connectivity.

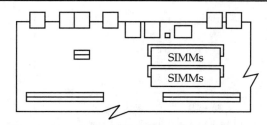

**Figure 28-8.**    *Location of DRAM SIMMs on the System 5000 series*

## 5380

The 5380 is an Ethernet router module for the System 5000 chassis. It takes up a single slot. The 5380 has the capability to connect to up to four of the 12 Ethernet segments located on the backplane of the 5000 and 5005 chassis. In addition, two slots are available for additional net modules, for front-panel connectivity (see Figure 28-10).

The four cluster ports (routed backplane interfaces) can be assigned to any four of the 12 Ethernet backplane segments. Together with the dual-port Ethernet net modules, the 5380 can provide up to eight routed Ethernet interfaces.

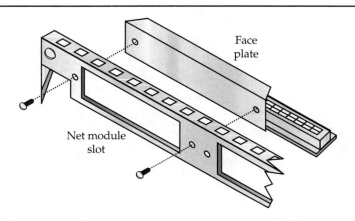

**Figure 28-9.**    *Net module slots with face plates removed*

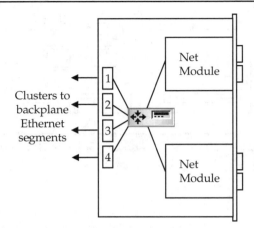

**Figure 28-10.** *A 5380 with backplane and frontplane connections*

**ACCESSING THE 5380** The 5380 can be accessed via a terminal session. This is accomplished by first connecting to the service port of the System 5000 or 5005 chassis, and then accessing the main connection menu. Once connected and the Enter Slot # (1-14) prompt is displayed, access the slot that houses the router module, by entering the command **c x**, where *x* is the slot number of the router module. This will establish a connection with the 5380, at which point the following menu should be displayed:

```
*************************************************************
Copyright (c) 1996
Bay Networks Inc.
All Rights Reserved.
Date: Wed Nov 8 12:33:04 EST 1996.
5380 Ethernet Router CMB Firmware V1.123
*************************************************************
*SERVICE PORT DIAGNOSTICS MENU*
c Connections menu
t Technician interface enable
e Engineering diagnostics
q Quit
Enter command:
```

To make connections to the backplane, enter choice **c**. To initiate a TI session with the router, enter choice **t**. Choice **e** is to enter the engineering diagnostics, and is not supported. Selecting **q** will break back out to the main connection menu.

**Note**  *Under some circumstances, connecting to the router slot from the main connection menu may result in being deposited directly into the TI (for instance, if the connection is terminated but the TI is still being accessed). To get back to the Service Port Diagnostics menu at any point, press CTRL-X.*

**BACKPLANE CONNECTIONS**  The 5000 series router can be configured to route between several different backplane connections. Choosing the backplane connections option opens another menu:

```
*CONNECTION DIAGNOSTICS MENU*
c show Connections
s change cluster Segmentation
a change backplane Attachments
p display ethernet Port statistics
g display ethernet Group statistics
-ESC Return to main menu
Enter command:
```

Here, the existing connections can be displayed and altered. By default, there are no backplane connections. Selecting choice **a** will allow the assignment of a cluster port (router interface) to a specific backplane segment:

```
Changing backplane attachments...
Enter cluster number (0 if done, 1 to 4)
```

Enter the cluster number here; the *cluster number* refers to the backplane router interface you want to attach to the backplane. Select one of the four backplane clusters, and you will be prompted for which backplane segment you want to attach the cluster port to:

```
Enter new backplane attachment (13 = disconnect, 1 to 12):
```

Select one of the 12 Ethernet segments. Selecting 13 disconnects the selected cluster port from the backplane entirely.

Cluster ports that are currently connected to a backplane segment can be partitioned, or segmented, on the backplane. Choose option **s**—change cluster Segmentation from the main connection menu:

```
Changing cluster segmentation...
Enter cluster number (0 if done, 1 to 4):
```

Again, select the cluster number (routed backplane interface) you wish to configure. You will be prompted to choose the port attachment type; in this case, whether the cluster port is to be connected or partitioned (segmented):

```
Enter new port attachment (1 = segmented, 2 = connected):
```

After you make the selections, option **c** from the main connection screen enables you to view the current status of the backplane connections:

```
Cluster Port       Backplane Status       Connection      MAC Address
------------       ----------------       ----------      ----------------
     1               Connected                 8          00-00-A2-00-10-00
     2               Segmented                 4          00-00-A2-00-20-00
     3               Connected                 7          00-00-A2-00-30-00
     4               Connected                12          00-00-A2-00-40-00
```

In this example, cluster port 1 is connected to backplane Ethernet segment 8; cluster 2 is assigned to segment 4, but is currently partitioned; cluster 3 is assigned to segment 7; and cluster 4 is connected to Ethernet segment 12.

## 5580

The 5580 is similar in architecture to the 5380, except that it supports connections to the backplane token rings rather than backplane Ethernet segments. It utilizes the same four-cluster-port design as the 5380, and the clusters connect to the backplane rings in a similar fashion.

**ACCESSING THE 5580**   Like the 5380, the 5580 can be accessed via a terminal session. This is accomplished by first connecting to the service port of the System 5000 or 5005 chassis, and then accessing the main connection menu. Once the Enter Slot # (1-14) prompt is displayed, access the slot that houses the router module, by entering the command **c** *x*, where *x* is the slot number of the router module. This establishes a connection with the 5580, at which point the following menu should be displayed:

```
*************************************************************
Copyright (c) 1996
Bay Networks Inc.
All Rights Reserved.
Date: Wed Nov 8 12:33:04 EST 1996.
5580 Token Ring Router CMB Firmware V1.123
*************************************************************
*SERVICE PORT DIAGNOSTICS MENU*
c Connections menu
```

```
t Technician interface enable
e Engineering diagnostics
q Quit
Enter command:
```

Enter **c** to make connections to the backplane, or enter **t** to initiate a TI session with the router. Choice **e** is selected to enter the engineering diagnostics, and is not supported. Selecting **q** will break back out to the main connection menu.

> **Note**    *Under some circumstances, connecting to the router slot from the main connection menu may result in being deposited directly into the TI (for instance, if the connection is terminated but the TI is still being accessed). To get back to the Service Port Diagnostics menu at any point, press CTRL-X.*

**BACKPLANE CONNECTIONS**    Choosing the backplane connections option opens another menu:

```
c show Connections
w change cluster Wrapping
sa change ring segment (4/9,5) Attachments
s change ring Speeds (4/16Mb)
d Display token-ring port statistics
-ESC Return to main menu
Enter command:
```

In the 5580, by default, all cluster ports (routed backplane interfaces) are in a wrapped state. They must be assigned to individual rings before they will attempt insertion. Of the four cluster ports, the first three clusters are statically associated with the first three backplane rings. The fourth cluster can be steered toward backplane ring 4 or 5 (see Figure 28-11).

Bear in mind that the token ring backplane can be split. (This is accomplished through the supervisory module.) When in a split state, rings 1 to 4 and 6 to 9 each extend only half the length of the 5000 chassis, while ring 5 extends the full length of the backplane. In this scenario, two 5580s (one on either side of the chassis) would have clusters associated with rings 1, 2, and 3 on the left side and rings 6, 7, and 8 on the right side. The 5580 on the left would then have the option of steering the fourth cluster toward ring 4 or ring 5, while the 5580 on the right would have the option of steering the fourth cluster toward ring 9 or ring 5 (see Figure 28-12). Within this scheme, both routers can use ring 5 to connect the two routed domains in the split environment.

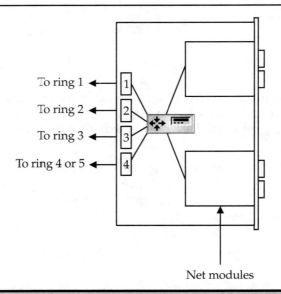

To ring 1

To ring 2

To ring 3

To ring 4 or 5

Net modules

**Figure 28-11.** *A 5580 with cluster/ring assignments*

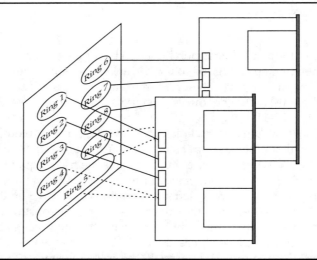

Ring 6

Ring 1

Ring 7

Ring 2

Ring 8

Ring 3

Ring 9

Ring 4

Ring 5

**Figure 28-12.** *Dual 5580s in a split backplane configuration*

To assign the cluster ports to the backplane rings, choose option **a**:

```
Changing cluster 4 ring connection...
Enter new ring connection (1 = ring 4/9, 2 = ring 5):
```

Remember in this case that clusters 1 to 3 are always associated with rings 1 to 3 or 6 to 8, depending on whether the backplane is split and the size of the chassis; only cluster 4 will be offered as an option. By entering 1, the cluster will be associated with ring 4 or ring 9, depending on the backplane configuration and the slot location of the 5580; entering 2 will associate the cluster with ring 5.

Just as the Ethernet clusters can be partitioned, the token ring clusters can be wrapped from the backplane without losing their ring association. Simply choose the **w** option from the main connection menu:

```
Cluster Port       Status      Ring Connection      Ring Speed      MAC Address
------------       -------     ---------------      ----------      -----------------
      1            Connected          1             16 Mb/s         00-00-A2-C5-AF-E2
      2            Connected          2             16 Mb/s         00-00-A2-C5-AF-E3
      3            Wrapped            3              None           00-00-A2-C5-AF-E4
      4            Connected          5             16 Mb/s         00-00-A2-C5-AF-E5
Changing cluster wrapping...
Enter cluster number (0 if done, 1 to 4): 0
```

A cluster number can be entered here; it will be followed by a prompt for the new cluster state:

```
Enter new port attachment (1 = wrapped, 0 = connected):
```

The cluster can now be wrapped, or connected. Notice that the ring speed is currently set to *None* in the preceding example. Ring speed must be configured manually, by choosing the **s** option from the main connection menu:

```
Changing ring speeds...
Enter cluster number (0 if done, 1 to 4):
```

Once the appropriate cluster has been selected, the ring speed can be chosen:

```
Enter new ring speed (1 = 4Mb/s, 2 = 16Mb/s):
```

Ring speed must, of course, match that of the backplane ring. Once selected, the appropriate ring speed will be displayed when viewing the token ring port cluster assignments.

**5380 AND 5580 ANNUNCIATOR PANEL**   Both the 5380 and 5580 have a similar bank of LEDs displayed on their annunciator panels. These LEDs indicate module- and backplane-specific information (see Tables 28-12 through 28-15).

| LED | Color | Status |
|---|---|---|
| S1-S12 (5380) | Green | Cluster attachment detected on the corresponding segment. |
| Ring 1-9 (5580) | Green | Cluster attachment detected on the corresponding ring. |

**Table 28-12.**   *Segment Connection LEDs*

| LED | Color | Status |
|---|---|---|
| Run | Green | System software is executing. |
| Boot | Green | System is initializing. |
| Diag | Amber | Diagnostics have failed. |
| Net1 | Green | Net module 1 is present and operational. |
|  | Amber | Net module 1 is present but has failed. |
| Net2 | Green | Net module 2 is present and operational. |
|  | Amber | Net module 2 is present but has failed. |
| BP | Green | Backplane connection detected. |
|  | Amber | One or more of the router backplane connections has failed. |
| PPX | Green | Unit is connected to the PPX bus. |
|  | Amber | PPX connection failure has occurred. |

**Table 28-13.**   *PPX Arbiter LED*

| LED | Color | Status |
|-----|-------|--------|
| A-D | Green | Unit is transmitting on PPX rail A-D. |

**Table 28-14.**    *PPX Transmit LED*

| LED | Color | Status |
|-----|-------|--------|
| A-D | Green | Unit is the arbiter for the indicated PPX rail. |

**Table 28-15.**    *Module Status LEDs*

The LEDs can be used as an indication of router operations or, in the event of a failure, the type of failure the router is experiencing (see Table 28-16 and 28-17).

| Condition | Run LED | Boot | Diag | Annunciator |
|-----------|---------|------|------|-------------|
| Router is running successfully. | Green | Off | Off | Green |
| CMB diagnostic test in progress. | Off | Off | Off | Amber |
| Router is resetting. | Flashing green | Off | Off | Amber |
| Router diagnostic test in progress. | Flashing green | Off | Off | Amber |
| Router is initializing successfully. | Off | Green | Off | Amber |

**Table 28-16.**    *LEDs in a Normal Router Operation*

| Condition | Run LED | Boot | Diag | Annunciator |
|---|---|---|---|---|
| Router is initializing with a diagnostic failure. | Off | Green | Amber | Amber |
| Router is running with an interface failure (cluster or net module). | Green | Off | Amber | Green |
| Diagnostics have failed; fatal error detected. | Off | Off | Flashing amber | Amber |
| Diagnostics have failed; diagnostics halted. | Flashing green | Off | Amber | Amber |
| PPX failure has occurred during diagnostics. | Flashing green | Off | Flashing amber | Amber |

**Table 28-17.**    *Router Failure LED Indicators*

**EXITING THE TI**    A TI session, once established, can be exited in one of two ways:

- Log out and then type press CTRL-T. This closes the TI session and backs out to the main connection menu of the 5000 chassis, where you can make a connection to any one of the 14 occupied slots.

- Press CTRL-X, which backs out of the TI session and brings up the Service Port Diagnostics menu, from which you can access the backplane connections menu.

## 5380 and 5580 Net Modules

The 5380 and 5580 net modules provide a variety of front-panel-routed LAN and WAN connections. The following net modules are available for the 5000 series router modules:

- **Dual-Port Ethernet**    Outfitted with four Ethernet ports, two of which can be active at any one time, two AUI connectors, and two 10BaseT RJ-45 connectors. These ports operate at 10Mbps only, half-duplex.

- **100BaseT**    Comes with two ports: one 100BaseT RJ-45 connector and one 40-pin MII connector with a 4-bit bus for use with an external transceiver. The maximum length for the MII cable is one meter. The 100BaseT connection can operate in half- or full-duplex mode.

- **Dual-Port Token Ring**   Has two DB-9 token ring STP ports, which operate at either 4Mbps or 16Mbps.

- **Dual-Attached Fiber FDDI**   Supports a single DAS connection, with a PHY A and PHY B. Each FDDI net module also has an 8-pin modular bypass port. FDDI net modules come in the following varieties:

  Multimode fiber
  Single-mode fiber
  Multimode fiber on PHY A, single-mode fiber on PHY B
  Single-mode fiber on PHY A, multimode fiber on PHY B

- **Dual-Port Synchronous WAN**   Has two synchronous ports, capable of supporting V.35, RS232, RS422 balanced (RS449 or RS530), and X.21 connections.

- **Quad-Port ISDN BRI**   Provides four 8-pin connectors, each capable of supporting a single BRI connection providing two 64K B data channels, and one 16K D channel for signaling purposes.

- **Multichannel E-1 (MCE1)**   Provides a single E-1 connection, as well as a connector for an external clocking device.

- **Compression Coprocessor**   Does not provide any additional front-panel ports. It provides hardware compression functionality, in 32 and 128 contexts.

## 5780

The 5780 provides connectivity to the ATM backplane with a single virtual interface. Unlike the 5380 and 5580, the 5780 does not use net modules and, in fact, has no front-panel connections whatsoever. The purpose of the 5782 is to establish a UNI connection across the backplane, to act as a one-armed router for any ELANs that have been created on the ATMSpeed Centillion MCP modules, such as the 5724M or the 5720M (see Figure 28-13).

In these cases, recall that the System 5000 ATM backplane is split (slots 2 to 7, and slots 8 to 13), and that to provide a routed interface for both sides of the chassis, either a front-panel ATM connection needs to be established between the left and right sides of the 5000BH chassis, or more than one 5780 is needed (one for each side).

The 5780 essentially provides the same functionality as an ARE/OC-3 link module ILI, without the need for an external router; the single backplane connection can be configured as a UNI port, and the unit can be configured with multiple LAN Emulation Clients (LECs).

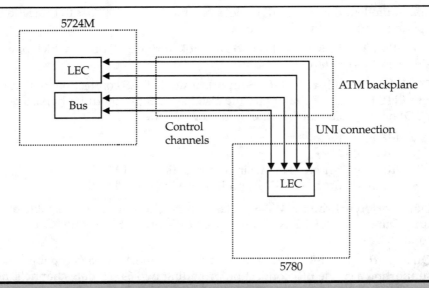

**Figure 28-13.**   *Logical view of a 5780 interacting with a 5724M*

# Router Software

All Nortel Networks routers utilize the Gate Access Management Entity (GAME) operating system, which acts as the basis for all system software versions. Each router must be configured to boot the system image software from a specific boot medium, most often a PCMCIA flash card. Depending on the type of router, this flash card may be installed in one or more of the router's processor cards (as with a chassis-based router, such as the BLN or BCN), can be installed in a bay located in the front panel (as with a stand-alone or stackable unit, such as the AN), or may be internal to the device (as with some of the early hardware versions). The boot mediums that are available to the Nortel Networks router platform are described in the following sections.

## Boot Mediums

In almost all cases, the boot medium for the router is a flash storage card, which is inserted either through the front or back panel (in the case of the AN, ANH, or ASN), or on an individual card (in the case of the BLN, BLN-2, BCN, and Series 5000 router modules). This flash can be accessed as a file system volume from Site Manager, or through the TI. (Instructions on accessing and manipulating the TI can be found later in this chapter.)

At least one boot medium must be present for the router to successfully boot; in the case of the BN and Series 5000 modules, which communicate across the PPX, only one flash card is required for all modules to boot from, though redundant boot mediums may be implemented, as long as they are all running the same code versions.

Some of the older AN and ANH routers cannot be equipped with a removable flash card; these devices hold their images on an internal flash SIMM. This SIMM can be mounted as a file system volume.

## Boot Images

The *boot image* for each router is the system software that it executes as its runtime image. It is a compressed executable file, containing both the GAME operating system and the protocols. These boot images will have different names, depending upon the router platform being used:

- **bn.exe**   Backbone node (BLN, BLN-2, BCN) boot image
- **asn.exe**   Access stack node (ASN) boot image
- **arn.exe**   Access remote node (ARN) boot image
- **afn.exe**   Access feeder node (AFN) boot image
- **an.exe**   Access node (AN) and access node hub (ANH) boot image
- **s5000.exe**   5380, 5580, and 5780 boot image; also 5780 ARE

## The Boot Process

Each router type follows a specific boot procedure, during which the unit is initialized and then finds and loads its image file and configuration parameters.

## BN and ASN

The BN and ASN families each follow a similar boot procedure. Upon initial startup, the units perform bootup diagnostics. Once diagnostics are completed, they request their system software over the PPX rails (this communication occurs over the SPEX cable, in the case of the ASN). If the image is located and loaded, then the device communicates across the PPX (SPEX), searching for configuration parameters with the filename "config." Upon finding this file, the device loads the configuration parameters.

If the image is requested across the PPX or SPEX cable, but isn't found, the unit then attempts to find the file on a local flash volume. If it does find it, it loads the image from there. If not, it sends the request over the PPX rail again. Likewise, when searching for the config file across the PPX or SPEX and it is not found, the unit then looks for a file named "config" on its local flash volume, even if it received its image file from a different unit.

Once the system software and configuration parameters are fully loaded, the system is initialized and ready to process data.

## The AN and ANH Models

The AN and ANH model routers were designed for use at remote sites. For this reason, their initial boot sequence is different from that of the BN or ASN models, using one of the three methods described next to obtain configuration parameters. The ASN, however, can also be configured to use the same boot procedures.

**EZ INSTALL**   Using EZ Install, The AN and ANH, upon powerup, run diagnostic testing. Once this is complete, the device sends a request for an IP address across the synchronous connections to the remote router, using BootP. This request is attempted first out COM1 and then out COM2, using the following protocols:

- Nortel Networks point-to-point
- Frame Relay Annex D
- Frame Relay link management interface (LMI)
- Frame Relay Annex A

This is a proprietary BootP, which will be serviced by the remote router. The router receiving it will provide an IP address to the requesting router. After the IP address is obtained, the AN or ANH sends another request for the location of the config file and/or a boot image from the BootP server (this is an actual BootP, serviced by a BootP server, and not the remote router) across both synchronous ports, and, upon locating it, loads the config file using TFTP. Once this is done, the AN or ANH either loads its image file or, if the image file is not indicated, boots its system software from its local flash.

**NETBOOT**   Using NetBoot, the router issues a BootP request to a preconfigured BootP server. The BootP server sends back the location of the TFTP server, as well as the path and location of the requested files. Upon receipt of this information, the router uses TFTP to load the files.

**DIRECTED NETBOOT**   Similar to NetBoot, only the IP address of the TFTP server (as well as the path and location of the desired files) is predefined, so that the router, upon bootup, simply attempts to TFTP the files from the TFTP server directly.

The current boot method can be viewed from the TI with the following command:

```
 [1:1]$ getcfg
Boot Options:
     boot image=local
     boot config=network
NetBoot Parameters:
     Slot 1:
```

```
XCVR21..None
XCVR22..None
COM31..EZ-Install
COM32..EZ-Install

Slot 2:
XCVR21..None
XCVR22..None
COM31..EZ-Install
COM32..EZ-Install
```

The reason for this scheme is that, since the AN and ANH are very often positioned at remote sites, they can be serviced from the central site and then simply connected to the WAN, whereupon they obtain their IP address and config file, and then boot locally and initialize with minimal configuration necessary at the remote site. If this procedure is not desirable, the AN and ANH can also be configured to obtain their config files locally, thus eliminating the need for a BootP/TFTP server at the remote end.

If you want to change the location of the boot and/or config file, issue the following commands from the TI:

## TO BOOT LOCALLY

```
[1:1]$ bconfig image local
[1:1]$ bconfig config local
```

## TO EXECUTE A NETBOOT

```
[1:1]$ bconfig image network
[1:1]$ bconfig config network
```

## TO EXECUTE A DIRECTED NETBOOT

```
[1:1]$ bconfig image network 200.20.10.14 /tftpboot/anh.exe
[1:1]$ bconfig config network 200.20.10.14 /tftpboot/site151.cfg
```

Applying a -d flag following the **bconfig** command will set the options to the factory defaults (EZ-Install):

```
[1:1]$ bconfig -d image
[1:1]$ bconfig -d config
```

**CONFIGURING BOOT INTERFACES**   The minimum configuration to the interface over which the router will boot can be applied through use of the **ifconfig** command, which allows the configuration of an IP address (if used, such as in the case of NetBoot or Directed NetBoot), as well as synchronous port configuration. Of course, another option is to not boot locally or across the WAN, but instead boot from the LAN; LAN interfaces can also be configured with this command:

[1:1]$ ifconfig -s[*slot-number*][*options*][*interface*][*ip-addr*][*subnet-mask*][*next-hop-addr*]

With this command, a slot number is selected (-s2 indicating slot 2, for instance), followed by optional switches (see Table 28-18).

**Note**   *If the -fr switch is not chosen, the default will be Wellfleet Standard.*

The *interface* option specifies the interface that will service the transfer. XCVR1 indicates the Ethernet interface, while COM1 or COM2 indicates either synchronous port. An IP address and subnet mask can then be assigned to the interface. *next-hop-addr* is the IP address of the next-hop router, if the request will pass through a router:

```
[1:1]$ ifconfig -s1 -fr com31 200.20.10.1 255.255.255.0 200.20.10.2
```

This example configures COM1 (slot 3, which accounts for the designation com31) for frame relay with the default data-link control management interface type of annex D, with an IP address of 200.20.10.1 and a mask of 255.255.255.0. A next-hop router is defined with IP address 200.20.10.2.

## Files Located on the Storage Medium

The flash memory on the different router platforms will contain a series of files associated with that unit. These include the runtime image, configuration files,

| Switch | Purpose |
|---|---|
| -d | Deletes the IP configuration on the interface and resets it to EZ-Install |
| -fr | Specifies frame relay for COM1 or COM2. The data-link control management interface type can also be selected:<br>-annexd (default)<br>-annexa<br>-lmi |
| -int_clk | Sets COM1 or COM2 to internal clocking at 1.25Mbps |

**Table 28-18.**   *Optional Command Switches Used with Ifconfig*

event log files, and others. Table 28-19 provides a complete list and describes their functions.

**Note** *By default, the router boots from the config file named Config, but can be instructed to boot from a configuration file with any name from the TI. To have a router boot automatically from a configuration file you have created, simply name the file **config** when it is completed. A backup of the original config file can be made, and stored on the flash as well. Remember that without some sort of valid config file, the router cannot boot. A template of the original config file comes on the flash using the filename TI.CFG. This file is there as a failsafe in case something goes wrong with the running config. For this reason, the ti.cfg file should never be deleted! The space it consumes is minimal, and it assures that a valid configuration file to boot from always is available. The preceding reference to aliases refers to commands that invoke long, or multiple, TI commands.*

| Filename | Function |
|---|---|
| an.exe/asn.exe/bn.exe | The bootable runtime image files |
| asnboot.exe | Upgrades the bootPROM on an ASN |
| freboot.exe | Upgrades the bootPROM on an FRE |
| asndiag.exe | Upgrades the diagnostic PROM on an ASN |
| frediag.exe | Upgrades the diagnostic PROM on an FRE |
| config | A default configuration file; when booted, all routers, by default, attempt to boot using the configuration file named config |
| debug.al | A source file containing predefined aliases |
| install.bat | A script file, which facilitates the initial IP configuration of a single IP interface so that the router will be accessible via Site Manager for further configuration |
| ti.cfg | Identical to the original config file; if the config file becomes corrupted or lost, this provides a valid configuration file to boot from |
| ti_asn.cfg | Holds the same function as ti.cfg, but is specific to the ASN |
| ti_arn.cfg | Holds the same function as ti.cfg, but is specific to the ARN |

**Table 28-19.** *Nortel Networks Router Files*

## Software Release Policy

With code version 12.10, a new software release policy was implemented. The purpose of this is to organize the software releases better, deliver new versions of system software on a predictable schedule, and make determining which software releases contain new features and fixes easier. Once code is released, it follows two distinct development paths: one to ensure that stability is maintained during the implementation of new features, and the other to develop the new functionality itself. The different code gradations indicated in the naming structure are as follows:

- **Major Releases (12.00, 13.00, etc.)**    A rollup of all new features, functionality, and fixes, as well as any significant changes in software architecture and enhancements that have occurred through maintenance, feature, and revision releases. No new features or functionality are introduced into Major Releases.

- **Maintenance Releases (12.01, 12.02, etc.)**    Provide a series of software bug fixes for the current Major Release. No new software or hardware features are introduced.

- **Feature Releases (12.10, 12.20, etc.)**    Introduce added functionality, in the form of new features and/or new hardware support; may also include bug fixes from the current Maintenance Release.

- **Revision Releases (12.01 [Rev.4], etc.)**    A bug fix or series of bug fixes that is integrated with any currently supported Major Release, Feature Release, or Maintenance Release.

   Major Releases occur roughly every 12 months or so, and provide a stable package of features and functionality introduced since the prior Major Release. Maintenance Releases generally occur about every 3 to 4 months after the first Major Release occurs. Feature releases are relatively new and are designed to give customers quicker access to new features and hardware support. Feature Releases occur approximately every 4 months. Be aware, however, that Feature Releases are often one of the first iterations of the feature in question; for a mature version of the feature set in question, a Major Release should be considered, if available. Revision Releases occur on a case-by-case basis, because they are often initiated to resolve specific customer issues.

# Upgrading System Software and PROMs

To upgrade the system software, it must be transferred to a bootable media (the flash). This is accomplished via TFTP. Upgrading the Nortel Networks router is not overly complicated, but it is a good idea to have a few details in order before commencing, such as the hardware requirements (for example, flash space and BootPROM version), the current software version that is running on the router, and the hardware configuration of the router that is to be upgraded.

# Checking Hardware Requirements

The first thing to check prior to upgrading the router's system software is the amount of flash memory. Make sure enough space exists to accommodate the image file. Remember, there must be enough *contiguous* free space to support the image. It is possible to have enough free space on the flash to contain the new software but not enough contiguous free space. If this is the case, you must reclaim the space by using the **compact** command.

Determine whether any of the hardware requires a certain software or PROM upgrade; certain hardware is supported only by certain software revisions. This information can be easily obtained from the release notes for the product in question.

Determine what your memory requirements are; depending on which protocols and how many will be installed on the router, the amount of memory required will vary. The memory requirements for each executable can be monitored via Image Builder, which can give you the total decompressed size.

## Identifying the Current Software Version

Sometimes an upgrade to a certain code revision requires that the router already be running at a specific code version. You can obtain the code version currently running on the router by issuing the **stamp** command from the TI.

## Identifying the Hardware Configuration

Determine the hardware configuration, including the link modules, FRE cards, and slot and stack assignments. Complete any necessary hardware upgrades prior to upgrading the system software.

## Determining the PROM Version

Depending on which new software features or hardware are going to be used, the router may require a specific PROM version. This may need to be upgraded prior to any upgrade of the system software. The PROM version can be determined in one of two ways:

**OBTAINING THE PROM VERSION VIA SITE MANAGER**    The PROM version can be obtained through Site Manager, by selecting Tools | Statistics Manager from the main Site Manager window. This opens the Statistics Manager window, which will display the router's current configuration.

Next, choose Tools | Quick Get. This opens the Quick Get Facility window, which will display a series of MIB values. Scroll through the available MIBs and select the top-level object group wfHardwareConfig. This displays a new series of MIB instances. Select the object group wfHwTable. Descend through the tree to the instance wfHwBootPromRev or wfHwDiagPromRev (depending on the PROM you are looking for). After you find the instances, select the MIB to query and, in the Quick Get window, choose Retrieve Request.

The BootPROM version will be displayed as eight hexadecimal numerals in a 32-bit display. The first four characters are major revisions, and the last four are minor revisions.

*The value must be converted from hexadecimal to decimal format. A version 9.xx router will appear as 0x00090000.*

### OBTAINING THE PROM VERSION VIA THE TI
To obtain the PROM version from the TI, enter the following command:

```
[1:1]$ g wfHwEntry.19.*
wfHwEntry.wfHwBootPromSource.1 = (nil)
wfHwEntry.wfHwBootPromSource.2 = "rel/12.00/freboot.exe"
wfHwEntry.wfHwBootPromSource.3 = "rel/12.00/freboot.exe"
wfHwEntry.wfHwBootPromSource.4 = "rel/12.00/freboot.exe"
wfHwEntry.wfHwBootPromSource.5 =  "rel/12.00/freboot.exe"
```

The output indicates different slot numbers. (wfHwEntry.wfHwBootPromSource.2, for instance, indicates slot 2).

*Slot 1 in this case does not return a value, because the router is a BLN and has an SRM in slot 1. In a BN chassis, slot 7 will also show a NUL value. In any AN product that does not utilize a SRM, no NULL value will appear.*

Diagnostic PROM versions can be obtained with the following command:

```
[1:1]$ g wfHwEntry.16.*
wfHwEntry.wfHwDiagPromSource.2 = "/harpdiag.rel/v6.00/wf.pj/harpoon.ss/image.p/freediag.exe"
wfHwEntry.wfHwDiagPromSource.3 = "/harpdiag.rel/v6.00/wf.pj/harpoon.ss/image.p/freediag.exe"
wfHwEntry.wfHwDiagPromSource.4 = "/harpdiag.rel/v6.00/wf.pj/harpoon.ss/image.p/freediag.exe"
wfHwEntry.wfHwDiagPromSource.5 = "/harpdiag.rel/v6.00/wf.pj/harpoon.ss/image.p/freediag.exe"
```

## PROM Upgrade Feature Support

Consult Table 28-20 to determine whether a PROM upgrade is necessary.

You can upgrade a router BootPROM either by erasing it and reprogramming the PROM components (burning the PROM), or by physically removing the PROM and replacing it with an upgraded PROM. Table 28-21 outlines when this may be necessary.

| Router Model | PROM Version | PROM Filename | PROM Features | If PROM Is This Version... | Reason for PROM Upgrade |
|---|---|---|---|---|---|
| AN/ ANH | 8.00 | anboot.exe | 4MB flash capability controller | Upgrade to 9.00 | 10.0 image may require more than 2MB flash. |
| | 8.10 | anboot.exe | Router-specific boot image name | No change | No new features beyond version 8.10 |
| | 9.00 | anboot.exe | None | No change | No new features |
| | 9.00b | anboot.exe | None | No change | No change |
| AN200 | 11.01 | an200boot.exe | Support for software version 11.01 | No change | No change |
| ARN | V1.17 | arnboot.exe | None | No change | No change |
| ASN | 8.00 | asnboot.exe | 4MB flash capability | Upgrade to 10.0 | 10.0 image may require more than 2MB flash. |
| | 8.10 | asnboot.exe | Router-specific boot image name. Supports SPEX-HS netmod | No change | No new features beyond version 8.10 |
| | 9.00 | asnboot.exe | None | No change | No new features |
| | 10.00 | asnboot.exe | None | No change | No new features |
| BN | 7.70/7.71 | freboot.exe | Support for FRE2 controller | Upgrade to 9.00 | 4MB flash capability; router-specific boot name |
| | 8.00 | freboot.exe | 4MB flash capability | Upgrade to 8.10 | 10.0 image may require more than 2MB flash. |
| | 8.10 | freboot.exe | Router-specific boot name | No change | No new features beyond version 8.10 |
| | 9.01 | areboot.ppc | ARE/ATM-specific feature | No change | N/A |
| VME | 8.00 | vmeboot.exe | 4MB flash capability | Upgrade to 8.10 | 10.0 image may require more than 2MB flash. |
| | 8.11 | vmeboot.exe | None | No change | Support for Quad Token board |

**Table 28-20.**    *Router PROM Compatibility Matrix*

| Router Model | PROM Version | PROM Filename | PROM Features | If PROM Is This Version... | Reason for PROM Upgrade |
|---|---|---|---|---|---|
| AFN | 3.03 | no filename | 4MB flash capability | No change | 10.0 image may require more than 2MB flash. |
| | 3.04 | no filename | Router-specific image name change | No change | No new features beyond version 3.04 |
| ARE | A0000 | areboot.ppc | Support for 5780 | No change | No change |
| S5000 | 11.02 | areboot.ppc | Support for software version 11.02 | No change | No change |
| | 11.00 | s5000boot.exe | Support for software version 11.0 | No change | No change |

**Table 28-20.** *Router PROM Compatibility Matrix* (continued)

## Upgrading the PROM

To actually burn the existing PROM with the new software, the new boot PROM software must be TFTP-transferred to the boot media of the router. This can be accomplished through Site Manager, using the Router Files Manager tool (Tools | Router Files Manager).

From the main Router Files Manager window, select File | TFTP. A pull-down menu will give the option to do a TFTP Put or a TFTP Get. A TFTP Put will be used in

| Router Model | PROM Replacement Method |
|---|---|
| AFN | Physical replacement |
| AN or ANH with motherboard Rev. earlier than 14 | Physical replacement |
| AN or ANH with motherboard Rev. 14 or later | PROM burned from TI |
| ASN, BLN, BLN-2, BCN, or ARE | PROM burned from TI |
| FN, LN, or CN | PROM burned from TI |

**Table 28-21.** *Router PROM Replacement Methods*

this case, opening the TFTP Put File Selection menu. In the Path field, enter the path on the Site Manager station where the PROM software resides. Add the file to the list of files to transfer, and then click OK.

Once the PROM software is on the flash, you can burn the PROM can by accessing the TI. Issue the following command:

[1:1]$ prom -w [*volume-number:BootPROM-source-file*][*slot-ID*]

For example:

```
[1:1]$ prom -w 2:freboot.exe 3
```

Multiple cards can have their PROMs upgraded simultaneously:

```
[1:1]$ prom -w 2:freboot.exe 3, 4, 5
```

This command erases the current PROM on slot 3, and then writes the contents of freboot.exe on flash volume 2 into the PROM on slot 3. The diagnostic PROM can be upgraded with the same procedure; simply substite the frediag.exe file (or the file appropriate to the specific router platform) for the freboot.exe file.

### Verifying the PROM Upgrade

After you burn the PROM with the new software, you can verify the upgrade from the TI by using this command:

[1:1]$ prom -v [*volume-number:BootPROM-source-file*][*slot-ID*]

For instance, the following code verifies that the PROM image on the prom in slot 3 actually does match the freboot.exe file on volume 2:

```
[1:1]$ prom -v 2:freboot.exe 3
```

 **Caution**   *During a PROM upgrade, be sure to avoid rebooting the router for any reason. Having a PROM upgrade interrupted can damage the PROM. Keep in mind also that, although the option exists to upgrade all PROMs on all cards within a BN chassis at once, doing so opens the possibility of damaging all the PROMs if anything, such as a power failure, interrupts the transfer.*

## Upgrading the System Software

After completing the previous considerations, you can transfer the software to the router's flash memory. To accomplish this, first transfer the router software from the software CD-ROM onto the PC or UNIX station.

## Transferring System Software to a PC

First, insert the CD-ROM into the PC's CD-ROM drive and launch Windows Explorer. Select the CD-ROM drive. Click the rtr_*xxx* directory, where *xxx* is the software version (rtr_1101, rtr_1200, and so on). Within this directory will be another series of router-model-specific directories. Select the directory associated with the router you will be upgrading. Copy the files in rtr_*xxx* to a destination folder on the PC.

## Transferring System Software to a UNIX Station

Insert the CD-ROM into the CD-ROM drive. If a CD-ROM mountpoint has not yet been created, then log in as **root** and create a root-level directory (**mkdir /cdrom**). Mount the CD-ROM drive on one of the following platforms:

### SUNOS ON A SPARCSTATION

```
mount -r -t hsfs /dev/sr0/ cdrom
```

### SOLARIS ON A SPARCSTATION

```
mount -F hsfs -o ro /dev/dsk/c0t6d0s0/ cdrom
```

### IBM WORKSTATION

```
mount -v 'cdrfs' "-r" /dev/cd0/ cdrom
```

### HP 9000

```
/etc/ mount /dev/dsk/c0t2d0/ cdrom
```

 *Solaris stations running the old vold daemon will automatically mount the CD-ROM in the longer form /cdrom/release/_xxx_yyy (where* xxx *is the software version and* yyy *is the Site Manager version).*

Change directories to the directory where the files will go, and then run the script to load the router software:

### SPARCSTATION

```
./copy.sh
```

### IBM WORKSTATION

```
./copy.sh
```

## HP 9000

```
./COPY.SH\;1
```

Once the software is transferred to either the PC or the UNIX workstation, the image can be loaded into Image Builder (if desired).

## Image Builder

Since the router software executable is, in reality, a series of executables, these files can be altered, to have components either added or removed. This is done with an application called Image Builder (see Figure 28-14), which is a component of Site Manager.

You can load images into Image Builder by selecting Tools | Image Builder from the main Site Manager window, and then selecting File | Open from the Image Builder toolbar. Choose the image you wish to manipulate. The Image Builder window will display a list of Available Components, as well as a list of Current Components.

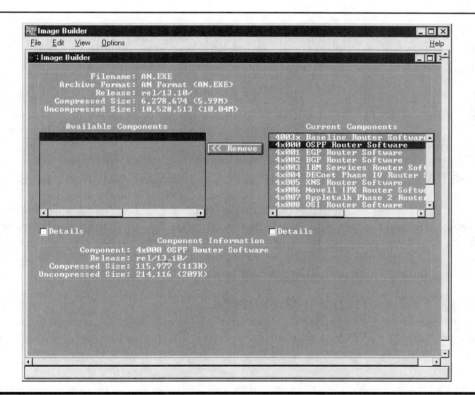

**Figure 28-14.**   *Using Image Builder*

Here you can conserve flash space by removing protocols that won't be used, or you can add back into the image any protocols that were previously removed. Image Builder will not allow the removal of any essential files.

## Loading the System Software to the Router

The image file is now ready for transfer to the router's storage medium. The procedure for this will vary slightly depending on whether the unit in question supports one flash medium or multiple flashes.

**IF THE ROUTER CONTAINS ONE FLASH MEMORY CARD**     You will most likely want to delete the current router software image, but before doing so, be sure to load the STR files into the router's memory. The current running software image may need to pull some of the STR files from the stored image, and may fail if the image has been removed without preserving the STR files. This can be done from the TI, while logged in as Manager:

```
[1:1]$ string load
```

After you do this, delete the previous image version from the flash. From Site Manager, choose Tools | Router Files Manager, and then, from the Router Files Manager window, select the image file and select Commands | Delete.

 **Caution**     *The flash must be compacted at this point to regain the flash space previously taken by the image file. However, the flash should not be compacted on an AN or ASN router that is configured for NetBoot! On an AN router that is not configured for NetBoot, flash compaction may take up to 12 minutes.*

**IF THE ROUTER CONTAINS MULTIPLE FLASH MEMORY CARDS**     Routers that support more than one flash card can have the new image transferred to the flash that does not contain the image that is currently running. This is helpful because it allows the user to upload the new image, and then verify that it is functioning properly, before actually removing the image that the router is currently running on. If the flash card being used for the upgrade transfer is new, it needs to be formatted. If it is already formatted, be sure there is enough space left onboard to contain the new image.

## Using TFTP to Transfer the Image

You can transfer files can be transferred with the Router Files Manager tool in Site Manager, using the TFTP command. First open the Router Files Manager tool (Tools | Router Files Manager) and then selecting the TFTP option (File | TFTP) from the main Router Files Manager window. The TFTP option yields a drop-down menu listing options to either Get or Put the file. A Put will be issued in this case.

**Note** *If the router being upgraded has only one flash, the BootPROM must be at version 8.10 or greater, or else the new image must be renamed boot.exe before the TFTP transfer. If the router being upgraded has multiple flash cards and the BootPROM is not at version 8.10 or greater, then the file must be transferred to an alternate flash and then booted using a named boot: [1:1]$ boot 2:bn.exe config.*

Verify that enough space exists on the flash to accept the new file, and then Select File | TFTP | Put File(s) from the toolbar. This opens a window called TFTP Put File Selection, in which you can choose the files you want to transfer. In the Path field, enter the path on the Site Manager station where the files reside. Then, you can add files to a list queued for the TFTP transfer. After you queue all the files that you want to transfer to the flash, you have the option of sending the files to one or multiple routers. Select the appropriate choice and then click OK. This initiates the transfer.

## Transferring Code via the TI

You can also transfer these files by using TFTP from the TI. Here is the command structure:

tftp [get | put][*address volume:filename*]

For example, to TFTP a file named sdlc.cfg from a remote router's volume 3 with IP address 200.20.10.12, you would issue the following command:

```
[1:1]$ tftp get 200.20.10.12 3:sdlc.cfg
```

This transfers the file to the current volume mounted on the router from which the command is being issued. Files can be transferred to a different volume (other than the current one) on the router issuing the command. For instance, to TFTP the same file, sdlc.cfg, but to volume 4 instead of the current volume, issue the following command:

```
[1:1]$ tftp get 200.20.10.12 3:sdlc.cfg 4:sdlc.cfg
```

## Updating the Config File

The config file can be updated in one of two ways: through Site Manager and through the TI. The existing config file must be loaded with the new software and then saved dynamically. For instance, in the TI, simply save the config file by using the **save** command:

```
[2:1] save config
```

This causes the config file that is now running with the new software to be saved in an updated format. Likewise, the file can be saved from Site Manager by selecting Tools | Configuration Manager | Dynamic, and then, once in the Configuration Manager main window, selecting File | Save. This save the config file with the new format.

 **Note**   *Although both methods will work, saving the config file from the TI does not update the MIB stamp that indicates the new version, as Site Manager does. The config file will be updated, but will still be reported as being the old version.*

## Verifying the Image

The **readexe** command from the TI will validate executable files before upgrading, and can be used after transfer to the flash memory to be certain that the file is intact, before booting from it. This command uses the following syntax:

readexe [*filename*]

For instance, to validate the diagnostic PROM image on a BCN router, the following command would be issued:

```
[2:1]$ readexe frediag.exe
Processing contents of '2:frediag.exe'...
-----------------------------------------------------------
 Module name: frediag.exe
-----------------------------------------------------------
      Validating header checksum... OK
      Validating image checksum.. OK
      Program execution address space:
      -----------------------------------------------------------
      Load Address: 0x0C000000  Size: 200265 Bytes    Entry point:   0x00000400
      PROM storage address space:
      ------------------------------------------
      PROM Load address:  0x00000000
      Input file information:
      -------------------------------
      Platform Key: (01010008)  BB M68000 Motherboard (FRE FRE2 FRE2_60)
      Workspace:  /harpdiag.rel/v4.00/wf.pj/harpoon.ss/image.p
      Compression:  OFF
      Revision:     4.0
```

```
Last Modified:      Friday February 3 15:25:22 1998
File type:          Executable file
Tool name:          Uasys Linker
```

## Checking the Application File Sizes

The load addresses and file sizes can be viewed for each application that is loaded dynamically. This is accomplished via the **loadmap** command, which is issued against a slot, or a series of slots:

```
[2:1]$ loadmap 4
---------------------------------------
Loadmap from SLOT 4:
---------------------------------------
    arp.exe
    tftp.exe
    snmp.exe
    ip.exe
    qsync.exe
```

# Upgrading the Data Collection Module

The DCM also may require an image upgrade from time to time. To run RMON against the BayStack routers, you should be running DCM software version 1.4.2, and router software version 12.00 or greater, though earlier versions are supported. The requirements for running RMON are outlined in Table 28-22.

| BayStack AN and ANH | BayStack ARN |
|---|---|
| Router software version 9.0 or greater | Router software version 11.02 or greater |
| DCM agent software version 1.4 | DCM agent software version 1.4.1 or 1.4.2 |
| | ARN BootPROM version 1.17 or greater |
| | ARN Diagnostic PROM version 1.30 or greater |
| | DCM Hardware Revision D or greater |

**Table 28-22.**    *Requirements for RMON*

*Enabling the DCM in an ARN with DCM software version 1.4 or earlier may disable the ARN.*

You can determine the current DCM agent software version through the TI by using the following commands for router software 11.00 or greater:

```
[1:1]$ g wfDCMEntry.wfDCMagentImageVersion.*
```

This will display the agent version:

```
wfDCMmw.wfDCMagentImageVersion.1 = "V1.4.2"
```

For router software 9.0 to 10.0x:

```
[1:1]$ g wfDCMmw.wfDCMAgentImageVersion.0
```

Since the hardware revision is important on the ARN router, this can also be determined through the TI:

```
[1:1]$ g wfDCMEntry.wfDCMhwRev.*
wfDCMEntry.wfDCMhwRev.1 = "D"
wfDCMEntry.wfDCMhwRev.2 = "D"
```

## Transferring the Code

Transferring the new agent image to the DCM is a two-step process:

1. Transfer the code to the flash memory card.
2. Transfer the code from the memory card into the DCM itself.

After you place the code onto a PC or UNIX workstation, you can transfer it to the flash by using Site Manager. This is accomplished in the same way as transferring an image or PROM upgrade. From the main Site Manager window, select Tools | Router Files Manager. From the Router Files Manager, select File | TFTP | Put file(s), and then enter in the Path field the path to the agent image on the Site Manager station. The file can then be transferred from the PC to the router flash.

Next, the agent image must be transferred from the flash into the DCM's flash memory. This can also be done via Site Manager. From the main Configuration Manager window, select Platform. A drop-down menu appears with two options regarding the DCM: DCM 10.0 or earlier, and DCM 11.0 and later. For this example, select DCM 11.0 or later | Global | Base Module DCM. This opens the Edit Base Module DCM Parameters window:

```
Edit Base Module DCM parameters                                          ☒

                                              ┌──────────────┐
   Configuration Mode: local                  │    Cancel    │
           SNMP Agent: LOCAL FILE             │      OK      │
                                              │   Values...  │
                                              │   Help...    │
                                              └──────────────┘
   Enable/Disable                       ENABLE
   Boot Option                          LOCAL
   Image Name
   Image Save Mode
   Configuration Mode                   LOCAL
   Save Configuration Info
   RMON Max Host
   RMON Default Host
   RMON Default Matrix
   RMON Object Support                  RMON2
```

Change the Enable/Disable state to Disable, in preparation for the download. Change the Boot Option from Local to Download, indicating that the code will be downloaded from the flash memory. The image name must be specified in the Image Name field. Once this is done, go to the Image Save Mode field and select the Save option (selecting No Save will cause the DCM to boot using the new software, but it will not actually save it to its own flash). Then click OK.

After you set up these parameters, return to the main Configuration Manager window and select Platform | DCM | Global to return to the Edit Base Module DCM Parameters window. There, set the Enable/Disable option back to Enable, to reactivate the DCM that will boot with the new software, and then save it to its flash. Once the software has been saved to the DCM's flash memory, set the Boot Option back to Local.

## Upgrading the DCM from the TI

Upgrading the DCM from the TI requires the use of a TI script called *dcmload.bat*. This script file must be present on the router's flash:

```
[1:1]$ dcmload
Do you want to download an image to the Base Module DCM
Or the Expansion Module DCM (b/e) [b]
```

The base module is used in router models AN and ANH, and also in the base module of the ARN. The ARN can also accept a DCM in its expansion slot. If the unit is an AN or ANH, then select the default choice **b** (base module). If the DCM is in an expansion slot, select **e**. The TI will prompt for the image name:

```
Specify DCM image name (volume:filename):
```

Enter the volume and filename (for instance, 1:in11_142.obj), and press ENTER. The following will be displayed:

```
Do you want DCM to save this image on its FLASH? (y/n) [y]
```

Select the default, **y**. Once this is done, the DCM begins the download, overwriting the old image.

# Chapter 29

## Technician Interface, Bay Command Console, and Router MIB

The Technician Interface (TI) can be thought of as a command line-interface (CLI) for routers, though it is commonly referred to as the TI rather than the CLI. It has a command set and the capability to poll and set individual MIB values. It is accessible through the console port (the SMR-L in the BN series routers) or via telnet. The TI is required for initial configuration of the router, because a valid IP address will need to be configured on at least one interface so that the router will be accessible via the configuration utility Site Manager.

# Essentials of the TI

Although the TI is a command-line interface of sorts, it is different in key ways (which may perhaps account for its designation as TI rather than CLI). The TI does not, by default, have the same style of command set often associated with a CLI; the TI has a limited number of predefined commands that can be issued from the initial TI. This command set may be augmented through the introduction of additional script files or through use of the Bay Command Console (BCC).

However, the TI can be used to poll any value contained within the Management Information Base (MIB), and thus can be a very useful tool even without the use of scripts. This process is discussed later in this chapter.

The TI runs automatically on the processor module of any slot in the chassis (or stack). If there are multiple slots or units in a stack, the TI becomes active on the first slot to finish its diagnostics.

## Getting to the TI Prompt

The TI prompt can be accessed via either an out-of-band connection or a Telnet session. To connect to the TI using a terminal, or using a PC running terminal-emulation software, an RS-232 cable is required. If connecting to a BLN, BLN-2, or BCN, the connector type found on the SRM-L is a 25-pin connector. An AN, ANH, or ASN utilizes a 9-pin connector. The VT-100 console configuration is as follows:

- 9600 baud
- 8 data bits
- No parity
- 1 stop bit

If PC terminal-emulation software is being used, set the terminal type to VT-100, and set flow control to either Xon/Xoff or none.

Upon establishing a connection with the TI, a login prompt is displayed. The login options are as follows:

- User (provides read-only access)
- Manager (provides read-write access)

By default, neither the User login nor the Manager login requires a password. Passwords, once configured, are case-sensitive.

INTERNETWORKING WITH NORTEL NETWORKS

> **Note** *To use telnet to access the TI, the router must be configured as a telnet server; likewise, to telnet from the router to any other devices (such as another router), the router must be configured as a telnet client. These options are not enabled by default. To be able to telnet to and from the router, telnet server and client functions must be configured. This is accomplished through Site Manager; from the main toolbar of the Configuration Manager window, select Protocols | Global Protocols | TCP | Create TCP. Select Create TCP. Once this is done, select Protocols | Global Protocols. From this menu, the options for Telnet Server and Telnet Client should be available. By selecting either and then choosing Create Telnet Server or Create Telnet Client, the router will be ready to serve either or both functions.*

## Dial-in Access

The TI can also be reached via a modem connection. This allows remote access by the network administrator and representatives from Technical Support, if necessary. Dial-in access is something that should be prioritized; if it is not configured currently, it is highly recommended that it be implemented at some point. Dial-in access may or may not be used by an administrator on a regular basis, but in any scenario where troubleshooting is required, it can be invaluable. Nortel Networks Technical Support Engineers can use this dial-in access to access the TI remotely, and this will cut down significantly on the amount of time spent troubleshooting.

**CONFIGURING FOR DIAL-IN ACCESS**    To set up the router for dial-in access, bring up the router in Site Manager and reconfigure the console port; the modem parameter, by default, is set to Disabled. Set this to Enabled.

Any Hayes-compatible modem should work for dial-in access to the Nortel Networks router. The modem parameters are as follows:

| Modem Parameter | Setting |
|---|---|
| Clear to Send (CTS) | On |
| Data Terminal Ready (DTR) | This may vary depending on the modem type. The DTR must be configured to require the modem to answer incoming calls. |
| Data Carrier Detect (DCD) | On while carrier is present (used to detect connects and disconnects). |
| Data Set Ready (DSR) | On |
| Ready to Send (RTS) | Ignore |
| Synchronous/Asynchronous Mode | Asynchronous |

| Modem Parameter | Setting |
| --- | --- |
| AutoAnswer | Set to On at $n$ rings, where $n$ is greater than 0, with DTR active. |
| Local Character Echo | Off |
| Supervisory Functions | Off |
| Baud rate | 9600 or less, but 9600 is recommended. |
| Data bits | 8 |
| Stop bits | 1 |
| Parity | None |

To connect the modem physically to the router's console port, the AN, ANH, and ASN models require a modem cable with a 9-pin D-sub plug to RS-232 modem plug. The BLN, BLN-2, and BCN models require a modem cable with a 25-pin D-sub plug to RS-232 modem plug.

## Functions of the TI

The TI can be an excellent diagnostic tool. Its command structure is divided into four basic categories:

- System administration commands
- Flash system commands
- System restarts and log commands
- Internetworking commands

Upon first logging in to the TI, a prompt is displayed that looks something like this:

```
[x:y]$
```

The $x$ and $y$ variables may vary each time the unit is recycled, depending on whether there are multiple slots or units, and what kind of unit the router is. For instance:

- $x$ in this case will be the slot number on which the TI is currently running (or the unit in an ASN stack). Since the first slot or unit to finish diagnostics will run the TI, this may change. In an AN, or any other router that has only one unit, $x$ will equal 1.

- $y$ in this case is the port number to which the TI connection is made. This number will always be 1, except on an ASN, where it will be the slot number of the stack element.

# Basic TI Commands

TI commands may be broken down further into three main types of commands:

- Individual MIB lists, sets, and gets
- Individual TI commands using a command-line syntax
- Script commands

MIB lists, sets, and gets can be used to view and set individual MIB objects, attributes, and instances that are not designated read-only. (Sets may be performed on MIB instances.) The actual MIB object, as well as its attributes and instances, needs to be known to issue these commands. (The structures, as well as numerous examples, of these MIBs are included later in this chapter, in the section "The Management Information Base.")

Script files generally are code-dependant and provide a means of executing several MIB gets or sets by issuing a single command (instead of manipulating each MIB individually). These script files are available on the Bay RS CD-ROM and must be loaded onto the router to be used. This procedure is outlined later in this chapter, in the section relating to the TI scripts. Even without loading script files, the TI possesses a series of commands that can be issued. A list of these commands can be obtained by using the **help** command:

```
[12:2]$help
!          [<repeat count>]
alias      [<name> [("]<alias_value>["]]]
arrayenv   [-a] <variable name> "<string1>" ["<string2>" ...]
atmarp     table [<options>] <IP address>
bcc
bconfig    <image | config> <local | network> [<IP address> <pathname>]
bconfig    -d <image | config>
boot       [<vol>:<image_name>|- <vol>:<config_name>|-]
cd         [<vol>:][<directory>]
clear      <sub_commands> <flags>
clearlog   [<slot ID>]
commit
compact    <volume>:
copy       <vol>:<filename1> <vol>:<filename2>
cutenv     -s -d<delimiter> [-f<list>|-c<list>] <variable> "<text string>"
date       [<mm/dd/yy>] [<hh:mm:ss>] [<+|-><hh:mm>]
delete     <vol>:<filename>
diags      [<slot ID>]
dinfo
dir        <vol:>
disable    <entity> <option>
echo       [["]<string>["]]
enable     <entity> <option>
enumenv    <start #> [+<incr.> <variable name> [<variable name> ...]
exec       [-load|-unload] <command name>
export     {<variable name> ...}
```

```
firewall   <sub_command>
format     <volume>:
fwputkey   [<key_string> <ip_address>] | [clearkey]
get        {<obj_name>|<obj_id>}.{<attr_name>|<attr_id>|*}[.{<inst_id>|*}]
getcfg
getenv     [<variable name>]
gosub      :<label name>:
goto       :<label name>:
help       [-all|<command>]
history    [n]
if         "<string1>" [<=>|<!=>] "<string2>" [then]; command(s) ;
ifconfig   [-s] [-d|-enable|-disable] <xcvr>|[-r4|-r16] <mau>
           [<IP addr> <mask> [<Next Hop>]]
ifconfig   [-s] [-fr [-annexd|-lmi|-annexa]] | [-int_clk] | [-d|-enable|
           -disable] <com> [<IP addr> <mask> [<Next Hop>]]
instenv    <variable prefix> <mib-object name> [<mib-instance-pattern>]
ip         <sub_command> <flags>
ip6        <sub_command> [<options>]
ipsec      <sub_command> [<options>]
isdb <sub_command> [-s<slot>] [-c<connector>] [-p<port>] [<vol>:<filename>]
kexit
kget  <sub_command>
kpassword
kseed
ksession
kset  <sub_command> [<flags>]
ktranslate <old_npk>
let        <var. name> = <expression>
list       [[<instances> [<obj_name>]]]
loadmap    [<slot list> | all] [<filepath>]
log        [<vol>:<logfile>] [-d<date>] [-t<time>] [-e"<entity>"] [-f<severity>]
           [-s<slot ID>] [-p[<rate>]] [-c<code #>]
log        [-x|-i] [-e"<entity>"] [-f<severity>] [-s<slot ID>]
log        -z [-s<slot ID>]
logout
mibget     [-n] [-p <pattern>] <object> <attribute var. array> <inst. id>
           <value var. array> <next_inst var.>
more       [on | off] [# of lines per screen]
mrinfo     [-r retry_count] [-t timeout_count] multicast_router
mtrace     [-M] [-O] [-U] [-s] [-w wait] [-m max_hops] [-q nqueries]
                [-g gateway] [ -e extrahops ] [-S statint] [-t ttl]
                [-r resp_dest] [-i if_addr] source [receiver] [group]
octetfmt   <variable name> <format option> <MIB object>
on         ERROR :<label name>:
osidata    -s <SLOT> -t <lsp_l1 | lsp_L2 | path_L1 | path_L2 |
                        adj_L1 | adj_L2 | adj_ES> -i <ID>
partition create|delete [<vol>:]
password   [<login-id>]
pause      <seconds>
permit     [ -file   [<vol>:]<filename> ] |
           [  <command>   [<attribute>] ] |
           [  <mib object> ]
```

```
ping        <-IP| -IPV6| -IPX|-OSI|-VINES|-AT|-APPN> <hostname|address>
            [-t<timeout>] [-r<repeat count>] [-s<size>] [-p] [-a<address>]
            [-m<mode_name>] [-iifindex] [-v] [-n]
pktdump     <linenumber> [-s<start>] [-c<count>]
printf      <format string>  <p1> <p2> ... <pN>
prom        [-v|-w] <vol>:<ROM Update File> <slot ID> [<slot ID> ...]
readexe     <vol>:<filename>
record      open [-fileonly] [-pause]  <vol>:<filename>
            record pause [on|off]
            record close
reset       [<slot ID>]
restart     [<slot ID>]
return       :<label name>:
revoke      <command> [<attribute>]
rsvp        <sub_command>
run         <vol>:<filename> [<p1> [... <p9>]]
save        {config|aliases|perm} <vol>:<filename>
save        log [<vol>:<logfile>] [-d<date>] [-t<time>] [-e"<entity>"]
            [-f<severity>] [-s<slot ID>]
securelogin
set         {<obj_name>|<obj_id>}.{<attr_name>|<attr_id>}.<inst_id> <value>
setenv      <variable name> "<text string>"
show        <entity> <option>
snmpserver view [view-name] [oid-tree] [included | excluded | list | delete]
            community [community-name] view [view-name] [RO | RW | list |         delete]

source      {aliases|env|perm} <vol>:<filename>
sprintf     <variable name> <format string>  <p1> <p2> ... <pN>
stamp
stop        <slot ID>
string      load|unload
system
tarp    <sub_command> <flags>
telnet      [-d] [-e escape_char] [hostname|address [port]]
tftp        {get|put} <name|address> <vol>:<file_spec> [<vol>:<file_spec>]
type        [-x] <vol>:<filename>
unalias     {<alias name>|*}
unmount     <volume>:
unsetenv    [<variable name> ...| [-l] [-g] *]
verbose     [on | off]
xmodem      rb|sb [ylwpn] filename...
wfsnmpkey <key_string> [encryption_alg_id]
wfsnmpmode <proprietary(3) | trivial(1)>
wfsnmpseed <community> <manager> [-|<val1>] [-|<val2>] [-|<val3>]
            [-|<val4>][-|<val5>]
```

This chapter covers the majority of these commands; the preceding listing constitutes the more widely used TI commands. The BCC may be reached by using the **bcc** command (the BCC is covered later in this chapter). Many TI commands are also accessible from the BCC, and some of the TI commands not covered in this section are addressed in the discussion of the BCC.

The TI help feature may also be used to get help on a specific command. This is accomplished by using the following syntax:

```
[12:1]$ help <command>
```

This command gives helpful information regarding specific commands and their syntax.

TI commands can be repeated by entering ! at the TI prompt. This repeats the last command that was entered. The previous command can be repeated numerous times by typing ! *x*, where *x* is the number of times to repeat the command.

The **history** command may also be used to review command; enter the following command:

```
[12:1]$ history
```

This displays the last 20 commands that were entered. Commands to repeat may be selected from this list, by entering the **history** command followed by the number of the command to repeat:

```
[12:1]$ history 11
```

Previous commands may be cycled through by pressing the up arrow while logged in to the TI; this causes a history of the last commands entered to cycle past. Once the desired command appears, press ENTER to repeat the command.

> **Note**    *If a command is running and you want to abort it for any reason, press CTRL-C, which halts the last command and returns control to the TI prompt.*

If too much text is scrolling by while in the TI, the number of lines displayed at a time can be altered through use of the **more** command:

```
[12:1]$ more
  More Mode : ON
  Lines per screen: 24
[12:1]$ more on 15
  More Mode: ON
  Lines per screen: 15
```

After the specified number of lines is displayed, text stops scrolling and a prompt appears, giving you the option to scroll more of the text.

## Assigning a Password

A single password will be distributed to the Non-Volatile RAM (NVRAM) of all processor modules in the router, so even if a board is removed or replaced completely, the password information will remain intact. There are two levels of login access: User (read-only) and Manager (read-write). The password for User may be changed from the User prompt, however. Changing the Manager password requires being logged in as Manager:

```
[9:1]$ password Manager
Changing password for Manager.
New Password:
Retype new password:
Manager password changed.
```

## Setting the Date and Time

The date and time can be important to maintain on the Nortel Networks router, because the time and date are stamped on the event log entries. This can be extremely useful when troubleshooting, to determine when failures occurred and how long they may have lasted. The time in the Nortel Networks router is kept on a 24-hour clock. The offset is the difference between the current time and Greenwich Mean Time (GMT). Altering the GMT offset will change the timestamps of messages in the event log. The following commands apply:

```
[9:1]$ date
```

displays the date and time,

```
[9:1]$ date 12/25/99 08:00
```

changes the date and time to 8 A.M., 12/25/99, and

```
[9:1]$ date 12/25/99 08:00 -5
```

changes the date and time with the GMT time zone offset.

**DISPLAYING THE SOFTWARE VERSION**    The **stamp** command displays the current software version:

```
[4:1]$ stamp
Image:      rel/13.10/
Created:    Mon Nov 23 21:16:46 EST 1998
```

## Manipulating the Directory Structure

From both Site Manager and the TI, you can access flash memory cards, display their directory structure, and manipulate their files. Each flash memory card is considered its own separate volume. In the AN or ANH, this volume is always 1:, because only one storage medium is present (in AN1 units, the flash SIMM is considered volume 1). In an ASN, the volume is equivalent to the unit's assigned Slot ID. BN family routers may contain multiple flash cards, each housed within a separate FRE card. These may be displayed and accessed as separate volumes. For instance, to access the flash volume in slot 3 of a BLN, enter the following command:

```
[1:1]$ cd 3:
Mounting new volume
Device label
Directory 3:
New Present Working Directory: 3:
```

Entering the **dir** command displays the files present for the current volume:

```
[1:1]$ dir
Volume in drive 4: is
Directory of 4:
File Name            Size       Date       Day             Time
Freboot.exe          173924     01/28/99   Thurs.          14:24:19
Frediag.exe          230393     01/28/99   Thurs.          14:24:41
bn.exe               11608869   01/28/99   Thurs.          14:27:02
install.bat          147228     01/28/99   Thurs.          14:28:32
ti.cfg               134        01/28/99   Thurs.          14:28:35
config               3664       01/30/99   Sat.            09:04:20
config2              4276       01/29/99   Fri.            10:43:22
16777216 bytes - Total size
4608678    -  Available free space
4504521    -  Available contiguous space
```

In this case, the flash size is 16MB. A slight discrepancy exists between the amount of available free space and the amount of available contiguous space. A possible cause is that some configuration files or other files were deleted, and the flash was never compacted to reclaim the lost space (see the next section, "File Storage and Manipulation").

Files can be displayed by using the **dir** command, using volumes and wildcards. For instance, **dir 3:** displays the files on volume 3:. Wildcards may be used, such as **dir *.exe**, which displays all executable files on the current volume. The **?** character may also be used, such as in the case of **dir ???.cfg**, which displays all three-letter files ending in a .cfg extension.

## File Storage and Manipulation

The AN, ANH, ASN, and ARN router models each supports a single flash card, and therefore a single volume. The BLN, BLN-2, and BCN each supports one flash volume per FRE processor card. Each of these volumes can be used for storage, as well as redundancy.

The file system on the flash does not use a FAT system for file allocation. Instead, each file has a Beginning Of File (BOF) and End Of File (EOF) statement. Each EOF points to the BOF of the next file. This system has two implications:

- No way exists to recover deleted files.

- Deleting files from the flash doesn't automatically reallocate the space for storage. Since the EOF of any file points to the BOF of the next file, whatever that file may be, any noncontiguous space on the flash isn't regained merely by deleting the file (see Figure 29-1).

The old data remains on the flash (even after deletion), and the EOF of the previous file merely bypasses it and points to the BOF of the file following the deleted file. This

INTERNETWORKING WITH
NORTEL NETWORKS

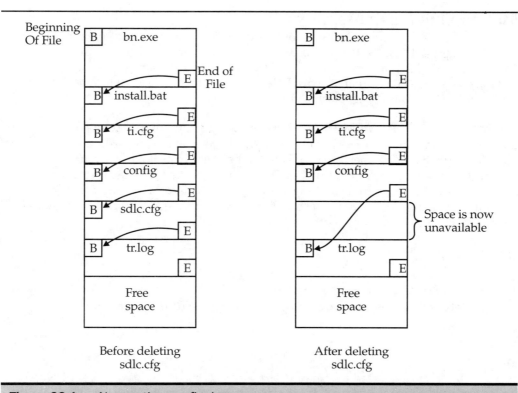

**Figure 29-1.**    *Noncontiguous flash space*

space can be recovered, however, through a process called *compacting* the flash. Compacting the flash can be accomplished with the following command:

```
[1:1]$ compact <volume>:
```

where <volume> is the flash volume number:

```
[1:1]$ compact 1:
Compacting file system on volume 1:   ...
This may take several minutes…Please wait...
100% complete
Compaction completed
```

At this point, any free space between files that was cleared with the **delete** command has been reallocated and is available for use.

## Maintaining Flash Memory

The flash card is a memory card with onboard EEPROM chips. They come in different memory sizes: 4MB, 8MB, and 16MB, and some of the very early ones came in a 2MB size. For a 4MB flash card to be supported by the router, it must be running system software version 8.00 or greater. Nortel Networks routers have been tested with IBM, Intel, and AMD series II 4MB flash cards.

**FORMATTING FLASH MEMORY**    Nortel Networks routers ship with flash memory that already contains the necessary files and system software. New flash cards purchased outside Nortel Networks need to be formatted before use, just like any other storage volume (such as a floppy or hard drive). This is accomplished with the **format** command, as shown next. Just as with formatting a floppy disk or hard drive, any files that exist on a flash card are lost when the flash is formatted. These files can't be recovered. The flash format is not compatible with PC laptop PCMCIA slots.

```
[1:1]$ format 1:
```

This formats the flash volume number 1:.

The status of the flash can be displayed by using the **dinfo** command:

```
[1:1]$ dinfo
VOL   STATE        TOTAL SIZE   FREE SPACE    CONTIG FREE SPACE
2:    FORMATTED    4194304      1020732       721721
3:    FORMATTED    4194304      3180855       3179840
```

**PARTITIONING THE FLASH**     The flash memory may also be partitioned into various, smaller volumes. Compacting the flash to regain space from deleted files is done on a partition-by-partition basis in this case. Flash memory cards must be at least 4MB in size to accept a partition, and you need system software version 8.10 or greater. Partitioning is accomplished by using the **partition** command:

```
[2:1]$ partition create 1:
```

This creates a partition on flash volume 1:. A flash partition will not exceed half the total flash space. Consult the following example:

```
[1:1]$ dinfo
VOL  STATE       TOTAL SIZE   FREE SPACE    CONTIG FREE SPACE
1:   FORMATTED   4194304      4194270       4194270
[1:1]$ partition create 1:
Partition created
[1:1]$ dinfo
VOL  STATE       TOTAL SIZE   FREE SPACE    CONTIG FREE SPACE
1a:  FORMATTED   2097152      2097118       2097118
1b:  FORMATTED   2097152      2097020       2097020
```

Flash cards may be partitioned in this manner, but the boot image and config file must reside on flash partition *a*.

## Booting from the TI

From the TI, the router may be booted and may be pointed at specific images and/or configuration files. This is accomplished by using the following syntax:

```
[1:1]$ boot <vol>:<boot image> <vol>:<config file>
```

For example, to boot from image bn.exe on volume 2:, using the configuration file sdlc.cfg on volume 3:, the following command would be issued:

```
[1:1]$ boot 2:bn.exe 3:sdlc.cfg
```

Entering a dash in place of either the image or configuration filename causes the router to boot from the default file. The default file in this case with be an.exe, asn.exe, or bn.exe for the image file, and the default configuration file config. For instance:

```
[1:1]$ boot - sdlc.cfg
```

INTERNETWORKING WITH NORTEL NETWORKS

In this example, the volume is absent, which causes the router to use the current volume. So, in this example, the router will boot from the default image on the current volume, using the configuration file sdlc.cfg, also residing on the current volume (since a different volume is not specified for the config file, either).

## Running Diagnostics

Hardware diagnostics may also be run from the TI. You can run a series of diagnostics on either the whole chassis or a subset of ILIs, using the **diags** command, which uses the following syntax:

```
diags <slot number>
```

For instance, to run diagnostics on slot 5, the following command would be issued:

```
[2:1]$ diags 3
```

Diagnostics may also be run on a series of ILIs simultaneously, using the following command structure:

```
[2:1]$ diags 3-5        To run diagnostics on ILIs 3, 4, and 5
[2:1]$ diags 3,5        To run diagnostics on ILIs 3 and 5 only
```

Running the **diags** command causes the specified slot to undergo a cold-restart. This involves the slot running CPU, backbone, and link diagnostics, as well as reloading the system image and config file.

> **Note** *Simply issuing the **diags** command without specifying a slot number causes **diags** to be run on the entire system, including a cold-restart of the entire system.*

**RESETTING THE SLOT**   Sometimes, it is necessary to reset a single slot, which is done by issuing the following command:

```
[2:1]$ reset 4
```

This example resets slot 4. A reset reloads images and configuration files, but does not perform diagnostics.

Similar to the **diags** command, the **reset** command can be used on a grouping of ILIs:

```
[2:1]$ reset 2-5  To reset slots 2 through 5
[2:1]$ reset 2,5  To reset slots 2 and 5 only
```

## Using Scripts

TI scripts can be stored on the flash memory, to be loaded for use with the TI. Script files come in many varieties, grouped by specific technologies. TI scripts are not available by default—they must be loaded to be used. To load script files, use the **run** command against the volume containing the script files:

```
[2:1]$ run setpath 4:
```

This causes the system to search for scripts on volume 4:.

Alternatively, the following command causes the system to prompt the user for the script volume:

```
[2:1]$ run 4:setpath
Mounting new volume...
Device label:
Directory 3:
NVFS File System
VOL   STATE            TOTAL SIZE     FREE SPACE     CONTIG FREE SPACE
2:    FORMATTED         4194303        1018458           205450
4:    FORMATTED         2097152         72955            41246
Please enter the volume ID that contains the script files.
More than one volume may be entered; each separated by a semicolon.
Format:      <vol>: [;<vol>:...]
Example: 2:;3:;4:
Enter volume(s) [2:]: 4:
```

Script files essentially are a series of TI commands that allow a command string to be entered, rather than polling individual MIBs, which can become quite complicated. The output of script files appears in a list format, to display statistics or configuration information, instead of being displayed as a series of MIB values. Scripts are primarily used to display information regarding protocols and their current operating state (such as to monitor IP circuits or frame relay circuits), or to enable and disable circuits, protocols, lines, and services. With new iterations of code, more scripts are being integrated into the Kernel so they can be accessed directly from the TI.

**Note**    *Scripts are widely available but rarely used, even when there is a good deal of excess flash memory. In the absence of the BCC, script files can make network troubleshooting much easier for the administrator, as well as obtaining technical support if the router needs to be accessed remotely. Script files are usually stored on a secondary flash volume.*

# The Event Log

Perhaps the single most valuable troubleshooting tool available on the Nortel Networks router platform is the event log. Events on the router are logged on each processor module and are stored on a first-in first-out (FIFO) 64K memory buffer, allowing for 4,000 entries per slot. These log events are sorted in chronological order.

Router events fall into many different categories, from normal protocol operations, to errors and faults. For this reason, the event log can, in many cases, give an indication as to what went wrong in the event of a failure. Router event logs are preserved during warm-boot, but are lost in the event of a cold-boot.

**Note**    *The log is lost when you hot-swap a module, or run **diags** on it, which causes a cold-boot.*

## Viewing the Event Log

The event log may be viewed from the TI, by using the **log** command. The following syntax is used:

```
log <switch>
```

The switch in this case may be any of the following switches or combination of switches:

- **-d<date>**   The date in *mm/dd/yy* format; displays only log entries from the specified date and time.

- **-t<time>**   The time in *hh:mm:ss* format; displays only log entries from the specified time.

- **-e<entity>**   The −e switch is followed by the entity for which you want to view logged events. The entity is always in all uppercase letters, and if a space is required, the entity must be in quotes. For instance:

```
[2:1]$ log −eATM
```

- **-f<severity>**   The severity switch is followed by a series of flags that indicate which levels of severity should be displayed from the event log. The following flags apply:
  - **f**   Fault
  - **w**   Warning
  - **i**   Informational
  - **t**   Trace
  - **d**   Debug

For instance, to poll the log for severity levels, using the informational, fault, and warning flags, the following command would apply:

```
[2:1]$ log —ffwi
```

The first **f** in the command is the **–f** switch itself, and the second **f** is the fault flag.

- **-s<slot_number>**   Allows you to poll events on a single slot only.
- **-p<rate>**   By applying this switch to the **log** command, the log will be monitored, displaying new event log messages every five seconds, by default, which can be changed by entering the rate in seconds. For instance, to poll the log every 20 seconds for ATM events of a severity level of faults, warnings, and debugs, the following command would be issued:

```
[2:1]$ log —eATM —ffwd —p20
```

- **-c<code_number>**   Allows the log to be polled for specific event codes. These codes are available in the manual *Event Messages for Nortel Networks Routers*.

The following is an example of event log output:

```
[2:1]$ log
# 1477: 01/29/1999 22:25:48.425  WARNING   SLOT 12   ATM_LE          Code:   34
LEC: LE-ARP checking timed out reverifies for LEC #20

# 1478: 01/29/1999 22:26:47.511  INFO      SLOT 12   TELNET          Code:    3
Connection Manager received connection request from 200.20.150.123,1904.

# 1479: 01/29/1999 22:26:47.515  INFO      SLOT 12   TELNET          Code:    9
Session Manager initializing.
Session Manager up for 200.20.150.123,1904 connection.

# 1480: 01/29/1999 22:26:47.621  INFO      SLOT 12   TCP             Code:    6
TCP Opened: 200.20.150.1,23 - 200.20.150.123,1904 TCB: 0x18f6b80

# 1481: 01/29/1999 22:26:50.128  INFO      SLOT 12   TI              Code:   62
User User logged in from 132.245.152.123 port 1904
```

This log output shows a stray ATM_LE (ATM LAN Emulation) warning, followed by log entries from the telnet session established with the router's TI, and then the execution of the login as User.

## Using the Event Log as a Troubleshooting Tool

If a problem exists in the network, and you suspect that it exists on the router, *save the event log*! The entries in the event log sometimes can be difficult to interpret, but even so, it may be of help if you need to contact the Technical Solutions Center. If a trouble ticket needs to be opened, the TSC likely will ask for the event log, because it can facilitate troubleshooting enormously.

By default, the event log creates a file containing the event log messages. On a BN product (BCN, BLN, or BLN-2), this is a 64K file, per slot. In the case of an AN product, a 32K file is reserved for event log messages (for the ASN, this is a 32K file per unit in the stack). Once the 64K or 32K have been filled, the log will wrap and new events will begin overwriting the old ones. This configuration can be altered so that after the allotted space is filled, the log events are written to a file saved on the local flash memory, and the 64K/32K memory begins to be filled again. Each time the allotted memory fills, a new file is written. This can be very useful if you are trying to capture event log messages related to an event that occurs only every few days or so.

**Note**    *This feature can't be configured through Site Manager; AutoSave must be enabled through the TI.*

By default, the AutoSave feature is disabled. It is enabled by setting the wfSerialPortAutoSaveNumFiles entry to a value between 1 and 99; when disabled, this entry has a value of 0, so resetting it to 0 disables AutoSave. After you enable AutoSave, it continues to save the log until the number of saved log files equals the value specified in wfSerialPortAutoSaveNumFiles.

**SAVING LOG FILES**    If the flash memory card to which the LOG files are being saved runs out of room, the router will continue to attempt to save those files, but the attempt to save will fail. At that point, you need to delete from the flash card the LOG files that you no longer need, and then reclaim the space by using the **compact** command.

The BN, AN/ANH, and ARN platforms have only one MIB instance of wfSerialPortEntry, designated as 1. The following example shows how to set up AutoSave on a BN router. The ASN platform has four instances of wfSerialPortEntry, one for each Slot ID. AutoSave can be configured on any one (but not more than one) of the wfSerialPortEntry instances corresponding to an existing ASN in the stack. So, if you have two ASNs stacked, you can configure AutoSave by issuing one of the the following commands:

```
[1:1]$ wfSerialPortEntry.33.1
```

or

```
[1:1]$ wfSerialPortEntry.33.2
```

wfSerialPortEntry.33.3 or wfSerialPortEntry.33.4 may not be used in this case, because ASN number 3 and 4 aren't there.

The order LinkNode (LN) platform also has four instances of wfSerialPortEntry, but only instance 1 corresponds to the LN router's console port. Therefore, to configure AutoSave on the LN router, you must configure the necessary MIB sets to wfSerialPortEntry.33.1 and wfSerialPortEntry.34.1.

The following are the two MIB attributes that must be set for AutoSave to be enabled:

```
wfSerialPortAutoSaveNumFiles OBJECT-TYPE
       SYNTAX    INTEGER(0..99)
       ACCESS    read-write
       STATUS    mandatory
       DESCRIPTION
             "Number of times AutoSave will save the log
         0 - disable the AutoSave log"
       DEFVAL    { 0 }
       ::= { wfSerialPortEntry 33 }

   wfSerialPortAutoSaveVolume OBJECT-TYPE
       SYNTAX    DisplayString
       ACCESS    read-write
       STATUS    mandatory
       DESCRIPTION
             "Volume, to which AutoSave will save logs
         Example:  'A:' or '2:'"
       ::= { wfSerialPortEntry 34 }
```

In the following example, a get on *wfSerialPortEntry.33.\** shows that the AutoSave feature is initially not configured on the BN router. After doing two MIB sets, AutoSave is enabled and configured to save up to 99 log files on flash volume 4.

```
[2:1]$ get wfSerialPortEntry.33.*
wfSerialPortEntry.wfSerialPortAutoSaveNumFiles.1 = 0

[2:1]$ set wfSerialPortEntry.33.1 99;commit

[2:1]$ get wfSerialPortEntry.33.*
wfSerialPortEntry.wfSerialPortAutoSaveNumFiles.1 = 10

[2:1]$ get wfSerialPortEntry.34.*
wfSerialPortEntry.wfSerialPortAutoSaveVolume.1 = (nil)

[2:1]$ set wfSerialPortEntry.34.1 "4:";commit

[2:1]$ get wfSerialPortEntry.34.*
wfSerialPortEntry.wfSerialPortAutoSaveVolume.1 = "4:"
```

**LOG FILES SAVED WITH AUTOSAVE**     The following example shows the log files created automatically by AutoSave. AutoSave uses the format of auto*x*.log when saving a log file, where *x* corresponds to the number of log files saved thus far, including the one currently being saved. In the following directory listing of flash volume 4:, the last log file created has 0 bytes, because the flash card on slot 4 ran out of room, and AutoSave was not able to write to the log file it created:

```
[2:1]$ dir
 Volume in drive 4: is
 Directory of 4:
File Name            Size      Date        Day      Time
------------------------------------------------------------
mping.bat            506    03/04/1998   Wed.     16:36:08
Nortel1.log       260616    07/02/1998   Thurs.   18:52:18
flt1019.log       233612    10/19/1998   Mon.     09:24:21
flt1031.log       260808    10/31/1998   Sat.     14:16:54
log1              260696    10/31/1998   Sat.     18:54:18
auto1.log         260772    11/02/1998   Mon.     14:21:14
auto2.log         260924    11/02/1998   Mon.     15:26:56
auto3.log         261628    11/02/1998   Mon.     15:33:16
auto4.log         260828    11/02/1998   Mon.     16:22:35
auto5.log         260612    11/02/1998   Mon.     17:56:42
   .
   .
   .
auto75.log         95932    11/02/1998   Mon.     20:38:24
auto76.log           852    11/02/1998   Mon.     20:41:08
auto77.log            16    11/02/1998   Mon.     20:41:28
auto78.log             0    11/02/1998   Mon.     20:41:59

20971520 bytes    -   Total size
       0 bytes    -   Available free space
       0 bytes    -   Contiguous free space
```

The following log entries show AutoSave attempting to save a log but finding that no room exists on the specified flash card to do so:

```
# 3032: 11/02/1998 11:20:08.937  DEBUG SLOT 4 NVFS           Code:  63
Volume 4: NVFS manager is opening file 'auto89.log' for writing

# 3049: 11/02/1998 11:20:18.953  DEBUG SLOT 4 NVFS           Code:  62
NVFS transaction timer expired, will close outstanding file

# 3050: 11/02/1998 11:20:18.960  DEBUG SLOT 4 NVFS           Code:  64
Volume 4: NVFS manager is closing file 'auto89.log'
Volume 4: Open file didn't have a directory entry???
```

## Xmodem for Out-of-Band File Transfer

The **xmodem** command is used to perform out-of-band file transfers (transfers via a dial-up session); this can be useful in the event that either all IP interfaces are down on the router or all IP paths to the router are down when the file transfer must be done remotely. This command uses the following command syntax: **xmodem [transmit/receive type] [switch] [filename]**. For example:

[12:2]$ xmodem rb –y sdlc.cfg sdlc2.cfg

is used to receive two binary files, named sdlc.cfg and sdlc2.cfg, in a YModem batch protocol transfer. This command uses the following variables.

### RECEIVE/TRANSMIT TYPE

- **rb**   Receive binary; overwrites files without prompting. By default, files are padded using CTRL-Z (0x1A) pad, making the file size a multiple of the frame size. Using the **–y** switch disables this.
- **rt**   Receive text.
- **sb**   Send binary.
- **st**   Send text.

### COMMAND SWITCHES

- **y**   Selects YModem batch protocol for sending files; if a list of files is specified, they files are sent in sequence. If receiving, and YModem batch protocol is requested by the sender, it is automatically adopted. This is the recommended mode. 0x1A padding is removed at the receiving side in this case.
- **m**   Selects Modem7 batch protocol for sending.
- **k**   Uses 1K packets on transmit.
- **c**   Selects CRC mode on receive.
- **l**   Do not write to system log.
- **w**   Wait 15 seconds prior to initiating startup handshake.
- **n**   Allows CAN-CAN aborts during midtransfer.

# The Management Information Base

Although the MIB is not recommended for major configuration changes and is primarily used for troubleshooting purposes, minor configuration changes can be made using MIB sets from the TI interface. This can be extremely useful if a Site Manager session can't be established for whatever reason, but the router is still accessible through a console, telnet, or a dial-in session.

The Nortel Networks recommendation is to use Site Manager to make configuration changes. Site Manager is programmed with the correct MIBs to set for each configuration change, as well as the sequence in which they must be executed. Site Manager also has a list of which values are valid. If configuration changes are to be made by directly altering the MIB values, the correct MIB must be changed and the proper value must be entered. Setting the wrong MIB, or setting the correct MIB with the wrong value, could potentially cause a big problem on the network. Sometimes, however, Site Manager can't be used, and under these circumstances, the MIB may need to be altered manually.

**USING MIB SETS TO CONFIGURE THE ROUTER**   All MIB sets affect only the configuration currently running in the router's memory; this means that if the router is power-cycled prior to saving the configuration changes to flash memory, those changes will be lost. If the configuration becomes corrupted after making configuration changes, power-cycling the router will cause it to boot up with the known good default config file. It is a good practice to make certain that the router will boot correctly with the new configuration, before you save it to config, by saving the changes to flash using a filename other than config, and then testing the new configuration file by executing a named boot:

```
[2:1]$ boot - newconfig.cfg
```

If the router boots, and the changes made to the configuration are working, the configuration may then be saved to the config file. Before you actually overwrite config, however, it is also a good practice to save the old config under a different filename, so it will be available in case something goes wrong. Execute this command after the configuration changes have been made:

```
[2:1]$ save config 1:newcfg.cfg
```

The following command boots from the new configuration, to make sure that the new configuration is working:

```
[2:1]$ boot - 1:newcfg.cfg
```

The following command copies the old config file to a new filename for use as a backup. If the new configuration fails for any reason, the file oldcfg.cfg can be changed back to **config**.

```
[2:1]$ copy 1:config 1:oldcfg.cfg
```

The following command saves the current configuration changes as the default config:

```
[2:1]$ save config config
```

The example assumes the flash card to which the configuration file is saved is in slot 1 of the router. If the flash card is on a different slot, substitute all instances of 1 with the correct slot number.

## Introduction to MIB

Basically, MIB is a system for storing and accessing configuration and operational information regarding network hardware, such as switches and routers. Two types of MIB exist:

- **Standard MIBs**   Specified by RFCs and implemented across many different vendors' platforms
- **Private MIBs**   Implemented only on a specific vendor's platform

The Nortel Networks routers support both types of MIBs, although this chapter discusses only the Nortel Networks router MIBs. Figure 29-2 shows where the Nortel Networks (Wellfleet) MIBs reside on the MIB tree.

The Nortel Networks router MIBs are accessed and manipulated during configuration and statistics gathering, either directly via the TI or indirectly via Site Manager or Site Manager's built-in MIB Walk utility. Using the TI commands **list**, **get**, and **set** (abbreviated to **l**, **g**, and **s**), the router administrator can list the Nortel Networks

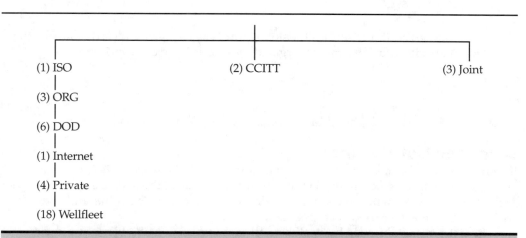

**Figure 29-2.**   *The MIB tree*

INTERNETWORKING WITH NORTEL NETWORKS

router MIBs and their associated instances, get the current values of specific MIBs, and set the values of specific MIBs. Site Manager provides a GUI to the router administrator and performs the necessary **get** and **set** commands when parameters are altered. The MIB sets that Site Manager performs on the router can be seen by viewing the router's log and looking at the SNMP entity entries. The following example shows how to do this via TI:

```
[2:1]$ log -fftwdi -eMIB
```

Each MIB follows the format *object.attribute.instance*. The MIB object describes a particular function of the router via a collection of various attributes associated with the object. An example of a MIB object is wfCSMACDEntry, which is the Nortel Networks router MIB for an Ethernet interface. Some of the attributes associated with wfCSMACDEntry are wfCSMACDState, wfCSMACDEnable, wfCSMACDFramesRxOk, and wfCSMACDFramesTxOk. Configurable attributes have read-write access, while others, such as counters or status, have read-only access. For example, wfCSMACDEnable is a configurable attribute. Conversely, the wfCSMACDState attribute is set by the router and can't be set by the router administrator.

The MIB instance specifies a particular occurrence of a MIB object. For example, there can be multiple sync interfaces on the Nortel Networks router. The MIB instance specifies which sync interface on the router is being described. The MIB instance can take many different forms, depending on the specific MIB object specified. For example, the MIB instance for wfCSMACDEntry takes the form **<slot #>.< connector #>**. So, to examine this particular MIB for slot 3, port 2, the following command is used:

```
[2:1]$ g wfCSMACDEntry.*.3.2
```

This produces all the attributes for slot 3, port 2, by using a wildcard value for the attribute. A specific attribute can be targeted by entering the appropriate value:

```
[2:1]$ g wfCSMACDEntry.3.3.1
```

which returns attribute 3 (the CSMACD state) for slot 3, port 2.

## Using the List Command

The **list** command lists all the MIB objects supported on the router if issued by itself. If a MIB object is specified with the **list** command, it lists all the MIB attributes for that MIB object. If the **–i** switch is used in addition to a MIB object, the command lists the MIB instances for the MIB object specified.

The **list** command issued by itself lists all the supported MIB objects and their location in the MIB tree, written in dotted-decimal notation. The following example represents only the first screen of output after issuing the **list** command (the rest of the output has been omitted):

```
[2:1]$ list
wfCSMACDEntry = 1.3.6.1.4.1.18.3.4.1.1
wfCSMACDAutoNegEntry = 1.3.6.1.4.1.18.3.4.16.1.1
wfFddiEntry = 1.3.6.1.4.1.18.3.4.4.1
wfFddiSmtEntry = 1.3.6.1.4.1.18.3.4.15.1.2.1
wfFddiSmtExtEntry = 1.3.6.1.4.1.18.3.4.15.1.3.1
wfFddiSmtActionEntry = 1.3.6.1.4.1.18.3.4.15.1.4.1
wfFddiMacEntry = 1.3.6.1.4.1.18.3.4.15.2.2.1
wfFddiMacExtEntry = 1.3.6.1.4.1.18.3.4.15.2.3.1
wfFddiPathEntry = 1.3.6.1.4.1.18.3.4.15.3.2.1
wfFddiPathExtEntry = 1.3.6.1.4.1.18.3.4.15.3.3.1
wfFddiPortEntry = 1.3.6.1.4.1.18.3.4.15.4.2.1
wfFddiPortExtEntry = 1.3.6.1.4.1.18.3.4.15.4.3.1
wfFddiPortActionEntry = 1.3.6.1.4.1.18.3.4.15.4.4.1
wfFddiXLineCfgEntry = 1.3.6.1.4.1.18.3.4.15.5.1.1
wfFddiXLineEntry = 1.3.6.1.4.1.18.3.4.15.5.2.1
wfFddiXSmtEntry = 1.3.6.1.4.1.18.3.4.15.5.3.1
wfFddiXMacEntry = 1.3.6.1.4.1.18.3.4.15.5.4.1
wfFddiXPortEntry = 1.3.6.1.4.1.18.3.4.15.5.5.1
wfBrTp = 1.3.6.1.4.1.18.3.5.1.1.1.1
wfBrTpFdbEntry = 1.3.6.1.4.1.18.3.5.1.1.1.2.1
wfBrTpAggrStats = 1.3.6.1.4.1.18.3.5.1.1.1.3
wfBrTpInterfaceEntry = 1.3.6.1.4.1.18.3.5.1.1.3.1
```

## DETERMINING MIB ATTRIBUTES THROUGH THE LIST COMMAND

The following example shows the output of the **list** command when used with a specific MIB object name. It is a list of all the attributes associated with the MIB object wfCSMACDEntry. The attributes can be referenced either by their ASN.1 (Abstract Syntax Notation) name or their numerical name. For example, wfCSMACDEntry. wfCSMACDEnable.* and wfCSMACDEntry.2.* both refer to the same wfCSMACDEntry attribute and produce the same output:

```
[2:1]$ l wfCSMACDEntry
wfCSMACDDelete = 1
wfCSMACDEnable = 2
wfCSMACDState = 3
wfCSMACDSlot = 4
wfCSMACDConnector = 5
wfCSMACDCct = 6
```

```
wfCSMACDBofl = 7
wfCSMACDBoflTmo = 8
wfCSMACDMtu = 9
wfCSMACDMadr = 10
wfCSMACDOctetsRxOk = 11
wfCSMACDFramesRxOk = 12
wfCSMACDOctetsTxOk = 13
wfCSMACDFramesTxOk = 14
wfCSMACDDeferredTx = 15
wfCSMACDLateCollnTx = 16
wfCSMACDExcessvCollnTx = 17
wfCSMACDBablErrorTx = 18
wfCSMACDBufErrorTx = 19
wfCSMACDLcarTx = 20
wfCSMACDUfloTx = 21
wfCSMACDFcsErrorRx = 22
wfCSMACDAlignErrorRx = 23
wfCSMACDLackRescErrorRx = 24
wfCSMACDTooLongErrcrRx = 25
wfCSMACDOfloRx = 26
wfCSMACDMerr = 27
wfCSMACDCerr = 28
wfCSMACDHardwareFilter = 29
wfCSMACDTxQueueLength = 30
wfCSMACDRxQueueLength = 31
wfCSMACDTxClipFrames = 32
wfCSMACDRxReplenMisses = 33
wfCSMACDCfgTxQueueLength = 34
wfCSMACDCfgRxQueueLength = 35
wfCSMACDAlignmentMode = 36
wfCSMACDUnAlignedFrames = 37
wfCSMACDLineNumber = 38
wfCSMACDLateCollnRx = 39
wfCSMACDModule = 40
wfCSMACDActualConnector = 41
wfCSMACDLastChange = 42
wfCSMACDOutQLen = 43
wfCSMACDIntProcessings = 44
wfCSMACDTxProcessings = 45
wfCSMACDRxProcessings = 46
wfCSMACDTxCmplProcessings = 47
wfCSMACDTxQueueReductions = 48
wfCSMACDSingleCollisionFrames = 49
```

```
wfCSMACDMultipleCollisionFrames = 50
wfCSMACDInternalMacTxErrors = 51
wfCSMACDLineCapability = 52
wfCSMACDEtherChipSet = 53
wfCSMACDRxSymbolErrors = 54
wfCSMACDInternalMacRxErrors = 55
wfCSMACDConfigurableSpeed = 56
wfCSMACDRxFlushes = 57
wfCSMACDTxDeadlocks = 58
wfCSMACDBoflRetries = 59
wfCSMACDBoflTmoDivisor = 60
wfCSMACDTurboBoflDebug = 61
```

The following command will list the current MIB instances that exist for a particular MIB object. This particular command is useful for determining which Ethernet interfaces are configured on the router and what their associated MIB instances are.

```
[2:1]$ list -i wfCSMACDEntry
inst_ids = 2.1
```

**UTILIZING MIB GETS IN THE TI**  The **get** command gets the value of a specific MIB attribute for a specified MIB instance. The wildcard asterisk (*) can be used to specify all MIB attributes or all MIB instances; however, the asterisk can appear only once in a **get** command. For example, the **get** command could be used to get the values of all the MIB attributes for a specific MIB instance (the first entry that follows) or to get the values of a specific MIB attribute for all the MIB instances (the second entry), but not both at the same time:

```
[2:1]$ get wfCSMACDEntry.2.*
```

or

```
[2:1]$ get wfCSMACDEntry.*.1.1
```

will both work; the first command provides attribute 2 for all slots and ports, while the second command provides all attributes for slot 1, port 1. The following command is an example of invalid use of the wildcard value:

```
[1:2]$ get wfCSMACDEntry.*.*
```

**USING WILDCARDS FOR MIB INSTANCES**   The following command gets the value of the specified MIB attribute for all MIB instances. This particular command is useful for determining which Ethernet interfaces are up and which are down.

```
[1:2]$ get wfCSMACDEntry.3.*
wfCSMACDEntry.wfCSMACDState.2.1 = 1
```

**USING WILDCARDS WITH MIB ATTRIBUTES**   The following command will get all the attributes and their values for a specified MIB instance. This particular command is useful for gathering information about a specific Ethernet interface, such as the number of errors received or transmitted.

```
[2:1]$ get wfCSMACDEntry.*.2.1
wfCSMACDEntry.wfCSMACDDelete.2.1 = 1
wfCSMACDEntry.wfCSMACDEnable.2.1 = 1
```

Port is enabled.

```
wfCSMACDEntry.wfCSMACDState.2.1 = 1
```

Port state is up.

```
wfCSMACDEntry.wfCSMACDSlot.2.1 = 2
wfCSMACDEntry.wfCSMACDConnector.2.1 = 1
```

Connector is slot 2, port 1.

```
wfCSMACDEntry.wfCSMACDCct.2.1 = 2
```

Circuit number is 2.

```
wfCSMACDEntry.wfCSMACDBofl.2.1 = 1
wfCSMACDEntry.wfCSMACDBoflTmo.2.1 = 5
```

Breath Of Life (BOFL) is enabled with a timeout of 5.

```
wfCSMACDEntry.wfCSMACDMtu.2.1 = 1518
```

MTU is 1518.

```
wfCSMACDEntry.wfCSMACDMadr.2.1 = x00 x00 xA2 x00 xA0 xF3
```

The interface MAC address is 00-00-A2-00-A0-F3.

```
wfCSMACDEntry.wfCSMACDOctetsRxOk.2.1 = 257829606
wfCSMACDEntry.wfCSMACDFramesRxOk.2.1 = 488253
wfCSMACDEntry.wfCSMACDOctetsTxOk.2.1 = 52983237
wfCSMACDEntry.wfCSMACDFramesTxOk.2.1 = 201909
```

Total number of both octets and frames received and transmitted on the specified Ethernet interface.

```
wfCSMACDEntry.wfCSMACDDeferredTx.2.1 = 286
```

Total number of deferred transmits (packets that could not be sent due to a collision on the Ethernet).

```
wfCSMACDEntry.wfCSMACDLateCollnTx.2.1 = 0
wfCSMACDEntry.wfCSMACDExcessvCollnTx.2.1 = 0
wfCSMACDEntry.wfCSMACDBablErrorTx.2.1 = 0
wfCSMACDEntry.wfCSMACDBufErrorTx.2.1 = 0
wfCSMACDEntry.wfCSMACDLcarTx.2.1 = 0
wfCSMACDEntry.wfCSMACDUfloTx.2.1 = 0
wfCSMACDEntry.wfCSMACDFcsErrorRx.2.1 = 0
wfCSMACDEntry.wfCSMACDAlignErrorRx.2.1 = 0
wfCSMACDEntry.wfCSMACDLackRescErrorRx.2.1 = 0
wfCSMACDEntry.wfCSMACDTooLongErrorRx.2.1 = 0
wfCSMACDEntry.wfCSMACDOfloRx.2.1 = 0
wfCSMACDEntry.wfCSMACDMerr.2.1 = 0
wfCSMACDEntry.wfCSMACDCerr.2.1 = 1
```

Ethernet errors, such as late collisions, excess collisions, frame check sequence (FCS) errors (also called cyclic redundancy check, or CRC, errors), alignment errors, and so forth.

```
wfCSMACDEntry.wfCSMACDHardwareFilter.2.1 = 2
wfCSMACDEntry.wfCSMACDTxQueueLength.2.1 = 32
wfCSMACDEntry.wfCSMACDRxQueueLength.2.1 = 32
wfCSMACDEntry.wfCSMACDTxClipFrames.2.1 = 0
```

Frames that were clipped due to congestion or lack of resources.

```
wfCSMACDEntry.wfCSMACDRxReplenMisses.2.1 = 0
wfCSMACDEntry.wfCSMACDCfgTxQueueLength.2.1 = 0
wfCSMACDEntry.wfCSMACDCfgRxQueueLength.2.1 = 0
wfCSMACDEntry.wfCSMACDAlignmentMode.2.1 = 3
wfCSMACDEntry.wfCSMACDUnAlignedFrames.2.1 = 0
wfCSMACDEntry.wfCSMACDLineNumber.2.1 = 102101
```

The CSMACD line number.

```
wfCSMACDEntry.wfCSMACDLateCollnRx.2.1 = 0
```

Number of late collisions received.

```
wfCSMACDEntry.wfCSMACDModule.2.1 = 0
wfCSMACDEntry.wfCSMACDActualConnector.2.1 = 0
wfCSMACDEntry.wfCSMACDLastChange.2.1 = 35
wfCSMACDEntry.wfCSMACDOutQLen.2.1 = 0
wfCSMACDEntry.wfCSMACDIntProcessings.2.1 = 0
wfCSMACDEntry.wfCSMACDTxProcessings.2.1 = 0
wfCSMACDEntry.wfCSMACDRxProcessings.2.1 = 0
wfCSMACDEntry.wfCSMACDTxCmplProcessings.2.1 = 0
wfCSMACDEntry.wfCSMACDTxQueueReductions.2.1 = 0
wfCSMACDEntry.wfCSMACDSingleCollisionFrames.2.1 = 0
wfCSMACDEntry.wfCSMACDMultipleCollisionFrames.2.1 = 0
wfCSMACDEntry.wfCSMACDInternalMacTxErrors.2.1 = 0
wfCSMACDEntry.wfCSMACDLineCapability.2.1 = 1
wfCSMACDEntry.wfCSMACDEtherChipSet.2.1 = 0
wfCSMACDEntry.wfCSMACDRxSymbolErrors.2.1 = 0
wfCSMACDEntry.wfCSMACDInternalMacRxErrors.2.1 = 0
wfCSMACDEntry.wfCSMACDConfigurableSpeed.2.1 = 2
wfCSMACDEntry.wfCSMACDRxFlushes.2.1 = 0
wfCSMACDEntry.wfCSMACDTxDeadlocks.2.1 = 0
wfCSMACDEntry.wfCSMACDBoflRetries.2.1 = 5
wfCSMACDEntry.wfCSMACDBoflTmoDivisor.2.1 = 1
wfCSMACDEntry.wfCSMACDTurboBoflDebug.2.1 = 0
```

**Note**  *The **set** command sets a MIB attribute with a specified value. After the **set** command is issued, the **commit** command must be issued for the MIB changes to take effect. You can issue the **commit** command separately, or append it to the **set** command, by using a semicolon after the **set** command. In the following example, both **set** commands will be committed:*

```
[2:1]$ set wfCSMACDEntry.2.1.2 2;commit
```

*Or the commands may be separated:*

```
[2:1]$ set wfCSMACDEntry.2.1.2 2
[2:1]$ commit
```

*A single commit after many sets will commit all MIB sets.*

# Setting Parameters Through the MIB

Again, Nortel Networks generally doesn't recommend that you configure the router using the MIBs. At times, however, doing so may be unavoidable, and it's good to know how to make changes through the MIB in the event that only the TI can be accessed. The following sections describe some of the procedures that may be useful to execute from the TI.

# Configuring an IP Default Route

The MIB for static routes on the Nortel Networks router is wfIpStaticRouteEntry. It is used to configure all forms of static routes, including a default route. The following are the attributes for the wfIpStaticRouteEntry MIB:

- **wfIpSrCreate**   Creates or deletes the static route entry. Setting this attribute to a value of 1 creates the static route instance. Setting it to 2 deletes the static route instance.

- **wfIpSrEnable**   Enables (activates) the static route if the value of this MIB attribute is set to 1. If it is set to 2, the static route is disabled (deactivated). The default is enabled.

- **WfIpSrIpAddress**   The destination IP network address for which the static route is being created.

- **WfIpSrIpNetMask**   The mask for the destination IP network address.

- **WfIpSrCost**   The cost associated with the static route. The higher the cost, the less desirable the route is.

- **WfIpSrNextHopAddr**   The IP address of the next-hop router.

- **WfIpSrNextHopMask**   The mask for the IP address of the next-hop router.

- **WfIpSrPreference**   The preference associated with the static route. If the router is presented with multiple routes to the same destination, it selects the route with the highest preference. Routes with a low preference are used only if no better routes are available.

- **WfIpSrIpAddressRt**   The Route Identifier assigned to the static route by the router when the static route is configured. This value is automatically set by the system and can't be changed.

- **wfIpSrValid**   A value of 1 indicates the static route is valid. A value of 2 indicates the static route is invalid and therefore not being used. An invalid route is a misconfigured route.

- **wfIpSrUnnumCct**   The circuit number associated with the unnumbered circuit.

A default route can easily be added via the MIBs. The following example adds a default static route to the 0.0.0.0 network, with a mask of 0.0.0.0 and a next hop of 10.1.5.1 with a next-hop mask of 255.255.255.0. This example assumes that no other static routes have been configured. The number following all the zeros in the MIB string (number 1 in this case) is called the *Route Identifier*. It correlates to the first static route, the second static route, the third static route, and so on. If static routes already exist, use the next available Route Identifier number. To determine what static routes exist already, issue the following MIB list string:

```
[2:1]$ list -i wfIpStaticRouteEntry
```

If the response is None, then no static routes are configured on the Nortel Networks router. If, however, multiple static routes exist, the last number in the instances (the Route Identifier) will be different. The Route Identifier starts with 1 and increments by one for each static route instance. For example, if five static routes are configured, the last static route instance listed will end in 5.

The following MIB sets may be used to add a default route when no other static routes currently are configured on the router. If additional static routes are present, consult the example immediately following this one:

```
[2:1]$ set wfIpStaticRouteEntry.1.0.0.0.0.0.0.0.0.0.1 1;commit
[2:1]$ set wfIpStaticRouteEntry.6.0.0.0.0.0.0.0.0.0.1 10.1.5.1;commit
[2:1]$ set wfIpStaticRouteEntry.7.0.0.0.0.0.0.0.0.0.1 255.255.255.0;commit
```

The following MIB sets may be used to add a default route in the presence of five additional static routes. Notice in the first set that the last digit is a 6 rather than a 1, as it was in the last example. This is to accommodate the presence of the existing routes.

```
[2:1]$ set wfIpStaticRouteEntry.1.0.0.0.0.0.0.0.0.0.6 1;commit
[2:1]$ set wfIpStaticRouteEntry.6.0.0.0.0.0.0.0.0.0.6 10.1.5.1;commit
[2:1]$ set wfIpStaticRouteEntry.7.0.0.0.0.0.0.0.0.0.6 255.255.255.0;commit
```

For Bay RS versions prior to 12.00, the subnet mask for the next hop must be set explicitly, as shown in the preceding example. However, with Bay RS 12.00 and higher, the code assumes that the next-hop mask is the same as the mask used on the local interface that connects to the same subnet as the next hop. If you try to set the next-hop mask, TI returns the following error message:

```
set: Object does not exist or is not writeable.
```

## Configuring an IP Static Route

The same procedure outlined in the preceding section relating to adding a default route is used for adding a static route through the MIBs. The only difference is that the destination IP address and destination mask will be something other than 0.0.0.0 and 0.0.0.0. The following example configures a static route to a destination network of 155.34.5.21, with a destination mask of 255.255.255.0 and a next-hop IP address of 10.1.5.1 with a next-hop mask of 255.255.255.0. This example also assumes that a default route is already configured, so the Route Identifier used is 2.

```
[2:1]$ set wfIpStaticRouteEntry.1.155.34.5.21.255.255.255.0.2 1;commit
[2:1]$ set wfIpStaticRouteEntry.6.155.34.5.21.255.255.255.0.2 10.1.5.1;commit
[2:1]$ set wfIpStaticRouteEntry.7.155.34.5.21.255.255.255.0.2 255.255.255.0;commit
```

For Bay RS versions prior to 12.00, the subnet mask for the next hop must be set explicitly, as shown in the preceding listing. However, with Bay RS 12.00 and higher, the code assumes that the next-hop mask is the same as the mask used on the local interface that connects to the same subnet as the next hop. If you try to set the next hop mask, TI returns the following error message:

```
set: Object does not exist or is not writeable.
```

## Adding an IP Address to an Existing Interface

MIBs may change over time, so the exact commands used to accomplish certain things may change from one code version to the next. For instance, the IP MIBs changed with Bay RS 12.00. So, the actual MIB sets required depend on what version of code the router is running.

### ADDING AN IP ADDRESS WITH CODE VERSION 11.03 OR LOWER   With Bay RS 11.03 and earlier, the following MIB sets will configure another IP address on a circuit with one IP address configured already. The additional IP address is 10.5.1.3, with a mask of 255.255.255.0. The circuit already has a configured IP address of 24.1.1.1, with a mask of 255.0.0.0. The number following the IP address in the following instance is the circuit number of the interface. In this case, the circuit number is 2. Having more

than one IP address configured on one interface is call *multinetting*. Multinetted IP addresses have the same circuit number.

```
[2:1]$ list -i  wfIpInterfaceEntry
inst_ids = 24.1.1.1.2
```

Once the information is obtained, perform the set:

```
[2:1]$ set wfIpInterfaceEntry.6.10.5.1.3.2 255.255.255.0;commit
[2:1]$ list -i wfIpInterfaceEntry
inst_ids = 1.1.1.1.2
         10.5.1.3.2
```

**ADDING AN IP ADDRESS WITH CODE VERSION 12.00 OR HIGHER**    With Bay RS 12.00 and higher, the same thing as previously described is accomplished with the following MIB sets:

```
[2:1]$ list -i  wfIpIntfCfgEntry
inst_ids = 1.1.1.1.2
[2:1]$ set wfIpIntfCfgEntry.6.10.5.1.3.2 255.255.255.0;commit
[2:1]$ list -i wfIpInterfaceEntry
inst_ids = 1.1.1.1.2
         10.5.1.3.2
```

## Changing an IP Address

The only way to change an IP address is to delete the IP interface and re-add it. Generally, this is done using Site Manager in Local or Remote mode, because changing an IP address can affect Site Manager's connectivity to the router. For instance, if an end station 3.3.3.2 is telnetted to the 2.2.2.2 Ethernet interface of the router. However, if the address 1.1.1.1 is to be changed, deleting it will bring down connectivity to the 2.2.2.2 interface via the WAN. End stations on the 2.0.0.0 network will still be able to access the Nortel Networks router via the 2.2.2.2 interface, though.

If changing the IP address on the Nortel Networks router must be done via the MIBs, then it must be done using a two-step process. The first step is to configure the new IP address on the desired interface while leaving the old address intact; having more than one IP address associated with an interface is called *multinetting* and is a valid configuration. After you configure the new IP address, telnet to this new IP address to make sure that it is working okay. Then, you can delete the old IP address by using the following instructions.

To delete an IP address using a code version prior to 12.00 execute the following command:

```
[2:1]$ set wfIpInterfaceEntry.1.1.1.1.1.3 2;commit
```

 *The IP address instance is in the form <IP address>.<circuit number>, which in this example is <1.1.1.1>.<3>, or 1.1.1.1.3.*

To delete an IP address using Bay RS 12.00 and higher, use the following command:

```
[2:1]$ set wfIpIntfCfgEntry.1.1.1.1.1.3 2;commit
```

## Adding an IP Adjacent Host

Certain protocols require adding an *adjacent host entry*, which is essentially a static ARP entry. For instance, PPP requires an adjacent host entry because it doesn't support ARP. An adjacent host entry also is required with group mode frame relay in a hub-and-spoke (not fully meshed) environment.

The following example adds an adjacent host entry for 10.2.0.1, with a mask of 255.255.0.0, to the router's 10.2.0.2 local interface:

```
[2:1]$ set wfIpAdjacentHostEntry.5.10.2.0.1 255.255.0.0;commit
[2:1]$ set wfIpAdjacentHostEntry.4.10.2.0.1 10.2.0.2;commit
```

In a group mode frame relay environment, the spokes need to have IP adjacent host entries for all the other spokes in the frame relay network if you want connectivity either between spoke routers or between an end station at a spoke router site and another spoke router. The configuration of the IP adjacent host is the same as in the preceding example, except the MAC address is the local data link connection identifier (DLCI) number. The local DLCI number can be seen by issuing the **show fr pvc** script command.

## Viewing the IP Host Cache (ARP Cache)

To view the entries in the IP host cache on a Nortel Networks router, enter the following TI command:

```
[2:1]$ list  -i wfIpNetToMediaEntry
```

To see the MAC address associated with a particular entry in the IP host cache, use
the **get** command on the wfIpNetToMediaEntry MIB using the associated instance. The
following is an example of viewing the IP host cache:

```
[2:1]$ list -i wfIpNetToMediaEntry
inst_ids  = 2.132.245.155.2
                  2.132.245.155.5
[2:1]$ list wfIpNetToMediaEntry
wfIpNetToMediaIfIndex = 1
wfIpNetToMediaPhysAddress = 2
wfIpNetToMediaNetAddress = 3
wfIpNetToMediaType = 4
[2:1]$ get wfIpNetToMediaEntry.2.*
wfIpNetToMediaEntry.wfIpNetToMediaPhysAddress.2.132.245.155.2 =
        x00 x00 xA2 xF6 xEB x61
wfIpNetToMediaEntry.wfIpNetToMediaPhysAddress.2.132.245.155.5 =
        x00 x00 xA2 xCB x2B xE0
[2:1]$ get wfIpNetToMediaEntry.3.*
wfIpNetToMediaEntry.wfIpNetToMediaNetAddress.2.132.245.155.2 = 132.245.155.2
wfIpNetToMediaEntry.wfIpNetToMediaNetAddress.2.132.245.155.5 = 132.245.155.5
```

Other ARP MIBs are wfArpIntfEntry and wfIpBaseHostEntry.

## Clearing the IP Host Cache (ARP Cache)

The MIB can also be used to clear the router's ARP cache. This is accomplished with a
series of MIB sets, as explained in this section.

**Note**   *The following procedure to clear the IP host cache will bounce IP on the interface. If it
is not convenient to do this, then instead of clearing the entire ARP cache, just mark
invalid the entry you want to remove; marking an entry invalid does not delete it, it just
causes the router to not use it, thus requiring the router to re-ARP to create a new entry.*

The following text is the actual MIB for the IP host cache:

```
wfIpInterfaceHostCache OBJECT-TYPE
        SYNTAX   INTEGER {
                     cacheoff(1),
                     cache120(120),
                     cache180(180),
                     cache240(240),
                     cache300(300),
                     cache600(600),
                     cache900(900),
                     cache1200(1200)
```

```
              }
ACCESS   read-write
STATUS   mandatory
DESCRIPTION
        "Whether the Host Cache (Address Aging) is on or not.
        A Range of discrete values is specified as well as a
        value meaning  don't age"
DEFVAL   { cacheoff }
::= { wfIpInterfaceEntry 15 }
```

By default, Nortel Networks routers do not age out the ARP cache. To flush the entire ARP cache, set the preceding MIB to 120 seconds, which will flush the ARP cache after two minutes. Then, after the host cache gets flushed, set the MIB back to a value of 1, which configures the router to no longer flush the ARP cache. If you want the ARP cache periodically to flush automatically, leave the MIB set to 120 seconds (or one of the other available values listed). If the network is constantly undergoing changes, with stations changing their IP addresses, you should set the wfIpInterfaceHostCache MIB value to age out. To minimize the extra traffic on the network that this will cause, set the host cache timeout timer to 1,200 seconds, which is 20 minutes.

The following is an example of how to flush the Nortel Networks router ARP cache for addresses that were resolved on interface 131.42.15.14 (circuit #3):

```
[2:1]$ list -i wfIpInterfaceEntry
131.42.15.14.3
[2:1]$ set wfIpInterfaceEntry.15.131.42.15.14.3 120;commit
```

After you enter the preceding command, wait about two minutes and then return to the previous value:

```
[2:1]$ set wfIpInterfaceEntry.15.132.245.155.3.1 1;commit
```

The following steps outline how to remove a single host cache entry without interrupting network traffic:

```
[2:1] list -i wfIpNetToMediaEntry
inst_ids  = 2.10.245.155.2
                2.10.245.155.5
                2.10.245.155.6
```

Perform the **set**:

```
[2:1]$ set wfIpNetToMediaEntry.4.2.10.245.155.6 2;commit
```

INTERNETWORKING WITH
NORTEL NETWORKS

and then verify the change:

```
NortelRouter>list -i wfIpNetToMediaEntry
inst_ids  = 2.10.245.155.2
                 2.10.245.155.5
```

After you do this, try pinging the host that was removed from the cache:

```
[2:1]$ ping 10.245.155.6
IP ping: 10.245.155.6 is alive (size = 16 bytes)
```

Now, check the host cache again; the entry should have been inserted back into the table:

```
[2:1]$ list -i wfIpNetToMediaEntry
inst_ids  = 2.10.245.155.2
                 2.10.245.155.5
                 2.10.245.155.6
```

# Verifying the Simple Network Management Protocol Configuration

One of the most common reasons that you'll need to access the TI specifically to make changes is if Site Manager can no longer initiate SNMP communication with the router, meaning that you can't make changes with Site Manager. This situation may arise due to an error in the SNMP configuration, and you may need to alter the configuration from the TI to reestablish a Site Manager session.

If Site Manager is unable to connect to the Nortel Networks router, you need to check the SNMP configuration. Perhaps the Site Manager station is using the wrong SNMP community name, or perhaps the Site Manager station is not configured as an authorized SNMP Manager on the Nortel Networks router. The wfSnmpCommEntry MIB deals with the community names configured on the Nortel Networks router and their associated access level. The wfSnmpMgrEntry MIB stores information about the SNMP Managers authorized to connect to the Nortel Networks router. The complete MIB descriptions for the Nortel Networks router SNMP MIBs can be found in the snmp.mib file located in the Site Manager/Mibs directory of the Site Manager station. The following are the MIB attributes for wfSnmpCommEntry:

- **wfSnmpCommDelete**    A value of 1 creates a community name instance; a value of 2 deletes the community name instance.

- **wfSnmpCommIndex**   An integer index assigned to the community name. Each community name is assigned a unique index, starting with an index value of 1.

- **wfSnmpCommName**   The community name string. By default, the "public" community name is the only community name configured.

- **wfSnmpCommAccess**   The access level associated with the community name. A value of 1 indicates read-only access; a value of 2 indicates read-write access.

The following are the MIB attributes for wfSnmpMgrEntry:

- **wfSnmpMgrDelete**   A value of 1 creates a SNMP Manager instance; a value of 2 deletes the community name instance.

- **wfSnmpMgrCommIndex**   The community index of the wfSnmpCommEntry MIB instance that this SNMP Manager is associated with. This determines whether the SNMP Manager has read-only access or read-write access.

- **wfSnmpMgrAddress**   The IP address of SNMP Manager.

- **wfSnmpMgrName**   An optional descriptive name assigned to the SNMP Manager. For example, if the SNMP Manager belongs to John Doe, the SNMP Manager name could be configured as "JohnDoe".

- **wfSnmpMgrTrapPort**   The UDP port number to which the Nortel Networks router will send traps. By default, the UDP port is 162. The SNMP Manager is assumed to be listening for traps on that UDP port.

- **wfSnmpMgrTraps**   The types of traps the Nortel Networks router will send to the SNMP Manager. A value of 1 = none; 2 = generic traps only; 4 = specific traps only; and 7 = all traps. The default is 2.

## Checking the SNMP Community Name Configuration

The following commands will determine which community names have read-only access and which have read-write access:

```
[2:1]$ get wfSnmpCommEntry.4.*
```

This returns the SNMP access levels for all the community names configured on the Nortel Networks router. Any values equal to 1 mean the community name has read-only access. If the value is 2, the community name has read-write access.

To determine the community name that is associated with read-write access, first get the community index number that is associated with an access level of 2. Then, use the community index in the following **get** command to get the community name string:

```
[2:1]$ get wfSnmpCommEntry.3.<community index>
```

For example, to create a new SNMP community name with read-write access, the following commands would be issued:

```
[2:1]$ set wfSnmpCommEntry.3.<an index not already used> "the new community name";commit
[2:1]$ set wfSnmpCommEntry.4.<the index used above> 2;commit
```

## Checking the SNMP Manager Configuration

The following command lists the IP addresses of all the end stations authorized to connect to the Nortel Networks router by using SNMP. Because Site Manager communicates with the Nortel Networks router by using SNMP, these are the only stations authorized to connect to the Nortel Networks router via Site Manager. By default, the Nortel Networks router creates a wfSnmpMgrEntry of 0.0.0.0. An IP address of 0.0.0.0 means "all IP addresses," and thus any end station can connect to the Nortel Networks router by using Site Manager. After the initial configuration is complete, it is a good idea, for security purposes, to specify explicitly which IP addresses have read-write access, and to give the 0.0.0.0 IP address read-only access.

```
[2:1]$ get wfSnmpMgrEntry.3.*
wfSnmpMgrEntry.wfSnmpMgrAddress.1.0.0.0.0 = 0.0.0.0
wfSnmpMgrEntry.wfSnmpMgrAddress.1.172.35.3.4 = 172.35.3.4
wfSnmpMgrEntry.wfSnmpMgrAddress.2.172.35.3.5 = 172.35.3.5
```

If Site Manager can connect to the Nortel Networks router, but can't make any changes, then Site Manager is probably connecting to the Nortel Networks router with a read-only community name. If Site Manager will not connect to the Nortel Networks router using the read-write community name, then the SNMP Manager entry on the Nortel Networks router most likely has read-only access configured, when read-write access is desired. If read-write access is desired, you need to create an SNMP Manager entry with read-write access. The wfSnmpMgrEntry MIB instance is of the format <community index number associated with either read-only or read-write access>.<IP address of the SNMP Manager>. In the following example, a community index of 1 is associated with read-only access, and a community index of 2 is associated with read-write access.

```
[2:1]$ set wfSnmpMgrEntry.1.1.172.35.3.5 2;commit
[2:1]$ set wfSnmpMgrEntry.1.2.172.35.3.5 1;commit
```

As you can see from the output of the preceding **get wfSnmpMgrEntry.3.\*** command, the 172.35.3.4 SNMP Manager is configured for read-only access, whereas the 172.35.3.5 SNMP Manager is configured for read-write access. To give the SNMP Manager entry for 172.35.3.4 read-write access, you first should delete it, and then re-create it by using the read-write community index. You could leave the read-only SNMP Manager entry and just add the read-write entry, if desired, but that would make the router configuration less understandable and more complicated to manage. If both entries do exist, the access level granted to the SNMP Manager is determined by the SNMP community name used to connect to the Nortel Networks router.

## Checking the State of SNMP

If Site Manager still can't connect to the Nortel Networks router and the SNMP community names and managers are configured properly, the problem may be related to SNMP on a global level. The SNMP object can be checked through the MIBs to make sure SNMP is working properly.

The following command checks whether SNMP is enabled or disabled. If the value returned is 1, SNMP is enabled. If the value is 2, SNMP has been administratively disabled.

```
[2:1]$ get wfSnmp.1.0
wfSnmp.wfSnmpDisable.0 = 2
[2:1]$ set wfSnmp.1.0 1;commit
[2:1]$ get wfSnmp.1.0
wfSnmp.wfSnmpDisable.0 = 1
```

## Determining Which IP Addresses Relate to Frame Relay DLCI Numbers

When you are troubleshooting a frame relay problem by using either a console, telnet, or dial-up session, it is not immediately obvious (if the scripts are not loaded) which IP address corresponds to which DLCI number. To determine this, first determine all the DLCI numbers by issuing the following command:

```
[2:1]$ list -i wfFrVCircuitEntry
```

For each DLCI, find out the associated circuit number:

```
[2:1]$ get wfFrVCircuitEntry.*.<DLCI #>
```

Next, find out all the IPs associated with the circuit numbers. The output will give the IP address and circuit number (for example, 134.141.2.3.1, where 1 equals the circuit number).

```
[2:1]$ list -i wfIpInterfaceEntry
```

Further verify by matching the IP addresses with the circuit name of the frame relay circuit:

```
[2:1]$ get wfCircuitNameEntry.3.*
```

## Checking Router Memory

If you suspect a problem related to the router running out of memory, you should query the following two MIBs:

- **wfKernelEntry**  Shows how much memory is being used, the router processes that are using memory, how much memory the processes are using, and whether any problems occurred when allocating buffers.

- **wfKernParamEntry**  Shows how much total memory a slot has, and how that memory is broken down into local and global memory. The router uses local memory to store its image and routing tables, and uses global memory to store buffers for frames.

The descriptions of both of these MIBs can be found in the GAMESTAT file in the MIBs directory of the Site Manager directory.

| | |
|---|---|
| WfKernelEntry wfKernelSlot | The router slot the processor board is installed in. For the AN, ANH, and ARN, this will be a value of 1. |
| wfKernelMemorySize | The total number of bytes of allocable memory. |
| wfKernelMemoryFree | The total number of bytes of memory that has not been allocated yet. |
| wfKernelMemorySegsTotal | The total number of kernel memory segments. |
| wfKernelMemorySegsFree | The total number of kernel memory segments that have not been allocated yet. |
| wfKernelMemoryMaxSegFree | The size of the largest kernel memory segment available. |
| wfKernelBuffersTotal | The total number of packet buffers. |
| wfKernelBuffersFree | The total number of available packet buffers. |
| wfKernelTasksTotal | The total number of tasks (router processes) currently running on the router. |
| wfKernelTasksInQueue | The total number of tasks waiting to be scheduled to run. |

```
wfKernelTimersTotal
wfKernelTimersActive
wfKernelBufOwnerTask1
```

Note that there will be a series of entries here regarding the Buffer Owner Task and Memory Owner Task for 1 through 10, ending with the following entry, and continuing as follows:

| | |
|---|---|
| `wfKernelMemOwnerTask10`<br>`wfKernelMemOwnerTask10Size`<br>`wfKernelAliasBuffsDropped` | The number of alias buffers dropped due to a lack of copy buffers. |
| `wfKernelBallocFail` | The number of times a buffer couldn't be allocated **via g_balloc**, a routine to allocate buffers to a process, because the free buffer pool was empty. Router processes need to store packets in packet buffers while they are being processed. |
| `wfKernelReplenEmpty` | The number of times the free buffer pool was emptied via **g_breplen**, a routine to allocate buffers to a link module's driver transmit queue or receive queue. For example, outgoing packets must be stored in buffers while waiting to be transmitted onto the line. Incoming packets must also be stored in packet buffers while waiting to be processed by the MAC driver. |
| `wfKernelMemoryFreeLow` | The low watermark of the number of bytes of available memory. |
| `wfKernelAliasNoMembers`<br>`wfKernParamEntry`<br>`wfKernParamSlot` | The router slot the processor board is installed in. For the AN, ANH, and ARN, this will be a value of 1. |
| `wfKernParamTotMem` | The total number of bytes of memory on the processor board. |
| `wfKernParamLocMem` | The total number of bytes of memory on the processor board that has been configured as local memory. Local memory is where the router image and routing tables are stored. |
| `wfKernParamGlobMem` | The total number of bytes of memory on the processor board that has been configured as global memory. Global memory is where the router keeps its packet buffer pools. |

# Bay Command Console

The BCC is the next generation of the TI. The BCC has integrated the concept of script files, providing a more user-friendly interface for purposes of configuration. The goal of the BCC is to allow users the same configuration flexibility from the TI as is available through Site Manager, while still retaining the ability to poll individual MIB instances for purposes of statistics checking and troubleshooting.

The BCC is not inherently present when the Bay RS is loaded; like the script files, the BCC must be loaded onto the router before it can be accessed.

The BCC is accessed from the Technician Interface by entering the **bcc** command:

```
[12:2]$bcc

     Welcome to the Bay Command Console!
     * To enter configuration mode, type config
     * To list all system commands, type ?
     * To exit the BCC, type exit

bcc>
```

The BCC has two modes: the initial BCC mode, and BCC configuration mode. Both of these BCC formats are covered in the following sections.

## BCC Configuration Mode

The BCC configuration mode is used to modify the router configuration more extensively from a console, dial-in, or telnet session than would normally be available. The BCC uses a command structure that has more in common with the Accelar CLI than with the TI, and it is accessed by using the **config** command:

```
bcc> config
Reading configuration information, please wait . . . done.
box#
```

The **box#** prompt indicates the root context level used by the BCC; like the Accelar, the BCC can be used to enter different contexts and to apply commands from a new context instead of entering the context for each command. To get a sense of how this works, examine the command list from the root context, by using the **?** command:

```
box# ?
Sub-Contexts:
   atm              fddi            ipx             serial          virtual
   backup-pool      ftp             isdn-switch     snmp
   board            hssi            mce1            telnet
   console          http            mct1            tftp
   ethernet         ip              ntp             token-ring


Parameters in Current Context:
   build-date       description     location        system-name
   build-version    has             mib-counters    type
   contact          help-file-name  on              uptime


System Commands:
   ?                     display              ping
   back                  enable               pktdump
   bccSource             exit                 pop
   bconfig               format               prom
   boot                  getcfg               pwc
   cd                    help                 readexe
   clear                 help-file-version    record
   clearlog              history              reset
   commit                ifconfig             restart
   compact               info                 rm
   config                loadmap              save
   cp                    log                  securelogin
   cwc                   logout               show
   date                  lso                  stamp
   debug                 mget                 stop
   delete                mlist                system
   diags                 more                 tic
   dinfo                 mset                 type
   dir                   partition            unmount
   disable               password             xmodem
```

As the preceding example output shows, the command list is broken into three sections:

- **Sub-Contexts**   Contexts that branch from the current context. For instance, where OSPF parameters are a branch from the IP context, OSPF would be a subcontext of IP.

- **Parameters in Current Context**   Parameters that may be used within the current context. For instance, the command to check the current IP state is **ip state**. Therefore, state is one of the parameters available in the current context if IP is the current context.

■ **System Commands**   The BCC system commands that are available from all contexts.

# The BCC Command Set

The BCC has two basic command prompts: bcc>, which is accessed upon first entering the BCC, and box#, which is accessed by entering configuration mode, where the majority of the BCC configuration is accomplished.

Many of the commands from the bcc> prompt are also accessible from the TI; those are not covered in this section, but are covered in the earlier section regarding the TI specifically.

The following is a list of the BCC commands and their basic usage (more information on most of these commands is available either earlier in this chapter or in the second half of Chapter 28):

■ **back**   While in BCC configuration mode, allows the user to collapse the command prompt to the previous level and change the current context to it:

```
box# ethernet slot 2 connector 1
ethernet/2/1# back
box#
```

Here, the command level was changed to specify Ethernet slot 2, connector 1. Entering the **back** command returned back to the root, since only one level had been descended. If the prompt has been changed multiple levels, a specified previous level can be reached by entering the number of levels after the command **back**, such as in the following example:

```
box# ip
ip# ospf
ospf# back 2
box#
```

■ **Exit**   By entering the command **exit** , the router withdraws from the BCC and returns to the TI.

■ **bconfig**   Used to set up the router's boot configuration.

■ **boot**   Used to boot the router; by using flags, **boot** can also be used to boot the router using a specified image or configuration file.

■ **cd**   Change directory; used to change the current flash volume. For example, to mount flash volume 3, enter **cd 3:**.

■ **clear**   Used to clear the IP routing table (**clear ip route**) or the IP host cache (**clear ip arp**).

■ **clearlog**   Used from the TI or bcc> prompt to clear the log information. Useful for testing purposes, for which a clean slate can make specific log entries easier to locate.

■ **commit**   Used at the TI or bcc> prompt to activate a MIB set.

■ **compact**   Used at the TI or bcc> prompt to compact a flash volume after a file has been deleted; since the GAME operating system doesn't use a DOS file format, deleting a file doesn't recover the space it occupied without first executing a flash compact to make the free space contiguous.

■ **config**   Opens the BCC configuration mode if the user has initially logged in to the router as Manager. Configuration mode may not be entered if you are logged in as User. After the user enters configuration mode, the command prompt changes to the root prompt:

```
box#
```

■ **cp**   Used to copy the contents of one file into another. For example, to copy the contents of a file called sdlc.cfg in flash volume 2: to a file called sdlc2.cfg on flash volume 5:, the following command would be used:

```
bcc> cp 2:sdlc.cfg 5:sdlc2.cfg
```

**Note**   *From the TI, this command uses the syntax* **copy**, *rather than cp.*

■ **cwc**   Change working context. Used to change context within the command tree.

■ **date**   Used to set the date and time of the router.

■ **delete**   Used to delete files. This does not automatically recover the flash space; you first must use the **compact** command to make the flash space contiguous.

■ **diags**   Used to run diagnostics on the router hardware.

■ **dinfo**   Directory information; used to gather information about the flash volume. By default, this is the currently mounted volume, although another volume may be specified. This gives information regarding the flash, such as total space, used space, and free contiguous space.

■ **dir**   Used to display the contents of the current directory (mounted flash volume).

■ **disable**   Used from the BCC's configuration mode.

■ **display**   Used from the BCC configuration mode.

■ **enable**   Used from the BCC's configuration mode to counteract the **disable** command.

■ **exit**   Used to exit the BCC.

■ **format**   Used to format a router flash volume.

- **getcfg**   Used to display the current boot configuration of the router.
- **help**   Used to obtain help for a variety of TI and BCC commands, using the following syntax:

```
bcc> help ifconfig
```

- **help-file-version**   Used to display the current version of the BCC help file:

```
bcc> help-file-version
Help file 2:bcc.help, contains this version data:
  Data version is:     2.
  Creation date is:    1998 Dec 02  6:42:50 hrs.
```

- **history**   Used to obtain a list of the last series of commands entered at the router's command prompt.
- **ifconfig**   Used to configure initial IP information on an interface.
- **info**   Used in BCC configuration mode. Displays basic system information.
- **loadmap**   Used to display the load addresses and file sizes of each dynamically loaded application.
- **log**   Used to view the router event log entries.
- **logout**   Used to log off the router, terminating the TI session.
- **lso**   List object; used while in BCC configuration mode.
- **mbulk**   Gives a bulk column MIB get for a specified MIB object, attribute and instance. For example; *mbulk wfHwEntry.2*.
- **mdump**   Displays every individual MIB set used in the current running configuration.
- **mget**   Used to issue a MIB get, using the following command syntax: **mget {<obj_name> | <obj_id>} . {<attr_name> | <attr_id> | * } [ . {<inst_id> | *}]**. This is very similar to issuing a MIB get from the TI interface, using the **get** command.
- **mlist**   MIB list; used to list a series of MIB attributes associated with a specific MIB object, using the following command syntax: **mlist [instances | -i [<obj_name>]]**. This is similar to issuing the **list** command from the TI.
- **more**   Used to indicate whether the user will be prompted before scrolling information, and to define how many lines of text will be displayed before prompting.
- **mset**   MIB set; used to set individual MIB values, using the following command syntax:

**mset <obj_name> | <obj_id>}.{<attr_name> | <attr_id>}.<inst_id> <value>**
This is similar to setting a MIB value from the TI by using the **set** command.

■ **partition**   Used to divide a flash volume logically into multiple volumes.

■ **password**   Used to alter the password associated with Manager privileged mode.

■ **ping**   Can be issued from the BCC in the following formats, by utilizing the following flags:

```
bcc> ping -IP <IP Address>
```

The preceding pings a specific IP address. You may use the following flags:

■ **-p**   Path report; displays the hops taken by the ping packet

■ **-s**   The size of the ping packet

■ **-a**   The source address

■ **-v**   Displays ping statistics associated with Echo Request/Reply

```
bcc> ping -IPV6
```

The preceding pings using an ICMPv6 Echo Request. This command may use the same flags as the **–IP** switch, as well as the following:

■ **-iifindex**   Signifies the outgoing interface for the ICMPv6 Echo Request.

```
bcc> ping -IPX
```

The preceding issues an IPX ping, using the following formats:

```
bcc> ping -IPX 0xnnnnnnnn.0xhhhhhhhhhhhh           (hex)
bcc> ping -IPX nnn.nnn.nnn.nnn.hhh.hhh.hhh.hhh.hhh.hhh (decimal)
```

where *n* equals the network portion of the address and *h* equals the host portion of the address.

```
bcc> ping -OSI
```

The preceding issues an OSI Echo Request/Echo Reply handshake with the specified Network Service Access Point (NSAP) address.

```
bcc> ping -VINES
```

The preceding issues a VINES ping, using the following command format:

```
bcc> ping -VINES nnnnnnnnnn.sssss
bcc> ping -AT
```

which uses the AppleTalk Echo Protocol to issue an Echo Request to the address configured in the format network.nodeID.

```
bcc> ping -APPN
```

The preceding -APPN option executes the APING TP, which sends an Echo message to the APINGD TP running on the CP (or LU) specified.

- **pktdump**   Used to display packets captured during a packet capture (PCAP), using the following command syntax: **pktdump  <linenumber> [-s<start>] [-c<count>]**. The switches have the following meanings:
    - **s**   Indicates the first packet in the interface capture buffer to receive. If this switch is omitted, the first packet in the buffer is selected.
    - **c**   Indicates how many packets to display. If omitted, all packets are displayed.
- **pop**   Causes the BCC to jump back one context. For example, if the working context is ip/arp, entering the pop command will fall back to the ip context.
- **prom**   Used for updating the router PROMs.
- **pwc**   Print working context; used in BCC configuration mode to indicate the current command positioning in relation to the root context. For example, in the following listing

```
bcc> config
Reading configuration information, please wait . . . done.
box# ip
ip# ospf
ospf# pwc
box; ip; ospf;
ospf#
```

the BCC configuration mode is accessed, and then the IP and OSPF contexts are accessed. The **pwc** command is used to show the user where exactly the command line rests in relation to the root (box#). In this case, **box; ip; ospf**.

- **readexe**   Used to verify executable files such as image files that are located on the router's flash.

- **record**   Used to record all messages set by the user terminal to a file. This file must first be opened, and then must be closed after the recording is complete:

```
bcc>record open test.txt
bcc>record close
```

The recording can also be paused during the procedure and then resumed, by using the following commands, respectively:

```
bcc>record pause on
bcc>record pause off
```

The current recording status can be viewed by issuing the following command

```
bcc>record pause
```

which indicates whether the current recording is paused. Only one recording file may be open at any one time.

- **reset**   Used to reset a specific slot, or to reset the entire router, using the following command syntax: **reset [slot ID]**. If the Slot ID is absent, the entire router is reset. This causes the GAME image to be reloaded.

- **restart**   Used to restart a specific slot or to restart the entire router, using the following command syntax: **restart [slot ID]**. If the Slot ID is absent, the entire router is restarted. This command restarts the GAME image, but does not reload it.

- **rm**   Used from the BCC to remove a file from the flash volume. For instance:

```
bcc> rm 2:sdlc.cfg
bcc> rm 2:sdlc.cfg 5:sdlc2
```

- **save**   Saves the current configuration information using the specified filename.
- **securelogin**   Used to toggle secureid on and off for TI telnet sessions. A console session is required to execute this command successfully.
- **show**   Used to display certain router information, such as the state of IP circuits, frame relay PVCs, and so on.
- **stamp**   Used to display the current router system image version:

```
bcc> stamp

Image:      rev/13.01/B
Created:    Fri Dec 4 21:53:43 EST 1998
```

- **stop**   Used to halt a slot where the router uses the ACE hardware system, so that the unit may be hot-swapped. This command is not used with the newer FRE, FRE2, and ARE modules.
- **system**   Begins a new TI session, which is useful for changing the privileged mode (for example, from User to Manager) during a TI session without having to log off first.
- **telnet**   Used to initiate a telnet session from the router. For this to occur, the router must first be configured as a telnet client, if it is not already. This can be accomplished through Site Manager, the procedure for which is explained earlier in this chapter.
- **tic**   Allows the use of any TI command from the BCC. The syntax is *tic <TI command>*.
- **tftp**   Used to execute TFTP gets and puts from the BCC command prompt, or from the TI by using the following command syntax: **tftp {get | put} <address> <vol>:<file_spec> [<vol>:<file_spec>]**. This command can be used to transfer image files, configuration files, or other system files such as log files or script files.
- **type**   Prints a file in text format to the user terminal. The syntax for this command is **type [-x] <volume>:<filename>**. For example:

```
bcc>type 2:install.bat

File: 2:install.bat

######################################################################
#
#   Installation Script.
#   Copyright Bay Networks Communications Inc. 1993, 1994
```

```
#
#                    INITIALIZATION
#########################################################################
#
on error :EXIT:
more off

# Alias Definitions
alias menuprompt   "setenv menuprompt %1 "
alias menurange    "setenv menulo %1 ; setenv menuhi %2 ; setenv menudef %3; "
alias callmenu     "setenv menudisplay %1 ;  setenv menutype %2 ;  setenv menuarg
 %3 ; gosub :MENU_DRIVER: "
#                              chan          type                        slot
      mod        conn
alias set_linenum "let linenum = 00 + ((\$circuit_type/10)*100000) + (\$slot * 1
000) + (\$mod*100) + \$port"
alias set_linkmod  "setenv LOADATTR %1 ; setenv LOADOBJ wfLinkModules ; gosub :
SLOT_MASK:"
alias set_driver   "setenv LOADATTR %1 ; setenv LOADOBJ wfDrivers      ; gosub :
SLOT_MASK:"
alias set_protocol "setenv LOADATTR %1 ; setenv LOADOBJ wfProtocols    ; gosub :
SLOT_MASK:"

alias echoline     "echo \"-----------------------------------------------------
-----------------------\""

# Initialize defaults
.
.
```

The remainder of the output has been omitted, because the contents of the install.bat file are quite extensive. The **–x** switch is used to display the file in hexadecimal format, which is used to view binary files.

- ■ **unmount**   Used to unmount the currently mounted flash volume.
- ■ **xmodem**   Used to perform out-of-band file transfers.

For more details regarding the BCC, consult the .PDF document using BCC.pdf, located in the Release Notes/Router directory on the CD.

# The Complete Reference

# Chapter 30

## Basic IP Configuration on the Nortel Networks Router Platform

1001

The Internet Protocol (IP) is the most common third-layer protocol in use today. The purpose of this chapter is to give some basic IP information that will be useful in configuring IP networks: basic IP concepts, IP addressing considerations, subnet masking, as well as global and interface IP parameters.

# IP Overview

The IP protocol is a Layer 3 protocol that, when coupled with TCP (a Layer 4 protocol), provides reliable data stream connections for Internet and LAN communications. The IP protocol is described in RFC 791, while the broadcast mechanisms of IP are examined in RFC 919. IP uses the following features:

- **Layer 3 addressing**   IP uses a 32-bit logical Layer 3 addressing scheme, in a dotted-decimal format. These addresses are used to determine the Layer 3 routed path through the IP network.

- **Time to Live (TTL)**   To prevent a scenario in which an IP packet is caught in a network loop and traverses the network endlessly, a maximum TTL value is given to the packet; this value decrements by one each time the packet traverses a router. When the TTL reaches 0, the packet is discarded.

- **IP fragmentation**   If an incoming IP datagram is too large for the network that it must traverse (such as a large token ring or FDDI frame being routed onto an Ethernet network), IP datagrams may be fragmented into smaller pieces, to be reassembled by the recipient.

- **Type of Service (TOS)**   IP allows a Type of Service implementation, providing traffic prioritization and Quality of Service (QoS) attributes.

- **Options**   Options for an IP packet are contained within the IP header. Options may include such things as Internet time stamps, trace routing (tracing the route that an IP packet takes through the network), and security implementations.

## IP Frame Format

IP utilizes an IP header of 20 bytes or so (the actual size of the header may vary depending on which options are being used), containing information about the IP packet itself; for instance, the IP version, the length of the IP packet, and the TTL. The IP header consists of the following fields:

- **Version**   Refers to the actual format of the IP header, for instance, version 4 for IPv4.

- **Internet Header Length**   Indicates the length of the IP header in 32-bit format.

- **Type Of Service (TOS)**   Exists to provide a certain packet prioritization, allowing for a QoS to be implemented.

■ **Total Length** Indicates the total length of the IP datagram, including the IP header.

■ **ID** Assigned by the sender of the datagram and used at the receiving device for purposes of aiding in packet reassembly after IP fragmentation has occurred.

■ **Flags** Indicate whether a frame is fragmented. If fragmenting is permitted, the flags may also show whether any more fragments are coming (is this the last fragment?).

■ **Fragment Offset** Indicates a fragment's position in the original datagram.

■ **Time to Live (TTL)** Indicates the maximum number of router hops the packet may traverse before being discarded. The TTL value is decremented by one each time the datagram traverses a router.

■ **Protocol** Used to identify the upper-layer protocol (TCP, UDP, OSPF, and so on).

■ **Header Checksum** Runs a cyclic redundancy check (CRC) on the IP header only.

■ **Source IP Address** Indicates the source IP address in 32-bit format.

■ **Destination IP Address** Indicates the destination IP address in 32-bit format.

■ **Options** Used to indicate such things as security, tracing IP routes throughout the network, and Internet time stamps.

**IP HEADER AS SHOWN IN A SNIFFER TRACE** The following is an example of what the IP header may look like when captured in a sniffer trace:

```
IP: ------ IP Header ------
IP: Version = 4, header length = 20 bytes
IP: Type of service = C0
IP: 110. ....   = internetwork control
IP: ...0 ....   = normal delay
IP: .... 0...   = normal throughput
IP: .... .0..   = normal reliability
IP: Total length = 68 bytes
IP: Identification = 572
IP: Flags = 0X
IP: .0.. .... = may fragment
IP: ..0. .... = last fragment
IP: Fragment offset = 0 bytes
IP: Time to live = 1 seconds/hops
IP: Protocol = 89 (OSPF)
IP: Header checksum = 3834 (correct)
IP: Source address = [180.108.72.1]
IP: Destination address = [224.0.0.4]
IP: No options
```

Notice that the Protocol field identifies the packet as an Open Shortest Path First (OSPF) packet; the IP destination address is, in this case, a multicast group address aimed at all Shortest Path First (SPF) routers.

# The Transmission Control Protocol

In and of itself, IP does not provide reliable data delivery; IP datagrams can be discarded without any requirements for informing the sender or receiver, and are transmitted without any actual guarantee that they will arrive at their destination. Many applications require a reliable transport, however, and this reliability is accomplished at the transport layer (Layer 4 of the OSI model). Thus, the Internet Protocol and the Transmission Control Protocol (TCP) are layered in the protocol stack. TCP is a connection-oriented protocol and provides reliability in an IP network.

TCP (RFC 793) is a full-duplex protocol. Except during connection setup or negotiation, where certain packets may require acknowledgements before the process can continue, full-duplex operation is very often, if not most often, used by TCP. Such connections include a variety of TCP attributes:

- **Sequencing**   The concept of using sequence numbers helps ensure reliable connections. TCP uses a 32-bit sequence number that indicates the beginning of each packet transmitted. These sequence numbers are randomly generated by each end during session establishment, and each end of a session increments its sequence number by the number of bytes in each packet it sends. These sequence numbers differ between TCP peers, and each peer is responsible for maintaining its own sequence number as well as that of the peer, so that both TCP peers are able to determine that each packet was received.

- **Flow control**   Each TCP peer contains a buffer for incoming datagrams. To prevent these buffers from overflowing, resulting in data loss, a window size is set in each packet transmitted. This window size lets the remote TCP peer know how much space is left in the sender's buffer. If a packet is received with a window size indicating 0, then the receiving peer will wait before sending any more data, until it receives an indication that buffer space has been freed (it receives a packet with a window size of a non-0 value).

- **Streaming**   TCP uses the concepts of sessions or streaming, whereby communication between two devices appears conceptually as a stream of data, and not as individual datagrams.

- **Network adaptation**   TCP is able to dynamically determine the existing network delay times and account for these delays when transmitting and receiving. This is done by calculating a *round-trip Time (RTT)* and basing acknowledgement expectations on that calculation. This can prevent unnecessary retransmissions in a TCP/IP network, and adds robustness to the protocol.

# IP Addressing

IP addresses use a 32-bit, dotted-decimal format. To identify subnetwork and host portions of a given IP address, each address is also accompanied by a subnet mask (also in 32-bit dotted-decimal format). An IP address is a logical network layer address, which maps to a device's Layer 2 hardware address, and is used for purposes of managing traffic through the IP network.

## IP Network Classes

IP addresses are configured in a dotted-decimal format consisting of 4 octets ($x.x.x.x$). Of these 4 octets, a certain range of bits is used to identify the network number itself, which identifies the IP network, and the host field, which identifies specific hosts on the IP network.

The number of octets used for the network portion of the address will vary depending on the IP network number being used. IP network addresses are broken down into several logical groupings, known as *classes*. Each class of network uses a different number of octets for the network portion of the address range; since the network portion of an IP address remains static, the fewer octets used for the network portion of the address, the more flexibility exists for configuring greater numbers of subnets and host addresses. The three address classes used in private and public networks are known as Class A, Class B, and Class C networks, and each uses a different number of octets to define the network number:

| Network Class | Network Number (N) and Host Portion (H) |
|---|---|
| Class A | N.H.H.H |
| Class B | N.N.H.H |
| Class C | N.N.N.H |

As this list outlines, a Class A address provides a great deal of flexibility, because only the first octet defines the network number, whereas a Class C address provides only a single octet for defining hosts. The breakdown of IP network address classes is determined by examining the first 3 bits of the first octet (see Figure 30-1). If the first bit is set to 0, the address is considered a Class A address. If the first bit is set to 1 and the second bit is set to 0, the address is considered a Class B address. If the first two bits are set to 1 and the third bit is set to 0, then the address is considered a Class C address.

This scheme results in the following address ranges for each address class:

- **Class A addresses**    Utilize the first octet for the network portion, with the first bit set to 0. This results in a first octet of 1 to 126, inclusive, with 24 bits used for the host field. A first octet of 0 and a first octet of 127 have been reserved. A total of 126 Class A addresses exist, each capable of providing up to 16,777,214 host addresses.

- **Class B addresses**    Utilize the first 2 octets for the network portion, with the first bit of the first octet set to 1, and the second set to 0. This results in a first octet of 128 to 191, inclusive, with 16 bits used for the host field. A total of 16,384 Class B addresses exist, each capable of providing up to 65,534 host addresses.

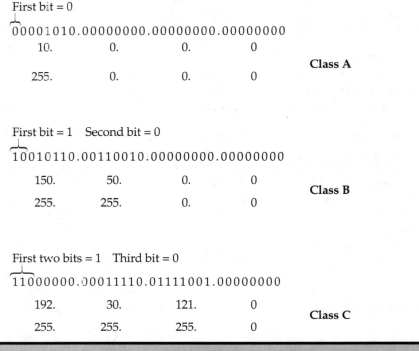

**Figure 30-1.**    *IP address classes*

■ **Class C addresses**    Utilize the first 3 octets for the network portion, with the first 2 bits of the first octet set to 1, and the third bit set to 0. This results in a first octet of 192 to 224, inclusive, with 8 bits used for the host field. A total of 2,097,152 Class C addresses exist, each capable of providing up to 254 host addresses.

In addition to the Class A, B, and C networks commonly used in public and private networks are the following two additional IP address classes:

■ **Class D addresses**    Used for multicast purposes; the first 3 bits of the first octet are set to 1, while the fourth is set to 0. The first octet is between 224 and 239, inclusive, while the remaining bits are used to specify multicast group addresses. Some examples of these multicast group addresses are as follows:

| Address | Residents |
|---------|-----------|
| 224.0.0.0 | Base multicast address (reserved) |
| 224.0.0.1 | All systems on subnet |
| 224.0.0.2 | All routers on subnet |
| 224.0.0.4 | Distance Vector Multicast Routing Protocol (DVMRP) routers |
| 224.0.0.5 | All SPF routers |
| 224.0.0.6 | All OSPF designated routers |
| 224.0.0.7 | ST (Internet Stream Protocol) routers (RFC 1190) |
| 224.0.0.8 | ST hosts (RFC 1190) |
| 224.0.0.9 | All Routing Information Protocol (RIP) version 2 routers |
| 224.0.0.10 | Interior Gateway Routing Protocol (IGRP) routers |
| 224.0.0.11 | Mobile agents |

■ **Class E addresses**   Set the first 4 bits of the first octet to 1, allowing for a first octet between 240 and 254, inclusive. This address range is currently reserved for future use.

## IP Subnetting

Because only three address classes are available for private use, the concept of using these address classes—which were essentially designed for small, medium, and large networks—quickly proved to be not flexible enough for practical networks. Consider that a single Class A address provides for over one million hosts; if multiple Class A addresses were used, then hundreds of thousands of host addresses would be wasted. To make network addresses more flexible, the idea of *subnetting* was introduced.

Class A, B, and C addresses each utilizes a *subnet mask,* which defines which portion of the host address is to be used for the subnetwork, and which for the hosts. By default, the subnet mask of an IP address covers only the portion of the address that is defined as the network number. This is called a *natural mask.* The natural masks are listed here:

| Address Class | IP Address | Natural Subnet Mask |
|---------------|------------|---------------------|
| Class A | 10.0.0.0 | 255.0.0.0 |
| Class B | 160.60.0.0 | 255.255.0.0 |
| Class C | 200.142.42.0 | 255.255.255.0 |

As the preceding examples show, the natural mask for each address class indicates where the network portion of the address ends and where the host portion begins. For purposes of defining the network only, and not individual hosts on the network, the host portion of each network is given a value of 0.

The network number is determined by masking the subnet mask against the IP address, performing a *logical AND,* whereby the mask is placed against the IP address, using the following rules:

- A value of 1 placed against a value of 1 results in a 1
- A value of 1 placed against a value of 0 results in a 0
- A value of 0 placed against a value of 1 results in a 0
- A value of 0 placed against a value of 0 results in a 0

By using this scheme, the subnet mask, when placed against an IP address, will result in a specific subnetwork number:

```
                 219              41              30              6

219.41.30.6:  1 1 0 1 1 0 1 1 . 0 0 1 0 1 0 0 1 . 0 0 0 1 1 1 1 0 . 0 0 0 0 0 1 1 0

255.255.255.0:  1 1 1 1 1 1 1 1 . 1 1 1 1 1 1 1 1 . 1 1 1 1 1 1 1 1 . 0 0 0 0 0 0 0 0

                 219         .      41        .      30        .      0
```

In this example, the IP address 219.41.30.6, using a subnet mask of 255.255.255.0, results in a network number of 219.41.30.0; the IP address in this case thus describes host number 6 on the 219.41.30.0 network.

Subnetting involves extending the existing subnet mask beyond the range of bits that are used to define the network portion of an address. For instance, the natural mask for a Class B address is 255.255.0.0, indicating that the first 2 octets are considered to be the network portion of the address. If, for instance, that mask is extended to 255.255.255.0, this indicates that a portion of the host bits (the third octet of the IP address) is to be used as part of the network address, and will not be used to describe hosts on the network. This extended portion of the network address is referred to as the *subnet:*

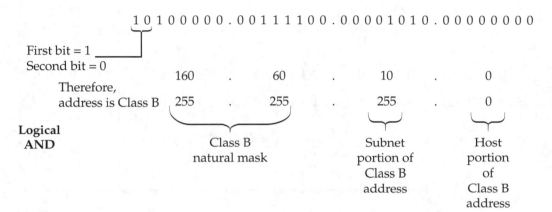

This concept allows a single IP network number (160.60.10.0 in this example) to be logically divided into a series of subnetworks. In the example of Class B address 160.60.10.0 being configured with a subnet mask of 255.255.255.0, the 160.60.0.0 network can be broken up into 254 different subnets, each with up to 254 hosts. Neither a subnet nor a host value of 255 can be used in this case; this results in a binary value of all 1's, which indicates a broadcast in IP networks.

## Complex Subnet Masking

Complex subnet masking involves extending a subnet mask only a portion of the available bits, and not the full octet. This is most commonly done when a Class C network number is being used, because only 1 octet is available as host bits, which means that an entire octet is not available for extending the network portion of the address. For instance, the Class C network 210.102.62.0 provides up to 254 hosts only; the subnet mask can't be extended an entire octet, because that would cover the entire host field, leaving no bits available to define actual host addresses.

To get around this, the subnet mask can be extended only a portion of the octet. Consider the following example, in which the address 210.102.62.0 is given a subnet mask of 255.255.255.224:

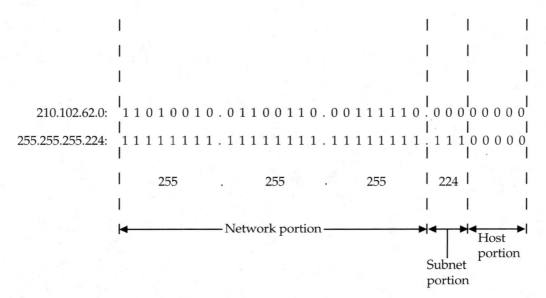

The last octet in this case has been split, whereby the first 3 bits have been masked to extend the network portion; the 8 bits that make up a single octet have the values 128, 64, 32, 16, 8, 4, 2, and 1 associated with them, moving from left to right (bits 128, 64, and 32 added together yields the value 224, accounting for the subnet mask of 255.255.255.224), while the remaining 5 bits can be used to define specific hosts on the individual subnets.

Complex subnet masking requires care and attention to detail; when either using a natural mask or extending the mask a full octet, the network portion, subnetwork portion, and host portion of an address are clearly defined. When performing complex subnet masking, the subnetwork and host portions of the address are combined. In addition, you must make sure that the individual bit ranges are not assigned a value of all 1's, because this would constitute an IP broadcast and is not an assignable address.

Consider again the preceding example of Class C address 210.102.62.0 with a subnet mask of 255.255.255.224; since 3 bits are available for assigning subnets, six different subnets can be defined (see Figure 30-2).

The available 3 bits (128, 64, and 32) yield subnets .128, .64, .32, .192, .96, and .160. A seventh subnet can be gained, as well, by enabling 0-value subnets via Site Manager and then also using subnet .0. However, not every router vendor supports this; thus, you must determine whether all routers in the network are capable of recognizing a .0 subnet, and if 0-value subnets are supported, you must ensure that the feature has been configured, if need be. A subnet of .224 is not valid in this case, because it would mean flipping all 3 bits in the subnet field, which indicates a broadcast address.

Using this scheme, the subnetwork and host values are combined in the last octet. For instance, using the same 210.102.62.0 address with the same 255.255.255.224 mask, host number 6 in the .192 subnet would appear as 210.102.62.198:

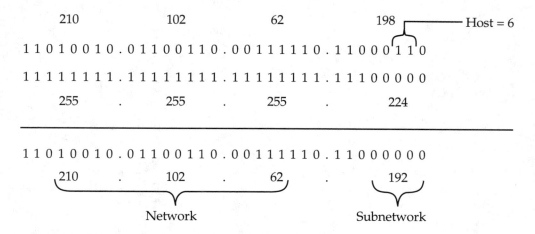

## Variable-Length Subnet Masking

Variable-length subnet masking (VLSM) refers to applying subnet masks of varying lengths to the same network number within the same physical network. For example, configuring two router IP interfaces with the same network number, but subnetting them differently (see Figure 30-3).

In this example, a router is configured with an IP address of 150.102.34.1, with a subnet mask of 255.255.255.0 on its Ethernet interface. The other interface on the same router, however, is a point-to-point WAN connection. Since only two hosts can exist on a point-to-point link (one for each router interface), using a mask of 255.255.255.0 and subnetting the third octet would waste 252 host addresses. To get around this, the point-to-point link is configured with the same network number, but a different subnet mask: IP address 150.102.34.253, with a subnet mask of 255.255.255.252. Masking the address in this way creates a subnet with only two hosts (only 2 bits are left unmasked, so only two hosts are available; a host of 0 indicates a network, not a host, and both bits can't be flipped, because this would constitute a broadcast for that subnet).

This is one of the more frequent applications of VLSM, but not all routing protocols support VLSM, most notably RIPv1.

# The Address Resolution Protocol

The Address Resolution Protocol (ARP) is used by IP devices to resolve which hardware address is associated with each IP address. For any device to transmit to a

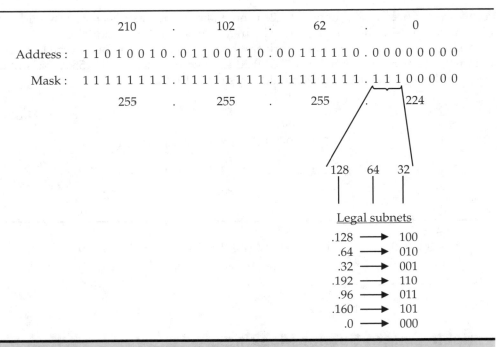

**Figure 30-2.**   *The six legal subnets, showing 0 as a possible seventh with a 3-bit mask*

destination IP address, the hardware address is required. An IP address is a unique, third-layer designation for each IP device, but ultimately it is used as a means of routing traffic throughout the IP network, and is not enough to allow communication between devices.

If an IP station needs to communicate with another IP device, it needs to know both the IP address and the MAC address of the destination. In many cases, the IP address may be known or already configured within the application being used. Alternatively, a Domain Name System (DNS) may resolve a name to the correct IP address, allowing the user to obtain the IP address of the destination server or device without needing to know it specifically. However the IP address is obtained, once it is acquired, the MAC address associated with it must be determined. This is accomplished by using ARP.

ARP utilizes a frame called an *ARP Request*, which is addressed to the destination IP address at the network layer, but uses an all-F's broadcast address as the destination

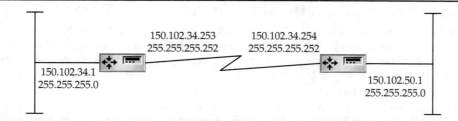

**Figure 30-3.** *A router configured with variable-length subnet masking*

at the MAC layer. This ensures that the frame will be received by each station within the broadcast domain. Each receiving station then checks whether the destination IP address in the frame matches its own (see Figure 30-4).

If a device receives an ARP Request with a destination IP address that matches its own, the device responds with an ARP Reply. The ARP Reply is directed specifically to the sender, whose IP and MAC addresses are both included in the ARP Request. The ARP Reply contains the destination device's MAC address, so that once the ARP Reply is received by the sender, transmission can begin in the form of a unicast directly to the destination.

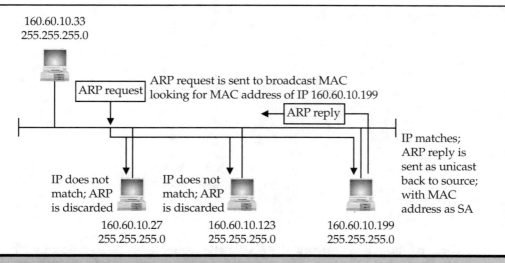

**Figure 30-4.** *ARP Request and ARP Reply*

## ARP and Destinations Outside the Broadcast Domain

Because an ARP is directed to a specific IP address, but uses an all-F's broadcast at the MAC layer, ARPs require special handing in a routed network. For example, the all-F's broadcast ensures that all devices *within* the broadcast domain receive the ARP Request, but devices that exist on separate networks or subnetworks behind a router can't be discovered by using ARP directly.

An ARP is used only on the destination network or subnetwork to resolve the specific destination. Thus, a station that must reach another station or server on a remote IP network or subnetwork will not ARP for the destination device's MAC address directly. Instead, it issues an ARP to its default gateway (if the default gateway does not already exist in its ARP cache). After the MAC address of the gateway is determined, the station then sends its data to the destination IP, using the default gateway's MAC address as the destination MAC. The router, upon receiving the data, checks the destination IP address to see what the actual destination IP is. If that IP network or subnetwork is associated with one of its interfaces, it issues an ARP for the destination IP address, and then sends the data, using its own MAC address as the source MAC and the destination device's MAC as the destination MAC (see Figure 30-5).

The router ARP cache can be viewed, to check for particular IP-to-MAC bindings that can be present. On the Nortel Networks router, this can be accomplished from the Technician Interface (TI) by issuing the **show ip arp** command:

```
[12:2]$show ip arp
   IP Address        Type       Physical Address
   ---------------   --------   --------------------
   132.245.135.1     Dynamic    00-00-A2-00-F7-FB-
   132.245.135.2     Dynamic    00-00-A2-C6-90-A2-
   132.245.135.3     Dynamic    00-00-A2-08-4A-DE-
   132.245.135.4     Dynamic    00-00-A2-0C-61-46-
   132.245.135.9     Dynamic    00-00-A2-0C-61-3A-
   132.245.135.10    Dynamic    00-00-A2-C6-99-E1-
   132.245.135.12    Dynamic    00-00-A2-0C-61-3E-
   132.245.135.33    Dynamic    00-00-A2-6D-B7-89-
   132.245.135.34    Dynamic    08-00-20-9A-58-CB-
   132.245.135.35    Dynamic    08-00-20-9A-AA-22-
Dynamic   00-00-A2-86-F3-B0-
```

In an active production network, the ARP cache would likely be significantly larger than what is displayed here, but this is the general format you would expect to see; particular entries can be sought out from the list as part of the troubleshooting process, if the situation so requires.

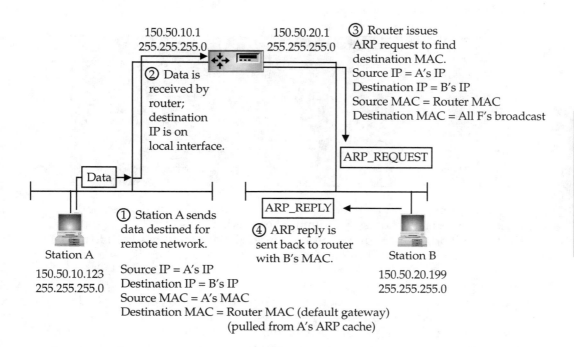

150.50.10.1
255.255.255.0

150.50.20.1
255.255.255.0

③ Router issues
ARP request to find
destination MAC.
Source IP = A's IP
Destination IP = B's IP
Source MAC = Router MAC
Destination MAC = All F's broadcast

② Data is
received by
router;
destination
IP is on
local interface.

ARP_REQUEST

Data

ARP_REPLY

① Station A sends
data destined for
remote network.

④ ARP reply is
sent back to router
with B's MAC.

Station A

150.50.10.123
255.255.255.0

Source IP = A's IP
Destination IP = B's IP
Source MAC = A's MAC
Destination MAC = Router MAC (default gateway)
(pulled from A's ARP cache)

Station B

150.50.20.199
255.255.255.0

INTERNETWORKING WITH
NORTEL NETWORKS

**Figure 30-5.**    *IP traffic being sent to a remote IP network*

# Configuring the Internet Protocol

Configuring IP on the Nortel Networks router platform is accomplished by selecting
the protocol for the given interface and then, if required, fine-tuning the IP parameters
on both a global and interface level.

## IP Configuration Basics

Regardless of which type of interface is being configured on the router, at some time,
Configuration Manager (see Appendix A) will open the Select Protocols window and

prompt you to select the protocols that you want the interface to run. If you select IP, a window labeled IP Configuration will open:

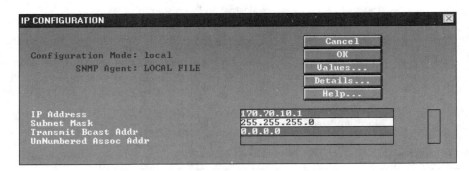

Here, you are prompted for an IP address, subnet mask, broadcast address, and unnumbered associated address, if IP unnumbered is being used.

The transmit broadcast address must be specified; by default, this is set to 0.0.0.0, which indicates that the host portion of whatever IP address and mask were configured will be set to all 1's. So, in the case of the address 110.32.1.1/24, the broadcast address would be 110.32.1.255.

IP Unnumbered is sometimes used on the Point-to-Point Protocol (PPP) and other point-to-point connections, to avoid having to use an IP address (and potentially an entire subnet) for a connection that has only two hosts. IP Unnumbered associates the point-to-point interface with another, existing IP address on another interface on the router. This can include a circuitless IP address, covered later in this chapter.

Clicking the Details button opens an interface-specific IP configuration window; the parameters found in this window are also accessible from the main Configuration Manager window by selecting Protocols | IP | Interfaces. These parameters are covered later in this chapter, in the section "IP Interface Configuration." Once the initial IP information is configured, click Done to close the IP Configuration window.

# Global IP Configuration

By selecting the IP protocol in the Select Protocols window, IP is automatically enabled both globally and on the interface being configured. When IP is selected as a protocol, it is loaded and will run with a series of default global parameters. You may need to alter these parameters, depending on the design of the network.

## Accessing and Altering Global IP Parameters

After you select IP as a protocol for at least one interface, the global IP parameters are accessible from the main Configuration Manager window by selecting Protocols | IP | Global. This opens the main Edit IP Global Parameters window:

```
Edit IP Global Parameters                                               [X]

                                                    ┌─────────────────┐
    Configuration Mode: local                       │     Cancel      │
            SNMP Agent: LOCAL FILE                   ├─────────────────┤
                                                     │       OK        │
                                                     ├─────────────────┤
                                                     │    Values...    │
                                                     ├─────────────────┤
                                                     │    Help...      │
                                                     └─────────────────┘

    Enable                      ENABLE                                  ▲
    Forwarding                  FORWARDING
    Arp Forwarding              FORWARDING
    Nonlocal ARP Source         DROP
    Nonlocal ARP Destination    DROP
    Default TTL                 30
    RIP Diameter                15
    Routing MIB Tables          ROUTE
    Zero Subnet Enable          DISABLE
    Estimated Networks          0                                       ▼
```

From this window, you can alter IP parameters that relate to all IP interfaces. Values that are changed in this window will apply to all configured IP interfaces and any IP interfaces that may be added in the future. A list of these parameters, as well as their meanings and possible contexts, are as follows:

- **Forwarding**   Allows the forwarding of all IP packets, which means that any IP packets not destined for that interface specifically (such as an OSPF interface receiving an OSPF Hello packet addressed to the OSPF group address 224.0.0.5) will be routed to the proper destination. If this option is disabled, the interface processes IP packets for which it is the destination, but does not forward any other IP packets. This can be useful for setting up a management station that does not require access to the rest of the network.

- **ARP Forwarding**   Should be set to the same value as the Forwarding parameter. A state of Enabled actually indicates that IP *is* forwarding, and that an incoming ARP, if not destined for the router specifically, will be dropped. A state of Disabled actually means the ARP will be processed if it is destined for the router interface, and will be forwarded across the other IP interfaces on the router.

- **Nonlocal ARP Source**   An ARP originating from an invalid source will be dropped; this parameter can be set either to Drop, in which case the packet is simply dropped, or to Drop and Log, in which case the source address of the invalid ARP will be logged.

- **Nonlocal ARP Destination**   Defines whether an incoming ARP with a source and destination address on different networks will be dropped or forwarded to the destination network.

**Note**   *If the Nonlocal ARP Destination parameter is set to Accept, the IP Interface parameter Proxy must be set to Enable if you want the router to send an ARP Reply in place of the actual destination (proxy ARP).*

- **Default TTL** Indicates the default TTL that will be assigned to all IP packets originating from the router. This value decrements by one each time the packet traverses another router, and will discarded when this value reaches zero.

- **RIP Diameter** Defines which metric denotes infinity within the RIP network; by default, this value is 15, meaning that this is the maximum hop count permitted, with a metric of 16 indicating infinity. If this value is altered in a RIP environment, all routers within the RIP domain must be identically configured.

- **Routing MIB Tables** No longer in common use; it specifies which MIB statistics to store regarding the routing table: the routing table, the forwarding table, neither, or both. This does not refer to the actual routing and forwarding table, only MIB statistics related to them. The Routing option does not support VLSM, but is MIB II-compliant, while the Forwarding option does support VLSM, but is not MIB II-compliant. If no VLSM is being used, select Routing; if VLSM is being used, select Forwarding. If both need to be monitored, select both, but be aware that this requires a greater amount of memory. This parameter is not supported in any Bay RS version greater than 7.70.

- **Zero Subnet Enable** By default, a subnet value of zero is invalid. This can be changed by setting this parameter to Enable; however, this can potentially cause problems on the network if some devices interpret the Zero Subnet field as a broadcast address.

- **Estimated Networks** Gives the option to preallocate memory for the routing table, instead of having the memory allocation occur dynamically. This can improve performance, but you must take care in configuring to avoid allocating either not enough memory or too much memory. By default, enough memory is allocated to allow for 500 (40,000, if ISP mode is being used) routing table entries, and anything beyond that must be dynamically allocated. The number configured should indicate the total number of networks that will be used, including subnets. The range is from 0 to 2,147,483,647.

- **Estimated Hosts** Used in conjunction with the Estimated Networks parameter, this parameter defines the estimated number of hosts. The default and range values are the same as the previous parameter.

- **Enable Default Routes for Subnets** Defines whether a default route will be used if the destination network or subnet is unknown. If this parameter is enabled, the default route must actually be present in the routing table.

- **Maximum Policy Rules** Indicates the maximum number of IP policy filters that can be applied on the router. By default, this value is set to 32; if more than 32 Accept and Announce policies combined need to be configured, this value needs to be increased.

- **Route Filter Support** Indicates whether IP route filters will be supported.

- **RIP Maximum Equal Cost Paths**   If the Multiple Next Hop Calculation Method is set to utilize a specific multipath method, then this parameter will define how many equal-cost multipaths are considered. The default is 1, with a range between 1 and 12, inclusive.

- **Multiple Next Hop Calculation Method**   Indicates whether equal-cost multipath will be used. By default, this feature is disabled. If enabled, an IP multipath method must be selected from the following options:

  **Round Robin**   Involves sending traffic evenly across each of the paths, each in turn. The distribution in this case is on a packet-by-packet basis, even if those packets are from the same source and are going to the same destination. This allows for a very even spread of traffic and an efficient use of bandwidth, but it introduces the possibility of packets arriving out of order.

  **Source/Destination Hash**   Chooses a path based on the source and destination address, keeping the path used constant for different address pairings once a path has been selected for that transmission. This is one of the more widely used methods. It not only provides a good balance over the multiple paths, but also keeps packet flow between a particular source and destination constant, because the path will not change after it has been selected.

  **Destination Hash**   Chooses an equal-cost path based on the destination address. This method, while preventing out-of-order delivery, requires some design considerations to prevent any one line from being overtaxed.

- **Enable ISP Mode Support**   Setting to Enable configures the router for ISP mode, allowing BGP to function as soloist, and disabling use of the forwarding tables on all IP interfaces.

- **IP OSPF Maximum Path**   If the Multiple Next Hop Calculation Method (previously described) is set to utilize a specific multipath method, then this parameter defines how many equal-cost multipaths can be considered within the OSPF domain. The default value is 1, with a range of 1 through 12, inclusive.

- **Percentage of ARP Buffer**   Describes the percentage of buffers used by ARP while resolving ARP Requests. The default is 100, indicating the full amount can be used.

# IP Interface Configuration

In addition to making global IP changes, specific parameters can be altered at the interface level. IP interfaces may vary dramatically from interface to interface, depending on the interface type. For example, an Ethernet interface, Frame Relay interface, and SMDS interface each has different considerations. An Ethernet IP interface may be configured to use standard ARP for its address resolution method, while a Frame Relay interface may be configured to use inverse ARP. A Switched Multimegabit Data Service (SMDS) interface requires an E.164 group address to be configured in its MAC Address field, while an Ethernet interface may have the MAC Address field left blank. As a result, you must take care to ensure that the individual IP interfaces are configured correctly.

## IP Interface Parameters

The IP interface parameters can be accessed from Configuration Manager, by selecting Protocols | IP | Interfaces. This opens the main IP Interface List window:

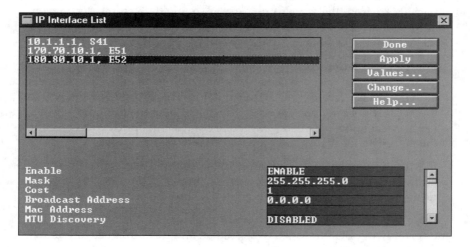

This window provides a list of all IP interfaces in the box located in the upper-left corner of the window. A list of IP parameters is also available from this window. The IP parameters include all IP parameters for all types of IP interfaces, so not every parameter listed is relevant to every type of interface; some options will not be available if the parameter is not relevant to the interface type. To select a specific interface, highlight the IP interface in the list of existing interfaces, and then manipulate the parameters located in the lower-right corner of the window. The following is a list of these parameters and when they are used:

- **Mask**   Indicates the 32-bit subnet mask that is associated with the interfaces being configured.

- **Cost**   Defines the RIP cost associated with the interface; by default, this cost is set to 1. This value can be changed, but you must make sure that the maximum RIP diameter (configured under IP Global Parameters) is not exceeded anywhere in the network as a result of increasing the cost.

- **Broadcast Address**   Specifies the broadcast address used by the IP interface; by default, this value is configured as 0.0.0.0, which causes the router to take the host portion of the address and set all host bits to 1. For example, a broadcast from an interface with an IP address of 150.50.10.0 with a mask of 255.255.255.0, using the default broadcast address, would be transmitted as 150.50.10.255—all hosts on the 150.50.10.0 subnetwork.

- **MAC Address**   Enables a user-defined MAC address to be configured. This is the MAC address that will be associated with the interface's IP address. If the circuit is an SMDS circuit, the E.164 address is entered here (for example, C19782412020FFFF).

- **MTU Discovery**   Allows the IP interface to send MTU Replies in response to MTU Probes (RFC 1063); this function allows the minimum MTU size for each transit network through which an IP packet must pass to be determined by the source, to prevent IP fragmentation.

- **AMR**   Allows the IP interface to issue ICMP Address-Mask-Replies in response to Address-Mask-Request messages (RFC 950 and RFC 1009)

- **ASB**   Indicates whether All Subnets Broadcast messages will be flooded on the interface; an All Subnets Broadcast is a message formatted as a broadcast for an entire network number, including any subnets. For example, an interface with IP address 150.50.10.0/24 would consider 150.50.255.255 (or, alternately, 150.50.0.0) to be an ASB.

- **Address Resolution Type**   Depending on the interface type, different forms of address resolution can be used. The following are the available options:

  **ARP**   The Address Resolution Protocol, where a broadcast ARP Request is used to determine the MAC address associated with a specific IP address.

  **INARP**   Inverse ARP, which is used on Frame Relay circuits as a means of minimizing traffic. In an Inverse ARP environment, a Frame Relay circuit issues an Inverse ARP for each newly advertised data link connection identifier (DLCI) number that it receives, to obtain the IP address of the remote interface. Once this is done, the Inverse ARP entries do not age out unless the circuit goes down, obviating the need to send multiple Inverse ARP Requests.

  **ARPINARP**   Enables both ARP and Inverse ARP.

  **X.25 DDN**   Enables ARP function for X.25 defense data network connection.

  **X.25 PDN**   Enables ARP function for X.25 public data network connection.

  **X.25 BFE DDN**   Enables ARP function for X.25 Blacker Front End defense data network connection.

**PROBE**   Enables HP Probe on Ethernet interfaces.

**ARPPROBE**   Enables both ARP and HP Probe on the interface.

**ATMARP**   Used in Classical IP (CLIP) environments to resolve IP-to-ATM address bindings.

- **Proxy**   Defines whether the IP interface will respond to ARPs destined for a remote network (proxy ARP). If this parameter is set to enable, ARP must be the selected ARP method for the interface, as well.

- **Host Cache**   Defines how long an ARP entry will remain in the host cache without being refreshed before it ages out of the cache and must be relearned; by default, this parameter is set to Off, indicating the host cache entries do not age out. This parameter may be set to Off, 120, 180, 240, 300, 600, 900, or 1200. The numeric values in this case are the number of seconds an entry can remain idle before being aged out of the cache.

- **Udp Xsum On**   Enables or disables User Datagram Protocol (UDP) checksum on the IP interface.

- **TR End Station**   Enables or disables token ring source-route bridging (SRB) end station support. For more information regarding token ring and source route bridging, consult Chapter 25.

- **SMDS Group Address**   Available only if an SMDS circuit is being configured; provides a MAC-layer multicast address for the IP interface. The E.164 address given by the SMDS provider should be entered here (for example, E12032270080FFFF).

- **SMDS ARP Request Address**   Available only if an SMDS circuit is being configured; provides an ARP Request multicast address for the IP interface. The E.164 address given by the SMDS provider should be entered here (for example, E12032270223FFFF).

- **FRB Broadcast**   Used for Frame Relay circuits only; the frame relay broadcast address supplied by the Frame Relay provider should be entered here.

- **FRM Cast 1 DLCI**   Used in a Frame Relay network where OSPF is being used as the routing protocol, providing a multicast address for all OSPF routers. The address should be filled in per the Frame Relay subscription agreement.

- **FRM Cast 2 DLCI**   Used in a Frame Relay network where OSPF is being used as the routing protocol, providing a multicast address for all OSPF designated routers (DRs). This address should be filled in per the Frame Relay subscription agreement.

- **Redirect**   Enables and disables ICMP redirects; enabled by default.

- **Ethernet Arp Encaps**   Observed only if the IP interface is also an Ethernet interface. The Ethernet encapsulation type for ARP may be set to Ethernet, SNAP, or both.

- **Slot Mask**   Used for determining which slots are capable of supporting circuitless IP; by default, all slots are enabled, signified by a series of 1's equaling the total number of router slots. For instance, a backbone link node (BLN), by default, would have a slot mask of 11111. Setting any slot to 0 disables circuitless IP support for that slot.

- **Enable Security**   Must be set to Enable if IP security is selected as a protocol, and security will be used on the interface. This activates the optional IP security parameters. The next 17 IP interface parameters—Strip Security, Require Out Security, Require In Security, Minimum Level, Maximum Level, Must Out Authority, May Out Authority, Must In Authority, May In Authority, Implicit Label, Implicit Authority, Implicit Level, Default Label, Default Authority, Default Level, Error Label, and Error Authority—are related to IP security and are not covered in this book.

- **Forward Cache Size**   Indicates the total number of entries that can exist in the IP forwarding table. By default, this value is set to 128, but can be configured between 64 and 2,147,483,647, inclusive. When an IP interface receives an IP datagram, it checks the forwarding table to see whether the destination is already in its cache; if it is, the datagram may be forwarded without having to do a route lookup. This can increase performance, but increasing the cache size also means increasing the amount of memory allotted to the forwarding cache, so creating a cache that is too large may drain too many resources, depending on the total amount of available memory.

- **Unnumbered Associated Address**   If IP Unnumbered is being used, lists the IP address of the interface with which the unnumbered interface is associated.

- **Unnumbered Associated Alternate**   If an alternate IP address is being used for an IP unnumbered interface, lists the alternate address if the interface associated with the primary IP fails.

- **ATM ARP Mode**   Relates to Classical IP (CLIP) and indicates whether the ATM interface will be acting as an ATMARP client or as an ATMARP server.

- **ARP Server ATM Address Net Prefix**   Each CLIP network requires an ATMARP server; if the interface being configured is the ATMARP server, the 13-byte NSAP prefix of the interface can be entered here. If the ATMARP server is remote, enter the 13-byte NSAP prefix of the ATMARP server.

- **ARP Server ATM Address User Part**   Each CLIP network requires an ATMARP server; the End System Identifier (ESI) and selector byte of the ATMARP server are configured in this field.

- **Registration Refresh Interval**    Indicates the amount of time between ATMARP registration refreshes; this is dependent on whether the interface being configured is acting as an ATMARP client or as an ATMARP server. For ATMARP clients, this value should be set to 900. ATMARP server interfaces should be configured for 1,200 (seconds).

- **SSCS Type Field**    For use with an IBM ATMARP server, this parameter may need to be enabled; by default, it is set to 0, thus disabling it. Configuring the hex value to 0x00200000 enables the feature.

- **TR End Station ARP Type**    Determines the type of Explorer packets used to determine the source-routed path to a destination. By default, set to Spanning Tree Explorer (STE); the interface may alternately be set to All Routes Explorer (ARE).

# Circuitless IP

A circuitless IP address exists on the Nortel Networks router, but is not associated with any particular interface. This feature can be useful for creating an IP address used to manage the router, providing an IP address that can be reached even if one or more of the physical interfaces or circuits goes down (provided at least one is still active). A circuitless IP address can also be useful for use with an IP Unnumbered circuit, providing a unique IP for the unnumbered interface that is not associated with any other IP interface.

## Creating a Circuitless IP

Creating a circuitless IP is accomplished through Configuration Manager, by selecting Protocols | IP | Circuitless IP. If no circuitless IP exists currently, the option Create will be present. Selecting this option opens the IP Configuration window, in which the circuitless IP address is configured via the following parameters:

- **IP Address**    The 32-bit dotted-decimal IP address the circuitless IP will use.

- **Subnet Mask**    The subnet mask associated with the circuitless IP address.

- **Slot Mask**    Defines which slot or slots the circuitless IP can run on; at least one slot must be selected or else the circuitless IP will not be able to initialize. If multiple slots are selected, another valid slot may take over the circuitless IP if the slot currently running it fails. System Resource Modules (SRMs) are not eligible to run circuitless IP. Configure the mask so that slots that can run circuitless IP are set to 1, and those that cannot are set to 0. The leftmost value indicates slot 1.

## Selecting a Protocol

Once the IP address, subnet mask, and slot mask are configured, click OK and the Select Protocols window will appear:

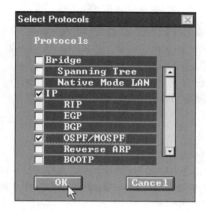

This window provides a subset of options available in the Select Protocols window that is associated with selecting protocols for a particular interface. Here, the options are IP, BGP, OSPF/MOSPF, and BootP. IP is selected by default for obvious reasons; the other protocols can be added in accordance with the network environment in use.

# IP Unnumbered

In addition to using VLSM to limit the number of wasted host addresses when configuring a point-to-point link, IP unnumbered is another technique to prevent utilizing an entire subnetwork to support the two hosts involved in a wide-area PPP connection.

Instead of giving a connection its own IP address, IP unnumbered associates the interface with another IP address already in existence on the router. This can be any valid IP address configured on any router interface.

To configure IP unnumbered, select IP as one of the protocols in the Select Protocols window when prompted during the initial interface configuration. Once this is done, click OK and the IP Configuration window will appear, prompting you for an IP address, subnet mask, broadcast address, and an option for an Unnumbered Associated Address, which is grayed out by default. To access the Unnumbered Associated Address field, enter an IP address of 0.0.0.0 in the IP Address field and then click OK. This causes the Unnumbered Associated Address field to become active, with a default IP address of

0.0.0.0; this is accompanied by a warning box stating that the Associated Unnumbered Interface can't be "0.0.0.0". Click OK to acknowledge the warning, and then enter the IP address of one of the existing interfaces or the circuitless IP address.

# Configuring IP Traffic Filters

IP traffic filters can be very useful in an IP network, particularly when two geographically distant sites are connected via a WAN. The administrator may want to either prevent certain traffic from crossing the WAN, or allow only certain traffic to pass, and drop everything else. Traffic filters can also be used to filter out unwanted protocols or IP address ranges from the local LAN.

## IP Traffic Filter Basics

Before you can add an IP traffic filter, you must create a template and then apply that template to the interface on which you want to implement the filter. A single interface can support multiple filter templates.

To add a traffic filter, you first have to create the templates. To do this, you must select the appropriate circuit, because the filter will be associated with a specific circuit, and is not a global parameter. After you select the Traffic Filters option from the main Configuration Manager window by selecting Protocols | IP | Traffic Filters, a window displaying the filters appears, but you aren't given any opportunity to alter or add to the existing filters.

To access the traffic filter template, click the interface on which you want to configure the filter (for example, XCVR1). This opens the Edit Connector window, if you've already configured the initial interface (if not, you are prompted to select a protocol for the interface, and then prompted to select the initial protocol parameters). From the Edit Connector window, select Edit Circuit, which opens the Circuit Definition window. Select Protocols | Edit IP | Traffic Filters, which opens the IP Filters window:

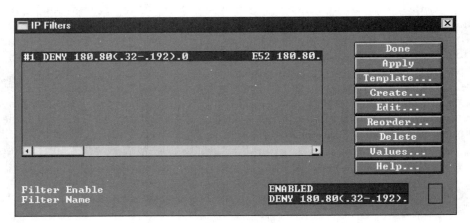

By default, no traffic filters are configured, so none are listed in this window. Several options are available to the right, including Template, Create, Edit, and Reorder. To create the first filter template, select Template.

## Creating a Template

Clicking the Template button from the IP Filters window opens the Filter Template Management window, in which new filter templates can be created, and existing templates can be edited or deleted. Since this is the first template and no others currently exist, click Create to open the Create IP Template window:

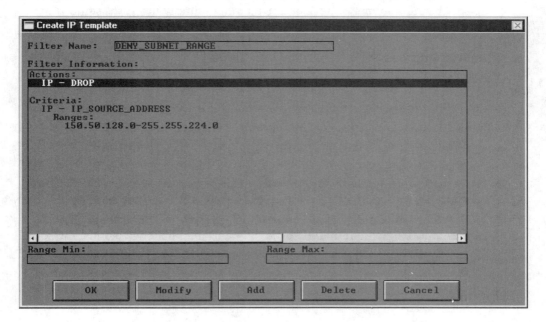

You create and configure the IP traffic filter template in this window. The template is blank, by default, so you need to define the parameters associated with it. These parameters include the Criteria, Range, Action, IP Destinations, and IP Interfaces. Each of these categories contains its own set of parameters that must be configured, and each is discussed in the following sections. Assign a name to the traffic filter template in the Filter Name field (this is an arbitrary string of characters, used to keep the filters unique from a management standpoint) and then begin filling in the template variables.

### Filter Criteria

The criteria are the set of attributes that IP traffic will be matched against. If the criteria are met, then the IP packet is considered a match by the traffic filter, and the appropriate action is taken. If the criteria are not met, then the packet will be compared against any other filters that are in place, and then finally forwarded without any action if no match is established.

New criteria are set by selecting Criteria | Add, which opens the following set of options:

- **Type of Service**   Allows the user to select a specified TOS as a match condition.
- **IP Source Address**   The IP source addresses that will be considered a match by the template; you will be prompted to add a range of IP addresses, although a range is not necessary. Source IP addresses can be checked on a specific host IP, a single subnet, a single network, or a range of any of these entities. To specify a single subnet or host, and not a range, simply insert the same value for both the Minimum Value and Maximum Value, as in this example:

| IP Source Address Type | Minimum Value | Maximum Value |
| --- | --- | --- |
| Host 150.50.10.1 | 150.50.10.1 | 150.50.10.1 |
| All hosts on .10 subnet | 150.50.10.0 | 150.50.10.0 |
| Subnets .128, .64, .192 | 150.50.64.0 | 150.50.192.0 |
| All subnets | 150.50.0.0 | 150.50.0.0 |

- **IP Destination Address**   Behaves in the same manner as the Source IP Address criteria, only the Destination IP Address is matched against, not the source.
- **UDP Frame (source/destination port)**   Selecting this option causes UDP frames to be singled out by the traffic filter and then matched against the source and destination UDP ports that you define. Some of the UDP ports in use today are listed here:

| UDP Port | Used By |
| --- | --- |
| 53 | Domain Name System |
| 67 | BootP Server |
| 68 | BootP Client |
| 69 | Trivial File Transfer Protocol |
| 137 | NetBIOS Name Service |
| 138 | NetBIOS Datagram Service |
| 139 | NetBIOS Session Service |
| 161 | Simple Network Management Protocol |
| 206 | AppleTalk Zone Information |
| 666 | Doom (ID Software) |

- **TCP Frame (source/destination port)**   Selecting this option causes TCP frames to be singled out by the traffic filter and then matched against the source and/or destination TCP ports that you define. A list of some of the TCP ports in use today appears in Table 30-1.

- **TCP or UDP Frame (source/destination)**   As some of the preceding tables indicate, certain port numbers are shared by both UDP and TCP packets; selecting this option prevents the need to create two separate criteria for each packet type in this event.

- **Established TCP**   Allows a TCP session that originated on the local side of the filter to be accepted when incoming from the destination, even though such sessions may not be permitted to originate from the destination. For example, a traffic filter configured on a router acting as the Internet gateway may be configured not to accept incoming traffic from unknown sources. However, if a telnet session were initiated from an internal address to an Internet address, the TCP session coming back from the remote device to the sender who initiated the telnet session should be accepted, whereas a telnet session actually initiated from the remote device should not be accepted.

| TCP Port | Used By |
|----------|---------|
| 20  | File Transfer Protocol (data) |
| 21  | File Transfer Protocol (control) |
| 23  | Telnet |
| 25  | Simple Mail Transfer Protocol |
| 53  | Domain Name System |
| 80  | Hypertext Transfer Protocol |
| 107 | Rtelnet |
| 137 | NetBIOS Name Service |
| 138 | NetBIOS Datagram Service |
| 139 | NetBIOS Session Service |
| 206 | AppleTalk Zone Information |
| 666 | Doom (Id Software) |

**Table 30-1.**    *Commonly Used TCP Ports*

- **User-Defined**  A user-defined criteria can be very useful; one particular instance of this that may come up in a Bay Networks environment is a user-defined criteria configured to match LattisSpan PDUs (refer to Chapter 7). By configuring the multicast group addresses used by the LattisSpan protocol (01-00-81-00-02-00 and 01-00-81-00-02-01), and then setting the action to Drop (explained shortly), LattisSpan PDUs can be prevented from passing between switch communities. This only needs to be done if bridging services are configured on the router; otherwise, LattisSpan PDUs will not pass through the router.

Configuring a user-defined criteria involves first selecting whether the match is based on the beginning of the IP header or the end of the header, and then selecting an offset to instruct how far into the packet to look, and a length that defines how far past the offset to look. After you define these parameters, the actual value to check for can be listed in the Minimum Value and Maximum Value fields.

## Range

If a criteria needs to be defined, whereby a range of values may be matched instead of a single, exact (for example, with a range of networks rather than a single, specific network), then a range can be defined here. The following parameters apply:

- **Add**  Adds a range of the selected criteria to the existing list.
- **Modify**  Allows the user to alter an existing range without needing to redefine the criteria altogether.
- **Delete**  Removes a range of criteria from the traffic filter template.

## Action

The Action defines how the IP packet will be treated if the defined criteria are matched. Several options can be used:

- **Log**  Logs the fact that IP traffic was received that matches the traffic filter criteria.
- **Detailed Log**  Provides more detailed log information regarding IP traffic which was received matching the specified traffic filter criteria.
- **Drop**  Indicates that any packet matching the traffic filter criteria will be dropped.
- **Accept**  Indicates the IP packet will be accepted. This action may possibly be used in conjunction with the Log or Detailed Log actions.
- **Forward to Next Hop**  Indicates that any incoming IP packet that matches the defined criteria should be forwarded to the next-hop router, which is also

defined here. When the Forward to Next Hop action is selected, a small window opens prompting for the next-hop IP address.

- **Drop If Next Hop Unreachable**   Works in tandem with the Forward to Next Hop option; if the Forward to Next Hop action is selected, and a next-hop router is defined, then this action causes the packet to be dropped if the next-hop router is not reachable.

- **Forward to IP Destination Address**   Causes the incoming packet to be forwarded to a specified IP address; this action causes the original destination IP address to actually be removed from the IP header and replaced with the IP address defined in this action. If this option is used, and further IP destinations need to be defined, this is accomplished by selecting the IP Destinations | Add.

- **Forward to Next Hop Interfaces**   Specifies that a frame that matches the criteria will be duplicated and forwarded to the interfaces that the user defines; when this action is selected, the user is prompted to enter an interface number. Once entered, the interface will be included on the interface list, visible in the template definition that dominates the window. If further IP interfaces need to be added, this is accomplished by selecting IP Interfaces | Add.

- **Forward to First Up Next Hop**   Ensures that all packets matching the criteria will be forwarded to a specified next hop. If this next hop is unreachable, the router will attempt each interface on the Forward to Next Hop Interfaces list, issuing ARP Requests out each interface in an attempt to reach each interface. If none can be reached, the packet is forwarded to the default destination, unless the Drop if Next Hop Unreachable action has been selected, in which case the packet will be dropped.

## IP Destinations

This option is used if additional IP destinations need to be added; this relates to the Forward to IP Destination action defined under Actions. If packets that match the filter criteria need to be forwarded to multiple destinations, those additional IP addresses can be defined here. If Forward to IP Destination was not selected as an action for the traffic filter, the IP Destinations options will be grayed out.

## IP Interfaces

This option is used if additional IP interfaces need to be added in relation to the Forward to Next Hop Interfaces action. In other words, if you wish to add any additional entries for Forward to Next Hop Interfaces, the IP interfaces option should be selected. If packets matching the filter criteria need to be forwarded out multiple interfaces, additional interfaces can be defined with this option. If Forward to Next Hop Interfaces was not selected as an action, the IP Interfaces option is grayed out.

# Creating the Traffic Filter

After you create the templates, you can add the actual filters. From the main IP Filters window, select Create to open the Create Filter window:

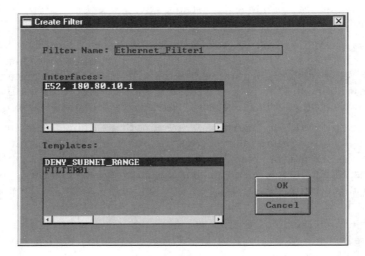

Here, an interface is selected, a name is applied to the filter, and a template is selected as part of the filter. Once this is done, click OK. Site Manager will return to the IP Filters window, and the newly defined filter will be visible in the IP Filter list.

## Prioritizing IP Filters

Multiple filters can be applied to a single IP interface. Therefore, you must be cognizant of the effect the filter order will have. The IP traffic filters are selected in turn, beginning with the first filter on the list. For example, it is common on wide-area links, particularly, to have a traffic filter that allows access from a specified remote site or specified devices, and another filter that drops everything else. If the "drop all" filter is placed before the "allow" filter, all IP traffic is dropped before the allow filter can ever be considered.

To change the priority of traffic filters applied to a specific IP interface, select the filter that you want to move either up or down the list, and then select Reorder from the main IP Filters window. This opens the Change Precedence window, which offers three options: Insert Before, Insert After, and a box labeled Priority Number. The Priority Number refers to the number of the entry in the filter list as it stands currently, and is used as a reference by the Insert Before and Insert After options. For example, an IP interface is configured with six traffic filters, number 3 is highlighted, and Reorder is selected. Selecting Insert Before, entering 4 as the Priority Number, and then clicking OK causes the selected filter to be moved to the position after the filter sitting in position 4.

# Configuring IP Adjacent Hosts

IP adjacent hosts may need to be created to establish IP connectivity with certain types of remote peers; an example of this might be older PPP implementations where a traditional ARP is not used. Another example would be Frame Relay in a non-fully meshed environment that is also running in group mode; the spoke routers in this scenario are unable to ARP for one another's MAC address.

In the preceding scenarios, some of the remote routers would be unreachable via a ping or telnet session due to the inability to ARP for the interface's MAC address. IP traffic will still pass through the routers, but the interface itself may be unreachable. To get around this, the remote router interfaces may be defined as IP adjacent hosts.

## Defining Adjacent Hosts

Defining the adjacent hosts is accomplished through Configuration Manager, by selecting Protocols | IP | Adjacent Hosts from the main window. This opens the IP Adjacent Hosts window. By default, no adjacent hosts are configured, so this window is grayed out for the most part. Click the Add button to open the IP Configuration window:

```
IP CONFIGURATION                                                    ☒

                                               ┌─────────────────┐
                                               │     Cancel      │
       Configuration Mode: local               ├─────────────────┤
             SNMP Agent: LOCAL FILE            │       OK        │
                                               ├─────────────────┤
                                               │    Values...    │
                                               ├─────────────────┤
                                               │    Help...      │
                                               └─────────────────┘

    IP Adjacent Host Address          150.50.20.2
    MAC Address, DLCI, VPI/VCI
    Host Encapsulation                ETHERNET
    Adjacent Host Address
    Remote Party Sub-Address
    Remote Party Type of Number       INTERNATIONAL
    Adjacent Host Type                DEFAULT
```

This is where you input the adjacent host information.

The following parameters must be configured for the IP adjacent host that you want to add:

■ **IP Adjacent Host Address**   The 32-bit IP address of the adjacent host that is to be added.

■ **MAC Address, DLCI, VPI/VCI**   This value varies, depending on the type of interface. The following parameters can be used:

> **Ethernet/Token Ring/FDDI Interfaces**   The hardware MAC address of the adjacent host.

**Frame Relay Interfaces**    The DLCI of the remote adjacent host.

**SMDS Interfaces**    The 64-bit SMDS address associated with the adjacent host.

**ATM Interfaces (PVC)**    For ATM PVCs, the VPI/VCI pair of the adjacent host.

**ATM Interfaces (SVC)**    For ATM SVCs (used in LANE or CLIP), the ATM address of the adjacent host.

**Host Encapsulation**    Defines the encapsulation type used; for Ethernet or any point-to-point connection, select Ethernet or SNAP. For X.25 interfaces, select PDN or DDN.

**Adjacent Host Address**    Referenced only if the interface is configured for PDN/X.25, DDN/X.25, or BFE/X.25, and should be configured with the X.121 address of the remote host.

**Remote Party Sub-Address**    Lists the subaddress used to establish an SVC with the adjacent host.

**Remote Party Type of Number**    Indicates the type of number used to establish an SVC with the adjacent host subaddress. Options are International and Unknown.

**Adjacent Host Type**    Defines the type of adjacent host: Frame Relay E.164, X.121, or DLCI.

# Troubleshooting IP on the Nortel Networks Router Platform

Troubleshooting IP problems on the Nortel Networks router platform can be done through Site Manager or through the TI by using the IP scripts and the MIB. The TI script and MIB commands are covered in this section.

## Troubleshooting IP by Using the Scripts

Unlike many other script files for the Nortel Networks router platform, the TI scripts for IP are part of the Nortel Networks router's kernel software and are available without copying any additional script files to the flash. The IP scripts are a quick and easy way to troubleshoot IP issues on Nortel Networks routers.

The **show ip** scripts are most useful in this regard; each **show ip** script uses the command syntax **show ip** *option* to display IP-related information. The following are some of the most commonly used **show ip** scripts, as well as a description of what they provide:

- **show ip adjacent hosts**   Displays the IP address and MAC address associated with each configured IP adjacent host. It also shows the IP address associated with the local IP interface on the same IP network as the IP adjacent host, the subnet mask, the frame encapsulation type used, and whether or not the IP adjacent host entries are valid.

- **show ip alerts**   Displays the circuit names, their associated IP addresses, and the state of the interface. Only circuits that are enabled but in a nonfunctional state are shown.

- **show ip arp** *IP-address*   Displays the ARP cache entries. For each entry, shows the IP address, associated MAC address, and whether the entry was dynamically learned or statically configured.

- **show ip base**   Displays the following IP global configuration information: the global state of IP; whether IP forwarding mode is enabled or disabled; whether the router is configured to use the zero subnet; the default TTL parameter setting; the RIP diameter parameter setting; the route cache size; the types of IP tables maintained by the router; whether a default route can be used for subnets; whether the use of route filters is enabled or disabled; the number of networks and hosts currently in the IP routing table; and the maximum policy rules that can be used for IP traffic filters:

```
[2:1]$ show ip base

Protocol:                      IP
State:                         Up
Forwarding Mode:               Enabled
Zero/All Ones Subnetting:      Disabled
Default TTL:                   30

RIP Diameter:                  15
Route Cache Size:              60
MIB Tables Maintained:         Route
Classless:                     Enabled
Route Filters:                 Enabled
Route pools contain 755 [est. 0] networks/subnets and 2 [est. 0] hosts.
Maximum policy rules per type per protocol: 32
```

- **show ip circuits** *circuit-name*   Displays the following for all IP interfaces or for a specific interface: the circuit name, circuit number, IP address, mask, and functional state.

The following output is the result of the **show ip circuits** command without using the argument *circuit-name*, which displays all configured IP circuits:

```
[12:2]$show ip circuits
Circuit   Circuit #   State      IP Address        Mask
--------  ----------- --------   ---------------   ----------------
ATMSR_1- 16           Up         150.50.10.2       255.255.255.0
414101.-
16
F101_BB  1            Up         150.50.20.130     255.255.255.252
E11-135- 2            Up         150.50.30.2       255.255.255.0
_32
E21-135- 3            Up         150.50.60.1       255.255.255.0
_64
4 circuit(s) found
```

■ **show ip disabled**   The output is the same as that displayed by **show ip circuits**, except that only IP interfaces that have been administratively disabled are displayed:

```
[12:2]$show ip disabled
Circuit   Circuit #   State      IP Address        Mask
--------  ----------- --------   ---------------   ----------------
E31-135- 4            Disabled 150.50.100.2  255.255.255.0
_96
1 circuit(s) found
```

■ **show ip enabled**   The output is the same as that displayed by **show ip circuits**, except that only IP interfaces that have been administratively enabled are displayed.

■ **show ip rfilters [export | import] [*protocol*]**   Displays the configured route filters for all routing protocols or for a specific routing protocol. The *protocol* option can be one of the following: **all**, **rip**, **ospf**, **egp**, or **bgp3**. The script displays the IP network address to which the route filter is applied; the mask describing the range of addresses the route filter acts upon; the routing protocol source that is affected by the route filter; the action the route filter will take; the IP address of the peer router; and the peer's autonomous system (AS) number.

■ **show ip rip**   Displays the IP interfaces RIP is configured on, the state of RIP on those interfaces, and whether RIP Supply and Listen are enabled or disabled.

The following output shows nine circuits: eight are configured for RIPv1 and the last is configured for RIPv2. Each is configured to both supply and listen to RIP advertisements, as well as to generate and listen for default routes. Each circuit number is listed (Ckt#), as well as whether the interface is using poison reverse or split horizon (all are using poison reverse), and whether each interface is configured to issue triggered updates (this is disabled on all interfaces).

```
[12:2]$show ip rip

                                 RIP    Def.Rt  Poison  RIP    Trig
 IP Interface    Ckt#   State    Sup/Lis Sup/Lis Reverse Mode  Updt TTL
 -------------   ----   -------  ------- ------- ------- ----- ---- ---
 160.60.10.2     6      Up       En/En   Gen/En  Poison  RIP1  Dis  1
 160.60.45.32    2      Up       En/En   Gen/En  Poison  RIP1  Dis  1
 160.60.135.41   3      Up       En/En   Gen/En  Poison  RIP1  Dis  1
 160.60.1.110    9      Up       En/En   Gen/En  Poison  RIP1  Dis  1
 160.60.100.2    18     Up       En/En   Gen/En  Poison  RIP1  Dis  1
 160.60.18.1     7      Up       En/En   Gen/En  Poison  RIP1  Dis  1
 160.60.60.1     18     Up       En/En   Gen/En  Poison  RIP1  Dis  1
 160.60.140.1    19     Up       En/En   Gen/En  Poison  RIP1  Dis  1
 160.60.150.14   25     Up       En/En   Gen/En  Poison  RIP2A Dis  1
 9 entries found
```

- **show ip rip alerts**   Displays the same information as **show ip rip**, except only the RIP interfaces with a state of Down are shown.

- **show ip rip disabled**   Displays the same information as **show ip rip**, except only the RIP interfaces that have been administratively disabled are shown.

- **show ip rip enabled**   Displays the same information as **show ip rip**, except only the RIP interfaces that have been administratively enabled are shown.

- **show ip routes [-A] [type** *local* | *bgp* | *egp* | *ospf* | *rip* |] | [*IP-network-address* | **find** *search-pattern*]   Displays the IP routing table. If the **–A** option is used, the entire routing table is listed, including routes that are not used. If the **type** option is used, only the routes learned via the routing protocol specified are shown. If an IP network address is given, only the route for that IP network is displayed. Finally, if a search pattern is given, only those routes matching the search pattern are displayed.

```
[2:1]$ show ip routes
  Destination      Mask          Proto  Age      Cost      NextHop Addr / AS
  -------------    -------------- -----  -------- --------  --------------------
  0.0.0.0          0.0.0.0        RIP    7        3         170.70.121.1
  10.0.0.0         255.0.0.0      RIP    8        3         170.70.121.1
  160.61.0.0       255.255.0.0    RIP    8        3         170.70.121.1
  160.66.0.0       255.255.0.0    RIP    8        3         170.70.121.1
  160.60.0.0       255.255.0.0    RIP    8        3         170.70.121.1
  170.70.1.0       255.255.255.0  RIP    8        2         170.70.121.1
  170.70.2.0       255.255.255.0  RIP    8        2         170.70.121.1
  170.70.5.0       255.255.255.0  RIP    8        2         170.70.121.1
  170.70.7.0       255.255.255.0  RIP    8        2         170.70.121.1
```

```
170.70.10.0    255.255.255.0    RIP   8    2              170.70.121.1
170.70.20.0    255.255.255.0    RIP   9    2         :    170.70.121.1
170.70.30.0    255.255.255.0    RIP   9    2              170.70.121.1
170.70.40.0    255.255.255.0    RIP   9    2              170.70.121.1
170.70.50.0    255.255.255.0    RIP   9    2              170.70.121.1
170.70.60.0    255.255.255.0    RIP   9    2              170.70.121.1
170.70.70.0    255.255.255.0    RIP   9    2              170.70.121.1
16 route(s) found
```

■ **show ip static**   Displays all the static routes configured on the router. The output shows the destination IP network; the destination IP mask; the cost of the route; the IP address of the next hop; whether the static route is valid; and whether the static route is enabled or disabled.

```
[12:2]$show ip static
 IP Destination  Network Mask      Cost      Nexthop          Valid Enabled
----------       -------------     --------  ----------------  ----- -------
180.80.10.0      255.255.255.0     1         180.80.42.7       Yes   Yes
1 entries found
```

■ **show ip stats [circuit** *circuit-name*]   For all IP interfaces or for a specific interface, displays the IP circuit name; associated IP address; the number of packets received, transmitted, and discarded by the interface; and the number of packets forwarded through the interface.

```
[2:1]$ show ip stats
                             In         Out                     In       Out
Circuit     IP Address     Receives   Requests   Forwards   Discards Discards
-------     ---------------- ---------- ---------- ---------- -------- --------
E21         145.214.15.1    112952     75831      0          0        0
1 entries found
```

■ **show ip stats cache [***circuit-name***]**   For all IP interfaces or for a specific interface, displays the IP circuit name; associated IP address; the total number of IP networks in the forwarding table cache; the number of times the IP routing table had to be consulted because an IP network was not available in the IP forwarding cache (cache misses); and the number of times an IP network was removed from the IP forwarding cache because the IP network timed out (cache removes).

```
[2:1]$ show ip stats cache
                             Cache     Cache    Cache
Circuit     IP Address      Networks   Misses   Removes
-------     ---------------- --------  -------- --------
E21         145.214.15.1    3          27       0
1 entries found
```

- **show ip stats datagrams** [*circuit-name*]   For all IP interfaces or for a specific interface, displays the circuit name; associated IP address; the number of datagrams dropped because they were received with header errors, address errors, or unknown protocol errors; the number of datagrams dropped because the IP destination was unknown; and the number of incoming and outgoing datagrams dropped due to lack of available buffers.

- **show ip stats fragments** [*circuit-name*]   For all IP interfaces or for a specific interface, displays the IP circuit name; associated IP address; the number of IP fragments received on the interface that required reassembly; the number of IP datagrams that were successfully reassembled; the number of IP datagrams the router failed to reassemble; the number of IP datagrams the router fragmented; the number of IP datagrams the router failed to fragment; and the total number of IP fragments created during the fragmenting process by this router.

```
[12:2]$show ip stats fragment ATMSR_1413101.19
                     Fragmnts Sucssful Failed  Fragmnt  Fragmnt   Total
Circuit    IP Address Received Reassem  Reassem Sent    Failed  Fragmnts
-------  -------------- -------- -------- -------- -------- -------- --------
ATMSR_1- 145.244.17.1    0         0        0      200914    0       599985
413101.-
19
1 entries found
```

- **show ip stats icmp client** [*circuit-name*]   For all IP interfaces or for a specific interface, displays the IP circuit name; the IP address; the number of ICMP Echo Requests received; the number of ICMP Echo Replies received; the number of ICMP Timestamp Requests received; the number of ICMP Timestamp Replies received; the number of ICMP Address Mask Requests received; and the number of ICMP Address Mask Replies received.

- **show ip stats icmp in** [*circuit-name*]   For all IP interfaces or for a specific interface, displays the IP circuit name; the IP address; the total number of ICMP messages received (including errors); the total number of ICMP messages received that had bad ICMP checksums; the total number of ICMP Destination Unreachable messages received; the total number of ICMP Time Exceeded messages received; and the total number of ICMP Parameter Problem messages received.

```
[2:1]$ show ip stats icmp in
                       ICMP    ICMP In  Destintn Rcv.Time Rcv.Parm
Circuit    IP Address  Received Errors  Unreach. Exceeded Problem
--------  ---------------- -------- -------- -------- -------- --------
E21      145.214.15.1    4168      0      3596       0        0
1 entries found
```

■ **show ip stats icmp misc** [*circuit-name*]   For all IP interfaces or for a specific interface, displays the IP circuit name; the IP address; the total number of ICMP Source Quench messages received; the total number of ICMP Source Quench messages sent; the total number of ICMP Redirect messages received; and the total number of ICMP Redirect messages sent.

```
[2:1]$ show ip stats icmp misc
                       SrcQunch Messages Redirect Messages Prohibit Prohibit
Circuit   IP Address      In       Out      In      Out       In      Out
-------  -------------- -------- -------- -------- -------- --------- --------
E21      145.214.15.1    0        0        0        0         0        0
1 entries found
```

■ **show ip stats icmp out** [*circuit-name*]   For all IP interfaces or for a specific interface, displays the IP circuit name; the IP address; the total number of ICMP messages generated by the router; the total number of ICMP messages not sent due to lack of buffers or some problem experienced on the router; the total number of ICMP Destination Unreachable messages generated by the router; the total number of ICMP Time Exceeded messages generated by the router; and the total number of ICMP Parameter Problem messages generated by the router.

```
[2:1]$ show ip stats icmp out
                       ICMP   ICMP Out Destintn Snd.Time Snd.Parm
Circuit    IP Address  Sent    Errors  Unreach. Exceeded Problem
-------  ---------------- -------- -------- -------- -------- --------
E21      145.214.15.1    574      0        2        0        0
1 entries found
```

■ **show ip stats icmp server** [*circuit-name*]   For all interfaces or for a specific interface, displays the same information as the script **show ip stats icmp client**, but shows statistics on ICMP messages generated by the router instead of received by the router.

■ **show ip stats security in** [*circuit-name*]   For all interfaces or for a specific interface, displays the total number of IP packets received that were dropped due to insufficient access rights based on the authority flag; the total number of IP packets received that were dropped due to an invalid security option format; the total number of IP packets received that were dropped due to an out-of-range classification level; the total number of IP packets received that were dropped due to a lack of an IP security label; and the total number of ICMP destination unreachable or communication administratively prohibited messages received.

# Troubleshooting IP Using the MIB

IP troubleshooting can also be accomplished from the TI by using the Management Information Base. This involves doing a series of MIB *gets* on a variety of IP-related MIB objects to obtain information about the router's current configuration and operational state. For more information regarding the TI, as well as the specific structure of the MIB and how to use them, consult Chapter 29. The following sections describe some of the more useful, commonly used MIBs for troubleshooting IP problems.

## Checking the IP State

The MIB can be used to examine the state of many IP-related parameters. In the following list, a series of MIB commands are described, each preceded by the **get** command (abbreviated to **g**, which the TI will parse as **get**). In each of the instances, a value of 1 or 2 will be returned, where 1 and 2 have the following meanings:

1 = UP (Enabled)
2 = DOWN (Disabled)

- **g wfIpBase.3.\*** Provides the current IP state on a global level.

- **g wfIpInterfaceEntry.3.\*** Displays the operational state of all IP interfaces for Bay RS versions prior to 12.00.

- **g wfIpIntfCfgEntry.3.\*** Displays the operational state of all IP interfaces for Bay RS versions 12.00 or greater.

- **g wfRipIntfEntry.3.\*** Displays the operational state of all IP interfaces that are configured to run RIP, when the router is running Bay RS versions prior to 10.00.

- **g wfRipInterfaceEntry.3.\*** Displays the operational state of all IP interfaces that are configured to run RIP, when the router is running Bay RS version 10.00 or greater.

- **g wfOspfGeneralGroup.3.\*** Displays the current operational state of the OSPF protocol at the global level.

- **g wfOspfIfEntry.3.\*** Displays the current operational state of all IP interfaces that are configured to run the OSPF protocol.

- **g wfOspfAreaEntry.3.\*** Displays the current operational state of all OSPF areas configured on the router.

- **g wfOspfNbrEntry.3.\*** Displays the current operational state of all OSPF neighbors configured on the router.

## Checking IP Statistics and Tables

The MIB can also be used to examine the IP routing tables, as well as a variety of other IP information. These MIBs are listed next, each preceded by the **get** command:

- **g wfIpBaseRtEntry.7.*** Displays the current IP routing table:

```
[2:1]$ g wfIpBaseRtEntry.7.*
wfIpBaseRtEntry.wfIpBaseRouteNextHop.0.0.0.0 = 160.61.11.1
wfIpBaseRtEntry.wfIpBaseRouteNextHop.10.0.0.0 = 160.61.11.1
wfIpBaseRtEntry.wfIpBaseRouteNextHop.145.12.0.0 = 160.61.11.1
wfIpBaseRtEntry.wfIpBaseRouteNextHop.145.140.0.0 = 160.61.11.1
wfIpBaseRtEntry.wfIpBaseRouteNextHop.145.201.0.0 = 160.61.11.1
wfIpBaseRtEntry.wfIpBaseRouteNextHop.160.61.1.0 = 160.61.11.1
wfIpBaseRtEntry.wfIpBaseRouteNextHop.160.61.2.0 = 160.61.11.1
wfIpBaseRtEntry.wfIpBaseRouteNextHop.160.61.8.0 = 160.61.11.1
wfIpBaseRtEntry.wfIpBaseRouteNextHop.160.61.9.0 = 160.61.11.1
```

- **g wfIpStaticRouteEntry.6.*** Displays all static routes that are currently configured on the router:

```
[12:2]$g wfIpStaticRouteEntry.6.*
wfIpStaticRouteEntry.wfIpSrNextHopAddr.180.80.130.0.255.255.255.0
.1 = 180.80.140.9
```

- **g wfIpNetToMediaEntry.2.*** Displays all MAC addresses that are currently contained in the ARP cache:

```
[2:1]$ g wfIpNetToMediaEntry.2.*
wfIpNetToMediaEntry.wfIpNetToMediaPhysAddress.2.190.90.15.2 =
        x00 x00 xA2 x06 xE0 xD8
wfIpNetToMediaEntry.wfIpNetToMediaPhysAddress.2.190.90.1.1 =
        x00 x00 xA2 xCB x2B xE0
```

- **g wfIpAdjacentHostEntry.3.*** Displays all IP addresses of configured adjacent hosts:

## Common IP Problems

In this section, some of the commonly encountered IP problems are described, as well as methods of dealing with those problems through the TI, by using the MIB rather than Site Manager. This can be useful if you are doing troubleshooting via a dial-in session or a telnet session at a location where Site Manager is unavailable.

**ROUTER IS NOT USING DEFAULT ROUTE**    In this scenario, the default route is present in the IP routing table, but the router can't ping devices on other subnets, although it is able to ping devices on other networks and reach the Internet. The problem in this case may be that the router is not configured to use a default route for subnets. This can be checked with the following command:

```
[12:2]$ g wfIpBase.14.0
```

If the value returned is 2, change it to 1 to enable the use of default routes for subnets:

```
[12:2]$ s wfIpBase.14.0 1;commit
```

**HOSTS ON SUBNET ZERO ARE UNREACHABLE**    In this scenario, all IP devices are reachable except those on subnet zero. The problem probably is that the use of subnet zero is not configured. This can be checked with the following command:

```
[12:2]$ g wfIpBase.10.0
```

If the value returned is 2, change it to 1 to enable zero subnet, by issuing the following command:

```
[12:2]$ s wfIpBase.10.0 1;commit
```

**RIP ROUTES MISSING FROM ROUTING TABLE**    In this scenario, RIP is enabled, but RIP routes are not appearing in the IP routing table. The problem may be that although RIP was selected globally, RIP is not correctly configured on one or more of the Bay routers for RIP Supply and RIP Listen. To check this parameter from the TI, issue the following commands:

```
[12:2]$ g wfRipInterfaceEntry.5.*    (RIP Supply)
[12:2]$ g wfRipInterfaceEntry.6.*    (RIP Listen)
```

If either entry is set to 2, then the parameter is disabled. Both the RIP Supply and RIP Listen parameters can be changed from the TI by setting the MIB value to 1:

[12:2]$ s wfRipInterfaceEntry.5.*instance* 1;commit
[12:2]$ s wfRipInterfaceEntry.6.*instance* 1;commit

**RIP DEVICES UNREACHABLE**    In this scenario, RIPv1 is working, but some devices are unreachable. Especially in a Class C network, make certain that the network number is not using subnet masks of different lengths, because RIPv1 does not support VLSM. First, check what routing protocol the interface is running:

```
[12:2]$ g wfRipInterfaceEntry.15.*
```

A value of 1, 2, or 3 will be returned, which have the following meanings:

1 = RIPv1
2 = RIPv2
3 = RIPv2 Aggregate

If RIPv1 is being used, the interface could be altered to run RIPv2, which does support VLSM. This is accomplished with the following command:

[12:2]$ s wfRipInterfaceEntry.15.*instance* 2;commit

### REPLACED DEVICE WILL NOT RESPOND TO PING AND IS UNREACHABLE

In this scenario, IP is working, but one particular device will not respond to pings, where the device in question was recently replaced due to a hardware failure. The replacement device was given the same IP as the old one, but now is unreachable, even through there is a valid link. The problem may be due to the fact that the router has an ARP cache entry that is now no longer valid. By default, Bay routers never flush their ARP caches, so the replacement device may still have the old device's hardware address associated with its IP address in the router's host cache. Bouncing IP globally will flush the ARP cache, accomplished with the following commands:

```
[12:2]$ s wfIpBase.2.0 2;commit
```

This command disables IP, and

```
[12:2]$ s wfIpBase2.0 1;commit
```

this reenables the IP protocol.

*If telnetted into the router TI, issuing the first command will disable IP, thus dropping the telnet session. A console session is required to bring up IP again in this scenario. Optionally, the value can simply be set to 1, because any change to a global protocol will cause the protocol to bounce, even if the MIB set merely sets the value to its current setting.*

Bouncing the IP interface will flush the ARP cache entries learned by that interface, which may be a less obtrusive way to clear the host cache on only the slot where the device resides. This is accomplished with the following commands:

[12:2]$ s wfIpInterfaceEntry.2.*instance* 2;commit
[12:2]$ s wfIpInterfaceEntry.2.*instance* 1;commit

Setting the IP ARP cache to flush also causes the individual ARP entries to be flushed, once the specified time has passed for each (the times will vary, because the timeout value applies to each individual entry); this will also cause the IP interface to bounce, however:

[12:2]$ s wfIpInterfaceEntry.15.*instance* 1200;commit

Table 30-2 lists the flush times that can be set.
The only nonintrusive solution is to mark the bogus ARP cache entry Invalid, which will allow the router to re-ARP for the MAC address:

[12:2]$ s wfIpNetToMediaEntry.4.*instance* 2;commit

**IP PACKETS ARE NOT BEING FORWARDED CORRECTLY**    In this scenario, the IP routing table has the correct next hop for a certain destination IP network, but IP packets are not being forwarded or are being forwarded to the wrong next hop. The problem may be that the slot IP routing tables are not synchronized between all the slots. If all the slot IP routing tables are not the same, IP packets may not be forwarded correctly. Check the IP routing table on each slot by using the following command, where *slot* is the number of the slot you want to verify:

ip routes -s*slot*    (code version 10.00 and above)

| Flush Value | Flush Time |
|---|---|
| 1 | ARP cache will never flush |
| 120 | After 120 seconds (2 minutes) |
| 180 | After 180 seconds (3 minutes) |
| 240 | After 240 seconds (4 minutes) |
| 300 | After 300 seconds (5 minutes) |
| 600 | After 600 seconds (10 minutes) |
| 900 | After 900 seconds (15 minutes) |

**Table 30-2.**    *IP ARP Cache Aging Timers*

If any discrepancies exist in the routing tables, either reboot the router or reset the slots that are out of sync.

 *If the router is running a code version prior to 10.00, debug must be used to view the routing table of a particular slot.*

**PINGS ARE SUCCESSFUL ACROSS THE ROUTER, BUT OTHER PROTOCOLS ARE NOT**    In this situation, end stations are able to ping across the router to devices on the Internet, but can't telnet, TFTP, FTP, or use HTTP to access the Web.

In this scenario, verify that the local router and the Internet service provider's router have the same MTU size configured on the WAN line they are communicating across. If the ISP's router is a Cisco router, the MTU size configured on the Bay router's WAN interface must be 11 bytes more than the MTU size configured on the Cisco's WAN interface.

**ROUTER IS BRIDGING ONLY, BUT REQUIRES IP TO MANAGE**    In this last scenario, the router needs to be configured to bridge all protocols. However, an IP address needs to be assigned to the router so that it is accessible via telnet and SNMP, so that it can be managed by Site Manager. This can be configured by using a feature called Host Only Mode. To configure this, three steps must be taken:

1. Check the Nortel Networks manual to make sure Host Only Mode is supported for your topology—not all topologies are supported.

2. Using Site Manager in either local or remote mode, change the IP global parameters Forwarding and ARP Forwarding to Not Forwarding.

3. Configure the same IP address and mask on all the interfaces.

After you complete these steps, save the configuration and then reboot the router with the new configuration.

# The Complete Reference

Nortel Networks

# Chapter 31

## OSPF Reference Guide

1047

Open Shortest Path First (OSPF) is a TCP/IP routing protocol that was created specifically for use in large IP networks. Since OSPF is a link-state protocol rather than a distance-vector protocol, it scales well, meaning it can handle large IP networks with little to no performance loss. This scalability is due to a fast convergence time and a lack of hop count restrictions. Distance-vector protocols, such as Routing Information Protocol (RIP), do not scale well. One reason why is that the larger the IP network, the longer it takes for distance-vector routing protocols to converge, that is, for all the routing tables in the network to contain all the necessary entries for proper routing of IP packets. Another reason why distance-vector routing protocols are not suitable for large-scale IP networks is that they have a maximum hop count limit, which effectively prevents the IP network from expanding beyond the hop count boundary. For example, RIP considers unreachable any network over 15 hops away. The trade-off for this scalability, however, is that OSPF is much more complicated than distance-vector routing protocols, consumes more router resources (CPU and memory), and requires much more consideration in the way of network design.

## OSPF Features

OSPF operates very differently from distance-vector protocols like RIP. Instead of advertising the entire contents of the IP routing table, OSPF advertises the link states, that is the up or down state of a router's network interfaces. Also, these advertisements are not broadcasts as they are in a RIP environment. Instead, they are multicasts, which only other OSPF routers listen to. Once the network has converged, OSPF only advertises changes in the link states. These features combined help to reduce the amount of routing protocol traffic in a large IP network.

Another difference between OSPF and distance-vector routing protocols is the way the best path to the destination network is chosen. RIP bases its decision on hop count: the lower the hop count, the better the path. This is a very simplistic view, however. Perhaps the path with the lower hop count involves crossing several slow WAN links. OSPF, on the other hand, makes its choices based on cost. Links with lower costs are considered more desirable and the path with the lowest cumulative cost is the best path.

OSPF can also handle several networking scenarios that many distance-vector protocols do not support. For instance, RIP version 1 does not allow for variable length subnet masking, which is the practice of associating multiple subnet masks with an individual IP network. The reason RIP1 does not support this is that it does not pass along the subnet mask information in its network advertisements. OSPF does advertise the subnet mask information; so variable length subnet masking is not a problem for it.

Another situation that poses a problem in a RIP1 environment is non-contiguous IP network numbers. This is the practice of separating a subnetted IP network, such as a class B network, with an entirely different IP network, such as a class C network. The issue commonly surfaces when a company wishes to connect its remote sites via WAN links and careful planning of the initial IP network was not done. Since it is usually too costly to reassign IP network numbers after an IP network is in place, creating non-contiguous IP networks is sometimes unavoidable. Fortunately, OSPF supports non-contiguous IP networks.

The key difference between OSPF and distance-vector routing protocols is that it is a Shortest Path First (SPF) protocol, meaning it gathers information about the network and computes the shortest, or best, path to all destinations. OSPF is also sometimes referred to as a distributed-database protocol. The terms are meant to describe how OSPF operates. Each OSPF router builds a database of all router links in the network, called the Link State Database (LSDB). Once the LSDB is built, OSPF runs an algorithm, known as Dijkstra's algorithm, against the LSDB in order to generate the shortest path to each destination in the network. The SPF tree created by Dijkstra's algorithm is from the perspective of the individual OSPF router running it, so each OSPF router's SPF tree will be different, depending on its location in the network.

OSPF utilizes the hello protocol to provide communication between OSPF routers in the network. Through these hello packets, OSPF routers discover one another's presence in the network. This, in turn, may lead to the forming of an OSPF adjacency, allowing the OSPF routers to exchange link state information and synchronize their LSDBs. All OSPF routers in an IP network must have synchronized LSDBs—that is, the LSDBs must contain the same information. After an OSPF Adjacency has been formed, OSPF routers continue to use hello packets as keep-alive packets to maintain their adjacent relationships.

This section provided a brief overview of the OSPF protocol. The following sections discuss the individual components of OSPF in greater detail. Additional information on OSPF can also be found in RFC 2178 (OSPF version 2).

## OSPF Network Types

Whether or not two OSPF routers form an adjacency depends on the network type configured on the routers' OSPF interfaces. Each of the various OSPF network types fall into the category of either point-to-point or multiple-access.

The OSPF routing protocol does not have the functionality to determine dynamically the type of network used; this must be configured on each OSPF interface. The following are the different types of OSPF networks:

- **Point-to-point**   Two routers connected point to point, with a single router at either end of the connection. Most commonly used in a T1, HSSI, or other PPP synchronous WAN connection.

- **Broadcast**   Encompasses most legacy LAN environments, such as Ethernet, Token Ring, FDDI, or SMDS (Switched Multimegabit Data Service). OSPF broadcast network environments involve many interconnected routers, intercommunicating through multicast messages.

- **Nonbroadcast multiple-access (NBMA)**   Multiple attached routers in an environment with no broadcast capability. Frame relay, for instance, may involve many interconnected remote sites; however, frame relay is inherently connection-oriented and does not provide a broadcast mechanism. In NBMA networks, OSPF control packets are sent to the IP address of statically

configured OSPF neighbors as unicast packets. ATM is another example
of an NBMA network.

■ **Point-to-multipoint**   Similar to NBMA networks, point-to-multipoint is often
defined in Group mode frame relay networks, both partially and fully meshed.
Like NBMA networks, adjacencies are formed across connections, and LSDBs
are exchanged by means of unicasts. Unlike NBMA networks however, OSPF
neighbors are learned dynamically.

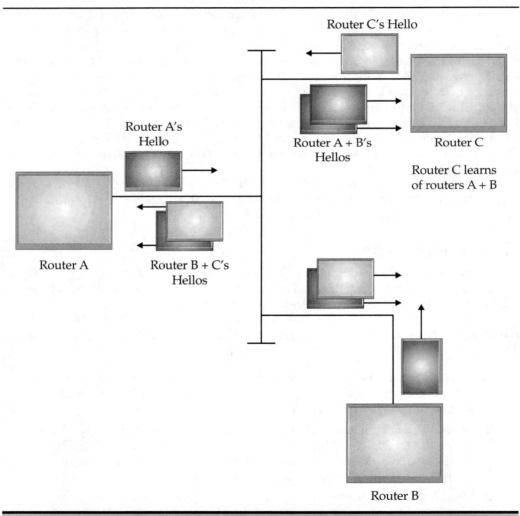

**Figure 31-1.**   *Routers exchanging Hello packets*

# Neighbors

OSPF routers periodically send out what are called Hello packets (see Figure 31-1), to identify one another on the same network. When a router interface receives a Hello packet from another router, that router is considered to be a *neighbor*. In a broadcast environment, a group of routers whose interfaces share a common network should all become OSPF neighbors:

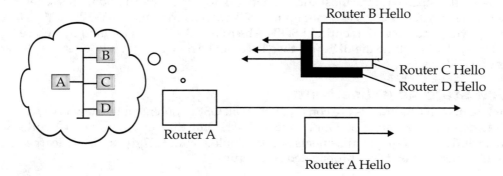

OSPF neighbors may or may not exchange link-state information directly. An OSPF router that detects its own Router ID listed in an OSPF neighbor's Hello packet assumes a bi-directional communication. (The router is aware of its neighbor and knows the neighbor has detected it as well.) Depending on the OSPF network type along with other factors, the two OSPF neighbors may then go on to form an OSPF adjacency.

# Adjacencies

The predominating factor in determining whether or not two OSPF neighbors form an adjacency is the type of OSPF network they communicate across. OSPF neighbors on point-to-point and NMBA networks always form adjacencies with each other. OSPF neighbors in a point-to-multipoint (Nortel Networks proprietary version) form adjacencies with the hub router but not with the other spokes. On OSPF broadcast networks, OSPF neighbors form adjacencies only with the Designated Router (DR) and the Backup Designated Router (BDR).

## Designated and Backup Designated Routers

The elected Designated Router (DR) and Backup Designated Router (BDR) exist on broadcast, NBMA, and point-to-multipoint (Nortel Networks proprietary version) networks. Point-to-point and point-to-multipoint (standard version) OSPF networks do not have a DR or BDR.

The DR and the BDR are just regular OSPF routers that take on the additional responsibility of distributing up-to-date topology information to all other OSPF routers within the same network. The DR accomplishes its job in the following way. All OSPF routers form adjacencies with the DR and BDR and exchange link state information (called Link State Advertisements, or LSAs) with them. The OSPF neighbors on networks where a DR exists do not form adjacencies or exchange LSAs with each other directly.

Both the DR and BDR assemble all received LSAs into a comprehensive network topology database, called the Link State Database (LSDB). While in the process of building its LSDB, the DR continually updates all of the OSPF routers on the same network it resides with the most current network topology information. This scheme keeps the transfer of LSAs to a minimum while still ensuring that all OSPF routers on the network end up with identical LSDBs. The role of the BDR is to stand by in case the DR fails, at which time the BDR will then become the new DR and take over the DR's responsibilities.

## Link State Advertisements

Link State Advertisements are constructed by all OSPF routers on the network. The LSAs describe the state of an OSPF router's links. Only directly connected networks are included in these advertisements because, unlike with RIP, dynamically learned routing information is not propagated (see Figure 31-2).

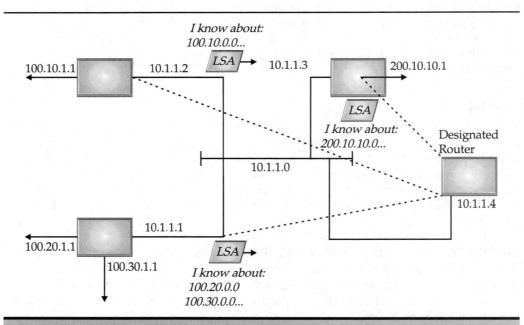

**Figure 31-2.**    *LSAs transmitted by individual routers over their adjacencies to the Designated Routers*

## Link State Database

By amassing all received LSAs together, the Designated Router builds its Link State Database. Once completed, the LSDB provides a topological picture of the OSPF network as a whole. It is important that the LSDB be identical on each OSPF router within the network since the routers use this information to determine routing paths through the network. If the LSDBs do not become synchronized throughout the network, it means a breakdown in router communication has occurred somewhere within the network. In order to achieve an agreed upon view of the network on broadcast networks, LSDB synchronization occurs via the DR. On point-to-point OSPF networks, where there is no DR or BDR, the OSPF neighbors form adjacencies with each other and synchronize their LSDBs directly.

# Dijkstra's Algorithm and the Shortest Path First (SPF) Tree

*Dijkstra's algorithm* is the algorithm run against the completes LSDB in order to derive the best path to all network destinations—the best path being the one with the lowest overall path cost. Cost in this case is predefined according to the link type (Ethernet, ATM, etc.), though it is a user. User configurable Dijkstra's algorithm will yield what is called a *SPF tree*. This logical tree defines the best path to all network points; at each branch of the tree, the lowest-cost path is selected (see Figure 31-3).

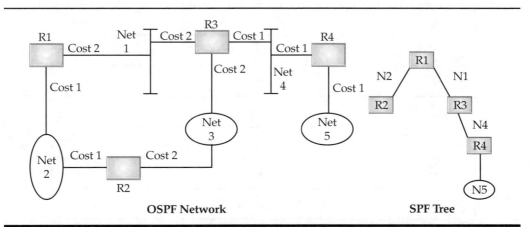

**Figure 31-3.** *An SPF tree generated by router 1 to reach Net 5*

Hello packets are transmitted periodically from each interface of the OSPF router. Hello packets are the mechanism by which OSPF routers discover each other, determine whether or not an adjacency can be formed, and maintain adjacencies once formed. A Hello packet contains the following information:

- The network mask of the interface transmitting the hello
- The Hello interval, specifying how often the Hello packets will be sent
- The Router Priority of the sending router
- The Dead Interval Timer, specifying how long the sender will wait after missing a Hello packet (after the Hello interval has expired) before breaking an adjacency
- The IP address of the Designated Router (if determined)
- The IP address of the Backup Designated Router (if determined)
- A list of all neighboring routers on the network, listed by Router ID

Here is a visual depiction of a Hello packet:

| Version # | 1 | Packet Length |
|:---:|:---:|:---:|
| Router ID | | |
| Area ID | | |
| Checksum | Authentication Type | |
| Authentication | | |
| Authentication | | |
| Network mask | | |
| Hello interval | Options | Router Priority |
| Router Dead Interval | | |
| Designated Router | | |
| Backup Designated Router | | |
| Neighbor #1 | | |

Here is an example of an OSPF Hello message as it might appear in a sniffer trace:

```
DLC:  ------DLC Header ------
DLC:  Frame 94 arrived at 10:01:31.801; frame size is 90 (005A hex) bytes.
DLC:  AC: Frame priority 0, Reservation priority 1, Monitor count 0
DLC:  FC: LLC frame, PCF attention code: None
DLC:  FS: Addr recognized indicators: 00, Frame copied indicators: 00
DLC:  Destination = BROADCAST FFFFFFFFFFFF, All Fs Broadcast
DLC:  Source = Station Wllflt005570
LLC:  ------LLC Header ------
LLC:  DSAP Address = AA, DSAP IG Bit = 00 (Individual Address)
LLC:  SSAP Address = AA, SSAP CR Bit = 00 (Command)
LLC:  Unnumbered frame: UI
SNAP: ------SNAP Header ------
SNAP: Type = 0800 (IP)
IP:  ------ IP Header ------
IP:  Version = 4, header length = 20 bytes
IP:  Type of service = C0
IP:  110. .... = internetwork control
IP:  ...0 .... = normal delay
IP:  .... 0... = normal throughput
IP:  .... .0.. = normal reliability
IP:  Total length = 68 bytes
IP:  Identification = 572
IP:  Flags = 0X
IP:  .0.. .... = may fragment
IP:  ..0. .... = last fragment
IP:  Fragment offset = 0 bytes
IP:  Time to live = 1 seconds/hops
IP:  Protocol = 89 (OSPF)
IP:  Header checksum = 3834 (correct)
IP:  Source address = [180.10.10.1]
IP:  Destination address = [224.0.0.5]
IP:  No options
OSPF: ------ OSPF Header ------
OSPF: Version = 2, Type = 1 (Hello), Length = 48
OSPF: Router ID = [0.0.0.10]
OSPF: Area ID = [0.0.0.1]
OSPF: Header checksum = C004 (correct)
OSPF: Authentication: Type = 1 (Simple Password), Value = hqospf
OSPF: Network mask = [255.255.255.0]
OSPF: Hello interval = 10 (seconds)
OSPF: Optional capabilities = X2
OSPF:     .... ..1. = external routing capability
OSPF:     .... ...0 = no Type of Service routing capability
OSPF: Router priority = 1
OSPF: Router dead interval = 40 (seconds)
```

```
OSPF: Designated router = [180.10.10.5]
OSPF: Backup designated router = [180.10.10.1]
OSPF: Neighbor (1)     = [0.0.0.20]
OSPF: Neighbor (2)     = [0.0.0.30]
OSPF: Neighbor (3)     = [0.0.0.40]
```

The above example is a Hello packet issued from Router ID 0.0.0.10, from Token Ring interface 180.10.10.1 to an all F's broadcast at the MAC layer, and to the OSPF multi-cast address 224.0.0.5 at the Network layer. The Designated Router and Backup Designated Router are identified (the sending interface is the BDR in this case). In this example, three neighbors are listed.

Hello packets are transmitted to either the multicast address of 224.0.0.5, directing them to all SPF routers in the case of a broadcast network, or to a statically defined neighbor address such as when the network is an NBMA network or if the packet is traversing a virtual link.

Hello packets ensure that bi-directional communication is in place between neighbors; this is indicated when a router receives a Hello packet and sees its own Router ID in the Hello packet neighbor list.

The function of the Hello packet differs depending on the network type. For instance, in the case of a broadcast network, the Hello packets are periodically transmitted to the 224.0.0.5 group multicast address described above, allowing the OSPF routers to discover each other dynamically as well as dynamically electing a Designated Router. On an NBMA network, OSPF routers are manually configured with each remote OSPF neighbor's IP address, and Hello packets are unicast to those neighbors.

## Sending Hello Packets on Broadcast Networks

Hello packets are sent out at certain intervals, defined by the Hello Interval parameter, and must be received at certain intervals as well, defined by the Router Dead Interval parameter. These parameters must match for all routers that are attached to the same network if an adjacency is to be formed and maintained.

On a broadcast network, Hello packets are transmitted every $x$ seconds, where $x$ is the Hello Interval. They are sent to the multicast group address of 224.0.0.5, except in the case of a virtual link (see the section on virtual links, further in this chapter), where the Hello packet is sent as a unicast, addressed to the virtual link's remote end.

## Receiving Hello Packets

The first things an OSPF interface checks an incoming Hello packet for (after verifying the packet headers) are the network mask, Hello Interval, and Router Dead Interval fields. If any one of these parameters is mismatched, the Hello packet is dropped; a mismatch in the network mask would indicate a misconfigured interface on the originator of the Hello, since all OSPF interfaces connected to the same network should have the same network mask. Likewise, a mismatched Hello Interval or Router Dead Interval would prevent a stable adjacency, and so there is no purpose in accepting the Hello. In the case of a point-to-point, or virtual link, the Router ID is examined instead of the network information. The reason in the case of a virtual link is that the IP information will always, by the nature of a virtual link, be mismatched. In the case of a point-to-point link, where a circuit is erected between two end points, a common network is implied already and no further examination of the IP network information is required.

Next, if the receiving OSPF interface is connected to a multiple-access network, it will check the source IP address in the IP header. (In the case of a point-to-point or virtual link, the Router ID is checked.) The receiving interface can then determine whether the incoming Hello is being transmitted from a known neighbor (see Figure 31-4). The interface checks its neighbor list and if the information contained in the Hello does not provide a match, then a neighbor listing is created with an initial state of Down. (See the section "OSPF Neighbors" found later in this chapter for more information on the different Neighbor states.)

Hello packets are also used to determine an OSPF neighbor state. For example, a router receiving a Hello packet from a neighbor with itself listed as a neighboring router is considered to have bidirectional communication with the sending neighbor, and a 2-Way state exists between them. This means that, if appropriate, an adjacency can be formed between the two neighbors. If a 2-Way state exists and a Hello is received that does not contain the receiving router in the neighbor list, then the neighbor state must be altered to a 1-Way state; under these circumstances, an adjacency is not possible.

Another way Hello packets are utilized is to elect the Designated Router and Backup Designated Router. During the election process, all eligible routers declare themselves to be the designated router. Then, after receiving a Hello from a neighbor with a higher Router Priority, an OSPF router announcing itself as the DR will change this information to reflect the neighbor as the DR. A neighboring router may, in this

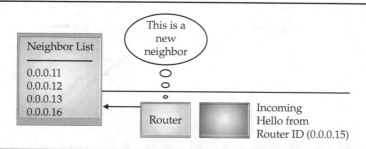

**Figure 31-4.**    *An OSPF interface comparing an incoming Hello to its neighbor list*

case, receive one Hello where the sending router declares itself the DR, then another Hello from the same router declaring a different router to be the DR. The receiving router in this case must update its DR information. Hello packets are used for the election of the Backup Designated Router as well.

# Hello Protocol in Nonbroadcast, Multiple-Access (NBMA) Environments

The Hello protocol functions a bit differently in nonbroadcast, multiple-access environments. Instead of sending Hello packets to the group multicast address of 224.0.0.5, OSPF routers in an NBMA network send Hello packets as unicast packets to the IP addresses statically configured in the OSPF neighbor list. Since Hello packets are the mechanism by which the DR and BDR are elected, each OSPF neighbor configured in the neighbor list must also be specified as either DR eligible or DR ineligible. All OSPF routers labeled as DR eligible transmit unicast Hello packets to each other in order to compete in the DR and BDR election process. All routers not eligible to become the DR respond to any Hello packets they receive with their own Hello packets and send periodic Hello packets to the DR and the BDR, once established. In a hub and spoke configuration, it is necessary to configure the Router Priority such that the hub router becomes the DR. Spoke routers should be marked DR ineligible since only the hub router has connections to all the OSPF routers in the NBMA network (Figure 31-5).

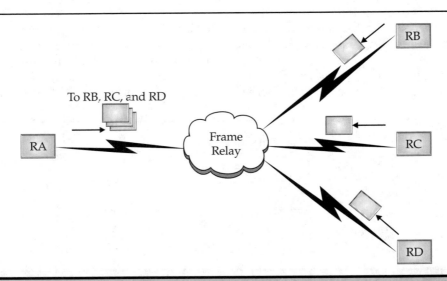

**Figure 31-5.**   *A Hello exchange over a nonbroadcast, multiple-access network*

# OSPF Neighbors

OSPF neighbors are either statically configured or determined through the transmission and receipt of Hello packets. Effectively, if a router receives a Hello packet from another router, then the receiving router is considered an OSPF neighbor. Since Hello packets are transmitted on an interface-by-interface basis, and not forwarded across interfaces, neighbors share a common network. A router may have neighbors residing in different networks, but only if it has interfaces in each of those networks.

Neighbors may form what are known as *adjacencies* to one another. Adjacencies are used for communicating link state information. A neighbor state, however, does not guarantee an adjacency. Adjacencies are formed only under specific circumstances, to be covered later in this chapter.

## Neighbor State Changes

OSPF routers on the same network may have differing link states. For instance, neighbors attempting to establish adjacencies enter different neighbor states than those which do not. The type of neighbor state indicates the type of relationship between two routers, and the current status of that relationship.

A list of the different neighbor states, and their meanings, follows:

**DOWN**   This state can only occur if the OSPF neighbor is statically configured. It is the state before any inter-neighbor communication occurs.

**ATTEMPT**   The Attempt state will exist only when the OSPF neighbor is statically configured. It indicates that the router has not seen a Hello from its OSPF neighbor.

**INIT**   The Init state is entered when a router receives a Hello packet from a neighboring router, but it hasn't yet been determined whether there is bidirectional communication with the neighbor because the receiving router is not listed in the neighbor's Hello packet. Once the neighbor receives a Hello packet from the receiving router, however, the neighbor will list the receiving router in its next Hello.

**2-WAY**   Once a router receives a Hello packet from its neighbor and sees itself listed in the neighbor's Hello, a 2-Way state is entered; bidirectional communication has been verified.

It should be noted that once the 2-Way state is reached, there will be no progression to the remaining states unless it has been determined that an adjacency must be formed. Progression to the ExStart, Exchange, Loading, and Full states will occur only between a router and its Designated Router and Backup Designated Router, between two routers on a point-to-point link, or between two routers connected by a virtual link. All other neighbor relationships will stop at the 2-Way state.

**EXSTART**   Once it has been determined that an adjacency must be formed, the first step is to establish a master/slave relationship between the two adjacent routers in order to determine which router will start the process of exchanging Database Description (DD) packets. The master sends DD packets and the slave responds, adopting the master's sequence number. The determining factor for the master/slave relationship is the Router ID; the router with the higher ID is the master.

**EXCHANGE**    During the Exchange state, DD packets are transmitted along the adjacency between the master and slave routers. Each Database Description packet contains an abbreviated view of the network link states, called Link State Advertisement headers. Only the headers are used instead of complete LSAs to cut down on overhead, since the LSAs may or may not be needed by the receiving router. The list of headers is compared against the receiving router's database, to determine if there are headers in a received DD packet that the receiving router has no corresponding link state information for; if so, then the full Link State Advertisements must be requested.

**LOADING**    Once the exchange of DD packets is complete, each router has compiled a list of Link State Advertisements that it is missing from its database. The missing entries are requested through the transmission of a Link State Request. In response to the Link State Request, a Link State Update is returned, containing the full Link State Advertisements. This information is added to the receiving router's Link State database.

**FULL**    Upon completion of the Database Description packet exchange and the exchange of Link State Advertisements, a Full state is reached, at which point both routers involved have identical Link State Databases. A Full state indicates a Full Adjacency has been achieved.

Again, bear in mind that the last four states, ExStart, Exchange, Loading, and Full are reached only when adjacencies are formed.

# Forming Adjacencies

When bidirectional communication is established, a decision must be made as to whether or not a full adjacency should be formed. This decision is made at the time bidirectional communication is first established and again if a topology change occurs, such as a failure of the DR. In the case where the Designated Router fails, the Backup Designated Router takes over as the new DR, a new Backup Designated Router is then elected, and adjacencies must be formed to the new BDR.

The rules for forming adjacencies are as follows:

- If the routers are on either end of a point-to-point link, an adjacency must be formed.

- If the router link in question is a virtual link, an adjacency must be formed with the Designated Router.

- If the router is the Designated Router or Backup Designated Router, an adjacency must be formed.

- If the neighboring router is the Designated Router or Backup Designated Router, an adjacency must be formed.

## Designated Router

In multi-access networks, a Designated Router is elected. The DR originates a Network Links Advertisement, which contains all the routers (itself included) in the network. The link state ID for the Network Links Advertisement will be the IP address of the DR interface that transmitted it. So that the DR can propagate its Network Links Advertisement, the DR, maintains adjacencies with all other routers on its network (see Figure 31-6).

The reason why the DR is used to synchronize LSDBs is that, depending on the number of routers in an OSPF multi-access network, it could become unwieldy from both a bandwidth and processor overhead perspective for all routers to exchange LSAs with every other router on the network. Since the synchronized LSDBs on all routers are identical, there is no real need to have each individual router synchronize its LSDB with all other routers, so instead the Designated Router acts as the representative for the network in this regard.

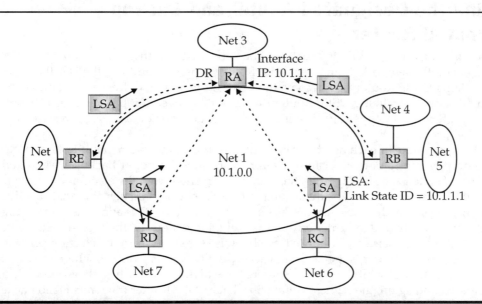

**Figure 31-6.**    *A Designated Router with adjacencies to all other network routers*

The Designated Router may potentially maintain a large number of adjacencies. In order to simplify the process of transmitting Network Links Advertisements and link-state updates to many routers at once, the DR sends these packets as multicasts to all other routers using the 224.0.0.5 address (AllSPFRouters), LSAs being sent to the DR or BDR utilize the multicast group address 224.0.0.6.

Should a router be elected as Designated Router, its interface state becomes *DR*. If the router becomes the Backup Designated Router, then its interface is changed to *Backup*. All other interfaces not in the DR or the Backup state should be listed as *DR Other*.

## Backup Designated Router

Since the role of the Designated Router is critical to network connectivity, a Backup Designated Router is also elected, so that a less disruptive cutover can occur in the event that the Designated Router is lost for whatever reason.

Router adjacencies, such as those maintained with the Designated Router, are also established and maintained with the Backup Designated Router. Should the Designated Router fail, the Backup Designated Router takes over the DR's responsibilities. There is a slight delay during the cutover process, however, while a new Backup Designated Router is elected and the new DR prepares to send Network Links Advertisements.

## Electing the Designated Router and Backup Designated Router

Upon initialization, an OSPF Router will become the DR if there are no other OSPF Routers on the network. If another OSPF Router is present and it is the DR, the initializing OSPF Router will become the BDR. If the network already has both a DR and DBR, the initializing OSPF Router defers to them even if it has a higher router priority. If several OSPF Routers initialize at once and no DR or BDR is present, an election process occurs.

First, the state of each neighbor is examined. If the state is 2-Way, then the router in question remains a potential candidate for Designated Router or Backup Designated Router. If state is not 2-Way, then the router is screened from the election process.

Of the remaining routers, the Router Priority is checked. *Router Priority* is a value that indicates how desirable a router is for the role of DR or BDR and is user configured. A Router Priority of 0 indicates a router is ineligible to become the Designated Router, and so all routers with a priority of 0 are likewise screened from the election process. The Designated Router is then selected according to Router Priority, where the highest value wins. In the event that OSPF Routers have identical priorities, the Router IDs are compared and again, the highest value wins. Each OSPF Router transmits Hello packets advertising itself as the DR. The receiving routers will compare the Router Priority in the received Hello with its own. If the router priority of the router that sent the Hello is greater than the router priority of the receiving router, the receiving router updates its DR parameter with the router ID of the router that sent the Hello. This DR will now be advertised by the receiving router in future Hellos.

The Backup Designated Router is then calculated; only routers that have passed through the initial screening process and have not declared themselves the Designated Router are eligible to become the Backup Designated Router. The BDR is chosen in the same way as the DR; by highest Router Priority, with ties broken by the highest Router ID.

Figure 31-7 shows three potential Designated Routers comparing Hello packets. The three have the following values:

| Router | Priority | ID |
|--------|----------|-----------|
| A | 10 | 0.0.0.10 |
| B | 10 | 0.0.0.20 |
| C | 100 | 0.0.0.30 |

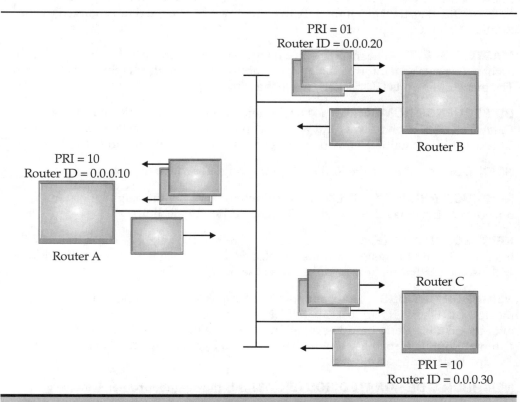

PRI = 01
Router ID = 0.0.0.20

Router B

PRI = 10
Router ID = 0.0.0.10

Router A

Router C

PRI = 10
Router ID = 0.0.0.30

**Figure 31-7.** *OSPF routers comparing router priorities and router IDs*

Notice that in this example, routers A and B have equal priority, but router B has the higher Router ID. Router C examines each Hello and, recognizing itself as having the highest priority, declares itself as the best candidate for DR. At the same time, routers A and B have compared the Router Priorities and found that router C does in fact have the highest priority. Router A and B insert Router C as the DR into their Hellos at this point, declaring it to be the best candidate until all OSPF routers agree. Since they are not eligible for the Designated Router position, Routers A and B each declare themselves as the Backup Designated Router. Through comparing Router Priority and Router ID, Router B is chosen as the BDR.

# Neighbor Information

Neighbor information is summarized in a Neighbor Data Structure; this structure contains all the information necessary to establish and maintain a neighbor adjacency. The different components of the Neighbor Data Structure follows:

**STATE**    This is the current level of the Neighbor state.

**INACTIVITY TIMER**    Should a Hello packet not be received in the expected time frame (defined as the Hello Interval), this timer will be triggered. It is defined by the Router Dead Interval parameter.

**MASTER/SLAVE**    The master/slave relationship is determined for the purposes of exchanging database information and is established during the neighbor state *ExStart*. The master transmits DD packets, while the slave responds.

**DD SEQUENCE NUMBER**    The DD Sequence number is used to identify the Database Description packets and will be incremented by the master each time a new DD packet is transmitted. Only one packet can be sent at any one time.

**NEIGHBOR ID**    This is the Router ID of the neighbor router.

**NEIGHBOR PRIORITY**    This states the Router Priority of the neighbor router (for purposes of Designated and Backup Designated Router election).

**NEIGHBOR IP ADDRESS**    This is the IP address of the neighbor router's local OSPF interface. Should the neighbor router be elected as the Designated Router, this address will also be used as its Router Links Advertisement Link ID.

**NEIGHBOR OPTIONS**    Here, optional OSPF capabilities are indicated. These may include ToS (Type Of Service) capabilities (which are generally not used). Other options include external routing capability, and whether or not the interface supports External Routing Capability or whether or not AS External Advertisements will be flooded to a specific area.

**NEIGHBOR'S DESIGNATED ROUTER**    This is the neighbor router's choice for Designated Router. It may or may not be itself.

**NEIGHBOR'S BACKUP DESIGNATED ROUTER**   The neighbor router's choice for the Backup Designated Router. It may or may not be itself.

**LINK STATE RETRANSMISSION LIST**   This lists the Link State Advertisements that have not been acknowledged. They will be retransmitted indefinitely until responded to or the adjacency fails.

**DATABASE SUMMARY LIST**   The compilation of Link State Advertisements for an OSPF area. This is sent in the Database Description packets.

**LINK STATE REQUEST LIST**   This is a list of Link State Advertisements currently missing from the router's Database Summary, compared to the Database Description packets from its neighbor. These missing entries are requested in the Link State Request packets.

# Database Synchronization

In order to ensure each OSPF router can correctly determine a valid path through the network, all SPF Routers must share a common database, which means the LSDB must be synchronized throughout the network.

LSDB synchronization occurs after the formation of an adjacency. The sections that immediately follow describe how OSPF routers synchronize their LSDBs.

## The ExStart State

In the ExStart State, the necessity for database exchange has been determined but has not yet proceeded. The master/slave relationship must be determined between the adjacent routers, after which the transfer of Database Description (DD) packets will commence. Here is an example of a DD packet:

| Version # | | 2 | | | | Packet Length | | | |
|---|---|---|---|---|---|---|---|---|---|
| Router ID | | | | | | | | | |
| Area ID | | | | | | | | | |
| Checksum | | | | | Authentication Type | | | | |
| Authentication | | | | | | | | | |
| Authentication | | | | | | | | | |
| 0 | 0 | | Options | 0 | 0 | 0 | 0 | 0 | I | M | MS |
| DD sequence number | | | | | | | | | |
| Link State Advertisement Header | | | | | | | | | |

The router with the higher router ID will send an initial DD packet with the I (initialize) bit set, indicating the exchange is about to begin; the M (more) bit set, indicating there will be more packets exchanged; and the MS (master/slave) bit set, indicating that it is the master and the receiving router should assume the slave role.

The receiving router, upon receipt of the initial DD packet will assume the role of slave and send back another empty DD packet, indicating to the sender that the packet was received and that the master/slave relationship has now been determined and acknowledged.

## Exchange

Once the master/slave relationship is determined, the actual exchange of Database Description packets commences. The master sends a DD packet containing a description of the current LSDB as it perceives it at that moment. The DD packet will contain a sequence number, as only one DD packet can be outstanding at any one time. It will also indicate whether or not there are more packets to come. (Upon transmitting the last DD packet in a series, the M [More] bit is set back to 0, indicating this is the last packet.) The slave receives each packet and compares it to the information currently contained in its own database, as shown here:

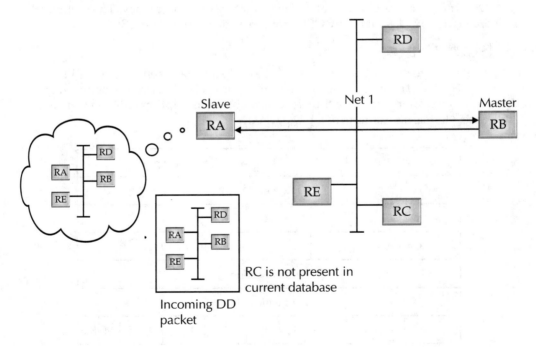

RC is not present in current database

Incoming DD packet

Database Description packets contain a series of Link State Advertisement headers; this is the information that is compared against the receiving router's current LSDB. If the received DD packet describes any link states that are not currently in the existing database, then these entries will need to be added. Since the DD packets contain only the Link State Advertisement headers and not the complete LSA, no new information is actually added at this time; the missing LSAs are compiled and will be requested specifically during the *Loading* state. If the received Database Description matches that of the existing database, and there are no further DD packets in the sequence, the databases are then synchronized.

# Loading

Once the list of LSA headers that are missing from a router's LSDB are determined, the actual LSAs must be requested so that the LSDB can be updated. This is accomplished with a Link State Request packet. The Link State Request may be sent at the conclusion of the Database Description packet exchange, or the two processes may be interleaved and the missing Advertisements requested as soon as their absence from the current database is noted.

Upon receiving a Link State Request packet, the receiving router then sends back a Link State Update:

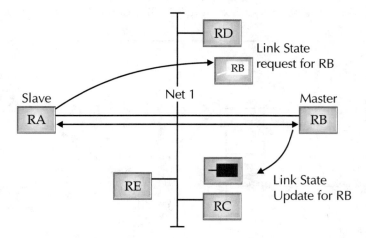

The Link State Update packet contains a string of Link State Advertisements, each with its own header describing the link state type, the Link State ID, and the Advertising Router. During convergence, a Link State Advertisement may be requested that has a lower sequence number than the LSA of the receiving router, as link state information may have changed during the packet exchange. Since the LSA with the higher sequence number is assumed to be the more recent, the receiving router sends this to the requesting router instead. The heretofore missing LSA entries are then added to the receiving router's LSDB.

# Full

A Full state is reached when each Link State Request has been satisfied and each Link State Advertisement contained in the Link State Update has been acknowledged with a Link State Acknowledgement containing the header of each LSA acquired (see the following section).

## Link State Acknowledgement Packet

To verify that all of the requested Link State Advertisements have been received and that they have arrived intact, the router that originally sent the Link State Request sends a Link State Acknowledgement in response to the update.

This Link State Acknowledgement contains a list of LSA headers for the LSAs that were received.

# An Example of Database Synchronization

For the purposes of this example, there are a total of eight OSPF routers in a single OSPF area. Routers F, G, and H have formed full adjacencies with Router A, the DR for the ATM portion of the network. (See Figure 31-8). Router B is aware of two other SPF

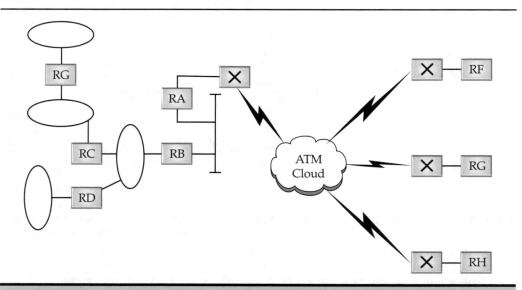

**Figure 31-8.**    *Two SPF routers, each aware of other SPF routers, sharing LS info*

interfaces through the Token Ring portion of the network. Bear in mind that, in this case, the OSPF interfaces that border the ATM network are Ethernet, not ATM, interfaces; the ATM cloud is invisible to the Ethernet network, so this is not an NBMA network but a Broadcast network.

Prior to the database synchronization, routers A and B have received one another's Hello packets. Each router has seen its Router ID listed in the other's Hello packet, so bidirectional communication has been confirmed, and a 2-Way state has been entered. Since, in this case, router A has determined itself to be the Designated Router, and router B has acknowledged Router A as the DR, an adjacency must be formed.

The ExStart state is entered. Since router B has a higher router ID, it assumes the master role (even though, since its Router Priority is lower, it is not the Designated Router). It transmits an empty Database Description packet to router A with the M, I, and MS bits flipped, telling router A that a DD packet exchange will now begin, that more packets will follow this one, and that router B is the master. In response, router A assumes the slave role, adopts router B's DD sequence number, and transmits an empty DD packet back to router B, acknowledging it is slave and ready to receive Database Description information.

Router B will now send the next DD packet, this time containing its list of known link states. Only, the Link State headers are sent; router A may already have full knowledge of some or all of the link states contained in the Database Description packet, and so there is no need to initially send the whole of the link state information.

Router A receives the DD packet and discovers that none of the Link State headers contained in the packet are present in its own database. However, the M bit is still flipped, indicating that router B has more DD packets to send. Router A notes the Link State headers it will need the full LSA for, and returns a DD packet of its own containing the headers of the link states that it is aware of:

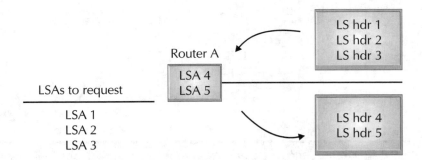

Router B learns that, likewise, none of router A's headers are currently in its own database. This exchange continues until the information has all been exchanged; the last DD packet sent by the master has the M bit flipped back to 0, indicating there are no more DD packets to follow.

Once this is complete, the master, drawing from its list of Link State headers that did not appear in its own database, transmits a Link State Request packet to router A, requesting the full Link State Advertisement information.

A Link State Update is sent from Router A to Router B in response. The Link State Update, contains the complete list of LSAs requested in the Link State Request. Once received, this new link state information is added to router B's LSDB. Likewise, router A then sends a Link State Request to router B, receives a Link State Update in response, and updates its own LSDB (see Figure 31-9). Database synchronization is now complete, and the two routers now have identical LSDBs. At this point, routers A and B are fully adjacent.

## Database Synchronization and Multiple Adjacencies

Taking the same example one step further, let us now introduce routers C and D. Router B is now fully adjacent with Router A, its Designated Router. Routers C and D

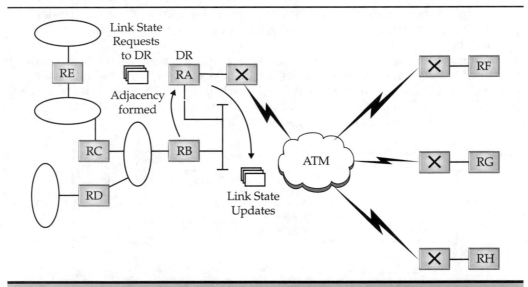

**Figure 31-9.**   *Routers A and B exchanging Link State Requests and Link State Updates*

share a common network with router B, but not with router A, though they all exist within the same OSPF area.

Routers B, C, and D all learn of each other via Hello packets. In addition, each router sees itself listed as a neighbor in the other router's Hello packets. Bidirectional communication is established between all three routers (see Figure 31-10). So a 2-Way state is reached between all routers. Router C is elected Designated Router.

Routers B and C and routers C and D enter the ExStart state to determine the master/slave relationships. Once determined, they enter the exchange state and DD packets are transmitted using the LSDB synchronization process.

In this case, router A and router B have synchronized their Databases, but routers C and D only have information about their own link states. Through the DD packet exchange during the Exchange state, however, router B exchanges its Link State Advertisement headers with router C, the Designated Router for that network, and Router C's LSDB becomes synchronized with Router B's. Router B updates router A at this point.

About Router D, through its adjacency with router C, learns of the rest of the network link states during database synchronization. At this point, Routers A, B, C, and D have identical LSDBs (see Figure 31-11).

INTERNETWORKING WITH NORTEL NETWORKS

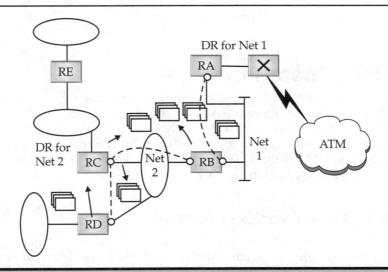

**Figure 31-10.** *Routers B and D exchanging Link State Requests and Link State Updates with router C, the elected Designated Router*

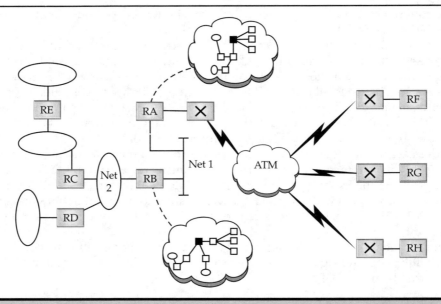

**Figure 31-11.** *All routers in both networks within the area are updated and synchronized*

# Link State Operations

Link State Advertisements contain information regarding directly connected networks only; an SPF router announcing its link state information will not describe any information about its neighbor's connections. By confining advertisements to only information the router has direct knowledge of, no SPF router will propagate incorrect information. SPF routers learn of the link states of routers that are not directly attached, but an SPF router advertises only its own link states.

## LSAs (Link State Advertisements)

Link State Advertisements are originated by each router within an Autonomous System. By collecting these LSAs, (an OSPF network under one administrative control) routers assemble a topological database of the network.

There are five different types of Link State Advertisements, each with a distinct function. Each of these LS types are listed in the following sections.

## LS Type 1: Router Links Advertisements

These LSAs are generated by all SPF routers. These advertisements describe the connection state of each of the router's interfaces within a single area. Each Router Links Advertisement includes a Link ID, the Link Type, and the Link Data. The Link Types that can be described by a Router Links Advertisement are as follows:

- **Link Type 1 (point-to-point)**    The local end of a point-to-point network type.

- **Link Type 2 (transit)**    A multiple-access network containing multiple SPF routers.

- **Link Type 3 (stub)**    Either a multiple-access network where there are no other routers present or, in the case of a point-to-point link, the remote end. (This Link Type should not be confused with the *stub area*, which will be described in greater detail later in this chapter.)

- **Link Type 4 (virtual link)**    A virtual link to the backbone area.

The Link ID and Link Data in these cases will vary, depending on the type of network (see Table 31-1).

In the case of a point-to-point link, a common network is implied, while in a virtual link, the IP information will not match and so the Router ID is used. In the case of a transit link, the DR will be used since that is where the router adjacency exists, while in the case of a stub link there are no adjacencies by definition (there are no other routers in that network), and so the network number is used.

For example, a Router Links Advertisement generated by an OSPF router with a Router ID of 0.0.0.10, and two interfaces (one interface with an IP address of 180.100.10.1,

| Link Type | Description | Link ID Information |
|---|---|---|
| 1 | Point-to-point link | The neighbor's Router ID |
| 2 | Transit link | IP address of Designated Router |
| 3 | Stub link | IP network number |
| 4 | Virtual link | The neighbor's Router ID |

**Table 31-1.**    *Link Types*

connected to a stub network, and the other a Frame Relay link configured with IP address 180.180.10.1) might look something like this when captured in a sniffer trace:

```
OSPF: Link State Advertisement #1
OSPF: Link state age         = 38 (seconds)
OSPF: Optional capabilities  = X2
OSPF:      .... ..1.      = external routing capability
OSPF:      .... ...0 = no Type of Service routing capability
OSPF: Link state type        = 1 (Router links)
OSPF: Link state ID          = [0.0.0.10]
OSPF: Advertising Router      = [0.0.0.10]
OSPF: Sequence number      = 22839371892, Checksum = 48AC
OSPF: Length            = 84
OSPF: Router type flags = 00
OSPF:          .... ..0.      = Non-AS boundary router
OSPF:          .... ...0 = Non Area border router
OSPF: Number of router links = 2
OSPF: Link ID     = [180.180.10.1]
OSPF: Link Data   = [180.180.10.1]
OSPF: Link type   = 2
OSPF: Number of ToS metrics   = 0, ToS 0 metric = 4
OSPF: Link ID     = [180.100.10.0]
OSPF: Link Data   = [255.255.255.0]
OSPF: Link type   = 3
OSPF: Number of ToS metrics   = 0, ToS 0 metric = 3
```

## LS Type 2: Network Links Advertisements

Network Links Advertisements are originated by the Designated Router on multiple-access networks. Each advertisement contains a Link State ID (described as the IP address of the advertising interface), the Advertising Router (described as the Router ID of the router sending the advertisement), the network mask of that interface, and a list of all other routers on that network by Router ID. The Designated Router floods these advertisements over each of its adjacencies. They remain within a single area only.

For example, suppose there is an OSPF Router (router ID 0.0.0.80), with an ATM connection to an ELAN that has four other OSPF LEC interfaces configured in it, where the advertising LEC is configured with IP address 180.80.10.1/24 the Network Links Advertisement generated by this router might look something like this in a sniffer trace:

```
OSPF: Link State Advertisement # 1
OSPF: Link state age     = 9 (seconds)
OSPF: Optional capabilities  = X2
OSPF:          ... ..1.      = external routing capability
OSPF:          .... .0   = no Type of Service routing capability
```

```
OSPF: Link state type        = 2 (Network links)
OSPF: Link state ID          = [180.80.10.1]
OSPF: Advertising Router     = [0.0.0.80]
OSPF: Sequence number        = 214298374932, Checksum = 487E
OSPF: Length                 = 48
OSPF: Network mask           = [255.255.255.0]
OSPF: Attached router (1)    = [0.0.0.10]
OSPF: Attached router (2)    = [0.0.0.20]
OSPF: Attached router (3)    = [0.0.0.30]
OSPF: Attached router (4)    = [0.0.0.40]
```

Here, the "Attached router" entries are the Router IDs associated with the remote OSPF LEC interfaces.

## LS Types 3 and 4: Summary Link Advertisements

Summary Link Advertisements (LS Type 3) are generated by Area Border routers. They describe destinations reachable outside a specific area, but still within the same Autonomous System. Summary Link Advertisements are passed from an Area Border to the Backbone area (0.0.0.0), and from the backbone to the other areas (see Figure 31-12).

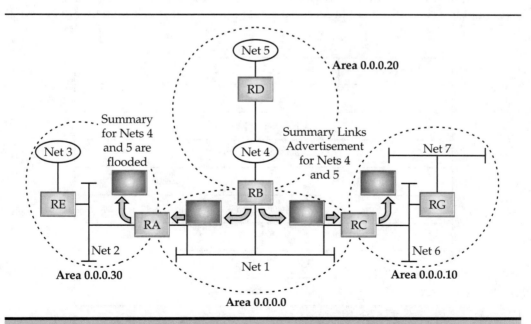

**Figure 31-12.** *A Summary Link Advertisement flooded across the backbone to other areas*

By default, a Summary Link Advertisement will be generated for each network in a specific area; however, in order to keep overhead low, the networks can be summarized so that the Summary Link Advertisement advertises a range of network addresses instead of the individual network addresses for each network.

Summary Link Advertisements (LS Type 3) describe routes to networks, while Summary Link Advertisement (LS Type 4) describe routes to AS Boundary routers. OSPF address summarization will be described in greater detail further on in this chapter.

The Area Border router is responsible for generating an AS Summary Links Advertisement when it receives Router Links Advertisements from an SABR. The ABR knows that the advertisements are from an ASBR because the SABR sets a bit in its Router Links Advertisements indicating this. Both LS Types 3 and 4 are flooded into adjoining areas, unlike LS Type 2 advertisements, which are flooded only within a single area.

## LS Type 5: AS External Link Advertisements

AS External Link Advertisements (LS Type 5) are generated by AS Boundary routers and are flooded throughout an entire Autonomous System with the exception of stub areas. These advertisements are similar in concept to Summary Link Advertisements, except that they advertise destination networks from other autonomous systems rather than other areas within the local AS. For example, RIP Routes learned from another AS would be flooded within the OSPF domain as LS Type 5 advertisements. Each AS External Link Advertisement describes a single route to a destination network external to the OSPF Domain:

| LS age | Options | 5 |
|---|---|---|
| Link State ID | | |
| Advertising Router | | |
| LS sequence number | | |
| LS checksum | Length | |
| Network mask | | |
| E | TOS | Metric |
| Forwarding address | | |
| External route tag | | |

Autonomous Systems and AS Boundary routers will be discussed in greater detail further on in this chapter.

## Link State IDs

As can be seen in the previous examples, each Link State type makes use of a Link State ID. However, what the Link State ID represents will differ depending on the Link State type. Table 31-2 outlines the Link State Ids, their corresponding values, and the link state types they are associated with.

## Flooding Link State Advertisements

When more recent Link State Update packets are received, the flooding procedure is initiated. Depending on the link state, and the LSA type, this is done in various ways.

In the case of AS External Link Advertisements and Summary Link Advertisements (LS Types 3 and 4), they are flooded out all OSPF interfaces, except virtual links and those interfaces connecting to stub areas.

Network and Router Links Advertisements will be flooded within a certain area. In this case, viable interfaces for flooding are any interfaces within the specified area, though not every neighbor within the area will receive the new advertisement. If the area in question is the backbone area, eligible interfaces include any virtual links.

| Type | Link State | Link State ID |
|------|-----------|---------------|
| 1 | Router Links Advertisement | The originating router's Router ID |
| 2 | Network Links Advertisement | The IP address of the network's DR |
| 3 | Summary Link/Network | The destination network number |
| 4 | Summary Link/AS Boundary router | The Router ID of the AS Boundary router |
| 5 | AS External Link Advertisement | The destination network number |

**Table 31-2.** *Link State Types and IDs*

The OSPF Router's decision-making process to flood or not to flood proceeds as follows: Prior to flooding, link state information neighbors are first examined to determine whether or not they need to receive it. If the advertisement is an AS External Link Advertisement or Summary Link Advertisement, then it is flooded out to all interfaces excluding virtual links and interfaces connected to stub areas. If it is any other type, however, then it is flooded only to neighbors who are in the Exchange state or greater. Furthermore, if the adjacency to a neighbor has not yet reached the Full state, then the Link State Request List associated with the adjacency is examined to see if an entry for the same advertisement already exists there. If it does, the advertisements are compared. If the new advertisement is older than the advertisement in the Link State Request List, then it will not be flooded to that neighbor and the next neighbor is examined. If the advertisements are the same, the request is removed from the Link State Request List (as it has already been acquired on another adjacency), and the next neighbor is examined. If the new advertisement is more recent, again, the advertisement is deleted from the LS Request List.

Link State information is not flooded back over the adjacency the advertisement was received from. If an advertisement has been received from a certain neighbor, it will not be flooded back to that neighbor; instead, the next neighbor will be examined.

At this point, a decision must be made as to whether or not to flood the information to each of the neighbors not yet eliminated by the screening process. To do so, two things are considered:

- Was the new advertisement received from the DR or BDR?
- Is the receiving interface the BDR?

If the answer to either of these questions is "Yes," then the advertisement is not flooded; If the answer is "No," then the advertisement is flooded.

## Validating Link States

It is possible under these circumstances for a router to receive two instances of a single Link State Advertisement. In these cases, the router must determine which of the two instances is the more recent (and therefore assumed to be more accurate). Observe the LSA header in the following diagram:

| LS age | Options | LS type |
|---|---|---|
| Link State ID | | |
| Advertising Router | | |
| LS sequence number | | |
| LS checksum | | Length |

For purposes of determining which LSA should be added to the LSDB, the LS sequence number, LS age, and LS checksum are used.

Upon the receipt of two instances of the same LSA, the LSA with the higher LS Sequence number will be considered to be the most recent. Should both instances share the same sequence number, then the LS checksum is calculated and the instance with the larger checksum is considered the more recent. If the checksums match, then each instance is checked to see if the LS age field is set to MaxAge, and if so, the instance bearing that value is considered the most recent. Lastly, if the two instances differ by more than the MaxAgeDiff value, then the smaller age is chosen. These rules hold true in the case of a Link State Request as well, since during convergence, an LSA requested in the Link State Request may actually have a lower sequence number than the LSA the receiving router is in possession of at that time. In these cases, the newer LSA is sent.

## OSPF Protocol Packets

The following is a list of the OSPF protocol packet types, along with their descriptions:

| Type | Packet name |
|------|-------------|
| 1 | Hello packet |
| 2 | Database Description packet |
| 3 | Link State Request packet |
| 4 | Link State Update packet |
| 5 | Link State Acknowledgement packet |

# Authentication

OSPF updates can be authenticated. A look at the OSPF packet header reveals an authentication field:

| Version # | Type | Packet length |
|-----------|------|---------------|
| Router ID | | |
| Area ID | | |
| Checksum | | Authentication type |
| Authentication | | |
| Authentication | | |

Authentication can involve a simple password scheme; this requires the configuration of a 64-bit field that will be inserted into the authentication field of the OSPF packet header. Upon receipt of an OSPF packet, the receiving interface will check the field to see if the password is consistent with its configured value. Authentication can take place on a variety of levels. For instance, passwords can be set on an area basis, on a network-by-network basis, or on both.

OSPF packets (such as LSAs, or Hello packets) not containing the proper value in the authentication field are ignored. This prevents routers from joining an incorrect area and also provides a certain amount of security, since the network will not be as vulnerable to having bogus route information from an external source used to upset the network.

## The Link State Database (LSDB)

By combining the information received from different LSAs, Designated Routers within a single area form an LSDB, then distribute the information contained in the LSDB to their OSPF neighbors. Since the LSDB will be used to formulate an SPF tree, an LSDB must be maintained for each area the router is a member of. The LSDB for an area will consist of Router Links Advertisements, Network Links Advertisements, Summary Link Advertisements, and AS External Advertisements. If the area is a stub area, then Summary Link Advertisements and AS External Advertisements are not included in the LSDB. Instead, a default route is generally used within stub areas.

## Inserting Link State Information into the LSDB

The OSPF routing table may need to be recalculated when new advertisements are added into the database. Should the new advertisement differ from information in the current database, then a recalculation must take place. The method of recalculation will differ depending on the LSA type. Consult the following list:

- **Router Links or Network Links Advertisement**   If the differing LSA is a Router Links Advertisement or a Network Links Advertisement, then the entire routing table must be recalculated. This will include the SPF tree for each area, not just the one where the change originated from. Boundary routers may belong to multiple areas; therefore, data that has taken the best path through one specific area may need to take a route through a different area if the primary path is cut off.

- **Summary Link Advertisement**   The best route to the range of networks affected by the change will need to be recalculated.

- **AS External Link Advertisement**   The best route that traverses an AS Boundary router must be recalculated.

## Multiple Adjacencies

An adjacency between two routers is local to a specific network. Since in an OSPF network, it is possible to have multiple paths to a destination, the possibility exists for two routers to be connected to more than one common network:

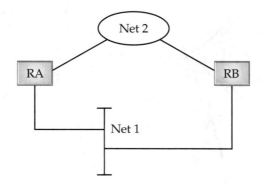

In a case such as this, a single adjacency is not sufficient; if router A is the Designated Router for both networks, then two adjacencies must be formed between the same two routers, one for each network.

## The SPF Tree

As mentioned earlier in the chapter, calculating the SPF tree involves determining a least-cost path from the router the path will be originating from. This is accomplished using Dijkstra's algorithm. While it is not entirely necessary to understand all of the inner workings of the algorithm, it is important from an OSPF design standpoint to truly understand how path costing will affect the building of the SPF tree and, therefore, the path by which data moves through the network. It is possible, through incorrect costing or careless design, for traffic to take an unintended and inappropriate route through the network, such as traffic bypassing an ATM link in favor of a 56K leased line.

To understand how the SPF tree is constructed, consider a network with six routers, routing between a total of 11 networks, three of which are *stub networks* (meaning that there are no other routers within those networks). Taking the network structure and reducing it to simply the routers and their interconnecting networks, the sample network can be viewed as shown in Figure 31-13.

Running Dijkstra's algorithm to build an SPF tree from router A involves the following steps:

- The first links to be examined are router A's directly connected links; the connections to router C by way of network 2 with a cost of 3, and to router B by

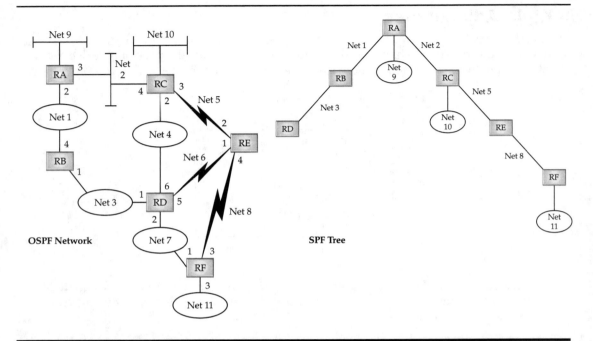

**Figure 31-13.** A network with six routers and three stub networks, and an SPF tree showing only the routers and networks interlinked

way of network 1 with a cost of 2. As this is the first iteration of the algorithm, the lower cost is accepted (router B by way of network 1), and added into the SPF tree. The path to router C is noted but not officially added or discarded at this time. As stub networks are not inserted in the first portion of the algorithm, network 9 is ignored.

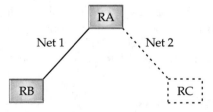

■ In the second step, since the path to router B has been chosen, router B's links are examined. Router B has only one link of consequence (since the path leading back to itself is discarded by router A). Router B's one link is to router D by way of network 3 with a cost of 1. There have been no further instances yet of router C, and the algorithm is not yet complete, so the link from router A to router C is still not officially added or discarded. The links from router D are examined:

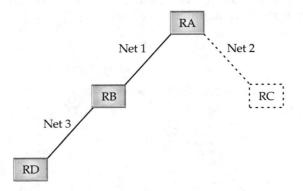

■ Router D has three links: to router C by way of network 4 with a cost of 6, to router E by way of network 6 with a cost of 5, and to router F by way of network 7 with a cost of 2. At this point, there have been two instances of router C; the two paths are weighed, adding the total path cost of each. In this case, the cost to router C via router A is 3, while the cost to router C via router B, then router D, is 9. The link from router D to router C is discarded, and the link from router A to router C is officially added to the tree. At this point, router E and router F are noted, but neither is officially added or discarded.

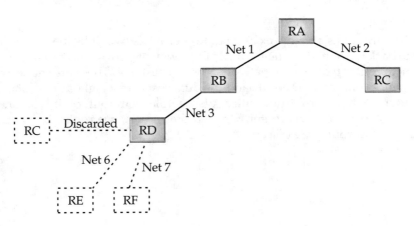

■ Since router C has officially been added to the SPF tree, its links are explored; router C has two links (aside from the link leading back to router A): one to router D by way of network 4 with a cost of 2, and another to router E by way of network 5 with a cost of 3. At this point, there is a second instance of router D and also of router E. The dual path costs are weighed: The total cost to router D by way of router B is 3, while the cost by way of router C is 5, and so the path to router D from router C is discarded. Likewise, the cost to router E by way of router B then router D is 8, while the cost to router E by way of router C is 6. The link to router E from router C is added, and the link from router D is discarded:

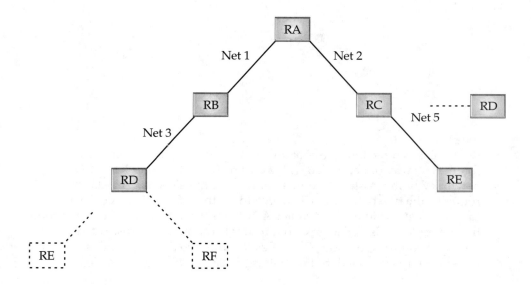

■ Router E's links are now examined. Router E has two links (not including the one back to router C); one to router D by way of network 6 with a cost of 1, and one to router F by way of network 8 with a cost of 4. These are the second instances of routers D and F, and the dual costs are weighed: The total cost to router D via router E from router A is 7, while from router B it is 3. Likewise, the cost to router F via router E from router A is 10; via router D, it is 5. The higher cost routes are discarded:

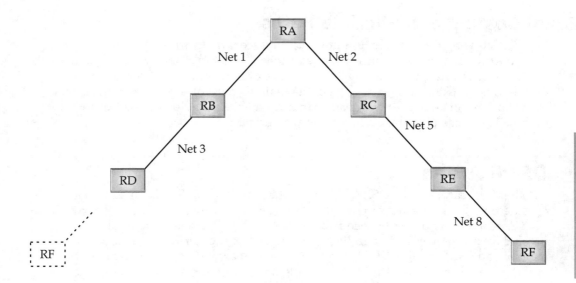

■ At this point, the shortest paths have been determined from router A to routers B, C, D, E, and F. Now the stub networks are added:

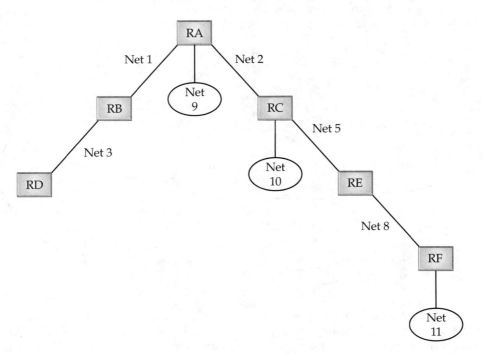

## Equal Costing and Multiple Paths

When calculating the SPF tree, it is possible for a scenario to arise where the path cost calculations along two branches are equal. While it is not mandatory according to the OSPF specification to acknowledge the presence of two or more equal-cost paths, the option to do so exists. The advantage of maintaining a list of equal-cost paths is that load-sharing can be done if both paths are known, whereas without this feature the path will be chosen arbitrarily on a case-by-case basis.

# OSPF Areas

Another key feature of the OSPF protocol is the logical breakdown of *areas*. An area is considered to be a logical grouping of routers, and may contain multiple IP networks.

The reason why one may need to break up an OSPF Network into multiple areas involve reducing overhead on individual routers. Each router within an area must maintain an LSDB of all of the link states within that area. If there are many routers within a single OSPF area, the LSDB residing on each router becomes quite large consuming a large portion of the router's memory resources. Likewise, processing a large number of LSAs can use up a significant amount of processor time. For these reasons, you may wish to configure multiple areas, keeping the LSDB small for each area and summarizing the information from other areas.

OSPF areas grouped together form what is called an *Autonomous System:*

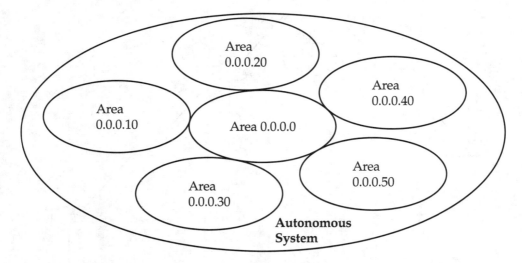

This scheme forms the basis for a sort of "hierarchical routing," in which routers perform different functions depending on their position within the network. Breaking an Autonomous System into multiple areas not only cuts down on CPU overhead and keeps memory requirements reasonable, it also reduces the impact of topology changes since all such changes will be advertised only within a single area and will not require a reconvergence of the entire network.

# Router Types

To accomplish full connectivity across multiple OSPF areas and Autonomous Systems, different routers perform different functions. For instance, a router connected to the backbone will behave differently than one that borders two Autonomous Systems. There are four different classifications of OSPF router, depending on the router's connection types.

## Internal Routers

*Internal routers* are those that have all interfaces within a common area. Routers with connections only to the backbone fall into this category. An internal router maintains a LSDB for its own area, but not for other areas (see Figure 31-14).

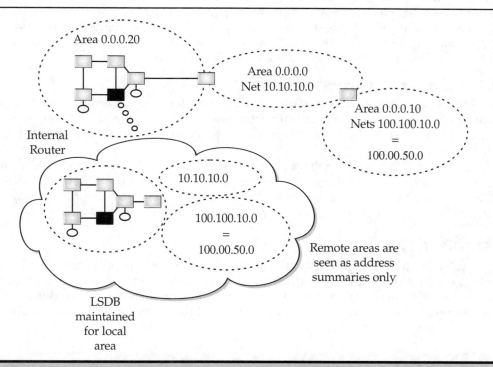

**Figure 31-14.**    *An internal router and its view of the OSPF network*

An internal router will run Dijkstra's algorithm against its own LSDB to create an SPF tree within its own area. If traffic is destined outside that area, the router need only be concerned with which area the data is destined for, not how it will be processed once it arrives there.

### Area Border Routers

An *Area Border router* is a router that has interfaces in multiple OSPF areas. It maintains an LSDB for each area to which it is attached and summarizes area information for distribution over the backbone to other areas. Area Border Routers must have an OSPF interface connected to the backbone area (0.0.0.0).

The Area Border router is capable of generating an SPF tree across multiple areas, so that when data is directed to it from one area, the router can select the shortest path to the destination area (or at least to the next area in the path leading to the destination area).

### Backbone Routers

A *backbone router* is one that has an interface connected to the backbone area (0.0.0.0). Since all areas must have a connection to the backbone area (either physically, or through a virtual link), many backbone routers will also be Area Border routers. Backbone routers will propagate the Summary Links Advertisements they receive throughout the backbone. Summary Links Advertisements are always sent from an area to the backbone, and then from the backbone, to the other areas.

### AS Boundary Routers

An AS Boundary router has interfaces in multiple Autonomous Systems. AS Boundary routers originate AS External Link Advertisements that are propagated throughout the Autonomous System. The path to each AS Boundary router must be known by each router within that AS.

An AS Boundary router will frequently border an OSPF Autonomous System and an Autonomous System using a networking protocol other than OSPF (such as RIP or BGP). Although both are under the same administrative control, networks running different networking protocols are considered separate autonomous systems.

## Backbone Area

Every OSPF network requires a backbone area. This area is defined as area ID 0.0.0.0. If only one area is configured, it must be area 0. Furthermore, any other areas configured within the OSPF network must have a connection to area 0. The reason for this is that area Summary Links Advertisements are flooded through the backbone area so all areas can learn of one another.

## Network Summaries

Network summaries are created by Area Border routers in OSPF networks containing multiple areas. These summaries are packaged in LSAs called Summary Link Advertisements. These advertisements are passed from area to area across the backbone area. They inform OSPF routers of networks accessible from neighboring areas, without providing the specific link state information about those areas. Using the information contained in a Summary Link Advertisement, an OSPF router can determine a routing path from the source router to the appropriate Area Border router, from that Area Border router across the backbone to the next Area Border router bordering the area where the destination lies. Then the receiving Area Border router can calculate the best path within its own area to the ultimate destination (see Figure 31-15).

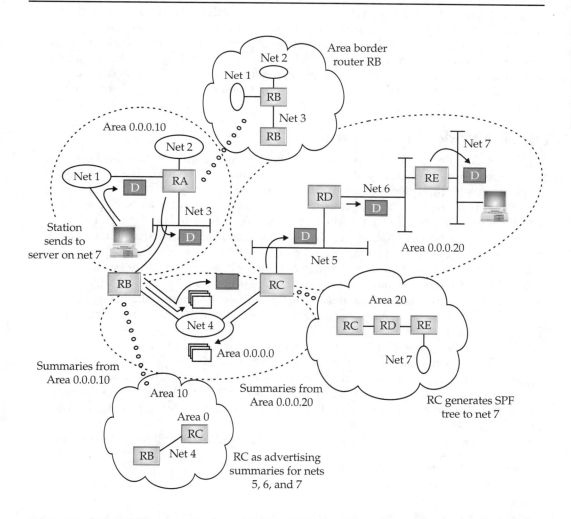

**Figure 31-15.**  *Path traced from the source to the backbone, Area Border router, and destination*

Summary Link Advertisements have a range of networks associated with them, which must be explicitly configured on the routers that originate them. Summary Link Advertisements are generated only by Area Border routers.

# Summary Link Advertisements

An Area Border router creates separate Summary Link Advertisements for each area it is connected to (i.e., each LSDB it maintains). Two separate LSA types are used in the case of a Summary Link Advertisement: Type 3 is used when the destination is an IP network, while Type 4 is used when the destination is an AS Boundary router.

It is the responsibility of an Area Border router to advertise the networks that it knows of, for each area that it is part of. These networks may be advertised separately (as they are by default), or they may be condensed into a range of networks in order to reduce overhead. In a well-designed OSPF network, each of the networks contained within an area can be condensed to a single network summary. This can drastically reduce the size of the LSDBs of routers receiving the Summary Link Advertisements, thus resulting in a smaller routing table.

# OSPF Network Summaries

Again, by default, every subnetwork in an OSPF network will be advertised separately by an Area Border router; a well-designed IP structure will result in fewer network summaries and, thus, demand less router resources.

In Figure 31-16, for example, four separate areas surround the backbone area of an OSPF network. OSPF area 0.0.0.0 (the backbone) consists of an ATM mesh. The surrounding areas contain Ethernet, Token Ring, and FDDI. Each area contains a range of IP networks: area 0.0.0.1 contains a range of subnets between 180.20.128.0 and 180.20.132.0, area 0.0.0.2 contains a range of subnets between 180.20.192.0 and 180.20.194.0, area 0.0.0.3 contains a range of subnets between 180.20.64.0 and 180.20.67.0, and area 0.0.0.4 contains a range of subnets between 180.20.32.0 and 180.20.34.0. This is an example of an OSPF network in which area summarization can be implemented.

To expand on our example, suppose that a network summary is created for area 0.0.0.1, where each subnet within the area is advertised in a single summary. To accomplish this, we must configure two values: the summary address and the summary mask. The summary address in this case will be the beginning of the range of subnetworks to be advertised, while the summary mask will define how far the range of summary addresses will extend.

In the case of area 0.0.0.1, the summary address and mask will have these values:

Summary address = 180.20.128.0
Summary mask = 255.255.224.0

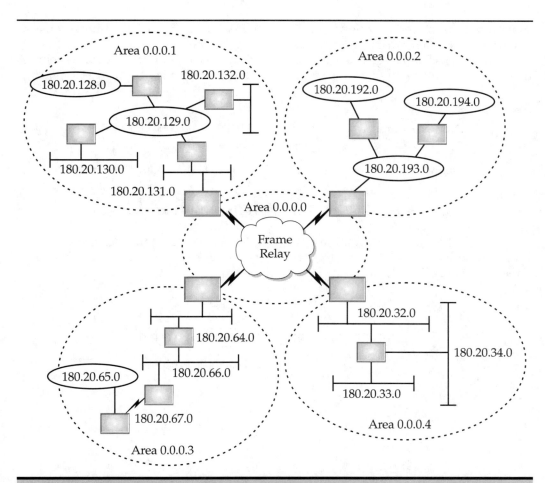

**Figure 31-16.**    *Four areas surrounding the backbone*

This combination results in an address summary for a range of subnetworks that will actually extend from 180.20.128.0 to 180.20.159.0, allowing for future growth within that area. Bear in mind that the summary mask and the subnet mask are two different things; all the networks in area 0.0.0.1 utilize a subnet mask of 255.255.255.0; this is for purposes of reserving the third octet of the network number as the subnet field. The summary mask is used to specify ranges of networks and subnets. The summary mask will be less than the actual subnet mask.

To get a sense of the summary address and summary mask relationships, it helps to understand how the values are broken down in binary, and how the mask is applied:

|  |  | 180 | . | 20 | . | 0 | . | 0 |
|---|---|---|---|---|---|---|---|---|
| Network number: | | 1011 0100 | . | 0001 0100 | . | 0000 0000 | . | 0000 0000 |
|  |  | 255 | . | 255 | . | 255 | . | 0 |
| Subnet mask: | | 1111 1111 | . | 1111 1111 | . | 1111 1111 | . | 0000 0000 |
|  |  | 255 | . | 255 | . | 224 | . | 0 |
| Summary mask: | | 1111 1111 | . | 1111 1111 | . | 1110 0000 | . | 0000 0000 |

In this example, the 255.255.224.0 summary mask covers the first two octets of the summary address (180.20, the network number), while the .224 portion covers the first three bits of the third octet:

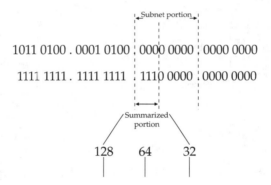

These three bits in the summary network address, in different combinations, will yield six subnets: .128, .192, .64, .32, .96, and .160.

This scheme also leaves five bits in the third octet of the summary address that are not specifically masked by the summary mask. In the example of area 0.0.0.1, by a summary address specifying the first bit in the third octet (180.20.128.0), combined with a mask of 255.255.224.0, will cover the range of subnets from 180.20.128.0 to 180.20.159.0. Once the address 180.20.160.0 is reached, the third bit in the third octet of the summary address is flipped, no longer matching the first three bits of the summary address of 180.20.128.0:

| 180 | . | 20 | . | 128 | . | 0 |

1011 0100 . 0001 0100 . 1000 0000 . 0000 0000
1111 1111 . 1111 1111 . 1111 1111 . 0000 0000

| 180 | | 20 | | 159 | | 0 |

1011 0100 . 0001 0100 . 1001 1111 . 0000 0000

Third
bit
will
flip

This is why the summary mask is lower than the subnet mask; within this scheme, if the summary mask were identical to the subnet mask, each subnet would need to be defined specifically in order to constitute a match (this is, in fact, the default setting) and each subnet would be advertised individually.

By planning the IP network structure of a multiple-area OSPF network, network summaries can be used to keep the LSDBs small. The following scheme can be applied to areas 0.0.0.2, 0.0.0.3, and 0.0.0.4 as well:

| Area Number | Summary Address | Summary Mask |
|---|---|---|
| 0.0.0.2 | 200.20.64.0 | 255.255.224.0 |
| 0.0.0.3 | 200.20.32.0 | 255.255.224.0 |
| 0.0.0.4 | 200.20.192.0 | 255.255.224.0 |

A sniffer trace of a Summary Advertisement passing into area 0.0.0.4 from area 0.0.0.1 would look something like this:

```
OSPF: Link State Advertisement # 2
OSPF: Link state age = 812 (seconds)
OSPF: Optional capabilities = X0
OSPF: .... ..0.    = no external routing capability
OSPF: .... ...0    = no Type of Service routing capability
OSPF: Link state type = 3 (Summary link (IP network))
OSPF: Link state ID = [180.20.128.0]
OSPF: Advertising Router = [0.0.0.80]
OSPF: Sequence number = 2367843297, Checksum = AA1C
```

```
OSPF: Length = 28
OSPF: Network mask = [255.255.224.0]
OSPF: Type of Service = 0 (routine), Metric = 1
```

In this trace, the summary address for area 0.0.0.1 is the Link State ID, while the summary mask is the network mask.

## Virtual Links

Due to the fact that address summaries are passed over the backbone area from one area to another, and never directly between areas, it is necessary for each area to have a connection to the backbone. However, under certain circumstances, it may be physically impossible for an area to contain a border router connected to the backbone area. In these cases, a virtual link must be configured.

The virtual link extends from an Area Border router in the non-contiguous area to an Area Border router connected to the backbone. It is not a physical link, but rather a least-cost path through the intermediary area (area 0.0.0.3, in this example). This will be treated as an unnumbered point-to-point link, over which an adjacency will be formed. Once this occurs, the virtual link will be included in the backbone Area Border router's Router Links Advertisements (router link Type 4), so that OSPF backbone information will also be flooded over the adjacency, to the noncontiguous area (see Figure 31-17).

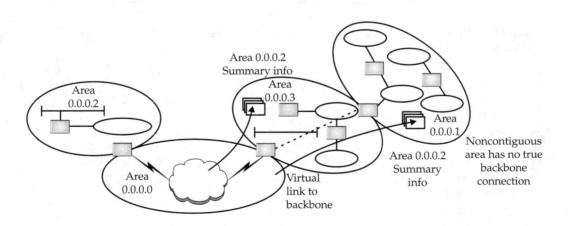

**Figure 31-17.**    *OSPF backbone information flowing over a virtual link that connects the noncontiguous area to the backbone*

Bear in mind that a cost is not configured for a virtual link; the cost in this case is defined as the total cost of the SPF path between Area Border routers. Likewise, when an unnumbered point-to-point link is used to connect virtual end-points, it may be impossible to determine the IP address of either interface. The IP addresses in this case are determined through the process of building the route table.

## OSPF Stub Areas

An OSPF *stub area* is an area that has only one path in and out. Since there is only one path out of the area, the calculation for best path to a remote area is not needed. Summary Link Advertisements, therefore, are not flooded into a stub area:

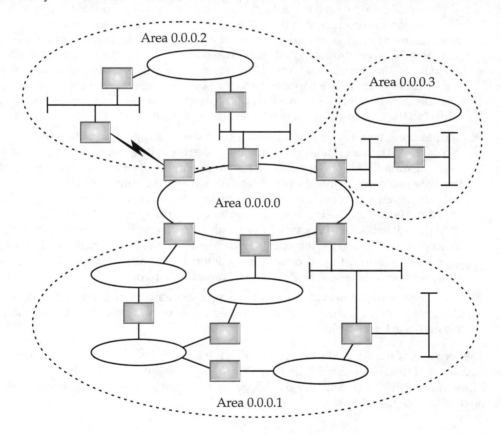

In a stub situation, a default route can be used instead of network summaries; all data to pass beyond the local area will take that route. Likewise, AS External Link Advertisements (LS Type 5) are not flooded into stub areas; the proper route to the AS Boundary router is determined when the data takes the default route out of the stub area.

# Route Table Calculation

The LSDB, amassed through the collection of LSAs, is used to make decisions regarding how best to route data through an OSPF network. This is accomplished using the following steps:

- First, the intra-area routes are computed; this process involves building an SPF tree for each area of which the calculating router is a member. The total cost for each path is determined.

- The route between areas is calculated next, using the Summary Link Advertisements. (The destination area is determined through the examination of Network Link Advertisements.) If the router is an Area Border router, only the summarizations received from the backbone are examined. Each advertisement originating from routers that border the destination network (contained in the Summary Link Advertisement) is checked to see if it has an interface in the source area. If not, it is passed over, and the next advertisement is examined. If there is a connection to the source area, then the path is considered valid and is given a cost of the distance to the Area Border router, added to the cost outlined in the advertisement itself.

- Should there be an Area Border router (or routers) supporting at least one virtual link, then a calculation is made to determine if the transit area (in this case, the area that is a non-backbone area) is capable of providing a shorter path than the one previously described. The transit area's Summary Link Advertisements are checked; if the Summary Link Advertisement has reached the MaxAge, or originated from the router doing the route table calculation, then the advertisement is passed over and the next one is considered. Should a lookup of a valid advertisement yield the destination net, the path is calculated to see if it is shorter than the previously determined path(s). If it is, the virtual link is chosen as the best route to the destination network.

- Should none of the previous steps yield a route to the destination network, AS External Link Advertisements are checked to see if the destination is reachable via an AS external link.

The location of the AS Boundary router(s) have already been determined at this point, as part of the AS External Link Advertisements present in the LSDB.

More information regarding AS Boundary routers, and external links, is included in the next section of this chapter.

# Autonomous Systems

OSPF areas grouped together form a single OSPF domain, known as an *Autonomous System*. The Autonomous System, or AS, can interface with another OSPF Autonomous System or with another network that is running an incompatible routing protocol (such as RIP or BGP). In the case of multiple OSPF Autonomous Systems, each AS possesses its own backbone area (0.0.0.0) and surrounding areas. In either case, the router that borders the two distinct Autonomous Systems is called the AS Boundary router.

## AS Boundary Routers

Though an AS Boundary router can border two OSPF Autonomous Systems, in practice these routers are more often used to provide access to networks that contain routing information that is not of an OSPF origin. AS Boundary routers (ASBR) originate AS External Link Advertisements (LS Type 5) describing the networks beyond the OSPF domain.

The AS External Link Advertisements are flooded without concern for the area structure. LS Type 5 advertisements are flooded to all areas, except stub areas (which do not receive external link information). A single AS External Link Advertisement is generated for each external route learned.

If a destination is located outside the Autonomous System, all routers within the AS must be able to reach the AS Boundary router. They must each learn of the presence and location of the ASBR, and so the ASBR announces its presence within the area that it is a part of. It does this by setting a bit in each of its Router Links Advertisements. Whenever an Area Border router receives one of these Router Links Advertisements and detects the altered bit, it propagates the information in its own Summary Link Advertisement. It does this by sending two Summary Link Advertisements for that area: a Type 3 Summary Link Advertisement, outlining its routes to networks within the area, and a Type 4 Summary Link Advertisement, describing a route to the AS Boundary router (see Figure 31-18).

The ASBR will advertise routes outside the Autonomous System as external routes to the OSPF domain.

## AS Summary Link Advertisements

A Summary Link Advertisement sent by an ASBR contains the following fields:

**LINK STATE ID**    This field indicates the external network number being advertised.

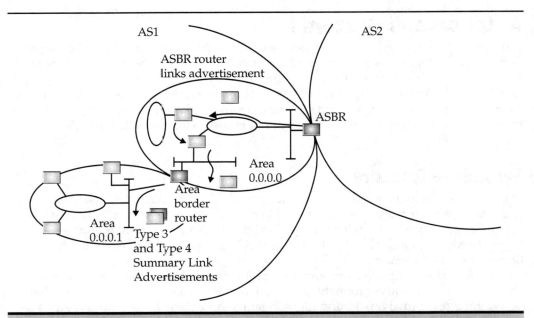

**Figure 31-18.**    *Summary Link Advertisement propagation from ASBR to area ABR*

**ADVERTISING ROUTER**    This field identifies the Router ID of the ASBR from which the AS External Link Advertisement originated.

**NETWORK MASK**    This field indicates the subnet mask associated with the external network being advertised.

**E-BIT**    This field specifies whether the external network being advertised is an external Type 1 network (with a Type 1 metric) or an external Type 2 network (with a Type 2 metric). A value of 0 indicates an external Type 1 network, and a 1 indicates an external Type 2 network.

**METRIC**    This field indicates the path cost to the external route in relation to the advertising AS Boundary router. In a Type 1 metric, this value is added to the intra-area path cost; in a Type 2 metric, this value is considered the total cost.

**FORWARDING ADDRESS**   This field provides the address where data destined for the network should be sent. When this value is set to 0.0.0.0, then the traffic in question will be sent to the ASBR (the advertisement's originator). When describing a default route, this value will be set to 0.0.0.0 and the network mask to 0.0.0.0.

**EXTERNAL ROUTE TAG**   This field is used to transfer information between OSPF and BGP routers; it is not used specifically by OSPF.

## OSPF External Routes

There are two types of external routes that can be described by an ASBR. Each uses a different metric:

- **Type 1 metric**   Total cost equals the sum of the internal and external costs.
- **Type 2 metric**   Total cost equals the cost advertised by the ASBR.

In the Nortel Networks implementation, a Type 1 metric is used to describe an external network that is directly attached to the AS Boundary router, while a Type 2 metric is used to describe remote external networks that are not directly attached.

## External Routes, Metrics, and Weights

OSPF considers external routes to be any of the following entities:

- RIP routes
- Static routes
- BGP or EGP routes
- Networks that are directly connected, but are not running OSPF
- Circuitless IP addresses that are not running OSPF

Each of these cases will result in an external route being advertised. In these cases, each route will also be given a relative weight by the Nortel platform, depending on the type of external route it is. This is because in OSPF it is possible for the same route information to be learned a number of different ways. The weight associated with the external route type will dictate which route is used. In each case, a preference is also applied to each external route type, since there may be circumstances where the route weight should be overridden. (Route weights are not configurable.) For the purposes of ideal external route determination, Route Preference is examined before weight.

Table 31-3 lists the external route types, along with their weights and default preferences. (Route preference is configurable, except in the case of OSPF intra-area routes, OSPF inter-area routes, and directly connected networks.)

In Figure 31-19, a RIP network borders an OSPF Autonomous System. There are three OSPF AS Boundary routers bordering the two routing environments, each with a different connection type to router A, a directly connected intra-area router. The three link types are an OC-3 connection, a DS-3 connection, and a leased 56K line.

The order of priority, in terms of path cost, from router A to routers B, C, and D, are the OC-3 link, followed by the DS-3 link, then the 56K line as a last choice. Each link has been assigned a path cost of 1, 2, and 6 respectively. External RIP routes are assigned a path cost of 1 each within the OSPF domain.

Bearing this in mind, the external advertisements will be propagated within the OSPF AS according to the following table. The information for each router is presented here in this form:

*external metric type/associated cost*

| Network Number | Router B | Router C | Router D |
|---|---|---|---|
| 1 | 1/1 | 2/4 | 2/6 |
| 2 | 2/2 | 2/4 | 2/6 |
| 3 | 2/2 | 2/3 | 2/5 |
| 4 | 2/3 | 2/2 | 2/4 |
| 5 | 2/4 | 1/1 | 2/5 |
| 6 | 2/4 | 2/2 | 2/5 |
| 7 | 2/4 | 2/3 | 2/3 |
| 8 | 2/5 | 2/4 | 2/2 |
| 9 | 2/6 | 2/5 | 1/1 |

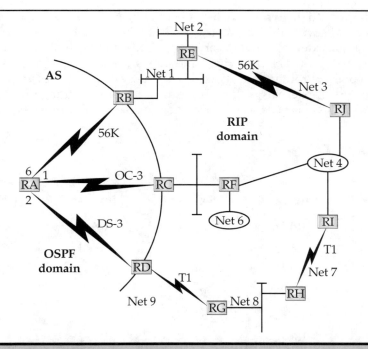

**Figure 31-19.**   *An OSPF/RIP external route*

| External Route | Weight | Preference |
|---|---|---|
| Directly connected network | 0 | 16 |
| OSPF intra-area route | 0 | 16 |
| OSPF inter-area route | 1 | 16 |
| OSPF Type 1 external route | 2 | 1 |
| BGP route | 32 | 1 |
| RIP route | 34 | 1 |
| EGP route | 35 | 1 |
| Static route | 36 | 16 |
| OSPF Type 2 external route | always worst | 1 |

**Table 31-3.**   *External Route Weights and Preferences*

Directly connected RIP networks are listed here with a Type 1 metric, and non-directly connected networks with a Type 2 metric. Each RIP hop count has a cost of 1.

This is how the external networks are advertised, but which router will take which route to which network? The following table shows the best routes to each network from the viewpoint of routers A, B, C, and D. Type-1 external routes are always selected over Type-2 externals, and routes learned via other routing protocols are selected over Type-2 externals. The information for each router is presented here in this form:

*Next hop router/associated cost*

| Network Number | Router A | Router B | Router C | Router D |
|:---:|:---:|:---:|:---:|:---:|
| 1 | RB/7 | RB/1 | RA/8 | RA/9 |
| 2 | RB/2 | RE/2 | RF/4 | RG/6 |
| 3 | RB/2 | RE/2 | RF/3 | RG/5 |
| 4 | RC/3 | RE/3 | RF/2 | RG/4 |
| 5 | RC/1 | RE/4 | RF/1 | RA/4 |
| 6 | RC/2 | RE/4 | RF/2 | RG/5 |
| 7 | RC/3 | RE/4 | RF/3 | RG/3 |
| 8 | RD/2 | RE/5 | RF/4 | RG/2 |
| 9 | RD/3 | RA/9 | RA/4 | RD/1 |

 *Although there may technically be a lower-cost route directly through the RIP network (as they are all assigned a path cost of 1), these (and others in this example) are Type 2 external route metrics. Type 2 is always considered the worst path and is always passed over in favor of an intra- or inter-area OSPF route.*

# Using Accept and Announce Policies

The advertising of external Type 1 and external Type 2 routes can be controlled in the OSPF environment through the use of Accept policies and Announce policies. These policies are configured on the OSPF interface; they determine which route information is to be used under which circumstances.

## OSPF Accept Policies

The OSPF Accept policies apply only to external Type 1 and external Type 2 network advertisements. A series of external routes may be advertised into the OSPF Autonomous System. In Figure 31-20, network 3 is not to be accessible via the OSPF

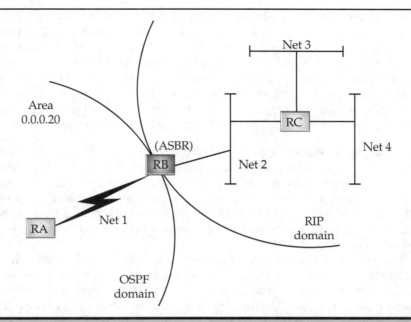

**Figure 31-20.**   *OSPF router A connected to an ASBR bordering a RIP domain*

domain, though all users in the RIP network must be able to reach it. By configuring an OSPF Accept policy for router A (the interface connected to the ASBR), network 3 can effectively be suppressed.

An OSPF Accept policy contains the following information:

- **Network(s)**   The network or networks that are to be singled out. When this parameter is configured on the Nortel Networks platform, the address and mask are specified, as well as a flag indicating whether the network number and mask represent a single network or a range of networks.

- **Action**   The action to be taken if an incoming route matches the network number or range defined in the policy. The options are Accept and Ignore.

- **Route Preference**   This is a metric (range 1-16). Should multiple routes to the same destination exist via different protocols (such as OSPF and RIP), this parameter defines which route should take preference and be inserted into the routing table. (The lower the value, the higher the route preference.)

■ **Rule Precedence**   This parameter is used when there are multiple Accept policies configured. In this scenario, an incoming route may match more than one policy, and so it must be determined which policy will be applied to the route: the higher the value, the greater the precedence. For instance, if one Accept policy accepts a series of networks, and a second policy drops all routes, then the rule precedence must place the Accept policy that accepts the predetermined routes before the second (drop all routes) policy is implemented. If rule precedence is equal, then the last created rule takes priority.

In this example, network 3 uses the network number 160.10.10.0, with a 24-bit mask. The Accept policy on router A has a Network value of 160.10.10.0, a Mask value of 255.255.255.0, and an Action value of Ignore. Once the policy is implemented, then no incoming routes from the external Type 2 network 160.10.10.0 will be entered into router A's routing table; these routes will, therefore, be unreachable by all networks attached to router A (except for router B, of course, which has no Accept policy configured for it).

Note that if router B were to have more networks directly connected to it within the OSPF Autonomous System, then those routers would, by default, receive advertisements for network 3, and would insert the route to network 3 into their routing tables. To completely suppress network 3 in this situation, you would need to implement Accept policies on all interfaces that might receive the external route advertisements.

## OSPF Announce Policies

Announce policies are configured only on the Autonomous System Boundary router, since only an ASBR will actually advertise non-OSPF routes into the OSPF domain. Taking the same example that was used previously, suppose again that network 3 is to be suppressed (see Figure 31-21), this time through the use of an Announce policy on router B (again the ASBR interface). The policy can use any of the following parameters:

■ **Network(s)**   The network to be affected by the Announce policy. This parameter may be a single network number or a range of networks. A value indicating a range of networks is identified by its attached flag.

■ **Action**   The action to be taken if an incoming route matches the condition defined in the policy. The options are Announce and Ignore.

■ **Rule Precedence**   This parameter is used when there are multiple Announce policies configured. In this scenario, a route may match more than one policy, and so it must be determined which policy will be applied to the route. A higher value indicates a higher precedence. If rule precedence is equal, then the last created rule takes priority.

■ **Remote Source**  The protocol that is the source of the routing information. The options are Any, Direct, Static, RIP, EGP, or BGP.

Here, network 3 uses the network number 160.10.10.0/24. The Announce policy on router B has a Network value of 160.10.10.0 255.255.255.0; the Action parameter is set to ignore. Such a policy will prevent router 3's incoming route from ever being advertised into the OSPF domain. In Figure 31-21, both network 2 and network 4 of the RIP domain are advertised into the OSPF domain; however, none of the OSPF routers will ever learn of network 3

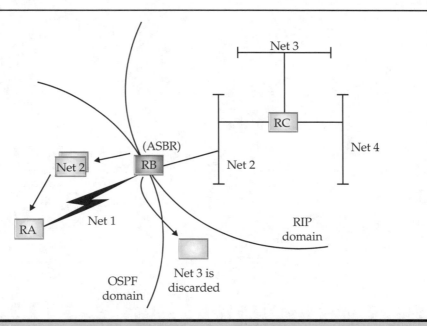

**Figure 31-21.**  *An OSPF Announce policy used to suppress network 3*

# The Complete Reference

Nortel Networks

# Chapter 32

## Configuring OSPF on the Nortel Networks Router Platform

# Initial OSPF Configuration

The initial Open Shortest Path First (OSPF) configuration occurs when the interface being configured is first set up. During the initial configuration of a LAN or WAN interface, the Select Protocols window opens, prompting the user for the protocols that the interface will utilize. If IP and OSPF are selected, then some basic OSPF parameters are prompted for during the initial configuration.

## Initial OSPF Configuration Example

For this example, a backbone link node (BLN) is being newly configured, which is going to run IP and OSPF. Two OSPF areas will be configured: the backbone area of 0.0.0.0, which all OSPF networks must have configured, and area 0.0.0.10. In this case, an ATM cloud constitutes the OSPF backbone, while the individual Ethernet legacy LANs constitute the different OSPF areas. The BLN in this example has two interfaces that are to be configured: one ATM interface, which will exist in the backbone area, and an Ethernet interface, which will exist in area 0.0.0.10 (see Figure 32-1).

### Configuring the Backbone Interface

In this example, the ATM interface will be assigned to the backbone area. After adding the initial LAN Emulation Client (LEC) service record and select the IP and OSPF protocols from the Select Protocols window, Site Manager prompts for some protocol-related information. The IP Configuration window will open, prompting for an IP address and subnet mask (see Figure 32-2).

For this example, the backbone area interface is in network 100.10.10.0/24, with an interface IP of 100.10.10.1/24. The Transmit Bcast Addr parameter is set to the default of 0, which indicates that the host field of the IP network to be broadcasted to will be set to all 1's. This will cause a broadcast to the 100.10.10.0/24 network, for instance, to use the format 100.10.10.255. After inputting this information, click OK. Enter the OSPF parameters in the Global OSPF Parameters window (covered in the following section) and then click OK. This opens a window labeled OSPF Area Address for Interface 100.10.10.1. By default, the area will be set to the backbone area of 0.0.0.0; in this case, because the interface will, in fact, be in the backbone area, you may accept the default. Click OK.

```
OSPF Area Address for Interface 100.10.10.1                            [X]

                                                    Cancel
                                                      OK
        Configuration Mode: local                   Values...
                SNMP Agent: LOCAL FILE              Help...


        Area Address                       0.0.0.0                      [ ]
```

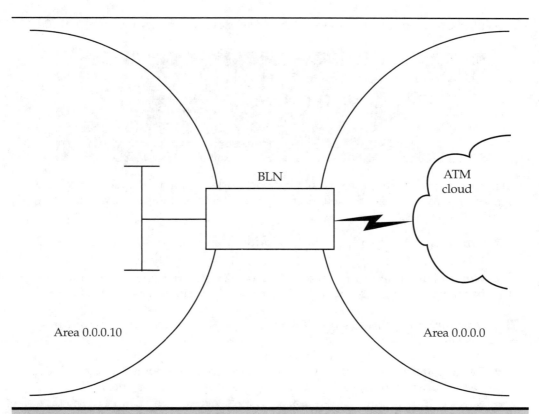

**Figure 32-1.** *OSPF network diagram, showing backbone area and area 0.0.0.10 with BLN*

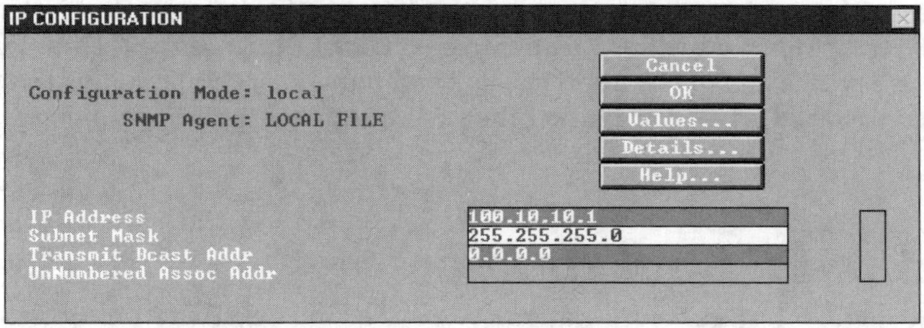

**Figure 32-2.** *The IP Configuration window*

Clicking OK opens a new window, labeled Broadcast Type for Interface 100.10.10.1:

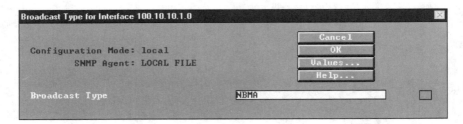

This dialog box defines the type of OSPF network in which the specific interface being configured will exist. By default, this parameter is set to Broadcast. The following network options exist:

- **Broadcast**   A network in which broadcasts are utilized, such as Ethernet or token ring legacy LANs.
- **Nonbroadcast multiple access (NBMA)**   A network that provides multiaccess but that doesn't use broadcasts. Such networks include X.25 and ATM.

 *When configuring an NBMA OSPF interface, OSPF neighbors must be configured manually.*

- **Point-to-point**   A network in which a direct point-to-point connection exists between two routers, such as a point-to-point synchronous line.
- **Point-to-multipoint**   A network using Nortel Networks' proprietary Frame Relay solution.
- **Point-to-multipoint (Std)**   A network, such as a standard Frame Relay hub-and-spoke configuration, that must be configured for the point-to-multipoint standard.

In this case, since the interface is an ATM interface, NBMA must be selected as the Broadcast Type. After you define this parameter, click OK. Since the ATM interface in the backbone area is an NBMA interface, its neighbors must be manually configured. This is accomplished when configuring the specific OSPF Interface parameters, which are covered later in this chapter.

# Global OSPF Configuration

During the initial interface configuration, when selecting OSPF as a protocol, Site Manager prompts for some basic OSPF parameters, such as the Broadcast Type and the Area ID. Many of the global OSPF parameters are set with default values, and are not specifically asked for at that time. To change these settings, from the main Site

Manager Configuration Manager window, select Protocols I IP I OSPF/MOSPF I Global. This opens the Edit OSPF Global Parameters window (see Figure 32-3).

# Fine-Tuning Global OSPF Parameters

The Edit OSPF Global Parameters window offers more detailed global OSPF parameters that affect the OSPF entity as a whole, across all interfaces, and are not specific to any one interface or area.

## Global Parameters

The global OSPF parameters may be accessed at any time after the initial OSPF configuration, by opening the Edit OSPF Global Parameters window from Configuration Manager, as just described (refer to Figure 32-3). The global parameters that you may alter in this window are as follows:

- **Router Id**  A unique identification for the OSPF router; this ID is included in all Hello packets transmitted out all interfaces on the router being configured. It is essentially a means of keeping OSPF neighbors unique, but when electing a Designated Router (DR), if the Router Priorities of the contending routers are all equal, the Router ID is used to break the tie (the higher Router ID is more desirable in this case). The Router ID uses a dotted-decimal format ($x.x.x.x$) and, by default, uses the IP address of the first OSPF interface configured.

- **AS Boundary Router**  Indicates whether the OSPF router being configured will border a separate autonomous system (AS) on any of its interfaces.

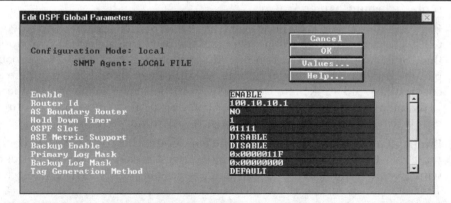

**Figure 32-3.**  *The Edit OSPF Global Parameters window*

Separate ASs are generally external, non-OSPF routing domains, such as Border Gateway Protocol (BGP) networks, or remote RIP or RIPv2 networks.

■ **Hold Down Timer**   Defines how frequently the Shortest Path First (SPF) algorithm may be run. The algorithm may be run once per $x$ seconds, where $x$ is the value defined as the Hold Down Timer. The default of 1 in this case allows the algorithm to run once per second, and no more.

■ **OSPF Slot**   The OSPF protocol may be run on any processor in any occupied slot of the router; the slot that is selected to run the protocol is known as the OSPF *soloist*. The OSPF Slot parameter dictates which slots are eligible to run the OSPF protocol. In the case of a BLN, for instance, which has five slots, the default OSPF Slot value appears as 01111. This value is a mask, applied against the five BLN slots. The slots in this case are numbered left to right, 1 to 5. A value of 1 indicates that the slot is eligible to run OSPF; a value of 0 indicates it is not. Since the System Resource Module sits in slot 1 of a BLN, slot 1 is masked at 0, by default, while the rest of the slots are masked with a 1.

**Note**   *When applying the OSPF slot mask, be aware that a slot may be masked with a 1 even if it is empty, and that, by default, all slots except those containing the System Resource Module are considered eligible. If any slots are empty, they should be set to 0; if an empty slot is selected to run OSPF initially, the protocol will not initialize. Likewise, if OSPF is running in a valid slot that later fails, it is possible that an empty slot may be selected as the backup, and OSPF will not recover.*

■ **ASE Metric Support**   May be either enabled or disabled; when enabled, the router uses the OSPF route weight as the OSPF metric in any type-2 external routes. (For more information regarding OSPF route weight and type-2 external routes, consult Chapter 33.)

■ **Backup Enable**   Each OSPF soloist has a backup soloist ready to take over OSPF protocol functions in the event that the primary soloist fails (provided the OSPF Slot parameter does not exclude all other slots). The Backup Enable parameter defines whether or not the backup soloist should also maintain a copy of the OSPF Link State Database (LSDB). Selecting Enable causes the slot to maintain a copy of the LSDB, which takes up more memory and resources, but provides a faster cut-over in the event of a primary soloist failure.

■ **Primary Log Mask**   Defines which OSPF messages should be entered into the router log. Clicking Values while this parameter is highlighted opens a secondary window in which the individual event messages may be selected or deselected. The following events may be logged:

■ **OSPF Trace/Info/Debug**   Selecting any of these three options indicates that Trace, Info, and Debug OSPF messages should be placed in the log. These may be polled from the TI, for instance, by issuing the command **log –ftid**.

■ **INTF State**   Log messages relating to the OSPF Interface state.

- **NBR State**   Log messages related to changes in OSPF Neighbor states.

- **LSA Self-Origin**   Log messages that indicate each time the router in question transmits a new Link State Advertisement (LSA). This includes the LSA type.

- **LSA Receipt**   Log messages that indicate each time the router in question receives a new LSA. This also includes the LSA type.

- **Route Change**   Log messages that are recorded whenever there is a change in the router's routing table.

- **Bad LS**   Log messages that may indicate several things, such as an acknowledgement for an LSA that was never sent, an LSA that was received but not requested, and so forth.

- **Less Recent LSA**   Log messages that indicate an LSA was received that was less recent than one already existing in the LSDB. Such a packet is rejected, because the information contained within is considered "out of date" even if it is identical to the existing entry for the link state.

- **More Recent LSA**   Log messages that indicate a self-originated LSA that is more recent than one existing in the LSDB.

- **Max Age LSA**   Once the Max Age is reached, an LSA is flushed. These messages may be recorded in the log.

- **Backup Log Mask**   The same series of parameters that apply to the log mask may also be applied to a backup log mask. This is configured in exactly the same way as the Primary Log Mask, with the same parameters.

- **Tag Generation Method**   Tag generation applies to OSPF and BGP interaction. This may be set to either 0, which indicates that a value of 0 (a null value) will be inserted into the tag, Autotag, which inserts a value compliant with OSPF/BGP interaction defined in RFC 1403, or Proprietary, which is used for debugging purposes and is not generally used in a production network.

- **RFC 1583 Compatibility Enable**   Enables or disables RFC 1583 compatibility. RFC 1583 refers to OSPF version 2, written in March 1994, which was obsoleted by RFC 2178, written in July 1997, which in turn was obsoleted by RFC 2328 in April 1998. RFC 1583 compatibility indicates the preference rules that are utilized when choosing among multiple AS external LSAs advertising the same destination. When the RFC 1583 Compatibility Enable parameter is set to Enabled, the preference rules used are those specified by RFC 1583. When set to Disabled, the preference rules prevent routing loops when AS external LSAs for the same destination originated from different areas (RFC 2178).

- **Multicast Extensions**   Indicates whether or not multicast forwarding is permitted on the OSPF router. The multicast forwarding options include the following:

  - **0**   No multicast forwarding
  - **1**   Intra-area multicast forwarding only

- **3**   Intra-area and interarea multicast forwarding only
- **5**   Intra-area and inter-AS multicast forwarding only
- **7**   Multicast forwarding throughout entire network
- **Multicast Timeout Value**   Defines the timeout value for multicast entries if Multicast Open Shortest Path First (MOSPF) is being used. The default is 500 seconds.
- **Multicast Max Queued Pckts**   Indicates how many multicast packets can be queued while calculating a multicast tree. The default is 64.
- **Multicast Dynamic TTL**   Indicates whether dynamic Time to Live values are calculated for each multicast instance in MOSPF.
- **Multicast Downstream IGMP Relay**   Specifies whether AS external routes should have the multicast bit flipped, indicating they are multicast-capable. By default, all autonomous system boundary router (ASBR) routes are multicast-capable. If a router needs to use unicast only, this feature should be disabled.

# OSPF Area Configuration

When configuring an OSPF network, different routers may exist in different areas, while some routers may have interfaces that exist in multiple areas at once (known as *area border routers*). Thus, each OSPF interface needs to have area parameters associated with it.

## OSPF Area Considerations

For purposes of OSPF area configuration, a router is designated as one of the following (see Figure 32-4):

- **Backbone router**   Connected to the backbone area 0.0.0.0.
- **Area Border router**   Borders more than one area; most likely the backbone area and another area or areas, but with the use of virtual links, a physical connection to the backbone is not required.
- **Internal router**   Exists in a single area only (which is not the backbone area).
- **Autonomous System Border router**   Borders two different autonomous systems.

The ASBR generally is used to border the OSPF domain and another, non-OSPF domain. However, each OSPF router needs to have the area-specific parameters on its interface; for instance, what area the interface is a part of.

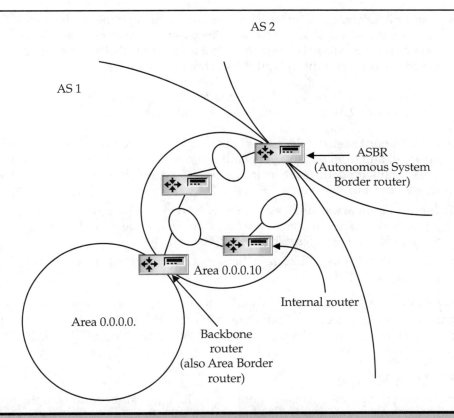

**Figure 32-4.** *Diagram showing a backbone router, area border router, internal router, and ASBR*

## OSPF Area-Specific Parameters

OSPF area parameters, listed next, are really a subset of the OSPF interface parameters, though they are area-specific:

- **Authentication Type**  Determines whether authentication is used to validate OSPF route information. By default, authentication is disabled, but may be set to Simplepassword. This indicates a simple password will be used for purposes of authentication. If OSPF information is received that does not contain the proper password, it will not be accepted.

**Note**  *Bear in mind that a simple password is visible in plain text in a sniffer trace.*

■ **Import AS Extern**   AS external routes are not flooded into stub areas. If the area being configured is a stub area, this parameter should be set to No. Otherwise, AS external routes are meant to flood to all other portions of the OSPF network, and the default of Yes should be used.

**Note**   *The backbone area is not, by nature, a stub area. For this reason, this option is not present for area 0.0.0.0, nor are the following three parameters.*

■ **Stub Default Metric**   Because a stub area has only one point of ingress and egress to and from the area, a default route is used at the area border router. This parameter defines the metric associated with that default route. Values range from 1 to 255, with a default of 1.

■ **Import Summaries**   Indicates whether Network Summaries are to be advertised into the stub area. With a default route being used, Network Summaries do not necessarily need to be used.

■ **Cost For PtP Links**   Indicates whether a cost will be calculated for point-to-point links.

If a specific area is configured as a stub area (it is configured to not import AS external routes and is assigned a Stub Default Metric), this will be reflected when the configuration changes are committed, by adding the designation STUB next to the Area ID in the OSPF Areas window.

## OSPF Area Ranges

Another option in the OSPF Areas window is the Ranges button, located to the right of the main area list. Clicking this button opens the OSPF Ranges window, shown in Figure 32-5.

*OSPF ranges* in this case refers to OSPF Network Summaries, a way of advertising groups of networks existing in one area into other areas, using only a single entry or a smaller subset of entries. This cuts down on both overhead and the amount of information that must be maintained in a router's database. For example, an area (area 0.0.0.10) consists of the IP networks listed in Table 32-1.

**Figure 32-5.**   *The OSPF Ranges window*

| Network | Mask |
|---------|------|
| 150.50.128.0 | 255.255.255.0 |
| 150.50.129.0 | 255.255.255.0 |
| 150.50.130.0 | 255.255.255.0 |
| 150.50.131.0 | 255.255.255.0 |
| 150.50.132.0 | 255.255.255.0 |
| 150.50.133.0 | 255.255.255.0 |
| 150.50.134.0 | 255.255.255.0 |
| 150.50.135.0 | 255.255.255.0 |
| 150.50.136.0 | 255.255.255.0 |
| 150.50.137.0 | 255.255.255.0 |
| 150.50.138.0 | 255.255.255.0 |
| 150.50.139.0 | 255.255.255.0 |
| 150.50.140.0 | 255.255.255.0 |
| 150.50.141.0 | 255.255.255.0 |
| 150.50.142.0 | 255.255.255.0 |
| 150.50.143.0 | 255.255.255.0 |

**Table 32-1.**    *IP Networks Present in OSPF Area 0.0.0.10*

By default, each of these networks is advertised individually into the backbone area; however, these networks may be summarized into a single range of networks, defined in the OSPF Ranges window in the following way:

| Network | Mask |
|---------|------|
| 150.50.128.0 | 255.255.240.0 |

Since only the first 4 bits in the third octet are masked, this indicates all subnets that fall within the range of this mask; the first bit is flipped and the next three are not in all cases, with only the unmasked bits changing with each subnet. Each subnet in this case, beginning with subnet .128, are included in the Network Summary. Once the entry is added, you will be returned to the OSPF Ranges window where the following parameters may be found:

- **Status**  Indicates whether the specified range will be advertised. By selecting the Do Not Advertise value, certain ranges of networks can be excluded when advertising networks or network ranges.

- **Metric**  The metric associated with the specified network range. If left at the default of 0, the receiving OSPF interface calculates the metric.

# OSPF Interface Configuration

Each OSPF interface must be configured individually, in addition to the global OSPF parameters that are specified. In the case of OSPF, each interface may exist in different areas, and may be of different OSPF network types. For this reason, you need to pay careful attention to what type of interface you are dealing with, and how that interface fits into the overall OSPF network design.

## Roles of the OSPF Interface

Although certain global OSPF characteristics apply, many specific OSPF functions are interface-specific. For instance, a router may have two interfaces, one Ethernet and one ATM, both of which are configured for OSPF; however, each interface exists in a different OSPF network type, broadcast (Ethernet) and NBMA (ATM). Likewise, each interface may be configured to be in a different area, with different metric costs and different MTU sizes, depending on the type of network.

For example, an ATM interface configured as an NBMA interface in area 0.0.0.0 needs to have OSPF neighbors manually configured, along with their IP addresses, so that Hellos may be exchanged via unicasts rather than the normal multicast group address. Conversely, a sync line configured as a PTP network type, placed in area 0.0.0.10, does not need to have its neighbors manually configured.

### OSPF Interface-Specific Parameters

OSPF interface-specific configuration is accomplished through Configuration Manager, by selecting Protocols | IP | OSPF | Interfaces. This opens the OSPF Interfaces window, in which the following parameters may be altered for each interface:

- **Area ID**   An arbitrary value used to give an OSPF area a unique identifier. It can be configured to be anything, as long as it follows the dotted-decimal format *x.x.x.x*. The only instance in which the Area ID is specifically dictated is in the case of the backbone area, which must always be set to 0.0.0.0.

- **Type**   Indicates the OSPF network type. The following options are included:

  - **Broadcast**   A network that uses broadcasts, such as Ethernet, token ring, or FDDI

  - **NBMA**   A network that may have multiple points of access, but does not use broadcasts, such as ATM or X.25

  - **Point to Point**   A network in which two routers are connected point to point, as is the case with a PPP connection

  - **Point to Multipoint**   A point-to-multipoint network that uses of Nortel Networks' proprietary Frame Relay solution

- **Point to Multipoint (Std)** A standard point-to-multipoint network, such as Frame Relay

- **Passive** Should be configured on the spoke routers in a Frame Relay hub-and-spoke (non-fully meshed) environment

- **Rtr Priority** Used to elect the Designated Router (DR). The highest Router Priority wins the election. The valid range for this value is 0 to 255, with a default of 1. A value of 0 indicates that the interface is not eligible to act as DR for that network, and thus is excluded from the election.

- **Transit Delay** The time it takes to route a packet over this interface. Since this will vary depending on the type of packet, this value is somewhat arbitrary.

- **Retransmit Interval** Defines the amount of time that will pass before retransmitting LSA information in the absence of an Acknowledgement. The default is 5 seconds, and may be configured between 1 to 3,600 (1 hour) seconds. The Retransmit Interval may be optimized for different OSPF network types; Nortel Networks makes the following recommendations:

| | |
|---|---|
| Broadcast | 5 |
| NBMA | 10 |
| Point-to-point | 10 |
| Point-to-multipoint | 10 |

- **Hello Interval** Defines how often Hello packets are transmitted from the interface. This value must be consistent with the rest of the OSPF network to which the interface is attached in order for an adjacency to form with the DR. Nortel Networks makes the following recommendations for Hello Interval values, depending on the type of OSPF network:

| | |
|---|---|
| Broadcast | 10 seconds |
| NBMA | 20 seconds |
| Point-to-point | 15 seconds |
| Point-to-multipoint | 15 seconds |

- **Dead Interval** Defines the amount of time that must pass without the receipt of a Hello packet before that router is considered to be down by its OSPF neighbors. For example, a router with area ID 0.0.0.10 is sending Hello messages at the interval defined by the Hello Interval. If its neighbors do not receive a Hello packet from Router ID 0.0.0.10 before the time specified by the

Dead Interval, then 0.0.0.10 is considered to be down. This value must remain consistent throughout the OSPF network with which the configured interface is associated. Nortel Networks makes the following recommendations for the Dead Interval, depending on the type of OSPF network:

| | |
|---|---|
| Broadcast | 40 seconds |
| NBMA | 80 seconds |
| Point-to-point | 60 seconds |
| Point-to-multipoint | 60 seconds |

- **Poll Interval**  Defines the maximum amount of time that may pass between sending Hello packets to inactive NBMA neighbors.

- **Metric Cost**  Indicates the metric cost associated with the OSPF interface. The valid range is from 1 to 65,535. Nortel Networks makes the following recommendations when assigning Metric Cost:

| | |
|---|---|
| 100Mbps Ethernet | 1 |
| ATM | 1 |
| Token Ring | 10 |
| 10Mbps Ethernet | 15 |
| E1 | 48 |
| T1 | 65 |
| 64Kbps | 1,562 |
| 56Kbps | 1,785 |
| 19.2Kbps | 5,208 |
| 9.6Kbps | 10,416 |

- **Password**  If an authentication type of simple password is being used, the password is defined here. Passwords may be up to eight characters long and are case-sensitive.

- **Mtu Size**  Maximum transmit unit size for the OSPF interface. This value may be from 1 to 10,000. In this particular case, an MTU of 1 indicates that the IP MTU for the physical interface will be used, while a value of 2 indicates the IP MTU for Ethernet will be used (1,500 bytes). Any value above 2 defines the actual MTU size in bytes.

| Note | *PPP lines should use an MTU size that is less than the size of the sync MTU (1,500 bytes).* |

- **Multicast Forwarding**   Determines how incoming multicasts are handled on the OSPF interface; the options are Blocked, where no multicasts are forwarded, Datalink Multicast, where the multicast is forwarded as a datalink multicast, or Unicast, indicating the packet will be converted to a unicast packet.

- **Mtu Mismatch Detect Enable**   In accordance with RFC 2178, the MTU field found in the Database Description packet indicates the largest IP packet the OSPF interface can receive, and problems will result if this size is greater than the MTU for which the physical interface itself is configured. Less-recent implementations of OSPF (RFC 1583) do not use this field.

## Neighbors

Depending on the OSPF implementation, the Neighbors option may or may not be used. OSPF neighbors are dynamically discovered in a broadcast network type; however, as in the case of an OSPF interface configured for a NBMA network type, OSPF neighbors must be added manually. Clicking the button labeled Neighbors opens the OSPF Neighbors window, where neighbors are configured individually.

The OSPF Neighbors window is grayed out the first time it is accessed for an interface, and new neighbors must be inserted by clicking Add. After clicking Add, the OSPF Neighbor Configuration for Interface *x.x.x.x* window opens, prompting for the IP address of the neighbor being added (see Figure 32-6). This information is requested because neighbors generally are determined through the receipt of OSPF Hello packets, which are transmitted to an OSPF group multicast address (224.0.0.5); since NBMA networks (such as ATM) do not use broadcasts per se, these Hello packets are sent directly to each neighbor as a unicast packet.

After you add the IP address of the neighbor, you don't need to do any further configuration; all other information that will be shared between the neighbors will be accomplished through the exchange of the Hello packets.

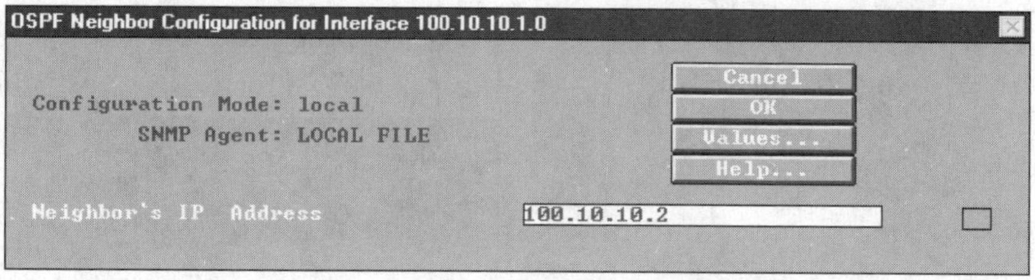

**Figure 32-6.**   *The OSPF Neighbors window*

# Accept and Announce Policies

OSPF Accept and Announce policies, unlike RIP Accept and Announce policies, relate only to a specific kind of route information: autonomous system external routes. These policies can be useful in determining how external route information is viewed within the OSPF domain. For instance, certain external route information may need to have the metric altered, or might possibly be suppressed altogether. The parameters associated with Accept and Announce policies differ, because Accept policies relate to incoming route information, whereas Announce policies relate to how received route information is advertised by the router using the Announce policy. The specifics of each policy type, as well as their parameters, are discussed in the following sections

## OSPF Accept Policies

OSPF Accept policies apply to external type-1 and external type-2 networks only. Therefore, any router may be configured with an OSPF Accept policy, except those that exist in a stub area, because external route information is not flooded into stub areas.

### Configuring an OSPF Accept Policy

OSPF Accept policies are configured by selecting Protocols from the main Configuration Manager window. From the drop-down menu, select IP | Policy Filters | OSPF | Accept Policies. This opens the OSPF Accept Policy Filters window, which is grayed out by default, because no policies currently exist. Click Add to open the OSPF Accept IP Policy Filter Configuration window (see Figure 32-7).

From this window, you create and define the OSPF Accept policy. Multiple instances of OSPF Accept policy filters may be created. The order in which these policies are

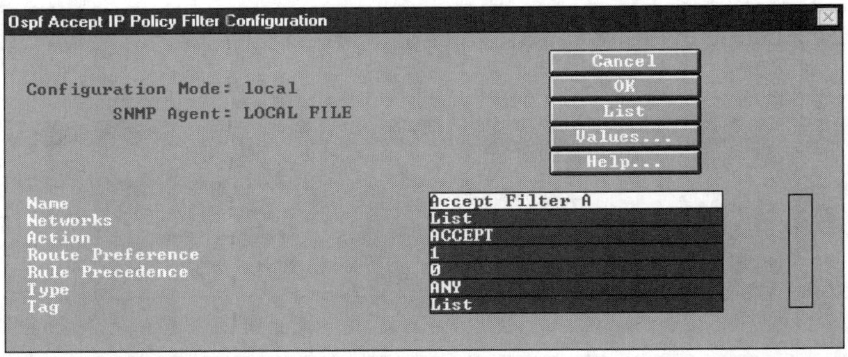

**Figure 32-7.**    *The OSPF Accept IP Policy Filter Configuration window*

observed may be dictated by the Rule Precedence settings (discussed shortly). The basic OSPF Accept policy parameters are as follows:

- **Name** An arbitrary name to easily identify the Accept policy being configured.
- **Networks** After highlighting this option, select the List option from the right-hand series of buttons. This opens the Policy Filters window, in which a series of networks, or ranges of networks, may be configured (see Figure 32-8).

The networks described here are the networks to which the Accept policy will be applied. For instance, in this example, two entries are configured:

| Network | Network Mask | Match Criteria |
|---|---|---|
| 150.50.10.0 | 255.255.255.0 | Exact |
| 160.60.128.0 | 255.255.248.0 | Range |

This configuration causes any incoming packet from network 150.50.10.0 to be identified and affected by whatever Accept policy has been created. Incoming packets from network 160.60.128.0 will be affected as well, but because Range was specified under the Match Criteria (using a mask of 255.255.248.0), any subnetwork beginning with 160.60.128.0 that falls within the bit mask of 248 will also be considered a match. This includes not only network 160.60.128.0, but also networks 160.60.129.0, 160.60.130.0, 160.60.131.0, 160.60.132.0, and 160.60.133.0, 160.60.134.0, and 160.60.135.0. This range of networks is also subject to the configured Accept policy.

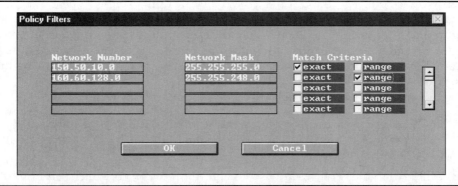

**Figure 32-8.** The Policy Filters window, displaying a specific network and a range

- **Action**    May be set to either Accept (the default) or Ignore. If ignore is selected, any route information about the described networks or network ranges is ignored. If Accept is chosen, then the accepted packet is subject to the rules outlined in the remainder of the Accept policy.

- **Route Preference**    Incoming route information may have its metric altered as part of the Accept policy; since the metric is used, in part, to determine the desirability of a route, adjusting the metric prior to the route being considered for insertion into the routing table may make the difference between the route being added or discarded.

- **Rule Precedence**    Allows a priority to be assigned to the current Accept policy; if multiple Accept policies exist, this setting enables you to label them in order of priority, so that they are applied in a predetermined order. For example, if two Accept policies are being used, one of which accepts certain routes and alters their metric, while the other ignores all incoming routes, the second policy would cancel the first if it were the first to be implemented. The higher priority is considered to have precedence in this case, so applying a Rule Precedence of 10 to the first policy and a precedence of 5 to the drop-all policy would ensure that the drop-all-routes policy is always implemented second, after the desired routes have been selected.

- **Type**    Identifies what kind of external route the policy applies to; the options are Type-1, Type-2, or Any, which includes both types of external routes.

- **Tag**    Selects potential tag values that may exist in external network advertisements. A value of 0 indicates any tag is considered a match.

# OSPF Announce Policies

OSPF Announce policies, like OSPF Accept policies, apply to either type-1 or type-2 external routes. Unlike OSPF Accept policies, however, OSPF Announce policies are configured on ASBRs only, because, whereas Accept policies pertain to incoming route information, and all routers except those that exist in stub areas are potential receivers of external route information, Announce policies pertain to actually announcing the external route information, which only the ASBR does.

The following rules apply to OSPF Accept/Announce Policies:

- OSPF Accept Policies are used to control which OSPF non-self-originated external routing information is stored in the routing table. This does not affect the LSDB and is therefore of local significance only.

- OSPF Announce Policies are used on an ASBR to control which self-originated external routing updates are placed in the LSDB. Announce Policies do affect what other routers learn, then, regarding the local boundary router's self-originated information only.

## Configuring an OSPF Announce Policy

To configure an OSPF Announce policy, open Configuration Manager and select
Protocols | IP | Policy Filters | OSPF | Announce Policies. This opens the main OSPF
Announce Policy Filters window, which, by default, is grayed out. Click Add to insert
the first policy filter. This opens the OSPF Announce IP Policy Filter Configuration
window (see Figure 32-9).

Here, the OSPF IP policy filter is defined. After one filter has been configured,
additional Announce policies may be added. The total number of policies (both
Announce and Accept combined) that may be configured for a single protocol is 32, by
default. This can be altered by selecting Protocols | IP | Global from Configuration
Manager and adjusting the Maximum Policy Rules parameter in the Edit IP Global
Parameters window.

To configure the actual Announce policy, define the specific attributes the policy
must match, as well as what action will be taken when a match occurs. Both attributes
are configured from the OSPF Announce IP Policy Filter Configuration window:

- **Name**    An arbitrary name used to identify the Announce policy being
  configured. If no name is selected, the designation Unknown Policy Name is used.

- **Networks**    After highlighting this option, select the List option from the
  right-hand series of buttons. This opens the Policy Filters window, in which you
  may configure a series of networks or ranges of networks (see Figure 32-10).

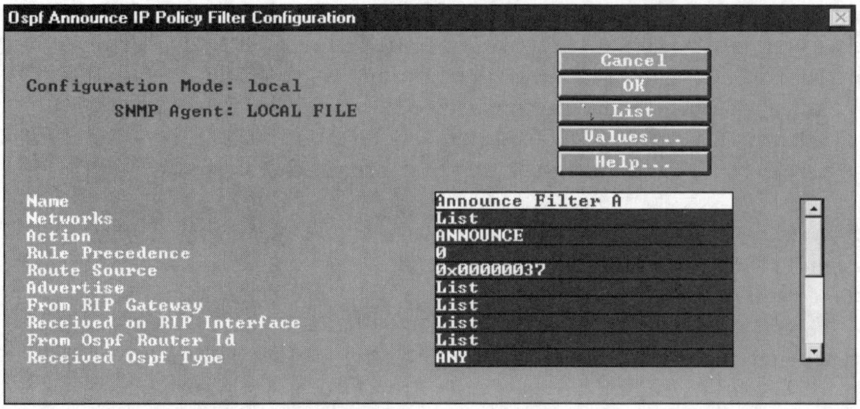

**Figure 32-9.**    *The OSPF Announce IP Policy Filter Configuration window*

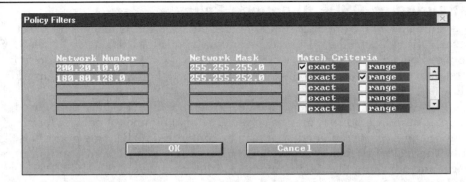

**Figure 32-10.**  *The Policy Filters window displaying a specific network and a range*

The networks described here are the networks to which the Announce policy will be applied. For instance, in this example, two entries have been configured:

| Network | Network Mask | Match Criteria |
|---------|--------------|----------------|
| 200.20.10.0 | 255.255.255.0 | Exact |
| 180.80.128.0 | 255.255.252.0 | Range |

This configuration causes any packet from network 200.20.10.0 to be identified and affected by whatever Announce policy has been created. Network 180.80.128.0 will be affected as well, but because Range was specified under the Match Criteria (using a mask of 255.255.252.0), any subnetwork beginning with 180.80.128.0 that falls within the range mask of 252 will also be considered a match. This includes not only network 180.80.128.0, but also networks 180.80.129.0 and 180.80.130.0, and 180.80.131.0. This range of networks also will be subject to the configured Announce policy.

*A network of 0.0.0.0 with a mask of 0.0.0.0 and an Exact Match Criteria will match the default route, whereas the same network and mask assigned a Range Match Criteria will match any route.*

Once the networks have been defined, the other policy parameters may be configured. The following parameters apply to OSPF announce policies:

- **Action**  May be set to Announce (the default) or Ignore. If Ignore is selected, any route information coming from the described networks or network ranges will be ignored. If Announce is chosen, then the accepted packet is subject to the rules outlined in the remainder of the Announce policy.

- **Rule Precedence**   Enables a priority to be assigned to the current Announce policy; if multiple Announce policies exist, this setting enables you to label them in order of priority, so that they are applied in a predetermined order. For example, if two Announce policies are being used, one that propagates certain routes and alters their metric, while the other ignores all incoming routes and does not announce them into the OSPF domain, the second policy would cancel the first if it were the first to be implemented. The higher priority is considered to have precedence in this case, so applying a Rule Precedence of 10 to the first policy would ensure that the drop-all-routes policy is always implemented second, after the desired routes have been selected.

- **Route Source**   Indicates the source of the route information that will be affected by this Announce policy. Highlighting this option and selecting Values opens a window in which you may select the route source types. The options are Direct, Static, RIP, EGP, or BGP. Selecting all of these options applies the Announce policy to any incoming route information.

- **Advertise**   Specific network identifiers may be configured to advertise in place of what is actually listed in the route advertisement if the match criteria for the Announce policy is met. Highlighting this option and selecting List opens a window in which the new route information may be configured. For example, an ASBR learns of RIP-sourced routes for network 150.50.0.0, which actually includes subnetworks 150.50.10.0, 150.50.20.0, 150.50.30.0, and 150.50.40.0, all of which have been aggregated by RIPv1. An Announce policy may be configured to match the incoming 150.50.0.0 from a RIP source, and then alternate Network IDs may be configured that define subnetworks 150.50.10.0, 150.50.20.0, and 150.50.30.0, but not 150.50.40.0. By specifying the actual subnet range and then excluding a particular subnet, the excluded subnet is never learned of within the OSPF domain (although it is still accessible from the RIP domain). Similarly, the opposite may be accomplished by replacing a series of subnetwork advertisements with a single aggregate entry.

**Note**   *Including a Network ID of 255.255.255.255 with a mask of 255.255.255.255 as the first network will cause the router to advertise all actual routes, in addition to any others configured in the list. Leaving the list blank causes the router to simply advertise the actual routes.*

- **From RIP Gateway**   An ASBR bordering a RIP domain may potentially be receiving RIP advertisements from several RIP routers on any number of RIP interfaces. By using this parameter, a list of RIP routers can be formed by IP address, whose advertisements will be considered by the Announce policy. For instance, if an ASBR is receiving RIP updates from router 1, router 2, and router 3, and the From RIP Gateway parameter is configured with a list including only routers 1 and 2, then router 3's advertisements will not be considered by the policy.

- **Received on RIP Interface**   If the remote AS is a RIP domain, and the ASBR has multiple interfaces within the RIP domain, then specific RIP interfaces can be targeted by the Announce policy by configuring their IP addresses into the list provided when this option is highlighted and the List option is selected. Leaving the list blank causes all RIP interfaces to be considered by the policy.

- **From Ospf Router Id**   If only routes from certain OSPF routers are to be considered, their IP addresses may be configured here. Clicking List opens another window in which a list of individual IP addresses may be defined. Leaving this list blank indicates that all incoming OSPF routes are considered.

- **Received Ospf Type**   Here, the types of routes that may be considered by the Announce policy are configured. These route types may include External Type-1, External Type-2, Internal, or Any.

- **Received Ospf Tag**   Uses the OSPF tag as a criteria match.

- **From Egp Peer**   If a Route Source of EGP is selected, then specific IP addresses of EGP Peers may be configured here. If a list of IP addresses is created, then only routes advertised by the specified EGP Peers are considered; otherwise, all EGP Peers are considered.

- **From Egp As**   Identifies to which AS the EGP Peers may belong to be considered by this policy. EGP must be configured as a Route Source for this parameter to be meaningful. If you configure the AS number(s) in the list provided by selecting List, only EGP routes that originate from the specified AS are considered. If left blank, every EGP AS is considered.

- **Received Egp Gateway**   Highlighting this parameter and then selecting List opens a window in which you may enter specific IP addresses. These addresses are considered the next-hop value for incoming route information, and only EGP advertisements that use one of the configured values on the list as its next hop will be considered by this policy. EGP must be selected as a Route Source.

- **From Bgp Peer**   If a Route Source of BGP is selected, then specific IP addresses of BGP Peers may be configured here. If a list of IP addresses is created, then only routes advertised by the specified BGP Peers are considered; otherwise, all BGP Peers are considered.

- **From Bgp As**   Identifies to which AS the BGP Peers may belong to be considered by this policy. BGP must be configured as a Route Source for this parameter to be meaningful. If you configure the AS number(s) in the list provided by selecting List, only BGP routes that originate from the specified AS are considered. If left blank, every BGP AS is considered.

- **Received Bgp Next Hop**   Highlighting this parameter and then selecting List opens a window in which you may enter specific IP addresses. These addresses are considered the next-hop value for incoming route information, and only BGP advertisements that use one of the configured values on the list as its next hop will be considered by this policy. BGP must be selected as a Route Source.

- ■ **OSPF Type**   Indicates what OSPF external advertisement type should be used for routes that match the Announce policy (in other words, how will routes that match this policy be announced). Options are Type-1, Type-2, and None. If None is selected, then a default type is used based on the route source. In this case, BGP, EGP, and RIP will default to type-2, while all other route sources will default to type-1.

- ■ **OSPF Tag**   Specifies which OSPF external route tag will match the Announce policy.

- ■ **BGP/OSPF Automatic Tag**   Enables or disables automatic tag generation for OSPF; if set to Disable, the value must be manually configured. If set to Enable, the tag value is automatically generated.

> **Note**   *If a value is specified, it overrides the value configured in the Tag Generation Method parameter of the OSPF Global Parameters window.*

- ■ **OSPF Metric**   Specifies the metric that will be associated with routes that match the policy. If set, the value replaces the actual value. If disabled, the value in the routing table is used.

# Troubleshooting OSPF

Troubleshooting OSPF can involve using Site Manager, scripts, or the TI. This section covers using both the scripts and the TI for purposes of OSPF troubleshooting. The primary things to check when dealing with an OSPF problem are the condition of the LSDB, the current OSPF interface states, neighbor states with neighboring OSPF routers, and the OSPF Area states.

## Examining the Area State

The OSPF Area state may be checked from a console, telnet, or dial-up session by using either the scripts or the MIBs directly. This can be useful for determining how many areas are configured, what type of area it is (stub or not), as well as its current state.

### Examining the Area State Using the Scripts

Using the scripts can be quite a bit simpler than using the MIB, if the proper scripts have been loaded. In general, a single script command often yields the same information as a series of MIB gets from the TI. Also, the output from a script command is displayed in a simple-to-interpret, clearly labeled format, whereas polling individual MIB objects can sometimes yield values that are difficult to interpret. The examples in this troubleshooting section will demonstrate this.

To check the Area state on the OSPF router by using the script commands, the following syntax is used: **show ospf area**. For each area configured on the router, this script displays the Area ID, the state, whether or not the area is a stub area, and the OSPF authentication type configured:

```
[2:1]$ show ospf area
OSPF Area Information
--------------------
                            Stub
Area ID         State       Area    Authentication
--------------- ----------  ----    --------------
0.0.0.0         Up          No      None

1 Area Entries
```

In the preceding example, a single area, 0.0.0.0 (the backbone area), is configured. Its state is Up, it is not a stub area, and OSPF authentication is not being used. A variety of other **show ospf** commands are available through the scripts, some of which are also covered in this "Troubleshooting OSPF" section. The OSPF Area state may also be examined using the MIB, as described next.

## Examining the Area State Using the TI

A variety of MIB variables exist that can be examined regarding the OSPF area. This is accomplished by polling the individual MIB instances. In the examples that follow, the first four MIB attributes and instances will yield much of the same information that is displayed by the **show ospf area script** command; the advantage to the MIBs is that they are already resident on the router, and do not need to be obtained and loaded, as the scripts do. Some of the more helpful TI commands for examining the OSPF Area state are as follows:

- **wfOspfAreaEntry.3.*** Indicates the state of all the OSPF areas configured on the router, where a value of 1 equals Up and a value of 2 equals Down:

  ```
  [2:1]$g wfOspfAreaEntry.3.*
  wfOspfAreaEntry.wfOspfAreaState.0.0.0.0 = 1
  ```

  The area in this case is Up. Only one area is configured in this case; if multiple areas were configured, they would all be listed (due to the wildcard value used for the instance). To target a specific area, select the actual area instead of using a wildcard.

- **wfOspfAreaEntry.4.*** Indicates the OSPF Area ID for each area configured on the router. This value is a 32-bit integer:

  ```
  [12:2]$g wfOspfAreaEntry.4.*
  wfOspfAreaEntry.wfOspfAreaId.0.0.0.0 = 0.0.0.0
  wfOspfAreaEntry.wfOspfAreaId.0.0.0.10 = 0.0.0.10
  wfOspfAreaEntry.wfOspfAreaId.0.0.0.20 = 0.0.0.20
  wfOspfAreaEntry.wfOspfAreaId.0.0.0.24 = 0.0.0.24
  ```

Again, the wildcard value indicates that all configured Area IDs are to be displayed. This can be useful, especially during a Telnet or dial-up session, when Site Manager connectivity has been lost and areas that have been configured on the router can no longer be easily referenced.

- **wfOspfAreaEntry.5.*** Indicates which OSPF authentication type is being used (if any). By default, no authentication is used. The output from this command yields a value of 0 (None) or 1 (simple password authentication):

```
[12:2]$g wfOspfAreaEntry.5.*
wfOspfAreaEntry.wfOspfAuthType.0.0.0.10 = 1
```

Simple password authentication is configured in this case. When dealing with OSPF networks that are utilizing authentication, remember that the simple password authentication is case-sensitive, and route information containing an incorrect password is ignored by the OSPF interface.

- **wfOspfAreaEntry.6.*** Indicates whether the area is configured to import AS external LSAs. Entering this MIB get results in a value displayed of either 1 (true, the default) or 2 (false):

```
[12:2]$g wfOspfAreaEntry.6.*
wfOspfAreaEntry.wfOspfImportASExtern.0.0.0.10 = 1
```

The area in this case is, in fact, configured to import ASE LSAs, which is the default setting.

- **wfOspfAreaEntry.8.*** Indicates whether the area is configured to import summary advertisements; the output from the get indicates either a 1 (true, the default), indicating yes, summary advertisements will be imported, or a 2 (false), indicating no, summary advertisements will not be imported (as is the case with a stub area). This MIB should be set to false only if the area is not configured to import AS external LSAs:

```
[12:2]$g wfOspfAreaEntry.8.*
wfOspfAreaEntry.wfOspfImportSum.130.30.1.0 = 1
```

Because this same router is configured to import AS external LSAs, it is also configured to import summary advertisements.

## Examining the Link State Database

All OSPF routers in an area must have a common view of the link state topology. All ABRs have this. They accomplish this by learning and maintaining a Link State Database (LSDB), which may be viewed by using either the scripts or the MIB from the TI. The contents of the LSDB is extremely important; since routing decisions will be made based on the LSDB, connectivity problems in an OSPF environment may be traced back to an LSDB that contains invalid information or that is missing certain entries.

Bear in mind that a single router may have to maintain multiple LSDBs, depending on how many areas the router is configured to be a member of. For instance, a router with four interfaces, in areas 0.0.0.0, 0.0.0.10, 10.0.0.1, and 0.0.1.50, must maintain four separate LSDBs, whereas a router configured with two interfaces, both in area 0.0.1.21, needs to maintain an LSDB only for one area.

## Examining the LSDB Using the Scripts

The contents of the LSDB of a router may be easily viewed by using the script commands, provided they have been loaded. If the router is an area border router, then more than one area's LSDB may need to be checked. The Area ID must also be known, since this value is utilized by this command. The Area ID may be obtained by using the command **show ospf area**. The script command for viewing the LSDB uses the following syntax: **show ospf lsdb <area-number>**.

For all Area IDs or a specific Area ID in the LSDB, this script displays the LSA type, the Link State ID, the Router ID of the advertising router, the autonomous system external (ASE) advertisement type, the metric (cost) for the ASE, the ASE forwarding address (next hop), the age (in seconds) of the LSA, and the sequence number of the LSA:

```
[12:2]$show ospf lsdb 130.30.1.0


OSPF LSDB
---------
OSPF Area:  130.30.1.0
LS Type   Link State ID   Adv Router     E  Metric  ASE Fwd Addr     Age   Seq Nbr
-------   -------------   -------------  -  ------- ---------------  ----  --------
STUB      130.30.1.16     130.30.152.75                              0     0
STUB      130.30.3.0      130.30.152.75                              0     0
STUB      130.30.161.0    130.30.152.3                               0     0
STUB      130.30.161.0    130.30.92.130                              0     0
STUB      130.30.152.32   130.30.152.3                               0     0
ROUTER    130.30.92.130   130.30.92.130                              740   80007ca3
ROUTER    130.30.92.134   130.30.92.134                              785   80005dce
ROUTER    130.30.92.172   130.30.92.172                              1539  800000c1
ROUTER    130.30.231.1    130.30.231.1                               1193  800031e2
ROUTER    170.70.10.129   170.70.10.129                              605   80006461
ROUTER    170.70.10.133   170.70.10.133                              517   80000d1d
NETWORK   130.30.152.3    130.30.152.3                               507   800005cd
NETWORK   130.30.92.3     130.30.152.3                               507   800018e2
NETWORK   130.30.92.131   170.70.10.133                              1717  800001cd
SUMMARY   160.60.0.0      170.70.10.129                              606   800066aa
SUMMARY   160.60.0.0      170.70.10.133                              1718  80000dd9
SUMMARY   160.60.64.0     170.70.10.129                              606   80006748
```

```
SUMMARY   160.60.64.0    170.70.10.133                              1718  80000dc6
SUMMARY   160.60.96.0    170.70.10.129                              606   8000403
AS_SUM    160.60.1.99    170.70.10.129                              607   80000dcb
AS_SUM    160.60.1.99    170.70.10.133                              1719  80000dbc
AS_SUM    160.60.13.15   170.70.10.129                              607   80003bed
AS_SUM    160.60.13.15   170.70.10.133                              1719  80000dd6
AS_SUM    160.60.13.24   170.70.10.129                              608   800009a2
AS_SUM    160.60.13.24   170.70.10.133                              1720  8000090d1d
```

This output displays an LSDB containing many different LSA Types; the entries indicate that the router interface associated with the requested Area ID is receiving intra-area advertisements as well as Network Summaries and Autonomous System Summaries. Table 32-2 translates what each LS Type in the LSDB means.

**ASE ADVERTISEMENT TYPE (E)**   There are two types of external advertisement types which may be listed, using the following values:

- 1 = Type 1 External Routes
- 2 = Type 2 External Routes

Another script command that is helpful for examining OSPF link states is the **show ospf ase** command, which utilizes the format **show ospf ase <link-state-ID>**. For all Link State IDs or a specific Link State ID, this script displays the Link State ID (the network number the ASE advertisement is advertising), the Router ID of the

| LSDB Indicator | Link State Advertisement Types (LS Types) |
|---|---|
| STUB | Stub link advertisement |
| ROUTER | Router link advertisement |
| NETWORK | Network link advertisement |
| SUMMARY | Summary link advertisement |
| AS_SUM | Autonomous system boundary summary link advertisement |
| AS_EXT | Autonomous system external advertisement |

**Table 32-2.**   *Link State Advertisement Types as Referenced in the TI*

originating router, the age of the ASE (in seconds), the metric (cost) of the ASE, the forwarding address the router should use to get to the network (gateway), the ASE type, and the tag. If the forwarding address is 0.0.0.0, then traffic is forwarded to the originating router.

```
[12:2]$show ospf ase 10.0.0.0

OSPF AS External Routes
-----------------------


     Link          Originating                      Forwarding
    State ID         Router       Age   Metric       Address     Type   Tag
--------------- --------------- ----- ---------- --------------- ---- --------
10.0.0.0        170.70.10.129    665        1 0.0.0.0              2   e0000000
10.0.0.0        170.70.10.133    577        1 0.0.0.0              2   e0000000
10.0.0.0        170.70.10.137    520        1 0.0.0.0              2   e0000000
10.0.0.0        170.70.10.141   1599        1 160.60.95.10         2   e0000000

4 matches
```

## Examining the Link State Database Using the TI

The LSDB information may also be examined by using the MIB from the TI. There are several commands that are useful for doing this, using the MIB object wfOspfLsdbEntry:

- **wfOspfLsdbEntry.1.***   Indicates the area the LSA was learned from:

    ```
    [12:2]$g wfOspfLsdbEntry.1.*

    wfOspfLsdbEntry.wfOspfLsdbAreaId.130.30.1.0.0.130.30.1.16.130.30.152.75 = 130.30.1.0
    wfOspfLsdbEntry.wfOspfLsdbAreaId.130.30.1.0.0.130.30.3.0.130.30.152.75 =  130.30.1.0
    wfOspfLsdbEntry.wfOspfLsdbAreaId.130.30.1.0.0.130.30.161.0.130.30.152.3 = 130.30.1.0
    wfOspfLsdbEntry.wfOspfLsdbAreaId.130.30.1.0.0.130.30.161.0.130.30.92.130 = 130.30.1.0
    wfOspfLsdbEntry.wfOspfLsdbAreaId.130.30.1.0.0.130.30.152.32.130.30.152.3 = 130.30.1.0
    ```

    The LSA type may also be examined, by checking the attribute wfOspfLsdbEntry.wfOspfLsdbType. This is accomplished by using the following MIB object/attribute, with a wildcard as the instance:

- **wfOspfLsdbEntry.2.***   Yields one of the following values for the LSA type:
    - **1**   Router link
    - **2**   Network link
    - **3**   Summary link

- **4** AS summary link
- **5** AS external link
- **6** Multicast link
- **15** Opaque link
- **16** Resource link

```
[12:2]$g wfOspfLsdbEntry.2.*
wfOspfLsdbEntry.wfOspfLsdbType.130.30.1.0.0.130.30.1.16.130.30.152.75 = 1
wfOspfLsdbEntry.wfOspfLsdbType.130.30.1.0.0.130.30.3.0.130.30.152.75 = 1
wfOspfLsdbEntry.wfOspfLsdbType.130.30.1.0.0.130.30.161.0.130.30.152.3 = 1
wfOspfLsdbEntry.wfOspfLsdbType.130.30.1.0.0.130.30.161.0.130.30.92.130 = 1
wfOspfLsdbEntry.wfOspfLsdbType.130.30.1.0.0.130.30.152.32.130.30.152.3 = 1
wfOspfLsdbEntry.wfOspfLsdbType.130.30.1.0.0.130.30.152.32.130.30.92.130 = 1
```

The preceeding output is truncated, showing only the Router Links advertisements. In a production environment, the list would be considerably longer, and would display a variety of LSA types.

Depending on the LSA type, different values may be described for the Link ID. For instance, a point-to-point link or virtual link defines the Link ID as the neighbor's Router ID; a transit link defines the Link ID as the IP address of the interface's DR; and the Link ID of a stub link will be defined as the IP network number. These values can be examined by using the following entry:

- **wfOspfLsdbEntry.3.\*** Doing a get on this value identifies what is being described by the LSA. The value of this MIB depends on the LSA type:

  - **1** The OSPF Router ID of the originating router, indicating a point-to-point link, or a virtual link
  - **2** The IP interface of the DR, indicating a transit link
  - **3** The destination network IP address, indicating a stub link
  - **4** The Router ID of the ASBR
  - **5** The destination network IP address

```
[12:2]$g wfOspfLsdbEntry.3.*
wfOspfLsdbEntry.wfOspfLsdbLSID.130.30.1.0.0.130.30.1.16.130.30.152.75 = 130.30.1.16
wfOspfLsdbEntry.wfOspfLsdbLSID.130.30.1.0.0.130.30.3.0.130.30.152.75 = 130.30.1.0
wfOspfLsdbEntry.wfOspfLsdbLSID.130.30.1.0.1.130.30.161.0.130.30.152.3 = 130.30.3.0
wfOspfLsdbEntry.wfOspfLsdbLSID.130.30.1.0.1.130.30.161.0.130.30.92.130 = 130.30.3.0
wfOspfLsdbEntry.wfOspfLsdbLSID.130.30.1.0.2.130.30.152.32.130.30.152.3 = 130.30.3.32
```

■ **wfOspfLsdbEntry.4.*** The following MIB attribute indicates the Router ID of the LSA's originating router, which can be useful for tracking down the source of LS information:

```
[12:2]$g wfOspfLsdbEntry.4.*

wfOspfLsdbEntry.wfOspfLsdbRouterId.130.30.1.0.0.130.30.1.16.130.30.152.245 = 130.30.152.75

wfOspfLsdbEntry.wfOspfLsdbRouterId.130.30.1.0.0.130.30.3.0.130.30.152.75 = 130.30.152.75

wfOspfLsdbEntry.wfOspfLsdbRouterId.130.30.1.0.0.130.30.161.0.130.30.152.3 = 130.30.152.3

wfOspfLsdbEntry.wfOspfLsdbRouterId.130.30.1.0.0.130.30.161.0.130.30.92.130 = 130.30.92.130

wfOspfLsdbEntry.wfOspfLsdbRouterId.130.30.1.0.0.130.30.152.32.130.30.152.3 = 130.30.152.3

wfOspfLsdbEntry.wfOspfLsdbRouterId.130.30.1.0.0.130.30.152.32.130.30.92.130 = 130.30.92.130

wfOspfLsdbEntry.wfOspfLsdbRouterId.130.30.1.0.0.130.30.152.64.130.30.152.3 = 130.30.152.3

wfOspfLsdbEntry.wfOspfLsdbRouterId.130.30.1.0.0.130.30.152.64.130.30.92.130 = 130.30.92.130

wfOspfLsdbEntry.wfOspfLsdbRouterId.130.30.1.0.0.130.30.152.96.130.30.152.3 = 130.30.152.3
```

■ **wfOspfLsdbEntry.5.*** The LSA sequence number. This is a signed 32-bit integer. Typical LSA sequence numbers are in the negative range. The larger the sequence number, the more recent the LSA. The router uses the LSA sequence number to remove old or duplicate LSAs.

```
[12:2]$g wfOspfLsdbEntry.5.*

wfOspfLsdbEntry.wfOspfLsdbSequence.130.30.1.0.0.130.30.1.16.130.30.152.245 = 80003d34

wfOspfLsdbEntry.wfOspfLsdbSequence.130.30.1.0.0.130.30.3.0.130.30.152.75 = 8000d237

wfOspfLsdbEntry.wfOspfLsdbSequence.130.30.1.0.0.130.30.161.0.130.30.152.3 = 800028de

wfOspfLsdbEntry.wfOspfLsdbSequence.130.30.1.0.0.130.30.161.0.130.30.92.130 = 80002387

wfOspfLsdbEntry.wfOspfLsdbSequence.130.30.1.0.0.130.30.152.32.130.30.152.3= 800027a3

wfOspfLsdbEntry.wfOspfLsdbSequence.130.30.1.0.0.130.30.152.32.130.30.92.130 = 80002873
```

■ **wfOspfLsdbEntry.6.*** Indicates the age of an LSA that is present in the LSDB (in seconds):

```
[12:2]$g wfOspfLsdbEntry.6.*

wfOspfLsdbEntry.wfOspfLsdbAge.130.30.1.0.0.130.30.1.16.130.30.152.75 = 723

wfOspfLsdbEntry.wfOspfLsdbAge.130.30.1.0.0.130.30.3.0.130.30.152.75 = 694

wfOspfLsdbEntry.wfOspfLsdbAge.130.30.1.0.0.130.30.161.0.130.30.152.3 = 712

wfOspfLsdbEntry.wfOspfLsdbAge.130.30.1.0.0.130.30.161.0.130.30.92.130 = 1334

wfOspfLsdbEntry.wfOspfLsdbAge.130.30.1.0.0.130.30.152.32.130.30.152.3 = 284

wfOspfLsdbEntry.wfOspfLsdbAge.130.30.1.0.0.130.30.152.32.130.30.92.130 = 1569

wfOspfLsdbEntry.wfOspfLsdbAge.130.30.1.0.0.130.30.152.64.130.30.152.3 = 283

wfOspfLsdbEntry.wfOspfLsdbAge.130.30.1.0.0.130.30.152.64.130.30.92.130 = 523

wfOspfLsdbEntry.wfOspfLsdbAge.130.30.1.0.0.130.30.152.96.130.30.152.3 = 1269

wfOspfLsdbEntry.wfOspfLsdbAge.130.30.1.0.0.130.30.152.128.130.30.152.3 = 623
```

- **wfOspfLsdbEntry.7.\***   The checksum of all the LSA fields except the age. The age is not included so that the age can be incremented without having to change the checksum.

```
[12:]$g wfOspfLsdbEntry.7.*
wfOspfLsdbEntry.wfOspfLsdbChecksum.130.30.1.0.0.130.30.1.16.130.30.152.245 = 0x6273
wfOspfLsdbEntry.wfOspfLsdbChecksum.130.30.1.0.0.130.30.3.0.130.30.152.75 = 0xc38d
wfOspfLsdbEntry.wfOspfLsdbChecksum.130.30.1.0.0.130.30.161.0.130.30.152.3 = 0x28d3
wfOspfLsdbEntry.wfOspfLsdbChecksum.130.30.1.0.0.130.30.161.0.130.30.92.130 = 0x2983
wfOspfLsdbEntry.wfOspfLsdbChecksum.130.30.1.0.0.130.30.152.32.130.30.152.3 = 0x2837
```

- **wfOspfLsdbEntry.9.\***   The forwarding address of the LSA; only applicable if the LSA type is an ASE:

```
[12:2]$g wfOspfLsdbEntry.9.*
wfOspfLsdbEntry.wfOspfLsdbAseForwardAddr.130.30.1.0.0.130.30.1.16.130.30.153.245 = 0.0.0.0
wfOspfLsdbEntry.wfOspfLsdbAseForwardAddr.130.30.1.0.0.130.30.3.0.130.30.153.245 = 0.0.0.0
wfOspfLsdbEntry.wfOspfLsdbAseForwardAddr.130.30.1.0.0.130.30.161.0.130.30.153.3 = 0.0.0.0
wfOspfLsdbEntry.wfOspfLsdbAseForwardAddr.130.30.1.0.0.130.30.161.0.130.30.164.130 = 0.0.0.0
wfOspfLsdbEntry.wfOspfLsdbAseForwardAddr.130.30.1.0.0.130.30.152.32.130.30.153.3 = 0.0.0.0
```

- **wfOspfLsdbEntry.10.\***   Describes the external route tag of the LSA; only applicable if the LSA type is an ASE:

```
[12:2]$g wfOspfLsdbEntry.10.*
wfOspfLsdbEntry.wfOspfLsdbAseTag.130.30.1.0.0.130.30.1.16.130.30.152.75 = 0
wfOspfLsdbEntry.wfOspfLsdbAseTag.130.30.1.0.0.130.30.3.0.130.30.152.75 = 0
wfOspfLsdbEntry.wfOspfLsdbAseTag.130.30.1.0.0.130.30.161.0.130.30.152.3 = 0
wfOspfLsdbEntry.wfOspfLsdbAseTag.130.30.1.0.0.130.30.161.0.130.30.92.130 = 0
wfOspfLsdbEntry.wfOspfLsdbAseTag.130.30.1.0.0.130.30.152.32.130.30.152.3 = 0
wfOspfLsdbEntry.wfOspfLsdbAseTag.130.30.1.0.0.130.30.152.32.130.30.92.130 = 0
```

- **wfOspfLsdbEntry.11.\***   Describes the external metric type of the LSA; only applicable if the LSA type is an ASE. The value returned will be either a 1 (type 1) or a 2 (type 2):

```
[12:2]$g wfOspfLsdbEntry.11.*
wfOspfLsdbEntry.wfOspfLsdbAseType.130.30.1.0.0.130.30.1.16.130.30.152.75 = 0
wfOspfLsdbEntry.wfOspfLsdbAseType.130.30.1.0.0.130.30.3.0.130.30.152.75 = 0
wfOspfLsdbEntry.wfOspfLsdbAseType.130.30.1.0.0.130.30.161.0.130.30.152.3 = 0
wfOspfLsdbEntry.wfOspfLsdbAseType.130.30.1.0.0.130.30.161.0.130.30.92.130 = 1
wfOspfLsdbEntry.wfOspfLsdbAseType.130.30.1.0.0.130.30.152.32.130.30.152.3 = 1
wfOspfLsdbEntry.wfOspfLsdbAseType.130.30.1.0.0.130.30.152.32.130.30.92.130 = 2
```

# Examining the OSPF Interfaces

Each OSPF interface exists within a specific area and must maintain an LSDB for that area. The OSPF interface also maintains adjacencies with the DR and BDR, as well as forming a neighbor state with neighboring OSPF routers. The OSPF interface state can be examined both through the scripts and through the MIB.

## Examining the OSPF Interfaces Through the Scripts

The OSPF interface state can be examined through the scripts by using the following command syntax: **show ospf interface**. For each OSPF interface configured on the router, this script displays the IP address of the OSPF interface, the Area ID the interface connects to, the type of OSPF link, the state of the OSPF interface, the metric (cost) associated with the OSPF interface, the router priority associated with the OSPF interface, and the DR and BDR for the Area ID the OSPF interface connects to:

```
[12:2]$show ospf interface

OSPF Interfaces
---------------
                                              Metric/
IP Address       Area ID       Type    State  MTU     Priority   DR  /  BDR
---------- --------------      -----   --------  -------  --------  ---------------
130.30.161.2    130.30.1.0    NBMA    DR Other  5         0    0.0.0.0
                                                          1    0.0.0.0
130.30.152.13   130.30.1.0    BCAST   BackupDR  1         10   130.30.152.3
                                                          1         130.30.152.13
130.30.152.62   130.30.1.0    NBMA    DR Other  4         0    0.0.0.0
                                                          1         0.0.0.0
3 Entries
```

**TYPE OF OSPF LINKS**    The Type field in the preceding output indicates the OSPF link type (point-to-point, broadcast, and so forth), defining the type of OSPF network the interface exists in. The OSPF link types are as follows:

- **PtoP**   Point-to-point network
- **BCAST**   Broadcast network
- **NBMA**   Nonbroadcast multiple access network
- **DFLT**   Misconfigured; the Type field should be changed to point-to-multipoint network

**STATE OF THE OSPF INTERFACE**    In addition, the State field can indicate a lot of information regarding the OSPF interface's current state. The following values may appear:

- **Down**    OSPF interface is in a nonoperational state. Check the data-link layer for problems.

- **Waiting**    The router is listening to Hello packets to determine the DR/BDR.

- **P to P**    The final operational state for a point-to-point OSPF link.

- **DR**    This router is the DR for the Area ID the OSPF interface connects to.

- **BackupDR**    This router is the BDR for the Area ID the OSPF interface connects to.

- **DR Other**    This router is neither the DR nor the BDR for the Area ID the OSPF interface connects to.

**ROUTER PRIORITY**    This value may be an integer between 0 and 255. The higher the number, the greater the router priority. If the router priority is 0, then the router is not eligible to become either the DR or the BDR.

## Examining the OSPF Interfaces Through the TI

The same OSPF interface information that can be obtained through the scripts can be obtained via the MIB, though a series of MIB gets need to be executed to gather the same information provided by the **show ospf interface** command. The following seven attributes provide the information displayed in the IP, Area ID, Type, State, Priority, and DR/BDR fields of the **show ospf interface** command:

- **wfOspfIfEntry.3.\***    Provides the current state of the OSPF interfaces configured on the router. For each interface, a value between 1 and 7 (inclusive) will be returned. These values indicate the interface state, with the following meanings:

  - **1**    Down. If the OSPF interface is down, check the state of the data-link layer. For example, the OSPF interface will be down if the state of the sync line is down.

  - **2**    Loopback. The interface has been placed into a loopback mode.

  - **3**    Waiting. The router is in the process of determining the DR and BDR by examining Hello packets.

  - **4**    Point to Point. The final state reached on a point-to-point link.

  - **5**    Designated Router. The router will form an adjacency with all other routers on the network segment, because this router is the DR for this network segment.

■ **6**   Backup Designated Router. The router will form an adjacency with all other routers on the network segment, because this router is the BDR for this network segment.

■ **7**   Other Designated Router. The router will form an adjacency with just the DR and BDR for this network segment, because this router is neither the DR nor the BDR.

```
[12:2]$g wfOspfIfEntry.3.*
wfOspfIfEntry.wfOspfIfState.130.30.161.2.0 = 7
wfOspfIfEntry.wfOspfIfState.130.30.152.13.0 = 6
wfOspfIfEntry.wfOspfIfState.130.30.152.62.0 = 7
wfOspfIfEntry.wfOspfIfState.130.30.152.94.0 = 7
wfOspfIfEntry.wfOspfIfState.130.30.152.126.0 = 1
wfOspfIfEntry.wfOspfIfState.130.30.152.130.0 = 1
wfOspfIfEntry.wfOspfIfState.130.30.92.2.0 = 1
```

■ **wfOspfIfEntry.4.***   Displays the IP addresses of the OSPF interfaces:

```
[12:2]$g wfOspfIfEntry.4.*
wfOspfIfEntry.wfOspfIfIpAddress.130.30.161.2.0 = 130.30.161.2
wfOspfIfEntry.wfOspfIfIpAddress.130.30.152.13.0 = 130.30.152.13
wfOspfIfEntry.wfOspfIfIpAddress.130.30.152.62.0 = 130.30.152.62
wfOspfIfEntry.wfOspfIfIpAddress.130.30.152.94.0 = 130.30.152.94
wfOspfIfEntry.wfOspfIfIpAddress.130.30.152.126.0 = 130.30.152.126
wfOspfIfEntry.wfOspfIfIpAddress.130.30.152.130.0 = 130.30.152.130
wfOspfIfEntry.wfOspfIfIpAddress.130.30.92.2.0 = 130.30.92.2
```

■ **wfOspfIfEntry.6.***   The results of a get on the preceding object/attribute provides a list of each area the OSPF interfaces connect to:

```
[12:2]$g wfOspfIfEntry.6.*
wfOspfIfEntry.wfOspfIfAreaId.130.30.161.2.0 = 130.30.1.0
wfOspfIfEntry.wfOspfIfAreaId.130.30.152.13.0 = 130.30.1.0
wfOspfIfEntry.wfOspfIfAreaId.130.30.152.62.0 = 130.30.1.0
wfOspfIfEntry.wfOspfIfAreaId.130.30.152.94.0 = 130.30.1.0
wfOspfIfEntry.wfOspfIfAreaId.130.30.152.126.0 = 130.30.1.0
wfOspfIfEntry.wfOspfIfAreaId.130.30.152.130.0 = 130.30.1.0
wfOspfIfEntry.wfOspfIfAreaId.130.30.92.2.0 = 130.30.1.0
```

■ **wfOspfIfEntry.7.***   Displays the OSPF network LAN/WAN type that the OSPF interface connects to. For each interface, a value between 1 and 6 (inclusive) will be returned, with the following meanings:

■ **1**   Broadcast. Should be used if the media supports broadcasting. Examples are Ethernet, Token Ring, FDDI, and Group Mode Frame Relay.

- **2** NBMA. Should be used for media that supports multiple connections, but has no broadcast capability, such as X.25 or ATM. OSPF neighbors must be configured manually if NBMA is selected.

- **3** Point-to-point. Should be used for media that supports only two connections. Examples include WAN Standard, PPP, and Frame Relay Direct Mode.

- **4** Point-to-multipoint—proprietary. Should be configured on the hub router in a Frame Relay hub-and-spoke (non-fully meshed) environment in which all the spoke routers are Nortel Networks routers.

- **5** Point-to-multipoint—standard (IETF). Should be configured on the hub router in a Frame Relay hub-and-spoke (non-fully meshed) environment if the hub router will be connecting to some or all non-Nortel Networks routers across the Frame Relay.

- **6** Passive. Should be configured on the spoke routers in a Frame Relay hub-and-spoke (non-fully meshed) environment.

```
[12:2]$g wfOspfIfEntry.7.*
wfOspfIfEntry.wfOspfIfType.130.30.161.2.0 = 2
wfOspfIfEntry.wfOspfIfType.130.30.152.13.0 = 1
wfOspfIfEntry.wfOspfIfType.130.30.152.62.0 = 2
wfOspfIfEntry.wfOspfIfType.130.30.152.94.0 = 2
wfOspfIfEntry.wfOspfIfType.130.30.152.126.0 = 2
wfOspfIfEntry.wfOspfIfType.130.30.152.130.0 = 2
wfOspfIfEntry.wfOspfIfType.130.30.92.2.0 = 2
```

- **wfOspfIfEntry.8.*** Indicates the configured OSPF router priority of the OSPF interfaces. The greater the number, the higher the router priority. On a multiaccess network, the OSPF routers with the highest priorities become the DR and BDR. By default, the router priority is set to 1. If the router priority is set to 0, the router is not eligible to become the DR and will not partake in the DR/BDR election process. The valid range is an integer between 0 and 255. If there is a tie during the DR election process, the router with the highest OSPF Router ID becomes DR and the next highest becomes BDR.

```
[12:2]$g wfOspfIfEntry.8.*
wfOspfIfEntry.wfOspfIfRtrPriority.130.30.161.2.0 = 0
wfOspfIfEntry.wfOspfIfRtrPriority.130.30.152.13.0 = 10
wfOspfIfEntry.wfOspfIfRtrPriority.130.30.152.62.0 = 0
wfOspfIfEntry.wfOspfIfRtrPriority.130.30.152.94.0 = 0
wfOspfIfEntry.wfOspfIfRtrPriority.130.30.152.126.0 = 0
```

- **wfOspfIfEntry.14.*** Displays the IP address of the OSPF interface's DR. The default is hex 00000000 (0.0.0.0).

- **wfOspfIfEntry.15.*** Displays the IP address of the BDR. The default is hex 00000000 (0.0.0.0).

- **wfOspfIfEntry.11.*** The OSPF Interface Hello Interval. Indicates how often the router transmits OSPF Hello packets. This timer must be the same on all OSPF routers connecting to the same IP network. A Hello timer mismatch prevents an OSPF adjacency from forming. The default value is 10 seconds.

```
[12:2]$g wfOspfIfEntry.11.*
wfOspfIfEntry.wfOspfIfHelloInterval.130.30.161.2.0 = 10
wfOspfIfEntry.wfOspfIfHelloInterval.130.30.152.13.0 = 10
wfOspfIfEntry.wfOspfIfHelloInterval.130.30.152.62.0 = 10
wfOspfIfEntry.wfOspfIfHelloInterval.130.30.152.94.0 = 10
wfOspfIfEntry.wfOspfIfHelloInterval.130.30.152.126.0 = 10
wfOspfIfEntry.wfOspfIfHelloInterval.130.30.152.130.0 = 10
```

- **wfOspfIfEntry.12.*** The OSPF Interface Router Dead Interval. Indicates how long the router will wait after not receiving a Hello packet from one of its OSPF neighbors before determining the router is down. The Dead Interval timer should be some multiple of the Hello Interval timer. All OSPF routers connecting to the same network have to be configured with the same Dead Interval timer. The default value is 40 seconds.

- **wfOspfIfEntry.17.*** An 8-octet numerical OSPF authentication key. If the OSPF authentication type is configured for simple password and the OSPF authentication key is less than 8 octets, then the router will left-justify the number and pad it with 0's to make an 8-octet number. The default is hex 0000000000000000 (0.0.0.0.0.0.0.0).

- **wfOspfIfEntry.18.*** The number of OSPF Hello packets transmitted by the OSPF interfaces.

- **wfOspfIfEntry.19.*** The number of OSPF Database Description packets transmitted by the OSPF interfaces.

- **wfOspfIfEntry.20.*** The number of OSPF Link State Request packets transmitted by the OSPF interfaces.

- **wfOspfIfEntry.21.*** The number of OSPF Link State Update packets transmitted by the OSPF interfaces.

- **wfOspfIfEntry.22.*** The number of OSPF Link State Acknowledgements transmitted by the OSPF interfaces.

- **wfOspfIfEntry.23.*** The number of OSPF Hello packets received on the OSPF interfaces.

- **wfOspfIfEntry.24.\*** The number of OSPF Link State Database Description packets received by the OSPF interfaces.

- **wfOspfIfEntry.25.\*** The number of OSPF Link State Request packets received by the OSPF interfaces.

- **wfOspfIfEntry.26.\*** The number of OSPF Link State Update packets received by the OSPF interfaces.

- **wfOspfIfEntry.27.\*** The number of OSPF Link State Acknowledgement packets received by the OSPF interfaces.

- **wfOspfIfEntry.28.\*** The number of OSPF packets dropped by the OSPF interfaces because the packets contained invalid data.

- **wfOspfIfEntry.30.\*** Indicates whether or not the OSPF interface uses multicast forwarding. On NBMA and PTP networks, multicasting forwarding is not necessary. A value of 1, 2, or 3 will be returned for each interface:

  - **1**  Do not do any multicast forwarding
  - **2**  Forward as a data link multicast
  - **3**  Forward as a data link unicast

- **wfOspfIfEntry.31.\*** Indicates whether or not the OSPF interface will flood opaque LSAs. A value of either 1 or 2 will be returned for each interface:
  - **1**  On
  - **2**  Off

# Examining the OSPF Neighbors

All OSPF interfaces form a neighbor state with other router interfaces connected to the same network. The state that exists between these neighbors determines the communication between them, and the failure of two OSPF neighbors to transition into the proper state will cause problems on the network.

Each OSPF router should have a list of neighbors associated with it, each neighbor in turn associated with a specific OSPF interface. These neighbor relationships can be examined either through the scripts or through the MIB, as are described in the sections which follow.

## Examining the OSPF Neighbors Using the Scripts

A list of OSPF neighbors, the OSPF interface the neighbors are associated with, and the current state that exists between the two neighbors can be displayed by using the following command syntax: **show ospf neighbors**. This displays all the OSPF neighbors, both dynamic and statically configured. The table that results shows the IP address of the local OSPF interface, the Router ID of the OSPF neighbor, the IP address of the neighbor's OSPF interface, the neighbor state, and the neighbor type:

```
[12:2]$show ospf neighbors

OSPF Neighbors
--------------
                                  Neighbor
   IP Interface   Router ID       IP Address        State      Type
   -------------- --------------  ---------------   ---------  --------
   130.30.152.13  170.70.10.129   130.30.152.1      Full       Dynamic
   130.30.152.13  170.70.10.133   130.30.152.2      Full       Dynamic
   130.30.152.13  130.30.152.3    130.30.152.3      Full       Dynamic
   130.30.92.4    170.70.10.129   130.30.92.2       Two Way    Dynamic
   130.30.92.4    130.30.152.3    130.30.92.3       Full       Dynamic
   130.30.92.136  130.30.231.1    130.30.92.130     Full       Dynamic
   130.30.92.136  170.70.10.133   130.30.92.131     Full       Dynamic
   130.30.92.136  170.70.10.129   130.30.92.132     Two Way    Dynamic
   8 dynamic neighbors


0 configured neighbors

OSPF Virtual Neighbors
----------------------

   Area Address     Router ID          State
   ---------------- ----------------  --------------

0 virtual neighbors
```

The output from this command provides information regarding the OSPF neighbor state; for more information regarding the specifics of the OSPF neighbor states, reference Chapter 31.

**OSPF NEIGHBOR STATE**    The OSPF neighbor state may be one of several values. The following is a list of the neighbor states, as well as a brief description of each:

- **Down**   Can only occur if the OSPF neighbor is statically configured. This is the initial state of an OSPF neighbor conversation.

- **Attempt**   Can only occur if the OSPF neighbor is statically configured. It means the router has not seen a Hello packet from the OSPF neighbor.

- **Init**   The router received a Hello packet from a neighbor, but the Hello packet did not include the Router ID for this router in its known OSPF router list.

- **Two Way**   The router received a Hello packet from a neighbor that includes the Router ID for this router in its known OSPF router list.

- **Exchange Start**   The routers are in the process of determining the master/slave relationship prior to exchanging LSDBs.

- **Exchange**   The routers are in the process of exchanging the Database Description packets and examining each other's LSDB.

- **Loading**   The routers are synchronizing their LSDBs by swapping entries that are missing.

- **Full**   The final state of an adjacency. The LSDBs are fully synchronized.

**OSPF ROUTER TYPE**   In addition to the neighbor state, a router type is displayed, indicating whether the neighbor was learned dynamically or was manually configured, as it would be in an NBMA network:

- **Dynamic**   The OSPF neighbor was learned. This occurs on broadcast and point-to-point networks.

- **Cfg**   The OSPF neighbor has been statically configured. This must be done in NBMA networks.

# The Complete Reference

Nortel Networks

# Chapter 33

## Routing Information Protocol and RIPv2

The Routing Information Protocol (RIP) is a legacy, Layer 3, routing protocol used in IP networks. This chapter discusses the workings of RIP, some of its design considerations, and the differences between RIPv1 and RIPv2. Although RIP is an older routing protocol, it is still in very common use and, particularly with the advent of RIPv2, is likely to remain in common use for quite some time.

# RIP

The Routing Information Protocol is a relatively simple, distance-vector routing protocol (as opposed to a link-state protocol, such as OSPF) for use in small to moderate sized IP networks. A distance-vector protocol is based on a table that contains all possible destinations in the system. Each destination has a metric for purposes of determining the desirability of the route. In a practical RIP setting, this metric is generally given a value of 1 for each router hop incurred.

Each router periodically sends an update packet out each RIP interface. These RIP updates are broadcast to the networks the interfaces are configured for, to be received by any other RIP routers that may exist on those networks. Contained in the RIP update is a list of all known networks, including networks that the router itself is directly connected to, and also those that the router has learned through updates from remote routers. Each network listing in the advertisement also includes the relative distance between that network and the router sending the update.

A router receiving such an update compares the entries found within it to its own; if an incoming entry has a distance metric associated with it that is less than that of an existing entry for the same network, then the route with the shorter distance replaces the previous route. This is the essence of a distance-vector protocol, and is essentially how RIP versions 1 and 2 function.

## RIPv1 Features

RIP version 1 is a routing protocol that is simple to design, configure, and maintain, as well as one that is not resource-intensive. Whereas in larger networks, the maximum hop count of 15 can become limiting, and reconvergence times can become lengthy compared to a link-state protocol. In smaller networks, RIP reconverges very quickly. Some of the advantages to running RIPv1 are the following:

- **Ease of configuration**    A RIPv1 network is relatively easy to design and implement; once installed, it is also relatively easy to maintain and troubleshoot.

- **Not resource-intensive**    RIP does not place the burden on CPU and memory that a more complex protocol does, such as Open Shortest Path First (OSPF) or

Border Gateway Protocol (BGP). As such, RIP is an ideal protocol for lower-end routers.

■ **Supports multiple paths between networks based on cost** RIP supports IP multipath, in which multiple paths to the same route can exist. In this scenario, route desirability is based on cost. This allows for flexibility in design and redundancy.

> **Note** *IP multipath is supported in software version 11.02 or greater.*

## RIPv1 Limitations

Because RIP was designed largely for small to moderately sized networks, it has some inherent limitations that make it inappropriate for large networks:

■ *RIPv1 is limited to networks whose router hop count does not exceed 15.* A router hop count of 16 or greater is considered to be unreachable and invalid by RIP. By default, RIP hop counts are given a cost of 1. This value can be altered (within the limit of 15 hops).

■ *RIPv1 uses fixed metrics for route comparisons.* It does not take into account the medium, bandwidth, or load of a configured RIP interface. Unlike OSPF, in RIP, an ATM interface with an OC-3 connection running at 20-percent utilization is considered the same metric as a 56K leased line running at 70-percent utilization.

■ *Networks in a RIPv1 environment must remain contiguous.* This is because subnet information is not conveyed in RIPv1 updates.

■ *Variable-length subnet masking (VLSM) is not supported in RIPv1 networks.*

■ *RIPv1 updates are broadcast periodically, rather than being directed to a multicast group address, which results in added overhead.*

# RIP Updates

A RIP *advertisement* is a packet containing route information. Each RIP update packet can advertise up to 25 destination networks. RIPv1 advertisements are sent as broadcasts and are directed to the broadcast address for the network on which the interface in question is configured. For instance, a RIP advertisement being sent out a RIP interface on the 130.10.0.0 network will be transmitted to the MAC broadcast address of FFFFFFFFFFFF, while at the IP layer, it will be directed to the 130.10.255.255 broadcast address to all hosts on the 130.10.0.0 network.

RIP updates are transmitted every 30 seconds, out of all RIP interfaces to the addresses just described. The routing information included in an update is a list of network numbers, each with an associated distance metric (hop count). This is the hop count that is seen by the router originating the advertisement:

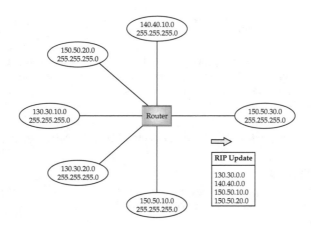

## Transmitting RIP Updates

As previously stated, a RIPv1 update is transmitted out each configured RIP interface on the router, every 30 seconds. These updates contain network information regarding all known networks, as well as their respective hop counts from the transmitting router. RIPv1 routers do not advertise the subnetwork portion of an address out an interface that belongs to a different network number. Thus, if a RIP interface is configured for the 150.50.10.0 subnetwork, other subnets on the 150.50.0.0 network will be advertised with the subnet portion included (150.50.20.0, 150.50.30.0, and so forth), but a network other than 150.50.0.0 will be advertised on that interface without the subnet portion. For example, network 140.40.10.0, in this case, would be advertised simply as 140.40.0.0.

## Cost

The cost associated with each network entry of the RIP update is calculated in the following manner: any network advertisements included in an incoming RIPv1 update have the cost of the ingress interface added to the cost defined in the advertisement itself. So, an incoming advertisement on an interface with the default cost of 1 assigned for network 150.50.0.0 with a cost of 2 will be given a cost of 3 when (and if) it is installed into the routing table.

If the advertisement received describes a route to a network that is already in the routing table, but which has a shorter metric, then it will replace the current entry for that network. If the paths are equal (i.e., if they have the same hop count), then a statically defined router weight is used to break the tie. If the weights are equal as well, then the first learned route will remain in the routing table.

**Note** *Local RIPv1 interfaces have a cost of 0, but for purposes of advertising a directly attached network in a RIPv1 update, the route is assigned a cost of 1.*

## Preventing Propagation of Invalid Routes

RIPv1 has two methods of ensuring that invalid routes do not propagate: *Split Horizon,* and *Poison Reverse.* In a RIP network, each router learns from its neighbors all routes that those neighbors know of. The updates sent by the neighboring routers are examined, and the advertisements contained within are compared against the current routing table. If any newly advertised routes are found to be valid, they are added into the routing table. If the updates list routes that already exist in the routing table, it verifies that those routes are still valid and prevents them from aging out prematurely. For this reason, it is important that the router does not advertise learned route information back out of the interface on which the route information was learned.

However, consider the example shown in Figure 33-1, which has the following three routers sharing route information:

■ Router A is configured with two token ring interfaces, one in network 150.50.10.0 and one in network 160.60.10.0.

■ Router B shares network 160.60.10.0 and also has an interface configured for the 170.70.10.0 network.

■ Router C shares an interface in network 170.70.10.0 and also has an interface configured in network 180.80.10.0.

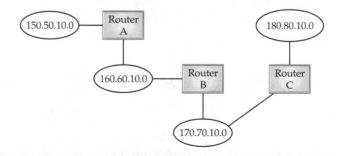

**Figure 33-1.**   *Three RIPv1 routers*

INTERNETWORKING WITH NORTEL NETWORKS

In this example, imagine that router A sends an update to router B containing route advertisements for networks 150.50.0.0 and 160.60.10.0. Router B receives this information and adds the 150.50.0.0 network into its routing table (the 160.60.10.0 network already exists in its routing table, with a metric of 0, because it has a direct connection to that network). Router B, then, when sending its update to router C, will include three advertisements: one each for networks 150.50.0.0, 160.60.0.0, and 170.70.10.0. Router C receives this update, examines the route advertisements, and installs entries for 150.50.0.0 and 160.60.0.0 into its routing table (again, the 170.70.10.0 network already is present, with a metric of 0).

Now, imagine that router A's interface configured for the 150.50.10.0 network has failed. Router A will no longer include network 150.50.0.0 in its RIP updates, so this route will eventually age out of the routing tables of routers B and router C—but only because a mechanism is in place to stop RIP routers from advertising learned routes out of the interfaces that the routes were learned on. If such a mechanism weren't in place, router C would include the 150.50.0.0 network in its update, and router B would receive the update, examine the route information, and validate the 150.50.0.0 route, even though it is no longer a valid route (see Figure 33-2).

Furthermore, router B would include the 150.50.0.0 in its update back to router C, which in turn would refresh the route in its route table; the route would then be perpetually passed back and forth, even though it is invalid. To prevent this from happening, RIP routers employ a method called *Split Horizon* or *Poison Reverse* when advertising updates.

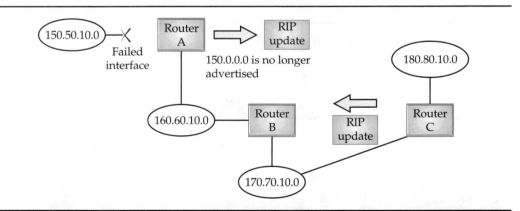

**Figure 33-2.**   *With no prevention mechanism, router B receives invalid route information from router C*

## Split Horizon

When a RIP router is configured for Split Horizon, it simply does not advertise route information back out of the interface it was learned on. So in Figure 33-2, for example, router C would never advertise the 150.50.0.0 network back to router B, because the 150.50.0.0 network would have been learned through an update received from Router B on the interface transmitting the RIP update in question. If router C were configured for Split Horizon, it would advertise only network 180.80.0.0 in an update transmitted to the 170.70.10.255 broadcast address, and not 150.50.0.0 or 160.60.0.0, even though those networks are present in its routing table.

> **Note**  *The 170.70.10.0 network would still be advertised; the transmitting interface would be configured for the 170.70.10.0 subnet, but the information would not have been "learned" on that interface. As long as router C's 170.70.10.0 interface were functioning, it would consider that network a valid route, and advertise it as such.*

## Poison Reverse

Poison Reverse accomplishes the same thing as Split Horizon, but in a different way. A RIP router configured for Poison Reverse advertises learned networks back out interfaces it learned them on, but it advertises them with a metric of 16, which makes them inaccessible. For this reason, in the previous example, router B would receive an update from router C with four networks advertised: network 180.80.0.0, with a metric of 1; network 170.70.10.0, with a metric of 1; network 160.60.0.0, with a metric of 16; and network 150.50.0.0, also with a metric of 16. Router B will install the 180.80.0.0 and 170.70.10.0 networks into its routing table, and will discard networks 160.60.0.0 and 150.50.0.0, because they have a metric of 16, which exceeds the maximum hop count for a RIPv1 network. In a network with a looped topology, Poison Reverse allows for faster route convergence than does Split Horizon.

> **Note**  *Router B will still receive updates containing valid advertisements for network 150.50.0.0 from router A, so the route will not age out as long as it is valid, and router B has an interface configured on the 160.60.10.0 network, so it does not need to rely on router C for this route information.*

## Subnet Masking

RIP interfaces advertise subnetworks in either of two ways. If a router has three RIP interfaces configured, all of which are on different subnetworks of the same network number, the subnetworks will be advertised, though their actual subnet masks will not be. If the interfaces are configured for different network numbers altogether, then the networks will be summarized, and their specific subnetworks will not be advertised.

## Example of the Subnet Portion of a Network Being Advertised

In Figure 33-3, router A has three RIP interfaces: one configured for network 130.30.10.0/24, one configured for 130.30.20.0/24, and one configured for 130.30.30.0/24. The transmitting interface in this case is 130.30.10.1. Assuming, for the sake of this example, that these three local interfaces are the only routes that router A currently knows about, interface 130.30.10.1 will transmit a RIP update to the broadcast address for its subnetwork, which is 130.30.10.255. This RIP update will contain three advertisements: 130.30.10.0, 130.30.20.0, and 130.30.30.0. Since the remaining two interfaces are configured with a network number that is the same as that of the transmitting interface, the subnetwork portion of the address is communicated in the RIP updates.

## Example of Route Summarization

In Figure 33-4, the same router A is again configured with three RIP interfaces, but the addressing scheme is different. In this scenario, the interfaces are configured for 130.30.10.0/24, 130.20.10.0, and 140.40.10.0. The transmitting interface in this example is again RIP interface 130.30.10.1.

In this example, as in the Figure 33-3, interface 130.30.10.1 sends a broadcast to its subnet broadcast address (130.30.10.255). The RIP update again contains three advertisements: 130.30.10.0, 130.20.0.0, and 140.40.0.0. However, because network 130.20.10.0 and network 140.40.10.0 are on different networks than the transmitting interface, their networks are summarized, and this time the subnetwork details are not included.

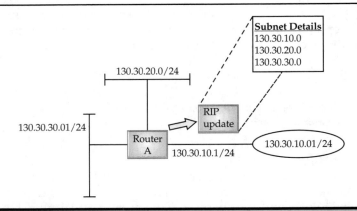

**Figure 33-3.**    A RIP with router A configured for three subnets on a common network

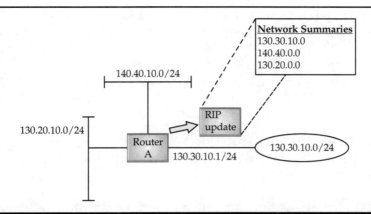

**Figure 33-4.**    *A RIP with router A configured for three different networks*

## RIP Subnetwork Advertisement

In the preceding example, there could have been a remote router with a series of other interfaces configured for other subnetworks of the 140.40.0.0 network. These subnetworks would always be advertised out of interfaces configured for the 140.40.0.0 network. The subnet mask, however, would not. When router A received an advertisement on its 140.40.10.1 interface describing the 140.40.20.0 network, only the subnet (.20) would be included; the subnet mask would not. Router A would apply its own mask to the incoming advertisement, as in a RIPv1 network, and all subnet masks would be assumed equal for a common network number. This is due to the fact that the RIPv1 specification was conceived before the RFC or IP subnetting, and at that time all masks were natural. The receiving interface would apply its own subnet mask information to any incoming advertisements for the network number it was configured for.

## Example of Successful Route Summarization

This example has three routers:

■  Router A is configured for subnetwork 150.50.10.0/24, on interface 150.50.10.1.

- Router B also is configured for subnetwork 150.50.10.0/24, on interface 150.50.10.2, as well as two other interfaces: 150.50.20.1, using the same 24-bit network mask (because all RIPv1 common networks must share a common subnet mask), and 150.40.30.1, which also uses a 24-bit mask.

- Router C also has an interface configured for subnetwork 140.40.30.0/24 on interface 140.40.30.2, and four other interfaces, configured for subnetworks 140.40.40.0, 140.40.50.0, 140.40.60.0, and 140.40.70.0.

**NETWORKS ADVERTISED BY ROUTER A**    Router A in this case only has one interface configured, so it will send updates containing one advertisement only; the 150.50.10.0 subnetwork.

**NETWORKS ADVERTISED BY ROUTER C**    Router C will send updates out each of its RIP interfaces, but for the sake of this example, only the update transmitted from interface 140.40.30.2 will be examined. This update will be broadcast to the subnet broadcast address 140.40.30.255. Since all of its interfaces are configured on a common network number, broken down into five subnets total, the update sent will contain five advertisements; 140.40.30.0, 140.40.40.0, 140.40.50.0, 140.40.60.0, and 140.40.70.0.

**NETWORKS ADVERTISED BY ROUTER B**    Router B will send updates out each of its RIP interfaces, but for the sake of this example, only the updates transmitted from interfaces 150.50.10.2 and 140.40.30.1 will be examined. The advertisement out interface 150.50.10.2 will be broadcast to the IP subnet broadcast address 150.50.10.255, and will contain three advertisements. Since one of its two other local interfaces is also configured for the 150.50.0.0 network, the individual subnet for that interface will be advertised; network 150.50.20.0 will be advertised along with 150.50.10.0. Router B also has an interface configured on subnet 140.40.30.0, and, as was outlined in router C's advertisements, router B has actually received an update from router C with five different subnets described on the 140.40.0.0 network. Router B, however, will not communicate these individual subnets when sending its update to router A. Since the 140.40.0.0 network is different from that of the transmitting interface (150.50.10.1, in this case), the subnetworks will not be advertised, only the network number, 140.40.0.0. So, router B's update to router A contains three entries: 150.50.10.0, 150.50.20.0, and 140.40.0.0.

Likewise, when router B sends its RIP update from interface 140.40.30.1, it will summarize its 150.50.10.0 and 150.50.20.0 subnets simply as 150.50.0.0, because if router A needs to route a packet to any of the 140.40.0.0 subnetworks, they are all available out router B's 140.40.30.1 interface. Therefore, no reason exists to describe them individually—they are summarized as 140.40.0.0, so router A knows that any traffic destined for any of the 140.40.0.0 subnets should be sent to router B.

This RIP information is shown in the following excerpt from a sniffer trace:

```
DLC: ------ DLC Header ------
DLC: Destination = BROADCAST FFFFFFFFFFFF, Broadcast
DLC: Source = Station <station MAC>
DLC: Ethertype = 0800 (IP)
DLC:
IP: ------IP Header ------
IP: Version = 4, header length = 20 bytes
IP: Type of service = 00
IP: 000. .... = routine
IP: ...0 ....  = normal delay
IP: .... 0...  = normal throughput
IP: .... .0..  = normal reliability
IP: Total length = 172 bytes
IP: Identification = 155
IP: Flags = 0X
IP: .0.. .... = may fragment
IP: ..0. ....  = last fragment
IP: Fragment offset = 0 bytes
IP: Time to live = 1 seconds/hops
IP: Protocol = 17 (UDP)
IP: Header checksum = 949B (correct)
IP: Source address (150.50.10.1)
IP: Destination address (150.50.10.255)
IP: No options
IP:
UDP: ------ UDP Header ------
UDP: Source port = 520 (Route)
UDP: Destination port = 520
UDP: Length = 152
UDP: Checksum B075 (correct)
UDP:
RIP: ------ RIP Header ------
RIP: Command = 2 (Response)
RIP: Version = 1
RIP: Unused = 0
RIP: Routing data frame 1
RIP: Address family identifier = 2 (IP)
RIP: IP Address = [150.50.10.0]
```

```
RIP: Metric = 1
RIP: Routing data frame 2
RIP: Address family identifier = 2 (IP)
RIP: IP Address = [150.50.20.0]
RIP: Metric = 1
RIP: Routing data frame 3
RIP: Address family identifier = 2 (IP)
RIP: IP Address = [140.40.0.0]
RIP: Metric = 3
```

The RIP entries following the RIP header in this case are the networks being advertised. In reality, there may be many more of these entries. Notice that in the preceding case, two networks are being described in two different ways: network 150.50.20.0/24, which is actually being described with the subnet address included, and network 140.40.0.0, which, in this case, is a representation of all five subnets of network 140.40.0.0 without the subnet information. The reason why the subnet portion is included in one advertisement and not the other, is that in the preceding trace, the 150.50.20.0 subnet shares the same network number that the advertising interface belongs to.

The broadcast address for the RIP advertisement is 150.50.10.255, which indicates that the RIP interface is configured for network 150.50.10.0 (the actual IP, also included in the trace as the source address, is 150.50.10.1). Within this network (150.50.0.0), the subnetwork is included, because this is a network that is configured locally on the router. Because the network 140.40.0.0 is an address that was learned from a remote source, the subnetwork is not included, and the network is summarized simply as 140.40.0.0.

## Variable Length Subnet Masking

In RIPv1, subnet information is not communicated in RIP advertisements. A RIPv1 interface advertises the subnetwork of a network only if the router is advertising those networks and subnetworks them from an interface with a common network number (for instance, advertising the 130.30.10.0 and 130.30.20.0 out an interface configured with IP 130.30.30.1/24). Consequently, any incoming advertisement for that same network number is assumed to share the same mask as the receiving RIPv1 interface. Thus, a RIP network must be designed in such a manner that subnet masks applied to a network remain consistent for that network. For example, consider a network in which three routers share interfaces on the common network of 150.50.64.0/19 (subnetwork .64 on the 150.50.0.0 network, with a mask of 255.255.224.0). Each RIP interface configured for that network will send its RIP updates to the IP broadcast address 150.50.95.255:

1001 0110 . 0011 0010 . 0100 0000 . 0000 0000

1111 1111 . 1111 1111 . 1110 0000 . 0000 0000

255  .  255  .  224  .  0

1001 0110 . 0011 0010 . 0101 1111 . 1111 1111

Mask Host bits  Host bits

64 + 31

150  .  50  .  95  .  255

Breaking down the binary value of the mask causes the first three bits of the third octet to be reserved for subnet information. The second bit is flipped, resulting in a subnet of .64. Before the broadcast address for that subnet can be obtained, the remaining five bits of the third octet must be flipped, along with the entire last octet. Flipping the last five bits yields a value of 31. When this is added to 64 (the flipped bit in the subnet field), the total is 95, so the broadcast IP address for subnet 150.50.64.0/19 is 150.50.95.255.

So, in this case, all RIP interfaces in the 150.50.64.0 subnetwork broadcast any updates they may have that are destined for the network to the all-F's broadcast at the MAC layer, and IP 150.50.95.255 at the network layer. Although this advertisement is broadcast to all hosts on the .64 subnet of network 150.50.0.0 (and, therefore, to all router interfaces also configured for the network), the subnet information is not actually communicated. This means that, although the RIP update is broadcast to the broadcast address of the subnetwork that the interface is configured for, the actual subnet mask is not defined anywhere in the RIP update.

In Figure 33-5, each router is configured on the network 150.50. However, router C has another interface, also on the 150.50 network, but with a different subnet mask than router A or router B: subnet mask 255.255.248.0. So, router C has an interface in subnetwork 150.50.64.0, and thus broadcasts its RIP update to the 150.50.95.255 address. The RIP updates are received by routers A and B.

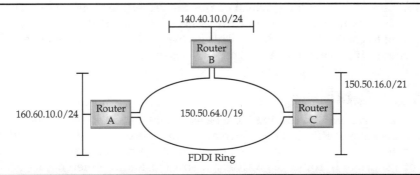

**Figure 33-5.**   *Three RIP routers sharing an interface on subnet .64; router C also has an interface on subnet .16 with a different mask*

Router A receives the RIP update from router C; this update contains the sending router interface IP (150.50.64.3) and the destination (150.50.95.255). It also contains two RIP advertisements: one each for networks 150.50.64.0 and 150.50.16.0. Router A examines the RIP advertisement and determines that router C knows of one network besides its local network, network 150.50.0.0, which is configured on one of router C's interfaces.

The reason that router A interpret router C's advertisement for network 150.50.16.0 as 150.50.0.0 is that RIP interfaces only communicate the subnet value, not the actual mask, when the network number is the same (150.50, in this case). Consequently, the receiving router then applies its local mask to the incoming network advertisement. So, when router A receives router C's advertisement for 150.50.16.0, it doesn't know that the mask should be 255.255.248.0, and thus it applies its own mask: 255.255.224.0:

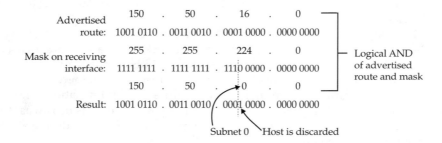

The .16 subnet falls outside the range of router A's specified mask for network 150.50.0.0. Because none of the first 3 bits in the subnet field is flipped, router A interprets this advertisement as a host on subnet 0, which is incorrect.

This example demonstrates why subnet masks must remain constant when being applied to a common network number. RIPv1 does not communicate any actual subnet mask information in its updates, which causes the preceding scenario to occur. If VLSM is absolutely necessary within a RIPv1 network, then RIP Accept policies can be configured to correct this condition. This is covered in greater detail later in the chapter, where RIP Accept and Announce policies are discussed.

## The Routing Table

Each RIP router generates a routing table based on the network information it receives in the form of RIP updates. Thereafter, this routing table is used by the router to determine the best route to get to any destination network. The routing table consists of a series of IP routes, as well as a metric (cost) and preference associated with each route (because route weights are statically defined in the router software, they are not included in the routing table generally). The following is an example of a RIPv1 routing table:

```
[1:1]$ show ip routes
Destination  Mask            Proto     Age   Cost   NextHopAddr
-----------  -------------   -------   -----  ----   ------------
150.50.0.0   255.255.0.0     RIP        11     3     170.70.10.3
160.60.0.0   255.255.0.0     RIP        20     2     170.70.10.2
200.20.1.0   255.255.255.0   LOCAL    1140     0     200.20.1.1
170.70.10.0  255.255.255.0   LOCAL    1145     0     170.70.10.1
140.40.0.0   255.255.0.0     RIP        15     3     170.70.10.3
        5 Routes in table
```

*Default routes can also be specified. A default route in this case causes the router to do a logical AND with the mask 0.0.0.0 and the network that is attempting to be reached. This results in the route 0.0.0.0, which will appear in the routing table in that format.*

## The Forwarding Table

Every IP interface has a certain amount of memory dedicated to its forwarding table. The purpose of the forwarding table is to act as a route cache for packets received on the interface in question. This eliminates the need to examine every route in the routing table each time a routing decision must be made. With software version 8.0 or higher, the structure of the forwarding table has been optimized for fast lookups, whereby unused routes are aged out of the forwarding table cache.

In Site Manager, the size of the forwarding table is defined by the Max Forwarding Table Size, as one of the interface parameters. The size of the forwarding table should depend on how much overall memory is available; larger forwarding tables can provide faster route lookups, if memory permits. More information on configuring this and other RIP parameters is available in Chapter 34.

**EXAMINING THE FORWARDING TABLE CACHE RESOURCES**　A quick way to check whether the current size of the forwarding table is accurate is to issue the following command from the TI:

```
[1:1]$ g wfIpInterfaceEntry.72.*
```

The output from this command shows the number of times a route was not found in the cache, due to overrun, and had to be obtained from the routing table instead. It does not specify the size of the cache or indicate how much larger it should be, but it does indicate that the cache is spilling over; based on this information, you must decide whether or not to increase the size.

**ROUTE PREFERENCE**　A route preference is associated with each RIP route in the routing table, to assign a value to each route for purposes of desirability. By default, each route preference that is learned within the RIP routing domain is set to a value of 1. This value can be altered, however, to select a preferred route path. Static routes can also be assigned user-configured preferences between the values of 1 and 16, where 16 is the most desirable route.

**ROUTE WEIGHT**    Route weight can be a factor in a network that is running multiple routing protocols. In situations where route preference is examined and found to be equal, route weight will be considered as the determining factor. Depending on the origin of the route information, it will be weighed differently; these route weights are static and are not user-configurable. Table 33-1 provides a list of RIP route weights and preferences.

## Keeping Networks Contiguous

For the same reasons previously outlined, network configuration within an RIPv1 environment must be contiguous. This means that in a RIP network, a single network number can be broken into many subnets, but those subnets must not be separated by a different network number, and can exist in only one portion of the network at a time.

Figure 33-6 shows four token rings and three routers. Ring 1 is configured for network 150.50.10.0, and is connected to RIP interface 150.50.10.1 on router A. Ring 2 is configured for network 170.70.10.0, and is connected to RIP interface 170.70.10.1 on router A, interface 170.70.10.2 on router B, and 170.70.10.3 on router C. Ring 3 is configured for network 160.60.10.0, and is connected to RIP interface 160.60.10.1 on router B. Finally, ring 4 is configured for network 150.50.20.0, and is connected to RIP interface 150.50.20.1 on router C.

| Type of Route | Weight | Preference |
|---|---|---|
| Directly connected networks | 0 | 16 |
| OSPF intra-area routes | 0 | 16 |
| OSPF interarea routes | 1 | 16 |
| OSPF type-1 external routes | 2 | 1 |
| BGP routes | 32 | 1 |
| RIP routes | 34 | 1 |
| External Gateway Protocol (EGP) routes | 35 | 1 |
| Static routes | 36 | 16 (by default) |
| OSPF Type 2 external routes | worst | 1 |

**Table 33-1.**    *RIP Route Weights and Preferences*

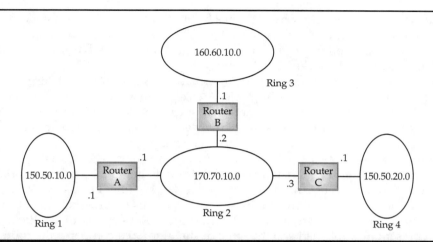

**Figure 33-6.**   *Four networks, one broken into two subnets, across four rings*

With RIPv1 implemented, this is an invalid network design. Although no subnetwork is actually repeated, the network number 150.50.0.0 exists on both router A and router C, even though the subnets are unique. Consider the routes that the three routers will build into their individual routing tables.

**ROUTER A**   Router A will receive updates from routers B and C. Router B's update will contain two network advertisements: the 170.70.10.0 network and the 160.60.0.0 network will be advertised, each with a metric of 1. Router C's update will also consist of two network advertisements: the 170.70.10.0 network and the 150.50.0.0 network, also with a metric of 1 each.

Router A will examine this route information, and must then determine which routes should be added into its routing table. Since no other instances of the 160.60.0.0 network exist, router A will install this route into its routing table. The 150.50.0.0 network, however, will be interpreted as a less-specific route to the 150.50.10.0 network, even though the 150.50.0.0 network has a greater metric (the local metric is 0). This route will be installed into the routing table, but as long as the local interface remains a valid RIP interface, the less-specific route with the greater metric will not be used. In this situation, an incoming route that is not destined for the 150.50.10.0 network, but instead the 150.50.20.0 network, will not be a match for the .10 subnetwork. However, the 150.50.0.0 route does constitute a match in this case. The 150.50.0.0 route will be used, and may result in the packet reaching its destination in some instances. However, particularly in cases where multipath is being used or a route is lost, keeping noncontiguous networks in a RIPv1 environment can create very unpredictable results.

**ROUTER B**    Router B will receive updates from routers A and C. Router A's update will contain two network advertisements: the 150.50.0.0 network and the 170.70.10.0 network. Router C's update likewise will contain two network advertisements: the 150.50.0.0 network and the 170.70.10.0 network.

Router B will also examine this route information, and must then determine which routes should be added to its routing table. A local route with a metric of 0 is already in its routing table for the 170.70.10.0 network, since it has a local RIPv1 interface configured for that network. In this case, however, it has received two updates containing advertisements for the 150.50.0.0 network.

Because two instances of the 150.50.0.0 network are being received as advertisements, router B will assume two paths exist to get to the same network: one each from routers A and router C. The network is summarized as 150.50.0.0, so router B has no way of knowing that these actually represent different subnets of that network that are accessible from two different routers. Router B assumes that the routes represent multiple paths to the same destination, so it compares the route preference (cost) of each; in this case, the 150.50.0.0 network was advertised from router A and router B with a cost of 1. Router B, upon receiving each, adds its own default cost of 1 to each route, giving each potential route a cost of 2. Because the cost is equal in this case, router B examines the route weight attributed to each. Both routes are RIP learned routes, so they are each given a weight of 34. Since the preference and weight are both equal for both routes, router B simply installs the first route that was received into its routing table.

**ROUTER C**    Router C will receive updates from routers A and B. Router A's update will contain two network advertisements: the 150.50.0.0 network and the 170.70.10.0 network. Router B's update will also include two network advertisements: the 160.60.0.0 network and the 170.70.10.0 network.

Router C will examine the route information, and must then determine which routes should be added to its routing table. Since router C currently has no entry for the 160.60.0.0 network, it installs this route into its route table with a metric of 2. However, much like the case in which router A received the advertisement from router C, the 150.50.0.0 network will be seen as a less specific route to the 150.50.20.0 network, although it has a higher metric. The route will be installed, but not used.

## RIP Timers

RIP has two methods of aging out route information that has become invalid:

- If 90 seconds pass (the equivalent of three RIPv1 update intervals) and no update has arrived that describes a route in place in the routing table, then the route is not removed from the routing table, but is assigned a metric of infinity (described as U in the routing table).

■ If 180 seconds pass (the equivalent of six RIPv1 update intervals) and no update has arrived to refresh the existing route, then the route is actually removed from the routing table.

**Note** *The amount of time that passes prior to a route being assigned a metric of infinity can be altered via the Timeout Timer parameter in Site Manager, by altering the Timeout Timer parameter. The amount of time that passes before a route is removed from the routing table altogether can be altered via the Holddown Timer value.*

## Topology Changes in the RIP Environment

When a RIP interface stops functioning, or a link fails, the problem obviously must be reflected in the RIP environment. For instance, if a RIP interface to IP network 150.50.0.0 configured on router A goes down, then router A must stop advertising knowledge of that network, and all other RIP routers must learn that network 150.50.0.0 is no longer accessible via router A.

This information is transmitted through the exchange of the RIP advertisements. If a router doesn't receive any RIP updates from a neighboring router, or if RIP updates are received but are missing entries, the receiving router may respond with a triggered update. Since the absence of route information indicates a change in the routed topology, the changed information must take precedence, and an update may be sent before the scheduled update time.

# RIPv2

RIPv2 is an extension of the RIPv1 specification. RIPv1 is a relatively older routing protocol and imposes some limitations on network size and design, but it also offers ease of use and reliability in smaller networks, so it was given some added functionality to overcome its original limitations, resulting in RIPv2. RIPv2 is defined in RFC 1723 (1994).

## RIPv2 Features

RIPv2 has a variety of features that were designed to improve upon those of the original RIP. In particular, the passing of subnet mask information was implemented; this feature allows for the use of VLSM with no need to configure Announce or Accept policies. RIPv2 features are described next.

**ROUTING DOMAIN**    RIPv2 routers can be configured for different *routing domains*, whereby routers in different domains do not exchange RIPv2 updates with one another. This helps to overcome some of the original scaling problems incurred by RIPv1, where the 15-hop limit dictates that the routed network cannot expand beyond a certain size.

**AUTHENTICATION**    Authentication of RIP updates was implemented in RIPv2. In this scenario, a RIPv2 interface receiving an update will first validate a simple password before accepting that update. This occurs on the first update only, after which future updates are accepted without being authenticated. The simple password can be up to 16 octets in length. The authentication feature allows a certain amount of security to be implemented, because false route information cannot be injected into the routing domain from an external source. Any false routes that do not carry the appropriate password will be ignored.        .

**ROUTE TAG**    RIPv2 routes described in a RIPv2 update may be given route tags so that routes originating from non-RIPv2 environments, such as OSPF or BGP, can be differentiated. (This feature is currently not supported.)

**SUBNET MASK**    The subnet mask is included in a RIPv2 update for each route contained within that update. So, rather than summarizing address ranges that are not local to the interface transmitting the update, each individual subnet is described by default. This can be changed through Site Manager; simply set the RIP-2 Aggregate to "summarize as RIPv1 does."

**NEXT HOP**    The next-hop address, by default, is the address associated with the interface that has transmitted the RIP update describing the route in question. This can be altered, however, in a RIPv2 update, although this feature presently is not supported on the Nortel Networks platform.

**MULTICASTING**    Unlike RIPv1 packets, which are sent to the network broadcast address (for the 180.80.10.0/24 network, this would be 180.80.10.255), RIPv2 uses a Class D multicast group address, as OSPF does. The address used is 224.0.0.9. This provides two advantages: it cuts down on overhead for routers not running RIPv2, and it allows RIPv1 and RIPv2 to operate independently.

## RIPv2 Updates

As just mentioned, RIPv2 uses a multicast group address for its updates. At the MAC layer, an update is addressed to an assigned MAC multicast address of 01-00-5E-00-00-09. At the IP layer, it is multicast to the address 224.0.0.9, which is reserved for all RIPv2 routers. RIPv2 updates also include an actual subnet mask for each advertised network:

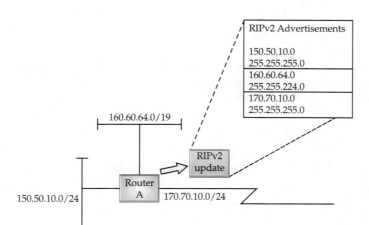

RIPv2 Advertisements

| 150.50.10.0 |
| 255.255.255.0 |
| 160.60.64.0 |
| 255.255.224.0 |
| 170.70.10.0 |
| 255.255.255.0 |

160.60.64.0/19

RIPv2 update

150.50.10.0/24    Router A    170.70.10.0/24

The following is another example of how a RIPv2 update might appear in a sniffer trace:

```
DLC: ------ DLC Header ------
DLC: Destination = BROADCAST 01005e000009, Broadcast
DLC: Source = Station W11flt00B211
DLC: Ethertype = 0800 (IP)
DLC:
IP: ------ IP Header ------
IP: Version = 4, header length = 20 bytes
IP: Type of service = 00
IP: 000. ....    = routine
IP: ...0 ....    = normal delay
IP: .... 0...    = normal throughput
IP: .... .0..    = normal reliability
IP: Total length = 188 bytes
IP: Identification = 323
IP: Flags = 0X
IP: .0.. ....    = may fragment
IP: ..0. ....    = last fragment
IP: Fragment offset = 0 bytes
```

```
IP: Time to live = 1 seconds/hops
IP: Protocol = 17 (UDP)
IP: Header checksum = 8B67 (correct)
IP: Source address = [150.50.10.1]
IP: Destination address = [224.0.0.9]
IP: No options
IP:
UDP: ------ UDP Header ------
UDP: Source port = 520 (Route)
UDP: Destination port = 520
UDP: Length = 152
UDP: Checksum = B075 (correct)
UDP:
RIP: ------ RIP Header ------
RIP: Command = 2 (Response)
RIP: Version = 2
RIP: Unused = 0
RIP:
RIP: Routing data frame 1
RIP: Address family identifier = 2 (IP)
RIP: .....Route tag = 0
RIP: .....IP Address = [160.60.64.0]
RIP: .....Subnet Mask = 255.255.224.0
RIP: .....Next Hop = 170.70.10.2
RIP: Metric = 2
RIP:
RIP: Routing data frame 2
RIP: Address family identifier = 2 (IP)
RIP: .....Route Tag = 0
RIP: .....IP Address = [170.70.10.0]
RIP: .....Subnet Mask = 255.255.255.0
RIP: .....Next Hop = 170.70.10.1
RIP:   Metric = 2
RIP:
```

**Note**   *In a token ring environment, the multicast address 01-00-5E-00-00-09 is not used, and an all-F's broadcast is used in its place.*

# General Features of RIP

The following features, IP unnumbered and IP multipath, are not specific to either RIPv1 or RIPv2, but, depending on the router software version being run, do work in either environment.

## IP Unnumbered

From an addressing standpoint, configuring point-to-point links can be costly. This is true particularly in RIPv1, where VLSM is not supported. Because the point-to-point connection basically constitutes a separate network, it must be assigned a network or subnet of its own just to support two hosts (the two router interfaces). To get around this limitation, Nortel router software version 9.0 or greater allows for unnumbered IP interfaces.

An unnumbered IP interface is configured with the IP protocol, but is not actually assigned an IP address. Instead, the interface is associated with an existing IP address that is already configured on the router. For instance, in Figure 33-7, router A has a LAN interface, configured with addresses 150.50.10.1, and router B also has a LAN interface, configured with addresses 150.50.30.1. Router A and router B are to be connected across a WAN via a leased PPP connection.

In this scenario, the sync line on routers A and B could be configured with IP addresses 150.50.20.1 and 150.50.20.2, but this would use the entire .20 subnet on the 150.50.0.0 network and, in a RIP environment, this network range could not be used again elsewhere in the network. With IP Unnumbered configured, both ends of the PPP link are configured for the IP protocol, but the interfaces are not configured with IP addresses. Instead, they are given the address 0.0.0.0 and a mask of 0.0.0.0. These unnumbered interfaces are then associated with existing IP addresses configured on other interfaces of the same router. For instance, router A's unnumbered interface is associated with IP address 150.50.10.1, and router B's unnumbered interface is associated with IP address 150.50.30.1.

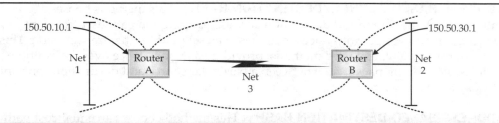

**Figure 33-7.** *Routers A and B, connected by means of a PPP link*

INTERNETWORKING WITH
NORTEL NETWORKS

The address with which the unnumbered interface is associated can be user-configured through Site Manager. An alternate interface can be specified as well, in case the first interface fails for any reason. In that event, the unnumbered interface will dynamically change its association to reflect the alternate address.

Bear in mind that the IP address with which unnumbered interfaces are associated is used as the source address for all packets transmitted from the unnumbered interfaces. Also, for obvious reasons, unnumbered interfaces can't be pinged or managed directly.

*If a circuitless IP is being used, it can be used for an IP unnumbered interface association. Interfaces configured for IP unnumbered do not use ARP, and at the data-link level, all packets are broadcast.*

# IP Multipath

IP multipath is a mechanism by which a router can maintain up to five equal-cost paths to the same destination within its routing table. This feature is available on all Nortel Networks routers at software version 11.02 or higher.

## IP Multipath

The alternate paths in an IP multipath environment can be maintained in the ways described next.

**ROUND ROBIN**    The *round-robin* method of IP multipath involves sending traffic evenly across each of the configured paths, each in turn. The distribution is on a packet-by-packet basis, even if those packets are from the same source and are going to the same destination. This allows for a very even spread of traffic and an efficient use of bandwidth, but it does introduce the possibility of packets arriving out of order.

**ADDRESS-BASED SOURCE/DESTINATION HASH**    This method chooses a path based on the source and destination address, keeping the path used constant for different address pairings once a path has been selected for that transmission. This is one of the more widely used methods, providing a good balance over the multiple paths while keeping packet flow between a particular source and destination constant, because the path will not change once it is selected.

**ADDRESS-BASED DESTINATION HASH**    This method chooses an equal-cost path based on the destination address. This method, while preventing out-of-order delivery, requires some design considerations to prevent any one line from being overtaxed.

**DISABLE**    This disables IP multipath.

# RIP Accept and Announce Policies

Accept and Announce policies can be configured on RIPv1 or RIPv2 interfaces, to adjust route information as it is either transmitted or received. Accept and Announce policies can, in many cases, be used to achieve the same goal. The main difference is that an Announce policy can be useful where the altered information will affect many remote routers, whereas an Accept policy is more appropriate if the information from many remote routers needs to be adjusted. As a general rule, determine first whether you can achieve your end goal could by using either policy type, and then determine which policy type will result in the least configuration and the least overhead.

## RIP Accept Policies

RIP Accept policies enhance the flexibility of the RIP protocol, and even eliminate some of the limitations, such as the lack of VLSM support in RIPv1. Accept policies allow a RIP interface to alter incoming routes in a variety of ways. For instance, Accept policies can instruct a particular RIP interface to listen only for certain networks, and exclude others. This can be useful as a security measure, because configuring an Accept policy to drop certain route information (and therefore never install it into the routing table) will cause a network to be inaccessible from that router. Incoming route information may also have its associated metric altered.

**AN ACCEPT POLICY EXAMPLE**   One example of an Accept policy is to allow the use of VLSM in a RIPv1 network. Consider the example we saw in Figure 33-5 of a RIPv1 network, configured with VLSM, in which three routers (routers A, B, and C) share interfaces on the common network of 150.50.64.0/19 (subnetwork .64 on the 150.50.0.0 network, with a mask of 255.255.224.0), and in which each RIP interface will send its updates to the IP broadcast address 150.50.95.255. Each router is configured on the network 150.50; however, recall that router C has another interface, also on the 150.50 network but with a different subnet mask (255.255.248.0) than router A and router B—subnet mask. So, router C has an interface in subnetwork 150.50.64.0 and therefore broadcasts its RIP update to the 150.50.95.255 address. The RIP updates are received by routers A and B.

Again, router A receives the RIP update from router C. This update contains the sending router interface IP (150.50.64.3) and the destination (150.50.95.255). It also contains two RIP advertisements: one each for networks 150.50.64.0 and 150.50.16.0. Recall that normally, in a RIPv1 environment, router A would examine the RIP advertisement and determine that router C knows of one network besides its local network, network 150.50.0.0, which is configured on one of router C's interfaces. In a RIPv1 environment (as shown in Figure 33-5), Router A would do this because the receiving interface normally applies its own mask to the incoming advertisement. In Figure 33-8, however, there is an Accept policy in place that causes router A to apply the correct mask, instead of its own mask, to the incoming route.

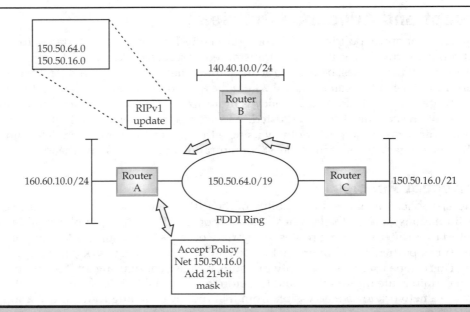

**Figure 33-8.**    *An Accept policy causes router A to apply the correct 21-bit mask to 150.50.16.0 only*

In our new example, the Accept policy instructs router A to detect all incoming route data for the 150.50.16.0 network and, if a match occurs, apply the 255.255.248.0 subnet mask to that data. Upon receipt of the RIP update from router C, router A will detect the route information for 150.50.16.0 and, rather than applying its own mask, apply the correct mask. Route 150.50.16.0 is a unique entry that does not already exist within the routing table, and it will be added with the appropriate metric.

## RIP Announce Policies

Announce policies can also be used to adjust route information in the RIP network. In this case, the configured policy is associated with outgoing updates rather than incoming updates.

**AN ANNOUNCE POLICY EXAMPLE**    Figure 33-9 shows two RIP networks in place within two corporations that have merged. The RIP networks are now to be joined via a WAN connection so that data and resources can be shared between the two sites. Individually, neither network exceeds the 15-hop count associated with RIP. However, when the networks are combined, one of the resulting routes does exceed the limit.

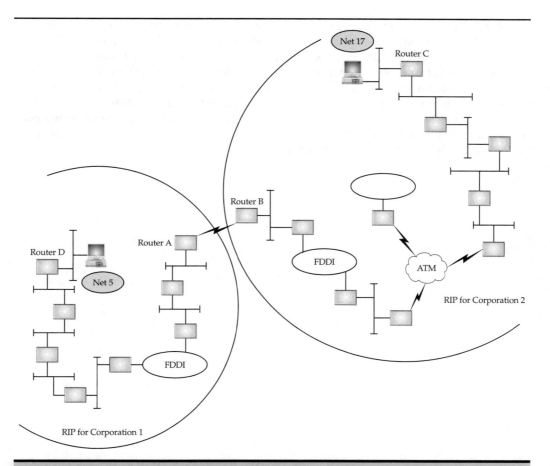

**Figure 33-9.** *Once the two corporate RIP networks are connected, the route between networks 5 and 17 exceeds the 15-hop count limit*

In this example, all routes are valid except that of network 5 when going to or from network 17. Any update from router C that describes the route to network 17 arrives at router D with a metric of 16, which, in the RIP environment, indicates a metric of infinity. The route therefore is never installed into the routing table. The same is true for routes travelling the other way; in this case, the route entry for network 5 will never be installed in router C's routing table.

As an alternative to redesigning a portion of the network, an Announce policy can be put into place on both routers A and B. For router A, the policy would target network 5. By the time an update containing an advertisement for network 5 were to reach router A, it would have a metric of 7. Since the route reaches router C with a metric of exactly 16, the Announce policy on router A would state that any update being advertised from router A across the WAN link to router B that includes a route advertisement for network 5 is to be given a metric of 6 rather than 7. When router C received an update from any router in network B describing the route to network 5, its metric will have been altered, allowing it to come in at a metric of 15. The route would be considered valid and installed into the routing table. The same type of policy would have to be configured on router B, to alter the metric for network 17.

# The Complete Reference

# Chapter 34

## Configuring RIP and RIPv2 on the Nortel Networks Router Platform

The Routing Information Protocol (RIP) is used by routers to share routing information. Through RIP, routers are able to advertise the networks they have knowledge of (either because the network is configured on a local interface or because the network was learned from another RIP router), and then place the routing information in a routing table, which is used to route data to the proper network. RIP as a routing protocol is relatively simple to configure and troubleshoot. The Nortel Networks router platform supports both RIP version 1 and RIP version 2, in addition to RIP Accept and Announce policies. The configuration of general RIPv1 and RIPv2 interface parameters is covered in this chapter, as well as some protocol-specific troubleshooting.

# Configuring RIP and RIPv2

The configuration for both RIPv1 and RIPv2 is much simpler than that of OSPF, or any of the more advanced routing protocols. This doesn't mean that RIPv1 and RIPv2 are less stable or less useful, but they are much simpler, thus requiring less configuration. In fact, if RIPv1 is to be used, selecting RIP as the routing protocol often is the only configuration requirement; it is enabled on all interfaces by default, and its default values are, in many circumstances, perfectly acceptable. RIPv1 does not have any means of authenticating route information, however, and authentication is a feature that you may want as a security measure. Furthermore, in RIPv1, all route updates are issued to an all-hosts broadcast IP address, which creates added overhead, and subnet masks are not communicated, which limits a single network number to a single subnet mask. RIPv2 addresses all three of these limitations.

Running RIPv2 does not require any significant additional configuration, because there is not a large inherent difference in the way the two protocols operate. As is described in Chapter 33, RIPv2 is an enhancement over RIPv1, not a truly different protocol. As such, the same parameters apply to both protocols, so the configuration of RIPv2 is not separate from that of RIPv1. The primary differences in the way the two versions operate are that, unlike RIPv1, RIPv2:

- Supports route authentication by means of a simple password.

- Utilizes a multicast group address for route updates instead of an all-hosts broadcast IP address.

- Communicates subnet mask information in route updates, thus allowing masks of different lengths to be used against the same network number.

These features of RIPv2 are also used in OSPF.

## Initial RIP Configuration

Unlike OSPF, RIP does not require any global protocol configuration; it is configured strictly on an interface-by-interface basis. Once RIP is selected as the routing protocol on an interface from the Select Protocols window during the initial configuration, Site Manager will prompt for an IP address and subnet mask. After you enter these values, no specific RIP parameters are prompted for. In fact, no distinction is made in the Select Protocols window between RIPv1 and RIPv2; the only option available for RIP-related protocols is simply RIP, because the two protocols share the same parameters. Once RIP has been selected, the RIP type may be selected on a per-interface basis.

# RIP Interface Configuration

RIP interfaces, by default, are configured to use RIPv1 with poisoned reverse and no authentication. In a LAN where other interfaces are also running RIPv1, these defaults will generally work. However, particularly given some of RIPv1's limitations, some of the interface-related parameters can be useful.

## RIP Interface Parameters

RIP is enabled globally automatically when the protocol is selected. However, the RIP method (RIPv1 or RIPv2) as well as many of the RIP-specific parameters may vary from network to network. For instance, a router with three interfaces, each running RIP, might have one interface running RIPv1 with the default interface values, one interface running RIPv2 with the default interface parameters, and one interface running RIPv2 with altered parameters (these must be consistent throughout the network that interface is associated with), such as timer values or possible Accept and/or Announce policies.

The basic RIP interface parameters are described in the following list; RIPv1 and RIPv2 use essentially the same parameters, so there is no second listing of RIPv2-specific parameters. All RIPv1 and RIPv2 parameters are accessible from Configuration Manager. Select Protocols | IP | RIP Interfaces to open the main IP RIP Interface Config window (see Figure 34-1).

- **RIP Supply**   Set to either Enabled or Disabled, this parameter dictates whether or not RIP updates will be transmitted from this interface.

- **RIP Listen**   Set to either Enabled or Disabled, this parameter dictates whether or not this interface will accept any incoming RIP updates.

- **Default Route Supply**   A default route is a route of 0.0.0.0, and if it is present in a router's routing table, it will be used for any destination route that is not currently known. Default routes may be defined statically, or they may be learned from a remote router if a default route is being advertised. The Default Route Supply parameter indicates whether or not a default route will be advertised by the interface being configured. This parameter may be set to any of the following:

    **Enable**   Advertises the default route only if it either is statically configured on the router or has been learned from a remote router and is in the routing table

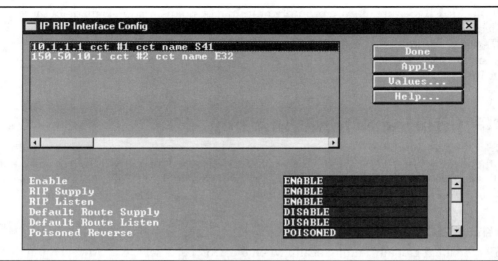

**Figure 34-1.**   *The IP RIP Interface Config window*

**Disable**   Prevents the route from being advertised even if it is in the routing table

**Generate**   Causes the router to advertise a default route from the interface being configured even if a default route is not present in the routing table

> **Note**   *If Generate is selected, the default route will not be present in the routing table of the advertising router, since it is being spontaneously generated for purposes of advertising only.*

- **Default Route Listen**   Indicates whether or not the interface being configured will observe incoming advertisements for a default route of 0.0.0.0. If set to Disable, a received default route will not be added into the routing table.

- **Poisoned Reverse**   By default, Nortel Networks' RIP implementation uses poisoned reverse as a means of preventing an interface from advertising learned routes back out the interface they were learned on. Poisoned reverse causes the routes to be advertised, but with a metric of 16, which labels the route as invalid so that it will never be added into the routing table of a receiving interface. This safeguard ensures faster route convergence when loops exist. Alternatively, this parameter can be set to Split, which indicates that Split Horizon will be used; Split Horizon causes the routes learned on a specific interface to not be advertised at all back out that same interface. Selecting Actual causes the routes to be advertised back out the learned interface, at the proper metric.

- **Time to Live**   Causes a TTL value to be inserted into the IP header of any outgoing RIP updates. The default TTL of 1 generally is fine, since RIP updates are only meant to be received by other local RIP interfaces, and are not meant to travel multiple router hops.

- **Broadcast Timer**   Indicates how often a RIP update will be sent; by default, RIP router interfaces transmit a RIP update every 30 seconds. This value can be adjusted from 5 to 86,400 seconds (24 hours), or, in the case of a dial-up line, 3,600 (1 hour) to 1,209,600 seconds (2 weeks). Each must be configured in increments of 5 seconds.

- **Timeout Timer**   Indicates how long will pass without receiving an update from a particular network before that network is considered no longer reachable (this does not actually remove the route from the routing table at this point; instead, it assigns it a metric of infinity (16), which causes it to be still present in the routing table, but unreachable). After the Timeout Timer value expires, the Hold Down Timer begins, and if that timer expires, the route is actually removed from the table. By default, this value is 90 seconds, which is three times that of the Broadcast Timer; this configuration dictates that a route is set to unreachable after three updates have been missed. If you intend to change this value, you should maintain a 3:1 ratio with the Broadcast Timer, so that the Timeout Timer is configured with a direct relationship to expected updates and is not just an arbitrary value.

- **Hold Down Timer**   Indicates the amount of time a route will remain in the routing table after it has been set to unreachable as a result of the Timeout Timer expiring. (This will set the metric to infinity.) By default, this value is set to three times the Broadcast Timer, as is the Timeout Timer. Under the scenario this creates, if three updates are missed, a network is set to unreachable in the routing table. If three more updates are missed, the route is actually removed from the routing table. If the Broadcast Timer and Timeout Timer have been adjusted, the Hold Down Timer may need to be adjusted also.

- **RIP Mode**   The specific RIP type is configured here. By default, RIPv1 is used, and only RIPv1 updates are transmitted or listened to. The other options are RIP2 and RIP2 Aggregate. The RIP2 option causes RIP version 2 to be used on the interface, and only RIPv2 updates will be sent or listened to. RIP2 Aggregate creates sort of a RIPv1/RIPv2 hybrid: the RIPv2 multicast address is used for purposes of sending updates, authentication may be used, and RIPv2 updates are listened for and accepted, but unlike the generic RIPv2, in which the specific subnet mask information is included in any advertisements, RIPv2 Aggregate causes the subnet information to be aggregated as it is in RIPv1; this allows for a simple configuration while still allowing for security and the use of a multicast group address for route information exchange.

■ **Triggered Updates**   Lists all RIP updates that are sent prior to the time scheduled by the Broadcast Timer, in response to some change in the network, such as a route's metric changing or a new update being received that reflects new route information.

> **Note**   *Triggered updates were not supported in code version 9.00 or prior.*

■ **Authentication Type**   Available in RIPv2 only, authentication is used via a simple password. If authentication is being used, this password is used to validate any incoming route advertisements. Incoming advertisements that do not have the proper password configured are ignored. This can prevent a scenario in which incorrect routing information is injected into the network, causing bogus routing tables to be created. Any intrusive routes introduced into the network that do not have the correct password associated with them are ignored.

■ **Authentication Password**   If authentication is being used with RIPv2, then the simple password is configured here. The password may be up to 16 characters and is case-sensitive.

■ **Initial Stabilization Timer**   Indicates how long a RIP interface will wait after initializing before it begins sending its own updates. This period should be long enough for the interface to learn the existing routes in the network. By default, it is set to 120 seconds, a period consistent with four RIP updates being sent by neighboring routers using the default Broadcast Timer value of 30 seconds. If the Broadcast Timer values have been altered, this parameter may need to be changed as well.

## RIP Accept Policies

RIP Accept policies are used to match incoming RIP route information, and then to either ignore those routes or adjust the route information in a manner described by the Accept policy. The most immediately obvious application of such a policy is to match incoming RIPv1 routes, and then have the Accept policy actually inject the subnet information into the route before adding it into the routing table.

An example of this is two remote sites running RIPv1 that are being connected for the first time via a point-to-point 64Kbps sync line; each site uses the same network address of 150.50.0.0. However, site A has been using a subnet mask of 255.255.255.0, while site B has been using a subnet mask of 255.255.255.224. In Figure 34-2, there are

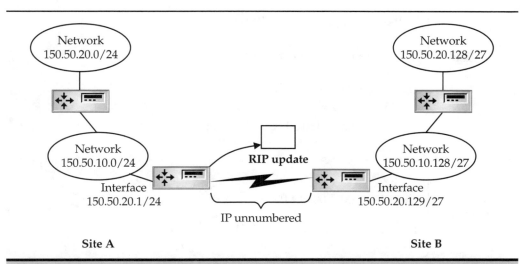

**Figure 34-2.**   _Variable-length subnet masking (VLSM) issues in an RIPv1 network, resolved by means of Accept policies_

INTERNETWORKING WITH NORTEL NETWORKS

two networks in site A (150.50.20.0 and 150.50.10.0) that must be advertised across the sync line to site B. Site B, in turn, must advertise two networks (150.50.20.128 and 150.50.10.128) back to site A.

The sync interface is using IP unnumbered in this case (where the sync interface utilizes an IP assigned to another local interface rather than a unique IP of its own), so site A's WAN interface utilizes IP address 150.50.20.1, and site B's WAN interface utilizes IP address 150.50.20.129.

The problem arises in RIPv1 because the two sides are applying different length subnet masks to the interfaces. Site A's RIP interface would see route information sourced from interface 150.50.20.129, which would be acceptable to Site A's interface, because it would apply its own subnet mask to the update and would interpret the update as having been sourced from host 129 on the .10 subnetwork of network 150.50.0.0. Although this is not correct, the update would at least appear to have come from an interface configured on the same subnet.

Site B's interface, however, would see updates coming across the wide area sourced from 150.50.20.1. Normally, Site B would apply its own 27-bit mask to these updates, and would interpret them as having been sourced from host 1 on the incorrect subnet:

$$
24\text{-bit mask} \begin{cases} 150 \quad \bullet \quad 50 \quad \bullet \quad 10 \quad \bullet \quad 0 \\ \\ 1001\ 0110 \bullet 0011\ 0010 \bullet 0000\ 1010 \bullet 0000\ 0000 \\ \\ 1111\ 1111 \bullet 1111\ 1111 \bullet 1111\ 1111 \bullet 0000\ 0000 \\ 255 \quad \bullet \quad 255 \quad \bullet \quad 255 \quad \bullet \quad 0 \end{cases}
$$

Network = 150.50.10.0

$$
27\text{-bit mask} \begin{cases} 150 \quad \bullet \quad 50 \quad \bullet \quad 10 \quad \bullet \quad 0 \\ \\ 1001\ 0110 \bullet 0011\ 0010 \bullet 0000\ 1010 \bullet 0000\ 0000 \\ \\ 1111\ 1111 \bullet 1111\ 1111 \bullet 1111\ 1111 \bullet 1110\ 0000 \\ 255 \quad \bullet \quad 255 \quad \bullet \quad 255 \quad \bullet \quad 224 \end{cases}
$$

◄─► Subnet mask is extended

Network = 150.50.10.0

This problem would hold true for any routes that site B received from site A, and for routes originating from site B going to site A. The problem could be resolved by using the Apply Subnet Mask option of the RIP Accept policy, indicating that each receiving router should apply the correct subnet mask to the incoming routes, and not the interface's own subnet mask, as would normally be the case in a RIPv1 network. The Accept policy illustrated in Figure 34-2, for example, causes site B's RIP to apply the correct 24-bit map to the incoming data.

## Functions of RIP Accept Policies

As demonstrated in the preceding example, Accept policies can be used to adjust subnet information; they can also be used to ignore routes from certain networks, which can be useful for implementing security in a network. In Figure 34-2, for example, such an Accept policy might indicate that any route advertisements for network 200.10.100.128 be ignored altogether. This would prevent any users at site B from communicating with that particular subnet, because those routes would never be inserted into the routing table, and therefore would never be propagated throughout site B.

To configure a RIP Accept policy, bring up Configuration Manager in Site Manager, and then, from the main toolbar, select Protocols | IP | Policy Filters | RIP | Accept Policies. This opens the main RIP Accept Policy Filters window, in which the individual RIP Accept policies can be configured. By default, 32 policies may be applied. This figure can be altered by changing the Maximum Policy Rule parameter in the Edit Global IP Parameters window. The following parameters may be configured:

■ **Name**    An arbitrary name to easily identify the Accept policy being configured.

■ **Networks**   Once the Networks option is highlighted, click the List button from the right-hand series of buttons. This opens the Policy Filters window, in which you may configure a series of networks or ranges of networks (see Figure 34-3).

The networks described here are the networks to which the Accept policy will be applied. For instance, in this example, two entries have been configured:

| Network | Network Mask | Match Criteria |
|---|---|---|
| 150.50.10.0 | 255.255.255.0 | Exact |
| 160.60.128.0 | 255.255.224.0 | Range |

This configuration causes any incoming packet from network 150.50.10.0 to be identified and affected by whatever Accept policy has been created. Incoming packets from network 160.60.128.0 will be affected as well, but because Range was specified under the Match Criteria (using a mask of 255.255.224.0), networks 160.60.129.0 through 160.60.159.0 will be considered a match as well. This range of networks will be subject to the configured Accept policy.

■ **Action**   Can be set to either Accept (the default) or Ignore. If Ignore is selected, any route information coming from the described networks or network ranges is ignored. If Accept is chosen, then the accepted packet is subject to the rules outlined in the remainder of the Accept policy.

■ **Route Preference**   Incoming route information may have its metric altered as part of the Accept policy. Since the metric is used, in part, to determine the desirability of a route, adjusting the metric prior to the route being considered

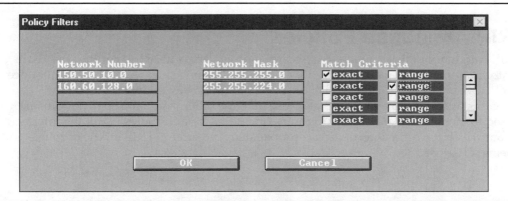

**Figure 34-3.**    *The Policy Filters window, displaying a specific network and range*

for insertion into the routing table may make the difference between the route being added or discarded.

- **Rule Precedence** Allows a priority to be assigned to the current Accept policy. If multiple Accept policies exist, this setting enables you to label them in order of priority, so that they are applied in a predetermined order. For example, if two Accept policies are being used, one that accepts certain routes and alters their metric, while the other ignores all incoming routes, the second policy would cancel the first if it were given a higher priority. The higher priority is considered to have precedence in this case, so applying a Rule Precedence of, for example, 10, to the first policy would ensure that the drop-all-routes policy is always implemented second, after the desired routes have been filtered out. The rule precedence may be between 0 and 1,410,065,408.

- **From Gateway** Indicates which routers incoming route advertisements must originate from in order to match the policy being configured. These gateways are configured by highlighting this parameter and then clicking List. For instance, if an IP address of 200.20.10.1 were configured, then incoming route advertisements from RIP interface 200.20.10.1 would be considered a match, and would therefore be affected by the Accept policy instructions.

- **Received on Interface** An Accept policy can relate only to specific interfaces. If you highlight this parameter and then click List, a window opens in which you can enter the IP addresses of the interface to which the Accept policy is to be applied. By default, no interfaces are configured, indicating that all interfaces are considered matches.

- **Apply Subnet Mask** Allows a subnet mask to be configured that will be applied to any route information prior to it being added into the routing table. This can be useful if VLSM is introduced into a RIPv1 environment.

## RIP Announce Policies

RIP Announce policies, much like Accept policies, can be used to alter the way route information is propagated through the network. In some cases, Accept and Announce policies can be used to accomplish the same things; however, depending on the circumstances, one may be simpler to use than the other. Announce policies can be used to include or exclude certain routes (including default routes), limit the interfaces from which the route information is propagated, and alter the RIP metric of routes being advertised.

## Functions of RIP Announce Policies

One common use of the Announce policy is to exclude certain routes from a router's route advertisements. When dealing with a point-to-point connection between two sites, if certain routes are to be excluded when advertising between sites, it would be simpler to create a RIP Accept policy at each router on either side of the point-to-point link, instructing them to ignore the routes. However, if a point-to-point link doesn't exist and certain routes need to be excluded, then a single Announce policy on one or two key routers may prevent the route from being propagated, while avoiding having to configure Accept policies on all the routers.

To configure a RIP Announce policy, bring up Configuration Manager and, from the main toolbar, select Protocols | IP | Policy Filters | RIP | Announce Policies. This opens the RIP Announce Policy Filters window, which is grayed out by default. Add an Announce policy by clicking Add, which opens the RIP Announce IP Policy Filter Configuration window (see Figure 34-4). The following parameters can be configured:

- **Name** An arbitrary name used to identify the Announce policy being configured.

- **Networks** Once the Networks option is highlighted, click List to open the Policy Filters window, in which you can configure a series of networks or ranges of networks (see Figure 34-5).

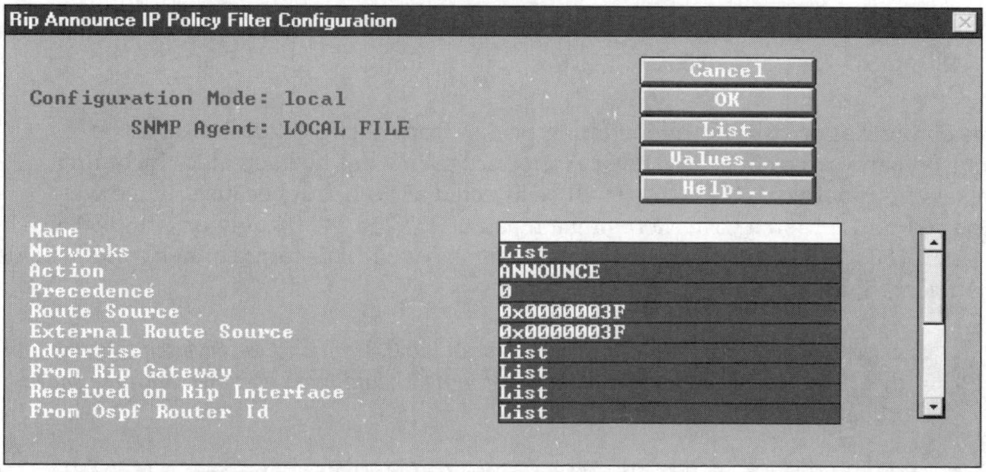

**Figure 34-4.** *The RIP Announce IP Policy Filter Configuration window*

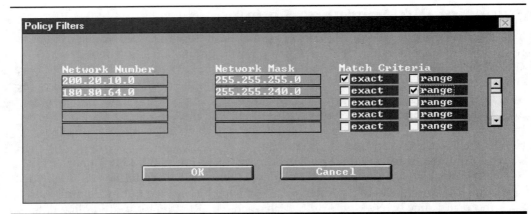

**Figure 34-5.** *The Policy Filters window, displaying a specific network and range*

The networks described here are the networks to which the Announce policy will be applied. For instance, in this example, two entries have been configured:

| Network | Network Mask | Match Criteria |
|---|---|---|
| 200.20.10.0 | 255.255.255.0 | Exact |
| 180.80.64.0 | 255.255.240.0 | Range |

This configuration causes any incoming packet from network 200.20.10.0 to be identified and affected by whatever Announce policy has been created. Incoming packets from network 180.80.64.0 will be affected as well, but because Range was specified under Match Criteria (using a mask of 255.255.240.0), networks 180.80.65.0 through 180.80.79.0 will be considered a match as well. This range of networks will also be subject to the configured Announce policy.

*A network of 0.0.0.0 with a Network Mask of 0.0.0.0 and an Exact Match Criteria will match the default route, whereas the same network and mask assigned a Range Match Criteria will match any route.*

■ **Action** Can be set to either Announce (the default) or Ignore. If Ignore is selected, any route information coming from the described networks or network ranges is ignored. If Announce is chosen, then the RIP packet is subject to the rules outlined in the remainder of the Announce policy.

■ **Precedence**   Enables a priority to be assigned to the current Announce policy; if multiple Announce policies exist, this setting enables you label them in order of priority, so that they are applied in a predetermined order.

■ **Route Source**   Indicates the source of the route information that will be affected by this Announce policy. Highlighting this option and clicking Values opens a window in which you may select the route source types. The options are Direct, Static, RIP, OSPF, EGP, or BGP. Selecting all of these options applies the Announce policy to any incoming route information.

■ **External Route Source**   Used with the OSPF routing protocol only and does not apply to RIP Announce policies.

■ **Advertise**   Specific network identifiers may be configured to advertise in place of what is actually listed in the route advertisement if the match criteria for the Announce policy is met. Highlighting this option and clicking List opens a window in which you may configure the new route information. For example, an incoming route that matches the Announce policy criteria, containing routes for several networks, may have certain network IDs either added or removed by altering this list, prior to being propagated.

**Note**   *Including a Network ID of 255.255.255.255 with a mask of 255.255.255.255 as the first network will cause the router to advertise all actual routes, in addition to any others configured in the list. Leaving the list blank causes the router to advertise the actual routes.*

■ **From RIP Gateway**   Indicates which remote routers any incoming route advertisements must originate from in order to match the policy being configured. To configure these gateways, highlight this parameter and then click List. For instance, if an IP address of 200.20.10.1 were configured, then incoming route advertisements from RIP interface 200.20.10.1 would be considered a match, and would therefore be affected by the policy instructions.

■ **Received on RIP Interface**   An Announce policy can relate only to route information received on specific interfaces. Highlighting this parameter and clicking List opens a window in which you can enter the IP addresses of the interfaces that will be considered by the Announce policy. By default, no interfaces are configured, indicating that all interfaces are considered matches.

■ **From OSPF Router ID**   If only routes from certain OSPF routers are to be considered by the Announce policy, their IP addresses can be configured here. Clicking List opens another window, in which you may define a list of individual IP addresses. Leaving this list blank indicates that all incoming OSPF routes should be considered.

■ **Received Ospf Type**    Used to configure the types of routes that will be considered by the Announce policy. These route types may include External Type-1, External Type-2, Internal, or Any. Unlike Accept policies, Announce policies may also consider internally obtained route information.

■ **Received Ospf Tag**    If OSPF has been identified as a Route Source, then this parameter indicates which tag values are considered to be matches for purposes of the Announce policy; by default, no tags are selected, meaning that all tag values are considered.

■ **From Egp Peer**    If EGP has been selected as a valid Route Source, then specific EGP peers can be selected for purposes of matching the policy. Highlighting this parameter and clicking List opens a window in which you may define the specific EGP peers.

■ **From Egp As**    Indicates that only route information sourced from the specified EGP autonomous system will be considered by the policy.

■ **Received Egp Gateway**    Highlighting this parameter and then clicking List opens a window in which you can enter specific IP addresses. These addresses are considered the next-hop value for incoming route information, and only EGP advertisements that use one of the configured values on the list as their next hops will be considered by the policy. EGP must be selected as a Route Source.

■ **From Bgp Peer**    If BGP has been selected as a valid Route Source, then specific BGP peers can be selected for purposes of matching the policy. Highlighting the parameter and clicking List opens a window in which you can define the specific BGP peers.

■ **From Bgp As**    Indicates that only route information sourced from the specified BGP autonomous system will be considered by the policy.

■ **Received Bgp Next Hop**    Highlighting this parameter and then clicking List opens a window in which you can enter specific IP addresses. These addresses are considered the next-hop values for incoming route information, and only BGP advertisements that use one of the configured values on the list as their next hop will be considered by the policy. BGP must be selected as a Route Source.

■ **Outbound Interfaces**    Limits the number of interfaces—and identifies which interfaces specifically—route information matching the policy's parameters will be advertised from. By excluding certain interfaces, you can ensure that incoming route information is hidden from the associated networks.

■ **RIP Metric**    Alters the RIP metric associated with route information matching the policy. This can be useful particularly in RIP networks that are being connected over a Wide Area, where combining the sites causes the maximum RIP hop count to be exceeded. A good positioning for such an Announce policy would be one of the WAN routers. Targeting the routes that will exceed the hop count, and then specifying a lower metric, will prevent the route metric from reaching a metric of 16—the point at which the network is considered unreachable.

# Troubleshooting RIP on the Nortel Networks Router Platform

As is the case with all Nortel Networks router platforms and protocols, RIP information and statistics can be gathered from the router TI by means of router scripts, and also via gets on the MIB. Each approach offers similar information, with the primary difference being the fashion in which the output is displayed. The TI scripts generally provide output in the form of a list or table, polling a group of statistics rather than one at a time, whereas the MIB gets are done individually, and usually provide their output in the form of a value that must be referenced to its appropriate meaning. Script files, however, generally need to be stored on the router flash and loaded, while MIB gets can be done from any router TI, regardless of whether any script files are present.

## Troubleshooting RIP Using TI Scripts

If the proper TI scripts are loaded, RIP information can be viewed from the TI by using the IP scripts that relate to the RIP protocol. Some examples of these commands are covered in this section; for more information regarding the mechanics of loading specific TI scripts, consult Chapter 29.

### Displaying RIP Interfaces

The RIP interfaces currently configured on the router can be displayed by using the **show ip rip** command, which displays the different RIP interfaces, their circuit number, and the current operational state:

```
[2:1]$ show ip rip
                                RIP      Def.Rt  Poison  RIP   Trig
  IP Interface  Ckt#  State  Sup/Lis  Sup/Lis Reverse Mode  Updt TTL
  ------------- ----- ------ -------- ------- ------- ----- ---- ---
  160.60.10.0   1     Up     En /En   Dis/En  Poison  RIP1  Dis  1
  160.60.20.0   2     Up     En /En   Dis/En  Poison  RIP1  Dis  1
  2 entries found
```

This output displays the two RIP interfaces configured on a router that is routing between subnet .10 and subnet .20 on the 160.60.0.0 network. Both interfaces are in the Up state. In addition, both are supplying and listening for RIP updates, are configured to listen for (but not supply) a default route, are configured to use poisoned reverse (as opposed to split horizon), are configured to use RIPv1, and have triggered updates disabled.

### Displaying RIP Alerts

By using the **show ip rip alerts** command, interfaces that are experiencing failures can be singled out, which can be useful particularly when many RIP interfaces are configured:

```
[2:1]$ sho ip rip alerts
                                    RIP     Def.Rt  Poison  RIP   Trig
 IP Interface   Ckt#   State     Sup/Lis Sup/Lis Reverse Mode  Updt TTL
--------------- ----   ----------- ------- ------- ------- ----- ---- ---
160.60.20.0      1     Down      En /En  Dis/En  Poison  RIP1  Dis  1
1 entries found
```

Here, one RIP interface is shown to be in a Down state. The output of this command lists only interfaces that are configured for RIP but currently in a Down state.

## Displaying the Timer Information

RIP timing information must remain consistent within a common IP network. For example, if one interface within a specified network has a Broadcast Timer of 30 (indicating that a RIP update will be sent every 30 seconds) and a Timeout Timer of 90 (indicating that three updates can be missed before the associated route or routes are deemed unreachable), while the other interfaces within the same network are configured with a Broadcast Timer of 60, then the first interface really would be able to miss only one update. By the time the second update is sent, 120 seconds will have passed, exceeding the Timeout Timer of 90 seconds. This can cause route information to bounce between being reachable and unreachable status at regular intervals; to ensure all timers are consistent, use the following command:

```
[2:1]$ sho ip rip timers
                       Broadcast TimeOut HoldDown
 IP Interface   Ckt# Timer     Timer   Timer
--------------- ---- --------- ------- --------
160.60.10.0      1    30        90      90
1 entries found
```

## Displaying Authentication Parameters

In the case of RIPv2, route authentication can be configured by means of a simple password. With Manager access, the password authentication information can be viewed with the **show ip rip auth** command:

```
[2:1]$ sho ip rip auth
 IP Interface   Ckt#   Type            Password
--------------- ----   ------          ---------
160.60.10.0      1     SimplePassword  ripnet
1 entries found
```

Passwords are case-sensitive, and must be consistent within a common network or subnetwork. If one interface is using uppercase letters in its authentication password, and the rest of the interfaces are not, then that interface's RIP updates will not be accepted by the other interfaces.

## Displaying the Route Table

The IP routing table can also be displayed from the TI. This table indicates each route, the protocol by which it was learned (the **show ip routes** command shows routes learned by any routing protocol, such as OSPF or BGP, as well as RIP learned routes), the age of the route, the slot it was learned on, the cost associated with the route, and the next hop on the way to that route:

```
[2:1]$ sho ip routes
Network/Mask          Proto   Age     Slot Cost  NextHop Address / AS
-------------------   ------  ------  ---- -----  ----------------/----
150.50.0.0/16         RIP     5       2    2      201.16.174.33
151.50.0.0/16         RIP     5       2    2      201.16.174.33
160.60.0.0/16         RIP     5       2    2      201.16.174.33
160.121.0.0/16        RIP     5       2    2      201.16.174.33
170.70.0.0/16         RIP     5       2    2      201.16.175.12
141.200.0.0/16        RIP     5       2    2      201.16.175.12
141.201.0.0/16        RIP     5       2    2      201.16.175.12
170.71.0.0/16         RIP     5       2    2      201.16.175.12
8 entries found.
```

Remember that "cost" in this case indicates the number of hops away the route is; by default, RIP gives a cost or metric of 1 for each router hop that must be traversed along the path to the route. Since RIP has a limitation of 15 router hops before a network is considered to be unreachable, a route with an associated cost of 16 is deemed an unreachable route.

# The
# Complete
# Reference

Nortel
Networks

# Part VIII

## Appendixes

# The Complete Reference

Nortel Networks

# Appendix A

## An Overview of Site Manager

ite Manager's main function is to provide a GUI interface for configuring Nortel Networks routers. It can also transfer files via the Trivial File Transfer Protocol (TFTP) to and from the router; download and save the router log; initiate pings from the router; reboot the router or reset slots; reallocate memory on router platforms that support that feature; view router statistics and Simple Network Management Protocol (SNMP) traps sent to the Site Manager station; and remove components of the router image to make it smaller. For an exhaustive description of all Site Manager's features, consult the Site Manager manual *Configuring and Managing Routers with Site Manager,* available on the Nortel Networks Web site at **http://support.baynetworks. com/library/tpubs/nav/router/bayrs.htm**.

Site Manager is a Nortel Networks router configuration and management tool. It is not a network management tool. Site Manager cannot manage any devices other than the Nortel Networks routers and it doesn't provide any type of network-bandwidth or network-protocol analysis.

Nortel Networks is moving toward Bay Command Console (BCC) as its primary router configuration tool, but BCC currently cannot configure all the protocols that Site Manager can. However, with each new release of Bay Router Software (Bay RS), more and more capabilities are added to BCC. Eventually, BCC will be able to configure anything that Site Manager can.

## Supported Site Manager Platforms

Site Manager runs on a variety of platforms. Before installing Site Manager, however, always check the *Site Manager Release Notes* for the minimum hardware requirements and supported operating systems for your particular version of Site Manager. If you don't have a copy of the *Site Manager Release Notes*, you can get one from the Nortel Networks Web site at the URL previously cited. Currently, Site Manager has been tested on Windows 95 and Windows NT; Solaris 2.5, 2.5.1, and 2.6; SunOS 4.1.4; IBM AIX 4.2; and HP-UX 10.20. Sun OS 4.1.4 support is being phased out, however, as of the time of publication, and the last version of Site Manager to support Sun OS 4.1.4 is 7.20.

## Connecting to the Nortel Networks Router Using Site Manager

Site Manager can connect to a Nortel Networks router as long as the following conditions exist:

- A compatible version of Site Manager is being used
- The Site Manager station can ping the router
- SNMP is enabled and functional on the router
- No SNMP Community Name or SNMP Manager restrictions are in effect on the router

## Connecting to the Router

If you are installing a Nortel Networks router that has never been configured, you first must make a console attachment to the router and then run the router installation batch file (called install.bat, or something similar, depending on the router platform). The purpose of running install.bat is to configure SNMP and an IP address for the router so that Site Manager can then connect to the router. All further configuration is done using Site Manager.

## Selecting a Configuration Mode

Connecting to the router using Site Manager is done by selecting Options |
Connections from the main Site Manager screen and entering the router's IP address and SNMP Community Name string. Once entered, click the router's IP address in the Well-Known Connections box on the Nortel Networks Site Manager main screen. When the connection is established, the status of the connection is displayed as UP. If a problem exists, the status of the connection is displayed as DOWN.

Once Site Manager connects to the router, you must select the type of configuration mode that Site Manager will use, starting by choosing Tools | Configuration Manager. The following are the four configuration modes from which to select:

- **Dynamic mode**   Used to make configuration changes that take place dynamically; Site Manager's Configuration Manager makes changes to the operating configuration in the router's memory. It does not make any changes to the configuration file stored on the router's flash card until the configuration is changed. If the changes made are undesirable, rebooting will return the router to an operating state that was active before the changes were made. As a precaution, always save to flash a backup copy of the current running configuration before you make any changes.

- **Local mode**   Used either to create a configuration file from scratch offline or to modify a preexisting configuration file that has been copied to the Site Manager station's hard drive. When you are done editing offline, the new configuration file must be uploaded to the router by using TFTP, FTP, or XMODEM. For the changes to take effect, the router must be rebooted with the new configuration file.

- **Remote mode**   Uses TFTP to copy a configuration file from the router flash card to the Site Manager station's hard drive. Changes are then made to this local copy. When you save the new configuration file, Site Manager uses TFTP to copy the new configuration file to the router's flash volume. For the changes to take effect, the router must be rebooted with the new configuration file. This is similar to local mode, except that in remote mode, Site Manager automatically takes care of downloading the current configuration file from the router and uploading the modified configuration file to the router.

■ **Cache mode**   The router copies the current router configuration to the hard drive of the Site Manager station. The cached configuration file is used to retrieve any necessary parameter values that Site Manager must get prior to performing requested configuration changes. Whenever Site Manager makes a configuration change to the current configuration in the router's memory, the changes are also applied to the cached configuration file, so that the cached configuration file and the running router configuration always remain identical. Cache mode is helpful if you want to make changes dynamically, but the Site Manager response time is slow.

When finished with Site Manager, select File | Exit.

*Although Site Manager has a "Windows-like" appearance, it uses windows for display purposes only; as such, you are recommended to close any Site Manager windows by choosing File | Exit rather than by clicking the Close button in the top-right corner, because, in some cases, using the Close button may close the window but leave the application running.*

# Viewing Router Statistics Using Site Manager

Site Manager can be used to poll the router for various types of interface and router statistics, using the Statistics Manager screen. To open the Statistics Manager screen, select Tools | Statistics Manager. Statistics Manager's initial window displays all the circuits configured on the router, along with the protocols running on those circuits.

## Using Screen Manager

To view other sorts of statistics, such as the status of all the IP circuits, first open the Screen Manager window by selecting Tools | Screen Manager. Highlight one of the available screens in the Default Screens box and click the Add button. Add as many screens as are desired. Use the up and down scroll bar arrows to cycle through all the available screens. If you change your mind and want to remove a selected screen from the Current Screen List, just highlight the screen and click the Remove button.

When you are finished adding screens, click OK. Then, select Tools | Launch Facility. Highlight the screen that will display the statistics that you want to view and click the Launch button. Statistics Manager contacts the router and does the necessary SNMP MIB queries to access the desired statistical information and display it onscreen in a table format. To close the screen and view another screen of statistics, select File | Exit in the Launch Facility window, and then highlight another screen and launch it by clicking Launch.

## Utilizing Multiple Screens

Multiple screens can be opened simultaneously for viewing, if desired. To open a new screen, highlight a different screen on the already-open Statistics Launch Facility window and click Launch. This opens another Launch Facility window, with the screen view that you indicated. After viewing, shut down the Statistics Launch Facility window by clicking Done.

Statistics Manager also provides a MIB Walk Utility called Quick Get, which enables you to poll the router for the current values of MIB objects that you select, and then display them onscreen. Quick Get can be accessed by selecting Tools | Quick Get from the Statistics Manager screen. To "walk the MIB tree," click the MIB objects displayed in the MIB Objects box of the Quick Get Facility window. Each time that you click a MIB object, Quick Get descends the router MIB tree. Eventually the MIB tree's "leaves" are reached, which are MIB objects that point to values. When a MIB object is selected and it becomes highlighted instead of bringing up more MIB subcategories to select from, then Quick Get has reached a MIB leaf that points to a value that can be displayed. To get the value of the MIB object, click the Retrieve Request button.

To view a description of the MIB object that is highlighted, click the Read Description button. To walk back up the tree, click the word Back in the MIB Objects box. To exit the Quick Get Facility window, click Done.

## Using Screen Builder

With a good understanding of the Nortel Networks router MIBs, custom screens can be defined by using Statistics Manager's Screen Builder utility. To access Screen Builder, select Tools | Screen Builder from the Statistics Manager screen. Create a new statistics screen by doing a MIB walk until the MIB value is displayed. Click the column number where the MIB value should appear onscreen, and then highlight the MIB object. The maximum columns per screen is nine. Enter a heading for the column and click Save Column. An asterisk (*) appears next to the column number when it has been saved. Continue selecting columns and MIB objects.

A column of total values can be created by selecting the column number, clicking the Total button, and selecting the columns you want Statistics Manager to add up. To see what the screen will look like, click the Preview button. After completing the new screen, click the Save button. Statistics Manager prompts you to enter the name of the new screen, a description of what it displays, and the display orientation. Click Save on the Statistics Save/Load screen to finish saving the screen. The screen can be tried by clicking the Load button. To close the Screen Builder Facility window, click Done. To close the Statistics Manager window, select File | Exit.

## Managing the Router's Flash Volume Using Site Manager

Site Manager provides a utility called Router Files Manager to enable you to manage the Flash Volume on the Nortel Networks router. Router Files Manager is accessed either by selecting Tools | Router Files Manager or by clicking the Files button. You can TFTP files to and from the router Flash Volume by selecting Files | TFTP and then selecting either Get File(s) or Put File(s).

TFTP Get File retrieves a file from the router's Flash Volume and places it on the hard drive of the Site Manager station. First, highlight the file that you want to get before choosing File | TFTP | Get File(s).

TFTP Put File uploads a file from the Site Manager hard drive to the router's Flash Volume. You are prompted for the filename and location on the Site Manager station's hard drive after selecting Put File(s). If multiple Flash Volumes are installed on the router, select the volume you want to manage by clicking the down arrow next to the displayed volume number.

Router Files Manager also provides the ability to copy a file, delete a file, compact the Flash Volume, format the Flash Volume, and refresh the Flash Volume directory listing onscreen. A new Flash Volume must be formatted before it can be used to store files. Compacting the Flash Volume makes all of its free space contiguous. Noncontiguous space on the Flash Volume is unusable. Refresh the Flash Volume directory listing after copying files to or deleting files from the Flash Volume. All of these Flash Volume management duties can be accessed by clicking the Commands pull-down menu from the Router Files Manager window and selecting either Directory (to refresh the display), Copy, Delete, Format, or Compact. To close the Router Files Manager window, choose File | Exit.

## Viewing/Saving the Router Log Using Site Manager

The Events Manager utility of Site Manager enables you to retrieve the router log, display it onscreen, and then save it to an ASCII file on the hard drive of the Site Manager station. To open the Events Manager window, either select Tools | Events Manager or click the Events button.

Set up the log filter so that Events Manager displays only the portion of the log that you want to see. If the log is being saved for a Nortel Networks Technical Support Engineer to analyze, be sure no log filters are configured. Choose View | Filters. Anything that is highlighted will appear in the log when it is displayed or saved, whereas anything not highlighted will be left out. To view the entire log, highlight Fault and Trace in the Severity box of the Filtering Parameters screen and click OK. Otherwise, limit the log display to just what is needed, by removing the highlight from the options listed in the Severity, Slot, and Entities boxes.

If a log is already displayed onscreen, to apply the new log filter, the display must be refreshed by selecting View | Refresh Display. To clear everything that is currently displayed onscreen, select View | Clear Window. Clearing the window is a good thing to do before instructing Events Manager to connect to a different router to display its log. To have Events Manager connect to a different router, select Options | Router Connection. You will be prompted to enter the IP address and SNMP Community Name of the router you want to connect to. This feature is useful when troubleshooting a problem involving multiple Nortel Networks routers.

## Retrieving the Log

To retrieve the router log, choose File | Get Current Log File, which displays the log onscreen. The Get Remote Log File option enables you to view a binary log file that has been saved on the router's Flash Volume. The Load Local Log File option enables you to view a binary log file stored on the hard drive of the Site Manager station. The Save Output to Disk option saves the log that is currently displayed onscreen to an ASCII file on the hard drive of the Site Manager station. Since the log is saved in an ASCII format, a text editor can be used to view a log file saved by Site Manager. A log file that has been saved via the Technician Interface (TI) on the router's Flash Volume is stored as a binary file, which cannot be viewed using a text editor.

When looking for a specific event in the log, choose Find | Find, which enables you to enter a keyword to search for in the log. If the keyword is found, Events Manager displays the log event message containing the keyword at the top of the display window. Choosing the Find Again option, instead, enables you to search for the next occurrence of the same keyword.

When finished viewing the log, close the Events Manager window by selecting File | Exit.

## Using Site Manager's Image Builder

Image Builder is used to remove portions of the Bay RS image, to reduce the size of the image. This is useful if the Flash Volume or amount of router memory (DRAM) is too small to store the entire version of the image. To access the Image Builder utility, select Tools | Image Builder.

When the Image Builder window opens, select the original image to work from by selecting File | Open. Image Builder will prompt for the filename and path. The software components that make up the Bay RS image are displayed in the Current Components box onscreen. To display the subcomponents, as well, click the Details box. The sizes of both the compressed and uncompressed image are displayed onscreen. As software components are removed, the size of the image will change. This way, the size of the image can be monitored, so that you know when you have removed enough of the image for it to fit on the Flash Volume or in memory.

Anything the router won't need to use can be removed by highlighting the software component and clicking the Remove button. To help determine what most of the software components are used for, a description of the component is displayed along with the component executable name. If unsure as to what a software component does, either find out by calling Nortel Networks Technical Support or simply leave it in place, if space permits.

When you are done manipulating the image, save the newly created smaller image by selecting File | Save As. You are prompted to enter the new name of the image executable. If the Save option is selected, Image Builder renames the original EXE image as a BAK file and saves the new image over the original one.

To alter a different image, select File | New. By default, Image Builder creates a text file called contents.txt that contains a list of the software components that make up the new image. This can be prevented by selecting the Options pull-down menu and deselecting the Generate CONTENTS.TXT when Saving option. When you are done, close the Image Builder window by selecting File | Exit.

## Using Site Manager to Verify the Configuration File

Site Manager's Report Generator utility can be used to determine whether a configuration file is valid or corrupted. A corrupted configuration contains invalid or missing information. To open the Configuration Report Generator screen, select Tools | Report Generator. Select the configuration file to analyze by clicking the Select File button and highlighting the configuration file stored on the hard drive of the Site Manager station. Next, tell Report Generator what name to give the report file it generates and where to put it. Then, click the Generate Report button. Report Generator indicates when it has finished generating the report.

A text editor can be used to view the report file. All the configuration parameters and their values will be displayed in the report. Report Generator marks any problems that it finds. You can also visually inspect the parameter values to make sure they contain the correct values. The report is also a convenient way to keep a hard copy of the configuration. After Report Generator is done creating its report, it automatically closes the Report Generator window.

## Viewing Traps Sent by the Router to the Site Manager Station

If the router is configured to send traps to the Site Manager station, they can be viewed by using Site Manager's Trap Monitor utility. To open the Trap Monitor window, select Tools | Trap Monitor. Before traps can be used, the Trap History file that contains the traps must be loaded by selecting File | Load History File from the Nortel Networks Trap Monitor screen. The contents of the History file are displayed onscreen. After the History file is loaded, new traps are dynamically displayed to the Trap Monitor screen as they are received.

Adjust what is displayed by selecting either View | Select Trap Types or View | Set Address Filters. The Select Trap Types option allows the selection of the trap severity to be displayed onscreen: Fault, Warning, Info, Trace, or Debug. The Set Address Filters option enables you to display only those traps sent by the routers listed by IP address in the filter.

After viewing the traps, they may be saved to a text file, which can be done by selecting File | Save Traps. Trap Monitor prompts for the filename to save the trap file as. After saving the traps, you also may want to clear the Trap Monitor display screen, by selecting View | Clear Window. To clear the contents of the History File, as well,

choose File | Clear History File. Close the Trap Monitor window by selecting
File | Exit.

# Running Multiple Versions of Site Manager on Windows Platforms

Normally, when attempting to install multiple versions of Site Manager on a
Management Station, the newly installed version of Site Manager will work fine, but
the old version will no longer run; the second Site Manager installation corrupts the
first Site Manager installation, because the installation wizard creates a siteman.ini file
in the Windows directory of the Site Manager station. Each version of Site Manager has
its own version of siteman.ini. For example, the siteman.ini file for Site Manager
version 12.00 is not the same as the siteman.ini file for Site Manager version 13.00. If
you attempt to run Site Manager with a different version of siteman.ini, it will not
work. When a new version of Site Manager is installed, the new version of siteman.ini
is copied to the Windows directory, overwriting the old version of siteman.ini.
Multiple versions of Site Manager can be configured to run on a single management
station, however, by following the steps in the next section.

## Installing Multiple Versions of Site Manager

Before installing the new version of Site Manager, rename the old version of
siteman.ini to **siteman.*ver***, where *ver* is the version number of the old Site Manager.
For example, if the old version of Site Manager is version 5.02, then rename siteman.ini
to siteman.502. Leave the renamed siteman.ini file in the Windows directory.

Now, install the new version of Site Manager as you normally would. After the
installation is complete, rename the siteman.ini file for the new version to **siteman.*ver***,
where *ver* is the version number of the new version of Site Manager. For example, if the
new version of Site Manager is 7.01, then rename the siteman.ini file to siteman.701.

Create a batch file for each Site Manager version, using a Windows edit utility. The
batch file will instruct the PC to change directory (CD) to the Windows directory and
copy the correct version of siteman.*ver* to siteman.ini. It then instructs the PC to CD to
the correct Site Manager directory and launch Site Manager, by running the Site
Manager executable wfsm.exe. Name the batch file **sm*ver*.bat**, where *ver* is the version
of Site Manager that it launches. For example, if the batch file will launch version 5.02
of Site Manager, name the batch file sm502.bat. The following is an example of a batch
file to launch Site Manager:

```
batch file SM502.bat
c:
cd c:\windows
```

```
copy siteman.502 siteman.ini
d:
cd \SiteMan\SM502
wfsm.exe
```

The first line of batch file SM502.bat changes to the C drive. Make sure this is done if multiple hard drives are installed in the Site Manager station. If you don't, this line can be left out. The next line instructs the PC to change to the Windows directory. The line that follows copies the correct version of siteman.ini (siteman.*ver*) to the siteman.ini. The fourth line causes the PC to CD to the D drive. On this particular Site Manager station, the different versions of Site Manager are saved on the D drive. If the Site Manager directory is located on the C drive, this line can be left out. The batch file then instructs the PC to CD to the directory that stores the appropriate version of Site Manager, which is \SiteMan\SM502 in this example. Once in the proper Site Manager directory, the batch file launches Site Manager by running wfsm.exe.

After setting up the Site Manager batch files, whenever you want to launch Site Manager, run the appropriate batch file for the desired version.

# Troubleshooting a Site Manager Connection to the Router

Site Manager uses SNMP MIB Gets and Sets to communicate with the router over a LAN or WAN. For this reason, Site Manager must establish an IP connection with the router and have the proper SNMP community strings defined. Site Manager cannot communicate with the router over a console connection.

## Checking IP and SNMP Connectivity

When troubleshooting a Site Manager connection failure, the first thing to check is whether or not the Site Manager station can ping the router, and vice versa. If there is no IP connectivity, then there can be no SNMP connectivity either.

If the Site Manager station cannot ping the router, make sure the IP interface on the router that Site Manager is attempting to connect to is up. Have other devices on the network attempt to ping the router. If they are successful, examine the Site Manager station.

### Ensuring Software and Image Version Compatibility

Once the Site Manager station can ping the router, and vice versa, try connecting via Site Manager again. If the Site Manager connection still fails, make sure you are using a compatible version of Site Manager for the version of Bay RS running on the router. The version of Site Manager that goes with a certain version of Bay RS is always six revisions less than the Bay RS version number. For example, if the router is running 13.01, then the version of Site Manager you should be running is 7.01.

Newer versions of Site Manager are backward-compatible with some older versions of Bay RS. Make sure to check the *Site Manager Release Notes* to find out which versions of Bay RS your version of Site Manager supports. When using an older version of Site Manager and attempting to connect to a Nortel Networks router running a version of Bay RS that is newer than what your Site Manager version supports, Site Manager will not be able to open the Configuration Manager window.

## Verifying the SNMP Configuration

When using a compatible version of Site Manager, the Site Manager station can ping the router, and the status in the Well-Known Connections box is UP, but Site Manager will not launch Configuration Manager, make sure you are using the correct SNMP Community Name string. By default, the SNMP Read/Write Community Name string is public. One of the first things that a network administrator does when setting up security on the Nortel Networks router is to change the SNMP Read/Write Community Name string.

If a copy of the router's configuration file is accessible, open it in Site Manager using local mode configuration and check the SNMP Community Name configuration. This can be done by selecting Protocols | IP from the Configuration Manager screen. Then, select the SNMP option and the Communities option. The configured SNMP Community Names will be listed in the SNMP Community List box. The level of access a configured Community Name string has can be determined by highlighting the Community Name string and selecting Community | Edit Community.

## Verifying the SNMP Managers List

If a valid SNMP Community Name string with read/write access is being used, make certain that the Site Manager station is listed as one of the configured SNMP Managers, by highlighting a Community Name in the SNMP Community List box and selecting Community | Managers. The IP addresses of the SNMP Managers authorized to contact the router using the SNMP Community Name that were highlighted are shown in the SNMP Managers box.

By default, the IP address displayed in the SNMP Managers box is 0.0.0.0. This means any Site Manager station with any IP address can connect to the router using the SNMP Community Name string highlighted on the previous screen. If, instead, individual host IP addresses are listed in the SNMP Managers box, make sure the IP address of the Site Manager station being used is listed there. If it isn't, Site Manager will not be able to connect to the router. Add the IP address of the Site Manager station by selecting Manager | Add Manager and then entering the IP address of the Site

Manager station. After making these changes to the router's configuration file, using Site Manager in local mode, transfer the updated configuration file to the router's Flash Volume by using TFTP, FTP, or XMODEM. The changes could also be made in dynamic mode if another Site Manager station is available that is able to connect to the router. If no other way is available, the new SNMP Manager can be added via the MIBs. How to check the router's SNMP configuration via the MIBs is explained later in this appendix.

### Enabling SNMP Globally

If Site Manager still cannot connect to the router, make sure SNMP is enabled globally on the router. The status of SNMP can be checked via the MIBs, if necessary. In addition to making sure SNMP is enabled, check the router log by issuing the **log -fftdwi -eSNMP** TI command, and look for any SNMP error messages. Something may have gone wrong when the router attempted to load SNMP.

If none of the preceding suggestions are effective, it is possible that either the router or Site Manager did not initialize correctly, and rebooting either the router or the Site Manager station may resolve the problem.

## Verifying the SNMP Router Configuration via the MIBs

If Site Manager is unable to connect to the Nortel Networks router, the problem could be with the router's SNMP configuration, or perhaps the Site Manager station is configured with the wrong SNMP Community Name. Another possibility is that the Site Manager station is not configured as an authorized SNMP Manager on the Nortel Networks router. The wfSnmpCommEntry MIB stores the Community Names configured on the Nortel router and their associated access levels. The wfSnmpMgrEntry MIB contains information about the SNMP Managers authorized to connect to the Nortel router. The complete Nortel Networks SNMP MIB descriptions can be found in the snmp.mib file located in the site manager/mibs directory on the Site Manager station.

The following are the most common MIB attributes for wfSnmpCommEntry:

- **wfSnmpCommDelete**   A value of 1 creates a Community Name instance, while a value of 2 deletes the Community Name instance.

- **wfSnmpCommIndex**   An integer index assigned to the Community Name. Each Community Name is assigned a unique index, starting with an index value of 1.

- **wfSnmpCommName**   The Community Name string. By default, the "public" Community Name is the only Community Name configured.

- **wfSnmpCommAccess**   The access level associated with the Community Name. A value of 1 indicates read-only access, and a value of 2 indicates read/write access.

The following are the most common MIB attributes for wfSnmpMgrEntry:

- **wfSnmpMgrDelete**   A value of 1 creates a SNMP Manager instance, while a value of 2 deletes the SNMP Manager instance.

- **wfSnmpMgrCommIndex**   The community index of the wfSnmpCommEntry MIB instance with which this SNMP Manager is associated. This MIB object determines whether the SNMP Manager has read-only access or read/write access.

- **wfSnmpMgrAddress**   The IP address of SNMP Manager.

- **wfSnmpMgrName**   An optional, descriptive name assigned to the SNMP Manager. For example, if the SNMP Manager (Site Manager station) belongs to the user named John Doe, the SNMP Manager Name could be configured as "JohnDoe" for easy identification.

- **wfSnmpMgrTrapPort**   The User Datagram Protocol (UDP) port number the Nortel Networks router will send traps to. By default, the UDP port is 162. The SNMP Manager is assumed to be listening for traps on that UDP port.

- **wfSnmpMgrTraps**   The types of traps the Nortel Networks router will send to the SNMP Manager. A value of 1 equals none, a value of 2, which is the default, equals generic traps only, a value of 4 equals specific traps only, and a value of 7 equals all traps.

## Checking the SNMP Community Name Configuration via the MIBs

The following command will help to determine which Community Names have read-only access and which have read/write access:

```
NortelRouter> get wfSnmpCommEntry.4.*
```

This MIB query returns the SNMP access levels for all the Community Names configured on the Nortel Networks router. Any value equal to 1 means the Community Name has read-only access. If the value is 2, the Community Name has read/write access. To determine the Community Name associated with read/write access, get the

Community Index Number for the Community Name with an access level value of 2. Then, use the Community Index Number in the following MIB query to get the Community Name string:

```
NortelRouter> get wfSnmpCommEntry.3.community index number
```

For example, to create a new SNMP Community Name with read/write access, the following commands would be issued:

```
NortelRouter> set wfSnmpCommEntry.3.a Community Index Number not
already used the new Community Name;commit

NortelRouter> set wfSnmpCommEntry.4.the Community Index Number used
above 2;commit
```

## Checking the SNMP Manager Configuration via the MIBs

The following command lists the IP addresses of all the end stations authorized to connect to the Nortel Networks Router using SNMP, and therefore Site Manager. By default, the Nortel Networks router creates a wfSnmpMgrEntry of 0.0.0.0. An IP address of 0.0.0.0 means "all IP addresses" and thus any end station can connect to the Nortel router by using Site Manager, as long as the correct Community Name is used. Many Nortel Networks router administrators, for security purposes, explicitly specify which IP addresses have read/write access to the router, and designate the 0.0.0.0 IP address to have read-only access.

```
NortelRouter> get wfSnmpMgrEntry.3.*
wfSnmpMgrEntry.wfSnmpMgrAddress.1.0.0.0.0 = 0.0.0.0
wfSnmpMgrEntry.wfSnmpMgrAddress.1.172.35.3.4 = 172.35.3.4
wfSnmpMgrEntry.wfSnmpMgrAddress.2.172.35.3.5 = 172.35.3.5
```

If Site Manager can connect to the Nortel Networks router, but can't make any changes, then Site Manager is probably connecting using a read-only Community Name. If Site Manager will not open the Configuration Manager screen when using a valid read/write Community Name, then most likely the IP address for the Site Manager station has been configured for read-only access.

An SNMP Manager entry with read/write access can be created for the Site Manager station via the MIBs. The wfSnmpMgrEntry MIB instance is of the following format:

*Community Index Number associated with read-only or read/write access.IP address of the Site Manager station*

In the next example, a community index of 1 is associated with read-only access, and a community index of 2 is associated with read/write access.

Refer to the output of the get wfSnmpMgrEntry.3.* command shown earlier. Notice that the 172.35.3.4 SNMP Manager is configured for read-only access, while the 172.35.3.5 SNMP Manager is configured for read/write access. To give the SNMP Manager entry for 172.35.3.4 read/write access, it must be deleted and then re-created using the read/write Community Index Number:

```
NortelRouter> set wfSnmpMgrEntry.1.1.172.35.3.4 2;commit
NortelRouter> set wfSnmpMgrEntry.1.2.172.35.3.4 1;commit
```

## Checking the State of SNMP via the MIBs

If Site Manager still can't connect to the Nortel Networks router, and the SNMP Community Names and Managers are configured properly, perhaps the problem is with SNMP on a global level. The following command checks whether SNMP is enabled or disabled. If the value returned is 1, SNMP is enabled. If the value is 2, SNMP has been administratively disabled.

```
NortelRouter> get wfSnmp.1.0
wfSnmp.wfSnmpDisable.0 = 2
NortelRouter> set wfSnmp.1.0 1;commit
NortelRouter> get wfSnmp.1.0
wfSnmp.wfSnmpDisable.0 = 1
```

# Performing Administrative Tasks Using Site Manager

Site Manager performs a variety of administrative tasks from the Administration pull-down menu from the Site Manager main screen, by selecting any of the following options:

■ **Boot Router**  Reboots the router using the image and configuration specified.

- **Reset Slot**   Causes the router slot indicated to reload its image and configuration. The other router slots will not be affected.

- **Clear Event Log**   Causes the router to clear the contents of the router log.

- **Router Date & Time**   Sets the router's clock to the date and time you define.

- **Ping from Router**   Initiates an IP, IPX, OSI, VINES, AppleTalk, or APPN ping from the router to the network address of another device.

- **Kernel Configuration**   Allows changes to the memory configuration on the ACE32 processor boards of the VME (Versa Module Eurocard) Nortel Networks routers, the FRE2 processor boards of the BN Nortel Networks routers, or the AFN, AN, ANH, and ASN Nortel Networks routers. (Although the VME product line has been discontinued by Nortel Networks, it is not unusual to find old VME routers still in operation at some customer sites.) Changing the memory configuration on any other router platform is not supported.

The memory of the Nortel Networks router (DRAM) is divided into global and local memory. Global memory is where the buffers reside, while local memory is where the operating image, configuration, and routing tables are kept. If the router is running out of buffers and there is plenty of local memory to spare, you can give some local memory to global memory to increase the number of buffers available.

# The Complete Reference

Nortel Networks

# Appendix B

## An Overview of SpeedView

peedView is a graphical-configuration and statistics-viewing utility that is used to set up and maintain the C100/C50/C20/5000BH platforms.

# SpeedView

SpeedView is an important application with respect to the C100/C50/C20/5000BH, because, unlike some of the other platforms, these devices cannot be configured through the command-line interface. The CLI of the C100/C50/C20/5000BH family is primarily for troubleshooting purposes and lacks the command set to accomplish even a basic configuration.

SpeedView is quite a bit simpler than its router-oriented counterpart, Site Manager; SpeedView comes with a configuration utility and a statistics-gathering utility.

## Versions of SpeedView

Not every version of image software is compatible with every version of SpeedView. With each new iteration of code, new functions may be introduced and new configuration options may be included. If these options are included in SpeedView, but not written into the current image version, it can cause the configuration to not be implemented correctly. Often, this will cause a configuration file to become corrupted, since the parameters are not being resolved correctly when the configuration file is created. If this happens, recovering the configuration file may be impossible, even if it is brought up with the correct SpeedView version, and it may have to be discarded.

As a rule of thumb, as long as the release number of the image software matches the SpeedView release number, they should be compatible. Table B-1 lists the corresponding versions of software in more detail.

| Image Software Release | SpeedView Release |
|---|---|
| 2.0.$x$ | 2.0.3 |
| 2.0.5.$x$ (Etherspeed MCP) | 2.0.5 |
| 2.1.07$x$ | 2.1.036 |
| 2.11.$x$ | 2.11.$x$ |
| 2.2.$x$ | 2.2.$x$ |
| 3.0.$x$ | 3.0 |
| 3.1.$x$ | 3.1 |
| 3.2.$x$ | 3.2 |
| 4.0.$x$ | 4.0 |

**Table B-1.**   *Compatibility Between Image Software and SpeedView*

# Connecting via SpeedView

SpeedView can be used to manage the Centillion family (excepting the C1x00 series switches) either by establishing a serial connection or through the Simple Network Management Protocol (SNMP). Prior to the introduction of SNMP communication in code version 2.1.070 (SpeedView version 2.1.036), the option of data link connection (DLC) communication also existed, although this connection option was eventually discontinued in favor of SNMP.

## Serial Connections

The serial connection is the simplest form of communicating with the Centillion via SpeedView, and was the primary means of configuration prior to code version 2.1.070, when SNMP communications were first supported. To establish a serial connection, simply connect the Centillion's serial cable to the device's Master Control Processor. If the Centillion is a C100/C50/C20, the MCP connector will be a small, round, 10-pin DIN connector. If a 5000BH is being configured, the MCP utilizes a standard 25-pin connector. Connect the other end of the cable to the PC's serial port.

The connection type must be specified within SpeedView itself; this is done by selecting File | Preferences from the main SpeedView map window (the default window when SpeedView is first launched). From the Preferences window, the connection type options can be selected:

Depending on the version of SpeedView being used, the options may vary; if you are using a release prior to SpeedView 2.1.070, the options will include a serial connection or a DLC. If the code version is greater than 2.1.070, the options include a serial connection or an SNMP connection, and in some cases, may include all three connection options—but a serial connection type will always be available regardless of

APPENDIXES

the SpeedView version being used. Select the appropriate COM port that the management PC is using for the serial connection (often COM 1, but not always). After you select the information, click OK to return to the main SpeedView window.

Serial communication allows you to manage only one switch at a time, and a direct serial connection must exist to the switch being managed. The advantage to using a serial connection is that IP connectivity to the switch doesn't have to exist for it to work, and all configuration and upgrades can be done over the serial connection. Therefore, a serial connection can be very useful if IP connectivity is lost, for whatever reason. A serial connection also allows for an emergency download if the switch experiences image corruption. The emergency download procedure is outlined later in this appendix.

## SNMP Communications

SNMP communications were introduced in code version 2.1.070, and SpeedView version 2.1.036. In addition to being much faster than a serial connection, SNMP communications with the switch allow for multiple switches to be modeled at one time, displaying all switches in the map window. This makes management of the switches much easier, because they can all be viewed and monitored simultaneously.

Since the switches are contacted by using their IP addresses when using SNMP, each switch must be configured with a valid IP address. Once this is done and all switches are reachable via that IP address (verifiable through a ping test), the individual switches must then be defined within SpeedView itself.

Depending on the version of SpeedView, creating the SNMP list is handled in different ways. In SpeedView versions 2.1.036 to 2.2.*x*, the SNMP list is edited from the Preferences window, reached by selecting File | Preferences. Here, you can add to the list the IP address of each switch you want to contact, and you can alter the SNMP community strings, if appropriate. Beginning with code version 3.0, switches are added by selecting Node | New | Switch from the main SpeedView window, which opens a window that displays the different types of Centillion switches that can be modeled:

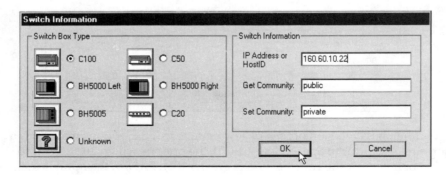

Select the appropriate type of switch by clicking the corresponding radio button. If one is not selected, and the default type of Unknown is kept, the Centillion type will be automatically detected and the correct icon chosen when the switch is discovered. Enter the correct IP address and community strings for the switch being added to the list, and then select OK. SpeedView will attempt to contact the switch that was entered. The switch will be added to the map at this time; if the discovery is successful, the new switch will be displayed with a green indicator. If the discovery fails, the switch is still displayed, but it is displayed with a red indicator. Once present in the map, all reachable switches are displayed with a green indicator, which will turn red if contact with the switch is lost.

# Upgrading the Centillion Image with SpeedView

SpeedView is also used to upgrade or downgrade the switch, and, like the switch configuration, either a serial connection or an SNMP connection can be used to perform the upgrade. The primary difference between the two methods is the speed at which the upgrade occurs; a serial upgrade can take up to 15 minutes to complete, whereas with SNMP the transfer takes only 1 or 2 minutes.

## Serial Upgrades

To perform the upgrade serially, choose the connection type and then discover the switch in SpeedView by selecting Map | Discover from the main SpeedView window. Once the switch icon appears, highlight it and then choose Switch | Download Software (Serial). This opens the Open window. Since the upgrade will be accomplished over the serial connector, no TFTP server is required, so you simply need to select the image, either by entering the path to the image and the image name, or by clicking the Browse button and browsing for the file. After you select the file, simply click Start Download, and the download will commence. A status is displayed, indicating the percentage of the upgrade that has been completed. Serial upgrades/downgrades take between 10 and 15 minutes. When the download is complete, you will be prompted to reset the switch.

 *When performing a serial or SNMP upgrade, do not interrupt the code transfer by recycling the switch or removing the cable. Interrupting the code transfer may corrupt the MCP's flash memory and may cause the unit to become nonfunctional.*

## SNMP Upgrades

Upgrading the switch using SNMP requires IP connectivity and a Trivial File Transfer Protocol (TFTP) server. SpeedView comes with its own TFTP server as part of the package, which you can launch by selecting Start | SpeedView | BootP & TFTP Server. The TFTP server window will appear; this may be minimized, but must be running for the upgrade to take place.

Be sure that the image file is in the right directory; when the TFTP server first launches, the first three lines that appear in the window will look something like this:

```
16:26:55   TFTP: Root Directory is c:\Program Files\SpeedView
16:26:55   BOOTP: BootP Server Initialized
16:26:55   TFTP: TFTP Server Initialized
```

The first line indicates where the TFTP server will look for the image file when it receives the TFTP request from the switch. If the image file is not in this directory, the upgrade will fail.

The upgrade procedure itself is not very different from a serial upgrade. Highlight the icon of the switch to be upgraded, and then select TFTP Download Software. A window opens in which you can define the TFTP server IP address and the image name. The TFTP server in this case is the IP address of the SpeedView station, because the TFTP software should be launched and running at this point. Enter the image name in the appropriate field. The path is not necessary in this case, since the TFTP server has the path to its root directory already defined, and will always look in that directory for the image name you specify. Once this is selected, click Start Download. After the download is complete, you will be prompted to reset the switch.

# Troubleshooting an SNMP Upgrade

If the SNMP upgrade fails, you can check a few things that commonly interfere with the procedure.

## Make Sure the TFTP Server Is Running

The BootP/TFTP server that is packaged with SpeedView does not launch automatically when SpeedView is launched. It must be launched individually and must be running while the upgrade is taking place.

## Check the Path to the Root Directory

When performing an upgrade, it is a good idea to alter the message verbosity level on the TFTP server, should something go wrong. This causes the server to deliver more detailed messages regarding what failed. To alter this level, open the BootP/TFTP server and select Options | Verbose Level | Debug. When the TFTP request is received, the TFTP server should make a note of any problems that occur (or indicate that the transfer was successful, if there were no problems). One of the most common errors that is received during an upgrade failure is Can't Open Local File. This indicates that the TFTP server received the TFTP request and looked for the file requested in its root directory, but could not find it. This may occur because the file was misspelled in SpeedView, or it may indicate some confusion as to where the file should be. To verify the root directory or change it to something else, open the win.ini file and scroll down to the section headed [BPTFTP]:

```
[BPTFTP]
ROOTDIR=e:\SpeedView
Editor=NOTEPAD.EXE
BootpFile=e:\SpeedView\BPTFTP\BOOTPTAB.TXT
Verbose=Summary
ProfileDir=e:\SpeedView\BPTFTP\
```

ROOTDIR is the directory where the TFTP server expects to find the image file. If this is altered, the PC does not have to be rebooted for the change to take effect; simply close the TFTP server and relaunch it.

## Check the Primary and Secondary IP Addresses

ATMSpeed MCPs which were manufactured more recently began implementing a single RJ-45 Ethernet connector on the front panel. This connection is meant to provide a way to contact the switch via Ethernet if the Centillion is fully loaded with ATMSpeed modules. The Centillion uses two IP addresses in this case: the primary IP address, which is used to communicate with the device through the Ethernet, token ring, and ATM host cards, and the secondary IP address, which is associated with the ATMSpeed MCP single Ethernet port. Although you can have both a primary and secondary IP address assigned to a single MCP, these IP addresses must be on different networks or subnets; otherwise, neither address will be reachable.

## The Emergency Download Procedure

Image corruption—whether the result of a failed upgrade or configuration upload, a power failure, or a sudden power surge—may cause corruption and prevent SpeedView from reaching the unit. In some cases, the C100/C50/C20/5000BH is able to attempt a recovery by requesting an emergency download. This will likely result in the configuration being lost, but the MCP is at least recoverable, and if a you have a backup copy of the configuration, you can simply reload it after the recovery is complete.

An emergency download can only be accomplished using a serial connection, so if the switch is not responding to SpeedView via SNMP, the connection type will need to be altered in the Preferences window before an emergency download can be attempted. No dialog box appears to indicate that an emergency download is being requested; select Map | Discover from the main SpeedView window. A small status window appears, indicating that SpeedView is attempting to contact the switch. If an emergency download is necessary, SpeedView will be unable to discover the unit. Let the discovery process time out, and then select the Switch option. At this point, if an emergency download is possible, the option Download Software (Serial) will no longer be grayed out, as it normally would be. Select it and then proceed with the upgrade procedure. A serial image upgrade can take anywhere from 10 to 15 minutes.

### Last Reset Cause Codes

In the event of a reset, SpeedView makes a note of the last reset cause. If a reset has taken place, or you suspect that a reset took place during off hours but aren't sure, the last reset cause code will be reported in the SpeedView Statistics window. This can be accessed by highlighting the appropriate switch and then selecting Switch | Statistics from the main SpeedView window. From there, select the System tab.

The SpeedView reset codes are listed in Table B-2.

## Making Configuration Changes via SpeedView

After a connection with the switch is established with SpeedView, the specific configuration can take place. To begin, do a map discovery by selecting Map | Discovery, and then highlight the switch icon you want to configure, and select Switch | Configure. Selecting these options opens the SpeedView configuration utility, where the system- and module-specific configurations are set.

| Code | Name | Description |
|------|------|-------------|
| 0 | Power On Reset | The last reset was caused by a chassis power on |
| 1 | Normal Operation | The switch is running normally after a power on |
| 2 | Watch Dog Reset | The switch was last reset due to a Watch Dog timeout |
| 3 | CLI Reset | The switch was reset from the CLI **reset** command |
| 4 | CLI Set Default | The switch was set to factory defaults from the CLI |
| 5 | SpeedView Reset | The switch was reset serially from SpeedView |
| 6 | SNMP Reset | The SNMP s5AgInfoReboot object caused a reset |
| 7 | SNMP Set Default | The switch was set to factory default via SpeedView using SNMP |
| 8 | TFTP Configuration Reset | A configuration was downloaded to the switch using TFTP and was reset to commit the change |
| 10 | Address error exception | Software crash |

**Table B-2.**  *Last Reset Cause Codes in SpeedView*

When a new switch is brought up in configuration mode for the first time, it is at its factory default settings and displays the blank configuration template. At this point, you can either configure the switch dynamically or introduce a saved configuration.

## Saving and Loading Configuration Files

If a Centillion switch is being configured for the first time, and the configuration already exists (either because the configuration was done offline, or because the MCP being configured is a replacement and the configuration is already saved), then the switch must still be brought up in configuration mode, to load the existing configuration from the SpeedView station to the switch. There are two basic methods for doing this:

- Bring up the switch in configuration mode by discovering the switch, highlighting the icon, and then selecting Switch | Configure. Once in configuration mode, select File | Load Configuration and then select the appropriate CFG file. This opens the new configuration for viewing, but does not apply the configuration to the switch. To actually commit the loaded configuration to the switch, select Switch | Download Configuration, which commits the loaded configuration to the switch's flash memory.

- Highlight the switch icon in the main SpeedView window and then select Switch | TFTP Download Configuration.

In either case, once the configuration download is complete, you are prompted to reset the switch so that the changes take effect.

## Dynamic Configuration

Rather than introduce an existing configuration to the Centillion switch, you can simply make the configuration changes to the default configuration template that is brought up the first time the switch is configured. After you make the changes, you can load the new configuration onto the switch by selecting Switch | Download Configuration.

Certain aspects of the SpeedView configuration take effect dynamically, while others require a reset of the switch. If a reset is required, SpeedView will prompt you for the reset by bringing up a dialogue box asking if you wish to reset the switch now. You will have the option to cancel out of this if you do not wish to reset the switch, however, configuration changes made prior to canceling out of a reset will be lost.

As a general rule, if a Centillion configuration change must be done, it is a good idea to plan on a switch reset.

## Offline Configuration

You can also make configuration changes offline, by opening an existing configuration (or blank configuration template) in SpeedView's configuration mode. To do this, from the main SpeedView window, select File | Offline Configure. When prompted, browse for or enter the filename of the configuration file you want to alter. This opens the file in configuration mode, where you can manipulate it without any danger of inadvertently introducing a dynamic configuration change to a production switch.

## Adding and Removing Modules

When doing an offline configuration, the default configuration template (or an existing configuration template) may need to have the chassis contents altered. This can be done in an offline configuration by selecting Configure | Add/Remove Module from the main configuration window (this option can be selected during a dynamic configuration as well, although SpeedView automatically detects new modules in a live configuration, so this option is superfluous in dynamic mode).

## SpeedView Module Indications

As stated in the previous section, SpeedView is able to detect changes between an existing configuration file and the actual configuration of the Centillion switch. For example, if a new module is added to an existing production switch, SpeedView makes a note of the new module when the switch is brought up in configuration mode. Likewise, if modules are removed, SpeedView will note the discrepancy.

SpeedView marks any differences between the existing configuration and the saved configuration when it displays the unit in configuration mode. For instance, if a C100 chassis contains an ATMSpeed MCP and three four-port ATMSpeed host cards at the time its configuration is saved, and then a 16-port EtherSpeed card is added to the chassis without any alteration to the existing configuration, the next time the switch is brought up in configuration mode, the EtherSpeed card will be displayed in the appropriate slot, but will be designated as a new addition, by bracketing the module name in asterisks, such as *M1-ENET-16*. The module will retain this designation until the configuration is loaded onto the switch, indicating that the administrator has noted the change and approved it.

Likewise, a new module can be added through SpeedView (usually in an offline configuration). When a new module is added in SpeedView (for instance, a four-port ATMSpeed host card), it is bracketed <M1-ATM-4>, which indicates that a new four-port ATMSpeed host card was added to slot 1 through SpeedView, but that this change has not been loaded onto the switch yet.

# Viewing Statistics

The second portion of the SpeedView utility involves statistic gathering. While each of these statistics and more can be gathered through a series of commands from the CLI (covered in the chapters pertaining to the configuration of various technologies on the Centillion platform), you can access a simple, easy-to-interpret statistics display by highlighting the switch you want to observe, and then selecting Switch | Statistics from the main SpeedView window. This opens the Statistics window, where the statistics are displayed. Statistics for Ethernet, token ring, and ATM can be found there.

# General Statistics

A variety of general system statistics are available from the System tab:

- **System**   Indicates the user-assigned name given to the system.
- **Status**   Indicates the operational status of the switch; either Up or Down.
- **Model**   Indicates the model number of the switch.
- **Serial Number**   Indicates the serial number of the switch.
- **Power Supply**   Indicates the number of power supplies residing in the switch.
- **MAC Address**   Indicates the MAC address of the switch.
- **Modules/Ports**   Indicates the number of modules and their associated ports installed in the switch.
- **SW Version**   Indicates the current operational run-time image.

## Status Enquiry Timer

The Status Enquiry portion of the System tab refers to ATM STATUS_ENQUIRY messages and their associated STATUS message responses. The following statistics can be obtained from this portion of the System tab:

- **Point-to-Point Calls**   Indicates the number of point-to-point calls currently in the switch status enquiry queue.
- **Sent Inquiries**   Indicates the number of STATUS_ENQUIRY messages sent.
- **Number of Retries**   Indicates the number of STATUS_ENQUIRY messages that were resent as a result of receiving no STATUS message in response.
- **Queue Size**   Indicates the size of the status enquiry queue.
- **Active Parties**   Indicates the number of active parties in the status enquiry queue, including point-to-multipoint calls.
- **Confirmations Received**   Indicates the number of STATUS messages received in response to STATUS_ENQUIRY messages sent.
- **Timeouts**   Indicates the number of instances where a STATUS_ENQUIRY message was sent, and no STATUS message was received in response before the timeout period. When this condition occurs, a RESTART message is sent, and the entire line is cleared of calls.
- **Calls Cleared**   Indicates the number of calls that have been cleared by a STATUS_ENQUIRY.

# Last Reset Cause

Upon a reset, SpeedView makes a note of the last reset reason, as well as other information related to the system reset. The following information can be viewed:

APPENDIXES

- **Last Reset EPC**   Indicates the specific exception program counter (EPC) code associated with the last time the device reset. The EPC gives a pointer to the routine that was running at the time the reset took place.

- **Last Reset Virtual Address**   Indicates the virtual address associated with the last reset.

- **Last Reset Cause**   Indicates the event associated with the last reset; this may indicate anything from an administrative reset (the device was reset from SpeedView or the CLI) to an image crash. A complete set of reset cause codes are provided earlier in this chapter, in Table B-2.

- **Last Reset Timestamp**   Indicates the time at which the last reset took place.

## Switching Mode Statistics

The Switching Mode tab indicates information regarding the switching mode associated with both Ethernet and token ring bridge groups, or Spanning Tree Group (STG)/VLAN combinations (in code version 4.0 or higher). The following information is available:

- **Switching Mode**   These two fields indicate the switching mode associated with the selected STG or bridge group. This information will indicate both the switching mode (transparent bridging, source route bridging, and so forth) as well as the Spanning Tree mode (IEEE Spanning Tree, IBM Spanning Tree, and so forth).

- **Spanning Tree Group**   Indicates the STG being viewed (earlier versions of SpeedView may indicate a bridge group). The specific group to view can be selected from the drop-down menu.

- **Bridge ID**   Indicates the Spanning Tree Group ID. The value is generated by SpeedView by using the STG priority and the switch's MAC address.

- **Root Bridge ID**   Indicates the MAC address of the device acting as root bridge for the selected STG.

- **Hello Time**   Indicates the interval (in seconds) between the transmission of Bridge Protocol Data Units (BPDUs) for the specified STG.

- **Max Age**   Indicates the amount of time (in seconds) that can pass without receiving a BPDU from a remote device before that device is considered down and a Spanning Tree topology change is indicated. This value is set by the root bridge.

- **Fwd Delay**   Indicates the forward delay for the specified STG; this indicates the delay (in seconds) between a Spanning Tree interface initializing and actually forwarding data. All devices should have assessed the spanning tree topology before forwarding.

- **Priority**   Indicates the priority of the switch for the selected STG. This value is used during the root bridge election. A lower value is considered to be a higher priority.

- **Bridge Num**   Indicates a Token Ring source-route-bridging-specific value, indicating the Bridge ID associated with the switch. This value is placed in the Routing Information Field (RIF) when source routing is being used. The bridge number is in hex.

## Ring and Segment Statistics

Information regarding token ring rings and virtual rings can be viewed from the Rings/Segments tab. Information is displayed on a port-by-port basis, in blocks of four. If you want to view additional ports, click the Next button. The following token ring statistics are available:

- **Rings/Segments**   Indicates the number of rings configured on the switch.

- **(V)Ring/Seg Number (hex)**   Indicate the different ring numbers and virtual ring numbers configured on the switch. A VRing refers to the Centillion's proprietary feature whereby multiple rings in a source-route bridging (SRB) environment that share the same number on the same switch are considered a single ring. The separate rings are transparently bridged between.

- **Spanning Tree Group Number**   Indicates the STG to which the ring belongs (or may indicate a bridge group in pre-4.0 SpeedView).

- **Module**   Indicates the module on which the specified ring resides.

- **Ports**   Indicates the ports on which the individual rings are configured. You can view additional ports by clicking the More Ports button.

## Static Station Statistics

Static stations, both Ethernet and token ring, can be viewed from the Static Stations tab. This displays information regarding the individual static station entries:

- **MAC Address**   Indicate the different MAC addresses associated with the static stations.

- **Module**   Indicate the different modules on which the individual static stations reside.

- **Port**   Indicate the different ports on which the individual static stations reside.

- **Static**   Indicates the MAC address entry type (static).

# ATM PVC Statistics

The ATM PVC tab provides statistics regarding Centillion CLCs (PVCs), as well as soft permanent virtual circuit (SPVC) information in SpeedView version 4.0 or greater. The following PVC information is available.

APPENDIXES

## Inter Switch PVC Status

The Inter Switch PVC status portion of the ATM PVC tab provides information regarding the current operational state of each PVC configured on the switch, as well as statistical information for each PVC. The following information is available for ATM PVCs:

- **ATM LAN ID**   Indicates the ATM LAN identifier for the specified PVC.
- **Circuit ID**   Indicates the unique circuit identifier for the specified PVC. This value is used to uniquely identify each PVC circuit from end to end.
- **FrameFwd**   Indicates the current forwarding state of each PVC. The state is indicated as either On or Off.
- **RemotePVC**   Indicates the current state of the remote PVC as either Up or Down. A value of Up means the PVC was successfully established.
- **RemoteMAC**   Indicates the MAC address of the switch on which the remote end of the PVC resides. Once the PVC establishment is successful, and the PVC is up and forwarding, the remote MAC address will be registered.

## SPVC Status/Statistics

Beginning with code version 4.0, soft PVC support was added to the Centillion. The SPVC operational status can be viewed from the ATM PVC tab:

- **Circuit ID**   Indicates the unique circuit identifier for the specified SPVC.
- **Last Release**   Indicates the reason for the last SPVC release.
- **Last Release Diag**   Indicates the value of the first 8 bytes of diagnostic information contained in the last release message for the specified SPVC.
- **Oper Status**   Indicates the current operational status of the specified SPVC. This will indicate either Active or Other.
- **Retry Timer**   Indicates the amount of time (in seconds) that can elapse without an SPVC being successfully established before it is considered to have failed and is retried.
- **Retry Failures**   Indicates the number of times an SPVC has failed while attempting to establish a connection with the destination border switch.
- **SPVC Call Failures**   Indicates the number of failed call attempts made while attempting to establish the specified SPVC.
- **Currently Failing SPVCs**   Indicates all SPVCs that have been configured, but have not successfully been established.

## SPVC Fails

The SPVC Fails portion of the ATM PVC tab indicates information regarding which SPVC circuits are experiencing failures (if any):

- **Circuit ID**   Indicates the unique circuit identifier for the failed SPVC.
- **Time Stamp**   Indicates when the failure occurred.

## IP Multicast Statistics

Beginning with code version 3.1, IGMP information can be obtained via SpeedView by accessing the IP Multicast tab:

- **IGMP Router Port List**   Has two tables associated with it that indicate all statically configured IGMP router ports (ports that lead to, or to which are attached, an IGMP router), as well as any that were learned dynamically (due to the receipt of IGMP Host Queries).
- **IGMP Group Address List**   Has two tables associated with it that indicate the statically configured IGMP multicast group addresses, which are either included or excluded (viewed by selecting either the Included or Excluded tabs), and a list of dynamically learned IGMP multicast group addresses.

## IGMP Timers

The IGMP timers indicate query, membership, and robustness information for the IGMP multicast groups. The following information is available:

- **Query Interval**   Indicates the IGMP Query Interval associated with the group.
- **Query Response Interval**   Indicates the expected Query Response Interval (responses to the IGMP queries).
- **Robustness**   Indicates the robustness value for the specified group. The robustness value indicates the packet loss tolerance associated with the group.
- **Membership Port Prune Interval**   Indicates the amount of time (in seconds) that can pass without a port receiving any IGMP reports before the port is removed (pruned) from the IGMP membership.
- **Router Port Prune Interval**   Indicates the amount of time (in seconds) that can pass without a port receiving any queries from its associated IGMP router before that router is removed (pruned).

## MPOA Client State

Beginning with code version 4.0, Multi-Protocol Over ATM support was added to the Centillion, when running Advanced code. When running MPOA, the Centillion switch supports an MPOA Client (MPC). MPC statistics can be viewed from the MPOA Client tab:

- **Actual State**  Indicates the current operational state of the resident MPC. This field will read either Up or Down.

- **Config Mode**  Indicates the resident MPC's configuration method; Automatic, meaning it obtains its configuration information from a LAN Emulation Configuration Server, or Manual, meaning the configuration information is manually configured by the administrator.

- **Setup Frame Time**  Used to define the threshold that must be reached before the MPC attempts to establish an MPOA shortcut. This value is used in conjunction with the Setup Frame Count value, the threshold being defined as the MPC receiving the Setup Frame Count number of frames within the Setup Frame Time.

- **Retry Time Max**  Indicates the maximum amount of time the resident MPC will wait (in seconds) for a reply to an outstanding request before it assumes the procedure to have failed.

- **Discontinuity Time**  Used in the event that either the MPC or its MPS reinitializes. Should this occur, the MPC will obtain a new value for this field to show that contact was lost to the MPS. This is used as an indicator that connection was lost between the MPC and MPS.

- **Setup Frame Count**  Define the threshold that must be reached before the MPC attempts to establish an MPOA shortcut. This value is used in conjunction with the Setup Frame Time, the threshold being defined as the MPC receiving a number of packets between the same source and destination IP address equal to the Setup Frame Count, within the amount of time (in seconds) defined by the Setup Frame Time.

- **Initial Retry Time**  Indicates the amount of time (in seconds) that an MPC waits after sending a Resolution Request, without receiving a Resolution Reply, before it reissues another Resolution Request.

- **Hold Down Time**  Indicates the minimum amount of time the MPC waits after a series of failed Resolution Requests before it restarts the resolution process.

- **Ctrl ATM Addr**  Indicates the control ATM address of the specified MPC; this address is used as the ATM address for the MPC when control connections (such as those to the MPC's MPS) are being established.

- **Data ATM Addr(s)**  Indicates the data ATM address(es) associated with the specified MPC. These addresses are used when establishing the actual MPOA shortcuts, and are associated with the individual host cards.

## MPOA Client Statistics

The MPOA Client statistics are obtained by clicking the MPOA Client Statistics button located on the MPOA Client tab of the Statistics window in SpeedView. The following MPC statistics are recorded:

- **IngressCacheTxTotalPackets**   Indicates the total number of ingress cache packets transmitted by the MPC.

- **EgressCacheTxTotalPackets**   Indicates the total number of egress cache packets transmitted by the MPC.

- **TxMpoaResolveRequest**   Indicates the number of MPOA Resolution Requests sent by the specified MPC.

- **RxMpoaResolveReplyAcks**   Indicates the number of MPOA Resolution Replies received by the MPC in response to an MPOA Resolution Request.

- **RxMpoaResolveReplyInsufECResources**   Indicates the number of times an MPOA Resolution Reply was received indicating that an egress cache entry could not be imposed on the Egress MPC due to a lack of resources on the Egress MPC.

- **RxMpoaResolveReplyInsufSCResources**   Indicates the number of times an MPOA Resolution Reply was received indicating that a shortcut could not be established with the Egress MPC due to a lack of resources on the Egress MPC.

- **RxMpoaResolveReplyInsufEitherResources**   Indicates the number of times a Resolution Request failed either because an egress cache entry could not be made on the Egress MPC due to a lack of resources or because the MPC did not have the resources to accept a shortcut (this statistic has a different MPOA code associated with it that does not distinguish between the two events).

- **RxMpoaResolveReplyUnsupportedInetProt**   Indicates the number of MPOA resolution failures that failed because the internetworking layer protocol being used is not supported. For example, currently, the Centillion MPCs support IPv4 only, and can't assist in resolving an IPX address.

- **RxMpoaResolveReplyUnspecifiedOther**   Indicates the number of MPOA Resolution Replies received with a failure code indicating Unspecified/Other.

- **RxMpoaImpRequest**   Indicates the number of MPOA Cache Imposition Requests received by the MPC from its MPS.

- **TxMpoaImpReplyAcks**   Indicates the number of MPOA Cache Imposition Replies sent back to the MPC's MPS in response to an MPOA Cache Imposition Request.

- **TxMpoaImpReplyInsufECResources**   Indicates the number of MPOA Cache Imposition Replies that were sent from the MPC indicating the imposed information could not be cached due to a lack of resources.

- **TxMpoaImpReplyInsufSCResources** Indicates the number of MPOA Cache Imposition Replies that were sent from the MPC indicating an incoming MPOA shortcut can't be accepted due to a lack of resources.

- **TxMpoaImpReplyInsufEitherResources** Indicates the number of MPOA Cache Imposition Replies that were sent from the MPC with a failure code indicating either a cache imposition could not be accepted due to a lack of resources, or a shortcut could not be accepted due to a lack of resources. This is a valid error code but does not specify which of the two events occurred.

- **TxMpoaImpReplyUnsupportedInetProt** Indicates the number of MPOA Cache Imposition Replies that were sent from the MPC indicating the cache information could not be accepted because it is related to an internetworking protocol that the MPC does not support. For instance, the MPS attempted to impose IPX header information on an MPC that supports IP only.

- **TxMpoaImpReplyUnsupportedMacEncaps** Indicates the number of MPOA Cache Imposition Replies that were sent from the MPC indicating the MAC layer encapsulation used is not supported by the MPC.

- **TxMpoaImpReplyUnspecifiedOther** Indicates the number of MPOA Cache Imposition Replies that were sent from the MPC with a code of Unspecified/Other.

- **TxMpoaEgressCachePurgeRequest** Indicates the number of MPOA Egress Cache Purge Requests transmitted by the MPC.

- **RxMpoaEgressCachePurgeReplies** Indicates the number of MPOA Egress Cache Purge Replies received by the MPC in response to a transmitted MPOA Egress Cache Purge Request.

- **RxMpoaKeepAlives** Indicates the number of MPOA Keep-Alive messages received by the MPC.

- **RxMpoaTriggers** Indicates the number of MPOA Trigger messages received by the MPC from the MPS.

- **RxMpoaDataPlanePurges** Indicates the number of MPOA Data Plane Purges received by the MPC.

- **TxMpoaDataPlanePurges** Indicates the number of MPOA Data Plane Purges transmitted by the MPC.

- **RxNhrpPurgeRequest** Indicates the number of Next Hop Resolution Protocol (NHRP) Purge Requests received by the MPC.

- **TxNhrpPurgeReplies** Indicates the number of NHRP Purge Replies transmitted by the MPC in response to an NHRP Purge Request.

- **RxErrUnrecognizedExtensions** Indicates the number of packets received by the MPC that had an error code indicating the extensions were not recognized.

- **RxErrLoopDetected**   Indicates the number of packets received by the MPC with an error code associated indicating a loop was detected on the network.

- **RxErrProtoAddrUnreachables**   Indicates the number of packets received by the MPC indicating that the internetworking destination address was not reachable via an MPOA shortcut and so no shortcut was initiated.

- **RxErrProtoErrors**   Indicates the number of packets received by the MPC with an error code indicating there were protocol errors.

- **RxErrSduSizeExceeds**   Indicates the number of packets received by the MPC with an error code indicating that the service data unit (SDU) size was exceeded.

- **RxErrInvalidExtensions**   Indicates the number of packets received by the MPC with an error code indicating invalid extensions.

- **RxErrInvalidReplies**   Indicates the number of replies to specific request messages that were incorrect.

- **RxErrAuthenticationFailures**   Indicates the number of packets received by the MPC with an error code indicating that an authentication failure took place.

- **RxErrHopCountExceeds**   Indicates the number of packets received by the MPC with an error code indicating the maximum hop count was exceeded.

## MPOA Client MPS ATM Addr Info

Clicking the MPOA Client MPS ATM Addr Info button at the base of the MPOA Client tab opens a smaller window labeled MPOA MPS ATM Addresses. This window consists of a single table, where each known MPS ATM address is listed. Commonly, this consists of a single address, but may consist of more.

## MPOA Client MPS MAC Addr Info

Clicking the MPOA Client MPS MAC Addr Info button at the base of the MPOA Client tab opens a smaller window, referred to as the MPOA Client MPS Information window. This window has a single table as well, which indicates the MAC-layer information associated with all known MPSs.

## Token Ring Port Statistics

Separate from the token ring segment/ring information, which is associated with individual ports, the actual physical port information can be viewed from the individual tabs associated with the TokenSpeed modules:

- **State**   Indicates the current operational state of the port; reads either Up or Down.

- **MAC Address**   Indicates the hardware MAC address associated with the token ring port.

- **Ring Num**  Indicates the ring number (in hex) associated with the specified token ring port. This is only of relevance in a source-route bridging or source-route transparent environment.

- **Speed**  Indicates the ring speed associated with the token ring port.

- **Connection**  Indicates the connection type associated with the token ring port; may be either Station, if the port is connected to a concentrator, Hub, if the port is connected to a station or server, or RI/RO.

- **Bridging**  Indicates the token ring switching mode; source route bridging, source route transparent, or transparent bridging.

- **Spanning Tree Group**  Indicates the STG (or bridge group, depending on the code version) associated with the specified port.

- **Bridge Port Priority**  Indicates the IEEE Spanning Tree port priority when utilizing a switching mode of either source-route transparent or transparent bridging.

- **Path Cost/Frame fwding/Hop count lim/SR brdcasting**  Indicates the port's current Spanning Tree parameters, if Spanning Tree is being used.

- **Frame count**  Indicates the number of frames that have passed over the specified port (both received and transmitted).

- **Frames xmit**  Indicates the number of frames that have been transmitted on the specified port.

- **Frames recv**  Indicates the number of frames that have been received on the specified port.

- **Mcsts xmit**  Indicates the number of multicast frames that have been transmitted on the specified port.

- **Mcsts recv**  Indicates the number of multicast frames that have been received on the specified port.

- **Error count**  Indicates the number of errors that have occurred on the specified port.

## Token Ring Errors

A list of Token Ring errors are also available in the Token Ring Port Statistics window; a list of specific token ring errors, their meanings, and possible causes can be found in Appendix C.

## ATM Port Statistics

ATM port statistics can also be viewed from the tabs associated with the individual ATMSpeed modules installed in the Centillion. The following statistics are available:

- **State** Indicates the current operational state of the ATM port; reads either Up or Down.

- **Speed** Indicates the operational speed of the ATM port. Depending on the type of connector, this may read 155Mbps (OC-3), 622Mbps (OC-12), or 45Mbps (DS-3).

- **Connection** Indicates the connection type for the port (OC-3, OC-12, or DS-3).

- **Frame Mode** Indicates the framing mode configured on the specified ATM port. May be SONET (Synchronous Optical Network), or SDH (Synchronous Digital Hierarchy), which is more commonly used in Europe.

- **Signal Detected** Indicates whether or not a valid SDH or SONET framing signal is detected on the ATM port. If no valid signal is detected, this reads Off.

- **Cells xmit** Indicates the number of cells transmitted on the specified ATM port.

- **Cells recv** Indicates the number of cells received on the specified ATM port.

- **Xmit cong errs** Indicates the number of cells that were slated for transmission, but that were clipped because there was no more room in the transmit buffer.

- **Rcv errs** Indicates the number of receive errors on the specified port. Not an error in and of itself, this counter is a culmination of the Header CRC errors and Unknown VPI/VCI errors.

- **Hdr CRC errs** Indicates the number of cell header CRCs (cyclic redundancy checks) that have failed, meaning the cell headers are not of the appropriate length. This could be caused by line corruption or signaling problems. Header CRC errors invalidate the affected cells.

- **Unknown** Indicates the number of unknown VPI/VCI errors received on the specified ATM port. In a PVC environment, this indicates an incoming PVC for which the receiving port has no record (if, for instance, one side of the link is configured for VPI/VCI pair 0/88, and the other side is configured for 0/81). In a LANE environment, these errors should not increment. If they do, it is generally a sign that one side of an SVC is being torn down, and the other side is not releasing the resources. In this scenario, the side that did release the SVC will attempt to reuse the VPI/VCI pair, only to have the remote side that did not release the resources refuse the call, stating the VPI/VCI pair is already in use. This will be recorded as an unknown VPI/VCI error.

- **Total LCV** Indicates the number of line coding violations detected on the specified ATM port. This error is associated with DS-3 interfaces only, and is recorded in 24-hour intervals.

- **Total PCV** Indicates the number of P-bit coding violations detected on the specified ATM port. This error is associated with DS-3 interfaces only, and is recorded in 24-hour intervals.

- **Total CCV**   Indicates the number of C-bit coding violations detected on the specified ATM port. This error is associated with DS-3 interfaces only, and is recorded in 24-hour intervals.

- **LOF Event**   Indicates a loss of frame on the specified ATM port. The value returned in this case will be a 1 or 2, where 1 indicates a loss of frame is occurring currently, and 2 indicates a valid signal.

- **LCD**   Indicates a cell delineation event on the specified ATM port. The value returned will be a 1 or 2, where 1 indicates a cell delineation event and a 2 indicated no LCD.

- **Received RAI**   Indicates a remote alarm was received on the specified ATM port.

- **Received AIS**   Indicates an AIS failure state is being received on the specified ATM port.

- **LOF**   Indicates a loss of frame on the specified ATM port; this generally occurs when signaling is lost on the port.

- **LOS**   Indicates a loss of signal on the specified ATM port; this generally occurs when signaling is lost on the port.

- **LBS**   Indicates the received signal is being looped back to the source.

- **SectionLOS**   Indicates a SONET section loss of signal detected on the specified port.

- **SectionLOF**   Indicates a SONET section loss of frame detected on the specified port.

- **LineAIS**   Indicates a SONET line alarm detected on the specified port.

- **LineRDI**   Indicates a SONET line remote detect indication on the specified port.

- **PathLOP**   Indicates a SONET path loss of pointer detected on the specified port.

- **PathAIS**   Indicates a SONET path alarm indication detected on the specified port.

- **PathRDI**   Indicates a SONET path remote detect indication received on the specified port.

- **SecBip8Errs**   Indicates the number of STS-3(c) frames received with BIP-8 errors.

## Ethernet Port Statistics

Ethernet port statistics can be viewed from SpeedView by selecting the tabs associated with the individual EtherSpeed host cards installed in the chassis. The following statistics are available:

- **State**   Indicates the current operational state of the specified port.
- **MAC Address**   Indicates the hardware MAC address associated with the specified port.
- **Speed**   Indicates the speed of the specified port (10Mbps/100Mbps).
- **PMD Type**   Indicates the PMD type of the port, such as 10BaseT, 100BaseT, 10Base-FX, and so forth.
- **Bridging**   Indicates the spanning tree mode associated with the specified port.
- **Spanning Tree Group/Brdge port priority/Path Cost/Frame fwding**   Indicate the STG (or bridge group, depending on the code version) associated with the port, as well as its Spanning Tree bridge port priority, and path cost if Spanning Tree is being used. Lastly, the Spanning Tree forwarding state is indicated (forwarding/blocking).
- **Octet count/Octet recv/Octet xmit/Frame Count**   Indicates the total octet count associated with the port, a breakdown of octets transmitted and received, and the total frame count.
- **Ucsts xmit/Ucsts recv/Mcsts xmit/Mcsts recv**   Indicates the number of packets received and transmitted by the specified port, broken down by unicasts received and transmitted, and multicasts received and transmitted.
- **Single colls**   Indicates the number of single collisions that have been detected on the specified ports. Ethernet collisions occur when multiple stations attempt to transmit simultaneously within the same collision domain.
- **Error count**   Indicates the number of errors detected on the specified port.
- **Xmit errs**   Indicates the number of transmit errors detected on the specified port.
- **Recv errs**   Indicates the number of receive errors detected on the specified port.
- **Align errs**   Indicates the number of alignment errors detected on the specified port. Alignment errors occur when a frame is received that does not contain the correct number of octets, and has failed its FCS check (described next). Alignment errors (especially when incrementing in conjunction with FCS errors) often indicates a mismatched duplex setting.
- **FCS errs**   Indicates the number of frame check sequence (FCS) errors detected on the specified port. FCS errors occur when a frame does not pass its frame check sequence, indicating the packet is no longer the same length that it was upon initial transmission. This often indicates a bad transmitter, a faulty cable, or a mismatched duplex setting.
- **Over size frm**   Indicates the number of frames received on the specified port that exceeded the maximum Ethernet frame length (1,500 bytes plus overhead). This can indicate a bad transmitter. Frames that have been fitted with 802.1Q

frame tags also exceed the maximum frame length, and may be interpreted as oversized frames if received on a port that does not support frame tagging.

- **Carrier sense** Indicates the number of carrier sense errors detected on the port. A carrier sense error indicates that the port temporarily lost carrier signal on the connected cable. This may indicate a remote port failure or cable failure.

- **Intl Mac xmit errs** Indicates the number of frames that were lost due to an internal MAC sublayer transmit error.

- **Intl Mac recv** Indicates the number of frames that were lost due to an internal MAC sublayer receive error.

- **Hub Port** Indicates the current operational state of a hub port; applies only to the hub ports residing on a 100Mbps Ethernet segment switch module.

*The statistics in the Statistics window do not update themselves automatically. To update the statistics through SpeedView, the option Statistics | Update must be selected from the main Statistics window.*

# The Complete Reference

Nortel Networks

# Appendix C

## Token Ring Errors

Token Ring errors can be broken down into three major categories; soft-isolating errors, soft-nonisolating errors, and hard errors.

# Soft-Isolating Errors

*Soft-isolating* errors are used to identify the transmitter, the receiver, and the cables and other devices that may lie between them. These are counted by the ""acted-on station"" only, because it will then flip the E (error) bit in the ED (ending delimiter) of the frame, thus preventing all other stations from recording the same error. This helps narrow down the offender, or source, of the error.

The fault domain, which defines where an error may have occurred, of a soft-isolating error consists basically of the station reporting the fault, the nearest active upstream neighbor (NAUN) of that station, and the physical layer components between the two of them. The three types of soft-isolating errors are line errors, burst errors, and A/C errors, and are outlined here:

| Error Type | Possible Cause | Response | Possible Source |
|---|---|---|---|
| Line | Token code violation detected by the station FCS error detected by the station; nondata bit detected between SD and ED fields | Flip the error detected bit to 1 so that the error can be isolated | A station entered or left the ring (most common cause); station receiver problem; NAUN transmitter failure; dirty line between station seeing the error and its NAUN |
| Burst | No clocking signals at a station's receiver; absence of any bit stream transitions for 5 half-bit times | Transitions are induced, error is reported, and stations downstream see transitions | A station entered or left the ring (again, the most common cause); station receiver problem NAUN transmitter failure; faulty cable |
| A/C | Two successive AMP frames are received with the A (address recognized) and C (copy) bits set at 0 | The A/C error counter goes up, the frame is fixed, and an error report is generated | The NAUN of the reporting station can't, for whatever reason, set the A bit and frame copied bit as they should whenever they receive an AMP frame; most likely cause is a bad transmitter upstream |

Line errors are normal in token ring, and are seen as stations leave and enter the ring. They are not "errors" in the true sense of the word, and are mostly informational. Burst errors may be interpreted in a similar way as line errors; they are normal, and most often caused by stations leaving and entering the active ring.

## Soft-Nonisolating Errors

Soft-isolating errors often point either to the NAUN or to physical layer problems. With soft-nonisolating errors, however, what actually caused the error isn't always as clear. These errors can still be valuable indicators, but generally require more investigation on the part of the administrator.

The types of soft-nonisolating errors are lost frame errors, receive congestion errors, frame copied errors, and token errors. These are outlined in this table:

| Error Type | Possible Cause | Response | Possible Source |
|---|---|---|---|
| Lost frame | Station TRR timer expires before the receipt of the ED of the frame transmitted (the frame was sent out on the ring, and never came back) | The lost frame counter is incremented, a report is generated, and the AM sees a token error | A burst or line error wiped out the ED of the frame; adapter failure |
| Receive congestion | A station sees that a frame is destined for it, but can't copy the frame because its buffer is full | The address recognized bit is set to 1, but the frame copied bit remains at 0; the error counter is incremented | The station can't maintain the current traffic rate |
| Frame copied | A station sees a frame come in with its address as the destination address (DA), but the address recognized bit has already been flipped | The frame copied error is incremented | A duplicate MAC address upstream resides on the ring |

| Error Type | Possible Cause | Response | Possible Source |
|---|---|---|---|
| Token | The AM sees a nonzero priority token (one that has given a station special priority) with the M bit set to 1; the AM sees a Data or MAC frame with the M bit equal to 1 (normally, this happens only after it passes the AM); the AM sees no token or frame in 10 milliseconds; the starting delimiter of a token OR frame is invalid | The token error counter increments and ring purge is initiated | A station leaving or joining the ring corrupted the token as it did so; line noise disintegrated the token |

## Hard Errors

Hard errors are hardware related. Stations are capable of detecting the following anomalies: wire faults, frequency errors, and ring signal loss. These are outlined in this table:

| Error Type | Possible Cause | Response | Possible Source |
|---|---|---|---|
| Wire fault | The DC current on the twisted pair is too high or too low for more than five seconds | The lobe wire fault bit of the ring status register is set and the station deinserts | Line shorted to ground |
| Frequency | The frequency of the incoming signal differs by more than 0.6% from the local oscillator | Counter incremented and monitor contention begins | The receiving station's internal clock is malfunctioning; the AM or any station between this station and the AM could have an internal clock that is malfunctioning |

| Error Type | Possible Cause | Response | Possible Source |
|---|---|---|---|
| Ring signal loss | The incoming signal is too weak or is out of phase with the local oscillator | After 200 milliseconds, the station enters contention mode; beaconing is likely | Faulty ring cable or faulty wiring; concentrator, transmitter, or receiver malfunction |

## More Hardware-Related Errors

In addition to the Hard Errors described in the previous sections, there are some other hardware-related errors that may come up. A list of them, as well as their meanings and possible causes, follow.

## Internal Station Error

Internal station errors are caused by:

- The incoming signal is too weak
- The incoming signal is out of phase with the local oscillator

The following is the response:

- After 200 milliseconds, the station enters monitor contention; likely to be followed by beaconing (a signal loss detected after monitor contention will trigger this)

and the possible causes are

- Broken ring cable
- Faulty wiring in concentrator
- Malfunction in transmitter/receiver

## Abort Delimiter

Abort delimiter is caused by:

- The signal being transmitted is not recognized

The following is the response:

- Transmission is cut by sending an Abort Delimiter frame in midtransmit; abort delimiter transmitted is incremented by 1

and the possible causes are

- NAUN has faulty transmitter
- Bad cable between reporting station and NAUN

## Streaming Errors

Streaming errors are caused by:

- Bit: A node is generating a bit stream that is writing over actual data.
- Frame: A node is sending a stream of frames that may be tokens, abort delimiters, or even data frames.

The following is the response:

- Monitor contention is triggered, probably followed by beaconing

and the possible cause is

- Logic or timer error internal to the station

## Ring Purge

A *ring purge* is a type of token ring MAC frame that wipes away everything that is currently on the ring. A ring purge is initiated under the following three conditions:

- The AM sees an error condition on the ring, such as a lost token or frame, a token ring process that didn't complete properly, or the occurrence of an active timing problem.
- The T (Any_Token) timer expires.
- The AM sees the M (monitor) bit set to 1 (M=1) in the Access Control field of a frame; this basically states that the data is looping the ring multiple times without being stripped.

The Active Monitor transmits a ring purge frame and waits for it to come back. If it returns, the ring is assumed to have stabilized, all timers are reset, and the neighbor notification process is initiated to bring the ring back to a normal state. If the Ring Purge frame does not come back, the token-claiming process begins. A Ring Purge MAC frame does not require the token for transmission.

## Abort Sequence

If something goes wrong during transmission, the abort sequence may be issued. This basically means that a station obtained the token and began transmission, but then detected some sort of problem with itself while still sending. It sends an abort sequence and stops transmitting immediately.

# Index

## E

## O

# About the CD

The CD included with this book contains three main types of information: release notes, example configuration files, and example sniffer traces.

- **Release notes**   The release notes are contained in the Release Notes folder off the CD's root. Within this directory is a series of subdirectories for each technology: Routers, Accelar, Centillion, and Centillion 1x00. Within each subdirectory is another series of directories labeled in accordance with the code version the release notes pertain to. In most cases, these release notes are in .PDF format; however, some of the older router release notes are in plain text format.

- **Example configuration files**   The example configuration files are in binary format and may be brought up as an offline configuration in either Site Manager or SpeedView. Each file is in a directory off the Configs directory. Each subdirectory name reflects what the example is meant to show. A short text file is also included with each configuration to further explain what the files contain. These configuration files may also be uploaded to a switch or router for testing purposes, provided the code versions match and the chassis contents are the same. All Centillion configuration files are in 4.0 format. The router configuration files were all built using Site Manager version 7.10. Because there is no offline configuration mode associated with Device Manager (the management platform for the Accelar) at this time, no Accelar configuration files are included on the CD.

- **Example sniffer trace files**   The example sniffer trace files are located in the Sniffer directory. Each file has a corresponding text file explaining how the trace was taken. All files are ATM sniffer trace files in ATC format, and they should be readable by any sniffer package capable of interpreting these file formats.

# WARNING: BEFORE OPENING THE DISC PACKAGE, CAREFULLY READ THE TERMS AND CONDITIONS OF THE FOLLOWING COPYRIGHT STATEMENT AND LIMITED CD-ROM WARRANTY.

## Copyright Statement

This software is protected by both United States copyright law and international copyright treaty provision. Except as noted in the contents of the CD-ROM, you must treat this software just like a book. However, you may copy it into a computer to be used and you may make archival copies of the software for the sole purpose of backing up the software and protecting your investment from loss. By saying, "just like a book," The McGraw-Hill Companies, Inc. ("Osborne/McGraw-Hill") means, for example, that this software may be used by any number of people and may be freely moved from one computer location to another, so long as there is no possibility of its being used at one location or on one computer while it is being used at another. Just as a book cannot be read by two different people in two different places at the same time, neither can the software be used by two different people in two different places at the same time.

## Limited Warranty

Osborne/McGraw-Hill warrants the physical compact disc enclosed herein to be free of defects in materials and workmanship for a period of sixty days from the purchase date. If the CD included in your book has defects in materials or workmanship, please call McGraw-Hill at 1-800-217-0059, 9am to 5pm, Monday through Friday, Eastern Standard Time, and McGraw-Hill will replace the defective disc.

The entire and exclusive liability and remedy for breach of this Limited Warranty shall be limited to replacement of the defective disc, and shall not include or extend to any claim for or right to cover any other damages, including but not limited to, loss of profit, data, or use of the software, or special incidental, or consequential damages or other similar claims, even if Osborne/McGraw-Hill has been specifically advised of the possibility of such damages. In no event will Osborne/McGraw-Hill's liability for any damages to you or any other person ever exceed the lower of the suggested list price or actual price paid for the license to use the software, regardless of any form of the claim.

OSBORNE/McGRAW-HILL SPECIFICALLY DISCLAIMS ALL OTHER WARRANTIES, EXPRESS OR IMPLIED, INCLUDING BUT NOT LIMITED TO, ANY IMPLIED WARRANTY OF MERCHANTABILITY OR FITNESS FOR A PARTICULAR PURPOSE. Specifically, Osborne/McGraw-Hill makes no representation or warranty that the software is fit for any particular purpose, and any implied warranty of merchantability is limited to the sixty-day duration of the Limited Warranty covering the physical disc only (and not the software), and is otherwise expressly and specifically disclaimed.

This limited warranty gives you specific legal rights; you may have others which may vary from state to state. Some states do not allow the exclusion of incidental or consequential damages, or the limitation on how long an implied warranty lasts, so some of the above may not apply to you.

This agreement constitutes the entire agreement between the parties relating to use of the Product. The terms of any purchase order shall have no effect on the terms of this Agreement. Failure of Osborne/McGraw-Hill to insist at any time on strict compliance with this Agreement shall not constitute a waiver of any rights under this Agreement. This Agreement shall be construed and governed in accordance with the laws of New York. If any provision of this Agreement is held to be contrary to law, that provision will be enforced to the maximum extent permissible, and the remaining provisions will remain in force and effect.

NO TECHNICAL SUPPORT IS PROVIDED WITH THIS CD-ROM.